Not Whether
But When

Not Whether But When

The U.S. Decision to Enlarge NATO

James M. Goldgeier

BROOKINGS INSTITUTION PRESS
Washington, D.C.

1775 Massachusetts Avenue, N.W., Washington, D.C. 20036
www.brookings.edu

Library of Congress Cataloging-in-Publication data

Goldgeier, James M.
Not whether but when : the U.S. decision to enlarge NATO / James M. Goldgeier.
p. cm.
Includes bibliographical references and index.
ISBN 0-8157-3172-8 (cloth)
ISBN 0-8157-3171-X (paper)
1. North Atlantic Treaty Organization. 2. United States—Foreign relations—1993—Decision making. I. Title.
JZ5930 .G65 1999
355'.031'091821—dc21 99-6674
CIP

9 8 7 6 5 4 3 2 1

The paper used in this publication meets minimum requirements of the American National Standard for Information Sciences—Permanence of Paper for Printed Library Materials: ANSI Z39.48-1984.

Typeset in Sabon

Composition by Betsy Kulamer
Washington, D.C.

Printed by R. R. Donnelley and Sons
Harrisonburg, Virginia

THE BROOKINGS INSTITUTION

The Brookings Institution is an independent organization devoted to nonpartisan research, education, and publication in economics, government, foreign policy, and the social sciences generally. Its principal purposes are to aid in the development of sound public policies and to promote public understanding of issues of national importance.

The Institution was founded on December 8, 1927, to merge the activities of the Institute for Government Research, founded in 1916, the Institute of Economics, founded in 1922, and the Robert Brookings Graduate School of Economics and Government, founded in 1924.

The Board of Trustees is responsible for the general administration of the Institution, while the immediate direction of the policies, program, and staff is vested in the President, assisted by an advisory committee of the officers and staff. The by-laws of the Institution state: It is the function of the Trustees to make possible the conduct of scientific research, and publication, under the most favorable conditions, and to safeguard the independence of the research staff in pursuit of their studies and in the publication of the result of such studies. It is not a part of their function to determine, control, or influence the conduct of particular investigations or the conclusions reached.

The President bears final responsibility for the decision to publish a manuscript as a Brookings book. In reaching his judgment on competence, accuracy, and objectivity of each study, the President is advised by the director of the appropriate research program and weighs the views of a panel of expert outside readers who report to him in confidence on the quality of the work. Publication of a work signifies that it is deemed a competent treatment worthy of public consideration but does not imply endorsement of conclusions or recommendations.

The Institution maintains its position of neutrality on issues of public policy in order to safeguard the intellectual freedom of the staff. Hence interpretations or conclusions in Brookings publications should be understood to be solely those of the authors and should not be attributed to the Institution, to its trustees, officers, or other staff members, or to the organizations that support its research.

Foreword

It is now ten years since the Berlin wall fell, bringing to an end the postwar division of Europe. After successfully defending the West for forty years, the North Atlantic Treaty Organization faced a daunting task after the dramatic events of 1989–91: how to reach out to former members of the Warsaw Treaty Organization and help them integrate into the prosperous and peaceful Western order. Among the most important and controversial of these post–cold war NATO initiatives was the decision to offer Poland, Hungary, and the Czech Republic full membership in the alliance. Supporters of this policy decision believed that they were erasing the line drawn in Europe in 1945 by Soviet dictator Josef Stalin and bringing these new market democracies into their rightful place in the West. Opponents meanwhile believed that the greatest post–cold war effort—turning Russia from enemy to partner—would be undermined beyond repair and that an effective military alliance would become unwieldy.

While proponents and opponents have written forcefully for and against enlargement since deliberations began in earnest in 1993–94, we have little information on how the Clinton administration actually developed the policy. In this book, James M. Goldgeier analyzes the process by which NATO enlargement became American policy. This account increases our understanding of the inner workings of the foreign policy bureaucracy, the influence of domestic politics, and the relationship between the executive and legislative branches of government. In addition, revealing the obstacles that NATO faced in carrying out this round of enlargement enables the author to provide insights into the constraints that face the alliance as it considers whether to include other Central and Eastern European states in the future.

This book is based largely on interviews conducted from 1997 to 1999 with more than 75 individuals who participated in the events described. The author thanks Graham Allison, Coit Blacker, Zbigniew Brzezinski, Nicholas Burns, Ashton Carter, Warren Christopher, Wesley Clark, James Collins, Lynn Davis, Paula Dobriansky, Thomas Donilon, Steven Erlanger, Charles Freeman, Daniel Fried, Alton Frye, Charles Gati, Leslie Gelb, Stephen Hadley, Richard Holbrooke, Robert Hunter, John Isaacs, Bruce Jackson, Richard Kugler, Anthony Lake, Michael Mandelbaum, Dick Morris, Leon Panetta, William Perry, Stephen Rademaker, Jeremy Rosner, Dennis Ross, John Shalikashvili, Strobe Talbott, Alexander Vershbow, Robert Zoellick, and the other men and women interviewed who asked that their names not be revealed.

This project benefited from early input by George Washington University professors David Auerswald, Steven Balla, Martha Finnemore, and Lee Sigelman, as well as from comments the author received during seminars at Georgetown University, the University of Maryland, the Council on Foreign Relations, the Brookings Institution, Stanford University, and the American Political Science Association 1997 annual meeting.

Leslie Gelb, Alton Frye, and Elise Lewis provided support through the Council on Foreign Relations International Affairs Fellowship Program. Michael Dobbs, Bennett Freeman, Michael Mandelbaum, Kori Schake, and Christopher Schroeder made special contributions to the research.

Robert Art, Michael Brown, Andrew Carpendale, Charles Kupchan, Steve Randolph, and Jeremy Rosner read the entire manuscript and provided useful criticism. Derek Chollet, Ivo Daalder, Katherine Goldgeier, and Richard Haass not only read the manuscript and offered valuable comments, but also spent many hours discussing the book with the author.

Funding for this book was provided by the George Washington University's Columbian School of Arts and Sciences Junior Scholar Incentive Award and the George Washington University Facilitating Fund. George Washington University's Institute for European, Russian, and Eurasian Studies and its director, James Millar, graciously provided travel money through the Roberts Family Foundation Fund and also provided funds for two outstanding research assistants, Michael Struett and Catherine Nielsen. Funding from the John M. Olin Foundation allowed the author to spend his 1998–99 sabbatical year here at the Brookings Institution to write the book. Candice Geouge, Lea Rosenbohm, and Monique Principi provided staff assistance. Susan Jackson and Myrna Atalla verified the factual content. At the Brookings Institution Press, Gary Kessler edited the manuscript, Vicki Chamlee proofread the pages, and Mary Mortensen provided an index.

The views expressed in this book are those of the author and should not be ascribed to any of the persons whose assistance is acknowledged above, or to the trustees, officers, or other staff members of the Brookings Institution.

MICHAEL H. ARMACOST
President

Washington, D.C.
September 1999

Contents

Not Whether
But When

CHAPTER ONE

Process, Politics, and Policy

On March 12, 1999, U.S. Secretary of State Madeleine Albright stood with the foreign ministers of Poland, Hungary, and the Czech Republic in the auditorium of the Harry S. Truman Library in Independence, Missouri. Albright chose the site because Truman was president in 1949, when America formally joined its Western European partners in alliance, and on this day she welcomed these three countries as the newest members of the North Atlantic Treaty Organization (NATO). The Czech-born Albright, herself a refugee from the Europe of Adolf Hitler and Josef Stalin, said quite simply on this day: "Hallelujah."[1]

Not everyone in the United States felt the same way. The dean of America's Russia experts, George F. Kennan, had called the expansion of NATO into central Europe "the most fateful error of American policy in the entire post-cold-war era."[2] Kennan was the architect of America's post–World War II strategy of containment of the Soviet Union, and like most other Russia experts in the United States, he believed that expanding NATO would damage beyond repair U.S. efforts to turn Russia from enemy to partner.

The U.S. decision to extend NATO membership to countries formerly belonging to the Warsaw Pact was highly controversial, and it was by no means inevitable. After the fall of the Berlin Wall in 1989 and the Soviet Union's collapse in December 1991, the Europe of the cold war—divided politically, militarily, economically, psychologically, and ideologically—had given way to a new Europe, one loaded with question marks. Would the United States remain engaged now that the main reason for its military presence on the continent after the end of World War II had vanished? Would the Europeans seek to create their own identity, extending their community in the West to the postcommunist states in the East? Would the Russians be part of this new order, or would they turn inward, only to reemerge later as a threat to the West once again?

NATO, created in 1949 to protect Western Europe against a possible Soviet attack, had faced off against the Warsaw Treaty Organization for most of the cold war. At its core was the treaty's collective defense provision—article 5—which stated that an attack on any member of the alliance would be considered an attack on all. The treaty also made clear that member states were committed to democracy, free markets, and peaceful resolution of disputes. NATO thus served both as an institution of shared interests (protection against Soviet attack) and as an institution of shared values (promotion of democracy and peaceful relations among the members). And in article 10 the alliance had declared at its founding that it could invite any European state to join, provided that the country furthered NATO principles and that it contributed to the security of the other alliance members.

With the collapse of the Eastern bloc, NATO had to decide whether it should extend the article 5 guarantee to new countries that wanted to join the West's premier security institution. Originally comprising twelve members (Belgium, Canada, Denmark, France, Iceland, Italy, Luxembourg, the Netherlands, Norway, Portugal, the United Kingdom, and the United States), NATO had added four more countries over the years: Greece and Turkey in 1952, West Germany in 1955, and Spain in 1982. A united Germany had reaffirmed its commitment as a full member of the alliance in 1990. In the aftermath of the cold war, the alliance now had an opportunity to reach out to its former adversaries—the countries of central and eastern Europe, Russia, and the other New Independent States (NIS) of the former Soviet Union. But reaching out did not necessarily mean extending a membership invitation.

The stakes were high as the United States and its allies considered the unprecedented step of considering these states for membership. Bringing some of these countries into NATO could guarantee the security of nations that had often been sacrificed to great power politics in the past, and it might extend Europe's zone of peace and prosperity from the west toward the east. But if Moscow viewed this expansion as a threat to Russia's core interests and ended its efforts to cooperate with the West, NATO's expansion would damage one of America and Europe's most important post–cold war interests: the development of a democratic, Western-oriented Russia.

When Bill Clinton took office in January 1993, the United States and its European allies had only just begun to address the new challenges. The war and genocide taking place in Bosnia added to the sense that NATO had not adequately addressed the difficulties of managing the post–cold war environment in Europe. And although the central Europeans had begun to press their case for joining NATO to ensure their own security in this new world order, few in the West had taken up their cause.

A year later, in January 1994, President Clinton stood in Prague with the central European leaders and vowed that it was no longer a question of whether NATO would enlarge, but simply a matter of when and how. Three-and-a-half years after those remarks, first in Paris with the signing of the NATO-Russia Founding Act in May 1997, and then in Madrid in July 1997, with the issuance of membership invitations to Poland, Hungary, and the Czech Republic, the United States and its European partners finally began to deliver on that promise.

One could just as easily have expected NATO to dissolve as to expand when the deliberations over its future began. The political philosopher Thomas Hobbes noted more than three hundred years ago that alliances typically disintegrate after the threat against which they were created has disappeared; a recent example in American history was the collapse of the Grand Alliance among the United States, Great Britain, and the Soviet Union soon after the defeat of Nazi Germany in 1945.[3] Clinton had won the presidency by focusing on the economy, not by promising to extend America's most solemn commitment to defend others. Except for a few officials within the German Ministry of Defense, Europeans showed no eagerness to expand NATO's membership. While Russian president Boris Yeltsin had spoken on occasion of Russia's potential desire to join the alliance, the elite in Moscow across the political spectrum were violently opposed to NATO's extension into central Europe.

Most important, if one looked at the executive and legislative branches in the United States in 1993, it was hard to find individuals who thought enlarging NATO was a good idea. With the cold war over and the lessons of the 1992 campaign fresh, only a handful in

Congress showed any interest in NATO's future, and even fewer were thinking in terms of new membership. Resources for foreign policy were diminishing. Meanwhile, those within the bureaucracy who worked on NATO or Russian affairs, particularly those at the Pentagon, were almost completely opposed to expansion. The military was not eager to extend a commitment to defend new members in the event of armed attack, feared the effect on U.S.-Russian security cooperation, and wanted to be sure that new members could make a contribution to Western security.

There were, however, certain features of the domestic and international environment that created a permissive environment for the few proponents of enlargement in the administration and in Congress to push their policy forward. First, the United States was so powerful vis-à-vis both the Europeans and the Russians that once it decided to follow through, there was little that could be done to prevent enlargement from happening. The failure of the Europeans to manage Bosnia led to their greater willingness to follow America's lead. While the Russians could complain about American actions, they were undergoing too much economic and military collapse to block these actions.

Second, within the United States no large organized domestic political constituency opposed expansion; while enlargement never became a big issue for the public, enlargement supporters were able to outorganize the community (largely academics and columnists) that opposed the policy. Had there been any powerful domestic constituencies organized against expansion, as there have been, for example, on trade issues, it is difficult to imagine President Clinton pushing forward with a policy that his military did not initially favor.

Still, in the face of intense bureaucratic opposition, particularly from the Pentagon, how did the few supporters of NATO enlargement within the Clinton administration prevail? What role did domestic politics play in the evolution of this policy? And why did a Republican-controlled Senate in a time of peace overwhelmingly consent to a Democratic president's initiative creating a new American defense commitment in central Europe?

It was America that drove the alliance throughout this process. The allies did have to support America's efforts, and the NATO-Russia Founding Act was vital for securing the policy in Washington and in Brussels. Without the Dayton Peace Accords of November 1995 that ended the fighting in Bosnia, and the reelection of Boris Yeltsin as president of Russia in July 1996, it is unlikely that the alliance would have sustained the enlargement effort, both because it would have been harder to justify and because the allies would have feared that Russia would end its Western orientation.

But despite needing allied support, all of the key decisions were made in Washington. The United States developed the program of military cooperation known as the Partnership for Peace. The United States decided on a two-track enlargement policy that would bring in new members but also create a formal agreement with Russia. The United States developed the substance of the NATO-Russia accord, although it asked NATO Secretary-General Javier Solana (with critical, if informal, U.S. assistance) to negotiate the accord to lessen hostility in Europe and in Russia. Finally, despite Italian and French interest in membership for Slovenia and Romania, America decided who would come into NATO in this first round of post–cold war enlargement. Thus to understand the development of NATO enlargement requires understanding the interplay of process, politics, and policy in Washington, D.C.

The American Foreign Policy Process

How do policies typically develop within the United States government? A core feature of decisionmaking in the executive branch is bureaucratic politics. Over time, scholars studying the inner workings of the bureaucracy have developed three central propositions about the behavior of government officials. First, the decisions that come out of the executive branch typically reflect a compromise reached through the interaction of representatives from different government agencies rather than being the product of any single interest. Different offices and individuals cut deals with one another to ensure that any outcome takes account of their own parochial interests. Add these deals together, and you get a policy acceptable to a range of government interests.

Second, in these negotiations these parochial interests are largely a reflection of organizational roles; in other words, where you stand depends on where you sit. Secretaries of defense will take a stance reflecting the interests of the military, whereas secretaries of commerce will fight for the interests of American business. Agencies and the offices within them have particular missions, and thus from cabinet members down to desk officers, an individual's approach to issues in many cases can be predicted based on that person's job title.

A third general proposition is closely tied to the second: how these individuals perceive what is at stake is also a reflection of bureaucratic role. Thus, argue proponents of the bureaucratic politics model, what you see also depends on where you sit. In a discussion of military intervention, for example, a Treasury Department official will see a threat to global markets, a State Department official will see a threat to diplomatic interests, and a Pentagon representative will think in terms of military missions.[4]

There are certain kinds of decisionmaking processes, such as the development of budgets, that lend themselves to a study of bureaucratic actors fighting for turf and protecting or seeking to expand missions and resources. The notion that compromises form based on interactions among individuals who reflect their agency or department interest is often quite powerful in these cases. But over the years analysts have put forward critiques of each of the three general propositions about bureaucratic politics.

First, critics have argued that the notion of decisionmaking as the product of bureaucratic bargaining does not account for the hierarchical setting in which decisions are made. National security advisers are more important than desk officers; most significant, the president is not one player among many but rather the one player who can trump the others. Bureaucratic politics may indeed drive many decisions that do not reach the president's radar screen or on which bureaucratic actors have outside supporters (for example, in Congress) who can constrain him. But when the president cares about an issue, decisions reflect his preferences rather than bureaucratic bargaining.[5]

Second, critics of the bureaucratic politics model argue that players take positions based on factors other than where they sit. Hawks and doves, for example, often form their general approach to policies long before they step into a government position. Individuals thus develop their beliefs about issues such as the proper role of military force during their earlier experiences, and these beliefs will shape their preferences once they assume office.[6]

Furthermore, one key official does not have a readily identifiable bureaucratic role to shape that person's preferences: the assistant to the president for national security affairs—better known as the national security adviser—who sits in the West Wing of the White House and who oversees a small staff that works directly for the president. As one scholar of American foreign policy has written, "This office enjoys an advantage over other bureaucratic organizations in the field of foreign affairs because it has no constituency other than the president himself. Indeed it was created for precisely the purpose of providing the president with assistance in framing national security policy from an organization that had no function other than that of serving him, no allies in Congress, and no bureaucratic interests or identity of its own to advance or protect."[7] Understanding the beliefs held by the national security adviser as well as that official's views of the president's needs is crucial for any analysis of American foreign policy.

Finally, there have also been a large number of studies drawing on psychological experiments that argue that prior beliefs color one's perceptions of a situation. Individuals have prior expectations providing them with "cognitive maps" that aid them in processing information. Because the limits of the human brain mean that we cannot process all of the information available to us when we make decisions, we take mental shortcuts in approaching most problems in life. Often when we confront a new situation, we draw analogies to experiences in our past. It has been common in the post–World War II period, for example, for policymakers to view conflicts through the lenses of the 1938 Munich accords that appeased German aggression; the 1941 Japanese surprise attack on Pearl Harbor; and, in the past two decades, the war in Vietnam. How decisionmakers define problems, assess stakes, and evaluate choices is greatly dependent on prior expectations shaped by the beliefs they hold and may not necessarily reflect bureaucratic position.[8]

In studying any decision, then, we want to be alert to issues of bureaucratic politics and beliefs, as well as to the level of presidential involvement. Did officials argue for or against a policy because of the agency they represented? Did individuals have longstanding beliefs about the issues that colored their perceptions of what was at stake? And how well did they understand what the president wanted and why he wanted it?

The Nature of Presidential Decisionmaking

Whatever one finds in the daily workings of the bureaucracy, no initiative as important as that of NATO enlargement can proceed without the involvement of the president. Initiatives like NATO enlargement, however, develop over a period of time in which at any given moment the nature of the policy is highly ambiguous, and the president may or may not be aware of where an issue stands in his own government.

Ambiguity is not an exclusive feature of the Clinton administration. When choosing from a menu, any president likes to pick the policy that least forecloses his future options, since he wants to have flexibility to change course if he desires.[9] It is also not unusual for presidents to show different levels of enthusiasm for a policy at different times and in different places. As scholar and practitioner Morton Halperin has written, "Because many issues come at him at once and from many different directions with many different pressures involved, a President's behavior is characterized, perhaps to a surprising extent, by . . . uncommitted thinking. He will often respond at any one time to whichever pressures are momentarily strongest, whether they come from particular elements in the bureaucracy, from foreign governments, or from his own domestic political concerns."[10]

These typical ambiguities have been exacerbated, however, by the personal style of William Jefferson Clinton. He is known by friends and foes alike for his ability to shift positions without hesitation. As Bob Woodward has written in his in-depth study of the Clinton White House, "[Presidential adviser George] Stephanopoulos knew that it was a mistake to assume that any one moment with Clinton, any one conversation, day, or even week reflected Clinton's true feelings or unchanging fundamental attitude about something."[11] And in foreign policy, the president's convictions were generally much weaker than his attitude toward domestic issues such as race relations or health care. Particularly in the first two years of his presidency, Bill Clinton left most foreign policy debates to his advisers so he could concentrate on his domestic agenda.[12]

Policy and Political Entrepreneurs

The ambiguities inherent in presidential decisionmaking provide opportunities for top-level individuals who are keen on pushing particular projects. These are the policy entrepreneurs who must know when the window is open for them to get their ideas on the agenda. Because these windows do not stay open, it pays, as scholar John Kingdon wrote, to "strike while the iron is hot."[13]

There were a number of "compelling problems" that opened the window for NATO enlargement. First was the general concern about instability in central and eastern Europe. In September 1993 National Security Adviser Anthony Lake stated that the administration's strategic vision centered on the enlargement of the community of democracies and market economies to promote peace and prosperity. But where? The central and eastern Europe region, located adjacent to the transatlantic community and showing prospects for success, was a perfect place to demonstrate that the administration could implement its vision. Second, the Clinton administration needed to show that America could continue to lead in the post–cold war world. The president's January 1994 trip to Europe, his first there since assuming office a year earlier, provided a window for demonstrating that the administration had a NATO policy, as did his trip six months later to Warsaw. Finally, Republican inclusion of NATO enlargement as part of the foreign policy plank in their September 1994 Contract with America pushed the window open even further as did continual pressure from the central and eastern Europeans and their supporters in the United States. NATO enlargement could fulfill both a political and policy need for President Clinton, if he had entrepreneurs who could take advantage of the opening.

What characterizes a policy entrepreneur? A policy entrepreneur needs both access and strong beliefs to outmaneuver a bureaucracy that opposes his way of thinking. If you do not have access to the president or to his top advisers, you cannot be an entrepreneur, especially on issues of strategic importance.[14] And strong beliefs lead to persistence, which can overcome bureaucratic lethargy. Morton Halperin has noted that part of what characterizes someone who can move a policy is also personality: "One must be willing to confront those who seek to usurp one's power and to deal with them in an ungentlemanly way. . . . A reputation for chutzpah also helps."[15]

One of the best means to outmaneuver the bureaucracy is through presidential speeches, and access and beliefs are central to using these opportunities. As former secretary of state Henry Kissinger described in his book on American foreign policy: "Many of his [the president's] public pronouncements though ostensibly directed to outsiders, perform a perhaps more important role in laying down guidelines for the bureaucracy. The chief significance of a foreign policy speech by the President may thus be that it settles an internal debate in Washington (a public statement is more useful for this purpose than an administrative memorandum because it is harder to reverse)."[16]

The Political Environment

Critics of NATO enlargement inside and outside the administration would argue that the president pursued this policy purely for political gain, to win the "Polish vote" and to outflank the Republicans who supported expansion.[17] Meanwhile, the top officials within the administration took great pains in interviews to argue that domestic politics were irrelevant. Neither of these arguments is correct. Political considerations are an inevitable part of crafting a major foreign policy initiative, particularly one that requires support from two-thirds of the Senate. But this fact of American democracy does not mean that the policy adopted had no strategic rationale.[18]

Even if explicit evidence of politics is lacking, we know they figure into the calculations of leaders who face the public at the polls and who also have other agenda items that are affected by how a given policy plays out.[19] The same officials who in interviews deny the role of politics usually add that they understood the political context within which the NATO enlargement decisions took place. And even if his foreign policy advisers were not always thinking about politics, the president and his political advisers surely were. There is nothing new about a story in which the president chooses from among the different options placed before him based in part on his own political calculus.[20] A key player in the enlargement story, National Security Adviser Anthony Lake, understood this well. As an academic writing in the 1980s, Lake and two coauthors wrote, "As politicians, Presidents must be sensitive (as national-security Cabinet members and their bureaucracies often are not) to broad public sentiment, and also to their partisan and electoral interests."[21]

Politics should be part of any good entrepreneur's calculation, especially if the policy requires presidential involvement.[22] The policy entrepreneur may be pushing a policy forward both because he is thinking of strategic interests *and* because he is thinking about partisan politics and winning elections. Policy entrepreneurs may also be political entrepreneurs. But this does not mean that a decision is made solely for domestic political reasons; rather, domestic political calculations are part of the set of inputs that lead to a policy initiative.

The most fruitful approach to policy is to understand how strategy and politics intersect, not which prevails over the other. Returning to our earlier discussion, it is also not enough to debate *whether* the president can dominate his bureaucracy or whether he is overly constrained by it. The issue is *how* individuals operating within highly ambiguous environments enable the president to dominate on issues of concern to him. They do so by operating in both the political and policy realms and by using such tactics as writing the president's remarks to prevail in bureaucratic debates. None of what takes place inside the executive branch occurs in a vacuum: political pressures shape the development of administration initiatives, even those that are developed to respond to strategic imperatives.

Entrepreneurship and NATO Enlargement

There are different types of entrepreneurial skills, including the ability to conceptualize a policy and the ability to enforce a decision. Conceptualization alone is insufficient to move the policy process. In his book on policy entrepreneurship, Bush administration official Richard Haass quoted his former colleague Condoleezza Rice as saying, "You don't have a policy unless you can get it done. You can have the best policy in the world on paper, it can be intellectually beautiful and elegant, but if you can't get it done, it never happened."[23] It is possible that one individual could possess both skills, but in the enlargement process, Anthony Lake played the role of conceptualizer and Assistant Secretary of State Richard Holbrooke was the enforcer. Lake and the president laid out the vision between September 1993 and July 1994, and Holbrooke then had the "chutzpah" to move the policy forward in the fall of 1994.

But even after Lake and Holbrooke had set up and pushed the policy forward, it still had to be implemented. Deputy Secretary of State Strobe Talbott, concerned about the effects of enlargement on U.S.-Russian relations, took over the policy in the spring of 1995 to run its two tracks: enlargement into central Europe and an agreement between NATO and Russia. And even after the success of this effort in 1997, with the signing of the NATO-Russia Founding Act in May and the NATO invitation summit in July, the policy still required support from two-thirds of the U.S. Senate. Not trusting the bureaucracy at the State

Department to run the process, the new national security adviser, Samuel R. Berger, tapped former National Security Council staffer Jeremy Rosner to run the ratification campaign. Assisted by key staffers on Capitol Hill and by lobbyists, Rosner's efforts overwhelmed the countervailing pressure by enlargement opponents seeking to build momentum against Senate consent.

Process, Politics, and Policy

Bureaucrats look out for their parochial office or agency interests. Policy entrepreneurs take advantage of "policy windows" to change an agenda in ambiguous settings. Presidents choose policies in an environment that is shaped and constrained by their political needs. But while process and politics are important, the substance of the policy is ultimately what all the debating and maneuvering is about.

NATO's enlargement provoked tremendous controversy because different individuals had markedly different visions of how best to shape the post–cold war environment in Europe. Some who favored enlargement were following in the footsteps of President Woodrow Wilson and believed that the development of democracies and market economies in central and eastern Europe could create peace and prosperity there. They believed that the prospect of membership in the West's premier security institution would be powerful incentive for elites to continue on the path to reform. Other supporters focused more on the need for stability along Germany's eastern border, fearing that unrest there might lead Germany to believe that it had to undertake unilateral security efforts in eastern Europe. Still other enlargement supporters had not rid themselves of the specter of the threat from Moscow and saw the end of the cold war as providing an opportunity to extend NATO's geostrategic reach should Russia ever again seek to dominate its European neighbors.

Passions ran just as strongly on the other side. Those who saw the end of the cold war as a chance to cooperate with Russia to reduce the dangers of nuclear war by safely dismantling and storing thousands of Russian nuclear warheads were appalled by NATO expansion; these opponents believed that Moscow would react to NATO's inclusion of former Warsaw Pact nations as a direct affront and would abandon its efforts to cooperate with the West. Still others thought NATO had become over time the most effective military alliance in history, and they feared that adding new states in the east would dilute its ability to deal effectively with problems that might arise in Europe and elsewhere.

Process, politics, and policy. The stakes were high, and proponents and opponents were equally passionate about their position on NATO enlargement. Examining in detail how the smaller number of proponents defeated the opposition, and why the politics favored enlargement supporters not only helps us understand the reason the United States developed this major initiative but also provides larger lessons for those seeking to understand how America makes its foreign policy choices.

CHAPTER TWO

The Partnership for Peace

As soon as the Berlin Wall fell in November 1989, NATO faced the need to maintain relevance in a post–cold war environment, one in which the Warsaw Pact would soon disappear. The discussions of NATO's mission during the talks on German unification in 1990 and then the development in 1991 of a new "strategic concept" to guide the alliance were important building blocks for the debate within the U.S. foreign policy bureaucracy in 1993 that led to a program of military outreach that would include all of non-NATO Europe in a new relationship with the alliance. That program was the Partnership for Peace, developed by senior U.S. diplomatic and military officials to give NATO the wherewithal to conduct peacekeeping operations. Peacekeeping outside of the territory of the member states was a different mission than defending countries against armed attack by a superpower, and the State Department and the Pentagon had different ideas about the requirements for the future, largely because the former focused on diplomatic outreach and the latter on military efficiency.

German Unification

NATO first began to address its post–cold war disposition during the talks on German unification in 1990.[1] The nature of these talks would directly affect later discussions between the United States and Russia over the legitimacy of NATO's enlargement. Although the formal deal struck between June and September 1990 over the terms of unification did not explicitly preclude NATO's further expansion, Moscow charged that NATO's later decision to include Poland, Hungary, and the Czech Republic violated the spirit of conversations among President George Bush, German Chancellor Helmut Kohl, Soviet President Mikhail Gorbachev, and their foreign ministers during this earlier period.[2]

Giving rise to the later criticism were the first statements on NATO and the East made by leading German and U.S. officials in January and February 1990, as they grappled with the fast-moving events that were leading to Germany's unification. On January 31, 1990, West German Foreign Minister Hans-Dietrich Genscher had declared, "What NATO must do is state unequivocally that whatever happens in the Warsaw Pact there will be no expansion of NATO territory eastwards, that is to say closer to the borders of the Soviet Union."[3] After a subsequent session at the State Department with U.S. Secretary of State James Baker, Genscher stated at a press conference, "What I said is, there is no intention of extending the NATO area to the East."[4]

Baker then repeated this language in Moscow in meetings with Mikhail Gorbachev and his foreign minister, Eduard Shevardnadze. Baker told Gorbachev that "there would be no extension of NATO's jurisdiction for forces of NATO one inch to the east." When Gorbachev later said, "Any extension of the zone of NATO is unacceptable," Baker replied, "I agree."[5]

But the Soviets did not cut a deal on unification in February 1990, when it may have been possible to receive such a pledge in writing. Once American officials realized the implication of Baker's remarks for the alliance's defense commitments, they started to back away and soon adopted NATO Secretary-General Manfred Wörner's idea of a "special military status" for what was then East Germany. When President George Bush and Chancellor Helmut Kohl met at Camp David in late February 1990, they agreed that while NATO forces would not extend to the territory of the former East Germany, all of Germany would be part of NATO's jurisdiction and the collective defense. Baker acknowledged at these sessions, "I used the term 'jurisdiction' before I realized that it would impact upon Articles 4 and 5 of the North Atlantic Treaty." (Article 4 provides for consultation in the event of a threat; article 5 states that an attack on any member will be considered as an attack on all.) Bush stated publicly at his press conference with Kohl,

"We share a common belief that a unified Germany should remain a full member of the North Atlantic Treaty Organization, including participation in its military structure."[6]

By the time the Soviets were ready to accede to the inevitability of German unification later in the spring, the U.S. and German positions had crystallized around full membership for a unified Germany. When Secretary Baker offered his "nine assurances" to Gorbachev in May 1990 to cement the deal, NATO was offering that none of its troops would be stationed in the former East Germany only while Soviet troops remained.[7] Kohl and Genscher then further clarified the Western position in meetings with Gorbachev in the Caucasus in July. As Genscher described the exchange in his memoirs (referring to the treaty articles on common defense and on the definition of NATO territory):

> Because it was important that Articles Five and Six of the NATO Treaty apply to all of Germany, I remarked that there must be no zones of different degrees of security in Germany—that is, NATO's security guarantees would have to apply to East Germany as well. This concern was finally established by a general consensus on the applicability of Articles Five and Six. . . . Gorbachev gave his approval, but not before remarking that no foreign troops could ever be deployed in these territories. The Chancellor accepted that restriction.[8]

During the treaty endgame in Moscow in September 1990, the parties included an agreed upon statement to provide more flexibility for non-German NATO forces in the eastern Länder. Paragraph three of article 5 of the treaty said that after Soviet troops left, "Foreign armed forces and nuclear weapons or their carriers will not be stationed in that part of Germany or deployed there." The "Agreed Minute" then added, "Any questions with respect to the application of the word 'deployed' as used in the last sentence of paragraph 3 of Article 5 will be decided by the government of the united Germany in a reasonable and responsible way taking into account the security interests of each contracting party."[9] Baker's chief negotiator for the treaty, State Department Counselor Robert Zoellick, has said that his goal was to ensure that NATO was not precluded from future transit across Germany if Poland ever became a member, although he acknowledges that few of his colleagues were thinking in such a long term. National Security Council (NSC) staffer Robert Blackwill wrote later, "Germany was given the sovereign right to determine how or when to apply the treaty's stricture against Allied troops being 'deployed' in the former GDR."[10]

There is no question that ambiguity abounded during the phases of this difficult negotiation. But Baker and Genscher's early comments concerned only Germany's position in NATO; after all, Germany was in no position to decide the fate of countries to its east.[11] And the deal reached in September 1990 provided more flexibility for the West in dealing with NATO's eastern orientation than did the language used earlier in the year.

NATO Reaches Out

To make the terms of German unification more palatable, NATO did declare at its London summit in July 1990 that it was becoming more of a political alliance rather than a military institution. After all, with the threat disappearing, what was NATO to do? Many people, both inside and outside Western governments, were concluding that NATO should declare victory and disband, and there was a growing clamor to replace the old alliance system with a new mechanism for collective security. An obvious place to start was the Conference on Security and Cooperation in Europe, which included all NATO and former Warsaw Pact members. Leading central Europeans, such as Czechoslovak President Vaclav Havel, called for an end to the blocs and for a greater role for this pan-European institution, the organization that had aided Havel and other dissidents in their struggle against the old regime.

For key Bush administration officials, such talk was frightening, since it was through NATO that the United States maintained its strong institutional ties to Europe and its leadership on the continent. The supreme allied commander of NATO was always an American, and the integrated military command at his disposal (overseen by the allied civilian leadership that the United States also dominated) gave the United States a powerful tool for shaping security affairs in Western Europe.

Seeking to maintain NATO's relevance, the Bush administration began the process of outreach to the East. At the 1990 London summit, NATO invited the six Warsaw Pact nations (Bulgaria, Czechoslovakia, Hungary, Poland, Romania, and the Soviet Union) to initiate regular diplomatic exchanges. A year later, Secretary Baker affirmed NATO's plans "to build partnerships with the countries of Central and Eastern

Europe and the Soviet Union."[12] Following through on this plan, NATO at its Rome summit in November 1991 unveiled the North Atlantic Cooperation Council (NACC). The NACC would establish ties with all former Warsaw Pact members and hold annual meetings at the ministerial levels. When the Soviet Union collapsed a month later, this body suddenly included nations from central Europe to central Asia. Representatives to the NACC had a formal mechanism through which to consult with NATO members in Brussels and the alliance's military headquarters in Mons, Belgium.[13]

At the Rome summit, NATO also unveiled a new "strategic concept" to continue the process begun in London the year before to remain relevant in a Europe no longer divided by the cold war. It noted, "Risks to Allied security are less likely to result from calculated aggression against the territory of the Allies, but rather from the adverse consequences of instabilities that may arise from the serious economic, social and political difficulties, including ethnic rivalries and territorial disputes, which are faced by many countries in Central and Eastern Europe." It spoke of the need for dialogue and cooperation with its former adversaries, and to ease concerns in the Soviet Union, it reiterated that "The Alliance is purely defensive in purpose: none of its weapons will ever be used except in self-defense."[14]

What neither the NACC nor the new strategic concept guaranteed, however, was the security of non-NATO members. And several high-level Bush administration officials began to put forward the idea of enlarging NATO into central Europe to provide greater security and stability. Secretary of Defense Richard Cheney, for example, had said in November 1992, "I, for one, would advocate that eventually we will want to expand NATO and move it to the East," and he referred specifically to Poland, Hungary, and Czechoslovakia (the latter had not yet split into two). And Secretary of State Lawrence Eagleburger declared in front of the NACC in December 1992 that the close partnership envisioned between NATO and these countries "could contribute to transforming the composition of the Alliance itself."[15]

Still, concern continued to grow in the 1992–93 period about the ability of NATO to respond to ethnic conflicts and border disputes in these territories to the east. In the Balkans, the bloodiest conflict of post-1945 Europe raged as NATO stood by and watched. While NATO advocates argued that the institution was never designed to go "out of area" and was created to protect its members (whose list did not include Bosnia or Croatia), critics wondered why NATO was still relevant if what appeared to be a more typical post–cold war conflict was outside its jurisdiction. And after all, NATO's 1991 strategic concept acknowledged that nations in the East seemed ripe for ethnic conflict now that the iron hand of communism had been lifted.

The Clinton administration came into office trying to figure out how to create multilateral frameworks for peacekeeping in this region and in others. But as the new American foreign policy team gathered in the spring of 1993 to put together a policy for Europe, it had no Bosnia policy; nor had the United States advanced in its thinking about resolving new problems in central and eastern Europe beyond the creation of the NACC and the 1991 strategic concept. For an administration concentrating on domestic affairs and uncomfortable with the use of force, there was neither much knowledge of nor interest in an organization like NATO.

The Clinton Administration Begins to Focus

Nothing focuses the foreign policy bureaucracy like a presidential summit. A president cannot go empty-handed to meet other heads of state, and the bureaucracy battles over precisely what course he will chart when he gathers with his counterparts. That is where this story begins—in June 1993, when U.S. Secretary of State Warren Christopher announced at the NATO meeting of foreign ministers in Athens, Greece, that allied heads of state would gather in Brussels six months hence. This trip would be President Clinton's first to Europe since taking office. Christopher's declaration provided a focal point for intensive discussion inside and outside the government about NATO's future, including discussions of the desirability of enlargement. In bureaucratic parlance, the January 1994 Brussels summit would serve as an action-forcing event.[16]

First Stirrings

In the first few months of his administration, President Clinton's policy for Europe seemed to start in Moscow. His top national security priority was assisting Boris Yeltsin's efforts at political and economic reform in Russia. A reformed Russia, after all, could mean lower U.S.

defense budgets, thus freeing resources for the president's cherished domestic programs.[17] But soon he became aware of competing priorities.

On April 21, 1993, President Clinton met one-on-one with a series of central and eastern European leaders, who were in Washington for the opening of the United States Holocaust Memorial Museum. The group included the highly regarded leaders of Poland and the Czech Republic, Lech Walesa and Vaclav Havel. These two, having struggled so long to throw off the Soviet yoke, carried a moral authority matched by few others around the world.

The president was busy that day negotiating with members of Congress on his spending bill, and he left his guests waiting at the White House for several hours. But the mood of the day had been set at the museum dedication, when Holocaust survivor Elie Wiesel and others drew parallels between ethnic cleansing in the Balkans in the 1990s with the events in Europe in the 1930s. Havel and Walesa finally saw the president during the afternoon in the Oval Office; other central and eastern European leaders each had ten minutes alone with the president and first lady during a reception before dinner. All argued to Bill Clinton that he had the historic opportunity to erase the line drawn through Europe by Soviet dictator Josef Stalin. As President Clinton remembered it shortly thereafter: "When they came here a few weeks ago for the Holocaust dedication, every one of those Presidents said that their number one priority was to get into NATO. They know it will provide a security umbrella for the people who are members." After the meetings, Clinton told Lake how impressed he had been with the passion with which these leaders spoke. Lake says Clinton was inclined to think positively toward expansion from that day on.[18]

The central and eastern Europe region was a natural place for the president to apply one of the few foreign policy themes he had enunciated during his campaign: since Western-style democracies do not go to war with one another, the United States should promote democracy and free market economies.[19] Lake had helped develop this approach, which had both ideological and political rationales. Lake and Clinton were intellectual heirs of Woodrow Wilson, believing that the expansion of international institutions and the promotion of freedom in economic and political affairs could increase global peace and prosperity.

Lake's career had been marked by a distinctly moral tone. He resigned from Henry Kissinger's National Security Council staff to protest American bombings in Cambodia. Later that decade, he served as director of the policy planning staff in the Carter administration, an administration that emphasized human rights abroad. "More than anyone I've ever known, Tony [Lake] is a moralist," one Clinton administration colleague told author Elizabeth Drew. "He believes passionately in the moral aspects of foreign policy—he's a true Wilsonian." And Lake himself has professed his determination to right wrongs around the globe. "When I wake up every morning and look at the headlines and the stories and the images on television of these conflicts, I want to work to end every conflict. I want to work to save every child out there," he said at a 1994 press briefing.[20]

Lake and others had developed democracy promotion as a Clinton campaign theme not just because it might create peace but also because they hoped to unite different wings of the Democratic party around foreign policy, and in particular, to bring conservative Democrats back into the fold after their defection during the Reagan and Bush years. Democracy promotion was a perfect centerpiece, since Democrats of all stripes could support it. Bringing central Europe into the leading Western military alliance could serve both the administration's strategic and political agendas, a double prize for any potential policy.[21]

Unfortunately, the success of reform in central and eastern Europe was by no means guaranteed. President Clinton came away from his April meetings in Washington clearly thinking about these issues: "We had a lot of other countries here for the Holocaust Museum delegation . . . leaders from Eastern Europe, leaders from at least one republic of the former Soviet Union, all of them having terrible economic challenges as they convert from a communist command-and-control economy to a market economy. . . . And in a world in which there is economic slowdown and difficulty, all leaders will have trouble having their policies be popular in a poll because they haven't produced the results that the people so earnestly yearn for."[22]

Creation of a Working Group

Using prospective NATO membership as a carrot to those implementing political and economic reforms would become one of the central arguments of the handful of enlargement proponents within the U.S. government. But it was hardly more than a passing thought for most officials when Christopher announced the NATO summit.

Christopher—using what his chief of staff Thomas Donilon calls "boilerplate language"—stated in Athens, "At an appropriate time, we may choose to enlarge NATO membership. But that is not now on the agenda." It was difficult enough just to schedule the presidential trip to Europe: Christopher had to lobby hard to get the White House schedulers to agree to it given the president's focus on domestic affairs, and Christopher writes that he was still making "some last-minute telephone calls to the White House" from Athens to get approval for the summit announcement. (Interestingly, given subsequent events, Lake fumed at his staff about the summit announcement because he believed the administration was not ready. But as one of them told him, the point of scheduling a summit was to get ready.)[23]

The main focus at Christopher's State Department regarding outreach to the East was how best to strengthen the North Atlantic Cooperation Council—the NATO institution that included all of Europe—to deal with what Bosnia suggested would be the key problem in central and eastern Europe: peacekeeping.[24] Christopher had begun to put these issues forward in February at a special NATO meeting in Brussels, essentially recycling ideas the Bush administration had been developing in 1991–92: "There can be no better way to establish a new and secure Europe than to have soldiers from Russia, Ukraine, Poland, Hungary, and the other new democracies work with NATO to address their most pressing security problems. We believe NATO and our Eastern colleagues should establish joint planning and training, and joint exercises for peace-keeping. Such cooperation can help ensure that all European peace-keeping operations are conducted in accordance with UN and CSCE [Conference on Security and Cooperation in Europe] principles."[25]

As Christopher prepared for his June NATO meeting in Athens, key officials were urging him to provide more muscle to the North Atlantic Cooperation Council as a way of demonstrating continued American leadership in Europe. Robert Hunter, soon to become U.S. ambassador to NATO, told Christopher that although the central Europeans would keep pushing to join NATO, if the United States began openly to discuss the possibility, these nations would never be satisfied with any initiatives short of membership. Hunter recalls that in his thinking at the time, "enlargement was a secondary matter," and he was emphasizing the North Atlantic Cooperation Council as the focus of U.S. policy.[26]

Dennis Ross had played a key role in NATO and Russian affairs in the previous administration and was still asked for his advice on these issues after becoming the State Department's special Middle East coordinator in June 1993. Ross suggested that Christopher should talk in Athens about the North Atlantic Cooperation Council's ability to serve as the action arm for NATO to support peacekeeping in the East. The NACC, argued Ross, would keep NATO vital and would hold out for the central and eastern Europeans (and even the Russians) the prospect that there was one Europe open to everyone.[27]

In Athens Christopher did outline a vision consistent with these ideas: "The NACC states should step up joint consultations, joint activities on peacekeeping, exchange of personnel, training in civil-military relations and joint exercises. . . . By our next meeting, we should agree upon an expanded NACC agenda, designed to draw post-Communist states more closely into the structure of security for the heart of Europe. At the same time, we should develop new ways for those European nations not in the NACC to participate in NATO work."[28] After being given substance by the bureaucracy in the fall of 1993, this program would become the centerpiece of the alliance's January 1994 meetings.

Despite Christopher's comment that NATO enlargement was not on the agenda, by announcing the coming summit, he forced the bureaucracy to face the issue. As the summit got closer, outside voices in favor of enlargement stepped up their rhetoric. Upon Christopher's return from Athens, administration officials established an interagency working group to prepare for the January 1994 summit and to recommend what the president should do there. Senior Director for European Affairs at the National Security Council Jenonne Walker chaired the group, which involved representatives from the National Security Council staff, the State Department, and the Pentagon. These included Walker's National Security Council colleague Charles Kupchan, State Department policy planners Stephen Flanagan and Hans Binnendijk, and Deputy Assistant Secretary of State for European Affairs Alexander Vershbow. From the Pentagon came Deputy Undersecretary for Defense Walter Slocombe; Director of Strategic Plans and Policy for the Joint Chiefs of Staff, General Barry McCaffrey; and Deputy Assistant Secretary of Defense Joseph Kruzel.[29]

According to a number of those present at the first meeting, Walker announced that there were two people in the White House who thought NATO expansion was a good idea—Bill Clinton and Tony Lake. Lake had written to his staff—in the margins of Christopher's Athens remarks that enlargement was not now on the agenda—"why not now?" Walker made clear to the working group members that she hoped to pull her boss back from this position to focus attention on the North Atlantic Cooperation Council. Before the first meeting, Walker had asked two of her staffers, Charles Kupchan and Barry Lowenkron, to write a paper that they entitled "Operationalizing NACC and a Draft NACC Charter." Their effort dovetailed with the thinking at the State Department and would serve as the basis for outreach to all former Warsaw Pact and former Soviet states.[30]

The working group would consider a number of issues relevant to NATO expansion, including criteria for admission, a timetable, and even the possibility of "associate membership" status for the leading candidates. But in the end sharp divisions within and across agencies precluded consensus on any of these. Instead, the group came to focus on a program that would fulfill the vision Christopher outlined in Athens to bring NACC states closer to NATO as well as to involve other European states in NATO affairs but that would not extend NATO's security guarantee to new countries. This program became known as the Partnership for Peace.

Why Partnership for Peace?

The development of the Partnership for Peace as the focus of America's NATO policy in the fall of 1993 was the result of typical bureaucratic politics. First, the partnership left ambiguous the future course of NATO's formal expansion, thus enabling both supporters and opponents of new membership in the alliance to support it, even as they continued to fight about the merits of expansion. The National Security Council staff and State Department's emphasis on inclusion and the Defense Department's desire not to weaken NATO led to the creation of a military-to-military program open to all states of the former Warsaw Pact and former Soviet Union as well as to traditional European neutrals, but with programs arranged bilaterally between NATO and each partner state, rather than through the multilateral North Atlantic Cooperation Council. Finally, at the working level, and even in some cases at the level of assistant secretary, those working on Russian or European affairs took positions that reflected where they sat.

There were two key features of the bureaucratic landscape that influenced the debates over NATO during this initial phase. First, at the National Security Council, the State Department, and the Pentagon, the parts of the bureaucracy dealing with former Soviet affairs had been formally split from those addressing European issues in the post–cold war period. This meant that those people responsible for western and central Europe no longer had to concern themselves with Russia and the other New Independent States on a daily basis, nor did they have bureaucratic incentives to develop programs across Europe. This would particularly affect the approach taken at the Pentagon, where the assistant secretary of defense for regional (later international) security affairs within the Office of the Secretary of Defense was responsible for NATO, the traditional neutrals (Austria, Switzerland, Sweden, and Finland), and the central and eastern Europeans, while the former Soviet states fell under the purview of his counterpart in the Office of International Security Policy. Similarly, at the National Security Council, there was a senior director for European affairs as well as one for Russian, Ukrainian, and Eurasian Affairs, and at the State Department, the ambassador-at-large for the New Independent States handled the non-Baltic former Soviet countries, which had been under the jurisdiction of the assistant secretary of state for European and Canadian affairs.

The second key feature of the bureaucracy in 1993 was that the ambassador-at-large for the New Independent States was Strobe Talbott—former roommate of Bill Clinton at Oxford. Talbott was the president's closest friend among his foreign policy advisers and the undisputed master of U.S. policy toward Russia. Talbott had developed a love for Russia through his study of language and literature, and his distinguished career had included translating Soviet leader Nikita Khrushchev's memoirs, authoring several books on arms control and foreign policy, and writing for *Time* magazine. He could write quickly and cogently, which gave him an advantage in an environment in which good writing was often in short supply. These skills and Talbott's access to the president made battling him on foreign policy a formidable challenge. Warren Christopher's chief of staff, Thomas Donilon, reportedly once said, "I may fight with him over Russia, but there's only one person in this building the President calls Sunday night to see how he's doing, and that person isn't Warren Christopher."[31] Talbott would prove to be central to the outcome of the bureaucratic bargaining in 1993, since his policy recommendation (which was based on the working group's consensus) was agreed to by Christopher and was approved by the president in October as the theme for the NATO heads of state summit.

The Pentagon Fleshes out Its Program

The seeds of the Partnership for Peace were planted in Europe, but not by Europeans. In June, General John Shalikashvili, the supreme allied commander in Europe (SACEUR), was growing concerned about the U.S. ability to remain in the driver's seat as NATO adapted to the post–cold war world. He asked his staff to look into the role that the allied commander in Europe had played in the past in the development of policy in Washington. "What I got was a blank stare," Shalikashvili says. "They came back and said, 'SACEUR doesn't play.' But I wanted to play." He believed that enlargement was inevitable at some point in the future, but he also saw the need for a compromise solution between those who wanted to enlarge right away and those who did not want to enlarge at all—a solution that would develop "patterns of cooperation" and that could also allow NATO to work with those, like the central Asians, who would never become NATO members. He recalls, "I wanted to avoid the experience of the NACC, which was just talk. We needed actual military contacts." As he looked at Bosnia, he was also concerned that there was no command structure for out-of-area operations that would have a headquarters flexible enough to absorb non-NATO members as well as the French, who had left NATO's integrated military command in 1966. In response to this latter problem, his staff would develop the Combined Joint Task Forces (CJTF), which would be unveiled at the NATO summit in January.[32]

In early July newly confirmed Assistant Secretary of Defense for Regional Security Affairs Charles W. Freeman Jr. went on a fact-finding trip to Europe. Freeman previously had been involved in Asian, African, and Near Eastern affairs and had most recently been U.S. ambassador to Saudi Arabia. Given the centrality of NATO to his new position, he wanted to gain a better understanding of the state of affairs in the U.S. relationship with Europe. Shalikashvili shared with Freeman his ideas about Combined Joint Task Forces and about training former Warsaw Pact militaries for potential peacekeeping.

On the plane home, Freeman has recalled, he wrote down on the back of an envelope a series of questions and answers, including, "If expansion is the answer, what is the question?" For Freeman, the question was not how to expand NATO, but how to build a security architecture to manage problems across Europe. Unlike his colleagues on the National Security Council staff and at the State Department, Freeman believed that the solution was not the North Atlantic Cooperation Council. In his view, the problem with the NACC was that it had the wrong membership list, since it included countries like Tajikistan that were not part of Europe, but not Sweden and Austria, which should have closer association with NATO. A few days after he got back, he invited his principal deputy, Joseph Kruzel, to his house for a drink to discuss what he had written on the back of the envelope. They discussed developing a document that states could sign in January 1994.[33]

At the end of July, two of Kruzel's assistants, Clarence Juhl and Don Herr, had drafted a paper entitled "Concept Paper: Charter of Association with NATO." A month later, the final draft was done, after Kruzel had discussed the paper with Shalikashvili. The paper argued that enlargement was an issue properly raised only at the end of a process of achieving NATO standards, when new members could be "contributors" rather than merely "consumers." From the Pentagon's standpoint, it did not make sense to talk about expansion until after NATO had established the type of military-to-military relationships that would enable new countries to integrate effectively into the alliance. According to one of his staffers, Kruzel told the central Europeans, "NATO membership isn't just something to keep the Russians out of Central and Eastern Europe; this is not just a guarantee for you. What can you do for Portugal if it's attacked?" Kruzel and Freeman also hoped that by forcing countries to pay their own way (as the architects of this program originally envisioned), some NACC members, particularly the central Asians who fell outside their bureaucratic portfolio, would not even bother to try to sign up. In fact, the secretary of defense's staff was proposing a selective program that would require countries to qualify for membership.[34]

Freeman needed to get Secretary of Defense Aspin on board, so he set up a meeting in Brussels with key allied officials as well as some of the European defense intellectuals who were there for the annual meeting of the International Institute for Strategic Studies. On September 11 Aspin joined Shalikashvili and NATO Secretary-General Manfred

Wörner at the residence of U.S. Ambassador to NATO Robert Hunter. Among those present from the U.S. government were Freeman, Kruzel, and Clarence Juhl.[35] At an afternoon session, which was attended only by the American officials, Freeman and Kruzel presented the ideas being developed for a "Peacekeeping Partnership," attributing their genesis to Shalikashvili. Shalikashvili then discussed the work his staff had done on Combined Joint Task Forces, and the group agreed that the combination of the two programs would provide the optimal answer to the question of how to carry out new military missions to NATO's east.

Two days later Freeman attended a session of the NATO summit working group back in Washington. He told his colleagues that Secretary of Defense Aspin and General Shalikashvili were opposed to expansion, because while they understood why membership served the interests of the central Europeans, they did not see how it served America's interests.[36] Among other problems, expansion in their view would dilute NATO's effectiveness, and Freeman announced that Aspin and Shalikashvili had agreed to an outreach program that could satisfy the bureaucracy's interests in peacekeeping. He made clear that the secretary of defense's staff wanted peacekeeping decisions made by the sixteen-member North Atlantic Council (NATO's highest political body) rather than the larger North Atlantic Cooperation Council. Freeman said that while the Pentagon could accept the idea of an open door to eventual expansion, his bosses rejected any discussion of NATO membership criteria at the January summit. But to ensure bureaucratic support for the new partnership, the outgoing chairman of the Joint Chiefs of Staff, General Colin Powell, called Shalikashvili (who was soon to return to Washington to replace Powell). Powell told Shalikashvili that he had to brief Jenonne Walker's interagency working group personally to sell the concept, which he did. Shalikashvili, however, was more inclined to take the State Department's position that the program should not exclude any members of the NACC, contrary to the thinking of the secretary of defense's staff.[37]

Pentagon officials were united in the view that it was not yet time to discuss expansion and that new membership was five to ten years in the future, particularly since they hoped to reap the benefits of the reduced threat from Russia. Deputy Undersecretary of Defense for Policy Walter Slocombe had articulated this view back in June in hearings before the Senate. In response to a question by Senator Carl Levin (D-Mich.)

about the desirability of discussing either a timetable or criteria for enlargement, Slocombe responded:

> As Secretary Aspin is fond of putting it, the success of Russian reform is the largest single factor affecting the demand for U.S. defense dollars, for it is that reform process that is started that forms the premise on the basis of which we can plan large reductions in our defense spending in the coming years. . . . It is certainly essential that over the course of the coming decade or so we build a system of broad European security embracing the former communist countries. Possibly in the long run that will involve expansion of the formal membership of NATO. There is a variety of reasons why that issue is not on the table right now. One of them is the complexities of the relationship between expanding membership in NATO, which began historically as an alliance against the Soviet Union, and our efforts to promote democracy and reform in Russia. The second is the very different positions of the different potential candidate countries. The third is whether, in fact, those countries are prepared to accept not only the benefits of NATO membership, but the burdens and responsibilities that go along with that.[38]

By September, with its new Peacekeeping Partnership (after the debacle in Somalia in October 1993 gave peacekeeping a bad name, a moniker developed earlier by Joseph Kruzel and Clarence Juhl—The Partnership for Peace—was adopted[39]), the Pentagon had a program that could build military relationships, involve all European countries, postpone the need to offer new security guarantees, and avoid confrontation with the Russians. For the military, concern about the cohesion of the alliance and about the wisdom of taking on new obligations during a drawdown period gave the partnership much more appeal than enlargement. As National Security Council staffer and partnership supporter Charles Kupchan would write after leaving the government, "The partnership was deliberately designed to enable member states to put off questions of formal enlargement and of NATO's ultimate disposition in post–cold war Europe."[40]

Fast-Trackers at the State Department

Over at the State Department, however, the debate over enlargement was by no means settled. A small group—led by Lynn Davis, the undersecretary for arms control and international security affairs; Thomas Donilon, the chief of staff; Hans Binnendijk, deputy director of the policy planning staff; and Stephen Flanagan, a member of the policy planning staff—began in August to advocate what became known in the department as the "fast-track" approach to membership for the central European nations of Poland, Hungary, the Czech Republic, and Slovakia. Christopher had asked Davis and Flanagan during the summer to lead the department's policy review on NATO's future.[41] While the fast-trackers envisioned that the first round of enlargement would take several years to complete, they believed that in January 1994 NATO should lay out criteria, put forward a clear timetable, and perhaps even float the prospect of "associate membership" to this first set of countries to put the process on a concrete path.

Richard Holbrooke has written of his former State Department boss, "Christopher reached his conclusions only after careful deliberations, which included not only the substantive officials responsible for the issue, but a core group of trusted senior aides, who sat in on almost every discussion. He would listen quietly, ask a few clarifying questions, more in the style of a judge than an advocate, and generally withhold his views until the end of the discussion."[42] Christopher held a series of lunches in September and October at which aides presented him with the pros and cons of expansion. Christopher listened as the fast-trackers pressed him to ensure that the January summit put the expansion process on track, saying, according to one of their opponents, that NATO should "strike while the iron is hot."[43]

From their perch on the policy planning staff, Binnendijk and Flanagan had been helping Davis shape her enlargement pitch to the secretary since the summer. Each had begun to articulate views on the subject long before. While a professor at Georgetown University in 1991, Binnendijk had argued that the alliance needed to start putting forward criteria to address "the principal issue that NATO faces in the 1990s: how and in what circumstances to expand so as to protect new democracies in the East."[44] A few months later, Flanagan, who was serving on the policy planning staff in the Bush administration, publicly floated ideas about expansion in an article in the *Washington Quarterly*, writing, "[N]o one is under any illusion that the membership issue will go away as long as NATO is perceived by Eastern states as the bedrock institution of European security." He laid out the basis for what would become a key element of the NATO expansion strategy: putting the onus for not drawing closer to the West on those countries themselves. As Flanagan argued, "Any European states outside the Alliance would not be excluded by a geostrategic gambit; rather states would exclude themselves from the new collective security pact by their failure to realize or uphold the expanded Alliance principles." In the piece he wondered whether NATO might lay out criteria "that would serve as the light at the end of the tunnel sought by Eastern states" (citing Binnendijk's 1991 piece as "illustrative" of how this might be done); he also suggested that an interim "associate" status might be possible.[45]

In September Flanagan wrote a memo for Davis, saying that the Partnership for Peace was not enough. Without the prospect of membership in a key Western institution, central and eastern Europe would lose the momentum for reform. NATO and the European Union (EU) were the premier institutions in Europe. The EU, absorbed in the internal problems associated with creating a monetary union, was likely to postpone its own expansion until well after the year 2000. Those arguing for a fast-track approach wanted to encourage states such as Poland and Hungary to continue on the path of reform—to adopt civilian control of the military, to build a free polity and economy, and to settle border disputes—by holding out the promise of NATO membership if they succeeded. And the prospect of NATO membership was a huge incentive for reformers in the East, since it would give them credibility with their populations, which were yearning to be part of the West, and might also assist them with membership in the European economic community, which they craved.[46] Flanagan argued that the United States had extended a security guarantee to Western Europe in 1949 to safeguard the postwar recovery, and it should do the same for the central and eastern Europeans after the cold war. By laying out a plan to put a first group of countries on a clear track to enter accession talks in 1996–97 and join the alliance in 1998, NATO could consolidate reform in the East.[47]

Two other State Department officials also helped provide ammunition to sway Christopher in favor of enlargement. Charles Gati, a specialist on central and eastern Europe who was serving on the policy planning staff, wrote a memo in September in which he argued that the new democracies were fragile, that the ex-communists were likely to gain power in Poland, and that if NATO helped Poland succeed in carrying out reforms, it would have a huge effect on the rest of the region.

Donilon took this memo straight to Christopher, who found the reasoning impressive. When the ex-communists did win parliamentary elections in Poland weeks later, Gati's words carried even greater weight.[48]

The other argument came from Dennis Ross. Because of his involvement in the German unification process and the development of the NACC, Ross attended two of Christopher's lunches on NATO. Ross reminded the group that critics had believed NATO could not successfully obtain full membership for a united Germany in 1990, but it did, and without damaging U.S.-Soviet relations. He suggested that NATO involve Russia in the expansion process rather than confront its former enemy, in part by laying out membership criteria that did not automatically exclude it. Ross argued that the previous administration's experience with German unification offered good reason to believe that the current administration could overcome problems with Russia, since he thought that managing the 1990 process was more difficult than managing NATO expansion with post-Soviet Russia.[49]

Outside Voices

During these internal deliberations, several key policy entrepreneurs outside the administration were also vocal in their support for NATO's enlargement to the East. Their public efforts gave the issue more salience because of their position and their access; these included German Defense Minister Volker Rühe, NATO Secretary-General Manfred Wörner; U.S. Senator Richard Lugar (R-Ind.), and RAND analysts Ronald Asmus, F. Stephen Larrabee, and Richard Kugler.

In 1992 the Army and Air Force had hired Asmus, an expert on Germany and on nationalism in central Europe, and Larrabee, a specialist on eastern Europe and Russia, to produce a report on the future of Europe. Working in Santa Monica, California, Asmus and Larrabee wrote a paper entitled "The Twin Arcs of Crisis," which emphasized the crises on NATO's periphery and NATO's need to adapt. The two authors then called on NATO expert Richard Kugler, a former Pentagon official and a RAND colleague working in Washington, to help write a public version.[50]

The Army and Air Force officials were incredulous when briefed on the "Twin Arcs" paper. They could not believe anyone serious would advocate NATO enlargement as part of a strategy of NATO reform.

But the RAND troika found a receptive audience outside the government as well as among the fast-trackers at the State Department. Their paper became "Building a New NATO," published in the fall in the influential journal *Foreign Affairs*. It created quite a stir. The article also served as the foundation for a series of briefings by the three that were central to administration deliberations between 1993 and 1996. After making the case for the "why" of enlargement in 1993, Asmus, Kugler, and Larabee proceeded to produce papers on the "how" (in 1995) and on the prospective cost (1996).[51]

The central thrust of "Building a New NATO" was that it was important to begin the process of eventual integration of the central Europeans into NATO and the European Community as they fulfilled certain criteria. Asmus, Kugler, and Larrabee argued that nationalism in the East would inevitably lead to security competition and instability that could not be isolated from western Europe and would almost certainly rejuvenate traditional German-Russian competition in the region. The NACC was not enough, they stated, since it was "essentially a holding operation that provides meager psychological reassurance." Most important, they believed that not only should NATO transform "from an alliance based on collective defense against a specific threat into an alliance committed to project democracy, stability and crisis management in a broader strategic sense," but it should also develop a charter with Russia to manage that relationship. The leading Western security institution could, they suggested, fulfill four key objectives: keep the United States involved in Europe; prevent Germany from having to address instability in the East on its own; stabilize central Europe; and use relations with Russia and Ukraine to help unify the continent. "NATO," they said, "must go out of area or it will go out of business."[52]

Although the article did not appear until the fall, the authors did a briefing at the State Department in August; Undersecretary of State Lynn Davis, their former boss at RAND, was receptive to their ideas, which were similar to those that Stephen Flanagan was giving her. Asmus, Kugler, and Larabee had also been distributing drafts of the article since the spring to a handful of people, including Senator Lugar and German Vice Admiral Ulrich Weisser, who was Defense Minister Rühe's planning staff director and who had become friends with the authors while on sabbatical at RAND in 1989. Weisser told Asmus that Rühe was moving in the same direction, and Lugar asked the RAND analysts to provide him with a briefing. Weisser, the RAND troika, and Lugar worked closely together to articulate a rationale for NATO enlargement in 1993.[53]

Rühe was without question the leading European proponent of NATO enlargement, and on this issue was publicly ahead of anyone in Washington (or in Germany, for that matter, since Chancellor Helmut Kohl and Foreign Minister Klaus Kinkel were much more hesitant, given their fears about the effect on Russia). Rühe was worried about instability to Germany's east and sought to include Poland in NATO so that Germany would no longer serve as the alliance's eastern border. As he would state later in the year, "Preemptive crisis management for us Germans means that we move the Western stability zone as far as possible to the East. It is not in Germany's interest to remain a state on the eastern fringes of the Western prosperity zone."[54] German scholar Reinhard Wolf argues that privately Rühe was nervous that weak states to Germany's east would provide little protection in case of renewed threat, which also led to the focus on Poland. As Weisser put it in an interview with Professor Stephen Szabo, "It was easier to defend Germany in Poland than in Germany." In fact, Rühe had little interest in countries further to the east, such as the Baltics.[55] Although Rühe remained important to the enlargement debate by funding the RAND group's next paper, his ability to influence the internal American deliberations waned over time because of his strong stance that Russia could never be a full member of the alliance, which was directly counter to the position that Strobe Talbott would argue successfully within the Clinton administration.[56]

Still, many of the phrases the German defense minister used in early 1993 would reappear in speeches given later by NATO and U.S. officials. In March 1993, in a speech to the renowned International Institute for Strategic Studies, he stated, "The Atlantic Alliance must not become a 'closed shop.' I cannot see one good reason for denying future members of the European Union membership in NATO."[57] (In September, at the International Institute for Strategic Studies meetings in Brussels just after the session at Ambassador Hunter's residence, Wörner would echo Rühe, saying, "NATO isn't a closed shop. In my view, the time has come to open a more concrete perspective to those countries of Central and Eastern Europe which want to join NATO and which we may consider eligible for future membership."[58]) Then, in a speech to the North Atlantic Assembly in Berlin in May 1993,

Rühe said, "To me . . . accession of new partners is not so much a question of 'if' as one of 'how and when.'"[59]

The most outspoken official voice in Washington in favor of enlargement during this time was Senator Lugar, who was one of the most intellectually respected members of Congress on foreign affairs. Over time his support would prove important to blunt elite criticism in the United States that pro-enlargement sentiment in the Senate stemmed largely from an anti-Russian bias. Along with Senator Sam Nunn (D-Ga.), Lugar had sponsored a program of U.S. assistance to provide for safe and secure dismantlement of nuclear weapons in Russia; but whereas Nunn would become one of the Senate's leading opponents of NATO enlargement, given his fear of the effect on Russian reform, Lugar believed that enlargement was not inconsistent with American interests in Russia. Already thinking about NATO's future when he read the draft article by Asmus, Kugler, and Larrabee, he gave a forceful speech on June 24, 1993 to the Overseas Writers Club. Laying out the problem of the "twin arcs of crisis," Lugar, using the RAND language, said, "The common denominator of all the new security problems in Europe is that they all lie beyond NATO's current borders. . . . NATO will either develop the strategy and structure to go 'out of area' or it will 'go out of business.'" He concluded, "It is now time for a new mission and new membership." Three days earlier, in remarks to a United States Information Agency press briefing, Lugar had promoted "heavy consideration" to be given "immediately" for NATO membership to Poland, Hungary, and the Czech Republic.[60]

Public support from prominent actors outside the government assisted those lonely few trying to push the issue from within. The other factor working in proponents' favor was that the central and eastern Europeans were not going to give up. Since they would keep pushing, they would maintain political pressure on the West, and they would keep raising fundamental questions. Was the West selling them out? Was the United States caving to Russian demands? If these countries were democratic, market-oriented, and peaceful, why should they not be included in the West's foremost alliance? Havel would state on a visit to Poland on October 21, "Any dialogue on associate or observer status is welcome but cannot exclude our eventual full membership. We will continue to express our opinion at the top of our voice. . . . The ghost of Yalta is not present but there is a danger of its re-apparition."[61]

Talbott Weighs In

Inside the State Department, however, bureaucrats dealing with Europe and with the New Independent States of the former Soviet Union expressed tremendous opposition to a fast-track approach and, in a number of cases, to any talk of expansion. Those who worked on NATO issues in the European Bureau's Office on Security and Political Affairs feared difficulties in managing the alliance if Clinton pushed hard on this contentious issue. Those who worked on Russia issues thought expansion would antagonize Russia and bolster nationalists and communists there. In mid-September, Yeltsin had written a letter to Clinton and other NATO heads of state in which he backtracked on positive remarks he had made in Warsaw in August on Polish membership in NATO. While still saying that he confirmed "the sovereign right of each state to choose its own method for guaranteeing its security," he argued that "relations between our country and NATO should be several degrees warmer than the relations between the alliance and Eastern Europe." He then suggested joint NATO-Russian security guarantees for the central and eastern Europeans.[62]

At the State Department the most important, powerful, and articulate proponent of a cautious approach to expansion was Strobe Talbott. Christopher had asked Talbott to comment on the pro-enlargement paper being circulated by Davis and Flanagan, and National Security Adviser Anthony Lake had done the same with Nicholas Burns, the senior director for Russian, Ukrainian, and Eurasian Affairs at the National Security Council. Talbott and Burns argued to both Christopher and Lake that any efforts to put expansion on a concrete track in January would impair the U.S.-Russia relationship, and they argued that Russia must have a place in European security arrangements. Moreover, given the domestic turmoil in Russia at that time—which included Russian President Boris Yeltsin's military assault on parliament—they argued that expansion might push Russia over the edge. But Talbott had little time to focus on NATO. Given his bureaucratic portfolio, Talbott was focusing almost exclusively on the Russian domestic political crisis and the endgame in negotiations on the Trilateral Accord that would remove nuclear weapons from Ukraine. For the moment, this left the field open to the fast-trackers in the attempt to sway Christopher.[63]

Christopher had to make a decision on what to recommend to the president for the January 1994 NATO summit. And in early October,

the fast-trackers believed that Christopher was moving in their direction (as did Lugar). On Saturday, October 16, at an internal NATO discussion lunch at the State Department, Lynn Davis pressed the case to Christopher that the NACC and the Partnership for Peace were simply not enough and that the administration needed to proffer a vision of a more inclusive NATO. While she was not arguing that NATO actually expand in 1994, she, Flanagan, and Donilon did believe that NATO had to make a firm political commitment at the summit to a concrete path toward enlargement. With Talbott in St. Louis for a conference on trade promotion between the United States and the New Independent States, the fast-trackers seemed to carry the day. Both Donilon and Davis say they left that meeting believing Christopher now supported their fast-track approach.[64]

When Talbott returned to Washington later that day, he learned of Davis's efforts, and he quickly sat down to write a paper reiterating the importance of a slow and vague approach to expansion. The next day he delivered a nine-page memo to Christopher's house, stating, "Laying down criteria could be quite provocative, and badly timed with what is going on in Russia. . . . My recommended bottom line is this: Take the one new idea that seems to be universally accepted, PFP [Partnership for Peace], and make that the centerpiece of our NATO position." Talbott argued that the administration should not put forward any criteria on NATO membership that would automatically exclude Russia and Ukraine, and that the administration could never manage the relationship if it did not offer Russia the prospect of joining the alliance at a future date. He firmly believed that Clinton should mention neither dates nor names at the NATO summit.[65]

How could the architect of America's Russia policy argue anything other than this position? With the situation grim in Russia and the stakes involved in reaching agreement on the removal of nuclear weapons from Ukraine, the surprise would have been if Talbott had supported Davis. Talbott would never waver from his ultimately successful efforts to ensure that the enlargement process never got ahead of the outreach to Russia.

Davis had left town after the Saturday lunch for Kiev in advance of Christopher's trip there later in the week, so Christopher called to tell her his decision. She says, looking back, "[The principals' recommendation] was not as forward leaning as I and Donilon and Flanagan had been recommending. But it was close. Strobe's position was based on the belief in the need to work the Russian side; it was not against my position but it placed the emphasis differently." Christopher told her that laying out criteria would lead to divisive speculation on who could meet them, and he had decided that neither some kind of intermediate status nor associate membership was a good idea. But he could support a statement that NATO intended eventually to enlarge. Christopher recalls that for him, "Shali's [General Shalikashvili's] enthusiasm for the Partnership for Peace was quite important. He saw it as laying a good foundation for expansion."[66]

The Principals Gather

When President Clinton's top foreign policy advisers sat down early in the week to make their recommendation, events had not been going their way. In addition to Yeltsin's assault on parliament, eighteen Americans lost their lives in Mogadishu, Somalia, and on October 12, the USS *Harlan County* turned back in the face of lightly armed Haitian security personnel.[67]

At that time Lake was the only one in favor of near-term expansion of NATO. He had asked his staff in the week before the mid-October principals meeting to give him reasons why the alliance should not enlarge.[68] After all, enlarging the alliance fit the larger conception of foreign policy that he had enunciated in his first major address at the Johns Hopkins School for Advanced International Studies on September 21:

> We have arrived at neither the end of history nor a clash of civilizations, but a moment of immense democratic and entrepreneurial opportunity. . . . The successor to a doctrine of containment must be a strategy of enlargement—enlargement of the world's free community of market democracies. . . . Unless NATO is willing over time to assume a broader role, then it will lose public support and all our nations will lose a vital bond of transatlantic and European security. That is why, at the NATO summit that the President has called for this January, we will seek to update NATO, so that there continues behind the enlargement of market democracies an essential collective security.[69]

The president then validated these words in his address to the UN General Assembly on September 27: "In a new era of peril and opportunity, our overriding purpose must be to expand and strengthen the world's community of market-based democracies. During the Cold War, we sought to contain a threat to survival of free institutions. Now we seek to enlarge the circle of nations that live under those free institutions."[70] For Wilsonians like Clinton and Lake, enlarging the community of democratic, market-oriented states could enhance America's national security.[71]

The principal drafter of both speeches was National Security Council staffer Jeremy Rosner, who would leave the government in 1994 and then return in 1997 to lead the administration's NATO enlargement ratification efforts. As legislative director at the National Security Council, Rosner had taken Lake on a series of courtesy calls on Capitol Hill in 1993. While working on the speech, they visited House Republican Newt Gingrich, who asked to see a draft. Gingrich then provided extensive editing suggestions. Gingrich spoke with Rosner about the opportunity for the "blue blob" of democracy to enlarge now that the "red blob" of totalitarianism had disappeared. According to historian Douglas Brinkley, Gingrich told the administration a number of times that congressional Republicans could never oppose policies designed to enlarge the "blue blob."[72]

The foreign policy team was in disarray as the principals gathered to discuss the January summit. Powell had officially retired on September 30, and Shalikashvili was just coming to town. Aspin never recovered from the military debacle in Somalia in early October, and he was on his way out the door for the next three months. With crises in Haiti, Bosnia, and Russia in addition, how could anyone focus on a long-term issue like NATO enlargement?[73]

At the time of the mid-October 1993 Principals Committee meeting, only a handful of people within the bureaucracy supported Lake's desire to move forward on enlargement. Some, like Lynn Davis, were in fact unaware during the fall that Lake supported NATO enlargement, given the position National Security Council staffer Jenonne Walker took at the working group meetings.[74] The consensus at the Principals Committee meeting coalesced around the Christopher/Talbott view, which also reflected the consensus that had emerged in the working group. With Lake favoring a faster track (and he was arguing for a faster track than enlargement proponents at State), and Secretary of Defense Aspin seeking to delay consideration of enlargement, Christopher sat in the middle. On Tuesday, October 19, Clinton approved the recommendation of his top advisers that at the January summit the alliance should formally present the Partnership for Peace as the centerpiece of NATO's outreach strategy, but that he should also make a statement announcing NATO's openness to eventual expansion.[75] At the time, many in the bureaucracy, says one official, saw the latter "as merely a throwaway line."[76]

The Ambiguity of Decision

The October 1993 Principals Committee meeting would be the last formal gathering of the president's top advisers to discuss the desirability of NATO enlargement. And rather than decide to enlarge NATO, they decided to emphasize the Partnership for Peace. Partnership proponents, such as Pentagon official Joseph Kruzel, believed they had put together the perfect alternative to enlargement and that the president had decided to back their approach.[77]

The decision to add a statement about NATO's open door, however, added an element of ambiguity and is the reason that consensus had emerged at the Principals Committee meeting. As Richard Holbrooke writes of these sessions in general:

> These meetings—somewhat misleadingly named because the real principals, the President and Vice President, rarely attended them—were supposed to be the primary decision-making forum in the Executive Branch. In theory, the views of senior officials, including any disagreements, were then brought to the President for final policy decisions. In fact, if a clear consensus was not reached at these meetings, the decision-making process would often come to a temporary halt, which was followed by a slow, laborious process of telephoning and private deal making. People hated to take their disagreements to the President; it was as though a failure to agree somehow reflected badly on each of them and consensus, rather than clarity, was often the highest goal of the process.[78]

Such was the case here. In 1993 the NATO summit working group had easily agreed on Partnership for Peace, but it could not agree on NATO enlargement issues such as criteria, a timetable, or "associate membership" status. In the end the principals agreed to what emerged from the working group and the memo from Talbott: put forward the Partnership for Peace and say something vague about NATO's eventual expansion. The Partnership for Peace was the one idea that had the support of all the major players, which was not true of any of the specific issues associated with expansion.

The nature of the Partnership for Peace program, as agreed on by the principals, also reflected compromises formed during the sessions of the working group. The State Department and National Security Council staff prevailed in their view of inclusiveness: all countries of the North Atlantic Cooperation Council, even the central Asian republics (countries that were of no interest to the secretary of defense's Office on Regional Security Affairs) could participate. General Shalikashvili had also supported this expansive view, since he hoped to make the NACC more meaningful. The partnership also enabled the European neutrals to draw closer to the alliance. But reflecting the concern within the Office of the Secretary of Defense that the new program not shift decisionmaking from the NATO members to the larger NACC, each partner would develop its own relationship bilaterally with NATO. The NACC was essentially dead, replaced by a program that was still inclusive but emphasized self-selection and rewards for reform.[79]

The consensus that emerged also reflected an idea that political scientist Graham Allison articulated many years ago: "Any proposal that is widely accepted is perceived by different men to do quite different things and to meet quite different needs."[80] In this instance, the different perceptions stemmed from the different attitudes toward enlargement, and the ambiguity over what a vague open-door statement meant is what created support throughout the bureaucracy for the October 1993 decision on the policy for the January 1994 summit.

Those opposed to NATO expansion, such as then Deputy Secretary of Defense William Perry and Assistant Secretary of Defense Ashton Carter, believed that the administration had decided to promote the Partnership for Peace while leaving any decisions on enlargement for later. Carter says that Defense Secretary Les Aspin and Deputy Assistant Secretary of Defense for NATO Affairs Joseph Kruzel shared this view at the time. Those in the middle, like Secretary of State Christopher, who were comfortable with signaling that the United States favored eventual expansion but did not want to do anything concrete in 1994 to set the process in motion, also saw the October decision as consistent with their preferences. Finally, the decision that Clinton should announce that NATO did intend eventually to expand pleased proponents of enlargement, like National Security Adviser Anthony Lake, State Department Chief of Staff Thomas Donilon, and Undersecretary of State Lynn Davis, since they believed that such a statement would help to move the process along.[81]

From the moment the participants went their separate ways, observers noticed that they interpreted the decision differently. Secretary of State Christopher's entourage, on its way to Budapest to brief the central Europeans (and then on to Moscow to explain the policy to Yeltsin), said the January summit would send the signal that NATO's door would open at some future date. Assistant Secretary of State for European Affairs Stephen Oxman, the senior official conducting the airborne press briefing, stated, "We believe that the summit should formally open the door to NATO expansion as an evolutionary process."[82] Meanwhile in Travemünde, Germany, attending a meeting of the NATO defense ministers to present the Partnership for Peace and gain allied support, Secretary of Defense Aspin stated,

> For those that are interested in NATO membership, I think the thing to best say is that this is a necessary step in order to get to NATO membership. . . . We are not, as you know, not promising anything at this point. What we are proposing is a partnership that will expand interoperability—joint operations—between NATO as an organization and these countries as individual countries. From that, there will certainly be a certain amount of security comfort that will come from that. But we, at this point, are not offering membership to those countries. . . . As [British Defense] Minister [Malcolm] Rifkind said in the meeting, NATO is not a club; it is a security organization. . . . I think that what we are proposing is that there be a Partnership for Peace. That this would be the process on which we would proceed for the next few—for the near term.[83]

As *New York Times* reporter Stephen Kinzer quickly realized, "Mr. Aspin's presentation, in fact, held out much less encouragement to the East Europeans than that of a State Department official traveling with Secretary of State Warren Christopher to Russia today."[84] According to another *New York Times* reporter, Lake called Aspin in a pique, saying the secretary of defense had veered from the script.[85]

A National Security Council staffer recalls that October 20, 1993, was by far his worst day on the job: Christopher and Aspin were out talking about the decision before the president could do so, each with different versions. And there had been no prior mention of the decision to members of Congress. Christopher did not clarify matters when asked at a news conference in Budapest about the seeming split between the State and Defense Departments. After repeating that "the expansion of NATO ought to be on the agenda of NATO at the December meeting but most importantly at the summit meeting in January," the secretary of state remarked, "There is no split between the State Department and Defense Department. The program we proposed to NATO was worked out jointly between Mr. Aspin and me and the members of the National Security Council. We didn't want to open NATO. I think Mr. Aspin's statement is one that I fully agree with and that is that at the present time countries that participate in the 'Partnership for Peace' would have a right to consultation which is similar to Article IV of the NATO Treaty."[86]

The simple fact was that at this point, there was no plan on enlargement, and principals still disagreed. They knew the president would say something about NATO enlargement on his trip to Europe in January. But no one was sure how much he would say and how specific he would be, since the president had not yet focused on his remarks. All that the president had done so far was to agree with his advisers' recommendation to unveil the Partnership for Peace while delivering some statement that NATO could eventually take in new members.

It is understandable then that a year later, when newly installed Assistant Secretary of State for European Affairs Richard Holbrooke announced that it was time to begin implementing the president's plan to enlarge NATO, his Pentagon colleagues were incredulous. How, they wondered, did the U.S. government get to that position given the outcome of the only meeting of foreign policy principals that had occurred on this subject? After all, for the Pentagon (as well as for Strobe Talbott, America's European allies, and the Russians), the Partnership for Peace was a brilliant solution to the problems of the new Europe. It resolved the issues of how to reach out to the central and eastern Europeans without providing a NATO security guarantee and of how to develop a new force structure for peacekeeping. The outcome of the October 1993 principals meeting, the bottom line of which was the Partnership for Peace as the centerpiece of NATO's outreach, was the

CHAPTER THREE

The Push to Enlarge

As the January 1994 summit of the NATO heads of state approached, U.S. officials did nothing to clarify the Clinton administration's position on enlargement. Aspin and Christopher each continued to put a different spin on the policy, and Christopher's own public and private comments appeared to be at odds with one another. Lake remained publicly invisible while pushing his staff to develop more concrete statements on enlargement as the date for the president's departure for the Brussels summit approached. Most important, the president's public remarks were highly ambiguous. Particularly after the shock of the December parliamentary elections in Russia—in which the party of ultranationalist Vladimir Zhirinovsky showed unexpected strength—Clinton struck an extremely cautious tone.

Given the contradictory signals, most people outside the administration read the October 19, 1993, decision as most of the bureaucracy had: the Partnership for Peace in lieu of enlargement. Critics pounced. Leading expansion proponents of previous administrations, such as former secretaries of state Henry Kissinger and James Baker, former national security adviser Zbigniew Brzezinski, and former State Department counselor Robert Zoellick, spoke out. Leaders in central Europe protested, especially Polish president Lech Walesa. And Americans of central and eastern European descent complained. Senator Richard Lugar (R-Ind.) and German Defense Minister Volker Rühe continued to apply rhetorical pressure (Lugar called the Partnership for

Peace "a band-aide offered in place of corrective surgery").[1] The critics pressed for the alliance to lay out criteria and a timetable for enlargement, arguing that the Clinton administration had failed to demonstrate leadership, was leaving in place a line in Europe drawn by Josef Stalin, and had caved to the Russians. Yeltsin's visible relief upon learning of the decision only fueled the complaints.

Administration Ambiguity

On November 30 Christopher spoke in Rome at the plenary session of the Conference on Security and Cooperation in Europe. Noting that the United States was proposing a Partnership for Peace, he also stated, "At the same time, we propose to open the door to an evolutionary expansion of NATO's membership."[2] Two days later, at a meeting of NATO foreign ministers in Brussels, he said, "With the Partnership for Peace, we can now deepen NATO's engagement with the East. . . . At the same time, we should signal that we envision an evolutionary expansion of the Alliance. . . . The Partnership is an important step in its own right, but it can also be a key step toward NATO membership."[3]

If Christopher's remarks were consistent with those emanating from the State Department briefing on the plane to Budapest in October, Aspin's echoed his earlier comments in Travemünde. On December 3 the secretary of defense gave a speech to the Atlantic Council in Washington. He argued:

> While [the Partnership for Peace] is no guarantee of NATO membership, active participation would likely be an essential condition of future NATO membership. There are big advantages to this approach. First . . . it does not redivide Europe. . . . Second . . . [it] sets up the right incentives. In the old Cold War world, NATO was an alliance created in response to an external threat. In the new, post-Cold War world, NATO can be an alliance based on shared values of democracy and the free market. . . . Finally, it puts the question of NATO membership for the partners where it belongs: at the end of the process rather than at the beginning of the process. After we have some experience with the partnership process, it will be much clearer who among the eligible nations genuinely want to buy into the NATO ideas of shared democratic values and cooperative security.

Then, in words that must have fueled tremendous concern in Prague and Warsaw, he added during the question and answer session, "This proposal certainly gives the Russians less heartburn than any other proposal that might add to NATO membership. This is a proposal which they have found very comforting, and they have been very supportive of it."[4]

Meanwhile, Christopher's private comments suggested that perhaps there was in fact little difference between the positions taken by the secretaries of state and defense. The Pentagon's view that the term "evolutionary" meant consideration of enlargement only "at the end of the process" appeared to be the prevailing one. Responding to Henry Kissinger's strong denunciation of the Partnership for Peace, Christopher told *Washington Post* columnist Jim Hoagland, "We cannot engage in a neo-containment of Russia. . . . If we tried neo-containment, it would be the surest way to unnerve our European friends." And in a slap at Lake's September 1993 speech on the administration goal of democratic enlargement, Christopher said that compared with the postwar doctrine of containment, "no single word will describe an activist internationalist policy."[5] In fact, Richard Holbrooke would later tell historian Douglas Brinkley that "Christopher just refused to use the 'E' word."[6]

The Critics

Throughout this process, the Clinton team was looking over its shoulder as two eminent strategic thinkers from previous administrations enunciated alternative concepts for European security. When asked in interviews which outside experts they read closely, all high-level officials gave the same answer: Henry Kissinger and Zbigniew Brzezinski. Kissinger complained in an op-ed piece on November 24, 1993, that "the Partnership for Peace would dilute what is left of the Atlantic Alliance into a vague multilateralism," and he called on NATO to offer Poland, Hungary, and the Czech Republic some form of "qualified membership," whereby they could become members but would not be included in the integrated military command. Brzezinski urged NATO members to sign a formal treaty of alliance with Russia and to lay out a more explicit path to full NATO membership for the leading central European candidates. Former secretary of state James Baker also made the case for a "clear road map" with "clear benchmarks" for the prospective members.[7]

Although the administration would publicly respond more often to Kissinger during this period, Brzezinski had a greater effect on policy. Lake and Holbrooke were the two leading policy entrepreneurs within the administration who pushed enlargement forward in 1994; Brzezinski was an important policy entrepreneur from the outside. Unlike Kissinger, whose criticisms could be viewed as partisan, Brzezinski represented those conservative Democrats who had grown disillusioned with the party during the 1980s. He operated not only through his public writings but also through his private contacts with administration officials; after all, when he was national security adviser in Jimmy Carter's administration, Warren Christopher was deputy secretary of state, Richard Holbrooke was assistant secretary of state for East Asian affairs, Anthony Lake headed the policy planning staff at the State Department, and Madeleine Albright served on the National Security Council staff. Brzezinski was successful in making the case for enlargement (as were Ronald Asmus, Richard Kugler, and F. Stephen Larrabee at RAND) because he articulated not only a rationale for expansion but also a place for Russia, something that Kissinger did not do. The two-track approach to expansion he articulated in December 1993 would become the policy that the administration would begin to develop in the fall of 1994.[8]

In the fall of 1993 Brzezinski met a number of times with Lake to share his ideas, and he also invited Lake to his home to meet central and eastern European leaders and to hear firsthand how important NATO enlargement would be to their prospects for reform. Since the debate at the White House focused more on "whether" than "how," these meetings with Brzezinski helped Lake to clarify his own thinking and emphasized to him the importance of keeping the process moving forward. Brzezinski argued that the United States could not have a policy for Europe that was static and kept in place a line drawn by Stalin while at the same time America had an active policy toward Russia. If Russia rejected NATO's attempts to codify a new relationship in the context of enlargement, the United States should make clear that this would be comparable to Russia's rejection of the Marshall Plan that had led to its isolation in Europe. Significantly, Brzezinski argued that Russia would be more likely to develop as a stable, democratic presence in Europe if the West removed all temptations for Moscow to reassert imperial control and precluded Russia's ability to intimidate its former satellites. As he would write the following year, "Russia will be more likely to pursue the good-neighbor option if a larger, more secure Europe promptly fills the potentially destabilizing geopolitical no man's land between Russia and the European Union."[9]

Lake was not yet convinced that the two-track approach was the right one. As he recalls thinking at the time, "NATO could become an enhanced defensive alliance if Russia went bad, or over a generation, it could become a Conference on Security and Cooperation in Europe with teeth that included Russia. Zbig wanted to work out a treaty with Russia separate from enlargement. To me, this was inconsistent with the concept of working for an undivided Europe."[10] The administration would not become comfortable with pursuing this separate track until the following fall and winter.

Summit Preparations

The two most important figures in the administration's policy toward expansion in the winter of 1993–94 were Anthony Lake and Strobe Talbott. In late December the president nominated the latter, his former Oxford roommate, to become deputy secretary of state. Talbott's goal was to take the reins of policy for "post–cold war structures," which implied that he would oversee American strategy toward both western and eastern Europe.[11] He told colleagues privately that the administration had its Russia policy, but it needed a Europe policy, and it needed for them to go together. In fact, he told his team working on the New Independent States that they needed to go on the Brussels and Prague legs of the January 1994 presidential trip to Europe to ensure that the U.S. message remained consistent when they then traveled to Moscow and Kiev.[12]

As Talbott's name was being put forward publicly for deputy secretary, Lake was reading the draft briefing memoranda for the president's trip. Lake's staffers were in general opposed to his desire to move expansion onto the near-term agenda, and several of them say he was completely dissatisfied on seeing their initial work. "Where's the vision?" Lake complained, when he saw that the memos emphasized Partnership for Peace (PFP) as the trip's headline (as had been agreed on in October); "What does the PFP do?" He demanded that they be rewritten, and National Security Council Russia hand Nicholas Burns says Lake made clear he wanted a presidential statement in January that would leave no doubt about the policy's direction. Whereas Talbott wanted to send a vague signal on enlargement in order not to upset the U.S.-Russia relationship, Lake wanted something concrete as a signal to both domestic and central European audiences that enlargement was on track.[13]

"No New Lines"

The emphasis in the administration's public remarks in early January was on the cautionary approach to enlargement articulated by Talbott, particularly given the unexpectedly strong showing of nationalists and communists in the December 1993 Russian parliamentary election. Private comments reflected the ongoing tensions between Lake and his fellow principals. The Pentagon continued to take the position that NATO policy should be sequential; countries would participate in Partnership for Peace for a number of years and then the alliance would consider the issue of expansion. At a United States Information Agency television call-in show on January 3, Chairman of the Joint Chiefs of Staff Shalikashvili stated, "Any other approach, I think, stands in danger of establishing a new division in Europe. And, after all, we have spent—I don't know, 40 years trying to break down divisions in Europe. And what a shame it would be if all of a sudden we would now be rebuilding divisions." He argued that "when the day comes when we wish to speak about extending membership," then the Partnership for Peace will have made the progress necessary to allow it to happen. At a press briefing the following day, he again said, "I think it is important that everyone understand—and I hope that our newfound friends in the East will understand—that the reason that partnership is defined as it is, is to avoid at all costs the establishment of a new line, a new division that in turn, then, would create new tensions and fuel new conflicts." As Aspin had enunciated in October and December, Shalikashvili said that those partners who made the most of the Partnership for Peace "at the end of that process will be in a much better position to seriously discuss with the Alliance the issue of partnership." He then added, in words that Clinton would make much more significant a week later, "If there is a point that I could make [it] is that in this whole discussion, it is useful to remember that we are talking so much less today about whether extension of the Alliance [should take place], but so much more about how and when." But again, Pentagon officials had a much different view of what "when" meant than did Lake or the enlargement proponents at the State Department, believing that the Partnership for Peace should operate for several years before the alliance even addressed expansion in a serious way.[14]

Inside the administration, the arguments for and against doing more at this time centered on this notion of "dividing lines." Those cautious about or opposed to expansion stressed that putting a few countries on a fast track merely moved the old line a little further to the east and would not only destroy the U.S.-Russian relationship but would also demoralize other eastern European countries.[15] Proponents, however, believed that not doing more would harm reform prospects in central Europe, embolden Russia to feel that it could "veto" the process, and leave a dividing line in place that reflected the world of 1945 rather than the world after 1989. In an exchange with reporters at the White House on January 4, President Clinton reflected all the tension and ambiguity in his policy, "[I]'m not against expanding NATO. I just think that if you look at the consensus of the NATO members at this time, there's not a consensus to expand NATO at this time and we don't want to give the impression that we're creating another dividing line in Europe after we've worked for decades to get rid of the one that existed before. What we want is a secure Europe and a stable Europe. And I think that the proposal that I put forward would permit the expansion of NATO, and I fully expect that it will lead to that at some point."[16]

That evening the president hosted a dinner with experts on European affairs. Vice President Gore attended, as did the foreign policy team and key domestic policy advisers David Gergen and George Stephanopoulos. Those invited to share their thoughts included presidential historian Michael Beschloss, economist Stanley Fischer, former National Security Council staffer Condoleezza Rice, investment banker Robert Hormats, and Russia experts Stephen Sestanovich and Michael Mandelbaum.[17]

Mandelbaum, later to become one of the leading critics of NATO expansion, was at the time a proponent of enlargement. He had argued back in September, "The inclusion of Poland—and of Hungary and the Czech Republic . . . [in NATO] would be good for them, good for the West and good for Russia too, provided that it is accompanied by a clear definition of a new NATO policy toward the former Soviet

Union."[18] According to one report, Mandelbaum complained at the dinner that the administration was dragging its feet on expansion because of the fear of its potential effect on Russia. Secretary Christopher reportedly replied, "The real reason is that we have not decided whether we are prepared to defend these countries. We haven't decided whether that's in our national interest."[19] Meanwhile, in contrast to Christopher's remarks, Lake had stated at a briefing that same day, "We are setting in motion a dynamic process which is explicitly opening the door—and one we hope that they walk through—to membership in NATO."[20]

Throughout this period the central Europeans and the ethnic communities in the United States were putting tremendous pressure on the administration to go beyond the Partnership for Peace. Jan Nowak, national director of the Polish American Congress and a prominent champion of Polish freedom since his days as a courier for the Allies during World War II, had responded quickly to Christopher's earlier remarks to Hoagland about the dangers of creating a new policy of containing Russia. In a letter to the editor in the *Washington Post*, Nowak wrote, "This important statement coming from the secretary of state may well be perceived in Moscow as a 'green light' for ambitions to restore the Russian empire and to regain its sphere of influence in East Central Europe."[21] In December Nowak and the Polish American Congress organized a massive letter-writing campaign to the White House. Back in October Havel had already raised the specter of Yalta, and in December Polish foreign minister Andrzej Olechowski visited Washington to lobby for enlargement in the wake of the Russian parliamentary elections. Kissinger, Brzezinski, the central Europeans, and leaders in the community of Americans of central and eastern European descent were all contributing to the growing sense outside the administration that the Partnership for Peace was inadequate to respond to the challenges of post–cold war Europe, and this in turn increased the fears inside the administration that it would have trouble projecting leadership.

Seeking Support

Facing a barrage of criticism from central Europeans as well as from Americans of central and eastern European descent, the president sought to gain the backing of these constituencies for the Partnership for Peace before heading for Europe. On January 6 Clinton sent Polish-born General John Shalikashvili; Czech-born Madeleine Albright, who was then U.S. ambassador to the United Nations; and Hungarian-born State Department adviser Charles Gati to central Europe to explain the administration's policy. There was still a debate in Washington before this trip about whether to promote the Partnership for Peace as a valuable program in its own right or as the transition step to membership. Albright—an enlargement proponent—settled the issue herself in her remarks on the trip, much to the chagrin of enlargement opponents back home. Seeking, as one central European official recalls, their "enthusiastic support for the PFP," Albright argued forcefully to the central European leaders that the Partnership for Peace would provide the best vehicle for these countries to gain future NATO membership. Albright repeated Shalikashvili's pretrip statement that expanding NATO was not a question of whether but when. Despite these assurances, Shalikashvili recalls that the meeting in Poland turned into a shouting match, and he and Albright asked to see President Walesa alone to calm things down. They succeeded, but Walesa remained unhappy about the direction of U.S. policy. In fact, a week later Walesa said, "It is difficult for me to hide my doubts and reservations. . . . The idea of a divided, confrontational Europe has revived."[22]

To present the NATO policy to a domestic audience, the administration chose Milwaukee, site of the one 1992 Clinton campaign speech on foreign policy and home to a large number of Americans of central and eastern European descent. Vice President Gore stood in for the president that day, after Clinton learned early that morning that his mother had passed away.

The *National Journal* reported that Alexis Herman (then a White House official in charge of public outreach) said she helped put together a group of twenty ethnic leaders to meet with Deputy National Security Adviser Samuel Berger the night before the speech. She recalled, "What I remember is the meeting we held in Milwaukee the day before the Vice President's arrival when Sandy Berger spent more than three hours in a dialogue on issues ranging from NATO expansion to the war in Bosnia." According to individuals present at the meeting, the community leaders were effective in making the argument to Berger that they were not asking the administration to pick winners and losers in the region; they were merely asking that countries have the chance to self-differentiate and that those who chose the path of reform should be rewarded.[23]

Gore's speech (written for the president to deliver) seemed designed to counter Christopher's comments about neocontainment and the ambiguity regarding the place of central and eastern Europe in American foreign policy—issues that had caused such an uproar from Jan Nowak and other leading figures in the ethnic community. The speech certainly was leaning farther forward than Christopher's comments only a few days earlier. Gore stated, "We did not spend years supporting Solidarity just to lose democracy in Poland. We did not celebrate the Velvet Revolution in Czechoslovakia just to see that birth of freedom die from neglect. . . . The new NATO must address the concerns of those nations that lie between Russia and Western Europe, for the security of these states affects the security of America. Let me say that again: The security of the states that lie between Western Europe and Russia affects the security of America." And he noted, perhaps responding to Polish foreign minister Olechowski's recent visit, "Especially after Russia's recent elections, those states are naturally concerned about whether they will again be rendered pieces of a buffer zone, prizes to be argued over by others."[24]

Unfortunately for the administration, critics continued to blast away. Former senior Bush administration official Robert Zoellick wrote on January 7 that the Partnership for Peace did not advance the ball much beyond the 1991 decision on the North Atlantic Cooperation Council (that he helped to create) and that the United States ought to put forward criteria that "would enable at least the Poles, Czechs, and Hungarians to qualify for NATO membership over the course of about three to six years." He argued that the problem in the administration was the imbalance in policy as it approached this comprehensive visit across Europe: "In his own determined way, Mr. Talbott is one of the few high U.S. foreign policy officials who has charted a course in his area of interest and fought to stick with it. The problem is that there has been no strong counterbalancing force making the case for a European policy separate from Washington's Russian calculations."[25]

The President in Europe

On January 8, 1994, Clinton left for Brussels. There he gave several speeches seeking to explain NATO's role and its future, including the relationship between the Partnership for Peace and expansion. On January 9 the president stated that "only NATO has the military forces, the integrated command, the broad legitimacy, and the habits of cooperation that are essential to draw in new participants and respond to new challenges." He then went on to explain his vision of the Partnership for Peace: "This Partnership will advance a process of evolution for NATO's formal enlargement. . . . The Partnership for Peace will not alter NATO's fundamental mission of defending NATO territory from attack. We cannot afford to abandon that mission while the dream of empire still burns in the minds of some who look longingly toward a brutal past. But neither can we afford to draw a new line between East and West that could create a self-fulfilling prophecy of future confrontation."[26]

The following day he was a bit more forceful in his speech at the NATO summit. Laying out the concerns of those arguing the need to help consolidate reform in central Europe, he declared, "The threat to us now is not of advancing armies so much as of creeping instability. . . . If democracy in the East fails, then violence and disruption from the East will once again harm us and other democracies." The Partnership for Peace, he added, "sets in motion a process that leads to the enlargement of NATO." Then, in comments that Lake says were designed to counter Kissinger's criticisms, Clinton declared, "It is the right thing to do at this moment in history. It leaves open the best possible future for Europe and leaves us the means to settle for a future that is not the best but is much better than the past." To the president, the best future would include a democratic Russia and Ukraine. When asked at a news conference if he could tell Poland, Hungary, Slovakia, and the Czech Republic that they were on a fast track, he answered,"I think I'll be in a position to tell them, number one, the purpose of the Partnership for Peace is to open the possibility of NATO's enlargement as well as to give all the former Warsaw Pact countries and other non-NATO nations in Europe the chance to cooperate with us militarily."[27]

During the summit, Secretary Christopher published an op-ed in the *Washington Post* seeking to articulate a rationale for the president's policy. According to several State Department officials, the op-ed had gone through numerous drafts during the previous month. Early in December, a week after Christopher's remarks in Rome and Brussels, Talbott sent a memo to Christopher's chief of staff, Thomas Donilon, expressing concern about the lack of any thesis in the draft publication, and he argued for the need to say more about deterring or managing future Bosnias.[28]

In fact, the op-ed stated that the key threat in the region was from "extremists" with "revanchist ambitions," who could undermine reform, and then made the case that the Partnership for Peace was the best program for addressing these issues. Continuing to stake out the middle ground, Christopher declared that while NATO had to adapt, it "will never add members at the expense of military readiness or effectiveness," and that while "there is long-term danger in keeping NATO as it is, there is immediate danger in changing it too rapidly."[29] A month of drafting within the State Department ensured that the final product had something for everyone.

Interestingly, despite all the misgivings about administration statements on the criteria for membership, Christopher's op-ed did discuss them (since, after all, these ideas were contained in the original 1949 treaty). Prospective members would have to demonstrate through their participation in the Partnership for Peace that they could "take on the mutual defense responsibilities of member states." Furthermore, he wrote, these countries would have to show that they adhere "to the principles of democracy, individual liberty and respect for human rights, the rule of law, the peaceful settlement of disputes, the inviolability of national boundaries."[30]

After the subsequent attention to when enlargement might occur, it is easy to forget that for the military in January 1994, both the Partnership for Peace and the Combined Joint Task Forces were extremely important programs in their own right, and Pentagon officials would concentrate the bulk of their attention after the summit on trying to implement these initiatives. The military believed that on-the-ground cooperation among NATO forces and these other militaries had the potential to reshape the European landscape. If any institutions had the power to block reform in former communist states, it would be the militaries, and if these militaries had incentives to cooperate with the West rather than to oppose it, the Pentagon believed this effort could prove invaluable. The goal was to create Western-style, civilian-controlled militaries that had transparent defense budgets and that could be in the forefront of integration into the Western community. When the experience of the partnership enabled countries to participate more effectively in the Bosnia Implementation Force two years later, the vision of the partnership proponents was borne out.[31]

Similarly, for the military the concept of Combined Joint Task Forces was a tremendously important one. How could NATO respond to problems that were not in the vital interest of all members and in which not all sixteen members wanted to participate militarily? The Combined Joint Task Forces proposal would allow the Europeans to develop their own capacities to use NATO to act in cases in which the United States declined to send troops, and it made acting out of area a real possibility. "Separable but not separate" forces would give NATO a flexibility it did not possess before. It would also head off any effort by the French to turn the Western European Union (the European Union's defense arm) into a competitor to NATO in the European security environment.[32]

Not Whether but When

Whereas the military was concentrating on developing these two important new programs, enlargement proponents had their eye on a different ball. State Department Chief of Staff Tom Donilon recalls that at the next stop on the January trip, as the team sat around a table in Prague discussing the president's forthcoming remarks at a news conference with the central European leaders, Lake complained that the Brussels leg had not satisfied his goal of signaling that the administration was seriously moving forward on enlargement.

Working with National Security Council staffers Jeremy Rosner and Daniel Fried, Lake and Donilon drew on language used earlier by Shalikashvili, Albright, and Gore. The result: Clinton declared in his prepared statement on January 12, "Let me be absolutely clear: The security of your states is important to the security of the United States. . . . While the Partnership is not NATO membership, neither is it a permanent holding room. It changes the entire NATO dialog so that now the question is no longer whether NATO will take on new members but when and how."[33]

To proponents such as Lake, the president's statement was critical, for it laid the basis to move the process along. Lake hoped that the alliance would address the "when" as soon as possible. For expansion skeptics, to whom "when" meant after the Partnership for Peace had created a new military environment in Europe, the president's words meant nothing specific and reflected, they believed, the outcome of the October 19 decision; they concluded that although the president had stated that expansion was theoretically possible, the administration would not undertake any actual effort at this time to expand the alliance. Their failure to recognize the importance of the president's remarks—at least as Lake and other expansion proponents interpreted them—would lead to their surprise later in the year that the process had been moving forward.

Nonetheless, it is a stretch to argue—as administration officials would in later years—that President Clinton had clearly stated an enlargement policy in January 1994 and that it was on track from there. Only a handful of people within the U.S. government believed in such a policy at the time, and most understood their job to be making the Partnership for Peace and Combined Joint Task Forces work. Even Clinton was still trying to figure out where his NATO policy stood. On the plane back to Washington after his stops in Kiev, Moscow, and Minsk, the president hardly gave his policy a ringing endorsement in an interview with reporters. "I'm more convinced than I was when I went there that the Partnership for Peace is the right idea at this time and that we're giving Europe a chance to have a different history than its past, and it's enormously significant," he said. "It's not something, as you all know, that just knocks you off your feet once you hear about it; we all know that. But the more I thought about it, the stronger I felt about it."[34]

Lingering Problems

On the January trip to Europe, Bill Clinton began laying out his vision of a unified, peaceful, democratic continent, a vision he took with him from Brussels to Prague to Moscow. But given the vagueness of the enlargement policy, he did not adequately prepare the Russians for the shift in emphasis away from the Partnership for Peace and toward enlargement that would come during 1994. Nor had the president and his advisers done anything to prepare Congress or the public for the development of the NATO enlargement policy.

Russia

In addition to the strong bureaucratic opposition to enlargement, the administration still had to reconcile its policy with its efforts to support

Boris Yeltsin. In October 1993, after his trip to Budapest, Secretary Christopher had visited Yeltsin at his dacha outside of Moscow. Christopher recalled in his book,

> Yeltsin became quite animated when I described the Partnership proposal. The Russians had been very nervous about the NATO issue in the run-up to our visit. Yeltsin had feared that we might try to bring some of the Central European states into NATO immediately, while working to keep Russia out. He called the Partnership idea a 'stroke of genius,' saying it would dissipate Russian tensions regarding the East Europeans and their aspirations toward NATO. I explained that we would explore possibilities for adding members to NATO in due course, but that any expansion would be long-term and evolutionary. 'This really is a great idea, really great,' Yeltsin said enthusiastically. 'Tell Bill that I am thrilled by this brilliant stroke.' In retrospect, it is clear that his enthusiasm was based upon his mistaken assumption that the Partnership for Peace would not lead to eventual NATO expansion.[35]

Small wonder Yeltsin made this assumption. One could paraphrase Christopher's remarks to the Russian president as "don't worry; we have found the perfect solution to your fears." And there is no indication that Clinton or his staff put it any differently in their visit to Moscow in January.

Yeltsin's own inconsistencies made administration management of the Russian problem more difficult during this period. In August 1993 he had stated in Warsaw that Russia would not object to Polish membership in NATO, which had intensified Polish efforts to promote enlargement. His September letter to NATO heads of state backtracking on these remarks only intensified the Polish desire to be included. With President Clinton in Moscow in January 1994, Mr. Yeltsin said, "[T]he time will come when Russia will be integrated and all the others will be integrated, but they will be integrated with one another in just one package, as they say. And this will bring security to everybody. But if you sort of dismember us, I mean, accepting us or admitting us one by one is no good. I'm against that—opposed. That is why I support the initiative shown by the U.S. President with respect to the Partnership for Peace."[36]

The Congress

During this period the administration also failed to lay any groundwork with Congress or the public to support NATO's eventual expansion. One National Security Council staffer recalls that the briefing memorandum that went to the president prior to the summit contained a section at the end entitled "Other Issues." Included under this heading was a one-word bullet: "Congress." Lake made no effort to consult congressional leaders on this issue, which was odd since any effort to amend the NATO treaty would require a two-thirds vote in the Senate. One high-level State Department official argues that because the administration had decided not to put things on a fast track and simply to announce an intention to expand, there was no need yet to reach out to Congress. This attitude seemed to prevail until late in the game, and critics would argue throughout the ratification process that the administration had made little effort after 1994 to take its case to Congress and to the public. One explanation, other than a general Clinton administration failure to consult adequately with Congress during this time, is that since no decision on enlargement had yet been made, the president and his staff had nothing to take to the American people or to Capitol Hill.[37]

Christopher did at least send a letter to members of Congress explaining the administration position after the meetings and trips in October 1993. He wrote, "We believe that the Summit also should make a statement of principle about NATO's intent to expand to include new democracies in Europe's East. We have decided that now is not the time to set a specific timetable for expansion of the Alliance, establish fixed criteria for membership, or identify 'preferred candidates,' as these steps could prove divisive and even destabilizing in the East. Rather, expansion should be an evolutionary process. The Partnership for Peace, while being an important initiative in its own right, is also an important part of the evolutionary process of NATO expansion." He reported that he had sent a letter to NATO foreign ministers on October 19 laying out this position, and he also noted that, "Our ideas received a particularly good response in Moscow." Finally, he added a pledge to "maintain close contact with you on all aspects of our preparations, and appreciate your suggestions, as we move toward the Summit in January." No officials from the administration or Capitol Hill can recall any close contact during this period.[38]

Electoral Politics

Administration critics would suggest later that Clinton supported expansion purely for political purposes, to win the "Polish vote."[39] Numerous foreign policy officials in the administration, who deny that domestic political considerations came up in their meetings on expansion, hotly dispute this claim. Lake says that although everyone knew the political context of the NATO enlargement debate, he never had "an explicit discussion" with the president about the domestic political implications of expansion.[40]

The lack of discussion in the foreign policy meetings on expansion does not mean that domestic politics were not a factor. Americans of central and eastern European descent are important constituencies in key Midwestern and Northeastern states, such as Illinois, Michigan, Pennsylvania, and New York. Strongly anticommunist, these groups had voted solidly Republican in the 1980s, but, as one observer has written, appeared to turn against Bush in 1992 in frustration with his hesitance about recognizing the rebellious Soviet republics the previous year. In 1992 Clinton won twelve of the fourteen states with the highest concentration of central and eastern European ethnic voters (9–18 percent of the electorate), which added up to 186 electoral votes, and Clinton reportedly told Alexis Herman before she was hired at the White House that he had "wide support from ethnic communities in 1992."[41] Candidate Clinton had given his key pro-democracy foreign policy speech in October 1992 in Milwaukee, and his advisers had chosen the same site as the venue of the January 1994 address explaining his NATO policy.[42]

Domestic politics probably played a role in the deliberations on enlargement during this period in a more complicated fashion than as a simple attempt to court ethnic votes in key Midwestern and Northeastern states. Politically, Clinton needed to demonstrate U.S. leadership. In 1993-94 his administration's policy in Bosnia was failing miserably, and this failure overshadowed every other foreign policy issue at the time. Some administration officials argue that one rationale for saying something decisive at the January 1994 NATO summit was precisely to show leadership in one part of Europe while the United States was doing so little in the Balkans.[43] Second, even if ethnic pressures did not drive the decision, Clinton would have alienated these vocal and powerful domestic constituencies had he decided against expanding NATO, and Republicans would have gained an issue to use both in congressional elections in 1994 and in the presidential campaign in 1996. If domestic politics did not dictate policy, they gave it more resonance for the White House, and they kept it on track from 1994 to 1996, as the administration sought to blunt potential Republican criticism. Both parties would use support for the policy for political purposes: Clinton's emphasis on enlargement in front of ethnic communities in places like Cleveland and Detroit in 1995–96 provides clear evidence of the perceived political value of NATO expansion, and Republicans included NATO expansion as one of the few foreign policy issues in their Contract with America during the 1994 congressional campaign.[44]

Moving Forward

President Clinton had opened a window to NATO enlargement with his statement in Prague that it was no longer a question of whether but when. Would anyone within the executive branch jump through it? Working separately, but toward the same end, first Anthony Lake and then Richard Holbrooke took advantage of presidential remarks to push the policy forward. Events within both the administration and Congress helped to alter the climate in 1994 and made the efforts of Lake and Holbrooke easier. First, personnel changes during the year made bureaucratic support for enlargement more possible than it had been in 1993. Second, enlargement proponents in Congress began introducing legislation designed to force the administration to commit to a timetable on enlargement and to provide assistance to the leading candidates. When Republicans included NATO enlargement as a plank in the Contract with America and then took control of both houses of Congress in November 1994, the political imperatives of the administration to stay out in front on this issue heightened.[45] What is remarkable about the movement that occurred inside the administration between January and October 1994 is that it happened in the absence of any formal decision meetings involving the president and his principal foreign policy advisers. Proponents had nothing more than lines in the president's remarks in Prague in January and in Warsaw in July to convince the bureaucracy in the fall of 1994 that it was time to begin implementing an enlargement strategy. But once opponents—particularly within the Pentagon—recognized by December 1994 that the president wanted to move forward (albeit gradually), they fell into line behind him.

The Summit Aftermath

For several months after Clinton's pronouncements in January, neither his advisers nor the bureaucracy paid much attention to NATO expansion. The Pentagon and the State Department had more pressing concerns, including the continuing denuclearization efforts in the former Soviet Union and the need to get the Partnership for Peace up and running. These were time-consuming affairs. Meanwhile, attention at the senior level shifted once again to Bosnia after the horrific February bombing of the Sarajevo marketplace. As Christopher writes, "Not only did this conflict occupy much of our time and energy, but psychologically we found it exceedingly difficult to focus on expansion while NATO groped for a way to stop the bloodshed in southern Europe."[46]

During this period officials sought to defend and articulate the policy enunciated during the president's trip to Europe in January, and the State and Defense Department positions reflected their respective bureaucratic interests. For the diplomats at the State Department, the key issue remained one of "line-drawing" and of not re-creating a political division in Europe, particularly one that left Russia on the outside. At the Pentagon, the main issues were security cooperation with Russia (and in particular, the efforts to dismantle Russian nuclear weapons) and the military contribution that new members might bring to the alliance.[47]

For partnership supporters in both buildings, avoiding new lines and ensuring that new members were "net contributors" led to continued defense of the decision not to put enlargement on a faster track. Testifying before the House Foreign Affairs Committee on January 25, 1994, Talbott argued:

> The issue of membership quite properly should be resolved once the question of the mission for NATO in the post–cold war era is decided. So there was, for reasons that I think were and remain very sound, a reluctance to rush into the question of membership until we had a clear idea of what the mission for the alliance should be. . . . If we were to adopt a course that said, early in

> 1994, led by the United States, NATO was going to expand the alliance and draw a new demarcation line, the line that now exists between the Federal Republic of Germany and Poland, and move that line to the East so that it would be between Poland and Byelorus [Belarus], we would be reinforcing one of the key elements of the cold war security order, namely the division of Europe.[48]

Critics continued to chastise the administration for dragging its feet. In the Senate, Richard Lugar complained about what he perceived as a "Russia-first" policy, and he stated in hearings held on February 1, "I am not adverse to line-drawing. I believe that expanded NATO membership should be a function of the alliance's own priorities."[49] In response, Assistant Secretary of State for European Affairs Stephen Oxman and Undersecretary of Defense for Policy Frank Wisner repeated the consensus in their agencies. Oxman reiterated that the administration did believe in an evolutionary process of expansion but could not lay out a timetable or criteria at that time. Wisner, meanwhile, remarked, "No nation to the East that would strive to have a partnership arrangement under the Partnership for Peace or, indeed, NATO association somewhere down the road could do so without making a real contribution to the common defense of the alliance, a contribution so clear in circumstances sensible enough that you, as Members of the Senate, would feel comfortable to extend the reach of the alliance, to extend the Article V coverage of the alliance to new areas."[50]

By far the most important occurrence within the bureaucracy at the time was the confirmation of Strobe Talbott as deputy secretary of state in February 1994. Both the Senate debate and his occupancy of this new office were critical in the evolution of his views on enlargement. His main objective in the fall of 1993 had been keeping concrete steps toward enlargement off the table, and he had succeeded. But his views began to change. The president had indicated his support for enlargement to occur at some point, both in his October 19 decision and then in his remarks in Prague in January. Talbott, as a loyal friend and public servant, would thus have to adjust to ensure that the policy was coordinated with the administration's Russia policy. In fact, from 1995 to 1997 Talbott emerged not only as one of the most articulate Clinton administration spokespersons for NATO enlargement, but also as the overseer of the effort to keep the enlargement train and the Russia train running on parallel tracks.[51]

Becoming deputy secretary played a key role in Talbott's evolution for two reasons. First, in the Senate floor debate preceding his confirmation vote, leading Republicans crucified him over the positions he had taken over the years, primarily in his writings for *Time*. Senator Jesse Helms (R-N.C.) stated that having examined Talbott's qualifications, "Frankly I was not thrilled by what I found." Senator John McCain (R-Ariz.), a leading voice on national security affairs, declared, "Ambassador Talbott's proclivity for zealously defending one's thesis beyond the bounds of logic and truth and wisdom will potentially endanger our national interests in a much larger area of the globe than he has heretofore had the opportunity to effect." Senator Mitch McConnell (R-Ky.) pronounced, "I have met very few people in my life who are as well educated and smart as Strobe Talbott who are so consistently wrong." And Senator Robert Dole (R-Kan.), who said he had been prepared to vote yes on the nominee, in the end decided, "Maybe it is time to say enough promotions for Strobe Talbott."[52] For an individual as talented and distinguished as Talbott, these remarks must have stung deeply. They certainly reflected the tense relationship between Republicans and Talbott that would continue throughout the process of NATO enlargement.

The Senate confirmed Talbott, but by a vote of only 66–31, with opposition from Senators Dole, Phil Gramm (R-Tex.), Helms, Trent Lott (R-Miss.), McCain, William Roth (R-Del.), and his future colleague, William Cohen, Republican from Maine. Since one of the major concerns for conservative Republicans was Talbott's views on Russia, his confirmation experience left him less room to articulate any opposition to enlargement based on the effect of the policy on Moscow. When Talbott later became in charge of the NATO enlargement policy's implementation, Republican senators continually voiced their (unsubstantiated) concern that he was willing to sell out NATO's effectiveness to appease Russia.[53]

Second, his promotion meant that Talbott would more regularly consider the broader European landscape and the needs of the central Europeans. As ambassador-at-large for the New Independent States, his bureaucratic portfolio had meant that his number one priority was the U.S.-Russian relationship and the efforts to assist Boris Yeltsin. As a deputy secretary who was taking over the portfolio of European architecture, Talbott had to give more attention on a daily basis to the need to harmonize America's Russia policy with its NATO policy.

Preparations for Warsaw

Just as the January 1994 summit had served as an action-forcing event, so, too, would the president's trip to Poland in July. In April Lake brought one of his staffers, Daniel Fried, a specialist on central and eastern Europe, to join him and Deputy National Security Adviser Samuel Berger for a discussion of how best to follow up on Clinton's January remarks and to prepare for the coming Poland trip. The visit to Warsaw had been offered to Walesa as a way of easing the Polish president's disappointment over the January summit. In their meeting, Lake asked Fried to put together a game plan on enlargement. When Fried reminded him of the bureaucracy's strong opposition to enlargement, Lake responded that the president wanted to move forward, and Lake needed an action plan to make it happen. For Lake, the strong advantage of being national security adviser was not having to go through the bureaucracy to reach the president.[54]

To write the policy paper, Fried brought in two colleagues: Nicholas Burns, the senior director for Russian, Ukrainian, and Eurasian affairs at the National Security Council, and Alexander Vershbow, who was then deputy assistant secretary of state for European affairs but who would shortly become the senior director for European affairs at the National Security Council. Fried had known Burns since the two worked together at the State Department during the tumultuous events of 1989. Despite his National Security Council portfolio on Russian affairs, Burns was not opposed to the idea of NATO expansion, which pleased Fried; Burns in turn appreciated that Fried accepted the need for a gradual approach and understood that the strategy had to include a place for Russia. Fried had known Vershbow since they had been graduate students together at Columbia University and valued his expertise on NATO. Vershbow had served as deputy U.S. permanent representative to NATO, and he was one of the few officials at either the State Department or the National Security Council who actually understood how NATO worked. This knowledge was crucial for thinking about *how* one went about enlarging a military alliance.[55]

Unlike many policy papers, which need clearance, or approval, from key people in each relevant government agency, this one went straight to

Lake, and he told this National Security Council troika to work outside of normal bureaucratic processes. Thus they sidestepped the need for the kind of bureaucratic bargaining that had occurred in the NATO working group in 1993. Before the president's Warsaw trip, Lake invited Talbott and State Department Policy Planning Director James Steinberg to the White House to discuss the draft paper with Fried and Burns. Talbott sought assurances that the proposed process would be gradual, consistent with the policy he had pushed the previous October.[56]

Meanwhile, key Pentagon officials continued to believe that the focus on the Partnership for Peace was still the right one, but they also understood that enlargement was going to occur down the road because countries that eventually met the criteria could not be told that the door was closed. In an address at the University of Virginia in May, Deputy Assistant Secretary of Defense Joseph Kruzel restated the prevailing view at the Pentagon regarding the beauty of the Partnership: "Bureaucracies constantly compromise; it is in their nature. One must sometimes hold one's nose and accept a compromise proposal as the best possible outcome between two groups that strongly hold two contrary opinions. No one likes such an outcome. The Partnership for Peace program is different from most compromise solutions, however, because it has produced better results than either of the alternatives it was intended to reconcile."[57] But he added, "The question that is constantly asked is when do we expect to admit new members to NATO. Officially, this question has never been answered because no one wants to create expectations. . . . President Clinton cannot say in 1994 that in 1999 they will be admitted. Thus, the official answer is that no promises can be made yet. The unofficial answer is that most people feel that new members will be allowed to join the alliance by the end of this century."[58]

For Partnership for Peace supporters, the president's main proposal in July was the so-called Warsaw Initiative, which would begin providing assistance in fiscal year 1996 to help non-NATO countries participate in partnership activities. Jeffrey Simon, an expert on central European militaries at the National Defense University, had told Kruzel in the fall of 1993 that the Partnership for Peace would cost money. Once the Pentagon had tried to start the partnership after January, Kruzel realized that his goal of having members fund their own participation was unrealistic. These countries simply did not have the resources to make use of partnership programs, from a presence at NATO military headquarters in Mons, Belgium, to joint exercises and training. Kruzel asked Simon for a memo. Simon's "Priming the Pump" paper made the case for authorizing $200 million. Lake, Christopher, and Perry approved half of that, with $25 million earmarked for Poland. Despite the misgivings of Kruzel and other Pentagon officials responsible for NATO affairs, those working on policy toward the New Independent States managed to garner $25 million for the countries of the former Soviet Union, thus winning the bureaucratic battle over whether the United States would actively seek to involve in the Partnership for Peace not merely the central and eastern Europeans, but Russia, Ukraine, and even the central Asians.[59]

Again, Clinton Speaks

Just as he had done in January, President Clinton moved the ball with his remarks before and during his trip to Warsaw in July. Tomasz Lis of Polish Television interviewed the president on July 1, 1994, and asked, "Could you make that step forward and say when and how?" Clinton responded, "Well, first of all, I have to make sure there is an agreement among the NATO members about what exactly the standards should be and the timetable. And they haven't all agreed. But I do want to make it clear that, in my view, NATO will be expanded, that it should be expanded, and that it should be expanded as a way of strengthening security and not conditioned on events in any other country or some new threat arising to NATO."[60]

Lis continued to press his case: "Will you give Poland and other Eastern European countries a clear timetable?" And Clinton, taking another small step forward, responded, "I think that a timetable should be developed, but I can't do that alone. . . . Earlier this year when I met with the NATO members, they felt very strongly that we should first have . . . these Partnership for Peace exercises . . . then see which people in the Partnership really wanted to become members and who was ready and then come back and meet and determine what the standards should be. So I think that probably won't be done until sometime next year, because of the feeling of all the NATO members about it." Interestingly, when Lis asked about the idea of a NATO-Russia treaty parallel with enlargement, President Clinton responded, "I don't know, I haven't thought of it in exactly those terms. . . . That's an interesting suggestion you made, but I haven't had time to think it through, so I can't comment on it."[61]

The White House was nervous about the treatment the
would receive in Warsaw, given Walesa's propensity to say ex
he felt and given the experience of Albright and Shalikashvi
ary 1994. But Walesa could not have been more gracious.
exchange with reporters after their meeting, Clinton n
beyond the bureaucratic consensus when he remarked, "I l
stated my support for the idea that NATO will expand. . .
NATO partnership to embrace, first, the Partnership for P
we would have a way of reaching out to all the nonmeml
cies in Europe. I did that as a first step toward expansion
also because, in my mind, I wanted to see whether there v
ing that Europe could be united and that these countri
pledge to respect one another's borders. . . . And now w t
do is to get the NATO partners together and to discuss
steps should be."[62] ni-

Several officials say the president made this comment re-
tiative, but enlargement supporters jumped at the op ber
sented. The NATO foreign ministers meeting schedul as
would be the logical place for such a discussion an ack.
another action-forcing event to keep an enlargemen State
Personnel changes on the National Security Council ct of
Department, along with the Republican introduction arge-
America during this time, assisted the few individua a new
ment to gain the upper hand and in moving the bu
position before the year was over. no was

Most important was the arrival of Richard H nadian
sworn in as assistant secretary of state for Euro merica's
affairs on September 13. Because of his past invo mbassa-
Asia policy and his hope in 1993 that he would b NATO
dor to Japan, Holbrooke had not given mucl d in Ger-
before his tenure as U.S. ambassador in Bonn. " EU mem-
many in September 1993," he has written, "I t urned me
bership was more important and would arrive Euro-mess
around was the realization that the EU, mired s, its inner-
(the common currency, the endless arguments invite any of
directedness, and its failure on Bosnia), was n Germany he
these countries in, at the earliest, before Minister of
became quite receptive to the arguments th were making
Defense Volker Rühe and RAND analyst Ro

ab
all 's security need for Poland's inclusion into the

pro was not Anthony Lake, NATO enlargement's biggest
rath administration, who sought Holbrooke's return, but
acco ott and Undersecretary of State Peter Tarnoff, who,
revit rooke, "had listed three priorities for the new job:
enlar ropean Bureau, shaping a coherent policy on the
ingly TO, and Bosnia."[64] Christopher had grown increas-
NATO ith what the European Bureau was producing on
and th ia. Holbrooke and Talbott had been close friends,
Talbott actically every day while Holbrooke was in Bonn.
right m convinced Christopher that Holbrooke was the
could ta , and Christopher promised Holbrooke that he
accordin enlargement policy at the State Department. And
and I ha e, "By the time I returned to Washington, Strobe
members ommon position: it was possible to bring new
wanted bu slower than the Kissingers and the Brzezinskis
Thus, a he Pentagon and some others desired."[65]
nents were s winding down in 1994, enlargement propo-
tion had ev situated within the bureaucracy. Talbott's posi-
although he rably from where it had been in October 1993,
ing to ensur leading figure within the bureaucracy work-
Russia train, largement train would not get ahead of the
concerned ab lelism that the fast-trackers had never been as
bott's evoluti ng.[66] Thus with Holbrooke's return and Tal-
Christopher l Department had moved from the position
October 1993 ed at the Principals Committee meeting in
The Nation was more favorable to NATO enlargement.
der Vershbow ouncil staff also had a new look, as Alexan-
torate. Lake un er to take the reins of the European Direc-
National Securi mportance of having people in place at the
viewing Vershbo who supported enlargement. When inter-
stood on the issu b, Lake asked him point-blank where he
would do the san gave the answer Lake was seeking. (Lake
the senior directo Blacker, who replaced Nicholas Burns as
Fried, who by now n affairs in the spring of 1995.) Daniel
be officially promo l of central European issues, was soon to
for central and east al assistant to the president responsible
n affairs. Because Fried, Vershbow, and

Burns were proposing a more gradual timetable than Lake had been considering the year before, the National Security Council and State Department positions had converged. By October 1994 the National Security Council troika's strategy paper laid out a game plan whose goal was to announce a timeline during Clinton's first term and seek to accomplish enlargement early in the second term. (In the paper they did not distinguish between an invitation summit and formal accession to NATO membership, which would turn out to be a two-year process between 1997 and 1999.)[67]

Pentagon officials remained concerned about the military dimension of expansion, and if they did not address the nuts and bolts of expanding the military alliance, the decision could not move from theory to practice. Slowly but surely Pentagon officials began to realize in September and October that the enlargement policy was not where they had understood it to be, and a series of public remarks followed by Holbrooke's first interagency meetings on NATO drove this home to them.

The Train Gathers Steam

On September 9, 1994, public remarks by both Vice President Al Gore and National Security Council staffer Vershbow jolted those who had been slow to realize the import of Clinton's Warsaw remarks. Addressing a conference in Berlin, Gore stated, "Everyone realizes that a military alliance, when faced with a fundamental change in the threat for which it was founded, either must define a convincing new rationale or become decrepit. Everyone knows that economic and political organizations tailored for a divided continent must now adapt to new circumstances—including acceptance of new members—or be exposed as mere bastions of privilege. . . . Beyond Partnership for Peace and NACC, several countries have already expressed a desire to become full members of the alliance. We will begin our discussions on this important question this fall."[68]

Holbrooke had provided much of the language for this speech. General Wesley Clark, who had succeeded General Barry McCaffrey as head of strategic plans and policy at the Joint Chiefs of Staff, recalls editing drafts three or four times to get the speech in line with where the Joint Chiefs saw the policy. He could not believe that it kept coming back stronger. Shalikashvili says that he too objected strenuously to the drafts that crossed his desk, because as he recalls, "it was too forward leaning on timing." Shalikashvili adds that Leon Fuerth, Gore's national security adviser, ignored his objections.[69]

Similarly, on September 8 Vershbow had also repeated the president's Warsaw language, stating that "the time has come for the NATO countries to begin to discuss among themselves the criteria and the timeline that may be associated with the expansion of the alliance."[70] One State Department official who opposed enlargement says that he complained to the National Security Council when he saw a memo circulating from Vershbow with this language in it. When Vershbow responded that he was simply repeating what the president had already said in Warsaw, this official then understood that the administration's stance was different than he had thought.[71]

Vershbow pushed the envelope during the September 8 interview in response to a question about whether NATO would enlarge before the year 2000. Stating publicly what the National Security Council troika had been writing privately in their "road map" paper, Vershbow remarked, "Well, I think that it would be a shame if NATO expansion were delayed as late as the very end of this century. I think that a more ambitious timetable is realistic. Without being precise, because this is something that has to be discussed within NATO, I can very well see the expansion of NATO occurring early in President Clinton's second term and perhaps, therefore, as many as four or five years before the enlargement of the European Union to the countries of Central and Eastern Europe takes place."[72]

Despite his own inclination toward expanding the alliance, Clinton understood the concerns about Russia's reaction. After all, his foreign policy had centered in large part on U.S. assistance for the Yeltsin government's reform program, and he did not want to undercut Yeltsin before the 1996 Russian presidential election. In late September Yeltsin came to Washington, and Clinton had a chance to tell him face to face that NATO was potentially open to all of Europe's new democracies, including Russia, and that it would not expand in a way that threatened Russia's interests. A major concern had been removed the month before, when Russian troops completed their withdrawal from the Baltics. According to several officials present, Clinton told Yeltsin over lunch at the White House that he had discussed NATO enlargement with key allied leaders, and he made sure Yeltsin understood that NATO would not announce any new members until after the Russian and American 1996 presidential elections. At the same time, Clinton wanted to ensure that any advances in the process that might take place in the meantime—during the NATO ministerials—would not surprise the Russian president.[73] Just as had many U.S. officials, Yeltsin may have recognized for the first time that America's expansion policy seemed to be shifting, and Russia's growing sense during the fall that the Partnership for Peace was not a substitute but a concrete path toward enlargement would lead to Yeltsin's harangue against NATO at the Conference on Security and Cooperation in Europe's Budapest summit in December 1994.

The Enforcer

With his statement in Warsaw and his conversation with Yeltsin in Washington, President Clinton had signaled his support for enlargement, even if he had not yet decided when it should occur. But few believed that enlargement was administration policy. And thus no one was acting to implement it, outside of the National Security Council troika's writing of a concept paper. A year earlier, one State Department official had said of the Clinton foreign policy team, "They make decisions and then they have absolutely no idea of how to get the bureaucracy to implement those decisions. . . . There is no enforcer."[74] With Richard Holbrooke's return to Washington in September 1994 as assistant secretary of state for European affairs, the president's NATO enlargement "policy" had an enforcer.

To make clear that he was in charge, Holbrooke held his first interagency meeting on NATO expansion at the State Department at the end of September, almost immediately after taking office. More than thirty officials came to the European Bureau's conference room, including three-star General Wesley Clark, Assistant Secretary of Defense Ashton Carter, Deputy Assistant Secretary of Defense Joseph Kruzel, National Security Council staffer Alexander Vershbow, Ambassador-at-Large for the New Independent States James Collins, and Stephen Flanagan from the policy planning staff. Holbrooke has recalled, "It emerged during the meeting that for many people at the Pentagon, the answer to the question when and how NATO would be expanded was 'never.'"[75]

Without having spoken to Lake or to the president, Holbrooke told the interagency group that there was a presidential policy to enlarge NATO that needed implementation. Holbrooke also made clear that Christopher had asked him to set up and run the mechanism to expand NATO.[76]

The new assistant secretary of state had a reputation for abrasiveness, and at this meeting, he demonstrated why. General Clark has recalled:

> Kruzel spoke first, since he was the policy guy, and said, "Why is this the policy? It's supposed to be an interagency process." Holbrooke crushed him like a bug. He said, "It is policy." Ash Carter walked out of the room. Then, as the meeting was about to conclude, I said, "I don't know that a decision has been made." Holbrooke said, "Anyone questioning this is disloyal to the country and to the president." My ears turned bright red . . . and I demanded that he take it back. The room stopped. I got ready to leave. Holbrooke took it back.[77]

The skeptics could not believe that Holbrooke was resting his whole case on remarks Clinton had made in Brussels, Prague, and Warsaw. As Carter recalls, "Why were these speeches so important?" To the Pentagon representatives, Clark was correctly disputing the history of the policy that Holbrooke was describing by waving these few sentences around in the air. Former secretary of defense Perry still refers to Holbrooke as having "presumed a decision had been made"; in Perry's view, Clinton had made no formal decision to that effect.[78]

After his dramatic outburst, Holbrooke, using, as Clark puts it, "problem solving 101," asked Clark to set up a meeting to brief this interagency group on what they would need to do to implement the policy. As a good military man, Clark could not say no. Through this request, Holbrooke enabled the Joint Chiefs of Staff to voice their concerns, but he would thus co-opt them into acting on this issue.[79]

At the Pentagon two weeks later, a team led by representatives from both the Office of the Secretary of Defense and the Joint Chiefs of Staff presented to the interagency group a briefing entitled "The Military Consequences of NATO expansion." As Holbrooke has remembered it, "Clark put this mountain of papers on the table and said, 'these are the NATO STANAGS [standardization agreements], and each country will have to meet all of them." The briefer from the Joint Chiefs, Colonel Steve Randolph, noted that there were 1,200 Atlantic Alliance standardization agreements, and while no country met all of them, the former Warsaw Pact armed forces had a long way to go to become compatible enough to work with NATO. Randolph also discussed issues of command structure, military doctrine, force structure, and infrastructure expansion. The Pentagon wanted to ensure that an enlargement of

NATO was not a hollow political gesture that weakened NATO's military effectiveness.[80]

Holbrooke, now playing "good cop," responded by saying that this briefing was exactly what the group needed, and he invited Pentagon officials to work with him to make the process a smooth one. Whereas some Pentagon officials sought to demonstrate with the briefing why it was impossible to move forward at that point, Holbrooke used it to lay out what steps were necessary to proceed. In fact, this briefing served as the basis for a briefing to the allies before the NATO foreign ministers meeting later in the year as well as for the NATO study on enlargement completed in September 1995.

But Bill Clinton's own secretary of defense could not believe a decision had been made. William Perry had been Les Aspin's deputy in October 1993, when the last meeting of the principals was held on this issue, and he was named to replace Aspin shortly after the president's January trip to Europe. Highly regarded, Perry had a distinguished career in academia, business, and government. Perry was known as a precise and thoughtful individual, perhaps reflecting his background in mathematics.[81]

Because he had no idea that enlargement had become presidential policy, Perry called for a meeting to clarify Clinton's intentions. On December 21, 1994, the president and his top foreign policy advisers gathered at the White House in the president's personal study. Perry argued for holding back and giving the Partnership for Peace another year to work before making a decision on enlargement. He wanted time to move forward on the NATO-Russia track and to convince Moscow that NATO did not threaten Russia's interests before the administration made a decision about proceeding with enlargement. As Perry and his assistant, Ashton Carter, have written, "While NATO could not declare itself closed to new members, we believed it was preferable to defer admission of new members from the former Warsaw Pact until Russia and other Eastern European nations had more opportunity to work with NATO. . . . The question was not whether NATO should expand, but when. We thought the question should be deferred until later in the decade."[82]

Shalikashvili recalls that he sided with Perry, but others argued that critics would say the United States had given Russia a veto. White House Chief of Staff Leon Panetta argued, "If you did Russia first, you would send a signal to the Central and Eastern Europeans that you are letting Russia call the play." But in Shalikashvili's view, the political costs in the short term for taking a Russia-first policy were well worth the long-term benefits of not re-creating a competitive division in Europe. Even as late as May 1995, when a reporter perceptively told him that he did not seem "in any great hurry to expand NATO," Shalikashvili responded, "I have argued that before we talk about an expansion we ought to have something like what I can modestly say I had some part in [originating], the Partnership for Peace, the development of a relationship between partners and the alliance that would bring them closer to us in a meaningful way, that would allow them to become more like us."[83]

Interestingly, Shalikashvili and Perry describe their recollection of the December meeting's outcome differently. Shalikashvili says, "That meeting was just about airing views; it was not a decision meeting." The former chairman of the Joint Chiefs remembers that only as the administration went forward with a two-track approach did he realize "that the administration had made a decision." Perry's recollection is that the president did clearly state that instead of the Perry policy, he endorsed the two-track plan that Lake and his staff, as well as the State Department, were now pushing within NATO—the plan that ultimately led to the May 1997 signing of the NATO-Russia Founding Act and the July 1997 NATO summit in Madrid inviting Poland, Hungary, and the Czech Republic to begin talks on accession to full NATO membership. Perry has written that Clinton and Gore "felt that right was on the side of the eastern European countries that wanted to enter NATO soon, that deferring expansion until later in the decade was not feasible, and that the Russians could be convinced that expansion was not directed against them."[84]

By the end of 1994 everyone in the administration finally understood that the president favored NATO's enlargement. But the president still had not answered two key questions: when would enlargement take place, and who would be invited to join? He did not answer the first until October 1996, and he did not decide the second until June 1997. To understand the logic behind that schedule requires us to turn our attention to the politics of enlargement.

CHAPTER FOUR

The Political Calendar

While politics played a secondary role in the 1993–94 administration deliberations that led to the NATO enlargement policy, they played a major role in determining how and when the United States and NATO would proceed. The looming 1996 Russian presidential election meant that, as President Clinton promised Boris Yeltsin in September 1994, NATO would not name names until after July 1996. But the 1996 American presidential election meant that "When" would be answered before November of that year, since otherwise Bill Clinton would get no political benefits from a policy he had been promoting for two years.

Politics was not just the "Polish vote." A second issue was leadership and the need for the Clinton administration to demonstrate that a Democratic president could conduct foreign and defense policy effectively. A third political issue—Russia—was the trickiest, forcing the administration into a delicate balancing act. As presidential adviser Dick Morris wrote after the 1996 election, "Russia became to the president's foreign policy what California was to his domestic political strategy: the one place he couldn't afford to lose."[1] But whereas the administration did not want to harm Russian reform or Yeltsin's reelection chances, the president also faced pressure not to be too soft on Russia. He could not be seen as caving to Russian threats, or Republicans would be swift to accuse him of being weak and of holding the central Europeans hostage to Moscow's interests. From the congressional elections of 1994 through the presidential elections of 1996, the administration had to navigate these crosscutting political currents of ethnic pressure, expectations of leadership, and the relationship with Russia.

The Congress

Part of Bill Clinton's political calculus was responding to demands from Congress. He did not want to let Republicans gain the upper hand with those communities in the United States that cared about the inclusion of central Europe in NATO. But just as a handful of individuals within the administration pushed NATO enlargement in 1994, also a handful of supporters of enlargement in Congress began to put together a legislative effort that was designed to prod the administration to move more quickly. In the House, Congressmen Benjamin Gilman (R-N.Y.) and Henry Hyde (R-Ill.) introduced legislation in the spring. In the Senate, the unlikely combination of liberal Paul Simon (D-Ill.) and conservative Hank Brown (R-Colo.) pushed for enlargement, as did Richard Lugar (R-Ind.) and William Roth (R-Del.). These efforts culminated in the inclusion of NATO enlargement as a plank in the Republican Contract with America in the fall 1994 congressional campaign and the passage of the NATO Participation Act a month later, which sought to provide assistance to specific countries to ready them for membership.

In Congress, supporters faced a challenge different from that of enlargement proponents within the administration. The legislative branch was not the setting of overwhelming opposition to the policy that existed in the executive branch, but rather was a setting, as one Senate staffer puts it, of "favorable indifference."[2] Outside of the few vocal supporters of enlargement, most members of Congress were largely ignorant of European security issues. They had generally positive thoughts about the alliance's role in the cold war, but in the electoral environment of 1992–94, there was absolutely no reason for the vast majority of congressional representatives and senators to spend much time on an issue about which few constituents cared.

By November 1994 a few vocal members of Congress were working toward the same ends as Lake and Holbrooke were inside the administration. Just as Holbrooke had been working in parallel but not in unison with Anthony Lake, however, key congressional enlargement supporters were working in parallel but not in unison with Holbrooke.

There was no administration support for congressional initiatives promoting funding for a first wave of countries to help them prepare specifically for membership, and this lack of support continued until after passage of the NATO Enlargement Facilitation Act in July 1996, which authorized the president to provide $60 million to help Poland, Hungary, and the Czech Republic make the leap to membership. Administration officials would claim that by naming names and declaring a timetable, the congressional legislation infringed on presidential prerogatives in foreign policy. But this lack of administration support (and in fact its vociferous opposition to the national security provisions of the Contract with America) fed congressional perceptions that President Clinton's statements of support for enlargement reflected no real commitment to the issue.

The effect of the initial legislation, the Contract with America, and the Republican takeover of Congress in the November 1994 elections should not be underestimated. A number of administration officials argue that Holbrooke effectively used this congressional pressure as another tool when discussing the need to move forward on a game plan for enlargement. The west Europeans, officials from central Europe, the Russians, and the ethnic communities in the United States all recognized that enlargement received a big push in the fall of 1994 within both the executive and legislative branches of the United States. This in turn would lead to the launching of NATO's study on enlargement in December 1994 and Boris Yeltsin's claim in Budapest shortly thereafter that the United States was plunging Europe into a "cold peace." Preventing the loss of the NATO enlargement issue to the Republicans, mollifying domestic and central European critics, and managing the allies and the Russians would mark the slow, but steady, Clinton administration efforts from October 1994 to October 1996.

The Congressional Legislation

In January 1994, just after the NATO summit, Stephen Rademaker, a Republican staffer on the House Foreign Affairs Committee, visited Brussels. Hearing the buzz about Partnership for Peace, Rademaker on his return suggested to his boss, Congressman Benjamin Gilman, the ranking Republican on the committee, that the partnership presented congressional Republicans with a real opportunity. It was either a brilliant program that might provide a path to membership, Rademaker told Gilman, or it was an unfortunate effort by the Clinton administration to set up a road block for the central Europeans. Given the Republican positions during the cold war regarding central Europe and NATO, Rademaker argued that Gilman should support the desire of the central and eastern Europeans to join the alliance. With a strong record of support for the captive nations during the cold war and a strong hostility toward Russia, Gilman, whose district included twenty-eight thousand Polish Americans, needed little persuading.[3]

On April 14 Congressman Gilman introduced HR 4210, the NATO Expansion Act of 1994, a bill providing a sense of Congress that Poland, Hungary, the Czech Republic, and Slovakia should enter NATO as full members by January 10, 1999 (the fifth anniversary of the NATO summit declaration on the Partnership for Peace) and authorizing the president to provide assistance to help them. The legislation was designed to respond to some of the criticism of Partnership for Peace, since it provided names, a timetable, and criteria for enlargement. Deferring to the privilege of the executive branch to conduct foreign policy, the president would be authorized, but not required, to provide assistance, including—for the first time in that region—military equipment. The act would also permit the president to assist other countries "emerging from communist domination" if he determined that they were on the track for NATO membership.[4] In a letter to his colleagues on April 22 (at about the same time Anthony Lake was asking his staff for an enlargement road map), Gilman wrote that "Partnership for Peace was a good start, but it is now time to go farther." The following month, Congressman Henry Hyde, whose Illinois district included a large number of Polish Americans, introduced the NATO Revitalization Act, calling for "benchmarks" and "a timetable for eventual membership for selected countries in transition." Hyde also named the Baltic countries in his legislation, urging that NATO include any nations that could meet the appropriate standards.[5]

Meanwhile, supporters in the Senate began to introduce their own legislation. On January 27, 1994, by the overwhelming margin of 94–3, the Senate had voted to support admission of countries that met the NATO standards, but this was viewed simply as backing for the president's comments in Europe. In the summer, several senators began ratcheting up the pressure to go beyond the Partnership for Peace. In June Senator Lugar said "PFP" stood for a "policy for postponement" and argued that NATO should not be hostage either to the EU or to Russia. Suggesting that the central Europeans should be on track to enter by 1998, Lugar declared, "The West must make plain to Russia that we are now discussing how to expand NATO, not whether to expand it. The best way to communicate that message is by agreeing on a schedule for associate and then full membership for the Visegrad states [Poland, Hungary, the Czech Republic, and Slovakia]."[6]

Several weeks later, Senators Brown and Simon introduced their version of the NATO Participation Act as an amendment to the Foreign Operations Appropriations Bill, and it passed handily on July 15, 1994, by an overwhelming margin. The act promoted the transfer of excess defense articles to Poland, Hungary, and the Czech Republic. But a lack of House support at the time meant that the Brown-Simon legislation was defeated in conference during the summer.[7]

Supporters kept the NATO Participation Act alive, and the administration fought to dilute it as much as possible. In a letter to House Foreign Affairs Committee Chairman Lee Hamilton (D-Ind.), dated September 8, State Department Assistant Secretary for Legislative Affairs Wendy Sherman wrote, "The bill [HR4210] is generally congruent with the Administration's view that NATO will expand. . . . We expect it will be some time before decisions on NATO expansion are taken." The administration was concerned, wrote Sherman, that the legislation benefited only four countries. She said that although the administration was delighted to have the authority to transfer defense articles to the region, it preferred that "references to particular states and specific timetables be deleted."[8]

The eventual passage of the NATO Participation Act came through the determined efforts of Senator Hank Brown. Brown, motivated largely by cold war beliefs that NATO should secure its victory over the Soviet Union by incorporating into the West those countries dominated for decades by Moscow, stymied two key pieces of legislation in September to promote his cause. After the House passed its Narcotics Technical Corrections Act and its State Department Technical Corrections Bill, Brown, exercising a senator's prerogatives, held them up in order to push two amendments, one being on Taiwan and the other being the NATO Participation Act. What emerged by early October was an amalgam of the Hyde, Gilman, and Brown-Simon efforts, and on October 7 and 8 the NATO Participation Act passed the House and Senate as Title II of the International Narcotics Control Corrections

Act of 1994. Becoming law on November 4 of that year, the act stated, "The United States, other NATO member nations, and NATO itself should furnish appropriate assistance to facilitate the transition to full NATO membership at an early date of full and active participants in the Partnership for Peace. . . . The President may establish a program to assist the transition to full NATO membership of Poland, Hungary, the Czech Republic, Slovakia and other Partnership for Peace countries emerging from communist domination."[9]

The Contract with America

In September 1994, 367 Republican members of Congress and congressional challengers stood on the steps of the Capitol and unveiled their ten-point Contract with America. The contract, emphasizing a conservative domestic agenda, had only one plank that referred to foreign policy. Included were three core Republican initiatives: constraints on multilateral peacekeeping efforts, ballistic missile defense, and NATO enlargement.[10]

Earlier in the summer of 1994, Congressman Richard Armey (R-Tex.) had put out the word among Republicans on Capitol Hill that he was developing the contract and was looking for politically popular legislation that was languishing. Hyde's and Gilman's staffs worked to put their earlier resolutions together into one package. Taking some of the policy language from Hyde's bill and the military equipment assistance sections from Gilman's, their staffs created the NATO enlargement legislation of the National Security Revitalization Act. Although drafts of the legislation had included the January 1999 date for entry proposed by Gilman in April 1994, the final version presented to the House early in 1995 merely read that Poland, Hungary, the Czech Republic, and Slovakia, if they stayed on track, "should be in a position to further the principles of the North Atlantic Treaty and to contribute to the security of the North Atlantic area in the near future, and, in accordance with Article 10 of such Treaty, should be invited to become full NATO members."[11]

Even this watered down version was too much for the administration, which engaged in a frontal assault on the legislation. In a *New York Times* op-ed in February 1995, Secretary of State Warren Christopher and Secretary of Defense William Perry wrote of the National Security Revitalization Act:

> The bill unilaterally and prematurely designates certain European states for NATO membership. NATO should and will expand. NATO expansion will strengthen stability in Europe for members and nonmembers alike. But new members must be ready to undertake the obligations of membership, just as we and our allies must be ready to extend our solemn commitments to them. Our present steady and deliberate approach to NATO expansion is intended to insure that each potential member is judged individually, according to its capacity to contribute to NATO's goals. That approach gives every new European democracy a strong incentive to consolidate reform. But if we arbitrarily lock in advantages now for some countries, we risk discouraging reformers in countries not named and fostering complacency in countries that are. Indeed, the effect of the measure before Congress could be instability in the very region whose security we seek to bolster. . . . In its present form, the bill unwisely and unconstitutionally deprives the President of the flexibility he needs to make the right choices for our nation's security.[12]

With Republicans looking for opportunities to stake out positions distinguishing themselves from the Clinton White House, on February 16 the House passed the NATO Expansion Act of 1995 by a vote of 241–181. Only four Republicans voted against the legislation. The language did not just authorize President Clinton to establish a transition program; it directed him to make Poland, Hungary, the Czech Republic, and Slovakia immediately eligible for assistance.

Despite the obvious reluctance to name names until after Yeltsin's 1996 election, the administration's response to enlargement supporters in Congress was curious. Lake supported a fast track. So did Holbrooke. Each sought to build on President Clinton's July 1994 Warsaw remarks about the need for criteria and a timetable. And yet neither did anything to reach out to enlargement supporters in Congress. Nor did their staffs. The lack of consideration for bridge building with legislators, so apparent in the memoranda prepared for the president before his 1994 trip, continued into 1995. It was reinforced by the continued misgivings regarding enlargement within the bureaucracy. Once the Democrats had taken a beating in the November 1994 congressional elections, the administration gave up any thought of working with Republicans on Capitol Hill to push an issue that the president claimed to support. And the Republicans were not making efforts of their own to reach out to the White House since they believed the elections gave them a mandate. This lack of consultation between the two branches of government would continue for another two years.[13]

Budapest and Beyond

If the administration was not moving fast enough or explicitly enough for Republicans on Capitol Hill, it was moving too fast for the Europeans and for the Russians. In Brussels for the North Atlantic Council ministerial, Holbrooke gave a background briefing for the press on December 1 in which he described the process of the previous two months: "In October of this year, the United States government got its act together. [The] Pentagon, NSC [National Security Council], State Department, all came together and came up with a clear, single position. . . . The U.S. position was formulated in October and then in late October and early November, we sent teams to Europe, joint State/Defense teams, to brief the British, French, Germans, the Dutch . . . and the Russians, and other interested parties." Christopher and Perry, he said, talked to their counterparts (although, as we know, Perry did not yet believe until later in December that the two-track approach was policy), and the president "personally was involved in at least three discussions of this with foreign leaders in the last month or two. . . . A year ago roughly, our position was you don't move forward on NATO because you might destabilize the former Soviet Union. And you don't move forward on the CSCE [Conference on Security and Cooperation in Europe] because that was an old Brezhnev left-over. . . . We flipped the process in the last few months. We are going to move forward on both."[14]

But there remained resistance both inside and outside the administration to the process that Holbrooke was leading. The September 8 remarks by National Security Council staffer Alexander Vershbow that membership early in the second term was conceivable may have reflected the National Security Council position, but others did not share this view. A senior administration official, asked about the Vershbow remarks at a press briefing on November 30, stated, "The person who spoke about 1997 was a little optimistic in how we were thinking about it. Indeed, it's, in our view, a more gradual process that begins with the kinds of discussions that I described earlier, which is for the partners to understand what it means to be a member of NATO. . . . In discussions that occurred between President Clinton and President Yeltsin in September, on this very point, they concluded that a reasonable path through this is, as the process begins, in that no one will be excluded. It will also be a transparent process—that is, there will be no surprises."[15]

The Europeans were not happy either about the push from Washington. According to one report, the German representative to NATO, Hermann von Richthofen, sent a telegram to the Foreign Ministry in Bonn earlier in November, complaining that "Washington was riding roughshod over its allies, negotiating terms of possible membership with the Eastern Europeans and presenting NATO with accomplished facts instead of consulting with them." Von Richthofen said publicly, regarding unilateral U.S. policies, "There was abandonment at short notice, without any consultation, of the 'Russia First' concept." And European Commission president Jacques Delors called these American efforts "premature and ill-timed."[16]

The Bear Roars Back

Seeking a chance to enhance the Conference on Security and Cooperation in Europe, the Russians hoped in the fall that a summit in Budapest would steer the security debate away from NATO and toward this other security institution in which they participated fully as a member equal to the other major powers. But the American push on enlargement in the second half of 1994 had shattered this hope. The Russian leadership believed during its discussions with the Americans in October 1993 and January 1994 that the Partnership for Peace had delayed consideration of NATO enlargement. Russian Foreign Minister Andrei Kozyrev reportedly told a group of Russian ambassadors in the spring of 1994, "The greatest achievement of Russian foreign policy in 1993 was to prevent NATO's expansion eastward to our borders."[17] Now the Russians were dismayed by the activities following President Clinton's summer 1994 trip to Warsaw and Berlin. Although the president had informed Yeltsin in September of his intentions to move ahead gradually and transparently, the administration's enlargement push in the fall of 1994 was too much for them to handle. Once the American briefings of allies in November produced a decision to move forward with a NATO study of the "how and why" of enlargement, the Russians in December 1994 abandoned their plans to sign their Partnership for Peace work program document.

President Clinton and his team were completely surprised by the Russian reaction in December. Part of the problem may have been the general overreliance in the relationship on one channel between the two governments, that between Deputy Secretary of State Talbott and his counterpart, Russian deputy foreign minister Georgi Mamedov. Furthermore, one senior State Department official says that the only time he saw Talbott disengage from Russia policy was between the September 1994 summit with Yeltsin and the December 1994 meeting in Budapest. Apparently Mamedov said nothing to foreshadow what was coming. But the Russian behavior in December had results: if the U.S. efforts after July had focused on getting enlargement moving forward, the period between December 1994 and May 1995 was devoted to repairing the damage with Russia.

As Secretary of State Christopher prepared for his NATO foreign ministers meeting on December 1, his team's main objective was dispelling notions that Bosnia was ripping the alliance apart and preventing success in other areas. At his briefing in Brussels, Holbrooke declared, "I understand completely why the press has been filled in the last week with stories saying Bosnia is wrecking NATO. But it is just not so. Bosnia is wrecking Bosnia. . . . We are not ignoring Bosnia. We are just trying to stress that while Bosnia is burning, we're still working on the larger structural issues which should prevent future Bosnias."[18] But who could have confidence in NATO's ability to deal with future crises if it could do nothing about the one it faced?

Christopher gamely attempted to promote the line that Bosnia did not diminish the enlargement initiative. In his opening statement to his fellow NATO foreign ministers, he stated, "The crisis in Bosnia is about Bosnia and the former Yugoslavia; it does not diminish NATO's enduring importance." And in the final communique of those sessions, the foreign ministers announced, "We have decided to initiate a process of examination inside the Alliance to determine how NATO will enlarge, the principles to guide this process and the implications of membership." Their goal was to complete this study before the end of the following year. The ministers made explicit that the study would not name names or declare a timetable.[19]

But Christopher and his fellow allied ministers had also believed that they had come to Brussels to witness Russian Foreign Minister Andrei

Kozyrev sign both his country's Partnership for Peace program document and one to establish a special dialogue between NATO and Russia. Holbrooke at his briefing had challenged those who claimed Russia had a problem with NATO: "Kozyrev is coming here today not to attack us, but to sign two agreements with us."[20] Christopher in his opening statement to the NATO foreign ministers echoed these remarks: "We welcome the agreement we will sign tonight on the NATO-Russia Individual Partnership Program."[21] But it was not to be. Kozyrev did attack NATO for forging ahead with enlargement, and he refused to sign.[22] Asked later in an interview if he had been surprised by Kozyrev's behavior, Christopher replied simply, "Yes, of course I was surprised."[23]

It is hard to believe after these events that President Clinton would be surprised by similar behavior from Boris Yeltsin at the Conference on Security and Cooperation in Europe summit in Budapest, but according to a number of his top aides, he was. The White House schedulers had compounded the president's problems by leaving him no time to meet with President Yeltsin bilaterally during the day. The White House opposition to presidential foreign travel that had made scheduling the January 1994 trip to Europe so difficult increased dramatically after the November 1994 election. The pull between domestic advisers who wanted him to attend to business at home and not go at all and foreign policy advisers who believed that his presence at the Budapest summit was important contributed to the disaster that awaited. The president's schedulers set up a reception for congressional leaders that evening, leaving their boss only seven hours for his Budapest summit visit.[24]

Clinton was careful to set the parameters of what NATO was doing in order not to provoke Russia. At a news conference in Washington with Ukrainian president Leonid Kuchma on November 22, he had remarked, "I believe we will have discussions in Budapest about how we might go about expanding NATO but not about when and which particular countries would be let in; I think that is premature."[25] Despite Clinton's efforts to circumscribe NATO's way forward, Yeltsin came to Budapest prepared to deliver a blistering attack. He signaled his intentions in remarks in Moscow as he boarded his plane for the trip: "Russia is against the North Atlantic Alliance expanding the sphere of its influence to the east, since NATO's boundaries will then approach the borders of the Russian Federation. . . . The two blocs we have left behind us would reappear in Europe and this would certainly not benefit European security."[26]

Although Yeltsin had stated his position, the president's team either did not listen or did not receive these pretrip remarks. In Budapest, President Clinton reminded his audience that enlargement was going forward regardless of opposition from Moscow: "We must not allow the Iron Curtain to be replaced by a veil of indifference. We must not consign new democracies to a gray zone. . . . NATO will not automatically exclude any nation from joining. At the same time, no country outside will be allowed to veto expansion. As NATO does expand, so will security for all European states, for it is not an aggressive but a defensive organization. NATO's new members—old members and nonmembers alike—will be more secure."[27] Yeltsin's response shocked those in attendance: "Europe, even before it has managed to shrug off the legacy of the Cold War, is risking encumbering itself with a cold peace."[28]

This dramatic outburst and a follow-on trip to Moscow by Vice President Al Gore, Secretary of Defense William Perry, and Deputy Secretary of State Strobe Talbott led to Perry's concern that NATO was unnecessarily upsetting Russia, since he still did not realize where the policy stood. He writes that he told Gore and Talbott that the "NATO communique was making policy—and unnecessary waves—when the president had not yet made a final decision on NATO expansion." On his return, he had the December 21 meeting at the White House that finally clarified for him that the Clinton administration, not the NATO bureaucracy, was pushing NATO enlargement.[29]

The Politics of Russia

According to Nicholas Burns, President Clinton's National Security Council Russia expert at the time, the president fumed at his staff on the trip home from Budapest.[30] Just as his secretary of state had reacted to Kozyrev's behavior, President Clinton was angry that he had no warning of Yeltsin's remarks. Yeltsin's attack at Budapest, followed by the Russian assault on Chechnya that month, and the growing problem created by Moscow's plans to complete a nuclear reactor deal with Iran put the administration in a difficult spot. While the president did not want the U.S.-Russian relationship to deteriorate, he came under assault from the Republicans for not confronting Yeltsin on issues like Chechnya and Iran.

If administration officials had given any thought to working with Republicans in the fall on fashioning an enlargement strategy (and according to numerous interviews, they had not), they certainly did not after Budapest. And despite the increasing Republican criticism, between December 1994 and May 1995, the administration worked not to get new members ready but to mend relations with Russia and get Moscow's agreement to participate fully in the Partnership for Peace.

Talbott may have become disengaged in the fall, but he reentered the picture with a vengeance early in 1995. Because of the bureaucratic divides at the National Security Council, the State Department, and the Pentagon, there was no individual at the assistant secretary level whose portfolio included both Europe and Russia. Controlling both the enlargement and the NATO-Russia tracks was bureaucratically possible in the Clinton administration only at a level above that of assistant secretary, and Deputy Secretary Talbott began in early 1995 to take the reins of the enlargement policy to put the two halves of the policy together.[31] With Holbrooke becoming more focused on the administration's problems in Bosnia, Talbott ensured that the Russia track came back in parallel with enlargement. Thus Talbott, the chief opponent of concrete steps on enlargement at the January 1994 summit, became the implementer of the two-track policy beginning in the spring of 1995.

The administration would spend the winter and spring trying to get the Russians back to their pre-Budapest position, an approach that succeeded by June, when Kozyrev finally signed the Partnership for Peace documents that he was expected to sign six months earlier. The Russian accommodation came after a series of intensive consultations between Talbott and Russian deputy foreign minister Mamedov. Essential to the successful conclusion of these discussions was the decision by President Clinton to travel to Moscow for the fiftieth anniversary celebrations of V-E day in May 1995. This decision, taken despite harsh criticism from Republicans that the president's visit was an endorsement of Russian policies in Chechnya and Iran, enabled the United States to get the Russia track back on line before the release of the NATO study on "how and why" in September 1995, which would in turn give enlargement another push forward.

NATO-Russia

By January 1995 many of the elements that would emerge later in the 1997 NATO-Russia Founding Act were already in play in administration deliberations. Some of the Russia experts inside the government had raised questions in the fall about whether a separate agreement between NATO and Russia would foreclose the possibility of Russian membership in NATO, but they had decided in the end that this should not be an issue. There was consensus that Russia would not gain a role in the NATO decisionmaking process in any NATO-Russia accord, nor would the United States engage with Russia on the issue of nuclear weapons stationing.[32]

According to press reports, Talbott put forward two ideas to Russian deputy foreign minister Mamedov in mid-January. One was a formal NATO-Russia accord that would fall short of being a treaty, so that Western parliaments and the Russian Duma would not need to ratify the arrangement. Second was the idea of a NATO-Russia standing commission that would have defined responsibilities but would not give Russia a "direct say" in NATO decisionmaking. As a senior official said at the time, "We fully understand that by the time NATO acquires a 17th member, there must be an agreed definition (of its relationship with Russia)."[33]

The following month, Mamedov reportedly responded to Talbott that Russia could accept NATO's expansion if two conditions were met: no nuclear weapons deployed on the territory of the new members, and no stationing of NATO troops on new members' territory either (conditions similar to those that the Soviet Union sought for the territory of the former East Germany during the 1990 talks on German unification). In response to Mamedov's implicit position that under certain conditions Russia could accept expansion, Yeltsin accused his foreign ministry of "gross blunders." Yeltsin's position had remained unchanged—no to enlargement—and he was not about to alter it before his 1996 election bid. Furthermore, as the Russian journalist who reported the story noted, since NATO was unlikely to deploy nuclear weapons or station troops on the territory of new members in the current benign environment in Europe, Mamedov's proposals did not require concessions by the West.[34]

While these talks in early 1995 laid a basis for future discussions, Russia could make no further moves on this front until after Yeltsin's reelection. Signs of Russian accommodation to enlargement would not play well with the Moscow political elite, and Russian engagement on the NATO-Russia track would not begin in earnest again until December 1996, when Yeltsin reemerged from his lengthy postelection illness. Yeltsin did agree at the May 1995 summit, however, to the U.S. request that Russia signal its willingness to move forward on participation in the Partnership for Peace.

The May 1995 Summit

In February Yeltsin had invited President Clinton to Moscow for the May V-E day celebration. The president faced tremendous pressure not to go. The Russian invasion of Chechnya in December 1994 had turned far more brutal than officials in Washington had imagined, and the initial decision to treat the invasion as a legitimate effort to preserve the territorial integrity of the Russian Federation would haunt the Clinton administration for some time. In January reports emerged that Russia was seeking to conclude its nuclear reactor deal in Bushehr, Iran. And there was always the concern about Yeltsin's behavior. As Chief of Staff Leon Panetta recalls, "The ups and downs with Yeltsin always played into [calculations about a meeting]. We never knew what he would hit us on."[35] After the reception accorded the president in Budapest, White House officials had to be even more concerned about how the president would be treated in Moscow.

President Clinton was playing a difficult balancing game in 1995: assuring the ethnic communities that NATO enlargement was moving forward and that Russia had no veto, but also assuring Yeltsin that he was moving slowly and transparently. In mid-January, Clinton had traveled to Cleveland, where he gave an impassioned defense of his enlargement policy in front of leaders from the central and eastern European ethnic community: "Now, in the aftermath of [the cold war] victory, it is our common responsibility not to squander the peace. We must realize the full potential of that victory. Now that freedom has been won, all of our people deserve to reap the tangible rewards of their sacrifice—people in the United States, and people in Central Europe. . . . We have taken the lead in preparing for the gradual, open, and inevitable expansion of NATO." But the president reiterated that he could not name names or lay out a timetable yet, and he called for "close, strong ties" between NATO and Russia "in parallel with expansion."[36]

Between March and May 1995, Clinton reportedly wrote Yeltsin a series of letters assuring the Russian president that NATO was not anti-Russian and explicitly mentioning that future Russian membership in NATO was possible.[37] He also agreed to go to Moscow for the summit.[38] This decision unleashed a firestorm of protest from Republicans on Capitol Hill. Senate Foreign Relations Committee Chairman Jesse Helms argued that this was "the latest in a series of ill-advised foreign policy actions . . . that will be perceived as an implicit show of support for the policies of the Russian government." Senator Mitch McConnell (R-Ky.) added that, given recent Russian activities, this decision sent "precisely the wrong message at precisely the wrong time."[39]

Given the seriousness of the politics of the Moscow visit, Clinton's public opinion guru, Dick Morris, took a poll before the trip to gauge public reaction on a variety of issues regarding U.S.-Russian relations. Morris says that the one and only NATO enlargement question he asked in a poll during his service for the president was included at the end of this survey. Interestingly, he asked respondents if they favored delaying NATO enlargement in exchange for Russia's agreement to kill its reactor deal with Iran. It is difficult to imagine that the public was informed on either issue, but Morris says the answer was a clear no.[40]

Just before the trip, Czech prime minister Vaclav Klaus met with Clinton and, according to a U.S. official, asked, "I want to know only one thing. Are you going to Moscow and allowing Yeltsin to slow up this procedure." Clinton responded, "No." Yeltsin asked the president three times during Clinton's Moscow visit to delay enlargement until after the year 2000, and each time the president turned him down. The U.S. team had anticipated the request, and they sought to ensure that Russia understood the American approach: enlargement was irreversible, but the United States would not humiliate Moscow in the process. The two tracks, administration officials argued, were to be "not linked, but parallel."[41]

At the summit Clinton and Yeltsin agreed to disagree on enlargement. At their joint press conference, Yeltsin stated, "We exchanged views on NATO issues. Today we better understand the interests and concerns of each other, and yet we still don't have answers to a number of questions—our positions even remain unchanged." Clinton added, however, "First of all, with regard to European security, while there was not an agreement between us on the details on the question of the expansion of NATO, Russia did agree to enter into the Partnership for

Peace. And I committed myself in return at the meeting at the end of this month to encourage the beginning of the NATO-Russia dialogue, which I think is very important. There must be a special relationship between NATO and Russia."[42]

From Clinton's standpoint, the summit was a success, especially given the previous meeting between the two presidents in Budapest. As Christopher recollects, "Yeltsin [at Budapest] was convinced that NATO was going pell-mell. We needed the president to go back to him to remind him of the gradual pace, and the president did persuade Yeltsin at the May 1995 summit that Russia should join the Partnership for Peace."[43]

In Moscow Clinton reiterated the need for enlargement to enhance the security of all countries in the region, and he offered to support the Russian position on amending the 1990 Conventional Forces in Europe Treaty to accommodate Russian concerns arising in the post-Soviet security environment. The summit had been a difficult one (the joint statement on European security was not agreed to until the night before departure), but it served its political and policy purpose for President Clinton as he steered his course between not humiliating and not appeasing Moscow. Clinton had beat back Yeltsin's requests for a significant delay on enlargement, but the United States was still being clear that it would not proceed with a timetable until after Yeltsin's coming election.[44] Within those constraints, the United States had to respond to continued domestic criticism that it was not moving forward quickly enough on enlargement, and attention turned again to that track.

NATO's Enlargement Study

The major sign that enlargement was moving forward again was the August 1995 publication in the *New York Review of Books* of Strobe Talbott's article "Why NATO Should Grow." Many people inside and outside the government saw this piece as Talbott's public expression of his conversion on enlargement. Talbott's opposition to concrete steps had shaped the policy in 1993–94, and his general concern about Russia led him to reassert control over the two-track policy in the spring of 1995. With the Moscow summit out of the way and Russia's accession to the Partnership for Peace in June, Talbott stated publicly that he was firmly behind the president's policy on enlargement. Laying out all the various rationales for NATO's foray east, Talbott signaled to his colleagues, to the allies, and to the Russians that the U.S. deputy secretary of state, the administration's point man on Russia, was no longer hesitant about proceeding.[45]

Talbott argued both for idealism and realism. Enlargement could provide the carrot to countries making the transition away from communism, and it could "extend the area in which conflicts like the one in the Balkans simply do not happen." But Talbott was tougher on Russia than many expected, making clear that NATO was ready as a hedge if things turned sour in Russia: "First, NATO is and will remain for the foreseeable future, including when it takes in new members, a military alliance and a collective defense pact; Second, among the contingencies for which NATO must be prepared is that Russia will abandon democracy and return to the threatening patterns of international behavior that have sometimes characterized its history, particularly during the Soviet period."[46]

Talbott, in control of Europe's post–cold war security architecture at the State Department, articulated in this piece the "why" of enlargement, a year and a half after the president first announced that NATO's expansion was only a matter of time. Normally, one might expect the rationale for a policy to be worked out before its announcement. And had this policy evolved along a formal decision path, that might have been the case. But it had not. No one seemed to have any hesitation to deliver speeches in 1994 and 1995 talking about the need to develop the rationale of a policy they claimed the president had enunciated in January 1994. Even the president, trying to make sure Yeltsin was comfortable with the pace, had announced at the May 1995 summit, "This whole year, 1995, was to be devoted for the rationale for expanding NATO and then determining how it might be done, with no consideration whatever of who would be in the included membership and when that would be done."[47] No longer was the central issue for the administration "when" NATO would enlarge (after all, if one was not prepared to answer the question, it was better not to raise it); now the issue was "how and why." Talbott now laid out the rationale: freezing the 1945 line in Europe was untenable; NATO could help consolidate reform and prevent future Bosnias; and it could defend its members if Russia reemerged as a threat.

Earlier in the year Secretary of Defense Perry had developed what became known as the "Perry Principles," the criteria by which NATO would judge the new members eligible: they had to make commitments to democracy and markets, to the sovereignty of others, to NATO's consensus decisionmaking, to developing interoperability in doctrine and equipment, and to the defense of the other allies. In September NATO released its enlargement study, building on the Perry Principles (and another study by Asmus, Kugler, and Larrabee at RAND) to lay out a set of criteria for new members to meet.[48]

The NATO enlargement study of September 1995 sent powerful signals both to the aspirants and to the Russians. To the aspirants, the study said that members would be judged on a case-by-case basis. While all members would be expected to observe the principles enshrined in the Washington Treaty of 1949, the study declared that "there is no fixed or rigid list of criteria for inviting new member states to join the Alliance."[49] This gave NATO an escape hatch if it wanted to delay accession to those aspirants who might meet all the criteria on a fixed list (for example, the Baltic nations of Lithuania, Latvia, and Estonia), and it also left ambiguous whether Russia might someday become a member. But to the Russians the study said the following: first, no country would have a veto; second, the alliance did not need to station troops on the territory of new members, but if it needed to, it would; third, new members would not be second-class citizens—they would have the full NATO security guarantee, including the nuclear umbrella.[50]

The study's discussion of new member requirements differed fundamentally from the Pentagon's approach back in 1994. In the October 1994 briefing for Holbrooke, Pentagon officials articulated the difficulty of enlargement given the need for new members to fulfill many of the NATO standardization agreements if they were going to enhance the overall security of the alliance. And they had argued in 1994 for putting the Partnership for Peace front and center to give aspirants a chance to develop the means necessary to become net contributors to the alliance's military capabilities. But the NATO study represented the victory of those who did not want to wait. Recognizing that the obstacles to readiness before accession were significant, the study scaled back expectations: "An important element in new members' military contribution will be a commitment in good faith to pursue the objectives of standardization which are essential to Alliance strategy and operational effectiveness. . . . There are at present over 1200 agreements and publications that new members should undertake to comply with. Compliance should be an evolutionary and controlled process to enhance Alliance operational effectiveness."[51]

The Importance of Dayton

NATO released its study as Richard Holbrooke's team was beginning its intensive efforts to find a solution to the war in Bosnia. The U.S. success in concluding the accords signed in Dayton, Ohio, later that fall gave U.S. and NATO officials more confidence to speak about the role of NATO enlargement in preventing future conflicts. Had the war continued to rage, it is difficult to imagine that the United States could have maintained alliance support for the inclusion of new members. Too many questions regarding NATO's relevance would have arisen, questions that largely disappeared when the NATO-led implementation force ended the Bosnian war.[52]

The Bosnian implementation force did not just prove that NATO could actually stop conflicts in Europe. It also demonstrated that NATO and Russia could work together. Putting together the agreement on Russian participation in the NATO force was not easy, and that such an agreement was reached was a result of the single-minded efforts of Secretary of Defense William Perry, with assistance from Assistant Secretary of Defense Ashton Carter and Deputy Secretary of State Strobe Talbott. Most officials working on Bosnia policy did not initially favor Perry's goal of including Russia. They believed that since the Russians were not militarily necessary and since they might be more trouble than they were worth, it was unnecessary, and perhaps counterproductive, to include them.[53] Perry and Carter argued forcefully that Russia had to be involved. As they have written, "We believed [those unsupportive of including Russia] were not seeing the forest for the trees; they failed to recognize that Russia was an indispensable part of the larger European security order of which the Bosnian peace was supposed to be a part."[54]

But Yeltsin in September 1995 had expressed disapproval of U.S. actions in Bosnia and once again had railed against NATO enlargement: "Why don't the Europeans themselves resolve this problem? That's why I am against NATO's enlargement. This is the first sign of what can happen. The first sign. When NATO approaches the borders of the Russian Federation, you can say that there will be two military blocs. This will be the restoration of what we have already had. . . . In that case, we will immediately establish constructive ties with all ex-Soviet republics and form a bloc."[55] Given Yeltsin's frame of mind, how could the United States get him to cooperate with a NATO-led military effort?

Clinton and Yeltsin met again at Hyde Park, New York, in October 1995. The location had been suggested by President Clinton's Russia advisers to evoke the spirit of Franklin Roosevelt's wartime cooperation with the Soviet Union. The administration was looking for any leverage to gain a favorable Russian response to participation in the Bosnian implementation force. Perry had already met once earlier in the month with his Russian counterpart, Defense Minister Pavel Grachev, in Geneva. The meeting had not gone well. Grachev had said to Perry, "You've got me by the neck. Either we are out of this or only in through NATO."[56]

At Hyde Park Yeltsin complained that the domestic political logic on each side was pushing in opposite directions. Clinton, he argued, needed to push NATO expansion forward as part of his coming electoral campaign. Meanwhile, Yeltsin argued, this effort would kill his own reelection.[57]

Despite his public rhetoric before the Hyde Park meeting, Yeltsin in New York agreed in principle to Russian participation in the implementation force, and the presidents left the details to their defense ministers. Perry then flew Grachev out to Fort Riley, Kansas, to witness a troop exercise and the exploding of an ICBM silo. On the flight back to Andrews Air Force Base in Washington, Perry indicated U.S. willingness to show flexibility on Russia's demands on adapting the Conventional Forces in Europe Treaty, which had been signed when the Soviet Union still existed.

At two subsequent sessions in Brussels, Perry and Grachev finalized the details and emerged with a plan by which the United States and NATO would retain command over all combat forces, but the Russians could say they were serving "with, but not under" NATO.[58] According to Holbrooke, Talbott remarked that "the Russians were unbelievably sanguine about being under American command in Bosnia, but NATO was still a four-letter word in Moscow."[59] For Perry, these sessions with Grachev were central to the future NATO-Russia relationship. He saw Christopher getting nowhere on a NATO-Russia charter; it was, Perry recalls, "an academic discussion with no practical nature." Serving together to implement the peace in Bosnia would show what could be done in practice and lead to a concrete NATO-Russia relationship.[60]

Time to Move Forward

In the fall of 1995 President Clinton signaled that NATO was ready to move ahead. In a speech in Washington at a dinner named for President Truman, he declared, "The end of the Cold War cannot mean the end of NATO, and it cannot mean a NATO frozen in the past, because there is no other cornerstone for an integrated, secure, and stable Europe for the future. . . . NATO has completed a study of how it should bring on new members. . . . [W]e have to move to the next phase in a steady, careful way, to consider who the new members should be and when they would be invited to join the alliance."[61]

Concluding the Dayton accords was central to embarking on the next phase. Had the U.S. efforts in Bosnia failed, NATO would have faced constant criticism such as that from *Washington Post* columnist Jim Hoagland the year before: "The visible gap between the alliance's rhetoric about unity and purpose, and its ability to act in a real crisis outside its original purpose of territorial self-defense, is growing."[62] U.S. officials clearly believed Dayton was critical as well. Holbrooke remarks in his book, "After Dayton, American foreign policy seemed more assertive, more muscular. This may have been as much perception as reality, but the perception mattered. The three main pillars of American foreign policy in Europe—U.S.-Russian relations, NATO enlargement into Central Europe, and Bosnia—had often worked against each other. Now they reinforced each other."[63] Christopher recalls, "As long as Bosnia was unresolved, it was a cloud that hung over our heads. It was more psychological than logical. But if NATO could not find a solution for Bosnia, then why think about enlarging it? Did NATO have a mission worth enlarging for if it could not solve Bosnia?"[64]

The ethnic community in the United States also took advantage of Dayton. Meeting with Holbrooke to get briefed on the accords, the Central and Eastern European Coalition, representing American ethnic groups, agreed to help sell Dayton on Capitol Hill. They believed that such assistance could help produce a favorable American response in 1996 to their own desires for an enlargement timetable, and Holbrooke apparently told one member of the coalition that Hungary's efforts in support of the Bosnia implementation force would have "a profound effect" on its chances for NATO membership. The ethnic community also kept the administration on an even keel after the victory of former communist Aleksander Kwasniewski over Lech Walesa in the November 19, 1995, presidential balloting in Poland. Lake; his staff director, Nancy Soderberg; and other officials quickly called a meeting with leading figures in the Polish American Congress to ask if they still supported Polish entry in NATO after the communist victory. Their response was emphatic: the election showed Polish democracy in action, and that democracy's future rested heavily on inclusion in the West. When Walesa himself emphasized this message personally to President Clinton several months later, he ensured that the United States remained steady on enlargement.[65]

On the congressional front, 1995 had been relatively quiet. The House in February had passed HR 7, the National Security Revitalization Act, the legislation that grew out of the foreign policy plank of the Contract with America, but the Senate had let it languish. While the Senate NATO Participation Act amendments pushed by Senator Hank Brown initially called for observer status in NATO's highest decision-making body—the North Atlantic Council—for those who became eligible for transition assistance, administration opposition led to this provision being dropped during the summer.[66] On September 21, 1995, the Brown amendments to the Foreign Operations Appropriations Act, HR 1868, were adopted by voice vote, but not much progress had been made by the Senate since November 1994. The 1995 act merely stated, "The provision of NATO transition assistance should include those countries most ready for closer ties with NATO . . . and should be designed to assist other countries meeting specified criteria of eligibility to move forward toward eventual NATO membership." An earlier draft naming Poland, Hungary, and the Czech Republic in the first group and Lithuania, Latvia, Estonia, Ukraine, Romania, Bulgaria, and Slovenia in the second, had been withdrawn.[67]

The tension continued between those who wanted to reward the countries making the greatest effort to join the West on the one hand and those concerned about inclusion and not drawing new lines on the other. Republicans in Congress were more eager to push the former, while the administration was on the whole still oriented toward the latter, at least in the demonstrated concern for Russia. But whereas the political pressure was not great in early 1995, by the end of the year it was becoming significant. Signaling the importance the issue would receive in 1996, the Polish American Congress sent a letter to members of Congress on October 5, 1995, accusing the State Department of an "all-out effort" to "kill" the original NATO Participation Act and complaining that by October 1995, the bill had failed to name names. The letter called the NATO study "purely theoretical with no practical significance to the countries." It continued, "Contrary to the State Department's claims, countries which are not designated in the first stage of expansion will not be discouraged by the gradual but specific progress of NATO expansion. They will be discouraged—and are discouraged—by the total lack of any progress."[68]

How "When" Gets Answered, and Why

A few weeks later, on October 30, 1995, Edward Moskal, president of the Polish American Congress, wrote a letter to President Clinton. In it he expressed concern about the administration's decision not to announce an enlargement timetable until the end of 1996. "Time is not on our side," he wrote, "and further delay may mean that the answers to your questions "When?" and "Who?" will be "No One" and "Never." He continued, "We look forward, Mr. President, to indications and actions on the part of your Administration that will dispel the growing perceptions of 19 million Americans with roots in Central and Eastern Europe, including 10 million Polish Americans, that the next Clinton Administration will continue a policy of deferring decisions on NATO enlargement, leaving the issue to your successor."[69]

The openness of the Clinton administration to appeals from Polish Americans stemmed in part from the perception that this constituency had supported Bill Clinton in 1992, after several elections of strong Republican support. Of the ten districts with the highest concentration of Polish Americans, Ronald Reagan had won seven in 1980 and nine in 1984. Although Bush also won nine of these in his race with Michael Dukakis in 1988, Clinton had taken seven of these districts in the 1992 campaign. (And he would go on to defeat Bob Dole in eight of them.) A poll taken in September 1996 showed that while Americans of central and eastern European descent did not show support for NATO enlargement at higher levels than other Americans (who were generally favorable), they felt more strongly about the issue and they were also significantly more likely to be aware of it.[70]

Growing Administration Confidence

At the NATO foreign ministers meeting in December 1995, Warren Christopher laid out the administration's plans for the next year. Finding a solution to the war in Bosnia had given the secretary of state growing confidence to speak forcefully and without embarrassment about enlargement.[71] In his opening remarks at a press conference in Brussels, the secretary of state declared,

> Today, the Alliance also began the next phase in the process of enlargement, a process that was launched by President Clinton at e NATO summit in January 1994. Beginning in early 1996, se partners who wish to pursue membership in NATO will l extensive consultation with the Alliance on what would be cted of them if they became members. NATO, in turn, will ler what it needs to do to prepare for enlargement—what be the responsibilities and consequences if an enlargement were taken. This process will take us through all or most ar. We will then consider steps to be taken thereafter at g next December.[72]

pproached, the administration decided that Christopher peech in central Europe on enlargement. The secretary considered Warsaw as a possible venue, but as Christo- he argument for Warsaw was that Poland was really at debate about NATO expansion; of the main candidates it had the most compelling claim, and Russia's angst was Choosing Prague would also be a powerful signal, but a e one."[73]

r's speech in Prague on March 20, 1996, was significant ns. First, the administration had spent a great deal of time ut the first wave of new members and about the Russian what about the countries in between? Although a com- and more formal) decision process would have included so-called "gray zone" from the start, numerous officials this was not an issue that had preoccupied them. As one Department official told me, "This issue was not policy relevant until we had made formal plans to move forward on the first wave."[74] Christopher writes, "For the first time, I suggested that the first wave of NATO expansion would not be the last, a crucial point that was to move to the center of the Administration's message after Poland, Hungary, and the Czech Republic were invited to join in July 1997."[75]

Second, Christopher signaled to those anxious about administration seriousness on moving forward that NATO enlargement was truly going to occur. He writes that the team "toyed" in the morning before the speech with using the word "inevitable," but they "decided it had a ring of arrogance about it."[76] Perhaps they did not realize that the president had told his Cleveland audience in January 1995 that NATO enlargement was inevitable, as had Defense Secretary William Perry in Munich in February 1996.[77] (Presumably U.S. senators would like to believe the administration would not prejudge their constitutional role by speaking of the inevitability of a treaty amendment!) Instead, building on the president's 1994 Prague remarks, Secretary Christopher declared, "NATO has made a commitment to take in new members, and it must not and will not keep new democracies in the waiting room forever. NATO enlargement is on track, and it will happen."[78] Christopher later called this speech a "turning point" that finally left "no doubt in central Europe, among our allies, or in Russia that NATO expansion would take place."[79]

The Dole Campaign

Republican presidential challenger Robert Dole sought to outfla President Clinton on enlargement in the areas the president had s diously avoided: naming names and setting a date. His team knew t the ethnic community was disappointed with Clinton's delays, and their vote appeared up for grabs, despite Clinton's success with t voters in the 1992 campaign.[80]

On June 4 Dole announced the introduction of the NATO En ment Facilitation Act at a press conference on Capitol Hill with Walesa. There, the senator accused Clinton of doing too much " ing and discussing" and not enough "acting."[81] The bill targete tance to a few countries, as compared to the 1994 Warsaw In which divided the pie among a large number of countries, r which almost undoubtedly were never going to become mer sum of sixty million dollars was authorized to help Poland, Hungary, and the Czech Republic, the countries deemed to have made the most progress toward meeting the criteria. But the act made no mention of dates for accession.[82]

Still, the president was not ready to bring himself to support the legislation. He wrote a letter to the chairman of the House Committee on International Relations, Congressman Benjamin Gilman, on May 9, declaring, "Your legislation specifically urges me to designate Poland, the Czech Republic and Hungary as eligible for assistance under the NATO Participation Act. These countries are indeed making substantial progress and I agree they will be strong candidates for early NATO membership when the Alliance decides to move forward. At this stage, however, writing into law a narrow list of countries eligible for special assistance could reduce our ability to work with other emerging democracies that are also making significant progress."[83]

Sensing an opportunity, Dole gave a major foreign policy address at the Philadelphia World Affairs Council in late June in which he hammered the president for holding the interests of central Europeans hostage to Moscow. Dole remarked, "In an era of tectonic shifts in world affairs, we must not continue to entrust American leadership to would-be statesmen still suffering from a post-Vietnam syndrome. . . . Russian officials have conducted a campaign of threats against NATO expansion, and President Clinton got the message. He deferred and delayed, placing the threats of Russian nationalists before the aspirations of democrats in countries like Poland, Hungary, and the Czech Republic." Seeking to stake his claim for moving faster than his opponent, Dole called for a summit in Prague in 1998, on the sixtieth anniversary of the appeasement at Munich, to bring in the new members.[84] Although the tragic bombing of the U.S. barracks in Dhahran, Saudi Arabia, occurred the same day and dominated the front pages, the campaign's press team worked hard to deliver the message to the ethnic community.

Passage of the Facilitation Act

When Boris Yeltsin had formally declared his candidacy in February 1996, polls showed him with single-digit support among his electorate.[85] For the Clinton-Gore team, a Yeltsin loss to Communist party leader Gennadi Zyuganov would have been a disaster, allowing the Republicans to accuse the first Democratic president since Jimmy Carter of bungling foreign policy and creating renewed threats for America. One can easily imagine that a Yeltsin loss would have brought a Republican taunt that "Reagan and Bush defeated Communism; Bill Clinton brought it back." Nothing could be done that might undermine Yeltsin's chances, so NATO could not be explicit about a timetable or names until the Russian president had been safely reelected.

Once Boris Yeltsin won reelection handily on July 3, 1996, and the fear of communist or fascist victory in Russia was behind them, both Congress and the administration could move forward more readily. On July 23 the House passed the NATO Enlargement Facilitation Act by an overwhelming 353–65 vote, and the Senate followed suit two days later, voting 81–16 in favor. Having passed earlier NATO enlargement acts either through a voice vote or through conference, senators were now on record in support of this policy. The administration finally began to work more closely with Congress. National Security Council staffer Daniel Fried and Senate Foreign Relations Committee majority staffer Stephen Biegun began to consult closely for the first time.[86]

In Congress the only suspense in the vote on the Facilitation Act was the position of Senator Sam Nunn (D-Ga.). Many Senate Democrats looked to Nunn for guidance on foreign and defense issues. Along with Senator Lugar, Nunn had championed legislation designed to help Russia dismantle and safely store nuclear materials, but Nunn had come to the opposite conclusion from his Indiana colleague on enlargement. Believing nuclear proliferation to be the central threat to American security, Nunn opposed NATO's expansion for precisely the same reason as had many senior officials in the Pentagon: he did not want anything to disrupt U.S.-Russian cooperation in this area. He had told NATO officials in June 1995 in Norfolk, Virginia: "Rapid NATO enlargement (at a volatile and unpredictable moment in Russia's history) will be widely misunderstood in Russia and will have a serious negative impact on political and economic reform in that country."[87]

Vigorous opposition by Nunn to the Facilitation Act might have swayed more than a few Democratic votes and sent a signal that Senate consent to a treaty amendment expanding NATO was up for grabs. Several Senate staffers and outside observers say Nunn was surprised that the Facilitation Act was coming up for a roll call vote. His staff had already worked out deals with other Senate staffers on certain provisions in the act. When voting commenced, Nunn voted in favor. So, then, did many of the Democrats, looking to follow his lead. Near the end of the roll call, however, Nunn switched his vote to "nay." Perhaps while not wanting to sway Democratic votes on legislation the administration no longer opposed, Senator Nunn ultimately could not support it.[88]

The Administration Lays Out a Timetable

There was a great deal of deliberation within the administration's foreign policy team about how to move forward without looking like they were pandering to the ethnic vote. Christopher was set to give a major speech in Stuttgart in early September 1996, and he argues that he, rather than the president, was to propose the next steps to "help remove our policy from the context of presidential politics."[89]

At Stuttgart Christopher announced that President Clinton believed a summit needed to be held to fulfill his January 1994 objectives. Calling on NATO heads of state to meet in the spring or early summer of 1997, the secretary declared that one purpose of the summit would be to issue invitations to those partners ready to begin negotiations for membership in NATO. He also called for a "formal charter" to be signed between NATO and Russia to lay out the nature of consultative mechanisms and for joint action.[90]

Despite the announcement of a summit for invitations, neither the president nor the secretary of state had said anything about a date for accession. A debate soon ensued within the administration about how far to go, and where to say it. On the diplomatic side, Strobe Talbott and other Russia experts felt that the president should not name a date, but rather should simply state that NATO intended to take in new members sometime during the second term. Talbott always worried about one track getting ahead of the other, and he feared that providing a specific date would make managing the process with the Russians more difficult. The administration had consistently opposed congressional attempts after 1994 to name names or set a date. Why should it abandon this approach now?[91]

There were, however, both strategic and political reasons for stating a date. For National Security Council staffers Daniel Fried and Alexander Vershbow—and their boss, Anthony Lake—setting a date would help push the envelope and lock enlargement in as a concrete policy. It would show seriousness to the central Europeans, who still feared that the answer to "when" was "never." And ever since the fall of 1994, administration officials had occasionally bandied about the idea of new members coming in on NATO's fiftieth anniversary, April 1999.

There were also good political reasons to provide a date. The administration could eliminate any advantage Dole had sought by making a commitment to including new members by 1998. Chief of Staff Leon Panetta argues that the political imperatives of naming a date in front of an ethnic audience were obvious.[92] Whereas some on the foreign policy side hoped that the location would be less overtly political, the White House chose Detroit, and its heavily Polish suburb of Hamtramck, for the only foreign policy event of Clinton's 1996 campaign.[93] President Bush's national security adviser, Brent Scowcroft, says of Hamtramck, the site of a Bush address on eastern Europe in 1989, "Its hallmark was patriotism, it had a high concentration of families with ties to Eastern Europe, particularly Poland, and it had lots of Reagan Democrat blue-collar workers."[94]

Talbott and his Russia team did not fight to oppose naming a specific date in October 1996 as hard as they had fought concrete steps on enlargement in October 1993. And on balance for the administration, the strategic benefits of putting NATO enlargement on a concrete path and the political benefits of taking credit for the policy with the ethnic community outweighed the concern about managing Russia. Thus, Clinton announced in Detroit,

> I came to office convinced that NATO can do for Europe's East what it did for Europe's West: prevent a return to local rivalries, strengthen democracy against future threats, and create the conditions for prosperity to flourish. . . . We have kept NATO enlargement on track. Now it is time to take the next historic step forward. Last month, I called for a summit in the spring or early summer of next year to name the first group of future NATO members and invited them to begin accession talks. Today, I want to state America's goal. By 1999, NATO's 50th anniversary and 10 years after the fall of the Berlin Wall, the first group of countries we invite to join should be full-fledged members of NATO.[95]

The president then stopped for lunch in Hamtramck at the Polish Village Café, where he enjoyed stuffed cabbage, pierogi, and sauerkraut.[96]

For nearly three years Bill Clinton had been attempting a difficult balancing act. In January 1994 he sought to lay out a vision of an undivided Europe, with a clear place for Russia, and had put forward the Partnership for Peace. The Pentagon was content with the Partnership for Peace, given its inclusiveness, its emphasis on creating military-to-military programs to assist the transition of the former Warsaw Pact nations to the West, and its lack of an article 5 security guarantee. But the central Europeans and the Republicans wanted more. They wanted a clear signal that those countries succeeding on the path of reform could formally join the West.

While President Clinton appears to have decided sometime in the spring or summer of 1994 that he really did intend for NATO to enlarge at some point, he could not move too fast or he would risk jeopardizing his policy to assist reform in Russia, the single most important national security objective for his administration. Yeltsin's precarious position and Russian outbursts toward enlargement pushed the president to go more slowly; central Europeans and Republicans pushed him to go faster. The president could not be seen as holding central Europe hostage to Moscow, but neither could he afford to undermine Yeltsin. As long as Bosnia raged, the United States could not hope to push the alliance to enlarge. Finally, any electoral benefits would come from those favoring enlargement; there is no American constituency that votes based on a concern about a good relationship with the Russians. So the period from 1994 to 1996 was quite delicate.

By October 1996 conditions had changed. Yeltsin had been reelected. The Dayton accords had brought peace to Bosnia. The president could thus go to Detroit and proclaim his intention that new members would enter NATO in April 1999. But the process was not over. The U.S. Senate still needed to provide a two-thirds vote to amend the 1949 Washington Treaty creating the North Atlantic Alliance. And while the Senate had voted overwhelmingly in favor of the enlargement process in July 1996, a real vote with real consequences had not been held. Some senators would want to be assured that Russia accepted this first wave of new members; others would fear any arrangement that gave Russia too much influence. All would want to believe that the costs of expansion would remain low. These are the issues that the Clinton administration had to address as it began the process of seeking Senate advice and consent.

CHAPTER FIVE

Advice and Consent

On April 30, 1998, by a vote of 80–19, the Senate approved the resolution ratifying NATO's addition of Poland, Hungary, and the Czech Republic, thus securing one of the major foreign policy achievements of the Clinton administration. A year earlier, the administration had set up a special office at the State Department, the sole job of which was to gain the Senate's support, and had chosen former National Security Council staffer Jeremy Rosner to run this campaign for ratification. Rosner had reason to be concerned about enlargement's prospects despite the Senate's 81–16 vote approving the 1996 NATO Enlargement Facilitation Act. After being named to his new position, Rosner read a 1933 book by W. Stull Holt that laid out the reasons for Senate defeats of treaties. The book culminated in an analysis of Woodrow Wilson's failure to gain consent for the Treaty of Versailles that would have led to U.S. participation in the League of Nations. Rosner had already demonstrated in his own 1995 book on executive-legislative relations that postwar periods have historically been times when Congress has asserted itself. Holt's treatise reminded Rosner that he faced a challenging landscape, since the Senate had been most likely to defeat presidents during times of peace and in periods of divided government, exactly the circumstances that Clinton faced.[1]

In the forty years after World War II, the Senate rejected only two of more than five hundred treaties that reached the floor (and both were minor issues).[2] But the cold war was now over, and with Republicans in control of the Senate, Rosner naturally worried that President Clinton would suffer a fate similar to that of Wilson. As Holt argued, "From the time political parties first appeared, senators in voting on treaties have inevitably felt the pressure of political motives. The temptation to defeat a treaty made by a president belonging to another political party was certain to be present. Either the treaty, if completed, might redound to his and his party's political advantage or the defeat of his foreign policy would produce an impression of ineffectiveness and thus be of advantage politically."[3]

Holt added another factor to his analysis that must have given Rosner pause: "Politics and the contest over the treaty-making power were not the only forces in the Senate operating against the Versailles treaty. A third, although relatively minor, factor was the personal hatred of Wilson that other senators besides [Henry Cabot] Lodge felt. Wilson aroused more hatred than any president since the days of Lincoln and Johnson."[4] And Bill Clinton probably aroused more hatred among the opposition than any president since Wilson, with the possible exception of Richard Nixon.

Many of the issues that played out in the NATO enlargement ratification process are those that have been central to Senate relations with the president since George Washington presented the first treaty to the Senate for its constitutionally mandated advice and consent. As Senator William Maclay, one of the first two senators from Pennsylvania, wrote in his private journal in discussing that first treaty, whereas the president "wishes us to see with the eyes and hear with the ears" of his advisers, the Senate wants to participate directly in negotiations in order to provide its advice. Barring that, it certainly wants the opportunity to amend a treaty put before it. While the president does not want a signed treaty tampered with to the point that other signatories object, the Senate has a constitutional right and duty. The framers believed that the Senate would be consulted before the president signed a treaty, but presidents have constantly sought to limit Senate influence.[5] Would an administration that had failed to consult Congress adequately on NATO enlargement from 1994 to 1996 change its approach in the face of necessity?

During these processes, individuals in the Senate can play a disproportionately significant role. As Holt wrote of Wilson's loss: "The outcome of this contest was to be decided chiefly by one man because of his powers as Republican leader in the Senate and as chairman of the Committee on Foreign Relations. This man was Senator Lodge."[6]

When the administration geared up its efforts in early 1997, it was a strong possibility that Senate Foreign Relations Committee Chairman Jesse Helms (R-N.C.) was poised to play the same role. He had single-handedly defeated President Clinton's nominee for ambassador to Mexico, William Weld, and he had thwarted administration attempts to pay United Nations arrears.

Essential to the overwhelming Senate vote in favor of enlargement was the belief among Republicans that supporting NATO enlargement was not consenting to a Clinton administration initiative. Rather, to them, it meant winning the administration over to a policy they had pushed since 1994. In Republicans' minds, they were not handing the president a victory; they were fulfilling Ronald Reagan's legacy. The fact that Senate Republicans and a Democratic White House perceived NATO enlargement as a product chiefly of their own efforts was crucial for the bipartisan support that each helped to create in this final phase.

Members of Congress often have tremendous freedom to act in foreign policy because most voters are not paying attention to these issues.[7] Despite the administration's effort to organize diverse constituencies to endorse NATO enlargement, most senators could have voted no without paying a steep electoral price. What the administration had to do was make it easy for senators to vote yes. It had first to gain agreement with Moscow on a NATO-Russia charter. Yeltsin's signature would help deflate the arguments of those who believed that NATO enlargement would destroy the U.S.-Russian relationship. Second, the administration had to gain internal agreement on who from central and eastern Europe should be included in this round of enlargement, and then gain the approval of both allies and the Senate for this choice. Third, the administration had to present a reasonable cost estimate: low enough that senators would not hear from constituents but not so low that conservatives would claim that the Clinton team was making a mockery of the military alliance.

NATO-Russia

Having waited until after Boris Yeltsin's July 1996 election to move forward concretely on expansion, the Clinton administration would then have to wait another six months finally to engage Russia on a formal charter. Yeltsin's health problems sidelined him for the entire second half of the year, and without Yeltsin, there would be no NATO-Russia agreement. No one else in the Russian government had either the incentive or the bureaucratic authority to assent to an accord with NATO. NATO enlargement was unpopular in Moscow, and Yeltsin had dominated Russia's policy toward the West. Only when he emerged from his illness during the winter, with the coming Madrid summit to issue invitations to new members staring him in the face, did Yeltsin give the word to Russian foreign minister Yevgeny Primakov to cut a deal.[8]

Within the Clinton administration, Deputy Secretary of State Strobe Talbott had been circulating a paper spelling out most of the elements he deemed necessary in a NATO-Russia agreement. Russia could not have a veto, and the new members could not be seen as "second-class citizens" in the alliance. This meant any Russian consultative mechanism had to have clearly defined limits, and it meant that language on the stationing of NATO troops had to be carefully chosen so that no one could doubt NATO's security guarantee to the new members. Meanwhile, Talbott understood (as Russian deputy foreign minister Georgi Mamedov had articulated in the winter of 1995) that Russia needed signals not only on troop deployments but also on the issue of nuclear weapons on the territory of the new members to reassure it that NATO enlargement did not increase Russia's insecurity. Otherwise, the two sides would never reach an accord.[9]

In December 1996 Vice President Al Gore and Prime Minister Viktor Chernomyrdin met in Lisbon for a meeting of the Organization on Security and Cooperation in Europe. (The December 1994 summit in Budapest had "upgraded" the Conference on Security and Cooperation in Europe to an organization.) In Lisbon the United States signaled that it was moving toward one element of the Russian position on another treaty—the Conventional Forces in Europe treaty that dealt with the deployment of military equipment in Europe. This treaty was of particular concern to the Russian military, which did not like the structure of the accord (among other problems they had with it). The treaty's limits were based on "Groups of Forces," Western and Eastern. Now the United States finally agreed with Russia that these groupings no longer made any sense and that the treaty should be adapted to place equipment limits nationally. The Western group, after all, was enlarging to include members from the Eastern group, and thus by the old limits, weapons on the territory of the new members would be counted in the same group as Russia's! This concession from the West to Russia to eliminate group limits in favor of national ones not only made sense for all parties, but it also allowed the United States to argue that any discussion of conventional force limits take place in the context of the negotiations to adapt the Conventional Forces in Europe treaty rather than in discussions of the NATO-Russia charter.[10]

In mid-December NATO made the first of two unilateral statements on its future disposition in the East that were designed to ease the way for a NATO-Russia agreement. At the NATO foreign ministers meetings in Brussels, Secretary of State Warren Christopher said, "We are declaring that in today's Europe, NATO has no intention, no plan, and no need to station nuclear weapons on the territory of any new members, and we are affirming that no NATO nuclear forces are presently on alert."[11] With the statement of the "three no's" in hand, Primakov now told the NATO foreign ministers that he was prepared to work with them on a charter. A private session that Talbott and his executive assistant, Eric Edelman, held with Primakov in London that month confirmed to them that the Russian foreign minister was finally becoming serious about concluding a deal.[12]

With Yeltsin's return to work in December, movement had been discernible. But an inability to engage substantively with Primakov left the Clinton team nervous about where they stood. In January 1997 Talbott met with Yeltsin chief of staff Anatoly Chubais to be sure that the presidential administration was informed. Talbott's team, which included officials from the State Department, National Security Council staff, and the Treasury Department, arrived at the Kremlin late at night, and as they entered Chubais's office, they saw that Yeltsin's daughter and closest confidant, Tatyana Dyachenko, was coming out. They took her presence as a sign that they would have Chubais's full attention.[13]

Talbott told Chubais that NATO enlargement was going to happen, and he said that Russia had to make sure that it did not look like Moscow had lost. Chubais told Talbott that this issue was Primakov's to work, and he also told the U.S. team that enlargement was making life tough for the reformers. Chubais told Talbott that Russian membership in other Western clubs would be important since Russia was being excluded from NATO.[14]

Also in January, the Clinton administration agreed that NATO Secretary-General Javier Solana would serve as the formal negotiator with Primakov to conclude a deal. Solana told Talbott that the United States should draft an agreement and he would sell it to the allies and to Russia. Talbott's original paper had been boiled down to a three-page outline by his executive assistant, Eric Edelman. In January this paper was given to a desk officer in the European Bureau, John Bass, to be expanded into language appropriate for a charter. Bass's draft then went to Solana, who shared it with the allies. As one senior administration official recalls, the allies complained that Solana had not changed one word, and Primakov was referring to Solana as the "American 'stukach' [stool pigeon]."[15] But Solana met with Primakov for five hours on January 20 in Moscow to discuss the initial work.[16]

In early March Talbott and Solana met in Brussels before the deputy secretary of state headed to Moscow. With Talbott was National Security Council European expert Alexander Vershbow. Discussing the issue of troop deployments on the territory of new members, Vershbow scribbled some language on a piece of National Security Council note paper. With Solana's concurrence, Talbott took the piece of paper to Moscow and xeroxed it for review by his team there. He then brought it back to Washington for approval by the Interagency Committee of Deputy Secretaries, chaired by Deputy National Security Adviser James Steinberg. Vershbow's scribbles became NATO's second unilateral statement of March 14—another crucial piece of the building block. Although Russia wanted a binding commitment that no foreign troops would be stationed on the territory of the new members, what it got was a pledge by NATO that "in the current and foreseeable security environment, the Alliance will carry out its collective defense and other missions by ensuring the necessary interoperability, integration, and capability for reinforcement rather than by additional permanent stationing of substantial combat forces."[17]

The United States had wanted NATO to issue the unilateral statements on nuclear weapons and on troop deployments before the Helsinki summit held between Presidents Clinton and Yeltsin in late March 1997. They feared that otherwise they would face accusations that they were selling out the central Europeans in private conversations with the Russians. Even so, critics scoffed at the limits the United States and its allies were placing as they proceeded with enlargement. Former secretary of state Kissinger complained, "I will hold my nose and support enlargement even though the conditions may be extremely dangerous. . . . Whoever heard of a military alliance begging with a weakened adversary? NATO should not be turned into an instrument to conciliate Russia or Russia will undermine it."[18] Still, while elites in central Europe constantly worried about this "quality of membership" issue, one central European commentator noted that the two unilateral statements would make NATO membership much more acceptable to segments of the population in the new member states that wanted neither nuclear weapons nor foreign troops on their soil.[19]

At Helsinki Yeltsin signaled that he was comfortable with what was emerging. Just as the October 1993 Principals Committee recommendation to President Clinton on the language regarding NATO's open door had been ambiguous enough to gain the support of proponents and opponents of enlargement, the document being worked out by NATO and Russia (which by now the Russians wanted with a name fancier than "charter") had enough ambiguity to become acceptable to both sides. Yeltsin defined his notion of what the parties were doing at his press conference in Helsinki: "We agreed on the parameters of the document. Namely nonproliferation of nuclear weapons to the new NATO members, nonproliferation of conventional weapons, nonuse of the military infrastructure left over from the Warsaw Pact in these countries of East and Central Europe, and the adoption of fundamental decisions solely with Russian participation. Finally, we agreed that this treaty would be binding on everyone."[20]

While the United States may have interpreted the framework differently, Clinton did offer Yeltsin several items to ease the pain. The presidents agreed to move forward on START III as soon as START II was ratified; START III would reduce the level of nuclear warheads on each side to between 2,000 and 2,500 by the end of the year 2007. Since the great disparity in resources meant that the United States could maintain much higher levels of nuclear weapons than could Russia absent an agreement, and since the Russian Duma objected to certain provisions in START II, this arms control effort was viewed in Washington as helpful to Yeltsin.

Fulfilling Chubais's January wish, Clinton also stated, "We will work with Russia to advance its membership in key international economic institutions like the W.T.O. [World Trade Organization], the Paris Club [group of Western creditors], and the O.E.C.D. [the group of advanced economies]. And I am pleased to announce, with the approval of the other G-7 nations [the Group of Seven advanced industrialized democracies], that we will substantially increase Russia's role in our annual meeting, now to be called the Summit of the Eight, in Denver this June."[21]

But the Helsinki meeting was not completely harmonious. Clinton repeated that President Yeltsin "made it clear that he thinks [NATO enlargement is] a mistake." And their joint statement on European security noted, "President Yeltsin underscored Russian concerns that NATO enlargement will lead to a potentially threatening buildup of permanently stationed combat forces of NATO near to Russia." Most important, Yeltsin was rebuffed when he sought a private "gentleman's agreement" that the Baltics would never come into NATO. Clinton reportedly responded that this was not only unacceptable to the United States, but it also was not in the interest of the "new Russia": "If you try to impose restrictions on who gets into NATO, you will impose a restriction on whether you yourselves get into NATO."[22]

Despite the disagreements, Clinton could confidently state at the joint news conference, "We didn't come here expecting to change each other's mind about our disagreement, but we both did come here hoping to find a way of shifting the accent from our disagreement to the goals, the tasks and the opportunities we share. And we have succeeded." Importantly, Yeltsin agreed that the document needed only the signature of the heads of state, not ratification by parliaments, and he and Clinton declared that Solana and Primakov would work to conclude the accord.[23]

While these formal negotiations had been proceeding, back in Washington an experts group sponsored by the New York-based Council on Foreign Relations had been meeting under the direction of Senator Richard Lugar (R-Ind.) to lay out a bipartisan approach to the NATO-Russia relationship. The president of the Council on Foreign Relations, Leslie Gelb, had asked Council Fellow Victoria Nuland, on leave from the State Department and formerly executive assistant to Strobe Talbott, to run the study. Talbott was pleased with the idea, hoping that a distinguished bipartisan group could broaden the base of those supportive of an accord. Talbott would also learn if this group would come to the same conclusions as had his team. In addition to Lugar and Nuland, the group included Ronald Asmus (in transition from RAND to the State Department), former State Department official Charles Gati, Richard Holbrooke, former and future administration official Jeremy Rosner, and James Steinberg, who was leaving his position as director of the State Department Policy Planning staff to become deputy national security adviser. It also included former high-level

Republican officials Brent Scowcroft, Stephen Hadley, Arnold Kanter, Peter Rodman, Paul Wolfowitz, Robert Zoellick, and Stephen Sestanovich, who would soon be joining the administration as its ambassador-at-large for the New Independent States.[24]

The report was released just before NATO heads of state were scheduled to meet in Paris with Boris Yeltsin to sign the NATO-Russia charter. In laying out the group's conclusions, Senator Lugar made clear that while the report sought to show that NATO and Russia could develop a relationship, it was also laying out what it deemed unacceptable—namely that Russia could not be allowed to turn NATO into a different entity, nor could it have a veto. These views were consistent with the internal administration positions. Lugar stated that the issue that most divided this illustrious group was how NATO should proceed following its first round of enlargement. Former Bush administration National Security Council officials Brent Scowcroft and Robert Blackwill, for example, urged that NATO initiate a formal pause after the first round of enlargement.[25]

On a visit to Germany in April, Yeltsin declared that on May 27, 1997, in Paris, the heads of state would sign a NATO-Russia agreement.[26] And so they did. In the "Founding Act on Mutual Relations, Cooperation and Security between the Russian Federation and the North Atlantic Treaty Organization," Yeltsin had received as much as he could have, given the realities of Russian weakness. He did not get a legal commitment from his counterparts, but he did get "an enduring political commitment undertaken at the highest level." Since this commitment came from the heads of state of sixteen democracies, Yeltsin could rightly state that the Founding Act "is a firm and absolute commitment for all signatory states." The two unilateral NATO statements of December and March were included. The Permanent Joint Council was created as a mechanism for consultation and possibly for joint action. Meanwhile, President Clinton enunciated the theme he had first spelled out on his trip to Europe in January 1994: "The NATO-Russia Founding Act we have just signed joins a great nation and history's most successful alliance in common cause for a long-sought but never before realized goal—a peaceful, democratic, undivided Europe. . . . From now on, NATO and Russia will consult and coordinate and work together."[27]

The signing of the Founding Act not only allowed the alliance to proceed with its Madrid summit, but it also significantly weakened the arguments of those who said the Russians would never accept enlargement. Yeltsin continued to state that Russia did not like enlargement and thought it a mistake of historic proportions, but he had shown that he too genuinely needed the relationship with the West to fight NATO's inevitable enlargement.

The main criticism the administration would face after the Founding Act was signed came not from those on the left who worried about Russia, but from those on the right who worried that Strobe Talbott had given away the NATO store. Recognizing this fear among conservatives, Talbott had given an address to the Atlantic Council just before the Paris ceremony in which he said of the two unilateral statements on nuclear weapons and on combat forces, "These are, I emphasize, reassertions of NATO's own policy, independently generated and promulgated; they are not negotiated limits on NATO's freedom of action."[28] Administration officials would stress throughout the year that the Permanent Joint Council gave Russia a voice in NATO affairs, but not a veto.

Having signed the Founding Act, the next step before Madrid was finally declaring which states would be invited to join in this first round of NATO enlargement. Although Poland, Hungary, and the Czech Republic had been the clear front-runners for some time (Slovakia dropped off the list because of its failures to proceed with political reform), other allies, as well as some United States senators, were arguing for a larger group. With the Russian accord safely in hand, the administration now had to gain agreement with the Senate and with allies on who should be invited, and this process was by no means an easy one.

The Who

Ronald Asmus, who in May 1997 had officially moved from RAND into the Talbott enlargement team as a deputy assistant secretary of state for European affairs, came up with a slogan for the administration's recommendation: Small Is Beautiful plus Robust Open Door. The issue was whether NATO should invite only Poland, Hungary, and the Czech Republic, or whether it should accede to the wishes of some allies and some senators and add one or two more countries, namely Slovenia and Romania in southeastern Europe.

Why did Asmus and his supporters at the State Department believe small was beautiful? First, if Slovenia and Romania were included, the administration would bring the Baltic issue to the fore immediately, since those countries would jump closer to the top of the list for a second round, given their progress on meeting political and economic criteria. Some would even argue that the Balts were further in front on reform than Romania, so why should they have to wait? But as Yeltsin had underscored for Clinton at Helsinki, moving NATO onto the territory of the former Soviet Union was an order of magnitude more serious for Russia than the move into central Europe. Conversely, not only had the United States never formally recognized Baltic inclusion in the Soviet Union, but also allowing Russia to intimidate any of the New Independent States in their sovereign choice of alliance partners was unacceptable to the administration and to Congress. Easiest for the administration would be to put the Baltic question off for as long as possible, a more likely task if the first round was limited to three. A second round that included Slovenia and Romania could postpone the question of former Soviet states even longer.

A second issue was how the Senate would view a larger number. Would those who already feared for NATO's future as a well-oiled military machine fear even more? What would be the added costs of an additional member or two? And were Slovenia and Romania really ready to join? Slovenia met the political and economic criteria, but its military capabilities were minimal given its small size. And Romania had only begun to consolidate political and economic reform with its elections in the fall of 1996. From the State Department's perspective, it was better to make sure that the first round included only those countries that raised no doubts in the eyes of the Senate.

The most important reason small was beautiful, however, is that it offered the greatest promise for a robust open-door policy. Asmus and others at the State Department feared that if the allied heads of state and the sixteen parliaments agreed to including five members in the first round, there would never be a second round. Everyone would congratulate themselves on a job well done and declare an end to the process. But President Clinton had pushed enlargement as part of a strategy of unifying Europe and had argued that this policy would not draw new lines. If so, a credible open door was integral to the policy, and State Department officials concluded that including three was optimal.

Others within the administration were more open to accepting four or five. The Pentagon had included Slovenia in its cost estimates, believing that it essentially fulfilled NATO's criteria, and some people in the Defense Department argued that it could serve as a land bridge to Hungary, which otherwise was not geographically connected to the alliance. The lack of infrastructure in Slovenia made this argument less impressive than it looked at first glance. Over on the National Security Council staff, Alexander Vershbow also believed in the strategic value of taking in a southeastern European country. Slovenia could send a signal to proponents of reform elsewhere in the Balkans that countries from that region could formally join the West if they chose the right path at home.

Vershbow, Asmus, and National Security Council central European expert Daniel Fried met to discuss what to recommend to their superiors, and they agreed to go with three. This time, the administration followed formal interagency procedures. The deputies met and agreed with three, as did the principals. The recommendation to proceed with Poland, Hungary, and the Czech Republic went to the president, who gave it his okay.[29]

As this process unfolded, the administration's handling of this issue with the other allies led to public complaints about U.S. diktat. The United States had made all of the important decisions on enlargement so far, but in this instance it announced a policy that was at odds with the public stance of a majority of NATO members. When the United States proposed the Partnership for Peace in October 1993, the program appealed to the allies as an ideal compromise. Even allied grumblings about the push to enlarge in October 1994 were contained by the recognition that no formal steps would occur until after Yeltsin's 1996 election. But on the issue of who should come into NATO, the majority of the allies were publicly in favor of more countries than the United States wanted, and thus the U.S. imposition of its will left a more bitter aftertaste than previous steps the Americans had taken on enlargement.

The administration's first mistake was postponing a decision until as close to Madrid as possible. Administration officials believed that if NATO let it be known months before the summit who was to be included, they would be inviting intense lobbying efforts to overturn the decision.[30] It did not seem to occur to them that leaving open the possibility that Slovenia and Romania might get in was just as likely to invite intense lobbying, and it did.

More important, the administration ignored the efforts by the French and Italians beginning in February 1997 to put together a NATO coalition favoring Romania and Slovenia. The French had strong cultural and historical ties to Romania, and the Italians were looking to strengthen NATO in their own neighborhood. Because France and Italy felt so strongly about their chosen countries, the administration did recognize that the choice was between three or five. Proposing to take Slovenia and not Romania would be such an affront to France that it was better to satisfy neither ally than to satisfy only one. By May, however, as the NATO foreign ministers gathered for their ministerial in Sintra, Portugal, France and Italy had generated support from seven other allies (Canada, Belgium, Luxembourg, Spain, Portugal, Greece, and Turkey) for their cause. While Germany and Britain were leaning toward the U.S. number, only Iceland openly supported the American efforts to limit the invitations to three.[31] How would the Clinton team get consensus on its position?

Before going further, the administration had to seek the advice of the Senate. And a number of senators favored including Slovenia. Senate Democrat Joseph Biden (Del.) believed strongly that the effect on the Balkans and the ability to provide a bridge to Hungary made Slovenia an obvious candidate. Inclusion of this former Yugoslav republic would signal others in that region that they were not doomed to be outside of Europe forever. Slovenia's neighbor, Croatia, might be particularly susceptible to arguments that better behavior might pay off down the road.[32]

President Clinton met in May and June with members of Congress. Many were promoting four or five countries instead of just three. Having been told by his advisers that the Senate was more likely to approve NATO enlargement with a smaller number, the president was puzzled. "How can you say they won't approve five?" he asked. "They're pushing it!"[33]

On June 11 a group of senators put out a letter supporting inclusion of Slovenia. That evening President Clinton, Vice President Al Gore, National Security Adviser Samuel Berger, and Secretary of State Madeleine Albright met with leading senators at the White House residence to discuss this issue. Senator William Roth (R-Del.) and others made a push for five. Several of those present from both the administration and Capitol Hill say there was a real give and take in the discussion. Finally, the senators told President Clinton that while many of them believed five was preferable, if he believed that three was better, they would accept that judgment.[34]

Then the administration stumbled. While it had consensus internally and with the Senate, it had not forged a consensus with allies. But since the president had decided on three, Defense Secretary William Cohen announced this decision as a done deal, and he argued that "a small initial group underscores that there are really going to be additional rounds." And once Cohen had laid out where the United States stood, presidential spokesman Mike McCurry backed him up: "The United States' position is firm. Our own military believes that NATO will better be able to absorb new members if we start with three, so there was a military reason to keep the number at three."[35]

The French did not give up. They continued to draw support from other NATO members. Nor did they hide their pique. As one French official asked at the G-7 summit in Denver the week after Cohen's announcement, "When exactly did the Americans go from leadership to hegemony?"[36]

But America had always been NATO's hegemon, and this was particularly true after the Europeans were unable to bring peace to Bosnia on their own in the early 1990s. Having shown in Bosnia that the Europeans depended on the United States, America continued to dominate the alliance's decisionmaking process. Thus just as it had driven the process since October 1993, from Partnership for Peace, to the push to enlarge, to setting a date for admission of new members, the United States now determined who would get into NATO in the first round of post–cold war enlargement.

To help ease the pain and to gain support from those allies disappointed in the outcome, the United States agreed to the following statement on the future, issued at the Madrid summit on July 8:

> With regard to the aspiring members, we recognize with great interest and take account of the positive development toward democracy and the rule of law in a number of southeastern European countries, especially Romania and Slovenia. The alliance recognizes the need to build greater stability, security and regional cooperation in the countries of southeast Europe, and in promoting their increasing integration into the Euro-Atlantic community. . . . At the same time, we recognize the progress achieved toward greater stability and cooperation by the states in the Baltic region who are also aspiring members.[37]

All that remained was convincing the United States Senate to support NATO membership for Poland, Hungary, and the Czech Republic. To that end, the smartest decision the administration had made was creating the NATO enlargement ratification office at the State Department. And of great help was the decision by Senate Majority Leader Trent Lott (R-Miss.) to create the Senate NATO Observer Group. The new State Department office and the Observer Group, together with help from the central Europeans and a bipartisan lobbying group known as the U.S. Committee to Expand NATO, would completely overwhelm any efforts by opponents to stop the enlargement train in its tracks.

The Administration's Campaign

In January 1997, as part of the transition from the first term to the second, the White House put together a paper on NATO enlargement. The view from 1600 Pennsylvania Avenue was that support for enlargement in Congress was broad, but thin. The administration had gone through a series of ups and downs from 1993 to 1996 as it sought Senate ratification of the Chemical Weapons Convention. (It was only successful in April 1997, after putting together a more organized effort.) The lesson of the chemical weapons battle was clear to many in both the administration and the Senate; if the White House did not have its act together, with a campaign run by one individual, a go-to person on all aspects of the Senate vote, then it might not get enlargement through.[38]

Not everyone was worried. The legislative affairs offices at the State Department and at the National Security Council argued that prior Republican support for the 1994 Contract with America and the 1996 NATO Enlargement Facilitation Act virtually guaranteed Senate ratification. But the politically savvy national security adviser, Samuel Berger, was concerned. So Berger brought back to the administration Jeremy Rosner, legislative director and speechwriter early in the first term and a person knowledgeable about Capitol Hill and public opinion. Rosner had written a book on congressional assertiveness in the post–cold war period, and he had been doing public opinion polling while out of government.[39]

Rosner was to run a NATO enlargement ratification office. But where? The White House or the State Department? Berger wanted Rosner to work out of the National Security Council, but Rosner argued that he should be based at the State Department. While the National Security Council had the clout of the White House behind it, from the State Department Rosner had more resources to carry out a large-scale operation. Rosner decided that the best option was to be "double-hatted," which meant being a special adviser to both the president and the secretary of state. Since he had close ties to Berger anyway, he would keep a strong White House link, while also having more control over what was occurring at the State Department. Despite fierce objections from the legislative affairs people, whose job it should have been to coordinate this effort, Rosner set up his office on the sixth floor of the State Department on March 5, 1997. His mission statement on the first day: the administration had to win by a larger than expected margin of victory; enlargement could not be at the expense of other interests, for example, Russia; the victory had to be overtly bipartisan; their work had to be overtly interagency; and the ratification effort could not have any ethical taints.[40]

Coming together inside the State Department in the spring of 1997, then, were two of the most effective outside proponents of NATO enlargement—Ronald Asmus as deputy assistant secretary of state for European affairs (who started formally on May 1) and Jeremy Rosner as the special adviser to the president and the secretary of state for NATO enlargement ratification. Both were young, highly energetic, and passionate about the issue. Most important for the administration's strategy, they were "new Democrats," which meant they worried about holding the center, not the left.

Working closely with Rosner was another talented and energetic individual, a foreign service officer named Cameron Munter. Munter had served in Poland in the late 1980s, when Daniel Fried was the Polish desk officer at the State Department. He was the Czech desk officer from 1989 to 1992 and in that capacity had come to know a Czech American who was heavily involved in affairs in that region—Madeleine Albright. In Prague from 1992 to 1995, Munter had worked closely with the deputy chief of mission, Eric Edelman, now Strobe Talbott's executive assistant. Albright, always nervous that career bureaucrats in the European Bureau's NATO office would undermine the administration's efforts, knew that Munter would serve her. So, while not having a normal job description for a foreign service officer,

Munter would spend the next year pursuing American constituencies that might endorse NATO enlargement.[41]

The most important decision White House officials had to make that spring concerned their strategy on Capitol Hill. Did they assume Republicans had to vote yes given their prior support for enlargement, as the legislative affairs people argued? That would mean targeting the message toward the Democrats and building support in from the left (a strategy dubbed "left-in"). Or did they assume Democrats had to support the president and target the message to Republicans (a strategy dubbed "center-out")? Many in the administration had long years of association with Democrats on Capitol Hill, never enjoyed reaching out to the same Republicans who were bashing the White House all the time, and argued strongly for a left-in approach. These individuals, like Deputy National Security Adviser James Steinberg—who had worked for Senator Ted Kennedy (D-Mass.) in the early 1980s—thought the White House needed to win over liberal democrats as well as the east coast elites who were so opposed to enlargement.[42]

Rosner and Asmus argued forcefully that the danger was from the right, not the left. Rosner argued that the administration did worst when it started on the left and tried to build support from there: gays in the military and health care were two examples. Meanwhile, said Rosner, the big successes stemmed from the center-out approach: Passage of the North American Free Trade Pact (NAFTA), welfare reform, and a balanced budget.[43] Rosner won.

Did it matter? It did because it affected how the administration would present enlargement. References to NATO as an institution based on shared values decreased. Now the emphasis would be on NATO's mission of collective defense. This was the NATO that Jesse Helms supported, which was not the NATO that Strobe Talbott had been talking about. Talbott, in fact, was worried when Rosner came on board that the new special adviser would be the voice for enlargement at the expense of Russia, and that the process would take a decidedly anti-Russian turn when it went to the Hill. He told Rosner, "I want you to approach this with two lobes of your brain, not just one."[44]

A Republican-oriented strategy was assisted immensely by the 1996 retirement of Senator Sam Nunn (D-Ga.). Had Nunn still been in the Senate and leading the charge against enlargement, the administration may have had to approach the issue differently. Nunn had a large following among Senate Democrats, who trusted his judgment on national security affairs. Had Nunn been arguing on the inside that NATO enlargement was the wrong strategy at the wrong time given a need to focus on stemming the proliferation of Russian nuclear weapons, a strategy seeking to build Republican support that took Democrats for granted would have been much less feasible.

Either way, the administration had to work more closely with Congress than it had from 1993 to 1996. With Rosner and Munter ensconced on the sixth floor at State in March, the campaign began to get organized. And later that month, Senate Majority Leader Trent Lott made their task easier by announcing his intention to create the Senate NATO Observer Group, which the administration astutely recognized was a vehicle for ensuring bipartisan backing, precisely what had been missing in 1919 when Woodrow Wilson sought to extend America's commitment to Europe through the League of Nations.

The Observer Group

On March 21, 1997, Lott proposed the creation of an observer group patterned after the Senate Arms Control Observer Group of the 1980s. He complained that the administration had delayed too long on important questions, and the time had come to name names. He argued that if the administration waited until 1998 to work with the Senate, ratification would be in doubt. To ensure that the Senate provided its advice and consent, Lott wanted a bipartisan group that would "join the administration in its negotiations on NATO enlargement and [would] cut across party lines and committee jurisdictions." He also asked that the group be part of U.S. delegations to Europe to "ensure that the Senate is in on the ground floor of the NATO enlargement process."[45]

The administration was prepared to meet many, although not all, of the Senate's demands. Secretary of State Albright, National Security Adviser Berger, and Defense Secretary Cohen had just agreed at one of their weekly lunches to urge the Senate to create such a group. Thus when Lott announced his idea, the administration could embrace it right away. Rosner informed Senate staffers that they could have meetings with anyone from the administration anytime they wanted, and the administration would provide them with regular briefings.[46]

Although Lott expressed typical Senate interest in being able to shape actual negotiations, there was a limit to what the administration was willing to countenance. The first and only real snag in the relationship between the White House and the Senate NATO Observer Group developed over the negotiations proceeding at exactly that moment: those between NATO and Russia on the Founding Act. The twenty-eight-member Senate NATO Observer Group was officially created on April 22, just weeks before the conclusion of the Founding Act. Staffers wanted drafts of the Founding Act, and they wanted to see the cable traffic between Europe and Washington. After all, Republicans believed Strobe Talbott was capable of destroying NATO to save the U.S.-Russian relationship. But State Department officials argued that this was a NATO document, and they could not give it to the Senate unless they had NATO's approval. Talbott briefed the Observer Group on May 15, but staffers argued to their Senate bosses that this was not enough. And when the Founding Act became available on the Internet before the administration had sent it to Capitol Hill, the Observer Group complained bitterly.[47]

Although the administration refused to allow Senate participation in negotiations and refused to let senators see cables on demand, they did provide a steady stream of briefings. In all, the Senate NATO Observer Group had seventeen meetings with administration and foreign officials, including the June 11 meeting with President Clinton to discuss who would be invited at Madrid, sessions with Albright and Cohen, and meetings with NATO Secretary-General Javier Solana as well as the leaders of Poland, Hungary, and the Czech Republic. Members of the group also accompanied the president to Paris in May 1997 for the signing of the NATO-Russia Founding Act and to Madrid in July 1997 for the NATO summit. Although the Europeans complained about the American inclusion of parliamentary representatives at Madrid, Senator William Roth and Congressman Gerald Solomon (R-N.Y.) had seats at the table as the heads of state negotiated the final document. Administration officials had been mindful of the fact that President Wilson had failed to take senators with him to the Paris peace talks, and they were determined not to repeat any of his mistakes.[48]

The Observer Group included Senate leaders Lott and Tom Daschle (D-S.D.), Jesse Helms and Joseph Biden, leading Republican national security senators John McCain (R-Ariz.) and Mitch McConnell (R-Ky.), current and future Armed Services Committee chairmen Strom Thurmond (R-S.C.) and John Warner (R-Va.), and longtime NATO enlargement backers Barbara Mikulski (D-Md.) and William Roth. Most important, it included some of the leading skeptics of enlargement: Kay Bailey Hutchison (R-Tex.), Daniel Patrick Moynihan (D-N.Y.), Ted Stevens (R-Alaska), and Paul Wellstone (D-Minn.).[49] Truly bipartisan and with enough skeptics to portray advice and consent as a process with real meaning, the Senate NATO Observer Group played a vital role in the campaign to enlarge NATO.

Challenges from Helms and Lugar

While the delegation was in Madrid, Senator Helms let it be known that he and his colleagues were not going to be pushovers. Helms had been skeptical about enlargement until recently, given his general concerns about what he saw as European unwillingness to share the burden in NATO. He had been swung in favor largely through the efforts of former British prime minister Margaret Thatcher, who had talked with the senator about the powerful pro-American sentiments of the three aspirants.[50] Even so, he was in favor of enlargement only if it proceeded on his terms.

Writing in the European edition of the *Wall Street Journal* on July 9, 1997, Helms argued, "The Clinton administration's egregious mishandling of NATO expansion is raising serious concerns in the U.S. Senate, which must approve any enlargement treaty." He criticized Strobe Talbott for talking about changing NATO from a military alliance into a "nebulous 'collective security' arrangement." NATO, he stated, is designed to prevent any state from achieving hegemony in Europe, and the likeliest candidate to pose such a threat is Russia. Helms stated that before the administration sent enlargement to the Senate for approval, it needed to do a number of things, including laying out a strategic rationale and not unduly limiting NATO's freedom of action, either by placing limits on troops or nuclear weapons on the territory of the new members or by giving the UN or Russia the right to veto NATO decisions. "NATO is a military alliance," Helms declared. "It must remain so or go out of business."[51]

Rosner immediately called Helms's staff from Europe to say he was ready to work with them to resolve the senator's concerns. Thus began a remarkable to and fro between Helms's staff and Albright's, culminating in the appearance by the secretary of state before the Senate Foreign Relations Committee in October to say precisely what the North Carolina Republican wanted to hear.[52]

Lugar writes to Berger

Conspicuously absent from the Senate NATO Observer Group was the Senate's most vocal proponent of NATO enlargement back in 1993: Indiana Republican Richard Lugar. Lugar's relationship with Lott had suffered ever since he had nominated Senator Thad Cochran (R-Miss.) for majority leader in 1996.[53] Now Lugar sought to get back in the game. Writing a ten-page letter to National Security Adviser Samuel Berger in late July, Lugar said that the lesson from the Chemical Weapons Convention campaign was the need for the White House to run a serious effort out of the National Security Council, not the State Department. In a swipe at the youthful Rosner, Lugar suggested that Berger put a "serious quarterback" in charge, and he argued that former U.S. ambassador to NATO Robert Hunter was the perfect choice to assist Berger. As columnist Robert Novak wrote, "With this, the no. 2 Republican on the Senate Foreign Relations Committee sought to bypass the secretary of state, the NATO Observer Group (consisting of congressional colleagues) and especially his committee chairman, Sen. Helms." The Senate NATO Observer Group, wrote Lugar, was merely "a vehicle by which the Senate leadership is seeking to maintain control of the issue."[54]

Although Albright and Talbott were friends of Hunter's, Berger decided to stick with Rosner and to keep him over at the State Department. There, Rosner and Asmus could begin to prepare the secretary for her public encounter with the Senate Foreign Relations Committee and put to rest Senate concerns about Russia and about the costs to the United States of enlarging NATO.

The To and Fro

Because the administration had decided on a "center-out" strategy, Albright would emphasize NATO's role as a military alliance that was not being diluted by enlargement or by the NATO-Russian Founding Act. Helms's staff had sent his first question to the State Department well ahead of the hearing. Rosner called back with an initial answer. It was not good enough. The staffs discussed further what would satisfy Helms.

Meanwhile, the administration needed to work out internal agreement on the answers Albright would give, particularly on NATO-

Russia. Talbott was out of town as Rosner and Asmus put together the testimony. Albright told them to accentuate that Russia had no veto and that the North Atlantic Council (NATO's political arm) was sacrosanct. Seeing the draft, Talbott worried about the tone. He added a paragraph on the positive role of the Permanent Joint Council.[55]

Helms's staff asked for further clarification. Getting it, they signed off on the proposed Albright response. Both sides were now ready.[56]

On October 7, 1997, Helms opened the hearings by saying, "[T]here's a right way and a wrong way to proceed with NATO expansion." Again he ascribed to Strobe Talbott a desire to change NATO from a defensive alliance to an organization involved in nation-building. In Helms's view, "Poland, Hungary, the Czech Republic and other potential candidate states don't need NATO to establish democracy. They need NATO to protect the democracies they have already established from external aggression."[57]

Albright made clear in her prepared statement that NATO had not given anything away. She stated, "I know that some are concerned that this relationship with Russia may actually go too far. You have asked me for an affirmation, Mr. Chairman, that the North Atlantic Council remains NATO's supreme decisionmaking body. Let me say it clearly: It does and it will. The NATO-Russia Founding Act gives Russia no opportunity to dilute, delay, or block NATO decisions."[58]

After her statement, Helms opened with his previewed question, confident of the answer he would receive: "Will you establish fire walls in NATO's relations with Russia and assure that Russia has neither a voice nor a veto in NATO discussions of issues such as arms control, strategic doctrine, and further alliance expansion? A pretty hefty question but I know you can handle it."[59]

The secretary, perhaps Helms's favorite administration official, had great appeal to him, given her background as a refugee from Hitler and Stalin. She began her carefully crafted response with the paragraph from Talbott: "We believe that the NATO-Russia Founding Act and the Permanent Joint Council it created offers real opportunities to develop a partnership between NATO and Russia through regular consultations and activities to build practical cooperation. . . . I believe that these elements of the NATO-Russia relationship, together with our bilateral efforts to integrate Russia more fully into the rest of the West, are beginning to bear fruit." But she then added, "At the same time, let me be very clear about your concern. The Founding Act and the Permanent Joint Council created as a result do not provide Russia any role in decisions the alliance takes on internal matters, the way NATO organizes itself, conducts its business, or plans, prepares for and conducts those missions which affect only its members, such as collective defense, as stated under Article 5."[60]

Shortly thereafter she stated, "So, let me just re-emphasize. I can assure you that the Permanent Joint Council will never be used to make decisions on NATO doctrine, strategy, or readiness. The North Atlantic Council [NAC] is NATO's supreme decisionmaking body, and it is sacrosanct. Russia will not play a part in the NAC or NATO decisionmaking and it will never have a veto over NATO policy. Any discussion with Russia of NATO doctrine will be for explanatory, not decisionmaking, purposes." Satisfied, Helms responded, "That is a good answer to my questions, and I appreciate it."[61]

Helms had told his staff as fall approached that he did not want any trouble during the Senate debate. He wanted all questions asked and answered well ahead of the floor debate. Seven hearings were held in October and November. In addition to the hearing with Albright to discuss NATO's strategic rationale, the committee held hearings with proponents and opponents on the pros and cons, with experts on the capabilities of the three invited countries, on the costs and on NATO-Russia, and finally, with invited guests from the public, including leaders from the Polish, Hungarian, and Czech ethnic communities.[62] Satisfied at the end, Senators Helms and Biden wrote their colleagues on November 10, "We are more convinced than ever that the enlargement of the North Atlantic Treaty Organization to include Poland, the Czech Republic, and Hungary is the correct policy for the United States to pursue."[63]

The Incredible Shrinking Costs

Perhaps even more than concerns about Russia, the issue that had the greatest possibility of producing Senate skittishness was the potential cost. Senators were not going to hear from constituents about the U.S.-Russia relationship. But they would hear from constituents if opponents could demonstrate that the costs to the United States of enlarging NATO were real and would take away from other cherished programs. As those inside and outside the administration began to put together estimates of the cost, supporters of enlargement would find they had a huge advantage: in the face of widely varying estimates, senators in the end could do no more than throw up their hands and hope that the lower estimates were right. Outside the handful of budget analysts who put the estimates together, no one had any real idea what the numbers meant. And the bottom line was that with no major military threats in Europe and a final analysis by the administration and by NATO that the infrastructure in Poland, Hungary, and the Czech Republic was better than expected, any estimate was believable. The biggest fear by some enlargement supporters—namely that conservatives would charge that the administration's low estimates signaled that enlargement was producing a hollow alliance—never materialized.

Largely because of the informality and ambiguity of the decision process in 1993–94, no systematic effort to assess costs was undertaken when the administration first began to consider enlargement. In the summer of 1995, shortly before his tragic death in Bosnia, Deputy Assistant Secretary of Defense Joseph Kruzel called RAND analyst Richard Kugler and asked, "Is this going to be hideously expensive?" Kruzel hired the RAND troika of Asmus, Kugler, and Larrabee to assess the costs and associated force requirements for enlargement. Since Kugler had close contacts within the Pentagon's budget office, he was able to draw on U.S. government estimates of the costs for specific needs and capabilities. Published in the fall of 1996, not long before Asmus was to join the State Department, the RAND troika's estimate of the costs of an enlargement designed to promote stability rather than defend Europe from a Russian invasion was $30 billion to $52 billion over the next ten to fifteen years. While this total figure might be cause for concern, Kugler in 1997 boiled it down for his audience: "For the average American, the annual cost is equal to the price of a candy bar."[64]

Because the RAND study drew heavily on Department of Defense cost projections, the Pentagon's own estimate was practically identical. Largely because of different assumptions about reinforcement needs, the Defense Department's estimate was slightly lower. As required by the 1997 Defense Authorization Act, the Department of State submitted this estimate in its "Report to the Congress on the Enlargement of the North Atlantic Treaty Organization." Not happy with the way the drafts of the report had been written, Deputy National Security Adviser James Steinberg and Deputy Secretary of State Strobe Talbott had asked Rosner, just coming on board as head of the NATO enlargement ratification office, and Asmus, awaiting his final security clearances before formally joining the government, to make the product more presentable to the Senate audience. Released on February 24, 1997, the report stated that total costs to allies and new members combined would be in the neighborhood of $27 billion to $35 billion from 1997 to 2009. The U.S. share of "direct enlargement costs" for the ten years following the 1999 admittance of the three would be only $150 million to $200 million a year. The report acknowledged, "These costs would, of course, increase if there were a dramatic increase in the threat or a decision by the United States to bear a larger share of the costs than would otherwise fall on our current allies or the new members."[65]

Critics complained that these estimates were deliberately low. Ivan Eland, formerly of the Congressional Budget Office and now at the CATO Institute—a conservative Washington think tank—called the Clinton administration study "fatally flawed."[66] Eland had prepared a paper for the House International Relations Committee in March 1996 while still at the Congressional Budget Office that, like the RAND study, laid out a range of options. Unlike the RAND approach, however, four of the five options Eland presented were "directed toward the threat of a resurgent Russia." He acknowledged, however, that "in the current environment, NATO can probably spend as much or as little as it likes on expansion."[67]

As the Senate geared up for its October 1997 hearings on the costs, Eland prepared another study. He argued that the Clinton administration's assumption of no current threat and no need to station NATO forces on the territory of the new member states "may prove problematic." As evidence he cited tension between Hungary and Serbia, Poland and Belarus, and Poland and the Russian enclave of Kaliningrad. Eland declared that even accepting administration assumptions, total costs were likely to be $70 billion over the decade after enlargement, with the U.S. paying at least $7 billion, and probably more if new members proved unable to pay their share.[68]

The Senate Foreign Relations Committee held its hearing on October 28. By then, NATO had come in with its own estimate, which was the lowest of all. And as Secretaries Albright and Cohen had told the Senate Appropriations Committee just the week before, the Pentagon had already lowered its earlier estimate on the grounds that the one released in February had included Slovenia and had underestimated the quality of military infrastructure in Poland, Hungary, and the Czech Republic.[69] As one administration official recalls, "The cost issue was becoming a problem when shrinking numbers made it seem that the books were being cooked."[70]

At the hearing Kugler and Undersecretary of Defense for Policy Walter Slocombe explained the RAND and Pentagon estimates; Eland was present to offer his. For senators, the basic problem in assessing the different estimates stemmed from different figures for "common budgets," "direct costs," and the like. At one point Slocombe explained that the NATO estimate was much lower because it only estimated the cost of the common budgets, not all the costs associated with expansion. When Senator Helms turned to Biden and asked if that was a good point, the senator from Delaware responded, "a good point that no one understands." He might as well have been speaking about the entire cost discussion.[71]

The Campaign

As the Senate finished with its hearings and prepared to schedule its debate and vote, the administration went into high gear. With help from key staffers working for senators on the NATO Observer Group who were supportive of enlargement—for example, Ian Brzezinski from William Roth's office, Michael Haltzel of Joseph Biden's staff, and Stephen Biegun of Jesse Helms's office—and important efforts by outside lobbyists, Rosner and his team pulled out all the stops. Their goal: transform enlargement from an ethnic issue to an American one; get endorsements from state and local governments, labor, business, veterans, Jewish organizations, and more. Supporters of enlargement engaged every conceivable group, and the opposition, which consisted largely of academics and columnists, with a sprinkling of organizations on the left and the right, had no chance. Opponents simply organized too little, too late to stop the momentum.

The Administration's Assault

For the year before the Senate debate in March 1998, Jeremy Rosner and Cameron Munter had traveled anywhere and everywhere to pick up support. They visited thirty states and targeted the editorial boards of the thirty papers with the highest circulation. From 1995 on the *Chicago Tribune* had opposed enlargement, with its last editorial to oppose expansion coming on February 1, 1998. Former chairman of the Joint Chiefs John Shalikashvili and former ambassador to NATO Robert Hunter were quickly dispatched to meet with the editorial's author, who was also given red carpet treatment when he visited Poland shortly thereafter. On March 13 the paper stated, "It is no small thing for a nation to enter into an alliance. . . . Neither is it a small thing for a newspaper to change its mind on an issue as momentous as NATO expansion. . . . Yet mindful of the historic opportunity this moment offers, that is what we do today."[72]

Rosner worried that labor groups and mayors would see this as guns versus butter, that veterans would fear that enlargement would dilute NATO, and that Jews would raise concerns about Poland. His office set out to ensure that no major group would oppose the administration. Labor leader John Sweeney was invited to a meeting with Secretaries Albright and Cohen, and Lech Walesa wrote him a letter reminding the AFL-CIO chief of his organization's longstanding support for Solidarity. Cameron Munter flew out uninvited to a U.S. Conference of Mayors meeting in San Francisco. Munter told the gathering that Secretary Albright had sent him because she wanted the American people involved, and by the way, this market was the fastest growing part of Europe. With assistance from the mayor of Detroit, Munter gained the endorsement of the Conference of Mayors. And Jewish organizations lined up behind the argument that securing democracy in Poland was the best guarantee for freedom of religion.[73]

In January 1998 the NATO enlargement ratification office laid out a week-by-week strategy to culminate in the expected Senate vote on March 20: who would go where, which foreign policy principals would speak when, how the president would play his part in the process. Not every event was a success. Rosner's appearance at Portland State University drew only five people; and the only mention he received regarding his appearance on public-access cable television the night of the Academy Awards was from Helms staffer Stephen Biegun. But the instant response machine, resulting in "blast-faxes" to Capitol Hill, briefings to senators on the presence of former KGB agents in central Europe before this issue could even become a concern, and increased delegations to Prague when public opinion polls showed low levels of support for enlargement in the Czech Republic, all paid off. The pitch to nonethnic organizations, based on the value of including the three new countries in the West, was usually successful. Jess Quintero, a local commander of the American GI Forum, a Hispanic Veterans Group representing ten thousand members nationally, said of Rosner, "He said that adding all those new voices would make Europe more stable . . . that our children and grandchildren, our cousins and their children, would be less likely to fight another war."[74]

Outside Help

The campaign to gain Senate support was not run merely from inside the administration. Outside the government, the main players were the U.S. Committee to Expand NATO, headed by Lockheed Martin Vice President Bruce Jackson, and the central European diplomatic corps, led by the ambassador from Poland, Jerzy Kozminski.

Partly because of Jackson's position at Lockheed Martin, critics of enlargement would argue that his committee and the general effort to support the policy were undertaken on behalf of U.S. defense manufacturers. These companies were certainly interested. Joel Johnson, the vice president for international affairs at Aerospace Industries Association, argued, "The stakes are high. Whoever gets in first will have a lock for the next quarter-century." Noting the possible $10 billion market for fighter jets, he added that "then there's transport aircraft, utility helicopters, attack helicopters, communications and avionics. Add them together and we're talking real money." Another report noted that with sales to a good, stable region with countries that did not abuse their citizens unlikely to be vetoed by Congress, this market was highly attractive.[75]

Inside industry and the U.S. government, consensus existed that NATO enlargement would be good for business. As Raytheon spokesman Barry French said, "The more there is standardization of military and defense systems that use standards that the US and NATO allies use, that would benefit US military contractors." The U.S. Department of Commerce concluded in its report on this market, "The potential for an increase in the number of NATO members and NATO emphasis on high technology equipment, along with the recent restructuring of forces, makes NATO an attractive option for U.S. firms supplying a wide variety of products and services. The implementation of the enhanced NATO's Partnership for Peace program and the expansion of the alliance to central Europe also provide increased business opportunities."[76]

Arguments that U.S. contractors might benefit from enlargement are not evidence that this issue swayed either the administration or the Senate to any significant extent, nor is it evidence that Bruce Jackson was shilling for Lockheed Martin. And the articles setting out to make these connections simply failed. In a *New York Times* article on enlargement, reporter Katharine Q. Seelye started by noting that "America's six biggest military contractors have spent $51 million on lobbying in the last two years." But she then had to acknowledge that "Not all of the lobbying has been for NATO expansion," and "No one contends that NATO is being expanded for the benefit of military contractors." Furthermore, most stories on potential buying sprees concluded that any spending was years away. *Business Week* concluded, "It looks like a bonanza waiting to happen. . . . But the bonanza may not arrive anytime soon." David Marcus of the *Boston Globe* also recognized, "For arms dealers, NATO expansion appears unlikely to rival the multibillion dollar bonanza in sales to Asia and the Middle East during the 1980s and '90s. Countries like Taiwan and Saudi Arabia have devoted amounts to weapons purchases that go far beyond Poland, Hungary, and the Czech Republic combined."[77]

Jackson's interest in the region went back decades. His father, working for U.S. intelligence during World War II, had hooked up with Jan Nowak, then a Polish courier for the Allies, who later became a high profile advocate for Poland's freedom during the cold war. During the enlargement debate, Nowak was the key figure from the Polish American community lobbying the administration. Jackson had held a senior position in the Defense Department during the Reagan administration, working for archconservative Richard Perle. Jackson saw enlargement as did the other conservative Republicans—a means to secure the victory of the cold war by bringing central Europe into the West and out of Russia's potential sphere of influence.[78]

In October 1996, shortly before the presidential election, Jackson (who was working on the Dole campaign) met with National Security Council staffers Alexander Vershbow and Daniel Fried and pitched his idea of a bipartisan committee to lobby for NATO enlargement. Jackson wanted to know if the administration was willing to work with them. Fried and Vershbow took the information to Berger, who asked

Rosner to find out who Jackson was. Rosner spoke to Jan Nowak, who told Rosner of his connection with Jackson's father.[79]

Jackson called Democratic lawyer Gregory Craig, who had worked for Senator Ted Kennedy (D-Mass.) in the 1980s and who would later join the administration as director of policy planning at the State Department (and then would serve on President Clinton's impeachment defense team). Jackson told Craig he hoped to form a committee evenly split between the two parties, and argued that even if they had different reasons for supporting NATO enlargement, they shared the same objective. Craig agreed. With Clinton's reelection and the retention of high-level Democrats in government, the U.S. Committee to Expand NATO would have a Republican tilt, but Jackson's goal was to have representatives from each of the administrations since Richard Nixon's. And he succeeded. The most important were Republican heavyweights Peter Rodman, Robert Zoellick, and Stephen Hadley, who could help sway votes on the Hill. And Julie Finley, head of the Washington, D.C., Republican Committee and a woman described by *Fortune* magazine as the "new Pam Harriman," hosted dinner after dinner for NATO expansion. From Senate staffers to administration officials to central European officials to members of the press, everyone describes these dinners as useful for providing senators and journalists the opportunity to meet officials from the three invited countries. It was no coincidence that the central Europeans who were invited were cosmopolitan, well dressed, and fluent in English; this sent a strong message that these countries were Western and deserved to be part of the club.[80]

The U.S. Committee to Expand NATO incorporated in November 1996 as a nonprofit organization, refusing to accept contributions from foreign nationals or corporations, and soon began working out of the offices of the American Enterprise Institute. The committee's strategy was similar to the one that Asmus and Rosner would push from the inside as "center-out": leave liberals like Paul Wellstone (D-Minn.) isolated on the left and conservatives like John Ashcroft (R-Mo.) alone on the right. If they could not capture the center, those worried about Russia and those worried about new missions would never be able to gain enough support to derail enlargement.[81]

In addition to the dinners, the U.S. Committee to Expand NATO spent a good deal of time with senators and their staffs. They had been involved in the planning for an observer group, and they had helped push for getting a Senate vote scheduled well before the congressional campaign season went into high gear. Hadley put together an impressive list of retired generals and admirals to endorse enlargement to counter possible criticism that this policy was not militarily sound. Working primarily inside the Beltway, the U.S. Committee to Expand NATO left no stone unturned in its effort to build a winning coalition. And most important from the standpoint of building a national campaign, the leading figures in the committee were neither ethnic Americans nor Democrats.[82]

The Polish Campaign

The groups representing Americans of central and eastern European ancestry had formed a coalition, which met every Wednesday to plot its lobbying strategy. But in terms of broad-based, grassroots organizational efforts, the most important single figure in the central and eastern European lobbying community was Polish ambassador to the United States Jerzy Kozminski. Kozminski, a quick study of the American political scene, had as early as 1994 started to map out a campaign to figure out which local constituencies could affect individual senators, and he had increased his efforts as soon as President Clinton gave a date for new members in his October 1996 Detroit speech. Kozminski had met often with Congressman Benjamin Gilman and Senator Hank Brown in 1994, as they developed legislation designed to push enlargement onto a fast track. And just as useful, he had begun to hone his arguments for Poland's accession. Whereas in 1993-94 the Poles had been stressing the dangers of a security vacuum in central Europe, by 1997-98 Kozminski's pitch had ten points centering on the integration of Poland in the West and arguing that enlargement would even strengthen Polish-Russian relations.

Kozminski's strongest card in seeking to build coalitions at the state and local level to pressure senators was the simple fact that state legislatures and trade organizations typically include Polish Americans. Calling or visiting these Polish Americans, Kozminski sought their assistance, with arguments not emphasizing NATO's expansion but focusing on bringing Poland back into the West. Each of the eight officers in the Polish embassy in Washington was assigned a job relating to congressional staffers, think tanks, press or regional operations and was assisted by the Polish consulates in Los Angeles, New York, and Chicago. The embassy's actions were also assisted by the Polish American Congress, which worked its own contacts.

When Senator Joseph Biden said early on that his constituents did not care about NATO enlargement, a staffer at the Polish embassy tracked down a Polish American on the Wilmington City Council. The city council endorsed enlargement. When Senator Robert Torricelli (D-N.J.) leaned against enlargement, busloads of Polish Americans organized by the New Jersey Polish American Congress appeared at one of his local offices to express their feelings. Torricelli voted in favor. In July 1997 Polish Americans set up a dinner for two hundred leading Hawaiians in honor of the visiting Polish ambassador, who had taken a day or two of his vacation to get in some work. The senators from Hawaii would support enlargement.[83]

It was not just Kozminski but the Czech and Hungarian ambassadors as well who traveled throughout the United States to build support. After the Madrid summit in July 1997, the three met weekly with Jeremy Rosner to discuss their strategy. Aleksander Vondra, the Czech ambassador, visited thirty states in one year, speaking at universities, world affairs councils, and chambers of commerce. In October 1997 Vondra called for a meeting of Czech American leaders at which Rosner spoke and Albright dropped by.[84] Czech Americans pale in comparison to their Polish brethren in terms of electoral weight, but the Czech-born secretary of state and the highly regarded Czech president Vaclav Havel certainly played a role in helping the cause of the central Europeans.

Public Opinion

In addition to the numerous endorsements by specific organizations, opinion polls had shown that Americans generally favored enlarging NATO. A study conducted by the Pew Research Center for the People and Press in January 1997 showed that 45 percent favored expansion and 40 percent were opposed. For the 20 percent who had followed the debate, the margin in favor was even higher, 54 percent to 37 percent. Another poll taken in September 1996 by the University of Maryland's Program on International Policy Attitudes suggested that 62 percent favored expansion to include the three new members. These University of Maryland pollsters argued that their numbers were higher than Pew's because they asked directly about Poland, Hungary, and the Czech Republic, rather than referring to central Europe. This general sentiment could only help enlargement's cause, although as one administration official noted at the time, "Foreign policy issues like this tend to be decided less by general public opinion than by highly organized segments of opinion. All the pressure, in terms of organized pressure, is in favor of expansion."[85]

Public Opposition

Enlargement opponents always open their interviews by saying senators told them their arguments were better than those of the proponents, but that they had little chance to win. In the face of a well-organized campaign that gave senators every reason to vote yes, the opponents gave them little reason to vote no. If business, labor, state and local governments, Jewish organizations, veterans groups, and Americans of central and eastern European descent endorsed enlargement, who opposed it? The academic community, several respected former government officials, and the *New York Times* were the most important.

Enlargement opponents argued that enlargement would end cooperation with the Russians, that enlarging NATO meant weakening it, and that the Senate would never make a commitment to lay down American lives for Warsaw or Prague, that is, the same kind of arguments that the Pentagon made in 1993–94 when stating its case that the Partnership for Peace better served American interests than expanding NATO. The most vocal and prominent individuals who campaigned against enlargement were former senator Sam Nunn, former Clinton 1992 campaign adviser and Johns Hopkins University professor Michael Mandelbaum, and *New York Times* foreign affairs columnist Thomas Friedman. As with William Perry and Nunn, Mandelbaum and Friedman could not believe that the United States was willing to sacrifice U.S.-Russian security cooperation to bring untested countries into NATO. Where was the administration's sense of balance, they would ask.

Mandelbaum argued that NATO was and should remain a military alliance, and the only reason for a military alliance to expand was to contain a threat. The only potential threat was Russia, but given its weakened state, expansion was unnecessary. Furthermore, since enlargement of the alliance would lead to Russian hostility, it would create precisely the threat that everyone hoped to avoid.[86]

Mandelbaum was joined by most of his academic colleagues, particularly those who studied Russia and feared the effect on Russian democracy. Longtime student of U.S.-Russian relations John Lewis Gaddis noted, "[H]istorians—normally so contentious—are in uncharacteristic agreement: with remarkably few exceptions, they see NATO enlargement as ill-conceived, ill-timed, and above all ill-suited to the realities of the post–Cold War world. Indeed I can recall no other moment in my own experience as a practicing historian at which there was less support, within the community of historians, for an announced policy position."[87]

It is not so remarkable that the academic community was so united on this issue, believing NATO enlargement to be a terrible idea. After all, those working on NATO or Russian affairs in the bureaucracy had been united in their opposition as well during the internal deliberations of 1993–94, and many remained opposed. But the Senate of the 1990s certainly did not care what these academics thought, particularly given the lack of interest in foreign policy on Capitol Hill. Nor did they seem to care that the *New York Times* mounted a vociferous campaign against enlargement. Leading the charge at the *Times* was foreign affairs columnist Thomas Friedman, who accused the Clinton administration of expanding NATO to win ethnic votes and argued that NATO would ruin any attempts to control Russian nuclear weapons. Since START II was more important to the United States than a security guarantee for Poland, Friedman argued, NATO enlargement was a blunder of monumental proportions.[88]

Linking the Russian Duma's failure to ratify START II directly to NATO's expansion was a flimsy argument, given the evidence. The Duma's position on START was based on a number of factors, including a belief in Russia that it was part of Mikhail Gorbachev's sellout of Soviet interests, concern about the American position on ballistic missile defense, communist opposition to Boris Yeltsin, as well as a reaction to NATO enlargement.[89] Conversely, the Russian view that enlargement was another sign that the West was taking advantage of its weakened state did create hard feelings. Even if the United States had avoided explicit promises on expansion during the talks on German unification, the Russians believed at the time that the United States wanted to create a new order in Europe in which Russia was a partner. Moscow was profoundly disappointed when the United States sought to make NATO the foundation of the new Europe.

Friedman and Mandelbaum were right that enlargement was not risk free, and good U.S.-Russian relations were a top national security priority for the United States in the post–cold war world (as Bill Clinton had believed from the start of his administration). But part of the reason they never got any traction was that the benign strategic environment of post–cold war Europe combined with Yeltsin's willingness to sign a NATO-Russia accord mitigated the concerns in the Senate about the Russian reaction.

Other opponents, such as political scientist and former Clinton National Security Council staffer Charles Kupchan, had been confident earlier in the process that the Senate would never consent to enlargement: "In the America I live in, political willingness to send troops into harm's way has been steadily shrinking since the Cold War's end, not expanding. . . . [A]s soon as debate on the Senate floor gets serious and turns to dollars and lives, the rest of the country will suddenly pay attention. Overnight, NATO expansion becomes a big loser."[90] If senators had believed that they were sending troops into harm's way, Kupchan would have been correct. The possibility that Poland or the Czech Republic would actually need defending seemed remote, and thus neither the Senate nor the public truly had to face this question.

The editors of the *New York Times* were strongly opposed to enlargement, and many outsiders complained that it was extremely difficult for enlargement supporters to have their say on the op-ed pages of the paper. *Times* reporter Steven Erlanger recalls, "Sources I trusted said that the *New York Times* was shut to the other side. And I passed that message along to the editorial board to do with as they liked. . . . There was a 'Chinese wall' between the editorial side and the reporting side. I found disturbing the complaints that the paper was not open to different points of view."[91]

Several highly regarded former government officials were appalled by the idea of NATO enlargement, but they were too few, and they were too late. When George F. Kennan, father of the containment doctrine and the dean of America's Russia experts, says a policy is "the most fateful error of American policy in the entire post–cold-war era," as he did of enlargement, people usually listen.[92] And few probably knew that Kennan had opposed NATO's creation in the late 1940s.[93] But the critique of enlargement by Kennan and other highly respected individuals, including former arms control negotiator Paul Nitze and former supreme allied commander in Europe John Galvin, were not part of an organized campaign, and thus they got lost in the face of the effort by enlargement proponents.[94]

Former senators Howard Baker (R-Tenn.) and Sam Nunn, former national security adviser Brent Scowcroft, and Council on Foreign Relations Vice President Alton Frye hoped to slow the process down by arguing that countries should have to join the EU before they could even think about becoming NATO members. NATO "is not a club" they said, and "a cornerstone is not a sponge. The function of a cornerstone is to protect its own integrity to support a wider security structure, not to dissipate its cohesion by absorbing members and responsibilities beyond prudent limits."[95] This argument, later pushed in the Senate debate by Daniel Patrick Moynihan (D-N.Y.), ran into opposition because of doubts that the Europeans would play a leading role in the inclusion of central Europe into the West and the fact that EU membership had never before been a prerequisite to joining NATO.

The opposition groups with the most experience organizing on Capitol Hill came from the left, and they knew from the start that they faced an uphill battle. The Council for a Livable World, founded back in 1962 by physicist Leo Szilard in the aftermath of the Cuban Missile Crisis, formally decided to oppose enlargement in February 1997 on the grounds that their issues—namely arms control and the need to dismantle Russian nuclear weapons—were affected. This was the same position that had been taken by Secretary of Defense William Perry and Senator Nunn. Realizing that the center was lost to supporters, the Council for a Livable World sought to build a coalition from the wings that was big enough to stymie expansion, following, in their president John Isaacs' words, the "Noah's Ark principle—for every group on the left, one group on the right." So when they brought in Americans for Democratic Action on the left, they brought in Phyllis Schlafly from the right.[96]

There were simply not enough votes on the wings, however, and many traditional Senate arms control supporters faced countervailing pressures. Isaacs says that some of his organization's best Senate friends—Russell Feingold (D-Wis.), Richard Durbin (D-Ill.) and Frank Lautenberg (D-N.J.)—told him that, given the political pressure they faced, they could not vote against enlargement.[97] Susan Eisenhower, longtime activist on behalf of U.S.-Russian relations and granddaughter of the former president, put together a letter from distinguished citizens, including former senators Bill Bradley (D-N.Y.), Gary Hart

(D-Colo.), and Sam Nunn, as well as Russia experts across the ideological spectrum, such as Michael Mandelbaum, Marshall Shulman, Jack Matlock, and Richard Pipes. But enlargement supporters then countered with several of their own. As Mandelbaum, one of enlargement's most persistent and articulate opponents after 1995, acknowledged, "You can't beat something with nothing, and we had no troops."[98]

The Senate Debates

On December 17, 1997, National Security Adviser Samuel Berger and Assistant to the President for Legislative Affairs John Hilley sent a memo to President Clinton entitled "Strategy for Completing Ratification of NATO Enlargement." It said that while things were going well, "Many supporters, particularly Democrats, remain lukewarm. Clear signs of your personal commitment will be essential to nail down the necessary votes. Even if we have the needed two-thirds votes, we will face difficult battles over reservations on such issues as cost, Russia, NATO cohesion, war powers, and future rounds of enlargement." Berger and Hilley noted that the campaign was in place: "We [have] organized an instant response capability to coordinate administration reactions to events, press stories, and events on the Hill." Attached to the memo was a week by week schedule, starting with the State of the Union Address on January 27, 1998, and including speeches by cabinet officials, op-eds by leading former officials, appearances on talk radio, and editorial board events. The White House expected the vote to occur in mid-March.[99]

As March approached, the administration could be pleased with what it had done right. It had included senators on the delegations to Paris and Madrid in 1997 to witness the signing of the NATO-Russia Founding Act and the issuance of invitations to Poland, Hungary, and the Czech Republic. Members of the Senate NATO Observer Group had received the briefings they asked for from the leading administration, NATO, and central European officials. Albright's staff had worked closely with Jesse Helms's staff to ensure his support. And the NATO enlargement ratification office, the U.S. Committee to Expand NATO, and the central Europeans and their supporters in the United States had produced a wide array of endorsements for senators trying to decide which way to vote.

The administration had also worked closely with Senate staff on the resolution of ratification on which the senators would vote. When NATO expanded to include Greece and Turkey in 1952, West Germany in 1955, and Spain in 1982, the resolutions were clean and simple. Some in the administration and on Capitol Hill argued that the best way to avoid troublesome amendments was to do the same here. But Helms's staff said no. They argued that the resolution had to answer Helms's concerns: why was NATO important; why does this enlargement serve U.S. interests; how does NATO retain its integrity; what would the process be for future candidacies; and how would NATO ensure that these new members were not second-class citizens. Within the administration, Rosner convinced his colleagues that a clean resolution would not be possible, and he worked closely with Senate staffers to produce a resolution that both branches of government were comfortable with.[100]

As reported out of the Foreign Relations Committee by a 16–2 vote—with liberal Minnesota Democrat Paul Wellstone (worried about Russia) and conservative Missouri Republican John Ashcroft (opposed to new missions) the only dissenters—the resolution contained seven declarations and four conditions. The declarations included language on NATO's purpose and the supremacy of the North Atlantic Council in decisionmaking, clarity regarding the Senate position that new members would be full members, and language on the limits of the NATO-Russia accord, as well as a reminder that any future rounds of enlargement had to be approved by two-thirds of the Senate. Through these conditions, the Senate sought to box in the administration on mission, cost, and Russia. Central to NATO's strategic concept, argued the Senate, was collective defense, and any revisions required administration consultations and briefings with them. The addition of new members could not increase the overall percentage of America's share in the NATO common budget. And the Permanent Joint Council could explain NATO positions to Russia but could not be used for joint decision making.[101]

March Madness

The initial debate in the full Senate got off to a bad start. Lott suddenly decided to bring NATO enlargement to the floor as filler in the midst of a battle with the administration over an education bill sponsored by his colleague Paul Coverdell (R-Ga.). Lott was exasperated with Democratic efforts to derail a bill he cared about, and his actions demonstrated the low public interest senators felt about enlargement: "I feel very strongly about this Coverdell A+ bill. . . . So I am determined we are going to get this bill up. We are going to consider it without a lot of extraneous matters. And I do want to observe that, as majority leader, I do still think the majority sets the agenda. I get to call up the bills, not somebody else. . . . [F]rom this administration and from my colleagues on both sides of the aisle, I am going to look for a little help and a little cooperation on issues that I think are important."[102]

NATO supporters audibly groaned when Lott tied the debate on new members to his pique on the education bill. Here was one of the major foreign policy initiatives of the post–cold war era, and the Senate was providing no sense of gravitas. Senator Biden, bemoaning the way that the NATO discussion was being "used as filler" stated, "The Senate's inability to alert the public that this major debate was underway lends an air of credibility to the unfair criticism that we have not adequately and fully and seriously taken into consideration the pros and cons relating to expansion." His colleague Paul Wellstone added, "This vote on NATO is not about what our position is on NATO. It is about saying we thought we were going to have a debate on education."[103]

The president then gave an address to the Senate on March 20 in which he asked it to approve the protocols on accession to membership. Lott not only failed to show for the event, but he pulled the resolution off the floor one hour later. Seventeen Senate enlargement opponents had earlier in the month asked for a delay until after June 1, ostensibly to give the Senate more time to debate the issues, but that was clearly not the reason for Lott's actions. The majority leader proclaimed, "Until the Senate indicates a willingness to stay focused and we get a little cooperation and don't have to have a filibuster fight and cloture vote on every bill, then it will just have to come up later."[104]

The Real Thing

Clinton had written a letter to Senator Lott on March 14, just before the first debate, arguing that the pause sought by the seventeen senators was "unnecessary and unwise." He reiterated that the core mission of NATO was collective defense, and he put U.S. costs at $400 million over ten years. He also said that no decisions or commitments had yet been made on when invitations would be extended for a second round or to whom. And he promised to consult with Congress before doing so.[105]

The administration did not have to wait until June. In the last week of April, the Senate debated and voted on enlargement. Senator Lott announced on April 27, "There will be no other issue that will be debated today or tomorrow or Wednesday other than NATO enlargement so that senators will have a chance to focus, and so that the news media will feel this debate has been focused, and we can give it the consideration that a historic treaty of this nature deserves."[106]

Opponents of enlargement laid out the potential problems. Wellstone and Moynihan raised concerns about the effect on Russia, and Moynihan proposed that EU expansion should come first. Senator John Warner (R-Va.), who believed that NATO was being diluted but recognized he could not stop the first round, sought a commitment to a mandatory pause before NATO moved to initiate a second round. Ashcroft, opposing NATO's involvement in peacekeeping missions like the one in Bosnia, offered an amendment that would restrict the alliance to defense of the territory of member states. Tom Harkin (D-Iowa) and Ted Stevens (R-Alaska) raised concerns about costs.

Because Senator Helms was ill (and in fact scheduled to enter the hospital on May 1), it fell to the leading Democrat on the Foreign Relations Committee, Joseph Biden, to manage the floor debate. Helms made a statement on the first day in which he reminded his colleagues he had warned the administration that the policy had to be done the "right way" and he declared satisfaction with the results. Furthermore, he added, the three new members saw the purposes of the alliance primarily as an instrument of collective defense, and they shared his views on Iraq, Cuba, and China.[107]

From there Biden took over, responding quickly to each and every concern. He was aided by a Government Accounting Office report that had concluded that "the Department of Defense's assessment of the NATO cost report was reasonable" and the fact that the U.S.-Russia relationship had not come apart despite NATO's push to enlarge. Arguments that the Senate had not debated the issue sufficiently were countered by the 552-page compilation put together by the Foreign Relations Committee of the hearings that had been held in the fall. Biden also added that the Senate NATO Observer Group "in my twenty-five years in the Senate was granted unprecedented access to the decision-making process." He argued that Warner's mandatory pause was unnecessary, since the Senate had to provide its advice and consent before any future rounds, regardless of what the administration or NATO sought to do. And as for Moynihan's proposal that the EU should expand first, Biden stated, "If this is designed as a killer amendment, it is a good strategy, but the logic of it I am lost in trying to comprehend. I find no logic to it, other than it being a killer amendment. You might as well attach an antiabortion amendment to the treaty. That would kill it." Given the proclivities of the Congress recently, he hastened to add, "I don't want to give anybody any ideas."[108]

Warner and Ashcroft

The administration was most concerned about two amendments, Warner's proposed pause and Ashcroft's restriction on mission. Warner had made his unhappiness about enlargement clear, arguing that as an alliance, NATO should only take in new members if they contributed to the military mission. He failed to see how the three prospective members served that purpose. And he introduced a letter from former government official Paul Nitze that ended, "In the present security environment NATO expansion is not only unnecessary; it is gratuitous. If we want a Europe whole and free, we are not likely to get it by making NATO fat and feeble."[109]

Warner knew he could not stop enlargement. And what harm would it do to mandate a three-year pause? After all, even leading former administration officials were suggesting that NATO would need time to digest the first round. Former administration officials Warren Christopher and William Perry had written in October 1997, "No additional members should be designated for admission until the three countries now in the NATO queue are fully prepared to bear the responsibilities of membership and have been fully integrated into the alliance military and political structures."[110]

The administration, which had fought congressional initiatives earlier in the enlargement process on the grounds of infringement of presidential prerogatives, made the case that Warner's amendment was unnecessary, given the Senate's constitutional prerogatives on advice and consent. They were worried a mandated pause would send a signal that the door was shutting after round one. The amendment appealed to many senators who were uncomfortable with the first round, and members of the Armed Services Committee wanted to support their future chairman. Although defeated, Warner's amendment garnered forty-one votes, thus securing more than the one-third necessary to prevent a second round. Despite their loss, those who had sought a formal pause thus had reason to be confident that the administration would lose its appetite (as it, in fact, did) for promoting a second round of enlargement anytime soon.[111]

Although the Warner amendment received the most public attention, the administration was secretly more worried about Ashcroft's proposed restrictions on NATO's mission. Ashcroft opposed administration efforts in Bosnia, precisely the type of peacekeeping missions that the United States had sought to make more effective by developing the Partnership for Peace and Combined Joint Task Forces. Ashcroft's amendment stated that "the United States will only support a military operation under the North Atlantic Treaty that is commenced on or after the date of adoption of this resolution of ratification if the operation is intended for the purpose of collective self-defense in response to an armed attack on the territory of a NATO member; or in response to a threat to the territorial integrity, political independence, or security of a NATO member."[112]

NATO would not be able to go out of area. And Senate restrictions might invite other NATO parliaments to legislate similar restrictions. As Senator William Roth would argue in opposition, "This amendment is not only unnecessary, it is dangerous. By attempting to define and restrict the missions that NATO can and should undertake, it risks foreclosing the ability of the United States to seek NATO's assistance in confronting future threats to the transatlantic community of nations."[113]

Given Republican sentiments regarding Bosnia, peacekeeping, and the threat of the "UN-ization" of NATO, it appeared Ashcroft might be able to gain support. As on other issues, however, NATO supporters maneuvered effectively, and in the end Ashcroft committed a tactical blunder that killed his amendment.

The administration acted quickly. Talbott called Kissinger to ask for his assistance. Asmus worked with his former colleagues at RAND to enlist their support. NATO's supreme allied commander, General Wesley K. Clark, called senators to argue against the amendment, as did now U.S. ambassador to NATO Alexander Vershbow.[114]

Meanwhile, a member of Senator Jon Kyl's (R-Ariz.) staff, David Stevens, had worked previously at the Pentagon in the Bush administration under Stephen Hadley, now a prominent member of the U.S. Committee to Expand NATO. They had helped develop NATO's 1991 strategic concept. With Hadley's help, Stevens put together an amendment that was less restrictive than Ashcroft's but that would give senators the opportunity to put their stamp on the planned 1999 revision of the earlier strategic concept. Reminding everyone that "NATO is first and foremost a military alliance," the Kyl amendment laid out a more expansive view of the common threats: the rise of a state with hegemonic aspirations, rogue states and nonstate actors with the ability to deliver weapons of mass destruction; threats to the supply of vital resources; and ethnic or religious conflict in the North Atlantic area. The amendment passed 90–9 and allowed senators to say that they would be vigilant regarding revisions to NATO's strategic concept even if they rejected Ashcroft.[115]

Ashcroft waited until late in the day Thursday, April 30, to begin his debate on mission. He hoped that perhaps this might delay the vote into the following week, thus giving opponents of expansion more time to work on colleagues. But Lott was not going to let it happen, and he made his position clear on the floor: "I believe maybe a Senator or two indicated that they didn't know we were going to try to finish this bill this week. I think I have said all along that we should have a focused, unobstructed debate, but the intent was to complete it Wednesday or Thursday. Here we are on Thursday at almost 4 o'clock. I talked to Senator Daschle, and we are agreed that we are going to finish NATO enlargement either at a reasonable hour this afternoon, or a late hour tonight, or tomorrow, or Saturday, but we are not going to leave this week until we finish NATO enlargement."[116]

Ashcroft went to Lott to ask for four hours to debate his amendment. By waiting until late in the day in an attempt to kill expansion outright, he had overplayed his hand. Lott offered his colleague one half-hour. Ashcroft balked. Lott's office asked Biden to table the amendment, which he did after being assured of the Republican leader's support. The motion to table succeeded by an 82–18 margin. The most serious Senate restriction on enlargement had been killed.[117]

The Final Vote

The resolution of ratification (altered only slightly from the version reported out of the Foreign Relations Committee in March by amendments such as that of Senator Kyl) finally went before the Senate on the evening of April 30, 1998, five years after Bill Clinton had met with Lech Walesa and Vaclav Havel during the opening of the Holocaust museum. Supporters had lost some on the left and right over Russia, cost, and mission. Two skeptics, Jeff Bingaman (D-N.M.) and Kay Bailey Hutchison (R-Tex.) in the end voted yes. Democrat Patrick Leahy (Vt.) decided that he could not decide, and thus he voted no. Bringing the resolution to the floor, Lott cited the forty hours of debate, the statements from fifty Senators, and the consideration of twenty amendments. And with urging from Senator Robert Byrd (D-W.Va.), Lott called on senators to sit at their assigned desks and cast their vote in turn. So they did, supporting the resolution of ratification by an 80–19 margin (Senator Kyl was absent), thus ensuring that America's support for NATO enlargement, a policy desired by so few back in 1993, had now become official.[118]

CHAPTER SIX

Implications

The development of the U.S. initiative to enlarge NATO reminds us that the decision process is often just that—a process—rather than a specific moment. My numerous interviews with enlargement opponents within the administration and with enlargement proponents outside of it have created the overwhelming recollection that in October 1994 Assistant Secretary of State for European and Canadian Affairs Richard C. Holbrooke pushed forward an enlargement policy that was no more than theory to that point. This jumpstart occurred a year after the only formal high-level meeting on enlargement among President Clinton's top advisers, who at the time did not agree on a NATO enlargement strategy, and in October 1994 the number of committed supporters of enlargement within the administration still did not reach double digits. Furthermore, although by the fall of 1994 the administration had essentially decided to pursue the two-track approach to enlargement that would take shape over the next three years, it still had not answered the essential questions of when, how, who, or even why. The answers to those questions came over time, and they were not fully answered until the Senate consented to the policy by its vote on April 30, 1998.

Revisiting the Bureaucratic Politics Model

The process taking place in the 1993–94 period offers several lessons about American foreign policy decisionmaking. If the question is whether policy outcomes inside the executive branch reflect presidential dominance over the foreign policy apparatus or the pulling and hauling of bureaucratic interests, the answer is: when the president gets involved, he wins (unless the bureaucracy can get outside actors, for example, Congress, to constrain him). From June until October 1993, from the establishment of the NATO Interagency Working Group to the recommendation for the January 1994 NATO summit put forward by the president's top foreign policy advisers, compromises formed by discussions among individuals from the National Security Council, the State Department, and the Pentagon produced the policy. From January until October 1994, however, it was not bureaucratic wrangling but presidential dominance that proved critical. Had the president opposed enlargement, the handful of people seeking to move the issue forward could never have prevailed. But through his remarks in Warsaw in July 1994 and with Yeltsin at the White House in September, Clinton had signaled that he supported enlargement, even if he kept his options open by not committing to the "when."

There was much Bill Clinton had not done by the summer of 1994. The president had not decided on a timetable for enlargement. The president had not decided which countries should be in the first group. He had not decided how to include the Russians in the process. But he had decided that, in principle, NATO enlargement was the right policy to pursue.

Had Bill Clinton tried in 1994 to answer any questions regarding when, who, and how, he would have engendered major opposition from most of his top foreign policy advisers. Only National Security Adviser Anthony Lake and probably Ambassador to the United Nations Madeleine Albright would have supported him.

What he had done by signaling that NATO enlargement was only a matter of time, however, was to give the handful of supporters enough help to outmaneuver the overwhelming opposition inside the executive branch. That handful, led by Lake, and then joined by Holbrooke, drove enlargement not through a series of decision meetings but through presidential language. First, at Lake's urging, President Clinton stated in Prague that it was no longer a question of whether NATO would enlarge, but when. And six months later, in Warsaw, the president urged the NATO partners to get together to discuss the next steps. In one sense, then, Holbrooke's critics were right. During his confrontation with Pentagon officials in September 1994, he was not armed with the results of a formal decision. Rather he was waving around lines from Clinton's speeches and remarks from news conferences. But since the president's remarks reflected his general support for enlargement, Holbrooke was ultimately correct: those who did not take Clinton's words seriously badly misunderstood what occurred in 1994. And once the bureaucratic opponents of NATO expansion realized that Holbrooke had the support of the president, vice president, national security adviser, and secretary of state, they had no choice but to fall into line behind the policy. Presidents do trump bureaucracies, particularly if they have policy entrepreneurs who can act decisively at critical moments. And the policy entrepreneurs did not come solely from within the administration; former national security adviser Zbigniew Brzezinski and RAND analysts Ronald Asmus, Richard Kugler, and F. Stephen Larrabee provided important intellectual firepower that, along with what Stephen Flanagan at the State Department and Daniel Fried, Alexander Vershbow, and Nicholas Burns at the National Security Council produced, helped Lake and Holbrooke press ahead.

As we have seen, there are different aspects of policy entrepreneurship crucial for the understanding of policy development. Lake conceptualized the policy, but he did not implement it, although the paper written by his three staffers on the "road map to enlargement" was later followed almost as scripted. As one of those staffers put it, however, NATO enlargement as it existed in that paper was only a "stealth policy" in the summer of 1994. It would remain one until Holbrooke came back to enforce the "decision" within the bureaucracy. No one was going to act on the president's remarks unless someone told them to do so. That is what Holbrooke did. He assembled his colleagues from the National Security Council, the State Department, and the Pentagon and told them: President Clinton has stated his policy; our job now is to act on it.

In part, this division between the National Security Council and the State Department on the functions of conceptualization and implementation reflected Lake's view of his role, which emphasized providing input but not taking action and which was distinctly different from that of some of his predecessors, like Henry Kissinger and Zbigniew Brzezinski.[1] From the State Department, Holbrooke woke up the bureaucracy. The State Department continued to lead the implementation of the policy after 1994; Deputy Secretary Strobe Talbott put together the two tracks of the policy from 1995 to 1997, and Special

Adviser Jeremy Rosner coordinated the efforts that followed to win Senate consent.

The two entrepreneurs, Lake and Holbrooke, are the reason enlargement developed when it did. Had bureaucratic politics defined the process, the outcome would have been what it was in October 1993: the Partnership for Peace program, a compromise acceptable to all the major players. But the momentum for NATO enlargement continued because Lake pushed the policy from his office in the West Wing, because Secretary of State Warren Christopher brought Holbrooke back from Bonn to serve as his assistant secretary of state for European affairs, and because the president favored enlargement. All of the activity from October 1993 to October 1994 that put the policy on track occurred outside of any bureaucratic bargaining, not because of it. When Holbrooke sat down with his colleagues in September and October 1994, he was not reopening a discussion of the issue; rather he was presenting his counterparts with a fait accompli. Essentially, the administration position on enlargement in the fall of 1994 was close to that pushed by Stephen Flanagan and Lynn Davis within the State Department a year earlier, particularly with regard to the timetable. But whereas Flanagan and Davis lost in the formal interagency arguments, their position won through the efforts of Lake and Holbrooke in 1994.

Holbrooke's task in the fall of 1994 was made easier by the perceptible shift that had occurred within the bureaucracy during that preceding year. The number of enlargement proponents may not have increased significantly, but their location had. Lake had altered his staff and now had two committed enlargement supporters in key positions: Alexander Vershbow as his senior director for European affairs and Daniel Fried as the shaper of policy toward central and eastern Europe and who in January 1995 would become formally the senior director for these regions. Holbrooke was no longer in Bonn but rather was the bureaucratic enforcer back in Washington, and thus Chief of Staff Tom Donilon had the muscle he needed to help Christopher shape the State Department position. Holbrooke also had an advantage within the bureaucracy, because while the Pentagon objected, this was a political, not a military, decision. No one was asking the Pentagon to achieve a military objective. The president was using a military alliance to fulfill a diplomatic and political agenda. The Partnership for Peace and the Combined Joint Task Forces were sufficient to achieve the military's goals, but in the fall of 1994 Holbrooke was asking for the military's professional advice about what was required to expand the alliance—not whether it was a good idea—and so that is what they had to provide.

Most important, Strobe Talbott, while the key voice for not letting the enlargement process get ahead of the NATO-Russia track, was becoming committed to the emerging presidential policy. Talbott, in fact, would spend far more time working on enlargement as its implementer than either Lake or Holbrooke ever did as the policy entrepreneurs who pushed it along at the beginning. Critics feared that Talbott's talents and his "Friend of Bill" status would mean that Russia would continue to trump central Europe. Brzezinski told a reporter in 1995, "My concern is that there are too many people studying the timetable in the Holbrooke train. There is a danger that it could get stuck in the station, while the Talbott train moves forward."[2]

Both Talbott and Perry, in fact, were model public servants, even though they still harbored misgivings about a policy they feared could damage the U.S.-Russia relationship and might make cooperation on a range of issues more difficult (most important for Perry, on nuclear weapons control). Once they realized that enlargement was presidential policy (and Talbott understood this sooner than Perry), they both worked to ensure its success rather than to undermine it. Because of the splits in the organizational charts between European and Russian affairs at the National Security Council, State Department, and Department of Defense, no single senior director or assistant secretary had the portfolio to run both the enlargement and Russia tracks, and it would be the deputy secretary of state who would do so. Meanwhile, the driver of the most remarkable example of NATO-Russian cooperation in the post–cold war period—Russian participation in the NATO-led implementation force in Bosnia—was Secretary of Defense Perry, who along with Talbott hoped that on-the-ground cooperation between NATO and Russia after December 1995 could demonstrate that a NATO-Russia track was no chimera.

Positions and Beliefs

A classic model of bureaucratic politics tells us that where individuals stand depends on where they sit, and that how they perceive a situation also depends on their bureaucratic role. The NATO enlargement policy process suggests that while bureaucratic position is crucial for understanding the orientation of officials at lower levels, the higher up you go, the more longstanding beliefs rather than a particular job title prove critical in many cases. Furthermore, how individuals perceived the decision of October 1993 and the import of presidential remarks in 1994 was dependent not on bureaucratic position but on attitude toward the policy; proponents perceived administration backing for enlargement much sooner than did opponents.

At the Pentagon and the State Department, bureaucratic roles did motivate individuals at the working level in the NATO and the New Independent States offices. Both civilians and military personnel at the Department of Defense worried that taking in new members would dilute the effectiveness of a military alliance developed among advanced industrialized democracies and might revive the Russian military threat that had disappeared with the collapse of the Soviet Union in 1991. The military also worried about NATO's article 5 security guarantee, both in terms of committing American troops to the defense of new countries and in terms of the military requirements for that commitment. Within the Office of the Secretary of Defense, battles over who was eligible for Partnership for Peace and then over funding assistance to help countries participate in the program had raged between the Office of Regional (International) Security Affairs, which was not interested in the New Independent States, and the Office of International Security Policy, whose section on Russia and the New Independent States fought for inclusion of "its" countries first in the Partnership for Peace and then in the Warsaw Initiative funding effort.

At the State Department, meanwhile, bureaucratic roles also affected how individuals behaved. Officials in the European Bureau's Office on Security and Political Affairs worried that enlargement would make management of the alliance more difficult; since there was no enthusiasm among the other fifteen NATO partners, except within the German Ministry of Defense, these individuals assumed that a push for enlargement would be a huge headache when they had to convince the European allies of the merits. And in the newly created office on the New Independent States, there was uniform opposition to enlargement for fear that it would isolate the Russians in Europe, undermine Yeltsin's efforts at reform, and generally damage U.S.-Russian relations.[3]

The best example of the notion that "where you stand depends on where you sit" was Strobe Talbott. His influence on Christopher in October 1993 led to the recommendation to the president that avoided naming names, laying out a timetable or criteria, or developing a notion of associate membership status, and yet he was the individual most responsible for Christopher's decision to bring Holbrooke back to Washington in 1994. While interviews with numerous colleagues paint a complex and contradictory picture of his evolution, part of the Talbott story must lie in his promotion from ambassador-at-large for and adviser to the secretary of state on the New Independent States (NIS) to deputy secretary of state in February 1994. Once he became responsible for overseeing European security "architecture" and the management of affairs from the Atlantic to the Urals, his views of enlargement as a key part of the administration's strategy for Europe evolved.

One problem with the bureaucratic politics model is that, a priori, it may be difficult to predict which way a bureaucratic role should tilt. For example, should the military be more likely to oppose new missions and new obligations, or in time of doubt about budgets, should the military be expected to seek new missions and obligations? Similarly with bureaucrats in the NATO offices. It is easy after the fact to ascribe their reluctance on enlargement to their bureaucratic role, but they might just as easily be expected to support enlargement on the premise that they would see it as increasing NATO's relevance in the post–cold war world. Even making a case then that at the working level individuals acted according to job title is not unambiguous.

The relevance of the bureaucratic politics model decreases as the attitudes of officials at the highest levels, for whom individual beliefs seem to be a more critical factor than particular position in the bureaucracy, are examined. In the NATO enlargement decision, the most important belief was the place of U.S.-Russian cooperation in the hierarchy of American foreign policy objectives in the eastern half of Europe. Those who viewed the U.S.-Russian relationship as the single most important objective, far outranking other U.S. priorities in the region, either flatly opposed expansion or believed it could only be considered well down the road. It was not William Perry's appointment as secretary of defense that shaped his attitude, but his long-held beliefs on the paramount importance of reducing the nuclear threat emanating from Russia. From his academic position at Stanford's Center for International Security and Arms Control, Perry had written forcefully on the subject, as had Assistant Secretary of Defense Ashton Carter at Harvard. As they recall, "The ideas and commitments reflected here [in our book] began . . . with work we did well before we began this period of government service."[4] (Even Strobe Talbott, who articulated views as ambassador-at-large in 1993 consistent with his bureaucratic role, had developed those attitudes during years of writing about Russia and the need for ending the antagonism in the U.S.-Russian relationship, attitudes that long predated his government service.)[5]

Informed by their longstanding beliefs, Perry and Carter believed that the Partnership for Peace was the best way of ensuring that cooperative security with militaries and governments throughout the region would continue, including in those states in Eastern Europe or the former Soviet Union that were unlikely to become NATO members. They have written, "We argued in 1995 that NATO's Partnership for Peace was the best foundation for NATO's eastward policy, and we continue to believe this today. . . . But attention was diverted from PFP [the Partnership for Peace] in 1995 by the question of NATO membership."[6]

On the other side, the early enlargement enthusiasts, such as Anthony Lake, Madeleine Albright, Thomas Donilon, Lynn Davis, and Stephen Flanagan, did not view the U.S.-Russian relationship as paramount, but rather as one interest among a number of important American foreign policy objectives in the region. It would be hard to predict from bureaucratic position whether a State Department chief of staff or presidential national security adviser would oppose or support NATO enlargement; what is crucial to understand is that for these individuals, assisting reform in central Europe and demonstrating U.S. leadership were at least as important as the continued security cooperation with Russia. Albright's deep personal commitment to the region and her first-hand understanding of the historical problems caused by German/Russian competition in central and eastern Europe led to her strong support for enlargement. Early in the first term—holding cabinet rank as the U.S. ambassador to the United Nations—she would have been a more influential voice in the decision process had there been formal Principals Committee meetings bringing her to Washington from New York.

For President Clinton, a trade-off between wanting to support reform in central and eastern Europe as well as reform in Russia likely introduced a problem that scholars refer to as "value complexity." What does one do if pursuing one objective seems adversely to affect the pursuit of another important objective? If an individual were oriented toward making one of these issues a priority over the other, as Perry did with Russia or Lake did with central and eastern Europe, then value complexity was not as large a problem. But for President Clinton, whose top national security objective was reform in Russia but who wanted to support Walesa and Havel for diplomatic and political reasons, this trade-off should have been quite difficult.

Psychologists tell us that when faced with the problem of competing objectives, individuals often convince themselves that there is no contradiction, that they can, in the words of one senior official discussing the two tracks of this policy, "walk and chew gum at the same time." Numerous administration officials said in interviews that President Clinton did not view these objectives as contradictory; he did not view NATO enlargement as anti-Russian, and, his advisers say, he believed he could convince Yeltsin of his attitude. He was certainly conscious of the trade-off, however, since he told Yeltsin in 1994 that he would delay being explicit about the NATO enlargement timetable until after the 1996 Russian presidential elections.[7]

Believing Is Seeing

Because there was never a single moment at which one could say definitively, "The President has now decided to enlarge NATO," participants saw the course of events in 1993–94 very differently, depending on their attitudes. Their responses to the question, "When did you believe that the decision to expand NATO had been made?" demonstrate that what you see depends on where you stand. Most enlargement supporters, such as Anthony Lake, Thomas Donilon, and Lynn Davis, cite the period between the October 1993 Principals Committee meeting and Clinton's trip to Europe in January 1994 as the time when the decision was made. They are incredulous that anyone failed to see the importance of the president's comments in Prague. The answers of opponents, however, generally range over the second half of 1994, depending on when they finally realized that Clinton was serious. Some officials understood things had shifted after the president's remarks in July in Warsaw; others, like General John M. Shalikashvili and Lieutenant General Wesley Clark at the Joint Chiefs of Staff, realized the policy was moving after their objections to Vice President Al Gore's September 1994 Berlin speech were dismissed. William Perry and Ashton Carter say they did not realize expansion was seriously on the table until after the Holbrooke interagency meetings in September and October 1994, and they only fully understood that enlargement was policy after the informal foreign policy team meeting with the president on December 21, 1994.

In fact, in interviews, Perry and General Shalikashvili remembered in vivid detail that December 1994 meeting with the president and their efforts to delay consideration of enlargement. Lake has no recollection of the meeting, nor does any of his staff. Christopher remembers Perry's concerns but not the meeting, nor does any of his staff. Why? Probably because Perry and Shalikashvili only learned then that enlargement was moving forward, which imprinted the meeting in their memory, whereas Lake and Christopher had believed the decision was taken months, if not a year, before. To the latter, the meeting was so much less significant that they cannot even recall it.[8]

The interpretations of when NATO enlargement was decided vary so widely because the president and his top advisers did not make a formal decision about a process for expansion or a timetable. Lake acknowledges, "My sin was not having a more *formal* process in the fall of 1993. I thought the policy was in place in December [1993]. I was surprised at Holbrooke's need to confront the Pentagon later. In the fall of 1993, Somalia, Haiti, Bosnia, and other issues dominated events. I was focused more on these short term crises than the process on longer term strategic issues, although we were addressing them."[9] Interestingly, Elizabeth Drew reports that on October 19, 1993 (the day Clinton approved his advisers' recommendation for the January 1994 summit), Secretary Christopher and Vice President Gore met with the president in the Oval Office and "Clinton complained that the national security system wasn't working well enough and that he had-n't been adequately involved in the decisions. Clinton also said he thought there should be more Principals meetings—that the Deputies Committee was stretched too thin."[10]

The when, who, how, and even why came over time, and only the decision on "who" seems to have been made through a formal decisionmaking process. In January 1994, when the president first said he expected the alliance to take in new members, no consensus existed among his top advisers on the difficult questions of when, how, and who, and this lack of consensus continued to exist for some time: "how" emerged in the 1995 NATO study; Clinton answered "when" in his campaign speech in Detroit in October 1996; and the administration decided the "who" in June 1997. In early 1994 then, Clinton's advisers could as reasonably believe that his remarks amounted to no more than a vague statement that NATO might someday expand as they could believe that the president wanted to begin moving forward *now*. No wonder proponents and opponents—at the highest levels of the U.S. government—cite dates spanning more than a year when picking the moment when President Clinton decided to enlarge NATO.

The Pros and Cons of the Policy Process

Scholars often disparage bureaucratic compromises as leading to suboptimal outcomes: the need to give something to everyone leads to bad policy. The enlargement process shows, however, that bureaucratic wrangling can at times produce better policy outcomes than individual agencies would create on their own.

For example, the Partnership for Peace was a better program as a result of the compromises reached among the National Security Council staff, State Department, and Pentagon. Had the individuals working on NATO in the Office of the Secretary of Defense had their way, the Partnership for Peace would have excluded the countries of the former Soviet Union, leaving them out of the effort to create a new military environment in Europe. Had the State Department's efforts to "operationalize" the North Atlantic Cooperation Council prevailed, it would have created another multilateral institution in Europe that—as one Pentagon staffer has recalled Principal Deputy Undersecretary of Defense for Policy Walter Slocombe arguing in the fall of 1993—would then have moved "at the speed of the slowest ship." The program that emerged, which included all countries of the North Atlantic Cooperation Council plus the European neutrals but allowed each country to develop its own individual partnership with NATO, stemmed from the compromises reached in the interagency working group.

Similarly, the two-track approach to enlargement was better than its alternatives. Those promoting concrete steps on enlargement in January 1994—Anthony Lake at the White House and Lynn Davis at the State Department—did not provide an explicit enough place for Russia in the process. Similarly, the effort by William Perry and General John Shalikashvili to get the NATO-Russia track in place before proceeding with enlargement would have given Russia too much of a voice in NATO's efforts in central Europe. The "road map to enlargement" paper produced in 1994 by Daniel Fried, Alexander Vershbow, and

Nicholas Burns at the National Security Council was successful in part because it was produced outside of bureaucratic channels, but also because it reflected a consensus forming at the National Security Council and the State Department that enlargement and a NATO-Russia track would have to proceed in parallel for the policy to be effective.

The interagency efforts on both the Partnership for Peace and the two-track policy demonstrate, however, that the post–cold war effort to create separate offices managing European and Russian affairs has been misguided. Those responsible for European affairs no longer have any bureaucratic incentive to concern themselves with America's Russia policy. Previously, the National Security Council's senior director for European affairs and the assistant secretary of state for European affairs had to worry about Russia on a daily basis. Now, they can leave that task to the National Security Council's senior director for Russian, Ukrainian, and Eurasian affairs and to the State Department's ambassador-at-large for the New Independent States. The division has been less of a problem at the National Security Council, because the three senior directors (for Europe, central Europe and Russia) have shared a balcony in the Old Executive Office Building during the Clinton administration and have kept in constant contact. This was not true at the State Department. If the United States is serious about its objective of a unified Europe, its bureaucracy should be configured so that the Europe policy and the Russia policy are produced in the same place.

The Costs of Informality

It is shocking that the secretary of defense and the chairman of the Joint Chiefs of Staff were surprised to find out that the White House believed that it had already put in motion a policy on a major strategic issue. The fact that Perry needed to call a meeting on December 21, 1994, to get clarification that the push to enlarge was coming not from NATO bureaucrats but from the White House is remarkable. The concerns held by Secretary of Defense Perry and General John Shalikashvili were serious: that enlargement would damage the denuclearization efforts in Russia or that it would diminish the effectiveness of the alliance. Thus these reservations should have been raised with the president before, not after, a decision had been made.

The lack of formality led to the failure to cover all the bases early in the process. For example, there was no real consideration in 1993–94 of the so-called "gray zone"—that is, those countries that would not get into NATO in the first round. Any comprehensive policy that sought to enlarge NATO and to create a new relationship with Russia should have considered how best to manage the relationships with the other central and eastern European aspirants before embarking, but those issues were not addressed until 1996 at the earliest. Similarly, a new initiative to increase America's defense commitment should have had a cost estimate done in the early deliberations. One should want to know the projected costs before embarking on a policy, not after the policy has been decided. Had the projected costs turned out to be much higher, decisionmakers could have factored that into a decision.

The lack of administration consultation with congressional enlargement supporters until 1997 is disturbing because it meant that there was no real public debate held until after membership invitations had been issued. In addition to needing Senate consent, the administration should have wanted congressional support to build the case that there was a broad base of Democrats and Republicans who wanted NATO to enlarge. But the administration was distrustful of Republicans, particularly after 1994, and congressional Republicans wanted to promote enlargement as part of their efforts to distinguish their positions from those of the White House. Neither had any real incentive to work with the other, and this gave rise to a sentiment widely expressed in 1997–98 that senators would have to vote in favor of enlargement because U.S. credibility was on the line at that point but not because they had engaged in detailed discussions with the administration from 1994 to 1996.

There were a number of reasons why the process was not more formal. The national security adviser had to deal first with the crises in front of him—in Bosnia, Haiti, Somalia—and long-term issues naturally are harder to focus on. Meanwhile, Perry, who had his own immediate issues of denuclearization, did not know he needed a meeting with the president until it was too late. Most important was the president: Clinton not only wanted to keep his options open (typical of a president), but he also wanted to keep foreign policy away from his day-to-day affairs as much as possible.

Conversely, some might argue in the end that the division between the principal foreign policy advisers was not that great. After all, what Perry and Shalikashvili argued was not that enlargement should never happen but that it should only happen at the end of the process that the

Partnership for Peace was designed to develop: military-to-military cooperation that would increase the capabilities of these countries to perform missions with NATO. And since it did take five years to complete the first round of NATO's post–cold war enlargement, was there any meaningful difference in the end between their vision and that of the "fast-trackers?" Yes, because had the enlargement process not been put on track in 1994, NATO would never have completed its work internally, with the aspirants, and with Russia in the time frame that it did. It would never have begun that process in the fall of 1994 had the partnership proponents prevailed.

Still, it is only through formal meetings that a president is likely to hear first-hand the diverse opinions and concerns of his senior advisers. Lake's focus on crises, which is typical of any high-level government officials given the tremendous burdens they face every day, and President Clinton's lack of foreign policy focus in 1993–94 led to a decision process that only haphazardly addressed many of the core issues of NATO's enlargement.

Some people may remain frustrated at still not knowing either *the* moment of decision or President Clinton's underlying, ulterior motive in enlarging NATO. However, many policies—even those as significant as this one—develop in an ambiguous fashion. This ambiguity is hardly unique to the Clinton administration, although the president's proclivity to avoid firm commitments added to it. White House meetings often leave participants, as well as those they inform, with conflicting understandings of what the administration has decided, as happened in October 1993. Policy entrepreneurs use presidential statements to push forward an issue that remains highly contentious in the bureaucracy. Each step alone seems trivial. But cumulatively they can result in momentous policies.

As for motive, Lech Walesa and Vaclav Havel may well have made a huge impression on a president open to emotional appeals when they sought his support for NATO expansion into central Europe in April 1993. Still, given that Clinton cared so much about the fate of Russian reform, Walesa's appeal to bring Poland and other central European nations into the West could hardly have been sufficient. Rather, Clinton's motive was probably more complex, and in all likelihood he has only a vague idea of when he himself made the formal commitment to proceed with enlargement. For Clinton the appeal by the central Europeans to erase the line drawn for them in 1945, the need to demonstrate U.S. leadership at a time when others questioned that leadership, and his own Wilsonian orientation toward spreading democracy all played important roles. He convincingly articulated many times during his presidency a vision of a unified, peaceful, democratic Europe.[11] But none of this would have mattered had the politics been different: if key constituencies had mounted opposition to enlargement as they had against free trade issues, it is hard to imagine that President Clinton could have gone ahead with a policy that the Pentagon did not initially favor. And the potential political appeal to white, ethnic voters in the Midwest and Northeast—voters the Democratic party lost to Reagan and Bush in the 1980s—was not lost on the policy entrepreneurs who pushed for NATO enlargement.

Politics

Finding evidence of the influence of domestic politics on the Clinton administration's decision to enlarge NATO is not easy, particularly since the foreign policy officials take such great pains to insist that domestic politics had no influence. And even Clinton's political guru Dick Morris dismissed the importance of ethnic votes when asked if he did polling on enlargement. "Neither I nor the president ever believed there is such a thing as a Polish vote," Morris said. "There is a white vote, a black vote, a Jewish vote, and a Hispanic vote. No other ethnic group votes as a bloc."[12]

Morris also describes in his book *Beyond the Oval Office* the relationship between the political and foreign policy sides of the White House (and one that fits well with what staffers on the National Security Council have recalled):

> The president's episodic interest in foreign policy in the early days of 1995 was reflected in the organization of his White House. The NSC staff, headed by Tony Lake and Deputy National Security Adviser Sandy Berger, was separated by a castle moat from the rest of the White House staff. Even [Leon] Panetta had very little to do with foreign issues, and George Stephanopoulos often complained to me that he was 'shut out' of what the NSC staff was doing on important decisions. . . . If the White House staff had limited access to the NSC, you can imagine how little access I had. Whenever I came too close to NSC issues, the foreign policy

> staff honked like geese on a pond, warning one another of an approaching dog. Tony Lake, deeply idealistic but highly territorial, thought political advice was unchaste.[13]

Several National Security Council staffers said in interviews that Lake grew visibly upset if they even joked about ethnic votes when discussing NATO enlargement.

As we have seen, however, politics played an important role in several aspects of the enlargement process. First of all, Lake's own interest in democracy promotion stemmed not just from his Wilsonian approach to international politics but also from the 1992 Clinton campaign efforts to find issues that could garner support among conservative Democrats. Bill Clinton did in fact do extremely well in districts with high concentrations of Americans of central and eastern European descent compared with his unsuccessful Democratic predecessors in the 1980s, and this point was not lost on Lake and Holbrooke, the policy entrepreneurs. Republicans sought to make inroads in this support through the 1994 Contract with America and during the Dole presidential campaign, but the Clinton White House always did enough to keep the issue for itself.

The policy was not ultimately a policy until the president announced a date for the accession of new members and until he had received Senate consent, and in both cases politics were important. From 1994 to 1996, domestic pressure had kept the policy on track: the continual criticism of respected strategic thinkers like Kissinger and Brzezinski, the public disappointment of Walesa and Havel with the Partnership for Peace, the campaign by Polish Americans and others in the ethnic community, and the legislative efforts by House and Senate Republicans. The politics of Russia meant that the president could not name names or declare a timetable until after July 1996, but it is no accident that Bill Clinton stated while campaigning in Detroit two weeks before the election that new members should enter the alliance in 1999. What he did not want was the phenomenon Senator Barbara A. Mikulski (D-Md.) often described to the president and others in the administration: "[My great-grandmother] kept on her mantelpiece three pictures: one of my Uncle Joe when he made the police force, the other Pius XII, and the other [Franklin Delano] Roosevelt. But after Yalta and Potsdam, my great-grandmother turned the picture of Roosevelt down because she felt the betrayal of Poland."[14]

Politics in the Senate

With the cold war over, it would be difficult enough for a president to gain congressional approval for a major foreign policy initiative. As congressional scholar James M. Lindsay argues, "Put simply, the collapse of the Soviet Union made obsolete the foreign-policy consensus on which presidential leadership in foreign affairs rested for four decades and emboldened members of Congress to challenge the White House over the direction of U.S. foreign policy."[15] Add to that Republican control of both houses of Congress, and a Democratic president could have expected to face an uphill battle to gain approval for the enlargement of NATO, as Bill Clinton did on issues like fast-track trade authority and funding for the United Nations.

As we have seen, there were a number of factors that led to the overwhelming Senate vote in favor of this policy. The national campaign organized by the administration's NATO enlargement ratification office, and supplemented by the efforts of leading members of the Senate NATO Observer Group, by the central Europeans and their ethnic supporters, and by Republican heavyweights on the U.S. Committee to Expand NATO, meant that all the political signals pointed toward support for enlargement. The columnists and academics who opposed enlargement on the op-ed pages and in leading journals had no comparable campaign. The pro-enlargement campaign occupied the political center and could not be defeated by the efforts of a few organizations on the left and right wings. The academics were as united in opposition as the bureaucracy had been but failed because the politics favored proponents not opponents and because they were not well organized.

A second major factor was the perception of Senate Republicans that they—not Bill Clinton—had been the engine driving enlargement. The attitude of Congressman Gerald Solomon (R-N.Y.) was widely shared: "It was Congress itself that had led the way on the enlargement issue."[16] Senator Richard Lugar (R-Ind.) had spoken forcefully in favor of enlargement before the administration did. Republicans had written enlargement into the Contract with America in 1994. Republicans had driven the legislative process from 1994 through the passage of the NATO Enlargement Facilitation Act in 1996. Senate Republicans claimed as much ownership of this issue as the administration did, which made their consent in April 1998 more likely than if they had seen this as a Democratic initiative.

Drawing lessons from Woodrow Wilson's failure to gain consent to the Treaty of Versailles in 1919 and finally realizing the folly of not consulting with Congress from 1994 to 1996, the Clinton administration consciously sought to include Senate Republicans in the ratification process in 1997-98. Lindsay noted, "When the Treaty of Versailles was signed in 1919, it enjoyed considerable support on Capitol Hill, though not in the form . . . in which it was submitted. Wilson, however, refused to accept the modified language that would have secured the two-thirds majority needed for approval." Wilson also did not take senators with him to Paris.[17] The Clinton administration took members of Congress to Paris and Madrid in 1997 and then worked closely with Senate staffers to put together a resolution of ratification that both branches of government could support.

For Senate Democrats who may have been skeptical of the administration's approach, by 1998 it was difficult to vote against an initiative the president had been touting for several years. Senator Joseph Biden (D-Del.) said of Congress at one of the NATO hearings in October 1997,

> We cannot make foreign policy. We can initiate things like Nunn-Lugar. . . . But, ultimately, we basically react in the area of foreign policy. If we had our way, I could make the argument that continuing the Partnership for Peace, which turned out to be much more robust and much more successful than I think anyone thought it would be at the outset, may arguably have been a better way to go, and that to continue that process and beef it up before you move to expansion, if you move to expansion, would have been better. But we are where we are.[18]

To overturn enlargement, senators would have needed a good reason. And with the NATO-Russia Founding Act signed and the cost estimates appearing quite low, it was hard for opponents to generate momentum against the policy. As leading enlargement opponent Michael Mandelbaum argued, "It passed because everyone was convinced that the stakes were low. Senators could persuade themselves that it didn't matter. This was a free vote for senators."[19]

No Debate?

Many opponents bemoaned the lack of visible public debate for such a major foreign policy initiative. But why would the public be interested in what appeared to be a low-cost extension of a defense commitment in a benign strategic environment? Had there been a real military threat to Poland, with the possibility of real U.S. military action, the public would have likely been more engaged.

In fact, there were a large number of congressional hearings on the issue, and the president did speak many times on the subject, albeit in forums with interested audiences. The general lack of public attention was not a new phenomenon. In 1949 *New York Times* columnist James Reston decried the complete disinterest of the public in NATO's creation, which had been an unprecedented step that overturned George Washington's admonition in his Farewell Address not to become involved in entangling alliances. Reston wrote, "When the Senate Foreign Relations Committee completed hearings on the North Atlantic Treaty this afternoon the question thoughtful observers here were asking was whether the lack of excitement over this legislation indicated public acceptance, public indifference, public ignorance or all three." Similarly, when Greece and Turkey were proposed for membership in 1952, the Senate Foreign Relations Committee held only one hearing, which lasted one and one-half hours. When the resolution was brought to the floor on January 29, only six senators were present, and all six voted in favor after a ten-minute discussion. Although the Senate later decided it needed to go through the process again in a more serious vein with a vote by the full body, the issue was not subject to tremendous scrutiny.[20]

The Future

In the end, groups with three different orientations provided the support for NATO's first round of enlargement into central Europe. Each was fixated on solving a different historical problem. The first group, conscious of the historical lessons of the first half of the century, worried about the revival of 1930s Germany. These individuals believed that the chief threat to peace in central Europe was the renationalization of German foreign policy, and they did not want Germany to believe that instability to its east was likely and would have to be dealt with unilaterally. Peace in Europe for these multilateralists depends on Germany's ties to the Western community and on its being embedded in regional institutions. The answer to the potential German problem was to move the eastern border of NATO to the eastern border of

Poland, thus centering Germany in the alliance rather than leaving it on the flank. German Defense Minister Volker Rühe (the earliest enlargement proponent among Europe's official elite) and RAND analyst Ronald Asmus promoted this rationale, and they heavily influenced U.S. Ambassador to Germany Richard Holbrooke.

The second group—the consolidators—focused on preventing future Bosnias, and they often reiterated that enlargement would "do for Europe's East what NATO did for Europe's West."[21] Seeing the potential for numerous border conflicts, they sought to provide NATO enlargement as a reward for adoption of Western political and economic norms. This group believed that creating democracy, a market economy, civilian control over the military, and border treaties would lead to peace and prosperity that would then be consolidated by NATO. Those taking this approach included President Clinton, National Security Adviser Anthony Lake, and, over time, Deputy Secretary of State Strobe Talbott.

The final group, steeped in the lessons of the cold war, was interested not primarily in reassurance in Germany or central Europe but rather in deterrence. To these individuals, the chief threat was the possibility of a future attempt by Russia to re-create an imperial security zone in central and eastern Europe in a bid to achieve hegemony in Europe. The answer to this problem was to enlarge NATO to protect the central and eastern Europeans and to fulfill NATO's core mission as a military alliance. The hedgers included former national security adviser Zbigniew Brzezinski; former secretary of state Henry Kissinger; Senator Hank Brown (R-Colo.), the key pro-enlargement legislator in the Senate until his retirement in 1996; and Senator Jesse Helms (R-N.C.), chairman of the Senate Foreign Relations Committee.

The Paradox of Enlargement

Any coalition that includes Richard Holbrooke, Strobe Talbott, Henry Kissinger, Tony Lake, and Jesse Helms is ripe for dissolution.[22] Whereas divergent threat perceptions made a large coalition favoring round one of enlargement possible, these same perceptions make future rounds much more difficult. The multilateralists, seeking to reassure the Germans, wanted to include Poland, cared much less about Hungary and the Czech Republic, have almost no interest in the Baltics, and do not want to provoke Russia. Round one satisfies them. The consolidators are eager to assist the central Europeans, but they do not want

Russia to feel isolated. They tout the open door as a way of reassuring the Russians that they too might someday get in, but they do not want to extend NATO in a way that sabotages efforts at reassuring Russia that the West is interested in stability, not provocation. This group is most conflicted about NATO's future since the logic of the position is to keep enlarging (Lake's original objective), but many, as good liberals, do not want to push Russia into a corner (Talbott's concern). Meanwhile, the hedgers want to keep Russia down and deterred, and some thus want to continue to press forward while Russia is weak. But even this crowd is wary of going too far, too fast, since they want to preserve NATO as an effective military alliance.

The paradox of enlargement, however, is that the first round only makes sense if NATO delivers on the Clinton administration's open-door promise in the future. Taking in the first three countries and then stopping merely redraws the line in Europe a bit further to the east and undermines Clinton's initial rationale, which was to make NATO the foundation of a unified, democratic, peaceful Europe. But while the logic of the policy suggests that the process continue, future rounds will be even harder for NATO to achieve than the first one, because the diverse coalition is likely to fracture. Three contentious issues were finessed during the Senate debate of 1998: the reaction of Russia, the potential financial costs, and the concerns about dilution of the alliance. Once the NATO-Russia Founding Act was signed in Paris in May 1997, it was difficult for critics to make the case that Russia found enlargement unacceptable. Once the Pentagon examined the existing infrastructure, and given the benign strategic environment, projected costs became much less than expected. Finally, those who feared that NATO would lose its character if it grew too large and would simply become another Organization for Security and Cooperation in Europe were comfortable with accepting three new members, as opposed to four or five.

Each of these issues is harder to finesse as NATO looks beyond the first round. While Slovenia and Romania (and Austria and Sweden, for that matter) are not particularly threatening to Russia, any second round puts the Baltic issue to the fore. The Russians time and again have stated their vitriolic opposition to inclusion of any former Soviet republic. But if Lithuania came to meet alliance membership criteria, why should its claim be less valid than those of others? Those who supported enlargement in round one despite misgivings regarding the effect on Russia, however, would fear any future rounds that raised a Baltic candidacy, which Russia would view as highly provocative.

Similarly, more members mean more costs. The U.S. Senate made clear during its ratification debate that it did not want the United States to spend significantly more on NATO than it already does. Finally, those who fear the end of NATO as a collective defense organization (and its transformation into a collective security pact) will want to see what effect the three new members have on the alliance, which will lengthen the time between the first and second rounds.

The administration understood early in 1999 how little enthusiasm existed on Capitol Hill and in Europe for another round of enlargement. Since no one cared as much about enlargement at the highest levels of the U.S. government as Anthony Lake, his absence from the administration in the second term meant that at the NATO fiftieth anniversary summit, the alliance merely reiterated that the door is still open, that a new "Membership Action Plan" would help aspirant countries know if they are making progress, and that NATO will review the open door process at a summit in 2002. In other words, the Clinton administration left enlargement's future to its successor.[23]

Just as Bosnia was important as round one developed, so will Kosovo be for round two. Warren Christopher and others were right that if NATO could not solve Bosnia, it could not justify enlarging to solve other Bosnias. And U.S. leadership in 1995 to bring peace to a conflict that had raged for four years made the Europeans more willing to accede to U.S. demands on NATO policies regarding the how, the when, and the who of enlargement. The United States would have been unlikely to convince anyone that NATO needed to enlarge in the absence of a solution to the war in Bosnia.

One effect of the war in Kosovo will be to exacerbate enlargement skeptics' concerns about costs, about Russia's reactions, or about the implications of an alliance that numbers more than twenty. Paying for the war and reconstruction will crowd out money for other purposes. The Russian public's and elite's reaction to NATO's attack on Yugoslavia has caused greater despair among those who already feared that a new cold war would ensue in Europe because of expansion. And talk of the difficulties of fighting war by committee will raise doubts that a larger alliance can function as an effective military machine.

Furthermore, the administration sold enlargement to the Senate not on the "consolidation" rationale but using the argument of the "hedgers." NATO, the administration assured Senate Republicans, was at its core a military alliance designed to defend against armed attack. The attack on Yugoslavia to stop ethnic cleansing is precisely the new mission that Senator John Ashcroft (R-Mo.) sought to preclude with his proposed amendment to the resolution of ratification. Those in the Senate who accepted the administration's claims that NATO is primarily a collective defense organization will be harder to convince in the future, given the Kosovo mission.

In the end then, the first round of NATO enlargement answered some questions and left others unanswered. The United States did demonstrate during the process that it still led the alliance, and it reassured Germany that its eastern border would remain stable. NATO also granted Poland, Hungary, and the Czech Republic the security they have never known. And finally, NATO demonstrated through enlargement (as it did by conducting the war against Yugoslavia) that it is as much an institution of shared values as it is an alliance to defend shared interests.

What NATO's 1999 enlargement left unanswered is first, what the future holds for the NATO-Russia relationship and second, what will happen to the countries that still aspire to NATO membership. These two questions hold the key to a future Europe that is undivided, peaceful, and democratic. A truly cooperative relationship between a new NATO and a new Russia requires that NATO convince Russia that neither taking in new members nor adopting new missions are directed against it; it also requires that Russia convince NATO that it will stay on the right track politically and diplomatically. The Permanent Joint Council provided for in the NATO-Russia Founding Act has done little because NATO is still unsure that it wants to give Russia a real voice in NATO's affairs and because Russia fears that participation will give a green light to NATO to act.

As for those still aspiring to NATO membership, the decision by President Clinton and his NATO colleagues in April 1999 to announce that they would conduct a review of the open-door process no later than 2002 has postponed the issue of a second round for the next president of the United States to address. While it was Bill Clinton who argued that NATO could serve as the foundation for a unified, peaceful, and democratic Europe, it will be the next administration that in fact decides if NATO's future enlargement is not a question of whether, but of when and how.

Notes

Chapter One

1. See Thomas W. Lippman, "NATO Embraces 3 from Warsaw Pact," *Washington Post*, March 13, 1999, p. A18.

2. George F. Kennan, "A Fateful Error," *New York Times*, February 5, 1997, p. A23.

3. Thomas Hobbes, *Leviathan*, edited by Richard Tuck (Cambridge University Press, 1996), p. 119. Modern proponents of this view include political scientists Kenneth Waltz and John Mearsheimer.

4. There are many useful studies of the decisionmaking process. These include Richard C. Snyder, H. W. Bruck, and Burton Sapin, *Decision-Making as an Approach to the Study of International Politics* (Princeton University Press, 1954); Richard E. Neustadt, *Presidential Power: The Politics of Leadership with Reflections on Johnson and Nixon* (John Wiley & Sons, Inc., 1976); Warner R. Schilling, Paul Y. Hammond, and Glenn H. Snyder, *Strategy, Politics, and Defense Budgets* (Columbia University Press, 1962); Samuel P. Huntington, "Interservice Competition and the Political Roles of the Armed Services," *American Political Science Review*, vol. 55 (March 1961), pp. 40–52; Paul Y. Hammond, "The National Security Council as a Device for Interdepartmental Coordination," *American Political Science Review*, vol. 54 (December 1960), pp. 899–910; Bernard C. Cohen, "Foreign Policy-Making: Modern Design," *World Politics*, vol. 5 (April 1953), pp. 377–91; Graham T. Allison, *Essence of Decision: Explaining the Cuban Missile Crisis* (Little, Brown, 1971); Graham T. Allison, "Conceptual Models and the Cuban Missile Crisis," *American Political Science Review*, vol. 63 (September 1969), pp.

689–718; Graham T. Allison and Morton H. Halperin, "Bureaucratic Politics: A Paradigm and Some Policy Implications," *World Politics*, vol. 24 supplement (Spring 1972), pp. 40–79; Stephen D. Krasner, "Are Bureaucracies Important? (Or Allison Wonderland)," *Foreign Policy*, vol. 7 (Summer 1972), pp. 159–79; Robert J. Art, "Bureaucratic Politics and American Foreign Policy: A Critique," *Policy Sciences*, vol. 4 (December 1973), pp. 467–90; Morton H. Halperin with Priscilla Clapp and Arnold Kanter, *Bureaucratic Politics and Foreign Policy* (Brookings, 1974); Halperin and Kanter, eds., *Readings in American Foreign Policy: A Bureaucratic Perspective* (Little, Brown, 1973); Jonathan Bendor and Thomas H. Hammond, "Rethinking Allison's Models," *American Political Science Review*, vol. 86 (June 1992), pp. 301–22; David A. Welch, "The Organizational Process and Bureaucratic Politics Paradigms: Retrospect and Prospect," *International Security*, vol. 17 (Fall 1992), pp. 112–46; I. M. Destler, *Presidents, Bureaucrats, and Foreign Policy: The Politics of Organizational Reform*, rev. ed. (Princeton University Press, 1974); Edward Rhodes, "Do Bureaucratic Politics Matter? Some Disconfirming Findings from the Case of the U.S. Navy," *World Politics*, vol. 47 (October 1994), pp. 1–41; Alexander L. George and Juliette L. George, *Presidential Personality and Performance* (Westview Press, 1998).

5. See, for example, Krasner, "Are Bureaucracies Important?" pp. 168–69; Welch, "The Organizational Process and Bureaucratic Politics Paradigms," p. 132; Bendor and Hammond, "Rethinking Allison's Models," p. 316; John W. Kingdon, *Agendas, Alternatives, and Public Policies*, 2d ed. (HarperCollins College Publishers, 1995), p. 31.

6. On these points, see Glenn H. Snyder and Paul Diesing, *Conflict among Nations: Bargaining, Decisionmaking, and System Structure in International Crises* (Princeton University Press, 1977), p. 512; Krasner, "Are Bureaucracies Important?" p. 165; Welch, "Organizational Process and Bureaucratic Politics," p. 131; Robert Jervis, *Perception and Misperception in International Politics* (Princeton University Press, 1976)

7. Francis E. Rourke, *Bureaucracy and Foreign Policy* (Johns Hopkins University Press, 1972), p. 26.

8. On this issue, see, for example, Deborah Welch Larson, *Origins of Containment: A Psychological Explanation* (Princeton University Press, 1985); Yuen Foong Khong, *Analogies at War: Korea, Munich, Dien Bien Phu, and the Vietnam Decisions of 1965* (Princeton University Press, 1992), pp. 10, 20–21; James M. Goldgeier, "Psychology and Security," *Security Studies*, vol. 6 (Summer 1997), pp. 137–66. For good overviews of the sources of perceptions, see Jervis, *Perception and Misperception*; Philip E. Tetlock, "Social Psychology and World Politics," in D. Gilbert, S. T. Fiske, and G. Lindsay, eds., *Handbook of Social Psychology*, 4th ed. (McGraw Hill, 1998), pp. 868–912.

9. See Warner R. Schilling, "The H-Bomb Decision: How to Decide Without Actually Choosing," *Political Science Quarterly,* vol. 76 (March 1961), pp. 24–46, for a set of similar questions.

10. Halperin, *Bureaucratic Politics*, p. 82.

11. Bob Woodward, *The Agenda: Inside the Clinton White House* (Simon & Schuster, 1994), p. 185.

12. See, for example, Alexander L. George and Eric Stern, "Presidential Management Styles and Models," in George and George, *Presidential Personality and Performance*, p. 244; Elizabeth Drew, *On the Edge: The Clinton Presidency* (Simon & Schuster, 1994), pp. 28, 139.

13. Kingdon, *Agendas*, p. 170. On entrepreneurs jumping through windows, see also Jeff Checkel, "Ideas, Institutions, and the Gorbachev Foreign Policy Revolution," *World Politics,* vol. 45 (January 1993), pp. 271–300.

14. For a similar discussion, see Destler, *Presidents, Bureaucrats, and Foreign Policy*, p. 58.

15. Halperin, *Bureaucratic Politics*, p. 223.

16. Henry Kissinger, *American Foreign Policy*, 3d ed. (Norton, 1977), pp. 22–23. On speeches, see also Richard Reeves, *President Kennedy: Profile of Power* (Simon & Schuster, 1993), p. 195; Warren Christopher, *In the Stream of History: Shaping Foreign Policy for a New Era* (Stanford University Press, 1998), pp. 8–11.

17. Many senior officials from the State Department and Pentagon who opposed the policy made this argument in interviews, as did outside critics such as Johns Hopkins University Professor Michael Mandelbaum. Staffers for congressional Republicans who supported enlargement but who were critical of the Clinton administration also argued in interviews that the president pursued this policy purely for political reasons. For a public articulation, see, for example, Thomas Friedman, "NATOwater," *New York Times*, May 19, 1997, p. A15; comments by Canadian prime minister Jean Chretien in John F. Harris, "Tape Catches Choice Words about Clinton," *Washington Post*, July 10, 1997, p. A24.

18. Robert J. Art, "Bureaucratic Politics and American Foreign Policy: A Critique," *Policy Sciences*, vol. 4 (December 1973), p. 469.

19. Halperin, *Bureaucratic Politics*, pp. 63–64.

20. On this point, see Art, "Bureaucratic Politics and American Foreign Policy," p. 475.

21. I. M. Destler, Leslie H. Gelb, and Anthony Lake, *Our Own Worst Enemy: The Unmaking of American Foreign Policy* (Simon & Schuster, 1984), p. 167.

22. Here I differ from Kingdon, who sees "the policy stream" and the "political stream" as conceptually distinct. See Kingdon, *Agendas*, p. 141.

23. Richard N. Haass, *The Bureaucratic Entrepreneur: How to Be Effective in Any Unruly Organization* (Brookings, 1999), p. 41.

Chapter Two

1. The story is well told in Philip Zelikow and Condoleezza Rice, *Germany Unified and Europe Transformed: A Study in Statecraft* (Harvard University Press, 1995); Elizabeth Pond, *After the Wall: U.S. Policy toward Germany* (New York: Priority Press Publications, 1990); Stephen F. Szabo, *The Diplomacy of German Unification* (St. Martin's Press, 1992); Szabo's review of Zelikow and Rice, in *German Politics and Society*, vol. 15 (Winter 1997), pp. 130–39; Michael R. Beschloss and Strobe Talbott, *At the Highest Levels: The Inside Story of the End of the Cold War* (Little, Brown, 1993); James A. Baker, *The Politics of Diplomacy: Revolution, War and Peace, 1989–1992* (G. P. Putnam's, 1995); George Bush and Brent Scowcroft, *A World Transformed* (Knopf, 1998); Hans-Dietrich Genscher, *Rebuilding a House Divided* (New York: Broadway Books, 1998); Robert D. Blackwill, "German Unification and American Diplomacy," *Aussenpolitik*, vol. 45 (1994), pp. 211–25; Alexander Moens, "American Diplomacy and German Unification," *Survival*, vol. 33 (November-December 1991), pp. 531–45.

2. For a good discussion of the different American and Russian views, see Angela E. Stent, *Russia and Germany Reborn: Unification, the Soviet Collapse, and the New Europe* (Princeton University Press, 1999), pp. 141, 225; Jonathan Eyal, "NATO's Enlargement: Anatomy of a Decision," *International Affairs*, vol. 73 (1997), p. 699. See also Michael Mandelbaum, *The Dawn of Peace in Europe* (New York: Twentieth Century Fund, 1996).

3. Szabo, *Diplomacy of German Unification*, pp. 57–58.

4. Zelikow and Rice, *Germany Unified,* p. 176.

5. Ibid., pp. 180–83.

6. Bush and Scowcroft, *A World Transformed*, pp. 239–41, 255; Zelikow and Rice, *Germany Unified*, pp. 184, 215; Michael R. Gordon, "The Anatomy of a Misunderstanding," *New York Times*, May 25, 1997, p. D-3. For an analysis of the Russian attitude on NATO expansion in this context, see Stent, *Russia and Germany Reborn,* pp. 141, 225.

7. On the nine assurances, see Baker, *Politics of Diplomacy*, pp. 250–51.

8. Genscher, *Rebuilding a House Divided*, p. 429.

9. Jonathan Osmond, *German Reunification: A Reference Guide and Commentary* (Longman, 1992), pp. 289–90.

10. Blackwill, "German Unification," p. 222; interview with Robert Zoellick, October 1998.

11. Robert L. Hutchings, *American Diplomacy and the End of the Cold War: An Insider's Account of U.S. Policy in Europe, 1989–1992* (Washington, D.C.: Woodrow Wilson Center Press, 1997), p. 290ff.

12. James Baker, "The Euro-Atlantic Architecture: From West to East," Berlin, June 18, 1991, in Department of State Dispatch, June 24, 1991, vol. 2, p. 440.

13. Jeffrey Simon, "Does Eastern Europe Belong in NATO?" *Orbis*, vol. 37 (Winter 1993), pp. 29–31; for a discussion of the new strategic concept associated with these efforts, see Hutchings, *American Diplomacy*, p. 293.

14. *NATO Handbook* (Brussels: 1995), pp. 237, 242.

15. RFE/RL Research Report, November 13, 1992, p. 63. Secretary Eagleburger's Parting Remarks to North Atlantic Cooperation Council, Brussels, December 18, 1992, *Foreign Policy Bulletin*, vol. 3 (January-April 1993), p. 116.

16. Christopher makes this same point in his book; see Warren Christopher, *In the Stream of History: Shaping Foreign Policy for a New Era* (Stanford University Press, 1998), p. 10. In the Athens speech, Christopher sought the summit by the end of the year. See his intervention at the North Atlantic Council ministerial meetings, "U.S. Leadership after the Cold War: NATO and Transatlantic Security," June 10, 1993, Department of State Dispatch, June 21, 1993, vol. 4, pp. 448–51.

17. See Christopher's remarks at his confirmation hearings, January 13, 1993, reprinted in *In the Stream of History*, p. 30.

18. See Elizabeth Drew, *On the Edge: The Clinton Presidency* (Simon & Schuster, 1994), pp. 119, 126, 132–35; The president's comments are from William Jefferson Clinton, "The President's News Conference," June 17, 1993, *Public Papers of the Presidents of the United States, 1993*, Book I (Government Printing Office, 1994) pp. 868–69. Material on this paragraph also comes from my interview with Anthony Lake (May 1997) and other U.S. government officials and with a central European official who was present at one of the meetings. See also Zbigniew Brzezinski and Anthony Lake, "For a New World, a New NATO," *New York Times*, June 30, 1997, p. A11. Clinton's references to these meetings over a long period of time reveal their importance to his thinking. In addition to his comments at news conferences in April and June, he referred to the meetings again in January 1994 just prior to the summit. See William Jefferson Clinton, "Exchange with Reporters Prior to Discussion with Prime Minister Ruud Lubbers of the Netherlands," January 4, 1994, *Public Papers of the Presidents of the United States, 1994,* Book I (Government Printing Office, 1995) pp. 5–6.

19. For the foreign policy campaign speech, see "Excerpts from Speech by Clinton on U.S. Role," *New York Times*, October 2, 1992, p. A21.

20. Drew, *On the Edge*, p. 141. Press briefing by Anthony Lake and General Wesley Clark, The White House, Office of the Press Secretary, May 5, 1994. For similar Lake remarks, see Antonia and Anthony Lake, "Coming of Age through Vietnam," *New York Times Magazine*, July 20, 1975, pp. 9ff.

21. I have discussed the political dimension of the October 1992 campaign speech and subsequent interest in democracy promotion with several high-level Clinton administration officials.

22. "Excerpts from President Clinton's News Conference," *Washington Post*, April 24, 1993, p. A16.

23. Interview with Thomas Donilon (September 1997). Warren Christopher, "U.S. Leadership after the Cold War," Department of State Dispatch, June 21, 1993, vol. 4, p. 450. On the last-minute calls, see Christopher, *In the Stream of History*, p. 131. The aside about Lake comes from an interview with a member of his National Security Council staff.

24. See also Gerald B. Solomon, *The NATO Enlargement Debate, 1990–1997: Blessings of Liberty* (Praeger Press [published with CSIS], 1998), p. 28.

25. Warren Christopher, "NATO and U.S. Foreign Policy," Brussels, February 26, 1993, in Department of State Dispatch, March 1, 1993, vol. 4, p. 120.

26. Interviews with Robert Hunter (September 1998), Thomas Donilon (September 1997), and other U.S. government officials.

27. Interviews with U.S. government officials.

28. Christopher, "U.S. Leadership after the Cold War," pp. 450–51.

29. On the working group, see Debra A. Cook and others, "Partnership for Peace: The Vector for European Security," Discussion Paper Series 97–002, (National Security Program, JFK School of Government, Harvard University, 1997), p. 15.

30. Walker's position is depicted in Solomon, *The NATO Enlargement Debate*, p. 28, and confirmed by interviews with working group participants.

31. Steven Erlanger, "Russia Vote Is a Testing Time for a Key Friend of Clinton's," *New York Times*, June 8, 1996, p. A1. On Talbott's career, see also Elaine Sciolino, "Clinton's Specialist on Russia to Fill No. 2 State Dept. Post," *New York Times*, December 28, 1993, p. A1; Michael Dobbs, "Strobe Talbott and the 'Cursed Questions,'" *Washington Post Magazine*, June 9, 1996, pp. 11ff.

32. Interviews with John Shalikashvili (July 1998) and other U.S. government officials. On the drawbacks of the NACC, see Hutchings, *American Diplomacy*, pp. 291–92. For a discussion of the ways in which the supreme allied commanders have influenced policy, see Robert S. Jordan, ed., *Generals in International Politics: NATO's Supreme Allied Commander, Europe* (University Press of Kentucky, 1987).

33. Interviews with Charles Freeman (August 1998) and other U.S. government officials.

34. See Solomon, *The NATO Enlargement Debate*, p. 28; interviews with Charles Freeman (August 1998) and other U.S. government officials. The Framework Document issued by NATO at the 1994 summit stated that partners "will fund their own participation in Partnership activities, and will endeavor otherwise to share the burdens of mounting exercises in which they take part." *NATO Review*, vol. 42 (February 1994), p. 29.

35. See Solomon, *The NATO Enlargement Debate*, p. 32; Charles Aldinger, "Aspin Told NATO Must Quickly Decide Future," Reuters, September 11, 1993; Cook and others, "Partnership for Peace," p. 6.

36. For a similar argument about U.S. interests see also Adam Garfinkle, "Losing One's Head over NATO," *Quadrant*, vol. 41 (September 1997), pp. 65–68.

37. Interviews with John Shalikashvili (July 1998), Charles Freeman (August 1998), and other U.S. government officials.

38. *Department of Defense Authorization for Appropriations for Fiscal Year 1994 and the Future Years Defense Program*, Hearings before the Senate Committee on Armed Services, pt. 4, 103 Cong. 1 sess. (Government Printing Office, 1994), pp. 80, 97.

39. On the link between Somalia and the name change, see Drew, *On the Edge*, p. 404. This was confirmed by interviews with U.S. government officials.

40. Charles Kupchan, "Strategic Visions," *World Policy Journal*, vol. 11 (Fall 1994), p. 113. This interpretation is also consistent with my interviews with William Perry (June 1997), Ashton Carter (May 1997), Graham Allison (May 1997), and other U.S. government officials. On the development of Partnership for Peace, see, for example, Catherine McArdle Kelleher, *The Future of European Security: An Interim Assessment* (Brookings, 1995); Philip H. Gordon, ed., *NATO's Transformation: The Changing Shape of the Atlantic Alliance* (Lanham, Md.: Rowman & Littlefield Publishers, Inc., 1997); and Gale A. Mattox, "The Debate over NATO Enlargement," paper prepared for the International Studies Association Annual Meeting, Toronto, March 19, 1997.

41. Christopher, *In the Stream of History*, p. 128.

42. Richard Holbrooke, *To End a War (*Random House, 1998), p. 80.

43. Descriptions of the lunches and the quote from the participant come from interviews with State Department officials. Supporting the evidence from my interviews is Michael Dobbs, "Wider Alliance Would Increase US Commitments," *Washington Post*, July 5, 1995, pp. A1, 16.

44. Hans Binnendijk, "NATO Can't Be Vague About Commitment to Eastern Europe," *International Herald Tribune*, November 8, 1991, p. 6.

45. Stephen J. Flanagan, "NATO and Central and Eastern Europe: From Liaison to Security Partnership," *Washington Quarterly*, vol. 15 (Spring 1992), pp. 142, 149–50.

46. NATO's role in promoting reform in central and eastern Europe had been publicly discussed in the Bush administration not only by Flanagan but also by Deputy Assistant Secretary of Defense Alberto Coll in "Power, Principles and Prospects for a Cooperative International Order," *Washington Quarterly*, vol. 16 (Winter 1993), pp. 5–14.

47. Interviews with Thomas Donilon (September 1997), Lynn Davis (August 1998), and other State Department officials.

48. Interviews with Thomas Donilon (September 1997) and other U.S. government officials.

49. Ibid.

50. On the role of this group, see Stephen F. Szabo, "Neither Yalta nor Versailles: The German-American Design for a New NATO," unpublished paper, March 1998. I have also confirmed these events through interviews.

51. Ronald D. Asmus, Richard L. Kugler, and F. Stephen Larrabee, "Building a New NATO," *Foreign Affairs*, vol. 72 (September/October 1993), pp. 28–40; Asmus, Kugler, and Larrabee, "NATO Expansion: The Next Steps," *Survival*, vol. 37 (Spring 1995), pp. 7–33; Asmus, Kugler, and Larrabee, "What Will NATO Enlargement Cost?" *Survival*, vol. 38 (Autumn 1996), pp. 5–26. In his book, former secretary of state Warren Christopher cites the importance of the first article. See Christopher, *In the Stream of History*, p. 129, footnote 2; see also Bruce Clark, "How the East Was Won," *Financial Times*, July 5, 1997, p. 3.

52. Asmus and others, "Building a New NATO," pp. 31–32, 37.

53. See Szabo, "Neither Yalta nor Versailles"; Reinhard Wolf, "The Doubtful Mover: Germany and NATO Expansion," in David Haglund, ed., *Will NATO Go East? The Debate over Enlarging the Atlantic Alliance* (Kingston, Ont., Canada: Queen's University, Centre for International Relations, 1996), pp. 197–224. The story also was confirmed by my interviews with individuals inside and outside the administration.

54. "Bonn Wants East in Updated NATO," *International Herald Tribune*, October 8, 1993, p. 6.

55. Szabo, "Neither Yalta nor Versailles," pp. 11–12; Wolf , "The Doubtful Mover," p. 206. Szabo also argues that Rühe was also looking for an issue that could bring him greater visibility within Germany and on which the defense ministry rather than the foreign ministry could take the lead.

56. For representative comments, see Volker Rühe, "Shaping Euro-Atlantic Policies: A Grand Strategy for a New Era," *Survival*, vol. 35 (Summer 1993), p. 134. On Kohl's shifts, see Eyal, "NATO's Enlargement," p. 704.

57. See Rühe, "Shaping Euro-Atlantic Policies," p. 135; the article is an edited version of the March speech.

58. Quoted in Frederick Kempe, "NATO Head Urges Alliance to Expand Membership to Ex-Warsaw Pact Nations," *Wall Street Journal*, September 13, 1993, p. A11.

59. Solomon, *The NATO Enlargement Debate,* p. 30. Wörner repeated this phrase in December 1993 at NATO meetings in Brussels. See Roger Cohen, "NATO and Russia Clash on Future Alliances," *New York Times*, December 10, 1993, p. A15.

60. Richard G. Lugar, "NATO: Out of Area or Out of Business," speech to the Overseas Writers Club, June 24, 1993. Speech as released by his office. Parts of the speech are also quoted in Stanley Kober, "The United States and the Enlargement Debate," *Transition*, December 15, 1995, p. 6. For the point about membership for the three, see Lugar's remarks at the USIA Foreign Press Center briefing on the future of NATO, June 21, 1993.

61. Jane Perlez, "Czech Leader Pushes for an Open NATO," *New York Times*, October 22, 1993, p. A8.

62. Letter published in Czech newspaper *Mlada Fronta Dnes*, December 2, 1993, p. 6, and reprinted in Foreign Broadcast Information Service, *Daily Report: Soviet Union*, December 3, 1993, p. 6. For more on Yeltsin, see Roger Cohen, "Yeltsin Opposes Expansion of NATO in Eastern Europe," *New York Times*, October 2, 1993, p. A4; William Drozdiak, "East European Bids to Join NATO Soon Seen in Jeopardy," *Washington Post*, October 6, 1993, p. A24.

63. Interview with Nicholas Burns (May 1997) and other U.S. government officials.

64. Interviews with Thomas Donilon (September 1997), Lynn Davis (August 1998), and other officials present at the meeting; on Lugar, see Solomon, *The NATO Enlargement Debate*, p. 29.

65. The quotes from the memo are in Michael Dobbs, "Wider Alliance Would Increase U.S. Commitments," *Washington Post*, July 5, 1995, pp. A1, 16. See also Michael R. Gordon, "U.S. Opposes Move to Rapidly Expand NATO Membership," *New York Times*, January 2, 1994, pp. A1, 7. The sequence of events was confirmed by interviews with nearly all of the State Department officials involved.

66. Interviews with Warren Christopher (December 1998), Lynn Davis (August 1998), and other U.S. government officials. On Davis's trip, see Thomas W. Lippman, "US Aides to Visit Ukraine," *Washington Post*, October 15, 1993, p. A33.

67. For a discussion of the swirl of events, see George Stephanopoulos, *All Too Human: A Political Education* (Little, Brown, 1999).

68. Interview with one of Anthony Lake's staffers (1999).

69. Anthony Lake, "From Containment to Enlargement," *Vital Speeches of the Day*, vol. 60 (October 15, 1993), pp. 14–16; for background on the speech, see Douglas Brinkley, "Democratic Enlargement: The Clinton Doctrine," *Foreign Policy*, vol. 106 (Spring 1997), pp. 111–27. For similar remarks by Lake, see Thomas L. Friedman, "Clinton's Foreign Policy: Top Advisor Speaks Up," *New York Times*, October 31, 1993, p. A8.

70. William Clinton, "Reforming the UN," *Vital Speeches of the Day*, vol. 60 (October 15, 1993), p. 10.

71. Lake liked to describe himself as a "pragmatic neo-Wilsonian" to demonstrate that he understood the limits to America's ability to change the world. See, for example, David Stout, "After Lake's Long Service, Both Sides Find Him Hard to Define," *New York Times*, March 18, 1997, p. B6; Jason DeParle, "The Man inside Bill Clinton's Foreign Policy," *New York Times Magazine*, August 20, 1995, pp. 33ff.

72. The discussion of blue and red blobs comes from Brinkley, "Democratic Enlargement," p. 118.

73. On the disarray of the team, see Drew, *On the Edge*, pp. 356–57.

74. Interview with Lynn Davis (August 1998).

75. Some sources say the Principals Committee meeting was held on October 18; others say October 19. All agree the president's concurrence came on Tuesday, October 19. See, for example, Elaine Sciolino, "U.S. to Offer Plan on a Role in NATO for Ex-Soviet Bloc," *New York Times*, October 21, 1993, pp. A1, 31; Michael Gordon, "U.S. Opposes Move to Rapidly Expand NATO Membership"; Dobbs, "Wider Alliance."

76. Interviews with U.S. government officials.

77. For a good discussion of the Pentagon's view on the Partnership for Peace, see Thomas W. Lippman, "Busy First Days in the Job Suit Secretary Perry Just Fine," *Washington Post*, February 7, 1994, p. A15.

78. Holbrooke, *To End a War*, p. 81. Similarly, in his study of the hydrogen bomb decision, Warner Schilling wrote, "There are many occasions when the necessary amount of cooperation can be achieved only by the device of avoiding disagreement, that is, by postponing the consideration of issues over which long and determined conflicts are certain to be waged." Warner R. Schilling, "The H-Bomb Decision: How to Decide Without Actually Choosing," *Political Science Quarterly*, vol. 76 (March 1961), p. 40.

79. On the bureaucratic debates, see Kupchan, "Strategic Visions," p. 122, endnote 4.

80. Graham T. Allison, *Essence of Decision: Explaining the Cuban Missile Crisis* (Little, Brown, 1971), p. 178.

81. Interviews with William Perry (June 1997), John Shalikashvili (July 1998), Anthony Lake (May 1997, October 1998), Thomas Donilon (September 1997), Lynn Davis (August 1998), and other U.S. government officials.

82. Quoted in Sciolino, "U.S. to Offer Plan." Oxman was identified as the briefer by my interviews with several individuals who were on the plane.

83. "Aspin's News Conference of October 20, 1993," from United States Information Agency Wireless File, October 22, 1993; "Partnerships Will Help NATO in New Role, Aspin Says," USIA Wireless File, October 22, 1993; for report on briefing, see Stephen Kinzer, "NATO Favors U.S. Plan for Ties with the East, but Timing Is Vague," *New York Times*, October 22, 1993, pp. A1, 8.

84. Kinzer, "NATO Favors U.S. Plan," p. A1.

85. Elaine Sciolino, "3 Players Seek a Director for Foreign Policy Story," *New York Times*, November 8, 1993, pp. A1, 12.

86. "Christopher, Jeszensky Hold Joint Press Conference," USIA Wireless File, October 22, 1993.

Chapter Three

1. Quoted in Gerald B. Solomon, *The NATO Enlargement Debate, 1990–1997: Blessings of Liberty* (Praeger Press [published with CSIS], 1998), p. 29.

2. "The CSCE Vision: European Security Rooted in Shared Values," Department of State Dispatch, vol. 4, December 13, 1993, p. 861.

3. "Strengthening the Atlantic Alliance through a Partnership for Peace," State Department Dispatch, vol. 4, December 13, 1993, pp. 857–58.

4. "Remarks by Secretary of Defense Les Aspin to the Atlantic Council," Federal News Service, December 3, 1993.

5. Jim Hoagland, "Christopher: Working from the Shadows," *Washington Post*, November 30, 1993, p. A25.

6. See Douglas Brinkley, "Democratic Enlargement: The Clinton Doctrine," *Foreign Policy*, vol. 106 (Spring 1997), p. 121.

7. Henry Kissinger, "Not This Partnership," *Washington Post*, November 24, 1993, p. A17; Zbigniew Brzezinski, "A Bigger—and Safer—Europe," *New York Times*, December 1, 1993, p. A23; James A. Baker III, "Expanding to the East: A New NATO," *Los Angeles Times*, December 5, 1993, p. M2.

8. Interviews with U.S. government officials.

9. Zbigniew Brzezinski, "Normandy Evasion," *Washington Post*, May 3, 1994, p. A23.

10. Interview with Anthony Lake (October 1998).

11. See Daniel Williams, "Talbott Set for No. 2 Job at State," *Washington Post*, December 28, 1993, pp. A1, 4.

12. Presidential spokesperson Dee Dee Myers echoed these goals of the trip on January 5, "Overall, the President's going to focus on the challenges and opportunities in Europe on this trip—specifically, to reestablish our ties to Europe through NATO and the EU; to reach out to Eastern and Central Europe through the Partnership for Peace; to continue to work on denuclearization issues in both Russia and the Ukraine; to reaffirm our support for the continued democratic and market economic reforms in Russia during our stops there; and finally, to continue to develop an overall policy towards Europe that integrates strategic economic and security concerns." "Background Briefing by Senior Administration Officials," The White House, Office of the Press Secretary, January 5, 1994.

13. Interviews with Nicholas Burns (May 1997) and other NSC staffers.

14. Press briefing by Chairman of the Joint Chiefs of Staff General John Shalikashvili, The White House, Office of the Press Secretary, January 4, 1994. The remarks at the U.S. Information Agency call-in show of January 3, 1994, were shown to me by a State Department official.

15. At a briefing on January 5, for example, a senior official stated, "Our concern is not just with the Russian reaction, which has received most press attention, but the tensions and apprehensions that would be aroused in all the countries that didn't think they were on a fast track to membership if we either identified now who we expect to be NATO members, or by some kind of wink and nod implied who we expect to be NATO members in the first tranche."

"Background Briefing by Senior Administration Officials," The White House, Office of the Press Secretary, January 5, 1994.

16. William Clinton,"Exchange with Reporters Prior to Discussions with Prime Minister Ruud Lubbers of the Netherlands," January 4, 1994, *Public Papers, 1994,* Book I, pp. 5–6.

17. Morton M. Kondracke, "Clinton's NATO Policy: Another Allied Retreat," *Roll Call*, January 6, 1994, p. 6.

18. Michael Mandelbaum "Open the Ranks to Eastern Europe," *Washington Post*, September 6, 1993, p. A23. He argued that enlargement would help change NATO from a defensive alliance to "a broader security community capable of contributing to the establishment of democracy and the maintenance of peace from the English Channel to the Pacific coast of Russia." On Senate questioning of these arguments in light of his later opposition, see *The Debate on NATO Enlargement*, Hearings before the Senate Committee on Foreign Relations, 105 Cong. 1 sess. (Government Printing Office, 1998), pp. 78–79.

19. Kondracke, "Clinton's NATO Policy," p. 6. The State Department had been using this language for some time. In a speech to the Atlantic Council back in August, Assistant Secretary of State for European Affairs Oxman had stated, "The heart of NATO membership is the mutual-collective-defense agreement embodied in Article 5 of the Treaty of Washington. Are the allies prepared to extend this security guarantee and commit their troops to defend the countries of Central and Eastern Europe?" Cited in Stanley Kober, "The United States and the Enlargement Debate," *Transition*, December 15, 1995, pp. 6–7.

20. Elaine Sciolino, "U.S. is Scrambling for a Strategy on Eve of Clinton European Trip," *New York Times*, January 5, 1994, p. A3.

21. Jan Nowak, "Letter to the Editor, The New Duchy of Moscovy," *Washington Post,* December 7, 1993, p. A24.

22. Interviews with John Shalikashvili (July 1998) and other U.S. government officials; also an interview with a central European official present at some of the meetings. See also Solomon, *The NATO Enlargement Debate*, p. 46.

23. Dick Kirschten, "Ethnics Resurging," *National Journal*, February 25, 1995, p. 485; Interviews with two participants from the session.

24. "Forging a Partnership for Peace and Prosperity," Department of State Dispatch, January 10, 1994, vol. 5, pp. 13–16.

25. Robert B. Zoellick, "Set Criteria for NATO Membership Soon," *International Herald Tribune*, January 7, 1994, p. 6.

26. William Clinton, "Remarks to Future Leaders of Europe in Brussels," January 9, 1994, *Public Papers, 1994,* Book I, p. 11.

27. William Clinton, "Partnership for Peace: Building New Security for the 21st Century," Department of State Dispatch Supplement, January 1994, vol. 5, pp. 3–4; Clinton, "The President's News Conference in Brussels," January

11, 1994, *Public Papers, 1994,* Book I, p. 29; interview with Anthony Lake (May 1997). The day before, at a news conference, Clinton seemed a bit more forceful when he said, "By providing for the practical integration and cooperation of these diverse military forces, the Partnership for Peace will lead to the enlargement of NATO membership and will support our efforts to integrate Europe." William Clinton, "Building Peace and Security through Partnership and Cooperation," Department of State Dispatch Supplement, January 1994, vol. 5, p. 11.

28. Interviews with State Department officials.

29. Warren Christopher, "NATO Plus," *The Washington Post*, January 9, 1994, p. C7.

30. Ibid.

31. Interviews with Pentagon officials; for the vision embodied in the PFP, see Charles Kupchan, "Strategic Visions," *World Policy Journal*, vol. 11 (Fall 1994), p. 113.

32. Interviews with John Shalikashvili (July 1998) and other U.S. government officials. On CJTF, see Catherine McArdle Kelleher, *The Future of European Security: An Interim Assessment* (Brookings, 1995); Nora Bensahel, "Separable but Not Separate Forces: NATO's Development of the Combined Joint Task Force," prepared for the Annual Conference of the International Security Studies Section of the International Studies Association, Norfolk, Virginia, October 24–25, 1997.

33. William Clinton, "The President's News Conference with Visegrad Leaders in Prague," January 12, 1994, *Public Papers, 1994,* Book I, p. 40.

34. William Clinton, "Interview with Reporters Aboard Air Force One," January 16, 1994, *Public Papers, 1994,* Book I, p. 90.

35. Warren Christopher, *In the Stream of History: Shaping Foreign Policy for a New Era* (Stanford University Press, 1998), pp. 93–94. See also Mary Curtius, "US Plan for NATO Is Less Than Central Europeans Sought," *Boston Globe*, November 7, 1993, p. A14.

36. William Clinton, "The President's News Conference with President Boris Yeltsin of Russia in Moscow," January 14, 1994, *Public Papers, 1994,* Book I, pp. 50–58; the quote is from p. 57.

37. Interviews with U.S. government officials.

38. The letter was shown to me by a congressional staffer. The last sentence in the paragraph is based on interviews with senior administration officials.

39. For representative remarks on this issue, see Thomas L. Friedman, "NATOwater," *New York Times*, May 19, 1997, p. A15; Edward N. Luttwak, "Don't Offer the Alliance to Those We Can't Protect," *Washington Post*, July 6, 1997, p. C3; comments by Canadian prime minister Jean Chretien in John F. Harris, "Tape Catches Choice Words about Clinton," *Washington Post*, July 10, 1997, p. A24.

40. Interviews with Anthony Lake (May 1997) and U.S. government officials.

41. Dick Kirschten, "Ethnics Resurging," *National Journal*, February 25, 1995, pp. 484–85.

42. "The 1992 Campaign: Excerpts from Speech by Clinton on U. S. Role," *New York Times,* October 2, 1992, p. A21.

43. For a good articulation of these points, see also Stephen Sestanovich, "The Collapsing Partnership: Why the United States Has No Russia Policy," in Robert Lieber, ed., *Eagle Adrift: American Foreign Policy at the End of the Century* (New York: Longman, 1997), pp. 169–70.

44. For the transcript of the Cleveland speech, see Department of State Dispatch, January 16, 1995, vol. 6, pp. 27–31.

45. For a similar perspective, see Solomon, *The NATO Enlargement Debate*, p. 68.

46. Christopher, *In the Stream of History*, p. 227. For a discussion of the focus at the Pentagon, see Ashton B. Carter and William J. Perry, *Preventive Defense: A New Security Strategy for America* (Brookings, 1999), pp. 1ff.

47. Perry would say in September 1994, for example, "No other country in any other era had 20,000 nuclear weapons. All of our thinking with regard to Russia has to keep that fact front and center." See Stephen Kinzer, "Russia in NATO? Germany and the U.S. Differ," *International Herald Tribune*, September 10, 1994, p. 2.

48. Strobe Talbott, *U.S. Policy toward the New Independent States*, Hearing before the House Committee on Foreign Affairs, 103 Cong. 2 sess. (Government Printing Office, 1994), pp. 19–20.

49. Richard Lugar, *The Future of NATO*, Hearings before the Subcommittee on Coalition Defense of the Senate Armed Services Committee and the Subcommittee on European Affairs of the Senate Foreign Relations Committee, 103 Cong. 2 sess. (Government Printing Office, 1994), pp. 12, 16.

50. Ibid., p. 27.

51. Interviews with U.S. government officials.

52. *Congressional Record*, vol. 140, February 22, 1994, pp. S1541, S1560, S1572–73. See also Steven Greenhouse, "Senate Confirms Talbott as State Department Deputy," *New York Times*, February 23, 1994, p. A9.

53. Interviews with many of Strobe Talbott's associates and friends.

54. Interviews with U.S. government officials.

55. Interviews with Nicholas Burns (May 1997), Alexander Vershbow (April 1997, November 1998), and Daniel Fried (April 1997, October 1998).

56. Interviews with U.S. government officials.

57. Joseph J. Kruzel, "Partnership for Peace and the Future of European Security," in Kenneth W. Thompson, ed., *NATO and the Changing World Order: An Appraisal by Scholars and Policymakers* (Lanham, Md.: University Press of America, 1996), p. 29.

58. Ibid., p. 37.

59. Interview with Jeffrey Simon (January 1999) and U.S. government officials; see also Solomon, *The NATO Enlargement Debate,* p. 63.

60. William Clinton, "Interview with Tomasz Lis of Polish Television," July 1, 1994, *Public Papers, 1994,* Book I, p. 1187.

61. Ibid., pp. 1187–88.

62. William Clinton, "Remarks Following Discussions with President Lech Walesa of Poland and an Exchange with Reporters in Warsaw," July 16, 1994, *Public Papers, 1994,* Book I, pp. 1205–06.

63. On Holbrooke's preference for EU enlargement first, see his letter to the editor, "Correspondence," *World Policy Journal* vol. 14 (Winter 1997/98), p. 100.

64. See Richard Holbrooke, *To End a War* (Random House, 1998), p. 57.

65. Holbrooke letter to the editor. Interviews with State Department officials.

66. On Talbott and the different interpretations of his behavior, see Dobbs, "Wider Alliance Would Increase US Commitments," *Washington Post*, July 5, 1995, pp. A1, 16.

67. Interviews with U.S. government officials.

68. Department of State Dispatch, September 12, 1994, vol. 5, pp. 597–98.

69. Interviews with John Shalikasvili (July 1998) and Wesley Clark (January 1999). This recollection coincides with the memories of others at the Joint Chiefs of Staff.

70. Worldnet interview with Alexander Vershbow, "Partnership for Peace Off to a Very Fast Start," USIA Washington Files, September 8, 1994. See also Solomon, *The NATO Enlargement Debate*, p. 67.

71. Interview with a State Department official.

72. Worldnet interview with Alexander Vershbow; see also Daniel Williams and R. Jeffrey Smith, "U.S. Moves to Expand NATO Expansion but Delays Key Choices," *Washington Post*, November 6, 1994, p. A10.

73. Interviews with Nicholas Burns (May 1997), Ambassador-at-Large for the New Independent States James F. Collins (May 1997), and other U.S. government officials.

74. See Mary Curtius, "Mass. Man Is Clinton's Invisible Adviser," *Boston Globe*, September 18, 1993, p. A4.

75. Interview with Richard Holbrooke (May 1998).

76. On this point, see also Christopher, *In the Stream of History*, p. 228.

77. Interview with Wesley Clark (January 1999). The story was also reported by Michael Dobbs in "Wider Alliance." These versions are confirmed by interviews with numerous officials present at the meeting. On Holbrooke's style, see Marjorie Williams, "Mr. Holbrooke Builds His Dream Job," *Vanity Fair*, October 1994, pp. 128–40.

78. Interviews with William Perry (June 1997), Ashton Carter (May 1997), and other officials present at the meeting.

79. Interview with Wesley Clark (January 1999).

80. Interviews with Wesley Clark (January 1999), Richard Holbrooke (May 1998), and other officials who attended the meeting.

81. On Perry, see, for example, Art Pine, "Low-Key Perry Being Asked to Master High-Flying Job," *Los Angeles Times*, January 25, 1994, p. A26; Douglas Jehl, "Pentagon Deputy Is Clinton's Choice for Defense Chief," *New York Times*, January 25, 1994, p. A1.

82. See Carter and Perry, *Preventive Defense*, pp. 29–31. Also, interviews with William Perry (June 1997), John Shalikashvili (July 1998), Leon Panetta (November 1998), and other U.S. government officials.

83. Claudia Dreifus, "Who's the Enemy Now?" *New York Times Magazine*, May 21, 1995, section 6, p. 34; Interviews with John Shalikashvili (July 1998) and Leon Panetta (November 1998).

84. Interviews with John Shalikashvili (July 1998) and William Perry (June 1997). In his description of the meeting in his book, Perry does not include Shalikashvili among the attendees. See Carter and Perry, *Preventive Defense*, p. 31. The quote is from p. 32.

Chapter Four

1. Dick Morris, *Behind the Oval Office: Getting Reelected against All Odds* (Los Angeles: Renaissance Books, 1999), p. 250. For a good discussion of the various political issues, see Stephen Sestanovich, "The Collapsing Partnership: Why the United States Has No Russia Policy," in Robert J. Lieber, ed., *Eagle Adrift* (New York: Longman, 1997), pp. 163–77.

2. Interview with a Senate staffer (1998).

3. See Michael Dobbs, "Wider Alliance Would Increase US Commitments," *Washington Post*, July 5, 1995, pp. A1, 16, on the composition of Gilman's district. Other material in the paragraph comes from my interview with Stephen Rademaker (June 1998).

4. HR 4210, "NATO Expansion Act of 1994," *Congressional Record*, vol. 140, 103 Cong. 2 sess., April 15, 1994, pp. E666–67.

5. The letter was shown to me by an interviewee. The Hyde Bill is in the *Congressional Record*, vol. 140, 103 Cong. 2 sess., May 5, 1994, pp. H3151–52. See also Gerald B. Solomon, *The NATO Enlargement Debate, 1990–1997: Blessings of Liberty* (Praeger Press [published with CSIS], 1998), pp. 48–49.

6. Solomon, *The NATO Enlargement Debate*, p. 49.

7. Ibid., p. 65.

8. The letter was shown to me by an interviewee on Capitol Hill.

9. *Congressional Record*, vol. 140, 103 Cong. 2 sess., part II, October 7, 1994, p. S14883.

10. John B. Bader, *Taking the Initiative: Leadership Agendas in Congress and the Contract with America* (Georgetown University Press, 1996), pp. 185–86.

11. HR 7, National Security Revitalization Act, Committee on National Security, House of Representatives, 104 Cong. 1 sess. (Government Printing Office, 1996).

12. Warren Christopher and William J. Perry, "Foreign Policy, Hamstrung," *New York Times*, February 13, 1995, p. A19.

13. Interviews with administration officials and congressional staffers.

14. Interviews have identified Richard Holbrooke as the briefer for this session with the press. Background briefing by a senior administration official, U.S. Mission to NATO, Brussels, December 1, 1994, Department of State, Office of the Spokesman.

15. Press briefing by a senior U.S. official, Conrad Hotel, Brussels, November 30, 1994.

16. Craig R. Whitney, "Why Europe Is Careful Not to Scold the Bear," *New York Times*, January 2, 1995, p. A6; "Cracks Are Appearing in the Alliance's Cohesion," *Financial Times*, December 2, 1994, p. 3; AFP, December 7, 1994, in Foreign Broadcast Information Service, *Daily Report: West Europe*, December 8, 1994, p. 24.

17. Martin Walker, "Clinton's Secret Successes," *Washington Post*, September 4, 1994, p. C1.

18. Background press briefing by a senior administration official at U.S. Mission to NATO, Brussels, December 1, 1994.

19. Warren Christopher, "A Time for Historic Challenge for NATO," Department of State Dispatch, December 19, 1994, vol. 5, p. 829; Warren Christopher, "North Atlantic Council Final Communique," Department of State Dispatch, December 19, 1994, vol. 5, p. 833.

20. Background press briefing by a senior administration official at U.S. Mission to NATO, Brussels, December 1, 1994.

21. Warren Christopher, "Time of Historic Challenge for NATO," pp. 831–32.

22. See Bruce Clark and Laura Silber, "Russia Warns NATO on Rapid Move Eastwards," *Financial Times*, December 2, 1994, p. 1.

23. Interview of Warren Christopher by Andrea Mitchell of NBC and Steve Hurst of CNN at NATO headquarters, Brussels, December 2, 1994, Department of State, Office of the Spokesman press release. On Kozyrev's behavior, see also George Melloan, "A Drop-in Guest for Yeltsin's Budapest Bash," *Wall Street Journal*, December 5, 1994, p. A15.

24. His foreign policy advisers also wanted President Clinton to attend to sign the Start I agreement with Ukraine. Numerous government officials dis-

cussed with me the difficulties of scheduling Budapest. For the president's schedule that day, see presidential documents online at "Weekly Compilation of Presidential Documents," December 12, 1994, vol. 30, pp. 2483–84. (http://www.access.gpo.gov/su_docs/executive.html [June 23, 1999]).

25. William Clinton, "The President's News Conference with President Kuchma of Ukraine," November 22, 1994, *Public Papers of the Presidents of the United States, 1994,* Book II (Government Printing Office, 1995) p. 2115.

26. ITAR-TASS, December 4, 1994, in Foreign Broadcast Information Service, *Daily Report: Soviet Union*, December 5, 1994, p. 4.

27. William Clinton, "1994 Summit of the Council of Security and Cooperation in Europe," Department of State Dispatch, December 12, 1994, vol. 5, p. 813.

28. Moscow Russian Television Network, December 5, 1994, Foreign Broadcast Information Service, *Daily Report: Soviet Union*, December 5, 1994, p. 4.

29. See Ashton B. Carter and William J. Perry, *Preventive Defense: A New Security Strategy for America* (Brookings, 1999), p. 31. The December 21 meeting is described in the previous chapter.

30. Interview with Nicholas Burns (May 1997).

31. Interviews with U.S. government officials.

32. Ibid.

33. R. Jeffrey Smith and Daniel Williams, "U.S. Plans New Tack on Russia-NATO Tie," *Washington Post*, January 16, 1995, p. A1. See also Elaine Sciolino, "U.S. and Russia at Odds, Despite Talks," *New York Times*, January 19, 1995, p. A6, for a discussion of the Christopher/Kozyrev meeting in Geneva on NATO-Russia on January 18.

34. Alexei Pushkov, "Reacting to NATO Expansion, Russia Should Take Its Time," *Moscow News*, March 24, 1995, p. 5. For a more elaborate proposal, see Yuriy Davydov's article in *Segodnya,* March 24, 1995, in Foreign Broadcast Information Service, *Daily Report: Soviet Union*, March 24, 1995, p. 6.

35. Phone interview with Leon Panetta (November 1998).

36. William Clinton, "The U.S. and Eastern Europe: Forging New Partnerships," Department of State Dispatch, January 16, 1995, vol. 6, pp. 28–29. For a discussion of the audience, see Dick Kirschten, "Ethnics Resurging," *National Journal*, February 25, 1995.

37. Steven Greenhouse, "U.S.-Russian Intersection: The Romance Is Gone," *New York Times*, March 27, 1995, p. A6; Steven Greenhouse, "Clinton to Tell Yeltsin that NATO is Not Anti-Russian," *New York Times*, March 14, 1995, p. A6; Michael Dobbs, "U.S. Offers Assurances on NATO," *Washington Post*, May 7, 1995, p. A1.

38. On this decision, see Carla Anne Robbins, "Clinton's V-E Day Visit Next Week to Bring Him to a Russia Many Aides Term Less Dependable," *Wall Street Journal*, May 5, 1995, p. A14.

39. Ann Devroy and Daniel Williams, "U.S.-Russia Summit Set for May 9," *Washington Post*, March 21, 1995, p. A1. See also Thomas W. Lippman, "Russia-Iran Atomic Deal Irks US," *Washington Post*, February 11, 1995, p. A1; "Radioactive Politics," *Christian Science Monitor*, February 24, 1995.

40. Phone interview with Dick Morris (June 1998).

41. R. W. Apple Jr., "Clinton's Moscow Visit: A Climate of Mutual Doubt," *New York Times*, May 7, 1995, p. A16; Dobbs, "Wider Alliance"; interviews with U.S. government officials confirmed the Yeltsin request.

42. "Remarks by President Clinton and President Yeltsin in a Joint Press Conference," The White House, Office of the Press Secretary, May 10, 1995.

43. Interview with Warren Christopher (December 1998).

44. On this latter point, see Chrystia Freeland and Bruce Clark, "Summit Fails to Narrow Gap over NATO," *Financial Times*, May 11, 1995, p. 2; interviews with U.S. government officials.

45. Strobe Talbott, "Why NATO Should Grow," *New York Review of Books*, August 10, 1995, pp. 27–30.

46. Ibid., pp. 28–29.

47. "Remarks by President Clinton and President Yeltsin," May 10, 1995. Similarly, the senior U.S. official who had conducted the press briefing at the Conrad Hotel in Brussels on November 30, 1994, just before the North Atlantic Council announcement of the NATO study had said, apparently with a straight face, "President Clinton has stated quite clearly that it's no longer a question of whether NATO will expand, but when and how. And we very much look forward to this ministerial as a time in which NATO will itself agree to begin formal discussions with the partners in the Partnership for Peace on how and why NATO needs to expand"; Holbrooke had put forward a statement on Europe's post–cold war disposition in early 1995. See Richard C. Holbrooke, "America: A European Power," *Foreign Affairs*, vol. 74 (March/April 1995), pp. 38–51.

48. See Perry's remarks at the Wehrkunde, Munich Conference on Security Policy, February 5, 1995, "The Enduring Dynamic Relationship That Is NATO," *Defense Viewpoint*, vol. 10 (http://www.defenselink.mil/speeches/1995/s19950205-perry.html [March 1999]). See also William C. Mann, "Decision on NATO's Expansion Toward Russia Expected by December," *Associated Press*, June 21, 1995; Ronald D. Asmus, Richard L. Kugler, and F. Stephen Larrabee, "NATO Expansion: The Next Steps," *Survival*, vol. 30 (Spring 1995), pp. 5–26. Because of the unpopularity at the Pentagon with their earlier study, the RAND troika initially received funding for this study from the German Ministry of Defense, an unprecedented step at the RAND corporation.

49. *Study on NATO Enlargement*, September 1995 (http://www.fas.org/man/nato/natodocs/enl-9502.htm [March 1999]). The quote is from paragraph 7.

50. This last point was emphasized at the press briefing on the study. See Michael Dobbs, "Ex-Soviet Bloc Nations to Get NATO Umbrella," *Washington Post*, September 29, 1995, p. A22.

51. *Study on NATO Enlargement*, paras. 74, 77.

52. The best studies of the Dayton accords are Richard Holbrooke, *To End a War* (Random House, 1998), and Ivo H. Daalder, *Getting to Dayton: The Making of America's Bosnia Policy* (Brookings, 1999).

53. Interviews with William Perry (June 1997), Ashton Carter (May 1997), and other U.S. government officials.

54. See Perry and Carter, *Preventive Defense*, pp. 36–37. I also discussed this in interviews with William Perry (June 1997), Ashton Carter (May 1997), and other U.S. government officials.

55. "Press Conference with President Boris Yeltsin," September 8, 1995, as published by Federal Information Systems Corporation, Official Kremlin International News Broadcast.

56. Interview with Ashton Carter (May 1997); see also Carter and Perry, *Preventive Defense*, p. 38.

57. Interview with a senior U.S. administration official.

58. On the details of this ingenuous plan, see Carter and Perry, *Preventive Defense*, pp. 43–44.

59. Holbrooke, *To End a War*, p. 214.

60. Interviews with William Perry (June 1997), Ashton Carter (May 1997), and other U.S. government officials.

61. William Clinton, "Sustaining American Leadership through NATO," Department of State Dispatch, November 6, 1995, vol. 6, p. 814.

62. Jim Hoagland, "NATO: A Sweet, but Misleading, Song," *Washington Post*, November 15, 1994, p. A19.

63. Holbrooke, *To End a War*, p. 359.

64. Interview with Warren Christopher (December 1998).

65. Interviews with leaders of the Central and Eastern European Coalition and with U.S. government officials.

66. Solomon, *The NATO Enlargement Debate*, pp. 75–76.

67. *Congressional Record*, vol. 141, 104 Cong. 1 sess., August 10, 1995, pp. S12297–98; *Congressional Record,* vol. 141, 104 Cong. 1 sess., September 21, 1995, p. S14090.

68. Solomon, *The NATO Enlargement Debate*, p. 87.

69. The letter was shown to me by an interviewee.

70. The districts are the following: New York 30, Wisconsin 4; Illinois 3, 5, 6 and 13; Michigan 10, 12, and 16; Pennsylvania 11. On the presidential vote, see Michael Barone and Grant Ujifusa, *The Almanac of American Politics* (Washington, D.C.: National Journal), editions published in 1981, 1985, 1991 and 1997. Poll by the Program on International Policy Attitudes of the University of Maryland on the Internet (http://www.fas.org/man/eprint/nato_pipa.html [March, 1999]).

71. Interviews with State Department officials.

72. Warren Christopher, "NATO: Building a New Security Structure for

Europe," Department of State Dispatch, December 1995, vol. 6, p. 907. See also his remarks at the North Atlantic Council that day, "NATO: Reaching Out to New Partners and New Challenges," Department of State Dispatch, December 1995, vol. 6, p. 902.

73. Warren Christopher, *In the Stream of History: Shaping Foreign Policy for a New Era* (Stanford University Press, 1998), p. 399.

74. Interview with State Department official.

75. Christopher, *In the Stream of History*, p. 400.

76. Ibid., p. 401.

77. William Clinton, "The U.S. and Central and Eastern Europe: Forging New Partnerships," Department of State Dispatch, vol. 6, January 16, 1995, pp. 27–31. On Perry's remarks, see "U.S. Backs NATO Growth," *New York Times*, February 5, 1996, p. A9.

78. Warren Christopher, "A Democratic and Undivided Europe in Our Time," Department of State Dispatch, March 25, 1996, vol. 7, p. 135.

79. Interviews with U.S. government officials. The quotes are from Christopher, *In the Stream of History*, p. 399.

80. Interviews with Dole campaign advisers.

81. Michael Dobbs, "Dole: Widen Alliance Faster," *Washington Post*, June 5, 1996, p. A26.

82. *Congressional Record*, vol. 142, 104 Cong. 2 sess., June 4, 1996, pp. S5756–57. See also Solomon, *The NATO Enlargement Debate*, p. 100; "Republican Internationalism," *Washington Times*, July 25, 1996, p. A18.

83. *Congressional Record*, vol. 142, 104 Cong. 2 sess., July 23, 1996, pp. H8118–19.

84. Excerpts from the speech were printed in the *New York Times*, June 26, 1996, p. A14.

85. Alan Philps, "Polls Point to Disaster for Yeltsin Campaign," *Daily Telegraph*, February 17, 1996, p. 8; Victoria Clark, "Yeltsin Can Win Again, But He Needs a Miracle," *Guardian*, February 18, 1996, p. 26.

86. Interviews with administration and Senate staffers.

87. Carol Giacomo, "Is the Tide Turning against NATO Expansion?" *Reuters*, June 28, 1995; Sam Nunn, "The Future of NATO in an Uncertain World," July 15, 1995, *Vital Speeches of the Day*, 1995, p. 585; on Nunn, see also Michael Dobbs, "Enthusiasm for Wider Alliance Is Marked by Contradictions," *Washington Post*, July 7, 1995, p. A1.

88. Interviews with Senate staffers and lobbyists.

89. Christopher, *In the Stream of History*, p. 452; interviews with National Security Council staffers and State Department officials.

90. For the speech, see Christopher, *In the Stream of History*, pp. 456–66.

91. Interviews with State Department officials and National Security Council staffers.

92. Phone interview with Leon Panetta (November 1998).

93. John F. Harris, "Campaign '96—Clinton Vows Wider NATO in 3 Years," *Washington Post*, October 23, 1996, p. A1.

94. George Bush and Brent Scowcroft, *A World Transformed* (Knopf, 1998), p. 48.

95. "Remarks by the President to the People of Detroit," The White House, Office of the Press Secretary, October 22, 1996.

96. Alison Mitchell, "The Democrat," *New York Times*, October 23, 1996, p. A20; Bush had done the same in 1989, describing it as "small-town America at its best." See Bush and Scowcroft, *A World Transformed*, p. 52.

Chapter Five

1. W. Stull Holt, *Treaties Defeated by the Senate: A Study of the Struggle between President and Senate over the Conduct of Foreign Relations* (Johns Hopkins University Press, 1933); Jeremy D. Rosner, *The New Tug-of-War: Congress, the Executive Branch and National Security* (Carnegie Endowment for International Peace, 1995). On the typical peacetime conflicts between the two branches, see also Bruce W. Jentleson, *With Friends Like These: Reagan, Bush, and Saddam, 1982–1990* (W. W. Norton, 1994), p. 247.

2. James M. Lindsay, *Congress and the Politics of U.S. Foreign Policy* (Johns Hopkins University Press, 1994), pp. 79–80.

3. Holt, *Treaties Defeated by the Senate*, p. 13.

4. Ibid., p. 306.

5. *The Journal of William Maclay: United States Senator from Pennsylvania, 1789–1791* (New York: Albert and Charles Boni, 1927), p. 128; Holt, *Treaties Defeated by the Senate*, pp. 27, 31, 275; Ralston Hayden, *The Senate and Treaties 1789–1817: The Development of the Treaty-Making Functions of the United States Senate during Their Formative Period* (MacMillan & Company, 1920), pp. 6, 22.

6. Holt, *Treaties Defeated by the Senate*, p. 258.

7. For a good discussion of this point, see Lindsay, *Congress and the Politics of U.S. Foreign Policy*, p. 34.

8. On the problem of Yeltsin's absence, see Angela E. Stent, *Russia and Germany Reborn: Unification, the Soviet Collapse, and the New Europe* (Princeton University Press, 1999), pp. 225–26.

9. Interviews with U.S. government officials.

10. Ibid.

11. For the statement, see Warren Christopher, "Fulfilling the Founding Vision of NATO," Department of State Dispatch, vol. 7, December 9, 1996, p. 601. See also William Drozdiak, "NATO Pledges Not to Put Nuclear Arms in New Member States," *Washington Post*, December 11, 1996, p. A16.

12. Craig R. Whitney, "Russia Tells NATO It Accepts Offer on a Formal Link," *New York Times*, December 12, 1996, p. A1; interviews with U.S. government officials.

13. Interviews with U.S. government officials.

14. Ibid.

15. The quote comes from an interview with a senior administration official. The other material in the paragraph comes from that official and other high-level U.S. government officials.

16. David Hoffman, "Russian, NATO Chief Open Talks on Alliance's Expansion Plans," *Washington Post*, January 21, 1997, p. A12.

17. Interviews with senior U.S. government officials. See also Craig R. Whitney, "NATO Says It Won't Base New Forces in the East," *New York Times*, March 15, 1997, p. A6. The NATO-Russia Founding Act is in *NATO Review*, vol. 45 (July-August 1997), pp. 7–10. The unilateral statement is on page 9.

18. Quoted in William Drozdiak, "Poland Urges NATO Not to Appease Russia: The Smell of Yalta Is Always with Us," *Washington Post*, March 17, 1997, p. A13.

19. Michal Mocek, "Helsinki Has Revived the Spirit of Understanding," *Mlada Fronta Dnes*, March 22, 1997, p. 12, in Foreign Broadcast Information Service, *Daily Report: East Europe*, March 24, 1997, p. 19 (http://wnc.fedworld.gov [October 1998]).

20. See Antonina Yefremova, "Summit Meeting: Positive Compromise," *Rossiyskaya Gazeta*, March 25, 1997, p. 7, in Foreign Broadcast Information Service, *Daily Report: Soviet*, March 24, 1997 (http://wnc.fedworld.gov [October 1998]).

21. "Clinton and Yeltsin and How They Failed 'Three Fundamental Challenges'," *New York Times*, March 22, 1997, p. A6.

22. See David Hoffman, "For Yeltsin, Business Prospects Outweighted NATO Threat," *Washington Post*, May 27, 1997, p. A1. Yeltsin's request and Clinton's response were confirmed by interviews with senior U.S. government officials. Michael Dobbs, "For Clinton, Sticking with Yeltsin Sealed Agreement on NATO," *Washington Post*, May 27, 1997, p. A11; Alison Mitchell, "Summit Talks End with Agreements, But Not for NATO," *New York Times*, March 22, 1997, p. A1.

23. Alison Mitchell, "Summit Talks End with Agreements," p. A1. See also "Clinton and Yeltsin," *New York Times*, p. A6.

24. Information on the group's genesis comes from interviews. For a list of the members, see *Russia, Its Neighbors, and an Enlarging NATO*, report of an independent task force sponsored by the Council on Foreign Relations, Richard G. Lugar, chairman (Council on Foreign Relations, 1997), pp. 8–12.

25. See Richard Lugar speech at the National Press Club, May 5, 1997, available on Lexis-Nexis Academic Universe. See also comments at the end of the report *Russia, Its Neighbors, and an Enlarging NATO*.

26. William Drozdiak, "Yeltsin, in Germany, Says He'll Sign NATO Pact Next Month," *Washington Post*, April 18, 1997, p. A21; on Kohl's role, see Stent, *Russia and Germany Reborn*, pp. 222–23.

27. The NATO-Russia Founding Act, *NATO Review*, July-August, 1997. See the remarks of both presidents at the signing ceremony, "Remarks by President Clinton, French President Chirac, Russian President Yeltsin, and NATO Secretary-General Solana at NATO-Russia Founding Act Signing Ceremony," The White House, Office of the Press Secretary (Paris, France), May 27, 1997.

28. Strobe Talbott, "NATO, Russia and Transatlantic Security in the 21st Century," a speech given to the Atlantic Council of the United States, May 20, 1997.

29. The discussion of the debate on who should be invited comes from interviews with officials from the National Security Council staff, the State Department, and the Pentagon.

30. Interviews with U.S. government officials.

31. See Steven Lee Meyers, "U.S. Now at Odds with NATO Allies on New Members," *New York Times*, May 30, 1997, pp. A1, 9.

32. Interviews with a member of Senator Joseph Biden's staff.

33. Interviews with U.S. government officials.

34. Interviews with administration and Senate staffers.

35. William Cohen, news briefing, Office of the Assistant Secretary of Defense (Public Affairs), Department of Defense, June 12, 1997 (http://www.defenselink.mil/news/Jun1997/t06131997_t612cohe.html [January 1999]); Cohen had made similar comments the day before. See his June 11, 1997, news briefing (http://www.defenselink.mil/news/Jun1997/t06131997_t611enrt.html [January 1999]). Also see William Clinton, "Statement by the President on NATO Enlargement," The White House, Office of the Press Secretary, June 12, 1997 (http://www.pub.whitehouse.gov/ [January 1999]). For McCurry's quote, see Philip Shenon, "For Now, U.S. Insists on Limiting New NATO Members to 3," *New York Times*, June 13, 1997, p. A6.

36. Steven Erlanger, "Yeltsin Basks at Summit; Some Europeans are Cool to U.S.," *New York Times*, June 21, 1997, p. A6. See also "Three Nations Defy U.S. on Expansion of NATO: France, Germany, Canada Stand Firm," *Sun-Sentinel*, June 14, 1997, p. A17.

37. Craig R. Whitney, "3 Former Members of Eastern Bloc Invited into NATO," *New York Times*, July 9, 1997, pp. A1, 8; for a good discussion of the issues, see Jonathan Eyal, "NATO's Enlargement: Anatomy of a Decision," *International Affairs*, vol. 73 (October 1997), p. 706.

38. Interviews with administration officials and Hill staffers. On the Chemical Weapons Convention debacle of 1993 to 1996, see Amy E. Smithson,

"Playing Politics with the Chemical Weapons Conventions," *Current History*, vol. 96 (April 1997), pp. 162–66.

39. Rosner, *The New Tug-of-War*.

40. Interviews with Jeremy Rosner (June 1998, December 1998) and other U.S. government officials.

41. Interviews with U.S. government officials.

42. Ibid.

43. Ibid.

44. Interviews with several State Department officials.

45. Trent Lott, "The Senate's Role in NATO Enlargement," *Washington Post,* March 21, 1997, p. A27.

46. Interviews with U.S. government officials.

47. Interviews with administration and Senate staffers.

48. For a list of the meetings, see Senate Foreign Relations Committee Report on the Protocols to the North Atlantic Treaty of 1949 on Accession of Poland, Hungary, and the Czech Republic, Exec. Rpt. 105–14, 105 Cong. 2 sess., March 6, 1998 (Government Printing Office, 1998) pp. 31–32. Other information comes from interviews with U.S. officials.

49. For a list, see Senate Report on the Protocols, March 6, 1998, pp. 30–31.

50. Interview with a Senate staffer.

51. Jesse Helms, "New Members, Not New Missions," *Wall Street Journal Europe*, July 9, 1997, p. 6.

52. This relationship was discussed in Dana Milbank, "SNOG Job," *New Republic*, May 25, 1998, pp. 14–15; confirmed by my interviews with administration officials and Senate staff.

53. On the Lugar-Cochran relationship, see Jennifer Senior, "Cochran Set to Quit Race if Lott Retains Huge Lead," *Hill*, May 29, 1996, p. 1; Timothy J. Burger, "Lott Trounces Cochran to Win Majority Leader," *Roll Call*, June 13, 1996, p. 1.

54. Robert Novak, "Weld Becomes Power Struggle for Lugar, Helms," *Chicago Sun-Times*, September 18, 1997, p. 35; "Lugar's Secret Alliance with the White House," *Weekly Standard*, September 15, 1997, p. 2. These events were confirmed by interviews with administration officials and Senate staffers.

55. Interviews with U.S. government officials.

56. Interviews with administration officials and Senate staffers. See also Milbank, "SNOG Job."

57. Jesse Helms, "Strategic Rationale for NATO Enlargement," and "The Madrid Summit—New Members, Not New Missions," *The Debate on NATO Enlargement*, Hearings before the Senate Committee on Foreign Relations, 105 Cong. 1 sess. (Government Printing Office, 1998), pp. 1, 3–4, respectively.

58. Madeleine Albright, "Statement of Hon. Madeleine Albright, Secretary of State," *The Debate on NATO Enlargement*, p. 11.

59. Helms, *The Debate on NATO Enlargement*, p. 18.

60. Albright, *The Debate on NATO Enlargement*, p 18.

61. The entire exchange is in *The Debate on NATO Enlargement*, pp. 18–19.

62. All of these hearings are included in *The Debate on NATO Enlargement*.

63. Jesse Helms and Joseph Biden, "Helms-Biden Letter to Senate Colleagues on NATO Enlargement," November 10, 1997 (http://www.fas.org/man/nato/congress/1997/97111303_wpo.html [June 1999]).

64. The RAND study appeared first in *Survival*, vol. 38 (Autumn 1996) and is reprinted as Ronald D. Asmus, Richard L. Kugler, and F. Stephen Larrabee, "The Costs of NATO Enlargement," in Philip H. Gordon, ed., *NATO's Transformation: The Changing Shape of the Atlantic Alliance* (Lanham, Md.: Rowman & Littlefield Publishers, Inc., 1997), pp. 177–200. Kugler's comment is in Richard L. Kugler, "Costs of NATO Enlargement," Strategic Forum, National Defense University, Institute for National Strategic Studies, no. 128, October 1997.

65. Department of State, "Report to the Congress on the Enlargement of the North Atlantic Treaty Organization: Rationale, Benefits, Costs and Implications," February 24, 1997 (http://www.fas.org/man/nato/offdocs/us_97/wh970224.htm [March 1999]).

66. Ivan Eland, "The High Cost of NATO Expansion: Clearing the Administration's Smoke Screen," CATO Policy Analysis no. 286, CATO Institute, October 29, 1997.

67. Ivan Eland, "The Costs of Expanding the NATO Alliance," Congressional Budget Office paper prepared for the House International Relations Committee, March 1996, p. 25.

68. Eland, "The High Cost of NATO Expansion."

69. Thomas W. Lippman, "Initial NATO Expansion to Cost Less than Estimated, Officials Say," *Washington Post*, October 22, 1997, p. A6.

70. Interview with a senior administration official.

71. For the exchange, see "Statement of the Hon. Walter Slocombe, Undersecretary of Defense for Policy," *The Debate on NATO Enlargement*, p. 144.

72. See *Chicago Tribune* editorials of May 14, 1995, sec. 4, p. 2; October 8, 1995, p. A20; March 24, 1996, p. A18; February 1, 1998, p. A18; and March 13, 1998, p. A24; See also Milbank, "SNOG Job"; Milbank's account was confirmed by my interviews with U.S. government officials.

73. Interviews with U.S. government officials.

74. Carla Anne Robbins, "How Little-Debated Expansion Plan Will Alter NATO," *Wall Street Journal*, March 12, 1998, p. A20; Milbank, "SNOG Job"; interviews with U.S. government officials.

75. Martin Walker, "US Set for Big Arms Sales," *Guardian*, July 5, 1997, p. 16; Joanna Spear, "Bigger NATO, Bigger Sales," *World Today*, November 1997, pp. 272–74.

76. David L. Marcus, "NATO Plans Draw Arms Contractors," *Boston Globe*, March 23, 1997, pp. A1, 38. Department of Commerce, "European Diversification and Defense Market Assessment: A Comprehensive Guide for Entry into Overseas Markets," 2d ed. (September 1997), p. 325. The report was prepared by the department's Bureau of Export Administration's Office of Strategic Industries and Economic Security.

77. Katharine Q. Seelye, "Arms Contractors Spend to Promote an Expanded NATO," *New York Times*, March 30, 1998, pp. A1, 6; Stan Crock and Karen Lowry Miller, with James Drake and Mia Trinephi, "Weapons, Anyone?" *Business Week*, international edition, June 2, 1997, p. 22; Marcus, "NATO Plans Draw Arms Contractors." For other pieces demonstrating the strong interest of U.S. firms in central Europe, see Tom Ferraro, "Arms Makers Eye NATO Expansion as Bonanza," *Hill*, May 13, 1998, p. 29; David Ruppe, "Lockheed Tutored NATO Prospects on Acquisition," *Defense Week*, August 18, 1997, p. 8; Jeff Gerth and Tim Weiner, "Arms Makers See Bonanza in Selling NATO Expansion," *New York Times*, June 29, 1997, p. 1; Bill Mesler, "NATO's New Arms Bazaar," *Nation*, July 21, 1997, pp. 24–28.

78. Interviews with members of the U.S. Committee to Expand NATO, administration officials, and Senate staff.

79. Interviews with U.S. government officials.

80. Information in this paragraph is drawn from interviews with individuals representing each of the groups mentioned. On Finley, see "Washington's New Pam Harriman Is a Republican: Now Serving Politics, Policy, and Canapes," *Fortune*, September 7, 1998, p. 98.

81. Interviews with members of the U.S. Committee to Expand NATO.

82. Interviews with several members of the U.S. Committee to Expand NATO, Shalikashvili (July 1998), and U.S. government officials. See also Dan McLean, "Unusual Alliances Shape Senate NATO Debate," *Hill*, October 22, 1997, p. 11.

83. Interviews with a central European official and U.S. government officials. On the Torricelli incident, see Steven Thomma, "NATO Expansion Debated," *Record* (Bergen County), April 30, 1998, p. A17.

84. Interview with a central European official.

85. Michael Dobbs, "Clinton Prepares NATO Sales Pitch," *Washington Post*, March 13, 1997, p. A26. The Pew poll, "Public Indifferent about NATO Expansion," was taken January 9–12, 1997 and published January 24, 1997 (http://www.people-press.org/natorpt.htm [August 1998]). The PIPA poll, "Americans on Expanding NATO: A Study of U.S. Public Attitudes," taken in September 1996 and published on February 13, 1997 (http://www.fas.org/man/eprint/nato_pipa.htm [August 1998]). An earlier poll, "American Public Opinion Report—1995," was taken by the Chicago Council on Foreign Relations (http://www.ccfr.org/publications/opinion opinion95.html [June 1999]).

86. See, for example, Michael Mandelbaum, "Statement of Dr. Michael Mandelbaum," *The Debate on NATO Enlargement*, pp. 72–73.

87. John Lewis Gaddis, "History, Grand Strategy and NATO Enlargement," *Survival*, vol. 40 (Spring 1998), p. 145.

88. For Friedman op-eds on NATO, see, for example, the *New York Times*, April 9, 1995, p. A15; April 26, 1995, p. A25; May 10, 1995, p. A23; June 9, 1996, p. D15; July 24, 1996, p. A25; April 14, 1997, p. A17; April 28, 1997, p. A15; May 19, 1997, p. A15; February 10, 1998, p. A21; March 3, 1998, p. A19; March 31, 1998, p. A23; April 28, 1998, p. A19. He continued this charge after the new members formally joined. See Friedman, "The Doomsday A-List," *New York Times*, March 16, 1999, p. A27.

89. See Ashton B. Carter and William J. Perry, *Preventive Defense: A New Security Strategy for America* (Brookings, 1999), pp. 84–85.

90. Charles A. Kupchan, "It's a Long Way to Bratislava: The Dangerous Fantasy of NATO Expansion," *Washington Post*, May 14, 1995, p. C1.

91. Interview with Steven Erlanger (December 1998).

92. George F. Kennan, "A Fateful Error," *New York Times*, February 5, 1997, p. A23.

93. For Kennan's general opposition, see, for example, George F. Kennan, *Around the Cragged Hill: A Personal and Political Philosophy* (W. W. Norton & Company, 1993), pp. 223–24.

94. See, for example, Jim Hoagland, "NATO: The Case for Holding Back," *Washington Post*, June 22, 1995, p. A31. Another official was former Reagan appointee Fred C. Ikle. See his "How to Ruin NATO," *New York Times*, January 11, 1995, p. A21.

95. Howard Baker Jr., Sam Nunn, Brent Scowcroft, Alton Frye, "NATO: A Debate Recast," *New York Times*, February 4, 1998, p. A23. See also their op-ed, "Will Expansion Undercut the Military?" *Los Angeles Times*, March 26, 1998, p. B9.

96. Interview with John Isaacs (December 1998).

97. Ibid.

98. Interview with Michael Mandelbaum (November 1998).

99. This memorandum was shown to me by a U.S. government official.

100. Interviews with Senate staffers and administration officials. For the Greece and Turkey resolution, for example, see *Congressional Record*, vol. 98, 82 Cong. 2 sess., January 29, 1952, pp. 587–88.

101. See Senate Protocols to the North Atlantic Treaty of 1949 (Exec. Rpt. 105–14), pp. 32ff; Steven Erlanger, "Key Senate Panel Passes Resolution to Expand NATO," *New York Times*, March 4, 1998, pp. A1, 4.

102. *Congressional Record*, vol. 144, 105 Cong. 2 sess., March 18, 1998, pp. S2171–72.

103. Katharine Q. Seelye, "Senate Struggles to Pay Attention to the Remapping of NATO," *New York Times*, March 19, 1998, p. A7.

104. Eric Schmitt, "Lott Abruptly Postpones Senate Action on NATO Expansion," *New York Times*, March 21, 1998, p. A5.

105. The letter was shown to me by a Senate staffer.

106. *Congressional Record*, vol. 144, 105 Cong. 2 sess., April 27, 1998, p. S3605.

107. Ibid., pp. S3603–04.

108. The GAO report is "NATO Enlargement: Requirements and Costs for Commonly Funded Projects," GAO/NSIAD-98-113, March 6, 1998 (http://www.fas.org/man/gao/nsiad98113.htm [May 1998]). The Foreign Relations report is *The Debate on NATO Enlargement*; *Congressional Record*, April 27, 1998, p. S3638; *Congressional Record*, vol. 144, 105 Cong. 2 sess., April 30, 1998, p. S3824.

109. *Congressional Record*, April 27, 1998, p. S3606; see also *Congressional Record*, vol. 144, 105 Cong. 2 sess., March 19, 1998, p. S2271.

110. Warren Christopher and William J. Perry, "NATO's True Mission," *New York Times*, October 21, 1997, p. A27.

111. *Congressional Record*, April 30, 1998, p. S3844.

112. Amendment 2318 is in *Congressional Record*, vol. 144, 105 Cong., 2 sess., April 29, 1998, p. S3793.

113. *Congressional Record*, April 30, 1998, p. S3861.

114. Interviews with U.S. government officials.

115. *Congressional Record*, April 27, 1998, p. S3657. Background information came from interviews on Capitol Hill and from interview with Hadley (February 1999).

116. *Congressional Record*, April 30, 1998, p. S3843.

117. Ibid., p. S3862. Background information came from interviews with Senate staffers.

118. Ibid., pp. S3857, S3905–3907. The Resolution of Ratification is in the *Congressional Record*, vol. 144, 105 Cong. 2 sess., May 4, 1998, pp. S4217–20.

Chapter Six

1. See I. M. Destler, Leslie H. Gelb, and Anthony Lake, *Our Own Worst Enemy: The Unmaking of American Foreign Policy* (Simon & Schuster, 1984), pp. 238–39, 244, 265. On general distinctions between State and NSC, see Ichak Adizes, "The Internal Conflict over Foreign Policy," *Wall Street Journal*, December 22, 1981, p. 20.

2. Michael Dobbs, "Wider Alliance Would Increase US Commitments," *Washington Post*, July 5, 1995, pp. A1, 16.

3. Interviews with U.S. government officials.

4. Ashton B. Carter and William J. Perry, *Preventive Defense: A New Security Strategy for America* (Brookings, 1999), p. v. See also Ashton B. Carter, William J. Perry, and John D. Steinbruner, *A New Concept of Cooperative Security* (Brookings, 1992); Graham Allison, Ashton B. Carter, and Philip Zelikow, "The Soviet Arsenal and the Mistaken Calculus of Caution," *Washington Post*, March 29, 1992, p. C3; William J. Perry, "Measures to Reduce the Risk of Nuclear War," *Orbis*, vol. 27 (Winter 1984), pp. 1027–35.

5. For a sample of Talbott's writings, see, for example, Strobe Talbott, *Deadly Gambits: The Reagan Administration and the Stalemate in Nuclear Arms Control* (Knopf, 1984); Strobe Talbott and Michael Mandelbaum, *Reagan and Gorbachev* (Vintage Books, 1987); Strobe Talbott and Michael R. Beschloss, *At the Highest Levels: The Inside Story of the End of the Cold War* (Little, Brown 1993).

6. Carter and Perry, *Preventive Defense*, p. 58. Interviews with William Perry (June 1997) and Ashton Carter (May 1997).

7. See Alexander George, *Presidential Decisionmaking in Foreign Policy: The Effective Use of Information and Advice* (Westview Press, 1980) for a good discussion on value complexity. Also, the particular trade-off involved in this case is discussed in Stephen Sestanovich, "The Collapsing Partnership: Why the United States Has No Russia Policy," in Robert J. Lieber, ed., *Eagle Adrift* (New York: Longman, 1997). Other material comes from interviews with numerous high-level administration officials.

8. Interviews with William Perry (June 1997), John Shalikashvili (July 1998), Anthony Lake (October 1998), Warren Christopher (December 1998).

9. Interview with Anthony Lake (October 1998).

10. Elizabeth Drew, *On the Edge: The Clinton Presidency* (Simon & Schuster, 1994), p. 336.

11. See, for example, Martin Walker, "Clinton Cleaves to Roosevelt's Dream," *Guardian Weekly*, March 23, 1997, p. 6.

12. Phone interview with Dick Morris (June 1998).

13. Dick Morris, *Behind the Oval Office: Getting Reelected against All Odds* (Los Angeles: Renaissance Books, 1999), p. 245. Elizabeth Drew also describes how Lake kept presidential adviser David Gergen out of big foreign policy meetings. See Drew, *On the Edge*, pp. 363–64.

14. "Special White House Briefing from Madrid: Senate NATO Observer Group Meeting," Lexis-Nexis Academic Universe, accessed November 1998. Numerous officials recount how she told this story to Bill Clinton and others. And General Wesley Clark says that Holbrooke told this story during the interagency meeting of September 1994 when arguing why the United States had to enlarge NATO. Interview with Clark (January 1999).

15. James M. Lindsay, "End of an Era: Congress and Foreign Policy after the Cold War," in Eugene R. Wittkopf and James M. McCormick, eds., *The*

Domestic Sources of American Foreign Policy: Insights and Evidence, 3d. ed. (Lanham, Md.: Rowman & Littlefield, 1998), p. 173.

16. Gerald B. Solomon, *The NATO Enlargement Debate, 1990–1997: Blessings of Liberty* (Praeger Press [published with CSIS], 1998), p. 135.

17. James M. Lindsay, *Congress and the Politics of U.S. Foreign Policy* (Johns Hopkins University Press, 1994), p. 16.

18. *The Debate on NATO Enlargement*, Hearings before the Senate Committee on Foreign Relations, 105 Cong., 1 sess. (Government Printing Office, 1998), pp. 253–54.

19. Interview with Michael Mandelbaum (November 1998).

20. James Reston, "Public Debate on Treaty Far Short of Expectation," *New York Times*, May 19, 1949, p. 10. On the minimal efforts on Greece and Turkey, see, for example, William S. White, "Senate Unit Backs Greece and Turkey for Atlantic Pact," *New York Times*, January 16, 1952, p. 8; White, "6-Man Senate Votes 2 into NATO," *New York Times*, January 30, 1952, p. 4. For the later vote, see White, "Senate Reaccepts Greece and Turkey: Votes 73 to 2 for Admission into Atlantic Treaty—Taft Deserted by Followers," *New York Times*, February 8, 1952, pp. 1,7.

21. William Clinton, "Remarks by the President at NATO Summit Send-Off by America's Veterans," The White House, Office of the Press Secretary, July 3, 1997. See also Strobe Talbott, "Why NATO Should Grow," *New York Review of Books*, August 10, 1995, pp. 27–30.

22. A good article on the "odd bedfellows" written by Jeremy Rosner when he was out of the government is "NATO Enlargement: What Will the Congress and Public Say?" *Armed Forces Journal International*, April 1997, p. 8.

23. On the need for a credible open door, see Javier Madariaga Solana, "NATO's Future: Growing the Alliance," *Economist*, March 13, 1999, pp. 23–28. On the difficulties of further expansion because of the declining salience of the notion of "the West," see James Kurth, "NATO Expansion and the Idea of the West," *Orbis*, vol. 41 (Fall 1997), p. 555–67. The Washington Summit Communique and the Membership Action Plan, both of which were released on April 24, 1999 (http://www.nato.int/docu/pr/1999/p99-064e.htm [April 1999] and http://www.nato.int/docu/pr/1999/p99-066e.htm [April 1999]).

Index

Praise for *The Diamond Eye*

"Kate Quinn amazes me. With each new book she reaches new heights in her craft as a writer of page-turning plots and prose. *The Diamond Eye* is a remarkable story filled with heart, intrigue, breathtaking drama, and, perhaps best of all, meticulously researched details that prove that history provides the absolute best raw material for storytelling. Like her sniper subject Lyudmila Pavlichenko, Kate Quinn has brilliantly hit her mark—this is a stunning novel about a singular historical heroine."

—Allison Pataki, *New York Times* bestselling author of *The Magnificent Lives of Marjorie Post*

"An absorbing, exhilarating thrill ride of a novel that explores an extraordinary real-life woman—plucked from the shadows of history—who went to unimaginable lengths to protect her homeland and her family, and in doing so, learned who she really was. At the beginning, *The Diamond Eye* burns slowly, drawing you meticulously and inescapably into the world of a humble university student who will, against all odds, become a world-class sniper. By the time you hit the middle of the book you'll be fully immersed in Lyudmila's dark, complicated world of duty, sacrifice, motherhood, and love against the odds. This is a book that reminds us, in the most beautiful and heart-wrenching fashion, that beneath our differences, all of us—across culture, nationality, and time period—have at our core the same basic desires: to live, to love, and to protect that which we hold dear. A stunning, immersive tour de force by one of the best historical fiction writers working today. Meticulously researched, deftly plotted, and executed with a thrilling blend of action and heart, *The Diamond Eye* is a masterpiece."

—Kristin Harmel, *New York Times* bestselling author of *The Forest of Vanishing Stars*

"A sparkling gem of a story about a fabulous and fascinating woman. Lyudmila Pavlichenko's journey from history student and mother to sniper and national hero is beautifully rendered by Kate Quinn in this utterly absorbing novel."

—Natasha Lester, *New York Times* bestselling author of *The Riviera House*

"The brilliant Kate Quinn is at the top of her game with an unexpected historical heroine to root for. The young Russian mother and war hero will steal your heart by stealth—just as she stole the heart of Eleanor Roosevelt, America's most celebrated First Lady. You'll be wowed by this unlikely tale of love and lasting friendship that transcends ideology. It kept me reading late into the night!"

—Stephanie Dray, *New York Times* bestselling author of *The Women of Chateau Lafayette*

"From blood-soaked Russian battlefields to the White House Rose Garden, Kate Quinn takes expert aim at one of history's forgotten heroines to bring us a story that will pull you in from the very first sentence. *The Diamond Eye* is her best yet!"

—Alix Rickloff, author of *The Way to London*

"Readers can all but smell the gun smoke in *The Diamond Eye*, so thoroughly does Kate Quinn immerse you in the grim and gray world of the Russian front—and in the psyche of her remarkable real-life heroine, Mila Pavlichenko. Quinn's page-turning account of Mila's transformation from student to sniper measures the unimaginable toll of pulling the trigger, portraying with power and compassion Mila's urge not to kill, but to protect. Unputdownable!"

—Bryn Turnbull, author of *The Woman Before Wallis*

"A riveting, authentic story of a Soviet woman who becomes a sniper during World War II. In page-turning prose, Kate Quinn illuminates the tale of Mila Pavlichenko, who, after killing more than three hundred of Hitler's most formidable officers, comes to the United States to promote America's entry into the war. With vivid characters, unforgettable battle scenes, and moments of intense humanity and love, *The Diamond Eye* is a master class in historical fiction. It will leave you breathless, choking on tears."

—Elena Gorokhova, author of *A Train to Moscow*

"*The Diamond Eye* is another winner from Kate Quinn. A historian-turned-sniper who falls in love in war-torn Russia and then befriends Eleanor Roosevelt—what's not to love? The thrilling showdown at the end is not to be missed!"

—Kaia Alderson, author of *Sisters in Arms*

"In *The Diamond Eye*, Kate Quinn introduces us to her fiercest heroine yet, Mila Pavlichenko, a celebrated female sniper for the Red Army who displays death-defying courage, skill, and wisdom. As readers follow her into the trenches of World War II, they will feel the adrenaline rush each time she pulls the trigger. Be forewarned: once you start reading, you'll not be able to stop turning the pages. Exquisitely told, this is what makes Kate Quinn such a powerhouse in historical fiction."

—Renée Rosen, *USA Today* bestselling author of *The Social Graces*

"An epic journey with history's deadliest female sniper from the trenches of the Russian front to the halls of American power, *The Diamond Eye* is an enthralling page-turner brimming with emotion and excitement. Kate Quinn writes with a diamond eye for detail."

—Taylor Adams, author of *No Exit* and *Hairpin Bridge*

"Kate Quinn is not one to be daunted by complex storytelling. In *The Diamond Eye,* she takes aim at the colorful life of the most well-known sniper you've never heard of. Though most of us cannot relate to standing on the battlefield, Quinn weaves humanity and emotional depth through the narrative, giving the reader a target we can relate to: the human experience, rife with grief, loss, love, wit, anguish. She does this, in part, by posing a compelling dilemma in need of solving, allowing us insight into what Lady Death values most: loyalty. Even if it means concealing a dark secret or two . . ."

—Sarah Penner, *New York Times* bestselling
author of *The Lost Apothecary*

"Mila Pavlichenko is not a born killer, but a shy bookworm with a love of history who discovers she's an excellent sharpshooter. Kate Quinn brings to life a little-known woman in history who took the world by storm and then quietly faded into the background. *The Diamond Eye* catapults the reader from one harrowing moment to the next in an edge-of-your-seat read laced with humor, friendship, love, and literature that will leave the memory of Lady Death alive and thriving in our hearts forever."

—Eliza Knight, *USA Today* bestselling
author of *The Mayfair Bookshop*

"*The Diamond Eye* is quintessential Quinn—a tough-as-nails heroine, the highest of stakes, and a rip-roaring conclusion. Even as I turned the pages late into the night, I was also learning about Russia and the eastern front of World War II, and the surprising truths about being a sniper. A transporting, gripping read."

—Kerri Maher, author of *The Kennedy Debutante*
and *The Paris Bookseller*

"Few authors are able to craft stories as immersive and compulsively readable as Kate Quinn's, and her latest is no exception. *The Diamond Eye* is a sparkling new gem in Quinn's already impressive bibliography. Quinn recaptures the Russian intrigue—the utter magic—of *The Huntress* in Mila's story. The characters and setting are vibrant and compelling, and the reader can't help but root for Quinn's heroine from start to finish. A brilliant tale by a master storyteller."

—Aimie K. Runyan, bestselling author
of *The School for German Brides*

THE DIAMOND EYE

ALSO BY KATE QUINN

The Alice Network
The Huntress
The Rose Code

The Empress of Rome Series

Lady of the Eternal City
The Three Fates (novella)
Empress of the Seven Hills
Daughters of Rome
Mistress of Rome

The Borgia Chronicles

The Lion and the Rose
The Serpent and the Pearl

Collaborative Works

A Day of Fire: A Novel of Pompeii
A Year of Ravens: A Novel of Boudica's Rebellion
A Song of War: A Novel of Troy
Ribbons of Scarlet: A Novel of the French Revolution's Women

THE DIAMOND EYE

A Novel

KATE QUINN

wm

WILLIAM MORROW

An Imprint of HarperCollins*Publishers*

This is a work of fiction. Names, characters, places, and incidents are products of the author's imagination or are used fictitiously and are not to be construed as real. Any resemblance to actual events, locales, organizations, or persons, living or dead, is entirely coincidental.

HarperCollins books may be purchased for educational, business, or sales promotional use. For information, please email the Special Markets Department at SPsales@harpercollins.com.

FIRST EDITION

Library of Congress Cataloging-in-Publication Data has been applied for.

ISBN 978-0-06-294351-4 (hardcover)
ISBN 978-0-06-322614-2 (international edition)

22 23 24 25 26 LSC 10 9 8 7 6 5 4 3 2 1

To all the writers who managed to produce a book during the COVID-19 lockdown—to all the creators who managed to make art in the middle of a pandemic. It was really tough, wasn't it?

In the summer of 1942,
as the world was locked in war against Hitler,
a woman crossed the sea from the Soviet Union to the United States.

She was a single mother, a graduate student, a library researcher.
She was a soldier, a war hero,
a sniper with 309 kills to her name.

She was Russia's envoy, America's sweetheart,
and Eleanor Roosevelt's dear friend.

Her story is incredible. Her story is true.
Meet Lady Death.

PROLOGUE

August 27, 1942
Washington, D.C.

He stood with a pocketful of diamonds and a heart full of death, watching a Russian sniper shake hands with the First Lady of the United States.

"Whoever heard of a girl sniper?" the marksman heard a photographer behind him grumble, craning for a look at the young woman who had just disembarked from the embassy limousine. She'd seemed to flinch at the barrage of camera flashes like muzzle fire, averting her gaze and walking in a phalanx of Soviet minders up the steps of the White House. The photographer snorted, scoffing, "I say she's a fake."

Yet we couldn't resist coming here for a look at her, thought the marksman, idly flipping his falsified press badge. A delegation from the Soviet Union arriving for the international student conference that was Eleanor Roosevelt's latest goodwill project—it wouldn't have merited more than a few lines of newsprint, much less rousted a lot of hungover journalists and photographers out of their beds before dawn and sent them scurrying, pens in hand, to the White House gates, if not for that girl in her crisp olive-green uniform.

"Did they say she had seventy-five kills on the Russian front?" a *Washington Post* journalist wondered, rummaging through his notes.

"I thought it was over a hundred . . ."

"Higher," said the marksman in the Tidewater Virginia drawl he'd grown up with. He'd long since ironed his soft southern vowels out into a flat mid-Atlantic cadence that could belong anywhere and nowhere, but he often let Virginia creep back into his tone, depending on who he was talking to. People trusted a southern accent, and they found themselves trusting the marksman: a loose-jointed man of medium height, medium hair between brown and blond, a bony face, and mud-colored eyes, usually jingling a clutter of uncut diamonds in his trouser pocket. He didn't like banks; anyone who hired him paid in cash, which he then promptly converted to jewels. Lighter than cash, easy to hide—just like bullets. He was thirty-eight years old and had been operating for nineteen years and more than thirty marks. It added up to a lot of diamonds, and a lot of bullets.

"How does a girl like that kill over a hundred Nazis?" a columnist at his side was speculating, still watching the Russian woman on the front steps of the White House, standing to one side in a cluster of dark-suited embassy men as the First Lady welcomed the rest of the Soviet delegation. "Wasn't she a librarian or a schoolteacher or something?"

"Russkies let women in their army, apparently . . ."

Their medical battalions, maybe, the marksman thought. *But even the Reds don't make women into snipers.*

Yet he was here to see for himself, wasn't he? Wanting a look at the woman whose sparse biography he had already committed to memory: Lyudmila Pavlichenko; twenty-six years old; fourth-year history student at the Kiev State University and senior research assistant at the Odessa public library—before the war. After the war, thirteen months of continuous fighting against Hitler's forces on the Russian front.

Nickname: Lady Death.

"Dammit, how many kills *was* it on her tally?" The *Washington Post* journalist was still searching his notes. "Was it more than two hundred?"

Three hundred and nine, the marksman thought, but he didn't believe a word of it. This little junior librarian/schoolteacher was no trained killer. She was a trick pony stuffed with Soviet propaganda, handpicked for the student delegation, and the marksman could see why. A pretty brunette with lively dark eyes and a neat, photogenic face above her bemedaled uniform, nothing like the sort of mannish freak Americans would expect of a Russian female soldier. The Soviets needed American aid; they needed good press coverage on this delegation to American shores, so they'd selected the most winsome candidates they could find. Front and center, this girl sniper who looked so small and appealing beside that tall bony bitch Eleanor Roosevelt.

"Congratulations on your safe arrival in America." The press corps clustered close enough to hear the First Lady's cultured, silver-spoon voice easily as she addressed the Soviet delegation, see the flash of her horsey teeth. "On behalf of my husband the President, welcome to the White House. He looks forward to meeting you all at a later time and invites you to spend your first days in America's capital under our roof. You are some of the first Soviet guests to be hosted in the White House, a historic moment in the friendship between our nations."

She began ushering the Russians inside, and that was that. It wasn't even six-thirty yet, the skies above the capital barely flushed with sunlight as the pack of journalists, photographers, and one lone innocuous assassin began to disperse. "Never thought I'd see the day a Russian sniper got welcomed to the White House," a grizzled columnist grumbled. "FDR will rue the day."

He won't be alive to do it, the marksman thought, eyes still on Mila Pavlichenko's neat dark head as she followed the First Lady toward the doors of the White House. *In nine days—the last day of the international conference—President Roosevelt will be dead.*

"I can see the headlines now," the *Washington Post* reporter muttered, scribbling in his pad. " 'Russian Female Sniper Receives Warm White House Welcome.' "

The marksman smiled, jingling his pocketful of diamonds again. Ten days from now, all the headlines would scream RUSSIAN FEMALE SNIPER MURDERS FDR!

Notes by the First Lady

The President was intending to greet the Soviet delegation with me as they arrived, but he had a fall this morning. I'd just entered with a knock, carrying a packet of memoranda and reports for him to read, and I saw the valet lose his grip as he transferred my husband from his bed. Franklin fell hard on the carpet of his bedroom. Had it happened in public he would have roared with laughter as though it were all a prank, a Charlie Chaplin pratfall, and set about regaining his feet with some hearty, bracing joke. Since he was in the privacy of his bedroom, he allowed his face to twist in agony. I always feel I should look away in such moments—watching the proud facade of President Franklin D. Roosevelt crack with frustration in response to his body's failings feels like a violation.

I reassure Franklin when he is sitting upright again, tell him to take his breakfast at leisure, and offer to greet the Soviet delegation alone. The President already has a packed schedule; I can at least take on this first task. I see the gratitude, even as he makes a joke about his fall. "Better in here than out where all the jackals can see."

"They wouldn't dare cheer," I say lightly.

"But they'd pray I never got up."

Something about his tone bothers me, but he's already reaching for his morning newspapers, girding himself for the day ahead. To the world he appears invincible: a voice full of golden confidence trickling honey-thick from the radio, a profile like a ship's prow cleaving the world, with a jutted cigarette holder rather than a bowsprit. Only a few see the iron will that keeps his facade in place, keeps his body moving ever forward, keeps his enemies at bay.

I hope, moving into the morning light to greet the Soviet delegation—a block of dark-suited inscrutable men, and one unexpected serious-eyed young woman (they say she is a sniper?)—that it will be enough.

FIVE YEARS AGO

November 1937

KIEV, SOVIET UNION

Mila

CHAPTER 1

I was not a soldier yet. We were not at war yet. I could not conceive of taking a life yet. I was just a mother, twenty-one and terrified. When you're a mother, panic can engulf you in the blink of an eyelash. All it takes is that instant when your eye sweeps a room for your child and doesn't find him.

"Now, Mila," my mother began. "Don't be angry—"

"Where's Slavka?" I hadn't even pulled off my patched gloves and snow-dusted coat yet, but my heart was already thudding. There was my son's half-constructed block factory on the floor of the apartment, there was the small worn pile of his books, but no sturdy dark-haired five-year-old.

"His father dropped in. He knew he had missed the appointment—"

"Nice of Alexei to acknowledge that," I gritted. The second appointment I had set up to have our divorce finalized; the second appointment my husband had missed. Each time it had taken me months to scrape up the required fifty-ruble fee; weeks to get an appointment with the backlogged office; then hours waiting in a cold, stuffy corridor craning my eyes for a glimpse of my husband's golden head . . . all to lead to nothing. Anger smoldered in the pit of my stomach. Any Soviet citizen already spent entirely too much time waiting in lines as it was!

My mother wiped her hands on her apron, her big dark eyes pleading. "He was very sorry, *malyshka*. He wanted to take Slavka out for a treat. He's hardly seen the boy these past few years, his own son—"

Whose fault is that? I wanted to retort. I wasn't the one keeping our son out of Alexei's life. My husband was the one who decided only a month or two after giving our son the name of Rostislav Pavlichenko that marriage and fatherhood weren't really to his liking. But my mother's kind, pretty face looked hopeful, and I bit back my hot words.

Mama's voice was soft. "Maybe there's a reason he keeps missing these appointments."

"Yes, there is," I stated. "To make me dance on his string."

"Maybe what he's really hoping for is to reconcile."

"Mama, not again—"

"A *doctor*, Mila. The best surgeon in Ukraine, you said—"

"He is, but—"

"A man on his way up. Rooms of his own rather than a communal apartment, a good salary, a Party member. Not things to throw away." My mother launched into the old argument. She hadn't approved of how Alexei and I had come together; she'd said it happened too fast and he was too old for me and she was right—but she also wanted me safe and warm and fed. "You always said he's no drunk and never once hit you," she went on now. "Maybe he's not the man you dreamed of, but a surgeon's wife won't ever stand in a bread queue, and neither will his children. You don't remember the hungry years, you were just a little thing . . . but there's nothing a woman won't put up with to keep her babies fed."

I looked down at my worn gloves. None of what she said was wrong, I knew that.

I also knew that a part of me was afraid to let my little boy be alone with his father.

"Mama. Where are they?"

THE SHOOTING RANGE wasn't much, just a converted storage space: bars on the windows, a small armory, a line of wooden shields with targets, men on a firing line standing with braced feet and pistols raised or lying on their bellies to fire rifles . . . and in the middle, a tall blond man with a small boy: Alexei Pavlichenko and little Rostislav Alexeivich. My stomach flipped in relief.

"Every man should know how to shoot," I could hear Alexei telling our son as I came closer. He was showing Slavka how to hold a rifle far too large for him, and his voice had that expansive cadence I remembered so well. There was nothing my husband liked better than explaining things to people who knew less than him. "Though inborn abilities are required to be a true expert, of course."

"What kind of abilities, Papa?" Slavka was round-eyed, looking up at this golden stranger he hardly knew. A man who had walked out of his life without a backward glance when he was just six weeks old.

"Patience. A good eye. A steady hand, and a precise feel for the tool in your grip. That's why your papa's such a good shot—he has a surgeon's touch." Alexei flashed a smile downward, and Slavka's eyes got even rounder. "Now you try—"

"Slavka," I called, striding down the firing line, careful to keep behind the shooters. "Give that rifle back. You're too young to be handling weapons that large."

Slavka started guiltily, but Alexei didn't look surprised to see me or my thunderous face. "Hello there," he said easily, brushing a lock of fair hair off his tall forehead. He loomed a head above me: thirty-six, lean and golden, his teeth showing white in his easy smile. "You're looking lovely, *kroshka*."

I didn't bother asking him not to call me that—he already knew it made my hackles rise. For about one week during our marriage I had found it adorable when he called me his *bread crumb*—"Because you're such a little bit of a thing, Mila!"—but it hadn't taken me long to realize a crumb was something that could be flicked away into a dustbin. A piece of trash.

"You shouldn't have taken Slavka out without me," I said instead, as evenly as possible. The pulse of fear was still beating through me, even at the sight of my boy safe and sound. I didn't really think Alexei would try to steal our son away from me, but such things weren't unheard of. At the factory where I'd worked when Slavka was a baby, one of the lathe operators had wept and raged when her former husband swooped their daughter out of school and took her off to Leningrad without any warning. She never got the girl back; her husband had too many Party friends in his pocket. These things *happened.*

"Relax, Mila." Alexei's smile broadened, and that was when the fear in my stomach started curling into anger. He knew I'd been afraid; he knew, and he rather enjoyed it. "Who's going to teach a boy to shoot if his father doesn't do it?"

"I know how to shoot, I can—"

"Anyway, it doesn't matter." Another amused glance. "You're here now. Here to spoil the fun!"

I saw him throw a wink over my head to some friend behind me. *Women!* that wink said. *Always spoiling a man's fun, am I right?* I busied myself pulling off my gloves and disentangling myself from my winter coat, aware I was the only woman standing on the firing line. Females stood at the back, applauding when their brothers or boyfriends or husbands sank a shot. From Lenin on down, Soviet men have always talked a good game about women standing shoulder to shoulder with their men in every field society had to offer, but when it came to children being tended, dishes being scrubbed, or applause being given, I had always observed that it was still female hands doing most of the tending, scrubbing, and clapping. Not that I questioned such a thing overly much: it was simply the way of the world, and always had been.

"Mamochka?" Slavka looked up at me anxiously.

"Give that weapon back, please," I said quietly, brushing a hand over his hair to make it plain I wasn't angry at him. "You're too little for a rifle that size."

"No, he's not," Alexei scoffed, taking the weapon. "Baby him like that and you'll never make a man of him. Watch me load, Slavka . . ."

Alexei's hands moved swiftly, loading the TOZ-8. It was his hands

I'd noticed first, when I saw him at that dance—a surgeon's hands, long-fingered and precise, working with absolute skill and focus. *What, you can't say no when a tall blond man smiles at you?* my mother scolded when she learned I was pregnant—but it wasn't Alexei Pavlichenko's height or his charm or even his hands that had drawn me into his arms. It was his skill, his focus, his drive—so different from the boys my age, all horseplay and careless talk. Alexei hadn't been a boy, he'd been a man over thirty who knew what he wanted—and what he wanted, he trained for; aimed for; *got.* I'd seen that in him that first night, young and laughing as I was in my flimsy violet dress. Barely fifteen years old.

A mother nine months later.

I sent Slavka to hang up my coat at the back of the room, then turned back to Alexei. "You missed the appointment." Fighting to keep my voice even. I was not going to sound shrill; it would just amuse him. "I waited nearly three hours."

He shrugged. "It slipped my mind. I'm a busy man, *kroshka*."

"You know they require us both to be there in order to finalize the divorce. You don't want to be married to me, Alexei, so why won't you show up?"

"I'll make it up to you," he said, breezy, and one of his friends farther down the line chuckled, seeing my face.

"She doesn't want you to make it up to her!" Laughter rippled behind me, and someone muttering, *I'll let her make it up to me!* Alexei grinned over my head.

"I'll set another appointment to finalize the divorce," I said as coolly as I could manage. "If you can just be there, it will all be over in a matter of minutes." I didn't like the mess I'd made of my own life, a mother at fifteen, estranged within months, and potentially divorced at twenty-one—but better to be divorced than to be stranded in this limbo of the last six years, neither married nor unmarried.

"Ah, don't get all prune-faced, Mila. You know I like to tease."

Alexei gave me a playful dig in the ribs. Only it was a dig that hurt through my wool blouse. "You're looking well, you know. Glowing, almost . . . Maybe there's a reason you want this divorce? A man?"

He was still teasing, still playful, but there was an edge behind the words. He didn't really want me anymore, but he didn't like the idea of anyone else wanting me, either. Much less having me.

"There's no one," I said. Even if there had been someone else, I wouldn't have told him—but there wasn't. Between university classes and studies, Komsomol meetings and caring for Slavka, I was getting by on about five hours of sleep a night. Where was there the *time* for a new man in my life?

Alexei turned the rifle over between his hands, still looking at me. "You're in your third year of studies now?"

"My second." The history department at Kiev University, and my student card had been hard-won after a year of studying at night while working shifts as a turner lathe operator at the arsenal factory. Back then I'd been operating on about four hours of sleep a night, but it was all worth it. All for Slavka, for his future and mine. "Alexei, if I can get another appointment—"

"Alexei!" someone called further down the firing line, looking me over. "This the little wife?"

My husband brought me under his arm with a quick squeeze. "Tell her what a good shot I am, Seryozha. She's not impressed with me anymore. Just like a wife, eh?" Alexei saw the look on my face and leaned down to nuzzle my ear. "Just teasing, *kroshka,* don't bristle."

"Your man's good, watch him with the TOZ-8!"

"Just a simple single-shot rifle," Alexei told me as I wriggled out from under his arm. "We call it the Melkashka."

"I know what it's called." I was no expert, but I'd been to the range before with the factory shooting club; I knew something about firearms. "TOZ-8, good 120 through 180 meters—"

"TOZ-8, muzzle velocity 320 meters a second, good from 120 to 180 meters," Alexei said, not listening. "Sliding bolt here—"

"I know. I've handled—"

He raised the rifle, took careful aim, and the crack of the shot sounded. "See? Nearly dead center."

I bit my tongue hard enough to hurt. I wanted to turn my back, gather up my son, and storm out of here, but Slavka was dawdling by the coat hooks listening to two men having some loud political discussion—and I didn't want to depart without some kind of guarantee. A guarantee that the next appointment I set to finalize our divorce, Alexei would *be there.*

"You never used to spend much time at the range. What made you want to get so good at it?" I pushed out a note of grudging admiration for his marksmanship. "You're a surgeon; you know what happens to muscles and organs when they take a bullet. You used to tell me about patching wounds like that."

"Soon there will be war, don't you know that?" Reloading the Melkashka. "When that day comes, they'll need a gun in every hand."

"Not yours." As long as I could remember, my father had been shaking his head and saying, *One day there will be war,* but it hadn't happened yet. "If war comes, *you* won't be a soldier."

My husband frowned. "You think I'm not capable?"

"I mean a surgeon like you is too valuable to waste on the front line," I said quickly, recognizing my mistake. I hadn't lived with Alexei in so long, I'd forgotten how to flatter his pride. "You'll be running a battlefield hospital, not pulling a trigger on command like a blind monkey."

His frown disappeared, and he raised the rifle. "A man sees chances in war, Mila. Chances he doesn't get in ordinary life. I intend to be ready."

He fired off another shot, not quite hitting the bull's-eye. "Good shot, Papa," Slavka said breathlessly, running back up.

Alexei ruffled his hair. Two young girls at the back were watching, winding their curls around their fingers, and maybe my husband saw their admiration, because he squatted down beside his son and said, "Let me show you."

That was the very first thing he'd said to *me.* To little Mila Belova, just past her fifteenth birthday and careening happily through a drafty dance hall, entranced by the music and the laughter and the violet dress swirling about my legs. I was dancing with a girlfriend, both of us eyeing the boys showing off across the room, and then the song changed to something slower, more formal . . . and a toweringly tall man with fair hair pulled me neatly away from my girlfriend and into the curve of his arm, saying, "Let me show you . . ." Later he spread his coat on the grass outside the dance hall for me to sit and told me he meant to be a great man someday. *I'll make the name Pavlichenko resound from Moscow to Vladivostok.* He'd grinned to show he was joking, but I knew he wasn't. Not really.

I can see it now, I'd replied, laughing. *Alexei Pavlichenko, Hero of the Soviet Union!* He burned bright with ambition, so bright he'd dazzled me. Looking at him now in the winter dimness of the shooting range, remembering how he'd taken my hand soon afterward and guided it as he whispered *Let me show you something else* . . . well. I could still admire the fire of ambition in him, much as I disliked him, but I couldn't feel even a flicker of the old bedazzlement.

"No, no," Alexei was telling Slavka, impatience lacing his voice. "Don't let the butt sag, sock it back against the shoulder—"

"He's too little," I said quietly. "He can't reach."

"He's seven years old, he can hold a rifle like a man—"

"He's five."

"Head up, Slavka, don't be a baby. Don't *cringe*!" he snapped.

"Sorry, Papa." My son was struggling to support the heavy birch stock, trying so hard to please this golden father he hardly ever saw. "Like this?"

Alexei laughed. "Look at you, jumpy as a rabbit." He put his finger over Slavka's chubby one on the trigger, pulling. My son flinched at the report, and Alexei laughed again. "You're not scared of a little bang, are you?"

"That's enough." I took the rifle away, pulling Slavka against my side. "Alexei, Slavka and I are going now. And if I set another appointment to finalize the divorce, kindly be there."

I spoke too curtly. I should have been soft, said *Please be there* or *Won't you be there?* The cautious wordsmithing of a woman stepping lightly around a man who has the upper hand, and might use it to lash out—no poet ever agonized over the crafting of a sentence more carefully.

Alexei's eyes took on a hard glitter. "You should be thanking me, *kroshka*. Who else is going to make this puppy of yours into a man?" A glance down at Slavka. "I remember when he was a baby and I'd come back from twelve hours of surgery to find him still awake and crying. *He can't sleep,* you kept whimpering, *he can't sleep.* Not like me, I can sleep anywhere." A glance at me, and Alexei dropped his voice to a murmur, just between us. "What does that tell me, Mila?"

"I can't imagine what you mean." I could feel Slavka trembling as he pressed against my side, uncomprehending but nervous. He wanted his toy train, I could tell—he wanted his grandmother's cramped, cozy apartment, the gleam of the samovar, the spoonful of jam she'd give him off a ladle. I just wanted him out of here, and I began to hand Alexei the Melkashka so I could leave, but his words stopped me.

"This boy doesn't sleep like me, that's all. Doesn't have my hair either, or my eyes . . ." Alexei shrugged, still speaking softly. "A man might wonder things, about a child like that."

"He takes after my father," I said icily.

"He takes after someone." Alexei sank his hands in his pockets, airily unconcerned. "Maybe that's why you want to get rid of me,

Mila. Not a new man in your life; maybe a man you've had in your life since before we met—"

"Go get my coat, *morzhik*," I interrupted sharply, sending Slavka toward the back of the room with a little push.

"—because I look at that boy with my name, and I wonder." Alexei watched our son—*our son*—drag off uncertainly toward the row of pegs again. "I really do wonder."

I still had the Melkashka in my hands, birch stock sticky from Slavka's nervous fingers. I felt my nails digging into the wood and wanted to sink them into Alexei's high-cheekboned face. I wanted to scream that I'd had no one before him and he knew it, because I'd gone straight from the schoolroom to his bed to pushing his baby out of me. But I knew the moment I lashed out at my husband, he'd seize my wrists and squeeze just a little too hard, chuckling, *Women! Always throwing tantrums . . .*

"Your face!" Alexei shook his head, grinning. "*Kroshka*, it was a joke! Don't you know how to laugh?"

"Maybe not," I said, "but I know how to shoot."

I raised the rifle, spun, aligned my aiming eye and front-sight and rear-sight with the farthest wooden target across the range, and squeezed the trigger. My ears rang, and as I lowered the Melkashka I imagined exactly where I'd sunk my shot: the bull's-eye, inside every one of my husband's shots. But—

"Good try," Alexei said, amused. "Maybe next time you'll even hit the target."

A burst of hoots from his watching friends. My cheeks burned. *I know how to shoot,* I wanted to lash out. I'd gone to the range a few times with the factory shooting club, and I'd done just fine. I hadn't dazzled anyone, but I hadn't missed the target either—not once.

But today I'd missed. Because I was flustered, angry. Because I'd been trying to wipe that smile off Alexei's face.

"Look at you, serious little girl with your great big gun." Alexei clipped the Melkashka out of my hand, chucking me under the chin like I was a naughty child, only this clip snapped my head back hard enough to sting. "You want to try again, *kroshka*? Jump for it!" He held it far over my head, smiling, a glint in his eye. "Jump!"

Other men along the firing line began laughing, too. I heard someone call *Jump for it,* coucoushka*! Jump!*

I wouldn't jump for the rifle. I turned to Slavka, coming back to the line with my coat, and began shrugging into it. "I'll let you know when I get another appointment, Alexei."

"Have it your way." Shrugging, he began to load the Melkashka again, flashing a smile at the two girls on the watching line. I saw them smile back. That's the thing with young girls: they're easily impressed. By lean height and golden hair, lofty ambition and devouring dreams. I used to be like that. But now I was twenty-one, an angry mother with the smell of gunsmoke on her hands and cheeks that burned in humiliation, no longer impressed by surface shine on bad men.

SLAVKA'S MITTENED HAND clung tight to mine as we walked through the darkening streets of Kiev. The iron-colored sky overhead sent snow spiraling down to catch in my lashes. "Put your tongue out and catch a snowflake," I told my son, but he was silent. "Hot pelmeni with sour cream when we get home?" I tried next, but he just kept trudging through the muddy snow, shoulders hitching now and then.

"*Morzhik,*" I cajoled softly. It meant *little walrus*—a name I'd given when he was still nursing at my breast. He'd certainly fed like one.

"Papa doesn't like me," Slavka mumbled.

"It isn't you, *morzhik.* Your papa doesn't really like anybody, even me." Feeling my fingers tremble with anger in my patched gloves. "We're not going to see your papa anymore, Slavka. You don't need a papa. You have your babushka, your dedushka." My parents, who hadn't approved of my separation from Alexei, but who had still taken me back in, doted on Slavka with all their hearts, cared for him so I could work a lathe in a factory and study for my exams. "And you have me, Slavka. Your mama, who is always proud of you."

"But who will teach me to shoot? I need a papa to . . ." Slavka floundered. He was only five; he didn't understand those phrases Alexei had flung around today: *be a man, make this puppy into a man, baby him too much.* He just understood that somehow his father had found him wanting.

I looked down at his dark head. "I will teach you."

"But you missed," my son blurted.

I had missed my shot. Because I'd made a mistake, let myself be goaded. But there wouldn't be any more mistakes—I couldn't afford them. I'd already made one colossal error when I fell into the arms of the wrong man, and my entire life had nearly tumbled off its tracks. Now I had a son, and if I made another mistake, his life would come tumbling down with mine. I drew a long breath and let it out. "I won't miss again. Not ever."

"But . . ."

"Rostislav Alexeivich." I addressed him formally, drawing him to a halt by a streetlamp and going to one knee in the snow, holding his small shoulders. My heart thudded again. I'd missed the wooden target at the range, but I couldn't make a mistake here. "From this day, I will be your papa. I'll be your papa and your mama both. And I will teach you everything you need to know to be a fine man someday."

"But you can't."

"Why not?" He looked uncertain, and I pressed. "Do you know what it means to be a fine man, Slavka?"

"No . . ."

"Then how do you know I can't teach you? Women know fine men when we see them." Especially after clashing with men like Alexei. "No one better to teach you to be a good man than a good woman, I promise."

Slavka just looked back in the direction of the gun range, snow veiling those long dark lashes. "You can show me how to shoot?" he whispered.

"Maybe I missed today, but that doesn't matter. Your mama goes to the shooting club sometimes already. Well, with a little more practice I can qualify for the advanced marksmanship course." I hadn't even considered it before—with a full course load at the university already, who would add on a three-times-weekly class in the finer points of ballistics and weaponry? Shooting was just a casual hobby, something I did to prove I was a proper civic-minded joiner in state-approved recreational activities. I'd gone because my friends were going; we'd fire a few rounds after work or after Young Communist League meetings, then we'd go off to a film or more likely I went home to care for Slavka. I'd never taken it very seriously.

That was about to change, I decided. An advanced marksmanship badge—now *that* would wipe the smirk off Alexei's smug face. More important, it would make Slavka believe I was more than just his soft, fond, loving mamochka. Because I had so much more to teach him than shooting, to make a fine man of him. To work hard, to be honest, to treat the women in his life better than his father ever did . . . But that marksmanship badge—yes. That would be a good place to start.

Besides, I recalled that edged, possessive glint in Alexei's eyes as he looked at me. Not wanting me himself, but not really wanting anyone else to have me, either.

Maybe it would be no bad thing if I knew how to defend myself better than I did now. Knew how to defend my son.

"He said I was a *baby*," Slavka burst out. "I'm not a baby!"

My heart squeezed and I hugged him tight. "No, you aren't." *You're not a baby; your father is a bastard. But we don't need him, you and me.* My son had me, and I would give him everything. An apartment of our own someday; a wall of bookshelves; a future. I didn't need my name to resound forever like Alexei dreamed of doing; I didn't need fame or greatness. I just wanted to give my son the life he deserved.

So no more mistakes, that flinty internal voice said. And I promised myself: *Not today. Not tomorrow. Not ever.*

CHAPTER 2

Silence, please." A human saber of a man with a scar on his brow and two St. George Crosses glittering on his chest came striding into the courtyard before the Osoaviakhim marksmanship school, surveying the double line of students arrayed in our new blue tunics. He allowed the stillness to stretch until a few flecks of snow came down from the steely sky, until we were shifting uneasily in our boots, then spoke again in a voice like a rifle shot. "I have heard that you all shoot quite well. But a good marksman is still not a sniper."

For the love of Lenin, I thought, borrowing my father's frequent exhortation whenever my sister and I plagued him. I wasn't here to be a *sniper,* I was here to take the advanced marksmanship course and get my badge. Prove myself worthy of being my son's father as well as his mother. I glanced down at the schedule requirements I'd been handed when I showed up this morning for my first day: twenty hours of political classes, fourteen hours of parade ground drill, two hundred twenty hours of firearms training, sixty hours of tactics . . . it all looked reassuringly academic, which soothed me. I was a history student—I preferred it when action and violence were strictly confined to the pages of a book.

But now the scarred instructor pacing up and down was talking about *snipers.*

"Um—" The girl next to me—there were only three females in this class—raised her hand. "I'm not here to be a sniper. I'm here so I can join higher-level competitions, qualify for USSR Master of Sport."

"In peacetime you will shoot targets in competitions," the instructor said calmly. "But one day there will be war, and you will trade wooden targets for enemy hearts."

Another one like my father, always shaking his head and saying, *When there is war.* Oddly, it relaxed me: I was already very used to men who taught every skill through a lens of how it might be useful in wartime, but the girl who had asked the question looked chastened. She put her hand down, and the instructor continued speaking, eyes raking the double line of students. "A *sniper* is more than a marksman. A sniper is a patient hunter—he takes a single shot, and if he misses, he may pay for it with his life."

That was when I felt myself straightening. Did all these courses and hours of study really boil down to something as simple as *Don't miss*?

Well. That I understood.

"I do not waste instruction on idiots or hooligans," the instructor went on, snow crunching under his boots. "If in one month you have not convinced me that you can acquire the skills and cunning required of a sniper, you will be dismissed from the course."

I stood up even straighter. Because I knew right then and there that if he sent anyone home, it wouldn't be me.

DON'T MISS.

Two years of firearms coursework and drilling squeezed in around my university classes: I'd put in two hours at Kiev University's Basic Archaeology and Ethnography lecture, then struggle into my blue tunic for two hours of Wednesday-night practice assembling and disassembling the Mosin-Nagant army rifle ("Called what, Lyudmila Mikhailovna?" "The Three Line, Comrade Instructor."). I'd go straight from a Komsomol meeting at which we indignantly discussed the German bombing of Guernica in Spain, then put in three hours on the Emelyanov telescope sight ("Break it down for me, Lyudmila Mikhailovna." "It's 274 millimeters with a weight of 598 grams, two regulating drums . . ."). Two years, and all the courses and drilling—the memorization of ballistics tables, the practice hours learning the

Simonov model and the Tokarev model versus the Melkashka and the Three Line—all boiled down to one thing.

Don't miss.

"That construction site," our scarred instructor would say, pointing at a three-story building half raised on Vladimir Street. "What positions could you take to neutralize the site foreman running up and down the plank walkways from floor to floor?" I'd list off every doorway, every line of sight, every window, and then feel tears prick my eyes when he pointed out the window aperture, the stairwell, and the third-floor ledge I'd missed. "Be better," the instructor told me icily. "Come back here in two days and examine how the site has changed: every new wall in place, every window boarded up, every new internal wall that has appeared. Life has a rapid pace, but not through telescopic sights—something is always receding into the background or coming into the foreground, so you must gain the whole picture through the tiniest of details."

I jerked a nod. The instructor had spent twice as long on my mistakes as anyone else's—the other two girls just got a nod!—and I could feel the flush rising out of my dark blue collar. He seemed to sense it, turning his back in scorn. I felt my eyes narrow, and two days later I spent three hours memorizing every single change on that building site, not missing one when I rattled them off in class.

Don't miss. I had those words stamped on my bones, and there were so many chances to miss in this life—to *fail.* As a mother I was forever struggling to hit on the perfect way to raise my son: not too indulgent, not too strict. As a student I was forever struggling to hit the balance that would keep me at the top of my class: flawless note taker, prepared exam taker, dedicated researcher. As a woman of the Soviet Union, I was forever struggling to hit the ideals of my age: productive worker, happy joiner, future Party member. So many gray spaces between those tiny moving targets, so many ways to fail . . . But when I stormed into the firing range after my latest university lecture, asking myself angrily how I could have only managed a Good on a history exam rather than an Excellent, I could put it aside knowing that here, at least, hitting the target was simple—a matter of black and white, not murky gray. You hit the bull's-eye or you missed it.

"A game," the scarred instructor called. He'd begun taking our class into the countryside on Saturdays for lessons on camouflage—how to hide in tangled brambles or stands of trees, or during the wintertime, in drifts of snow. It was winter again now; we'd had a half hour's break for lunch under a cluster of ice-hung birches, stamping our boots, the boys passing flasks of something to warm the belly. Our instructor produced a sack of empty lemonade bottles and was rigging them on their sides in cleft sticks, narrow necks facing toward us as we scrambled upright and got into line with our rifles. "This game's called *bottle base*," he said, rising from his squat and coming to join the line. He set up his own shot methodically, and when he fired, a series of gasps and whistles went up: he had blown out the bottle's base without touching its neck or sides. "Can anyone match that?" he challenged, eyes glinting under the scar.

I could have sworn his eyes stopped on me, deliberate and taunting, but I stood leaning quietly on my rifle and let the younger boys scramble forward. I analyzed their misses: they were shooting too fast, eager to impress.

"You don't want to try, Lyudmila Mikhailovna?" The instructor's voice came at my shoulder, breath puffing white in the frigid air. "Or are you going to hang back posing like a fashion plate?" I had a new winter coat, dark blue with a collar of black fur my mother had painstakingly trimmed from an ancient moth-eaten scarf and restitched to cuddle around my neck like a friendly sable, and the class had been teasing me all morning that I looked too fine and fancy to be toting a weapon.

I ignored the instructor's dig, nodding at the boys as they blasted away. "I'm not joining in because they're showing off. That's not what a rifle is for."

"That could spring from a good instinct," he said. "Showing yourself—that's dangerous for a sniper. You're only invulnerable as long as you're unseen."

"I'm going to be a marksman, not a sniper."

"So you're not hanging back out of good instincts, then. You're not wary of showing off; you're just . . . afraid you'll lose. Afraid to *miss.*"

I gave him a level look and went to kneel at the firing line, sinking back on my right heel, socking the rifle into the hollow of my shoulder. Index finger on the trigger, the comb of the butt against my cheek, rifle supported with the strap under my bent elbow as I rested on my left knee and slid my hand closer to the muzzle to steady even further. I stared through the telescopic sight at the bottle in its cleft stick. Even with fourfold magnification, it looked no bigger than the period at the end of a sentence—a full stop in bold type. But I didn't stop. I fired, and in the flash of the shot I remembered the way I'd missed the target when Alexei watched me.

But this time when I lowered the rifle, I saw that the base of the bottle had been blown away in a diamond-sparkle of broken glass scattered across the snow . . . and the neck was intact.

"Well done," my instructor said calmly. "Can you repeat it?"

I felt a grin spreading across my face, barely hearing the applause of my classmates. "Yes."

That was the first day I heard it: the song a rifle could sing in my hands, its stock hard against my shoulder, my finger curled through the trigger. I'd somehow slipped away from my jockeying classmates and their flashy antics and found myself in a place of silence—an island in that raucous atmosphere of fun and games. I blocked everything out, the whole world, all so I could hear the song the Three Line was singing in my hands.

That afternoon I blew the base out of three bottles in a row, setting up every shot with painstaking care, not chipping a single bottle neck. I waited for my instructor to say something—*Scorn that, I dare you*—but he came for me with a fond, surprising hug. "Well done, my long-braided beauty," he said, giving my waist-length plait a tug. "I knew you'd win."

I blinked. "You did?"

"From whom much is given, much is demanded," he quoted. And the day I graduated from his course over a year later, he gave me an autographed copy of his booklet "Instructions for Sharpshooters" inscribed simply: *Don't miss, Lyudmila Pavlichenko.*

"Quite an achievement, *malyshka,*" my father said that evening when I came home and proudly showed my certificate. "My daughter's become a dangerous woman."

"Hardly, Papa." I kissed him on both cheeks: my solid, reliable father in the gabardine service jacket he still preferred to wear even though his military days were long behind him, the Order of the Red Banner worn proud on his breast, hands folded around a steaming cup of tea at the kitchen table. He'd been helping Slavka with his schoolwork, I could tell. My father had helped me with my schoolwork at this table too, as long as I could remember. Even if he didn't get home from work until midnight, he always made time to sit with his children, look over their assignments, and hear their problems—even when we drove him to distraction and he groaned, *For the love of Lenin, you're driving an old man mad!*

Slavka was running his fingers over the round seal crest on my marksmanship certificate. "I can teach you whenever you like," I said, tugging him into my lap and kissing his chocolate-dark hair, the same as mine and Papa's. "Shall we go to the range?"

"Maybe when I'm a Young Pioneer," he said very seriously. "When I get the red kerchief."

"When you're older," I agreed. It didn't distress me that he wasn't eager to learn yet. I had the skills when he was ready; that was what mattered. "Let's see that assignment, *morzhik.* Plant biology, I always liked that at your age. Can you name me all the parts of a leaf?"

I listened to his earnest voice until my slender, beaming mother came home, swooping to exclaim over my certificate. She was proud but a little baffled: "What is such a thing good for, *malyshka*?"

"It taught me not to miss," I said honestly.

"At targets?"

"At anything."

AND THAT IS my secret, if you're curious. You are, aren't you? Everyone is, when they first meet me. Even Eleanor Roosevelt wondered, when we met later on the steps of the White House in August of 1942. I could see it in her eyes: How does a girl like *me*—a mother, a student, an aspiring historian—become a sniper and kill hundreds of men? What's her secret?

Hardly anyone comes right out and asks me. Partly they're afraid I'll be annoyed and add them to my tally—but it's more than that. People love war heroes, but such heroes are supposed to be clean, honorable, white-cloaked. They fight in the open, in the sunlight, face-to-face with their enemies. They deal death from the front. When someone (especially a woman) earns their stars as I have done, people shiver. Anyone who walks in the night, melts into shadows, looks through telescopic sights at an unwary face—at a man who doesn't know I exist, even as I learn that he nicked himself shaving this morning and wears a wedding ring—when I learn all that and then pull a trigger so he is dead before he hears the report . . .

Well. Anyone who can do that over and over again and still manage to sleep at night must surely have a dark side.

You are not wrong to think that.

But you are wrong about *who* has such a dark side, waiting to be tapped. You think that surely someone like me is a freak of nature, gnawing a rifle in her cradle, hunting at five and killing wolves at eight, emerging from the wilds of Siberia (it's always Siberia) fully formed. Americans especially loved to imagine me that way—one of those icy Russian women of dark myth, crawling with bloodied teeth and bloodied hands from some snowbound hellscape: a killer born.

Then you meet me: little Mila Pavlichenko with her wide smile and her bag crammed with books, a student from Kiev only too happy to tell you how she wants to be a historian someday and show you pictures of her adored, chubby-cheeked son—and you are crestfallen. This is Lady Death? This is the girl sniper from the frozen north? How disappointing.

Or . . . and this is your second reaction, the one you won't ever voice . . . how unsettling. Because if a twenty-six-year-old library researcher has such a dark side to her moon, who else does?

I don't know.

I know only that mine awoke when I realized there was no room in my life for mistakes. When I realized I could not miss, not ever. When I heard a rifle sing in my hands as I buried a bullet through the neck of a bottle and sent the base flying into diamond shards . . . and realized who and how I could be.

CHAPTER 3

June 1941
Odessa

Patriotic memoirs have become all the fashion—as the Party would say, they are popular, edifying, and good for public morale (if also somewhat sleep-inducing). But if I were ever to write my memoir. I'd have to modify my story a good deal, or just leave parts out altogether, because there are many, many things about the life of Lyudmila Pavlichenko that would never make it into any memoir. Or at least not the official version.

For example, my account of the day war broke out in the Soviet Union. An official memoir might say, "The day Hitler invaded, I was attending a Komsomol meeting and reflecting on my duties as a future Party member."

The truth? The unofficial version? I was a student in Odessa, and I was at the beach.

"You have *beaches*?" I can just imagine Americans wrinkling their noses. They think Russia is nothing but a vast waste of snow glittering under the white nights—no coasts, no summer days, only ice and wolves. Really, does anyone look at a map? Odessa is farther south than Paris, Munich, or Vienna—and that June day was beautiful, the sky clear and hot, the glittering expanse of the Black Sea stretched flat and shining to the horizon.

I hadn't intended to go swimming, but my friend Sofya rapped my knuckles the day before, both of us enduring the last hour of an endless shift at the front desk of the Odessa public library. "Vika and Grigory are finally back from Moscow, and we're all going to the beach."

"I'm working on my dissertation." I was flipping through my notes at the desk, since we had no patrons to wait on. Not long after getting my advanced marksmanship certificate, I'd passed my fourth-year university exams, all Excellent to Good. I took my results out and looked at them whenever I needed a little internal fortitude. Mila Pavlichenko might have become a mother at fifteen, but her life was firmly back on course, chugging along like a patient little train hitting a predetermined progression of stations. First stop: graduating from Kiev University. Second stop: this assignment to the Odessa public library as a senior research assistant while I sent money home for Slavka every week. Next stop: finishing my dissertation . . .

"The sea, Mila," Sofya cajoled. "It's calling your name, you horrid little bookworm."

"Bogdan Khmelnitsky is calling my name."

"Do not quote your dissertation at me. I do not want to hear one more word about Bogdan Khmelnitsky, the Ukraine's accession to Russia in 1721—"

"—actually 1654."

"—or the activities of the Pereyaslav Council."

"It is *fascinating history*," I said a little huffily. All the library staff were well acquainted with my dissertation topic by now, but somehow no one was excited by it. Sofya regularly threatened to toss my dog-eared pages into the incinerator; I threatened to cram her lipstick up her nose; it was that kind of friendship. "Without the alliance of the Cossack Hetmanate to the centralized Russian state, we would never see a properly unified nation of—"

"Mila, no one cares. Come swimming tomorrow."

So here we were at the beach, striped towels spread out under the sun, a fraying basket full of lemonade bottles parked in the sand. Children careened past shrieking, sand flying up from their feet, but I just flopped back in my navy blue swimsuit that sagged at the thighs. Face turned to the sky, I drowsed to the sounds of the waves, dreaming of the day my dissertation would be done, my degree would be awarded, and I would become a historian in Moscow. I'd have an apartment not far from Gorky Park, where I would take Slavka ice-skating, buy him sugar-dusted ponchiki in a paper cone . . .

"Let's go to the opera tonight," Sofya was saying, flicking sand off her legs. "*La Traviata*—Vika's got extra tickets."

"I've been loaned from *Swan Lake* to fill out the opera dancers for the Act II gypsy dance," Vika said, rolling her eyes. She was a demi-soloist at the Odessa ballet, newly returned from the Bolshoi school in Moscow; she wasn't even twenty, but she had one of those flowery nicknames dancers get—"the Nightingale" or "the Dragonfly," I couldn't remember which. I thought she looked more like a dragonfly, all bug eyes and endless twiggy limbs. "I hate those little ballets in operas," Vika complained. "Substandard choreography—"

"Snob," her brother Grigory teased, flicking sand at her. All of us found Vika a bit of a trial at times, but we adored her twin, who was also a dancer but wasn't so everlastingly *precious* about it. "Let's get dinner after the opera. I'm always so hungry after I get the greasepaint and tights off, I could eat Vika's toe shoes."

"Everything makes you hungry," Sofya scolded, giving me a pang because it was something I was always telling Rostislav. My boy, nine years old now, sturdy and dark and bouncing, forever running up to show me a stone striated with quartz; a whorl in a slab of bark that looked like Comrade Stalin's profile; a baby frog cradled in his gentle hands. I hadn't seen him in months, since leaving Kiev to take up the researcher position at the Odessa library. I didn't have to close my eyes to see him on the train platform with the rest of my family, clinging to my hand. "You could take me with you," he pleaded. "I could help with your work."

"It won't be for long, *morzhik*," I promised, hugging him tight, trying not to cry. I'd never been separated from him for so much as a fortnight, and this would be at least four months. But it would put me on the path toward the future I'd planned so carefully: the apartment in Moscow, the post as a historian; the independence and security. "It's for you," I told my son. "It's all for you—" and heaved my bag of books onto the train before I could break down crying.

And now here I was at the beach on a beautiful day, and it wasn't as beautiful as it could have been because my son was so far away.

Vika was still complaining. "Ballet variations in operas are just a lot of swishing about in red petticoats. A waste of my training—"

"Give it a rest, Vika. You're not being asked to perspire over a lathe in a factory!"

"Ugly sweat work either way!"

"I worked a lathe in a factory," I protested. "It wasn't ugly. Almost beautiful, actually." The days when Slavka had been a baby, barely weaned—as I'd worked the lathe, brushing tungsten dust out of my tight-braided hair and wondering if I'd ever be able to go back to school again, I realized how lovely I found the sight of those blue-violet metal shavings curling out from under the blade.

"Beautiful?" Vika looked scornful.

"No matter how hard the metal, it yields to human strength," I retorted. "Everything does. All you have to do is devise the right weapon."

The dancer snorted, but her twin raised his eyebrows. "Speaking of weapons—"

"I'm not going to shoot a hole in a playing card to win you a bet," I said, heading him off at once. I took regular range practice after earning my advanced certificate, to keep my skills sharp, but I still didn't like showing off. Shooting deserved more respect than that.

"Come on, Mila!" Grigory grinned, dimples showing. He'd been flirting with me all day, and he was certainly good-looking, with those marvelously muscled legs all dancers had . . . but he was still a boy, just eighteen. There was so much difference between eighteen and twenty-four! Becoming a mother so young meant that by the time I'd gone back to school, my fellow students were all five or six years my junior—at times I felt like an old crone in comparison. I went out to plenty of dances and parties now, but none of the men I met there had ever become a long-term prospect. The university boys who invited me to films after Komsomol meetings had nothing more in their minds than fun, whereas I had a child and a future to plan for. As for the older men I sometimes met, they were too trenchantly set in their own futures, and they made it clear they expected me to give up mine if our romance got serious.

Romance later, I told myself whenever the pangs of loneliness stung too sharp. *University degree now.* Once a few more mistake-free stops on my train journey had been safely logged, once the matter of my still-pending divorce had been finalized . . . Alexei hadn't showed up for the third divorce appointment any more than he had for the first two, but when I had a little breathing room after university to finally settle all that, then I could turn an eye to finding a suitable man to share my life and Slavka's. When my feet were on firmer footing there would be time for men, family, more children—all the rest of it.

When you're young and you've known nothing but peace, you assume there will always be time for everything.

"Let's get lunch." Sofya gave me a swack with her towel. "Or I'm going to eat Vika, bony mosquito legs and all. Come on . . ."

That day! A cluster of sandy, laughing young people buttoning summer dresses and old jackets over damp swimsuits, packing up their towels and trailing off to the cheburek café on Pushkin Street. Waiting for a platter of flaky fried meat pastries to arrive, mouths watering; Vika announcing she wasn't going to eat anything because if she gained so much as a gram she'd lose her title role in next year's *Cavalry Maiden*; her brother telling her if she kept complaining about grams and kilos he'd drop her on her head in their next pas de deux; Sofya sipping cold birch juice through a straw; me remembering a footnote I needed to add to my dissertation. All of us surrounded by the noisy, happy clamor of café diners and beach-goers, sticky children and their sunburned mothers. The last day, the last *moment*, before it all went to hell; before the wheel turned and flung all of us into the air, our careful plans shivered into diamond shards and raining down around us. Vika wasn't going to dance the Cavalry Maiden next year; Grigory wasn't going to partner her through any more grand jetés; Sofya would have no sunny afternoons to linger over pale green birch juice, and I wasn't going to defend my dissertation on Bogdan Khmelnitsky, the Ukraine's accession to Russia in 1654, and the activities of the Pereyaslav Council. Within the year, half the people at our table would be dead.

All because of an announcement blaring loud from a speaker on the street just outside, cutting off the café chatter like a knife, informing everyone that at four this morning, Germany had invaded the motherland.

We all froze as if we had been shot. Outside it was the same, all heads turned toward the speaker, listening to Comrade Molotov. *Each of us must demand from himself and from others the discipline, organization, and self-sacrifice worthy of a true Soviet patriot, in order to provide for all the needs of the Red Army, the Navy, and the Air Force, in order to ensure victory over the enemy.* He sounded agitated, but firm. *Victory will be ours!*

He didn't speak long. Just long enough to rearrange the world.

The buzz of conversation started immediately, but the four of us looked at each other around the table, stunned. *Slavka,* I thought. *Slavka . . .* No one moved until our platter of sizzling hot chebureki arrived on the table with a bottle of straw-pale wine, and suddenly we were all talking.

"How far have they advanced?" Sofya sounded sick. "The Hitlerites?"

"I'll enlist," said Grigory.

"You will not," snapped Vika, eyes more buglike than ever with shock. "They won't conscript artists—will they?—so don't go throwing yourself in front of the guns."

"Maybe I can enlist on the medical side," Sofya said, trying to sound brave but only sounding scared. I just stared at my plate. *Slavka* . . . war brought such horrors into the lives of children. Bread lines, bombing raids, queues that stretched for blocks. My parents still spoke of the last war, and the terrible hardships that followed . . .

Vika slammed to her feet, glaring daggers at her brother. "I still have to dance in *La Traviata* tonight, invasion or not. I'll see you all afterward."

"Vika—" Her twin rushed after her, leaving Sofya and me staring at each other.

"We may as well go to the opera tonight," my friend said at last. "Whatever happens, it's not happening yet. Not here."

But over the horizon—yes. Not so far over the horizon, either. I'd learn later that German air raids had pierced as far as Kronstadt near Leningrad; Sevastopol in the Crimea. Outside the café, Pushkin Street was filling up, people gathering under the speaker to argue.

Yet there were still mothers heading toward the beach with excited children, couples ambling hand in hand along Marine Boulevard. It was still a beautiful summer afternoon; no one wanted to skip their plans for the cinema, the theater, the concert hall just because of the outbreak of war. I couldn't decide if it was blind stubbornness or just the Russian way, putting your head down and simply marching ahead, and I still couldn't decide that night when Sofya and I settled in our seats in Box 16 of the dress circle at the Odessa theater, watching over the stage as the hushed opening strains of Verdi's *La Traviata* whispered out over the theater. Such a beautiful theater, all gilded moldings and huge crystal chandeliers—a theater for *us*, ordinary students and citizens, when once people like me would have been left to scrabble at the door while the aristocrats swept inside.

But I couldn't enjoy the opera, the soprano with her white frills and vocal fireworks, the swooning tenor. I stared blindly at the stage, hands flexing in my lap, my thoughts a jumble of random images laced with the ribbon of Comrade Molotov's radio-flattened voice. My son eating hot blini with sour cream and apple jam . . . *German troops have entered our country, without making any demands of the Soviet Union and without a declaration of war . . .* The orderly rows of files I took such pleasure in organizing at the library . . . *They have attacked our borders in many places . . .* The nods from my history professors when I answered a question correctly: "Exactly right, Lyudmila Mikhailovna" . . . *Hostile aerial attacks and artillery barrages have also taken place . . .* Blue-violet shavings of implacably hard metal curling out from under a blade; a shot rocketing from my triggering finger to the center of a target . . .

The curtain descended to a crash of applause. Act I was over, the soprano had renounced love in favor of life (or had she?), and I'd barely heard a note. All I knew was that something was building in my chest, building with implacable steadiness, and suddenly I couldn't breathe, couldn't think, couldn't sit here through Act II and Vika's strutting entrance in her red petticoats. "I need to go," I told Sofya brusquely and rose from my seat, pushing down the great stairs toward the outside until I was taking in great gulps of the warm night air. I stood on the steps of the opera house for a moment, my blue crepe de chine dress stirring about my knees, then began to walk.

I found myself down by the bay, fingers curling and uncurling around the rail overlooking the sea. On the summer stage of Marine Boulevard nearby, a brass band was playing a military march, the notes nightmarishly cheerful. The water glittered, and dimly I could see the outlines of the Black Sea Fleet warships out in the bay. Gunboats, destroyers, an old cruiser that had been re-equipped as a minelayer . . . I wondered if any of them would be here within the week. I wondered if anyone out walking and laughing and clapping along to the band's drumbeats would be here within the week, either, or if it would all be uniforms and grim faces.

This beautiful world. This nighttime wonder that was my city, my country. Slavka's world, the one I wanted to show him, build for him, pour into his hands. Overrun by German thugs with their ranting little toothbrush of a dictator and their smug dreams of world superiority.

"Were you Soviets any better?" a half-drunk American journalist asked me later. "Some nerve you've got, feeling righteous, wanting to make the whole world commie . . ."

There are things my homeland can apologize for. We have a long way to go, and we train ourselves to see not the world around us, but the world as it will become, knowing that world is still a ways away. But whatever our faults, I will never apologize for fighting the war that came to our doorstep in 1941. Germany invaded *us*. Germany wanted *our* oil, *our* cities, *our* flag added to their imperial crown. They wanted to see their damned eagles staked high, from the blue and gold palaces of Leningrad to the icebergs of Lake Baikal, and what we wanted was of no importance, so they invaded. The first shots fired were theirs, the first boots crossing borders were theirs, and if we rolled over and let them do it, my Slavka would be mass-churned into the Hitler Youth and taught to salute a monster.

Is Germany truly so surprised that every mother, every father, every *soul* born in this vast icy land of ours objected to that fate?

Are you?

The anger that had kindled in my stomach upon hearing the announcement of war was burning higher, becoming fury as I thought of swastikas flying over Odessa. The fury clawed and coiled, liquid and molten at the core of me, a tangible white-hot thing being manufactured in the fires of some monstrous factory. Enough rage to churn a sea to boiling fury.

What use is it being angry? whispered the voice of doubt inside me as I stared out at the calm water. *Students like you are no use during a war.* The voice sounded very much like Alexei's. I could imagine him saying *A man sees chances in war, Mila . . . but not little bookworms like you. Go roll bandages.*

And I could—finish my dissertation, dig tank traps, enlist to work at the nearest hospital. Stick to the careful plan, stick to the roles I knew: the library staffer, the researcher, Slavka's mother. These were roles I could fill with never a mistake.

But here, unlike in England and France and America, a woman's fight was not limited to hospitals. And I had more in me than filing and note-taking and far too much seventeenth-century Ukrainian history. *No matter how hard the metal,* I'd told Vika that afternoon, *it yields to human strength. All you have to do is devise the right weapon.*

I *was* a weapon. I'd learned to shoot, after all. And I'd vowed to be Slavka's father as well as his mother.

In times of war, fathers go fight for their children.

So I let out a shaky breath, went home to my student digs for my passport, student card, and marksmanship certificates, and went—still in my crepe de chine dress and high-heeled sandals—to enlist.

CHAPTER 4

My memoir, the official version: When I arrived at the front on Bessarabian soil, I was impressed by the efficiency and organization of the Red Army officers, and I took on my new duties with stoicism and resolve.

My memoir, the unofficial version: When I arrived at the front, it was a complete and utter disaster and so was I, because I'd gone to war without saying goodbye to my son.

"NO TIME TO come home?" my mother cried through the telephone line, hearing me say it. "It's not so long a journey—"

"Nearly five hundred kilometers, Mama." I blinked fiercely, keeping the wobble out of my voice. "I leave tomorrow. I didn't know it would be so soon."

"Surely you didn't have to enlist yet." She was weeping, and I heard my father in the background: *Give her peace, our daughter knows her mind.*

The line was silent for a moment, and then I heard his quiet voice. "Did you have trouble enlisting, *malyshka*?"

"A little. The first military registrar I went to wouldn't even look at my certificates." He'd muttered something about women who wanted to be soldiers but had no idea how hard it was and tossed me unceremoniously out of the office.

"They don't know Belov women," my father said, adding somewhat ominously, "Do I need to have a word with someone for you?"

He could, I knew. My father was a good, kind man, devoted to the Party and to his family, but he was also not a man to be crossed, ever.

As the saying goes, he knew people—the kind of people who organized one-way trips into rivers, gulags, or vats of concrete. It was the reason Alexei had married me when I was fifteen: my father informed him I was pregnant, then informed him he would do the right thing by me, and Alexei probably reflected it was better to say yes than to lose his thumbs. Surgeons need thumbs.

But I didn't want my father pulling strings to get me to the front. "I found another enlistment officer, Papa." A much more amiable fellow than the first, though I'd still been asked *Does your husband have any objection to your volunteering for the Red Army*? At least the officer hadn't made me go get some piece of paper from Alexei. If he had, I might have wrecked the office.

"Don't pack too much," my father cautioned. "All you need in war is dry socks, a good pair of boots, and something to read. And be sure—"

"For the love of Lenin, Papa!" I borrowed his own words to tease him. "Stop fretting. I have plenty of socks, and I packed my dissertation." Somehow I couldn't bear to leave it behind. Curling my fingers tight around the handset, I made myself add, "I'm . . . I'm sorry I didn't come home first to say goodbye, then enlist afterward. I could have, but—"

"Harder to leave once you've had Slavka's big eyes fixed on you," my father said.

I bit my lip savagely. "Yes." How would I ever be able to tear myself away if I had my son clinging to my waist, sobbing and begging me: *Mamochka, don't go, don't go, please* . . . And what kind of mother would I be then—a mother who wouldn't fight for her child, for the world she wanted her child to grow up in?

"I'm proud of you, *malyshka*." My father's rumble brought tears to my eyes. I cuffed them away. "When you get to the front, just remember—"

"*Belovs don't retreat,*" we both chanted, and that gave me enough strength to bid goodbye to Slavka over the telephone.

What a little life I had in Odessa—packing it away took almost no time at all. Goodbyes to my library colleagues and to my professors; hugs to Sofya. Just a few short days after my enlistment, I found myself crammed into a military train full of jostling new recruits—some in uniform, most still in civilian dress. I searched the car hopefully for another woman and saw none. My heart sank under the lace-edged collar my mother had insisted on stitching to my sturdiest traveling dress to make it pretty. The soldiers around me looked friendly enough, but—

"Here!" A slender hand waved from a bench by a window, and I saw a lanky blonde in a too-big overcoat. "Olena Ivanovna Paliy," she said briskly as I fought my way through. "I'll watch while you sleep if you do the same for me. Personally I'd rather arrive at the front without getting pawed."

I put out my hand. "Lyudmila Mikhailovna Pavlichenko. Mila."

"Lena." She made room for me on the bench by the window, scowling at a big red-haired soldier who tried to squeeze down between us. "Find somewhere else, *blyat*," she said with a casually obscene gesture, and I backed her up with a steely look. We might not know each other yet, but we were two women traveling alone in a compartment full of rowdy young men—such alliances are fast, practical, nearly primal. "Medical battalion for me," Lena Paliy went on. "Last week I was a second-year student in the Odessa medical institute, slicing up shriveled blue corpses on the dissection table. You?"

"Last week, alphabetizing periodicals. Tomorrow"—I thought of my marksmanship badges—"I can be useful wherever they put me, if they just give me a rifle."

"You'd think more women would be here besides us." Lena took a beet out of her pack and began to eat it raw. "Hitlerites pouring over the border like roaches, and we're the only two skirts in this train? Makes you ashamed to be female. If girls want to stay home and cower behind their soup kettles while the men fight, let them move to

England. Prance around Piccadilly with Princess Margaret Rose and put their hair in pin curls."

I grinned, deciding I was going to like Lena Paliy.

The train chugged slowly out of the station, snaking west toward the steppe. The gleaming surface of the Dniester estuary soon shone off to the right, then the string of stations. Shabo, Kolyesnoye, Sarata, Artsyz, Hlavani . . . I choked down a wave of homesickness. *What am I doing so far from everything I love?* But I stamped down on that thought before it could flower into self-pity. *Slavka. This is for him.*

A long night—Lena dozed first as I kept watch; then I put my forehead against the glass and took my turn. An even longer day to follow; more strange depots; more unfamiliar towns. Lena and I traded stories; I admired the scarf her mother had knitted; she admired my picture of Slavka. "Cute," she said, touching his round baby face. "And his father?"

"Not so cute. A real bastard, in fact."

"I sense a story." Lena made a *tell-me* gesture, and I normally wasn't so forthcoming with new people, but I found myself recounting the tale: fifteen-year-old Mila Belova at her first dance, the tall fair-haired man who pulled her away from her girlfriends into a two-step and said, *Shall I show you?*

"That's all it took?" Lena raised her eyebrows. "Must have been some dance."

I grimaced. "Any ordinary night, I'd have danced with him once and gone back to my friends. But right before my eyes, he saved a life."

Alexei and I had circled the dance floor only twice when a stranger by the wall suddenly bent over, red-faced with vodka, eyes wide with panic, choking on something. His friends didn't know it was serious, guffawing even as he slipped to his knees clawing at his throat—but Alexei knew. He melted through the crowd to the man's side and flipped him on his back on the hot dance floor, trying to expel whatever was choking him. By the time I fought my way through the crush, he'd shoved his pristine sleeves up and was yanking a fountain pen and a small knife from his pocket. Seeing me, he tossed the pen into my hands and barked, "Take it apart, give me the barrel!" even as he was seizing a bottle of vodka from the nearest table and using the icy liquor to sterilize the penknife. I went to my knees beside Alexei, heart thudding, and saw he was very calm. He took the disassembled fountain pen, tossing his handkerchief at me. "When I tell you, mop up the blood."

And he cut into the man's throat just under the Adam's apple, down to the windpipe in one firm stroke, and I was mopping blood, terrified but moving under that cool voice, and he was fashioning a breathing tube from the hollow fountain pen, and the man wasn't dying. All because of the steady, long-fingered hands of Alexei Bogdanovich, Dr. Pavlichenko, whose name I didn't even learn until an hour later, when we were sitting under an oak tree in the cool, shadowed garden outside the dance hall, the patient taken away to the hospital.

"You're good in a crisis, little—what's your name? Mila?" Taking my hand in both of his, twining it in those long fingers in a way that rendered me completely breathless.

"I'm not so little," I said, hoping he wouldn't guess my age, feeling relieved when he smiled.

"No, I can see you're not."

("That was a lie," I told Lena. "He made a very accurate guess how old I was, which was too young, which was exactly the age he liked.")

"How did you do that surgery?" I'd pressed. "Save that man?"

"I'm a surgeon. It's what surgeons do." He smiled. "Though I'll be more than a surgeon someday."

"What do you want to be?"

"Great," he said simply. "I'll make the name Pavlichenko resound from Moscow to Vladivostok someday." He grinned, to show he was joking, but I knew he wasn't. Not really. He burned bright with ambition.

"I can see it now," I answered, laughing. "Alexei Pavlichenko, Hero of the Soviet Union . . ."

"Has a nice ring to it." He laughed too, looking at me. "And what do *you* want, Lyudmila?"

Hearing the story, my new friend Lena whistled. "And you swooned into his arms like a plucked lily?"

"More or less." Barely fifteen, poised somewhere between raiding orchards with the local boys and studying for my advanced exams—neither the bookish girl who dreamed of university nor the sunburned mischief-maker who was the best shot in the neighborhood with a slingshot stood a chance against a tall golden Viking who pulled me into his orbit to help him save a life, then asked me *what I wanted.* I did what any girl would have done: leaned in and kissed him before my nerve gave out, and maybe I was caught off guard by how fast everything moved after that, how quickly buttons were slipping free and clothes disappearing, but I was too eager, too dazzled to want to pull away.

"Nine months later," I told Lena now, "there was Slavka."

She whistled again. "And the blond bastard?"

"Moving up in the world. He's the best surgeon in the region, I'll give him that." I'd had to contact him a year or so ago for some piece of paper required for my student enrollment: *Does your husband have any objection to your registration at the University of Kiev?* He'd been amiable enough as he wrote out a brief confirmation that we had not lived together in years. He didn't ask anything about Slavka, just pulled my wrist toward him asking if I'd give him a kiss *for old times' sake.* I'd wanted to say something cutting, but I didn't dare because I needed the paper he'd just written out. So I just smiled tightly, avoiding the kiss, and he grinned and held the paper over my head. *Jump for it,* kroshka*!* And I actually did jump, because I had to, and he only made me jump three times before he let me have it. The thought of that still made my toes curl in shame.

"Let's not talk about him anymore," I told Lena, swallowing the anger I always felt thinking about Alexei. Rage was no use to a mother, a student, a future historian, and productive member of society, and it certainly wouldn't help me be a calm and effective soldier, either. Alexei was the past, the war was the future, so I nudged Lena with my shoe and said, "Your turn."

"I've got a blond bastard or two in my past . . ." She launched into some colorful story that pushed Alexei out of my mind, hopefully for good.

Nearly forty-eight hours of cold, malodorous discomfort and aching bones before we were decanted from the train: three in the morning, pushing and shoving to line up on a strange railway siding, shivering in the cold damp. Shouted into rough order, we began the long trek down a dirt road. By seven, my feet were blistered inside my canvas lace-ups and I smelled dense pine, tree sap . . . and gunsmoke. The smell of war, or at least my war. My father said his time at the front had smelled of mud and wire, but perhaps every war smells different.

Mine was trees and smoke and blood.

Since that day, I have never gotten it out of my nose.

THERE IS A sameness to how war stories begin, isn't there? The story flows like a film, with suitably themed music. The proud recruit; the family farewells; the donning of the uniform—the music swells, tender and poignant. The taking of the soldier's oath; a dramatic moment—something with patriotic brass is called for. Then the training period as the wide-eyed new recruit learns to handle their weapon—put it to a military march, lots of drums. By then the recruit (and his audience, as he tells this story) is ready for battle.

But I arrived on Bessarabian soil among the rear units of the 25th Chapayev Rifle Division in the middle of utter chaos. There was no time for proper training or measured appreciation of the different moving moments of my initiation; there was barely time to gulp a dish of buckwheat porridge to the sound of far-off machine-gun fire. Mud squelched underfoot, and trees looked down like silent sentinels on the dirty tents, the rattling trucks, the soldiers rushing back and forth like ants. I changed into the uniform that was flung at me, rattled my oath off, and signed my life and body away to the Red Army, absorbing the information that I'd become a soldier of the 54th Stepan Razin Rifle Regiment, 1st Battalion, 2nd Company.

"Goodbye, civilian life," said Lena, cramming her new forage cap over her hair. "Not very many of us, are there? I wonder if that's because it's early days, or because they're sticking the women behind desks or into the hospital battalions?"

I knew there weren't *many* women in the Red Army, but I hadn't expected to be the only one in 2nd Company. I'd always got along well with men; most of my friends growing up were boys, and they accepted me as one of them without question. But it's one thing to run with a pack of boys through a world that was still half women, and another thing to find yourself the lone woman in an entire company of loud, boisterous, overexcited young men, hardly any other females in sight. "Cut my hair," I asked Lena suddenly, pulling my new cap off. "Chop it short at the neck."

"It's nice hair," she objected as I unpinned my thick plait.

"We won't have time here to keep long hair washed and combed." I stamped down the regrets—I was a middling sort of woman, not tall or short, not fat or thin, but the heavy chocolate-brown hair that rippled to my waist was beautiful. *Hair grows back,* I told myself. "Just hack it off, Lena. It's not only the washing—my father said once that the women who get along best in the army are the ones who don't draw attention to being female. Short hair. All business. No flirtation."

"One of the boys." Lena began sawing at my thick plait. "Right. Whack mine off next."

We sheared each other, hurled our severed braids ceremoniously into the nearest campfire, and traded rather grim smiles as they sizzled and stank. "Look after yourself," I told my new friend as she was shunted toward the medical battalion. "Eyes in the back of your head until you make yourself some friends who will watch your back." We didn't have to say why. All women know why.

"You too, Mila." Lena waved over one shoulder as she departed, and with her gone, the officers in my battalion seemed even less certain what to do with the only remaining female in the batch of new recruits. I found myself standing in front of a lieutenant barely old enough to shave, trying to explain that I already knew how to shoot—news he greeted like a mortician confronted by a corpse that had arrived on the slab already embalmed.

"You know how to shoot?" he repeated for the third time. "Well, maybe you think you do. War isn't women's business. I'll petition the battalion commander to transfer you to a medical battalion."

"I would be wasted as a medical orderly, sir." But I was waved off to the command post of the 1st Battalion, where I had the same conversation all over again, and then again when I fetched up—exasperated and stamping in my khaki tunic and new trousers—at the desk of a long-faced, lugubrious-looking captain. "You can shoot?" He looked at my various certificates. "Are you any good?"

"Try me, Comrade Captain," I replied. "A rifle with telescopic sights—"

He pushed his cap back on his thinning hair. "We have no sniper rifles."

"A standard Three Line, then?" Thinking back to the scarred instructor and his lessons handling the Mosin-Nagant rifle.

"We don't have those either, Lyudmila Mikhailovna. Not enough for the new arrivals." I could have been annoyed at the captain's use of my name, but he didn't curl his tongue around it the way I'd already heard some of the officers do. Captain Sergienko was gray, stalky, perhaps thirty years old and looking fifty, and he spoke my name like a man who was two weeks into a war and already felt like he hadn't slept in a year.

"How will I fight then, Comrade Captain?" My helmet clamped awkwardly under one arm, I looked at my artificial leather boots, two sizes too big, and had the distinct thought: *All dressed up, and no way to fight.*

"For you new recruits, the main weapon for now will be the shovel."

A shovel.

Not really a dramatic moment, is it? There isn't a sweeping Prokofiev theme for a new recruit heroically digging trenches. But that was my entrance to the 25th Chapayev Rifle Division: a shovel rather than a rifle, and a disorganized scramble into a mass retreat rather than a headlong sprint toward glory.

One of the many ways in which real life is not like a film.

I WOULDN'T SHOOT a single bullet for nearly a month—and most of that month is only fragments in my memory. Clarity came to me with a trigger; before that it was chaos and clods of earth, confusion and clotted blood. Perhaps it's different for the generals, the men commanding large military units who look at nice clean maps and see the bigger picture, the whole machine. For us cogs, only the earth directly under our boots is clear. I'd been flung headfirst into a welter of attacks and counterattacks, surges and retreats—I marched, I obeyed every order shouted at me, I learned to stop flinching at the sound of artillery overhead. What I didn't learn was how to fight, even as battles raged the entire length of our borders. There was no time to catch my breath or even learn the name of the man marching beside me, much less fight.

Fragments.

I remember the regiments traveling in the day and in the night once we began the scrambling retreat across the Black Sea steppes—trucks, horse-drawn carts, on foot. I remember tumbling down to sleep at night fully dressed, too exhausted to watch my back, though it didn't matter because in such chaos the men in my company had no energy to register that Comrade Private Pavlichenko was female, much less do anything about it. I remember the steppe as it looked on the warm summer nights, spread out on both sides of the road like an opened book—and how it looked in the day, booming with cannon volleys, pricked everywhere by fires, the smell of burnt gunpowder lingering bitterly in the nose. I remember civilians retreating with us, whole caravans of factory workers and equipment; farmers prodding herds of livestock from the collective farms; women and children trudging along with laden baskets and knapsacks, shuddering whenever a Focke-Wulf droned overhead.

I remember digging trenches with small sapper spades by the light of the moon, as long-range enemy artillery crackled. I remember realizing I'd been at the front a full month and hadn't yet written my father. *Belovs don't retreat*—yet we were retreating, burying our dead in bomb craters as we went. We were retreating in swaths all along our own diminishing border, falling back before the swastika.

I remember a field of wheat going up in billowing sheets of flame under a flight of German bombers; remember the twisted shells of burnt towns and fire-bombed machinery. The Junkers flying overhead would line up a cratered road crammed with walking families and strafe directly down the center—as my company was ordered off into the trees for cover. One blood-laced twilight, a rawboned woman whose cart had just been bombed to splinters spat at me when I came back to the road with the rest of my company. "To hell with you," she hissed. "Why aren't you fighting these bastards?" I remember lowering my eyes, shouldering my pack, and falling into formation, unable to say a word.

I remember the fear. *Push it away, push it down*, I told myself, but there was no pushing it away, it was everywhere: we lived fear, breathed fear, ate and drank and sweated fear. Every drone of German planes overhead could mean my end, and I had nothing to defend myself with but a *shovel.*

That changed on a July morning along the shattered, cratered hellscape that marked the Novopavlovsk to the Novy Artsyz line. The artillery fire had been sounding in waves; for the moment my regiment was dug in. *Dug in,* a pretty term for *hiding,* sheltering in makeshift trenches and stands of splintered trees, hunkering down on our heels every time another wave of deafening fire rolled through like the footsteps of a giant. The man sheltering next to me in our dugout slit of a trench was little more than a boy, freckled and earnest, fiddling so constantly with his rifle that I wanted to box his ears. Another surge of shellfire crashed; I laced my hands behind my neck and lowered my head, hissing at the boy to keep his head down. "Ride it out," I shouted over the din, nearly choking on my own reflexive terror, "the attacks come in waves, it's like childbirth—" but he just gave me a puzzled look. Of course he did; what a useless analogy to give a man, and I hunted for another one, but suddenly his face was a sheet of blood. He touched his forehead, looking even more puzzled, and I saw the side of his head had been cratered like an egg. He toppled slowly into me; I tried to support him, but he was too heavy, sliding down into the mud.

Leaving his blood-slicked rifle in my shaking hands.

THE SOVIET DELEGATION: DAY 1

August 27, 1942

WASHINGTON, D.C.

CHAPTER 5

If she's ever held a rifle in her life, the marksman thought, watching the supposed girl sniper disappear into the White House after the First Lady, *I'll eat my damn hat.*

The doors closed behind the Soviet delegation, and that was that. "When do we get a crack at the Russkies?" the *Washington Post* journalist wanted to know, riffling his notes. "They're not going to make us wait until the student conference kicks off, are they?"

"There will be a press assembly tonight at the Soviet embassy." The marksman dialed up his Virginia drawl, turning away from the White House in its rosy dawn glow. "Save your questions till then. Unless you scored an invitation to the White House welcome breakfast this morning."

"You got one? Lucky son of a gun . . ."

The marksman smiled. Luck had nothing to do with it; the men who'd hired him for this job moved in high circles, and they'd made sure his name (the name on the immaculately falsified press badge, anyway) was on the list. "Why do you need to see the girl up close?" they'd grumbled. "You need to frame her, not date her."

"I'll need to know how to pull her aside when the time comes," the marksman replied. "If she'll be easy to distract or difficult. If I'll need to bribe someone in her delegation to give me access to her, and if so, who. And I'll only have a week, from the day the Soviet delegation arrives to the last day of the conference, to figure all this out."

"Sounds like a lot of work" the answer had been, and the marksman shrugged. In truth, he'd always rather enjoyed the elbow grease involved in a new job: settling into a well-planned cover identity, backing that identity up with solid research, *living* the job if necessary. He remembered that time in 1932 when he'd worked four solid months in an insurance office to get access to a mark . . . sold a lot of honest insurance, too. Putting those hours in *was* work, no question—meticulous, frequently boring work. But he'd always figured there were two kinds of men in this business: good shooters who thought pulling a trigger was the job and only did enough work to research a skin-deep cover, sweating the whole time . . . and pros to whom the deep cover *was* the job, who put in enough hours and research that they didn't have to sweat by the time it came to pulling a trigger.

He knew which type he was.

"Still a lot of trouble to take for a patsy," his higher-ups' flunky had complained.

Says the man who won't end up in handcuffs if this all goes south, thought the marksman. "Just keep making sure my press-pass name clears all the security and ends up on all the necessary guest lists and travel passes," he'd said, and at least there hadn't been any trouble *there.* He could usually find his own ways to gain whatever access a job needed—after nineteen years, he had a stable of contacts and informants he could pay for just about any information or paperwork—but the men he was working for now could accomplish a great deal more with a little backroom hand-waving.

He had a meeting with his employers in thirty minutes, in fact—or rather, his employers' flunky. It wasn't necessary, but they wanted reassurances, and he had an hour or so to kill before heading back here for the welcome breakfast, where the bucktoothed First Lady would host the Soviets and a handful of press in the small dining room on the first floor of the White House. Idly, the marksman wondered what Mila Pavlichenko was doing now. Was she awed to be standing under that fabled roof or sneering at the capitalist Western decadence of it all? Was she reviewing her cover story about her supposed 309 Nazi kills, or feeling lost, floundering, far from home? He hoped the latter. Lonely women were easy to pick off. He'd targeted quite a few over the years.

He wasn't sure yet whether he'd need to kill her or not. Whatever option proved simplest: all professionals knew that the simpler any plan was, the better. Because as soon as bullets began singing, even the best-laid plans went awry. A certain amount of improvisation was inevitable. Whether he ended up leaving her body as a suicide-note confession on the last day of the conference, or merely fixed a frame around her and let her Soviet-inflated reputation put the noose around her neck, one thing was certain.

When you planned to assassinate a president, you timed it when a Russian sniper was in town to take the fall for you.

The marksman jingled his pocketful of uncut diamonds as he flagged down a passing cab. "The Lincoln Memorial," he told the cabbie, rolling down the window to appreciate the warm morning breeze. The forecast for the week ahead predicted nothing but blue skies, hot days, and perfect late-summer weather. *Miss Pavlichenko, enjoy your first visit to America while it lasts.*

Notes by the First Lady

As I show the Soviet delegation up the White House stairs to their guest rooms, my mind is still lingering over Franklin's words to me this morning after his fall: "They'd pray I never got up." An extra twist on the word they, *beyond his usual amused irony. Bitterness? Worry? I ponder that as I usher Lyudmila Pavlichenko to the rosy chamber that will be hers during her visit.*

My husband has detractors and rivals, of course. Every president is hated. The man who has won an unprecedented third term is hated by more than most. He usually laughs such hatred off . . . but he was not laughing this morning.

Is there a particular cabal of enemies which has him worried?

I blink, startled out of my thoughts as the young Russian woman—who has so far said not a single word—moves across the bedchamber to the window, where the morning light shines through the glass. For an instant I think she is going to exclaim over the view of the gardens flowering below, but instead she yanks the shades down with a snap. "Is something wrong, my dear?" I ask.

She says something in Russian, looking composed enough as she folds her hands at her waist, but I sense discomfiture. "She says she prefers not to have uncovered windows at her back, Mrs. Roosevelt," the interpreter translates helpfully.

Ah. They say she is a sniper—I didn't know what to make of that. In truth, I still don't. But she thanks me for my hospitality through the interpreter and I examine those opaque dark eyes, I wish I could ask her: How do you know when an enemy is lurking? How do you know if it is just nerves or genuine danger?

How do you know if there is a target on your back?

FOURTEEN MONTHS AGO

June 1941

THE ODESSA FRONT, USSR

Mila

CHAPTER 6

M*y memoir, the official version: Every woman remembers her first.*

My memoir, the unofficial version: Those words mean very different things for me than most women.

"I SEE YOU'VE managed to get PE sights for that rifle." Lugubrious-looking Captain Sergienko nodded at the weapon now registered in my name. "Have you fired it yet?"

"Yes, Comrade Captain." I kept my eyes forward, wondering why I'd been called to the command post in the long, slanting light just before dark.

He studied me. I shifted in my boots, realizing my lips were dry enough to crack, that my chopped hair was filthy. The Chapayev division had reached the Tiraspol fortified district and dug in. Not a bad place to turn and fight: earthworks, reinforced concrete, and stone firing points; dugouts; deep trenches; machine guns and artillery of our own. The line of Russian defense, strung like a necklace across the throat of Alexandrovka, Buyalyk, Brinovka, Karpova, Belyayevka . . . Had I really been at war less than six weeks? I blinked that thought away.

Sergienko's voice brought me back to myself. "Have you hit anyone you've lined up in those sights?"

"I don't know, Comrade Captain. It hasn't been that kind of shooting." I'd fired like a good soldier—when I was told, blindly, over the lip of trenches and behind trees, as the Chapayev division continued its retreat. You couldn't see what you were firing at in such moments;

you fired because you were being fired on, not because you had anything in your sights. I didn't know if I'd hit anyone; I knew only that I was less afraid when I had the comforting weight of a rifle in my hand. Nonsensical, really—having a weapon didn't make me invulnerable—but I felt less helpless. I couldn't push my fear away, but I could push it into my weapon.

"Come with me," Sergienko said, and I followed him out of the command post through the mess of crates and tents, makeshift desks and earth plowed into bulwarks, some ways distant to a bombed-out peasant hut where he could point toward the far end of Belyayevka. Among the distant overgrown trees was a large house with a ridge-roofed porch, gleaming in the setting sun. "You see?"

I nodded. Two officers in sandy-gray uniforms came out onto the porch; I could see the gleam of their insignia, their pudding-basin helmets. Not Hitlerites; Romanians—Germany's ally. So close. I had not yet seen an enemy so clearly; until now they had all been shadowy shapes on the other side of trenches, helmeted outlines in the cockpits of planes strafing overhead. These two men weren't even half a kilometer away. Standing there on a porch in the sunshine, *scratching* themselves, having a laugh. Our invaders.

The fear banked constantly in my stomach began to curl again. I usually felt the fear cold and blue-violet as a shaving of tungsten twisting under a lathe, but this time the metal of it was forging from blue to red. Fear to rage.

"That's likely their staff headquarters," the weary-looking Captain Sergienko was saying. "You showed me your certificates; from our records you're the only one yet who's come in with an advanced marksmanship course already under her belt. Now that we've a moment to breathe"—*between retreats*, he didn't say, but he might as well have—"let me see what you can do."

I was already unslinging my rifle.

Sergienko stood back, watching. I felt the pulse beating under my jaw as I began setting up to shoot at the two men. *Targets,* I told myself, but couldn't ignore the reality that these weren't painted circles on a range or glass bottles in cleft sticks.

They are enemies, the anger inside me said, stoking higher as I moved through my preparations. *Invaders.* I hadn't asked them to come here. I hadn't asked them to ally with Germany, to make grandiose plans for renaming Odessa *Antonescu* once they captured it; to purge any territory they captured of Jews and Gypsies, Ukrainians and Russians, because we were racially undesirable. I hadn't asked for any of this. I wanted to stay home, cuddle my son, finish my damned dissertation. I didn't necessarily want the other side dead; I only wanted them *gone.* But they weren't going, and so help me, I would settle for dead.

I never stopped moving, never hesitated. What hesitation can there truly be, after three weeks of desperate retreat under enemy fire? I just exhaled my rage and let training take over.

A good shooter moves without haste, every movement as deliberate as a clock's hour hand ticking over. *One* . . . Take the first cool, measuring glance through the sights, the moment the soul falls silent and the eye takes control. *Two* . . . Estimate the horizontal sight line; I saw it cover the shoulders of the officer at the top of the porch steps. *Three* . . . Use that benchmark to calculate distance, the equation I'd learned in my shooting course employed in a blink: four hundred meters. *Four* . . . Sliding Ball L light bullets into place. *Five* . . . Finding a firing position in the bombed-out farmhouse where we stood: trying a belly-down angle—not possible; trying a kneeling position behind the half-shattered wall with the stones supporting my rifle's barrel—better. *Six* . . . Settle in: weight resting on the heel of the right boot, left elbow on bent left knee, hold it until you are still, until you are stone, until frost could gather on your lashes. *Seven* . . . Adjust the rifle strap under the elbow, let it carry the weapon's weight. *Eight* . . . Find the target again through the sight, adjust for wind.

Nine . . . Find the trigger, take aim. *Ten* . . . Breathe in. *Eleven* . . . Breathe out.

On *twelve* the clock strikes midnight and the finger squeezes the trigger.

I looked at the invaders through my sights, and on the exhale I fired.

Seven shots later I lowered the rifle, realizing my ears were ringing and my shoulder stung from the recoil. Captain Sergienko lowered his binoculars, looking at me. "You got the rear officer with your third shot, and the front officer with your fourth—even though they were off the porch and scrambling fast by then."

"I saw." My voice seemed to be coming from very far away. I realized my hands were trembling and gripped the rifle's stock harder. When I looked at the captain, his face was still overlaid with the lines of my sights, as though it had burned itself inside my eyes.

The captain looked through his binoculars at the Romanian staff headquarters again. There seemed to be quite a lot of activity swarming that porch now. "Good shooting."

"Not really." My face burned. "It should only have taken me two bullets."

"But you still downed both men." Sergienko looked reflective, retreating from the farmhouse now and beckoning me with him. The Romanians might calculate where my shots had come from and fire back on this position. "I've got feral Siberian boys who can put a bullet through a squirrel's eye at half a kilometer, but when I asked them to show me what they could do, they all froze when it came to firing on a man for the first time. You know the science of it—ballistics, trajectories, all that. More important, you knew how to let the science carry you through when it came to fire on a human target. You might have missed, but you didn't hesitate. That's rare in new recruits."

"It's just training," I said. "I've had some already; the others haven't. That's all."

"Training? Not instinct?"

Sergienko was a smart man, but even he (like many, as I was soon to learn) was inclined to be fanciful about a sniper's *instinct*, about *feeling it in the blood*, about how it was all *in the gut*. Rubbish. I was a good library researcher because I'd learned how to file, catalog, and organize; I was a good shooter because I'd learned range calculation and distance estimation, and knew how far a rotating bullet would drift laterally from muzzle to target. I could do this not because of some inborn instinct, but because I had studied and drilled and practiced until training *became* instinct. I was a good sniper because I was a good student. "Training," I repeated, with a belated salute.

"And you can do it again? I can use long-distance shooters."

"I can do it again." Even after five missed shots, I knew I could. Because I'd trained to be *perfect*, and perfection had become a habit too strong to allow missteps. Life so rarely allowed a woman to be perfect, much less a mother, much less a single mother, much less a single mother in the Soviet Union, which was a beautiful place but not precisely a forgiving one . . . so when I was lashing myself inside for missing an exam question or a chance at a student conference, I could at least go to the range and know that there, I wouldn't miss a thing.

And that compulsion not to miss was so strong, I'd put two live targets down today without hesitation.

I hadn't stopped to examine the enemy faces through my sights, but their features must have made an impression despite me, because I saw them now in my mind's eye with sickening clarity. The first officer had been close-shaven, hawk-nosed; the second had been swarthy with the beginnings of a paunch. Enemies—but perhaps they had also been husbands, fathers. All the quirks and talents, weaknesses and foibles that made up two unique human lives, extinguished in seconds by two bullets.

Suddenly I wanted to put my head between my knees, but I couldn't do that in front of my commanding officer. I swallowed the bile rising in my throat and took a glance over one shoulder toward the building I'd targeted—a building now swarming, so I imagined, with panicked Romanian officers. *Invaders,* I reminded myself again. And despite my moment's queasiness I knew that the next time I fired on my enemies, I wouldn't miss.

"Can you use me, Comrade Captain?" I asked. "As a sniper?"

My scarred instructor had often used that word. This was the first time I spoke it.

"Oh, yes." Sergienko strung his binoculars over his arm, looking suddenly so serious my heart began to thud. "There's just one thing."

"W-what?"

"Seven shots on two Nazis! You need to conserve cartridges, Lyudmila Mikhailovna. Such waste!" His scowl held for a moment, then cracked to a somewhat lugubrious smile. For the first time in weeks, I found myself laughing. A shaky laugh, but still a laugh. Laughter at the front—I hadn't known such a thing could feel so good, be so necessary.

"I'll get it right next time, Comrade Captain." I saluted, smiling but kicking myself, too. Seven shots for two marks—my instructor would have scratched his scar and asked if I wouldn't mind aiming for Moscow next time instead of Paris. "Two lives, two bullets next time."

"Do try. They'll be crawling back soon, and there's no one but us to stamp on them."

"America," I said, because there were rumors: the Americans would join the war, they'd send troops to the east to take pressure off our lines. But Captain Sergienko shook his head.

"The Americans would rather leave us to rot. It's all on us." He nodded dismissal, turning to head toward his command post, but then turned back to me. "You've opened your tally today, sniper. Let the record show that L. M. Pavlichenko's tally now stands at two."

"No," I heard myself say.

My captain raised his eyebrows.

"These two were test shots." They still counted—I'd never forget them—but it hadn't been official, not yet. And I wanted it to be clear that I didn't care about padding a tally at all costs, counting lives like coins. That was another kind of showing off, and I still didn't like it. Maybe this was the moment the midnight side of my moon started to wax from crescent to full, but making some game out of my skills was still distasteful to me. I just wanted to do a job and repel this invasion, not build myself a reputation. "Sniper-Soldier Pavlichenko will open her tally tomorrow."

CHAPTER 7

My memoir, the official version: Before an attack, you steel yourself with thoughts of the motherland and Comrade Stalin.

My memoir, the unofficial version: Before an attack, you usually feel sick.

THE PRE-BATTLE FIT of gloom—everyone has their own way of combating it. Most of the men in 2nd Company with me relied on a stiff belt of vodka, a bracing exchange of the dirtiest jokes possible, and a rousing chorus or two of "Broad Is My Native Land" or "Over There Across the River." I liked to pull my now-dog-eared dissertation out of my pack and leaf through it. There was something wonderfully soothing about Bogdan Khmelnitsky when I was about to come under shellfire.

A state of siege had been declared in my lovely city of Odessa; it was nearly September, and my sniper's tally was—well, it had been officially opened and I'd been adding to it almost every day, becoming accustomed to that dark and bloody-handed work without too many innate lurches between fear and anger, queasiness and perfectionism. But today I was off with the rest of 2nd Company, not on one of those routine sorties that made up so much of war, but something different.

Smoke drifting over water, screams echoing across the flat plain of the isthmus between the Khajibeisk and Kuyalnik estuaries. The 3rd Battalion was pinned down, hammered by three days of shelling, cut down to no more than four hundred defenders. Romanians spilled over the plain, a sandy-gray mass firing wherever they saw movement, grappling and clawing with anyone they could drag out of the half-destroyed fortifications. Someone was shouting orders; the scream of artillery overhead turned the words to nonsense. I slipped and scrambled into a half-dug trench with a makeshift parapet, set up with my rifle, began taking shots—and almost as soon as I began, the thunder of guns died away.

A silence fell then, drifting across the bloodied ground like the smoke. The Romanians had faded away, fallen back to regroup. Why do these strange pauses fall in the middle of furious fights? Battles seem to be living things, creatures that need to breathe as much as the soldiers who are fighting them. When these silences fall, the impulse is to huddle where you are with your head down, but only novices freeze. The experienced cram a hasty lump of bread down, unfasten trousers for a quick piss, check their ammunition with hands that their friends pretend not to see shaking. I wiped my rifle down and reloaded, flexing my trembling fingers. The man beside me had done the same and then pulled a battered copy of *War and Peace* from his knapsack and calmly propped it against his rifle sights.

"*War and Peace*?" I heard myself asking, bizarrely conversational. "You couldn't bring anything more ironic to war?"

He turned a page. "Wanted to see how the Battle of Austerlitz turned out."

"Napoleon won. Hope that doesn't spoil the book for you." I couldn't remember the reader's name—a blade-thin Siberian, black hair razored brutally close to his skull. "I never finished *War and Peace.* Never got past the New Year's Eve ball."

The Siberian raised his eyebrows. My taste in literature was clearly being judged.

"I prefer history to novels." I shrugged. "Give me a good account of the seventeenth-century Polish-Lithuanian Commonwealth/ Ottoman Empire conflict any day."

The Siberian returned to his book, but I saw the corner of his mouth quirk. "Philistine," he said. I opened my mouth to reply—a vigorous philosophical discussion on the merits of imaginative fiction versus historical documentation seemed like just the way to pass the time in a muddy trench in between artillery attacks—when a strange skein of sound brought my head and the Siberian's whipping round in unison.

The Romanian infantry was advancing again, not spreading out across the steppe, but packing forward in dense columns, feet swinging high to the drums as if they were on parade . . . and they were *singing.* Officers strode between the gaps in the columns, unsheathed sabers on their shoulders; on the left flank I saw a priest in a gold-embroidered gown, three church banners billowing behind. He was shouting, urging the men on under the heartbeat of the drums and the massed roar of the hymn.

Seven hundred meters away.

I marked my field of fire, calculations sliding liquid-quick through my brain: a fence at the edge of a cornfield, six hundred meters; some wolfberry thickets closer, five hundred meters . . . the dull roar of the hymn grew louder, and our mortar battery launched a strike. I saw earth fountain up against the sky among the gray columns, but the living closed ranks and marched over the dead. Bayonets lowered and the blades gleamed like shivers of trapped lightning. I made a quick count—perhaps two thousand bayonets, coming for my stripped-down regiment of four hundred. The priest kept on shrieking, and as my pulse pounded, I wondered what he was saying.

"*Vive l'empereur?*" guessed the dark Siberian at my side, as though reading my mind.

" 'Long live the emperor'? Why—"

He brought up his rifle, and as I did the same, I realized what he meant. Napoleon's troops had roared *Vive l'empereur!* as they marched in massed columns exactly like this, under eagles not so different from Hitler's eagles, closing ranks around the dead and rolling inexorably toward Tolstoy's heroes at Austerlitz . . . and they had marched in the same columns, screamed the same cries against Russians when Napoleon decided to invade the motherland.

Well, we all knew how *that* had turned out.

The rage was stirring in my stomach again, doing its work to drown the fear. Two thousand bayonets were coming right toward me, and my terror died. I waited just until they passed that fence by the cornfield and opened fire.

Click, click, click. Midnight struck on the clock with every second that passed. I was aware of the Siberian beside me firing calm and fast, rifle propped on the thick spine of *War and Peace.* I realized I'd run through all my cartridges; when I called *Out!* he pushed a bag of his own at me, a yellow-tipped Ball D heavy bullet gripped between his teeth, and I reloaded and kept firing. *Got the priest,* I heard someone grunt on my other side.

How long did we lie there firing, our four hundred against their two thousand? Suddenly the sun was setting, lighting the feathered grass of the steppe to flame, and my ears hurt again with the boom of Romanian artillery laying down cover fire. The Romanians were stumbling back over their own wounded, and for the first time in what felt like hours, I lifted my eyes from my sights. I saw those hatched sight lines over my vision again, seemingly burned over anything I saw out of my right eye.

"What—" I began, and that was when a stray mortar shell screamed into the parapet of the trench, not two meters away. My rifle blasted into pieces, ripped straight out of my hands; I heard my own cry of agony that was all for my damaged weapon and not my own flesh. I saw a glimpse of the Siberian leaping toward me as I crumpled into the trench.

A fall of earth slid down over me, and then there was a familiar voice saying, "Wake up, sleepyhead."

I peeled up my gummy eyelids and saw the blunt thin face of Lena Paliy, my friend from the train.

"No, you can't get up," she said, her voice sounding curiously distant—my ears were buzzing as though my head were a beehive. "No, your rifle didn't make it. No, you are not *fine*, it is not *just a sprain*, you have a concussion and damaged eardrums, and your joints and spine got such a rattling, you're going to be stumping around like Baba Yaga for at least a week."

"What can you tell me that starts with *yes*?" I asked peevishly, realizing I was flat on my back in a hospital cot.

"*Yes*, you can go back to your division soon. *Yes*, you are going to do everything Lena Paliy tells you, because she is the best orderly in this medical battalion. *Yes*, you are an idiot for sneaking about under the moon like Lady Midnight." Lena grinned at my frustration, relenting. "You're in the field hospital, Mila. Your regimental mates dug you out and carried you here."

"They shouldn't have, not for a concussion and damaged eardrums," I grumbled. "If I were a man, they'd have told me to shake it off, not rushed me to a stretcher."

"Probably," Lena agreed. "But now that you're here, be sensible and look after your health."

"Fate and fortune grant us health," I quoted my mother. "For everything else, we wait in line."

"Oh, shut up and enjoy the quiet. We're far enough back from the front lines, you'd hardly know there was a war on."

I wondered what had happened to the Tolstoy-reading Siberian, but Lena said no one else had been brought in with me. I wouldn't know till I got back to the front, so I stretched my toes under the clean sheets, wincing as my neck lit up with sparks of pain. Long rows of cots stretched across the floor, and I smelled antiseptic over the coppery tang of old blood. I had the cot on the end, by a window; outside swayed a tangle of tree branches, as if the hospital had been erected near some abandoned orchard. Wind rustled the leaves, and there was a flutter of wings . . . little gray sparrows, black-headed starlings. Outside the world was tilting toward autumn, and for some reason that made my eyes fill up with tears. The last thing I remembered from the front was the hot spread of the steppe, those massed columns of fanatically singing enemies under the banner of their shrieking priest.

They will never stop, I thought. *Not ever. Not until they're all dead—or so many of them dead that the living can no longer clamber over the corpses.*

"The attack—" I began, but Lena forestalled me.

"Pushed back. That one, at least. They keep coming like roaches, of course."

And my division was still there, fighting without me.

"So," Lena said, seeing how my eyes had filled, "you're starting to rack them up, sniper."

"Who told you that?"

"It's getting around. A woman sniper, that's different. What is it now, twenty on your tally?"

"Twenty-one." I swiped at my eyes. Even that small movement sent a jolt of pain through my spine. "Officially."

"What do you mean, *officially*?" Lena pulled out a pack of Litka cigarettes. "Is it twenty-one or not?"

"It's not like picking apples, and just counting how many are in your basket," I flared. "The only marks added to the official tally are the ones someone else has verified, or the ones that I've verified by bringing back dog tags or papers from—"

She struck a match. "From the bodies?"

"Yes." A part of my new assignment that I loathed, but it had to be done, so I did it. "If there isn't verification, the mark isn't added to my tally. And sometimes I can't tell if I've hit a target or not, so those aren't added, and neither are the ones I hit when I'm fighting alongside my whole company. It's not—clean-cut. It's twenty-one official, and I don't even know how many unofficial." I waited for her to ask if it bothered me. She didn't, just silently offered a cigarette. I shook my head. "I don't smoke."

"I don't, either." She inhaled with a sigh of satisfaction, sitting down on the end of my bed.

I moved my feet for her, feeling another wrench of pain along my back. "Don't you have other patients?"

"I'm on break. And there's a captain on the second floor I'm avoiding until he's done with his rounds. Drooling for a frontline wife, thinks I don't know he has the real thing back in Moscow." She made a certain face. "Officers can be such shits."

I made a noise in agreement, glad not to be talking about tallies and kills anymore. "The rank-and-file boys aren't nearly as bad, are they?" When Lena and I cut our hair on first arriving at the front, we'd both been bracing ourselves for being outnumbered by the men in our companies, but they hadn't turned out to be the problem. You developed your own way of dealing with fellow soldiers: Lena's, I could see, was deft avoidance and blunt profanity; mine was a kind of breezy, no-nonsense toughness I'd perfected as a tomboy running with the local boys. Do it right, and the men in your company came to look at you as a kind of honorary male: cheerful, sexless, useful in a crisis. (The uniform helped, too. Much to the disappointment of the American press I'd meet later, a woman soldier's uniform in the Red Army was not tight, svelte, or alluring. It had all the grace of a potato sack, but itchier.)

No, it was the officers who turned out to be the problem, not the rank-and-file soldiers. Those damned shiny lieutenants and captains who regarded female soldiers as a perk of rank—they'd come prowling whenever they heard a new woman had arrived at the front. There's nothing quite like sitting in a dugout with a needle file, working on the bolt mechanism of your rifle, only to see some amorous bit of brass with three or four bars on his collar come sniffing around with a gleaming smile, a bar of chocolate, and an indecent proposal.

"Have the officers come at you yet?" Lena asked, thoughts clearly mirroring mine. "Or are they just marginally smart enough to steer clear of a woman with more than twenty kills?"

"I've got a good captain. Sergienko shoos the officers off the women in his battalion."

"Some don't like hearing no, regardless what a fellow officer says," Lena warned. "They'll slither at you when his back's turned, so keep your eyes as sharp as your sights."

"Same for you." I struggled to sit up, catching the hiss of pain in my teeth. "Any other news while I've been out?"

"Odessa's changed, from what the locals say. Sandbags in the streets, antiaircraft guns in the squares, windows taped up. No holiday people swanning into the resorts."

I remembered that beautiful day on the beach, the crowded café filled with laughter. "What else?"

Lena hesitated. "Lots of casualties," she said briefly. We traded another set of looks; I took her hand in mine and gave a silent squeeze. Defeatism wasn't allowed; you couldn't go about griping that the motherland was losing to the Hitlerites . . . but Lena had only to count the dead passing through, and I had only to count the waves of artillery fire booming over the steppe. Easily three enemy salvos to every one of ours.

"Looks like I'd better head back to the front and nab a few more," I said, trying to keep my voice even.

"Bag a few for me." She squeezed my hand back, then stubbed out her cigarette in a discarded bottle cap. "I'd better get moving. Hopefully the captain with the wandering eye has gone creeping back to his sewer by now. I'll be back in a few hours—maybe even with mail. Letters find us a lot easier here, closer to the city."

Four letters caught up with me within the week. Darling Mama, scolding me not to drink untreated water on the march, enclosing a precious scribbled scrap from Slavka that began *Dear Mamochka* and brought me to tears . . . Quiet Papa, telling me about his days in the army: *Belovs have always been lucky in battle.* My family was such a long way away from me now, evacuated to Udmurtia—they might as well have been writing from Paris, or the moon.

Another letter from Sofya in Odessa: *Did you hear Vika's twin enlisted in the tank corps? Vika says men who are dancers are usually boneheads, but she never thought her brother was the biggest bonehead of them all. I should dash to the library now; I'm boxing up the more valuable scrolls in case of evacuation. The place is humming!*

For a moment I smelled not antiseptic and blood, but the Odessa library's scent of old leather, parchment, books. My favorite smell in the world. At the front with my rifle, Mila the student seemed very far away, but here I could feel her with me, shuffling note cards and pencils in her bag, organizing her research according to color-coordinated tabs. How had that woman ended up here, with her ears ringing and her spine aching from mortar fire? All that woman wanted was an orderly life with no mistakes in it; to ride the train chugging through her life right to its end because she couldn't afford to miss any more stops.

Well, I'd stepped off that train and found myself on a different set of tracks, with a different set of targets. Only here, the cost if I missed was much higher.

The sterile, stuffy air in the ward suddenly choked me. I reached out an arm and managed to push open the window by the bed, drinking in the breeze. The unpruned branches of the tree outside were nearly knocking on the sill. I broke off a leaf, smoothing along its veins, and picked up my son's letter. He was about to go on his first hike with the Young Pioneers; he was so proud of that new red kerchief that he even wore it to bed, and he was worried he wouldn't fit in with the country lads who knew everything about the woods. *I'm a city boy, Mamochka, I don't know anything about trees and plants . . .*

"What kind of trees are those outside?" I asked the nearest nurse, pointing to the window. She answered, and I wrote Slavka back in a firm hand, stopping now and then to wipe my eyes. *Darling* morzhik, *I will help you learn all about trees and plants. Your mamochka is never too busy for you, even at the front! Enclosed please find a leaf clipping from a pear tree: see the oval leaves, the pattern of the veining? Now you'll know it again when you see it. It belongs to the scientific classification of* . . . I paused, not sure what kind of scientific classification this type of pear tree was, but I was going to find out. I might be hundreds of kilometers away from my son, but I'd make him feel like his mama was still watching.

I sealed the letter and the leaf inside with a kiss, and then wrote another to my family. And this one told them I'd become a sniper-soldier and that I planned to take down a thousand Germans and then return home with pride. Somehow I had to be the woman who wrote both kinds of letters and did not fail at either. The mother and the sniper both, succeeding at both.

"GOOD TO SEE you back with us," Captain Sergienko greeted me when I finally located the command post near a half-destroyed village. Nearly two weeks after I'd been shipped out with the other wounded, I'd cajoled Lena into getting me released and cadged a lift on a truck headed for the Kuyalnik and Bolshoi Ajalyk estuaries. Another half day to find the command post in the mess of dugouts, carts, trucks, and shattered buildings that comprised the front line, but here was my captain with his familiar gray face, looking three-quarters dead as opposed to only halfway there.

I saluted. "Comrade Private L. M. Pavlichenko reporting."

"You are out of uniform, Lyudmila Mikhailovna." I looked down at myself, startled, but he handed me a little gray cardboard box. I opened it and saw two brass triangles. "You're no longer a private, but a corporal. Congratulations."

A thrum went through me, a tangled mix of pleasure—how proud my father would be!—and disquiet. *You are being promoted over corpses.* Quietly I attached the triangles to the raspberry-colored parade tabs on my collar, listening as my captain gave me a list of the dead: the commander of my platoon, thirty other men from my battalion. They couldn't even be replaced with soldier recruits, but with volunteer sailors from Sevastopol, not a lick of infantry experience among them . . . My stomach sank with every new bit of bad news.

"There's a new rifle waiting for you," my captain finished, "given the destruction of your old one. We've received directives for snipers from the high command of the Odessa defense district, and that"—his voice shifted into official cadences—"is to occupy the most advantageous positions for observation and firing, to give the enemy no peace, to deprive him of the opportunity to move freely in the lines closest to the front—and to disrupt and degrade all enemy morale, good order, and discipline among the ranks." Sergienko's face didn't look at all lugubrious now. It looked fierce, and I could feel my still-sore spine stretch hungrily in response. That list of the dead had brought rage curling back through me, where it had slept muted under the pain of the concussion, the weariness, the longing for my son. "We don't have many qualified as snipers," my captain went on, "so look for new recruits who can be trained. For one, you'll need to find yourself a partner." Snipers worked best in pairs, watching each other's backs.

"Yes, Comrade Captain." I saluted, already itching to get my hands on the new rifle. I'd known my last weapon so well she'd felt like an extension of my own flesh; I'd have to get to know this one. I'd modified my old Three Line to suit my exact firing style, removing the wood along the whole length of the handguard groove so it no longer touched the barrel; filing down the tip of the gunstock. Once I did the same for the new rifle and got off some practice rounds, we'd be friends . . .

"Lyudmila Mikhailovna?" Sergienko added as I turned to leave.

"Yes, Comrade Captain?"

He looked me hard in the eyes. "Good hunting."

Two words that helped me put away the mother, the daughter, the student, and let the sniper unfurl her wings.

CHAPTER 8

My memoir, the official version: Rank conveys privileges.

My memoir, the unofficial version: Being known as someone who can put a bullet through a target's eye at five hundred meters also conveys privileges.

"OUT," LENA TOLD the half-naked man in the banya's steam room. "Or face the wrath of the deadliest shot in Odessa."

He rose from the pine bench, towel around his waist, ruffling a hand through sweat-damp blond hair. "Can I at least get dressed?"

"I'm not shooting anyone just so I can get a bath," I protested to Lena, but she was already tossing the tall man his clothes. Civilian clothes, I was glad to see. At least it wasn't an officer or a fellow soldier she was ruthlessly ejecting.

"I usually like to know a woman's name before she sees me with my pants off," he complained good-naturedly as he padded out.

I laughed, and he grinned at me as Lena dragged me into the steam, though not without a cheerful ogle at the fair-haired man's gleaming shoulders.

"I'm having a bite of that when I'm done," she decided, bolting the door from the inside. "Now, strip off and soak in this heat till your hip loosens up."

"No doctor I've ever met said a long steam in the banya did anything for a wrenched hip, Lena Paliy." I eased down my trousers, hissing at the pain in the joint. "You're just using me to get first crack at the bathing facilities."

"Too fucking right, Mila Pavlichenko. You know how long it's been since I've visited a proper banya?" Lena shimmied out of her uniform like a snakeskin, flopping down naked on the long wooden bench. "You're welcome."

The warm baritone of the man we'd ejected came floating through the door. "You ladies just came off the Gildendorf attack?"

"This morning," I called back, stretching out on the bench opposite Lena. The attack had been done by noon, the enemy driven out from Gildendorf and the Ilyichevka state farm, where my company had been happily settling themselves when I came limping in using my rifle as a crutch. Stripped out of my clothes, I could now see the huge black bruise covering my entire flank.

"I can't believe you fell out of a damned tree," Lena scolded, closing her eyes.

"I still pulled off my shot." I parked my Finnish combat knife within arm's reach—not that I believed I'd need it, but only an idiot would strip naked in a camp full of men and not have a weapon at hand. Sweat was already running freely down my face in the dark, enclosed space.

The baritone voice through the door again: "Are you the woman sniper who took out the entire machine-gun nest?"

"Four shots." Quite a bit of preparation had gone into those four shots: a day to reconnoiter the site, then a morning wedging into a maple tree with a clear line of fire over the Gildendorf cemetery to the road—but the result was one dead adjutant, two dead machine gunners, and one final armor-piercing bullet through the breech of the MG 34 to render it useless before my regiment advanced down the road. "They were using telescopic sights—the entire day before, our boys couldn't so much as wiggle a finger without seeing it shot off." I'd seen three men from my company go down, boys I'd traded jokes and smiles with over evening mess tins.

"How many is it now on your tally?" Lena asked after a half hour's silence, rolling her neck.

I massaged my shooting hand, reflexively checking that the post-shooting tremors had worked themselves out. September was more than half over; fighting was continuous and my nights had been busy. "Officially, forty-six." I still disliked that question. I didn't want to count the dead; I didn't do this for bragging rights. It was simply a job I had to do. And I was doing it. Suddenly the heat felt stifling, and I sat up. "Let's sluice off."

In the village where I was born, my family always went to the banya together: my parents and sister and me all sitting in the steam, then everyone racing out to plunge whooping into the icy stream—or if the stream was frozen, the nearest snowbank. No snow here yet, and I wasn't plunging into any stream naked with an entire regiment around, so Lena and I rinsed off in the bolted changing room with pails of icy water. The man outside called through the door again, just as Lena upended a bucket over my head.

"Not to lurk around your bath, ladies, but one of the corporals just came by and left a rather nice pile of gifts for L. M. Pavlichenko."

"Gifts?" I sluiced icy water off my steaming skin, shivering. The good kind of shivering, the banya's magic where hot met cold and sweat met ice, and your flesh remembered it was violently, beautifully alive. Buried in the dust and blood of the front, making do with tepid washes out of a basin, I hadn't realized how much I'd needed this. I gave my head a shake, feeling the dust and dried blood stream out to puddle at my feet.

"Don't think that's getting you in here, lover boy," Lena shouted through the door, turning around so I could upend a pail over her in turn. "This door's staying shut till we're dressed—"

"I guess you don't want this nice cake of bath soap, then. I can certainly—"

"Give me that!" Lena wrenched the door open, just far enough for a big brown hand to pass the soap through.

"Quite a motley assortment here," he continued as the door closed again. "Another bar of soap, a little flask of scent, a pear from the farm's orchard . . . the note says: *From the men of 2nd Company.*"

Not courting gifts, simply the kind of small luxuries given in wartime as a thank-you. My eyes pricked as I lathered up the cake of soap. My job now was to take lives—I sometimes forgot that I was also saving them. My company had been able to march up that road today without being mowed down by machine-gun fire, because of four shots fired by my hand. I'd forgotten that for a moment, but the men hadn't. Their rough, simple thank-you felt better than the suds lathering my skin.

"You must be one of the civilian guides," I called through the door to the man outside, soaping my hair. "Do you know what's happening in the rest of the eastern sector?"

He gave me the results of the attack as I finished washing my hair. "My company is south a ways from Gildendorf," he finished. "What's a name like Gildendorf doing so near Odessa, anyway?"

I smiled, rinsing off. "That's very interesting, actually—"

"You'll be sorry you asked," Lena groaned, stealing my soap.

"I found out the town was settled eighty years or so ago by German settlers—hence the Teutonic influence. You can see it in the local nomenclature on their gravestones," I added, brightening at the bit of historical trivia I'd managed to glean.

"Gravestones?" The baritone voice now sounded bemused. "When were you sightseeing cemeteries in between taking out machine-gun nests?"

"When I was reconnoitering the best position to fire. I've been reading *Combat in Finland*; you know in the Karelian forests, the Finnish snipers did target shooting from trees? Very interesting. It's why they got the nickname *cuckoos*—"

"You're the one who's cuckoo." Lena pitched my shirt at me, and I pulled it over my scrubbed, glowing skin.

"—so I found a graveyard," I went on over her, still talking through the door. It had been so long since Mila the student had had a chance to emerge from her cave, instead of Mila the sniper (when I was fighting) or Mila the mother (when I was writing letters home). "Germans, I tell you, those settlers couldn't even dig graves without putting them all in fanatically straight lines like rulers. I staked out with my rifle in the tree, right over the tombstone of Bürgermeister Wilhelm Schmidt, who died in 1899—"

"Would that explain this fetching outfit piled at the door?" Definitely laughter in the baritone voice now. "I've seen camouflage before, but this stuff . . ."

"I worked all night on that!" Bits of netting and brown sackcloth and old green uniform material, cut painstakingly into ribbons and sewn down all over my jacket—I'd remembered my lessons from the scarred instructor, who used to disappear into a meadow in a pair of unspeakable yellow-green hooded overalls sewn with leaves, and challenge the class to spot him. We'd give up after an hour, eyes aching, and he'd invariably pop up from a bush three feet away, smirking. I hadn't had a chance to use my camouflage skills on the steppe, since there was hardly anything to camouflage in*to,* but the wooded areas around Gildendorf had given me trees and foliage to hide among. "And you shouldn't laugh at it, because I got the machine-gun nest."

"Then she fell out of the tree," Lena called through the door.

"Nine meters." I buttoned up my shirt, yanked my trousers and belt into place. "Right on the tombstone of Bürgermeister Wilhelm Schmidt, died 1899."

"Next time you read a book that tells you to climb trees dressed like a Finnish cuckoo," Lena said, "don't assume you can *fly* like one."

I made a face and swung out of the bathhouse, carrying my boots. Leaning up against the banya wall was my pack with my hat, the little packet of wolfberry leaves I hadn't been too busy to pick for Slavka, and my rifle, twined in maple leaves and vines to disguise her sharp clean lines. I slung her over my shoulder, then looked up at the man I'd been chatting with through a door. He'd shrugged into dilapidated boots, old trousers, and an even older shirt missing a button at the throat, and he looked about thirty-five in contrast to all the uniformed boys of nineteen and twenty. Definitely one of the local civilians drafted as army scouts.

"A nine-meter fall?" He looked me over, searching for damage, and I found myself looking him over, too. Tall, broad-shouldered, laugh lines around the eyes . . . "You're lucky that hip's not broken."

I shrugged. "Injuries happen." It's only new recruits who look at the wounded and think, *That can't happen to me.* A soldier who's been under fire thinks, *That could happen to me, so I need to be more careful.* And a soldier who has seen comrades die regardless of how careful they were thinks, *This will someday happen to me—but not* today, *if only I can get out of here.*

Lena came out of the banya still toweling her hair, and she gave the fair-haired man a loud smack of a kiss. "That's for cutting your bath short, *zaichik.*"

He looked at me with a raised eyebrow. "Well worth it if I get one from the lady sniper, too."

I laughed, stood on tiptoe, and slung an arm around his neck. "Why not?" I didn't ever respond to the flirtations of fellow soldiers, but civilians were something different. It had been a long time since I felt admired, felt complimented, felt *female,* so I planted a kiss on his cheek. He turned his head, diving after my lips unashamedly, and I pulled back with a grin before his mouth could land on mine. He smelled like pine.

Lena wolf-whistled, scooping up the little pile of gifts by the door. "Come on now, or we'll miss the chow line!" I let her drag me off and winced again as the pain in my hip flared.

"Lover boy wasn't wrong when he said you could have broken that. You need a partner, Mila. Someone to cover your back, lend a helping hand when you have to dive out of sniper nests."

"I haven't found one yet." I'd gone looking in my battalion, following Sergienko's orders to find recruits who could be trained as snipers, but I hadn't found anyone I wanted at my back longer than one night's sortie. A boy from Kiev shot well but moved like an ox; a lanky Leningrader had the keenest eyes I'd ever come across, but couldn't stop flinching when he pulled the trigger.

"Forty-six kills . . ." Lena pulled the golden pear from my pile of presents and inhaled its fragrance. "You're living on borrowed time. Get a partner, or next time you fall on a gravestone, it might end up being your own. So, can I eat this pear?"

FOURTEEN MEN, ALL sizes, all ages: my new recruits stood in a rough cluster, laughing, looking about for their officer. I let them wait, resting my still-sore hip against a crate of shells, flipping through the signed instruction booklet from my old instructor. The word was we'd be transferring soon, retreating through Odessa, but not yet—and I'd received another set of orders about training up new marksmen, this time handed down from General Petrov himself. He wanted more snipers, and he wanted them soon. *You can't train a sniper in just three or four days,* I'd protested, only to hear from a sour-faced major standing behind Sergienko: *You have a week.*

I eyed the men before me over the top of my manual, dubiously. A few were riflemen orphaned from slaughtered platoons and folded into new companies, but two-thirds were volunteer sailors from Sevastopol. I had my doubts that any man in wide-legged pants who was more used to a pitching deck than the smooth, brutal heft of a Mosin-Nagant was going to have a marksman's eye.

The biggest of the sailors finally called to me. "You're serving here too, *kukulka*?"

"Yes," I said, still perusing the manual.

"Smashing medic they've given us, eh, boys?" I couldn't see him winking at his friends, but I could just about feel it. "Let's get acquainted, beauty—I'm Fyodor Sedykh, and your name is?"

I made a mark with my pencil. "Lyudmila Mikhailovna."

"Well, Lyuda, don't frown. Be nice! It won't do you any harm."

I had a sudden flash of Alexei saying *Give me a smile!* I shoved the memory out of my head, but my voice came out with an icier edge as I said, "I'll *be nice* when you all stand at attention and announce your presence to the commander as you are supposed to do in accordance with the military code."

He blinked. "Where's the commander?"

"I'm the commander."

"Quit having us on, Lyuda, that's no way to—"

I unfolded fully, lowering the manual so they could see my corporal's tabs and raising my voice to my father's bellow. "*At. Attention.*"

A dark-haired man stepped from the back and came to, smartly. A long silence fell; I tried not to hold my breath. Then the sailor named Fyodor Sedykh stepped into line beside the first man, still looking puzzled, and one by one the rest fell in.

"You're here because snipers will be needed in the push to come," I continued, walking the line, meeting each pair of eyes one by one. Some blue and some brown, some insolent and some curious. "Let's see if you have what it takes. Cartridges over there, take five each." I came to the last recruit, the one who had come to attention first. "Let's start with you." He was older than the others, nearer thirty-five than twenty-five, a compact razor of a man pared down to sinew, bone, and whiplike tendon. His cap sat on black hair razed down to stubble like a winter wheat field, and when he met my gaze, I knew him.

"Did you get past Austerlitz in *War and Peace*?" I asked the Siberian I'd last seen in the trenches before I was first wounded.

He gave a single nod, not smiling, but there was a smile folded into the corners of his eyes.

I nearly smiled back. "Name, Private?"

"K. A. Shevelyov." His voice was quiet, steady, educated.

"Let's see what you can do." I stood back as he began loading in swift movements. I already knew from our first meeting in the trenches that he could shoot, but I wanted the others to see him following my orders. "Then the rest of you, starting with Fyodor over there with the smart mouth." A smile, to let him know I was willing to joke as long as he fell in line. "If any of you are any good, I'll take you with me on a sortie and see how you do in the field."

"If you're Pavlichenko," Fyodor challenged, "are you the one with a tally of forty-six?"

"Fifty-one. Load your rifles."

They began to load, some looking impressed, some looking resentful. Either way, I knew they were mine.

PARAPHRASING TOLSTOY SHOULDN'T be allowed, but I can't help it: unsuccessful hunts are all alike; every successful hunt is successful in its own way. (I didn't finish *Anna Karenina* any more than I finished *War and Peace,* but even I knew the first line.) A successful day for a sniper might involve ten kills or a tense standoff with no kill at all. An unsuccessful day for a sniper is the day you miss and end up dead. So the eternal question—*What is it like, to be a sniper?*—has no answer. Every day was different. If it was a day I lived, it was a good day.

But what is it like*?* I could hear my trainee snipers asking, silently. I saw that question in Eleanor's eyes a year later—even the First Lady of the United States wasn't immune to morbid curiosity. *What is it like, Lyudmila?*

You are asking too, aren't you?

All right. Come with me.

Watch now, as I take you on a sortie. Not a particularly important sortie—I didn't bag an adjutant that night or a Gestapo colonel carrying secret plans from Hitler. I'll take you along on the night where I found my partner, the other half of my dark moon—for a sniper, a discovery far more important than the night you meet your true love. Husbands, as I have had cause to know, cannot always be trusted. A sniper puts her life in the hands of her partner, night after night after night. He had better be someone she trusts more than a husband.

I'd sited the hideout earlier during the day, everything reconnoitered down to the last blade of grass. A thicket of shrubs—one hundred and fifty meters long, twelve to fifteen wide—in the broad no-man's-land stretching beyond our front line, the narrow end piercing the Romanian defensive line like a spear, ending in a shallow gully near the enemy's second echelon.

"Machine gunners?" The recruit I'd decided to take along tonight kept his voice quiet as we set out from the dugout in the hour after midnight.

"Raise your spade, and our gunners will lay down fire for us to retreat." That was all we said, ghosting along in the warm night from the dugout to the thicketed hideout. Slithering like shadows under the cloudless sky, hauling our rifles and our bags of cartridges. An hour to cover six hundred meters.

Watch now, as my recruit and I do our homework. The dull, painstaking part no one imagines when they think of this dark work done under a dark sky. This isn't like the demonstration Captain Sergienko asked me to give in the bombed-out farmhouse; and it isn't like my stakeout in the maple tree, either, where I'd camouflaged myself to blend into the leaves. This is ground that has to be prepared, and that means hours in the pitch-black digging trenches and small parapets, reinforcing them with stones and turf—because snipers are more likely to fire from hidden ground positions than lofty rooftops or trees, contrary to popular belief. Then the hours of lying down in our nests, placing rifle barrels to find optimal stability, testing the direction of the wind, calculating the distances. And then the wait, two of us folded into the torn earth as the stars wheel and the enemy sleeps. The waiting is where green snipers show their inexperience; they fidget and rattle their cartridges, break down enough to reach for their cigarettes. The dark Siberian lies quiet an arm's length away, calm-blooded, his eyes just a gleam in the starlight.

Watch now as dawn comes. As movement stirs the enemy like heat roiling the surface of a soup kettle, soldiers walking about, calling to each other, thinking themselves safe. The field kitchen sets up, officers give loud orders, a medical station swarms with the gleaming white smocks of medics. One gesture to my new recruit—I'd target the left flank, he'd take the right. A returning nod.

Watch now as the day warms. Fingers flex, loosening, becoming pliant. The heart stirs. The sun climbs. The rifle sings softly to me, and artillery fire rumbles overhead. I begin the countdown to twelve, to my midnight.

Watch.

The first kill is mine. A Romanian officer in a cloth kepi topples over; the Siberian snaps off his first shot before my first target has even finished falling, and I see a second officer stagger. Our shots are masked in the rumble of artillery; for a moment no one can see who or what is dropping their officers, and we pick off two more before they all begin to panic. I fire and fire and fire, the Siberian racking shot after shot at my side, and it isn't until machine-gun rounds begin to thrash the thickets around us that we pull up and slide back into the brush, raising our spades for covering fire.

Back behind our own lines, gasping from the final sprint, I look at my companion. "Seventeen shots, sixteen kills. You?"

"Seventeen shots, twelve kills." The first words he'd spoken in the last twelve hours, and he sounds angry at himself for those five shots that missed.

"I took seven bullets to drop my first two. It happens." We settled in the dugout in the steel-gray morning light, stripping and cleaning our rifles. "Congratulations—your tally is opened."

A nod, and he went back to oiling the barrel. His hands were trembling just slightly; he was trying to hide that from me.

"Hold your hand out," I said.

He hesitated.

I held up my own so he could see it was shaking. "Nervous tension," I said. "It comes on after the sortie is done, but it goes away." I'd learned that by now, but he hadn't yet. "You weren't shaking when there was shooting to be done, were you?" I asked gently.

"No. But I still missed five shots." He didn't scowl, but his face darkened. "I've hunted since I was a child. I haven't missed like that since I was eight years old."

"Firing at a human being for the first time—it's not the same as firing at a deer. There's no pretending it is."

"I've fired at men, too. Hundreds of times with my battalion, aimed at hundreds of enemies."

"This is different. The way *we* kill, you see their faces. If they've washed that morning, if they're meticulous with their uniform or sloppy; if they've had a haircut recently." I was the one to hesitate now. "It's—intimate. You feel that afterward."

"Not during?"

"Not for me. When waiting in a hideout . . ." I hesitated again. "I don't feel any emotions then. I fold into place, and I wait there. Telling my rifle to be sure and steady."

"You talk to it?"

"Oh, yes. I know her better than I know myself. She's a little more ornery than my last rifle, a little fractious." I kissed the barrel's cool black metal. "But she's reliable."

He looked at me. He smelled of gunsmoke, and so did I. "Do you see their faces afterward?"

"Not anymore." Not often, anyway.

"But you still—" Nodding at the tremor in my hand.

"I know enough now to know it goes away in a little while. Same as the eye fatigue." I rummaged for my cigarette case. "This helps. I didn't used to smoke, but my friend Lena said it would only be a matter of time, and she was right." I lit up, drawing the calming smoke into my lungs.

"This helps, too." He pulled a flask from inside his breast pocket, offering it to me.

"Get yourself a cloth-covered flask." I swigged. The rough vodka tasted like pine sap. "You don't want the metal glinting, giving away your position."

"Rifle, flask, knife, two ammunition pouches—" He ticked his way through a list of a sniper's gear. "No helmet?" Glancing at my bare head.

"Not for me. Shell damage during that Romanian attack with the priest—my ears aren't quite what they were." Almost, but not quite, and *almost* was a drop-off as deadly as a Caucasus ravine for someone like me who dealt in fractions. When you lived by *Don't miss,* there was no room for *almost.* "A sniper has to become all ears, and a helmet makes it harder for me to detect faint sounds." I laid my rifle aside. "Hand?"

He held it up, fingers stone-still. His eyes smiled.

"Good." We sat, passing his flask back and forth, looking over the busy encampment. The battalion would be pulling up stakes and retreating through Odessa very soon now. Word was we'd be merging with two other battalions from the 54th. There'd be a big push then.

"Will you be my partner?" I asked simply.

He answered just as simply. "Yes, Pavlichenko."

"If you've got my back out there, you can call me Mila." I offered him a cigarette. "What's your name, K. A. Shevelyov?"

"Konstantin Andreyvich." He lit up, drawing down a curl of smoke. "Kostia."

Watch, now. That's a day in the life of a sniper. One hunt. Twenty-eight kills. And I'd found my my partner, my shadow, my other half.

CHAPTER 9

My memoir, the official version: On the morning of the second day of October, our mighty military machine moved crisply into action at Tatarka, organized and efficient.

My memoir, the unofficial version: It was about as organized and efficient as a monkey shit-fight in a zoo.

THE MORTAR BATTALIONS and rocket installations struck the invaders first—a roar as deafening as a dragon's, and the huge yellow blazes of flame enveloping the enemy positions to the west and southwest of Tatarka might have come from a dragon, too. I went in with the rest of my battalion a few hours later, across black earth baked into a hellish dreamscape. Dugouts, communication passages, firing points, all surrounded by tall grass and hazel bushes and wild apple trees—everything scorched into ash. My squad of newly trained marksmen followed me in silence. They'd boasted before the battle of how many enemies they'd take down, but now in the face of victory they were white-faced. There is nothing pleasant in such a horrifying triumph of death over life, even the death of a hated enemy. Half my men vomited when they first smelled the strange sweetish aroma of the dead.

"Look at it all," I told them quietly, stepping over the smoldering fragments of a gun placement. "But then forget it. Because we will have to do it all again." All this fire and blood had bought us only a kilometer and a half of ground, and the Romanians still had eighteen divisions to our four.

That was the battle, and I fought in it, and when I read accounts of it, I could remember the broader strokes. But Tatarka would forever be bound up for me not in a battle, but in a girl named Maria.

"The Kabachenko homestead." Captain Sergienko's thumb marked it out on the map. "Overlooking the road from Ovidiopolye to Odessa, not far from the railway tracks, used as a command post by the enemy machine-gun battalion. They've abandoned it for now. You and your squad"—nodding at me—"take two hundred cartridges each, hold it as long as you can." He went on to divvy up the other advance posts, and I went to prepare my informally grouped squad. I was a sergeant now, and of the fourteen men I'd been given to train, I'd cut four. Of the ten left, I had eight decent shooters, and two who might make real snipers.

They were singing as they swung along behind me toward the Kabachenko homestead—"Merry Wind," from the Vaynshtok film *The Children of Captain Grant*. "Never saw that one," I remarked to Kostia, who was padding along in his usual place at my elbow, and he gave me his silent smile. He was my partner now, and he was rarely more than an arm's length away from me, but I still knew nothing about him except that he'd come from Irkutsk and now had a tally of thirty-six. He didn't boast of his numbers or his kills any more than I did—that, even more than his sharp eyes and wolf-prowl tread, was what told me I'd chosen my partner well. War highlights the true essence of every person, and as little as I knew about Kostia, I knew his essence was bedrock.

The homestead was single-storied with a red-tiled roof, an orchard spreading beyond up a gentle slope. Secure that slope and we could keep a watch on the road, fire on any who advanced . . . My squad split around the burnt-out wreck of an enemy truck and overturned motorbike, an armored transport with a torn track. The woman who answered my knock at the door looked fifty, erect and bitter-eyed in a gray headscarf. "I don't often see soldiers in the command of a woman," she answered my greeting stiffly. "Serafima Nikanorovna. Come in." She must have known we'd have to come in and avail ourselves of her stores regardless of whether she invited us or not, but she made a rigid little gesture of welcome anyway. "Of course you may share what we have."

What they'd had, before the fascists came, was one of those beautiful little farms you see all over the countryside: a cozy farmhouse with a husband and wife, sons and daughter, all tending the vegetable garden, the chicken coop, and the pigpen. Then the enemy had come, and they'd rifled the vegetables, rounded up the chickens, and slaughtered the pigs. As for the family, the two sons had been beaten black and blue, the father had an arm in a clumsy sling, and the daughter was sitting wrapped in shawls beside the window, staring vacantly at the field behind the homestead. One of my men approached her with a friendly bow—the young ox named Fyodor Sedykh who had first challenged me, and the next best shot I had after Kostia—but she shrank away with a wordless cry. Fyodor, a nice boy and not too bright, withdrew with a puzzled look as the girl's mother gave him a sharp glance.

"Our military units all withdrew from this area in September." Serafima's voice was hard as she slapped down a plate of sauerkraut and salted pickles. "They left us to the mercy of the fascists. I made my Maria hide behind the pigpen, but the invaders found her anyway. My Maria, who used to dream of going to Odessa and becoming an actress in films. They—" The girl's mother broke off abruptly, looking at me with furious eyes. "Four of them. Four. Where were you then, Comrade Sergeant?"

I wanted to tell her the war wasn't lost; that it was just beginning. I wanted to tell her we had been holding the line at Odessa for over two months; that thousands of invaders had died trying to take the Black Sea steppes. But the words crumbled to dust on my tongue. I stood and let her harangue me as long as she wanted, and when she was done, I crossed to the window where seventeen-year-old Maria sat with her eyes like fields of ash. She'd shrunk from Fyodor, but she let me kneel beside her.

"Maybe you can help me with something, Maria," I said quietly, unfolding a handkerchief from my pocket. It held a handful of different leaves, which I now laid across her lap. "I'm collecting samples from the trees here to send to my son. He's learning all about plants in the Young Pioneers, but I'm no country girl and I don't know what kind of trees these came from. This one here—is that birch?"

Her voice was a bare whisper. "Black alder."

"And this one?"

"Chalk pine."

"And that?"

"Sessile oak." She named the rest for me, one by one, as her mother watched, and my men.

"Thank you, Maria." I tucked the leaves away for later, for when I could put aside the sniper and write to Slavka. "May I show you something?"

She nodded like an old, old woman. The pang that went through me was so far beyond pain, so far beyond grief, it left me breathless. Gently I took her hand where it lay in her lap.

"See the black streaks there on the slope?" I pointed to the field beyond the window. "That's from the rocket shells of our Katyushas. They can burn fascist soldiers down to black cinders. We don't bury them, Maria. We let their dust vanish into the earth, so no one will remember their faces and names. That's the way invaders ought to die."

Her eyes pierced me. May I never see such a look in the eyes of my own child. No mother should see such a thing. "Are you a good shot, Sergeant?" the girl asked.

"Yes. I've got a rifle with special gun sights."

A breath everyone in the squad seemed to hold together, and then:

"Kill them," said Maria. "However many you see, kill them all."

• • •

MURDERESS. SLAYER OF innocents. Cold-blooded killer. Later some of the American journalists called me that. To them, a woman who had overcome her natural feminine sympathies to become a sniper must be nothing but an icy front-line murderer, hunting poor defenseless German soldiers who were after all only following orders of their own. I wanted to tell those self-righteous typewriter warriors the truth: *You* didn't look into the eyes of Maria Kabachenko after she had been pinned down by four men who invaded her country, then her home, and then her flesh. *You* didn't see the desperate, grieving fury in her gaze. *You* didn't hold her clutching hands in yours as she begged you, *Kill them all.*

If you had, you would have done what I did. Squeezed her hands back, with all the gentleness in your soul, and then with every drop of rage you could summon, say: *I promise I will.*

I shot five when my squad ambushed three motorcycles with sidecars. I dropped eight more when we stopped two enemy trucks rumbling past; Kostia took out the wheels and I picked off the invaders as they spilled from the cabs. My men dug a trench at the foot of the slope behind the homestead, past a hillock overgrown with wild roses, and I lay there between Kostia and Fyodor when we watched Romanian tanks roll past; heard the dragon roar of our artillery opening fire on them, and then picked off the survivors retreating back across the slope. Every day I brought a handful of leaves and flowers for Maria to identify, and as she told me the names, I told her how many I'd downed that day. For her, I would care about my tally. Because every day, I saw her smile.

"I'll pray for you," she whispered when she heard we'd be returning to our battalion tomorrow. "Our Lord Jesus Christ will protect you."

I don't believe in God, I nearly said. Like most city families, mine had always put its faith in the state and the motherland rather than in empty religious trappings. Even if I had been devout, as remote rural families like this still often were, this war and its horrors would have killed my faith stone dead. But I squeezed Maria's hand and thanked her for her prayers.

"Do you believe, Kostia?" I asked my partner that night. Everyone had gone to bed except those on watch—and us. I'd wandered out to sit in the long grass before the darkened house, savoring the crisp autumn air, and Kostia followed with a jug of the cloudy home brew Maria's mother had uncorked for everyone this evening. Leaning back on our elbows in the grass, rifles lying alongside us like pet dogs, stars wheeling diamond-silent overhead . . . it was the kind of night to talk about God, about souls, about the great mysteries.

A long silence as my partner rolled a stem of grass between his fingers. "I believe in books," he said finally.

"Just books?"

"Books—and friends."

"But you're a loner like me." Fyodor and the others were always wrestling and joking in a pack like friendly dogs, but Kostia could usually be found by himself, reading or tending his rifle in his own patch of silence. I was the same way. I liked company, I liked to laugh, but after a point I needed solitude.

"We're loners," Kostia said. "But we have friends who would die for us. And we'd die for them."

I wondered what merry Sofya was doing right now back in Odessa, or prickly Vika. "I don't think my friends from before the war would know me anymore." Mila the library researcher was a long way from Mila the soldier.

"You'd start talking about Bogdan Khmelnitsky." A smile gleamed briefly in Kostia's shadowed face. "Then they'd know you."

I laughed, picking up the jug of home brew. At supper that night, we'd drunk it out of cut-glass goblets Serafima had proudly taken out from a chest that had somehow escaped the German raid. Now I swigged directly from the jug and coughed. "I swear this is tank fuel."

"Give it over." Kostia took a long swallow, looking back up at the slow dance of stars. "What do you believe in, Mila?"

I thought about that, feeling the burn of rough liquor in my throat. "Knowledge, to light the path for humankind," I said at last. "And this"—patting my rifle—"to protect humankind when we lose that path."

"You lead us down the path," Kostia said, "I'll have your back."

THE 1ST BATTALION had driven the enemy out of Tatarka, but my squad and I found ourselves in the thick of the fighting when we rejoined the ranks, flung headlong against three enemy battalions by the railway line. Bombs were falling like summer rain all around our trench; half-deafened and half-blinded, I was struggling with my rifle's dust-fouled bolt when something sang very close to my ear, a silver chime of warning. And suddenly I couldn't see; blood was ribboning down my face, sewing my left eye closed, sliding over my lips. I tasted copper and salt.

Just need one eye to shoot, I thought sluggishly, still tugging at my fouled bolt. The blood kept coming, and I wasn't hearing anything at all out of my left ear. Dimly, I watched my hands drop the rifle and fumble for the first-aid kit at my belt; I managed to clap a wad of bandaging to my face but winding it round my head seemed impossible. If this din would let up, this dust—I couldn't *see*—

"Mila." Kostia's voice, very calm. "Look at me." My partner pressed what was apparently a cut in my hair above the forehead; pain went through me in a bolt. He wound the bandage around my head, and I wanted to joke: *You've had my back—now you have my head!* But everything around me was sinking into fog. And for the second time, I woke up in a hospital cot.

"Want a souvenir, sleepyhead?" Lena dropped a blackened piece of jagged-edged metal into my hand. "That's what sliced your scalp open."

I looked down at the mortar splinter, hardly bigger than a matchstick. A little lower and it would have gone through my eye socket—I'd be one of the hundred and fifty of my regiment who would never leave Tatarka.

"Who's gone?" I asked Lena, folding my fingers around the splinter. "Who died this time, while I was unconscious?"

She lit a cigarette, gaunt and gray-faced after what I could only imagine were frantic, endless hours tending the nonstop flood of wounded. "Private Bazarbayev took a bullet to the heart."

One of my sniper trainees. He hadn't been very good, but he'd tried—how hard he'd tried. I felt the metal splinter's sharp edges dig into my palm as my fingers tightened. "Who else?"

"Your company commander—what was his name?"

"Voronin." A good man, one of the few officers I liked. I remembered a trench-side discussion once about favorite museum collections; the young officer had waxed eloquent about the Scythian-gold collection at the Hermitage, and I'd told him about the archaeological excavation I'd been lucky enough to attend after my first year at university. Just one brief hour in which I'd talked tenth-century grave barrows and the Kostromskaya stag, feeling like a student rather than a soldier. And now he was gone, and I'd be carrying my rifle to yet another hasty funeral between sorties, marked by a few mumbled words and a red plywood star.

"Kostia?" I asked, dreading the answer. "Is he—"

"Promoted to corporal. He's been underfoot looking in on you, whenever he's not leading sorties."

"He should have stitched me up on the front line rather than rushing me here," I grumbled. But at least my makeshift squad was in good hands while I was gone. "When can I go back?" I tried to rise from my cot, but a wave of dizziness nearly flattened me. Lena reached out with one finger and pushed me down onto my pillow.

"When I need two hands to shove you back down and not my pinkie, you can go back. At least a week."

"A *week*—"

"Are you that eager to add to your tally? I hear you're over a hundred now."

I was. Well over a hundred. But the last thing I wanted to do was discuss my tally. "Lena, speak to the doctors. They can sign off on—"

She drew a long hard pull on her cigarette, reached into her pocket for a battered compact, and held the mirror up to my face. I hadn't looked at myself in so long, and I recoiled at the sight. My cheeks were gaunt, my eyes shadowed in their sockets; a patch of hair had been shaved away to treat the splinter wound, which marched parallel to my hairline in a centipede of black thread. The area had been daubed with brilliant green antiseptic. I looked like . . .

"Death," supplied Lena. "You're not going anywhere, Mila, because you look like death."

I pushed the mirror away. "I am death." To over one hundred invaders, anyway. *Not enough,* the thought whispered.

Too many, whispered an answering thought.

Lena pocketed the compact, rising. "You can still be killed, Lady Death," she threw over one shoulder as she resumed her rounds.

"Lady Death?" I said to Kostia when he visited the following day. I'd braced myself for a lot of "thank goodness you're not dead" heartiness, but my partner just pulled up a stool without a word, leaning his rifle against my bed. "Why did Lena call me that?"

"They're all calling you that." He looked at the dried flowers I'd scattered across half the sheet: the latest batch of samples for Slavka. "Iris, chamomile, rhododendron," he said, naming them.

I began folding each one into its own piece of paper, marking the name in large clumsy letters. My hands weren't quite steady yet, so maybe Lena was right that I needed more time. Before anyone else I'd have been embarrassed of those shaking hands, but not my partner.

"Lady Death—like Lady Midnight, Baba Yaga's servant?" Polunochnitsa, servant of the fabled witch in the old lore before the revolution swept away superstitious myths.

"Was she your favorite from the old stories?"

"I preferred Lady Midday. But really they're the same thing. I wrote a paper once on how such pre-revolutionary folkloric figures represented the opposing faces of pre-Soviet womanhood." Tucking another dried flower into its envelope. "It got a grade of Excellent."

"Of course it did." My partner's trigger-calloused fingers sorted through some dried daisies. "When I was growing up, I thought my father was old man Morozko."

"You thought your father was Father Frost?"

"He was a Baikal fur trapper . . . He came to Irkutsk only once a year with the first snows, and he sprouted knives from everywhere like icicles. He always left in a huge violent gust like an avalanche."

"He sounds noisy. Winter is quiet." It was the first time Kostia had ever said anything about his family. "You're Morozko, not him."

Kostia smiled under his eyelids. He picked up my hand where it lay among the scatter of flowers, unfolding my fingers and then folding them back inside his own, and he pulled it against his chest. He didn't say anything—he just held my hand against his tunic, where I could hear the steady beat of his heart.

Gently I disengaged my fingers and sat back. I didn't say anything, either, just looked at him with steady regret. This wasn't like flirting with that fair-haired scout for a lark—I was Kostia's sergeant, and maybe a difference in rank didn't stop most officers from fraternizing with their inferiors, but it didn't sit right with me. Even more important, he was my *partner,* the one I relied on above all others during the deadly dance in no-man's-land every night. I didn't dare introduce any chaotic rush of new passions into that delicate, critical balance, or we both might end up dead. So I just let the silence fall and gave a small shake of my head.

"Let's get you up and walking," Kostia said as if nothing had happened, and helped me off the cot so I could totter around the room. By the next day I was standing alone, peaked cap crammed over my battered, bandaged head, limping determinedly outside. The medical battalion had been stationed at what had once been a rural schoolhouse; skirting the cots and the rushing doctors, the stretchers with burned men and unconscious men and moaning men clutching stumps of arms and legs, I managed to find my way to the garden surrounding the schoolhouse.

Just days ago the autumn sun had been shining bright from a blue sky, warming the whole vast surface of the steppe. Now winter was coming in a bluster of lead-colored clouds and cold northern gusts, old man Morozko stealing closer on snow-scented feet. Even here, as far back from the front lines as we were, I could hear the rumble of guns.

I turned away from the sound, inhaling the smell of fresh-turned earth and wild roses. Juniper grew here straight as a green wall; tulips and roses bloomed in the borders—despite all the bombing and shelling, someone was looking after this garden. I gave silent thanks to whatever soul cared enough to nurture this humble patch of flowers in such a living hell. I picked up a fallen red-gold leaf for Slavka, nearly falling in my dizziness, and tried to uncurl it in my hand. It broke, dry and dead. I dropped it, feeling another wave of weakness, wondering why I was fighting so to stay upright. Why not just fall, lie down, close my eyes? I was *tired*. When I got back to the fight, I'd have to rekindle the rage and carry on, but for now it was ash in my stomach, dead and cold after three and a half months of sorties and battles. I sat on a garden bench and pulled out my dissertation, hoping dear old Bogdan Khmelnitsky would cheer me up, but I couldn't make my eyes focus on the words. The letters crawled off the page like ants, and the heading that little library researcher Mila Pavlichenko had typed with such pride earlier this year was now half-obscured by a bloodstain.

For the life of me, I couldn't tell you whose blood it was.

A purring sound slid into my one good ear, and I looked up to see a khaki-colored staff car ooze through the open gates toward the school. A flurry of uniforms; by the time they came marching toward the front doors, I had stuffed my dissertation pages back into my pack, limped up the drive, and drawn myself up at attention. It wasn't the first time I'd clapped eyes on Major General Ivan Yefimovich Petrov, commander of the coastal army, but this was the first time I'd seen him so close. Perhaps forty-five, red tinges in his hair, bags under his eyes . . .

I expected him to sweep past, but one of his officers caught sight of me, whispering something, and the general halted. "Pavlichenko, yes? I've heard your name—the woman sniper."

I saluted. "Yes, Comrade Major General."

He surveyed me. "A head wound, I see."

"On October 13, with the 1st Battalion at Tatarka."

"Are you being treated well?" He nodded at my assent. "Well, get ready to move, Lyudmila Mikhailovna. We're off to Sevastopol, orders of the supreme command."

Shock rocked me to the soles of my feet. I'd known the retreat from Odessa was coming, but hearing the order become official was a different thing entirely. "We're not going to surrender Odessa to the enemy? They'll raze it to the ground." My beautiful Odessa of the sparkling sea and blue skies, the striped umbrellas and outdoor cafés. The city I'd helped defend, holding my firing lines, taking my shots. I stared at the commander of the coastal army in stark horror, and I saw a flicker of sympathy in his gaze. It hurt his soul too—he just hid it better.

"It's the duty of a soldier to carry out orders to the letter." He gave me a clap on the shoulder, surprisingly gentle. "My orders to you now? Don't mope, have faith in victory, fight bravely. How many in that tally of yours?"

"One hundred and eighty-seven," I said dully. The enemy attacked in such dense ranks, I could nearly get two with one bullet. Who knew what my real tally was when the battles and the skirmishes and the unconfirmed shots were added to my official sorties, but officially I was at 187.

Low whistles from the staff behind General Petrov, and his grip on my shoulder tightened approvingly. "That's champion," he said. "Sevastopol needs that rifle. We'll cross the sea and defend the Crimea." I could see him visibly searching for something stirring to say, something to put fire in the blood, but the general looked as exhausted as I felt. "Everything will be fine," he said at last. "You'll see."

Off he swept with his entourage, going to survey the wounded, evaluate morale—and probably, oversee this evacuation of his military units to Sevastopol—leaving me standing frozen before the useless fragrant borders of flowers.

WE WOULD LEAVE by sea, and that meant retreating through Odessa itself to the port.

I begged to be released so I could travel with my squad, but was refused. Kostia and my men left in advance of me; I departed with the medical battalion, which had been loaded onto road transport, skulking in the falling dark under the camouflage fire of the rearguard battalions, which would remain in their trenches until the last. "Retreating," I spat to Lena. "We're fucking cowards." I'd never used such a word in my life, but I felt as though I were choking on a throatful of thorns.

"Not so loud," Lena hissed. "Do you want to be shot for defeatism? They've executed more important people for less." She was called off to rebandage an amputee on a truck, and I knew she'd be too busy with the wounded to listen to me brood. I had nothing to occupy me but putting one foot in front of another as I took what was perhaps my last look at the city I loved.

How changed it was since the day I'd taken a train out of here to the front. The autumn twilight covered the parks and boulevards like a shroud, but the shroud couldn't hide how many buildings gaped roofless, how many black holes instead of windows looked down like mournful eyes on the retreating defenders. Our column halted at an intersection blocked by artillery wagons, and with a start I saw the two-storied enlistment office where I'd gone to join the Red Army. Only the building wasn't there anymore, just collapsed beams and soot-blackened walls, the twisted bones of the iron staircase I'd tripped up in my crepe de chine dress, bent on seizing fate by the throat.

"Mila?"

A voice called me from the silently watching onlookers. Turning, I saw a woman hugging herself against the cold night, wrapped in a too-short coat. For a moment I didn't recognize her, but then I registered the protuberant eyes and endless dancer's legs. "Vika?" I blinked, and with a word to my lieutenant, stepped out of the column to join her. I hadn't seen her since the day war broke out, the day she'd pirouetted in red petticoats with the opera ballet.

"You're retreating?" she said, sounding stunned.

"Withdrawing to a place of better strength," I said, repeating the official line, hating it.

"Retreating." Her voice flattened out. "Abandoning Odessa."

"At least I'm fighting," I flared. "Didn't you dancers get evacuated to safety? Must be nice to be a Bolshoi-trained demi-soloist." I knew I was being unfair, but her contempt stung me.

"I've quit the ballet. My brother, I—" Vika drew an unsteady breath. "Grigory's dead. He didn't even make it two months in the tank corps."

Her twin, her dance partner, her other half. “I’m sorry,” I said, regretting my sharpness.

“Sofya’s dead too. A stray bomb.”

“Sofya?” I whispered, feeling my stomach wrench.

“She wanted to be a teacher,” Vika said tonelessly. “She had all these didactic little studies on group play that were going to encourage cooperation in the four-to-seven age group. Who kills someone like that, Mila? A *teacher*? Or a boy like my brother, who could dance the Bluebird variation like an angel?”

“Fascists,” I said. Fascists had now killed half the little quartet who’d been sitting at the Pushkin Street café that afternoon war broke out. I’d thought the rage banked in my stomach had subsided to ash, but it turned over in a flicker of renewed heat as I saw Vika’s bleak eyes.

My column was starting to move; the blockage with the artillery carts had been cleared. “Take care,” I told her awkwardly. “Can’t let the invaders stop the Dragonfly from dancing. Or was it the Nightingale? The Star?”

“Does it matter? No one needs dragonflies and stars now. What we need is killers.” She gave a bleak smile. “At least we have you.”

The dancer turned and walked up the shattered street, head erect, toes turned out, and I continued my retreat toward the sea.

The port looked like Babylon before the fall: army trucks swarming everywhere, tractor units pulling howitzers and tanks, thousands upon thousands of soldiers. The water was choked with ships from the steamer service and the Black Sea Fleet; in the pitch-dark I shuffled up the gangplank of the *Zhan Zhores,* which loomed before me like a long black wall rising sheer above the quay. The heaving mass of wounded funneled below, down to the crew mess room. I sat clutching my pack and fighting waves of dizziness as the tugs began leading the vessel away from the wharf, the ship shuddering like a whale lumbering toward the open sea. Through the porthole I saw leaping flickers of red and gold—Odessa's huge portside warehouses were aflame. Deliberate, to leave nothing to the fascists, or an accident with the gas cans? Either way, no one was rushing to put the fires out. There was no one left; everyone who could leave Odessa was abandoning her. My last sight of the city where I'd enlisted as a soldier was to watch it going up in flames as I slunk away over the Black Sea.

My rage rose, and rose, and rose.

"Comrade," the third mate scolded, seeing me take out my cigarettes in shaking hands. "No smoking down here."

"Then tell me where," I snarled. The mess room already smelled of sweat and nervousness, the air loud with shouts and the shuffle of boots. My skin crawled, crying out for solitude.

"Quarterdeck, at the stern."

"Quarterdeck? What's that? How do you have a quarter of a deck?" He began some deeply technical answer; I exhaled the last of my patience. "Tell me. Where. I can *smoke*."

He saw the look on my face. "The back of the ship, at the top."

I fought my way through the crowd out of the mess room, continuing above deck to the smoking area. Sailors and medical orderlies stood in clusters, smoke curling upward. We weren't just leaving Odessa, I thought—we were leaving Gildendorf, the Kabachenko homestead, Tatarka; the battlefields that had turned me into what I was now. Whatever that was. Sergeant Pavlichenko, as I heard every day? The woman sniper, as General Petrov had called me? Lady Death, as Lena called me? I shook the names away on the wind, squinting over the dark ocean toward where Odessa was vanishing like a mirage.

"May I borrow your binoculars?" I asked the nearest man, and then dismay froze me to the deck as he turned.

"Little Mila," said Alexei Pavlichenko, looking down at me with that amused flick of his mouth. "Look at you."

THE SOVIET DELEGATION: DAY 1

August 27, 1942
WASHINGTON, D.C.

CHAPTER 10

The marksman sat on a grassy verge overlooking the Lincoln Memorial, fanning himself with his hat. His employer was late, but Washington types liked to play such games, to remind you how important they were. The marksman tipped his face to the sun, covertly observing the trickle of visitors trailing in and out of the huge marble edifice. It was early, but a handful of tourists were already coming out to beat the summer heat: a family clutching brochures, some vacationing parents dragging sullen teenagers, a couple wandering hand in hand to look up at the giant contemplative marble figure inside.

A shadow fell across the marksman's hands. "Did we have to meet here of all places?" a peevish voice demanded.

The marksman replaced his hat, smiling. "What, overlooking a monument to another president who was assassinated?"

"Keep your voice down." The new arrival was middle-aged, balding, packed into an expensive suit with a faint pinstripe and a blue pocket square.

"No one's listening." It was why the marksman preferred to do this sort of thing outside. In the middle of a broad expanse of grass, not a soul in earshot, surrounded as they were by the bustle of a busy city, no one would pay attention to the idle chatter of two men lounging on a warm morning. "Sit down."

Pocket Square spread out a handkerchief to protect his suit from the grass, sitting with bad grace. The marksman didn't know his name, or the name of the men behind him who'd selected him as the go-between. The marksman didn't care, either. It wasn't his business who his customers were or what drove them to pay for death. As long as they paid promptly and kept their mouths shut, none of the rest mattered. "Well?" Pocket Square demanded.

"I'll know more after the White House breakfast in an hour, but the girl and the rest of the delegation are already scheduled for a press conference this evening," said the marksman. "My name is on the list of attending press?"

"Yes, but my employers don't see any reason for you to attend."

"I need to establish myself on the fringes of this delegation as a security-vetted and innocuous part of the scenery, so I can cozy up with someone who can get me access to the girl when the time comes." It wasn't the usual way he worked—normally the marksman put more distance between himself and his targets, worked through layers of anonymous informants—but with a presidential target in his sights, he wanted as few people and complications built into the plan as possible. Perhaps superstitiously, he wanted his own eyes on everything. "I'll need a list of the attending delegation members—not her fellow students, they'll be in the spotlight, but the little people."

"You'll get it." Pocket Square mopped his face. The day was already heating up, but even if it had been cold, the marksman suspected he'd be sweating. Some people just didn't have the nerves for assassination. "When are you going to—do it?"

"September fifth. The last day of the conference."

"But you can guarantee success?" Pocket Square pressed.

"No." Death was never guaranteed. "Failing the desired outcome, I can guarantee embarrassment, public outrage against the President and his Soviet guests. I was given to understand this would be an acceptable secondary outcome."

"For some of my bosses," Pocket Square muttered.

"The America Firsters will be pleased enough, and so will the anti-Soviets." The marksman smiled at the other man's startled expression. It wasn't hard to figure out who, in this carnivorous capital city, would want Franklin Delano Roosevelt dead. Even popular presidents had enemies, and FDR was no exception: American fascists who loathed *President Jewsevelt*; bitter political rivals in Congress; isolationist tycoons who opposed war with Germany; Communist-hating millionaires so rabidly anti-Marxist that even beating Hitler wasn't worth allying with Stalin—not to mention righteous idealists who saw any third-term president as a tyrant in the making. Who knew what occasion or event had brought enough seething men together, what match had lit the wick as they aired their grievances, what events had stoked the flames until someone was brave enough to whisper the word *assassination* . . . but it had happened, and the marksman's telephone had duly rung with an offer.

Pocket Square now looked positively ashen. "You can't possibly know who they are. The greatest care was—"

"They're suits," the marksman said calmly. "Men in expensive suits who want the world to run in their favor. That's always who hires me—some shadowy compact of powerful discontented suits. And they know I can get the job done."

He rose, giving a mental tip of his hat to the distant marble figure of President Lincoln inside the monument. A theater performance spattered with presidential blood and brains; now that had been an assassination with style. "If you'll excuse me," the marksman told his employer's flunky, "I have a breakfast to attend."

Notes by the First Lady

I have very little time before the welcome breakfast for our Soviet guests, but I look through an invitation to address the U.S. Committee for the Care of European Children, examine the minutes of a meeting of the advisory committee of the American Federation of Negro College Students, review the schedule for the commissioning of a new battleship in the Brooklyn Navy Yard, read over a report from the Civil Aeronautics Administration concerning the use of women in their CAA pilot training, and check on Franklin. He's sitting up in bed where he always takes his breakfast, old blue cape thrown over his pajamas, breakfast tray set to one side with its scatter of toast crumbs and coffee dregs. Newspapers litter the bed—he always takes the Baltimore Sun, *the* Washington Post, *the* Washington Times-Herald, *the* New York Herald Tribune, *and the* New York Times *with his breakfast—and on the floor by his bedside table is the Eleanor basket, where I leave reports and communications earmarked for his attention. He groans sometimes—"More homework, Eleanor?"—but he knows he cannot see everything and counts on me to fill the gaps. He's already gone through the notes I left earlier, and he must be about to get dressed, because I hear the valet rustling in the wardrobe. Franklin is sitting with his eyes closed, face set in exhausted, determined lines.*

I know what he's doing. He's imagining himself as a boy back on the family estate in Hyde Park, standing with his sled at the top of a snowy hill overlooking the Hudson far below. In his mind he tips over the brow of the hill and careens down, wind rushing past his face, steering every curve in a shower of diamond-bright snow crystals. At the bottom he brakes to a halt, throws the rope of his sled over one arm, and strides back up on strong young legs. He relives that hill, that exhilaration, that climb, until it is real and the vigor of it flows through him.

Normally he saves this memory for restless nights, using it to calm his mind and bring sleep. This morning he has taken it out to banish weakness before he faces the day ahead. This morning he has need of it. His lean strong hands brace his weight on the bed—it is like he is braced for a bullet.

What is it you fear? *I want to ask.* What—or who? *But the gong sounds below, and I tiptoe away to welcome our Soviet guests.*

ELEVEN MONTHS AGO

September 1941
THE SEVASTOPOL FRONT, USSR
Mila

CHAPTER 11

My memoir, the official version: I hadn't seen Alexei Pavlichenko for at least three years before enlisting in the Red Army. I'd write it that way not because I wanted to lie, but because then I could dispense with him in one line, and not waste the page space that real life had allotted him.

Because in my memoir, the unofficial version? That rot-gut, oily-tongued bastard turned up in the middle of the war like what the Americans would call a bad penny. The most unwelcome penny in the world.

I STOOD GAZING at him, large as life and three times as unpleasant on the deck of the ship bound for Sevastopol, my stomach suddenly roiling. "Look at you," he said, and noted the rank on my collar. "Sergeant? I hope you didn't steal your boyfriend's tunic just to keep warm, *kroshka*. There are penalties for impersonating rank!"

I'd forgot how tall he was. Most of the soldiers on the *Zhan Zhores* looked disheveled and weary from the retreat, but Alexei's uniform was crisp, his cap perched on his fair hair at a rakish angle. "This is my uniform," I said as coolly as I could manage. "I am a sergeant."

"Not bad, I suppose, for such a little girl." He didn't ask about Slavka. I didn't want him to ask—I didn't want him anywhere near our son—but it still made my blood boil that he had not even a stray thought for the beautiful boy he'd fathered. That Slavka meant so little in his eyes. He wore a lieutenant's triangles on his collar—of course he was an officer; of course he outranked me.

"Medical battalion?" I made myself ask. He must have enlisted in

Odessa around the same time I did. Surgeons of his skill were worth their weight in silver at the front.

"That's right. I told you once, didn't I? A man sees chances in war—this is mine." He nodded out to the black expanse of sea ahead of us. "I have a good feeling about Sevastopol. Great things lie in wait, you'll see."

So confident, not a doubt in the world. He must have seen hellish things if he'd had months in the hospitals of Odessa, operating on battle wounds from dawn to dusk, but clearly it had made very little impression. He hadn't gone to war to heal his wounded countrymen or preserve this land for his son to grow up in—he'd gone to war for a chance to rise. He clearly still had his dreams of greatness. "Alexei Pavlichenko, Hero of the Soviet Union?"

My voice came out hard and mocking. He frowned. He was used to seeing me deferential, pleading, frustrated—the wife who hated to ask him for things and kept having to ask him for things anyway. The little woman who jumped when he told her to. He was used to having the upper hand over me . . . but not anymore. I'd seen too much blood and terror in the last few months to be impressed by a man with a mean streak. He could still make me seethe, but he couldn't make me tiptoe, and he could no longer make me jump. Alexei leaned on his elbow against the ship's rail, and he looked like he was seeing me now. "Chapayev division?" he guessed. "We'll be seeing more of each other in Sevastopol."

"I doubt it." I couldn't resist a jab. "Unlike doctors, I don't operate safe behind the lines."

Another frown. "But you're in the medical battalion, yes?"

"No." I smiled at him. "I'm a sniper."

He laughed. "Nice to see you've finally developed a sense of humor, *kroshka*."

I shrugged. If he was stupid enough to miss the rifle slung over my shoulder, that was not my problem.

"No joking, now." Alexei's smile disappeared. "You're not a rifleman."

"Why not?"

"That's no position for women, even in war. No matter what the state says."

"Tell that to all the enemy dead I put in the ground while defending Odessa."

I threw it at him, wanting to see the surprise in his face. Instead he just chuckled. "Aren't you all grown up. Still want to borrow my binoculars, for one last look at Odessa?" He held them high up in the air, over my head. "Jump, little Mila!"

I didn't stop to think. I slung the rifle off my shoulder, nipped the barrel through the loop of his binoculars, and with a wrench and a twist flipped them out of his hands over the ship's rail. "Jump for them yourself," I said, hearing them splash far below, and turned to go.

Not so fast I didn't see the flash of anger go through his eyes, didn't hear his final words behind me. "Still can't take a joke, can you?" His voice laughed, but there was real anger underneath. "Still pretending *you* aren't a joke."

"One hundred and eighty-seven dead enemies know I'm no joke," I shot back, and stalked off across the quarterdeck.

Alexei Pavlichenko here. My heart pounded. My husband, back in my life after years of barely thinking of him at all. On the same ship, headed to Sevastopol.

It doesn't matter, I told myself, going below. I wasn't afraid of him, not anymore. And in the chaos of the front it would be easy to avoid each other. I could stay out of his way and he—if he was smart—would stay out of mine.

Surely.

SEVASTOPOL. I CAME to the white city with my red hands and my battered heart, and I stood in wonder. It wasn't even a quarter of the size of bustling, cosmopolitan Odessa, but its public gardens and lanes of red-gold trees were still untouched by war. The stone walls of the ancient twin forts guarding the entrance to the main bay hadn't yet been pocked by German mortars; the blue dome of St. Vladimir's Cathedral gleamed whole and pristine. People strolled the streets after work, went to public baths, bought tickets to see *Tractor Drivers* or *Minin and Pozharsky* at the local cinemas. A beautiful city—and one I quickly tired of, because I couldn't get *out* of it.

First I was ordered to recuperate with the medical battalion until my scalp wound healed. Then to my exasperation, I couldn't find a single officer who could tell me where my regiment had *gone.* "You can't just lose an entire regiment," I protested to a harried-looking staff officer. "Did you lose the whole coastal army as well?"

"That is defeatist talk," he said stiffly. "Don't you have friends in high places, Pavlichenko? Go talk to *them.*" But October was over by the time Major General Petrov arrived in Sevastopol along with his staff at the coastal defense command post, and more days yet before I could obtain even a three-minute meeting.

"Greetings, Lyudmila Mikhailovna." He was doing about eight things at once, white dust of the Crimean roads still frosting his general's stars, but he smiled through the pince-nez perched on his nose. "How are you feeling?"

I was yearning for Kostia and my squad like a missing limb, but that wasn't what he was asking. "Fully recovered, Comrade Major General." My stitches were out, and my hair was already growing back over the shaved area around the scar. If I placed my cap carefully, you'd never know it was there.

"So, are we going to beat the Nazis in Sevastopol?"

"Absolutely, Comrade Major General."

"I'm making you a senior sergeant, and I want you commanding a sniper platoon when you rejoin your regiment. Which is"—followed by some murmuring from an aide—"somewhere on the road between Yalta and Gurzuf. See the staff headquarters for your documents, and the quartermaster for winter gear." He hesitated. "Make sure you get a pistol."

"I have my rifle, Comrade Major General—"

"Get a Tula-Tokarev for close quarters. Eight shots. Seven for the enemy, if they come on you by surprise. The last one . . ." His face was suddenly stony. "It's the Hitlerites we're fighting now, not the Romanians. Germans don't take snipers prisoner; they shoot them on sight. And for the women . . ."

Better not to be taken alive. The unspoken words hung in the air like drops of ice. Was that what awaited me in Sevastopol—death at my own hand, to avoid gang rape and execution? Even with my tally of one hundred and eighty-seven dead enemies behind me, a thread of fear wormed through my stomach. I'd done all my shooting in flat steppes where visibility was excellent, and my targets had been thickly bunched, easily flustered Romanian soldiers. This was the Crimea, a dense wooded country full of secrets, and my targets were Hitlerites. Highly trained Germans captained by fanatical officers drilled into hatred of anyone who didn't belong to their master race. Who shot or starved captured Russian soldiers in their prisoner-of-war camps rather than treat them like the British or French soldiers. Who would rape a woman to death if they caught her alive, just for the sin of stepping outside *Kinder, Kirche, Küche* to kill an enemy who had invaded her country.

I swallowed, saluting. "I'll make sure I'm never without a pistol from now on, Comrade Major General."

Nearly another week before I could rejoin my regiment in the Mekenzi Hills—the third defense sector, lying between the Belbek and Chornaya Rivers, more than twenty kilometers outside Sevastopol. I made my way first by truck in a group of new arrivals, then on foot as they dropped me at a nest of dugouts and thickly forested paths, asking directions from the rushing soldiers around me. I was longing to see Sergienko's familiar lugubrious face and tease him about how if he got any grayer he'd look embalmed, but I got a shock at the command post.

"Captain Sergienko has been gravely wounded and dispatched home. Comrade Lieutenant Grigory Fyodorovich Dromin commands the battalion now." Before I could manage more than an inhalation of shock and grief for my captain, I was meeting his successor. Dromin was new, slim, immaculate, and thirty-five; not one hair on his smooth head did anything but shriek *fresh meat.*

He flicked through my documents as I saluted. "You wish to become a platoon commander, Comrade Senior Sergeant? Are you really up to it?"

"That's not for me to decide, Comrade Lieutenant," I said evenly, "but senior command."

"Which senior command do you mean? I am your senior commander, and I am opposed to women occupying field positions in the army."

At least he *said* it. Plenty of officers thought the same thing but refused to admit it. They just smiled when they saw women arrive in their commands, then refused to make use of them.

"You're a sniper, apparently." Dromin tossed my documents back. "Fire away at the Nazis by all means. But commands will be issued by those who are supposed to issue them."

"Who would that be, Comrade Lieutenant?" I couldn't resist replying.

"Men, of course. Proper officers."

He would have dismissed me from his presence right then and there, but a laughing voice came from the rear of the command post where a cluster of officers was working. "Give her a platoon, Dromin. Or do you want to argue with General Petrov?" A man unfolded from a too-small stool, and for a moment I thought it was Alexei and nearly recoiled. A junior lieutenant, tall and fair-haired—but he wasn't my husband, though he did look familiar. "She already had an unofficial squad," the lieutenant continued, leaning against my new battalion commander's table. "Give her more men and call it a proper platoon."

"Do we really believe this nonsense about one hundred and eighty-seven kills?" Dromin spoke as though I wasn't there. "If she had even a quarter that many, she'd have an Order of the Red Banner by now."

"Petrov still gave her a platoon." Cheerfully. "Fork it over or go argue with him."

The lieutenant smiled at me, and I realized who he was: the fair-haired man at the banya outside Gildendorf, the one I'd kissed on the cheek. He'd been in civilian clothes, so I'd assumed he was a scout or a guide . . . that was the only reason I'd let myself flirt with him. Now here he was in the damned *command post.* I felt myself flush, not even bothering to hope that he didn't remember. His eyes were sparkling. He remembered, all right.

I was only too happy to obey Dromin's curt dismissal, marching out with eyes fixed on the middle distance. The bickering continued behind me, and I distinctly heard: ". . . Petrov's little pet, she's probably warming his bedroll—" My face flamed as I stamped through the unfamiliar mess of trenches, communication passages, machine-gun emplacements. New front line to defend, new enemies to understand, new terrain to learn, and now a new commanding officer who thought I was a front-line whore. An impression for which I had only myself to blame. Well, if lieutenants wouldn't traipse around dressed like civilians . . .

The army sappers had constructed good, deep dugouts in the thickly forested hills. Making my way down the winding trail leading me to the lines of 2nd Company, still swallowing my embarrassment down like hot coals, I heard a whoop and found myself suddenly seized in bearlike arms. "Mila! Mila, there you are—!" I saw the broad beaming face of that young ox Fyodor Sedykh as he set me back on my feet. "We thought maybe the Romanians got you after all. I told Kostia—"

I turned from Fyodor and registered my partner's still, carved face. "Kostia," I said, and his arms came round me like a band of iron. I hugged him back hard, only pulling back to look him over. He was thinner than when I'd seen him last, and his trigger hand was bandaged. "You're wounded?" He shrugged, and then Fyodor was drawing us both down by the nearest stove.

"It's a tangle out here," he said frankly, heating some water in a mess tin for tea. I sat on an upturned crate, my shoulder hard against Kostia's as he rewound the bandage on his hand. "Second Company's down by half. We came up against the Hitlerites at the end of October near Ishun—beat them back, but their mortars and Messers ground us down, and we were being deployed almost on the open steppe. Too exposed; that was where Sergienko got it. Direct hit on the battalion command post; completely shattered his leg."

"Will he make it?" Throat tightening for the man who'd elevated me to sniper; kept his amorous fellow officers from pestering me; given me my first promotion.

"He'll make it, but he won't walk again. It's a desk for Sergienko now."

At least he'd survive this war. I already missed my calm, competent captain—badly—but at least he was *alive.* "And the regiment?"

Fyodor passed out the tea along with some precious hoarded sugar and plain biscuits. "Down to six, seven hundred."

Six or seven hundred, from the three thousand it would have been in peacetime. "And my squad?" I asked, taking Kostia's injured hand and tying off the wrapping, since he was having trouble doing it one-handed. In my pack I'd brought gifts for each and every one of the men I'd trained, bought while waiting in Sevastopol—mostly flasks of brandy or bars of chocolate, though for Fyodor I had a tin of his favorite sardines in oil, and for Kostia a secondhand copy of Tolstoy's *Sevastopol Sketches* bought in a bookshop, remembering his much-battered *War and Peace* . . . but now my heart clutched, realizing I hadn't seen any of the other men I'd trained. The Kiev boy with the acne-scarred face, the lanky sailor from Minsk . . . "How many are left?"

Kostia spoke for the first time. "Us."

I'd commanded ten, I thought sickly. Now I had two. These Germans were a different kettle of fight. "When can we get more men?" I said more to myself than the others. "More men, more rifles . . ."

"I'll see what I can get for you," a cheerful voice said behind me, and when I looked over my shoulder, I was surprised to see the big blond lieutenant. Any last lingering hope that he didn't remember me shriveled as he said, "You look different with dry hair, Pavlichenko."

"So do you," I said stiffly. "Comrade Lieutenant."

"I was on leave when we last met, hence the civilian clothes. I didn't transfer to 2nd Company until I arrived in Sevastopol—Comrade Lieutenant Kitsenko, at least in the command post." He offered a hand. "Off-duty, Alexei."

The name made me blink. It wasn't his fault he was a tall, blond, blue-eyed lieutenant like my husband, but did he have to be named Alexei, too? Then I blinked again, as Kostia jumped up with a broad grin and embraced the new arrival as though they were brothers.

"You'll get your platoon," Kitsenko told me, thumping Kostia's back with a friendly fist and coming to sit on an old oil drum. "Dromin's just kicking and squealing. He knows he can't argue with Petrov."

"Thank you, Comrade Lieutenant." He was being friendly, but I couldn't help wondering if his had been the voice speculating that I was General Petrov's bed warmer. All because of one careless kiss . . .

"My friends call me Lyonya," Kitsenko said with a grin, feinting at Kostia, who slipped the mock punch and threw one back. "And you're Lyudmila Pavlichenko. When I met up with Kostia here, I asked him about this brunette vision I'd seen come out of a bathhouse like Venus from a clamshell, and Kostia told me all about you."

The breezy flattery caught me off guard, but not as much as this unexpected camaraderie. "How do you two know each other?"

"Met years ago in Donetsk, in technical school," Kitsenko said, reaching for a biscuit. "I see this skinny kid from Irkutsk come prowling into the classroom like a nervous wolf—"

"Everyone in the class poking fun at my accent," Kostia said. "Except him—"

"Oh, I made fun of your accent, too. Siberian vowels that could cut ice. But I thought, *That's a feral little bastard that will be useful in a hockey scrum; let's be friends.*"

"And then an ox from Leningrad said my mother was a whore, and Lyonya broke his nose." Kostia shook his head, still grinning, and I stared. I hadn't heard my silent partner volunteer so many words in—well, ever. "So I invite this big-city boy here to Irkutsk to visit, that fall—"

"—and his father took us on a hunt, and I saw *that* was the real wolf," Kitsenko finished, shuddering. "Something out of Baba Yaga's nightmares."

I wondered how one man could be a lieutenant and the other a corporal considering they must have joined around the same time, but Kostia said, "Lyonya took the accelerated course for middle-rank officer corps under the coastal army general staff."

"And now I get to give him orders," Kitsenko said with another feinted punch. "Now let's hear about you, Lyudmila Mikhailovna. If you've got a hundred and eighty-seven scalps, why haven't you earned an Order of Glory or two?"

"I don't do it for glory," I said, not quite able to keep the edge out of my voice.

"She does it for the liquor." Fyodor laughed, passing a cup of the rot-gut army vodka. "Not to mention the luxury accommodations around here."

Kitsenko smiled but persisted. "Really—why not a single decoration on that tunic?"

I shrugged, but Fyodor answered for me. "Sergienko passed her name up for commendations, but they must have died on someone's desk. Someone over his head, who didn't like our Mila here—"

"Someone who didn't feel like pinning stars on a woman's tunic," Kostia observed.

"They'll get used to the idea," said Kitsenko. "You know Comrade Stalin's ordered three all-female combat regiments formed in the Red Air Force, under Marina Raskova? They'll be pinning red stars and gold stars on hundreds of ladies by the new year." He smiled at me, frank and admiring. "You'll get your share, Mila."

I paused, looking at him over my mug of tea. "Sir," I said at last, wondering how not to give offense, but wanting this line drawn here and now before his flirtatious first impression of me turned into an assumption that I was *available.* "Kostia and Fyodor call me *Mila.* They've guarded my back, and I've guarded theirs. We've killed together, fought together, bled together. I don't give my nickname unless it's to a brother in arms."

"Then until we bleed together," Kitsenko said without rancor, and raised his mug of tea in salute. "I imagine Sevastopol will give us the opportunity."

He was certainly correct about *that.*

CHAPTER 12

My memoir, the official version: I was given the responsibility of recruiting and training a proper platoon of snipers—the first woman of the Red Army so honored.

My memoir, the unofficial version: I have no idea if I was the first Red Army woman to lead a platoon, but someone in the propaganda office decided it sounded better that way, so there I was with my ragtag little band of fumble-fingered amateurs that was absolutely nothing like a proper platoon.

A REAL RIFLE platoon would be fifty-one troops commanded by a lieutenant and a deputy senior sergeant, the men beneath them divided into four sections each with their own sergeant. There would be a mortar section, a dispatch rider, clear lines of organization. Mine was a handful of raw recruits grudgingly pointed in my direction by Lieutenant Dromin, who culled them from the marine infantry battalions when reinforcements arrived in November. The scene played itself out exactly as it had when I was given my first batch of trainees: the men argued with me about whether or not I was their commander; they argued about whether I had or had not killed one hundred and eighty-seven enemies; they argued about whether or not women belonged on the front line. But frankly you have heard enough of that sort of thing by now, and so had I, so let us move on to the point when they were listening, more or less, and I had a platoon, more or less.

Although I nearly didn't have any corporals to help me lead it, because Fyodor and Kostia were both no help at all with the new recruits that first day. In fact they considered it hugely amusing to sit back and watch me get my temper up stamping all over the new men, and I threatened to send the pair of them up to Dromin for laughing at their commander. "I wasn't laughing," said Kostia, statue-faced, his eyes dancing, and as for Fyodor, he could barely be peeled guffawing out of the mud. I made them dig latrines for three hours.

So I had riflemen under my command again, but there weren't many proper sorties to get them seasoned. The first half of November was a series of furious skirmishes trying to push back against the Hitlerites, who had fortified Mekenzia in hopes of using it as a base to push toward the rear of the city's defenders. They were now driving like an arrow for Sevastopol, which meant not sniper work but blind firing, counterattacking under heavy mortar fire . . . weeks of German attacks and our own counterattacks, not only when we were at Mekenzia but all up and down the defensive lines of Sevastopol.

"Twenty-five days," Kostia said, and I heard the speculation in his voice. Twenty-five furious days the Fritzes had attacked Sevastopol, never wavering, never faltering until they'd pushed us back a few precious kilometers. The attackers around Odessa would never have had such steely will, not under the rain of death we were pouring down.

"They'll have to regroup now," I said, scanning no-man's-land through my binoculars: a neutral strip laced on either side with trenches, communication passages, machine-gun nests, minefields, antitank ditches. "Things will be quiet for a bit. So you know what that means."

Kostia pointed out the spot I'd already marked, along the high ridge of the Kamyshly gully. It wouldn't be a crossing point ordinary troops could make without withering fire pouring down, but snipers at night? I nodded. "There."

"They'll be sending theirs through, too," Kostia noted. "Scouts, reconnaissance teams." But the first man my platoon and I barreled into on evening patrol was one of our own, not a Hitlerite.

The forest here was like a maze once we were past the excavated stretches of trenches and barbed wire. It sprang to life in a living tangle of juniper, hornbeam, garland thorn, wild rose—plants I could identify by sight now, after gathering so many leaves and flowers for Slavka. I'd been leading my platoon along the ridge, where we'd just flushed a dozen German submachine gunners armed with Schmeissers. Though out of our range, they hastily retreated, and we had no orders to follow minor patrols. For the sake of training, I had the men target-shoot at the distant gray dots of German uniforms until they vanished into the trees. Gunsmoke was still wreathing the hills, the last shots resounding around the gullies, when a white-haired man melted out from a thicket.

Fyodor snapped his rifle up, but I shoved the barrel down. The old man's hands were raised, showing what looked like a Soviet passport; he was shouting, "Friend! Friend!"

"If you're a friend," I called without moving a step, "what are you doing on the military lines of the 54th Regiment, and how did you get past the enemy lookouts?"

"It's not difficult." He spat into the leaves at his feet. "The Germans are afraid to venture too far into the woods, and I know the hidden tracks. I've been a ranger here for thirty years."

"A ranger?" I echoed, dubious. In his gray civilian jacket and knapsack, his white beard growing dense and scraggly nearly up to his eyes, that thin stooped figure looked more like an elderly wood sprite than a woodsman.

"I was." The old man met my eyes, and his whole face screwed up in a paroxysm of grief. He swiped at his eyes before the tears could fall, saying gruffly, "I'm known as Vartanov here. And if you listen to me, I can give you the German staff headquarters at Mekenzia."

THERE'S A HOUSE. Caterpillar armored transports with aerials beside it, machine guns on the roofs of the cabs, tractor-borne cannons, motorbikes with sidecars. That's the one."

"Troops?" I asked.

"The usual gray-green uniforms." The ranger hunkered on his heels in one of our watch trenches, shoveling down a dish of hot barley porridge. "Others in short black jackets, berets."

"Tank crew." I made a note. "Who's giving the orders overall?"

"Big officer, about forty, pale eyes. Parade tunic, braided silver epaulets, black-and-white cross under the collar. Every morning he comes out to wash at the pump and go through his calisthenics. They have everything at their pleasure, those Krauts." Vartanov's face rippled, hatred passing deep under the surface. "But they're afraid of Russians."

"Why?"

Vartanov's eyes went to my weapon, never more than an arm's length away. "I'm told there are rifles with special sights."

"That's true," I said, neutral.

"Then use them." He scraped up the dregs of the porridge from his mess tin. "It's not far from here—through the forest, about five kilometers using a shortcut. I'll show you."

I exchanged glances with Kostia. He drew me aside with a flick of his eyes.

"Trap?" He put the question bluntly, and it was a distinct possibility. Not all the local populace here was loyal to the motherland; even with news spreading of how Germans treated our civilians and captured soldiers, some rural idiots saw the Hitlerites as liberators who might save them from Comrade Stalin's food shortages. I had no desire to get walked into an ambush and shot.

"We'll take this to the head of reconnaissance," I decided. "We get firm confirmation of this man's allegiance and identity, I'll risk taking him out to reconnoiter."

Kostia's face tightened. "Not alone."

"We need a guide," I said. "The front lines are stabilizing; the Krauts likely won't mount another major assault for weeks. It's time to send the platoon out hunting." And there was no way to start them off if I didn't know the ground, didn't know how to navigate this dense forest that stood like a green wall and rustled in the unruly wind from the sea.

So, two days later, approval secured and Vartanov's identity and loyalties satisfactorily vouched for, the old ranger and I moved into the Mekenzi Hills at first light.

He passed through the trees like a ghost, following a nearly invisible hunter's track. I wound along behind him through the bent sycamores, wondering how I was going to shoot in these trees. Good for hiding—better than the brutally wide-open steppe—but not for sharpshooting. What were my bullets supposed to do, zigzag between tree trunks?

"Pavlichenko," Vartanov grunted, sounding out my name. "You're Ukrainian?"

"I'm Russian," I answered levelly. These questions of nationality always irked me. We were all Soviets, weren't we?

Another grunt. I doubted Vartanov agreed, but at least he didn't argue. "From the bent sycamore to the well is eighty-five meters," he said, forking right, and as I followed, a garland thorn snagged my jacket. Yanking loose, I froze to hear a flock of tomtits take off noisily from the nearest tree. "Careful," the ranger hissed, and moved off through the growth again like an eel. By the time the sun rose we'd reached Mekenzia, and I climbed into the nearest tree with my binoculars.

German trucks and mouse-colored uniforms moved ant-like along the road stretching between Mekenzia and the village of Zalinkoi. Among all the Teutonic gray I saw the Crimean Tartars with the white armbands of the Politsei, the pro-Hitler collaborationist force, guarding the barrier at the cordon. At noon a field kitchen appeared, and my mouth watered at the smell of potato stew and ersatz coffee.

"There," Vartanov murmured from the ground below, and I saw the officer. I knew enemy decorations better than the old ranger—through my binoculars I saw the tabs of an artillery major and a recipient of the Knight's Cross. I watched him light a cigar and set off by car toward Cherkez-Kermen. *Main staff headquarters probably up there,* I thought. Colonel General Erich von Manstein himself might be residing there, not that I'd get a shot at *him*. But this smug major with his morning calisthenics and his silver epaulets—yes. *You are mine,* I told him as his car jounced away over the road.

I sketched the homestead on a rough firing map, jotted the distances, began calculating the wind. *Speed medium, four to six kilometers per hour.* "What's all this?" Vartanov said, looking at my figures when we were retreating safely back toward no-man's-land. "This is about wind?"

"The rifle fires the bullet, but the wind carries it." I quoted the old proverb. "We choose that position, we have a breeze from the side blowing at a ninety-degree angle. At 100 meters from the target, the horizontal lateral correction for a sniper is several milliradians. Now, in locations high above sea level"—I brightened, unable to resist the technical tangent—"the atmospheric pressure changes and the distance of the bullet's trajectory and flight increases. But in hills under 500 meters in height, and here we're at 310, one *can* ignore a longitudinal wind as long as one takes the lateral into consideration, since it can cause significant—"

Vartanov had that wary, hunted look the Odessa librarians used to get when I started talking about Bogdan Khmelnitsky.

I sighed. "You calculate the wind so you can make allowances in your aim and not see your shot blow off target."

"Why didn't you say so?" He sounded offended. "I can take down a buck at two hundred meters; I know how to compensate for wind!"

"I'm sure you can, but there's still value in understanding the science behind it."

He waved that off. "This time of year, expect strong blows from the north and northeast. You'll attack tomorrow?"

No sense waiting, I thought. We could bag the entire nest here with a little luck and some cool heads . . . not a job for my whole platoon, though. Some of them had barely mastered their ballistics tables, much less cross-wind calculations, and this would be tense, precise work.

"Take the dark one," Vartanov said, reading my mind. "Your partner. He's the only one among you who moves quietly."

"Him, and Fyodor Sedykh, and Burov." The best of my sailor recruits. "I'll borrow a couple of hand-to-hand types from my reconnaissance officer as well, in case we get rushed."

"And me," said Vartanov.

I stopped beside a tangle of garland thorn. "You aren't a soldier of the Red Army, dedushka," I said gently. "I can't take civilians hunting."

"That homestead the Germans turned into their headquarters was mine." The ranger's eyes over the thicket of beard were like knives glinting from underbrush. "I lived there with my son and his wife, my own wife and my younger children. We had a banya, a barn, greenhouses, we all worked dawn to dusk; I couldn't tell you where the war even was, or what it was about. I was off to the municipal authority offices ten days ago, to register some supplementary expenses—and that was the day a party of Hitlerite scouts came along, lined my family up alongside my house, and shot them all." There were tears in his eyes, but he wouldn't let them fall. "I will be there to watch those beasts die, with your permission or without."

Slowly I reached for the rifle slung across his bent shoulder. He let it fall into my hands. An old Berdan II, almost an antique. I looked the ranger in the eye. "You can borrow a Mosin-Nagant from one of my platoon. I can spare you twenty rounds to get comfortable with her before tomorrow."

He bared his teeth. "I'll only need ten."

WATCH NOW, AS a party of seven shooters approaches the village at first light the following morning.

Kostia isn't at my side for once, and he's not happy about it. He doesn't argue with my orders to stay with the less-experienced platoon members, but there's a line sharp as a whip cut between his dark brows. "I'm staying with the old man," I say, nodding at Vartanov. "If after all this he ends up playing us false, I'll put him down. If he's everything he says he is, he's still the newest to a firefight and I want to be there to steady him. You steady the others. Shoot true—" and Kostia nods, slipping away through the shadows. It's strange having him leave my side. He's become like another limb since we found each other after Odessa; I'd be less uneasy if I settled in for duty without my shadow than without Kostia. He and the rest of the platoon take position fifteen paces to my left; I take my place in the middle with Vartanov, and the two extra soldiers I borrowed from the reconnaissance officer plant themselves fifteen paces to my right: a triangle of fire we'll pour down on the Nazis. Wind at right angles to my position; I correct the dial of the lateral on the tube of my telescopic sight and quietly pass instructions down the line. Vartanov follows my every movement, eyes glittering.

Watch now. The Germans gather at the same time, the same place, the same numbers. For the love of Lenin, their iron adherence to schedules and rules may have conquered empires but it makes them prey to a lynx pack like us. The sun climbs, the mobile kitchen comes out at 11:37 on the dot, the men cluster . . . at least sixty officers and specialists.

A sniper platoon's commander always fires first, signaling the rest. My rifle sings, sending her first hot gift through the eye of an officer berating a private in a loud voice, and he's barely begun to crumple before shots begin to thunder to my right and left.

Watch now as the Nazis fall like scythed rye. They're pinned under three points of fire: my side-line shooters all work from the outside in; I target anyone coming out of the middle, and Vartanov aims for anyone crossing left or right toward my zone. They came to the mess line without their weapons, too tightly packed to run, and I feel not a drop of pity. It was this crew that murdered Vartanov's family, and if my tiny band of seven lets up for even a moment, we'll be charged, overrun, and outnumbered eight or nine to one. If that happens, my men will all be executed. As for me, I'll be gang-raped and then executed, if I don't manage to shoot myself first . . . but that's not our fate today, because we're winning this, numbers be damned.

The artillery major charges out of the house, still in his singlet from his daily calisthenics, and a bullet drops him between the eyes. I think it's Vartanov's. The old ranger is firing slow but steady beside me, teeth bared in his harsh old face. Kostia across the way is snapping shots with cool precision like the block of ice he is. My platoon trainees and the borrowed reconnaissance soldiers are aiming and reloading without hesitation, and I am so proud of them all. Not one of them hesitates. They're my men, my pack of deadly, silent, soft-prowling lynxes.

Watch now, and don't blink—it's all over in moments. Close to fifty dead on the ground, another dozen fled into the nearest truck and careening away. We do a fast raid of the headquarters, stripping whatever we can find in the way of staff papers for our officers to analyze, supplies to supplement our meager rations, an MP 40 submachine gun we can turn back on its makers. Then we're fleeing into the trees. Fyodor lumbers along with soft whoops as though he has just won a football game, the great ox, and Kostia glides like a shadow at my elbow again, and Vartanov is weeping as he runs, but he never stops smiling.

And neither do I.

WE WOULDN'T BE able to cross no-man's-land and return to our barracks until nightfall, so we made camp at a place Vartanov had marked for me on our reconnaissance run: a plank shack half dug into the earth, protected by a stand of conifers and prickly juniper. We were nearly there, blowing from a kilometer and a half's worth of sprinting, when a buck crashed through the underbrush ahead. "No time to go after it," I said as it disappeared, before any of the men could start dreaming of fresh game.

"Never mind venison, I'd take it just to put on the wall." Fyodor watched the crown of antlers disappear into the trees, wistful.

"A sniper doesn't have to kill everything in sight," I retorted as we moved back into a jog.

"Hunt to fill your soup kettle and put a pelt on your bed, not just to put a trophy on your wall," Vartanov grunted unexpectedly. "The forest is like a temple: observe the old customs, be respectful, don't kill for amusement, and the woods will reward you for it."

"I don't believe in forest spirits, but I don't enjoy hunting animals. They're defenseless against these." I patted my rifle as I ducked under a low-hanging sycamore branch. "It's not like the days when the boyars went out with spears. At least with that kind of duel, the animal had a fighting chance."

"We just slaughtered fifty men from the cover of shadows." Kostia spoke for the first time all morning. "We certainly didn't give them a fighting chance."

"But we're at war, and wars are mankind against mankind. Not innocent beasts."

Vartanov bared his teeth again. "Those men we killed today were beasts."

To my surprise, someone had already lit a campfire outside the plank shack when we reached it. "I was off duty, so I offered to meet your sniper party," Lieutenant Kitsenko called, brushing pine needles from his breeches as he rose. "See if you recovered any critical intelligence."

"You're avoiding the command post," Kostia guessed, thumping his friend on the arm as we pressed inside.

"All right, I'm trying to get away from Dromin before I jam the officious little sprat headfirst into a tank turret." Kitsenko looked to me. "Good hunting today?"

"Not bad." I grinned, and he grinned back. I could hear Lena's appreciative whistle in my head: *That's a smile!* "You can stand watch, Comrade Lieutenant," I suggested as my men began making themselves comfortable all around the shack. "We can't cross back until nightfall, and my platoon needs sleep."

Kitsenko watched as we all flung ourselves down on the pine needles and stretched out. Fyodor was already yawning hugely and I felt an answering yawn climb up my own throat, the fast-running blood of the long night and tense morning giving way to that sudden familiar exhaustion that fell on my platoon after action like a curtain. "All the waiting and watching you do, staking out a shot." Kitsenko looked thoughtful. "I hadn't realized that could be so tiring."

"The most exhausting thing in the world is being on high alert for hours." I thumped my pack down, leaning against it for a pillow. "A sniper's eyes get tired from focusing so much."

"One eye, or both?"

I laughed. "Good snipers don't close one eye—you just focus on the dominant one; it fights eye fatigue. But fatigue happens anyway after awhile, and the eye starts slipping in and out of focus." Like mine were doing now. I yawned. "If you don't mind, Comrade Lieutenant, I'm going to pass out for a bit." And I did, until late afternoon when I peeled my gummy lids open and saw that a thick autumn mist like milk had rolled through the trees.

Kitsenko was digging a firepit under Vartanov's instruction, my other men were rising and yawning, and I couldn't remember the last time I felt so pleased. My platoon was coming together: we'd had a successful night; no one had died or even been injured. Days like today were days to treasure. I looked over at Kostia, still sleeping an arm's length away with his head on *War and Peace*—he took it everywhere, even on hunts—and gave him a poke. "Come on, you. Let's see what goodies we got off the Germans—unless your officer friend already had a rummage?"

"You think I'd risk annoying a woman who can drill an eye socket at 300 meters?" Kitsenko asked. "I leave the honors to you, Comrade Senior Sergeant."

All the men gathered round as I opened up the artillery major's pack, and moans of ecstasy rose. Biscuits, bars of chocolate, tins of sardines, a log of salami the size of my forearm, a liter-and-a-half flask of brandy . . . I looked up to see my platoon gazing at me soulfully like starving puppies and raised my eyebrows at Kitsenko.

He scratched his jaw. "You take that back to the command tent, and it'll be confiscated. So we clearly have no choice but to—"

"Eat every bite?" I tossed a tin of sardines at Fyodor. "You heard the lieutenant, boys. Eat up."

Nothing makes a party sing like the knowledge that death awaits you tomorrow, but you've dodged it today. In no time Vartanov was boiling water over the fire in a mysteriously procured pot, tossing in pea puree cubes to make soup; hunks of ration bread were being toasted on sticks. Kostia set up a proper table on a big flat rock and sliced the salami. I took charge of the brandy, dividing it into standard-issue tin mugs as we all gathered around the rock and the men looked at me in the dancing firelight. "Well done, lads," I toasted them, sitting between Kostia and Vartanov. "May we always have such luck."

"To Lady Death and her pack of devils," Kitsenko answered, raising his own mug. "I've never seen anything in my life as terrifying as you lot melting out of the trees this morning with your rifles. Well, except the time I walked into the latrine and saw Dromin's bare ass shining like a searchlight; *that'll* drive a man screaming into the night."

A laugh went around the rock, and we bolted the brandy as one. It fired its way down to my stomach, and I closed my eyes in dreamy peace as the first spoonful of soup slipped down my throat, and the jokes and laughter began to fly. *I could die here,* I found myself thinking. *I could die here and at least I would be happy.* And I opened my eyes, drinking the rest of my soup and wondering when it was that I'd started to think of death as something not just possible, but inevitable.

The men were ahead of me, done with their soup and now sucking down the sardines, chins slick with oil. The brandy had clearly gone to Vartanov's head; he was proclaiming, "'S easy to find your way among trees, even you townies . . . trees are like *people*, each has its own soul . . ." When the last scrap had been eaten, Fyodor stripped to his undershirt and rose to challenge one of the reconnaissance soldiers to a wrestling match as catcalls rose. I smiled and rummaged further into the German major's pack, gnawing on a bar of chocolate as I turned over the packet of papers.

"What did you find?" Kitsenko leaned to look over my shoulder.

The spiky German script was hard to read, but I could make out the man's name. "Klement Karl Ludwig von Steingel." His decorations spoke of a career that had led through Czechoslovakia, France, Poland.

"That's a lot of war under one man's belt," Kitsenko said. "All that, and then he came here."

"Here he came, and here he stays," Kostia said from my other side.

"Kostia!" someone called from the campfire. "Come give Fyodor a run, you mangy wolf—"

"Who are you calling mangy?" Kitsenko challenged even as my partner rose and began stripping off his jacket. "Tear his arms off, Kostia! Just you wait," the lieutenant added low-voiced to me. "Everyone will bet on that ox Fyodor because he's twice as big."

The two stepped in to circle each other, my partner smiling faintly. "I'll wager a chocolate bar the young ox takes it!" Vartanov called across the fire.

"I'll take that bet," Kitsenko called back, adding for my ears, "Now watch our wolf eat him alive."

"You've played this game before," I said as Kostia began to circle round Fyodor, hands poised, eyes alert. Fyodor was the size of a boulder, but he was fleshy and rash; my sparely built partner wasn't much taller than me, but he was made out of tungsten and patience.

"You know how many classmates we rooked out of their pocket money with this game when we were students? Every Moscow golden boy with a Party bigwig for a daddy thought he could wipe the floor with the skinny kid from Siberia." Kitsenko rested his elbows on his drawn-up knees. "By the time they spat out a tooth or two and learned how wrong they were, we'd have raked in bets at five-to-one."

I watched Kostia side-slip a rush from Fyodor and come back in an armlock that doubled his opponent's wrist up behind his back. "So you were the bookie and he took the punches?"

"Oh, we both took the punches. Moscow golden boys with Party bigwig daddies don't like losing, so usually Kostia and I would end up in another fight when the official one was over. But we'd still come out of it with more rubles than bruises."

I smiled. "That's friendship."

"The best."

His glance held mine just a touch too long. *Don't flirt with officers,* I reminded myself, and was glad when Kitsenko jumped up to shout encouragement to my partner: "Go for his knees, Kostia!" Kostia threw a bow back, and I smiled. I couldn't help but like Kitsenko for bringing such an unexpected light side out of my taciturn other half.

Biting off another square of chocolate, I went back to the German officer's pack again and found something more disquieting: a photograph. A pretty, fair-haired woman with her arms around two gawky boys, all beaming at the camera. On the back was a woman's writing: *Mein Herz! Mit Liebe, Anna*. There was a packet of letters in the same feminine script, and another in a man's writing—the major had written his wife back, but not had time to post the letter. Even Nazi devils had families who loved them. I wondered how Anna would feel, if she'd known about Vartanov's murdered family and whatever other crimes her husband had committed here.

A roar went up around the fire. I looked up in time to see Kostia flip Fyodor neatly on his face, pinning that huge arm behind him. Fyodor tapped out, and Kostia handed him up with a grin. Swiping his jacket from the ground, he waved off calls for a rematch and shadow-boxed briefly with Kitsenko, who was then hauled off to an arm-wrestling match with old Vartanov. My partner flopped beside me again, growing still as he saw the photograph in my hand.

"I wonder when she'll get news of her husband's death." I tilted the picture. "Or how he died."

Kostia slung his jacket over shoulders that had already begun prickling with gooseflesh in the chilly mist. "Handsome family."

"It's not their fault their father came here and walked into my sights." I grimaced, looking at the major's young sons: perhaps fourteen and sixteen years old, standing proud in Hitler Youth uniforms. "Will we end up fighting them, if this war goes on long enough?"

"If it comes to that." Kostia did up the last of his buttons "I didn't ask them to come here and fight me. Any more than I asked their father."

The wrestling and catcalling died down around the fire now, as twilight fell. Once it was full dark we'd have to douse the firepit and be on the move, but a soft lull descended as purple dusk hovered. "Who's got a song?" Kitsenko asked from the other side of the fire, and Vartanov began to sing in a cracked but still strong bass—a minor-key ballad in a Russo-Armenian dialect I could barely understand. One of my sailor recruits responded with a melancholy sea chantey; then unexpectedly Kostia's low baritone rose. "*The pale moon was rising above the green mountain . . .*" Startled, I realized he was singing in English. I spoke some English—my mother had taught languages at the local grammar school—but not enough to understand all the verses. Something about *Amid war's dreadful thunder, her voice was a solace and comfort to me . . .*

"What was that?" I asked my partner when he finished, and Kitsenko began singing "The Women of Warsaw" in a resonant tenor.

" 'The Rose of Tralee.' " Kostia poked at the fire with a stick. "My grandmother used to sing it."

"She spoke English?"

He hesitated, then lowered his voice even further. "She was American."

"*What?*"

Kostia said something long and fluent in English, smiling at my surprise. "An Irish girl from New York who came over with a missionary group in czarist days. She'd read too much Tolstoy, had romantic ideas about Russian snows and white nights . . . Of course she fell in love with the first Siberian revolutionary she came across, and married him." He leaned back on one elbow. "She lived a long time, past the revolution. I learned English from her."

"Is that her copy of *War and Peace* you lug around everywhere?" I guessed.

Kostia looked at me, face abruptly serious. "Mila, I don't tell people about this. Even my grandmother kept it hidden. She and my mother made sure all our documentation was lost when the family moved to Irkutsk, so it's not on record anywhere."

I could understand why. Contact with foreigners who had counter-revolutionary purposes—it was something the authorities took seriously. Just receiving an innocuous letter from the decadent West could be enough to land you in an interrogation room, much less having blood ties to a capitalist nation. America wasn't exactly a friend to the motherland, especially now when they were dragging their heels on offering even a lick of support against the Hitlerites. "Does anyone else know?"

My partner nodded across the fire at Kitsenko, still singing as the men beat time. "Only Lyonya."

That surprised me. "He's that trusted a friend?"

"The best," Kostia said, echoing what Kitsenko had said to me earlier.

"Well, I won't tell, either." I bumped Kostia's shoulder with my own, not knowing how to answer such a tremendous gesture of faith except to make light of it all.

"Just don't go singing 'The Rose of Tralee' where any of the other officers can hear, eh?"

He smiled.

"So where exactly is New York?" I asked, mentally searching a map of the American east coast. "North of Washington, but where?"

"I'm not too sure. I'd like to see someday. Where do you want to go, after the war?"

There is no after *for me,* I thought. *I won't be going anywhere but a grave.*

It was the first time I let myself admit what I'd come to believe: that I was never going to make it home. That this war, at least for me, was the end of the road.

CHAPTER 13

My memoir, the official version: Snipers must be calm in order to succeed.

My memoir, the unofficial version: Snipers must make themselves calm in order to succeed, and that is why women are good at sharpshooting. Because there is not a woman alive who has not learned how to eat rage in order to appear calm.

"NO," LIEUTENANT DROMIN snapped at me. "You cannot have that relic Vartanov in your platoon. The motherland is not so desperate we will stuff decrepit old grandfathers into uniform and send them tottering out toward the enemy on canes."

I took another long, calm swallow of fury, keeping my voice reasonable. "He has requested permission to join, and his knowledge of the local terrain makes him invaluable." My written petition to accept the old ranger into my platoon had been denied, and I was at the command post to plead his case. "It was with his scouting assistance that my men wiped out twelve Hitlerites in no-man's-land over the last two days."

"I heard the resulting mortar attack from the other side," Lieutenant Kitsenko said from where he was leaning against Dromin's desk. "Quite a concert they put on. Bit heavy on the brass; blame Wagner for that—"

"Who?" Dromin said irritably. "Never mind," he added as Kitsenko opened his mouth.

Kitsenko just laughed, arms folded across his chest, cap pushed at a cheerful angle over a rumple of fair hair. I remembered Lena saying *I'm having a bite of that!* when she eyed his shoulders outside the banya, and I was trying not to notice the shoulders now. If you get distracted by a man's shoulders, it's better if he's not the new commander of your company in the middle of a war zone, and it's even better if you're wearing a nice dress so you can be admired back. I was just back from a morning's hunt and was wearing my camouflage jacket, which had been draped and stitched all over with tendrils of garland thorn, so I looked like an ambulatory bush.

"I say let Vartanov in if he's keen to serve," Kitsenko was saying. "Maybe he last saw service under Catherine the Great, but who cares? If there's still sap in the tree, it may as well wear a uniform."

"Your company, your decision," Dromin said with an air of washing his hands of the matter. "On your head be it when he dodders off a cliff. As for you, Comrade Sergeant Pavlichenko . . ." I could see his eyes wandering with distaste over my camouflage and my rifle, which had been bundled and thorn-twined until it looked like a load of kindling. Clearly he did not find my horticultural couture appealing, and clearly he thought I should care about this. "You will represent 2nd Company tomorrow afternoon at the command post of the 54th Regiment in the Kamyshly gully, when Major General Kolomiets will be presenting government awards."

Dromin had a spiteful gleam in his eye, and I bit back a curse. An afternoon ceremony meant I'd get no sleep after a night spent scouting, digging, and camouflaging a nest in no-man's-land, and a morning spent tensely waiting for a shot. Instead of toppling into my bedroll I'd have to get sleeked up in my parade uniform and make the trek across the gully all so I could stand and yawn through hours' worth of speeches . . .

But I'd have Vartanov in my platoon, and he was worth losing a few hours of sleep. "Thank you, Comrade Lieutenant," I said, saluting smartly, and rustled out in my leafy splendor.

Kitsenko came out behind me and sauntered along at my side. "I'll give you a ride in the staff car tomorrow," he said. "I've been sent along to the ceremony as well. Giving you a lift will make up for all the droning."

"Why do you want to give me a lift?" I swatted a tendril of garland thorn out of my eye.

"So I can steal a kiss," he said. "Last time you kissed me. I feel I should return the favor."

"I knew that kiss was going to come back and haunt me," I retorted.

"Hopefully your daydreams, not your nightmares. Would you shoot me if I laid a smack on you, Comrade Senior Sergeant Pavlichenko?" Kitsenko went on, grinning.

"I might." I paused to yank some of the vines off my shoulders, making my tone polite but unyielding. Flirtation is all very well in a more civilized place—intermission at the opera, say, while wearing yellow satin instead of a shrub. For a moment I wished that was exactly where I was. But we weren't at the opera, and I didn't have the excuse now of not knowing he was my superior officer. "Thank you, Comrade Lieutenant, but I can make my own way to the ceremony tomorrow."

"Are you sure? I've always wanted to attend an awards ceremony with a hedge on my arm. We'll be a very dashing couple; I sprig up nicely as a spruce."

My lips twitched despite myself, so I busied myself pulling more bits of camouflage off. "Thank you for speaking up for Vartanov back there. He'll be delighted to learn he can officially join as a soldier of the Red Army." Actually, Vartanov had no love for the Red Army, the motherland, or anything else he considered an oppressor of the Ukrainian people, but he hated Hitlerites more than he hated Comrade Stalin. "He's longing to kill fascists," I added with complete honesty.

"I like the old bastard," Kitsenko said cheerfully, hands in the pockets of his overcoat. "He could sneak up behind Father Frost and cut his throat, you can tell. Glad he's on our side. What's that?" he continued as I disentangled a flask and a rubber tube from my ammunition pouch. "An enema bag?"

"Another tool from the sniper's bag of tricks. Vartanov showed me a trail down to a very small section of no-man's-land—it overlooks a dirt road running within half a kilometer of the German front line. When I fill this with water"—I held up the flask—"and then bury it in the earth around my nest and run a tube through the mouth of the flask up to my ear, I can hear the rumble in the ground that means motorcycles or staff cars are approaching up the road." I'd lain all night and half the morning next to Kostia in a shallow trench, covered by a scrim of wild rose vines and hornbeam bushes, passing the tube back and forth until we heard the vibrations of a good-sized convoy. "Kostia and I shot the wheels out on the staff car and downed three officers and a gunner."

"You really are terrifying. Are you sure I can't kiss you?"

I was tempted to let him, remembering that he'd smelled like pine, and it annoyed me that I remembered that so clearly. "Quite sure." I resumed walking, trailing vines.

"Why not?" He kept pace easily at my side. "Do you not like junior lieutenants?"

"I shoot junior lieutenants. I shot one this morning. Iron Cross, acne."

"Is it junior lieutenants named Alexei, then?"

"The man I married at fifteen is a junior lieutenant named Alexei, Comrade Lieutenant, and I'm not very fond of him." I hadn't seen hide nor hair of Alexei Pavlichenko since arriving in Sevastopol—no surprise given that he'd be up to his elbows in blood and disinfectant in the hospital battalion. As long as I didn't get wounded, surely I wouldn't *have* to see him again. Now there was an incentive to dodge German bullets.

"My nickname is Lyonya," Kitsenko pointed out. "Because my mother wanted to name me Leonid and not Alexei, and *Lyonya* was how she got around my father. If you'd use that, there shouldn't be any negative associations with my name."

"Nicknames are for—"

"Comrades in arms, yes. Do I need to rustle up a battle for us to march into by tomorrow noon?" My company commander squinted at the sky as if checking the hour. "The timing's tight, but—"

"Comrade Lieutenant, I prefer not to fraternize with officers," I said firmly. "I mistook you for a civilian when we first met, but that doesn't change the fact that regulations—"

"I prefer not to fraternize with sergeants. Just exceedingly lovely hedges. I dated a hawthorn for a while; oooh, she was prickly. I had better luck with a viburnum, but her affection withered. A garland thorn, now—"

"Good afternoon, Comrade Lieutenant . . ." and I marched into the latrine where he couldn't follow, before he could see that despite myself, I was smiling.

"DEATH BY DRONING." It doesn't matter whether you're attending a Komsomol discussion of "The Communist Youth of Tomorrow" or an Order of the Red Banner presented in honor of the gallant defense of Odessa: any meeting of officials held anywhere in the motherland always includes speeches. I used to think that no one could beat Soviet men for endless speeches, but when I came to America, I realized men of *all* nationalities like the sound of their own voices, especially the kind of man who spends long hours behind a podium. Whether in a Washington park or a Sevastopol battle zone, it's all the same: after the first speech you're afraid the boredom will kill you; after the fifth speech, you're praying it will.

To keep awake at the awards ceremony the following day, I mentally thumbed through the pages of my dissertation and wondered if there was any way, here on the front line, to get it retyped. Too many trenches and sniper nests had left the pages soft and creased, and my section introducing the Pereyaslav Council had been splattered with blood when Kostia took a splinter wound across the back of his neck. He hadn't been badly hurt—he stripped off his jacket and offered up his neck so I could stitch the cut myself, disinfecting the needle with vodka so he wouldn't have to register at the medical battalion—but my poor dissertation, like Bogdan Khmelnitsky, had been through the wars . . . I snapped out of my musing when it came time to deliver my own (short!) speech of congratulations on behalf of 2nd Company.

Lieutenant Kitsenko delivered a longer speech, just the right combination of official language and wry wit, which brought grins to faces. He was good at that, as I'd had a chance to observe by now. It was a rare officer who could be friendly without losing his authority, and I was willing to concede Kitsenko had the gift. I'd seen him break up a brawl between a cluster of soldiers with fast efficiency, and rather than put them all on punishment duty, he delivered a combination lecture of scolding and joking that had them half laughing, half cringing, and vowing like naughty children that no, Comrade Lieutenant, they'd never do it again, Comrade Lieutenant.

The speeches were over at last, and then it was just watching ribbons and stars being pinned to tunics. One of the decorated soldiers was a woman, a pretty machine gunner who had helped five hundred fascists into their graves. *Good for you,* I thought approvingly, watching her beam as the Order of the Red Banner was fixed to her breast. Then the line shifted, and I saw Alexei Pavlichenko in line to be honored. I wasn't sure what ribbon or star they were pinning to his tunic, but there was something about *exceptional efficiency in the restoration of the wounded to the front lines* and I saw the pleased curve of his lips. Of course he'd been decorated. Men like Alexei always got the right kind of awards. He'd climbed fast at his hospital as a civilian; he'd climb fast in the hospital battalion as a lieutenant.

I made a quick escape when the assembly was dismissed. Somehow I knew Alexei would be looking for me—he'd have lined me up like a trick shot the moment he saw me step forward to make my speech—and I made a bolt into some tangled brush at the side of the makeshift parade ground. "Mila?" His voice floated over the air, the voice that still had the power to make my teeth grit, and I sank down noiselessly against a toppled tree. I'd outwait him, sit here until he got tired of the game and went back to his battalion. After so many stakeouts I could outwait Father Time, much less an irksome husband.

I didn't dare smoke until I saw Alexei's fair head move away. Lighting up and inhaling gratefully, I remembered what a prig I'd been when I came to the front, turning my nose up with a sniffy *I don't smoke.* I looked back on that woman—the library researcher, the graduate student, the aspiring historian—and barely knew her. I'd been nearly six months now in the school of war.

"This is the first time I've ever seen a woman smoke a pipe," Kitsenko said behind me. I could have told him I preferred to be alone, but if I was sitting with my company commander, my husband couldn't hunker down if he found me, so I didn't object when Kostia's friend leaned against the tree at my side. It had nothing, absolutely nothing, to do with his shoulders.

"Where'd you get that?" he asked, nodding at the pipe in my hand as he took out a pack of cigarettes.

"Vartanov. He gave it to me after our first sortie." It was an old Turkish pipe carved of pear root, with an amber mouthpiece—a beautiful thing, clearly the last object of value he possessed. I preferred cigarettes, but he'd offered it with such fierce, tremulous pride, I knew better than to give it back. It was a decoration earned and won; I'd take it over Machine Gunner Onilova's Order of the Red

Banner any day. "I'm trying to learn how to pack it, so I can at least use it where he can see."

"Isn't that shag tobacco a bit strong?" Kitsenko lit up a Kazbek cigarette.

"I've got used to it."

"It's funny," Kitsenko said, exhaling smoke into the frosty sky. "Good-looking women usually don't smoke pipes."

"In other words, I must be ugly and unusual." I said it with a grin, because I was feeling anything but ugly right now. In fact I was feeling delightfully feminine for the first time in months. Maybe since we'd first laid eyes on each other, flirting at the banya's door.

"The fact that you're *unusual* is well known to the entire 54th by now." Kitsenko blew a smoke ring. "The question of looks, well, that's complex. Ideals are dictated by time, fashion, custom. For me"—he looked at me very seriously—"I've never met a prettier hedge."

I couldn't help it; I burst out laughing. He punched the air as though he'd won a victory lap.

"Why are you trying so hard with me?" I asked, still laughing, giving up on the pipe. "There may not be many women in the regiment, but there are enough. And they're all softer targets than me."

"Less interesting targets."

"Why?" I took the cigarette he offered. "Do you have some romantic idea about snipers? Felling the woman who's felled more than two hundred men?" I was starting to encounter this notion among some of the more idiotic young officers. Some vaguely articulated notion that a woman who had killed so many in cold blood had to be, I don't know, hot under her knapsack?

"That's the thing." Kitsenko surveyed me, thoughtful. "A woman sniper with two hundred marks in her tally—it conjures up a very specific image. And you . . ."

"I match your imaginings?"

"Not in the slightest. I pictured someone a bit like Kostia's half sister. I met her last year when I visited him in Irkutsk; no idea how I survived the experience. You'll have to get Kostia to tell you about his complicated family history, but his father didn't exactly marry his mother. The old man lives out on Lake Baikal with a pack of Kostia's half brothers and sisters, one of whom came to Irkutsk for flight school—"

"Is this going somewhere, Comrade Lieutenant?" I asked, out to sea.

"Bear with me. So Kostia and I bumped into this half sister Nina in Irkutsk; he barely knew her himself, but he introduced me. That girl just about gave me nightmares. Little feral thing with eyes like razors, practically picking her teeth with a human bone, absolutely capable of tearing your throat out with her bare hands. That," Kitsenko concluded, "is the kind of woman you imagine when you hear the words *woman sniper with two hundred kills*. Some wild thing from the Siberian wastes with icy eyes and no more conscience than a wolf."

"What leads you to conclude that?" I tilted my head. "Why imagine *that's* what a woman sniper would be—cold, unemotional, savage? You don't know me or any other woman sniper, so what makes you think we have to be a certain way? Look a certain way?"

"It's just surprising to meet a woman with two hundred lives to her name and find a history student with the world's most boring dissertation in her pack and the softest brown eyes ever to paint crosshairs on a man's heart."

I didn't know what to say to that, except that my own heart was thumping in a way it usually didn't bother to do unless I was just back from a hunt. "How do you know anything about my dissertation?" I finally managed to say. "For your information, it is not at all boring."

"Your dissertation is famous throughout the entire *company*, Sergeant. Brave men leap into live fire zones when they see you haul it out. Soldiers with the Order of Lenin falter and grow pale—"

"Insulting my dissertation, now that's a sure way into a woman's bedroll!"

His smile quirked. "Did you miss the bit about your eyes?"

"Even if you have very pretty compliments about my eyes, I'm not interested in being anyone's front-line fling. For all I know, you've got a wife at home, or a fiancée, or a whole string of would-be-either."

"I'm not seeing any other hedges at the moment, on my honor. I'm a very monogamous sort of shrub."

"They all say that."

"I suppose they do," he admitted.

"Then sometimes if you say no, they threaten to demote you."

"I won't do that, Lyudmila. If you say no from now until the war's end, I won't do that." He cocked his head. "You've really been threatened with *demotion* if you didn't—"

"Of course I have." Twice, in fact. I'd been less concerned with being demoted and more concerned about being raped by my own officers if I continued to say no. Such things happened. Lena patched those women up afterward in the hospital battalion, but of course no report was ever made.

"With your record, you should have been standing up with that little machine gunner getting an Order of the Red Banner of your own, not fending off demotion from your own officers." For the first time since I'd met him, this lighthearted lieutenant looked angry. It took the form of a cloud with him, as though rain gusts had rolled behind those blue eyes and broad high cheekbones and crystallized into a storm front. "I'll put your name up. With a tally like yours—"

I shrugged, drawing deep on the cigarette. "I'll take any decoration I've earned, but that's not why I do it."

"Why do you do it, then?"

"Really, now. Would you ask any of the men that?"

"I would, and I do," he said, surprising me. "I ask all new men why they volunteered, if they did. I want to know who the patriots are, who are the fanatics are, who the desperate are . . ."

"But they'll all say the same thing. *I do it for Comrade Stalin and the motherland.*"

"Yes, but it's how they say it—that still tells me something." He nudged me. "So why did you enlist?"

"For Comrade Stalin and the motherland," I intoned.

He gave me a serious look, waiting. I hesitated.

"For my son." That I admitted it surprised me. Hardly anyone outside my platoon knew I had a son. I didn't talk about Slavka; *couldn't* talk about him. It felt like I was soiling him, bringing his name into this reeking world of death and mud and gunsmoke. "If I don't fight, he won't have a world to grow up in."

Kitsenko tapped ash off his cigarette. "Do you have a picture?"

I pulled it out, surprising myself again. "My Slavka." A formal photo taken when he was seven, sitting upright with his favorite wooden boat clutched in his hands, dark hair brushed sleek. "He looks nothing like that now," I said softly. "So much taller, getting gawky . . . at least he was when I last saw him. Who knows how much he's changed by now?" If I was killed here—and more often these days, I thought *when* I was killed here—I'd never learn the answer to that question.

If Lieutenant Kitsenko had attempted to put his arm around me then, I would have bristled and snarled like a badger. He just gazed at the photograph, pretending not to notice me fighting for self-control. "A beautiful boy," he said, handing the photograph back when I had my face straightened out. "He looks like you."

"I . . ." Another fight to push the tears back as I tucked my son's picture back into my breast pocket. "I promised him I'd think about him every day. But days go by when I don't think of him at all. Does that make me a bad mother? Even—" I had to stop, breathing unsteadily. "Even when I'm collecting leaves and flowers to send him in my letters, I don't think about him. I *can't* think about him, not here. He doesn't *belong* here. So I put him away in a locked room in my mind, and I seal it off."

"You do what you have to. We all do." Kitsenko cocked his head down at me. "How old is he?"

"Nine." I could see Kitsenko doing the math. "I was very young when he was born, yes." Hearing my voice grow brittle as I dashed at my eyes. "Too young."

"I couldn't help notice a Lieutenant Pavlichenko in the receiving line for a decoration." My company commander exhaled smoke. "Your former husband?"

I didn't answer, not wanting to get into the complicated history of the divorce that never quite happened. I just took a long, savage draw of smoke down into my lungs. We leaned against the tree side by side until the last of the voices faded in the distance, the last of the cars drove away, and then Kitsenko tossed his cigarette butt down and ground it out. "I'll give you a lift back."

"I'll make my own way." If Kostia rode back with his company commander, everyone would know they were friends when rank wasn't in the way. If I rode back with my company commander, everyone would assume he was sleeping with me.

"I'll drop you off two hundred meters from camp so you can walk in alone," he said, reading my mind perfectly.

I hesitated. "Thank you."

His cheeks creased. "About that kiss—"

"You're not getting a kiss!"

"Is that a wager? Remember, I used to be a bookie."

"You'll have to catch me off guard, and I'm never off guard."

"I'm patient. You can't always have that rubber tube in your ear."

"Sneaking up on a trained sniper to steal *anything* she doesn't want to give you seems quite a stupid idea to me." I saluted. "Good luck with that, Comrade Lieutenant."

"Ah, but you're smiling . . ."

CHAPTER 14

My memoir, the official version: At ten past six in the morning of December 17, 1941, ten days after the Americans entered the war, the Hitlerites unleashed a fury of artillery and shellfire on Sevastopol's defense positions. The intent was to split our defensive front and come out at Sevastopol in four days exactly—on December 21, the sixth-month anniversary of war between Germany and the Soviet Union.

My memoir, the unofficial version: My luck ran out.

FLICKERS, LIGHT AND dark. Pain, dark red and midnight black. Confusion, a muffling blanket.

I couldn't move.

—armored transport approaching, followed by two battalions of riflemen and submachine gunners—The crackle of the report comes in from the military outposts. The men of my company flow into position. Orders—from Dromin? From Kitsenko? *Soldiers in the sniper platoon to stand with the machine gunners. Pavlichenko*—that's Kitsenko speaking, his hand on my shoulder, eyes blue sparks in a gunsmoke-grimed face—*you take the concealed trench covering the flank, aim for machine-gun nests and mortar crews . . .*

I blinked blood out of my lashes. I still couldn't see, couldn't move. I lay on my stomach, pinned flat.

—The machine-gun nest, take it out—The order, screaming out in a voice that cracks hysterically over the din. More screams as the armored transport vehicle slinks into the clearing on its caterpillar tracks, the machine gun chittering like some malevolent insect behind the armored shield on the cab roof, crawling toward the broken

trunk of a young elm and raking 1st Battalion's trenches with bullets. I hear a roar of crashing timber from a trench giving way, a man shrieking in pain . . .

I blinked blood again. Something trickled across my side, something weighted me down across the back. Kostia. Where was Kostia? My platoon? *Kostia.*

—let me come with you, Kostia shouting directly into my ear to be heard over the din, catching my arm as I head for the concealed trench, but I point him back toward the platoon. *You have the platoon, take them*—Vartanov open-mouthed, trying not to tremble in the din and smoke of his first pitched battle; some of the others looking on the verge of bolting unless they have a steadying hand. *Kostia, TAKE THEM*—and I dive into the shallow trench half covered by the fallen leaves of an acacia tree. The armored transport droning forward, spitting death; I rack a round into place and line up my shot, and I have less than sixty seconds . . .

Blink, blink. I lay pinned in the dark like a butterfly to a board, tasting blood and iron on my lips, but my mind helpfully produced the calculations I'd run in a matter of frenzied seconds just a few minutes—hours? days?—before. *Heads of the machine gunners over two meters above ground level; rifle propped on a twenty-centimeter parapet; between aiming line and weapon horizon, a 35-degree angle . . . distance of two hundred meters to moving target; bullet traveling two hundred meters in .25 seconds; in that time target would have traveled four meters . . . adjust windage drum on sights . . .* Calculations had coiled and crossed as my internal clock wound the shot-count down to midnight.

—Fire. My bullets spanging through the eye slots of the armored shield; one body falling—two. A German lieutenant actually climbing out of the cab to see what has hit his gunners. What does he have to fear, after all, when he is covered by the shield and all the Soviet fire

is coming from the trenches in front? My bullet comes from the side, takes him in the temple . . .

Blink. I still couldn't see, but I tried to get my hands under me, push myself up. A wave of pain roared up my spine, flattening me into the earth. Dirt, was I still on the ground, in my trench, or—?

—*Scharfschütze, Scharfschütze*—is that the German word for sniper; is that the cry going up from the command post of the German reconnaissance battalion? Gunfire suddenly thrashing the trees over my head, German bullets plucking the ground, trying to find my hiding place. I grab my rifle and roll up out of my trench to the left, once, twice—there's another, deeper sniper's nest dug just a few paces over; one more roll and I'll drop into it—

But the world drops on me first, a shell that rips the air and swats me sideways like a swipe from some massive clawed beast. I have time, feeling myself flung up among the clods of earth and shards of trees branches to think *No, no, not wounded* again—

But I am. Which I realize when the veiling cold brings me back to full consciousness, when I blink the blood from my eyes, and finally come back to my torn body in the falling grip of night.

THE FIRST THING that really came into focus was my rifle. My Mosin-Nagant with her shining lines looped in camouflaging layers of garland thorn . . . the wooden stock was cracked in half, the barrel bent, the telescopic sight shivered into splinters of metal and glass. She'd never fire another a shot, my lovely rifle who had sung to me so sweetly, and I pulled her shattered body against me and began to weep numbly. I could move my arms but nothing else—the crown of an acacia tree overhead had been torn loose by shellfire and plunged down to pin me against the ground. The pain stabbed between my spine and my right shoulder blade; I couldn't tell if it came from impaling branches or mortar wounds, but I couldn't rise or wriggle or reach around to stanch my own bleeding. I could only lie in the mud clutching my broken rifle, icy twilight falling softly around me like a pitiless mist, and feel blood pooling under me as the daylight faded. My undershirt and tunic were drenched.

So quiet. The trees rustled almost noiselessly; the tide of battle had clearly swept on toward the next sector—I could hear shellfire echoing from somewhere distant. *My platoon,* I thought, my regimental mates—how many were dead this time? How far had the Fritzes managed to push? If the Germans found me here, I'd never be able to put a bullet through my brain before they took me—I couldn't reach down past my own shoulder; the TT pistol at my belt might as well have been in Moscow.

This is where I die, I thought, still clutching my useless rifle. Trees tossing overhead against the winter sky, stripped black and leafless from mortar fire, casting strange shadows on the ground in front of my blurring eyes . . . I saw my mother leaning toward me to smooth the hair off my face; then the twist of shadow turned into my father, saying sternly, *Belovs don't retreat!* I wanted to tell him I'd tried, that I was still a Belov even if I had to drag Alexei's *Pavlichenko* behind me like a poisoned anchor—but my father was gone before I could tell him, and it was Slavka who now stood before me. My little walrus in his red Young Pioneers kerchief, turning toward me with his hands full of all the dried leaves and flowers I'd sent him. *Mama?* No more plump walrus cheeks; the bones of his face were coming through to show the adolescent he'd soon become, but I'd never see it. I'd never see *him*, not in this life. I was bleeding out.

"Slavka—" I managed to get through my blood-gritted teeth, but when I blinked he was gone. He was gone, and I saw a man's dark shadow, the sun's last shiver of daylight touching a gleam off his helmet. Lieutenant Kitsenko, an overcoat over his uniform and a submachine gun slung over one shoulder.

"Mila," he was saying. "*Mila,* tell me where it hurts—"

Everywhere. Soldiers behind him, but they were just shadows helping shift the splintered acacia. *Don't bother,* I wanted to tell them, *I'm done.* Maybe I'd finally get a medal, something posthumous my son could remember me by.

"Don't talk horseshit, you're not allowed to die yet." Kitsenko again, turning me over and sliding his arms under my knees and shoulders. "You haven't submitted the necessary paperwork to your company commander, and that's me, so dying's going to have to wait. Hold steady—" and he was lifting me up, carrying me back toward the trenches.

"*Fuck.*" Lena Paliy's tired exhortation came at me the same instant I felt shears slitting seams down my back, my coat and undershirt peeling away like a bloody carapace. "It's dug clear down her back—"

"I can have her at the medical battalion in twenty minutes. Fighting in my sector's lulled." Kitsenko again. "I have Dromin's car."

"That prick lent you his car?"

"Let me put it this way: if you bandage her fast and I drive faster, I can have it back before he realizes it was ever gone."

Jouncing over shell-pocked roads, my strapped torso a blaze of agony. Kitsenko's hand on my lolling head when he could spare it from the wheel. "Come on, Mila, you're not letting a few splinters take you down . . . talk to me, tell me about Bogdan Khmelnitsky. If you die, who's going to drone at me about the Pereyaslav Council?"

A brief side-slip into unconsciousness, and then the shadowed hell of Medical Battalion 47, a complex maze of bandaging rooms, isolation wards, and sickrooms dug into underground tunnels like a kingdom of moles. "She needs blood—" a doctor's voice, weary. "Fuck, how many more coming in? The blood reserves are—"

I don't need blood, I tried to say, *I'm dying.*

Kitsenko was rolling up his sleeve. "I saw her tags; we're the same blood type. Tap a vein."

"She'd be better off getting stabilized and dispatched to unoccupied territory. The next transport ship—"

"My company loses Lyudmila Pavlichenko, they'll riot. Get her an operating table, then a bed here."

"But—"

"You need blood? Her whole battalion will be in here rolling up their sleeves, just *keep her here.*" An operating theater: blinding lights overhead, four surgeons slaving over four separate tables. The last thing I saw as I was wheeled in, before I tumbled down a tunnel of darkness, was a man shrieking as a burly aide held him down and an artery gouted; an exhaustion-slumped surgeon turning with blood down the front of his smock. Even with my hearing receding into the black after my eyesight, I recognized the voice: "*Kroshka*, what are you doing here?"

Oh, for the love of—

And I was gone.

THE FIRST FACE I saw when I woke up was Alexei Pavlichenko's, and I recoiled so hard he nearly had to peel me off the ceiling.

"Not very flattering, *kroshka.*" He put a hand to the base of my throat and pushed me back flat on the hospital cot, sitting closer beside me than I would have liked. Of course, if he'd been sitting on a bed in Vladivostok he would have been closer than I liked. "Considering I saved your life three nights ago."

I started to say that it was Kitsenko and Lena who had saved my life—he by carrying me out of the front lines, she by strapping me up so I didn't bleed out on the way here—but I went into a fit of coughing instead, every cough a stab of agony. Alexei took my pulse as I coughed, counting beats, watching me hack with a detached expression.

"How bad is it?" I managed to gasp out at last. "My wound?" I had about as much strength as a kitten; my elbows were pocked with needle marks from blood transfusions; and my back and shoulder felt like they'd been dipped in acid, but if it was three days later, I didn't seem to be dying very fast. I yanked up my blankets, realizing that I was freezing cold.

"A splinter the length of your foot plowed from your right scapula to your spine," Alexei said matter-of-factly. "A few centimeters deeper, you'd be dead or paralyzed. I dug it out, stitched you up, pumped blood into you."

"Thank you," I said, in part because he paused pointedly, in part because he'd without doubt done a fine job. Alexei Pavlichenko might be a bastard, but he was also a superb surgeon.

"It was the blood loss that nearly did you in," he continued, noting my various vital signs. "That lieutenant who brought you in, he dropped about a liter straight into your veins . . . who is he?"

I ignored that, trying to sit up. "The German attack, is it—"

"Ongoing, but we're holding them off. Von Manstein won't be toasting the new year in Sevastopol as he planned."

"When can I get back to my company?"

Alexei pushed me back down. "It'll be two weeks before your stitches are even out."

"Ten days," I rasped. "On the eleventh I start ripping them out with the nearest broken bottle."

"You would, wouldn't you?" My husband regarded me, thoughtful. "On the boat I thought you were having me on, all that guff about one hundred and eighty-seven kills. I've heard things since then . . . You weren't joking after all, were you?"

I pressed my lips together, looking up at the ceiling.

"What is it now, *kroshka*? Over two hundred? Considering the little breadcrumb I once married, I can hardly—"

"You will please address me by my rank, Comrade Lieutenant Pavlichenko."

"Just teasing, you never could take a joke—"

"Is our problem patient making a nuisance of herself?" Lena, to my intense relief, breezed up with a basin of water. "I'll check her stitches, Comrade Lieutenant, they need you back in the operating theater."

Another long thoughtful look, and Alexei strode off in a parade-ground swing. His absence seemed to widen and lighten the whole room; suddenly I was aware of the other cots in my row, the patients stone-still or thrashing under their blankets, the smell of antiseptic and copper. Suddenly I could draw a deep breath, even if it made my stitches feel as though they'd been doused in fuel and set alight.

"All the surgeons in the battalion, why is he the one who ends up working on me?" I demanded, coughing again.

"Because he asked to be alerted if you were brought in. All the doctors do that for the soldiers they know. Same with the orderlies—why do you think it's always me checking your stitches? Speaking of which, turn over." Lena helped me onto my side, pretending she didn't notice the hiss of pain I couldn't suppress. "So that's the husband, eh? He's a looker. Half the women in the medical battalion are trying to get in his pants."

"They can have him." I braced, feeling the cold air on my naked back, the bandages unwinding. "Does he ever give you any trouble?"

"I have a feeling I'm too old for him," Lena said, very dry. "He's always chasing the young, dewy, wide-eyed ones. He did pretty work on these stitches, though, I'll say that. The other surgeons, if they're young they're inexperienced, and if they're old they're drunks. Your Alexei did twenty-hour shifts this past week and never fumbled a single incision."

Cold conceited bastards make good surgeons, I thought. "The attack—do you know anything about 2nd Company? My platoon?"

"Your partner came by to give blood, stalking around like a wolf until they said you weren't going to bleed out on him. He left to take command of the platoon, but he gave me this for the moment you woke up." Lena passed me a folded square of paper. "The casualties."

Bless you, Kostia. I scanned the names in his handwriting, which was small and square. I'd never seen it before—strange how you could fight beside someone for months, know every intimate detail about them from how they yawned to how they exhaled to how they tapped their fingers against a thigh to expel fear, yet not know what their handwriting was like . . . I breathed shaky relief. Only one death, my youngest recruit, and the rest unscathed except for minor wounds. Old Vartanov had made it, and thickheaded Fyodor, and Kostia . . . and me.

I still didn't entirely believe I'd made it. I'd been so sure my time was up.

"You'll heal faster than you have any right to," Lena was saying cheerfully, bandaging me back up. "You lead a charmed life, you lucky bitch."

"Charmed." I eased back into my hard pillow, closing my eyes. I loved Lena, but right now I didn't want to talk to anyone, even her. *Lucky.*

It was something people kept saying, over the next week. Vartanov said it, tugging his gray beard: *The feet of a lynx and the luck of the devil!* Fyodor said it, wringing my hands between his huge paws. The rest of my platoon said it when they managed to trek in on their off-hours, giving news from the front. "Don't you say it," I warned Kostia when he appeared. "Don't you tell me how *lucky* I am."

The corner of his mouth tilted, and he unslung a gleaming Mosin-Nagant from his shoulder. "Your new rifle. I insisted on a Three Line. They tried to stick you with a Sveta."

"Who on earth thinks a rifle with a muzzle flash like a searchlight is a good weapon for a sniper?"

"That's what I said." He sat at the foot of my bed without another word, taking out his Finnish combat knife and needle file. I could see he'd already put considerable time into making it battle-ready. He'd watched me strip and oil my old rifle hundreds of times; he knew I'd removed the wood along the length of the handguard groove so that it no longer touched the barrel; he knew I preferred to insert padding between the receiver and the magazine; he knew I kept the tip of the gunstock filed down. I nearly wept, watching his hands work, and felt the words hovering at the tip of my tongue: *When I get out of this bed and take that rifle up, I'm going to die.*

But I couldn't say it to Kostia; he was my partner, my shadow, the one who was supposed to keep me from dying. When my fate came for me, he was going to blame himself—so I let the words wither, letting myself sink instead into Kostia's snow-soft silence whenever he visited my hospital cot, sliding in and out of a doze, feeling the comforting weight of the new Three Line's barrel against my leg as he worked on it through each of his visits, patiently making it mine. When a leader has doubts about herself in wartime, even if she's just a sergeant, she can't reveal them to her men. I'd learned that, leading my platoon.

I shouldn't reveal such doubts to my officers, either, but Kitsenko had a way of surprising things out of me.

"You're not dying," he said from the doorway on my sixth day in hospital, startling me as I frowned at a bowl of broth. "Have some chocolate," he added, taking out a paper-wrapped bar as he came to sit on a too-low stool by my cot. "Proper Belgian stuff. One of my sergeants plucked it from the pack of a dead German lieutenant yesterday afternoon. I pulled rank unashamedly and stole it for you."

I blinked, surprised to see him here. "The German attack, aren't you—"

"The attack on the 54th eased yesterday. I'm free and easy until they come pulsing back at us like the maggots they are." His face was grained and his uniform rumpled and splattered as though he'd come right from the front lines, but his smile was still cheerful as he looked down at me. "You're not dying," he repeated, unwrapping the chocolate for me.

"Why do you keep saying that?"

"Because when I was hauling you off the front lines, you wouldn't believe me. Kept muttering, *I'm dead, I'm dying.* I thought I'd try to pound the truth into you now that you're a bit more conscious. You're not dying," he finished, and broke a square off the bar.

I slipped it into my mouth. Belgian chocolate, the real stuff, not the chalky blocks of army chocolate I was used to. The sweetness in my mouth brought tears to my eyes. "Maybe this time didn't kill me," I found myself saying, almost inaudibly. "The next one will."

I expected him to say something hearty: *You'll bag many more for the motherland, don't you worry!* Or perhaps I'd get a stern reprimand about defeatism. Instead he broke off another piece of chocolate and pushed it at me, asking, "How do you figure that?"

I chewed, swallowed. Tucked my ragged hair behind my ear. "They say the third wound kills you."

"Who's *they*, and who says *they* know everything?"

"You know what I mean."

"Well, your count's off. This is already your fourth time injured."

"The first two don't count." An impatient shake of my head. "A concussion, then a strained hip . . . those were little nothing wounds. The last one was the first, really. Now this. The next one—"

"But last week you were convinced you'd be dead on this one," Kitsenko pointed out. "So it sounds to me like you're changing your story. Are you so determined to be a martyr that you've forgotten how to count?"

I tried giving him a sour look, but it was hard with a mouth full of chocolate.

"You're not dying," he said. "What can I say to make you believe that?"

"I can't—shake it." My voice came out thready, uneven. "Maybe it's not the number of wounds. Third, fourth . . . at some point, I'm done. My luck's almost out."

"I don't think that's how luck works, Pavlichenko." He pushed his cap back on his rumpled fair hair. "You're not issued a certain amount, like bread in the chow line."

"Run the numbers," I said brutally. "I can calculate wind shifts by the milliradian; you think I can't run the odds on whether I'll ever see my son again?"

"I think you have a good many more dead Nazis to go before that has any chance of happening." Kitsenko pushed another square of chocolate into my hand. "Here. My mother always said when a woman is upset, give her chocolate and tell her she's beautiful. In your case, I think I can amend that to give you chocolate and tell you you're dangerous. You are beautiful," he added, "but something tells me you'll be more comforted by the thought that you're still dangerous. And that the Hitlerites know it."

Maybe the compliment shouldn't have mattered at a moment like this, but it did. I hiccupped a laugh.

"We all have that feeling from time to time," he added. "The feeling that we're doomed. It comes and goes, like fever. I had it when I first came to the front—I thought the first battle would kill me, and I'm still here. Kostia had a bad patch in Odessa at the end, he told me, convinced he'd be cut down before the evacuation."

"He didn't tell me that."

"He needs to be invincible for you, just as you are for him. And now you're having a bad case of the forebodings, and that's perfectly natural. You've dealt so much death, you feel it breathing at your shoulder."

"You're going to tell me it's *not* breathing at my shoulder?"

"It's breathing at all our shoulders. We could all die tomorrow. So eat your chocolate, Pavlichenko." He gave me the last square. I rolled it around my mouth, savoring the last drop of sweetness, not sure what to feel. Except . . . lighter, a very little. For everyone else—my family, in my letters; my men, in my platoon; even Kostia, in our partnership—I had to be invincible. But before Kitsenko, I could be afraid. Be tired. Be *human*.

The relief of that stabbed so sweetly.

"Mila," I said at last.

"What?" He linked his hands between his knees.

"We've fought together now." I lay back in my hard cot. "Call me Mila."

He smiled. "If you call me Lyonya."

THE SOVIET DELEGATION: DAY 1

August 27, 1942
WASHINGTON, D.C.

CHAPTER 15

Say, Mrs. Pavlichenko, can we call you Lyudmila? *Pavlichenko,* that's a mouthful!"

The marksman watched the hungry ripple of curiosity that rose up as the girl sniper entered the first-floor White House dining room. Another barrage of camera flashes—he hid his face behind his own borrowed camera—and through the lens he saw her flinch. Lyudmila Pavlichenko was not a tall woman, and she looked smaller now that she'd changed out of her olive-drab uniform into a blue-sprigged day dress that probably passed for stylish in Moscow. The marksman watched her eyes drift over the smart frocks of the sleek Washington women in the room, their pearl necklaces, their carefully set waves and curls; for an instant the Russian girl's hand stole up to her bluntly chopped hair.

Timid, the marksman filed away, still fiddling behind the camera to hide his face. *They'll eat her alive.*

"I hope you have all rested." The First Lady stepped forward with a gesture of welcome for the whole Soviet delegation as the dark-suited men filed in behind their girl sniper, trying not to gawk at their surroundings. The room was big despite its being called the *small* dining room, with a glittering chandelier, gracious molded ceilings, and tall windows draped in elegantly tied-back curtains. Interpreters on both sides murmured introductions, and the marksman paid close attention to the murmurs of Russian. He didn't speak the language well, but he could understand it. Useful for when he had to sit through American Communist Party meetings, waiting for a chance to pick off the latest Red agitator who had sufficiently alarmed someone in Washington or New York. Arranging fatal accidents for American

Marxists had paid the bills nicely in its day—not so much now that the Soviets were allies . . .

Although the people he worked for weren't at all convinced they should *remain* allies, a prospect which the marksman thought might mean a great deal of future employment.

The First Lady continued, gesturing everyone toward the long table with its forest of china, crystal, and silver. "I thought you might begin your acquaintance with the American way of life by trying a traditional American breakfast."

"Is there always this much food at an American breakfast?" the marksman heard the head of the Soviet delegation mutter in Russian as everyone took their places. The dishes had already been laid out: fried eggs, grilled bacon and sausage, marinated mushrooms, jugs of cold orange juice, and carafes of hot coffee. "What are those, oladi?"

"Pancakes," Mila Pavlichenko murmured back, also in Russian. The marksman had angled himself into a seat two down from her, where he could hear her clearly but she'd have no view of *his* face at all. "Americans call oladi *pancakes*. Don't stare, or they'll think we're yokels."

"The one they're staring at is you. Maybe they think you're the yokel." The head of the Soviet delegation sounded peevish, and the marksman hid a smile as chatter erupted across the table. The Soviets had sent two other Russian students turned soldiers to attend the international conference, both of whom sat at this table, along with a phalanx of minders and embassy staff—but they were all blocky charmless men in dark suits, and no one was interested in them. All the eyes were on the girl sniper, who had started to empty the marmalade pot into her cup of tea, then stopped with a deprecating little shrug as she realized her neighbors were staring.

"I wish they'd stop calling me the *girl sniper*," the marksman heard her mutter in Russian as she took a slug of tea laced with marmalade. "Only in America can you be a soldier and twenty-six, and still be a *girl*."

Thin-skinned, the marksman noted, crunching bacon, increasingly glad that he was here to make his own evaluation of Lyudmila Pavlichenko. Normally he'd have obtained any information he needed about her from some well-bribed third party; kept a careful layer of distance between himself and a patsy being set up for a fall. But with a top-shelf cover identity in place thanks to powerful backers, not to mention a throng of avid newsmen and glittering Washington functionaries to keep the girl from focusing on one more innocuous face at a table of loud strangers . . . well, he'd thought it merited the slight risk. He could already feel his internal sketch forming of this pretty Soviet propaganda pony: who she was, what made her tick, how to pull her strings. He didn't think it would be much of a challenge.

"A woman at the front lines, serving as a soldier!" A slim blonde leaned across the table toward the Russian side, eyes avid. "You can't imagine how strange that is to American women. I suppose the measure was only passed to defeat Hitler, desperate measures for desperate times and all that?"

"On the contrary," the girl sniper replied in Russian once the question was translated. "Our women were on a basis of equality long before Hitler rose. Our full rights were granted from the first day of the revolution—that is what makes us as independent as our men, not the war."

Practiced, thought the marksman, as her words were translated into English. Naturally she would be. Soviet envoys were always stuffed with canned answers and memorized slogans.

"Do you miss borscht, Lyudmila?" one of the First Lady's aides asked, leaning across the orange juice and bacon.

"Nobody in their right mind misses beets," Lyudmila Pavlichenko said through the interpreter, and got a laugh.

Funny, thought the marksman, in some surprise. He hadn't anticipated a sense of humor.

More questions began to fly. "I understand you rode in on the

Miami-Washington train this morning, Lyudmila—first time on an express? Were you shocked how fast it was?"

"The only thing I was shocked by was the sign on the carriage saying FOR WHITES ONLY." The girl sniper forked a mushroom off her plate. "It's a strange thing to see in a country that started with 'All men are created equal.' "

Prickly, thought the marksman. He was fairly certain the head of the delegation gave her a kick under the table, but she just chewed her mushroom, looking bland. The interpreter looked relieved when the blonde leaned forward with another question.

"Tell me, are unmarried women allowed in the Red Army? I noticed you were *Mrs.* Pavlichenko."

Married, the marksman noted. He wondered where the husband was.

"I can't imagine Soviet husbands being any more keen than American ones about the idea of their wives heading off to war." The blonde chuckled. "Men! My husband fusses so much when I'm off to chair a committee meeting, you'd think I *was* abandoning him for the Russian front!"

"Some husbands don't like much of anything a wife does," said the girl sniper. More chuckles around the table.

"I don't know about that." The First Lady spoke up unexpectedly. "If I decided to head for the Russian front, I imagine my husband would simply say, 'Don't get yourself killed, Eleanor, and bring back some Nazi scalps for the office.' "

The girl sniper laughed—before the interpreter murmured a translation. *Understands English,* the marksman thought with yet another flicker of surprise. And clever enough not to advertise the fact.

"I say, Mrs. Pavlichenko, you're doing well for your first trip to the USA," a hearty-looking man across the breakfast table boomed. "Look at you, managing that silverware like a pro!"

Lyudmila Pavlichenko's voice grew edged. "Thank you," she said brightly. "We just received silverware in the Soviet Union last week. Up until now it's all been stabbing our food with sticks!"

Angry, the marksman thought, fairly certain she'd got another kick under the table. He watched her apply herself to her plate again, spearing her sausage with more force than necessary. *Behave yourself and smile,* the delegation head muttered in Russian, and she just gave back a narrow-eyed stare. *Very angry, in fact,* the marksman amended. Not so smooth and controlled as he'd assumed a propaganda poster girl would be. Lyudmila Pavlichenko didn't want to be here, didn't like smiling on command, and hated idiotic questions.

The marksman smiled, making a note of that. *Be angry, little girl,* he thought, sipping his coffee. *Lose your temper, lose your poise, lose your script. The angrier you look over the week to come, the more these people here will be willing to believe you pulled the trigger on their president.*

Notes by the First Lady

Franklin will be interested to learn that our Soviet guests speak more English than they let on—or at least the young woman does. "Those rascals," he'll say, chuckling around his cigarette holder. I'll enjoy painting the scene for him later—not for nothing do they call me the President's eyes and ears. He'll pretend his fall this morning did not happen, he'll wave away any suggestion of mine that the ill will of his enemies might be worrying him, and he'll ask me to talk. "Describe it, Eleanor!"

How often has he said that, drumming his lean fingers on the arm of his chair, eyes bright and ravenous to understand, to absorb, to learn? Often I tell him entirely more than he wants to hear, and he becomes annoyed about my persistence in the matter of my pet causes, but that has never stopped him from asking for my descriptions or me from giving them.

So I watch the Soviets over the breakfast table, compiling impressions for my husband even as I think of a thousand other things that will demand my attention the moment I am released from this room (the column I need to finish, the letter to Hick, the planned banquet for the National League of Women Voters, following up with the fund for Polish relief . . .). Our Russian friends are dignified, grave, conscious of making a good impression—yet under the dignity I sense fragility. The Soviets did not only send students for my international conference, and they did not send granite-hard Soviet supermen, either. They sent war-weary veterans who have suffered. Look at us, *they are saying with every move and every gesture.* We eat bacon and pancakes with the same delight you do; we laugh at the same jokes you do; we plan and hope and dream just like you do . . . and we're being bled dry by Hitler's tanks and bombs and planes. See us as the allies you call us. Help us.

That is the real purpose of their visit, of course. To make us understand how much they need aid, how much they need a second front . . .

And there are those here in Washington who will do anything—anything at all—to stop Franklin from giving it to them.

NINE MONTHS AGO

December 1941

THE SEVASTOPOL FRONT, USSR

Mila

CHAPTER 16

My memoir, the official version: Being a woman in the army has its difficulties. In male company one must be strict: no flirting, no teasing, no games, not ever.

My memoir, the unofficial version: Well. About that . . .

"STOP," I WHEEZED, wiping at my eyes. "My stitches are killing me."

Kostia and Lyonya paid absolutely no attention. They were fighting a mock duel up and down the ward, brandishing rolls of bandaging for sabers and bedpans for shields. "Yield, you cur!" Lyonya shouted with some Errol Flynn sweeps of the bandage roll—something told me he'd managed to sneak a look at a forbidden Western film reel or two. The entire ward was cheering: patients calling encouragement from their cots, Lena and the other orderlies staggering with mirth in the doorway. I tried to catch my breath and went off in another fit of laughter. I couldn't remember when I'd laughed so much.

Kostia and Lyonya couldn't visit me more than every few days, but when they did, elaborate high jinks always seemed to ensue. Last time Kostia taught us some labyrinthine dice game with a set of caribou-bone dice carved from a buck he'd shot when he was nine, and Lyonya fleeced us both out of every ruble we had before we figured out he was cheating. The time before that I was in need of a blood transfusion, and Lena ran a line directly from Kostia's elbow into mine while Lyonya told ghoulish stories about night-walking *upyr* who sucked blood to survive: "Mila, keep an eye out if you start growing fangs. Of course Kostia won't be able to tell, not with those wolf incisors . . ."

And today—

"Disarmed, you villain!" One of Lyonya's wild parries sent Kostia's bedpan buckler flying, and my partner gave a ghastly scream as the bandage-roll sword plunged dramatically toward his gut. He folded up around it, collapsed across the foot of my cot, and writhed there for a while in some obliging death throes as Lyonya took a bow and the ward cheered. A month ago I'd have sworn my taciturn partner had no gift for horseplay; now I applauded his dramatic demise as loudly as anyone else.

"You'd better not be too dead," I told him. "I still need a partner when I get out of here."

"And I need to make sure you have a platoon to come back to." Kostia looked at his watch, rolled upright, and retrieved his cap. "I should get back. Your rifle's almost battlefield ready," he added.

"Can't wait to get back to it." I lay drumming my heels under the sheets, thinking of my men heading out to hunt without me to look after them. "Tell the boys to look sharp." I watched wistfully as Kostia thumped Lyonya's shoulder and padded noiselessly out. "Aren't you going, too?" I asked Lyonya as he flopped into the chair by my cot.

"I'm not on this nocturnal schedule you *upyrs* are, thank goodness. How does anyone accomplish anything at three in the morning besides brooding over old mistakes?"

I began rotating my arm and shoulder to get some of the motion back, something Lena had encouraged even if it did make my stitches pull painfully. "What mistakes do you have to brood over?"

"I was married once," he said unexpectedly. "Divorced within a year. Do you think less of me?"

"That depends on why you divorced."

"Oh, I was young and stupid." He shook his head, rueful. "Eighteen years old, letting my mother push me into marrying the girl next door. I knew nothing about women, not even to tell Olga she was beautiful and hand her chocolate when she was crying, and after a few months it seemed like all she did was cry. We both realized it was a mistake, so we parted ways before there were any children to get hurt. Olga's an engineer now, with another husband and two babies. We're friendly enough when we meet."

"How civilized," I said, thinking of Alexei's mocking *Jump for it!* My stitches pulled again, and I flinched.

"I know you married young, too." Lyonya leaned back in his too-small chair, elbow hooked around the back. "What went wrong?"

"He decided being a husband and father wasn't for him." I hesitated. "If he hadn't . . . well, I'd have left him anyway, eventually. He was bad for my son, and he made me feel small."

"You are small. A pocket-sized sniper." Seeing me strain for a harder stretch through my shoulder, Lyonya caught my wrist—his fingers overlapped my narrower bones easily—and gave a slow, firm tug. "But I've seen you when your Lieutenant Pavlichenko comes by on rounds. You shrink around him; I don't like to see it. Here, tell me when it hurts . . ."

I gasped, feeling the torn muscles stretch. "I don't like to feel it, believe me."

Lyonya released my wrist when I nodded, and I eased back into my pillow, not wanting to talk more about Alexei. Lyonya steered the conversation into happier waters for another half hour or so, then glanced at the time. "I should go. Allegedly I'm a lieutenant with serious responsibilities; I need to go shirk them for a while so Dromin will have an excuse to glare at me."

I laughed. Lyonya leaned close to speak into my ear.

"Your former husband is hovering at the door. Shall I steal that kiss now, to make him jealous?"

I choked back another laugh, tempted. "No."

"Worth a try." Lyonya sauntered off whistling, fair hair gleaming under the harsh hospital lights, and I turned hastily on one side and pretended to go to sleep before Alexei could come over and begin making conversation. I heard him standing over my cot for a long moment, though. Just breathing.

What do you want? I thought, listening as he finally strolled away.

Lena, coming to sit by my cot on her break, was blunt. "He wants to know if you're tossing the bedroll with Lyonya or Kostia or both. He's grilled all the nurses and orderlies about you three."

"It's none of his business," I protested. "And why does no one believe I might just be doing my *job,* not hopping in and out of bedrolls?"

"Because men are worse gossips than old women, that's why. The rumor is you're screwing both of them." Lena gave me a shrewd look. "So, which one's the lucky fellow?"

"Neither, and you know it. For the love of Lenin, I just had a foot-sized splinter excised from my back."

"You could have either one of them, and *you* know it. Amazing they haven't started punching each other."

"They wouldn't. They're friends." Lyonya was the only one I knew who could crack Kostia's silence, bring out his elusive, tilted grin. "And they're *my* friends. Nothing more."

"Kitsenko's got plenty to do in the command tent without hustling up here every other day, with gifts." Lena nodded at the little vial of scent my company commander had brought on his last visit, wrapped in a lace-edged handkerchief. "Red Moscow, not cheap. First a liter of his own blood, then perfume . . . He'd be bringing you diamonds if he had 'em. He's courting, Lady Midnight."

"You're an advocate for front-line romance now?" I leaned forward so she could check my stitches. "After all our talks about fending off officers?"

"Fending off the asses and the brutes, yes." Her fingers were icy; it was the eve of the new year, and the weather had turned biting. The only comfort in this bitter chill was that the Germans with their soft Bavarian childhoods would be feeling it far worse than we were. "The officers who think they're entitled to have us flop on our backs if they so much as crook a finger, those are the ones to run from. But if a nice, decent fellow comes asking, I don't always run." She waggled her eyebrows. "Or at least I run slow enough so they can catch up."

"I hope you're careful."

"I tell them straightaway they can glove it up or they can put it back." She tugged my smock over my stitches. "It's nice having a warm body to curl up with now the nights are cold, Mila. Give it a try. Either your lieutenant or your Siberian would be thrilled down to their socks if you climbed under their blankets."

"Kostia doesn't—"

"Don't even *pretend* to be one of those stupid women who doesn't notice when a man's head over heels!"

"But he's my partner," I said softly. Hard to explain the bond between sniper partners to someone who wasn't one. When we fell in at each other's side at the dark hunting hour after midnight, we didn't just move in unison: we breathed in unison, thought in unison, felt our blood beat in unison like a pair of soft-padding lynxes sliding through snow. We lived by the heartbeat whisper of *Don't miss*. Introduce anything to disrupt that perfect working partnership, and one or both of us might make some infinitesimal, lethal error—might end up tossed in a hastily dug grave with our names misspelled on a red plywood star. *No.*

"Your lieutenant, then. He's a dish, and no mistake." Lena spritzed herself with Red Moscow. "Now, you'll be out of here in two days. Promise me you'll try to go at least a week without getting blown up again?"

"I don't walk in front of mortar splinters just to keep you in suturing practice, Lena Paliy." I didn't tell Lena my superstition that the next wound would kill me. She'd just smack me with a bedpan.

That didn't mean I wasn't still feeling it, though: the hovering dread, the gray certainty that my luck had run out. *Don't be a coward,*

I lashed myself fiercely, but I didn't think it *was* cowardice, precisely. Put a Hitlerite in my sights, I knew I wouldn't freeze pulling the trigger. No, this was just a matter-of-fact voice in the back of my head, saying, *Get as many as you can now; do as much as you can now—because your sand has almost run through the hourglass.*

Well. Would that be so terrible, if Mila Pavlichenko did not survive this new year of 1942, did not live to see the age of twenty-six? I'd have done my part for my homeland, fought as long and as hard as I knew how. My son could be proud of me, and he would grow up with my mother and father, cherished with all the love I wouldn't be there to give him.

And if Germans overran the motherland and subjected everyone I loved to live under a swastika, I'd never see it.

I was discharged in a steel-gray twilight a few days into the new year. Buttoning up my uniform, I saw how it hung loose on me, and in the sliver of mirror I could see how grained and ashy my skin had grown. "You look pretty," Alexei said from just behind me. "Do you have much of a scar?"

"You're losing your touch, Alexei." I arranged my cap over my hair, feeling the puckered ridge on my scalp from my last trip to the hospital battalion. "Telling a woman she looks pretty while bringing up her scars."

"At least this one doesn't show, under that uniform." He came a step closer. "You could show me, you know. Later, maybe. After dinner."

"The scars under my uniform are none of your business. You are never, ever, going to see them." I made a point of not stepping away from him. Alexei had done that so often when we were married; moved just a hair too close so I felt the urge to back up. I was done backing up. "If you'll excuse me, Comrade Lieutenant." Turning away from the mirror.

"I'm trying to compliment you, *kroshka*." His hand dropped to my arm; he sounded irked. When Alexei Pavlichenko exerted himself for a woman, he expected his efforts to be greeted with smiles. "Can't you appreciate that?"

"And I have invaders to target." Yanking away. "Can't you appreciate that?"

He laughed, the indulgent sound raking my ears. "Mila, really. You should—"

"Be going? Yes." I straightened my collar, lifting my chin. "I don't want your compliments. I don't want your dinner invitations. I don't want anything from you at all."

"You want that blond lieutenant instead?" Alexei asked, conversational. "Maybe I should give him a few tips. How to handle the girl sniper . . . it's been a while, but I still remember what makes you writhe and moan."

Rage made me light-headed as I strode off down the corridor with its harsh-flickering lights. Around the corner I had to stop and steady myself against the wall, shoulder throbbing. Beating the rage into submission didn't help; the wound kept beating in a pulse of pain I felt right down to my feet. It really wasn't done healing. If this had been peacetime, I'd have been given another week in bed, but if it had been peacetime, I wouldn't need it. The second German assault had been pushed back, at the cost of 23,000 dead, wounded, or missing . . . but there would be another soon enough. I stood there mentally framing my husband's smirking face with imaginary telescopic sights as he chuckled and said, *Just teasing, Mila!*—now that would be a shot I wouldn't miss. I mentally pulled that trigger until the dizziness of rage passed. Then I made my way aboveground from the dugout medical center.

As I shaded my eyes in the fading winter light, I saw a mud-splattered official car pulled up by the entrance. Lyonya leaned against it, reading a battered Gorky novel. "I thought I'd drive you back to 1st Battalion's lines," he said when he saw me. "Have dinner with me when we get there?"

And I shoved Alexei's jeering voice out of my head and said simply, "I'd like that."

EVEN A COMPANY commander doesn't get much in the way of living quarters on the front line. Lyonya had a private dugout like a tiny cellar, earth walls and packed dirt floor and three layers of logs overhead for a ceiling he had to stoop under . . . and when I saw how he'd made it ready, all that came out of me was a quiet "Oh."

"It's not much," he said anxiously, hovering at the entrance. He'd knocked a table together out of rough planks and covered it with a canvas drape for a tablecloth; the battery-powered lamp showed dinner laid out on tin plates—the kind of front-line feast that meant a week's worth of bartering and trading of favors had taken place. Black bread and hard salami, a can of meat stew, soft-cooked potatoes in a mess tin, vodka . . . In the middle was a 45mm shell case he'd turned into a vase, crammed with green fronds of juniper and sprays of maple twigs glowing with red-gold leaves. "I thought you could send them to your son later—I know you collect leaves and flowers for him."

I lowered my face toward the sprigs, inhaling winter, feeling suddenly short of breath again. *He's courting,* Lena had said.

Yes, it appeared he was.

"What would you have done if I hadn't agreed to dinner?" I asked, raising my face.

"Invited Kostia," said Lyonya. "I've heard he's a *great* lay."

Laughter spluttered out of me, breaking the tension, and I let him pull out a stool for me at the makeshift table. "I'm starving."

"Good, because you're officially off duty tonight."

"But—" I hadn't seen my company yet, or my platoon, or been back to my usual dugout.

"You can wait till tomorrow night to go stalking back into no-man's-land, Comrade Senior Sergeant." Lyonya forestalled my objections, spooning meat stew onto my plate. "Tonight you'll eat well and get a good night's sleep, orders from your company commander. And that's the last thing I'm saying as your company commander tonight."

"Why is that?" I dug into the feast.

"When I propose marriage after dinner," Lyonya explained, "I'd prefer the offer not be overlaid with any sense of obligation, coming from a lieutenant to a sergeant. Vodka, my one and only?" he offered as I choked on a mouthful of stew.

"You can't be serious." I managed to swallow the chunk in my mouth, which was more gristle than stew meat. A dinner invitation and flowers were one thing; I knew he was hoping to romance me into his bedroll, but— "You're proposing *marriage*?"

"No," he said, pouring vodka for us both. "I'll do that later, on a full stomach."

"You're teasing," I decided.

He looked across the table through the lamplight. "You dazzle me," he said.

My hand stole up to my chopped, stick-dry hair. "You've known me six weeks."

"You dazzled me within six seconds, Mila."

I knocked back my vodka, chasing it with a bite of black bread and salami. "It's too soon. I've only known you—"

"Then say no. I'm still going to ask. Later," he added, swallowing his own portion of stew down. "Right now I'm nervous. Most fellows feel nervous at this point, but I feel fairly certain I'm the only fellow in history proposing marriage to a woman who has personally dispatched over two hundred men."

I laughed again, despite myself. "How do you always do that?"

"Propose marriage to homicidally gifted women?"

"Make me laugh."

"I display a distressing tendency to levity and bourgeois sentimentalism, or so my Komsomol leader told me, growing up. I will never rise high in the Party unless I strive for objectivity in my personal relations, rather than mirth."

"Clearly a hopeless case."

"At thirty-six? Utterly."

I smiled, relaxing despite myself, vodka unfurling in my stomach. I couldn't remember the last time dinner had been taken for pleasure, with conversation and leisure in mind, rather than a simple refueling exercise between bouts of dealing death. "Tell me something, Lyonya." Deciding on a change of subject, something a little less weighty than marriage proposals and kill counts. "As an officer, would you have any idea where I could get access to a typewriter here at the front?"

"A typewriter?" He addressed the winter bouquet on the table. "Give a woman a romantic dinner; she wants a typewriter . . ."

"I want to retype my dissertation. It has blood all over it—"

The crash overhead nearly deafened me. The shriek of mortars—normally I was impervious to the sound of German artillery, but two weeks in hospital away from the clangor of the front line had softened my ears. Maybe softened my spine too, because at the scream of shellfire overhead, I erupted out of my chair as if I had been electrified, grabbing desperately for my rifle, which wasn't there.

"Mila—"

The table rocked as I dived under it, clamping my arms to my ears, heart hammering through my chest.

"Mila—"

I couldn't tell if there were more mortars coming; my damaged ears were ringing and roaring. I shuddered, my eyes screwed shut. Were the German bastards starting again so soon? Did nothing *stop them*?

"*Mila*." Warmth around me, a voice vibrating low and soft beside my ear. He sounded calm, but his muscles were tense. "It's not an attack, just the Hitlerites giving us a little night music. Trying to keep us scared."

I'm not scared, I tried to say, but the words jammed in my throat. What an idiotic thing to say, anyway—I was clearly afraid; I was under a table with my arms around my ears. My company commander had had to *crawl under the table after me.* I felt his arms tight around my shoulders, gripping me against his chest. I'd felt such relief in hospital when I'd realized I didn't have to hide my fears from him . . . but I was out now, I was supposed to be recovered, not still cowering and petrified. Such a wave of shame swept through me that I nearly sank through the floor like a *domovoi,* one of those old hearth spirits people made offerings to in the days before the revolution, before education and rationality conquered fear and superstition. Except of course, such things are never conquered, no matter what the Party says.

"I'm sorry," I muttered, trying to pull away, trying to shrivel into my collar, but Lyonya just tucked me more firmly into his shoulder.

"Believe me, I'm the frightened one here. I was right behind you getting under the table."

We were both huddled against the floor now, the canvas drape of the makeshift tablecloth curtaining off the rest of the world. My heart was still racing in misplaced alarm; I peeled my hands off my ears and watched my fingers sink into the front of Lyonya's jacket instead. "They're—they're not attacking."

"Doesn't sound like it."

I listened hard. Boots walking past outside, the occasional low laugh, the clink of tin cups. A company going about its evening routine, no screams or shouts or chatters of machine-gun fire. "Don't tell them," I whispered into his jacket. "The company, the men and the officers, don't—"

"Don't tell them what?"

"I—this." Lyudmila Pavlichenko curled in a shaking ball. The girl sniper, sniveling under a table.

"You've killed more than two hundred men while looking them square in the face as you pulled the trigger." Lyonya's hand moved over my hair. "No one thinks you're a coward."

I do. "Do I still dazzle you?" I managed to say harshly.

I could feel him smile against my temple, pressing his lips over my ear. "Utterly."

We disentangled, climbing out from under the plank table. The tin plates were safe, but the shell-case vase had been knocked over, the winter bouquet scattered on the dirt floor. "It's all right," Lyonya said, but I scrambled to retrieve the juniper fronds, the maple twigs. Those bright leaves like fire cupped in my still-shaking hands, jammed into a 45mm shell case—if that wasn't wartime life in a nutshell, I didn't know what was. A stray frond of beauty here and there, jammed into something mass-produced and violent, usually toppled and trampled underfoot before too long. Dead and withered tomorrow, but still glowing with life today.

Like us.

I was still trembling when I reached up and pulled Lyonya's face down to mine. "Do you have something?" I asked, and kissed him. He tasted of vodka and pine.

"Something?" He was already kissing me back, hands in my hair, both of us lurching against the dugout wall.

"You know." I pried at his collar; he pried at mine as his mouth traveled down my jawline. A button spanged off the table. "Do you have—"

"I don't have a ring," he confessed. "It was hard enough getting a loaf of decent bread and a damned can of stew."

"For the love of—" I pushed him into the chair, climbed into his lap, put my forehead against his so we were eye to eye, dark eyes drowning in blue, and locked my other hand around his belt buckle.

"I will not get *pregnant* on the front line, Lyonya. Do you *have something*?"

"Oh," he said. "Yes," he added, producing a small packet from somewhere.

"Good," I said, and our mouths nailed back together as my jacket and then his hit the floor. Maybe this wasn't a good idea, not with my company commander, not after knowing him less than two months, but I had no idea if we'd be alive next week or not. *This,* I thought, kicking off my boots, *give me this while I'm still alive to enjoy it.*

"I've never had to disarm a woman before bed," Lyonya murmured into my collarbone, tossing aside my combat knife, my pistol, my belt with its ammunition pouches, pulling me back into his lap in the chair as trousers were shoved away. It was too cold to be naked like this, we were both shivering despite the little dugout stove, breath pluming in the air between us and melting again in every kiss. He was broad-shouldered, long-flanked, his hair soft under my hand, his wide hands steadying my hips as I tore the little packet open.

"It's been a while," I murmured as we fitted ourselves together, thinking despite myself of the boy last year with whom I'd enjoyed a laughing romp on a visit to the Lenin All-Union Academy of Agricultural Sciences. That had been good fast fun, a little perfunctory, nothing serious on either side. There was nothing fast or perfunctory here. Lyonya smiled into my eyes the entire time, palms sliding the length of my spine, my throat, the back of my neck, our bodies rocking breast to breast in silence, the prosaic muddy world of the regiment moving by outside in its nailed boots.

I love you, his lips murmured soundlessly into mine, and his hand against my throat must have felt the stutter-stop of my pulse in response to those simple, terrifying words, because he smiled and said it out loud so I couldn't mistake him: "I love you," simple and stark as he moved in me, as my eyes brimmed. The terrifying lock of our eyes didn't break until the end, when he saw me biting my lips fiercely as the tide built in us both. He put his broad hand to my mouth and let me cry out into it, stifling his own shout in my shoulder.

We clung silently after, still coiled together in the chair. "Marry me," he whispered against my throat. "Marry me, Mila."

"I can't," I muttered, still trembling in his arms.

He pushed my hair back. "Do you trust me?"

"Yes, but—" There was a conversation we'd need to have, but did it have to be now? "Do we have to talk about the future, Lyonya? Can't we just—"

Can we have this? Just this, for now? Because I felt more alive than I'd felt in months.

"We'll work on the marriage part." He kissed my temple as we began to disentangle. "I'll ask you again tomorrow. In the meantime, do you want to sleep over?"

"Sleep *over*, like we're on holiday? We're in a dugout. Shells may cave the roof in at any moment."

"Well, you can't say it doesn't add excitement . . ."

CHAPTER 17

M*y memoir, the official version: Lieutenant Kitsenko sent in an application to our superiors to formalize our new relations in the official way. It would need to be stamped and signed by Lieutenant Dromin and the regimental commander, then given the regimental seal of approval and filed for implementation at the staff headquarters of the 25th Chapayev Division.*

My memoir, the unofficial version: "Lyonya, we should talk . . ."

"YOU'RE STILL MARRIED?" my new lover repeated for the third time.

"Only technically." I took a deep breath, trying to calm the flutter in my stomach—we were sitting at the rickety little table in his dugout, two days after our first night together, and the topic I'd been dreading was spilling out all over the table like a messy, invisible oil slick. "The divorce was never finalized."

Lyonya scratched his jaw. "But divorces are so easy to get."

"My father made things complicated." I sighed. "He can be old-fashioned . . . He didn't entirely approve of my leaving Alexei. Papa let me move home but asked me to wait and think about the divorce, make sure it was the right choice. I let it go because I thought Alexei would divorce *me,* one of those no-fuss postcard legal splits—what I should have realized was that having an absentee wife he didn't have to support suited him just fine." All the freedom in the world to mess about with young girls and then say mournfully, *I can't marry you,* kroshka, *I've already got a marital noose around my neck.* "Then before I knew it, Slavka was four and the new laws came through." The laws requiring payment of a fifty-ruble fine, and the presence of both parties before officials to dissolve the marriage. I explained how Alexei had missed every appointment I set.

"So you put it off till later?" Lyonya guessed. "When things weren't so busy?"

"But when you're juggling a child and factory work and night school, and then university classes, and then a researcher job, well, things are *always* busy." There had never been a day I thought, *Now is just the right time to pay money I can't spare to wrangle my husband whom I can't stand into an office he'll pretend he can't find, to sign papers he has no intention of signing.* And it hadn't made any difference to my daily life or Slavka's, whether Alexei was divorced from me or merely separated.

Only now I was sitting opposite a man who wanted to marry me . . . and I felt myself wanting to say yes. I scanned Lyonya's face, looking for signs of anger, but he leaned across the table and kissed me, smiling. "This does put a wrinkle in my wedding plans, I admit."

"You're not upset?"

"Upset? I'm relieved. I thought maybe you didn't *want* to marry me. If it's just a matter of a still-living husband, well, I can work with that."

I raised an eyebrow. "What, do you mean to kill him?"

"I'm not ruling it out," Lyonya said cheerfully, going to the stove to heat up some tea. "It would cost the Red Army a good surgeon but save on the paperwork. And if he's such a schoolgirl-chasing swine, we'd be doing the world a favor."

"It's not funny," I protested, but found myself laughing anyway. It was Lyonya's gift, I'd already come to realize—he could bring laughter like a stray thread of sunshine to brighten even the most shadowed room. He grinned over his shoulder, and I grinned back, propping my chin in my hand. "What really isn't funny is that you started all that front-line marriage paperwork for nothing," I said, enjoying the sight of his broad back under his uniform tunic. "What's that, sixteen pages in triplicate?"

"I'm sure there's another sixteen pages I can fill out in triplicate, which formalize a nonlegal front-line union so you can billet here with me. I'll find out."

I wrinkled my nose. "Surely there isn't paperwork to document who's living as your dugout girlfriend?"

"*Milaya,* this is the Soviet Union." Lyonya pushed a tin mug into my hand—tea, hot and sugared just the way I liked it. "There's paperwork for everything."

"For the love of—"

"Don't worry, we'll handle Alexei one way or another—later. For the moment, I'm due back at the command post." Lyonya bent down and kissed the corner of my mouth. "See you in the morning. Kill lots of Nazis. Don't die."

He kissed me again, so hard the tea nearly went flying, and then he swung out whistling. "Sixteen pages in triplicate," I muttered, but I couldn't stop smiling. In the face of Lyonya's jokes, Alexei and our strung-out legal status didn't seem like such a mountain. And even if it took another few months to wrangle the divorce, I had Lyonya here and now. It had been only a few days, but I'd already grown addicted to sleeping beside the solid warmth of his body, the arms that wrapped me up when I blew in cold and snowy from a night huddled in a sniper's trench, the pot of water he always had ready on the potbelly stove for me to wash my chilled face and aching hands.

"Can I kill these wretches, Comrade Senior Sergeant?" old Vartanov grumbled as I came to join my platoon. He waved at the handful of new recruits he was teaching to fieldstrip their SVT-40 rifles. "Worthless, every one of them. Younger than new butter."

I surveyed the new men, looking for the resentful gleam in the eye that meant trouble, but they all seemed either cowed or awed at the sight of me. "You used to be younger than new butter, remember."

"When I was that young and dim, Russia still had a czar."

"Well, things have improved since then."

"Have they?" Vartanov wondered.

"Of course they have!"

He tugged at his ragged beard. "I don't know, Comrade Senior Sergeant. The little men are still out here taking the bullets while the big men sit safe and dry. That doesn't change no matter who's in charge."

"Shut *up,* Vartanov." I headed him off before he could slide into one of his patriotic Ukrainian moods and start making not-too-veiled anti-Soviet jabs. "Again," I called to the new recruits, and had the old ranger strip the Sveta as I called out the stages. "Detach the ten-cartridge box . . . Remove the breech cover . . . See how he releases the catch and puts his weapon down with sights upward? Then push the cover forward—left hand, there . . ." Patiently I walked them through it. "Again, on your own. You'll be able to do this in the dark soon enough."

"Not *very* soon," Vartanov muttered as they fumbled back into motion. "You tell that commander of yours to get us some better recruits."

I waited to see if the mention of Lyonya would come with a leer or a wink, but it didn't. I'd been bracing for mockery or obscene jokes, dreading the moment I'd hear jeers from my platoon—I'd guarded my reputation for so long, been so careful not to cross that line—but so far, my men seemed to be taking it in stride.

As if reading my mind, Vartanov said, "The boys feel like they can rest easy now you've got an officer in your bedroll, Lyudmila Mikhailovna."

"It's not their business, Comrade Corporal," I said coolly. But I couldn't deny I was relieved. Maybe this could all be managed without fuss, after all. If anything, I seemed to be getting *fewer* impudent looks or flirtatious remarks than I was used to.

"Having a young woman walk around a war zone without knowing who she belongs to, that unsettles the lads." Vartanov was surely the only man in my platoon who'd dare be so blunt with me, but age had its privileges, even on the front lines. "You settled it, now they can settle down."

For the love of Lenin, I thought. *Men.* "Again," I called to the new boys with their Svetas. Away they went, fumble, fumble, fumble.

"Kostia's back, by the way," Vartanov added, wincing as he saw a breech cover drop off a Sveta into the grass.

"Kostia?" I hadn't seen my partner since his last visit to the hospital—the morning after coming back from Lyonya's quarters for the first time, smiling and floating and undeniably kiss-flushed, I'd found my new rifle propped up in the dugout where I usually slept, polished to a diamond gleam, with a note in Kostia's small square writing. *Yours,* it said simply. And then Fyodor told me my partner had put in for a little of his long-overdue leave now that the German assault had finally tailed off, and had headed into Sevastopol as though an entire Panzer division was on his tail.

"He's back," Vartanov repeated, scratching his rough white beard. "Wouldn't say he's in the best mood. I've never seen a boy that hungover, and I've seen a few in my day."

"Tell him to come find me when you see him." I knew why my partner had taken off, but there wasn't anything to say about it, so I just called out to the new recruits: "Again—" and began thinking about a foray into no-man's-land tonight, maybe taking Vartanov for a lookout, when an orderly appeared with a message: I was to report to the regimental command post at once.

I half expected to see Lyonya there, but it was Major Matusyevich and a sturdy red-faced colonel introduced as the commander of the 79th Naval Rifle Brigade. They took my salute, the colonel eyeing me curiously. "They say you're the best shooter in the division, Comrade Senior Sergeant Pavlichenko. Your picture's on the divisional board of honor."

That was news to me. He went on.

"A first-rate German rifleman has appeared in our defense sector.

Over the past two days, five of our men have been killed—three soldiers and two officers, one the commander of our 2nd Battalion. All single shots to the head."

I could feel every nerve in my body prick. "His nest?"

A shrug. "Our best guess, he's tucked himself somewhere in the wreckage of the bridge over the Kamyshly gully."

I felt myself smile, the kind of smile Lyonya had never seen. The kind of smile no one saw, except maybe Kostia, because it was the smile I wore only when the count went down to midnight and it was time to fire. "I know that bridge."

I knew it because I'd marked it as a sniper's paradise. The gully in the middle of no-man's-land was covered in reeds and overgrown, splintered apple orchards, two slopes rising up from the stream meandering down the center. The steep, pine-furred southern slope was held by our division; the gentler northern slope was held by units of the Germans' 50th Brandenburg Infantry Division . . . and the two high sides of the gully were spanned by a bombed-out railway bridge. A span or two survived on either side, giving way to nothing but soaring air in the central section, concrete pilings topped by a spider's web of tangled, twisted metal overlooking the ravine.

"He'll have found a place on one of the surviving spans and hidden among the metal wreckage." There was a map on the table; I tapped the place. "Six hundred, eight hundred meters . . . perfectly possible for a good shot. He's been able to fire at leisure if he's up there."

"Can you put an end to it?"

I looked up, still smiling. "Yes."

"GERMAN SHARPSHOOTERS." LYONYA sounded matter-of-fact. "I'm not surprised they're starting to turn up."

"Why?" My fight was such a narrowly focused thing, I saw little more than what was in my sights—or at most what was directly embroiling my company, my regiment, my division. Lyonya's war, seen from the company command post, had a wider angle.

"The first assault on Sevastopol, the Hitlerites expected to bull straight through our defenses." Lyonya pushed aside the remnants of our supper, which the orderly had fetched from the mess kitchens, and unrolled a map. "Their second assault, they realized how we've dug in—they've had to reexamine their situation. We're a first-rate fortress here, so they'll be bringing in specialists to nibble at morale. In the command post we're hearing talk of German snipers being sent in from Poland, even France."

"Who do you think he is?" Kostia's voice sounded behind me. I turned and saw my partner leaning against the doorjamb like a dark shadow. His black eyes were a little sunken but steady. "This German sniper."

"I don't care who he is." I shrugged. Some icy-eyed Alsatian who grew up hunting boar on his family estate; some fanatical flaxen-haired Reich soldier who had burned through a special training course so he could take his place on that shattered bridge and pick us off—what did it matter? "He's mine."

"You're not going alone," Lyonya protested.

"No." I looked at my partner. "Kostia, would you rather I asked Fyodor or Vartanov?"

It was a careful question, and I needed a blunt answer. If he felt awkward with me now, if he couldn't be my other half as soon as we went hunting, it would be no good out there. If that was the case, I needed to hear a no, and I needed to hear it now before it got either of us killed.

Kostia took the third place at the table with Lyonya and me, looking at the map. "We stake it out tomorrow. Get him the old Russian way—"

"Cunning, persistence, patience," I finished with my partner in unison. I couldn't stop the smile that broke over my face. Lyonya pushed a glass of vodka across the table with a tilted grin. Kostia drank it in a neat swallow and bent back over the map, drawing my attention to a spot on the bridge's northern end. The two of us put our elbows on the table and our heads together and made our plan, while Lyonya sat back and watched us work, contributing the occasional observation. And when the hour before dawn arrived and the car rolled around that would carry Kostia and me to the command post of the 79th Naval Rifle Brigade, Lyonya loaded it with our kit bags and rifles, buttoned my overcoat for me, scolded Kostia for not taking down his earflaps until Kostia swatted at him and the two men started shadowboxing in the dugout. "Quit it," I scolded, swatting them both, and Lyonya stopped, merriment fading as he caught Kostia's shoulder.

"Watch her out there," my lover said. "Watch her for me."

"Always," my partner said, and there was a moment of silence I interrupted with a cough.

"No long goodbyes," I said briskly, "it makes the heart sad in wartime!" and we piled out outside. But when the car bore us away, I had the strangest sensation in my life—the sensation, new to me, of leaving someone behind to worry through the night. Heading off to fight as a man who loved me stood with his hands balled in his pockets and fear for my life flickering in his eyes as he watched me go.

And then I forgot all about Lyonya, because that was what I had to do.

KOSTIA AND I stared at the bridge for three straight hours before either of us said a word. "Tricky," he said at last.

"Just when I got used to shooting among trees," I answered, thinking of the Crimean forest tracks Vartanov had taught me to walk like a shadow, but this was something new: crumbling arches of bridge topped by charred timbers, splintered sleepers, twisted railroad tracks rising to spear the whitened sky. My partner and I lay our stomachs on the snowy earth on the other side of the ravine, camouflage smocks pulled over our heads, eyes hawk-slitted through our binoculars.

"He's there," Kostia said.

"Not now."

"No, he's got his shot and he's gone till nightfall. But he's been firing from a nest up there."

"Lazy." I let my binoculars trace a tangle of corkscrewed metal beams. "He's fired from that position two days running. I'd have found a new nest by day two." A good sniper didn't form habits. Habits got you dead.

"Germans like patterns." Kostia's binoculars traced the bridge. "It's worked for him twice. He'll think he can get one more."

"I'm thinking his nest is there—" I pointed.

"—or there." Kostia pointed to another spot.

"Agreed. One of those."

We wriggled back on our elbows, carefully, till we were back behind our own lines. I sat up, rolled my neck, arched my back to stretch out the aches of a long stakeout. Kostia pulled out our night rations: a heel of rye bread each, with two strips of rosy fatback sprinkled with salt and ground black pepper. We chewed, both still looking in the direction of the bridge.

"Trench?" he said at last, swallowing the last of his bread.

"Trench," I agreed. "And you know who else we need."

Kostia looked at me and grinned, his teeth a sudden gleam of white under the quarter moon. "Ivan?"

"Ivan."

The colonel of the 79th was dubious, but he agreed to lend us a team of sappers. Hidden in the frosty thickets of juniper and hazelnut bushes, the men dug out a trench after nightfall, in the early hours of darkness when the day's shellfire had lapsed but before the German sniper would return to his nest after midnight. "It's deep enough," one complained, chafing the blisters on his hand from spading the frozen earth.

"Eighty centimeters deep, ten meters long." I waved my papers. "I've done the calculations."

"I'll show you what you can do with your calculations," the man mumbled.

"I've reached 226 right now in my sniper's tally," I remarked. "Keep talking if you want to be 227."

Trench dug, Kostia and I unfolded a metal frame and canvas drape over it and spent a full eight hours camouflaging it with twigs, brush, and armfuls of snow. And we worked on another little sniper's trick we'd long ago nicknamed Ivan. "He doesn't have much in the way of personality," I said, standing back and surveying our work.

"Don't criticize Ivan," Kostia said. "He's my brother in arms."

"Speaking of which . . ." I held up my rifle, the one my partner had customized for my hands, my eyes, my habits while I was laid up. "I didn't have a chance yet to thank you for this. It's perfect, Kostia."

"Let's get 227 with it," he said, the smile back in the corners of his eyes, and we crawled into our nest.

The best time for a sniper begins an hour and a half after midnight. That's when a shooter usually moves into position, and my partner and I were fully concealed in our trench and lying in wait for the German sniper to move onto the bridge and make for his nest. But the night passed and dawn broke through our binoculars, and finally we looked at each other. "Go back?" Kostia asked, because the German wouldn't move on his nest now, in the light of day. I envisioned Lyonya's dugout, the potbellied stove, the mess tin of hot potatoes and stew he'd put down for me while I peeled out of my uniform. The compress he'd prepare for the still-healing scar on my back.

I shook my head, looking across the ravine at the bridge. "I'm staying until we bag him."

"I'll keep watch till midmorning. You sleep."

I hesitated to curl against Kostia the way I usually did, but my winter uniform—thick underwear, tunic, padded vest and trousers, overcoat, white camouflage smock—didn't do much for warmth beyond keeping you from freezing to death. I curled into Kostia's back and slept till he woke me and took my place, alternating through the day until the sun fell again, the shrinking moon rose, and we were both back at our binoculars. *Come on, you Kraut bastard.*

Another long, empty night. Another morning alternating sleep and watch, relieving ourselves in an empty can as the other politely turned away. Lyonya would be ripping the floor of his dugout to bits pacing, I thought, but I couldn't abandon the stakeout—not yet. "What if he's dead?" I asked as another midnight rolled over the ravine. "What if our side finished the sniper off in the forest somewhere after he retreated from his last sortie here?"

Kostia passed me a pinch of dry tea and a lump of sugar wrapped in foil. Chew the sugar and the tea together, it helped keep you awake on a long stakeout, and without pouring tea into your belly that you'd have to pee out into a can. "You want him badly," my partner observed. "More than the usual target."

"Yes." I thought about why for a half hour or so. Kostia and I could have four-sentence conversations that stretched over hours; there was no need to hurry in a sniper's nest. "I don't have any ridiculous notion that what snipers do is unfair," I said finally. "The Hitlerites invaded and then started exterminating us—we're stopping them however we can. They already have the upper hand in so many ways. So I don't have time for anyone who says firing on them from the shadows might not be fair."

"No one says that," Kostia observed, and he was right. A few weeks in the chaos and cruelty of the front lines was enough to turn even the most ardent lover of fair play into a soldier who would do *anything* to beat back the swastika. The whole notion of what constituted a fair fight wasn't a question to be entertained during a brutal invasion; it was an academic argument for peacetime. But I was an academic at heart, and in long empty nights like this, theoretical questions still sometimes floated through my mind.

"A sniper against a sniper . . ." I paused, thinking for another silent half hour. Kostia waited, chewing tea. "This is about as close to a truly fair fight—whatever that's worth—as we're going to see in this ugly war," I finished at last.

"It's two against one," Kostia pointed out.

"Fine, spoil my theory. It's not much of one anyway." And I was all right with that. I just yearned, looking at the bridge where I hoped to trap my enemy, to win this duel.

The moon climbed. The tea ran out; the bread ran out. Hunger raked at my stomach with steel claws, but I dozed despite myself, chin drooping as I squatted with my shoulder hard against the trench wall—and that was when Kostia touched my shoulder. I came awake with a snap as he pointed at the bridge.

Watch now. The duel begins.

The first frozen light of an approaching January dawn is just creeping over the bridge, barely enough to see the shadowed figure of a man picking his way through the iron tangle of beams. He's late, rushing but still keeping low—he vanishes almost as fast as he appeared in the first place, too fast for me to fire.

Kostia and I trade looks. He gestures with one thumb; I nod. My partner begins slithering on his stomach back along the trench toward the front line as I watch the bridge through my sights. Across the gully, the German sniper will be settling into his nest out of sight, setting up his own rifle, finding familiar markers to gauge today's kill shots. Only there won't be any. Mine should take him from below.

Half an hour ticks past as day brightens in utter silence. No chatter of mortar fire this morning as the guns on either side clear their throats; no fighters or bombers rising into the sky. The war has withdrawn from view, like a swan folding her wings. There is only a gully, and a sniper on either side of it. I put two fingers to my lips and let out a low, crooning birdcall Vartanov taught me. A moment later I hear Kostia answer with a whistle of his own.

I never take my eyes off the bridge, but my mind sees every move my partner makes, clear as day. He's pushing Ivan into position: a mannequin we fashioned with a stuffed torso on a stick, dressed in winter overcoat and a captain's helmet. From across the bridge, it should look like a Soviet officer has abandoned his post for a moment and gone to the edge of the ravine for a morning stretch.

Old trick, Kostia had said as we wrestled Ivan into a spare uniform.

Good trick, I'd responded.

The shot from the far side of the bridge sounds muted, a gong from a cracked bell. I see a brief glitter of light in the tangle of shattered iron beams, and my sights hone in. *There you are,* I think even as Kostia lets Ivan's stuffed body fall. *There you are, you Nazi bastard.* The German sniper sitting on the heel of his right leg, rifle propped in the crook of a bent branch, almost completely hidden by a metal beam. Through my sights I see him pull the bolt of his rifle, pocket the spent cartridge . . . and raise his head to look out of his nest.

Midnight, I think.

And fire.

"SO WAS HE a big name?"

"Very. Helmut Bommel, Iron Cross, 121st Infantry Regiment, 50th Brandenburg Infantry Division, Oberfeldwebel—" I let out a groan as Lyonya's hands worked at my aching feet. The minute he'd put me down after pulling me out of the staff car and hugging the breath out of me, he bore me off to his dugout, peeled me down to my undershirt, wrapped me in a blanket, and parked me beside the glowing stove, hunkering down on a stool to pull my feet into his lap.

"Stop squirming, *milaya,* your feet are like blocks of ice. How were you able to find out his name and rank?" Massaging my tingling toes.

"His soldier's book." The sniper's body had plummeted from the bridge to the ravine below like a falling star; Kostia had covered me with his own rifle as I slipped and slithered down the brush-choked gully to search the corpse for usable intelligence. "It said he'd fought in Poland, Belgium, and France, and that he served as a sniper instructor in Berlin. He had 215 kills," I said, thinking of that cold-stippled, rosy-cheeked face on the dead man lying among the frost-white reeds.

"What's that grimace for?" Lyonya's hands worked up to my calves, knotted and aching.

"I don't like looking at their faces afterward," I admitted.

"Lady Death is human after all." Lyonya smiled. "Don't worry, I won't tell the brass."

I snorted. "The colonel of the 79th? He assumed Kostia made the shot. Looked right past me and asked how he'd done it."

"Turn around, let me at those shoulders . . ."

I turned, groaning again as Lyonya's strong thumbs began digging circles beside my neck, carefully avoiding my still-healing shrapnel wound. "You never saw a man look more embarrassed than that colonel when Kostia jerked a thumb at me. Fell over himself asking, *How is it this Hitlerite has two decorations and you have none, Comrade Senior Sergeant Pavlichenko*? Then it was Dromin's turn to look embarrassed. Ouch!"

"Two days in a sniper's nest chewing dry tea at negative thirty degrees Celsius, and you grouse at a shoulder rub?" Lyonya pressed a kiss between my shoulder blades, letting his mouth stay there a long moment. "I was terrified for you, *milaya,*" he said quietly. "I'd rather fight a hundred Hitlerites with bayonets than pace the dugout wondering if some blasted sniper instructor with a copy of *Mein Kampf* over his heart is going to make you his two hundred and sixteenth."

I felt my shoulders tense. "Lyonya . . . I won't give it up if that's what—"

"No. I'm not asking that." He turned me so we sat face-to-face. I already knew his face so well: the broad, high cheekbones; the clear blue eyes; the mouth that quirked on one side. No quirk now. "Just—be cautious."

"I can't be cautious," I said honestly. "Caution makes you miss. You can be cautious or you can be good, and I'm very good."

"You are good, you little killer." He pulled me into his chest, rubbing my arms, which were still prickled with the bone-deep cold of two days in that trench. "The world is about to know it."

"What do you mean?"

"I think Dromin's days of sitting on your achievements are done. You"—Lyonya kissed the tip of my nose—"are about to become famous."

CHAPTER 18

My memoir, the official version: I was congratulated by General Petrov in the matter of the sniper duel, and he told me he hoped I would not rest on my victories but would continue to crush the foes of our socialist homeland. He also informed me that an account of the sniper duel would be broadcast throughout the Sevastopol defense district, and I would have my picture taken for some combat leaflets. I was pleased to comply, in the name of inspiring our brave soldiers of the Soviet Union.

My memoir, the unofficial version: Combat leaflets? For the love of Lenin.

I DON'T KNOW why anyone wants to become famous. It's utterly maddening. First the visit from the senior political officer, and then hordes of press, each visit more annoying than the last.

From the chirpy photographer of the coastal army newspaper *For the Motherland:* "You're very photogenic, Comrade Senior Sergeant. Try a smile—"

From the correspondent of *Beacon of the Commune*: "Details of the duel will be most helpful . . . Are you sure that's how it happened? Wasn't it a little more dramatic? Try to look more friendly for the camera—"

From the writer sent by *Red Crimea*: "How about a smile for your partner? I'm sure he helped you make that fateful shot!"

From the war cine-cameraman Comrade Vladislav Mikosha: "I'm looking for the right *angle* for this footage; I'm just not *seeing it*. Look, climb up that apple tree there and strike a pose with your gun. Big smile—"

"No," I snapped, finally cracking. "I'm not climbing up an *apple tree*, and it is a *rifle*, not a gun."

My lover and my partner were no help. Lyonya was laughing so hard he could barely stand; Kostia had to hold him up, eyes dancing. I shot them both a filthy look as the cameraman fiddled with his camera.

"Look," I said, trying to lay it out for a civilian, "I don't shoot from trees in Sevastopol, so any picture of me like that is misleading. And I can't answer questions about marksmanship, camouflage techniques, or my methods for hunting—anything printed in a newspaper will end up in enemy hands."

He gave a blithe wave. "We don't need technical details, Comrade Senior Sergeant, we need excitement! Tell us about the cold gray eye of the fascist oppressor as you locked gazes through your sights—"

"We didn't lock gazes through our sights. That isn't how this works."

"—tell me how you trembled with hatred for the invader Helmut Bommel before overcoming your rage to pull the trigger—"

"I don't feel rage when I pull the trigger. That would be distracting. You come to firing position with a heart at rest and the knowledge that you are in the right, and I guarantee that Helmut Bommel felt the exact same way." I gave Lyonya a *Help me* glance, but he just stood there, broad shoulders shaking with laughter.

"Look, Lyudmila Mikhailovna," the cameraman finally said, sounding amused, "I don't care what you felt when you pulled the trigger. People need heroes right now, and you've been picked for the role, so say a few nice things about how inspired you are by the bravery of your comrades in arms and the leadership of the Party and climb up in that damned apple tree with your rifle. And *smile*."

I bit my tongue. The whole circus was absurd, but he wasn't wrong about the need for heroes. I didn't think I was one, but maybe Slavka would read the accounts and be proud of his mother—who he hadn't seen now in more than a year. So I climbed the damned tree, posed with my rifle, and bared my teeth in what you might, in a charitable mood, call a smile.

At least after this it will all be done, I thought, ignoring the muffled chortles from Kostia and Lyonya as I tried to figure out what exactly "Put a heroic gleam in your eye!" meant. *They'll all go away and leave me alone.*

"Wrong, *milaya,*" Lyonya said when the stories came in. "I'm afraid this is only the beginning."

"They got it all wrong," I nearly wailed, pacing up and down the dugout as I read one of the newspaper clippings. "Listen to this: *In the pale light of dawn, Lyudmila saw her enemy behind a tree root . . .* They reset everything in the forest; apparently the bridge wasn't dramatic enough? . . . *Suddenly she caught in the lines of her sight the Hitlerite sniper's deadened eyes, flaxen hair, slab-like jaw . . .* That's not what he looked like, and I never tried to describe him anyway! *Life was decided in an instant—by a mere second, she beat him to the shot. Taking the Nazi sniper's notebooks, she read that more than 400 Frenchmen and Englishmen had perished at his fascist hands.* It was 215, not—"

"*Beacon of the Commune* put his tally at 600 Soviet lives alone," Lyonya said, reading away.

"Who is going to believe that?" I stuffed the clipping into the stove. "No German sniper has had a chance of racking up that many Red Army kills by this point in the war. Entrenched fighting and long sieges, that's where sharpshooting come into play. The Hitlerites have been here only half a year, and they've been pushing forward with tanks and aircraft, not digging in with telescopic sights. Positional fighting—"

"I love it when you start footnoting yourself about positional fighting." Lyonya tossed the clippings aside and tugged me into his lap. "You can take the sniper out of the student, but you cannot take the student out of the sniper."

"It's all absolute rubbish," I grumbled, thumping my head on his shoulder.

"They're propagandists, *milaya*. They deal in rubbish. They're determined to make you a heroine—"

I made retching noises.

"—and personally, I quite like the thought of marrying a heroine. You earn the glory, I bask. I've already been asked what it's like to live with the girl sniper herself—"

I groaned but could feel a smile starting to creep over my face. "What did you say?"

"I was very complimentary. I told them you were lethal on the battlefield yet an utter disaster in the kitchen, and what man could possibly want more in a wife?"

"You don't even know if I can cook or not—"

"I'm sure you have a box of recipes somewhere, and they're all beautifully footnoted. With blood splatter," Lyonya added, and as I exploded into laughter, he picked me up and slung me over one shoulder. "When can we get married?" he asked, tossing me down on his army cot.

"Later." I pulled him down on top of me, taking his face between my hands for a long kiss. "Come here . . ."

"Why later?" he asked afterward when both of us were still breathing hard, damp with sweat, our limbs interlocked. "Why not get things finalized with Alexei and marry me, Mila?"

My hand was still tangled in his hair, brushing slowly up and down from the soft strands at the crown to the short velvety buzz down his neck. "I love you, Lyonya—but are you sure I'm what you want? It's so soon . . ."

"It's been a month since you started here with me. A month in front-line time? That's a year in peacetime." He gave me a shrewd look. "I think you're just dragging your feet at the idea of facing Alexei about the divorce."

I was dragging my feet, and I hated that. I knew, I just *knew*, that Alexei would make trouble when I told him I wanted a divorce so I could marry someone else, and it felt unlucky to invite even a drop more trouble into life when Lyonya and I were already living in a war zone. "What's the rush?" I asked, ducking the subject. "What do we get by marrying that we don't have now?" I indicated the little world of the dugout: the stove that warmed our evenings; the table where we ate supper; this cot where we burrowed against the cold.

"If we were married, you'd get my pension if I die," Lyonya pointed out. "Come on, Lady Death—marry me for the money."

"Maybe you're trying to marry me for mine," I teased. "My ever-so-luxurious senior sergeant pension if I cap it here on the front line."

"I would like to know you're taken care of, after all this." That quirk of Lyonya's mouth. "Things get lean and hungry after wars. I'm eleven years older than you; I probably remember the hungry times after the last war a bit more clearly."

"Don't worry on that score." I traced the outer edge of his eyebrow. "I won't ever starve. My father knows people. The kind of people who never die of hunger, but make sure their enemies do."

"Then marry me so your father won't accuse me of despoiling his daughter and decide to take steps." Lyonya rolled onto his back, grinning, arm still around my waist. "Make an honest man of me before I'm found floating in a river."

"If a man ever ends up floating in a river on my behalf, *I'll* be the one who put him there, not my father!" I burrowed into Lyonya's shoulder. "Though Papa would probably like it if you ask for his approval."

"I'll make you a trade. I'll write to your father if you tackle Alexei."

I took a long breath. Yes, I could do that. I'd faced down far worse in this war than Alexei, so this heel-dragging was inexcusable. "I'd like a chance to write to Slavka first, get him accustomed to the idea. You haven't even met him, and he's part of any decision I make."

"I may not know him yet, but he's yours, so I'll love him, too." Lyonya quirked an eyebrow. "You don't think I'd refuse to raise a boy I hadn't fathered?"

I'd run across men before who felt that way. And Alexei hadn't even wanted to raise the boy he *had* fathered. But no, I didn't think Lyonya was like that. "Alexei left us," I said slowly, "and it hurt Slavka to grow up knowing his father didn't want him. If I bring someone else into Slavka's life and it goes wrong, he'll be hurt all over again. So you need to be sure, Lyonya. Are you?"

He plaited his fingers slowly with mine, one finger at a time. "I've been sure since the moment I met you, Mila. Why?"

"Because it's wartime. This isn't normal, this life we're leading." The only time we saw each other was a few hours in the evening: Lyonya was long asleep at midnight when I was tugging on my boots to head out into no-man's-land; by the time I returned with my rifle by noon or so and tumbled yawning into bed, he would be long gone on his lieutenant's duties. The only time we really saw each other was after twilight, when he came in from the command post and woke me up with "Dinner's here, *milaya*." We might have a few hours in bed after eating, but when he dropped off to sleep tonight I'd be climbing into my uniform and heading off to hunt with Kostia. "This isn't real life—yet we're talking about making a real life together." I made myself say it, the thing I feared. "What if we find out we don't suit each other in ordinary times? What do ordinary times even look like?"

"Well, I'll tell you." Still plaiting my fingers with his own. "I'd find work in Moscow—I have my electrical certification, technicians like me can always work. You'd finish your dissertation, get your degree, become a historian or a librarian. We would live on the same clock, go off to work at the same time every day. I'd put jam in your tea for you every morning while you packed us lunches, and if we worked close enough together, we'd meet on our lunch hour. And when Slavka comes home from school, he and I will bash hockey sticks around in Gorky Park." Lyonya smiled. "The only real difference in our lives, Lyudmila Mikhailovna, is that instead of asking 'How many Nazis did you kill today?' I'd be asking 'How many footnotes did you annotate today?' "

I sat up, pulling the blanket round my shoulders to hide my shiver. Not a shiver of cold—a shiver of *yearning*. I could see it, feel it, almost touch it: that shared apartment, the tea with jam, the lunches and games in the park. A golden, glorious *then* on the other side of our bleak, bloodstained *now*.

If there is a then, my thoughts whispered. Because it wasn't gone, that fear that still sometimes clutched my throat. The certainty that the next bullet would kill me . . . that all Lyonya's talk of the future was pointless, because the only future for me was a coffin.

"By the way—" Lyonya kissed the side of my neck. "I've rung the sergeant major to find you a parade uniform in the regimental stores."

"I spend most of my days dressed as a bush," I said. "What do I need a new parade uniform for?"

"FIRST TIME?" COMRADE Senior Sergeant Onilova condescended to ask. "I suppose I was nervous the first time I made a public speech. I've done so many now, I can't remember." She straightened her Order of the Red Banner; I wanted to say I'd seen them pin it on her for her machine-gun heroics, but I was too nervous. Nervous or not, my orders were clear: *On February 2, 1942, platoon commander Senior Sergeant Pavlichenko, L.M., is to leave the front line and join a conference of female activists in the defense of Sevastopol, where she is to give an address of up to fifteen minutes on the operations and activities of snipers.*

"A formal public address?" I'd said, highly dubious. "I shoot people from long distances away, doing my best never to be seen, and they want me to stand in front of a packed audience hall under glaring lights and give a speech? I mean, I'll try, but—"

"Shut up, Mila, you'll be brilliant," said Lyonya.

"The brass haven't thought this through at all. What if I fall on my face? What's *that* going to do for morale among female activists in the defense of Sevastopol?"

"The brass never think *anything* through, and you're not going to fall on your face. You shoot Iron Cross sharpshooters through the eye socket for a living; don't tell me you're afraid of a little public speaking."

"Not a bit," I lied. And here I was in the regimental commander's car, wearing a uniform skirt and stockings for the first time in eight months, nervously flicking through my talking points, which were looking stupider by the minute.

"You're the girl sniper, aren't you?" Onilova continued, looking mildly interested. "Don't tell me you have *notes*? Goodness, I haven't needed notes in ages. Don't read off your page, that's fatal. And don't hunch at the rostrum—"

She went on rat-a-tat-tatting like her machine gun, all the way from the front lines into Sevastopol, as I chewed my lip and picked at my stockings, which both sagged and itched. I should have been drinking in the sights of the city as the car rolled through its heart—it had been so long since I'd seen houses, spires, anything that wasn't olive-drab and made of metal and canvas—but I was too nervous. A whirl through the Teachers' House, where the conference was being held, and then suddenly I was in a hall full of women. Machine Gunner Onilova was carried off at once by a crowd of eager fans, but I stood staring. I hadn't seen so many women in one place in months: blue dresses and rosy blouses, long braids swaying against bony hips . . . and like drab spots among the finery, the severe uniform tunics of the servicewomen like me. Narrow-eyed lynxes in a crowd of gentle house cats.

Or maybe not *so gentle,* I thought, seeing the fierceness on the civilian women's faces as they gathered to sit. They were carrying on life in the middle of a siege, after all—they knew what the cost would be if the city fell. After some official droning from the brass, it was women getting up to speak, one after the other, and suddenly I was riveted. Some had notes like me; others extemporized as they told their stories. A yellow-kerchiefed woman taught a classroom full of children in a bomb shelter every day; a stout apple-cheeked matriarch put in twelve-hour shifts stamping out hand grenades. A woman who had lost her left arm in a bombing raid had still stayed in the city to work—she met her quota every day, she said fiercely, because it was her part to play in fighting the enemy. Her empty left sleeve was pinned to her dress like a decoration, worn as proudly as Onilova's Order of the Red Banner. I was supposed to follow her with a dry account of Nazis wiped out in Crimean forests?

When it came time to get up and address them, I had tears in my eyes. I crumpled my talking points in my hand and heard myself saying, "The thing you have to know in your bones is that you can never miss. Not ever, not in war, not in civilian life, or that mistake will be your downfall."

And I spoke from the heart.

"How did that go?" Lyonya asked when I returned.

"Dreadfully," I admitted. "I fumbled. I backtracked. I hemmed and hawed a great deal. But they gave me a round of applause anyway, and told me to kill a Hitlerite apiece in their name, and I promised I would. So I must have done something right." I began peeling gratefully out of the parade uniform, looking forward to my padded trousers and camouflage smock.

"You have the best legs on the front line," Lyonya admired, watching me carefully roll down my stockings.

"That is an unbacked supposition. How can you possibly know I have the best legs at the front without extensive gathering of further data?"

"I have no intention of gathering further data. No interest at all in seeing Kostia or old Vartanov in a skirt. Are you really going to kill one more apiece for all those women?"

"They'll hunt me down if I fail." I pulled up my trousers, buckling the belt around my hips. "They nearly asked me to bring them ears as proof."

"Women are bloodthirsty creatures. The English and Americans are utter fools if they think females are too delicate to send to the front." Lyonya handed me my boots. "So, your first public speaking engagement—that's a milestone."

"First?" I snorted, pulling out my heavy socks. "After my performance today, no one's ever going to put me in front of a crowd again."

Fate must really have had itself a laugh, there.

CHAPTER 19

M*y memoir, the official version: March 4, 1942. The day that . . .*

My memoir, the unofficial version: . . .

SPRING! I DON'T remember ever greeting a season's shift with more joy. A week ago had brought us storms of low clouds, flurrying snow, frost crunching underfoot. Today the snow had melted, the sun shone down, the temperature bloomed well north of zero. In the Crimean heights you could glimpse yellowed grass, new shoots of juniper, cypresses and cedars putting out bright green growth—I'd be able to start taking leaf and flower samples for Slavka again. I scanned the valley through my binoculars, nearly beaming.

"Spring means another assault soon," Vartanov growled at my elbow. "They've been quiet too long."

"Then let's shake them up." I had seven of my platoon with me today, because an entire group of Nazi snipers had nested themselves on a hilltop our maps had simply labeled No-Name Height. They'd targeted traffic on the dirt road passing below; half the personnel of a 45mm antitank gun had been downed yesterday, and answering with artillery fire just made the German sharpshooters change position and resume picking us off. "Take your boys, Lyudmila Mikhailovna," I was ordered—so here we were with almost the whole platoon.

"Eyes on our bushes," I ordered. Last night in Lyonya's dugout, Vartanov and Kostia and I had crammed in to make six decoy bushes, wiring long juniper branches together in bunches. *We look like brides making garlands,* Lyonya remarked, pitching in to help, *but with more khaki.* Kostia fired back with *You're the ugliest bride I ever saw, Kitsenko,* and I'd plunked myself down between them before they could start trying to arm-wrestle among the bushes, scolding *You two!* as Lyonya kissed my neck and Kostia lobbed a juniper frond at me. Lyonya had hugged me goodbye on the dugout steps at three in the morning when I set out, then more formally returned my salute when we stepped into the open. It was always like that: the minute we put a toe over the dugout threshold we were no longer lovers. We were regimental comrades who gave each other a formal farewell and a call of "Good hunting."

And now the long night of setting the trap was done, and I watched through my binoculars for the German snipers to take the bait: our decoy bushes, which would stick out like obvious decoys to the enemy who knew every centimeter of this hill by now, and who could be counted on to notice when six new bushes appeared on the slope overnight. And I couldn't stop myself from beaming when daylight broke, as the Hitlerites saw the conspicuous new brush we'd placed in the dead of night and began to thunder fire down on our wired juniper branches, which they assumed we'd brought to hide behind.

"There—" Kostia pointed out one of the hidden German sniper nests, tracking it from the downward angle of fire. "And there—and there—" And when the German fire ceased and the Nazi snipers put their heads up to survey the damage, a hail of Russian bullets greeted them.

"*Up!*" I shouted when everything went still. "*Forward!*" and we flowed up the last hundred meters of No-Name Height, over the top and down into the enemy trenches at the crown. Not just a complex of sniper parapets up here, but an entrenched net of communication passages and machine-gun nests, three MG 34 machine guns with loaded ammunition belts trained on the road below . . . Vartanov fired off a red flare, which meant *We've captured it*; a green flare bloomed in response on the Soviet side of no-man's-land, meaning *Well done!* The road below would soon be swarming with our troops, but my platoon looked at me, poised and hungry.

"Wait here," Kostia asked, "or clear it out?" There were undoubtedly more Hitlerites in there, who'd ambush us given half a chance.

I grinned at my partner. "Clear it out."

We tore through like methodical wolves, one dugout after another. Pitching hand grenades through doorways, shielding ourselves from the blast, then fanning through with snapped shots and wary eyes on each other's backs. A corporal with a Walther charged me with a shrill cry; I snapped my pistol up, but Kostia dropped the man with a thrust of his Finnish combat knife. A German captain went down after clipping Fyodor's earlobe with a wild shot. When we finally cleared out the underground staff quarters, we whooped with triumph to see a portable radio set with transceiver and batteries, rod aerial spearing through the dugout roof. "The reconnaissance officer will dance a jig," Vartanov chortled, disconnecting the radio for transport—a working enemy radio was such a prize, and here we had earphones, codebooks, and record books. I began dividing them for my men to carry, the blood beating in me: *Keep going, keep going.*

"Mila!" Kostia's shout came from the eastern side of the dugout, and rushing to his side, I saw the team of German submachine gunners, at least twenty, struggling up a narrow track through hazel bushes. My platoon closed around me, eight rifle butts hitting shoulders, eight barrels smacking parapets. I called out the calculations that had spliced through my head in a half second, finishing with *Adjust for downward aim, boys, don't miss*—and snapped the first shot off, bringing the storm of bullets down.

"How many did you get?" the young captain who relieved us from our position said a few hours later.

"Thirty-five," I said, and my platoon clustered around me with fierce cheers. I kissed every one of my men on both cheeks like a brother, too choked to speak. Lumbering Fyodor and my silent Kostia, who were both junior sergeants now, old Vartanov and the other men whom I'd nurtured from fumbling green recruits to cool, capable shooters . . . there wasn't a one who couldn't move like a shadow through brush or woods now; not a one who couldn't hold himself motionless in the dark and the cold for six hours straight if that was what the shot required. "Let the Germans bring that third assault," I yelled over the din as my shouting men carried me on their shoulders back toward our division. "Give my platoon the high ground and enough ammunition, and we'll stop the whole eastern advance in its tracks!"

"You'll be decorated for this one," Lyonya told me that night. "You and Kostia. Dromin is yowling like a kitten in a rain barrel, but he can't stop the awards coming down from Petrov. You'll soon have enough tin on your tunic to make a dinner service, *milaya*. How many does that make on your tally now?"

"Two forty-two." I went on tiptoe in my combat boots to kiss him. "Being in love is good for my shooting. I swear, every bullet zings along the right trajectory when I know I'm coming home to you . . ."

"For the love of Lenin, woman, did you just say you loved me as you *tallied your dead*? Classic Mila Pavlichenko." He kissed me back, and I nearly puddled down into my boots. "You've been awarded a leave pass for Sevastopol. I can take leave, too—what do you say to an afternoon in town?"

"A day off? Together?" I'd spent my last half day off trying to find Alexei at the hospital battalion, finally leaving a note for him that I wanted to discuss the finalization of our divorce as soon as possible. I still hadn't had any response, and I knew I'd have to go track him down, but I wasn't going to waste a leave pass on Alexei when I could spend it in Sevastopol with Lyonya.

It felt like the strangest thing in the world to walk with him along the winding waterfront path that weekend, an old floral skirt rippling around my knees instead of my greatcoat, Lyonya in an unraveling knitted jumper rather than his epaulets. Arm in arm like any ordinary couple enjoying a Sunday afternoon, looking at the sweeping expanse of the sea, stopping periodically to kiss the salt from each other's lips. He bought me a posy of early-blooming hyacinths, then rescued it when I started gesturing a little too vigorously at the Monument to the Sunken Ships: "Erected to honor the scuttling of the Black Sea Fleet during the Crimean War! I wrote a paper about that once. One of the few monuments from czarist days to eschew ostentation for simplicity—just that single granite column on a spire of rock, and the lapping waves all around. You know it was designed by—"

"I do not know who it was designed by, and I have a feeling there's nothing in the world that will stop you from telling me," Lyonya said, wrapping his arms around me from behind and resting his chin on top of my head as I chattered, waving at the monument.

"History lives all around," I concluded happily after Mila the student came out of hibernation with a really-quite-curtailed lecture on the works of Amandus Adamson and his influence on the Russian Art Nouveau style. "You can breathe it in on every street corner. Can we go to the museum on Frunze Street? One of the women at the conference told me there's a special historical exhibit. The first siege of 1854 through the revolution—"

"Life with you is going to mean trudging through a great many museums, isn't it?" Lyonya complained.

"—the factory exhibits! Did you know the lathe operators association has a special—"

"Yes, yes, I will take you to the damned museum . . ."

I WAS STILL thinking about the museum the next morning, after we'd returned to the front line. That evening I'd get back to my usual nocturnal habits, but for today I could wake up with the sun and wander outside in the spring sunshine to enjoy my breakfast like any ordinary soldier. Yawning, pondering the exhibit on Sevastopol's role in the revolution and wondering if there were parallels I could draw to my dissertation topic, I took my cup of lukewarm coffee and joined Lyonya, who was already sitting on a fallen log with his mess tin, teasing Kostia.

"My father does not transform into a wolf by the light of the moon," Kostia was saying as he sewed down a loop of shaggy netting on his camouflage smock. "You met him once, and you're convinced he's a *bodark*?"

"I swear he had incisors that lengthened whenever he smiled, and so did that sister of yours."

"*Half* sister—"

"The wolf half. Your family is all feral, you Siberian miscreant—"

They kept ribbing each other as I sat down on the log. Lyonya draped an absent-minded arm around my shoulders—*You soft southern boys wouldn't last a day on the Siberian taiga, Lyonya—I should order you to take your boots off, Kostia, I'll bet we'll find wolf claws instead of toes*—and I stole a wedge of black bread off Lyonya's mess tin, scattering crumbs for the Sevastopol sparrows. They hopped around my boots, twittering and pecking, utterly unafraid. How could such tiny, fragile things have no fear at all?

"Ah, the morning chamber music," Lyonya remarked as the usual scattering of long-range German artillery fire began. "Will it be Brahms or Wagner today?" We listened to the first shells explode, far in the rear. "Wagner," Lyonya decided as the second salvo appeared to fall short. "I'm definitely hearing the timpani come in."

I was laughing, Kostia was laughing, Lyonya was laughing as he gave my shoulders a squeeze and said, "How'd you sleep, *milaya*? You're not tired, are you?" and then a shell from the third German salvo exploded directly at our backs.

The three of us hit the ground, arms around heads. Lyonya's arm dragged me down beneath him as splinters and shrapnel tore the air. My ears rang, and I coughed as I was crushed between the hard earth and Lyonya's heavy chest. I unlaced my fingers from around my head and looked up when the din cleared.

"Mila?" Kostia was doing the same, looking around. He had a shrapnel cut on his forehead streaming blood, but he was already rising. Lyonya uncurled from around me with a groan, pulling to a sitting position against the log, and I crawled clear with my ears still buzzing.

"You half crushed me," I started to say, smiling, and then I saw the pallor on Lyonya's broad, handsome face. Saw the red wetness soaking his right shoulder, saw that something was wrong—terribly, horrendously wrong—with his right arm hanging limp inside its sleeve. Then my entire rib cage felt like it was collapsing on itself as I rose and caught sight of the red ruin of my lover's back.

Splinter wounds, driving deep through tunic and undershirt to the flesh below as he wrapped his body around me, to protect me.

"Listen to that brass section," he said, trying to smile, and then he toppled slowly sideways into the earth.

THE MEDICAL BATTALION again. I knew it so well now, it was like home. Only this time I wasn't the one being wheeled into the operating theater on a stretcher. "Lyonya, breathe, just breathe. You're in good hands now." My hand hadn't left his pale, sweating forehead on the entire jolting, rattling ride to this underground hell of disinfectant and glaring lights; now he was wheeled away from me and I felt his soft hair glide out from under my fingertips like a phantom.

Stupidly I started to follow and Kostia pulled me back. "Let the surgeon work." He'd helped me carry Lyonya to the first-aid station on a blanket, and now he was pulling me away.

"Blood," I babbled, remembering when it had been me who was wounded. "They'll need blood for him, we're the same type—" I tore my sleeve open, giving the nurse my arm for the needle. I'd have opened my veins with my teeth and funneled my blood right into Lyonya's body if they'd let me. He wasn't supposed to be injured, not a lieutenant who spent his days at the command post, and this wasn't even a proper assault—it was the morning *chamber music.* Why then was he *injured*?

"Mila." Kostia took me by the shoulders, his face blurring in and out, streaked with dried blood down one side like a harlequin mask. He had one sleeve pushed up too; the nurse was taking a pint of my blood and pint of my partner's into the operating theater. "We wait now."

And we waited. I paced the underground corridor; Kostia sat against a wall with his elbows on his drawn-up knees, frozen still as though he were on stakeout. Maybe there were others waiting with us; I don't know. I just paced, counting the minutes as they ticked past like beads of frozen amber.

And then two surgeons came out, gloved in blood up to their elbows.

"Bear up, Lyudmila Mikhailovna." The older man gave my hands a squeeze, face drawn. "His right arm had to be amputated. It was hanging by a single tendon."

My breath went in and out, but I couldn't breathe. Dimly I heard Kostia saying, "He can live without an arm."

The other surgeon spoke up then, and with dull shock, I saw it was Alexei. "What's much worse are the seven splinters in his back. I've taken three out, but the rest—"

I don't remember what happened then. I don't remember. I don't remember. I came back to myself in a room somewhere, sitting on a narrow cot. My hand fell to my holster automatically, and found it empty. "Where is my pistol?" I asked the nurse.

"Your weapon will be returned later when you aren't so—"

"No." With a wrench I managed to stand. "Give it back. Give it back right now."

"Mila, stop." Kostia's voice, Kostia's arms keeping me from lunging at the nurse.

"You think I'm going to shoot myself?" I screamed. "No. No, that won't happen." I stopped fighting, seizing my partner by the collar and yanking him toward me until our noses nearly collided. "Give me. My *pistol*."

Kostia got it for me. I could see the terrible doubt in his eyes, the tension that coiled through him—but I only buttoned it back into its holster with numb fingers. I didn't know how to be calm without a weapon at hand. I looked back up with swimming eyes. "Now take me to him."

My love lay white-bandaged and still in a curtained-off cot. So still. I went to my knees at his side, reaching out to touch his one remaining hand. "Lyonya." I tried to say it, clear and calm, but no sound came out, only my lips moving silently. His entire torso wrapped in bandages, his right arm ending in a gauze-capped stump just under the shoulder. His face was drained, empty, no sign of the laugh lines that crinkled his eyes or the humorous vitality that quirked his smile.

I unholstered my pistol, feeling Kostia tense again, but I only folded Lyonya's limp hand over it and then enclosed both between my own. It wasn't my Three Line, but it still knew the same song. "You're going to make it," I whispered, my eyes blurring. "And then I'll down another hundred Nazis just for the one who fired that mortar at you."

I squeezed his hand, but there was no answering squeeze. No flicker in the vacant face. Throat choked, I put my pistol on the nightstand and crawled onto the cot beside him, my head on his shoulder. I'd lain like that so many nights . . . no. Not so many. It had been only three months since we came together. Not enough time. Surely we were going to have more time. He would make it.

"He might wake," the nurse said, sounding flat. "You could try reading to him, speaking to him."

I tried. I tried so hard, but the only sound I could squeeze out was a strangled sob. I just lay shaking against Lyonya's shoulder. Kostia sat down on the other side of the cot, his eyes like black holes burned in snow, and I saw the same helplessness in his carved face. We were snipers; the world of silence and darkness was where we lived. This terrible place of bright lights and loud voices had us both flailing.

Seeing I still couldn't speak, Kostia reached into his pack and took out his battered, bloodstained *War and Peace*. His voice was hoarse as he began to read, translating the English edition to Russian. " '*Vera,' she said to her oldest daughter, who was clearly not a favorite, 'how can you have so little tact? Don't you see you aren't wanted here?*' "

Kostia kept reading as the nurse faded away and my tears began to slide. *You aren't wanted here,* I told death, breathing faint and inexorable over my shoulder. *You were supposed to take me. Not him.*

Death didn't care. He stood at my shoulder, implacable, immovable, as the hours of day slipped into night, as Kostia read and read and read, as Lyonya sometimes stirred in delirium and opened blind, blank eyes, and sometimes lay still as a headstone. Once he turned his head in my direction—I thought perhaps he smiled at me. Kostia stopped then, so hoarse his voice was almost gone.

I took Lyonya's hand between my own, kissed his papery cheek. "We're getting married," I whispered. "Remember?" He didn't move, didn't smile, didn't speak. Death kept on breathing at my shoulder. "I got the divorce. I can marry you now." Anything I could say to keep him here, keep him with me. "We can marry now. I'll marry you tomorrow."

I kept saying it long after he was gone.

THE SOVIET DELEGATION: DAY 1

August 27, 1942

WASHINGTON, D.C.

CHAPTER 20

The White House welcome breakfast was almost over. Teacups were being drained, smears of maple syrup were being mopped up, the buzz of chatter through the small dining room was dying away. The marksman was swirling the dregs of his coffee and laying silent plans when someone finally got up the courage to ask the girl sniper what everyone had been thinking since the moment she arrived.

"Mrs. Pavlichenko, I'm simply ravenous with curiosity . . . Is it true you are a . . . a *sharpshooter*? That you've, um, well"—no one wanted to say the word *killed*—"*dispatched* 309 enemies?"

The whole table fell silent then, and every American eye went to Lyudmila Pavlichenko. Some were disapproving, some disbelieving, all were curious. The marksman sat back in his chair, every bit as curious to see how she would reply.

The Russian girl's neat, pretty face showed no sign of annoyance. She turned a polite smile across the table and said through the interpreter, "Yes, it's quite true."

Bullshit, thought the marksman. He knew women who could shoot: backwoods wives who filled their family soup pots with whatever they could bag; society belles who enjoyed a little gossipy target practice before a three-martini lunch; sporty girls who lined their rooms with competition ribbons for marksmanship. But he did not believe a woman could shoot 309 men—and if she did, she'd be in handcuffs or a straitjacket. No woman could shoot 309 men and be capable of sipping tea with the First Lady, cool as a cucumber.

The buzz that swept the table sounded skeptical; evidently the marksman wasn't the only one with doubts. Eleanor Roosevelt, however, looked thoughtful, sitting with her chin resting in her hand. "Can you see their faces?" she asked.

Her interpreter, a young officer in lieutenant's epaulets, murmured a translation as the girl sniper answered. "Their faces, Mrs. Roosevelt?"

"Of the men you shot. If you had a good view of the faces of your enemies through your sights, but still fired to kill . . . well, it will be hard for American women to understand you, Lyudmila dear."

For a long moment, the girl sniper stared at the First Lady. Long enough for people to begin shifting in their seats, long enough to make the marksman's blood prickle in his veins. He had the urge to reach into his jacket for a weapon, but of course he hadn't brought so much as a pocket knife to the White House. Yet suddenly, here and now, he wished he had a gun.

"Mrs. Roosevelt," Mila Pavlichenko began, and with a jolt the marksman realized she was speaking in English. Her accent was marked, and she was clearly struggling to express herself correctly, but every word came slow, clear—and furious. "We are glad to visit your beautiful country. It is prosperous—you all live far from the struggle. Nobody destroys *your* towns, cities, fields. Nobody kills *your* citizens, your sisters and mothers, your fathers and brothers. I come from a place where bombs pound villages into ash, where Russian blood oils the treads of German tanks, where innocent civilians die every day."

She caught herself up, exhaled slowly as she marshaled her next words. No one moved, least of all the marksman.

"An accurate bullet fired by a sniper like me, Mrs. Roosevelt, is no more than a response to an enemy. My husband lost his life at Sevastopol before my eyes. He died in my arms. As far as I am concerned, any Hitlerite I see through my telescopic sights is the one who killed him."

A frozen silence fell over the room. Only the marksman's eyes moved as he looked around the table, cataloging responses. The Soviet delegation leader sat clutching his butter knife, looking like he wanted to saw off her head and bowl it through the window into the White House gardens. The smart Washington women in their frills and pearls looked appalled. The First Lady looked . . .

Embarrassed? the marksman wondered. Did that horsey presidential bitch look *embarrassed*?

"I'm sorry, Lyudmila dear," she said quietly, laying down her napkin. "I had no wish to offend you. This conversation is important, and we will continue it in a more suitable setting. But now, unfortunately, it is time to disperse. My duties are calling, and I understand you have a photographer waiting at the embassy."

She rose from the breakfast table, made some farewells, and was gone before the girl sniper could essay a response. "What did you say?" hissed the delegation leader. "We have orders not to offend them!"

"They offend *me*," Lyudmila Pavlichenko whispered back in furious nearly inaudible Russian. The marksman, looking after the First Lady's departure as though oblivious, strained to make out every word from two seats down. "I came here to help solicit aid for my comrades in arms, my friends at the front, men and women dying every day in their dugouts, and the President's wife sits there worrying that her husband's constituents won't find me *likable*?"

"Lyudmila Mikhailovna, you will obey directives—"

The back-and-forth hiss of Russian got too rapid for the marksman to follow, and the Soviet delegation was rising to leave anyway. Chairs were pushed back, pleasantries were exchanged in both languages, an aide hovered: "Mrs. Roosevelt has instructed me to give you a brief tour of the White House before you depart for the embassy . . ." The marksman faded into the departing throng of guests, turning to give one last thoughtful glance over his shoulder at the girl sniper. Color burned high and angry in her cheeks as she turned to follow the aide, and her eyes were molten.

For just one instant, the marksman wondered: *What if she actually* is *everything they say she is?*

Notes by the First Lady

"She put me in my place," I tell Franklin later ruefully. "No other word for it."

"I'd like to see the Russki who could do that." He grins.

"I wasn't intending to belittle her . . . if anything, it was American women I was thinking of less favorably. I want the Soviet delegation's time here to be a success, but the average Virginia housewife or Washington hostess will not make that easy for a woman like Mrs. Pavlichenko." I frown at myself as I pass my husband a new pen. It's not like me to stumble so with a guest, but my nagging worry about Franklin has me distracted this morning.

"Never mind American housewives. She'll have her hands full with the American press." He uncaps the pen, looking full of vim and vigor, which relieves me. "We'll see if she puts the journalists in their place at the press conference tonight."

He taps the pen against his leg brace, looking thoughtful even as we make notes for his upcoming tour of the western defense plants. He's wondering if the girl sniper can be useful in his crusade to swing public opinion in the matter of aid to the Soviet Union. He hopes she will be, not only because he wants his second front in Europe—and has been facing opposition to it given our setbacks in the Pacific—but because he has a most unusual liking for useful women. He collects us, and what a varied constellation of females we are. The shy, awkward wife he turned so efficiently into his eyes and ears . . . his impervious secretary Missy LeHand, who could organize that second front as efficiently as she organizes everything else in the White House . . . his labor secretary, Frances Perkins, the iron hand behind his New Deal, who dispatches strong men reeling from cabinet meetings . . .

Franklin's women. He collects us, admires us, hones us, and then he does not hesitate to use us up, burning through us body and soul until we flame out. If some part of us rises up in silent protest at such treatment—as it does sometimes in me, for things between us are not always easy—then it dies unspoken when we see that he burns himself up no less ruthlessly. We would all die for him, because he is killing himself for all of us.

Do they realize that, the men who are his enemies, who call him class traitor and communist lover and tyrant? The men he worries about now, whether he will admit it or not? Do they realize this man in leg braces is the bulwark against the fall of the West?

Or do they wish to topple him anyway, just so they can see the crash?

FIVE MONTHS AGO

March 1942

THE SEVASTOPOL FRONT, USSR

Mila

CHAPTER 21

My memoir, the official version: The funeral of my husband Lieutenant A. A. Kitsenko was attended by my entire platoon and all the officers of the 54th Regiment who were not on duty; the speeches were powerful and the salute heartfelt.

My memoir, the unofficial version: He was not my husband in law—I missed my chance for that, missed, *and the mockery of the loss cored me. But Lyonya was my husband in every way but law, and I knew I'd call him that until the day I died.*

"POST-TRAUMATIC NEUROSIS." ALEXEI Pavlichenko said it without bothering to examine me. "I'm giving you two weeks in hospital."

"This is absurd." I tried to push up from the chair.

He pushed me back down. "You nearly throttled the political instructor at Kitsenko's funeral."

I stared stonily, not speaking. The instructor had pressed into my face after the salute was fired over Lyonya's coffin, demanding to know why I hadn't fired my pistol with the rest. I'd seized him by the collar and grated, *My salute will be directed at the Nazis.* It was the only thing I remembered from the entire occasion.

"It took half your platoon to get you off him," Alexei continued. "He wants an apology. Your partner persuaded him you were suffering from shock."

"So why is a surgeon examining me, not a neuropathologist?"

"It doesn't take a specialist to identify post-traumatic neurosis. Besides, I told the man I was your husband, and so he should leave you to me." Alexei smiled easily, looking as golden and healthy as a sun.

"I know you wanted to finalize that divorce of ours, but we didn't quite get around to it, did we? And maybe that's not so bad. I'm in a position to help you here. I can make that political officer forget about the apology. If you ask nicely."

"I will walk to Vladivostok barefoot before I ask you for a thing." I wanted to leap up and sink my hands into his throat, but they were trembling too badly. I kept them clenched in my lap so he wouldn't ask to see them and I wouldn't have to admit they hadn't stopped shaking in three days.

"Two weeks' rest," Alexei went on, ignoring my venom. "Valerian root infusion and a bromide solution to calm your nerves—"

"Did you kill him?" I asked.

For the first time since I'd known him, Alexei looked truly startled. "What?"

"Did. You. Kill. Lyonya." The words jerked out in near gulps. "You had him on your operating table. You knew we wanted to marry. He comes in with seven splinters, and you can only get three of them out—" I stopped, rage boiling in my throat. The suspicion had haunted me since I saw Alexei coming blood-gloved out of the operating theater. "You son of a bitch, did you kill him?"

Alexei's face shuttered. I saw anger there, but a vast, exhausted sadness as well. "You think I'd do that? Murder a man on my operating table?"

I refused to look away. "Did you?"

"Look, maybe you think I was a shit husband, and maybe you think I'm a shit father—"

"You are a shit father," I hissed.

"—but you can *never* say I am a shit surgeon. I put in fifteen hours in that operating theater every day; you think I notice names and faces anymore? I didn't realize it was your golden-boy lieutenant until it was done. I broke the news to you myself as a *courtesy*—"

"You are never getting thanks from me. Not for doing your sworn duty by a wounded man. *If* you did—"

"I couldn't have saved him if he'd been hit by those splinters right on the operating table in front of me. Saint Nicholas the Wonder-worker couldn't have magicked them out of his lungs." Alexei pushed back from my chair. "Believe me or not, Mila."

He walked away, looking like the weariest man in the world. I simply sat there. My head ached dully. I didn't know whether to believe him or not. I barely knew what I was saying or seeing or thinking; I hadn't slept in three days and nights. When I tried, I just lay aching and exhausted on the cot in Lyonya's dugout, which I'd probably have to vacate soon for the new company commander.

"We have a bed for you, Comrade Senior Sergeant." An orderly helped me up when it was clear I wouldn't rise on my own. "Two weeks' hospital rest, starting now."

No, I thought. *I want to be out hunting. Killing the men who killed Lyonya.* But I wasn't up to it, and that was the terrible truth. The day of the funeral I came back to the dugout, ripping off my parade uniform for my camouflage smock, picking up my Three Line . . . and I realized my hands were trembling too badly to push a single bullet into the chamber. They kept spilling from my fingers as I tried. The rifle might as well have been a club, not my deadly midnight partner with her inaudible song. If I tried to take her out, I'd miss every shot I tried. I'd get myself or my platoon killed.

Get over it, Pavlichenko, I tried to tell my shaking hands as the orderly showed me to my cot—but all I could think was that if I hadn't dragged my damned heels on my divorce for so long, I'd be calling myself *Kitsenko* instead. "I should have married you," I whispered, sinking into the cot.

Too late now. Too late to marry him, too late to avenge him.

Too late for everything.

• • •

AT SOME POINT in the next two weeks, I realized the hand holding out my daily dose of valerian didn't belong to Lena or one of the nurses. It was a man's hand instead, tough and olive-skinned, with a sniper's calluses. "Hello, Kostia," I rasped, the scratch of my unused voice surprising me. He looked thinner, sunken-eyed, terrible. I looked down into my cup. "I wish it were vodka."

"I have vodka," he said, indicating his pack.

I nodded slowly. "Can . . . can we get drunk?"

He looked around. "Not here."

It was midafternoon, the orderlies and nurses mostly assisting the surgeons, the wounded lying quiet. "How long have I been here?"

"Nine days."

"The platoon?"

"They need you back."

I held up my hand. Still shaking. Every day I worked, I tried, and it wouldn't go away. "I want to be out there," I whispered. "But I can't. Not like this. I'll get you killed."

Kostia rose. "Let's get out of here. I borrowed a car."

"I can't drive." Alexei could, and he was very proud of that. But I'd never had cause to learn.

"I'll drive."

Kostia drove us fast and loose, rattling out toward the fourth defense sector. I knew where we were going before we were halfway there, and I bit the inside of my cheek savagely when the wall of Crimean limestone with its imposing iron gates loomed before us: the Fraternal Cemetery.

We entered through the southern side, parked, and began to climb on foot toward the ancient, bombed-out church at the crown of the hill. The church had been consecrated in czarist days to Saint Nicholas the Wonderworker, which made me think of Alexei's angry words. Now it wasn't a church, it was a ruin. I could have used the blackened, crumbled dome for a sniper's nest.

At the funeral over a week ago I'd had no eyes for the old graves with their white-and-black-marble stones, much less the new graves marked by nothing more than wooden stars. I took a long, steadying breath as I saw Lyonya's. It had been painted more carefully than the others, and the inscription was longer, his birth and death and full name inscribed in neat, square letters I recognized. "You did this?" I asked Kostia around the lump in my throat. He nodded, and I traced the lettering with a fingertip. "I wish it could say something about how he could make anyone laugh. Even me."

"He was my best friend in the world," Kostia said.

"Tell me." There was a tree stump beside the grave, wide enough for two. I sat down, pulling Kostia to sit beside me. "I—I want to hear more about him."

For a long time I didn't think Kostia would speak. "Boys can be cruel," he began finally. "*Konstantin Andreyvich Shevelyov*—everyone knew my father wasn't Andrei Shevelyov. My mother married him because my father was a hunter out on Lake Baikal, and by the time I was coming, she'd found out he had a wife and family back there, not that he'd ever told her when he came to Irkutsk to sell furs. But the boys all knew my father was mad old Markov out on the lake, and even when I went far away to school in Donetsk, someone found out and they all called my mother a whore and me a bastard." A breath. "Except Lyonya . . ."

My partner and I sat arm against arm on the stump, and in Kostia's spare, honed words I saw Lyonya as my partner had first seen him: a broad-shouldered, loose-limbed, golden young athlete, all hockey sticks and poorly graded tests, with a streak of kindness most golden young athletes utterly lacked.

"He was good at making friends," Kostia concluded quietly. "I never was. But that didn't matter, because I had him."

We'd been passing Kostia's flask of vodka back and forth as he talked. I took another swallow, gazing at the row of graves. Lyonya's was still heaped up, the earth black and tumbled, but it would soon be just another mound of drying earth topped by a forlorn fading star. I didn't have any flowers, so I took a heel of bread from my canvas gas-mask bag and crumbled it over the earth so the Sevastopol sparrows would circle and sing here. For my golden front-line husband.

Kostia poured a stream of vodka over the grave. "Rest in peace, brother."

I tried to reply, but my throat closed on the words. We fell into silence then, sitting in the cooling afternoon for more than an hour, passing the vodka again. The sparrows swooped down, fluttered, swooped away. Such a beautiful day.

"I heard you're a senior sergeant now," I said at last. Kostia nodded. "The platoon's yours."

He shook his head. "We need you, Mila."

I held up my hand. Still trembling. He put the flask into it and I drank, feeling the scorch down my throat and into my stomach. "You don't need me. You need someone who can shoot."

"We need *you*. Mila—"

"Stop." I gave him a sudden furious shove; he went off the stump but came to his feet at once, standing with his hands open and his eyes black and steady.

"You're the best." His voice was implacable as granite. "The Hitlerites fear you. The platoon believes in you. We need you back."

"I can't *shoot,*" I shouted, erupting to my feet and shoving him again. He braced, taking it. I hit him this time, a closed fist to his sternum, and he took that, too. "All I want is to kill them, and I can't *shoot—*"

"You have to," he said. "We need you."

I drained another long swallow from the flask and hurled it at his feet. "It's not that I'm afraid." My tongue fumbled the words, and I realized how hard the vodka had hit my empty, burning stomach.

"I didn't say you were." Kostia took a step closer. I slammed my fists into his chest again; he was my height; I didn't have to reach up. "Mila—"

My eyes were swimming. I staggered when I raised my hands again, looking down at the grave. "I was the one with the dangerous job. It was supposed to be *me*."

"It wasn't," my partner said simply.

"I'm going to get you all killed," I whispered.

"Then we die like Lyonya." I saw the tears in Kostia's black eyes then. "We die like soldiers."

"In agony, with iron splinters in our lungs?" My voice slurred. I was so drunk. Why didn't the vodka ease the pain?

"We die brave. Like him." Kostia reached out and took my shoulders, as much to steady himself as me. He could put it away like a Siberian, but he was drunk, too. "And you and me, Mila? We die shooting."

He pulled me into his chest as the sobs exploded out of us both. He wept into my neck and I wept into his, the two of us grappled together swaying over Lyonya's grave. I don't know how long it took that explosion of grief to tear itself free, only that we ended up back on the tree stump, leaning against each other, faces salt-streaked and chests still heaving, gulping the last of the vodka and watching twilight fall. In the darkness we kept on sitting in a sniper's silence, motionless as death. Which still hovered at my shoulder, breathing black and silent.

Kostia looked at me. "Comrade Senior Sergeant?" he asked formally.

I took a long breath and held up my hand. I hadn't slept in a week; my eyes were swollen to slits; I had a belly full of vodka, a heart full of hatred, and a soul full of grief—but my hand was steady as a rock.

"Tomorrow night," I told my partner. And I was back.

CHAPTER 22

My memoir, the official version: Thanks to the valiant spirit of the Red Army and the leadership of our brave officers, none of us believed Sevastopol would fall.

My memoir, the unofficial version: I remember the exact moment I knew Sevastopol was doomed.

A QUIET MARCH, April, May, when I hunted every night in no-man's-land and slept like the dead through the day . . . and then the sudden savage Nazi attack that claimed the Kerch Peninsula in mid-May; the massive air strikes afterward on the main naval base of the Black Sea Fleet, turning the city into a sea of fire and smoke—and then the main assault itself, long-awaited, long-dreaded, in the first week of June.

"Psychological attack," Kostia said as we watched the massive wave of German infantry advancing on the front line of our defenders. He was thinking, I knew, of the Romanians advancing in a Napoleonic column under their shrieking priest, looking to overwhelm us with fear as much as numbers.

I stared through my binoculars over the lip of the sniper trench where the two of us lay on our bellies, taking in the tanks sliding forward like centipedes, German riflemen with Mausers, submachine gunners with MP 40s, all half hidden by coils of black smoke from the dawn artillery bombardment. "New arrivals," I said, noting well-fed bodies in those Nazi uniforms, not yet whittled down by Russian cold and Russian resistance. "Imperial Germans. Probably transferred from Donetsk, the 17th Army." I tossed the binoculars, set my rifle into my shoulder, and saw an officer marching at the side of his troops, striding right into my sights. I fired, the rifle kicked, and down he went. "This batch won't be any luckier than the first two assaults last year."

I believed that. I was still in the grip of the agonized fury that had taken me in its jaws after Lyonya; I'd spent three months killing Hitlerites six nights a week and spending the seventh trying to write letters to Slavka, folding dried flowers into torn end pages of my dissertation. The third assault began, and I joined the firing with my platoon, and it didn't occur to me that we would lose.

But every day the hammer fell: five-hour mortar attacks, tanks and infantry columns pushing along the road that led toward the Mekenzi Hills railway station. Every day the Nazis nibbled at our defenses like the rats they were, pushing centimeter by centimeter toward the northern side of the main bay. Ten days, maybe eleven of continuous fighting, and I was staggering along a path in the Martynov gully, wondering where I could get a cold meal and an hour's sleep, when I nearly collided with a line of boys struggling along under the exhortations of the regimental Young Communist League organizer. "Comrade Senior Sergeant Pavlichenko," he hailed me. "Look lively, boys! Our very own girl sniper, a true hero of the motherland. How many is it now, Lyudmila Mikhailovna?"

"I don't know," I said wearily. Three hundred? Who cared?

"The Hitlerites fear the shadow of her rifle," the organizer told his boys, who just stared at me in exhaustion, white-eyed and blank-faced. They looked so young—surely some weren't any more than fourteen. I snapped off a salute, tried to smile, and the organizer's cheer suddenly broke. He put a hand to his mouth to hide its tremble, and I drew him aside.

"How bad in your sector?" I asked, low-voiced.

"The Fritzes have the entire Kamyshly gully," he muttered. "The railway station, Verkhny Chorgun, Nizhny Chorgun, Kamary . . . battles are raging around the Fraternal Cemetery."

My gut twisted. Lyonya's grave—it might be vandalized by Germans now, his red star splintered.

The Young Communist League organizer went on in a monotone. "This is all that's left of my lads—" waving a hand at the swaying, gray-faced line of boys. "I lost two-thirds of my entire league in nine days. We've no more ammunition coming in. Foodstuffs and water, well . . ."

We will lose, I realized then, gazing at those doomed boys in their deathly exhaustion, swaying under the scorching hot sun. They looked barely older than my Slavka, who in his last letter had told me he got an *Excellent* for Russian dictation and a *Good* for mental arithmetic; that he missed me and that he was making a book of all my plant samples—he was the best in his Young Pioneers troop at biology, Mamochka . . .

If my Slavka had been here in Sebastopol, he might have been carrying a rifle, because the city was going to fall.

"Do you have a word of encouragement for my boys?" the organizer begged. "Just a word?"

I had no encouragement, no hope at all. But I looked at those boys, making myself remember their faces, and I said, "I swear I will fight for you all till the last drop of blood."

"We swear—we so swear—we also swear." The oaths rippled from them like a wave of hot, dying wind through grain. We saluted each other and passed by, on our way to defend our city as it entered its death throes. When I returned to my platoon, and we faced the next wave of Nazi soldiers advancing in their smug, well-fed ranks, the wave of hatred that came over me nearly turned me blind.

"Don't aim for the first rank," I ordered my men. "Aim for the second, aim for the gut—and don't miss." Rifles began to spit bullets, and Hitlerites in the second ranks began to scream, doubling over; the third rank tripped on them, and the first rank turned as they heard the shrieks; the column lost its unity. "Keep it up," I shouted, sinking steel into one soft German belly after another—me, the woman who prided herself on clean, quick, merciful kills, shooting now to maim. "Break their focus. Make them hurt. Slow them *down.*"

They were going to take Sevastopol, but Mila Pavlichenko was going to make them pay for it.

It took nearly a month for the city to fall, and it took 300,000 German soldiers, over four hundred tanks, and more than nine hundred aircraft. But I wasn't there to see it.

On what turned out to be my last day of battle on the Black Sea front, I trekked wearily down from the heights of a shattered church I'd been using to pick off German spotters. They were like crows, nesting in trees, on hilltops, in upper floors of buildings—I should have had Kostia at my back, but we were spread too thin now to double up, and I saw him come down from the building across the street, face streaked in grime. "Got nine," he said.

"Got twelve." Not that it did any good. Shoot twelve spotters and twelve more took their place, calling strikes down on the city in walls of fire—Luftwaffe planes were now strafing individual cars and pedestrians on Sevastopol's ruined streets. The city where I'd walked arm in arm with Lyonya, admiring the Monument to the Sunken Ships and planning our future, had become a slaughterhouse. "Fyodor?"

"One block over, on the bakery roof."

We fell into step, rifles in the crook of our arms. Neither of us flinched at the crackle and boom of artillery thundering overhead, at the shrieks of the dying and the roar of collapsing masonry following it. This wasn't just the morning chamber music anymore; it was a symphony of death. A symphony that never ended.

We clambered up to the bakery roof where Fyodor Sedykh had wedged himself behind a chimney to pick off more spotters, Kostia pulling me up through the hole in the bombed-out roof as I called out, "Fyodor?" But my huge lumbering ox of a junior sergeant was beyond answering; an air strike had hit the roof, toppled the chimney, and pinned him in a welter of shattered beams and broken bricks. The whole lower half of his face was gone, but his eyes begged. Kostia and I went to him, either side of that big, hopelessly broken body, and Kostia took Fyodor's hands and murmured the question we all knew to ask, if a day like this ever came. Fyodor nodded, writhing, eyes not leaving mine, and I nodded back. "Hero of the Soviet Union Fyodor Sedykh," I rasped, "the honor has been mine—"

And I fired a single, merciful shot.

Kostia and I were too ravaged to weep as we climbed down from the shattered rooftop. We just clung to each other for a few numb seconds, then disentangled and made our way toward the regimental staff headquarters. There were only four left in my platoon besides us. "Check on Vartanov and the others," I told Kostia as we waited for new orders from the reconnaissance officer, and that was when a shell hit the dugout.

No time to shout a warning to my partner.

No time to shelter myself.

No time.

SWEAT. OIL. STUFFY air and unwashed bodies all around me. Even with my eyes still glued shut, I knew I was crammed into some claustrophobically small space, a space that buzzed my bones with the throbbing hum of churning diesel engines. I was panicking before I was even fully conscious.

"I thought you were dead," a voice said dully somewhere beside me.

I peeled my eyelids open. A low ceiling not far above me; a floor spread with cork mattresses and metal partitions, soldiers jammed everywhere they could sit, lie, or curl into fetal positions. Most were bandaged, all seemed to be staring with blank eyes at some unknown distance. Only there was no distance; this room was as windowless and cramped as the inside of a rifle's barrel. "Where are we?" I rasped, looking around to see a skinny corporal from 54th Regiment whom I'd chatted with in the mess line from time to time. "You're Misha—Comrade Corporal Sternov, right? Third company? Where—"

"Cruising underwater toward Tsemes Bay in Novorossiysk," he answered. "L-4—she used to be a minelayer, now she's a transport submarine. Captain Polyakov took her down at dawn—you've been out cold since they loaded you in here on a stretcher."

I couldn't make sense of what he was saying. Submarine? Dimly, I remembered hearing a rumor that a handful of submarines were coming into Sevastopol's bay with ammunition, fuel, and provisions, but no one knew anything more. If they'd arrived and unloaded, of course they would depart with as many wounded as they could carry . . .

Kostia. Vartanov. My platoon. I tried to sit up, and a wave of splitting agony cratered my head. I knew what it was: concussion, eardrum damage, shell shock. I heard a whimper that seemed to be coming from me, and reaching up, I found a row of neat stitches along my earlobe.

"Looks like a blast knocked you out and a splinter nearly took your ear off." Corporal Sternov looked at me a little spitefully. "I'd like to know who you've got in your pocket back in the medical battalion, getting on the evacuation list for a splinter wound."

Lena—was she here? "Do you know Lena Paliy? The best medical orderly in—"

"Dead, so I heard. Mortar fire on a first-aid station."

No, not Lena, *not Lena*. "My platoon." I moistened my cracked lips, trying to sit up despite my throbbing skull. "Sergeant Shevelyov, Corporal Vartanov—"

A shrug.

"Second Company?" Names of friends and comrades in arms fluttered through me like trapped bats.

"Probably all dead." With shocking suddenness, Sternov's face screwed up in a sob. "My company was overrun, too. I don't know if I'm the only one who . . ."

I reached out and took his hand, hardly aware of what I was doing. "I can't be here," I whispered. What was I doing here when my partner was back there, my men were back there, Lyonya's grave was back there? How could I have been magicked onto a stretcher and into a submarine, fleeing my doomed city like an underwater rat? If I'd been conscious when the evacuation order came through, I'd have fought with every bone in my body. I'd have pried myself off the stretcher and crawled back into Sevastopol on my bloodstained hands and knees. "I have to get back."

"You think they'll turn the submarine around just for you?" Sternov snarled tearfully. "Even Lady Death doesn't get that privilege."

"*Don't call me that!*"

He pulled away sullenly, tears still leaking. I turned over, facing the humming metal wall, and felt a sharp corner poke me. I'd been lying on my pack; probably the only reason it hadn't been stolen. My rifle was gone—that would have been tossed to someone still able to defend Sevastopol. The beautiful Mosin-Nagant Three Line Kostia had turned from a standard-issue rifle to a sniper's weapon just for my hands . . . but my shaking fingers found the rest of my things. The packet of letters from my family; Slavka's picture; my battered dissertation; the pear-wood pipe Vartanov had given me. And something else.

It slid out of the pack into my hands: a bloodstained, oil-smeared English copy of *War and Peace.* Kostia's. I'd seen him prop his rifle on it if there wasn't time to construct a parapet; he pulled it out to read on long stakeouts; he carefully tore a strip from its blank end pages to light our cigarettes when we were out of matches. We'd teased him that he loved it more than his babushka. "It was my babushka's," he retorted.

I didn't know if he'd left it with me as a farewell when I was carried off the battlefield for the last time, or if he'd died back there and some well-meaning orderly tucked it among my things as a memento. I didn't know, and maybe I never would know. My *partner.*

I doubled over weeping, clutching the book, as the submarine slid through the alien waters toward a safety I didn't want, away from a death I would have welcomed, abandoning everyone I loved.

"LYUDMILA MIKHAILOVNA, IS that you?"

I turned as I approached the Novorossiysk commandant's office. At first I didn't recognize the grim-faced, weary-looking man in his fine greatcoat and cluster of aides. Then I saw his rank and hastily saluted. "Comrade Major General Petrov, sir."

Twelve days since the submarine slid into Novorossiysk and off-loaded its wounded to the hospital wards, me among them. Just one day since I had been released from my cot there, told to come to the commandant's office and testify to my recovery—at least, testify that I had recovered enough to hold a rifle again. And here was Petrov himself, turning away from his idling staff car and coming toward me with a smile. I remembered meeting the man before evacuating Odessa, and I knew he'd been the one to put my name up for my first combat medal after the duel on the bridge, but we hadn't traded any further words. If he'd recognized my gaunt, unsmiling face with its centipede of stitches still marching up my neck and ear, he had a good memory.

He spoke baldly, no niceties. "You've heard?"

"Yes, Comrade Major General." The *Pravda* had printed the news yesterday: *By order of the Red Army Supreme command dated 3 July, Soviet forces have abandoned the city . . .* I'd been knocking on every door I could find for the last twenty hours, begging for information on Sevastopol's survivors. There had to be survivors. The rest of my platoon . . .

"Who else from Chapayev division made it out with you, Lyudmila Mikhailovna?" General Petrov had been there until the end, so I'd been told—evacuated with the rest of the top brass right before the city fell. I gave him all the names I could, the soldiers I'd been evacuated with on the submarine, the ones I'd seen in the hospital wards afterward. I saw him filing each one away. "I have one name for you, Comrade Senior Sergeant. Your doctor husband, Alexei Pavlichenko, was on the last transport out. Headed for Krasnodar, I think." A smile. "He's being decorated for his service to the wounded. A valiant servant of the Red Army."

"Valiant," I echoed. Kostia's quiet stoicism, Vartanov's bitter endurance, Lena's humor under fire—*they* were the valiant ones. But I couldn't deny Alexei's surgeon hands had probably saved hundreds if not thousands of lives, and the general clearly thought he had given me good news. So I nodded my thanks and asked the question I'd dreaded to ask. "The rest of my division, the ones in Sevastopol when I was evacuated at the end of June?"

"There is no more Chapayev division," Petrov said gently. "They fought to the end—burned their staff papers, buried their seals, threw their standards into the sea. The Hitlerites won't be parading your division's colors through Berlin as trophies."

My eyes filled with tears again; I managed to keep them from brimming over as I gave a stiff nod. The general managed a smile, more like a death's-head rictus. I remembered hearing a rumor that he'd tried to shoot himself rather than flee Sevastopol, and someone from his military council had prevented him. Just one of those wild army rumors that fly everywhere like chaff, but suddenly I believed this one. General Petrov looked haunted, a dead man walking. "Tell me, Comrade Senior Sergeant, have you received new orders?"

"Not yet." I had to swipe at my eyes, to my shame. "I hope to be posted back to the front as an officer."

Petrov's aide glanced meaningfully at the waiting car, but the general turned back to me. "An officer?"

"Yes. I think I've earned it by now." I shouldn't have been so blunt, but I was too drained to be anything but honest. "I've learned over this last year how to command troops, Comrade Major General. To think about them in combat, to be responsible for them. And I still haven't got even with the Nazis for the deaths of my friends." Lena, Fyodor, Lyonya. Oh, Lyonya. If I were an officer at my next posting, responsible for giving more of the orders, perhaps I could save more of my men next time. "The Hitlerites are still advancing. The things I saw done to civilians at Odessa and Sevastopol . . . The earth should burn under their feet."

The general surveyed me for a moment. "In three days, I'm leaving Novorossiysk for Moscow. You will accompany me—to receive your new posting."

CHAPTER 23

My memoir, the official version: Moscow was the perfect incarnation of the Soviet imagination encapsulated in stone and steel.

My memoir, the unofficial version: Moscow was huge, austere, and hellish. But my mother's eyes were the size of saucers when she laid eyes on it—and me.

"LOOK AT YOU: a war heroine, a lieutenant, *and* a Moscow girl!" Mama was skinnier than ever on wartime rations, but her long plait and bright eyes were the same as I led her into my quarters at the Stromyn Street hostel. I'd been living here since arriving in Moscow—more than a month now. "You should have seen your father when he heard about your Order of Lenin. He strutted to work like a rooster."

My eyes pricked. I wished my father could have come to Moscow too, but there was a pass only for one—and he couldn't have taken so much time from work, to travel more than a thousand kilometers simply for a visit. Nor could a child take that journey, and I took a deep stabbing breath before asking, "What did Slavka say?"

"Proud as punch." Mama stowed her wicker traveling case under the table. "And before you ask, he thinks I'm off visiting a cousin."

"Good," I jerked. If he knew I was back from the front, he'd plead to visit me, and I couldn't inflict that on him. I'd heard from other soldiers that it was devastating trying to visit your children if you could stay only a short while—they went completely to pieces when it was time to leave again.

"Oh, *malyshka,* don't cry. It's the right thing to do." Mama gave me the hug I was craving, folding me into her arms like a child. I leaned into that hug, and I felt the moment she gave a quick inhale, catching the scent of vodka I hadn't quite been able to scrub away from last night.

That was the other reason I'd asked her to leave Slavka home: I didn't want him to see that his laughing mamochka, the woman who checked his schoolwork and told him stories of Lady Midnight running errands for Baba Yaga, had become a woman of hard shining boots and pitiless brass stars, a woman without smiles. A woman who managed to sleep the night through only because of vodka.

But my mother didn't mention the vodka. "Such luxury," she said instead, admiring my room. "Sixteen square meters all to yourself! How long will you be here?"

"I don't know. They're giving me a sniper platoon in the 32nd Guards Parachute Division, but I don't have orders to the front yet." I'd had to bottle my frustration since coming to Moscow; now it spilled over as I began pulling out sliced black bread and pickles. "Mama, I'm stuck doing instruction duty at the local training center. When I'm not at a chalkboard, the secretariat of the All-USSR Young Communist League's central committee wants me doing *speeches*."

"And why shouldn't they?" Mama smiled. "You're a heroine, aren't you?"

"I'm not a speaker." That was what I told the secretariat, but he just waved my objections aside. *People need to be told about this war. Just do it with an optimistic note!*

Optimistic. As if there was an *optimistic* way to tell the story of losing my entire platoon . . . none of whom I'd heard any news of, no matter how often I beat on doors looking for information: *Konstantin Shevelyov speaks very good English, perhaps he came out of Sevastopol and was put to work as an interpreter at one of the embassies? Anastas Vartanov, is there any news of an old ranger from the Crimea?*

Nothing.

"I think you've been doing more than just making speeches and teaching ballistics!" My mother beamed, and for a horrible moment I thought she was going to ask if I had a man in my life. *No,* I nearly shouted, *I don't have a man. I go to sleep every night aching for Lyonya, and I think I always will.* But I caught my angry words before they could spill out. My mother didn't know about Lyonya; he'd been killed before I wrote to my family about him—I'd wanted to wait until the divorce from Alexei was final before telling my parents about a new son-in-law, and after he died, I couldn't bear to put his name to paper. Mama didn't know I was grieving, and she didn't seem, in any case, to be asking about romance, because she prompted, "The Lavrenyov pamphlet?"

"Oh," I said. "That."

That damned pamphlet, commissioned by the Red Army central board of political propaganda, part of the much-read Frontline Library series: the wartime heroics of sniper Lyudmila Pavlichenko, to be written by none other than famous novelist Boris Lavrenyov.

"What was he like?" Mama wanted to know. I'd been trying to lay out snacks for her, but she pushed me into a chair and insisted on slicing the salami herself. "I've always loved *The Forty-First*—so romantic! Did he interview you himself?"

Ha. The great man had looked me up and down through his iron-framed spectacles, cut me off in my first sentence, and explained to me his *Vision* for how to present my life to the masses. (He had a *Vision*. I sensed the capital letter.) "You're just like my Maryutka," he said kindly. "My heroine in *The Forty-First*, of course you know of her. Just a few details about you, and I'll finish the pamphlet in a week."

I admit I didn't react well. I was hungover, I was tired, and the self-satisfied flashing of the man's spectacles was making my temples throb. "I'm nothing like your dumb fictional factory girl," I'd told him flatly. "Your novel's entire premise is contrived, and if you think I want a hack like you writing about me—"

Things went downhill from there, if not quite downhill enough to cancel the pamphlet. It would release at year's end and I'd already had an advance look. *The girl sniper and I went down the boulevard on Commune Square one fine morning, the wind ruffling her cropped silky hair over her maiden's brow as we sat on a bench. Her delicate, high-strung face pulsed with a deep passion of character. Her eyes seemed sad, but sparked under my skillful questioning with a childlike eagerness.*

I wondered if that part was supposed to happen before or after I told him he was a prosy hack and he told me I was a rabid Ukrainian bitch.

"Before I forget, Lyuda—a letter came last week for you." Mama fished in her drawstring bag. "I'd have forwarded it on, but when I knew I'd see you so soon . . ."

I slit the envelope, unfolding the square of smudged paper as my heart began to thud. I'd traded family addresses with all my platoon; we swore to write to one another's families if one of us fell or was separated from the company. I'd dispatched letters to the families of all my men. Who was now writing to me?

Small square writing, familiar as my own pulse.

Mila,

I'm alive. Last evacuation out of Sevastopol, shattered knee. Recuperated in hospital ward in Krasnodar; about to be shipped to Moscow military district for reassignment. Where are you?

—Kostia

"Are you all right?" My mother's hand flew to my forehead. "You look so strange—"

"I'm all right, Mama." I looked up from my partner's letter with a smile that felt like it stretched all the way down to my toes. "You just brought me the first good news I've had in months."

Kostia alive. My partner, my shadow, my other half. Some dark bottomless ache in me eased, as though one of my legs had gone to sleep and now blood was flowing back through it, prickling me with the painful yet welcome sensation that it was still there and whole.

Kostia, alive.

I hugged my mother so hard her toes left the ground. "Put on the finest dress you've got in that bag, Mamochka. You're going to see everything in Moscow this week, starting with the ballet."

"Ballet!" Mama chuckled. "Remember your ballerina friend Vika? I heard she walked out of a starring role in Odessa to drive a T-34 in the tank corps! A ballerina becoming a tank driver, the things this war does to us. Thank goodness you're home from the front . . ."

I didn't tell her that all I wanted was to go back there. Collect my partner, get him assigned to my new platoon, and then go back to war. Because the job wasn't done yet, and right now I wasn't good for anything else.

"GOOD NEWS, LYUDMILA Mikhailovna! You're headed back to war."

I blinked exhaustion-gritty eyes, surprised. I had served a twenty-four-hour shift on instruction duty at the training center, done my rounds of the various personnel offices inquiring if Kostia had reached the Moscow military district yet, then helped organize four trucks of newly arrived weaponry. And now here I was summoned to the first secretary's office, looking at an entire cluster of men, some in uniform and some in suits. "My orders are in? Orders to the front?"

"Not that war." The secretariat laughed. "The most important war of all—the war of propaganda."

I stared at him in utter confusion.

"You're going too fast," a familiar voice said behind me, and I turned to see Alexei's smiling face. I hadn't seen him since Sevastopol or thought of him since Petrov told me he'd been evacuated. I'd assumed he was off polishing his shiny new decoration and angling for a better post. Now he was *here*?

"Hello, *kroshka*." He kissed both my cheeks in breezy greeting. "We're going to America."

THE SOVIET DELEGATION: DAY 1

August 27, 1942

WASHINGTON, D.C.

CHAPTER 24

If there was anything the marksman disliked, it was having to reassure nervous clients. *You want to be soothed, go see a headshrinker.* He didn't let his impatience show, strolling down a hot Washington sidewalk with Pocket Square, but he was annoyed. He'd already given the man an update this morning before the White House breakfast; a second meeting was excessive. He preferred to keep contact with his employers minimal, for God's sake—the fewer points of connection, the safer they'd all be. Yet here he was, being required to soothe and reassure.

"We need to *know*." Pocket Square glanced behind him, perspiring more than ever. He was already in agony because the marksman had refused to meet in some dark whiskey-scented bar to discuss all this, but bars had eavesdroppers, which was why the marksman kept his business discussions outside. "You said you'd know more after the welcome breakfast. Well?"

"Things are in hand." The marksman picked up the pace as they turned the final corner toward the Soviet embassy. In one hour, the Soviet delegation would address the nation on live radio.

"But we want *details*," Pocket Square hissed.

"You're paying me for results, not details." The marksman had already fleshed out his plan for September 5, the last day of the conference. That horsey bitch of a First Lady was intending to invite all the international students to a farewell reception on the White House lawn. The President would be in attendance, as would a full cadre of press . . . including the marksman, thanks to the strings Pocket Square's employers had already pulled behind the scenes. "Everything's in place on my end." Almost, anyway.

"What have you learned about the Red girl?" Pocket Square kept glancing around him, drawing glances from a pair of middle-aged women hurrying past with their shopping. "You can guarantee she'll take the fall?"

"No guarantees in this business." The marksman fed a little more Virginia drawl into his voice, soothing. "But your people were right to have me look into her. We couldn't ask for a better patsy."

Pocket Square peered up at the stony bulk of the embassy, now looming overhead. Journalists and photographers were already hurrying inside, showing their press badges to embassy security. "Is she really a sniper?"

"No." The marksman had had a moment's doubt at the end of breakfast, looking at Lyudmila Pavlichenko's furious face as she said *An accurate bullet fired by a sniper like me, Mrs. Roosevelt, is no more than a response to an enemy* . . . but on reflection he'd dismissed it. An angry woman didn't make a sniper. "She's a propaganda poster girl who gets flustered easily and loses her temper at idiotic questions, and God knows the press can be counted on to ask plenty of those. The Russkies made a mistake, cooking up the sniper cover story. They think it will make her admired, a war hero." In the Soviet Union maybe, but not in America, where pretty brunettes were supposed to bake cookies, not kill fascists. "Mrs. Pavlichenko won't be the sensation here that they're hoping for. Everywhere she goes, she'll be viewed as a freak and a monster."

In fact, he was counting on it.

"MRS. PAVLICHENKO—"

"Mrs. Pavlichenko—"

"Mrs. Pavlichenko—"

I tried not to flinch. Flashbulbs were going off in my face like grenades—had none of these journalists ever questioned soldiers before? Setting anything to explode with a flash of light in a battle veteran's face was just *asking* to get stabbed.

"Smile," the delegation head murmured. Three of us had been chosen for this delegation, all of us students, all of us soldiers, but he was in charge: Nikolai Krasavchenko, twenty-six and square and earnest. He'd fought well at Smolensk, but that wasn't why he'd been chosen to lead the delegation. He'd been chosen because he was a pompous young bore who could be counted on not to have a single original thought on this entire trip. *No surprises here,* I imagined them saying as they stamped approval on his folder. *Backbone of the Party!*

Maybe Krasavchenko was delighted to have been chosen, but not me. I'd stood (dumbfounded, incredulous, increasingly angry) through a great deal of droning about Eleanor Roosevelt's international student conference, that first night I heard about it in Moscow. How it provided Comrade Stalin with an opportunity to send students as the most progressive element of the population to speak out against fascism to the Americans . . . How we had been chosen among hundreds of candidates in the Moscow military district, not only as former students and current soldiers but as Young Communist League personnel . . . How we would advocate for our country, our party, and for the dire need of American aid . . .

"Smile," Krasavchenko repeated now, glaring at me. He wasn't happy about my angry outburst at the White House breakfast this morning, and his were the orders I was supposed to follow, so I faced the cameras and obediently pulled back my lips. The conference wouldn't begin for a few days; tonight's address to the American press would broadcast live over radio, from the embassy to the whole of America. I swallowed my nerves, looking out over a sea of cameras and chatter. This whole scene seemed as foreign to me as the moon. All I'd wanted was to find Kostia and go back to the fight, and instead I'd been packed off to a continent full of oblivious capitalists on a *propaganda mission*? Americans didn't like Russians. They called themselves our allies, but so far they were leaving us to die in the hundreds of thousands. How was anything I said at this press conference supposed to change that?

"A glass of water, *kroshka*?" Alexei murmured, hovering.

"I can get my own water. I don't require the delegation doctor to get it for me."

That was the post he'd landed: official physician for the Soviet delegation to Washington. "How did you manage to worm your way onto this mission?" I'd sputtered back in Moscow, still reeling from the surprise of seeing him again. "What does a student delegation need with a combat surgeon?"

"They want a Soviet doctor to attend to any of the delegation's health needs, another soldier with a sterling record, and I've done my share of general doctoring." Alexei had looked golden and confident in his immaculate uniform, not a smudge of Sevastopol's horrors on him. "As for how I got this assignment . . . well, naturally I kept my ear to the ground for any news of my wife." Straightening the Order of Lenin at my breast, fingers lingering on the proud red ribbon. "And naturally, a husband would wish to accompany his wife overseas if she were sent on such a long journey—"

"You are *trading on my name* to get out of frontline service and into a cushy post," I'd hissed, but there was no undoing it. Even halfway around the world, I wasn't going to be able to escape my husband.

And he'd been solicitous ever since: first in Moscow, those few frantic days we were all being briefed and prepared for the journey; then on the long flight from Moscow to Tehran and then to Cairo, cadging the seat beside me as I clutched the armrest during takeoff, offering to hold my hand if I felt afraid.

"What do you want?" I'd asked bluntly.

He just smiled. "Can't I tell my wife how brave she is? Your first flight; you're doing so well, *kroshka*."

"Oh, and you've flown on airplanes *so* many times, yourself," I scoffed. But his smile didn't waver, and after we flew from Cairo to Miami he knocked on my hotel room door and asked if I wanted to walk on the *beach*—"Let's get some sun on that pretty face." All this niceness was making me twitchier than a two-day stakeout.

I swatted him away now, looking back to the bank of microphones and cameras as we were herded into position. "If you three will take your seats, Mrs. Pavlichenko in the center . . ." I did as I was told, banishing my husband from my thoughts if not my presence. Krasavchenko was shuffling the pages of his statement on my right, at my left lounged Lieutenant Pchelintsev, our third student delegate, looking haughty. "You have coffee on your tunic," I said, and he nearly overturned his cup in his haste to brush himself off. I couldn't really dislike Pchelintsev—in some ways he wasn't so different from me, just an earnest university student before the war turned him down a different road and made him a sniper. But it was hard not to regard him a little cynically all the same, because he was three years younger than I and his official tally was half mine, but he was a senior lieutenant to my junior and he'd been made Hero of the Soviet Union and not just Chevalier of the Order of Lenin. I wasn't eaten up with jealousy for his gold star, but it was hard not to look at the burnished young Lieutenant Pchelintsev and wonder if I'd be where he was if I'd simply been born a man.

Hit four hundred on your tally, little boy, I thought the first time I met Pchelintsev's superior gaze in Moscow. *Then you can look down your nose at me.*

But it wasn't my impressive tally that had won my place here with Pchelintsev and Krasavchenko, and I knew it. I'd heard two of the Moscow suits arguing over my appointment while I was getting fitted for the uniform skirt I was now wearing: "Should have chosen that tank driver from the Leningrad literary program, Vassily Something. Who wants a woman on a delegation? Too emotional, too difficult to control."

"But this one's pretty, and she'll present the USSR in a more favorable light . . ."

"We're beginning." Krasavchenko's whisper across the table snapped me back to the present. "Remember, listen to our interpreter, not theirs."

And a lump rose in my throat as I saw Kostia take his place quietly before the table.

If Alexei could pull strings to get a position on the delegation, so could I—and I'd maneuvered to get my partner back at my side, the moment I'd heard Krasavchenko drone about bringing our own interpreters. I hadn't formulated any kind of plan, just blurted, "I can recommend an excellent interpreter, newly transferred to the Moscow military district. Decorated soldier and fluent speaker of English and Russian." Because if I was going halfway around the world with the possibility of new enemies in front of me and the certainty of at least one old enemy behind me, I wanted my partner at my back.

And here he was, my partner, almost unrecognizable in a pressed uniform and a clean shave, standing beside the delegation table, leaning on the cane he still needed after a splinter had nearly blown his knee apart in Sevastopol's fall. I willed him to look over and smile, but he was shuffling papers, adjusting his microphone. *After the press conference,* I thought. *We can finally talk*—but flashes were going off again all over the room as the broadcast began.

I shifted in my seat as the introductions rolled, trying to get rid of that feeling of being exposed, unarmed, locked in unfriendly gunsights. Krasavchenko seemed polished and at ease in this kind of setting; I'd rather be dressed as a bush with my Three Line in hand. But my way back to the front led through this tour. *The Americans need to be shown the truth of our struggle against Nazism,* we had been lectured in Moscow as we prepared for the trip. *Our need for reinforcements—that is the real purpose of your delegation, not merely sitting in sessions with international students. This directive comes all the way from Comrade Stalin.* A stern look all around. *We cannot miss this chance.*

My spine had straightened at that. Maybe I wouldn't have a rifle in hand, but apparently this mission still boiled down to the same directive: *Don't you dare miss.*

"Propaganda ponies," I heard an American journalist snicker in the front row as the broadcast rolled on, not bothering to whisper, since he assumed none of us could understand. "Let's see 'em go through their paces."

I put up my chin. *Yes, let's.*

At first it wasn't so bad. Krasavchenko read a statement: the dire plight of our country, the unity of our civilians. Pchelintsev read a statement: the readiness of the Red Army to strike back against the Germans. I read a statement—first some Party-approved fluff about greetings from Soviet womanhood, and then I was glad to get to the meat of it. "The Soviet people send thanks for your aid, but the struggle which our nation is leading demands more and more from us. We await active assistance and the opening of a second front." I heard Kostia's voice translating in a quiet murmur; saw pencils scratching as the journalists took notes. I straightened in my chair. "As a Russian soldier, I extend my hand to you. Together we must defeat the Nazi monsters." That was the end of my printed statement, but I added in English, with a smile, "Forward to victory!" A nice little slogan that could wrap up just about any speech. People need a signal that you're finished, and that they can clap now.

The ambassador opened the floor for questions, and I began marshaling facts and figures, though most questions would probably go to Krasavchenko.

But the questions were almost all for me, and they weren't about the war.

"Is it true your nickname is Lady Death?"

I began to say that another interpretation could be Lady Midnight, but I was already sensing that no one here wanted complicated answers; they wanted simple comments that fit easily into newspaper captions. "Yes," I said, through Kostia. I'd been instructed to use the interpreter for all questions, even if my English was up to it. (Because who knew what a volatile female might say, without a man to sift her words if she gets out of hand? I'd rolled my eyes at that, but on the whole I preferred to be underestimated by the press, so all to the better if they thought I spoke little English.) "I am sometimes called Lady Death. Also the lynx, for the way I move through trees."

"Lyudmila, can you take hot baths at the front?"

I blinked, surprised partly by the question and partly by the fact that he didn't bother using my rank. "What?"

"Baths," the man repeated, a lanky fellow from the *Washington Post*. "Hot." He mimed sweating.

I stared at him. "Yes, I get a hot bath two or three times a day, whenever I'm sitting in a trench and there's an artillery attack. That's a real bath for you, only it's a dust bath."

A ripple of surprised laughter answered my response. Then a man in a checked tie rose. "Are you women soldiers able to wear lipstick?"

I glanced at Krasavchenko. He made a little urging motion. "With bullets coming at you, you're more likely to reach for a rifle than a lipstick." Kostia translated me with an impassive face, but I could hear his buried amusement.

A woman journalist came next, pursing her lips at me. "Is that your parade uniform or your everyday uniform?"

"We have no time for parades at the—"

"The cut is very unflattering. That skirt length makes you look fat! Don't you mind?"

I let my breath out slowly as anger licked through me and leached the color out of the room. My briefing in Moscow had warned me:

Some Americans will be convinced a woman cannot do what you have done, Lyudmila Mikhailovna—that you're an actress prepped by propagandists. Disabuse them, but gently.

I'd already decided this morning at the White House breakfast that if the questions were insulting enough, I wasn't going to bother with *gentle*.

"I am proud to wear the uniform of my army," I answered the woman journalist. "It has been soaked by the blood of my comrades who have fallen in combat." A sudden, horrendous flash of Lyonya's blood drenching my tunic as splinters drove like spikes of ice into his lungs; of being spattered with the gray slurry of Fyodor Sedykh's brains when I put him out of his agony on a Sevastopol rooftop. *Breathe. Breathe.* "I wish you could experience a bombing raid, ma'am. Trust me, you would forget about the cut of your outfit."

I couldn't even see the next journalist through the blur of fury fogging my eyes, only hear the faint leer in his voice. "Lyudmila, what color of underwear do you prefer?"

Kostia didn't translate that. The embassy interpreter did, as my partner sat radiating cold rage and so Krasavchenko and Pchelintsev on either side of me. Oddly, that checked the furious beat of my pulse. Perhaps I had a platoon around me after all.

I looked at the journalist, and I smiled. It was the smile that made new recruits back up a few steps, if they had even a thimble of sense. "In Russia," I began, nodding at Kostia to translate, "you'd get a slap in the face for asking any such question. That's an inquiry for your wife or your mistress. I'm neither to you, newsman, so if you'd like to come closer, I'd be happy to give you a slap."

To my surprise, the room burst into outright guffaws. Even the man who'd asked the question shook his head ruefully, as if he knew he'd earned my sharpness. I didn't trust myself to say anything more, so I rose before the applause could cease. "We're done here."

I braced myself for a reprimand from the Soviet ambassador

as we retreated into the corridor, but he only gave me a look of grim amusement. "Well said, Lyudmila Mikhailovna. Washington cockroaches . . ."

"I feel I must apologize for our press." The serious tones of the First Lady made us all straighten. "They can be something of a trial." She was followed by a comet-like tail of White House secretaries and flunkies, and she wore a practical navy blue dinner dress. *I am a working woman,* that dress said, *not a clotheshorse.* Which was starkly at odds to the summation I'd heard in my Moscow briefing: *an aristocrat, a millionairess, a member of the exploiting class.*

Was she? This was our second meeting, and the first had not exactly ended well . . . but her smile was just as welcoming as it had been on our introduction this morning. If she was angry with me, she wasn't showing it.

"You are all invited to supper at the home of Mrs. Haabe, daughter of the former U.S. ambassador to the USSR," the First Lady continued, encompassing us all in her smile. "I thought perhaps you would like to proceed straight there."

A bustle of bilingual chatter erupted as details were discussed, and eventually I ducked out onto the nearest balcony for a cigarette, dying for a moment alone as much as the nicotine. Another party full of curious strangers, when the morning had begun with that awkward breakfast and then proceeded through an afternoon blur of meetings, photographs, speeches . . . I fumbled for matches and saw a silhouette of someone else on the balcony, already smoking—not holding a cigarette loosely between fingertips, but cupped in a reversed hand the way snipers smoked, to keep the spark from giving away your position. I lit up, took my first drag, and went to stand with my partner. Kostia was as still as a pillar, eyes going over the city. So many electric lights! Washington looked like a scatter of jewels in the dark. It should have been beautiful, but all I could think was that it ruined my night vision.

"Three," Kostia said at last.

"I make four," I answered. "Where are yours?"

He pointed to a rooftop across the way; to an upper window at a diagonal; to a street-corner phone box—all the best vantage points with direct lines of fire to where we stood. "Your fourth?"

I pointed almost directly up, at a sixth-floor window above us. "A good shot could make that, straight down between the window ledges."

"Crosswinds would make that tricky."

"I could make that shot. So could you."

There was so much I wanted to say. There should have been ample chance for us to talk—the hours of preparation in Moscow, the endless plane flights, those few days in Cairo where we'd all been trotted out for the British and American ambassadors and had our first whirlwind introduction to cocktail parties and cameras. But there had been no chance at all for Kostia and me to exchange more than a few hurried words. The first time I saw him, a mere two days after I'd proposed his name as delegation interpreter, the moment had taken me completely by surprise—he'd appeared at the secretariat's office, sun-darkened and gaunt, an Order of the Red Banner glinting on his chest. If we'd had a chance to fall on each other with a comradely hug and a few quiet moments to reflect on that last day in Sevastopol, all would have been well.

But we'd stood staring at each other, awkwardly—he barely seemed to recognize me in my new medals and skirted uniform; my eye was glued to the cane in his hand, the lines of pain whitening around his mouth—and the moment had passed. And ever since, there always seemed to be someone in the room, keeping us from talking: Krasavchenko rabbiting on about a Party memorandum, the British ambassador in Cairo wondering audibly if Pchelintsev and I were *actually* soldiers, Alexei glued to my side . . .

And now we finally had a moment alone, and we were pointing

out lines of fire to each other for imaginary duels. *Snipers,* I imagined Lyonya hooting, *you're all just a bucket of laughs!* A bolt of agonized longing went through me like a bullet. Without Lyonya, how would I ever remember how to laugh?

"You still have Vartanov's pipe?" Kostia asked unexpectedly, looking at the cigarette in my hand.

I drew the pipe out of my pocket; a good-luck talisman I still carried everywhere. "I never learned to smoke it properly, no matter how often he tried to show me." I stroked the amber mouthpiece, feeling my chest tighten. "You didn't say what happened to him."

"Shot in the thigh, the day before I was hit and evacuated. Femoral artery. He bled out before we could get an orderly."

I bowed my head for the old ranger, the way he could move through trees like a ghost. "The others? Burov, Volkonsky—" I listened as Kostia went down the list. I'd hoped maybe some would have been evacuated with him, but my heart sank as Kostia listed name after name. "Of the whole platoon, you're saying the only ones who lived . . ."

"Us." Just as he'd said when I rejoined him in Sevastopol after being evacuated from Odessa. "Just us."

How I wished for a bottle of vodka and a little privacy. We could have got utterly smashed as we did when Lyonya died, cried it out on each other's shoulders, grieved and raged and come out the other side. That was what you did when you lost your friends in war. But here we were on a Washington balcony, about to be called away any minute now for some blasted official function, and I didn't know how to fight through the grief that thickened the air between us like amber.

"Kostia," I began, not even sure what I was going to ask him. *I still have your copy of* War and Peace *if you want it? Do you forgive me for yanking you along on this trip, when you'd probably rather be at the front avenging our friends? Do you think I want to be here, either, with all the lights and the idiotic questions?*

"There you are." Krasavchenko's loud voice made us both jump.

"We're leaving for Mrs. Haabe's house, only the Cadillac won't hold the three of us delegates and the interpreters."

"I thought perhaps Mrs. Pavlichenko might travel with me," the First Lady was suggesting as I stubbed out my cigarette and came back inside, the frustration hastily wiped off my face. "I drove myself over, and my car has room for a passenger."

"Me?" I hadn't forgotten her words that morning: *It will be hard for American women to approve of you.* I'd taken that to mean that *she* didn't approve of me. So why was she inviting me to ride in her private car?

I looked at her now, really looked: such a tall woman, neat rather than fashionable, an air of energy around her like the crackle of a coming storm. Her teeth prominent, her eyes kind, her smile as she looked down at me unmistakably friendly. "I would welcome the chance to know you better, Lyudmila dear."

IT WOULD BE fair to say that I do not frighten easily. I'd lived through the siege of Odessa, I'd survived the fall of Sevastopol. I'd earned the nickname Lady Death.

Well, Lady Death had never been so certain she was about to die.

"Harry Hopkins will be present at dinner; he has been a great advocate of rapprochement between our countries." The First Lady rocketed her little two-seat convertible down the broad Washington avenues like she was piloting a tornado. We'd left the embassy Cadillac and both the Soviet and American security patrols behind at the first stoplight; it was all I could do to hang on and try to follow her English. Were presidents' wives allowed to do this? I tried to imagine Comrade Stalin's wife (should he have one) zooming around Moscow like an unescorted missile, and my imagination failed utterly. "Harry is keen to speak with you about the fighting at Leningrad, Odessa, and Sevastopol."

"I did not fight at Leningrad, Mrs. Roosevelt." I squeezed myself back into the seat as we approached a turn. For the love of Lenin, she had to slow down to turn, right?

"Wherever you've fought, he'll be glad to hear details." She threw the convertible around the curve very nearly on two wheels. I gripped the door handle. "He's long been advising the President that though you Russians may have withstood a blow of unprecedented German force, the time has come to offer help."

"Past time," I couldn't help saying, trying not to scowl.

"We do understand your country's dire need of a second front, Lyudmila dear." Mrs. Roosevelt's voice was mild but very firm, even as she flung the car down another long avenue. "Perhaps you are not aware of the difficulties we face in taking such a measure. We have our hands full in the Pacific—the fall of Singapore, the retreat from the Philippines. There are those who argue we must concentrate upon Japan, not split ourselves between the Pacific and Europe, and such concerns must be addressed."

I blinked. It was not something I had really considered—that the Americans too might be struggling to allot their resources in this war. They had so *many* resources that sending us aid had seemed a simple matter to me, something to be accomplished with the wave of a presidential hand. Of course it was not. In the dark, I felt myself reddening—maybe I'd knocked the First Lady off-balance at breakfast, but she'd done it to me now with a few deft words.

"A second front—it is an obsession with Red Army soldiers," I offered, struggling to find the right words in English. The words that would offer an olive branch for the narrowness of my focus, without apologizing for asking for what we *did,* after all, so desperately need from her country. "We are too close to the violence of the fight for objectivity. And of course I think like a sniper, focusing only on what is right in my sights—" I broke off again as a light turned red unexpectedly, and I braced myself before her stamp on the brakes sent me through the windshield.

"Naturally, your chief concern is for the men and women in the trenches at your side. And I would assure you that we have not forgotten them, either. At tonight's dinner, you'll find supporters of your cause, but you will also find detractors . . ." The First Lady took her hands off the wheel as she chattered, prominent teeth flashing, the very picture of a gossipy fifty-eight-year-old woman chattering about her grandchildren. Only she was breaking down anti-Soviet factions and which members I might expect to see at the dinner party, not stopping for breath when the light changed and she sent us bulleting off into the night again, at speeds I wasn't sure trains should be achieving much less automobiles. *The President's wife is a lunatic,* I thought, clutching the door for dear life. She threw me an amused glance as if she could tell what I was thinking, but I'd be damned if I asked her to slow down. And she didn't offer.

"Is your sniper's tally truly at 309?"

Yes. No. Maybe? I knew my official tally was over three hundred, but in the final chaotic days of Sevastopol's fall, I'd stopped taking note of official hits. Who had time for that with the German advance grinding forward? "But the Americans will want a specific number," the secretariat had insisted back in Moscow, so the number 309 was settled on. I didn't care enough to argue. My real count was probably over four hundred, but no one seemed interested in the complex answer over the simple one. "Three hundred and nine, *da*," I told the First Lady now.

"You know, your English will put you at an advantage at events like tonight's," she said, hurtling us through a yellow light without slowing. "It's really quite good. Where did you learn?"

"My first lessons came from my mother, when I was a child."

"Is she a teacher?"

"*Da*—" I caught my lip in my teeth as we scraped past a dark green Packard. "Is this interesting to you, Mrs. Roosevelt?"

"Americans want to like people," she said unexpectedly. "We want to like everybody. It's one of our better traits. But we need a reason, Lyudmila. You Russians with your statements and talking points—that's all well and good for policy meetings, but the American people want to know *you.* The young woman behind the official statements. Who your family is, what food you like—"

"What underwear I wear?" I couldn't help saying, and imagined Lena chuckling: *She might be the First Lady, but she's still a cheeky Yank! And you can't let cheeky Yanks have it all their own way.* "That is the kind of thing Americans want to know about me—my underwear?"

"They would appreciate a glimpse at the underpinnings of your character," Mrs. Roosevelt said tactfully. "Questions about the underpinnings of your clothing may of course be ignored."

"But things about my character, my family—these things are not relevant. Not to the public." I tried to find the words as the convertible pulled up with a screech of tires outside a stately Washington home, all redbrick and vast expanse of lawn. The windows blazed with light; I could see women in satin gowns moving on the other side of the glass; waiters with trays of hors d'oeuvres. "What is important is the reason I am here. You say your presidential adviser Mr. Hopkins wants the details of our fight—why does no one else?" My voice rose despite myself. "Why does your press not care? Why don't their readers?"

"Let them get to know you," Eleanor replied. "Make them care."

"And do not fail?"

"I hate to put it that way, Lyudmila dear, but you are not here long. It's a short window you have, to win over the American people."

"Don't worry, Mrs. Roosevelt." I looked at the cocktail party inside, drawing a steadying breath. "When I take aim at something, I do not miss."

Notes by the First Lady

She did well. No easy thing to walk into a Washington dinner party (oh, how those elegant cocktail-sipping matrons used to make my knees knock, as the young Mrs. Roosevelt!) and hold one's own under all those idle, curious eyes. In a foreign language, no less—her English is painstakingly grammatical, if accented.

It's near midnight by the time I bring our Soviet guests back to the White House. They trail into their bedrooms looking utterly exhausted, but I still have hours of work ahead tonight—a draft of the speech I'm to give at the Brooklyn Navy Yard, the text for the "My Day" column still to be finished. Franklin will already be asleep, or at least I hope so, because it will not do to have him brooding about cabals of enemies in the shadows and what they may or may not be planning. The best way to stop him brooding is to intrigue him, and I know just how to do it. Pausing in the darkened hall outside his bedroom, I nod to the Secret Service officer patrolling the corridor and scribble a note for the Eleanor basket, pushing it under the door for tomorrow morning's perusal. My feet ache as I head off to my own study, already flipping the pages of my Navy Yard speech, and I can't wait to take off my shoes.

You'll like Lyudmila Pavlichenko, *my note to Franklin reads.* And she has given me one of my ideas.

CHAPTER 25

The headline: SNIPER LYUDMILA PAVLICHENKO ENJOYED HER FIRST NIGHT IN WASHINGTON UNDER THE PRESIDENTIAL ROOF.

The truth: Sniper Lyudmila Pavlichenko learned that even under the presidential roof, she was not safe from people wanting her dead.

FOR A MOMENT I just stared at it: the folded sheet of plain paper that had been tucked into an unmarked envelope and slid under my bedroom door while I slept. No salutation, no signature, just blocky Cyrillic lettering blaring into my sleep-fuddled eyes.

GO HOME YOU COMMUNIST WHORE
OR YOU'LL DIE HERE

I realized, remotely, that my hand holding the paper was shaking. Not at the words—I'd been called a whore before; I'd certainly been threatened with death before. It was that someone had reached me *here,* in the White House. Had approached my bedroom at some point after I retired from last night's press conference and pushed their hate under my door for me to find as soon as I woke.

Whoever they were, they wanted me to know they could get to me. Even here.

I looked around the palatial bedroom where Mrs. Roosevelt had ushered me just yesterday morning. "Mr. Churchill stays here when visiting, and so does Princess Märtha of Norway." I wasn't impressed by royals, but I was certainly impressed to rest my head where Britain's prime minister had. A big bed with a rosy canopy; striped couches and lace-draped occasional tables; a vanity and a dressing room. A private bathroom all for me, which didn't have to be shared with eight Muscovite neighbors across the hall . . . I'd done some unabashed reveling last night in the big bathtub and then the bed's unbelievably soft pillows, reflecting how different it was from the muddy dugouts of the front line. In a bed like this, even someone like me could drift off to sleep feeling safe.

I looked back at the scrawled threats in my hand. *Not anymore.*

"You look rather grim," the First Lady greeted me when I came down to breakfast. Krasavchenko and Pchelintsev were already digging into their eggs and bacon. "Did you not sleep well, my dear?"

"Your friend Mr. Hopkins poured me many whiskeys last night as he asked about the Sevastopol front." I put on a bright smile, unfolding the newspaper.

"The reports of yesterday's press conference are really quite favorable," said the First Lady, pouring hot tea into a delicate china cup. "Elsa Maxwell gave you a lovely write-up in the *New York Post.* Listen: 'What Lieutenant Pavlichenko possesses is something more than just beauty. Her imperturbable calm and confidence come from what she has had to endure and experience. She has the face of a Madonna from a Correggio painting and the hands of a child, and her olive-colored tunic with its red markings has been scorched by the fire of fierce combat—' "

The florid words made me flush, and the next article—the one that described me as having *the icy eyes of a cold-blooded killer*—made me burn. One day in Washington, and I already had people who disliked me. No, worse than that—I pushed the newspaper away, feeling the crackle of paper in my pocket: *Go home you Communist whore or you'll die here.*

One day in Washington, and I was already watching my back.

"YOU WILL RETURN to the White House for the student conference in a few days," the Soviet ambassador told us all when we gathered in his office after another press conference at noon. "But from tonight on you will be housed near the embassy—a hotel a few blocks from here. You may have the afternoon today for sightseeing on your own, but this evening there is a performance at the national theater which the entire delegation will attend." Checking notes. "The opera is *Madama Butterfly*."

I hadn't attended the opera since *La Traviata* in Odessa on the day war broke out. I'd left at intermission then, not even staying to see Vika dance in the opera ballet. I wondered if Vika was still driving tanks or if she'd returned to her toe shoes and raked stages.

Or if she was dead. So many of the people I knew were now dead. And here I was going to the opera . . .

I felt a sudden violent need for fresh air and decided (once we were dismissed) on a walk through the city. High time I saw some part of America that wasn't glimpsed through a train window or over a bank of microphones—I couldn't get over how glossy and prosperous this city was. You'd never know there was a war on, looking at the men in gleaming shoes that had never been patched, the women in smart hats and ready-made frocks, the children with their plump well-fed cheeks. The shining automobiles, the buildings unmarked by bomb craters, the shops with no queues stretching out the doors . . . And I blended in here, passersby moving around me without a glance for my canvas shoes and lace-collared dress. I was just another window shopper, not the icy-eyed cold-blooded killer these people had read about with their morning coffee. Not a *Communist whore.*

I shook that thought away before it could darken the day. "Are you looking forward to the opera tonight?" I asked my minder gamely as he tramped along at my shoulder. "Do you like Puccini?"

"No, Comrade Pavlichenko. It is Western and therefore decadent."

I sighed. The delegation members had all been assigned minders, discreet Party men in heavy suits whose job it was to shadow us whenever we left the embassy. I'd made a token protest yesterday—what did they think I was going to do, defect? with my son still back home?—but the minder was mandatory, and mine was named Yuri Yuripov, who looked like a cement block in his gray wool coat, and had all the personality of a cement block, too. Having him trudge along behind me while I wandered a line of shops was like wearing a concrete bangle to the swimming pool. "What about some shopping, Comrade Yuripov? A few little luxuries for your wife in Moscow?"

He just stared at me stolidly. You didn't really expect a rollicking sense of humor from anyone who'd made a career in the NKVD, but the occasional smile would have been nice. *I bet he's a real thigh-slapper at parties,* I imagined Lena saying with a chuckle. I wished desperately that she was here instead. If she had been, she would have had her nose pressed up against the glass of the nearest boutique, ogling the dresses on the mannequins. *Look at this beauty,* she'd be crowing. *I'd look like Hedy Lamarr in that!*

"Yes, you would," I said aloud, lingering to look at the dress in the window: a yellow evening gown, heavy satin the color of buttery sunshine, scooped low at the front, skirt slinking toward the floor from a tight-molded waist. I couldn't take my eyes off that color—something a sniper would never wear; a color that painted you like a target. I'd spent an entire year trying to camouflage myself, blend in, and now suddenly I was yearning for color.

Well, why not? I had money in my pocket, all my army pay I'd never had the chance to spend, and Lady Death wanted some life for a change. Lady Midnight wanted to put on a little sunshine.

"Would you mind waiting out here?" I asked Yuri. "Or are you going to follow me into the dressing room?"

"No, Comrade Pavlichenko. That is not part of my directive."

"Small favors," I muttered, and went in. Coming out half an hour later with a shopping bag in hand, I saw an unpleasant sight: Alexei leaning up against the lamppost, smoking a cigarette with Yuri.

"Is the pretty lady out buying herself pretties?" my husband asked.

"What, you're going to report me for succumbing to Western decadence?" I retorted. "When half the men in this delegation raced out to buy lipsticks and nylons by the sack for both their wives in Moscow *and* their Bolshoi Ballet mistresses?"

"Everyone knows the perks of trips like these. Nylons and lipsticks are only the beginning." Alexei fell into step beside me. He'd already kitted himself out in a Western-style suit, a fine supple tweed that draped his long lean body with casual elegance. "There's one of those Hot Shoppes around the corner—a big improvement on the cheburek cafés in Odessa. Let me buy you a root beer." He glanced back as my minder fell into step a dozen feet behind us. "Yuri too."

"Root beer is not part of my directive," Yuri said stolidly.

"Mine either." I'd been told there was a park not far from here, so I reversed down Decatur Street instead. A sniper could look at only so many shop windows before yearning for trees and brush.

Or maybe it was cover I was looking for. The spot between my shoulder blades had been feeling itchy since I read that scrawled threat this morning, and now here was Alexei pressing me, too.

"Wait up, *kroshka*." My husband tagged along behind me, Yuri behind him. Thank goodness Alexei hadn't been deemed important enough to also have a minder (and oh, but that must be annoying him) or else it would have looked like I was leading a parade. "Have that root beer with me. You'll like it."

"What I *don't* like is taking anything from you, Alexei."

"You used to call me Alyosha. Not in public, but when it was just the two of us, and you weren't talking so much as moaning."

I stopped on the corner of Decatur and Blagden, nearly bumping into a woman with a patent leather pocketbook. "Alexei, what do you *want*? Why are you being like this?"

His eyes danced. "Being like what?"

I nearly shrieked. It wasn't fair that he could still get under my skin this way. It wasn't *fair*. "Forget it. I'm going for a walk in the park."

"Then I'll walk with you. Would you mind falling back out of earshot, Comrade Yuripov?" Alexei asked. "A man wants a private discussion with his wife, eh?"

Yuri fell back another twenty feet without consulting me. It wasn't broadly known in the delegation that Alexei was my husband, but clearly it was no surprise to the NKVD. I sighed, tempted to tell Alexei I'd rather walk out into a live fire zone than walk with him, but if my husband and I were going to have it out, better to do that away from the embassy. So I shrugged, taking a fast clip in the direction the hotel clerk had told me Rock Creek Park lay. I was expecting some tame stretch of city-bound grass, but it turned out to be a proper stretch of woods in the heart of the capital. What looked like miles of brush and boulders and trees, some clinging to their green needles, some weathering to red and gold autumn glory. Even trailing my irritating entourage, I couldn't help but be enchanted.

"Are you sure you wouldn't like a hamburger instead?" Alexei said, still ambling along at my side as I threaded in among the beeches and oaks. "I tried something called a Mighty Mo—charred meat and flavorless white bread, strangely addictive. I wouldn't mind trying more American food. Seeing more of this country . . ."

I ducked under a branch dipping over the path that barely deserved the name. "We're only in town another week or so."

"But this is just beginning for you, surely. You were approved by the Boss himself. That means there could be more trips overseas, more travel, more privileges . . . the wages of fame showering down on our family."

"Fame's fleeting." I ignored the *our*, still swinging my shopping bag at my side. "I intend to go back to the front. What are the odds I'll survive another year? My family will be the only ones to remember my name when I'm gone, and that's enough for me."

"The Party might have bigger plans for you." Alexei didn't seem fazed by the overhanging trees, he scrambled surefooted as a mountain goat up a slope toward a jutting rock. "Now that's a view!"

I scrambled up, ignoring his outstretched hand, and stood for a moment looking out over a steeper ridge below, all tangles of mountain laurel and the fluttering wing beats of thrushes. *What a perfect place for a stakeout,* I couldn't help thinking. You could lie flat up here with a rifle and pick anyone off on the slope below.

"How is Slavka?" Alexei asked, turning back his pristine cuffs.

"You have never once asked me how your son is doing." I turned to scramble back down from the rock, feeling all my senses tense at Slavka's name.

"I still have a right to know."

"Debatable." I resumed my brisk pace along the bending path. "He's healthy, if you must know. Excelling in his studies."

"It's been so long since I've seen him, but I'm sure he's growing up handsome. I always thought he had my eyes."

"I remember a time you said he looked nothing like you, and you asked me whether he was your son at all."

"I was an ass back then." Alexei gave a rueful grin, but I could hear the edge creeping into his voice. "Can you entirely blame me? Your father strong-armed me into a wedding I wasn't ready for; it was a choice between marrying you or worrying he'd send someone to cut my thumbs off. You wonder why I was just a little resentful about that? Having my hand forced?"

"No one *forced* you to seduce a girl barely fifteen years old." I heard my own voice scaling up.

"I'm saying I'm sorry, Mila." He made one of those little *calm down* gestures that made me want to hit him with the nearest blunt cement object. Right now, that would be Comrade Yuri Yuripov, trudging along behind doing his NKVD best to ensure that we didn't start divulging state secrets to the nearest elm. "I'm not here to quarrel with you," Alexei continued. "I'm here to make amends. I want to see our son when we return home."

I resumed my brisk pace. "No."

"Mila, a man can admit he's made mistakes. I wasn't a good husband and father then; let me make it up to you now. When all's said and done, Slavka's still my son."

Suddenly I was regretting this walk among the trees. There weren't the kind of crowds I'd envisioned, children playing, women with baby carriages, students with picnic lunches. Just a few hikers in the distance, spots of color in bright jackets, and a gangly birdwatcher with binoculars . . . but otherwise, not a soul among these sound-swallowing woods except Yuri. And I didn't think he'd interfere if Alexei tried to put hands on me. His directive was to stop me misbehaving, not get in between a husband and wife. I heard the babble of a creek somewhere close and pressed toward it. Running water meant open banks, and suddenly I wanted room to maneuver.

"Even you have to admit every boy needs a father," Alexei coaxed, seemingly unaware of my unease. "Someone to teach him how to play hockey, help him with his lessons—"

Lyonya would have shown Slavka how to do all that. It was so easy to see the future we'd never have, the three of us ice-skating on the pond at Gorky Park in winter . . . I gave a hard blink, willing the tears out of my eyes as I came out onto the creek bed. Not a deep current, more a winding stream littered with rocks, but there was a bridge spanning it to my left, ancient-looking arches slabbed together out of massive chunks of stone, and I made for it.

"You know Slavka needs a father. Why else did you take up with that lieutenant?" Alexei asked, reading my mind even if he couldn't see my face ahead of him. "But he's gone now, and that made me realize I let a good thing slip away."

I came to the middle of the bridge, looking out. A beautiful spot: huge trees spreading across either bank, the creek with its happy babble and scatter of stones, red-gold arches of autumn leaves fluttering overhead. Part of me marveled to see something so beautiful in the middle of a city, wilderness left pristine and perfect to restore a soul tired of stone buildings and pavement. And part of me was as wary as I had ever been, conscious of my husband beside me, his every move and glance.

"What do you want?" I asked at last, levelly. I knew perfectly well what he wanted, but I refused to make this easy for him.

"I want you back, Mila." Alexei laid his hand on the bridge parapet, palm up in invitation. "You, me, Slavka. A proper family again. And what better time for you and me to make a new beginning than on this tour?"

"No," I stated. "No a thousand times. No."

His smile didn't budge. "I know I'll have to win you back, *kroshka*. Court you properly, the way I should have done the first time."

"Aren't I a little old for you by now?" I'd seen the way his eyes followed the barely curved hips of the teenage girls we passed on Decatur Street.

"You were a girl then. Now you're a woman. A man gets to a stage in his life when he appreciates a woman—"

"When he appreciates a war heroine, you mean. A woman in line for privileges from the Party." If Alexei was already thinking about the overseas trips I'd earn if I survived the war, I was certain he was also thinking about a big apartment in Moscow; Party functions where caviar and champagne flowed; gifts and bribes and seats at the high table with glittering officials. Fame, comfort, wealth—maybe he'd rather have earned those things in his own right, but if it took hitching his troika behind a star rather than becoming one himself, he'd get out the harness and start buckling straps.

All he needed was for the mare to walk into the horse collar he was holding out.

"Imagine the life we'd have," he was saying softly, persuasively. "The gowns and jewels I'll give you, the privileges for Slavka—"

"I'm not as famous as you seem to think. This luxurious life you think is mine for the taking—"

"Ours for the taking."

"Even if it were possible"—I didn't believe my notoriety had any more staying power than the strike of a match—"why would I need you? Anything you promise for our son, I can already give him myself." I ignored Alexei's outstretched hand. "These privileges you're talking of, they all flow from *me*."

"Except the name." Something in his smile flickered. "The name under which you got famous, Mila. That's still mine."

"The world knows me as Lady Death, and I earned that myself. I don't owe you for your name."

"You owe me for something. Didn't I let you have your lieutenant in Sevastopol?"

Rage choked me momentarily. "*Let* me—"

"Anyone could see it wasn't going to last, so I let you have it. He was going to get the chop sooner or later, or you would, so I didn't make a fuss . . . and really most husbands wouldn't have been so understanding. But things are different now—"

A thrush exploded out from the nearby bushes as the birdwatcher with the binoculars came tromping along the bank, lenses flashing. I nearly jumped out of my skin at the sudden noise, and Alexei's smile widened just a little. "I'm going to divorce you the moment I get back to Moscow," I told him, wishing I hadn't shown any weakness, and reversed course back toward stolid Yuri on the bank. I wanted out of these woods. I wanted my private Washington hotel room. Somewhere both my husband *and* any anonymous hate-scrawling enemies could be safely locked on the other side of a stout door.

"You don't want that, Mila." I didn't turn, but I could hear the smile in Alexei's voice. The man it was impossible to anger, because he always knew best and was always in control. Always. "You don't know what you want."

That made me turn, even though I knew I shouldn't. His eyes sparkled. *Enjoy your little tantrum?* they asked.

"I want you to leave me alone," I snarled. "Because I will never, ever, *ever* take you back."

"I'm going to change your mind," he said softly. "And, *kroshka*, you're going to like it."

"I AM REQUESTING Dr. Pavlichenko be removed from the list of those attending the opera tonight," I told Krasavchenko in the embassy study he'd made his own. "I was instructed not to mention him publicly on this tour because the American press would disapprove of a woman who was separated from her husband. Very well, I want more distance between him and me on *all* forthcoming events."

Krasavchenko looked confused. "He made it clear to me that the two of you were considering reconciliation."

"*I* am not considering anything. *He* is pressing me when I am trying to focus on my duties, and *you* are to see that this stops."

I could see the look in Krasavchenko's gaze: *Look at her, overreacting just like a woman.* "If you would perhaps be calmer about this—"

"I am very calm, I assure you. Unless provoked, I am an exceptionally reasonable, calm, and quiet person. Dr. Pavlichenko, however, is beginning to provoke me. I guarantee that if he and I are in the same place, there will be a scene."

A sigh. "He will not attend the opera tonight."

"Thank you."

Just get through the conference, I told myself as I went back to my hotel room. Once I returned home and then to the front, Alexei would know my chances of surviving were too minimal to get much out of my fame before I was killed . . .

I paused, yanking a comb through my short hair, realizing it had been a while since I felt death's quiet shadow at my shoulder reminding me how little time I had left. I had this short space before battle consumed my life again; maybe it was all right to enjoy it for what it was: the long final breath before the last plunge down.

So enjoy the opera, I thought with a surge of tentative pleasure, and unwrapped the yellow satin dress I'd purchased from the boutique. The first pretty thing I'd bought myself in so long—I hung it up so the creases would fall out, then shimmied into my slip and spent some time powdering my face, applying lipstick. My hair was still cut short to the nape of my neck, but it had curl and shine in it again, and you could hardly see where it had once been shaved away from a splinter wound. I clipped it back on one side and let it fall on the other, over the ear that had nearly been ripped off by mortar fire and still showed stitch marks. Scars safely hidden, I pulled the dress over my head and reached behind me to do up the dozen little satin-covered buttons.

A knock sounded. Strange how you can know a man from his knock—Krasavchenko's knock was as self-important as he was; Alexei's knock insinuated, nearly curling itself under the door. Kostia's was almost inaudible, hardly more than a brush of knuckles. He didn't need to call out for me to know it was my partner.

"I'll be down soon." The room had only one small mirror; I stood twisting in front of it, trying to see my back. "Tell Krasavchenko I have to change."

Kostia's voice floated. "Why?"

I couldn't see my back. I blew out a frustrated breath. "Would you mind coming in?"

My partner came into the room, and the sight of him made my brows fly up: severe black-and-white evening clothes setting off his sun-swarthy face, the dark cane like a knight's sword rather than an aid to lean on. "I've never seen a wolf in black tie before," I joked.

He said nothing, just looked me over. I folded my arms over my yellow satin bodice, suddenly self-conscious. Strange to feel all this naked skin: bare arms; hair curling against bare neck; satin clinging to stockinged legs—my partner hadn't ever really seen me in anything but uniforms. I'd had an evening dress for the formal events in Cairo, but Moscow's idea of an evening dress and America's were very different. Kostia's face was carefully blank.

"I bought this without trying it on," I burst out, filling the silence. "The salesgirl assured me it would fit . . . I didn't think about the back."

I turned around. The back of the yellow satin dress plunged in a deep V, and as much as I twisted, I couldn't see how much of my back it revealed. "Does it show?"

The splinter wound that landed me in a hospital cot in Sevastopol had healed into a long, reddish, forked scar that snaked from my right shoulder blade to my spine. Lena had angled a pair of mirrors so I could see it. "Looks like a firebird clawed you," she'd said cheerfully. I'd never had cause before to feel self-conscious about it. Why would I? The only one to see it besides Lena had been Lyonya; he used to trace it when I fell asleep at night with my naked spine curled against his chest. Otherwise, my uniform covered the scar. All my clothes covered it—except this foolish dress I'd bought on impulse, because Lady Death wanted to look *pretty.*

No one would think *pretty*, looking at my scars framed between the panels of yellow satin. I could cover the scars in my hair, the scars on my ear, but not this. "Let them get to know you," the First Lady had counseled me in dealing with Americans—but they wouldn't want to get to know me if my battle wounds made them recoil.

"It shows, doesn't it?" I asked as the silence stretched.

My partner's voice came quietly, right behind me, close enough to prickle my skin. "Yes."

"I'll change. Tell Krasavchenko—"

Kostia's hands came down on either side of my waist. He bent his head, setting his mouth against the puckered skin of the scar, and stood there for a long year of a moment. "Wear it," he murmured into my skin. The kiss started at the blade of my shoulder and finished over my spine at the scar's tailing end. "Wear it with pride."

I stood utterly still, pinned in place, until I heard the quiet click of the door signaling he was gone.

THE MARKSMAN SLID onto the stool beside the tall fair-haired Russian silently nursing a vodka alone at the hotel bar. "Mind if I join you?" he asked in his bad Russian, flashing his falsified press ID. "You're Dr. Pavlichenko, right? The delegation physician." He'd plucked the name off the list Pocket Square had provided of the delegation's little people.

"The same," said Alexei Pavlichenko, clearly pleased to be recognized. "Sit, sit. It's always a pleasure to converse in my native language."

"Even as badly as I speak it, eh? I had the beat covering the American Communist Party a few years . . ." The marksman trotted out some pleasantries, letting the conversation eddy around the drinks. He didn't normally make contact with target-adjacent people like this—usually he operated by the rule that the fewer points of contact there were, the better—but he'd done enough research to talk like a newsman all night if necessary, and some careful changes in outward presentation (wig, shoe lifts, voice) meant Alexei Pavlichenko was very unlikely to recognize the marksman again once he'd reverted to his own accent and hair color.

"So, doc," he said after calling for another round of drinks, "I hear you're something of a war hero yourself. So why aren't you at the National Theatre with the others?"

The doctor's smile wavered. "One gets tired of these public events. All the press, the attention . . ."

You weren't invited. The marksman had already sat through the first act of *Madama Butterfly* tonight, keeping an eye on the Soviet delegation, which attracted more attention than the singers. At intermission they were urged onstage by the audience to take a bow. Lyudmila Pavlichenko, looking visibly nervous in yellow satin, had given a pretty speech through the interpreters about how pleased they all were to be in Washington, how dire the Russian need was for American aid . . . when the theater audience began passing the hat for donations to the Red Army, the marksman had risen in his seat and ambled back to the hotel where the delegation had been put up. Not just the delegation but their flunkies and minders.

"Say, about your name," the marksman exclaimed as if just struck. "It's the same as the lady sniper's. What are you, her brother, cousin—"

"Her husband." The doctor drank his vodka off in a quick motion.

"I thought she was a widow." Pretending bewilderment.

"It's complicated." A conspiratorial smile. "Aren't all things, with women?"

The marksman buried his own smile in his glass. He heard jealousy in the other man's voice, envy, spite, longing . . . that confrontation at Boulder Bridge *had* been a marital quarrel, then. He hadn't been entirely sure—bumbling around the banks of Rock Creek as a local birdwatcher hadn't gotten him near enough to eavesdrop, and he hadn't wanted to get close enough for anyone to see his face under the brim of his baseball cap—but the body language between the girl and the doctor had told its own intriguing story. Their meetup had surprised him. The marksman had been tailing the doctor that afternoon, not the girl—narrowing down his choice for who to approach on the delegation staff, what person could be used to fix the frame around Lyudmila Pavlichenko. And then to discover his top pick was her disgruntled, shunted-aside husband?

Sometimes fate dropped a gift in your lap.

Another round of drinks, and the marksman waited for them to hit before he leaned closer across the bar. "So, this student assembly . . ."

CHAPTER 26

The headline: THE INTERNATIONAL STUDENT ASSEMBLY OPENED TODAY WITH NEARLY FOUR HUNDRED STUDENTS FROM FIFTY-THREE COUNTRIES. LATIN AMERICANS, AFRICANS, ASIANS, AND EUROPEANS MINGLED IN HARMONY AND ENTHUSIASM.

The truth: The students from Bombay University nearly came to blows with the British Oxford contingent over the so-called Indian Question, and the only reason I didn't start swinging alongside the young man in the turban shouting, "We'll win independence eventually, you colonial curs!" was because Krasavchenko threatened to have me exiled to the Arctic Circle.

"MAY I STEAL you away, my dears?"

I blinked up at the First Lady, exchanging glances with Krasavchenko and Pchelintsev. The opening-day reception was far from over; the three of us stood with untouched plates of canapés and glasses of ubiquitous warm white wine like perfumed goat pee, besieged by questions from journalists, honorary guests from U.S. civic organizations, and fellow students. Krasavchenko was boring the ears off a White House aide; Pchelintsev was re-fighting all his Leningrad duels for an American general laden with medals; and I was fending off an avid society columnist who wanted to know what kind of makeup routine I followed at the front. "I bathe in the blood of my enemies," I wanted to tell her. "It's simply *wonderful* for the complexion!" But she would probably think I was being serious, because Americans seemed to assume all Soviets were as humorless as my minder, Yuri.

In other words, all was going much as expected, the first day of the conference. But now the First Lady was drawing the three of us aside. "Supper at the White House," she made our excuses for us, collecting Kostia along the way. I expected to be ushered into the familiar White House dining room and resolved that this time I wouldn't gape at the chandeliers and portraits and china—but we were led into a private oval-shaped study instead, and my jaw dropped for an entirely different reason.

In the center of the room, a man sat alone in a wooden chair with a high back, long-fingered hands resting on its wide arms, a tartan rug across his legs. "I'd like you to meet the President," the First Lady said simply.

I was already standing at attention, bracing without making the decision to do so. So were the others, all of us responding to the authority radiating out of that chair. The President's keen gaze passed over us as Kostia made introductions, and I knew he'd be able to produce our names and details a decade from now if he were asked. "Krasavchenko, Pchelintsev, Pavlichenko—how wonderful." He smiled, and I couldn't help smiling back as I stepped forward in turn to press that long, sinewy palm.

"I would hear the lady's experiences first." A courtly half bow from the chair. *You're a sniper with 309 kills,* I scolded myself. *Don't blush just because the American president is a charmer!* But for the love of Lenin, it was a close thing: I'd been told to expect a sharp mind and a strong will when it came to Franklin Delano Roosevelt, but I hadn't expected the warmth, the force, the unblinking attention as he aimed questions at me through Kostia. What fighting had I done; what actions lay behind my military decorations; how had my regiment fought? The press corps here found it hard to believe I did anything at the front but curl my hair for propaganda pictures; their president didn't bat an eyelash when I described how to dig a trench and wait six, seven, eight hours for the perfect shot. How our shortage of firearms was so dire that my first rifle came to me with the blood of its previous owner still wet on the barrel.

"Years of war," President Roosevelt said finally after grilling my fellow delegates in turn, "and our side hasn't succeeded anywhere in resisting their enemies as long as you Russians have done. Is it your military spirit, your training? The skill of your officers and generals? The unity between army and populace?" He tilted his head, looking at each of us in turn. "What would you say?"

"It's *will*," I answered when I saw Krasavchenko hesitate. "Because we hold and fight or we die. But no amount of willpower in the world matters if we have no bullets to shoot or rifles to fire."

"Tell me more," the President said quietly.

He'd won us all over in a matter of minutes. The First Lady's authoritative voice sounded in the background and chairs were pulled up; drinks poured; rough maps sketched with napkins and cocktail shakers as we talked and the President listened. "And how do you feel in our country?" he finished, looking from face to face again. "Are the Americans cordial toward you all?"

For an instant, I thought of the second hand-scrawled threat I'd received just yesterday morning: YOU'LL DIE SCREAMING YOU RED BITCH. Same scrawled Cyrillic, same handwriting as far as I could see, and they could apparently get to me just as easily in my Washington hotel as they could in the White House. I couldn't stop glancing over my shoulder now whenever I ventured outside, even if the Soviet ambassador shrugged and said it was likely nothing . . .

"We're greeted everywhere as welcome guests," Krasavchenko was assuring the President through Kostia. "You Americans are a very hospitable people!"

I wasn't going to bring up my death threats, but I couldn't resist saying in English, "Sometimes we are subjected to sudden attacks."

The President frowned. "Attacks?"

"From your reporters." I kept my face serious but let my eyes dance. "They are very persistent. They want us to bare everything."

President Roosevelt grinned. What a grin that man had. He liked women, we had been told in our reports in Moscow, and I could tell he liked me. He didn't think the cut of my uniform was unflattering at all. So I took a breath and said, "May I ask—"

"More active assistance for the Soviet Union?" he said, reading me without effort. "The opening of a second front in Western Europe to draw German divisions away from the banks of the Volga?"

I nodded. I knew that second front wasn't such an easy matter for him to put into motion as I'd first assumed when I arrived in this country, but neither would I pretend our need for it wasn't dire.

He looked pensive. "Mr. Stalin is already aware that it is difficult at present for us to render more active assistance to your country. We Americans are not yet ready for decisive action—"

"You acted decisively after Pearl Harbor," I couldn't help saying.

Another of those rueful grins. "Yet when it comes to expanding into a European front, we're held back by our need to aid our British allies. But in heart and soul"—another of those courtly bows from the chair—"we stand with our Russian friends."

"Well," Krasavchenko muttered later as we went down to our actual dinner and the President excused himself to another function, "that was useless."

"Did you think he'd put his hand on his heart and promise an army on the spot? If he had, I wouldn't have trusted him a centimeter." I smiled. "We're just students, not negotiators. All we can do is advocate. At least he listened, unlike his journalists."

Unexpectedly Kostia spoke up, his voice quiet over the muffled tread of our shoes on expensive carpet. "That's a man to follow into shellfire."

"He makes me think . . ." I paused, trying to find the words. "I might only be a student here, but I don't have to be useless. If one man like him can tow his nation single-handedly through a worldwide economic depression and then a worldwide war, I can learn to give speeches without feeling like a deer caught in klieg lights, can't I?"

Kostia didn't answer, but his eyes caught mine for the first time since the opera. There was something in his gaze now that scorched, and I couldn't stop my stomach from clenching in confused, chaotic response, even as we were ushered toward another long dining room table of White House officials and guests. The final day of this conference here would also mark six months since the day Lyonya had died . . .

I was relieved to turn away from my partner and take a seat beside the presidential adviser Harry Hopkins, who pulled out my chair with something of a twinkle in his eye. From our very first meeting he'd taken a liking to me, and despite my instinct to stay reticent with Americans, I'd taken a liking to him. He was another one, like his boss, who asked questions and actually listened to the answers. I'd been dropping as many facts as I could into that receptive ear. "What did you think of the President?"

"I am honored to call him an ally," I managed in my most gracious diplomatic tones, murmuring a *spasibo* to the server who filled my glass.

"Mrs. Pavlichenko, I've heard the tobacco company Philip Morris is offering you a contract," a woman called across the table. "They want to put your portrait on cigarette packets! What have you to say to that?"

"They can go to the devil," I said in English, abandoning the gracious diplomatic tone, and the table burst out laughing.

"Cigarette packets may only be the start of it," the First Lady murmured, and I cocked my head.

"What do you mean, Mrs. Roosevelt?"

"Oh, nothing." Her eyes positively danced. "I merely have an idea . . . and I believe the President, having met you all, is ready to agree to it."

THE SECOND AND third day of the conference. Long droning addresses, usually followed by heated debates. Answering questions about my uniform; trading university lecture stories with a bucktoothed girl from York and a smooth-cheeked boy from Beijing who barely looked old enough to shave. Applauding as the delegates adopted a Slavic Memorandum condemning German fascism. "So kind of them to conclude that fascism is bad," I whispered to Yuri. "I can't wait to inform Comrade Stalin of their decision. He'll be so relieved!" Even that didn't get a facial expression out of my minder, who continued to watch beady-eyed from the back of the room as flashbulbs went off.

The First Lady insisted on posing for photographs between Pchelintsev and me, taking our hands very firmly in her large, capable ones. Maybe her husband couldn't promise aid as quickly as we wanted, but she made sure no photographer left without that photograph of us all holding hands, a visible symbol of the Soviet-American military alliance.

"You're getting comfortable in the limelight at last," Alexei murmured on the conference's last day. The closing reception was being held on the green beside the White House; the warm, sunny evening threw my shadow ahead of me long and slanting. "Well done, *kroshka*."

"*Ta mère suce des ours*," I told him. A phrase I'd been taught by a French Canadian student on a cigarette break, when we'd been discussing how to get rid of handsy lecturers—a topic female university students could discuss across all global divides and language barriers. I'd taught her how to say *Put your pig paws back in your pockets* in Russian; she'd taught me *Ta mère suce des ours,* which apparently meant *Your mother sucks bears.* "It's even more insulting than it sounds in translation," she advised, and I grinned at Alexei's perplexed face now as I strolled off to join the group of students from Montreal. I was determined to enjoy this last reception. In Moscow it would have been an elaborate affair, white-draped tables and dark suits and long speeches, but the First Lady had made it all into a backyard party: students wandering the gardens with paper plates full of sandwiches and glass bottles of Coca-Cola, the sound of decadent, delicious ragtime drifting from an unseen radio. President Roosevelt had yet to join us, and I could sense a thrum in the crowd as the guests looked for him, but until he arrived, things could remain decidedly informal. I ended up telling a White House aide about my walk to Boulder Bridge in Rock Creek Park, blinking as the aide told me how President Roosevelt had once lost a signet ring there on a hike. "President Roosevelt was hiking?"

"This was his cousin President Teddy Roosevelt, forty years ago," the aide explained. "He lost a favorite ring there, so he put an ad in the paper: *Golden ring lost near Boulder Bridge in Rock Creek. If found, return to 1600 Pennsylvania Avenue. Ask for Teddy.*" He guffawed, and so did the students from Montreal. "The ring never turned up . . ."

I smiled, taking a deep breath to smell the fresh-cut grass, letting the aide press a sandwich into my hand—a sausage roll the Americans called a *hot dog.* American food looked Technicolor-bright to me, like it had been molded in plastic rather than cooked. "Not bad," I said, swallowing my first bite. "Actual dog?"

"Mrs. Pavlichenko, you're a card!"

"What? They eat worse than dog in Leningrad by now." As party chitchat went, that observation went over like a lead balloon, as the Americans liked to say, but Mrs. Roosevelt rescued me, smoothing the moment over.

"You know," she said, drawing me to one side, "I've been planning this conference a long while now. The idea was to promote American values in the context of international youth . . . but you Russians have changed that plan."

I took a sip of my Coca-Cola through a straw. Too sweet and too cold, like sucking on sugared razor blades. "How, ma'am?"

"All you delegates are eloquent"—ha, that was a lie; she was as bored by Krasavchenko's droning as I was—"but you Russians have a particular passion when you speak about the war, Lyudmila dear. It nearly hurts to listen to you."

"I am sorry if it *hurts* to hear truth," I began stiffly, but she put a pacifying hand on my arm.

"No, it's good if it hurts us. We Americans are used to viewing war from a distance—the privilege of living, as Chancellor Otto von Bismarck once said, with less powerful neighbors to the north and south, and nothing to the east and west but fish. Even the terrible attack on our own Pearl Harbor came thousands of miles away. You have helped put a visible face on the price of war viewed inside one's homeland. The bleeding and suffering of neighbors and loved ones in their own cities . . . You make it real and impossible to ignore. Thank you for that."

She paused, but I said nothing. I still wasn't entirely sure how to treat her, this observant lady who was so evidently bent on charming us all. President Roosevelt might have been a man of privilege, but his crippled legs had clearly left him with a keen understanding of suffering. I wasn't so sure about the First Lady. She was very friendly, very clever, very complimentary when she spoke of *putting a visible face* on war—but what did she know of it, really?

And I still hadn't forgotten her statement to me that first day over the breakfast table. Whether I could see the faces of my enemies through my sights, and whether that would make it difficult for Americans to like me.

She smiled, not offended by my silence. "It's my hope that our whole country will hear what you have to say."

"But we return to Moscow in a few days." I couldn't wait. This celebration on the White House green would be the end, and I was glad. The Washington journey might have had its pleasant moments, but I wanted home soil under my feet again. I wanted to know I was at least on the same continent as my Slavka.

"Your ambassador has yet to brief you officially, but other plans have been—" The First Lady broke off as Alexei bowed his way into our conversation.

"Do pardon me to the First Lady," he whispered in Russian with a bow over her hand. "I need to steal you away for a moment, *kroshka*. I've been asked to show you the Rose Garden before President Roosevelt arrives and the evening goes to chaos."

I was about to tell him that I had no intention of strolling any roses with him *ever*, but the First Lady broke in. She didn't speak any Russian beyond *da, nyet,* and *spasibo*, but she'd heard her husband's name. "Is he asking when the President is coming down?" she asked, looking at me. "He won't be able to drop by tonight as he planned, unfortunately. Some other business intruded—but never fear, you'll all have other chances to meet with him." She broke into a wide smile. "At my urging, the President has invited the entire Soviet delegation to extend their stay. You will tour more of our cities to give greater publicity to your fight against Hitler. Your ambassador tells me approval has just been granted from Moscow!"

In the face of her delight, I worked to keep the disappointment off my face. "How long is this visit extending, ma'am?"

"That will be decided later. The immediate plan is to send you all to New York City tomorrow morning, on the Washington–New York express." She lowered her voice. "I've requested that you especially, Lyudmila, get the chance to do more speaking. I think the American people will respond to a woman—and not merely to any woman, to *you*."

"I thought you were worried they would not approve of me," I couldn't help saying.

She smiled. "I think you have the power to change their minds."

"What's she saying?" Alexei asked in Russian. I ignored him, trying to match Mrs. Roosevelt's evident pleasure as my heart sank into my knees. I wasn't going home yet, after all.

POCKET SQUARE'S POCKET-SQUARE handkerchief was red today instead of blue, and his face was even redder. "Explain yourself," he hissed at the marksman without so much as a greeting. They'd met overlooking the Washington Monument today, clouds racing past the tip of the great stone spire, standing well out of earshot of the crowding tourists. "The conference done and not a shot fired! Did you lose your nerve or—"

"The President didn't attend," the marksman said calmly, tipping his hat to a pretty young mother steering her baby carriage toward the monument. "A last-minute schedule change." A great pity, because everything had been going like clockwork: the marksman poised to drift away from the cadre of photographers, disappear into the gardens, and begin setting up his long shot that would take Roosevelt between the eyes the moment the man appeared on the portico. That booby of a Russian doctor had been primed to lead his wife off to the Rose Garden so she would be suspiciously absent from the festivities once the shot was fired. "I'll lurk along behind, get some real good photographs of you two there for tomorrow's write-up," the marksman had promised him at the hotel bar; the doctor, full of vodka by that point, was so keen to see his own face in the paper alongside his wife's, he hadn't even needed the incentive of a folded bill or two. No notion he was being set up: the husbandly accomplice helping his assassin wife murder the president. Theirs would have made a pretty pair of mug shots in the papers, the marksman thought wistfully.

Ah, well.

"I warned you that even the best plans can go awry," he told Pocket Square, who was still apoplectic. "Fortunately the Soviet tour in the

United States has been extended, so we'll have plenty more chances while Pavlichenko's still here to take the fall. She's gone to New York; I'll need a copy of the new itinerary."

The marksman paused, frowning. The cover identity of a journalist had been a good one so far, but the First Lady seemed to have taken a liking to Lyudmila Pavlichenko, and if they appeared at events together on the road, then Eleanor Roosevelt would insist on *women* journalists. Another of the horsey bitch's peccadilloes, something about getting more females onto newspaper staffs. Like the world needed more yattering cows. "I may need a new cover," the marksman said, more to himself than to Pocket Square, and walked away from the stone needle of the Washington Monument without a goodbye. Lady Death was in New York City; there was plenty of time to plan.

"I WISH WE were in Stalingrad."

I spoke into the silence of the car, but even so, I wasn't sure Kostia could hear me over the wail of sirens, the rumble of motorbike engines from the motorcade that enclosed the Cadillac. Two vehicles had greeted our delegation at the train station in New York; Krasavchenko, Pchelintsev, and their minders had been shuttled through a tunnel of flashing cameras and shouting journalists to the first car, and I'd dived into the second with my partner as Yuri rode with the driver on the other side of the partition.

"I hear the Germans are storming for the Volga," I continued. "Pushing into the outskirts of Stalingrad." The Red Army soldiers would be falling back from street to street, skirmishing from rooftops and bombed-out buildings—perfect conditions for snipers. I could so clearly envision Kostia and me there, camouflaged against the rubble of shattered pipes and demolished walls, chewing dry tea and sugar, our rifle barrels twin eyes narrowed on the enemy.

Yet here I was in a Cadillac instead, moving at a crawl through the brightest, busiest city I'd ever seen. The closer we got to Central Park, the deeper the roar of the crowd became all around us. My heart was trying to climb up my throat. I'd thought Washington was overwhelming, but the noise in New York City had me wanting to dive into a foxhole.

And maybe my rising nerves had a little something to do with the *third* threatening note I'd found . . . this one waiting in my coat pocket as I boarded the train for New York City. Whoever it was had followed me from Washington—had been close enough to touch me—could have sunk a knife between my ribs rather than slipping a note into my pocket that read I'M GOING TO CORE YOUR SKULL WITH YOUR OWN RIFLE BARREL YOU MURDERING RED SLUT.

I didn't care that the embassy wasn't worried; that they'd wave it off as *another American crackpot.* I was being hunted, and I was weaponless on unfamiliar territory, and for a sniper that was terrifying.

And on top of all of that, I had to give a speech in this huge, cacophonous park crammed with people who would probably agree that I *was* a murdering Red slut.

"Lyonya told me you gave your first speech in Sevastopol." Kostia looked straight ahead, voice low and calm, but his shoulder was pressed into mine as though we were lying on our elbows in a trench, waiting for our shot. He knew about the threats, but I'd made light of them—I didn't want him seeing I was afraid. "How did you prepare then?"

"I asked Lyonya—" My voice caught on his name; I swallowed hard. "I asked how someone like me who shoots people from a distance, trying never to be seen, is somehow stuck under bright lights in front of a packed crowd, giving a speech."

"And he said?"

" 'Shut up, Mila, you'll be brilliant.' "

"He was right." Kostia looked at me squarely. "You'll always be brilliant."

"But—"

My partner raised his hand, holding it flat at eye level. I stopped speaking and raised mine. My pulse might be racing, but my hand was granite steady. Threats or no, crowd or no. Kostia smiled. Not with his mouth, but folded into the corners of his eyes, where only I could see it.

I couldn't resist a smile back, the strange chaos of conflicting emotions warring in my stomach again. Ease and awkwardness, tenderness and confusion, wariness and—

The Cadillac swung through the main entrance of Central Park, and the roar redoubled. Crowds were pressing all around, barely held back by the motorcade. I spared one look at them, then back to Kostia. Breathe in, breathe out. "You'll have my back?"

"From here to Stalingrad."

The car halted. "I wish I was armed," I groaned as the doors opened, and then I swung myself out, hoisting a smile into place. My ears roared at the noise; hands were pulling me forward and men in burly jackets lifted Kostia and me up onto their shoulders. They bore us along through the crowd up to the stage, where the mayor of New York was saying something through a microphone about the gargantuan struggle of the Russian people against the German fascists.

And then it was time for me to speak.

I looked out at a sea of faces, an ocean of cameras. *Don't fail,* I thought. *Don't miss.*

"Dear friends." I heard my voice soaring, as though it might carry all the way up to the spires of these vast skyscrapers. Kostia repeated my words into his own microphone, fierce and sonorous. "Hitler is making a desperate attempt to cripple our united nations before we

Allies do it to him. It is a matter of life and death for the freedom-loving people of every country to join forces and render assistance to the front. More tanks, more planes, more ordinance."

I spread my boots, clasped my hands at my back. I found the rage in me that a year at the front hadn't killed, and let it roar flame-red into my voice. I spoke in Russian, but even if these New Yorkers couldn't understand my words, they could understand my fire. My anger. My *will.*

You will aid us, I thought. *You will aid us in this fight, or I will die trying.*

I still stumbled in places. I still faltered. But it was better than the speech I'd given in Sevastopol, better than the statements I'd given for the Washington press conferences, and the scream of the crowd when I finished nearly blew my shell-damaged ears in.

Maybe they didn't think I was a murdering Red slut after all . . .

I stood on the stage with applause raining down on me like mortars, hearing thousands of Americans call my name, and I wondered for the first time if Alexei had been right. If this flash of fame I'd somehow accrued was something more than a matchstick's brief transitory flare.

CHAPTER 27

The headline: MAYOR FIORELLO LA GUARDIA OF NEW YORK CITY PRESENTED THE SOVIET DELEGATION WITH A MEDALLION STRUCK IN HONOR OF ALL WHO STRUGGLE AGAINST FASCISM, AND "BROAD IS MY NATIVE LAND" WAS SUNG BY PAUL ROBESON, WHOSE BASS IS AS DARK AND SHINING AS HIS VISAGE. BOTH TRIBUTES WERE ACCEPTED BY CHARMING GIRL SNIPER LYUDMILA PAVLICHENKO, WHOSE SPEECH WAS RECEIVED WITH ENTHUSIASM BY THE PEOPLE OF NEW YORK CITY. MRS. PAVLICHENKO PROCEEDS ON TO BALTIMORE . . .

The truth: When women become famous, it brings strange men out of the woodwork.

"YOUR ADDRESS WAS brilliant, Mrs. Pavlichenko, utterly brilliant!"

"Thank you, Mr. Jonson." I tried to remove my fingers from the man in front of me, but he seemed determined to wring them off my hand, eyes glowing with fervor over his starched collar and pinstriped suit.

"Quite as brilliant as the speech you gave in New York."

"Mr. Jonson, it was the same speech—"

"I first heard you in New York, and I followed to Baltimore just to hear you speak again!"

"How . . . dedicated!" My welcoming smile was slipping; I hitched it back in place as Kostia translated. Usually I tried to speak English when conversing at these receptions and parties, disliking the embassy's instructions about using the interpreter for all questions, but Mr. William Patrick Jonson—American millionaire, dedicated eccentric, owner of a metallurgical company, and apparently smitten with *the girl sniper*—had me diving to take refuge behind the dual shields of my native language and Kostia. Not that Kostia was much help; he was so entertained by my new suitor he was actually almost smiling. "I will hand you your molars on a wreath if you keep smirking," I warned him in Russian, still beaming at Mr. Jonson.

"Mr. Jonson wishes to know if you will visit his home on the outskirts of New York," Kostia said, straight-faced. "He has a fine collection of artwork by Russian avant-garde artists from the beginning of the twentieth century."

"Tell him he can jump into Baltimore Harbor."

"Mrs. Pavlichenko prefers the work of the Peredvizhniki artists," Kostia translated, "particularly Vasily Vereshchagin."

"I will *acquire* some Vereshchagin, Miss Pavlichenko, if only you will agree to visit." The American millionaire was still chafing my hand as though trying to warm it back to life from frostbite. "And then you can meet my mother—"

For the love of Lenin. "Mr. Jonson, I'm afraid I am leaving very soon. The Soviet delegation has been invited to spend a week at the President's family estate."

"She would love to meet your mother when she returns," Kostia translated. He was quivering with laughter by the time I managed to scrape free.

"Number 310 on my tally is going to be you," I promised Kostia in a whisper as we moved off through the thronged Baltimore reception room. "Because I'm going to *shoot you in the back* as soon as we are sent to Stalingrad after coming home from this circus."

"Lady Midnight, I'm always the one at *your* back."

We traded quick smiles. We weren't uncomfortable with each other, but we were *aware*; we were making conversation rather than slipping in and out of comfortable silence, and I heard myself saying brightly, "Are you coming to Hyde Park? If Alexei inveigled his way along, surely you can."

"Alexei's coming?" Hyde Park was where the Roosevelt country estate was located on the Hudson River; the First Lady had invited the Soviet delegation, the students from Britain, several from Holland and China . . . "I thought Krasavchenko agreed to leave him behind."

"He claims he needs to tend Pchelintsev's recent illness."

"Pchelintsev has hay fever."

"That's what I said, but did anyone listen to me?"

Alexei was right there with the rest of the delegation, squeezing himself up between Kostia and me when we all arrived at Hyde Park. I saw his eyes go narrow and acquisitive at the sight of the gracious colonial house with its pillars and porticoes, its surrounding acres of green lawn and waving trees. "Never mind having a dacha someday," he breathed, putting a caressing hand at the small of my back as the party crowded toward the entrance hall. "We'll have something like *this*. Spacious, well-appointed, near the woods for a little hunting . . . what do you think, *kroshka*?"

I moved away from his hand without saying anything, because words did no good. Clearly his plan was to wear me down with sheer persistence until I got so tired of refusing that I gave in. Insults didn't put him off; silence didn't put him off—and maybe he'd gotten a warning from the delegation not to make any embarrassing public fuss around me, but that left plenty of time away from cameras and American eyes to continue his campaign. *That's my wife,* he was always saying casually to the other delegation members. *We've been separated, but she was very young . . . you know how fickle young girls can be, eh? We get on so well now . . .*

Avoid him, I thought, looking around the vast green spread of the Roosevelt estate, the guest quarters where Yuri and the other minders were already tramping with the luggage. *At least there's plenty of room here to do it.*

The fresh country air should have been a restorative after the choking noise and smoke of New York and Baltimore, but somehow my dreams that first night were full of cobwebs and nightmares. Lyonya died in my arms, over and over, and when I twisted out of that dream, I fell into another where a shadowy figure stalked me through Washington's empty streets, snarling *Commie slut . . . Red bitch . . .* I woke up gasping, on the whisper of *You'll die here.*

"I am not going to die here," I said aloud into my shadowed bedroom. No crackpot could get his scribbled notes or his murderous intentions anywhere near this remote presidential hideaway surrounded by Secret Service and forest. But I knew I wouldn't sleep another wink, so as soon as the dawn broke, I tugged a flowered day dress over my head and slipped out of the house for a walk—only to run right into the cement pillar of Yuri.

"Really?" I exploded. "We're on the presidential retreat. Everything is entirely locked down—there is no way I could meet any undesirables on these grounds, even if I wanted to, *which I don't.* Can't you just sleep in for once and let me go on a walk alone?"

"That would countermand my directive, Comrade Pavlichenko."

Well, it had been worth a try. "Would you mind staying a bit back, then?" I sighed, and headed toward the gardens, away from the bustle of breakfast preparation I could already see at the main house as servants streamed in and out.

The surrounding park was laced with paths, beds of autumn flowers, gazebos for dallying, all standing sunlit and peaceful in the morning light against the surrounding darkness of the woods. I took a deep lungful of air, not realizing until now how badly I'd missed quiet—silence—space to breathe. Snipers are loners, after all, and between Yuri, the ever-present journalists, and my speaking schedule, I hadn't had much time to myself. My night terrors were melting away fast as I wandered toward the water; one bank was choked with reeds, while the other sported a bathing shed, a row of small boats, a small dock. At the end of the dock, looking out at the water—

"I should have known I'd find you out here away from everyone," I said to Kostia's back, wandering out to join him as I motioned Yuri to stay on the bank. My partner was smoking a Lucky Strike; we'd both taken to American cigarettes, so he lit another off his own and passed it to me. We stood looking over the water for a quarter hour's companionable silence, smoke drifting up from our cupped hands.

"Three," he said at last.

"Three," I agreed. "Bathing shed—"

"Back behind the tree line—"

"And among the reeds on the far bank." I narrowed my eyes at the spot, mentally planning a foxhole. "Hard to keep your weapon dry there."

"Good thing we don't have to shoot anyone this morning."

I finished the cigarette, grinding the butt under my heel as I looked at the row of small boats. "When I was a child in Belaya Tserkov, my sister and I took a flat-bottomed rowboat out on the river sometimes. We called it the *Cossack Oak*, pretended we were rowing to the North Pole to find Morozko." I remembered telling Kostia in Odessa how he reminded me of the winter god from old times, snow-silent and dangerous. I cleared my throat, nudging the nearest craft—a narrow leather-covered thing with two short paddles that I was fairly certain Americans called a canoe. "Shall we try it? The First Lady did say to make ourselves at home."

Kostia jumped down into the canoe before I was done speaking.

I took the seat behind him as he gave us a push off the dock. "Only room for two!" I shouted toward Yuri just in case he had any thought of joining us, and we got our paddles in a rhythm, aiming for deeper water. I enjoyed the burning in my shoulders even if I did favor the unscarred side, savoring the glassy expanse of water and the rustle of reeds. "Lyonya would have liked this," I found myself saying. I could almost see him here in the canoe with us, fair hair ruffling in the wind.

"He didn't like water," Kostia said over his shoulder. "I used to tease him about that."

"Oh." Something I hadn't known about the man I thought of as my second husband. In my mind's eye he reached out and tucked a lock of hair behind my ear. *There are a lot of things you didn't get a chance to know about me,* milaya.

And now I never would. I'd missed my chance—my second chance at love, the world giving me Lyonya after I'd made such a monumental mistake in my first attempt at marriage. You hardly ever got a second shot after missing your first; life as a sniper had taught me that, but the world had been kind enough to give me one and I'd missed that, too . . .

"Mrs. Roosevelt says there's a very fine library at the house," I said just to be saying something. "I could use some new books to read, to practice my English. Maybe we can find you something other than *War and Peace*."

Kostia's shoulders continued to flex and relax, flex and relax as he swept his paddle through the water. "I'm going back to Washington tomorrow."

I blinked. "You're leaving the delegation?"

"Only for a few days. I'll make a private fuss to Krasavchenko that it doesn't sit well with me, staying in a presidential palace built on the backs of the masses, and ask to go back to the embassy for the rest of the week." A brief thread of amusement laced his voice. "The real reason . . . I mean to take a day in New York City, on my way to catch the New York–Washington express."

"New York City?"

He stopped paddling, and the canoe drifted to a halt in the middle of the glassy mirror of water. "My grandmother. Remember the one I told you about?"

The American girl who had come to Russia before the revolution with a missionary group, full of romantic ideas about Siberian snows and white nights, marrying a revolutionary and staying behind. I nodded, remembering the night he'd trusted me with that story—a forest camp outside Sevastopol, celebrating with Vartanov and the rest of our platoon when they'd all still been alive and laughing. Strange to think I'd nearly forgotten Kostia was part American, though he'd spent the last few weeks among Americans, deploying his fluent English instead of his rifle.

"I have family in New York," Kostia went on, still sitting with his back to me. "Cousins I've never met. They probably don't know I exist. I've done some digging, very quietly. I know at least where my grandmother's sister lives. She's still alive, living in Ridgewood."

"Kostia, the risk . . ." He'd managed to conceal his American ties for so long, lost or destroyed all the relevant documention—clearly he'd passed all the background checks, to be allowed to join this delegation at all. If, after all that, it were found out he had undisclosed American relations . . . I didn't even want to imagine the consequences. They would assuredly be hideous.

"I won't have trouble getting permission to return to Washington alone—they don't assign minders for little fish like me. And I'll concoct a story about missing the last train, having to stay the night in New York City. They won't suspect."

"And—what? You'll just walk up to your great-aunt's house and knock on the door?"

"Maybe I'll knock. Or maybe I'll just walk the streets where my grandmother grew up." He hesitated. "I don't know."

I tried to imagine an Irish family in New York finding this sinewy Siberian wolf on their doorstep, a cousin from halfway around the world. *They'd better not slam the door on you,* I thought. "If you need a story I'll cover for you," I began, digging my paddle into the water again to turn us back toward shore.

"Careful," Kostia began, "it's got a very shallow draft—"

Too late. The canoe slewed sideways from my paddle, and before I knew it, I was in the drink.

The famous Lady Death and her sniper partner, Lyonya hooted fondly as Kostia and I floundered and splashed. *May I present the deadliest shots in Sevastopol!*

The water was barely up to chest height, so there wasn't much hurt but my pride as I surfaced spitting water. Yuri, on the bank, didn't move; his orders were to stop me from defecting, not drowning. Kostia righted the canoe, pushing back his soaked sleeves and tossing the paddles in before they could float away. "We'll tip that over again if we try to climb back in," I said, grabbing for my felt hat before it could sink. "Good thing the Hitlerites can't see us like this. They'd be dead of laughter, not lead shot."

Kostia tossed my soaked hat into the canoe too, angling the boat so it blocked out Yuri on the bank. My partner reached for my hand under the water and pulled it against his chest, then he bent his head and kissed me. He tasted like iron and rain, his other hand tangling briefly in my hair, and I felt the sniper-calluses of his trigger hand against my scarred neck before he pulled away.

"You already know," he said. "What I feel for you."

I did know. I'd known a long time.

"No reason to say it in Sevastopol." He untangled his hand from my hair, reaching for the canoe before it could drift away from us. "You were my sergeant. You were my partner. And you loved my friend." A pause. "It feels too soon, saying this to you now. Lyonya has only been dead six months."

Lyonya. I realized my hand had bunched into Kostia's wet shirt, and I pulled it away.

"I wish I could wait a year, wait until the grief is less. But we don't have a year. We barely have tomorrow." Kostia hesitated. The fire in him had always been leashed, banked; now it was blazing high in his gaze, almost too bright to look at. "I'm out of time, Mila. When we return to Moscow—in a week, two weeks, whenever it is—you'll be headed back to the front, and I won't. We'll be pulled our separate ways. So I have to say this now."

"But you're coming back to the front, too." I don't know how I fastened on that first when everything he said had cracked me and tumbled me like an earthquake, but the thought of rejoining the fight without him sent a pang of utter terror through me, pushing past everything else. "You're my *partner.* I'll ask to get you in my platoon, they'll transfer you—"

"Not with this knee. I couldn't make a two-kilometer march, much less an all-day advance. I'm done as a soldier. It'll be sniper instructor duty for me, and you'll be heading back to the fight." He pushed a strand of wet hair off my forehead. "It's too soon. I know that. But this is what we have. Before there's danger and bullets flying again, and we run out of life."

Lyonya, I thought. Kostia was thinking it, too.

"You still love him. You still miss him. So do I. Six months or six years or six decades, we'll still miss him." Kostia's eyes were black and still. "I wasn't even jealous, him winning you. You picked the best man I knew. I wasn't going to break with my friend over that, or my partner."

There was pain there in his voice, but well-buried. He'd paved it over at the time, matter-of-factly, because in his eyes it didn't matter that he'd lost. I remembered Alexei's narrow-eyed glance assessing every man who visited me in the hospital battalion: a dog keeping an eye on a discarded bone, not wanting anyone else to have it . . . while Kostia had just quietly gone on being my other half, being Lyonya's friend, keeping it complete: the three of us.

And now it was just the two of us, the ones who'd loved Lyonya best.

"That's all." Kostia blew out a long breath. "I'm just—I'm not waving you off to war without telling you I love you. "

I was shivering with cold and something else. My mouth burned. I reached out, tangling my hand in his shirt again, but unable—for the first time in our partnership—to look my shadow in the eye. "I feel it, too," I heard myself say, so quietly. "Maybe I've felt it for a long time. But I'm still . . . mourning my dead."

All my dead, not just Lyonya. Still fighting my way free.

Kostia's fingers folded over mine. "So am I."

He released my hand, took the canoe by its prow, and began towing it back toward shore.

"LYUDMILA!" MRS. ROOSEVELT'S voice suddenly sounded. I looked up as I crossed the lawn toward the big house and realized she was leaning out of a first-floor window. "What on earth happened?"

"Swimming," I said through chattering teeth, arms crossed across my soaked dress. "Without a bathing costume." Yuri, tramping along behind, hadn't offered me his coat. Wasn't part of his directive.

"It's far too cold for bathing," the First Lady scolded, sounding like my mother. "Come here at once."

I was too numb to resist. I followed the wave of Mrs. Roosevelt's hand toward the vestibule on the side, where she met me and began clucking. "You may stay outside," she told Yuri politely but unmistakably, and even he didn't say a word about his directive to the First Lady as she wafted me into her private quarters. I gave a disjointed explanation about the canoe, hesitating to walk on her exquisite carpets in my soaked shoes, but she shooed me into the attached bathroom and put a big soft towel into my arms. (American towels! I never ceased to marvel at their fluffiness. I was still undecided about hot dogs, but American towels, now . . .) "Undress here, I'll be right back."

"*Izvinite,* I can go to my room," I began, but there was no stopping her. By the time I came out of the bathroom, wrapped up in towels, leaving a pile of wet clothes on the edge of the First Lady's bathtub, she was back with a pair of pajamas and a sewing box. She smiled at my scarlet face, called a maid for my wet clothes, then turned with a matter-of-fact expression as if she was entirely accustomed to have half-naked Soviet snipers dripping on her Persian rugs. "Change into my pajamas, dear."

"W-we are not the same height," I said, teeth still chattering.

"No matter, I'll take a hem in the sleeves and legs."

"B-by y-yourself?"

"*Da,* my Russian friend. Or do you imagine that Roosevelt women are ladies of leisure who never lift a finger?" That was exactly what I'd thought, and she smiled again at my expression. "I assure you, American women know how to work! Now, into the bottoms first . . ."

I was still too bemused to argue as she tactfully turned her back to rummage through her sewing box, and I swam into the pajama bottoms. Heavy rose-pink satin, clearly never worn, with violets embroidered down the seams—I'd never seen anything so lovely in my life, just for *sleeping* in. Normally I slept in one of Lyonya's old shirts, or if it was cold, my winter uniform's woolen under-layers. I left the towel around my torso as the First Lady whipped out a tape measure and took the length of my arms. "You do not need to do this, ma'am," I assayed feebly, but she paid no attention at all, so I submitted to the measuring.

"Goodness," she said behind me, and I knew she was looking at the scar on my back. "What's that, Lyudmila?"

I felt Kostia murmuring against my spine, *Wear it with pride*—felt it so keenly, a shiver went over the entire surface of my skin. "The result of a scrap of metal," I said finally, unable to find the English words for *scar* or *splinter*. "Last December, Sevastopol."

"A mechanical accident?" Mrs. Roosevelt came back around to the front, folding her measuring tape. "Or did it come from fighting the Germans?"

"From battle."

"My poor girl," she said simply. "What dreadful things you've had to endure."

She hugged me. *Hugged* me—I hadn't been hugged since my mother embraced me on the train platform in Moscow. And it shattered me. I felt my shoulders shake, felt the First Lady's arms tighten around my back as I buried my face in her bony shoulder. I had so many broken pieces stabbing me inside, I didn't know what to do but dissolve into that hug and try not to weep. "I lost—so many," I managed to say around deep gulping breaths. Lyonya, Vartanov, Lena, my platoon . . . and now, when I went back to the front, I was going to lose Kostia. Not tomorrow, not the next day, but soon. We'd never fight together again.

The First Lady said nothing. She just held me until I stopped shaking, and then she passed me a handkerchief, just like Mama would have done. I laughed shakily. "You and my mother—you would like each other."

"I'm sure I would. She raised a fine daughter, after all." Mrs. Roosevelt stepped back, going to her sewing box to give me time to scrub at my eyes. "Is your mother pleased at your war record, Lyudmila?"

"She is proud," I said, perching on the edge of the bed as the First Lady seated herself on the other side and threaded a needle. "But she grieves for the history student she waved off to university." I hesitated, wondering if it was defeatist counterpropaganda to say what I wanted to say. "I grieve, too," I admitted finally.

"Do you?" Mrs. Roosevelt took up her scissors, measuring where to cut the too-long sleeves.

"People think I hate the Hitlerites," I said tiredly. "I do hate them. I have to. But I didn't ask to hate them. I grew up dreaming to be a historian, not of killing 309 fascists."

"I know it hurts you when you read articles that call you a killer. Don't look surprised; I saw your face when you read the accounts of your first press conference." *Snip* went her scissors; the ends of the cuffs fell away. "I advise you not to go into politics, where one has to get used to reading such things about oneself."

"You are used to it?" I couldn't help asking.

"If I worried about mudslinging, I would have been dead long ago." The First Lady folded the cut edges of satin over for a new hem. "But I was a shy girl, Lyudmila, and the sight of my name in newspapers once made me cringe. Eventually I grew into my role, but in those early days as a politician's wife . . . well, public criticism had a way of stinging. It takes time to grow a thick skin for insults."

"But your poll numbers are higher than the President's." I remembered hearing that in a Moscow briefing. She was rated "good" by 67 percent of Americans polled, as opposed to her husband's 58 percent.

"I've still been called impudent, presumptuous, meddling. A traitor to my class, a bucktoothed horror, a Negro lover, a Jew lover." She shrugged. "I have heard it all."

"Have they called you *a cold-blooded killer*?" I couldn't repeat the worse ones to her: *Red bitch, communist slut* . . .

" 'A cold-blooded killer with no mercy for the poor enemy soldiers who are merely following the orders of their senior command'?" Eleanor quoted. "I thought that one bothered you the most."

"What do these journalists think I should do, nicely ask all those enemy soldiers to leave? Do they think that would *work*?"

"I believe they didn't know what to think, meeting you. But they're beginning to change their tune, thanks to all your recent public appearances."

"What, because they are starting to get to know me? To like me?" My words came out mocking, but she nodded.

"Is that so impossible? I wasn't at all sure I would like you when I first met you, but I have gotten to know you . . . and now I do like you. The American people are beginning to do the same. Which is why, if you wish to help sway public opinion about sending American soldiers to Europe to aid the USSR, you should consider extending your speaking tour even further."

"I do as my delegation and the Party dictate," I said, heart sinking. Yuri wasn't the only one who had to follow a directive.

"I know you don't want to. I know you dislike the spotlight." The First Lady bit off a thread. "I disliked it, too. I remember my knees shaking the first time I gave a speech."

I could not imagine it, not at all. "How did you do it? Become good at it?"

"I reminded myself that you must do the thing you think you cannot do," she said simply. "Always. And generally you find out you can do it, after all."

"But what if you can't?" I burst out. "What if you fail?"

"You try again—"

"No." I shook my head, reflexive. "It does not work that way. You cannot count on the world giving you second chances when you fail."

She looked thoughtful. "Is that a rule you've made for yourself?"

"The most important rule there is." I quoted the words that breathed in my bones. "*Don't miss.*"

"Oh, my dear. That is no rule to live by."

"It is for a sniper!"

"You think such a rule is exclusive to snipers? *Most* women are haunted by the fear of missing. Of failing."

I blinked, taken aback. "It kept me alive."

"And clearly made you into a brave soldier, but a frightened woman." The First Lady laid down her needle, looking at me with those piercing eyes. "Everyone fails, Lyudmila. I've failed. My husband has failed—you think all his New Deal proposals were dazzling successes? He has proposed initiatives that have fallen flat; he has espoused positions for which he has rightly been condemned; he has hosts of enemies who would happily see him dead." A shadow crossed her face at that. "He has failed at more than most men ever try . . . but better that than not to try at all."

"He is a man," I said harshly, "and an American. He makes mistakes, and the world makes him the only three-term president in your history. The world is not so kind to a woman's mistakes."

"Agreed," she said, surprising me again. "Which is why we women are especially prone to believe we must never stumble. But constant perfection is something at which we will *always* fail, all of us. And despite what you may think, the world won't smite you for the occasional misfire. I daresay you didn't down every enemy you ever had in your sights on the front—yet you're still here, alive, wearing my pajamas. You lost the man you loved—yet I daresay you don't regret loving him, and you may very well have another chance for love someday, because you are very lovable." She picked up her needle and began stitching again. "If at first one doesn't succeed . . . well, I'll spare you the somewhat obnoxious little rhyme I learned in childhood, but *trying again* is something we Yanks believe in very strongly."

"In Russia we believe that if we fail, we die," I stated. "And I have seen nothing in this war to make me disbelieve that."

"But life isn't always going to be war, Lyudmila," she said gently. "And you'll do yourself a grave disservice if you live your every moment—not just your wartime moments, but your gentler ones—by a standard as harsh as *never miss*."

I stared at her, clutching the towel around me, shaken to my core.

"Now let's get these cuffs done." Clearly seeing my distress, the First Lady adopted a brisker tone, holding the pajama top up to my face. "This pink is a lovely color for you . . ."

An hour, a pot of tea, and a plate of biscuits later, there came a knock at the door. But we didn't hear it, because we were talking up a storm. "But to my understanding, women do not regularly serve in the Soviet military," Eleanor was saying. "Even in your own country, it is not entirely common. So how is it that you were able to make the choice to enlist so easily?"

"Because in my home, women are respected not just as females but as individuals." To my relief, the First Lady and I had moved into less sensitive topics of discussion: first color palettes and fashion disparities, then the differences between American and Soviet cinema, and now the complexities of serving in the military as a female. "We do not feel limitations because of our sex. That is why women like me took their places beside men so naturally in the army."

"You need to work this into your next speech. I would emphasize that word *individual*—we Americans are enamored with the idea of the individual, and assume you Soviets are all about the collective—"

The door opened, and I looked up at the creak of hinges. "What's this?" said President Roosevelt, looking amused.

I jumped to my feet, shedding biscuit crumbs. I was now wearing the towel around my lower half, upper body draped in the frivolous pink flower-embroidered top as Eleanor set the final stitches on the bottoms. I watched the American president look around his wife's room—pink satin scraps scattered over the bed, reels of thread everywhere, teacups drained to the dregs, a half-dressed Soviet sniper. "Hello, dear," Eleanor said tranquilly, as if she hemmed pajamas for foreign-born killers every day before dinner.

"This is one of those scenes," the President mused, rubbing his jaw with that sinewy hand, "that just defies description."

I began to apologize, side-slipping into Russian, but he burst out laughing. So did Eleanor. And then so did I.

When I went back to my own quarters in my pink satin splendor, I found my felt cap, which Kostia had scooped from the water into the canoe, carefully dried now and sitting on a chair beside the door. I folded it tight in my hands, heart thumping—but I could feel the First Lady's arms around me in a surprisingly strong hug, and my battered heart was cautiously exploring the words that still echoed through my bones in her forthright voice: *The world won't smite you for the occasional misfire.*

Notes by the First Lady

Something dear Lyudmila said today bothered me deeply. It was when she was departing for her own room, looking no more than sixteen in her pink pajamas and damp hair, and Franklin asked how she was liking Hyde Park. "I sleep well," she replied, straightforward as one of her bullets. "No one can harm me here."

She doesn't know Franklin, so she didn't see the shadow on his face as he answered jovially, "Or me."

When she is gone, I look at my husband and ask, "Who do you think would try to harm you?"

He shrugs the question aside with a tilted grin. "We'll be late for lunch."

"Another Zangara?" I make myself ask. "Another MacGuire?"

Zangara was the assassin who fired five shots at Franklin in Miami in 1933, seventeen days before his inauguration. MacGuire was the American Legion official at the head of a plot to depose my husband in 1934 and install a military dictator. Zangara killed the mayor of Chicago instead of my husband; MacGuire's coup folded and was disappeared into a flurry of House committee hearings. Those men failed.

But there have always been rumors that bigger names—industry names, Wall Street names, names any American would know—were behind both.

"Franklin—" I begin, pulse beginning to pound, but he is already silently taking himself away.

CHAPTER 28

The headline: THE SOVIET DELEGATION RESUMES THEIR GOODWILL TOUR THROUGHOUT THE CITIES OF AMERICA. MR. KRASAVCHENKO AND LIEUTENANT PCHELINTSEV WILL CONTAIN THEIR TRAVELS TO THE EAST COAST, BUT FAMED GIRL SNIPER LYUDMILA PAVLICHENKO HEADS TO DETROIT, CHICAGO, MINNEAPOLIS, SAN FRANCISCO, FRESNO, AND LOS ANGELES. SHE WILL BE ACCOMPANIED ON THE FIRST LEG OF HER JOURNEY BY NONE OTHER THAN THE FIRST LADY . . .

The truth: Thank goodness the presidential limousine had a driver, because if Eleanor Roosevelt proposed to get behind the wheel herself, I'd *walk* to the Midwest.

"I DO NOT understand," I complained as the limousine eased down the highway. "Why have me visit the headquarters of the Ford Motor Company if the workers would not even talk to me?"

"Of course they wouldn't talk to you." The First Lady chuckled. "Ford pays well, and they have a great deal to lose. They worry it will seem suspect if they show too much interest in a visitor from communist Russia, much less her notions about workers' rights!" Mrs. Roosevelt was already taking rapid notes from our tour through the aircraft works and our meeting with Mr. Ford. I came to America assuming the President's wife would be an idle society millionairess, but from what I could see the woman never stopped working. "Your speech went over well, I thought."

I was less certain, but I was already starting off this tour on a sour note: another of those ominous threats had found its way under my hotel-room door this morning. IT'S NOT ENOUGH TO LEAVE WASHINGTON, YOU MURDERING CUNT. GO HOME NOW OR YOU'LL GO HOME IN A BOX.

Was my enemy stalking me across the country now? Or was it someone inside the delegation? Darkly, I thought of Alexei. I wouldn't put it past him to try to terrify his own wife, just so she'd feel like fleeing into sheltering arms. If he thought *that* would work—!

"Five hours to Chicago," Eleanor said, interrupting my brooding, and I looked through the bulletproof glass at the flaming autumn trees by the roadside. Five hours . . . I wished I'd brought a book, like Kostia. He had a leather-bound copy of some poems by a Mr. Walt Whitman, on loan from the First Lady's library. "How is it?" I asked, slipping back into Russian.

"Perplexing." He had my English dictionary on his other knee and kept flipping back and forth between the two. The watery autumn sun slanted through the bulletproof window over his black hair. "What's *pokeweed*?"

"I don't know. I feel like I should get a sample of it for Slavka." I took a deep breath—no one in the car would understand us; neither the First Lady nor her secretary spoke enough Russian; the driver and guard were separated by a partition; the ever-present Yuri was riding in the security car behind us with Alexei (who had somehow talked himself onto my half of the tour)—but I was still shy to voice the question. "How was your visit to New York?" My partner had been at the Soviet embassy in Washington when we returned from the Roosevelt estate, but I hadn't dared ask a thing about his family within embassy walls. "Did you . . ."

His smile stayed invisible as he turned a page. "Yes."

"Lyudmila, do look out the window," the First Lady called. "This flat land in Michigan, does it remind you of your native steppes?" Kilometer after kilometer, the limousine rolled along as Eleanor pointed out the cities she knew from her coast-to-coast traveling.

She was proud of her country, I could hear it in her voice—certainly she thought it superior to anything found in Russia, which made me grin privately. The towns and cities ticked by, *Ann Arbor, Albion, Kalamazoo* . . . then the vast shores of Lake Michigan like a sea, and my eyes blurred as I remembered the Black Sea bordering Odessa.

"You're homesick," Mrs. Roosevelt said, reading my face with a glance. "You'll be home soon enough, my dear—and if we're lucky enough to see this war end soon, you'll be able to return to your studies rather than your platoon."

"I would be able to finish my dissertation." I sighed. "Would you like to see? A study of Bogdan Khmelnitsky, the Ukraine's accession to Russia in 1654—"

I could have sworn Kostia gave a cough of warning on my other side, but the First Lady listened with every appearance of fascination, only interrupting me to point out the high sand dunes that had begun to appear on the landscape the farther south we drove.

"It is a beautiful country," I admitted, leaning past her to look out. "You people here live in such peaceful conditions. I keep looking around and wondering where the bomb damage is . . . such a land of luxury."

"But?" she said, hearing the note in my voice.

"A land of destitution, too." I looked her in the eye. "I see enough of the poorer parts of your cities to know that American Negroes live very badly."

"It's true we have a long way to go," she acknowledged calmly. "America fights prejudice abroad but tolerates it at home. Segregation warps and twists the lives of our Negro population; that is beyond doubt. Things must change."

"How?"

"Work," she said, flourishing her pen. "It isn't enough to believe in equality and peace and human rights—one must work at it."

I grinned. "For an American millionairess you have a work ethic a Russian would approve of."

"And you have an ability to laugh that any American would approve of," the First Lady replied. "*Punch* cartoons and Hollywood would have us all believing that Soviets have no sense of humor."

"Life can be hard for us. We have to laugh at it." I remembered a joke my darling Lena had told me. "What did one German soldier say to the other when they reached the Russian front?"

"What?"

" 'Look at that cute Russian girl eyeing me over there.' His friend says, 'Why not go say hello?' His friend replies, 'Because she's eyeing me with her scope.' "

Eleanor laughed. More kilometers slipped by; conversation giving way to silence and then to drowsiness. At some point I dozed off, giving a great start when the limousine stopped. My eyelids were gummy, and I felt a weight against my shoulder—Kostia's dark head.

"You dropped off at the same time," Mrs. Roosevelt said, eyes crinkling down at me, and I realized I had fallen asleep with my head on *her* shoulder. "Wake up now, my darling," she continued as I sat upright, pink with embarrassment, thinking *Please let me not have drooled on the First Lady!* "We are in Chicago. A famous American poet once called it 'the city of the big shoulders,' you know."

"We have bad poetry in the Soviet Union, too," I consoled, and she burst out laughing.

DON'T THEY LOOK *fresh and rested,* the marksman thought sourly, watching Lyudmila Pavlichenko and the First Lady take the bunting-draped stage, waving to the cheering crowds below. He'd spent five hours following the presidential entourage in a shoebox-sized Packard, cramped and irritable—*he* hadn't arrived in Chicago bright-eyed and rested like the girl sniper.

A dazzle of flashbulbs went off, and the marksman noticed she no longer flinched as though grenades were exploding in her face. He'd thought she'd be more nervous, especially after he'd bribed a hotel maid to get another of his anonymous threats shoved under her door. In Washington, it had seemed to be working. She'd been visibly nervous at the opera, and at the conference reception she glanced repeatedly over her shoulder as though looking for her stalker. She'd looked off-balance, which was precisely his aim. But now she appeared poised and professional as she gave a short speech through her interpreter—and people were responding, damn it. The marksman had been convinced she'd never be the success the Soviets hoped for on this goodwill tour—asking an American audience to warm to a woman who had supposedly killed 309 men was absurd. But the audience here in Chicago was ecstatic.

"All right," he mused aloud under the hubbub of the crowd, jingling the little rocks of uncut diamonds in his pocket. "So she's a success." That just proved she was a seasoned propagandist, not a sniper. Only a professional could have pulled this off . . . and she'd charmed the First Lady, to boot. They kept putting their heads together in conversational lulls onstage, sharing some private joke. *Let's see how you're smiling by the time we hit Los Angeles,* thought the marksman. It was the new plan: slip into the cortege of hangers-on shadowing the presidential entourage as it snaked west and insert himself so that he became part of the scenery, unremarkable and unremarked upon. He'd already contacted Pocket Square, made sure his name passed the First Lady's security without a hiccup. No one would give him a second glance, and he'd have all the time in the world to stay in the background until they came to the City of Angels . . . where President Roosevelt, who had been making a private tour of the nation's defense plants, was scheduled to arrive for a joint appearance with his wife and Lyudmila Pavlichenko.

That was when the shot would now be fired.

And wouldn't the First Lady be surprised to see her new friend plummet from the heights, no longer a national heroine but a Soviet John Wilkes Booth. MRS. ROOSEVELT BEFRIENDS HER HUSBAND'S KILLER—that would be a headline worth reading.

The marksman realized, watching the two women leave the stage, that he was looking forward to that with a visceral, spiteful satisfaction. He hadn't felt much of anything about Lyudmila Pavlichenko when he first watched her disembark at the doors of the White House a few weeks ago, only a mild curiosity as he set about framing her for the assassination of the century.

Now, having been dragged all over the country tailing the Red bitch and already planning his next set of anonymously scrawled Cyrillic threats, he wanted to see her fall.

"MRS. PAVLICHENKO, SO delightful to gaze on your face again!"

At first I didn't recognize the man—linen suit, slightly pop eyes—but then I felt the damp, fervent fingers wringing mine, and remembered the millionaire I'd met in Baltimore. "Mr. Jonson, here you are . . . all the way from Maryland."

"I would have greeted you in Detroit," he said, starry-eyed. "But Mr. Ford's headquarters have very strict security."

"Don't they here?" I couldn't help asking. The First Lady and I had been invited to visit the Chicago Sharpshooters' Association; you'd think a firearms club would have more armed guards at the door. "How did you—"

"Oh, I bought a ticket. And I would buy a dozen for a chance to meet with you again. Would you like a handkerchief, it's very hot—"

"*Nyet.* Mr. Jonson—"

"William!"

"William, I have been asked to visit with the association chairman." I extricated my hands from his clammy ones and made my way toward the weapon racks, shaking off journalists piping *Mrs. Pavlichenko . . . Mrs. Pavlichenko . . .* like a chorus of baby birds. So many of them! I kept trying to put faces to names, but they were simply too numerous to keep straight.

"Smile for the camera, *kroshka*," Alexei murmured, managing to get his arm around my shoulder and turn me neatly toward the nearest flashbulb, thumb caressing the back of my neck. I shrugged him away with a warning glance and finally managed to find the head of the Sharpshooters' Association, waiting not too patiently to have his picture taken with me.

"What do you think of our American weapons, Miz Pavlichenko?" he harrumphed, and I wasn't surprised to see skeptical glances between the clubmen. Did they think I couldn't hear the whispers? *That girl they're calling a sniper doesn't know one end of a rifle from another . . .*

"Is this a M1 Garand?" I asked the chairman through Kostia, strolling along the club's gun racks. "Very similar to the Sveta we use on the eastern front—the diverting propellant gas through the port in the bore to unlock the breech." I took the self-loading rifle off the rack, gave it a quick inspection, lifted it to my shoulder to sight along its length. "Weaver sights, very nice."

Surprised looks, which I pretended not to see. "What do you think of this one, Miz Pavlichenko? Our M1903 Springfield."

"Yes, much more like the Three Line I used. I prefer a sliding bolt in field conditions. The nonautomatic safety catch here is very similar to the German army Mauser Zf. Kar. 98k, as well—"

I chatted about Soviet rifles and how they compared to various Allied models, urging the chairman to break the 1903 down with me so I could examine the trigger mechanisms and exclaim over the pull weight, the crispness, the feel of the hammerfall. The older men were grinning by the end. Even the watching corps of journalists looked grudgingly impressed, and William Jonson was starry-eyed. "Oh,

Mrs. Pavlichenko, how I wish you would favor us with a demonstration."

I hesitated. I'd always refused such invitations before today. I wasn't a trick pony performing on command; I was a soldier. A journalist in Detroit had compared me to some American circus shooter he called Annie Oakley, asking if I could shoot over my shoulder while looking at a mirror, and I told him that skills like mine weren't meant for big-top tents or party games. But these shooting club fellows looked so keen—the older men had the look of veterans, men who remembered what blood smelled like when mixed into mud, and the younger ones were so cherry-cheeked and innocent . . . yet they were the ones who'd go off to fight, if the First Lady's plan to sell the idea of a second front through me succeeded. Mrs. Roosevelt was speaking with an Army colonel on the other side of the room, but I could have sworn she gave me a tiny nod from the corner of her eye.

"*Nu ladno*," I said with a grin, and the men cheered.

My hands were trembling just a little by the time we'd hashed out the demonstration's details: 100 meters distance, prone unsupported, ten shots, ten minutes to shoot, iron sights. *You haven't fired a rifle for a month and a half*, the voice inside my head scolded. *A professional needs to shoot at least twice a week to keep in practice!* Was I supposed to defend my own reputation and the honor of the Red Army with rusty skills and an unfamiliar weapon?

"She'll need someone to shoot against," Kostia volunteered in English as we came to the range, unexpectedly. I blinked as a clamor of Americans jostled forward. "No, someone she'll have trouble beating. Another Russian." He grinned, provoking just the right chorus of laughs and catcalls. "If you'll lend me a 1903, I'll join Lieutenant Pavlichenko. Comrade Yuripov, would you care to join us?"

"That is not part of my directive," said Yuri against the wall.

"Our delegation doctor, then." Kostia gave a bland smile. "He fancies himself a keen shot."

My head jerked up as Alexei sauntered forward in his western pinstripes from the cluster of delegation hangers-on, taking a rifle from the nearest hand. "Delighted," he said in the English he was clearly making an effort to pick up on this tour.

"And I'll join you," William Jonson said eagerly, coming forward so fast he nearly tripped over his own shoelaces. "I fancy I can match any embassy doctor, ha-ha! Done a little pigeon-shooting in my boyhood, 'deed I did . . ."

"What are you doing?" I hissed to Kostia in Russian, but he just carried on loading his own rifle with a quick flash of his hands. We all took position, settling ourselves on the ground belly-down, and took five or six calibration shots to familiarize ourselves with our weapons, then waited for new paper targets: me lying between my husband and my partner; Mr. Jonson, who kept shifting his rifle's barrel with a carelessness that made me twitch; and a handful of the older Americans who proclaimed they had fought in the Great War. The call to begin went out, Lady Midnight began the countdown, and the world fell away.

Ten shots. My first went a few centimeters wide of the bull's-eye; from how the round landed, I could tell I'd jerked the trigger rather than squeezing it. I steadied myself, not letting the miss sting me. This wasn't the battlefield; death wouldn't claim me because I was a few centimers short of perfect. By the second shot, the unfamiliar rifle whispered, *There.* When I saw the bullet hit that time, I was grinning. Kostia was already sighting his third shot alongside me, an American with gray brush-cut hair just behind us. Kostia's 1903 and mine thundered in unison, and I knew that was a pair of bull's-eyes. Our hands flew in tandem, our rifles barked in tandem, and it was just like old times. No, better—cleaner, the smell of gunpowder unmarred by the smell of blood.

I didn't need ten minutes to make my ten shots. I didn't even need five.

Everyone rose as the last shots from the stragglers tailed in and crowded around the paper targets. Whoops went up as the hits were tallied. "Lady Death takes it!" I grinned, dusting off the front of my dress and wondering what my scarred firearms instructor would say if he could see his pupil now. Wondering if he was still training snipers in Kiev, if he still lived . . .

"Goddamn, I ain't lost a contest that bad since aught nine." The American with the gray brush-cut hair hair offered me a hand like oak. He'd come third, right after Kostia, and I could hardly understand his odd drawl. "I reckon your Siberian boy here could shoot the eye out of a muskrat at three miles if the wind was right, Miz Pavlichenko—and you could probably do it at five. I'd ask you to marry me, if I didn't have a missus at home already who wouldn't care for no Russki sniper gal bunking in her spare room. Care to raise a glass with me instead?"

"And me," gushed William Jonson, who hadn't even managed to hit the target most of the time. He lit up a Lucky Strike, waving it enthusiastically. "A wonderful demonstration, Mrs. Pavlichenko!"

Bottles of brandy and whiskey began appearing; up in the gallery with Colonel Douglas, the First Lady looked faintly disapproving. I waved up to her, unrepentant. This was a soldiers' gathering, a shooters' gathering, and for the first time since coming to America I felt honestly at home. One of the delegation flunkies bleated a reminder at me to let Kostia interpret rather than use my English, but I ignored him. I didn't want a filter between me and these men; I was done with filters. Out of the corner of my eye, I saw Alexei toss his 1903 aside with a curt gesture, and grinned. He'd come in fifth out of ten.

"Good try," I called to him in Russian. He glared and I fluttered my fingers, murmuring to Kostia, "Why *did* you invite him to join?"

"Because you were nervous," my partner returned. "But once he stepped to the line there was no way this side of the Arctic Circle you'd let him win."

I laughed, tossing down a shot of American whiskey that tasted like a wood fire. "I gutted him, didn't I?"

"Like a fish."

"Will you be able to give your usual speech tonight?" the First Lady asked as we settled back into the limousine, giving a disapproving shake of her head.

"It was not very much whiskey. Americans, they don't know how to drink. Forty milliliters is not enough for a proper toast." Just enough to warm my cheeks, which were still smiling from a half hour with the American shooters. The chatter over the glasses had all been war stories—they asked for mine from this year; I asked for theirs from the Great War—and then they had presented me with the mahogany box now sitting in my lap. "Have you ever seen anything so pretty?" I burst out, lifting the lid on my gift again: a pair of Colt M1911A1 pistols, brand new and gleaming, and two magazines with cartridges.

"In New York you were given a full-length lynx coat." The First Lady looked amused as I gleefully took one of the Colts out and began examining it right there in the passenger seat. "In Detroit, you were given six dozen roses. Yet you turn starry-eyed over a pair of pistols?"

"This is much better than the last time I got a pistol." That had been in Sevastopol, when General Petrov told me to keep the last bullet for myself rather than be taken alive and suffer what the Germans did to women snipers. I blinked that memory away, examining the various mechanism parts of my new Colt. "Ah, .45 caliber! Made by Browning, you know that? Adopted by your army in 1911, then by ours in the last war . . ."

Mrs. Roosevelt laughed. "Play with your new toy later, my dear. We're almost at Grant Park."

Maybe it was the whiskey, maybe it was having the reassuring song of a rifle back in my ears, or maybe it was the fact I'd finally, *finally* managed to wipe the serene look off Alexei's face—but something went through me when I found myself in the park on yet another flag-draped stage, looking out at yet another crowd of middle-aged men.

"The floor is yours, Mrs. Pavlichenko—"

"Lieutenant Pavlichenko, *spasibo.*" I stepped forward and began my speech, painting the war raging in my far-off home as Kostia translated. One of the men in the front row stood jingling his hands in his pockets, watching me with a cold gaze; a journalist stood fiddling with his camera and looking bored; a cluster of city officials were eyeing my uniform as though it were a costume. *None of you believe I've really fought in a war,* I thought. The men I'd met at the range today, they believed me. Many of them had been veterans; they knew a real soldier when they saw one pull a trigger. But these audiences I faced in city after city, these people I faced armed with nothing but my voice—what did they know?

Let them know now, I thought, and the thought for once was not bitter or angry. It filled me with a fierce pride.

"Gentlemen," I called sharp and loud, abandoning my planned speech. I waited until I had all the eyes that might have wandered, and then I planted my boots wide on the platform with a sound like a coffin knock, clasping my hands behind me in parade rest. "Gentlemen, I am twenty-six years old. At the front, I have already eliminated 309 fascist soldiers and officers. Don't you think, gentlemen, that you have been hiding for too long behind my back?"

I let the challenge hang in the air.

For an instant, the crowd was silent. Then a roar of applause drifted out across Grant Park, men surging to their feet, ladies waving their hats, journalists raising their cameras. I looked at Kostia, and meeting his eyes through the flashbulbs, I could have sworn I saw Lyonya at his shoulder.

He was smiling.

THE BITCH CAN *shoot.*

The marksman hadn't been able to think anything else since watching Lyudmila Pavlichenko sink ten superb shots at 100 meters with an unfamiliar weapon in three minutes. He'd gone through the motions of admiration with the rest of the crowd at the range, but the words had pounded through him over and over: *The bitch can shoot.*

He couldn't even tell himself he was watching a target shooter, a gun-club competitor. There was range expertise and there was *real* expertise, the cold kind practiced until it was part of the blood. He'd seen a flash of it when she first handled her rifle—and then she'd taken position on the firing line, and he'd seen Lady Death unhood her eyes. The sparkling brunette with her warm gaze had disappeared; the sniper with 309 enemies on her tally flared to life. By the time she sank that last bull's-eye, he believed she'd bagged every one of those kills on the eastern front.

God damn, the marksman thought numbly, watching her stand on this Grant Park stage as half of Chicago howled her name, *she's the real deal.* A hundred small impressions were slotting into place now: the way she held her cigarettes in a reversed, cupped hand, to keep the ember from showing; the way her eyes flicked as she entered new rooms, establishing exits and movement lines. Why hadn't he realized?

You didn't want to, the answer came. *You didn't think it was possible.*

Well, it was. Lady Death, here in the flesh. A pint-sized Russian woman who had just thrown back her head on an American stage and told every red-blooded man in that audience to stop hiding behind her back.

I would happily shoot you face-to-face, the marksman thought, watching her fierce eyes prowl over the wildly applauding crowd like those of a predatory lynx. *But tomorrow I have a president to kill in Los Angeles, and a slip of a Soviet girl to pin it on.*

CHAPTER 29

The headline: IN THE WAKE OF HER NOW-FAMOUS CHALLENGE TO THE CITIZENS OF AMERICA, LYUDMILA PAVLICHENKO TRAVELS TO THE CITY OF ANGELS. HOLLYWOOD ROYALTY THE LIKES OF DOUGLAS FAIRBANKS JR., MARY PICKFORD, AND CHARLIE CHAPLIN ARE LINING UP TO HOST THE GIRL SNIPER . . .

The truth: "You were wonderful in *The Mark of Zorro,* Mr. Fairbanks" was not my best conversational opening, considering the actor's drunken response was "That wash my father Douglash Fairbanksh Shenior."

"BRILLIANT AS ALWAYS, Mrs. Pavlichenko! Champagne?"

"*Nu ladno,* Mr. Jonson," I sighed. In a dinner jacket, no less, but he just looked even more pop-eyed and irritating. I hastily took the flute of champagne before he could seize my hand. "I did not think you would come to Los Angeles."

"I submitted a request to the First Lady herself! I had something very particular to ask you, and her people put me on the list today . . ."

I blinked, coming down from the now-familiar sensation of having shaken two hundred hands, posed for two hundred photographs, and answered two hundred inane questions. "Ask me what, Mr. Jonson?"

"Lyudmila, I've invited you to call me William," he chided.

"William, are you intending to hear every speech I give from Washington to Fresno? How much free time do you have?"

Too much, clearly. I bolted half my champagne, hoping it would kill the headache I'd been nursing since Chicago. I hadn't slept well after the Grant Park event—the First Lady assured me it had been a resounding success ("I wouldn't be surprised if Reuters reported that speech worldwide, my dear"), but ever since, I'd felt like I had spiders running down my spine. It wasn't even due to the appearance of yet another ugly note in my hotel room (I'M GOING TO RIP YOUR SPINE OUT AND CHOKE YOU WITH IT, YOU STALIN-LOVING BITCH)—I realized I was becoming almost inured to the hateful things. Given that whoever sent them was following me on the road, it seemed fairly obvious it was someone in the delegation, and even more obvious that that person was Alexei, and though I'd registered this suspicion with delegation security in no uncertain terms, I refused to be frightened by the notes anymore, *or* give my husband the satisfaction of confronting him. No, it wasn't the anonymous notes. Something else was bothering me, at a level so low I could hardly register it.

Something I'd seen, something I'd heard? On the front line I could keep watch so closely that not a single leaf's fall in the nightscape before me would pass unnoticed, but this tour had been such an avalanche of sights and sounds, something easily could have got lost in the hubbub. And I felt like something had, but couldn't put my finger on what.

"You know I am a widower, of course," Mr. Jonson was still yattering.

"I do? That is, yes, *da*—"

"And I read in the newspaper that you too were married. You lost your husband at Sevastopol—"

My second, unfortunately. Not my first. "Yes," I said, thinking how Lyonya would have roared with laughter at this entire exchange.

"Then, my darling Lyudmila, why should we not salve our mutual loneliness? If you would but make me the happiest of—"

"*Chto?*" My attention snapped back to the man who was now gripping my hand regardless of the empty champagne flute in it. "Mr. Jonson—"

"William!"

"Mr. Jonson, you are out of your mind."

"From the moment I saw you speaking in New York, my heart told me you were the only possible wife for me. Will you marry me?"

"YOU COULD ACCEPT his offer, you know."

I paused, buttered roll halfway to my lips. "Are you serious, Eleanor?" The First Lady had invited me to use her first name, but this was the first time I'd done so.

"Why not?" Across the small table from me, Eleanor unfolded her napkin. The delegation had taken to having meals privately after these receptions, since whenever the First Lady and I turned up to dine at a restaurant, the entire meal turned into hours of autograph signing. Kostia, Yuri, and the rest were already tucking in at the table across the private dining room. "Mr. Jonson is perhaps a trifle eccentric, but pleasant and well-bred," Eleanor went on. "He has not deceived you as to his background and prospects: he is a widower, he does in fact own a metallurgical company, his finances and reputation are sterling. Such men are investigated," she answered in response to my puzzled look, "when they begin following my entourage from state to state. Mr. Jonson's proposal of marriage may be sudden, but it seems sincere."

I snorted. "I have only met him a few times!"

"But to marry a gentleman of means who is madly in love with you—it's as much a guarantee of security and safety as the whims of fate give a woman." She smiled, reaching for her salad fork. "You would remain here in our country, and I would welcome the chance to continue our friendship."

"So would I, but—" I dropped my roll, rising to pick up a copy of the *Chicago Tribune* I had carried off the plane. "Look at this: *Mrs. Pavlichenko is in raptures over American food, eating five helpings at breakfast every morning.* Blatant lies. Where do they even get such things, and why are they obsessed with such nonsense?" I laid the paper down again, cheeks heating, fighting for the right words in English. "In your country I am the object of idle curiosity. A circus act, like a bearded woman. At home I am an officer of the Red Army. I have *fought*, and I am not a freak because I have fought. There are other women like me." I thought of what I'd told her about how Soviet women had full independence as human beings, not just as women. "This tour—this is my fight now. But soon I will go home, and I will go on fighting for the freedom and independence of *my* country. Not join yours, as much as I have grown to appreciate it."

I realized the other table had heard my outburst. Kostia's face was still, watching me. I flushed and sat back down, tearing my discarded roll into scraps. When I looked up at Mrs. Roosevelt, I saw a strange wistful smile on her face. I'd said there were no women like me in America—well, there were no women here like her, either. Was that why she had befriended me, why she had so liked the idea that I might stay in this country? Because she too felt like a circus act at times?

"We will forget Mr. Jonson," she said simply, pushing the breadbasket across the table. "I'll have his name struck off the list of any future events here, before I return to Washington."

"Thank you," I said, feeling rather embarrassed now for my impassioned words. "You aren't staying through the President's arrival?"

"Yes, about that . . ."

GOD DAMN THAT *Soviet bitch to hell and back,* thought the marksman. He'd just received word: President Roosevelt had quietly canceled his Southern California appearances. His tour of the nation's defense plants had been under a press blackout, but alert Washington operators already knew the President's special train had headed back toward the capital, and Pocket Square had duly telephoned with the update. Maybe it wasn't Lyudmila Pavlichenko's fault that the presidential cripple hadn't felt up to a press leg at the end of his private tour, but the marksman decided he'd blame her anyway. Lady Death was murdering his usually excellent luck on the job.

Idling through the hotel lobby, avoiding the NKVD minders and their stony eyes, he flipped through the remainder of the itinerary. Some Hollywood party; more speeches; then the trip to Fresno . . . *Fresno*, for Christ's sake. The marksman remembered a two-for-one job there a few years back, knocking off a couple of executives who'd been dipping in the company funds. Lousy town full of lousy farm hicks, and now he had to go *back*, after already trailing that woman from Detroit to Chicago to Los Angeles? That was a hell of a lot of travel considering how little he had to show for it: a lot of nights in anonymous hotels, a backache from so many hours behind the wheel of that tin-can Packard, and no damned shot at Roosevelt. He might as well have cooled his heels in Washington and waited for her to return, not run all over the country trying to manufacture a chance at a target that never showed up. And now fucking *Fresno.*

It's your own fault, he told himself, still fuming. Normally he *would* have stayed in Washington rather than follow the tour: kept well back, gathered any information he needed from third parties. Less contact, less trouble, less danger. But no, he'd decided on a more personal approach with this job. Had he really let *curiosity* get the better of him, after so many years of distant professionalism?

The Soviet delegation came rolling through the doors, back from the evening's reception. The marksman eyed Lyudmila Pavlichenko over the edge of his newspaper as she paused at the front desk. The night clerk passed over a sealed envelope; the girl sniper raised her eyebrows as she reached for a paper knife. The marksman sat forward a little, knowing exactly what words greeted her: WATCH YOUR BACK, SOVIET WHORE. He'd never seen her open one of his missives before. He hoped she'd blanch, tremble, look over her shoulder . . .

She rolled her eyes. It was unmistakable—she *rolled her eyes.* "Another one," she said in Russian to the blocky minder at her shoulder, balling up the letter and tossing it at him, and then she was sweeping off toward the hotel elevator. Heading upstairs to her luxurious whore's bed and a good night's sleep, no doubt. Having herself a good *chuckle.*

The marksman came to a sudden decision as she disappeared from sight. Tossing down his newspaper, he made for the hotel doors and the warm night outside. "Taxi," he told the bellboy curtly. No more orange groves, no more Beverly Hills chatter, and no goddamn Fresno: he was abandoning the Packard and his current cover identity and getting a flight back to Washington. Lady Death had to return to the capital at some point—he'd get her (and the President) then.

It occurred to him, settling into the taxi, that getting Lyudmila Pavlichenko now seemed just as important as getting FDR. Before, he'd left his plans open: frame her or kill her, whichever proved simpler.

He reckoned he'd just decided.

"ARE YOU TIRED of signing autographs yet?" Laurence Olivier gave me his trademark burning glance: every bit as handsome in person as he was on the screen. Lena would have had him up against the wall and his trousers down by now. His hand drifted to my lower back as he remarked, "I always thought autograph hunting was the most unattractive manifestation of sex-starved curiosity."

Slide your hand any lower, and you'll be drawing back a stump, I thought. A popping sound made me start, but it was only a champagne cork. Beside the wide French doors thrown open to the balmy California night, I could see the actress Mary Pickford throw her head back in laughter at something the silver-sequined Myrna Loy was whispering in her ear: this graceful Italianate house was packed to the rafters with film stars. Not that I knew who half of them were; I hadn't seen many Western films. My poor friend Sofya from Odessa, she'd have known every face after all her covert poring over Western film magazines—she'd have been thrilled to her toes for a chance to meet Mary Pickford at a Hollywood party. I'd just been bemused. And missing Sofya . . .

"Charlie Chaplin is throwing a bash for the delegation at Breakaway House—that's his home in Beverly Hills," the staff of the Soviet consulate had told me giddily that afternoon after a luncheon event, an embassy meeting, and a speech at a hotel overlooking the long blue rollers of the Pacific. "Now that the First Lady is away"—Eleanor had had to depart for Washington that morning, leaving me with a fond hug—"we'll have a chance for a little fun!" So far I'd had my hand kissed by Charlie Chaplin, my champagne poured by Tyrone Power, and my backside appreciated by Laurence Olivier.

I smacked his hand off as it drifted downward, but the Englishman didn't appear offended. He just laughed, tucking a strand of my hair behind my ear. "No need to be so tense and watchful, darling. You might get stabbed in the back at a Hollywood party, but no one's going to shoot you."

"Very clever, Mr. Olivier."

"Do call me Larry."

"*Nyet,*" I stated. The film star reminded me far too much of Alexei: the same glitter, the same charm, the same complete inability to hear the word *no.*

"Charlie's got a swimming pool at the bottom of the slope," Call Me Larry was purring, oblivious. "Why don't we slip away for a little private party while your friends are enjoying themselves?"

The Soviet consulate people certainly *were* enjoying themselves, taking over this sumptuous space with its French doors, its ink-black grand piano, its silver platters of hors d'oeuvres and ice buckets of champagne on every surface. Even Yuri was positively giggling as he watched Charlie Chaplin grip a bottle of champagne between his teeth and walk on his hands across the marble floors.

Hollywood people, I mused. If Americans sometimes seemed strange to me, these film stars seemed even stranger. Breezy, informal, not nearly as inclined to bristle at socialist ideas as guests at a Washington party . . . but they seemed to perform more than exist, and I wasn't sure they saw my uniform as anything more than one of the outlandish costumes they were all wearing.

Suddenly I wanted some fresh air. "Excuse me, Mr. Olivier"—peeling his hand off my hip again—"I need more champagne."

"Drink *me,* you darling little killer. I'm like a vintage wine—you have to swill me down before I turn sour!"

I managed to fight my way free, through the crowd on the terrace outside and toward the long, sloped lawn leading away from Breakaway House. "I see we're both looking for some quiet," Kostia said, melting out of the shadows in his silent way.

"At least Yuri's not breathing down my neck for once." My partner and I wandered down the long stretch of grass, which did indeed lead to a swimming pool far below. "Who'd have guessed he was so starstruck?"

"Apparently he used to shadow a Moscow bigwig with a liking for private showings of forbidden Western films," Kostia said.

We'd had our own private cinema showing tonight: *The Great Dictator,* Charlie Chaplin's most famous film, showed in his small personal theater. I'd seen some strange things in my life, but not much was stranger than watching a man strut and posture across a flickering screen, then turning and seeing the same man sitting on my right, all friendly smiles, watching for my reaction. I'd never seen a Chaplin film before; he seemed like an odd pop-eyed little man, not how I envisioned a film star.

"What did you think of *The Great Dictator*?" Kostia asked, reading my thoughts.

"I don't know if I can laugh at Hitler." I shortened my stride to match Kostia's slight limp, since he'd come outside without his cane. "Maybe we should—laughter makes men small. But I've seen too many Hitlerites coming at me with rifles and tanks to find them funny."

"You're philosophical," my partner observed.

"Only at noisy parties." I didn't feel alone in a sniper's nest at midnight, but I frequently felt alone in crowds—which was why I was here outside, and Kostia, too. That's where you find two snipers at a party: away from the crowd, in the dark, alone. And happy to be there.

"I hate almost all parties," Kostia confessed. I was still in uniform, but he was in black tie again. He'd left the jacket somewhere inside and his sleeves were pushed up, hands stuffed in his pockets.

"You didn't seem to hate this one so much when you had two film stars draped over you earlier," I couldn't help saying. Myrna Loy and Mary Pickford, learning that my interpreter was a sniper himself, had asked to see the hands of an expert marksman, had gushed over his calluses, had cooed like doves when he cracked walnuts effortlessly between his cast-iron fingers. "Myrna Loy was nearly sitting on your lap."

"Charlie Chaplin kissed your hand," Kostia pointed out. "And went down on one knee."

"That was embarrassing." The actor had proclaimed he was ready to kiss every finger on my hand for those 309 Fritzes I had put into the ground—and then he did it, lingeringly, damply, as cameras flashed and I resisted the urge to wipe my fingers on my uniform.

Another champagne cork popped in the distance. It made my partner and me tense briefly; we traded smiles and Kostia handed me down the half wall above the swimming pool at the bottom of the long lawn. The house at the top of the slope was barely visible from here; I saw bouncing shadows of half-drunk actors—I could have sworn I saw Yuri's square silhouette dancing on top of the piano—and heard the distant strains of "Song of the Volga Boatmen," undoubtedly being played in Soviet honor. The night was warm; autumn had already come to the Midwest, but it had yet to touch down in the City of Angels. The swimming pool shimmered only faintly in the dark; it was a new moon, almost no light at all. That didn't matter. Kostia and I, we could see in the dark like it was noon.

We sat down at the edge. I kicked off my heels so I could lower my feet into the cool water, and Kostia rolled up his trousers to do the same. "Your visit in New York," I began, thinking maybe he could tell me about his family now—no one in earshot here, much less anyone who could speak Russian—but he shook his head.

"Later."

I nodded, looking down at the water, dark blue and shimmering. I'd never seen a private swimming pool before, marble-tiled and sumptuous, all for one person to enjoy alone—or *not* alone. My heart ratcheted up into my throat, and I swallowed. "Let's swim."

I peeled out of my uniform, down to my new silky American underthings, and entered the water with a neat dive. Kostia shed his black-tie finery like a fish leaving its scales behind in a scatter of silver, slipping into the water seemingly without disturbing the surface. A second later I felt steel-strong hands link around my wrist and yank me into the deep end; I pivoted underwater and got my heels into his ribs, yanking free as an underwater laugh surprised me in a stream of bubbles. We thrashed and fought and finally fetched up gasping for breath on the far edge of the deep end, arms folded side by side on the lip of the pool, bodies hanging light in the water. My heart was still cannoning inside my chest.

"Your leg," I managed to say, nodding down through the ripples toward the livid scar I'd seen on his leg when he dived in. The gash gouged from the knee almost to the ankle. "From the end of Sevastopol . . . I know all your other scars but that one."

A drop of water slid down his sharp jaw. I resisted the urge to smooth it away. "Do you?"

"Of course I do. I was never more than a few meters away from you whenever you were wounded." I wasn't sure exactly what I was saying, just that I had to keep putting words into this dark, bottomless silence. "You didn't usually get hit badly enough to land in the hospital battalion; you were always luckier than me. But you got the bad cut on your trigger hand at the beginning of the Sevastopol siege—" I was talking too fast. Forcing myself to slow down, I nodded at the ridged line running along his thumb where it rested on the pool's tiled edge. "The slash from a German combat knife, clearing out that nest of snipers on No-Name Height." I reached up to touch the puckered seam running along the crown of his head under the razored-short hair. "And the splinter wound on the back of your neck, the one I stitched up for you in Sevastopol." Sliding my fingers across the jagged mark on his neck. I let my hand stay there, resting against his pulse. "Four near misses," I said quietly.

He didn't name my scars, but his hand found them under the water—sliding over the hip I'd wrenched outside Gildendorf; running up my spine along the forked shrapnel scar, up through my wet hair to find the splinter wound from Odessa, coming to rest on the side of my face, fingers brushing the ear that had had to be stitched back to my head. "Those are just the scars we can see."

Lyonya, I knew we were both thinking.

And then Kostia was looking at me through the dark, thinking *I love you.* He didn't need to say it for me to hear it. I took a deep, unsteady breath, looking down at the tiled ledge where my hand had found his and linked finger to finger.

"You're my partner," I said unsteadily. "You're my shadow. My other half. I trust you like no one else in this world. No one can do what we've done and not be closer than two humans can ever be, in this world or the next." My parents, my child, my friends, either of the men I'd called husband—none of them knew me like Kostia. No one would ever know Kostia like me.

His trigger-calloused forefinger caressed my knuckles. "You could have just said *I love you,* Lyudmila Mikhailovna."

"I do," I whispered. I loved Lyonya, too. Maybe I'd loved them both all along, my husband *and* my partner. Maybe it wasn't moving too soon; maybe it was *this has always been.*

The second kiss, slower and fiercer than the one by the canoe. "Why are we always in water when we do this?" I murmured as he pulled me against him through the silky ripples of the pool. He still tasted of iron and rain. We clung, coiled together, mouths locked, silent as a countdown. With Lyonya, things had been all jokes and laughter, even curled in bed; falling into Kostia felt like falling into a well down to the middle of the world. My fingers skated over his skin, satin over granite. He'd looked deceptively slight next to Lyonya's golden height and breadth, but naked in my arms, Kostia looked like he'd been forged rather than born, bolted together out of piano wire and iron rivets rather than tendon and muscle. My head fell back against the lip of the pool as his mouth found my breast, and that was when we heard tipsy shouts from the house above. Yuri's voice, calling my name—the delegation, tipsy and happy, was returning to the hotel.

Kostia gave a soundless wolf's snarl into my throat, and then we were breaking apart, splashing out of the pool as quietly as possible, wrestling back into our dry clothes. I gave him one last dark, drowning kiss, murmuring "Room 114" into his mouth even as I wrestled my damp limbs back into my uniform—thank goodness for sturdy gabardine that could withstand a Russian winter, much less a little Beverly Hills chlorine. A fast scoop of his own clothes and Kostia was limping back toward the house the long way, while I shoved my wet hair out of my face and shouted "I felt like a swim!" to the cross-looking Yuri as he tramped out of the shadows.

"It is not part of your directive to swim."

A drunken, weaving drive out of Beverly Hills, every centimeter of my skin singing like I was crawling on my elbows through no-man's-land again, feeling my partner in the seat in front of me like he was a missing limb, everyone around us drunk and oblivious in the crammed car . . . then I was in my hotel room in the dark, waiting, *alive*. I knew when he was there; he didn't have to knock. He was moving into the room like an arrow before I even had the door fully open, tumbling me to the floor in a midnight blackness that felt as bright as day. Grappling and pulling at each other, sniper eyes flaring, rifle-roughened fingers teasing out cries of response the way we'd once teased out ballistic arcs through icy winds. Folding our bodies together into a nest, a foxhole, like we'd done so many times—only this was a foxhole of crisp sheets and fierce warm arms and a silence so complex it wiped away the world.

No one spoke until nearly dawn, and then it was me, arm curled around Kostia's waist, his lips in my hair. "When I said I was still mourning my dead, I was really thinking, *What would Lyonya say if he saw us?*"

My partner's voice in the darkness was quiet. "I've been thinking that, too."

I knew he had. Our thoughts, in the few private moments to be found around the edges of this noisy, exhausting, exceedingly public goodwill tour, had probably been much the same. Thinking in somber reflection, in bitter grief, in tensile silence, imagining Lyonya's smiling face, holding entire unspoken conversations with the man we'd both loved.

"I think," Kostia said slowly, "he would be glad for us. He'd say no one should waste time if there's a chance to be happy."

"I was thinking the same thing," I whispered as Kostia's lips touched my temple, my scarred ear. "I can hear him saying it."

CHAPTER 30

The headline: WHO WOULD HAVE THOUGHT THAT AMERICA'S NEXT SWEETHEART COULD BE A SOVIET GIRL SNIPER WHOSE HAND (NOW KISSED BY HALF THE COUNTRY!) HAS ENDED THE LIVES OF 309 NAZIS? LYUDMILA PAVLICHENKO RETURNS TO WASHINGTON AFTER CONCLUDING HER TOUR OF THE WEST WITH CROWDED STOPS IN SAN FRANCISCO AND FRESNO . . .

The truth: I think San Francisco had a bridge. Fresno I don't remember at all, but even the people who *live* in Fresno probably don't care to remember it. The only thing that rose above my daze of quiet happiness at being with Kostia was the question the entire delegation asked the moment we returned to Washington: When can we go home?

"THE TOUR HAS been extended." The Soviet ambassador beamed, looking at the three student delegates who had been reunited. We had traded stories of our respective tours, and the stories had been largely the same . . . except that my leg of it had gotten considerably more newspaper coverage. Krasavchenko was the only one who looked pleased to be continuing in the public eye; Pchelintsev scowled openly, and I couldn't keep my face from falling. "My friends, this is good news," the ambassador protested. "You have accomplished the near impossible: shifted public opinion in the USA in favor of the USSR. Opposition to a second front is subsiding. We would be foolish not to capitalize on—"

"Send Lyudmila on the tour," Pchelintsev interrupted. "She's the one they want to see. Have her trot round the spotlights and send me to Stalingrad."

I looked at him. "If anyone's going to Stalingrad, it should be the better sniper, and that would be me."

The ambassador waved our objections aside. "No one is going to Stalingrad yet. Our directive comes from the Kremlin; we will continue on to Canada and then Great Britain . . ."

I wilted, hearing the details: we were to fly to Montreal, then Halifax, then Glasgow, then London . . . I saw a long line of receptions, dinners, and speeches stretching out in front of me. Would Slavka think I didn't want to come home to him? At this rate he'd be a man grown by the time I returned. "I serve the Soviet Union," I replied, sighing, when the ambassador paused for a response.

"Did you manage to say that without cursing?" Kostia asked later. He'd come to my room as discreetly as ever, knocking only after Yuri had trundled off duty. (What *did* Soviet concrete blocks do, off duty? Perhaps a little light reading: *Winning the War Against Capitalism*, I. K. Volkov, 9th edition.)

"Barely." I curled into Kostia's shoulder. We were lying in a mess of sheets, cold Washington sunlight slanting through the blinds, still damp with sweat from recent exertions. "Then I got a scolding because the ambassador somehow got wind of the marriage proposal I got from that ass Jonson, and feared I meant to accept it and defect!" I pleated the sheet between my fingers, shaking my head. "Imagine thinking I'd jump at the chance to stay in the United States."

"It's not so bad here."

I smiled. "If I have to eat another hot dog, I'll run shrieking around the Washington Monument. I want white nights, Kostia. I want ponchiki in a paper cone, all dusted with sugar. I want people who know about Bogdan Khmelnitsky and the Pereyaslav Council—"

"Mila, even in Russia no one knows about the Pereyaslav Council."

"They will once I finish my dissertation. If you can even read my dissertation anymore through the bloodstains and the gunpowder burns." I shook my head. "All my schooling would mean nothing if I stayed here—I could never be a historian, and that's all I've ever wanted to be. Yet even people like Mrs. Roosevelt seemed to think I'd be grateful to stay."

"Some people would." Kostia's voice sounded odd.

"Not people like us." I tugged my partner's head down for a kiss, but he'd gone utterly still. "Kostia . . ."

He reached over suddenly and turned on the radio. The sound of Kay Kyser warbling "Jingle, Jangle, Jingle" filled the hotel room as Kostia cranked up the volume, then rolled over in bed and pulled me beneath him. Laying his cheek against mine and his lips to my ear, he spoke in a voice that was barely more than a thread. "I want to tell you about New York."

I didn't know if my room was being listened to by our minders, but Kostia was taking no chances. He told me in the vaguest terms possible, in a nearly soundless whisper right into my eardrum so not even the most sensitive microphone could pick up his words . . . but the picture was clear enough.

He'd summoned up the nerve to knock on the door of his grandmother's sister in Ridgewood. He'd shown her photographs: his grandmother; his mother. He'd been welcomed, embraced, introduced to others.

It hadn't been explicitly said . . . but they would welcome him if he stayed.

He fell silent then, his face taut and stony, and I had no idea what I could say. There were too many things to say, all of them impossible. *How can you think of walking away from your country?*—but I could see why he was tempted. The motherland could be great, I believed that with all my soul, but I wasn't going to pretend in a moment like this that it wasn't a hard, unforgiving place to make a life. *You're in danger*—but Kostia knew that; he knew he risked a bullet even for revealing he had family here, much less for visiting them. And my final desperate question: *How can you be with me and then threaten to leave me?*—but that wasn't important. This was a life to consider, his life—I had flesh and blood in Russia pulling me back there by an invisible steel thread, but he didn't. His only blood family was here. His tie to Russia was . . . me.

He must have read the shock in my face. I couldn't voice anything, not here in this room where there might be wires and listening ears, so I only shook my head mutely. He switched off the radio, then leaned back to cup my face in his hands. I don't know what we might have said, but there was a key rattling in the lock, and suddenly the door swung wide.

Alexei Pavlichenko stood there with an armload of pink roses.

He could have been an illustration in a romantic novel. The suitor in a sharp suit, flowers in his arm, a charming half-smile on his handsome features. But the smile disappeared like a doused light, and a wave of dead anger swept over his face.

I was already near tears, brimming with various churning emotions. I did not, *not*, need Alexei added to the mix. "No," I snarled before he could say a word. "Not now. Not today. Not *ever*. I don't care what you want, just get out."

He stood looking at Kostia as if he were vermin. "How long have you been fucking your pet wolf behind my back, Mila?"

Kostia sat up slowly, the sheet sliding to his waist as he rested his elbows on his raised knees, and maybe my husband missed how that movement put my partner closer to his Finnish combat knife lying on the nightstand, but I didn't.

I threw the sheet back and got out of bed. My naked skin was crawling, but I refused to cower in the bed like a guilty wife caught in an illicit romp. "How did you get in here?" I knew I'd locked the door.

"I charmed the housekeeper into giving me a passkey. So I could leave these as a surprise." He tossed his armload of roses to the floor, a careless scatter of thorns and petals over the carpet. "I wonder how many other men you've paraded naked for in this room."

Kostia tensed behind me, silently asking me what I wanted. My fingers tapped against my leg twice, as if we were back in a sniper trench communicating in silence: *wait.* I stalked across the room naked, head held high, and pulled my robe off the wall hook. "Don't pretend you're jealous, Alexei. This grown woman's body of mine is ten or twelve years too old to arouse you." I knotted the sash about my waist with a snap. "Now get out."

"No." He took a step closer, turning away from Kostia now. Kostia hadn't moved from the bed, stone still and watching everything . . . but his combat knife had disappeared off the nightstand.

"I am the one saying no, Alexei." The storm of roiling emotions in me was tipping rapidly in favor of rage. From the damp-handed Mr. Jonson's blind insistence to Alexei's smug persistence to Laurence Olivier's hand returning over and over to my hip—why could I not seem to make anyone hear the word *no*?

"You're still my wife."

I made myself laugh in his face. "Who do you think you are? I'm the famous sniper; the war heroine; *America's sweetheart*. I'm the one being feted all over the *world*, helping Comrade Stalin get his second front. You're the delegation pill pusher. A dog being towed behind on a leash."

"Shut your mouth. You sound like a spoiled little girl having a tantrum."

"Spoiled little girl, is that all you can call me? What about all those lovely things you wrote in your unsigned notes? *Red bitch, murdering slut*—"

"Act like a slut, don't be shocked when you're called one." His eyes tightened. "But I didn't write those damn things. I answered enough questions about them from delegation security; I won't stand here and listen to you—"

"You had better listen to me, Alexei." Now I was the one to overrun him. He'd once loomed in my life like a mountain, the biggest obstacle I faced in making a new life. Now, after everything else I had confronted this last year and a half, he was a pebble. Yet that pebble was still lodged in my shoe, doing its best to prevent me from moving forward. I was done with it. "You're not my husband anymore, and as soon as we get back to Moscow, we *will* make it official. Because I'm the one with friends in high places now, and I will make you stop stalling."

He took one long stride toward me—and stopped, because Kostia was behind him. My partner, who had silently slid out of bed as I was speaking, angled himself to one side and moved the moment Alexei came at me. My husband froze. Kostia had never looked more like the old myth of Morozko, ice-silent winter standing frost-cold and naked, knife growing from his fist like an icicle, its razor tip resting gently over Alexei's jugular.

My husband started forward. Kostia pressed the knife a millimeter deeper, and a trickle of blood slid down Alexei's throat toward his snowy shirt collar. Alexei stopped, eyes moving from me to Kostia. "You know what?" he said. "Take her. Take her and choke on her."

Maybe now he'd finally leave me alone. Now that *he'd* decided he was done with me. Whatever I'd decided up till this moment didn't count, of course. Over the roaring in my ears I stretched out a foot toward the nearest discarded flower on the rug and kicked it toward him. "Get out, and take your cheap lousy bribe with you."

But the door slammed behind him and left Kostia and me staring at each other, and the rage drained away to leave me cold and shaking. I wanted Alexei to leave, and he finally had. I wanted Kostia to stay . . . and I had no idea, looking at his closed face, if he would or not.

THE MARKSMAN FELT his luck returning when he saw Alexei Pavlichenko bang into the hotel bar and call for a double vodka in a tone barely above a snarl before he even sank down on the barstool. The marksman ambled over, sifting his fingers through the uncut diamonds rattling in his pockets. "Bad day?" he asked in his execrable Russian.

Alexei glanced over. "The journalist," he said, visibly recalling their last conversation here. Nearly two months ago now, before the international student conference that had started all this off. "What's your name?"

The marksman showed his falsified press credentials. He was back to the journalist identity again, the one he'd backed with extensive research and cover from above. "I never did get those pictures in the White House Rose Garden of you and your wife," he said, just to be saying something. "You want to try again? The delegation's getting one last dinner at the White House before leaving, right? A nice photograph of you and the wife for the Sunday edition . . ."

"If you think that bitch needs more flattering press—" the doctor paused, eyes suddenly sharpening. "I've seen you before."

"Sure," said the marksman amiably. "Right here, couple of months ago."

"No. After that. Chicago, the sharpshooters' club. You're the one who was trailing after Mila like an idiot." A long moment. "You're *Jonson*." Alexei Pavlichenko blinked.

"No, I'm not," the marksman said, genuinely startled. The changes in his clothes, posture, hair, voice . . . he'd been so careful. He was good at disguises, damn it. He sank into each new cover like a bespoke suit. "Who's Jonson?" he asked, swirling the ice in his lowball glass.

"You are." The Russian doctor's eyes were flicking rapidly over the marksman's face. "Surgeons see bone and muscle, not hair color and posture. You're him."

And you're good, thought the marksman in some dismay. Lady Death certainly hadn't seen past William Jonson's dark wig with its receding hairline, the honking upper-crust voice, the eager-to-please scurry that put her would-be suitor two inches in height under the tall, ginger-haired, mustachioed newsman who had tailed behind her at so many public functions. Then again, he'd taken care that Lyudmila Pavlichenko never saw the newsman except as one more form hunched behind a camera across the room.

But the doctor had put two and two together. The marksman rattled the ice in his glass again. Kill him, bribe him, or find a way to use him?

"So which one are you?" Alexei Pavlichenko demanded. "William Jonson or—"

"There is a William Jonson," the marksman decided to acknowledge. A metallurgical businessman living as a near-total recluse in New York State. The man never went anywhere, he never met anyone, so his identity was useful whenever the marksman needed one that would come out both genuine and whistle-clean when investigated. A wig, a clean shave, and some expensive suits were all it took to match the out-of-date photograph.

"There's a rumor going around here that you proposed marriage to her. To my *wife*." Alexei was still looking at him as if waiting for the final punch line of a prank. "Was that a joke or—"

"I needed an excuse to follow the tour. Journalists don't typically follow even a presidential entourage all the way across the country, and ordinary citizens are liable to get asked some hard questions if they keep turning up." Even with all the backroom handwaving from Pocket Square's employers, making sure the First Lady's security passed the marksman without question onto any necessary lists, he'd wanted additional cover . . . and nobody looked as harmless as a lovestruck idiot who picked up more than his share of restaurant bills. Especially a lovestruck idiot who popped the question. "Besides," the marksman said with complete honesty, "I wanted a closer look at Lady Death." Squeezing that small hand with its trigger calluses, seeing the annoyance masked in those big brown eyes. Thinking how those eyes would flare in fear if they realized what was going on behind William Jonson's earnest pop-eyed stare. Thinking: *You have no idea, you Red bitch.*

Yes, the marksman thought—he had definitely let curiosity get the better of strict professionalism on this job. A bad thing, considering it was the biggest target of his career . . . Yet somehow he wasn't dismayed. This turn of events was going somewhere, he could feel it. Weeks of dead ends and failed plans were all leading here.

Alexei Pavlichenko sat back on his stool now, tilting the vodka in his glass. Sudden calculations going through that handsome head, without a doubt. "And why did you need to follow my whore wife?"

"Just looking to make a little trouble for America's Soviet sweetheart." The marksman leaned closer, still speaking in his bad Russian, feeling the pulse quicken. "Not everyone here wants her to go home a heroine, you know."

The doctor's gaze sharpened. "Really."

There it is, thought the marksman. And leaned closer.

CHAPTER 31

The headline: THE GIRL SNIPER AND HER COMPATRIOTS RETURN TO THE WHITE HOUSE FOR A FAREWELL DINNER AND PRESS APPEARANCE WITH PRESIDENT ROOSEVELT BEFORE DEPARTING OUR FAIR SHORES TOMORROW MORNING . . .

The truth: My last trip to the White House was not quite that uneventful.

THE WIND WAS blustering outside as the delegation gathered in the hotel court in black tie and evening finery: our final night in America. "Pretty fitting weather for Halloween, eh?" the concierge said.

"What's Halloween?" I asked, distracted by the delegation baggage piling up behind the front desk. Most of our things were already packed, ready for our flight to Halifax tomorrow morning. There was nothing left to do in this country but say our goodbyes to the President and the First Lady at tonight's White House dinner. Krasavchenko and the other men were already joking about getting a bottle or two of vodka here at the hotel afterward, since we'd have a long flight to Canada to sleep off any hangovers. I searched among them—Yuri, Pchelintsev, a glowering Alexei—but I didn't see Kostia.

"Mila."

I turned. My partner looked rumpled, his sleeves pushed up to his elbows, a dark shadow of stubble on his jaw. "You're not dressed for dinner," I said inadequately.

"I begged off," he said. "They have plenty of interpreters . . . I'm going for a walk."

Are you coming back? I thought, stepping closer. I couldn't read his face. I knew him so well and I couldn't read his face. "Take a coat," I said instead. "It's cold."

"Not to a Siberian." His eyes went over me like a kiss. I was back in my yellow satin dress, and I hadn't flinched when the elevator operator gasped at my scars.

"Will I see you later?" I meant my room—I wondered if he'd come to me after I was back from the White House dinner. Maybe if we were pressed skin to skin I could say all the things through our blood-bonded silence that I couldn't voice aloud . . . But as soon as the words were out, I realized it sounded like, *Will I see you tomorrow morning?* Would he be here, waiting for the embassy car to take us to the airfield, or would he be . . . gone? Here we were the night before departure, and I still didn't know. I knew he was avoiding me. I knew I couldn't beg. Beyond that—

"I don't know," he said. I stepped forward and kissed him in the middle of the crowded hotel court, long and desperately, and his hand came around my waist and touched the scar over my spine.

Then I broke away, ignoring the glances all around us, and joined the delegation for my last visit to the White House.

PRESIDENT ROOSEVELT RAISED his glass. "To new friends."

The delegation murmured in response, toasting. We sat in the same small dining room where we'd been welcomed to our first American breakfast. Had that really been only two months ago? When I first sat at this table, I'd been grieving, angry, resentful, convinced I'd hate America and all Americans. Well, I'd given speeches in more cities than I could count, in front of more journalists than there were stars in the sky, and I'd seen the beauty in rolling American hills, towering American skyscrapers, and friendly American faces. I no longer flinched to see my name in print, or a microphone standing in the circle of a spotlight awaiting my voice, or a crowd of eager faces turned up toward mine to listen. How very far Mila Pavlichenko had come.

Although I was still grieving and still angry, even if for different reasons.

"Are you quite all right, Lyudmila?" the First Lady asked in a low tone. She'd placed me on her right, the seat of honor. "You look strained."

"Quite all right, Eleanor." I saw Alexei looking at me from his place at the far end of the table, his gaze speculative rather than sullen—I hadn't spoken to him since he scooped his rejected roses off my rug and stormed out of my room. He'd probably decided he'd come out on top of it all . . . no one could beat Alexei when it came to twisting an argument around so *he'd* won it.

Three courses, more toasts, and then the President excused himself to the oval reception room, where the press would take some final photographs. I knew by now—though Eleanor certainly never said any such thing—that her husband would situate himself in an armchair in advance of the photographers, so they would find him at ease with his trademark cigarette holder clamped between his teeth, not struggling with his braces and cane. A respectful wait, then the Soviet delegation followed into the big oval room with its vaulted ceilings and graceful fireplace, beside which the President gave his famous fireside chats. One last bank of photographers and journalists flooded in, snapping pictures—not just of us but of the gifts we'd accrued during the goodwill tour. A long table had been piled with plaques, city seals, mayoral keys, commemorative albums of all the cities we'd visited. I smiled to see the mahogany box of the twin Colt M1911A1 pistols that had been given to me by the Sharpshooters' Association in Chicago, and the soft silver pile of the lynx coat I'd been awarded in New York.

"Two more gifts for you, Lyudmila." The First Lady drew me

aside, lowering her voice as Krasavchenko approached President Roosevelt for his farewell handshake. "I have many photographs of you by now, but I thought you might like one of me, to remember our friendship."

I blinked down at the framed picture she placed in my hand: an image of Eleanor in the black dress she wore tonight, seated at her desk like the hard-working woman she was, inscribed in her own hand. *To Senior Lieutenant Lyudmila Pavlichenko, with warm good wishes from Eleanor Roosevelt.*

My eyes prickled as I looked up from the picture to its smiling subject, and for a moment my own troubles faded away. "I will miss you," I said simply. "I will not miss hot dogs, or your press—" Casting a glance at the hubbub of journalists and flashbulbs all around. "But I will miss you, Eleanor. You have taught me so much."

"And you me," she said with a smile. "I'll miss all of you, even Mr. Krasavchenko and his rather endless anecdotes of his Komsomol days . . . but of everyone, dear Lyudmila, you're the one I wish I could keep."

You might be keeping my partner, I wish I could have said. *If he stays, look after him.* But I couldn't say that. If Kostia asked for asylum here, our delegation would be in utter uproar; it would have to look like he'd told no one of his plans. Besides, I knew I didn't have to ask the First Lady to extend a helping hand if he needed it. If there was one thing Eleanor Roosevelt knew how to do, with grace and tact and unending sympathy, it was how to *help*.

"One more gift arrived for you," she said with a mischievous smile, lightening the moment of farewell and passing me a flat silk box. Pchelintsev was now having his photograph taken with Roosevelt; I'd be next. "From a certain brokenhearted American suitor, once it was made clear to him that you would never accept his proposal!"

I eyed the case like it was a snake. What surprises had the damp-handed Mr. Jonson left for me now? When I lifted the lid, my gasp made the Soviet ambassador drift closer.

A collar necklace of tiny diamonds. Twin bracelets like bands of diamond lace. A brooch with hanging diamond tremblers to catch the light. A diamond ring like a drop of cold fire.

To Lyudmila with great love from W. P. Jonson, my businessman suitor had written on the accompanying card. *We will meet again.*

"I cannot take this," I began to say, but Eleanor shook her head.

"The man's covering note stated that he refused to take anything back."

"A fitting tribute to a heroine of the USSR," the Soviet ambassador said, looking envious. I made a mental note to offer the brooch to him for his wife or his mistress. That was the way things were done in the Soviet Union, and I was fairly sure it was the way things were done in Washington as well.

Alexei's voice sounded, sharp-edged and mocking on the ambassador's other side. "Try them on, Mila."

"Yes, do," Eleanor enthused. "For your final photograph." She looked innocently pleased, and for her I clasped the necklace around my neck, fastened a bracelet around each wrist, pinned the brooch to my yellow satin bodice, and tried on the ring. It ended up fitting my trigger finger, perfectly.

I looked at the handwritten card. *We will meet again . . .*

"Your American suitor picked well, Mila," Alexei said, still mocking. "Diamonds for a girl with a heart like a diamond."

"I would disagree," Eleanor said when I translated for her. "I think I have come to know something about snipers by now. An eye like a diamond, yes. But a heart"—she led me toward her husband for my final photograph—"for friendship."

"Agreed," President Roosevelt boomed, grinning around his cigarette holder, and for the last time I felt the clasp of that strong, sinewy hand. We turned toward the bank of journalists, smiling as flashbulbs went off, and before he released my hand, he gave it a final squeeze along with a low-voiced promise: "Go home, keep fighting, and tell your friends that America is coming."

THE MARKSMAN, METHODICALLY setting up behind a thicket of shrubs on the edge of the South Lawn, wondered why he'd given her the diamonds.

He'd get them back, of course, but why do it in the first place? He was finished with the William Jonson persona, at least as far as this job was concerned; there wasn't any need to extend the facade of the mooncalf suitor. Yet when he made his preparations for this evening, packing up his disassembled rifle into the case specially modified to look like a carrier for camera equipment, he'd gone on a whim to his private safe, pushed aside the uncut gems into which he routinely converted most of his cash payments, and reached for a jewelry case at the very back. Payment for a job back in 1927; some stockbroker's inconvenient wife. The marksman had made it look like an interrupted robbery; the grateful husband had paid him with the now-dead wife's diamonds, then gone on to collect the insurance and a dewy-fresh fiancée; everyone had gone home happy. Well, except the wife. The marksman remembered how her eyes had widened, the moment she realized he was going to kill her . . . Would Lady Death's eyes widen in the same way, when she faced his gun muzzle? On impulse, he took out the jewelry case, scribbled out an accompanying card, and sent it all off in the name of that booby William Jonson. A whim.

Maybe he hadn't been able to resist telling her *We will meet again.*

Or maybe he was old-fashioned. You gave a woman a present, after all, when you took her on a date. And wasn't this a date, in a way?

His hands had never stopped moving, assembling the rifle from its pieces. He'd separated from the other journalists as soon as they were admitted onto White House grounds; it shouldn't have been so easy, but it was. The Secret Service weren't on high alert for small functions like this, and his path had been smoothed for him by his shadow-suited employers, who made sure his name made the night's list and gave him the routes in advance where he would need to avoid security points as he melted into the gardens.

He checked his watch, timed down to the second. The Soviet delegation would be finishing up their last photographs in the oval reception room just inside the South Portico. After that they'd spill out onto the lawn, a last informal mingle with Halloween punch before everyone departed . . . and the President and his wife would wave farewell from just above the portico stairs.

The shot across the south lawn would be long, but he'd made longer. He just needed Mila Pavlichenko out of the way first . . . and if her husband did his part, that should be in about ten minutes.

I HAD THE feeling, once again, as if I had spiders crawling down my spine. We were all mingling on the South Lawn now, sipping cups of highly spiked Halloween punch for a final informal aperitif as the delegation's mountain of gifts was packed into the embassy cars pulled around front. Eleanor was spinning one of her amusing, informative anecdotes about the celebration of October 31 in America: costumes, harvest parades, candles placed in hollowed-out turnips or pumpkins . . . but I couldn't focus. That unsettled feeling was back, stronger than ever, and I couldn't shake it. I lit a cigarette and looked up at the moon rising over the tipsy, triumphant crowd of celebrating Soviets and eager journalists. The moon was waning gibbous—it had been months since the moon's phase was a matter of my nightly survival, but I still couldn't help tracking her wax and wane. The wind had died down; it wasn't cold by Russian standards, but the yellow satin dress was flimsy enough that I'd shrugged into my lynx coat before coming down to the White House lawn. I took another deep inhale of a Lucky Strike, watching the sparkle of Mr. Jonson's diamonds on my wrist in the moonlight.

We will meet again . . .

Where exactly did he think we were going to meet again, when tonight was my last in his country? I shook my head at my pop-eyed suitor, who had probably thought he was being very romantic. Anyone could have told him that the line between *very romantic* and *vaguely creepy* is not one you want to land on the wrong side of when you are courting a sniper. Kostia would split himself laughing.

Kostia. Surely he was the reason I felt so unsettled. I side-slipped a journalist cajoling *One more smile for the camera, Lady Death?* and turned back toward the columned portico of the White House's southern side. President Roosevelt had not, of course, followed us down the stairs to the lawn; he sat under the awning between the portico columns, chatting with someone or other. I could see the confident line of his profile all the way from here. If Kostia were with me, we'd be automatically assessing potential angles of fire.

"There," I said aloud, nodding at a series of hedges to the east of the lawn. "Better yet, there." A thicket of trees and shrubs on the other side, near the West Wing. I lifted my cigarette for another drag and stopped. Even here, even now, I turned my lit cigarette inside the curl of my palm, hiding the ember . . .

And it slid into my memory with a click: William Jonson in the sharpshooters' club in Chicago, laughing at himself for shooting so badly during the demonstration, lighting a Lucky Strike—which he held in a cupped, reversed hand, like a sniper.

It's not just snipers who smoke that way, I thought. Any battle veteran who had stood a night watch did. Had Mr. Jonson been a soldier? He was too young to have fought in the Great War. And he'd shot so badly in the demonstration, half his shots missing the target altogether . . .

Which is exactly what a trained sniper would do if he wanted to look like something else.

We will meet again.

"Mila!" Alexei was trying to get my attention from across the crowd, but Krasavchenko had waylaid him about something. My husband beckoned me, but I turned the other way, stubbing out my cigarette in the grass underfoot, looking up at President Roosevelt on the portico. I didn't know what I was doing, just that the sense of wrongness was stronger than ever, and my eyes were flicking back and forth between the potential lines of fire so automatically parsed by my sniper's eye (*an eye like a diamond*, Eleanor's voice whispered).

The hedges to the east; the trees and shrubs to the west. I hesitated.

"Lyudmila!" Eleanor sailed up to me, cheeks flushed with the night's chill. "Would you like more punch, or—"

I cut her off, something I'd never done before. "Get him inside," I said, pointing to the seated figure of her husband on the portico. "Inside, *now*—" and without waiting for a reply, I arrowed off toward the western side of the White House lawn. A white-aproned server stood at the edge of the grass with a tray, and among the glasses I saw a small paring knife for peeling lemon twists or taking the foil off wine bottles. I plucked the little blade off the tray and kept going, past the startled server and straight into the thicket of trees. I wasn't thinking, not in words. I was following something so deep I couldn't name it, or maybe I could. Maybe I already had, to Captain Sergienko when he asked if skills like mine were instinctive and I'd scoffed that it was simply training.

Well. Dozens of months of practice, hundreds of hours of training, thousands of shots fired under a blood moon on the other side of the world had all joined voices, singing a song down deep inside my veins.

And my feet followed it.

Notes by the First Lady

She gave an order. I find myself obeying it. Is it because the tone of absolute authority issuing commands will get feet moving whether they intend to or not?

Perhaps it is simply that when a woman with the name Lady Death looks suddenly and fearsomely alert, mortals formed of mere flesh and blood know it is time to run.

I hurry up the steps toward the South Portico, heart hammering, and I cannot help but think of that crisp night in Miami when a shot was fired at my husband's heart as he stood making a speech from his open car. That night. This one. Franklin's unspoken fears over the last few months—yes, he has been afraid. Of what? Of this?

I reach the top of the steps, and my husband looks toward me. His careworn face, etched with pain and humor, so alive. I call out quietly but urgently: "My dear, you are needed inside—" and then I turn to the nearest Secret Service officer.

I don't know what your diamond eye saw, Lyudmila, but do not miss.

CHAPTER 32

His luck was back; the marksman could feel it. His Packard was waiting for a quick, discreet getaway; it had already been vetted on the way in, and he thought he could manage to exit in the chaos after the shot. If not, people inside were already prepared with cover stories to smooth his way. He could hear the tick of the clock inside him, counting down toward the squeeze of the trigger.

Perhaps ten more minutes. The girl sniper would arrive, puzzled, directed by her husband: *I'll tell her that her precious partner is here to speak with her; she runs like a bitch in heat when he calls.* A fast, silent arm-bar from behind to choke her out without overt bruising, then the long-range shot toward the South Portico, where the President and the First Lady were both standing, heads bent close in some discussion. The marksman had already prepared his weapon: a Mosin-Nagant with PE sights, the same type Lady Death would have used on the front. He'd put in thousands of practice rounds on it—a good weapon, workmanlike, unfussy. The moment the President fell, the marksman would fire another shot, this one through Lyudmila Pavlichenko's unconscious mouth, and leave the rifle behind in her hand: an assassination-suicide. The newspapers would eat it up. Reaching for the rifle with gloved hands, he smiled as he loaded five rounds. He should only need two.

He didn't know why he looked up. It was too soon for her to be here yet, and not so much as a rustle of leaves or whisper of twigs had sounded against his ears. But some unknown trip wire twanged in his silent depths, far below the level of clocks or plans or even thought, and his head whipped around.

There she was: Lady Death gliding across the shadowed grass in rippling lynx fur, the glitter of his diamonds at her throat like stardust. Bleached silver in the faint moonlight, but her eyes pitch-black. They didn't widen in shock or take in his face in stunned disbelief. She knew. She already knew.

How did she—

His hand on the rifle twitched—he couldn't shoot her; the report would ruin everything—and in that instant's hesitation she moved shadow-fast. Not away, running for safety. *Toward* him. He lunged to meet her, and the two snipers collided under the gibbous moon.

IN THAT SPLIT instant I saw the skull under the face: William Jonson without the darkened hair, the eager gaze, the supplicant stoop in his shoulders. A coat hanger of a man considerably taller than Jonson, bony-shouldered, scoop-faced, with eyes like mud. And at his side, the long, glinting, unmistakable shape of a rifle's barrel and telescopic sights, aimed through the bushes toward the White House like a half-hidden snake poised to strike. A Mosin-Nagant.

One glance, and then we were grappling.

I got out a piercing, wordless shout before his fingers clamped over my mouth. I bit as hard as I could and heard his strangled curse. I nearly lost my grip on the paring knife in my hand; before I could bring it up in a fast stab between his ribs or into his throat, he flung himself sideways to shake me off. He didn't wrench free, but I lost my footing and went to my knees in the grass. He kicked once, twice, and I felt something in my side go white-hot. I gasped for breath, and then the inside of my head filled with sparks as he clubbed me across my bad ear.

Dimly, I felt him hauling me up by one arm. I fumbled inside my coat, feeling instinctively for the eight-shot Tula-Tokarev that hung at my belt in case I ever fell into enemy hands, the weapon I'd jam to my own temple before I ever let myself be taken alive. But I wasn't wearing the TT; I was in cocktail-party satin and diamonds halfway around the world from my battleground, and I wasn't supposed to be among enemies—yet I was. Here in the velvet heart of America's capital, Lady Death had finally fallen into enemy hands.

And President Roosevelt was sitting just a bullet shot away. Eleanor's husband, who had gripped my hand and said, *Keep fighting, and tell your friends that America is coming.*

Get him off the balcony, Eleanor. Get him off the balcony—

I felt the man lock his arm around my throat from behind, grip tightening like a steel band. My sight darkened. My lips parted but I didn't have enough air to scream.

I fumbled the paring knife in my numbing hand, and stabbed down hard and straight into the meat of his calf.

He shouted, arm loosening around my throat, and his shout disappeared into a chorus of whoops: Krasavchenko and Pchelintsev and the rest of the delegation, kicking off the round of heartily bawled patriotic songs without which no evening with Russians present can conclude. I managed to tear myself out of the slackening choke hold, gagging for breath, ripping the knife out of his leg with another savage twist. My enemy scrambled backward with a hiss of agony, head jerking toward the sound of Russian voices—they were loud, close, coming closer—and then he wavered another split second, eyes whipping back toward me as I struggled up to my knees with the little bloody knife still gripped in my hand.

My gaze flickered toward the White House portico. So did the marksman's. In the same split second we saw it was empty. Or rather, it was rustling with swiftly moving dark suits, but no seated figure with a cigarette holder. *Thank you, Eleanor,* I thought disjointedly, gripping the knife even as another verse from the half-drunk delegation roared skyward.

"Mila?" Even closer than Krasavchenko and the others, I heard Alexei's irritated voice. The bushes rustled, and I saw the decision pass through my enemy's mud-colored eyes. He scooped up his rifle and its case in one swift movement and half a heartbeat later was running jerk-legged and stumbling in the opposite direction.

I tried to stand and nearly collapsed. My side was on fire from where he'd kicked me—*cracked rib,* I could hear Lena diagnosing, *maybe two*—and my throat was ablaze with pain from his half-throttling. Worse was the dizziness from his blow across my head; the world wouldn't stop spinning. But I lurched to my feet and went reeling after the man who'd attacked me: my suitor William Jonson, who had given me diamonds; the man who had aimed a rifle exactly like mine at the American president on the grounds of the White House. Nothing made sense.

Except his note tonight—written, I realized hazily, in the same writing that had scrawled so many epithets in Cyrillic. His latest note, saying: *We will meet again.*

"Mila, I've been looking for you—" Alexei caught me by the arm as I came staggering out of the bushes onto one of the gravel paths. "I was going to tell you, Kostia is . . ." But my husband stopped, staring at the marks on my throat, the knife in my hand.

"The man we called William Jonson tried to kill President Roosevelt," I managed to say, and saw the look of utter horror on Alexei's face as I began half running and half stumbling after the man with the mud-colored eyes.

I SHOULDN'T HAVE done it that way. I should have stopped in my tracks and started screaming until White House personnel came running. But I'd already warned Eleanor; it was up to her and the Secret Service to shield the president now. The man who'd tried to kill him was getting away, fast, and I didn't want to waste even the precious moments it would take me to explain what had happened to White House security. And it wasn't in me to *stop and scream* when death reared its head around me and bullets threatened to sing—everything I'd learned in a year at the front told me not to stop and scream, but to run in silence.

So I went after him.

Alexei hurried along beside me as I arrowed through the dark gardens toward the front of the White House. My husband was pouring out words in a disjointed torrent—"He said he'd knock you out, get some embarrassing pictures of you like you were drunk. I just wanted to see you taken down a peg. I didn't know, Mila, I didn't know he was—" and even with my attention fractured into slivers, I took it in for what it was. If an assassin were looking for someone to take the blame for a presidential hit, a girl sniper from the Soviet Union fit the bill. And if you needed a way to get to that girl sniper, her disgruntled husband fit the bill, too.

"Mila, you have to believe me, I'd never be part of something like this, I don't have a damned *death wish*, I wouldn't piss about with American assassination plots—"

I kept thinking we'd run into presidential bodyguards, White House staff, whoever was responsible for protecting these grounds. NKVD would have had any assassin up against a wall and half his fingernails yanked out by now. But there was no knot of guards with a handcuffed figure, no matter how my eyes hunted, and I wondered if someone had taken care of that. A change of roster to clear his path . . .

Even so, he couldn't go far. These grounds were fenced.

And then I realized someone had taken care of that for him too, as I came out through the dark gardens to the front of the White House where the Soviet embassy cars were pulled up for our departure . . . and saw, beyond them, a blue Packard driving fast but not suspiciously fast for the entry gates.

Stop and scream—that's what I could have done, even then. But the car would be through the gates and gone before anyone could hear me out, and I was still in the grip of that raging imperative to *fight*, not stop. This man had been under my nose for weeks, and I'd missed him. Missed a threat to Eleanor's husband, to the whole fragile alliance that was the only thing that would save my homeland, and now I had him on the run. I couldn't have stopped myself going after him if he'd leaned out the driver's side window and shot me in the head; I'd still have crawled blood-blind and dying after that Packard.

So I whirled and grabbed Alexei by the lapels, feeling an instant's twisted howl of frustration that Kostia wasn't here at my side tonight of all nights. "Alexei," I panted, dragging him toward the nearest embassy car, where the White House stewards were loading up the last of the delegation gifts. "That man nearly made you into an assassination's patsy. Help me now and you become the hero instead."

I swear I saw calculation go through his eyes. Even now he was looking for the angle that benefited him most. "What—"

In the open trunk of the embassy car, I saw a familiar mahogany box: the twin pistols from Chicago, complete with two magazines of .45-caliber ammunition. I yanked the box out, slung it under my arm, banged the trunk, and stumbled around toward the passenger side. I'd never in my life had cause to regret not learning to drive, but I regretted it now. Too late. "Get the president into a bunker if he isn't already, and tell your people to ask who drove a blue Packard onto the grounds," I said to the nearest astonished White House steward, then collapsed into the seat. "Alexei," I roared, slamming the door, "get in and *drive*."

CHAPTER 33

The marksman swore when he realized the embassy car had caught up with him as he turned onto 16th Street. "What the hell do you think you're doing?" he asked her. She should have stayed on White House grounds; raised the alarm. She didn't have a weapon beyond a *paring knife*, yet she'd come after him anyway?

Well, he'd made a study of her over the last few months—that very first morning he'd seen how she lost her temper and her script when surprised.

The fingers on his shooting hand were bleeding from the marks of her teeth, and his leg was a roar of pain. He'd strapped it tight with his tie, stanching the blood for now, but she'd stabbed him deep: if he hadn't been limping too badly to run, he'd have easily beat her to his Packard and been gone into the night before she could follow. Rage was beating through him in unsteady pulses as he blew through a stoplight past Dupont Circle and saw the embassy car blow through the light, too.

You cocked it up, he told himself brutally. He'd ignored his own rules about keeping his distance; he'd underestimated her from the start and let it make him careless. And now the chance at Roosevelt was gone, and he *hated* to miss a mark. He caught himself wondering if she was the same way. He didn't think they had much else in common—he shot people for hire; she shot people because they'd invaded her home, and he was well aware of the difference there—but he would have bet every diamond in his pocket and around her throat that she hated to fail as much as he did.

He was the one who'd failed tonight. He'd never be the man who killed a president. Instead, he was the man running away from a woman armed with a paring knife.

He almost wished she had a gun. He'd never gone up against someone with skills like his own before.

"Not rolling your eyes at me now, are you?" he said aloud.

The car behind ghosted along in silence. No horn-blaring, no trying to force him off the road. Just following as the marksman blasted down 16th Street. This late at night, the Washington streets were clear enough to drive fast and smooth. The marksman looked at his fuel gauge. A full tank; he could make for the city limits and lose her on the highways.

But what was the fun in that?

He made a sudden, vengeful turn onto Decatur Street, knowing exactly where he was going.

"STOP HERE," I told Alexei, gripping one of the now-loaded Colt pistols in my lap. I was still loading the other, but it slithered off my lap and under the seat in a cascade of loose bullets as Alexei stamped too hard on the brakes. He'd seen what I'd seen: the Packard ahead, abandoned at the side of Colorado Avenue, driver's door open.

"Where did he go?" Alexei gripped the wheel, white-faced. He was still imagining his future, if it got out that he'd aided a would-be presidential assassin, however unwittingly. I didn't know if he was envisioning an American electric chair or a Soviet bullet, but I doubted he liked either prospect. "Why would—"

"He wants to lose me in the woods." Rock Creek Park loomed on the other side of the street, a dark wall of trees. I'd walked here before, with Alexei—the day I'd bought the yellow satin dress I was wearing now. I wondered if the man we were tailing had been tailing *us,* back then. If he'd picked this place for a reason: because he and I both knew it. I cursed, fumbling under the seat for the fallen pistol.

"Maybe he just ditched the car and doubled back into the city between buildings," Alexei was muttering, staring at the Packard.

"He's in the woods." Because it was what I would have done. And he hoped I'd follow. *We will meet again.*

I abandoned scrambling for the second pistol, swept up as many of the loose bullets as I could, and got out of the car.

"Mila—" Alexei began.

"Go back to the White House and tell the ambassador everything," I said. "Raise the alarm. If I come out of these trees, that man is dead. If I don't, *I'm* dead and they can pick up his trail from my body. Either way, the President is safe and you get to be the hero who carried the warning." And I slammed the door and began walking toward the trees.

For the love of Lenin, I asked myself, *what are you doing?* I could focus my eyes again, but my head still pulsed. My ribs throbbed with every step. I was in my stocking feet since I'd kicked off my flimsy heels; I was decked out in yellow as bright as a traffic light rather than my sniper's camouflage, and I had a weapon I'd never fired before . . . but I didn't stop walking toward the trees, not hurrying, watching every shadow, because if this man were smart he'd wait for me just inside the tree line in case I came crashing down the street and into the wall of woods without looking around me. But I wasn't going to do that. Even caught at a disadvantage like this, I still knew my trade, and I knew something now about my enemy. He'd been hunting me since I came to this city, and he'd been hunting Franklin Roosevelt, who wasn't my president but was still—as long as I'd pledged friendship to his wife, and as long as he'd pledged friendship to my country—under my protection. And this man who'd thrown a challenge down to me with his diamonds and his hate-filled notes wasn't a sniper like me. He wasn't even an assassin, because he hadn't killed anyone—not tonight, anyway. He was just another marksman, and I was Lyudmila Pavlichenko.

And with every step toward the trees, I felt my sniper self filling me back up. Maybe I wasn't at my best with my injured ribs and ringing head, and maybe I looked like just another Washington elite hurrying home from a dinner party—some politician's pampered wife swathed in dappled furs, diamonds glittering at her throat under the streetlights. But it was All Hallows Eve, when dangerous things supposedly walked the night . . . and the most dangerous of them here was me. A woman who wore a lynx pelt like the predator she was, who strode under the waning moon not with a socialite's bustle or a housewife's scurry, but with a gunslinger's glide, shoulders swaying easy, hips loose and rolling below, pistol swinging ready at her side. I pulled the diamonds from around my neck and wrists and stuffed them into my coat pocket so their sparkle wouldn't give me away, and as I slid from the paved surface of Colorado Avenue into the dark choir of trees, the glossy propaganda poster-woman so at ease in the national spotlight disappeared. Breathing through her skin was Lady Midnight, Lady Death, the woman who had terrified Nazi invaders from Odessa to Sevastopol.

Even if I'd been living soft on tour for two months, the muscles of my legs remembered what it was to clamber Kamyshly gully and No-Name Height under fifteen kilos of snipers' gear. My feet were being sliced and bruised beneath me, but I put the pain away along with the pain of my cracked ribs, finding the nearly invisible trail and noiselessly following its bend. I went slow, keeping low to the ground and taking cover behind every tree trunk and boulder, listening for the faintest rustle or creak that was out of place.

Where are you?

I remembered the way to Boulder Bridge perfectly, even in the blackness of night. I was edging past the jutting rock where I'd lingered the last time to gaze over the ridge, pressing through tangles of mountain laurel toward the bend that would lead to the creek and the stone bridge, when instinct raked the back of my neck with dark claws. The barest rustle of leaves, a faint slide of pebbles, the tiniest click of metal where no metal belonged in the tapestry of night noises—I threw myself flat on the earth without a second's hesitation.

An instant later the crack of a gunshot echoed through the dark, and I heard a bullet bury itself in a tree trunk just beyond me.

I rolled hard to my left and didn't stop. Another shot whined as I went into a tangle of mountain laurel, scrambled through it with twigs raking my face, and finally wedged myself in a ball behind a boulder of rough granite.

He's up on that rocky outcrop, I thought, mentally tracing the shot's angle. *The one where I stopped to take in the view. The one that made me think,* "What a perfect place for a stakeout."

IT WAS A perfect place for a stakeout. The marksman lay flat, the Mosin-Nagant's barrel braced, the ground spread below in a perfect arc. If she moved from behind that boulder in any direction, he'd split her through the eyes—at this distance he couldn't miss, even in the dark.

Now it was a waiting game. He almost called down to her, in sheer curiosity. But what was there to say? The question had been asked silently: *Which of us is better?* The answer would come at the tip of a bullet.

Again, he wished she had a gun. It would have made things more interesting.

HE HAD A Russian rifle; I had an American pistol. The irony was not lost on me. My Colt wouldn't be effective past fifty meters, but it was better than no firearm at all. I lay behind the boulder, going through the pockets of my lynx coat to verify what else I had: the paring knife, a handful of loose bullets, the discarded jewelry I'd pulled off at the tree line . . . and among the rattle of diamonds, a matchbox.

I heard a rustle of leaves as he moved in his nest and thought about trying for a shot—but in the dark, aiming uphill with an unfamiliar weapon, I'd have to expose myself to get clear aim, and that meant the marksman's shot was far more likely to hit than mine. He had picked this ground, not me; it favored him, not me, and I didn't want to tip my hand until the ground was mine. Right now he thought I was cowering here unarmed, the quivering fool who'd rushed blindly, rashly into the night after her enemy.

The air between us shivered with unsaid words. I almost called out to him—*Who are you? Why did you do this? Are you a fanatic or just a hired gunman*?—but there was no point. It didn't matter who he was or why he did this dark work. I'd been driven by war to find the midnight side of my moon; he'd followed his willingly. That was all I needed to know.

But I could still feel the pulsing beat of his curiosity all but touching me through the dark. He was watching, he was eager . . . and the time was now.

I squeezed my eyes shut and struck the entire bundle of matches to life by touch. Feeling the flare in my fist, I thrust my hand up above the rock and flung the burning handful out like a scatter of fireflies. The minute the marksman's night vision was wrecked by the flashes of light I was moving, eyes still shut, bursting out from behind the boulder and flinging myself down the slope toward the creek in the direction I'd already mapped out for my feet. His shot went off somewhere behind, nowhere near me; I heard him grunt, heard the uneven thump of his boots crashing off into the trees at the wrong angle. Heard what I thought was a gasp of pain and smiled at the thought of the knife wound through his calf. I opened my eyes then and went still against the nearest tree, listening with all my senses to the living dark. Distant crunching of leaves; the marksman was still pressing the wrong way, but he'd soon get his bearings.

The forest is like a temple, I remembered Vartanov saying. *Be respectful, and the woods will reward you.* I used every trick the old ranger had ever taught me about how to move through trees, making my silent way down to the creek and then stealing along its pebbled bank. I knew exactly where I needed to be.

The frozen moon slid out from behind a cloud, and I saw the dark arch of the bridge. I scrambled through the boulders and rocks of the bank, freezing water numbing my bruised feet in their shredded stockings, dead leaves clinging to the sodden hem of my furs, and then I was onto the bridge and moving across it at a flat sprint. If the marksman was already behind me, this was his chance to drill me between the shoulder blades—but there was only the burbling rush of the creek below as I melted off the bridge and down onto the far-side bank beside the stone arch.

It was near midnight and icy cold, the ground beside the water hard-frozen and glittering with frost, but I stripped off my lynx furs, dropping the loose bullets into the bodice of my dress. I gathered an armload of wet leaves and driftwood, casting it all on top of a rock beside the bridge and just above the water. I worked frantically fast, going still every time I heard a new sound. Once or twice a distant drunken shout came to my ears; once I thought I saw the outline of some passerby in the distant trees—this park wasn't completely deserted, even late at night—but it was too dark and cold for anyone but the odd tramp or troublemaker. However this duel finished between the marksman and me, there were no innocents here to get between us. I was almost grateful to him, for moving the game to an arena where we could fight things out alone.

I finished up my heap of leaves and driftwood under the bridge and tucked my coat around it to look like a woman huddling under the stone arch. I took the diamond brooch with its flashing tremblers (had I really put it on only a few hours ago at the White House, as Eleanor beamed over the table of gifts?) and pinned it to the fur collar, where it would catch the moonlight. I added the necklace and bracelets too, tucking them around the coat's sleeves, and stood back to examine the effect. *You're no Ivan,* I thought, remembering the dummy soldier Kostia and I had built together for the duel with the German sniper overlooking a very different bridge outside Sevastopol. *But you'll have to do.* From a distance, to my enemy's eyes, it would with luck look like I'd crossed the bridge, slid exhausted to hide underneath on the far side, and waited there trembling and praying for him to cross . . . unaware, of course, that my diamonds were catching the moonlight and giving away my position, stupid commie bitch that I was.

He was the stupid bitch, to come at me like this. To assume a real sniper would ever, ever enter a duel unarmed.

I found a big lightning-forked beech tree on the bank—plenty of foliage, perfect vantage point. I'd never mounted a stakeout in a satin evening dress before, but at least the bright yellow turned to gray in these deep shadows. I wriggled up into the tree, feet wedging painfully against the bark, and then I nested into a fork in the branches and turned myself to stone.

CURSING, LIMPING, AND increasingly cold, the marksman reminded himself that all she could do was hide. It was a smart trick with the matches—he'd gotten turned around in the dark, losing his night vision and arrowing off a good quarter mile in the wrong direction before getting his bearings—but he was back on her trail now, heading toward Boulder Bridge. Two months ago he'd stood on the bank of Rock Creek covertly watching the Russian woman argue with her husband on that bridge . . . Following her at the time, he'd noted how she wore no perfume that would linger in the air and make her trail easier to follow. She still wasn't wearing any, and he cursed, wishing she were.

He'd ceased enjoying himself. He wanted a beer and a painkiller for this leg; he wanted to telephone Pocket Square and tell him the job was off. He just wanted this duel done.

I WATCHED THE moon slide behind a cloud, plunging the world into midnight. The bridge was a dusky arch against the black silk rush of the water, and the cold sang a high freezing note, moving into my body like ice fronds creeping across the surface of a lake. An October night in Washington wasn't cold the way a Crimean January was cold, but without the lynx coat my bare flesh was marbling. I had to keep shaking out my hands, rubbing them together to keep them from trembling. My side burned. My throat ached. My legs cramped. My skin froze. I wished I had my Three Line rifle, not this unfamiliar pistol braced rock-steady in the crook of a tree branch. The last time I'd fought a duel I'd been padded in camouflage and wool with Kostia at my back, idly talking in the lulls about whether a face-off between two snipers constituted a fair fight. I yearned for a pinch of dry tea and a lump of sugar to chew; for a heel of black bread with strips of fatback and salt. I yearned for Kostia.

I held my position. I'd hold it all night if I had to.

A rumble of thunder sounded overhead in the rushing black clouds. Even as I prayed for rain not to fall, I adjusted my Colt against the branch and took aim at the central bridge stone. I got three shots off in the masking roll of the next crack of thunder—three shots weren't going to teach me enough about this weapon, her unique variations to the song they all sang in my hands, but it would have to be sufficient. My shots landed high; I was bracing my wrist up. I could compensate for that, but how much? A pistol was so unforgiving compared to a rifle; the tiniest movement could throw my shot off. For a sure hit, I would have to let him get close. Very close. Calculations split and slid through my mind as I shivered under the rising snap of the wind and thunder continued to peal.

And then I saw a limping shadow moving down the far side of the bank, and I went utterly still as the countdown began. Lady Midnight's countdown, the one I'd sung softly to myself from the days I'd been shooting at wooden targets to the day I killed my first enemies outside Odessa, all the way through 309 officially tallied kills and who knew how many unofficial ones, to *here*, to *now*, to this black, ghost-filled night on the far side of the world.

One . . . the first cool, measuring glance at the target, the moment the soul falls silent and the eye takes over.

Two . . . measuring the horizontal sight line; I didn't have telescopic sights tonight, but I could imagine the lines framing the marksman's shoulders as he stepped out of the trees.

Three . . . using that benchmark to calculate distance. Hardly any distance at all here, but still not close enough. My heavy .45-caliber bullet would drop fast as soon as it left the barrel, but I hadn't put in thousands of rounds of practice with this weapon to learn how fast.

Four . . . checking the bullet in the chamber.

Five . . . nestling the barrel forward a hair through the foliage as he stepped onto the bridge with his rifle leveled.

Six . . . watch him stop, watch him catch the flash of the diamonds just barely visible beneath the far arch of the bridge.

Seven . . . become stone, become ice, become so still frost could gather on me—all as I watched the President's would-be killer raise his weapon, satisfaction in every line of his body because he thought he had me dead in his sights.

Eight . . . final adjustment for wind, normally. No need here.

Nine . . . take aim.

Ten . . . breathe in.

Eleven . . . breathe out.

THE MARKSMAN WAS smiling as he fired, straight into the huddled heart of the lynx-fur mass. The girl sniper toppled on one side in the sluggishly moving stream, and he felt the slow, ecstatic beat of his heart as her arm flopped out. *Got you, you Red bitch.*

Then he saw the diamond bracelet slide off the fur sleeve without catching on a limp hand. Saw the fur collar gaping around a mass of pine needles. Saw the necklace he'd given her, wound around a sodden bundle of pine branches and sparkling up at him with a cold, merry light.

He looked wildly up from the dummy and saw the glitter. Not of diamonds, but of moonlight off a gun muzzle. *Oh, fu—*

TWELVE.

My shot took him clean through the right eye.

CHAPTER 34

I *want to go home.*

All my light-footedness was gone as I began making my way out of Rock Creek Park. Every ache and pain had flooded back into me the moment I slid half frozen and shaking with aftermath out of that lightning-forked beech tree. I'd still made myself wade down into the creek where the dead man had toppled, heave him onto his back, and go through all his pockets. No identification, no keys, not so much as a handkerchief or a book of matches to tell me who he was or where he'd come from—only his rifle, and a scatter of bullets and odd little rough rocks in one pocket, which I transferred to mine so I'd have something to show the Soviet ambassador. Shrugging my cold-marbled arms gratefully back into the sodden lynx sleeves, I stood for a moment looking down at the man I'd killed. Number 310, looking up at the sky with his blank, unremarkable face, the moon reflecting glossy and empty from his open eye. He looked surprised. They so often did. Even when you were the one used to dealing death, you were still surprised when it came for you.

What's your name? I wondered, looking down at him. And then in a sudden surge of exhaustion and distaste, I didn't care. I didn't care who he was or who he'd been working for. I didn't care about anything but going home and holding my son in my arms, cradling his beautiful head between my hands as I promised him on my life that I would never leave him again.

So I left the marksman behind, jamming the pistol that had killed him into my coat pocket and limping on my torn soles back toward the city street and the abandoned Packard. Once I got there, it was some six or seven kilometers back to the hotel on foot . . . I'd walked it before, swinging my yellow satin dress in its shop bag, but that had been on a warm day in comfortable canvas lace-ups, not in utterly shredded American stockings on a blustery midnight. But I'd have to walk it now; I couldn't drive and I didn't have a single coin for a taxi. Would the delegation have returned to the hotel by now, or were they embroiled in uproar at the White House? Had the White House even realized they'd had an assassin on their grounds, or—

"Mila!" Alexei's voice, sharp with alarm through the trees. "Is that you?"

"Alexei?" I pulled up, swaying with exhaustion—he stood just inside the tree line at the edge of the park, a silhouette against the shadowed saplings, streetlights not far behind. "Why didn't you go raise the alarm?" Even as anger went through me in a spasm, relief did, too. Now I could collapse into the embassy car and he could drive us wherever we needed to go to make our report. I'd make him a hero in the telling, just for that—give him all the credit he liked, as long as I could sit down.

"Is he dead?" Alexei asked, coming a step closer.

"Dead under Boulder Bridge," I said wearily, and that was when my husband shot me.

The bullet whisked through my hair. It should have sunk through my left eye socket but I'd seen his arm rise, seen the glint of metal where there shouldn't have been metal, and that dark claw-rake of instinct sent me lurching sideways before I'd registered what was happening, so the bullet grooved the tip of my ear instead of burying itself in my brain. There was nothing controlled this time about my flight; I went half scrambling and half galloping into the thicket of brush on all fours, crashing like a panicked deer.

"You're wondering how I got a weapon." Alexei's voice was shockingly conversational. "The Colt that fell under the seat . . . along with a few rounds of ammunition."

I fetched up behind a big half-rotted tree stump, both hands clamped over my mouth to stop my ragged gasps from escaping. The tip of my earlobe dripped hot blood down onto my shoulder. My husband had shot me. Alexei had *shot* me. And I wasn't even surprised. He knew he'd never win me back, and even if he had, he'd never have been satisfied living the rest of his life hanging on the arm of a more famous wife. Maybe he wouldn't have thought to kill me on his own, but the marksman had handed him a chance on a silver platter: either I'd have died in the duel with the President's would-be assassin and Alexei would get to raise the alarm alone, the grieving widower and heroic messenger—or I killed the marksman, Alexei killed me when I was exhausted and off guard, and the rest went according to script. Either way, he didn't have to share the glory with me, and he was free of his bitch wife.

Or maybe he hadn't even thought it through that much. Maybe he just wanted me dead and thought he could get away with it.

"Don't run, Mila." I heard Alexei reloading his Colt, and I scrabbled for my own in my sodden pocket. "I saw how wet that coat was. You'll freeze to death out here if you run, and it won't be pretty. I'll make it quick."

I got my pistol into my cold-numbed hand, frantically reloading, still fighting for breath. I risked a glance over the stump, and he was nowhere in sight. He wasn't stupid; he knew not to give me a silhouette. I'd be foolish to underestimate him simply because he wasn't the marksman I'd just left dead. My husband was no sniper, but he'd already winged me in near-total darkness, from thirty paces, with an unfamiliar weapon. And he was warm, rested, alert, committed; a man with dry clothes, sturdy shoes, and the prize of a lifetime—freedom, fame—within his grasp. Not an exhausted, half-frozen woman with two broken ribs and pulverized feet, who'd left a blood trail clear from Rock Creek while driving herself to the breaking point dispatching *another* man bent on killing her tonight.

For an instant, I felt my whole shivering body contract in on itself, and I understood why animals sometimes froze in a predator's path and waited with dulled eyes for death to claim them. I was so tired. I'd shot so many enemies in Odessa, in Sevastopol—now I'd crossed half the globe and I was still shooting enemies. When did they stop coming? When would I look around and see no one advancing to kill me? Could I just close my eyes and let it all stop?

But Alexei wasn't any enemy; he was the first enemy. The one I'd outgrown, the one I'd stopped being afraid of a long time ago when larger monsters entered my sights . . . but still the first. The one whose gaze had prickled me as I pulled a five-year-old Slavka away from him at the shooting range, the one who made me think perhaps it would be just as well if I learned to shoot. Not only so I had a father's skills to teach my son someday, but if the moment came to defend us.

Well. Here it was. Die here, and Alexei would try his best to swan home a hero and claim my son.

"Mila?" His voice sounded again, impatient, taut. "Don't play dead. I know I didn't hit you. If I had, you'd be screaming."

I drew a deep, slow breath. "You have no idea what makes me scream. In battlefield or in bed, you pathetic sad sack of a man."

I *felt* his surprise through the shadows. Him behind a rocky slope somewhere to the southwest of me; me behind my tree stump: this was another waiting game, like the one I'd played not even an hour ago with the marksman in his nest and me pinned behind a boulder. Only the marksman could have waited forever. I hadn't known his name, but I'd known he'd had a sniper's patience. I'd had to play my trick with the matches to change the game, change the ground, change the beat.

I no longer had any tricks up my sleeve, just a pistol and a few remaining shots. But this was an enemy I knew, right down to his bones.

"You'll never get away with killing me," I called into the dark. "Everyone in the delegation knows how I despise you. They'll never believe you had nothing to do with my death."

"I'm going to be the hero of the night," he called back. "Once I tell them where to find the man who tried to kill the president—"

"You're still just the messenger. They'll know I'm the one who took care of him. They'll fete me in Red Square with a citywide parade and make me posthumous Hero of the Soviet Union. You'll be playing second best even at my funeral."

"You're my wife." His voice rose, despite himself. I was getting to him. "That famous name you're boasting of, that's *my* name."

"Not anymore." I flexed my right hand, shaking out the tremors. "You dreamed of making your name famous, Alexei? You dreamed it would be known from Moscow to Vladivostok? You dreamed of Lieutenant Pavlichenko, Hero of the Soviet Union? Well, it's all coming true. But for me, not you." I hissed the words through the dark between us like a viper, sinking each one deep. He'd never listened when I said no, never heard when I begged *please*, but he'd hear this. Maybe it was the only thing he was capable of hearing: that his grand dreams had blossomed for someone else. "I didn't even want fame. All I wanted was to defend my home. I didn't want fame, but I still got it—not you. You're still just what you've always been: a dog eating scraps from someone else's table. You don't have a drop of real heroism in you. All you've ever been is a collection of pieces scavenged from someone else—mostly me."

I heard him breathing faster, felt the pulse of his anger rising. *If you were clever, Alexei, you'd abandon this madness and go back to the hotel,* I thought. *Leave me out here waiting; concoct a story to tell the delegation and get in front of whatever I might say.* But he wasn't going to do that. Whatever had pitched him over that final edge and made him want me dead—the sight of me in Kostia's arms, maybe, or the sight of my name in one too many newspaper headlines—he wasn't going to let me leave Washington alive. He'd made his choice, and he was in it till the end.

"How does it feel?" I taunted, voice rising. "Knowing that the Pavlichenko recorded in the history books won't be you? It'll be your child bride instead. It'll be *me.*"

The marksman wouldn't have broken at a schoolyard taunt. My husband did. I heard Alexei come out from behind the rocky slope to close the distance, saw his arm level, his teeth bared in a snarl of utter hatred—and I was erupting to my feet, bracing every exhausted muscle in my body behind the pistol as I fired once, twice, three times.

It happened in the space of a heartbeat, in the blink of a sniper's eye, in the flash of light off a diamond. He swayed—my husband, my first fear, my last shard of an outgrown life—and then he fell.

Alexei was dead.

I SUMMONED THE invisible steel, force, and spirit of Eleanor Roosevelt as I came into the hotel court at nearly two in the morning: my feet bloody, my face bruised and filthy, my sodden lynx furs wrapped over a destroyed satin gown. As my furious minder and half the delegation staff flooded toward me in a storm of Moscow suits and questions, I drew myself up as if I were six feet tall, pulled my coat collar around me like I'd seen Eleanor settle her famous fox stole, and put my hand out with all the absolute authority of the First Lady of the United States.

"Bit of a to-do with my husband," I said breezily, cutting off Yuri's *Where were you?* and Krasavchenko's *How dare you?* and Pchelintsev's *The First Lady said.* "I started feeling unwell at the White House, he offered as delegation doctor to drive me back early, and he ended up picking a quarrel and shoving me out somewhere near Rock Creek Park. The car's still there on Colorado and Blagden; it's full of delegation gifts, so I suggest you send someone to retrieve it. We will all assemble in Comrade Krasavchenko's room in forty-five minutes for a fuller report, but right now I intend to clean up."

The men parted for me as I made for the elevator, still spilling questions which I ignored. No one was saying anything about President Roosevelt or a hullabaloo at the White House, and that told me he was safe. Eleanor's husband was sleeping between crisp sheets right now, safe and sound . . . or perhaps he was hard at work at his desk despite the hour, and Eleanor was right there beside him. Making plans, perhaps, for when they could broach the matter of a second front to lend aid to my countrymen.

My glowering minder made to get into the elevator with me, and I put out my hand again. "Yuri," I said mildly, "*no*." And he stepped back and let the doors shut between us.

Tonight I'd survived two duels, countless minor injuries, and a seven-kilometer midnight walk on my shredded feet—yet the thing that nearly felled me was arriving at my hotel room two floors up and realizing I had no idea where the key was. I sagged against the door, shaking with exhaustion, wondering if I could curl up and go to sleep right here on the threshold—and then I nearly collapsed in a heap as the door opened inward and I fell right into Kostia's arms.

"Mila—" He gripped me, pulled me into the room and against his chest. My teeth were chattering too much to say anything, so I just clutched him. He was warm against me, granite-solid and night-silent in his dark shirt with the sleeves rolled up. He'd clearly let himself in with the key I'd given him days ago; waited for me in the chair by the desk where his borrowed copy of Walt Whitman lay facedown.

"You're h-here," I said, still shaking with cold, and the import of that struck me like a blow. He was *here*, not on his way to New York or to his family. He was here. With me, his face turned toward mine, not turned away to find a new future far from our homeland.

"I'm here," he said quietly, and that was all.

When I'd returned from my duel with the German sniper in Sevastopol, it had been Lyonya who peeled me out of my ice-stiffened clothes, wrapped me in a blanket, and began rubbing the life back into my cold feet and cramped shoulders. Now it was Kostia who stripped the creek-soaked lynx fur off my back, peeled away the destroyed yellow dress beneath it, and without comment laid aside my pistol and the little pile of diamonds all tangled up with loose .45 slugs and Alexei's wallet and ID. He didn't burst out with questions like the men downstairs; he just stripped me down and tucked me under the blankets, then crawled in and pulled me against him to warm me. "They said you hadn't come back from the White House, Mila. The First Lady told the ambassador you'd taken off running." His voice was normal, unconcerned, but I felt the tension humming through him like steel hawsers. Because unlike the men downstairs, he could recognize the aftermath of a sniper duel when he saw one.

I told him what happened. I'd go through it again in half an hour, for the benefit of the whole delegation, but this was a chance to get my facts in a row . . . figure out what I'd say, and what I'd leave out. Kostia pulled back when I finished, looked at me. I looked back, my teeth still chattering, reactions finally setting in now that I'd stopped long enough to let my guard down. "I killed Alexei," I repeated, stark and plain, not having to care if there were ears listening in this room. I couldn't stop shaking; I couldn't stop seeing his face. But I felt not one straw's worth of guilt. *He's gone. He's finally gone.* He wanted me, and if he couldn't have me, he wanted me dead, and now he was the one dead.

"You left them?" Kostia asked.

"Where they fell." I'd tell Krasavchenko and the Soviet ambassador where, and they could do what they liked about retrieving the bodies or leaving them to rot unidentified; involving the White House or not. Whichever way they decided to handle it, I knew it would be done with maximum discretion. This was one escapade by the Soviet girl sniper that would *not* be written up in any American newspapers.

The only thing I'd insist on, when I gave my briefing, was a full and comprehensive warning to Eleanor: *your husband has enemies who want him dead.* I'd taken care of one, but I was leaving American shores. She'd have to take over the watch.

But I trusted she could do it.

It occurred to me that when I pulled the trigger tonight—first on the marksman, then on Alexei—I had not once intoned my desperate prayer of *Don't miss.* Perhaps Eleanor's lesson had finally sunk home: the knowledge that even if I'd missed, I'd have gotten up, fired again, kept going until I succeeded. Until I saved the American president; until I saved myself.

Kostia was still looking at me, gaze urgent enough to burn. *What do you need?* he was telling me. *How can I help?* I just nestled into his chest, floating somewhere between warmth and cold, between the dregs of old fury and the restlessness of a finished hunt, burrowing into this oasis of warmth and safety before I'd have to rise and make my report. I saw the marksman lying in the creek, an enigma to the end. I saw Alexei's eyes staring up at the gibbous moon, empty as glass. I wondered what the official excuse would be when he failed to return to the Soviet Union. Would they say he'd defected or—

My eyes snapped suddenly wide at the word *defected,* half stupefied though I was by the warmth creeping through my limbs and the leak of adrenaline seeping out of them. "Kostia, where have *you* been tonight?" He'd skipped the farewell dinner and he'd clearly come to some decision during that time, but how?

"The Soviet embassy," he said into my shoulder blade. "I've been heading back there every week, whenever I had a few hours free. I needed a Cyrillic typewriter."

I blinked. "A Cyrillic typewriter?"

"I can't give you diamonds." Kostia nodded at the glittering heap on my desk, raising himself on one elbow to reach a pile of paper sitting on the nightstand. "All I could think of was this. I finished it tonight."

I snaked an arm out from under the coverlet to take the pages, reading the title at the top in neatly typed Cyrillic letters. " 'Bogdan Khmelnitsky, the Ukraine's accession to Russia in 1654, and the activities of the Pereyaslav Council: a student dissertation by Lyudmila Mikhailovna Pavlichenko,' " I read in astonishment. "You . . . you retyped my dissertation?"

"Pecked it out with two fingers." Kostia kissed the back of my neck. "You had blood all over the last one."

I wondered if this had been intended as a goodbye gift. Maybe, as he typed through my final footnotes tonight, he'd changed his mind about leaving. Or maybe finishing it had been a way to keep himself from turning toward the life that beckoned here.

Time enough to talk about that later, once we had real privacy.

"Thank you," I whispered, smoothing my hand over the pages. The marksman had given me diamonds. My husband had utterly ignored anything I told him I wanted, because he always knew better.

My sniper partner had retyped my dissertation with two fingers on a borrowed machine.

Kostia was sliding toward sleep in the way that snipers did, still full of questions, and full of tension too, but the body taking any opportunity for rest that it could. Careful not to wake him, I slid out of bed and into some fresh clothes, wondering if we'd all still be departing for Canada tomorrow or not.

As I stood sorting the bullets from the diamond jewelry and those odd little rough rocks I'd taken from the marksman's pocket, I found an unfamiliar lump. In Rock Creek Park, I'd automatically collected the shells from my shots that killed Alexei and the marksman—my hand had evidently swept up another lump of metal from the dead leaves. I blinked in bemusement at the modest gold signet ring with tiny dirtied chips of diamond, sized for a man's finger, metal dulled as though it had been buried from sunlight for decades. Inside the band were worn English letters—I couldn't make out the first, but the second was definitely an R.

I held it to the light, a memory nagging for a moment before it slipped into place: a White House aide on the mansion's lawn, telling me the story of President Teddy Roosevelt on a hike, losing a ring near Boulder Bridge forty years ago. Could this be it? I turned it over in my hand. It was a lovely thing, this marker from my final dueling ground. A sign, perhaps. I'd had two husbands, one in law and one in my heart; one who had fallen in Washington's woods where I'd never walk again, one who had fallen in Sevastopol where I might never walk again either unless it could be wrested out of Nazi hands. I should never have married the first husband, and time had stolen my chance of legally marrying the second.

I wouldn't make a mistake like either of those again. I wouldn't miss this third precious chance.

I leaned over Kostia, dozing so lightly, and folded the signet ring into his loose-curled hand. "When we get back to Moscow," I whispered softly, preparing to go meet with the rest of the delegation and pass on my full account, "marry me."

Notes by the First Lady

I watch my husband's chest rise and fall in sleep. He'll get far less rest than usual tonight—the hullabaloo behind closed doors, after Lyudmila's exit, was considerable, and there have been confused telephone calls winging back and forth from the Soviet embassy and Franklin's private line. The picture is far from complete, but one thing is clear: the immediate danger has been taken care of, thanks to the young woman who leaves our shores tomorrow.

Welcoming her to my home, I had no idea the service she would render me and this country. I only thought she might be of interest, another useful female of the type Franklin likes to collect and hone and use—use up, sometimes—in this great work of his.

Franklin's women. I am sure many books will be written about him someday, but I hope there will also be books about us. The woman who was his wife, his eyes and ears . . . the women who served on his cabinet and at his side in the White House . . . and the woman from a nation halfway around the world, a nation entirely foreign to us and sometimes frightening, who held no oath to him but nevertheless threw down her life in his defense.

I watch his chest rise and fall in the dark for another long moment, smiling. Then I close the door.

There is still much work to be done tonight before I find my bed . . . but a Russian bullet has given me peace and safety to do it.

CHAPTER 35

It was a long two months more before I found myself back on Soviet soil, disembarking from a four-engine B-24 Liberator bomber after an endless night flight from Glasgow to Vnukovo airfield. Twelve hours in the bomber's belly, the inside sparkling with frost like the Snow Queen's bedroom, the entire delegation wrapped in furs to the whites of our eyes and talking of the tour we'd finally, *finally* completed. But I wasn't thinking now of the glittering functions we'd attended in Montreal and London, Cambridge and Birmingham, Newcastle and Liverpool—not as we touched down at last in an enormous frosty field ringed by a blue belt of snowy woods. *Home,* I thought. I was supposed to be gone only one month—it had been four.

A lifetime.

Disembarking, gloved hand linked with Kostia's—I could feel the hard circle of the gold signet ring on his finger. My heart pounded as I saw shadowy figures breaking away from the waiting crowd, running toward the bomber. Pchelintsev was already embracing his wife, Krasavchenko kissing his father on both cheeks, but I had no thought for them. I could see my mother with her long plait, bundled like a round little owl . . . and breaking away from her, sprinting toward me, a smaller figure.

My hand tore from Kostia's as I broke into a run. I shed Lady Death behind me, I shed the famous sniper of a thousand photographs, I shed my proud hopes of seeing Allied soldiers in Europe soon to buoy our eastern front—I shed everything but the sight of the child running toward me, ten years old, lanky with growth, his face alight. I flung my arms around him and then my legs buckled underneath me and I crashed to my knees in the snow, holding my son in a hug like steel, weeping unashamedly into his hair.

Mila Pavlichenko was finally home.

EPILOGUE

Eleanor Roosevelt Arrives in Moscow

October 10, 1957

Mrs. Roosevelt, may I present Lyudmila Pavlichenko, Hero of the Soviet Union."

We looked at each other for a long moment—long enough for whispers to ripple through the Committee of Soviet Women clustered around us in the airless public hall. Fifteen years since the former First Lady and I had set eyes on each other. I took in the plain suit and black hat, the lines of grief that the loss of her extraordinary husband had carved on her face, and knew she was absorbing the changes time had wrought in me. I was forty-one now, no longer the angry young lieutenant who had eyed her so warily over the White House breakfast of eggs and bacon. My dark hair showed wings of gray at the temples, and my medals were pinned to a businesslike suit instead of an olive-drab uniform.

But I could feel my face cracking in a huge smile, a smile that mirrored in her face under the white hair. "Darling Lyudmila," she said, coming forward.

"Eleanor," I breathed, leaning into the embrace, and there was a ripple of applause as the two of us beamed at each other. Perhaps fifteen years was not so very long, after all. We had met once more during my English tour when Eleanor came to visit the Churchills, and we had corresponded when I returned to the Soviet Union. I'd sent a letter of condolence on the death of President Roosevelt ("Eleanor, I remember the press of his hand as though it were yesterday"); she'd congratulated me after the war on the news that as a fifth-year student of the Kiev State University history faculty, I'd finished my dissertation with a grade of Excellent ("Lyudmila, I confess I do not remember who Bogdan Khmelnitsky is, and I pray you will not tell me!")

And here she was in Moscow, a First Lady no longer but still a diplomatic force to be reckoned with, our positions reversed: now she was the one on a goodwill tour of my country.

There were speeches to sit through (there are always speeches); there were hands to be shaken (there are always handshakes); there were commemorative plaques to be presented (for the love of Lenin, no more plaques—where is a Hero of the Soviet Union to put them all?). But at long last the former First Lady and I were permitted to retire to my Moscow apartment, sitting with our feet up, drinking tea from the samovar in the corner, security details and NKVD minders alike waiting outside.

"You have a beautiful home, Lyudmila." Her eyes took in the apartment I'd been awarded: four whole rooms near the center of Moscow, not far from the Soviet Navy department where I'd worked, an entire wall filled with nothing but my books. "Does your son live with you?"

"He has a place of his own now. Graduated with distinction from Moscow University's law faculty." My Slavka, a young man now, so steady and kind, his dark hair and stocky build marking him a younger version of my father. Nothing, fortunately, like his own.

"He must make you proud." Eleanor studied me, stirring her tea. "You look happy, Lyudmila. I confess I worried that it might make you bitter—the fact that you never returned to the front, after your goodwill tour."

"It was determined that I would be of more use as a sniper instructor." Yes, I'd been bitterly disappointed at the time . . . but as Kostia pointed out, if I'd returned to sniping, I would probably have died in Stalingrad with so many other sharpshooters, and that would have been a great propaganda victory for the Germans. Instead I was assigned to train new snipers—and not just boys. Girls passed through my hands, cherry-cheeked girls like I'd once been, so fierce and burning bright. I'd poured my skills into them, told them how to manage the shakes in their hands when they made their first kills, and that shaking hands didn't mean they lacked courage. I taught them how to camouflage themselves and care for their weapons; how to scavenge battlefields for spare cloth, because the Red Army would never give them enough for their monthlies; how to avoid amorous officers and how to cross no-man's-land on lynx feet so silent that the long-dead Vartanov would have blinked tears of pride.

I taught them to try again without shame when they missed a shot. That failure was not always a death sentence.

I taught them everything I knew and I saluted them when they left me and I grieved them when they died . . . and the ones who lived, I hosted here in Moscow to drink vodka and trade stories of old nightmares and comrades in arms long gone, and we'd part with tears on our cheeks and smiles on our lips: the girl snipers who lived.

Maybe I could have added more Nazis to my tally, but more than two thousand women fought for their homeland as sharpshooters by the end of the war, and a good portion of them were trained by me. The tally of every woman I trained stands alongside mine, and as a woman of forty-one I cannot look back and see my switch from sniper to sniper instructor as a waste.

"Besides," I said now to Eleanor, smiling, "I wanted to be a historian, not a sniper. And I became one."

"Certainly you did—Lyudmila, are you putting *jam* in your tea?"

"It's the Russian way." I added a heaping spoonful of cherry jam to her cup. "I hope you'll have time on your visit to meet with the Committee of War Veterans?"

"Of course. You work with them now that you're retired from—what was your position again?"

"Research assistant in the Soviet Navy fleet history section." I'd retired a few years ago, my old war wounds acting up. All those concussions, all that shell shock, all that scar tissue . . . it sank deeper as I got older, rather than fading away. "But retirement is no reason to sit around doing nothing."

"I could not agree more," said the former First Lady.

Kostia slipped in then, still lean as a wire, his hair now iron gray, our dog bounding in front of him. He'd finished his war at my side, my shadow to the end, helping me train young snipers . . . and then he found himself at the Red Star Kennel helping train military dogs, who he said were much smarter than most military recruits. We had a big black Russian terrier puppy of our own now; Kostia romped with her all over Gorky Park every day, ignoring his old limp. "My husband," I introduced him as he came to drop a kiss on my hair and shake Eleanor's hand, but no more than that. For many reasons, Kostia kept a low profile.

"He looks familiar," Eleanor said thoughtfully as Kostia nodded farewell and took the dog into the next room for a brushing. "Was he on the Washington delegation?"

"Mmm," I murmured.

"Perhaps I'm thinking of your first husband . . . I didn't realize until later that *he* had accompanied the tour to Washington."

"Mmm." I smiled.

"You didn't paint a very flattering portrait of him, little as you told me." Eleanor's eyes regarded me calmly over the rim of her glass. "Perhaps it's no great tragedy that he didn't end up leaving with the rest of you."

"Mmm." Alexei Pavlichenko had officially died on tour of a burst appendix—all part of the frantic behind-the-scenes scurrying to make sure nothing from Rock Creek Park surfaced to embarrass either the Soviet delegation or the White House. Nothing at all, of course, was said of the marksman.

I still woke at night sometimes thinking of his mud-colored eyes, wondering what his name had been. Who had hired him. Eleanor and I had never had the opportunity to speak of such things, even when we met afterward in England.

Now . . .

"Remember that eccentric American businessman who proposed marriage to me?" I mused, stirring my tea. "I always wondered what became of him. Who his friends were, the people he worked with."

(It would be foolish to assume there were no listening ears tuned to hear this conversation. Eleanor and I might be friends, but our nations no longer were, much as that grieved me.)

"My husband had a good idea who your suitor's friends were," Eleanor said. "He spoke with a few of them, after your departure. There was a certain settling of accounts . . . I don't believe anyone gave much trouble after that."

Clearly not. If there were any further attempts on his life, they had evidently failed: he had sailed unharmed into a fourth term, after all. "I wish President Roosevelt could have lived to see the end of the war." I'd saved him from death on Halloween night of 1942, and he'd lived long enough to fulfill his promise that American soldiers would come to aid my countrymen . . . but he'd died before Hitler's fall.

"He might not have lived to see victory, but he lived long enough to ensure it." And Eleanor raised her cup to me, in silent thanks.

I raised mine in return. We held each other's eyes a long moment, and then we both began clattering our saucers like the middle-aged ladies we were. "Such good weather for your visit, Eleanor—"

"Yes, and I do hope I can see more of this country in your company while I am here, Lyudmila!"

"This time I will be *your* tour guide. There's so much I want to show you. Leningrad, Tsarskoye Selo, the Hermitage, and the Russian Museum . . . But for tonight," I said, "the opera. I have tickets for *Eugene Onegin,* since my friend Vika is dancing a variation in the ballroom scene. She was a tank driver in the war, you know—decorated three times for bravery, and now she's a Bolshoi ballerina."

"What extraordinary women your country produces," Eleanor observed.

"I'll introduce you to more of them." I knew so many now through my work with female war veterans: Vika, prickly and incorrigibly elegant despite the fact that she'd lost an eye during the final drive toward Berlin; a dark-haired Hero of the Soviet Union named Yelena Vetsina who had flown nine hundred bombing runs with the Night Witches . . . and best of all, my darling friend Lena Paliy. She hadn't died in the fall of Sevastopol after all. She'd turned up emaciated but alive after retreating into the hills from the German invasion, and now we went walking every month in Gorky Park to talk about old times. I was usually late, and she'd pound on my apartment door with a shouted, *Wake up, sleepyhead!*

"Vodka during the day?" Eleanor shook her head disapprovingly when I proposed a toast before we headed out. "Very bad habit, Lyudmila dear."

"You can't call yourself a veteran until you have at least one bad habit you can't kick." I grinned.

In truth, I have more than one. I drink too much, this I know. I wake at night gasping from the old memories of battle, or dreams where I am frozen in that lightning-split beech tree beside Rock Creek until the marksman comes to put a bullet through *my* eye instead of the other way round. On those nights Kostia has to hold me until the shudders subside, and on other nights I do the same when his own demons of war come snarling and red-clawed through the land of sleep to hunt for him. I still tense up whenever I hear anything that sounds like a shot, and I can't enter a room, a building, or an open space without parsing the movement lines and the potential threats. But that is the cost, as much as the old physical wounds that still sometimes cause me pain. The invisible wounds can hurt just as much—if not more.

The Party is encouraging me to write my memoirs. *A straightforward account of your heroics on the front line, Comrade Pavlichenko, with suitably stoic reflections on courage, duty, and the bright future of the motherland.* But, as I have frequently reflected in the years since my war concluded, there will be a great difference between any official account of my time in the Red Army and the version that lives in my memory. I can write honestly about the friends I lost, about my work as a sniper and the demands it places upon the soul. I can write about the extraordinary people I met on my goodwill tour from America to Canada to Britain, from Charlie Chaplin to Franklin Roosevelt, from Paul Robeson to Winston Churchill. I will not lie in my memoir . . . but there is much I will leave out.

Alexei Pavlichenko will not appear in those pages, except in a line or two as the infatuation of a foolish girl hardly out of childhood and the father of my son. Let him disappear from memory, from the pages of history, into the leaf mold of a Washington park.

Kostia will not appear in those pages, either, for very different reasons. Not long after we returned from our overseas tour, he had quiet word that his unofficial father, that Baikal fur trapper who had passed his diamond eye and savage skill to the son he'd fathered in Irkutsk, had been denounced for speaking against Comrade Stalin. It took half my diamonds—the uncut ones I'd scavenged from the marksman's pockets, and the bracelets from the jewelry set he'd given me in a duelist's challenge—to keep Kostia's name off the warrants that swept up the rest of his father's family, the sons and daughters who bore the name *Markov* and not *Shevelyov.* I keep the rest of my jewels in reserve, and Kostia lives quietly, not drawing on the fame that could be his as a decorated sniper and the husband of Lady Death. I sometimes look at him and wonder if he has regrets: the children we weren't able to have, the family he left behind in America . . . but if so, he never voices them. I hope I have been enough for him, and since he made the choice to yoke his life to mine, I have sworn to keep him safe. Red Army records may say I was intimate with my sniper partner, but the partner in my memoir won't be named as Konstantin Shevelyov. I'll give that title to one of my other platoon members instead—one of the men too long dead to gainsay my word—and I'll keep my husband anonymous.

And finally, there will be no word in my memoir of the muddy-eyed man who courted me, stalked me, and fought me in Rock Creek Park.

Because people love war heroes . . . but even in my own beloved homeland, war heroes are supposed to be clean and uncomplicated. Those urging me to write my memoir will want a patriotic young woman who fought to defend her country, a heroine to root for with a story clean and simple as a full moon—and I was that young woman, but I was more. My moon had a midnight side.

To the world, Lyudmila Pavlichenko's tally officially stands at 309, a list achieved without bloodthirstiness, every shot fired in simple defense of hearth and home. Only a few know that there was another duel fought under a waning moon on the other side of the world, a duel fought in rage and desperation and savage self-preservation against two very different men . . . and that my true tally stands at 311.

But that is my secret, a sniper's secret, and it dies with me. Eleanor knows, but I saved her husband's life, and perhaps our nations along with it, so she will take my secrets to her grave. So I put down my tea and head to my wardrobe with a smile. "I don't have that old yellow satin dress anymore, but let's see what I can rustle up to wear to the opera tonight . . ."

"I'm here to tack up a hem or let down a sleeve if you require it," said the First Lady.

AUTHOR'S NOTE

Odds are, you've never heard of Lyudmila Pavlichenko. A few years ago, I hadn't, either—it wasn't until my research into *The Huntress*'s Night Witch pilots that I ran smack into the astounding story of another Soviet war heroine: this celebrated library-researcher-turned-sniper who was responsible for 309 kills during World War II, took America by storm during a publicity tour in 1942, hobnobbed with Hollywood stars, and became White House besties with Eleanor Roosevelt. I knew at once that I had to write her incredible story.

The Soviet Union's record before, during, and after the war isn't pretty, so it's easy to forget that in the early days of World War II, they were the underdog. The Third Reich regarded Russians as racial undesirables fit only to be exterminated; Soviet soldiers were routinely slaughtered or starved if they were taken prisoner, unlike the more by-the-book treatment of French and English POWs. The Russians responded with equal savagery once the tide turned in their favor, but at the beginning of Germany's terrifying and overwhelming invasion, all the under-equipped Red Army could do was mount a fighting retreat, letting the harsh terrain and Russian winter do to Hitler what it had done to Napoleon. That strategy came at a horrifying cost: millions of Soviets died wearing down the German advance.

And many of those front-line lives at stake were women.

The USSR was the only Allied nation to employ women on the front line in their actively fighting military branches. Approximately 800,000 women served in the Soviet Armed Forces during the war, or about 5 percent of the total military personnel. They were more likely to be shunted into communications and medical personnel, but many managed to play a more active part: bomber pilots, like the Night Witches; tank drivers, like Mila's friend Vika—and snipers.

Hollywood has colored our view of sharpshooters. We imagine them as militarized serial killers; at best they're the odd man out on a squad of regular guys, the one described as having ice water in his veins—see Barry Pepper's Scripture-quoting sniper in Steven Spielberg's *Saving Private Ryan.* And the idea persists that killing from a distance, from hidden nests, is somehow dishonorable or unfair . . . but skilled marksmen have been used by every army since the invention of firearms (and before that the bow and arrow: think of the English archers bringing down French knights at Agincourt, or Robin Hood's Merry Men downing royal soldiers from hidden forest hideouts!). The use of snipers isn't a violation of the Geneva Convention, but the stereotype persists: snipers are cold-blooded, remote, pitiless. As Eleanor Roosevelt said when meeting Lyudmila Pavlichenko: If you have a good view of the faces of your enemies through your sights and still fire to kill, how can ordinary people approve of you?

But the woman known as Lady Death defies such stereotypes. She comes across in her memoirs and the anecdotes of her peers as warm, funny, charming, a bookworm, a loving mother, an introvert who savored her alone time but could nevertheless be the life of the party. She did not even have the requisite ice-blue or cold gray eyes most snipers are described as having!

She was no naïf who learned to shoot at the front; she arrived in uniform already an accomplished markswoman. Neither did she come from the kind of rural family where a daughter might be expected to wield a rifle right out of the cradle. She was Ukrainian (though she described herself firmly as Russian when asked), a city girl and a booklover whose ambition was to be a historian, but she enjoyed the occasional outing at the gun range with her friends—enjoyed it enough that she decided to apply for an advanced marksmanship course. Though she acquired her skills as a hobby, she lost no time volunteering them in her country's defense: a young woman went to the beach with her friends in the morning, heard the declaration of war at noon over lunch at a nearby café, and by nightfall was leaving *La Traviata* early to go enlist. It didn't take long for the girl from Odessa—the graduate student who had been finishing the world's nerdiest dissertation on Bogdan Khmelnitsky, the Ukraine's accession to Russia in 1654, and the activities of the Pereyaslav Council—to begin racking up a serous tally.

A sniper's official tally consisted only of confirmed kills, so Lyudmila's true list of enemy dead probably did not stand at the official 309: fighting in two desperate sieges, she would not have had time or opportunity to verify all of her kills, and the enemies she downed fighting as a soldier rather than a sniper wouldn't have been counted at all. Her true tally might have been less than the 309 eventually finalized for official purposes; it could also easily have been much more. What seems certain is that in less than eighteen months of fighting, Lyudmila Pavlichenko buried hundreds of enemies, was wounded at least four times, and earned the nickname Lady Death. Many of the feats described in this novel—her training of a platoon, the assaults on Gildendorf and No-Name Height, her recruitment of the ranger Vartanov whose family had been murdered, the Kabachenko homestead and the bond she formed with a young girl who had been raped by German soldiers ("Kill them all")—are drawn directly from the memoir Lyudmila wrote later in life.

Soviet memoirs are long on fact and short on emotion; it isn't the Soviet way to gush about feelings. Yet Lyudmila's response to becoming such an efficient taker of lives come through as far from ghoulish. Making her first two kills under the eye of Captain Sergienko, she didn't hesitate to down the two officers, yet admitted that firing on a target and firing on a human being were very different things. She disliked her own growing fame, viewing herself simply as a soldier with a job to do: the enemy were invaders who had been ordered to attack; she was a defender who had been ordered to push them back, and that was that. Her anger at the Germans flowered into hatred as she saw the damage Hitler's forces inflicted on her homeland, but Lyudmila still prided herself on clean kills and utter professionalism. The only time she gave the order to shoot to wound rather than to kill was in the final defense of Sevastopol, where it was the only way to slow down an overwhelming enemy.

The Russian front was pure hell: the casualty rates were appalling, the weather brutal, the troops ill trained and under-equipped, almost as likely to be shot by their own officers (if they showed a single sign of faltering) as by the Germans. Women soldiers had an especially tough time of it. Red Air Force women like the Night Witches served together in all-female regiments or were at least grouped with their sister pilots in mixed regiments, but Red Army women were vastly outnumbered by male soldiers and commonly regarded as sexual perks for the officers. Turning down a superior's advances could result in anything from physical assault to being left off lists for commendations and promotions. Lyudmila was intensely admired by the men in her company, whom she apparently handled with friendly but steely authority, but at least one source states that she incurred resentment for turning down men who outranked her. This could explain her lack of military decorations early in her fight . . . until a three-day duel with a German sniper catapulted her to fame.

Detractors disputed both that fame and her achievements. Even now, some insist that Lyudmila Pavlichenko was a fake, a pretty propaganda-department brunette with a memorized story designed to inspire the masses. Such claims nitpick at the inaccuracies in her memoir's timeline, insist that the kind of platoon she described leading wasn't yet formed, and cite her refusal to demonstrate her sharpshooting skills in America as proof she didn't actually have any.

To me, Lyudmila Pavlichenko comes across as the real deal. Her memoir bears the stamp of Soviet propaganda, but her technical recall of a sniper's skills, weapons, and routine is exactly where her voice is the most precise and vividly individual. There are inaccuracies in her timeline, but a woman piecing her memories together through the fog of war and the PTSD of multiple battlefield concussions is bound to get a few details wrong. The kind of sniper platoon she described leading didn't exist yet in the Red Army, but Lyudmila was fighting in the early days of the war when everything was slapdash, and she was probably making up procedure as she went along. As for her on-tour *nyet* whenever she was asked to shoot on command (except for one gun-club demonstration in Chicago), her reasons come through loud and clear in her memoir: Lady Death scorned the idea of being trotted out like some show-pony circus shooter, and she absolutely refused to reduce her deadly skills to a parlor trick.

Her war wasn't all mud, blood, and pain. Lyudmila had a sense of humor, which shines through when she recounts butting heads with oblivious superior officers or relaxing with her platoon in an evening of song, vodka, and scavenged treats after a successful raid. And despite her mandate of no fraternizing with male colleagues, she broke her own rules for a spectacularly romantic front-line love affair.

At twenty-four, Lyudmila had already endured a minefield of a love life. She says extremely little (and nothing good) of her first husband Alexei Pavlichenko, the older man who seduced and impregnated her after a dance when she was barely fifteen. Lyudmila's only comment about Alexei, after he abandoned her and their son Rostislav, is: "Fortunately, my son is nothing like his father." As a single mother she remained focused on her work, her education, and her son—so romance hit like a thunderbolt when she met a tall, funny, good-looking Red Army lieutenant in Sevastopol. Enter Lyonya Kitsenko, the man who wooed and won the most dangerous woman on the Russian front.

Kitsenko is frequently described as her junior sergeant and fellow sniper, her partner with whom she hunted night after night as part of a lethal, inseparable team—but Lyudmila described him as the lieutenant who commanded her company. My conjecture is that two men may have been confused, and that Lyudmila was romantically involved with both her company commander and her sniper partner at different points. Thus I separated the two and described Kitsenko as Lyudmila did: Lieutenant Alexei Arkadyevich Kitsenko, nicknamed Lyonya, her superior officer and eventually second husband. Whether they were legally married or not (he is not listed on her grave as her spouse), Lyudmila regarded Lyonya as her husband in every way that counted: they had a whirlwind courtship culminating in the attack where Lyonya carried the wounded Lyudmila off the front line, gave blood for her surgery, visited throughout her recovery, and invited her to dinner in his dugout (complete with flowers in a shell-casing vase!) the day she was released. He proposed that night; he and Lady Death were inseparable from then on.

It was the best time of Lyudmila's war. She wrote that love was good for her shooting; while she was coming home to Lyonya she seemed to hit every target she aimed at, including the tense three-day duel where she and her sniper partner (to whom I gave the name of Konstantin Shevelyov, a name later crucial in her life) outwitted a German sharpshooter. But after barely three months together, Lyonya was hit by mortar fire right before Lyudmila's eyes. He died in her arms hours later, and she nearly went mad from grief. She wasn't able to return to shooting until she and her sniper partner grieved together at Lyonya's grave. Then she returned to the front lines with a new fury: as she later told Eleanor Roosevelt, every German in her sights after that might as well have been the man who killed Lyonya.

Sevastopol fell months later, and Lyudmila likely would have been killed there (women snipers in the Red Army had about a 75 percent chance of dying in combat) had she not been wounded and evacuated a few weeks before. Despite her wish to return to the front, the propaganda department had other ideas. A missive had recently landed on Stalin's desk from Washington, D.C., inviting a deputation of Soviet students to join Eleanor Roosevelt's international student conference, and the Boss saw an opportunity: Lady Death was headed to America.

She certainly felt like a fish out of water, and the White House welcome breakfast did not go well: Lyudmila's terse response to the First Lady's comment about how a woman sniper could be relatable to Americans is drawn directly from her memoir, as are her responses to the astonishingly asinine questions she was asked at her first press conference. But one woman turned things around for Lyudmila: the First Lady, who offered her Soviet guest a ride in her convertible to that evening's dinner party. Though her driving apparently alarmed Lady Death more than an entire panzer division, it signaled the beginning of an unlikely friendship.

It was Eleanor who introduced Lyudmila and her fellow delegates to FDR for a private meeting where they could discuss the hoped-for second front in Europe, and who escorted her on part of her subsequent goodwill tour around America. The idea of a First Lady and a Russian sniper becoming friends may seem wildly improbable, but many of their scenes in *The Diamond Eye* are taken directly from Lyudmila's memoir: their discussions on American segregation (which appalled Lyudmila, as did British colonialism in India); Lyudmila falling asleep in the presidential limousine with her head on Eleanor's shoulder; Lyudmila tumbling out of a canoe at the Hudson estate and ending up in the First Lady's bedroom as Eleanor hemmed a pair of pink pajamas for her and they chatted for so long that FDR had to retrieve the unlikely BFFs for dinner!

Under Eleanor's wing, Lyudmila found her feet in the spotlight. She met everyone from Charlie Chaplin to Woody Guthrie (who wrote a song for her, "Miss Pavlichenko"—find it on YouTube!) and became a passionate public speaker, never forgetting her mission of asking for American aid on behalf of her fellow soldiers. In Chicago she brought an audience roaring to their feet with the speech that cemented her fame: "Gentlemen, I have killed 309 fascist invaders by now. Don't you think, gentlemen, that you have been hiding behind my back for too long?"

Eleanor and Lyudmila bid goodbye at a farewell dinner at the White House in October 1942. They continued to correspond for the next fifteen years, as FDR carried through on his promise to send American soldiers to Europe and Mila finished her war as a sniper instructor. In 1957, the widowed Eleanor came to the USSR on a goodwill tour of her own, and the former First Lady and the former sniper embraced with cries of welcome.

My author notes usually take time to explain where my fictional characters weave in with the historical ones. *The Diamond Eye* is different, because nearly every person named comes straight from the historical record. Lyudmila's fellow delegates Pchelintsev and Krasavchenko; her officers General Petrov, Lieutenant Dromin, and Captain Sergienko; her platoon mates Fyodor Sedykh and old Vartanov; her Odessa friend Sofya and medical orderly friend Lena Paliy . . . all real. My only substantial fictional additions to the record are Vika, the ballerina turned tank driver (a heroine I have in mind for a future novel!), and Kostia Shevelyov, who is a fictionalized composite of two real men.

I have taken some liberties with the historical record to serve the novel. A few of Lyudmila's front-line adventures were condensed and reordered: the Romanian attack with priests was slightly moved up, and her subsequent recovery moved to the hospital battalion rather than back in Odessa. The first sortie she fights with Kostia was fought with another recruit, and Lyonya is introduced earlier in *The Diamond Eye* than he appeared in real life—his time with Lyudmila was so limited, I couldn't resist bringing him onstage sooner! Some events on the goodwill tour are also reordered: Lyudmila's meeting with Laurence Olivier likely didn't happen until she went to England, and FDR's private tour of U.S. defense plants ended somewhat earlier and wasn't intended to coincide with any of Lyudmila's California press engagements.

Wherever I have conflicting information, such as the exact name of Lyudmila's regiment or the precise evening of the Soviet delegation's White House farewell, I have used Lyudmila's version—likewise, I generally use her spellings of location names and Russian names, which may appear differently in modern maps and transliterations. Some of the facts and figures she quotes may not be accurate, but they are the facts and figures she would have believed were accurate at the time, so I have used them. There are also incidents in Lyudmila's memoir which I have chosen to leave out, like a meeting with Stalin that probably didn't happen. It has been something of a delicate dance to treat Lyudmila Pavlichenko's memoir as the concrete original source of its heroine's memories, yet also a document with which the propaganda office took some liberties.

Her memoir contains tantalizing gaps and silences which I've filled in with artistic license. Lyudmila states that she last saw her husband Alexei Pavlichenko three years before war broke out, and she makes no further mention of him. Likely he was one of the millions of Russian men who disappeared into the Red Army and died on the front—there is some evidence suggesting he was a doctor, so I brought him into the novel as a combat surgeon. His ultimate fate was unknown, so I crafted what I felt was a suitably satisfying end for the man who seduced a fifteen-year-old and abandoned her and their child.

The other place I filled in a historical gap is around Lyudmila's sniper partner, and around her final husband Kostia Shevelyov. Lyudmila's partner is named in her memoir as Fyodor Sedykh: such a relationship would have been as intimate as a working relationship could possibly be, yet she makes no mention of him after Sevastopol. Likewise, the man who became her husband after the war is a complete blank: we know nothing about Kostantin Shevelyov except his birth and death dates. Why does her memoir contain so little about two men who would have been so important to her?

I gave her a reason: Konstantin Shevelyov had good cause to fly under the radar, and his famous wife was doing her level best to keep him out of her own limelight. In the carnivorous Stalinist regime, there could be any number of reasons a man might want to lie low. Thus I turned Kostia into Lyudmila's sniper partner so I could introduce Lady Death's final husband into the story and pay homage to the records that indicate a romantic link between her and her partner, but also gave him a background that explains why she might list another name as her partner.

Lastly, the marksman: there was no known plot against President Roosevelt in 1942, though he narrowly escaped assassination in 1933 when Giuseppe Zangara fired on him from a crowd in Miami, and he also managed to escape being deposed the following year by a shadowy cabal (allegedly including some of America's most prominent heads of industry) who hoped to replace him with a military dictator. By 1942, Roosevelt still had plenty of enemies who would have celebrated his death: isolationists, American fascists, political rivals who believed him a traitor to his race and class, and anti-communists who saw even a wartime alliance with the USSR as treason. Creating the marksman also allowed me to make sense of one of the most bizarre episodes of Lyudmila's goodwill tour: the American millionaire William Jonson who fell in love with her on her tour, followed her from city to city, proposed marriage, and sent her a spectacular set of diamond jewelry with a note stating: "We will meet again." According to Lyudmila's memoir, they did not. But this was too good a story to ignore, so in my version they do meet again: first at the White House (which had *much* less stringent security in the forties than it does today) and then in Rock Creek Park, a stretch of wilderness slicing through the nation's capital that has swallowed its share of bodies over the years. Murdered Washington intern Chandra Levy disappeared there for a year, despite modern search capabilities. Another park mystery is the lost ring of Teddy Roosevelt, which fell off during a presidential hike in 1902. It remains missing to this day, and I enjoyed crafting a possible fate for it, too!

I owe heartfelt thanks to many people who helped in the writing, researching, and production of this novel. My mother and husband, this book's first cheerleaders. My wonderful critique partners Stephanie Dray and Stephanie Thornton. My beta readers and marvelously knowledgeable subject matter experts: Erin Davies and Outlaw, Charles F. A. Dvorak, Annalori Ferrell, Elena Gorokhova, and Shelby Miksch. My agent Kevan Lyon and editor Tessa Woodward, and the marvelous team at William Morrow. I would be lost without you all!

I would also have been lost without Lyudmila herself. I recommend her engrossing autobiography *Lady Death: The Memoirs of Stalin's Sniper* for those wishing to know more about this fascinating woman. The English translation by David Foreman (Greenhill Books) proved invaluable in the research and writing of this novel. Lyudmila Pavlichenko was far more than a killer of men, and she paid a price for her tremendous courage. Although she survived her war, finished her dissertation, and achieved her dream of becoming a historian, she saw many of her friends die, she struggled with PTSD, and she outlived Kostia . . . but she devoted her later years to war veterans, recorded her story for posterity, and died in the arms of her beloved son, surrounded by family and swearing at death until the very end.

It's sometimes said that World War II was won with British intelligence, American steel, and Soviet blood. This sweeping generalization bears a kernel of truth. Since the USSR became America's enemy in the Cold War so soon after WWII's end, it's easy to forget that without them, the war against the Axis powers might have been lost. Of all Hitler's mistakes, his colossal Napoleonic error in taking on the USSR was perhaps the most pivotal: without the eastern front soaking up so much of Germany's manpower, the Allies might never have prevailed. The cost of that victory was millions of Red Army dead as Soviet blood gave American steel and British intelligence time to turn the tide. In *The Rose Code* I wrote about the war through the lens of British intelligence. *The Diamond Eye* is seen through the lens of Soviet blood—one woman's fight to stanch its flow, first with her rifle and then with her voice as she crossed an ocean to bring American steel home to help her countrymen.

HISTORIC PHOTOGRAPHS

Lyudmila Mikhailovna Pavlichenko
(© Shim Harno [Mr Robert Kemp] / Alamy)

Lyudmila Pavlichenko, propaganda photograph, Sevastopol, early 1942

Sniper platoon commander Lyudmila Pavlichenko with her troops (32nd Guards Parachute Division), Moscow military district, August 1942 (Courtesy of Greenhill Books)

Lyudmila Pavlichenko and Eleanor Roosevelt, USA tour, 1942 (© ITAR-TASS News Agency / Alamy)

Lyonya Kitsenko and Lyudmila Pavlichenko,
Sevastopol, January 1942

FURTHER READING AND ENTERTAINMENT

Nonfiction

Alexeivich, Svetlana. *The Unwomanly Face of War,* trans. Richard Pevear and Larissa Volkhonsky. Random House, 2017.

Cook, Blanche Wiesen. *Eleanor Roosevelt, Volume 3: The War Years and After, 1939–1962.* Viking, 2016.

Fitzpatrick, Sheila. *Everyday Stalinism: Ordinary Life in Extraordinary Times: Soviet Russia in the 1930s.* Oxford University Press, 2000.

Fitzpatrick, Sheila, and Yuri Slezhine, eds. *In the Shadow of Revolution: Life Stories of Russian Women from 1917 to the Second World War.* Princeton University Press, 2000.

Glantz, David, and Jonathan M. House. *When Titans Clashed: How the Red Army Stopped Hitler,* revised and expanded ed. University Press of Kansas, 2015.

Goodwin, Doris Kearns. *No Ordinary Time: Franklin and Eleanor Roosevelt—The Home Front in World War II.* Simon & Schuster, 1995.

Markwick, Roger D., and Euridice Charon Cardona. *Soviet Women on the Frontline in the Second World War.* Palgrave Macmillan, 2012.

Nikolaev, Yevgeni. *Red Army Sniper: A Memoir on the Eastern Front in World War II.* Greenhill Books, 2017.

Obratztsov, Youri, and Maud Anders. *Soviet Women Snipers of the Second World War.* Histoire and Collections, 2014.

Pavlichenko, Lyudmila. *Lady Death: The Memoirs of Stalin's Sniper,* trans. David Foreman. Greenhill Books, 2018.

Vinogradova, Lyuba. *Avenging Angels: Soviet Women Snipers on the Eastern Front (1941–45).* Quercus, 2017.

Wacker, Albrecht. *Sniper on the Eastern Front: The Memoirs of Sepp Allerberger, Knight's Cross,* reprint ed. Pen and Sword Military, 2016.

YouTube

"Lyudmila Pavlichenko—The Extraordinary Sniper." Dubistic, September 23, 2016. https://www.youtube.com/watch?v=rYnnBpxsI7s&ab_channel=dubistic.

"Lyudmila Pavlichenko Speech in New York City." Pietrossino, YouTube, February 12, 2010. https://www.youtube.com/watch?v=jDO6n7GuslA&ab_channel=pietrossino.

Film

Battle for Sevastopol, 2015 biographical war film.

Enemy at the Gates, 2001 war film.

ABOUT THE AUTHOR

KATE QUINN is a *New York Times* and *USA Today* bestselling author of historical fiction. A native of Southern California, she attended Boston University, where she earned bachelor's and master's degrees in classical voice. A lifelong history buff, she has written four novels in the Empress of Rome Saga and two books set in the Italian Renaissance before turning to the twentieth century with *The Alice Network, The Huntress, The Rose Code,* and *The Diamond Eye*. All have been translated into multiple languages. She and her husband now live in California with three black rescue dogs.

MANUAL OF THE GRASSES OF THE UNITED STATES

A. S. Hitchcock

Second Edition
Revised by AGNES CHASE

IN TWO VOLUMES

VOLUME ONE

DOVER PUBLICATIONS, INC.
NEW YORK

Published in Canada by General Publishing Company, Ltd., 30 Lesmill Road, Don Mills, Toronto, Ontario.
Published in the United Kingdom by Constable and Company, Ltd.

This Dover edition, first published in 1971, is an unabridged republication of the second revised edition, as published by the United States Government Printing Office in 1950 as U. S. Department of Agriculture Miscellaneous Publication No. 200. The first edition of the work was published in 1935.
For convenience in handling, the text is published in two volumes in this paperback edition.

International Standard Book Number: 0-486-22717-0
Library of Congress Catalog Card Number: 70-142876

Manufactured in the United States of America
Dover Publications, Inc.
180 Varick Street
New York, N. Y. 10014

MANUAL OF THE GRASSES OF THE UNITED STATES

By the late A. S. HITCHCOCK,[1] *principal botanist, Division of Plant Exploration and Introduction;* second edition revised by AGNES CHASE, formerly *senior botanist* and later *collaborator, Division of Plant Exploration and Introduction, Bureau of Plant Industry, Soils, and Agricultural Engineering, Agricultural Research Administration,* and *research associate, United States National Museum, Smithsonian Institution*

VOLUME I

VOLUME II

INTRODUCTION

Of all the plants of the earth the grasses are of the greatest use to the human race. To the grasses belong the cereals, sugarcane, sorghum, and the bamboos; and, since they furnish the bulk of the forage for domestic animals, the grasses are also the basis of animal industry.

USES OF GRASSES

The grasses furnish the principal breadstuffs of the world and a large part of the food of domestic animals; they are also used in the industrial arts and extensively as greensward and ornamentals in parks and gardens.

FOOD GRASSES

The most important food plants for the human race are the cereals, including wheat, corn (maize), rice, barley, rye, oats, and many kinds of grain sorghums. For primitive peoples the seed of certain other grasses, such as pearl millet, common millet, broomcorn millet, Japanese millet, and African millet (ragi), have played an important role. The seeds of the cereals are also extensively used as feed for domestic animals.

FORAGE GRASSES

Forage grasses are used for hay, pasturage, soiling, and silage.

HAY GRASSES

The grasses together with clovers and alfalfa are the basis of permanent

[1] Died December 16, 1935.

meadows. The most important perennial grasses used for tame hay are: Timothy (*Phleum pratense*), redtop (*Agrostis alba*), orchard grass (*Dactylis glomerata*), meadow fescue (*Festuca elatior*), smooth brome (*Bromus inermis*), and Johnson grass (*Sorghum halepense*). A few other species are used occasionally or rarely: Rhodes grass (*Chloris gayana*), Dallis grass (*Paspalum dilatatum*), desert wheatgrass (*Agropyron desertorum*) and crested wheatgrass (*A. cristatum*), velvet grass (*Holcus lanatus*), Natal grass (*Rhynchelytrum repens*), tall oatgrass (*Arrhenatherum elatius*), and slender wheatgrass (*Agropyron trachycaulum*). Some of the grasses used primarily for pasture are also occasionally used for hay.

Market hays from grasses usually consist of timothy, prairie grasses, Johnson grass, or grain (wheat, oats, and wild oats). The prairie hays are divided into upland prairie and midland prairie. The species of most importance in the upland prairie are *Agropyron smithii* and *Stipa comata* (northern Great Plains), *Andropogon gerardi* and *A. scoparius* (eastern Great Plains), *A. saccharoides* (Texas), and *Panicum virgatum* (Kansas to Texas). Midland prairie is invariably composed of *Spartina pectinata*. Tussock sedge (*Carex stricta*) is harvested in large quantities on the marshes of Wisconsin for use as packing hay.

For temporary meadows the grasses most used are the cereals, which, with wild oats, furnish the grain hay of the Pacific coast, the sorghums, including Sudan grass, and millet (*Setaria italica*).

PASTURE GRASSES

The more common grasses used for permanent pasture are: Kentucky bluegrass (*Poa pratensis*), Bermuda grass (*Cynodon dactylon*), redtop (*Agrostis alba*), colonial bent (*A. tenuis*), orchard grass (*Dactylis glomerata*), smooth brome (*Bromus inermis*), Italian ryegrass (*Lolium multiflorum*), perennial ryegrass (*L. perenne*), meadow fescue (*Festuca elatior*), Dallis grass (*Paspalum dilatatum*), carpet grass (*Axonopus compressus* and *A. affinis*), Canada bluegrass (*Poa compressa*), and sheep fescue (*Festuca ovina*). Many of the meadow grasses mentioned above are also used for pasture.

Temporary pasture is furnished by the cereals and by rescue grass (*Bromus catharticus*), Italian ryegrass, and Sudan grass.

Two grasses, important in the tropics but in the United States grown only in southern Florida and southern Texas, are Guinea grass (*Panicum maximum*) and Para grass (*P. purpurascens*).

SOILING GRASSES

Grasses used for soiling are for the most part the cereals, millet, and other annual grasses used for temporary meadows, and in addition but only locally, pearl millet (*Pennisetum glaucum*), teosinte (*Euchlaena mexicana*), and Napier or elephant grass (*P. purpureum*).

SILAGE GRASSES

Any grass may be cut and stored in silos, but corn (maize) and sorghum are the ones most used.

RANGE GRASSES

A large number of grasses make up much of the wild pasture, known in the West as the range, only the more abundant and valuable of which are recognized by stockmen as important. Probably the best known range grass is buffalo grass (*Buchloë dactyloides*), a sod-forming "short grass" dominant over much of the Great Plains. Throughout the same region two tufted short grasses, blue grama (*Bouteloua gracilis*) and hairy grama (*B. hirsuta*), are abundant. In Texas the dominant grass over much of the range is curly mesquite (*Hilaria belangeri*), a sod-former similar to buffalo grass.

In the prairie region of the Mississippi Valley and in the eastern part of the Great Plains certain "tall grasses" in earlier days furnished excellent hay and pasture, but in recent times these fertile grasslands have been broken up for cultivated fields. The more important tall grasses are big bluestem (*Andropogon gerardi*), little bluestem (*A. scoparius*), switch grass (*Panicum virgatum*), side-oats grama (*Bouteloua curtipendula*), and Indian grass (*Sorghastrum nutans*).

The marsh hay of the northern Mississippi Valley consists of bluejoint (*Calamagrostis canadensis*), reed canary grass (*Phalaris arundinacea*), and a few other wet-land species.

The forage grasses of the Great Basin include species of *Poa, Festuca, Bromus, Aristida,* and *Stipa.* In the Southwest, the gramas, species of *Bouteloua,* dominate the range. A large bunchgrass, sacaton (*Sporobolus wrightii*), and alkali sacaton (*S. airoides*) furnish much forage.

A few of the many nutritious species found in the Northwestern States are greenleaf fescue (*Festuca viridula*), bluebunch fescue (*F. idahoensis*), pinegrass (*Calamagrostis rubescens*), slender wheatgrass (*Agropyron trachycaulum*), California bromegrass (*Bromus carinatus*), and in the semiarid regions bluebunch wheatgrass (*Agropyron spicatum*).

GRASSES IN THE INDUSTRIAL ARTS

The most important species of the industrial arts group is sugarcane (p. 740). This might be included among grasses that furnish food, but sugar is a manufactured product.

The chief fiber-producing grasses are esparto (*Lygeum spartum* and *Stipa tenacissima*), also known as alfa, natives of Spain and north Africa. The leaves and stems are utilized in paper making. The pith of the cornstalk and the oil of the corn grain find many uses in the arts.

Certain aromatic grasses furnish essential oils used in perfumery. The best known are lemon grass (*Cymbopogon citratus*), citronella grass (*C. nardus*), and vetiver (*Vetiveria zizanioides*).

The bamboos, the largest of the grasses, are of vast importance in the Indo-Malay region and are receiving increasing attention in the United States. The larger kinds reach a height of 30 meters and are 15 to 25 or 30 centimeters thick below, tapering to the summit. The culms or stems are very strong and are used in building houses and bridges. When the stems are split, flattened out, and the partitions at the joints removed they make very durable boards, a foot or more wide, for floors and walls. Rafts and floats are made of the hollow stems closed at the joints by natural airtight partitions. With the partitions removed bamboo stems furnish water pipes or conduits. Sections of the stem closed at one end by the partition form convenient vessels for holding water. Much of the furniture and many of the utensils and implements used by the Malays are made wholly or in part of bamboo. Slender bamboo stems are familiar to us in the form of fishing rods and walking canes. Shoots of *Phyllostachys edulis, Sinocalamus beecheyanus,* and other species of bamboo are a choice vegetable in the Orient and an expensive dainty in the United States. Paper and rayon are made from the culms of some species.

Brooms are made from the seed heads of broomcorn, a variety of sorghum. Leghorn hats are made of a kind of wheat straw cut young and bleached. Straw of rice and oats is used for matting and for hats.

Starch and alcohol are made from the grain of maize, wheat, and other cereals. The stalks, grain, and cobs of maize furnish a great variety of products, such as wallboard, glucose, oil, red rubber, and corncob pipes.

SOIL-HOLDING GRASSES

Grasses used to hold soil in place and prevent erosion possess strong creeping rhizomes.

Sand-binding grasses in addition are able to grow up through the deepening sand. The most effective sand binders for seacoast drifting sand are the European beachgrass (*Ammophila arenaria*) and its American relative (*A. breviligulata*). The dunes of the Netherlands, southwestern France, northern and western Denmark, and other parts of Europe and areas on Cape Cod are planted with beachgrass. These fixed dunes act as barriers, protecting the land behind them. The land now occupied by Golden Gate Park, once an area of drifting sand, was first held in place with beachgrass and later planted to shrubs and trees. *Calamovilfa longifolia* and *Redfieldia flexuosa* are effective native sand binders on sand dunes of the interior.

Grasses with strong rhizomes are used to hold the sides of cuts and banks and to protect them against erosion. Bermuda grass in the South and quackgrass (*Agropyron repens*) in the North have been used successfully for this purpose. Rhizome-bearing species of *Elymus* and *Agropyron* have been used in the Northwest to hold railroad embankments along the Columbia River.

Shallow-water marshes and lagoons are in many places being converted into dry land by native plants growing therein that accumulate soil and gradually raise the level of the bottom. Grasses, especially species of *Spartina* and *Phragmites*, play an important part in the process. Artificial plantings of *Spartina townsendii* have been used with great success in the south of England, northern France, and in parts of the Netherlands to convert marshes and mud flats along the coast into dry land.

GRASSES FOR LAWNS AND GOLF COURSES

The lawn is a most important part of a well-planned landscape, park, or garden. For the humid regions of the Northern States, Kentucky bluegrass, also used for pasture, is the best-known lawngrass. Rough bluegrass (*Poa trivialis*) is often used as a lawngrass in shady places. In the Southern States Bermuda grass takes the place of bluegrass. Two other species are prominent as grasses for lawns and putting greens, creeping bent (*Agrostis palustris*) and colonial bent (*A. tenuis*). Along southern coasts St. Augustine grass (*Stenotaphrum secundatum*) and centipede grass (*Eremochloa ophiuroides*) are planted, being propagated by cuttings. Some of the fescue grasses are used in mixtures for lawns. These are red fescue (*Festuca rubra*), sheep fescue (*F. ovina*), hard fescue (*F. ovina* var. *duriuscula*), and shade fescue (*F. rubra* var. *heterophylla*).

ORNAMENTAL GRASSES

Among typical ornamentals the plumegrasses, giant reed (*Arundo donax*), Ravenna grass (*Erianthus ravennae*), eulalia (*Miscanthus sinensis*), and pampasgrass (*Cortaderia selloana*) are the most popular for parks and large areas. Dwarf bamboo (*Bambusa multiplex*) is used for hedges in the South, and the smaller species of *Phyllostachys* for masses of evergreen foliage. *Pseudosasa japonica*, an aggressively spreading hardy bamboo, is rather common in parks. Fountain grass (*Pennisetum setaceum*) and blue fescue (*Festuca ovina* var. *glauca*) are used for borders. Ribbon grass (*Phalaris arundinacea* var. *picta*) is a familiar grass in old gardens. Basket grass (a variegated form of *Oplismenus hirtellus*) will fall in long festoons from hanging baskets.

DISTRIBUTION OF GRASSES

One of the most widely distributed of the families of flowering plants, the grasses are found over the land surface of the globe, in marshes and in deserts, on prairies and in woodland, on sand, rocks, and fertile soil, from the Tropics to the polar regions and from sea level to perpetual snow on the mountains.

The different grasses, like other kinds of plants, thrive best under certain conditions of soil, moisture, temperature, exposure, and altitude.

The conditions under which a plant normally grows is its habitat. Some species are narrowly restricted in their habitat—being found only in sand or on rocks, in salt marshes or on alpine summits, for example, whereas others are tolerant of wide variations of habitat. Red fescue (*Festuca rubra*) is an example of wide distribution of a species tolerant of a variety of habitats. It is found from the Arctic regions south at low altitudes to Georgia and central California and in the mountains farther south, and from the seacoast marshes to mountain tops.

Each species is found growing over a rather definite geographic area, but within this area it is confined to its particular habitat.

In mountain regions altitude is an important factor in modifying range, each species thriving within certain limits of altitude. Species found at high altitudes in one range of mountains may reappear at about the same altitude on other ranges. Certain grasses growing at low levels in the north are found in the mountains and at increasingly higher elevations southward.

The geographic range is of importance and is given in some detail for each species in the manual. The range as given is based upon the study of a vast amount of material, both in the herbarium and in the field. For convenience in keeping the records of distribution a series of outline maps, one for each species or variety, has been prepared in the grass herbarium of the United States National Herbarium. The known range of each species is indicated upon these maps by a dot on each State from which specimens are in the herbarium or have been examined by the author. (A few extensions of range have been found since the maps were engraved. These are included in the text.) Local floras, lists, and records of distribution have been checked, and efforts have been made to verify the records that seemed to indicate an extension of range. Other herbaria have been visited or have lent specimens, and many correspondents have submitted specimens for verification. No additions have been made without a study of the specimens. But it must be borne in mind that dots (representing specimens) necessarily indicate where the different specimens have been collected, therefore where botanists have been. Absence of a dot in a state does not necessarily mean the species in question does not grow in that state.

The ranges of native species are usually fairly well defined and continuous. A species of the Coastal Plain extends, for example, from New Jersey to North Carolina or from Virginia to Florida and Texas, without a conspicuous break. Mountain plants extend along mountain ranges where similar conditions prevail. Some species have in the main a continuous range but are found also in isolated and distant localities. *Bouteloua hirsuta* extends over the Great Plains east to Wisconsin and Louisiana, and again occurs abundantly and apparently native on Sanibel Island, Fla. Some Coastal Plain species appear again around the head of Lake Michigan. In these cases it is probable that the species do not occur in the intermediate areas.

Certain arctic or northern species also show interrupted range, being found within the limits of the United States only on isolated mountain tops. The arctic grass, *Phippsia algida*, for example, is known within the United States only from alpine summits in Colorado. What appear to be interrupted ranges along the northern or southern borders are mostly due to extensions into this country from the main ranges in Canada or Mexico.

The distribution of recently introduced species is often very erratic. A single introduction may maintain itself or even spread considerably for several years before coming to the notice of botanists. Introduced species often travel rapidly along railroads by means of cattle cars, or they spread as impurities in the seed of crop plants. That seeds may travel great distances through the air has been shown by experiments in which airplanes have collected seeds, insects, and other objects at varying heights in the atmosphere. For example, spikelets of *Paspalum dilatatum* and *P. urvillei* were taken at altitudes up to 5,000 feet in Louisiana.

Grasses introduced into cultivation may spread or "escape" from cultivation and become established over wide areas. Kentucky bluegrass (*Poa pratensis*) and the ryegrasses (*Lolium perenne* and *L. multiflorum*) are familiar examples. Johnson grass is an excellent forage grass, but if it escapes into cultivated fields may become a troublesome weed.

Other cultivated grasses, such as the grains, frequently spread from fields but are unable to maintain themselves for long. Eulalia (*Miscanthus sinensis*) has been cultivated for ornament in the eastern part of the United States for many years. Recently it has shown a tendency to spread by seed. It is now becoming a nuisance in some localities because of its aggressiveness in old fields.

MORPHOLOGY OF GRASSES

The organs of grasses undergo many modifications or departures from the usual or typical structure. A knowledge of the structure and modifications of the organs, especially of the parts of the spikelet, is essential for the interpretation of relationships.

VEGETATIVE ORGANS

In size grasses vary from minute species only 2 or 3 cm. high to the giant bamboos 30 m. tall. The vegetative organs, however, consist, in all cases, of root, stem, and leaves. A single unbranched stem with the attached leaves is a shoot.

ROOT

The roots of grasses are fibrous with little modification. The primary root persists only a short time after germination, its place being taken by secondary roots produced from the nodes of the young culm. Besides the original root system at the base of the plant, secondary roots are often formed from nodes above the ground as in maize (prop roots), or from the nodes of creeping culms (rhizomes or stolons). Roots are never produced from the internodes of the culms.

STEM

The jointed stem of a grass, called a culm, is made up of a series of nodes and internodes. The internode is hollow (wheat), or solid (maize); the node or joint is always solid. The culm may branch at the base as in wheat (stools) or above the base as in *Muhlenbergia*. Creeping culms, modified for propagation, may be below ground (rhizomes) or above ground (stolons). The lower internodes may thicken into corms (timothy, species of *Melica*, *Arrhenatherum elatius* var. *bulbosum*), sometimes referred to as bulbs. Perennial grasses may form a sod or mass of individuals by means of rhizomes or stolons, or they may form a crown or tuft by the continual formation of upright branches within the lower sheaths.

LEAF

The leaves are borne on the culm in two ranks, one at each node. The leaf consists of sheath and blade. The sheath envelops the culm above the node, the margins overlapping (open) or infrequently united into a cylinder for a part or a whole of the distance to the summit (closed).

The blades are typically flat, narrow, and sessile. In dry regions they are usually involute or convolute; in tropical shade they are often comparatively short and wide (lanceolate, ovate, or elliptic); in most of the bamboos they are narrowed into a short petiole articulate with the sheath.

Some grasses (especially the Hordeae) bear, one on either side at the base of the blade, appendages known as auricles. At the junction of the blade and sheath on the inside is a membranaceous or ciliate appendage called the ligule. The region on the back of the leaf at the junction of the sheath and blade is called the collar.

PROPHYLLUM

At the point where a branch shoot originates from a main shoot (in the axil of a sheath), there is produced on the side next to the parent shoot a 2-keeled organ (the first leaf of the shoot) called the prophyllum. At first the prophyllum completely covers the bud but later opens as the shoot develops. The organ is usually concave between the keels toward the parent shoot but clasps the new shoot by its margins.

FLORAL ORGANS

The floral organs of all flowering plants are modified shoots. The flowers of grasses consist of stamens and pistils with no floral envelopes or perianth, except as they are represented by the lodicules.

THE INFLORESCENCE

The unit of the grass inflorescence is the spikelet. The spikelets are nearly always aggregated in groups or clusters which constitute the inflorescence. The tassel of maize, the spike or head of wheat or timothy, and the panicle of the oat or bluegrass are examples of inflorescences.

The simplest inflorescence is the raceme, in which the spikelets are pediceled along an axis. The typical raceme, as in *Pleuropogon*, is rare in grasses. Modified spikelike racemes are characteristic of *Paspalum*, *Digitaria*, and allied genera, in which the spikelets are paired and short-pedicellate, and of most Andropogoneae, in which the spikelets are paired, one sessile, the other pedicellate. The inflorescences of the groups mentioned may best be considered as specialized panicles.

The spike differs from the raceme in having sessile spikelets. In the Hordeae the spikes are symmetrical, in the Chlorideae they are one-sided.

The panicle is the commonest kind of grass cluster. In this the spikelets are pediceled in a branched inflorescence. The panicle may be open or diffuse, as in *Panicum capillare*, or contracted, as in millet. Compact panicles, especially if cylindric like timothy, are called spikelike panicles.

Numerous small inflorescences may be aggregated into a large or compound inflorescence. Many Andropogoneae have compound inflorescences, for example, the broomsedge (*Andropogon virginicus*).

Panicles often expand at the time of flowering (anthesis). Such expansion or spreading of the branches and branchlets is brought about by the swelling of motor organs (pulvini) in the axils of the inflorescence.

Sometimes the ultimate branches of an inflorescence are sterile instead of bearing spikelets. The sterile branchlets of *Setaria*, *Pennisetum*, and *Cenchrus* are modified into bristles around the spikelets.

THE SPIKELET

A typical spikelet consists of a short axis (rachilla) on which the flowers are borne in the axils of 2-ranked imbricate bracts. The spikelet is, therefore, a reduced modified shoot in which the rachilla is a stem bearing at each node a reduced leaf (bract). The flowers are secondary reduced shoots borne in the axils of the bracts, the first bract (palea) on the secondary shoot being a modified prophyllum and the stamens and pistil being modified leaves or bracts. The bracts of the lowest pair on the rachilla, being always empty, are distinguished as glumes. The succeeding bracts are called lemmas (flowering glumes of some authors). The glumes and lemmas represent the sheath of the leaves, the blades not developing (in proliferous spikelets the parts are partially developed into typical leaves). The lemma, palea, and included flower are called the floret. The branchlet bearing the spikelet is the pedicel.

The spikelet may be reduced to a single floret (Agrostideae), sometimes with a prolongation of the rachilla behind, as in *Calamagrostis*. In *Andropogon* a fertile spikelet is paired with a sterile one in which the pistil or both pistil and stamens are wanting. The upper florets of the spikelet are often reduced in Festuceae, and the lower lemmas may be empty in some genera (*Uniola, Blepharidachne*). In *Melica* and *Chloris* the upper florets may be reduced and form a club-shaped body. In *Phalaris* there is one fertile floret with a pair of sterile florets below, each reduced to a small appressed scale. In *Lamarckia* and *Cynosurus* there are prominent sterile spikelets mixed with the fertile ones.

In Paniceae the spikelet has a perfect terminal floret and below this a sterile floret, consisting of a sterile lemma similar to the glumes, either empty or with a hyaline palea or sometimes with a staminate flower.

In a few grasses (*Amphicarpum, Chloris chloridea*) there are, in addition to the usual inflorescence above ground, cleistogamous spikelets borne on underground culms.

RACHILLA

The axis bearing the florets, the rachilla, usually disarticulates between the florets when the spikelet is more than 1-flowered. In many species of *Eragrostis* it is continuous, usually bearing the persistent paleas, after the remainder of the florets have fallen. When the rachilla disarticulates the break is usually just below the florets so that the rachilla joint remains attached as a little stipe back of the palea. The disarticulation is near the middle of the internode in *Trichoneura* and *Festuca subuliflora*. The rachilla disarticulates just above the floret in *Phragmites*, the rachilla remaining as a plumose stipe below it. The rachilla is short-villous or pilose in many genera of Aveneae (the callus of the floret often pilose also).

In some genera with 1-flowered spikelets (*Calamagrostis, Cinna, Cynodon*) the rachilla is prolonged behind the floret as a slender, often villous, stipe or bristle, and in several genera with several-flowered spikelets (*Koeleria, Poa*) it is prolonged beyond the uppermost floret.

GLUMES

The glumes are usually similar in shape and texture, the first often smaller and with fewer nerves. Rarely the first glume is longer than the second (species of *Aristida*). The first may be much reduced or wanting (*Axonopus, Paspalum, Digitaria*). Rarely both glumes are wanting (*Leersia, Reimarochloa*). In *Eriochloa* the first glume is reduced or wanting, the first rachilla joint being a hard ring below the spikelet. In Andropogoneae the first glume is usually indurate, sometimes strongly so. In some Hordeae the glumes are bristlelike.

LEMMAS

The lemmas in the more primitive grasses are typically similar to the glumes but may be variously modified. In *Panicum* the fertile lemma is much harder than the glumes; in Andropogoneae they are much thinner than the glumes, often hyaline. The indurate cylindric lemma of *Stipa* and *Aristida* bears a sharp callus at base, formed by the oblique articulation with the rachilla.

PALEA

The palea is mostly 2-keeled and often concave between the keels. It is homologous with the prophyllum. Sometimes the 2 nerves of the palea are so close together as to appear like a single nerve (*Cinna*); sometimes the 2 nerves are marginal and widely separated as in rice. The keels may be ciliate (*Eragrostis*), bearded (*Triplasis*), or winged (*Pleuropogon*). The palea is much reduced or wanting in species of *Agrostis*. Usually the palea falls with its lemma, but in many species of *Eragrostis* it persists upon the rachilla after the fall of the lemma.

FLOWER

The flower proper consists of the stamens and pistil. The stamens are usually 3 but may be 1 to 6, rarely more. The slender filaments bear 2-celled anthers which are basifixed but so deeply sagittate as to appear versatile. The pistil is 1-celled, with 1 ovule; the styles are usually 2 but may be 1 or 3; the stigmas may arise from a single style or directly from the ovary. The style of *Zea* is greatly elongated and stigmatic over much of the exserted surface.

The lodicules are small organs found at the base of the flower outside the stamens. There are usually 2, rarely 3, the function of which is to open the floret at anthesis by their turgidity. They probably represent much reduced divisions of a perianth.

Typically the grasses are adapted to cross-pollination, but many species are cleistogamous in part. The axillary inflorescences of some species (*Panicum clandestinum* and allies, *Leersia oryzoides*) are enclosed in the sheaths and are self-pollinated. The florets of wheat expand for only a short time, when cross-pollination may take place, but for the most part are self-pollinated.

The fruit of the grasses is usually a caryopsis, in which the single seed is grown fast to the pericarp, forming a seedlike grain. In a few genera (*Sporobolus, Eleusine*), the seed is free from the pericarp. The caryopsis may be free from the lemma and palea, as in wheat, or it may be permanently enclosed, as in the oat and in the Paniceae. The grain (caryopsis) may enlarge during ripening and greatly exceed the glumes, lemma, and palea, as in maize and *Pennisetum glaucum*.

The embryo lies on the side of the caryopsis next to the lemma, and can be easily seen as an oval depression (the "germ" of maize and wheat). The hilum is the dot or line opposite the embryo which marks the point of attachment of the seed to the pericarp. The part of the caryopsis not occupied by the embryo is the endosperm, or nourishment for the germinating seed.

CLASSIFICATION OF GRASSES

A natural classification of plants is one in which the different kinds or species are arranged in groups according to their resemblances as shown by their structure, especially (in the grasses and other flowering plants) by the structure of their flowers. The plants of today represent a cross section of the lines of descent from countless generations that have preceded them. It is generally accepted that there has been much variation during the evolutionary process, and that all living plants are genetically connected through their lines of descent. Some of the gaps in present-day knowledge of relationship are filled by fossil remains, but relatively few of the ancestors of living plants are represented by fossils. Knowledge of the ancestry of the kinds of plants now on the globe is necessarily very incomplete. Hence, ideas of the relations of groups to each other are largely inferences based upon morphological resemblances. Those individuals which are so much alike as to appear to be of one kind, with, presumably, a common ancestor in recent geological times, are regarded as belonging to the same species. The species is the unit of classification. For convenience, species are grouped into genera and genera into families. For example, the white oak, red oak, black oak, and other kinds or species of oak belong to the oak genus (*Quercus*), all the species of which have one character in common —the fruit is an acorn. The oak genus, the beech genus, the chestnut genus, and a few allied genera are grouped together as a family.

The grass family (Gramineae or Poaceae) is one of the largest in number of genera and species, and, among flowering plants, is probably the largest in the number of individuals and is one of the most widely distributed. Some genera, such as the bluegrasses (*Poa*), the bromegrasses (*Bromus*), and the immense genus *Panicum*, contain numerous often closely allied species. Some genera contain but a few species or only one.

When an attempt is made to classify a group of related variable species the question always arises whether there are several closely related but distinct species or a few distinct species, each of which shows great variation. It is but natural that botanists should differ in their conclusions. This explains in part the different classifications of the same group given by botanists of different periods or even of the same period. A satisfactory classification depends upon the study of abundant material both in the field and in the herbarium. By observation in the field one learns the range of variability of a species, while in the herbarium one can compare plants from different localities, interpreting the dried specimens in the light of field experience.

In the classification of variable species it is found convenient sometimes to separate variants as varieties. A variety comprises those individuals of a species that show a definite tendency to vary in a certain direction, but which are connected with the species by rather numerous intergrades. Sometimes a variety is founded on a single variation which is distinct but trivial, for example, pubescent specimens of a glabrous species. A variation supported by a distinct geographical range or even by a distinct habitat is given greater weight than is a variation found in a few individuals growing among plants of the typical form.

The study of a vast amount of material in field and herbarium during some 40 years has resulted in the recognition of relatively few varieties, the intergrades proving to be more numerous than fairly clear-cut variants. Well-marked varieties are given a separate paragraph in the text, but are not usually given in the keys. Less well-marked varieties are given in the paragraph with the species. Many additional forms are indicated in a descriptive statement without being formally recognized as species or varieties. For example, under *Digitaria gracillima* appears, "A tall plant with * * * has been called *D. bakeri* (Nash) Fernald"; and under *Eriochloa michauxii*, "a form with * * * has been described as *E. mollis* var. *longifolia* Vasey."

The arrangement of the genera in this manual is, in general, from the simple to the complex. It is, of course, impossible to arrange all the genera in linear sequence and at the same time represent a gradual increase in complexity because plants have not developed in a single line, but have diverged in all directions, their relationships being a complex network. The highest genus of one tribe may be much more complex than the lowest genus of the next tribe above. On the average the Bambuseae seem to be the most primitive and the Tripsaceae the most complex. A grass with a spikelet consisting of glumes and several florets, the lemmas and glumes being similar and resembling bracts, is a primitive form. Grasses with spikelets in which the parts are reduced, enlarged, or much differentiated, are derived or complex forms. Derived forms may be simple from the reduction of parts and yet not be primitive. In the main the genera of grasses fall readily into a few large groups or tribes, but several genera of uncertain affinities are, for convenience, placed in the recognized tribes on artificial characters, with the hope that further study and exploration will bring to light their true relationships.

The grasses of the world (some 600 genera) have been grouped into 14 tribes, all of which are represented in the United States.

SCOPE OF THE MANUAL

The manual includes descriptions of all grasses known to grow in the continental United States, excluding Alaska. There are 169 numbered genera and 1,398 numbered species. Of these, 46 genera and 156 species are introduced, mostly from the Eastern Hemisphere.

In addition to the numbered species, which may be considered permanent constituents of the flora of the United States, there are 16 genera and 120 species that are known only as ballast plants, or as waifs, or are only rarely cultivated. These appear not to be established and are mentioned, without numbers, in paragraphs appended to their nearest allies. They are not included in the keys.

The manual is based mainly on the material in the United States National Herbarium, the grass collection of which is the largest in the world, numbering more than 320,000 sheets. In addition, all the larger collections of grasses in the United States have been consulted and the curators have lent specimens for study and have aided in other ways. Many smaller collections have contributed information, especially on the ranges of species. The cooperation of the Forest Service, United States Department of Agriculture, has been invaluable. The Forest Service maintains in its Washington office a range-plant herbarium consisting of the collections made by forest officers, especially those located in western national forests and forest experiment stations. The grasses of this range-plant herbarium have been examined and have furnished important data on distribution.

Many botanists throughout the country have rendered valuable assistance in recent years by contributing specimens that have added species previously unknown from the United States, have extended ranges, and have helped to solve the position of puzzling species and varieties.[4]

Nearly all the numbered species are illustrated.[5] About half are accompanied by a map, giving the distribution of that species in the United States.

To aid the users of this work in pronouncing the Latin names the accented syllable is indicated. The accent mark is used to show the accented syllable without reference to the length of the vowel.

GRAMINEAE (POACEAE), THE GRASS FAMILY

Flowers perfect (rarely unisexual), small, with no distinct perianth, arranged in spikelets consisting of a shortened axis (rachilla) and 2 to many 2-ranked bracts, the lowest 2 being empty (the glumes, rarely one or both obsolete), the 1 or more succeeding ones (lemmas) bearing in their axils a single flower, and, between the flower and the rachilla, a second 2-nerved bract (the palea), the lemma, palea, and flower together constituting the floret; stamens 1 to 6, usually 3, with very delicate filaments and 2-celled anthers; pistil 1, with a 1-celled 1-ovuled ovary, 2

[4] The more important are: A. A. Beetle, from California; E. E. Berkeley, from West Virginia; H. L. Blomquist, from North Carolina; W. E. Booth, from Montana; Clair Brown, from Louisiana; V. H. Chase, from Illinois, Arkansas, and Idaho; Earl Core, from West Virginia; R. A. Darrow, from Arizona; R. J. Davis, from Idaho; Charles C. Deam and J. E. Potzger, from Indiana; H. I. Featherly, from Oklahoma; M. L. Fernald, from Northeastern States and Virginia; A. O. Garrett, from Utah; L. N. Goodding, from the Southwest; F. W. Gould, from Arizona and California; C. R. Hanes, from Michigan; H. D. Harrington, from Colorado; Bertrand Harrison, from Utah; R. F. Hoover and John Thomas Howell, from California; T. H. Kearney, from Arizona; John and Charlotte Reeder, California to Michigan; and W. A. Silveus, from Texas and other Southern States.

Jason R. Swallen, Curator, Division of Grasses, U.S. National Museum, has given valuable assistance. The bibliography is based on the catalog of grass names maintained in the Division of Grasses, this catalog being the work, over some 35 years, of Cornelia D. Niles, bibliographer. F. A. McClure, bamboo specialist, U.S. Department of Agriculture, contributed the economic notes on bamboos and has aided in the elucidation of the native species of bamboos.

[5] The drawings illustrating the genera (previously published in the U. S. Department of Agriculture Bulletin 772, the Genera of Grasses of the United States . . .) and nearly half of the others were made by Mary Wright Gill; the rest were drawn by Edna May Whitehorn, Frances C. Weintraub, Leta Hughey, and Agnes Chase. The last-named made most of the spikelet drawings. In each case the specimen from which the drawing was made is cited, for example (Nash 2198, Fla.).

(rarely 1 or 3) styles, and usually plumose stigmas; fruit a caryopsis with starchy endosperm and a small embryo at the base on the side opposite the hilum.

Herbs, or rarely woody plants, with hollow or solid stems (culms) closed at the nodes, and 2-ranked usually parallel-veined leaves, these consisting of 2 parts, the sheath, enveloping the culm, its margins overlapping or sometimes grown together, and the blade, usually flat; between the 2 on the inside, a membranaceous hyaline or hairy appendage (the ligule).

The spikelets are almost always aggregated in spikes or panicles at the ends of the main culms or branches. The perianth is usually represented by 2 (rarely 3) small hyaline scales (the lodicules) at the base of the flower inside the lemma and palea. The grain or caryopsis (the single seed and the adherent pericarp) may be free, as in wheat, or permanently enclosed in the lemma and palea, as in the oat. Rarely the seed is free from the pericarp, as in species of *Sporobolus* and *Eleusine*. The culms of bamboos are woody, as are also those of a few genera, such as *Olyra* and *Lasiacis*, belonging to other tribes. The culms are solid in our species of the tribes Tripsaceae and Andropogoneae and in several other groups. The margins of the sheaths are grown together in some species of *Bromus*, *Danthonia*, *Festuca*, *Melica*, *Glyceria*, and other genera.

The parts of the spikelet may be modified in various ways. The first glume, and more rarely also the second, may be wanting. The lemmas may contain no flower, or even no palea, or may be reduced or rudimentary. Rarely, as in species of *Agrostis* and *Andropogon*, the palea is obsolete.

The division of the family into two subfamilies is somewhat artificial. The tribes Zoysieae, Oryzeae, Zizanieae, and especially Phalarideae, do not fall definitely into either of the recognized subfamilies. They are placed as indicated largely for convenience.

DESCRIPTIONS OF THE SUBFAMILIES AND KEYS TO THE TRIBES

SUBFAMILY 1. FESTUCOIDEAE

Spikelets 1- to many-flowered, the reduced florets, if any, above the perfect florets (except in Phalarideae; sterile lemmas below as well as above in *Ctenium*, *Uniola*, and *Blepharidachne*); articulation usually above the glumes; spikelets usually more or less laterally compressed.

Key to the tribes of Festucoideae

Plants woody, the culms perennial. Spikelets several-flowered........ 1. BAMBUSEAE (p. 27)
Plants herbaceous, the culms annual (somewhat woody and persistent in *Arundo*).
  Spikelets with 2 (rarely 1) staminate, neuter, or rudimentary lemmas unlike and below the fertile lemma; no sterile or rudimentary floret above......8. PHALARIDEAE (p. 547)
  Spikelets without sterile lemmas below the perfect floret (or these rarely present and like the fertile ones, a dissimilar pair below and a rudimentary floret above in *Blepharidachne*).
    Spikelets unisexual, falling entire, 1-flowered, terete or nearly so. 10. ZIZANIEAE (p. 561)
    Spikelets perfect (rarely unisexual but then not as above), usually articulate above the glumes.
      Spikelets articulate below the glumes, 1-flowered, very flat, the lemma and palea about equal, both keeled. Glumes small or wanting........ 9. ORYZEAE (p. 556)
      Spikelets articulate above the glumes (rarely below, but the glumes, at least one, well developed).
        Spikelets 1-flowered (or the staminate 2-flowered) in groups (short spikes) of 2 to 5 (single in *Zoysia*), the groups racemose along a main axis, falling entire; lemma and palea thinner than the glumes.................................. 6. ZOYSIEAE (p. 482)
        Spikelets not as above.
          Spikelets sessile on a usually continuous rachis (short-pedicellate in *Leptochloa*

and *Trichoneura;* the rachis disarticulating in *Monerma, Parapholis, Hordeum, Sitanion,* and in a few species of allied genera. See also *Brachypodium* in *Festuceae.*)

Spikelets on opposite sides of the rachis; spike terminal, solitary. 3. HORDEAE (p. 230)

Spikelets on one side of the rachis; spikes usually more than 1, digitate or racemose........ 7. CHLORIDEAE (p. 491)

Spikelets pedicellate in open or contracted, sometimes spikelike, panicles, rarely racemes.

Spikelets 1-flowered (occasionally some of the spikelets 2-flowered in a few species of *Muhlenbergia*)........ 5. AGROSTIDEAE (p. 313)

Spikelets 2- to many-flowered.

Glumes as long as the lowest floret, usually as long as the spikelet (sometimes shorter in *Sphenopholis*); lemmas awned from the back (spikelets awnless in species of *Trisetum, Koeleria, Sphenopholis,* and *Schismus*). 4. AVENEAE (p. 280)

Glumes shorter than the first floret (except in *Dissanthelium* with long rachilla joints, and in *Tridens strictus*); lemmas awnless or awned from the tip or from a bifid apex........ 2. FESTUCEAE (p. 31)

SUBFAMILY 2. PANICOIDEAE

Spikelets with 1 perfect terminal floret (disregarding those of the few monoecious genera and the staminate and neuter spikelets) and a sterile or staminate floret below, usually represented by a sterile lemma only, 1 glume sometimes (rarely both glumes) wanting; articulation below the spikelets, either in the pedicel, in the rachis, or at the base of a cluster of spikelets, the spikelets falling entire, singly, in groups, or together with joints of the rachis; spikelets, or at least the fruits, more or less dorsally compressed.

Key to the tribes of Panicoideae

Glumes membranaceous, the sterile lemma like the glumes in texture.

Fertile lemma and palea thinner than the glumes. Sterile lemma awned from the notched summit........ 11. MELINIDEAE (p. 569)

Fertile lemma and palea indurate or at least firmer than the glumes. 12. PANICEAE (p. 569)

Glumes indurate; fertile lemma and palea hyaline or membranaceous, the sterile lemmal ike the fertil e one in texture.

Spikelets unisexual, the pistillate below, the staminate above, in the same inflorescence or in separate inflorescences........ 14. TRIPSACEAE (p. 789)

Spikelets in pairs, one sessile and perfect, the other pedicellate and usually staminate or neuter (the pedicellate one sometimes obsolete, rarely both pedicellate). Lemmas hyaline........ 13. ANDROPOGONEAE (p. 737)

DESCRIPTIONS OF THE TRIBES AND KEYS TO THE GENERA

TRIBE 1. BAMBUSEAE

Culms woody, perennial, usually hollow; spikelets 2- to several-flowered, in panicles or racemes, or in close heads or fascicles; often 1 or more sterile lemmas at base of spikelet; lemmas usually awnless; blades usually articulated with the sheath, flat, rather broad. Only one genus, *Arundinaria,* is native within our limits. Several species of this and other genera are cultivated in the Southern States.

TRIBE 2. FESTUCEAE

Spikelets more than 1-flowered, usually several-flowered, in open, narrow, or sometimes spikelike panicles (rarely in racemes); lemmas awnless or awned from the tip, rarely from between the teeth of a bifid apex; rachilla usually disarticulating above the glumes and between the florets.

A large and important tribe, mainly inhabitants of the cooler regions. The lemma is divided into several awns in *Pappophorum* and its allies, is deeply 2-lobed in *Triplasis* and in a few species of *Tridens,* 3-lobed in *Blepharidachne,* several-toothed in *Orcuttia*, and slightly 2-toothed in *Bromus* and in a few other genera, the awn, when single, arising from between the teeth. The paleas are persistent upon the continuous rachilla in many species of *Eragrostis*. *Scleropogon*, *Monanthochloë*, *Distichlis*, *Hesperochloa* and a few species of *Poa* and *Eragrostis* are dioecious. *Gynerium*, *Cortaderia*, *Arundo*, *Phragmites*, and *Neyraudia* are tall reeds. In *Blepharidachne* there is a pair of sterile florets at the base of the single fertile floret, and a rudiment above. In some species of *Melica* there is, above the fertile florets, a club-shaped rudiment consisting of 1 or more sterile lemmas. In *Uniola* there are 1 to 4 sterile lemmas below the fertile ones. In *Melica imperfecta* and *M. torreyana* there may be only 1 perfect floret.

Key to the genera of Festuceae

1a. Plants dioecious, (sometimes monoecious), the sexes very dissimilar, the pistillate lemmas with 3 long twisted divergent awns, the staminate lemma awnless or mucronate. 41. SCLEROPOGON.
1b. Plants with perfect flowers, or, if dioecious, the sexes not dissimilar in appearance.
2a. Lemmas divided at the summit into 5 to several awns or awnlike lobes.
Awnlike lobes 5. Inflorescence an erect raceme or simple panicle........ 36. ORCUTTIA.
Awns 9 or more.
Awns unmixed with awned teeth; all the florets falling attached, their awns forming a pappuslike crown, the lower 1 to 3 fertile; panicles narrow.
Spikelets 3-flowered, the first floret fertile; awns 9, plumose, equal. 40. ENNEAPOGON.
Spikelets 4- to 6-flowered, the lower 1 to 3 fertile; awns numerous, not plumose, unequal........ 39. PAPPOPHORUM.
Awns mixed with awned teeth; florets not falling attached, the rachilla disarticulating between them; panicles somewhat open........ 38. COTTEA.
2b. Lemmas awnless, with a single awn, or, if with 3, the lateral awns minute.
3a. Tall stout reeds with large plumelike panicles. Lemmas or rachilla with long silky hairs as long as the lemmas.
Leaves crowded at the base of the culms........ 27. CORTADERIA.
Leaves distributed along the culms.
Lemmas naked. Rachilla hairy........ 28. PHRAGMITES.
Lemmas hairy.
Rachilla naked........ 26. ARUNDO.
Rachilla hairy........ 29. NEYRAUDIA.
3b. Low or rather tall grasses, rarely more than 1.5 m. tall.
4a. Plants dioecious, perennial.
Plants densely tufted, rather coarse, erect from short rhizomes; lemmas scabrous; grasses of dry mountain slopes........ 11. HESPEROCHLOA.
Plants not densely tufted, spreading by stolons or extensively creeping rhizomes; lemmas glabrous; grasses of salt or alkaline soil.
Plants low, stoloniferous; spikelets obscure, scarcely differentiated from the short crowded rigid leaves........ 20. MONANTHOCHLOË.
Plants erect from creeping rhizomes; spikelets in narrow simple exserted panicles. 21. DISTICHLIS.
4b. Plants not dioecious (except in a few species of *Poa* with villous lemmas and in an annual species of *Eragrostis*).
5a. Spikelets of two forms, sterile and fertile intermixed. Panicle dense, somewhat one-sided.
Fertile spikelets 2- or 3-flowered; sterile spikelets with numerous rigid awn-tipped lemmas; panicle dense, spikelike........ 24. CYNOSURUS.
Fertile spikelets with 1 perfect floret, long-awned; sterile spikelets with many obtuse sterile lemmas; panicle branchlets short, nodding.... 25. LAMARCKIA.
5b. Spikelets all alike in the same inflorescence.
6a. Lemmas 3-nerved, the nerves prominent, often hairy.
7a. Inflorescence a few-flowered head or capitate panicle overtopped by the leaves or partly concealed in them. Lemmas toothed or cleft; low plants of the arid regions.
Inflorescence hidden among the sharp-pointed leaves, not woolly; plants annual (Chlorideae)........ 114. MUNROA.
Inflorescence a capitate woolly panicle, not concealed; plants perennial.
Lemmas cleft either side of the midnerve to near the base, the lower two

sterile, the third floret fertile, the fourth reduced to a 3-awned rudiment.......... 37. BLEPHARIDACHNE.

Lemmas 2-lobed but not deeply cleft, all fertile but the uppermost. 33. TRIDENS.

7b. Inflorescence an exserted open or spikelike panicle.

8a. Lemmas pubescent on the nerves or callus (except in *Tridens albescens*), the midnerve usually exserted as an awn or mucro.

Nerves glabrous. Callus densely hairy; lemmas firm; panicle large, diffuse. 19. REDFIELDIA.

Nerves hairy at least below, the lateral ones often conspicuously so.

Palea densely long-ciliate on the upper half.......... 34. TRIPLASIS.

Palea sometimes villous but not long-ciliate on the upper half. Perennials.......... 33. TRIDENS.

8b. Lemmas not pubescent on the nerves nor callus (the internerves sometimes pubescent), awnless.

Glumes longer than the lemmas; lateral nerves of lemma marginal, the internerves pubescent.......... 18. DISSANTHELIUM.

Glumes shorter than the lemmas; lateral nerves of lemma not marginal, the internerves glabrous.

Lemmas chartaceous; grain large, beaked, at maturity forcing the lemma and palea open.......... 17. DIARRHENA.

Lemmas membranaceous; if firm, the grain neither large nor beaked.

Spikelets subterete; palea longer than the lemma, bowed out below. 16. MOLINIA.

Spikelets compressed; palea not longer than the lemma, not bowed out below (except in *Eragrostis oxylepis* and *E. sessilispica*).

Lemmas truncate; spikelets 2-flowered.......... 15. CATABROSA.

Lemmas acute or acuminate; spikelets 3- to many-flowered. Rachilla continuous, the paleas persistent after the fall of the lemmas (rachilla disarticulating in Sect. Cataclastos). 14. ERAGROSTIS.

6b. Lemmas 5- to many-nerved, the nerves sometimes obscure.

Spikelets with 1 to 4 empty lemmas below the fertile florets; nerves obscure; lemmas firm.......... 22. UNIOLA.

Spikelets with no empty lemmas below the fertile florets; nerves usually prominent; lemmas membranaceous (firm in a few species of *Bromus* and *Festuca*).

Lemmas flabellate; glumes wanting; inflorescence dense, cylindric. Low annual.......... 35. NEOSTAPFIA.

Lemmas not flabellate; glumes present; inflorescence not cylindric.

Lemmas as broad as long, the margins outspread; florets closely imbricate, horizontally spreading.......... 13. BRIZA.

Lemmas longer than broad, the margins clasping the palea; florets not horizontally spreading.

Callus of florets bearded.

Lemmas erose at summit, awnless.......... 9. SCOLOCHLOA.

Lemmas bifid at summit, awned.......... 31. SCHIZACHNE.

Callus not bearded (lemmas cobwebby at base in *Poa*). Lemmas not erose (slightly in *Puccinellia*).

9a. Lemmas keeled on the back (somewhat rounded in *Poa scabrella* and its allies).

Spikelets strongly compressed, crowded in 1-sided clusters at the ends of the stiff, naked panicle branches.......... 23. DACTYLIS.

Spikelets not strongly compressed, not crowded in 1-sided clusters.

Lemmas awned from a minutely bifid apex (awnless or nearly so in *Bromus catharticus* and *B. brizaeformis*); spikelets large.......... 2. BROMUS.

Lemmas awnless; spikelets small.......... 12. POA.

9b. Lemmas rounded on the back (slightly keeled toward the summit in *Festuca* and *Bromus*).

Glumes papery; lemmas firm, strongly nerved, scarious-margined; upper florets sterile, often reduced to a club-shaped rudiment infolded by the broad upper lemmas. Spikelets tawny or purplish, usually not green.......... 30. MELICA.

Glumes not papery; upper florets not unlike the others.

Nerves of lemma parallel, not converging at summit or but slightly so.

Spikelets in racemes.
Racemes short, dense, overtopped by the leaves; spikelets awnless........ 8. SCLEROCHLOA.
Racemes elongate, loose, exserted; spikelets awned or mucronate........ 10. PLEUROPOGON.
Spikelets in open or contracted panicles.
Nerves prominent; plants usually rather tall, growing in woods or fresh-water marshes........ 7. GLYCERIA.
Nerves faint; plants low, growing in saline soil. 6. PUCCINELLIA.
Nerves of lemma converging toward the summit, the lemmas narrowed at apex.
Lemmas awned or awn-tipped from a minutely bifid apex (awnless in *Bromus brizaeformis*); palea adhering to the caryopsis.
Spikelets in open to contracted panicles; stigmas borne at the sides of the summit of ovary........ 2. BROMUS.
Spikelets nearly sessile in a strict raceme; stigmas terminal on the ovary........ 3. BRACHYPODIUM.
Lemmas entire, pointed, awnless or awned from the tip (minutely toothed in *Festuca elmeri* and *F. gigantea*).
Spikelets awned (awnless in a few perennial species); lemmas pointed........ 4. FESTUCA.
Spikelets awnless.
Second glume 5- to 11-nerved; spikelets mostly 1 cm. or more long; lemmas broad.
Florets persistent on the continuous rachilla, the caryopsis falling free........ 32A. ECTOSPERMA.
Florets falling together with the joints of the articulate rachilla........ 32. VASEYOCHLOA.
Second glume 1- to 3-nerved; spikelets smaller; lemmas 5-nerved, membranaceous, not pointed.
Spikelets on slender pedicels in compound panicles; perennials........ 12. POA.
Spikelets on thick short pedicels in simple panicles; annual. Rachilla disarticulating at the base, forming a stipe to the floret above.... 5. SCLEROPOA.

TRIBE 3. HORDEAE

Spikelets 1- to several-flowered, sessile on opposite sides of a jointed or continuous axis forming symmetrical spikes (not 1-sided, but spikelets sometimes turned to one side in some species).

This small but important tribe, found in the temperate regions of both hemispheres, includes our most important cereals, wheat, barley, and rye. The rachis is flattened or concave next to the spikelets, or in some genera is thickened and hollowed out, the spikelets being more or less enclosed in the hollows. In *Triticum* and its allies there is 1 spikelet at each node of the rachis; in *Hordeum* and its allies there are 2 or 3 at each node. In *Lolium* and its allies the spikelets are placed edgewise to the rachis, and the first or inner glume is suppressed except in the terminal spikelet. The rachis of the spikes disarticulates at maturity in several genera. In some species of *Elymus* and especially in *Sitanion* the glumes are very slender, extending into long awns, in the latter genus sometimes divided into several slender bristles. The spikes are rarely branched or compound, especially in *Elymus condensatus*. In this tribe the blades of the leaves usually bear on each side at the base a small appendage or auricle.

Key to the genera of Hordeae

1a. Spikelets solitary at each node of the rachis (rarely 2 in species of *Agropyron*, but never throughout).
2a. Spikelets 1-flowered, sunken in hollows in the rachis. Spikes slender, cyclindric; low annuals.

Lemmas awned; florets lateral to the rachis.......... 53. SCRIBNERIA.
Lemmas awnless; florets dorsiventral to the rachis.
First glume wanting.......... 51. MONERMA.
First glume present, the pair standing in front of the spikelet...... 52. PARAPHOLIS.
2b. Spikelets 2- to several-flowered, not sunken in the rachis.
Spikelets placed edgewise to the rachis. First glume wanting except in the terminal spikelet.......... 50. LOLIUM.
Spikelets placed flatwise to the rachis.
Plants perennial.......... 42. AGROPYRON.
Plants annual.
Spikelets turgid or cylindric.......... 44. AEGILOPS.
Spikelets compressed.
Glumes ovate, 3-nerved.......... 43. TRITICUM.
Glumes subulate, 1-nerved.......... 45. SECALE.
1b. Spikelets more than 1 at each node of the rachis (solitary in part of the spike in some species of *Elymus*).
Spikelets 3 at each node of the rachis, 1-flowered, the lateral pair pediceled, usually reduced to awns.......... 49. HORDEUM.
Spikelets 2 or more (sometimes solitary in *Elymus*) at each node of the rachis, alike, 2- to 6-flowered.
Glumes wanting or reduced to 2 short bristles; spikelets horizontally spreading or ascending at maturity. Spikes very loose.......... 48. HYSTRIX.
Glumes usually equaling the florets (reduced in *Elymus interruptus*); spikelets appressed or ascending.
Rachis continuous (rarely tardily disarticulating); glumes broad or narrow, entire. 46. ELYMUS.
Rachis disarticulating at maturity; glumes subulate, extending into long awns, these and the awns of the lemmas making the spike very bristly........ 47. SITANION.

TRIBE 4. AVENEAE

Spikelets 2- to several-flowered in open or contracted panicles, or rarely in racemes (solitary in *Danthonia unispicata*), glumes usually as long as or longer than the first lemma, commonly longer than all the florets; lemmas usually awned from the back or from between the teeth of a bifid apex, the awn usually bent, often twisted, the callus and rachilla joints usually villous.

A rather small tribe widely distributed in both warm and cool regions. In our genera the rachilla is prolonged beyond the upper floret as a slender stipe (except in *Aira* and *Holcus*). The lemma is awnless or nearly so in *Schismus*, two species of *Trisetum*, one species of *Koeleria*, and in most of the species of *Sphenopholis*. *Koeleria* and *Sphenopholis* are placed in this tribe because they appear to be closely allied to *Trisetum* with which they agree in having oblanceolate glumes about as long as the first floret.

Key to the genera of Aveneae

Florets 2, one perfect, the other staminate.
Lower floret staminate, the awn twisted, geniculate, exserted.... 63. ARRHENATHERUM.
Lower floret perfect, awnless; upper floret awned.......... 64. HOLCUS.
Florets 2 or more, all alike except the reduced upper ones.
Articulation below the glumes, the spikelets falling entire.
Lemmas, at least the upper, with a conspicuous bent awn; glumes nearly alike. 57. TRISETUM.
Lemmas awnless or (in *S. pallens*) the upper with a short awn; second glume much wider than the first.......... 56. SPHENOPHOLIS.
Articulation above the glumes, the glumes similar in shape.
Lemmas bifid at apex, awned or mucronate between the lobes. Spikelets several-flowered.
Awns conspicuous, flat, bent. Spikelets 1 cm. or more long.......... 66. DANTHONIA.
Awns minute or nearly obsolete.
Spikelets 8 to 12 mm. long.......... 65. SIEGLINGIA.
Spikelets not more than 5 mm. long; awns, when present, slender, rounded. 54. SCHISMUS.
Lemmas toothed, but not bifid and awned or mucronate between the lobes.
Glumes 2 to 3.5 cm. long, 7- to 9-nerved; spikelets 2-flowered, or with a rudimentary third floret, pendulous. Plants annual.......... 61. AVENA.

Glumes not more than 1 cm. long, 1- to 5-nerved; spikelets not pendulous.
Spikelets 3- to several-flowered, 1 to 1.5 cm. long .... 62. HELICTOTRICHON.
Spikelets 2-flowered (or 3-flowered in *Trisetum cernuum*), mostly less than 1 cm. long.
Lemmas keeled, the awn when present from above the middle.
Rachilla joints very short, glabrous or minutely pubescent; lemmas awnless or with a straight awn from a toothed apex .... 55. KOELERIA.
Rachilla joints slender, villous; lemmas with a dorsal bent awn (awnless or nearly so in 2 species) .... 57. TRISETUM.
Lemmas convex, awned from below the middle.
Rachilla prolonged behind the upper floret; lemmas truncate and erose-dentate at summit.
Awn slender, not jointed .... 58. DESCHAMPSIA.
Awn clavate, jointed near the middle .... 60. CORYNEPHORUS.
Rachilla not prolonged; lemmas tapering into 2 slender teeth .... 59. AIRA.

TRIBE 5. AGROSTIDEAE

Spikelets 1-flowered, usually perfect, in open, contracted, or spikelike panicles, but not in true spikes nor in 1-sided racemes.

A large and important tribe, inhabiting more especially the temperate and cool regions. The articulation of the rachilla is usually above the glumes, the mature floret falling from the persistent glumes, but in a few genera the articulation is below the glumes, the mature spikelet falling entire (*Alopecurus*, *Cinna*, *Polypogon*, *Lycurus*, and *Limnodea*). The palea is small or wanting in *Alopecurus* and in some species of *Agrostis*. In a few genera the rachilla is prolonged behind the palea as a minute bristle, or sometimes as a more pronounced stipe (*Brachyelytrum*, *Limnodea*, *Cinna*, *Gastridium*, *Calamagrostis*, *Ammophila*, *Lagurus*, *Apera*, and a few species of *Agrostis*). In some genera the rachilla joint between the glumes and the lemma is slightly elongated, forming a hard stipe which remains attached to the mature fruit as a pointed callus. The callus is well marked in *Stipa* (especially in *S. spartea* and its allies) and in *Aristida*, the mature lemma being terete, indurate, and convolute, the palea wholly enclosed. In many genera the lemma is awned either from the tip or from the back, the awn being trifid in *Aristida*.

Key to the genera of Agrostideae

Glumes wanting. Low annual .... 73. COLEANTHUS.
Glumes present (the first obsolete in *Muhlenbergia schreberi* and sometimes in *Brachyelytrum* and *Phippsia*).
1a. Articulation below the glumes, the spikelets falling entire.
Spikelets in pairs in a spikelike panicle, one perfect, the other staminate or neuter, the pair falling together .... 78. LYCURUS.
Spikelets all alike.
Glumes long-awned .... 77. POLYPOGON.
Glumes awnless.
Rachilla not prolonged behind the palea; panicle dense.
Glumes united toward the base, ciliate on the keel; inflorescence not capitate and bracteate .... 76. ALOPECURUS.
Glumes not united, glabrous; inflorescence capitate in the axils of broad bracts. 85. CRYPSIS.
Rachilla prolonged behind the palea; panicle narrow or open, not dense; glumes not united, not ciliate on the keel.
Panicle narrow; lemma with a slender bent twisted awn from the bifid apex. 75. LIMNODEA.
Panicle open, drooping; lemma with a minute straight awn just below the entire apex (rarely awnless) .... 74. CINNA.
1b. Articulation above the glumes.
Fruit dorsally compressed, indurate, smooth, and shining, awnless .... 88. MILIUM.
Fruit laterally compressed or terete, awned or awnless.
2a. Fruit indurate, terete, awned, the nerves obscure; callus well developed, oblique, bearded.
Awn trifid, the lateral divisions sometimes short, rarely obsolete (when obsolete no

line of demarcation between awn and lemma as in the next).... 92. ARISTIDA.
Awn simple, a line of demarcation between the awn and the lemma.
Awn persistent, twisted, and bent, several to many times longer than the fruit.
Edges of lemma overlapping (rarely only meeting), enclosing the palea; callus sharp-pointed, usually narrow and acuminate........................... 91. STIPA.
Edges of lemma not meeting, exposing the indurate sulcus of the palea, this projecting from the summit as a minute point; callus short, acutish.
90. PIPTOCHAETIUM.
Awn deciduous, not twisted, sometimes bent, rarely more than 3 or 4 times as long as the plump fruit; callus short, usually obtuse .... 89. ORYZOPSIS.
2b. Fruit thin or firm, but not indurate; callus not well developed.
Lemma firm, subindurate at maturity, bearing a long delicate straight awn just below the tip; palea about as long as the lemma, the naked rachilla produced back of the palea.. 70. APERA.
Lemma thin or membranaceous.
3a. Glumes longer than the lemma (nearly equal in *Agrostis thurberiana* and *A. aequivalis*).
Panicle feathery, capitate, nearly as broad as long; spikelets woolly.
81. LAGURUS.
Panicle not feathery; spikelets not woolly.
Glumes compressed-carinate, stiff-ciliate on the keel; panicle dense, cylindric or ellipsoid.. 79. PHLEUM.
Glumes not compressed-carinate, not ciliate.
Glumes saccate at base; lemma long-awned; panicle contracted, shining.
80. GASTRIDIUM.
Glumes not saccate at base; lemma awned or awnless; panicle open or contracted.
Floret bearing a tuft of hairs at the base from the short callus; palea well developed, the rachilla prolonged behind the palea (except in *Calamagrostis epigeios*) as a hairy bristle.... 67. CALAMAGROSTIS.
Floret without hairs at the base or with short hairs (nearly half as long as the lemma in *A. hallii*); palea usually small or obsolete (developed and with a minute rachilla back of it in Nos. 1 to 3).
71. AGROSTIS.
3b. Glumes not longer than the lemma, usually shorter (the awn tips longer in *Muhlenbergia racemosa* and *M. glomerata*).
Lemma awned from the tip or mucronate, 3- to 5-nerved (lateral nerves obscure in a few species of *Muhlenbergia*).
Rachilla prolonged behind the palea; floret stipitate; glumes minute or obsolete.. 87. BRACHYELYTRUM.
Rachilla not prolonged; floret not stipitate................. 82. MUHLENBERGIA.
Lemma awnless or awned from the back.
Floret bearing a tuft of hairs at the base from the short callus; lemma and palea chartaceous, awnless.
Panicle spikelike; rachilla prolonged................................ 68. AMMOPHILA.
Panicle open; rachilla not prolonged............................ 69. CALAMOVILFA.
Floret without hairs at base.
Nerves of lemma silky.. 84. BLEPHARONEURON.
Nerves of lemma not silky.
Caryopsis at maturity falling from the lemma and palea; seed loose in the pericarp, this usually opening when ripe; lemma 1-nerved.
83. SPOROBOLUS.
Caryopsis not falling from the lemma and palea, remaining permanently enclosed in them; seed adnate to the pericarp.
Panicle few-flowered, slender, rather loose; glumes minute, unequal, the first often wanting. Low arctic-alpine perennial.
72. PHIPPSIA.
Panicle many-flowered, spikelike; glumes well developed, about equal.
Panicle short, partly enclosed in the sheath; low annual.
86. HELEOCHLOA.
Panicle elongate; perennial........................... 82. MUHLENBERGIA.

TRIBE 6. ZOYSIEAE

Spikelets subsessile in short spikes of 2 to 5 (single in *Zoysia*), each spike falling entire from the continuous axis, usually 1-flowered, all perfect, or perfect and staminate together in the same spike; glumes usually firmer than the lemma and palea, sometimes awned, the lemma awnless.

This small and unimportant tribe is known also as Nazieae. In *Zoysia* the spikelets are single and have only 1 glume, this coriaceous, much firmer than the lemma and palea, the palea sometimes obsolete.

Key to the genera of Zoysieae

Spikelets single; first glume wanting........ 94. ZOYSIA.
Spikelets in clusters of 2 to 5; first glume present.
  Spikelets bearing hooked spines on the second glume, the group forming a little bur. 93. TRAGUS.
  Spikelets not bearing hooked spines, the second glume mostly cleft and awned.
    Groups of spikelets erect, the inflorescence not 1-sided........ 95. HILARIA.
    Groups of spikelets nodding along one side of the delicate axis........ 96. AEGOPOGON.

TRIBE 7. CHLORIDEAE

Spikelets 1- to several-flowered, in 2 rows on one side of a continuous rachis, forming 1-sided spikes or spikelike racemes, these solitary, digitate, or racemose along the main axis.

A large and rather important tribe, confined mostly to warm regions. The group is heterogeneous, the only common character of the genera (aside from the characters that place them in Festucoideae) being the arrangement of the spikelets in 1-sided spikes. *Chloris* and the allied genera form a coherent group, in which the spikelet consists of 1 perfect floret and, above this, 1 or more modified or rudimentary florets. *Leptochloa*, *Eleusine*, and their allies, with several-flowered spikelets, are more nearly related to certain genera of Festuceae. The spike is reduced to 2 or 3 spikelets or even to 1 spikelet and is sometimes deciduous from the main axis (*Cathestecum* and Sect. Atheropogon of *Bouteloua*). In *Ctenium* there are 2 sterile florets below the perfect one.

Key to the genera of Chlorideae

Plants monoecious or dioecious. Low stoloniferous perennial........ 115. BUCHLOË.
Plants with perfect flowers.
  1a. Spikelets with more than 1 perfect floret.
    Inflorescence a few-flowered head or capitate panicle hidden among the sharp-pointed leaves. Low spreading annual........ 114. MUNROA.
    Inflorescence exserted.
      Spikes solitary, the spikelets distant, appressed, several-flowered.... 99. TRIPOGON.
      Spikes more than 1 (sometimes 1 in depauperate *Eleusine*).
        Spikes numerous, slender, racemose on an elongate axis.
          Rachilla and callus of floret glabrous or nearly so; glumes acute, less than 5 mm. long........ 97. LEPTOCHLOA.
          Rachilla and callus of floret strongly pilose; glumes long-acuminate, about 1 cm. long........ 98. TRICHONEURA.
        Spikes few, digitate or nearly so.
          Rachis of spike extending beyond the spikelets........ 101. DACTYLOCTENIUM.
          Rachis not prolonged........ 100. ELEUSINE.
  1b. Spikelets with only 1 perfect floret, often with additional imperfect florets above or below.
    2a. Spikelets without additional modified florets, the rachilla sometimes prolonged.
      Rachilla articulate below the glumes, the spikelets falling entire.
        Glumes unequal, narrow........ 107. SPARTINA.
        Glumes equal, broad, boat-shaped........ 106. BECKMANNIA.
      Rachilla articulate above the glumes.
        Spike solitary, slender, arcuate........ 102. MICROCHLOA.
        Spikes 2 to many.
          Spikes digitate; rachilla prolonged........ 103. CYNODON.
          Spikes racemose along the main axis; rachilla not prolonged.
            Spikes slender, divaricate, the main axis elongating and becoming loosely spiral in fruit........ 105. SCHEDONNARDUS.
            Spikes short and rather stout, appressed, the axis unchanged in fruit. 104. WILLKOMMIA.

2b. Spikelets with 1 or more modified florets above the perfect one.
Spikelets with 2 sterile florets below the perfect one; second glume bearing a squarrose spine on the back; spike single, arcuate........ 108. CTENIUM.
Spikelets with no sterile florets below the perfect one; second glume without a squarrose spine.
Spikes digitate or nearly so.
Fertile lemma 1-awned or awnless........ 110. CHLORIS.
Fertile lemma 3-awned........ 111. TRICHLORIS.
Spikes racemose along the main axis.
Spikelets distant, appressed; spikes slender, elongate........ 109. GYMNOPOGON.
Spikelets approximate or crowded, not appressed; spikes usually short and rather stout.
Spikelets 3 in each spike, the 2 lateral staminate or rudimentary; spikes falling entire........ 113. CATHESTECUM.
Spikelets 2 to many (rarely 1) in each spike, all alike; spikes falling entire or persistent, the florets falling........ 112. BOUTELOUA.

TRIBE 8. PHALARIDEAE

Spikelets with 1 perfect terminal floret and, below this, a pair of staminate or neuter florets (1 sometimes obsolete in *Phalaris*).

A small tribe of about 6 genera, 4 of which are found in the United States. In *Phalaris* the lower florets are reduced to minute scalelike lemmas closely appressed to the edges of the fertile floret. In *Hierochloë* the lateral florets are staminate and as large as the fertile floret.

Key to the genera of Phalarideae

Lower florets staminate; spikelets brown, shining........ 116. HIEROCHLOË.
Lower florets neuter; spikelets green or yellowish.
Lower florets consisting of awned hairy sterile lemmas exceeding the fertile floret. 117. ANTHOXANTHUM.
Lower florets reduced to small awnless scalelike lemmas, much smaller than the fertile florets........ 118. PHALARIS.

TRIBE 9. ORYZEAE

Spikelets 1-flowered, perfect, strongly laterally compressed, paniculate; glumes reduced or wanting; palea apparently 1-nerved; stamens 6.

A small tribe whose affinities are not evident. It includes rice, the important food plant.

Key to the genera of Oryzeae

Glumes minute; lemma often awned........ 119. ORYZA.
Glumes wanting; lemma awnless........ 120. LEERSIA.

TRIBE 10. ZIZANIEAE

Spikelets unisexual, the pistillate terete or nearly so; glumes shorter than the lemma, usually 1 or both obsolete, the pedicel disarticulating below the spikelet. Glumes well developed in *Pharus*, a tropical genus placed in this tribe provisionally.

A small tribe of uncertain affinities, aquatic or subaquatic grasses (except *Pharus*) of no economic importance except the Indian rice (*Zizania*).

Key to the genera of Zizanieae

Blades elliptic, 2 to 4 cm. wide........ 125. PHARUS.
Blades much longer than wide.
Culms slender; plants low; staminate and pistillate spikelets borne in separate inflorescences.
Inflorescence a few-flowered raceme; floating aquatic........ 124. HYDROCHLOA.
Inflorescence a panicle; plants stoloniferous........ 123. LUZIOLA.
Culms robust; plants tall; staminate and pistillate spikelets borne in the same panicle.
Pistillate spikelets on the ascending upper branches, the staminate on the spreading

lower branches of the panicle; plants annual or perennial........ 121. ZIZANIA.
Pistillate spikelets at the ends, the staminate below on the same branches of the panicle; plants perennial........ 122. ZIZANIOPSIS.

TRIBE 11. MELINIDEAE

Spikelets disarticulating below the glumes, these very unequal, the first minute, the second and the sterile lemma equal, membranaceous, strongly nerved, the latter bearing a slender awn from the notched summit; fertile lemma and palea thinner in texture, awnless.

A tribe of about a dozen genera represented in the United States by an introduced species, *Melinis minutiflora*.

TRIBE 12. PANICEAE

Spikelets with 1 perfect terminal floret and below this a sterile floret and 2 glumes; fertile lemma and palea indurate or at least firmer than the glumes and sterile lemma, a lunate line of thinner texture at the back just above the base, the rootlet protruding through this at germination; articulation below the spikelet.

A large tribe, confined mostly to warm regions, and containing relatively few economic species. The first glume is wanting in some genera, such as *Paspalum*, and rarely the second glume also (*Reimarochloa*). The spikelets are usually awnless, but the glumes and sterile lemma are awned in *Echinochloa* and *Oplismenus*, and the second glume and sterile lemma in *Rhynchelytrum*. In *Eriochloa* and in some species of *Brachiaria* the fertile lemma is awn-tipped. In *Setaria* there are, beneath the spikelet, 1 or more bristles, these representing sterile branchlets. In *Pennisetum* similar bristles form an involucre, falling with the spikelet. In *Cenchrus* the bristles are united, forming a bur. The spikelets are of 2 kinds in *Amphicarpum*, aerial and subterranean. The culms are woody and perennial in *Lasiacis* and *Olyra*.

Key to the genera of Paniceae

Spikelets of two kinds.
  Spikelets all perfect, but those of the aerial panicle rarely perfecting grains, the fruitful spikelets borne on subterranean branches........ 146. AMPHICARPUM.
  Spikelets unisexual, the pistillate above, the staminate below on the branches of the same panicle. Blades broad, elliptic........ 147. OLYRA.
Spikelets all of one kind.
  Spikelets sunken in the cavities of the flattened corky rachis........ 131. STENOTAPHRUM.
  Spikelets not sunken in the rachis.
    1a. Spikelets subtended or surrounded by 1 to many distinct or more or less connate bristles, forming an involucre.
      Bristles persistent, the spikelets deciduous........ 143. SETARIA.
      Bristles falling with the spikelets at maturity.
        Bristles not united at base, slender, often plumose........ 144. PENNISETUM.
        Bristles united into a burlike involucre, the bristles retrorsely barbed. 145. CENCHRUS.
    1b. Spikelets not subtended by bristles.
      Glumes or sterile lemma awned (awn short and concealed in the silky hairs of the spikelet in *Rhynchelytrum;* awn reduced to a point in *Echinochloa colonum*).
        Inflorescence paniculate; spikelets silky........ 142. RHYNCHELYTRUM.
        Inflorescence of unilateral simple or somewhat compound racemes along a common axis; spikelets smooth or hispid, not silky.
          Blades lanceolate, broad, thin; culms creeping........ 140. OPLISMENUS.
          Blades long, narrow; culms not creeping........ 141. ECHINOCHLOA.
      Glumes and sterile lemma awnless.
        2a. Fruit cartilaginous-indurate, flexible, usually dark-colored, the lemma with more or less prominent white hyaline margins, these not inrolled.
          Spikelets covered with long silky hairs, arranged in racemes, these panicled. 128. TRICHACHNE.
          Spikelets glabrous or variously pubescent but not long-silky (somewhat silky in *Digitaria villosa*).

Spikelets in slender racemes more or less digitate at the summit of the culms. 129. DIGITARIA.
Spikelets in panicles.
Fruiting lemma boat-shaped; panicles narrow........ 127. ANTHAENANTIA.
Fruiting lemma convex; panicles diffuse........................... 130. LEPTOLOMA.
2b. Fruit chartaceous-indurate, rigid.
Spikelets placed with the back of the fruit turned away from the rachis of the racemes, usually solitary (not in pairs).
First glume and the rachilla joint forming a swollen ringlike callus below the spikelet.. 132. ERIOCHLOA.
First glume present or wanting, not forming a ringlike callus below the spikelet.
First glume present (next to the axis); racemes racemose along the main axis.. 133. BRACHIARIA.
First glume wanting; racemes digitate or subdigitate...... 134. AXONOPUS.
Spikelets placed with the back of the fruit turned toward the rachis (first glume, when present, away from the rachis) of the spikelike racemes or pedicellate in panicles.
Fruit long-acuminate; both glumes wanting................ 135. REIMAROCHLOA.
Fruit not long-acuminate; at least one glume present.
First glume typically wanting; spikelets plano-convex, subsessile in spikelike racemes.. 136. PASPALUM.
First glume present; spikelets usually in panicles.
Second glume inflated-saccate, this and the sterile lemma much exceeding the stipitate fruit.. 139. SACCIOLEPIS.
Second glume not inflated-saccate.
Culms woody, bamboolike; fruit with a tuft of down at the apex. 138. LASIACIS.
Culms herbaceous; no tuft of down at the apex of the fruit. 137. PANICUM.

TRIBE 13. ANDROPOGONEAE

Spikelets in pairs along a rachis, the usual arrangement being one of the pair sessile and fertile, the other pedicellate and staminate or neuter, rarely wanting, only the pedicel present; fertile spikelet consisting of 1 perfect terminal floret and, below this, a staminate or neuter floret, the lemmas thin or hyaline, and 2 awnless glumes, 1 or usually both firm or indurate.

A large tribe, confined mostly to warm regions. The rachis is usually jointed, disarticulating at maturity, with the spikelets attached to the joints. In a few genera it is thickened. Sometimes the racemes are shortened to 1 or 2 joints and borne on branches, the whole forming a panicle (as in *Sorghum* and *Sorghastrum*) instead of a series of racemes. In a few genera the spikelets of the pair are alike. In *Trachypogon* the fertile spikelet is pedicellate and the sterile one nearly sessile. The most important economic plants in this tribe are sugarcane and sorghum.

Key to the genera of Andropogoneae

1a. Spikelets alike, all perfect. (See also *Arthraxon* and *Sorghastrum* in which pedicellate spikelets are not developed.)
Spikelets surrounded by a copious tuft of soft hairs.
Rachis continuous, the spikelets falling; the spikelets of the pair unequally pedicellate.
Racemes in a narrow spikelike panicle; spikelets awnless.................. 148. IMPERATA.
Racemes in a broad fan-shaped panicle; spikelets awned............ 149. MISCANTHUS.
Rachis breaking up into joints at maturity with the spikelets attached; one spikelet sessile, the other pedicellate.
Spikelets awnless.. 150. SACCHARUM.
Spikelets awned.. 151. ERIANTHUS.
Spikelets not surrounded by turfs of hairs; racemes few................ 152. MICROSTEGIUM.
1b. Spikelets unlike, the sessile perfect, the pedicellate sterile (sessile spikelet staminate, pedicellate spikelet perfect in *Trachypogon*.
2a. Pedicel thickened, appressed to the thickened rachis joint (at least parallel to it) or adnate to it; spikelets awnless, appressed to the joint.

Rachis joint and pedicel adnate. Annuals.
Perfect spikelet globose; sterile spikelet conspicuous.............. 164. HACKELOCHLOA.
Perfect spikelet oblong; sterile spikelet minute.......................... 162. ROTTBOELLIA.
Rachis joint and pedicel distinct, the sessile spikelet appressed to them, its first glume lanceolate.
Racemes subcylindric; rachis joints and pedicels glabrous, much thicker at the summit, the spikelets sunken in the hollow below; sterile spikelet rudimentary. 163. MANISURIS.
Racemes flat; rachis joints and pedicels woolly, not much thicker at the summit; sterile spikelet staminate or neuter.. 161. ELYONURUS.
2b. Pedicel not thickened (if slightly so the spikelets awned), neither appressed nor adnate to the rachis joint, this usually slender; spikelets usually awned.
3a. Fertile spikelet with a hairy-pointed callus, formed of the attached supporting rachis joint or pedicel; awns strong.
Racemes reduced to a single joint, long-peduncled in a simple open panicle. 158. CHRYSOPOGON.
Racemes of several to many joints, single.
Primary spikelet subsessile, sterile, persistent on the continuous axis after the fall of the fertile pedicellate spikelet.............................. 160. TRACHYPOGON.
Primary spikelet sessile, fertile; pedicellate spikelet sterile. Lower few to several pairs of spikelets all staminate or neuter........................ 159. HETEROPOGON.
3b. Fertile spikelet without a callus (a short callus in *Hyparrhenia*), the rachis disarticulating immediately below the spikelet; awns slender.
Blades ovate. Annual... 153. ARTHRAXON.
Blades narrow, elongate.
Racemes of several to many joints, solitary, digitate, or aggregate in panicles.
Lower pair of spikelets like the others of the raceme.......... 154. ANDROPOGON.
Lower pair of spikelets sterile, awnless. Racemes in pairs on slender flexuous peduncles.. 155. HYPARRHENIA.
Racemes reduced to one or few joints, these mostly peduncled in a subsimple or compound panicle.
Pedicellate spikelets staminate.. 156. SORGHUM.
Pedicellate spikelets wanting, the pedicel only present...... 157. SORGHASTRUM.

TRIBE 14. TRIPSACEAE

Spikelets unisexual, the staminate in pairs, or sometimes in threes, 2-flowered, the pistillate usually single, 2-flowered, the lower floret sterile, embedded in hollows of the thickened articulate rachis and falling attached to the joints, or enclosed in a thickened involucre or sheath or, in *Zea*, crowded in rows on a thickened axis (cob); glumes membranaceous or thick and rigid, awnless; lemmas and palea hyaline, awnless. Plants monoecious.

This small tribe of seven genera is scarcely more than a subtribe of Andropogoneae, differing chiefly in the total suppression of the sterile spikelet of a pair, the fertile spikelet being pistillate only and solitary; staminate spikelets paired. It is also known as Maydeae.

Key to the genera of Tripsaceae

Staminate and pistillate spikelets in separate inflorescences, the first in a terminal tassel, the second in the axils of the leaves.
Pistillate spikes distinct, the spikelets embedded in the hardened rachis, this disarticulating at maturity... 167. EUCHLAENA.
Pistillate spikes grown together forming an ear, the grains at maturity much exceeding the glumes.. 168. ZEA.
Staminate and pistillate spikelets in separate portions of the same inflorescence, the pistillate below.
Spikes short, the 1- or 2-flowered pistillate portion enclosed in a beadlike sheathing bract. 165. COIX.
Spikes many-flowered, the pistillate portion breaking up into several 1-seeded joints; no beadlike sheathing bract.. 166. TRIPSACUM.

DESCRIPTIONS OF GENERA AND SPECIES

TRIBE 1. BAMBUSEAE

1. ARUNDINÁRIA Michx. CANE

Spikelets 8- to 12-flowered, large, compressed, the rachilla disarticulating above the glumes and between the florets; glumes unequal, shorter than the lemmas, the first sometimes wanting; lemmas papery, rather fragile, about 11-nerved, acute, acuminate, mucronate or awn-tipped; palea about as long as the lemma or a little shorter, prominently 2-keeled, deeply sulcate between the keels; rachilla joints rather thick, appressed-hirsute; stamens 3; caryopsis narrowly elliptic, terete, 1 to 1.2 cm. long. Shrubs or tall reeds with extensively creeping horizontal rhizomes 5 to 10 mm. thick, the woody perennial branching culms erect, 2 to 5 m., sometimes to 8 m., tall and 2 cm. thick, freely branching, the flowering branchlets borne in fascicles on the main culm or on primary branches, their sheaths bladeless or nearly so, flowering shoots also arising from the rhizomes, their sheaths bladeless; flowering at infrequent intervals, usually each species over a wide area simultaneously, the flowering period apparently continuing for about a year; the flowering culms apparently dying after setting seed; sterile branches numerous and repeatedly branching, the basal shoots and primary branches with 6 to 10 loose, papery culm-sheaths with narrow rudimentary blades 2 to 20 mm. long, not petiolate at base, and 4 to 10 large petiolate tessellate blades toward the ends, their sheaths overlapping, the upper blades crowded, the lower papery sheaths finally falling, the leaf-sheaths bearing several flat scabrous bristles at the summit, these readily falling in age. Type species, *Arundinaria macrosperma* Michx. (*A. gigantea*). Name from Latin *Arundo*, a reed.

Primary branches erect or nearly so, the individual culm with its branches oblong-linear in outline; spikelets usually rather loose; lemmas appressed-hirsute or canescent, at least toward the base, greenish tawny to bronze-russet.......... 1. A. GIGANTEA.
Primary branches ascending at an angle of about 45°, the individual culm with its branches broadly lanceolate in outline; spikelets rather compact; lemmas glabrous or obscurely pubescent at base only, usually livid-purple.......... 2. A. TECTA.

1. Arundinaria gigantéa (Walt.) Muhl. GIANT CANE. (Fig. 1.) Culms as much as 2 cm. thick and 2 to 8 m. tall, smooth; lower sheaths about half as long as the internodes, finally falling, the upper 6 to 10 sheaths striate, tessellate, usually hirsute, becoming glabrous or nearly so, densely ciliate, canescent at base, the 10 to 12 bristles at the summit 5 to 9 mm. long, these often borne from the margin of a rather firm auricle, this sometimes prominent but often obscure or wanting, a dense band of stiff hairs across the collar; ligule firm, scarcely 1 mm. long; blades of main culm and primary branches 15 to 27 cm. long, 2.5 to 4 cm. wide, rounded at base (petiole 1 to 2 mm. long), strongly finely tessellate, acuminate, pubescent to glabrous on the lower surface, puberulent to glabrous on the upper, the margin finely serrulate; blades of ultimate branchlets much smaller, often crowded in flabellate clusters, commonly glabrous or nearly so; flowering branchlets finally crowded toward the ends of the branches, the racemes or simple panicles with few to several spikelets on slender angled pedicels 2 to 30 mm. long, hirsute to nearly glabrous; spikelets 4 to 7 cm. long, about 8 mm. wide, mostly 8- to 12-flowered, rather loose; glumes distant, acuminate, pubescent, the lower minute, sometimes wanting; lemmas broadly lanceolate, keeled, mostly 1.5

FIGURE 1.—*Arundinaria gigantea*. Flowering shoot, × ½; summit of culm sheath, outer and inner face, showing auricles and ligule, and two views of floret, × 2. (Swallen 6717, Miss.)

to 2 cm. long, sometimes tapering into an awn 4 mm. long, ciliate, appressed-hirsute to canescent, rarely glabrous except toward the base and margins, faintly to clearly tessellate; rachilla segments densely hirsute; palea scabrous on the keels. ♃ —Forming extensive colonies in low woods, river banks, moist ground, southern Ohio, Indiana, Illinois, Missouri, and Oklahoma to North Carolina, Florida, and Texas, mostly above the Coastal Plain. Livestock eagerly eat the young plants, leaves, and seeds, and canebrakes furnish much forage. The young shoots are sometimes used as a potherb. The culms are used for fishing rods, pipestems, baskets, mats, and a variety of other purposes. Early travelers speak of the abundance of this species and state that the culms may be as much as 2 or even 3 inches in diameter. It is said that the plants are easily destroyed by the continuous grazing of cattle and by the rooting of swine.

2. Arundinaria técta (Walt.) Muhl. SWITCH CANE. (Fig. 2.) Similar to *A. gigantea*, the culms usually not more than 2 m. tall, the sheaths more commonly as long as the internodes; auricle at summit of sheaths only rarely developed, the bristles 2 to 6 mm. long, a very short firm erose to ciliate membrane across the collar; blades on the average a little longer and narrower; inflorescence similar, the spikelets 3 to 5 cm. long, 6- to 12-flowered, relatively compact and less compressed than in the preceding; glumes obtuse to acuminate, often glabrous or nearly so; lemmas scarcely keeled, 12 to 15 mm. long, glabrous or minutely canescent at the base, rarely very faintly tessellate toward the summit; the rachilla strigose. ♃ —Forming colonies in swampy woods, moist pine barrens and live oak woods, and sandy margins of streams, Coastal Plain, southern Maryland to Alabama and Mississippi. Two collections from northwest Florida appear to be intermediate between the two species.

A great many exotic species of bamboo have been introduced into cultivation in the United States, particularly from China, Japan, India, and Java. *Arundinaria, Bambusa, Cephalostachyum, Chimonobambusa, Dendrocalamus, Gigantochloa, Guadua, Indocalamus, Lingnania, Oxytenanthera, Phyllostachys, Pleioblastus, Pseudosasa, Sasa, Schizostachyum, Semiarundinaria, Shibataea, Sinarundinaria, Sinobambusa, Sinocalamus,* and *Thamnocalamus* are the principal genera represented. In southern Florida the commonest introduced species are *Bambusa multiplex* (Lour.) Raeusch., *B. bambos* (L.) Voss,[6] *B. vulgaris* Schrad. ex Wendl., and *Sinocalamus oldhami* (Munro) McClure ("*Dendrocalamus latiflorus*" of California and Florida gardens). Farther north, where the minimum winter temperatures are lower, *Arundinaria simoni* (Carr.) A. and C. Riv., *Phyllostachys aurea* A. and C. Riv., and *P. bambusoides* Sieb. and Zucc. are the commonest, and in regions where the winters are still more severe *Pseudosasa japonica* (Sieb. and Zucc.) Makino is the species most commonly found in cultivation in the open air; escaped in Philadelphia. In California, *Sinocalamus oldhami, Bambusa multiplex,* and several species of *Phyllostachys* are about equally popular. The most recent systematic treatment of the species of bamboo cultivated in the United States is that of Rehder.[7]

[6] Contributed by F. A. McCLURE; see also McCLURE, F. A. THE GENUS BAMBUSA AND SOME OF ITS FIRST-KNOWN SPECIES. Blumea Sup. 3. (Henrard Jubilee vol.): 90–112, pl. 1–7, 1946; and YOUNG, R. A. BAMBOOS IN AMERICAN HORTICULTURE. Nat. Hort. Mag. 1945: 171–196; 274–291; 1946: 40–64; 257–283; 352–365, illus.

[7] REHDER, ALFRED. MANUAL OF CULTIVATED TREES AND SHRUBS. Ed. 2, 996 pp. New York. 1940.

FIGURE 2.—*Arundinaria tecta*. Flowering and leafy shoot, × ½; spikelet and floret, × 2. (Chase 5881, Va.); summit of culm sheath, outer and inner face, × 2. (Amer. Gr. Natl. Herb. 498, Va.)

TRIBE 2. FESTUCEAE

2. BRÓMUS L. Bromegrass

Spikelets several- to many-flowered, the rachilla disarticulating above the glumes and between the florets; glumes unequal, acute, the first 1- to 3-nerved, the second usually 3- to 5-nerved; lemmas convex on the back or keeled, 5- to 9-nerved, 2-toothed, awned from between the teeth or awnless; palea usually shorter than the lemma, ciliate on the keels. Low or rather tall annuals or perennials with closed sheaths, usually flat blades, and open or contracted panicles of large spikelets. Standard species, *Bromus sterilis* (type species, *B. secalinus*). Name from *bromos*, an ancient Greek name for the oat, from broma, food.

The native perennial species of bromegrass form a considerable portion of the forage in open woods of the mountain regions of the western United States. *Bromus carinatus*, California brome, and its more eastern ally, *B. marginatus*, are abundant from the Rocky Mountains to the Pacific coast. Before maturity, they are relished by all classes of stock. Horses and sheep are particularly fond of the seed heads. *Bromus anomalus*, *B. pumpellianus*, and *B. ciliatus*, of the Rocky Mountain region, are abundant up to 10,000-11,000 feet altitude, and are of first rank for all classes of stock. Several other species are nutritious but are usually not abundant enough to be of importance in the grazing regions. The most important species agronomically is smooth brome, *B. inermis*, a native of Eurasia, which is cultivated for hay and pasture in the northern part of the Great Plains. It is more drought-resistant than timothy and can be grown farther west on the Plains, but does not thrive south of central Kansas. It is recommended for holding canal banks. Also called smooth, awnless, and Hungarian brome. Rescue grass, *B. catharticus*, is cultivated for winter forage in the Southern States from North Carolina to Texas and in the coast district of southern California.

The annuals are weedy species introduced mostly from Europe. The best known of these is chess, *Bromus secalinus*, a weed of waste places sometimes infesting grainfields. Formerly it was believed by the credulous that under certain conditions wheat changed into chess or "cheat." Chess in a wheatfield is due to chess seed in the soil or in the wheat sown. This species is utilized for hay in places in Washington, Oregon, and Georgia. On the Pacific coast the annual bromegrasses cover vast areas of open ground at lower altitudes where they form a large part of the forage on the winter range. They mature in spring or early summer and become unpalatable. Those of the section Eubromus are, at maturity, a serious pest. The narrow, sharp-pointed minutely barbed florets (or fruits) with their long rough awns work into the eyes, nostrils, and mouths of stock, causing inflammation and often serious injury. Sometimes the intestines are pierced, and death results. On the Pacific coast, *B. rigidus*, the chief offender, is called ripgut grass by stockmen, and the name is sometimes applied to other species of the section.

Spikelets strongly flattened, the lemmas compressed-keeled...... Section 1. Ceratochloa.
Spikelets terete before anthesis or somewhat flattened, but the lemmas not compressed-keeled.
  Plants perennial........ Section 2. Bromopsis.
  Plants annual. Introduced, mostly from Europe.
    Awn straight or divaricate, sometimes minute or obsolete, not twisted and geniculate; teeth of the lemma sometimes slender but not aristate.
      Lemmas broad, rounded above, not acuminate, the teeth mostly less than 1 mm. long........ Section 3. Bromium.
      Lemmas narrow, with a sharp callus, gradually acuminate, bifid, the teeth 2 to 5 mm. long. Awns usually more than 1.5 cm. long.... Section 4. Eubromus.
    Awn geniculate, twisted below; teeth of the lemma aristate. Section 5. Neobromus.

Section 1. Ceratochloa

Lemmas awnless or nearly so.......... 1. B. CATHARTICUS.
Lemmas awned, the awn more than 3 mm. long.
  Panicle branches elongate, slender, drooping, bearing 1 or 2 large spikelets at the end, the lowermost naked for as much as 10 to 15 cm. Sheaths smooth; Washington and Oregon.......... 2. B. SITCHENSIS.
  Panicle branches not greatly elongate.
    Panicle branches ascending, rather stiff, naked below, bearing 1 or 2 large spikelets. Washington.......... 3. B. ALEUTENSIS.
    Panicle branches short and ascending or longer and drooping, with some short branches at the base.
      Blades canescent, densely short-pilose, 2 to 5 mm. wide, often involute; panicle narrow.......... 4. B. BREVIARISTATUS.
      Blades not canescent, glabrous to puberulent or sparsely pilose, mostly 5 to 12 mm. wide.
        Sheaths strongly to sparsely retrorsely pilose; blades 4 to 12 mm. wide; lemmas usually pubescent, the awns mostly less than 7 mm. long; plants perennial. 7. B. MARGINATUS.
        Sheaths scaberulous to pilose.
          Plants annual or biennial; culms mostly 30 to 100 cm. tall; spikelets rather open at anthesis, the rachilla joints relatively long; awns 7 to 15 mm. long.
            Spikelets 6- to 10-flowered; second glume shorter than the lowest lemma. 5. B. CARINATUS.
            Spikelets mostly 5- to 7-flowered; second glume nearly or quite equaling the length of the lowest floret.......... 6. B. ARIZONICUS.
          Plants perennial; awns mostly less than 15 mm. long.
            Culms erect, mostly 80 to 120 cm. tall; panicle mostly open; spikelets rather glossy, loose, the rachilla joints relatively long.......... 9. B. POLYANTHUS.
            Culms subgeniculate and leafy at base, mostly 25 to 70 cm. tall; panicle rather dense; spikelets closely flowered.......... 8. B. MARITIMUS.

Section 2. Bromopsis

1a. Creeping rhizomes present; lemmas awnless or short-awned; panicle erect, somewhat open, the branches ascending.
  Lemmas glabrous.......... 10. B. INERMIS.
  Lemmas pubescent near the margins.......... 11. B. PUMPELLIANUS.
1b. Creeping rhizomes wanting (base of culm decumbent in *B. laevipes*).
  2a. Panicle narrow, the branches erect.
    Lemmas glabrous or evenly scabrous.......... 12. B. ERECTUS.
    Lemmas appressed-pubescent on the margins and lower part.......... 13. B. SUKSDORFII.
  2b. Panicle open, the branches spreading or drooping.
    3a. Lemmas glabrous.
      Blades broad and lax, more than 5 mm., at least some of them 10 mm., wide (var. *laeviglumis*).......... 20. B. PURGANS.
      Blades narrow, not more than 6 mm. wide.......... 23. B. TEXENSIS.
    3b. Lemmas pubescent.
      4a. Lemmas pubescent along the margin and on lower part of the back, the upper part glabrous.
        First glume 3-nerved; plant mostly pale or glaucous. Culms decumbent at base. 17. B. LAEVIPES.
        First glume 1-nerved, or only faintly 3-nerved near the base; plants dark green.
          Ligule prominent, 3 to 5 mm. long; lemmas narrow; awn usually more than 5 mm. long.......... 18. B. VULGARIS.
          Ligule inconspicuous, about 1 mm. long; lemmas broad; awn 3 to 5 mm. long. 19. B. CILIATUS.
      4b. Lemmas pubescent rather evenly over the back, usually more densely so along the lower part of the margin (glabrous in *B. purgans* var. *laeviglumis*).
        Panicle branches short, stiffly spreading; blades short, mostly on lower part of culm.......... 14. B. ORCUTTIANUS.
        Panicle branches lax or drooping; blades along the culm, mostly elongate.
          Panicle small, drooping, usually not more than 10 cm. long. Spikelets densely and conspicuously pubescent.
            Sheaths and blades sparsely pilose to subglabrous; blades mostly 2 to 4 mm. wide (rarely 5 to 6 mm.).......... 24. B. ANOMALUS.
            Sheaths and blades (except uppermost in some) conspicuously pubescent; blades 5 to 10 mm. wide.......... 25. B. KALMII.

Panicle larger, usually erect, the branches more or less drooping. Blades mostly wide and lax.
Ligule 3 to 4 mm. long; blades pilose above, scabrous or smooth beneath; panicle large, open, the slender branches long, drooping. 16. B. PACIFICUS.
Ligule short; blades pubescent or pilose on both surfaces, or glabrous or scabrous.
Blades densely short-pubescent on both surfaces............ 15. B. GRANDIS.
Blades more or less pilose or glabrous.
Sheaths, at least the lower, retorsely pilose (rarely glabrous in *B. purgans*) blades mostly more than 5 mm. wide.
Sheaths shorter than the internodes. Nodes 4 to 6.... 20. B. PURGANS.
Sheaths as long as or longer than the internodes.
Second glume 5-nerved; nodes 6 to 8; sheaths without flanges at the mouth........ 22. B. NOTTOWAYANUS.
Second glume 3-nerved; nodes 10 to 20; sheaths with prominent flanges at the mouth........ 21. B. LATIGLUMIS.
Sheaths glabrous; blades mostly less than 5 mm. wide.... 26. B. FRONDOSUS.

Section 3. Bromium

Panicle contracted, rather dense, the branches erect or ascending.
Lemmas glabrous........ 37. B. RACEMOSUS.
Lemmas pubescent.
Spikelets compressed; lemmas rather thin and narrow........ 31. B. MOLLIFORMIS.
Spikelets turgid; lemmas rather thick, broader........ 30. B. MOLLIS.
Panicle open, the branches spreading.
Awn short or wanting; lemmas obtuse, inflated (see also short-awned forms of *B. secalinus*). 27. B. BRIZAEFORMIS.
Awn well developed.
Foliage glabrous........ 28. B. SECALINUS.
Foliage pubescent.
Branches of the panicle rather stiffly spreading or drooping, not flexuous; awn straight. 29. B. COMMUTATUS.
Branches lax or flexuous, usually slender, but rather stout in *B. squarrosus*.
Spikelets inflated, 5 to 8 mm. or even 10 mm. wide; awns flattened, strongly divergent, about 1 cm. long; panicle branches stout but flexuous, bearing 1 or 2 spikelets........ 33. B. SQUARROSUS.
Spikelets not inflated, usually less than 5 mm. wide, if more the spikelets pubescent; awn not strongly flattened, straight or somewhat spreading.
Panicle 8 to 11 cm. (rarely to 15 cm.) long; branches and pedicels conspicuously flexuous or curled; lemmas pubescent........ 36. B. ARENARIUS.
Panicle 15 to 25 cm. long (smaller in depauperate specimens), the long branches spreading or drooping, somewhat flexuous but usually not curled; lemmas glabrous or scaberulous.
Palea distinctly shorter than its lemma; awn flexuous, usually somewhat divergent in drying; spikelets rather turgid........ 34. B. JAPONICUS.
Palea about as long as its lemma; awn straight or nearly so in drying; spikelets thinner and flatter, scarcely turgid........ 35. B. ARVENSIS.

Section 4. Eubromus

Panicle contracted, erect; awn 12 to 20 mm. long.
Culms pubescent below the dense panicle........ 39. B. RUBENS.
Culms glabrous below the scarcely dense panicle........ 40. B. MADRITENSIS.
Panicle open, the branches spreading.
Second glume usually less than 1 cm. long; pedicels capillary, flexuous. 41. B. TECTORUM.
Second glume more than 1 cm. long; pedicels sometimes flexuous but not capillary.
Awn about 2 cm. long; first glume 8 mm. long........ 38. B. STERILIS.
Awn 3 to 5 cm. long; first glume about 15 mm. long........ 37. B. RIGIDUS.

Section 5. Neobromus

A single species........ 42. B. TRINII.

SECTION 1. CERATÓCHLOA (Beauv.) Griseb.

Annuals, biennials, or perennials; spikelets large, distinctly compressed; glumes and lemmas keeled, rather firm.

1. **Bromus cathárticus** Vahl. Rescue grass. (Fig. 3.) Annual or biennial; culms erect to spreading, as much as 100 cm. tall; sheaths glabrous or pubescent; blades narrow, glabrous or sparsely pilose; panicle

Figure 3.—*Bromus catharticus*, × 1. (Peebles, Harrison, and Kearney 1271, Ariz.)

Figure 4.—*Bromus sitchensis*, × 1. (Piper 3013, Alaska.)

open, as much as 20 cm. long, the branches as much as 15 cm. long, naked at base, in small plants the panicles reduced to a raceme of a few appressed short-pediceled spikelets; spikelets 2 to 3 cm. long, 6- to 12-flowered; glumes acuminate, about 1 cm. long; lemmas glabrous, scabrous, or sometimes pubescent, acuminate, 1.5 cm. long, closely overlapping, concealing the short rachilla joints, awnless or with an awn 1 to 3 mm. long; palea two-thirds as long as the lemma. ⊙ (*B. unioloides* H. B. K.)—Cultivated in the Southern States as a winter forage grass. Escaped from cultivation or sparingly introduced in waste places throughout Southern States and rarely northward. Known also as Schrader's bromegrass. Introduced from South America.

2. Bromus sitchénsis Trin. (Fig. 4.) Stout smooth perennial; culms 120 to 180 cm. tall; sheaths glabrous; blades elongate, 7 to 12 mm. wide, sparsely pilose on the upper surface; panicles large, lax, drooping, 25 to 35 cm. long, the lower branches (2 to 4) as much as 20 cm. long, naked below for as much as 10 or 15 cm., few-flowered; spikelets 2.5 to 3.5 cm. long, 6- to 12-flowered, the rachilla joints longer than in *B. catharticus*, exposed at anthesis; lemmas scabrous, sometimes hirtellous toward base; awn 5 to 10 mm. long. ♃ —Woods and banks near the coast, Alaska to Oregon.

3. Bromus aleuténsis Trin. ex Griseb. (Fig. 5.) Culms rather stout, erect from a usually decumbent base, 50 to 100 cm. tall; sheaths sparsely retrorse-pilose or glabrous; blades sparsely pilose, 5 to 10 mm. wide; panicle erect, loose, 10 to 20 cm. long, the branches rather stiffly ascending, bearing 1 or 2 (rarely 3) spikelets, the lower as much as 10 cm. long; spikelets 2.5 to 3.5 cm. long, 3- to 6-flowered; glumes subequal, the first 3-nerved, the second 5- or indistinctly 7-nerved; lemmas broadly lanceolate, 7-nerved, scarious-margined, smooth to scabrous-

FIGURE 5.—*Bromus aleutensis*, × 1. (Evans 550, Alaska.)

pubescent, about 15 mm. long; awn mostly about 1 cm. long. ♃ —Open ground, Aleutian Islands to the Olympic Mountain region.

4. Bromus breviaristátus Buckl. (Fig. 6.) Erect tufted perennial; culms 25 to 50 cm. tall; sheaths canescent to densely retrorse-pilose; blades narrow, becoming involute, canescent and also pilose with spreading hairs, mostly erect or ascending, often only 1 to 2 mm. wide; panicle narrow, erect, 5 to 15 cm. long, the branches short, appressed, often bearing only 1 spikelet; spikelets 2 to 3 cm. long; lemmas appressed-puberulent; awn 3 to 10 mm. long. ♃ (*B. subvelutinus* Shear.)—Dry wooded hills and meadows, Wyoming to British Columbia, eastern Washington, Nevada, and California.

5. Bromus carinátus Hook. and Arn. CALIFORNIA BROME. (Fig. 7.) Erect annual or mostly biennial; culms mostly 50 to 100 cm. (occasionally to 120 cm.) tall; sheaths scabrous to rather sparsely pilose; blades flat, mostly 20 to 30 cm. long, the lower shorter (those of the innovations numerous), scabrous or sparsely pilose, mostly 3 to 10 mm. wide; panicle mostly 15 to 30 cm. long, with spreading or drooping branches, in small plants much reduced; spikelets (excluding awns) 2 to 3 cm. long, mostly 6- to 10-flowered, the florets in anthesis not or scarcely overlapping, exposing the relatively long rachilla joints; glumes acuminate, the first 6 to 9 mm., the second 10 to 15 mm., long; lemmas minutely appressed-pubescent to glabrous, about 2 to 2.5 mm. wide as folded, 10 to 20 mm. long; awn 7 to 15 mm. long; palea acuminate, nearly as long as the lemma, the teeth short-awned. ⊙ —Open ground, open woods, and waste places, at low and middle altitudes, common on the Pacific coast, British Columbia to Idaho and California; New Mexico and Baja California. The species is extremely variable in size, in shape of panicle, and in pubescence, and intergrades freely with the following.[8]

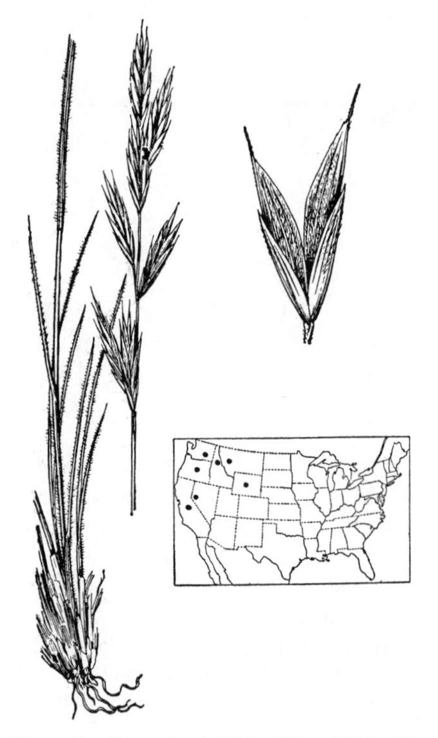

FIGURE 6.—*Bromus breviaristatus*. Plant, × ½; spikelet, × 5. (Nuttall, Rocky Mts.)

6. Bromus arizónicus (Shear) Stebbins. Annual, similar to the preceding, commonly shorter; panicle mostly

[8] For variability in *Bromus carinatus* see HARLAN. J. R., Amer. Jour. Bot. 32: 142. 1945. For proposed varieties see SHEAR, C. L., U. S. Dept. Agr., Div. Agrost. Bul. 23. 1900. See also STEBBINS, G. L., TOBGY, H. A., and HARLAN, J. R., Calif. Acad. Sci. Proc. 25: 307–321. 1944.

FIGURE 7.—*Bromus carinatus*, × 1. (Hitchcock 2704, Calif.)

stiff, erect and relatively narrow; spikelets mostly 5- to 7-flowered; glumes less unequal, the second often equaling the length of the lowest lemma; lemmas hirsute toward the margin, occasionally sparsely so across the back, the teeth of the apex 0.7 to 2 mm. long. ☉ —Open, mostly arid slopes and valleys, western Texas; Arizona to middle California and Baja California. Plants short-lived, flowering in the early spring rains and dying after seeding.

7. **Bromus marginātus** Nees. (Fig. 8.) Perennial, sheaths mostly conspicuously retrorsely pilose; blades commonly pubescent, 6 to 12 mm. wide; panicles usually less open than in *B. carinatus;* spikelets mostly

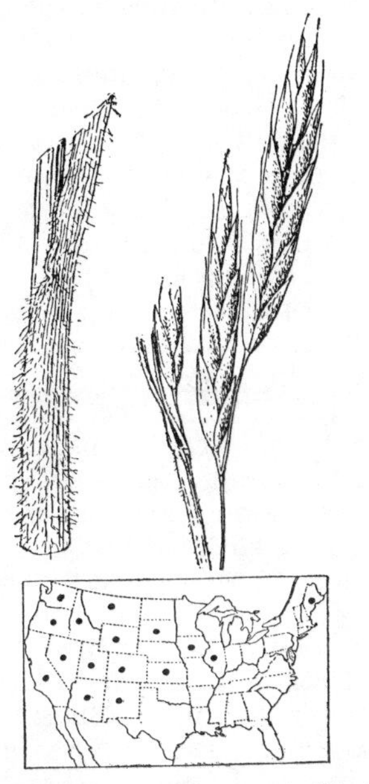

Figure 8.—*Bromus marginatus*, × 1. (Hunter 555, Oreg.)

closely flowered, lemmas more strongly pubescent, awns usually less than 7 mm. long. ♃ —Open woods, open or wooded slopes, meadows, and waste places, British Columbia and Alberta to South Dakota, New Mexico, and California, mostly on the eastern slope; adventive in Maine (in wool waste); introduced in Illinois, Iowa, and Kansas. Variable, intergrading with *B. carinatus* and scarcely distinct, though extremes are very different in appearance.

8. **Bromus marítimus** (Piper) Hitchc. Perennial; culms stout, 25 to 70 cm. tall, geniculate at base with numerous basal shoots; sheaths smooth or scaberulous; blades mostly 6 to 8 mm. wide, scabrous; panicle mostly 10 to 20 cm. long, the branches short, erect; spikelets 3 to 4 cm. long. ♃ (*B. marginatus maritimus* Piper.) —Near the coast, Lane County, Oreg., to Monterey County, Calif.

9. **Bromus polyânthus** Scribn. (Fig. 9.) Perennial; culms robust, mostly 90

Figure 9.—*Bromus polyanthus*, × 1. (Chase 5349, Colo.)

to 125 cm. tall; sheaths glabrous; blades 6 to 15 mm. wide, scabrous; panicles commonly 15 to 25 cm. long, the branches ascending; spikelets glabrous or scaberulous, somewhat glossy, rather loose at anthesis; awns 4 to 6 mm. long. ♃ —Open or sparsely wooded slopes, foothills, moist ground, Montana to Washington, south to Texas and California (Yosemite National Park); Kansas (experiment station).

Bromus laciniatus Beal. Tall slender perennial; blades flat; panicles 20 to 30 cm. long, open, drooping; spikelets flattened, about 3 cm. long, mostly purplish; lemmas keeled, awned. ♃ (*B. pendulinus* Sessé, not

Schrad.)—Occasionally cultivated for ornament; Mexico.

SECTION 2. BROMÓPSIS Dum.

Perennials; panicles mostly open; spikelets rather elongate, subterete or slightly compressed before flowering; florets closely overlapping.

10. Bromus inérmis Leyss. SMOOTH BROME. (Fig. 10.) Culms erect, 50 to 100 cm. tall, from creeping rhizomes; ligule 1.5 to 2 mm. long; blades smooth or nearly so, 5 to 10 mm. wide; panicle 10 to 20 cm. long, erect, the branches whorled, spreading in flower, contracted at maturity; spikelets 2 to 2.5 cm. long, subterete before flowering; first glume 4 to 5 mm. long, the second 6 to 8 mm. long; lemmas 9 to 12 mm. long, glabrous or somewhat scabrous, rarely villous, obtuse, emarginate, mucronate, or with an awn 1 to 2 mm. long. ♃ —Cultivated as hay and pasture grass, especially from Minnesota and Kansas to Washington and California, occasionally eastward to Michigan and Ohio and south to New Mexico and Arizona, now running wild in these regions; introduced along roads and in waste places in the northern half of the United States; occasionally southward. Also used for reseeding western mountain ranges. Introduced from Europe.

FIGURE 10.—*Bromus inermis*. Plant, × ½; spikelet, × 2½. (Deam 11633, Ind.)

11. Bromus pumpelliánus Scribn. (Fig. 11.) Resembling *B. inermis;* culms 50 to 120 cm. tall, from creeping rhizomes; sheaths glabrous or pubescent; blades rather short, mostly glabrous beneath, scabrous or somewhat pubescent on upper surface; panicle 10 to 20 cm. long, rather narrow, erect, the branches short, erect, or ascending; spikelets 7- to 11-flowered, 2 to 3 cm. long; first glume 1-nerved, the second 3-nerved; lemmas 10 to 12 mm. long, 5- to 7-nerved, pubescent along the margin and across the back at base, slightly emarginate; awn mostly 2 to 3 mm. long. ♃ —Meadows and grassy slopes, Colorado to the Black Hills of South Dakota, Idaho, and Alaska; introduced in Michigan. BROMUS PUMPELLIANUS var. TWEÉDYI Scribn. Differing in having lemmas more densely pubescent. ♃ —Alberta to Colorado.

12. Bromus eréctus Huds. Culms tufted, erect, 60 to 90 cm. tall, slender; sheaths sparsely pilose or glabrous; ligule 1.5 mm. long; blades narrow, sparsely pubescent; panicle 10 to 20 cm. long, narrow, erect, the branches ascending or erect; spikelets 5- to 10-flowered; glumes acuminate, the first 6 to 8 mm., the second 8 to

10 mm. long; lemmas 10 to 12 mm. long, glabrous or evenly scabrous-pubescent over the back; awn 5 to 6 mm. long. ♃ —Established in a few localities from Maine to New York; also in Washington, California, Wisconsin, West Virginia, Kentucky, and Alabama; introduced from Europe.

Bromus ramósus Huds. Tall slender perennial; blades flat; panicles 15 to 25 cm. long, open, drooping; spikelets 2 to 3 cm. long, lemmas 12 to 15 mm. long, awned. ♃ —Introduced in Washington; Europe.

13. Bromus suksdórfii Vasey. (Fig. 12.) Culms 60 to 100 cm. tall; panicle 7 to 12 cm. long, the branches erect or ascending; spikelets about 2.5 cm. long, longer than the pedicels; first glume mostly 1-nerved, 8 to 10 mm. long, the second 3-nerved, 8 to 12 mm. long; lemmas 12 to 14 mm. long, appressed-pubescent near the margin and on the lower part of midnerve; awn 2 to 4 mm. long. ♃ —Rocky woods and slopes, Washington to the

Figure 12.—*Bromus suksdorfii*, × 1. (Type.)

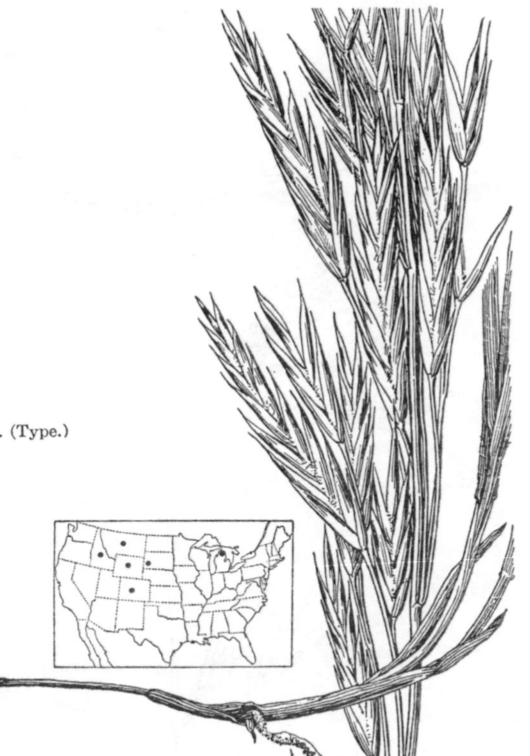

Figure 11.—*Bromus pumpellianus*, × 1. (Umbach 453, Mont.)

southern Sierra Nevada of California; Nevada (Lake Tahoe).

14. Brómus orcuttiánus Vasey. (Fig. 13.) Culms 80 to 120 cm. tall, erect, leafy below, nearly naked above, pubescent at and below the nodes; sheaths pilose or more or less velvety or sometimes glabrous; blades rather short and erect; panicle 10 to 15 cm. long, narrow-pyramidal, the few rather rigid short branches finally divaricate; spikelets about 2 cm. long, not much flattened, on short pedicels; glumes narrow, smooth, or scabrous, the first 6 to 8 mm. long, acute, 1-nerved, or sometimes with faint lateral nerves, the second 8 to 10 mm. long, broader, obtuse, 3-nerved; lemmas 10 to 12 mm. long, narrow, inrolled at margin, obscurely nerved, scabrous or scabrous-pubescent over the back; awn 5 to 7 mm. long. ♃ —Open woods, Washington to California; Arizona.

Bromus orcuttianus var. hállii Hitchc. Blades soft-pubescent on both surfaces; glumes and lemmas pubescent. ♃ —Dry, mostly wooded

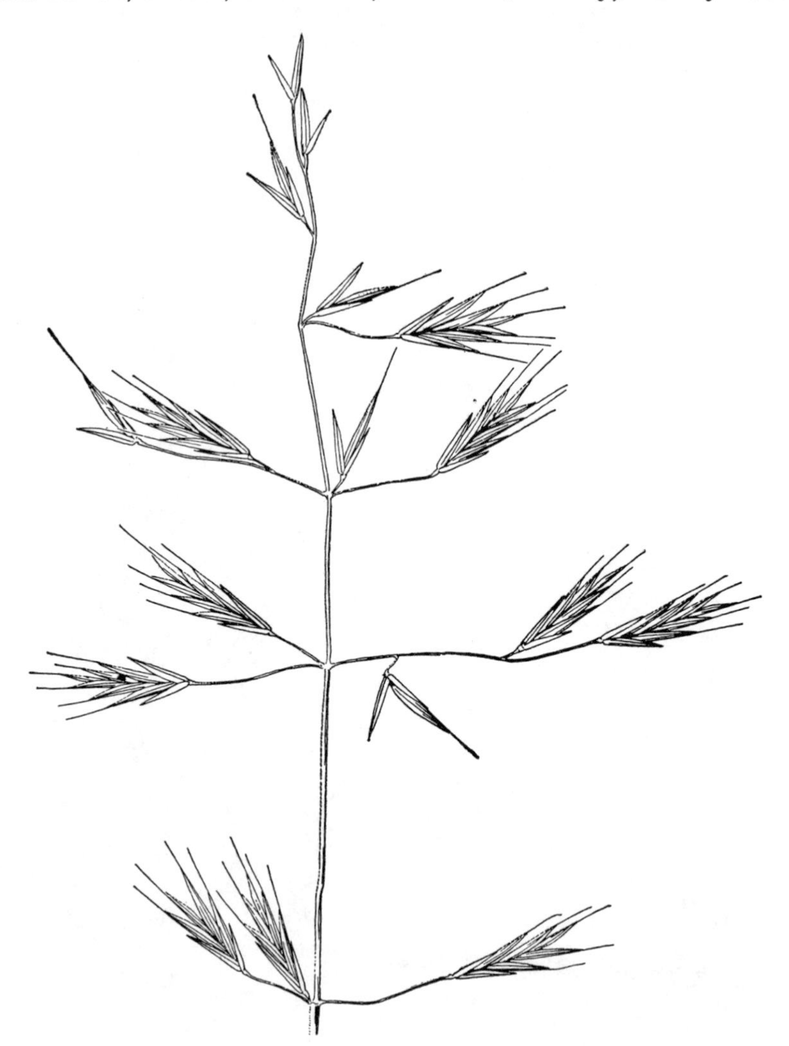

Figure 13.—*Bromus orcuttianus*, × 1. (Type.)

ridges and slopes, 1,500 to 3,000 m. elevation, California.

15. Bromus grándis (Shear) Hitchc. (Fig. 14.) Culms 1 to 1.5 m. tall; sheaths softly retrorsely pubescent; blades elongate, rather lax, spreading, densely short-pubescent on both surfaces; panicle 15 to 20 cm. long, broad, open, the branches slender, drooping, naked below, the lower usually in pairs, as much as 15 cm. long; spikelets 2 to 2.5 cm. long, on subflexuous pedicels; first glume usually distinctly 3-nerved, the second 3-nerved; lemmas 12 to 15 mm. long, densely pubescent all over the back; awn 5 to 7 mm. long. ♃ —Dry hills at moderate altitudes, Monterey and Madera Counties, Calif., south to San Diego.

FIGURE 14.—*Bromus grandis*, × 1. (Johnston 1407, Calif.)

FIGURE 15.—*Bromus pacificus*, × 1. (Elmer 1957, Wash.)

16. Bromus pacíficus Shear. (Fig. 15.) Culms 1 to 1.5 m. tall, stout, erect, pubescent at the nodes; sheaths sparsely pilose; ligule 3 to 4 mm. long; blades sparsely pilose on upper surface, scabrous or smooth beneath, 8 to 10 mm. wide; panicle very open, 10 to 20 cm. long, the branches slender, drooping; spikelets 2 to 2.5 cm. long, coarsely pubescent throughout; lemmas 11 to 12 mm. long, the pubescence somewhat dense on the margin; awn 4 to 6 mm. long. ♃ —Moist thickets near the coast, southern Alaska to western Oregon.

17. Bromus laévipes Shear. (Fig. 16.) Light green or glaucous; culms 50 to 100 cm. tall, from a decumbent base, often rooting at the lower nodes; sheaths and blades glabrous; ligule 2 to 3 mm. long; blades 4 to 8 mm. wide; panicles broad, 15 to 20 cm. long, the branches slender, drooping; first glume 3-nerved, 6 to 8 mm. long, the second 5-nerved, 10 to 12 mm. long; lemmas obtuse, 7-nerved, 12 to 14 mm. long, densely pubescent on the margin nearly to the apex and on the back at base; awn 3 to 5 mm. long. ♃ —Moist woods and shady banks, southern Washington to California.

FIGURE 16.—*Bromus laevipes*, × 1. (Amer. Gr. Natl. Herb. 866, Calif.)

18. Bromus vulgáris (Hook.) Shear (Fig. 17.) Culms slender, 80 to 120 cm. tall, the nodes pubescent; sheaths pilose; ligule 3 to 5 mm. long; blades more or less pilose, to 12 mm. wide; panicle 10 to 15 cm. long, the branches slender, drooping; spikelets narrow, about 2.5 cm. long; glumes narrow, the first acute, 1-nerved, 5 to 8 mm. long, the second broader, longer, obtuse to acutish, 3-nerved; lemmas 8 to 10 mm. long, sparsely pubescent over the back, more densely near the margin, or nearly glabrous; awn 6 to 8 mm. long. ♃ —Rocky woods and shady ravines, western Montana and Wyoming to British Columbia and California. Two scarcely distinct robust varieties have been described: *B. vulgaris* var. *eximius* Shear, a form with glabrous sheaths and nearly glabrous lemmas, Washington to Mendocino County, Calif.; and *B. vulgaris* var. *robustus* Shear, with pilose sheaths and large panicle, British Columbia to Oregon.

FIGURE 17.—*Bromus vulgaris*, × 1. (Chase 4945, Wash.)

19. Bromus ciliátus L. FRINGED BROME. (Fig. 18.) Culms slender, 70 to 120 cm. tall, glabrous or pubescent at the nodes; sheaths glabrous or the lower short-pilose, mostly shorter than the internodes; blades rather lax, as much as 1 cm. wide, sparsely pilose on both surfaces to glabrous; panicle 15 to 25 cm. long, open, the branches slender, drooping, as much as 15 cm. long; first glume 1-nerved, the second 3-nerved; lemmas 10 to 12 mm. long, pubescent near the margin on the lower half to three-fourths, glabrous or nearly so on the back; awn 3 to 5 mm. long. ♃ —Moist woods and rocky slopes, Newfoundland to Washington, south to New Jersey, Tennessee, Iowa, western Texas, and southern California (San Bernardino Mountains); Mexico. *B. richardsoni* Link is a form that has been distinguished by its larger spikelets and lemmas and more robust habit, but it grades freely into *B.*

FIGURE 18.—*Bromus ciliatus*. Plant, × ½; spikelet and floret, × 5. (Hitchcock, Vt.)

ciliatus and can scarcely be ranked even as a variety. This is the common form in the Rocky Mountains.

20. Bromus púrgans L. CANADA BROME. (Fig. 19.) Resembling *B. ciliatus;* nodes mostly 4 to 6; sheaths, except the lower 1 or 2, shorter than the internodes, more or less retrorsely pilose, or sometimes all glabrous; blades elongate, 5 to 17 mm. wide, narrowed at base, and without flanges or auricles; pubescence of lemma nearly uniform, sometimes more dense on the margins, sometimes sparse and short on the back or scabrous only. ♃ —Moist woods and rocky slopes, Massachusetts to North Dakota, south to northern Florida and Texas.

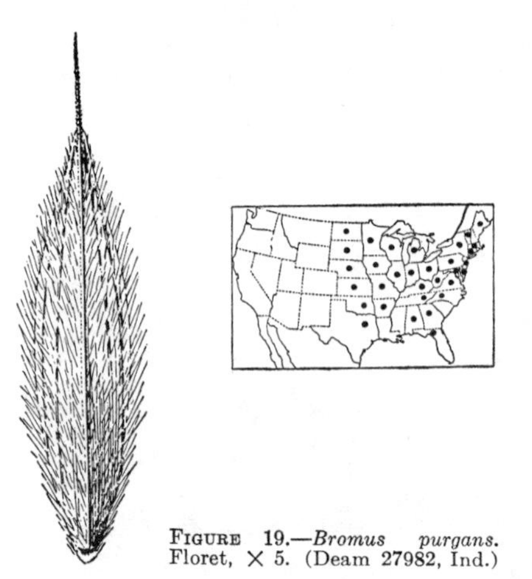

FIGURE 19.—*Bromus purgans.* Floret, × 5. (Deam 27982, Ind.)

BROMUS PURGANS var. LAEVIGLÚMIS (Scribn.) Swallen. Culms stout, leafy, mostly more than 1 m. tall; sheaths shorter or longer than the internodes, glabrous to pubescent, not strongly pilose; blades elongate, as much as 1 cm. wide or even wider; panicle large, open; lemmas glabrous or nearly so. ♃ —Woods and river banks, rare. Known from Quebec, Ontario, Maine, Vermont, Connecticut, New York, Michigan, Wisconsin, Maryland, West Virginia, and North Carolina.

21. Bromus latiglúmis (Shear) Hitchc. (Fig. 20.) Differing from *B. purgans* in having usually 10 to 20 nodes; sheaths overlapping, more or less pilose, especially about the throat and collar; base of blades with prominent flanges on each side, these usually prolonged into auricles. Where the ranges of *B. purgans* and *B. latiglumis* overlap, the latter flowers several weeks later than the former. ♃ —Alluvial banks of streams, Quebec and Maine to North Dakota, south to North Carolina and Kansas.

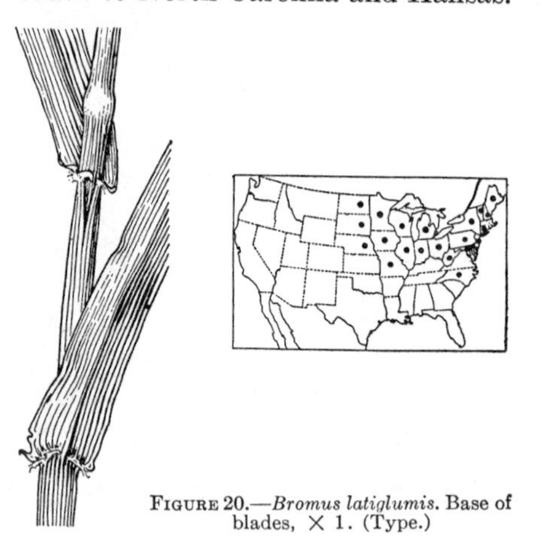

FIGURE 20.—*Bromus latiglumis.* Base of blades, × 1. (Type.)

BROMUS LATIGLUMIS f. INCÁNUS (Shear) Fernald. Culms 1 to 2 m. tall, decumbent below, mostly somewhat weak and sprawling; sheaths densely canescent; panicles rather heavy. ♃ —Low woods, Indiana, Illinois, Michigan, and Maryland.

22. Bromus nottowayánus Fernald. (Fig. 21.) Resembling *B. latiglumis,* but with fewer nodes; sheaths mostly longer than the internodes, usually retrorsely pilose, without flanges at the mouth; ligule very short; blades elongate, 6 to 13 mm. wide, pilose above, some sparsely so beneath; panicles 12 to 22 cm. long, the slender branches drooping, the pulvini inconspicuous; first glume 1- to 3-nerved, the second 5-nerved; lemma 8 to 13 mm. long, densely appressed-pilose, the awn 5 to 8 mm. long. ♃ —Rich woods, Indiana and Illinois; Maryland to North Carolina; Tennessee; Arkansas.

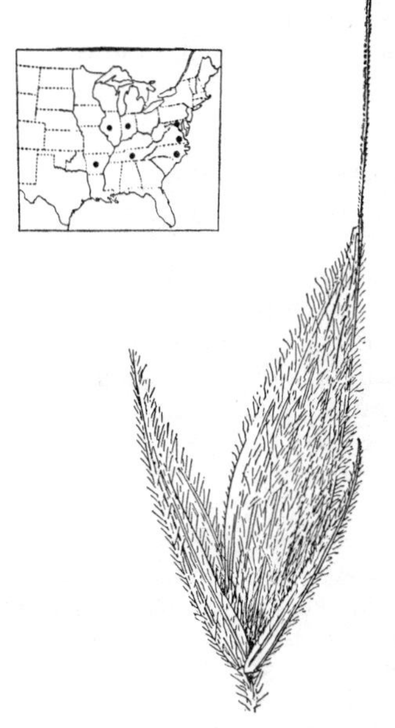

FIGURE 21.—*Bromus nottowayanus*. Glumes and lower floret, × 5. (Type number.)

23. Bromus texénsis (Shear) Hitchc. (Fig. 22.) Culms slender, mostly solitary, 40 to 70 cm. tall; sheaths much shorter than the internodes, softly retrorsely pilose; blades pubescent on both surfaces, rarely gla-

FIGURE 22.—*Bromus texensis*, × 1. (Tracy 8881, Tex.)

brous, mostly 3 to 6 mm. wide; panicle mostly not more than 12 cm. long, few-flowered, drooping; lemmas scabrous to nearly smooth; awn 5 to 7 mm. long. ♃ —Among brush, Texas (Bexar County and Corpus Christi) and Cochise County, Ariz.; apparently rare; northern Mexico.

FIGURE 23.—*Bromus anomalus*, × 1. (Pammel, Colo.)

24. Bromus anómalus Rupr. Nodding brome. (Fig. 23.) Culms slender, 30 to 60 cm. tall, the nodes pubescent; sheaths sparsely pilose to glabrous; ligule about 1 mm. long; blades scabrous, mostly 2 to 4 mm. wide; panicle about 10 cm. long, often less, few-flowered, drooping; first glume 3-nerved, the second 5-nerved, lemmas about 12 mm. long, evenly and densely pubescent over the back; awn 2 to 4 mm. long. ♃ (*B. porteri* Nash.)—Open woods, Saskatchewan to North Dakota and south to western Texas, southern California, and Mexico.

Bromus anomalus var. lanátipes (Shear) Hitchc. More robust, with woolly sheaths and usually broader blades. ♃ (*B. porteri lanatipes* Shear.)—Colorado to western Texas and Arizona.

Figure 24.—*Bromus kalmii*, × 1. (Chase 1866½, Ind.)

25. Bromus kálmii A. Gray. (Fig. 24.) Culms slender, 50 to 100 cm. tall, usually pubescent at and a little below the nodes; sheaths usually shorter than the internodes, pilose or the upper glabrous; blades usually sparsely pilose on both surfaces, 5 to 10 mm. wide; panicle rather few-flowered, drooping, mostly 5 to 10 cm. long, the branches slender, flexuous, bearing usually 1 to 3 spikelets; first glume 3-nerved, the second 5-nerved; lemmas 7 to 10 mm. long, villous over the back, more densely so near the margins; awn 2 to 3 mm. long. ♃ —Dry or sandy ground and open woods, Maine to Minnesota and South Dakota, south to western Maryland and Iowa. Called wild chess.

26. Bromus frondósus (Shear) Woot. and Standl. (Fig. 25.) Culms erect to weakly reclining, 80 to 100 cm. tall; sheaths glabrous or the lower pilose; blades pale green, scabrous, mostly less than 5 mm. wide, occasionally to 10 mm., rarely wider; panicle open, drooping, the slender lower branches naked below; first glume 2- to 3-nerved; lemmas pubescent all over, rarely nearly glabrous. ♃ (*B. porteri* var. *frondosus* Shear.) —Open woods and rocky slopes, Colorado, Utah, New Mexico, and Arizona.

Section 3. Brómium Dum.

Annuals; spikelets subcompressed; glumes and lemmas comparatively broad, elliptic or oblong-elliptic. Introduced, mostly from Europe.

27. Bromus brizaefórmis Fisch. and Mey. Rattlesnake chess. (Fig.

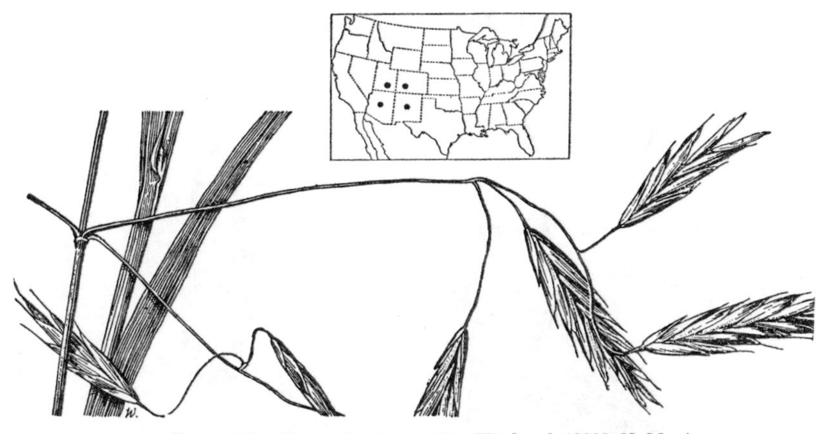

FIGURE 25.—*Bromus frondosus*, × 1. (Hitchcock 13282, N. Mex.)

26.) Culms 30 to 60 cm. tall; sheaths and blades pilose-pubescent; panicle 5 to 15 cm. long, lax, secund, drooping; spikelets rather few, oblong-ovate, 1.5 to 2.5 cm. long, about 1 cm. wide; glumes broad, obtuse, the first 3- to 5-nerved, the second 5- to 9-nerved, about twice as long as the first; lemmas 10 mm. long, very broad, inflated, obtuse, smooth, with a broad scarious margin, nearly or quite awnless. ⊙ —Sandy fields and waste ground, Canada and Alaska; occasional from Washington, Montana, and Wyoming to California, rare eastward to Massachusetts and Delaware; introduced from Europe. Sometimes cultivated for ornament.

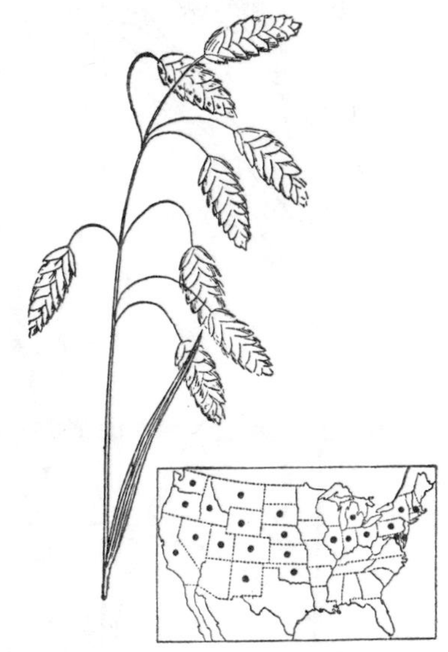

FIGURE 26.—*Bromus brizaeformis*, × ½. (Leckenby 40, Wash.)

28. Bromus secalínus L. CHESS. (Fig. 27.) Culms erect, 30 to 60 cm. tall; foliage glabrous or the lower sheaths sometimes puberulent; panicle pyramidal, nodding, 7 to 12 cm. long, the lower branches 3 to 5, unequal, slightly drooping; spikelets ovoid-lanceolate, becoming somewhat turgid at maturity, 1 to 2 cm. long, 6 to 8 mm. wide; glumes obtuse, the first 3- to 5-nerved, 4 to 6 mm. long, the second 7-nerved, 6 to 7 mm. long; lemmas 7-nerved, 6 to 8 mm. long, elliptic, obtuse, smooth or scaberulous, the margin strongly involute at maturity, shortly bidentate at apex, the undulate awns usually 3 to 5 mm. long, sometimes very short or obsolete; palea about as long as lemma. ⊙ —Introduced from Europe, a weed in grainfields and waste places, more or less throughout the United States. Also called cheat. Occasionally utilized for hay in Washington and Oregon. In fruit the turgid florets are somewhat distant so that, viewing the spikelet sidewise, the light passes through the small openings at base of each floret. BROMUS SECALINUS var. VELUTÍNUS

FIGURE 27.—*Bromus secalinus*. Plant, × ½; spikelet and floret, × 5. Chase, Ill.)

(Schrad.) Koch. Spikelets pubescent. ⊙ —Oregon (Corvallis, The Dalles). Europe.

The species of the group containing *Bromus secalinus*, *B. commutatus*, *B. mollis*, and *B. racemosus* are closely allied, differentiated only by arbitrary characters. The forms are recognized as species in most recent European floras and this disposition is here followed.

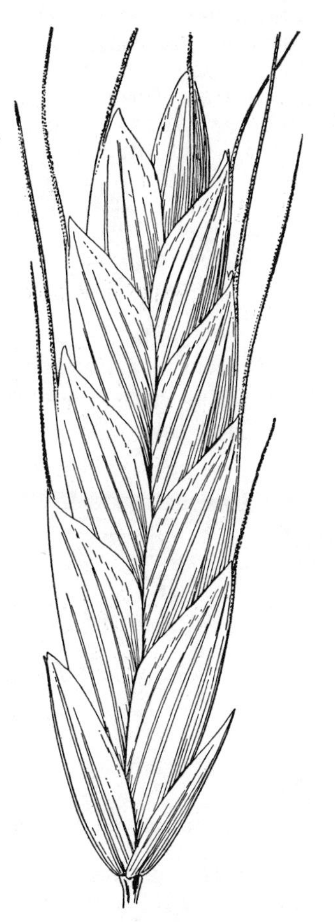

FIGURE 28.—*Bromus commutatus*, × 5. (Amer. Gr. Natl. Herb. 890, Va.)

29. Bromus commutátus Schrad. HAIRY CHESS. (Fig. 28.) Resembling *B. secalinus*, but the sheaths retrorsely pilose; the blades more or less pubescent; lemmas at maturity less plump and more overlapping; awn commonly somewhat longer. ⊙ —Introduced from Europe, a weed in fields and waste places, Washington to California, Montana, and Wyoming, eastward through the Northern States, thence less commonly southward. BROMUS COMMUTATUS var. APRICORUM Simonkai. Lemmas pubescent. ⊙ —Washington, Nevada, and California; rare. Introduced from Europe.

30. Bromus móllis L. SOFT CHESS. (Fig. 29.) Softly pubescent throughout; culms erect, 20 to 80 cm. tall; panicle erect, contracted, 5 to 10 cm. long, or, in depauperate plants, reduced to a few spikelets; glumes broad, obtuse, coarsely pilose or scabrous-pubescent, the first 3- to 5-nerved, 4 to 6 mm. long, the second 5- to 7-nerved, 7 to 8 mm. long; lemmas broad, soft, obtuse, 7-nerved,

FIGURE 29.—*Bromus mollis*, × 1. (Hall 258, Calif.)

coarsely pilose or scabrous-pubescent, rather deeply bidentate, 8 to 9 mm. long, the margin and apex hyaline; awn rather stout, 6 to 9 mm. long; palea about three-fourths as long as lemma. ⊙ —Weed in waste places and cultivated soil, introduced from Europe, Canada, and Alaska, abundant on the Pacific coast, occasional eastward to Nova Scotia and south to North Carolina. This has been referred to *B. hordeaceus* L., a distinct European species.

FIGURE 30.—*Bromus molliformis*, × 1. (Chase 5564, Calif.)

31. Bromus mollifórmis Lloyd. (Fig. 30.) Culms erect, mostly 10 to 20 cm. tall, sometimes taller; lower sheaths felty-pubescent, the upper glabrous; blades narrow, the upper surface with scattered rather stiff hairs; panicle 2 to 4 cm. long, ovoid, dense, few-flowered; spikelets oblong, compressed, 12 to 18 mm. long; glumes about 6 mm. long, the second broader, loosely pilose, the hairs spreading; lemmas thinner and narrower than in *B. mollis*, closely imbricate, about 8 mm. long, appressed-pilose, the margin whitish; awn from below the entire apex, 5 to 7 mm. long; palea a little shorter than the lemma; anthers 0.4 mm. long, about as broad. ⊙ —Open ground, southern California; Texas (College Station); introduced from Europe.

32. Bromus racemósus L. (Fig. 31.) Differing from *B. mollis* in the somewhat more open panicle and glabrous or scabrous lemmas. ⊙ (Including what in this country has been called *B. hordeaceus glabrescens* Shear, *B. hordeaceus* var. *leptostachys* Beck, and *B. mollis* f. *leiostachys* Fernald.)—Weed in waste places, chiefly on the Pacific coast and east to Montana, Colorado, and Arizona; a few points from Wisconsin and Illinois to Maine and North Carolina; introduced from Europe.

Bromus scopárius L. Resembling *B. molliformis;* culms 20 to 30 cm. tall; sheaths soft-pubescent; blades glabrous, scabrous or sparingly pilose; panicle contracted, erect, 3 to 7 cm. long; spikelets about 1.5 cm. long, 3 to 4 mm. wide; lemmas about 7 mm. long, narrow, glabrous; awn 5 to 8 mm. long, finally divaricate. ⊙ —Introduced from Europe in California (Mariposa), Virginia (Newport News, on ballast), and Michigan (Schoolcraft).

Bromus macróstachys Desf. Annual; culms erect, 30 to 60 cm. tall; panicle narrow, compact, consisting of a few large coarsely pilose, awned spikelets about 3 cm. long. ⊙ —Wool waste, Yonkers, N. Y., and College Station, Tex. Sometimes cultivated for ornament. Mediterranean region.

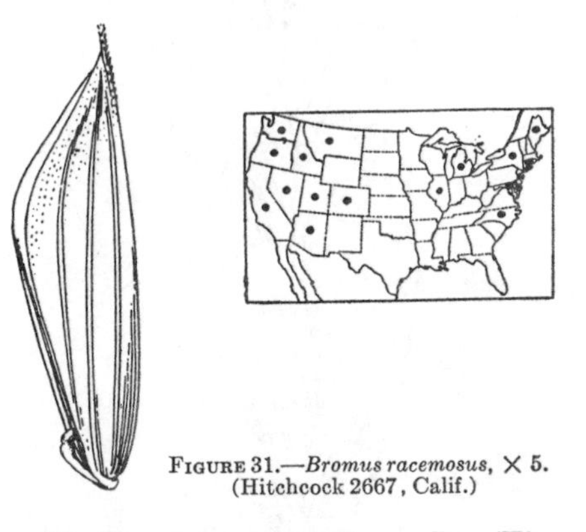

FIGURE 31.—*Bromus racemosus*, × 5. (Hitchcock 2667, Calif.)

33. Bromus squarrósus L. (Fig. 32.) Culms mostly 20 to 30 cm. tall, erect; sheaths and blades softly and densely pubescent; blades 5 to 15 cm. long, 2 to 4 mm. wide, usually erect; panicles nodding, the relatively coarse, short branches subverticillate, flexuous, bearing 1 or 2 large spikelets; spikelet about 2 cm. long, 5 to 8 mm. wide, somewhat inflated; awns flat, spreading or recurved, about 1 cm. long. ⊙ —Waste places, Michigan and North Dakota. Introduced from Europe.

34. Bromus japónicus Thunb. JAPANESE CHESS. (Fig. 33.) Culms erect or geniculate at base, 40 to 70 cm. tall; sheaths and blades pilose; panicle 12 to 20 cm. long, broadly pyramidal, diffuse, somewhat drooping, the slender lower branches 3 to 5, all the branches more or less flexuous; glumes rather broad, the first acute, 3-nerved, 4 to 6 mm. long, the second obtuse, 5-nerved, 6 to 8 mm. long; lemmas broad, obtuse, smooth, 7 to 9 mm. long, 9-nerved, the marginal pair of nerves faint, the hyaline margin obtusely angled above the middle, the apex blunt, emarginate; awn 8 to 10 mm. long, usually somewhat twisted and flexuous at maturity, those of the lower florets shorter than

FIGURE 32.—*Bromus squarrosus*, × 1. (Hanes 688, Mich.)

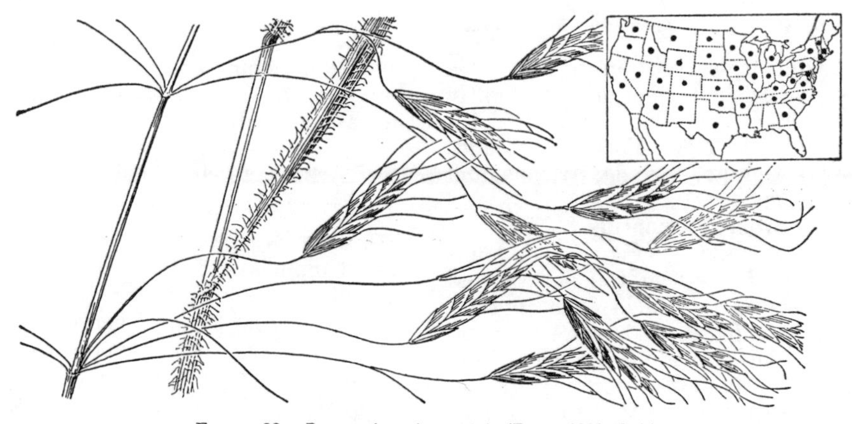

FIGURE 33.—*Bromus japonicus*, × 1. (Deam 6833, Ind.)

the upper; palea 1.5 to 2 mm. shorter than the lemma. ⊙ (*B. patulus* Mert. and Koch)—Weed in waste places, Vermont to Washington, south to North Carolina and California; Alberta; widely distributed in the Old World, whence introduced.

BROMUS JAPONICUS var. PORRÉCTUS Hack. Differing only in straight awns. ⊙ —New York to Utah and New Mexico infrequent; more common from Maryland to Alabama. In some mature panicles both straight and flexuous-divergent awns occur. In *B. japonicus* before maturity the awns are straight and identity is often uncertain. Specimens of this have been distributed as *B. japonicus* var. *subsquarrosus*.

35. Bromus arvénsis L. (Fig. 34.) Resembling *B. japonicus*, foliage downy to subglabrous; spikelets thinner, flatter (less turgid), often tinged with purple; lemmas acute, bifid; awn

FIGURE 34.—*Bromus arvensis*, × 1. (Gray, Md.)

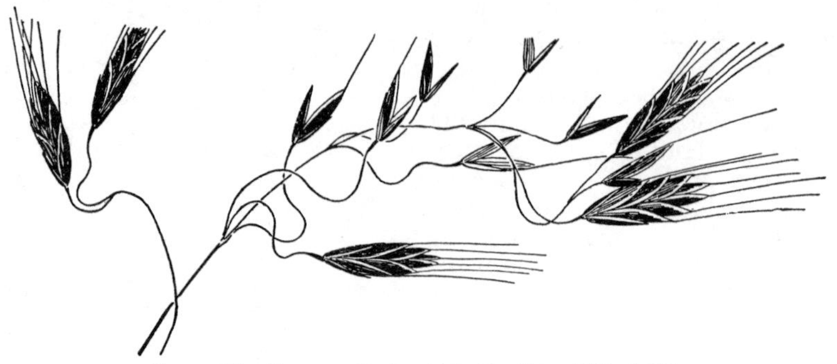

FIGURE 35.—*Bromus arenarius*, × 1. (Pendleton 1459, Calif.)

straight or nearly so in drying; palea as long as the lemma or only slightly shorter. ⊙ —Open ground, cultivated soil, New York, Maryland; North Dakota, Nevada, Arizona, and California.

36. Bromus arenárius Labill. AUSTRALIAN CHESS. (Fig. 35.) Culms slender, 15 to 40 cm. tall, sheaths and blades pilose; panicle open, pyramidal, nodding, 8 to 11 (rarely 15) cm. long, the spreading branches and pedicels sinuously curved; glumes densely pilose, acute, scarious-margined, the first narrower, 3-nerved, 8 mm. long, the second 7-nerved, 10 mm. long; lemmas densely pilose, 7-nerved, 10 mm. long; awn straight, 10 to 16 mm. long. ⊙ —Sandy roadsides, gravelly or sterile hills, Oregon, California, Nevada, and Arizona; adventive at Philadelphia, Pa.; introduced from Australia.

Bromus alopecúros Poir. Weedy annual 20 to 40 cm. tall; foliage softly pubescent; panicle narrow, dense, 5 to 10 cm. long; spikelets short-pedicellate, about 2 cm. long, the glumes and lemmas softly pubescent, the awn of the lemma, flat, twisted at the base, spreading, 1.5 to 2 cm. long. ⊙ —Adventive in waste ground, Ann Arbor, Mich. Mediterranean region.

SECTION 4. EUBRÓMUS Godr.

Tufted annuals; spikelets compressed; glumes and lemmas narrow, long-awned; first glume 1-nerved, the second 3-nerved; lemma 5- to 7-nerved, cleft at the apex, the hyaline teeth 2 to 5 mm. long; floret at maturity with a sharp hard point or callus. Introduced from Europe.

37. Bromus rígidus Roth. RIPGUT GRASS. (Fig. 36.) Culms 40 to 70 cm. tall; sheaths and blades pilose; panicle open, nodding, rather few-flowered, 7 to 15 cm. long, the lower branches 1 to 2 cm. long; spikelets usually 5- to 7-flowered, 3 to 4 cm. long, excluding awns; glumes smooth, the first 1.5 to 2 cm. long, the second 2.5 to 3 cm. long; lemmas 2.5 to 3 cm. long, scabrous or puberulent, the teeth 3 to 4 rado, and New Mexico; in the ern States from New England Illinois to Virginia and Arkansas.

. Bromus rúbens L. Foxtail ss. (Fig. 38.) Culms 15 to 40 cm. puberulent below the panicle; ths and blades pubescent; panicle , compact, ovoid, usually 4 to 8 long, usually purplish; spikelets 11-flowered, about 2.5 cm. long;

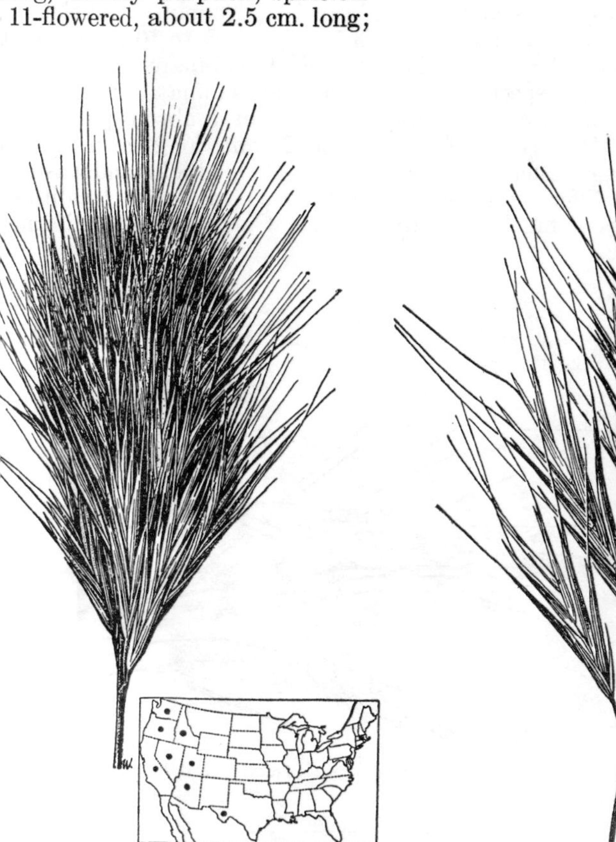

38.—*Bromus rubens*, × 1. (Blankenship 36, Calif.)

Figure 39.—*Bromus madritensis*, × 1. (Eastwood, Calif.)

lume 7 to 9 mm. long, the second 12 mm. long; lemmas scabrous arsely pubescent, 12 to 16 mm. the teeth 4 to 5 mm. long; awn 22 mm. long, somewhat spread- maturity. ⊙ —Dry hills and ste or cultivated ground, Wash- n to southern California, very lant over extensive areas, and to Idaho, Utah, and Arizona; ; Massachusetts.

40. Bromus madriténsis L. (Fig. 39.) Resembling *B. rubens*, but the culms smooth below the less dense panicles; sheaths mostly smooth; blades puberulent to glabrous; panicle 5 to 10 cm. long, oblong-ovoid (in dried specimens more or less fan-shaped); lemmas a little longer than in *B. rubens*, the teeth 2 to 3 mm. long; awn rather stout, 16 to 22 mm. long. ⊙ —Open ground and waste places, Oregon and California; less common than *B. rubens*. Occasionally cultivated for ornament.

41. Bromus tectórum L. Downy chess. (Fig. 40.) Culms erect or spreading, slender, 30 to 60 cm. tall;

mm. long; awn stout, 3.5 to 5 cm. long. ⊙ (*B. villosus* Forsk. not Scop.; *B. maximus* Desf., not Gilib.) —Common weed in open ground and waste places in the southern half of California, forming dense stands over great areas in the lowlands, occasional north to British Columbia and east to Idaho, Utah, and Arizona; rare in the Eastern States, Maryland, Virginia, Mississippi, Texas, introduced from Mediterranean region. Distinguished from the other species of the section by the long awns. BROMUS RIGIDUS var. GUSSÓNEI (Parl.) Coss. and Dur. Differing in having more open panicles, the stiffer, more spreading lower branches as much as 10 to

12 cm. long. ⊙
rigidus, growing in
Washington to Cali
zona; more common
in middle and north

38. Bromus stéri
Resembling *B. rigi*
culms 50 to 100 cm.
bescent; panicle 10 t
branches drooping;
3.5 cm. long, 6- to 1(
lanceolate-subulate,
mm. long; lemmas 1
scabrous or scabro
teeth 2 mm. long;
long. ⊙ —Field
introduced in a f
British Columbia

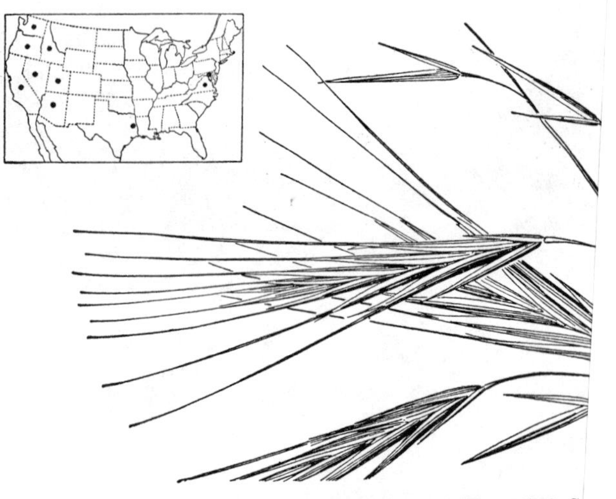

FIGURE 36.—*Bromus rigidus*, × 1. (Tracy 4702, C

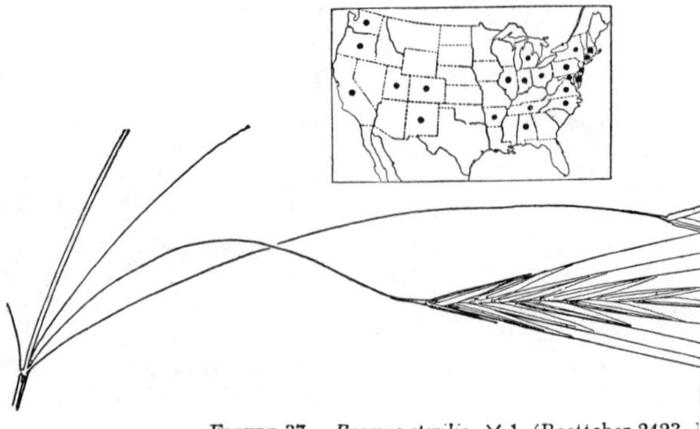

FIGURE 37.—*Bromus sterilis*, × 1. (Boettcher 2423,

FIG

fir
10
to
lon
18
ing
in
ing
abu
eas
Te

FIGURE 40.—*Bromus tectorum*. Plant, × ½; spikelet and floret, × 5. (Chase 2051, Ind.)

sheaths and blades pubescent; panicle 5 to 15 cm. long, rather dense, soft, drooping, often purple; spikelets nodding, 12 to 20 mm. long; glumes villous, the first 4 to 6 mm. long, the second 8 to 10 mm. long; lemmas lanceolate, villous or pilose, 10 to 12 mm. long, the teeth 2 to 3 mm. long; awn 12 to 14 mm. long. ⊙ —Along roadsides, banks, and waste places, common on the Pacific coast, especially in Washington and Oregon; Alberta, and here and there throughout the United States as far south as South Carolina and Texas. BROMUS TECTORUM var. GLABRÁTUS Spenner. Differing in having glabrous spikelets. ⊙ (*B. tectorum* var. *nudus* Klett and Richter.)—About the same range as the species, less common.

SECTION 5. NEOBRÓMUS Shear, as subgenus.

Annual; lemmas lanceolate, deeply bifid, the teeth aristate; awn twisted, geniculate. Approaches *Trisetum*.

FIGURE 41.—*Bromus trinii*, × 1. (Eastwood, Calif.)

42. Bromus trínii Desv. CHILEAN CHESS. (Fig. 41.) Culms 30 to 60 cm. or even 100 cm. tall, erect or branched and spreading below, often pubescent at the nodes; sheaths and blades pilose-pubescent to nearly smooth; panicle 8 to 20 cm. long, narrow, rather dense, erect, the branches erect or the lower more or less spreading or flexuous; spikelets narrow, 1.5 to 2 cm. long, 5- to 7-flowered; glumes lanceolate, acuminate, the first mostly 1-nerved, 8 to 10 mm. long, the second mostly 3-nerved, 12 to 16 mm. long; lemmas 5-nerved, 12 to 14 mm. long, pubescent, acuminate, with narrow teeth 2 to 3 mm. long, the teeth aristate; awn 1.5 to 2 cm. long, twisted below, bent below the middle and strongly divaricate when old. ⊙ (Including *B. trinii* var. *pallidiflorus* Desv.) —Dry plains and rocky or wooded slopes, Oregon, California, and Baja California, rarely eastward to Colorado; introduced from Chile.

BROMUS TRINII var. EXCÉLSUS Shear. Differing in having larger spikelets, 7-nerved lemmas, and divaricate but not twisted or bent awns; teeth of the lemma acuminate, but not aristate. ⊙ —A little-known form from the Panamint Mountains, Calif., and Emory Canyon, Lake Mead, Ariz.

3. BRACHYPÓDIUM Beauv.

Spikelets nearly sessile, several- to many-flowered, the rachilla disarticulating above the glumes and between the florets; glumes unequal, sharp-pointed, 5- and 7-nerved; lemmas firm, rounded or somewhat flattened on the back, 7-nerved, acuminate, awned or mucronate; palea as long as the body of the lemma, concave, the keels pectinate-ciliate. Annuals or perennials with erect racemes of subsessile spikelets. Type species, *Bromus pinnatus* L. (*Brachypodium pinnatum* (L.) Beauv.) Name from *brachys*, short, and *podion*, foot, alluding to the very short pedicels.

Eurasian species introduced in the United States; two American species only; Mexico to South America.

1. Brachypodium distáchyon (L.) Beauv. (Fig. 42.) Annual, branching and geniculate at base, 15 to 30 cm. tall; nodes pubescent; sheaths and blades sparsely pilose to subglabrous; ligule, 1.5 to 2 mm. long, pubescent; blades flat, 2 to 6 cm. long, 3 to 4 mm. wide; raceme strict, the segments of the axis alternately concave; spikelets 1 to 5, imbricate, 2 to 3.5 cm. long, excluding the awns, 5 to 6 mm. wide; florets closely imbricate; lemmas scabrous, the slender scabrous erect awn 1 to 2 cm. long. The spikelets resemble those of some species of *Agropyron.* ⊙ —Open ground, Arapahoe County, Colo., Humboldt, Sonoma, and Marin Counties, Calif.; on ballast, Camden, N. J., and Portland, Oreg. Sparingly introduced from Europe, but spreading in Marin County, Calif.

Brachypodium sylváticum (Huds.) Beauv. Perennial, 60 to 100 cm. tall; blades to 25 cm. long and 1 cm. wide; raceme 12 to 20 cm. long, the spikelets 4 to 5 cm. long, subterete, the lower distant, the upper closely imbricate. ♃ Occasionally cultivated for ornament and in grass gardens. Europe.

Brachypodium caespitosum (Host) Roem. and Schult., a tall, leafy perennial, with racemes 8 to 12 cm. long of overlapping spikelets 2.5 to 3 cm. long, the lemmas imbricate, strongly nerved, glabrous, the awns about 5 mm. long. Introduced from Turkey; has been grown at the experiment station, Tucson, Ariz.

Brachypodium pinnatum (L.) Beauv., similar to the preceding, but with pubescent nodes, scabrous laxer foliage, and narrower spikelets with hirsute lemmas. Introduced from Rumania; has been grown in the Grass Garden, Beltsville, Md. The results of both trials are as yet inconclusive.

Figure 42.—*Brachypodium distachyon.* Plant, × ½; glumes and floret, × 5. (J. T. Howell 23186, Calif.)

4. FESTÚCA L. Fescue

Spikelets few- to several-flowered (rarely 1-flowered in some of the spikelets of a panicle), the rachilla disarticulating above the glumes and between the florets, the uppermost floret reduced; glumes narrow, acute, unequal, the first sometimes very small; lemmas rounded on the back, membranaceous or somewhat indurate, 5-nerved, the nerves often obscure, acute or rarely obtuse, awned from the tip, or rarely from a minutely bifid apex, sometimes awnless. Low or rather tall annuals or perennials, the spikelets in narrow or open panicles. The blades are sometimes somewhat auriculate as in the Hordeae. Standard species, *Festuca ovina.* Name from *Festuca,* an old Latin name for a weedy grass.

Many of the perennial species of fescue are important forage grasses in the grazing regions of the West. *Festuca arizonica,* Arizona fescue, of northern Arizona and *F. idahoensis,* Idaho fescue, of the region from Colorado to central California and northward, are important, though they become rather tough with age. *F. viridula,* greenleaf fescue, locally called mountain bunchgrass, is an outstanding grass in subalpine regions of the Northwestern States, and *F. thurberi*, Thurber fescue, is important in similar regions from Colorado to Montana. *F. ovina*, sheep fescue, is a good grazing grass though not abundant, but its variety *brachyphylla*, alpine fescue, furnishes much of the forage above timber line from the Rocky Mountains westward. *F. occidentalis*, western fescue, in open woods up to 10,000 feet in the Northwest, and *F. rubra*, red fescue, widely distributed at various altitudes in the West, are valuable in proportion to their abundance.

The most important cultivated species is *F. elatior*, meadow fescue, a native of Europe, used for hay and pasture in the humid region, especially in Tennessee, Missouri, and Kansas. *F. ovina*, and its allies, and *F. rubra*, are cultivated to a limited extent in the Eastern States as lawn or pasture grasses, usually in mixtures.

Plants annual........ SECTION 1. VULPIA.
Plants perennial........ SECTION 2. EUFESTUCA.

Section 1. Vulpia

1a. Spikelets mostly more than 5-flowered. Lowest lemma 4 to 5 mm. long, the margin inrolled, not scarious........ 1. F. OCTOFLORA.
1b. Spikelets mostly less than 5-flowered (sometimes 6-flowered in *F. dertonensis* and *F. sciurea*). Lemmas usually scarious-margined.
  2a. Panicle narrow, the branches appressed.
    Lemmas appressed-pubescent over the back, about 3 mm. long........ 2. F. SCIUREA.
    Lemmas glabrous, scabrous or ciliate, not pubescent over the back.
      Lemmas ciliate toward the apex........ 3. F. MEGALURA.
      Lemmas not ciliate.
        First glume two-thirds to three-fourths as long as the second. 4. F. DERTONENSIS.
        First glume much shorter than the second, 1 to 2 mm. long........ 5. F. MYUROS.
  2b. Panicle rather short, the branches and often the spikelets spreading (scarcely spreading in *F. arida*).
    3a. Spikelets glabrous.
      Pedicels appressed; lower branches of the panicle usually finally reflexed; spikelets usually 3- to 5-flowered........ 6. F. PACIFICA.
      Pedicels or nearly all of them finally reflexed, notably those of the upper part of the main axis; branches of the panicle reflexed; spikelets mostly 1- or 2-flowered. 10. F. REFLEXA.
    3b. Spikelets pubescent, the pubescence on glumes or lemmas or on both.
      4a. Pedicels appressed or slightly spreading; lower branches of panicle usually spreading or reflexed.
        Lemmas glabrous; glumes pubescent........ 7. F. CONFUSA.
        Lemmas pubescent.
          Lemmas hirsute; glumes glabrous or pubescent; lower branches of panicle spreading or reflexed........ 8. F. GRAYI.
          Lemmas woolly-pubescent; glumes glabrous; panicle nearly simple, the branches scarcely spreading........ 9. F. ARIDA.
      4b. Pedicels and panicle branches all finally spreading or reflexed.
        Glumes glabrous; lemmas pubescent........ 11. F. MICROSTACHYS.
        Glumes pubescent; lemmas pubescent........ 12. F. EASTWOODAE.
        Glumes pubescent; lemmas glabrous........ 13. F. TRACYI.

Section 2. Eufestuca

1a. Blades flat, rather soft and lax, mostly more than 3 mm. wide.
  Lemmas awned, the awn usually more than 2 mm. long.
    Floret long-stipitate, the rachilla appearing to be jointed a short distance below the floret........ 14. F. SUBULIFLORA.
    Floret not stipitate.
      Lemmas indistinctly nerved; awn terminal; blades 3 to 10 mm. wide. 15. F. SUBULATA.
      Lemmas distinctly 5-nerved; awn from between 2 short teeth; blades 2 to 4 mm. wide. 16. F. ELMERI.

Lemmas awnless or with an awn rarely as much as 2 mm. long.
  Spikelets oblong to linear, mostly 8- to 10-flowered and more than 10 mm. long. 17. F. ELATIOR.
  Spikelets ovate or oval, mostly not more than 5-flowered, less than 10 mm. long.
    Lemmas acuminate, sometimes with an awn as much as 2 mm. long, membranaceous, distinctly nerved, 6 to 9 mm. long 18. F. SORORIA.
    Lemmas awnless, obtuse to acutish, rather firm, indistinctly nerved.
      Lemmas 5 to 7 mm. long, acutish 19. F. VERSUTA.
      Lemmas about 4 mm. long, relatively blunt, rather turgid.
        Spikelets loosely scattered in a very open panicle with long slender branches. 20. F. OBTUSA.
        Spikelets somewhat aggregate toward the ends of rather short branches of a less open nodding panicle 21. F. PARADOXA.

1b. Blades involute or if flat less than 3 mm. wide (sometimes flat in *F. californica*, but firm and soon involute).
  Ligule 2 to 4 mm. long or longer. Lemmas awnless or cuspidate.
    Lemmas 7 mm. long 22. F. THURBERI.
    Lemmas 4 mm. long 23. F. LIGULATA.
  Ligule short.
    Collar and mouth of sheath villous. Culms tall and stout (rather short in var. *parishii*). 25. F. CALIFORNICA.
    Collar and mouth of sheath not villous.
      Panicle branches densely ciliate on the angles. Blades about 1 mm. wide, flat or folded 26. F. DASYCLADA.
      Panicle branches not ciliate on the angles.
        Culms decumbent at the usually red, fibrillose base, in loose tufts. Awn of lemma shorter than the body; blades smooth 28. F. RUBRA.
        Culms erect.
          Lemmas 7 to 10 mm. long, scabrous. Culms densely tufted, rather stout, usually scabrous below the panicle; lemmas acute, rarely short-awned. 24. F. SCABRELLA.
          Lemmas mostly not more than 7 mm. long.
            Lemmas awnless (see also *F. arizonica*).
              Lemmas 6 to 7 mm. long; culms slender, loosely tufted. 27. F. VIRIDULA.
              Lemmas about 3 mm. long 31. F. CAPILLATA.
            Lemmas awned.
              Awn as long as or longer than body of the lemma; blades soft, glabrous, sulcate 29. F. OCCIDENTALIS.
              Awn shorter than body of the lemma; blades slender, numerous, usually scabrous.
                Blades mostly not more than half as long as the culms; panicle narrow, often almost spikelike, few-flowered, mostly less than 10 cm. long; culms mostly less than 30 cm. tall 30. F. OVINA.
                Blades elongate; panicles 10 to 20 cm. long, somewhat open; culms 30 to 100 cm. tall.
                  Awn 2 to 4 mm. long 32. F. IDAHOENSIS.
                  Awn short or obsolete 33. F. ARIZONICA.

SECTION 1. VÚLPIA (Gmel.) Reichenb.

Slender annuals; lemmas awned; stamens usually 1, sometimes 3; flowers usually self-pollinated, but young panicles are found with anthers and stigmas exserted. Some of the species, especially numbers 7 to 13, resemble each other closely. The differences, though small, appear to be constant, hence the recognizable forms are maintained as species, rather than reduced to varieties under leading species.

---

1. Festuca octoflóra Walt. SIX-WEEKS FESCUE. (Fig. 43.) Culms erect, usually 15 to 30 cm. tall, sometimes as much as 60 cm.; blades narrow, involute, 2 to 10 cm. long; panicle narrow, the branches short, appressed or spreading; spikelets 6 to 8 mm. long, densely 5- to 13-flowered; glumes subulate-lanceolate, the first 1-nerved, the second 3-nerved, 3 to 4.5 mm. long; lemmas firm, convex, lanceolate, glabrous or scabrous, 4 to 5 mm. long, the margins not scarious; awn commonly 3 to 5, sometimes to 7 mm. long. ⊙ —Open sterile ground, New York to Florida, Illinois, Kansas, and Texas; Idaho, Washington. The species and its varieties are found throughout the United States.

FESTUCA OCTOFLORA var. TENÉLLA (Willd.) Fernald. Mostly smaller; panicle usually nearly simple; spike-

FIGURE 43.—*Festuca octoflora*. Plant, × ½; spikelet, × 5. (Chase 1776, Ind.)

lets smaller; first glume 2.3 to 4 mm. long, awns 1 to 5 mm. Distinctions not constant, many intermediates occur. ⊙ —Canada and Connecticut to Washington, south to Virginia, Tennessee, and Oklahoma; Georgia, Alabama, Texas; Colorado, Nevada, and New Mexico.

FESTUCA OCTOFLORA var. GLAÚCA (Nutt.) Fernald. Panicle shorter and denser than in most specimens of var. *tenella;* awn of lemma from minute to 2 mm. long. Intergrades with var. *tenella.* ⊙ —Indiana, Arkansas, Nebraska, Kansas, Oklahoma, and Texas.

FESTUCA OCTOFLORA var. HIRTÉLLA Piper. Commonly rather low and densely tufted; foliage sometimes pubescent; panicle usually rather dense; lemma hirtellous or pubescent, sometimes strongly scabrous only; awns mostly 2 to 4 mm. long. Intergrades with *F. octoflora* and with var. *tenella.* ⊙ —British Columbia to Baja California, east to Kansas and Texas; Florida.

2. Festuca sciúrea Nutt. (Fig. 44.) Culms erect, 15 to 50 cm. tall; blades less than 1 mm. wide, often capillary, soft, mostly involute, 1 to 10 cm. long; panicle narrow, 5 to 20 cm. long; spikelets 4- to 6-flowered, 4 to 5 mm. long; first glume 2 mm. long, the second 3.5 mm. long; lemmas 3 to 3.5 mm. long, sparsely appressed-pubescent; awn 6 to 11 mm. long. ⊙ —Open ground, New Jersey and Maryland to Florida, west to Oklahoma and Texas.

FIGURE 44.—*Festuca sciurea.* Panicle, × ½; spikelet, × 5. (Reverchon, Tex.)

3. Festuca megalúra Nutt. FOXTAIL FESCUE. (Fig. 45.) Culms 20 to 60 cm. tall; sheaths and narrow blades glabrous; panicle narrow, 7 to 20 cm. long, the branches appressed; spikelets 4- or 5-flowered; first glume 1.5 to 2 mm. long, the second 4 to 5 mm. long; lemmas linear-lanceolate, scabrous on the back especially toward the apex, ciliate on the upper half; awn 8 to 10 mm. long. ⊙ —Open sterile ground, British Columbia to Baja California, common in the Coast Ranges of California, east to Montana and Arizona; introduced in a few localities eastward; Guatemala; Pacific slope of South America. In mature lemmas the cilia may be obscured by the inrolling of the edges; moistening the floret will bring the cilia to view.

FIGURE 45.—*Festuca megalura.* Panicle, × 1; spikelet, × 5. (Leiberg 150, Oreg.)

4. Festuca dertonénsis (All.) Aschers. and Graebn. (Fig. 46.) Resembling *F. megalura*, the panicles on the average shorter, usually less dense; glumes longer, the first about 4 mm. long, the second 6 to 7 mm. long; lemma lanceolate, scabrous on the back toward the apex, 7 to 8 mm. long; awn 10 to 13 mm. long. ⊙ — Dry hills and meadows, British Co-

FIGURE 46.—*Festuca dertonensis*. Plant, × ½; spikelet, × 5. (Palmer 2041, Calif.)

lumbia to southern California, Arizona, and Texas; rare as a waif in the Eastern States; introduced from Europe. This species has been referred to *F. bromoides* L. by American authors.

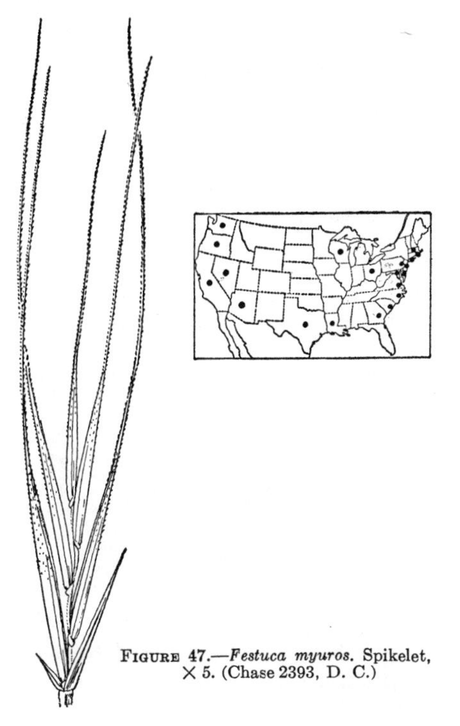

FIGURE 47.—*Festuca myuros.* Spikelet, × 5. (Chase 2393, D. C.)

5. Festuca myúros L. (Fig. 47.) Differing from *F. megalura* chiefly in the absence of cilia on the lemma; panicle usually smaller, first glume 1 to 1.5 mm., the second 4 to 4.5 mm. long. ☉ —Open ground, Coastal Plain, Massachusetts to Texas; Ohio; Wisconsin; Pacific coast, Washington to southern California; Arizona; Mexico and South America; introduced from Europe.

6. Festuca pacífica Piper. (Fig. 48.) Culms erect or geniculate at base, 30 to 60 cm. tall; blades soft, loosely involute, glabrous, 3 to 5 cm. long; panicle 5 to 12 cm. long, the lower branches solitary, somewhat distant, subsecund, spreading, 1 to 3 cm. long; spikelets 3- to 6-flowered; first glume subulate-lanceolate, about 4 mm. long, the second lanceolate-acuminate, about 5 mm. long; lemmas lanceolate, glabrous or scaberulous, 6 to 7 mm. long; awn 10 to 15 mm. long. ☉ —Open ground, mountain slopes, and open woods, British Columbia to

FIGURE 48.—*Festuca pacifica.* Panicle, × 1; floret, × 10. (Type.)

Baja California, east to western Montana and New Mexico.

FESTUCA PACIFICA var. SÍMULANS Hoover. All spikelets reflexed or divergent at maturity. ☉ —Kern and Kings Counties, Calif.

7. Festuca confúsa Piper. (Fig. 49.) Resembling *F. pacifica;* sheaths retrorsely pilose; foliage pubescent; spikelets usually 2- or 3-flowered; glumes hirsute with long spreading hairs; lemmas glabrous. ☉ —Dry hillsides, Washington to southern California.

8. Festuca gráyi (Abrams) Piper. (Fig. 50.) Resembling *F. pacifica,* often somewhat stouter; sheaths and sometimes blades pubescent; glumes glabrous to sparsely villous; lemmas pubescent, puberulent or sometimes villous. ☉ (*F. microstachys* var. *grayi* Abrams.)—Open ground and rocky slopes, Washington to southern California and Arizona.

9. Festuca árida Elmer. (Fig. 51.) Culms erect or spreading, mostly less than 15 cm. tall; sheaths and blades

FIGURE 49.—*Festuca confusa*. Plant, × 1; spikelet, × 5. (Type.)

FIGURE 50.—*Festuca grayi*. Plant, × ½; spikelet, × 5. (Pringle, Ariz.)

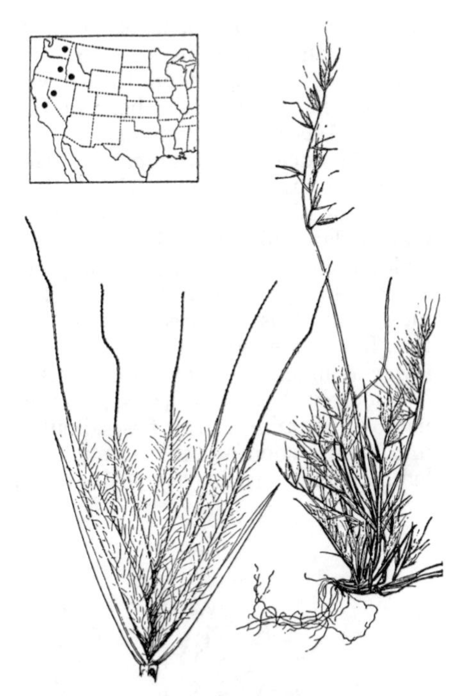

FIGURE 51.—*Festuca arida*. Plant, × ½; spikelet, × 5. (Type.)

glabrous, the blades loosely involute, mostly less than 4 cm. long; panicle narrow, 2 to 5 cm. long, the branches appressed or the lowermost somewhat spreading; glumes about equal, glabrous, 5 to 6 mm. long; lemmas densely woolly, about 5 mm. long; awn 5 to 10 mm. long. ☉ —Sandy or dry ground, rare, eastern Washington and Oregon, southwestern Idaho, northeastern California, and western Nevada.

10. Festuca refléxa Buckl. (Fig. 52.) Culms 20 to 40 cm. tall; sheaths glabrous or pubescent; blades narrow, flat to subinvolute, 2 to 10 cm. long; panicle 5 to 12 cm. long, the solitary branches and the spikelets all at length divaricate; spikelets mostly 1- to 3-flowered, 5 to 7 mm. long; first glume 2 to 4 mm. long, the second 4 to 5 mm. long; lemmas glabrous or scaberulous, 5 to 6 mm. long; awn usually 5 to 8 mm. long. ☉ —Mesas, rocky slopes, and wooded hills, Washington to southern California, east to Arizona and Utah.

11. Festuca micrôstachys Nutt. (Fig. 53.) Resembling *F. reflexa;* glumes glabrous; lemmas pubescent. ☉ —Open ground, Washington to California; rare.

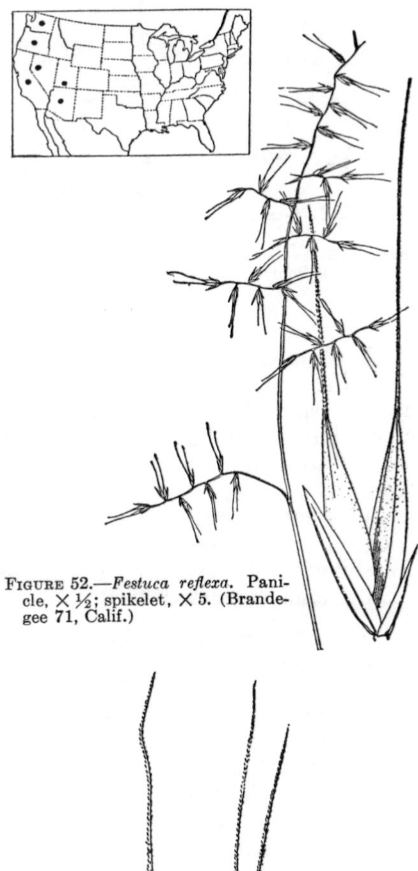

FIGURE 52.—*Festuca reflexa*. Panicle, × ½; spikelet, × 5. (Brandegee 71, Calif.)

FIGURE 53.—*Festuca microstachys*. Spikelet, × 5. (Allen, Calif.)

12. Festuca eastwoodae Piper. (Fig. 54.) Resembling *F. reflexa;* glumes hirsute; lemmas hirsute, the awn 4 to 5 mm. long. ⊙ —Open ground, Oregon, Arizona, and California; rare.

FIGURE 54. — *Festuca eastwoodae.* Panicle, × ½; glumes, × 5. (Type.)

FIGURE 55. — *Festuca tracyi.* Panicle, × ½; glumes, × 5; floret, × 5. (Type.)

13. Festuca trácyi Hitchc. (Fig. 55.) Resembling *F. reflexa;* glumes rather sparsely hispid-villous, the first 1.5 to 2 mm. long, acute, the second 3 to 4 mm. long, obtusish or abruptly acute; lemmas glabrous, about 4 mm. long; awn 4 to 7 mm. long. ⊙ —Open rocky ground, Washington (Bingen) and California (Kings and Napa Counties).

SECTION 2. EUFESTUCA Griseb.

Perennials, culms simple, stamens 3.

14. Festuca subuliflóra Scribn. (Fig. 56.) Culms erect, slender, 60 to 100 cm. tall; blades flat (or loosely involute in drying), lax, pubescent on the upper surface, those of the culm mostly 2 to 4 mm. wide, those of the innovations narrower; panicle loose, lax, 10 to 20 cm. long, nodding, the branches drooping, the lower naked at base; spikelets loosely 3- to 5-flowered, the rachilla pubescent or hispid, the internodes of the rachilla as much as 2 mm. long; floret long-stipitate, the rachilla appearing to be jointed a short distance below the floret; glumes very narrow, acuminate, the first 3 to 4 mm., the second 4 to 5 mm., long; lemmas scaberulous toward the apex, 6 to 8 mm. long; awn somewhat flexuous, 10 to 15 mm. long. ♃ —Moist shady places from sea level to 1,000 m., British Columbia to northern California, mostly near the coast. Peculiar in the stipitate base of the lemma. Aspect of *F. subulata.*

15. Festuca subuláta Trin. BEARDED FESCUE. (Fig. 57.) Culms erect, mostly 50 to 100 cm. tall; blades flat, thin, lax, 3 to 10 mm. wide; panicle loose, open, drooping, 15 to 40 cm. long, the branches mostly in twos or threes, naked below, finally spreading or reflexed, the lower as much as 15 cm. long; spikelets loosely 3- to 5-flowered; glumes narrow, acuminate, the first about 3 mm., the second about 5 mm., long; lemmas somewhat keeled, scaberulous

FIGURE 56.—*Festuca subuliflora.* Panicle, × ½; spikelet, × 5. (Howell 19, Oreg.)

FIGURE 60.—*Festuca sororia.* Panicle, × ½; floret, × 5. (Baker 36, Colo.)

18. Festuca sorória Piper. (Fig. 60.) Culms erect, loosely tufted, 60 to 90 cm. tall; blades flat, thin, smooth except the scabrous margins, 3 to 6 mm. wide; panicle loose, open, nodding, or sometimes somewhat condensed, 10 to 15 cm. long, the branches solitary or in twos, naked below; spikelets rather loosely 3- to 5-flowered; glumes lanceolate, the first about 3 mm., the second about 5 mm. long; lemmas membranaceous, somewhat keeled, scaberulous or nearly smooth, the nerves evident but not prominent, the apex tapering into a fine point or an awn as much as 2 mm. long. ♃ —Open woods, 2,000 to 3,000 m., southern Colorado and Utah to New Mexico and Arizona.

FIGURE 61.—*Festuca versuta.* Panicle, × ½; spikelet, × 5. (Johnson, Tex.)

19. Festuca versúta Beal. (Fig. 61.) Culms slender, 50 to 100 cm. tall; blades flat, mostly 2 to 5 mm. wide; panicle open, 10 to 15 cm. long, the spreading lower branches bearing a few spikelets above the middle; spikelets 2- to 5-flowered; glumes narrow, acuminate, nearly equal, 5 to 6 mm. long; lemmas firm, obscurely nerved at maturity, 5 to 7 mm. long, acute, awnless, rarely awn-tipped. ♃ (*F. texana* Vasey; *F. johnsoni* Piper.)—Shady banks, Arkansas, Texas, and Oklahoma.

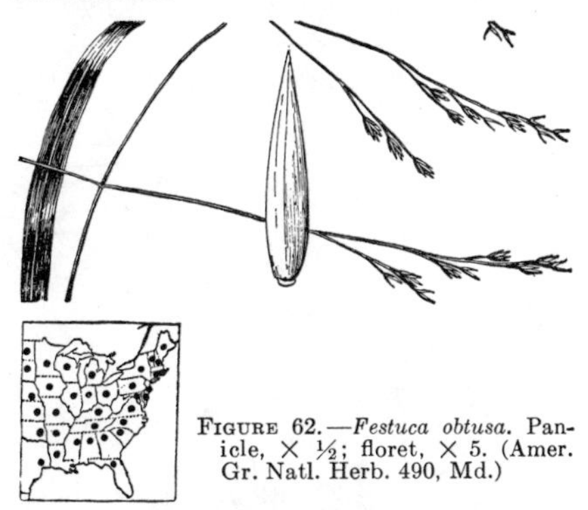

FIGURE 62.—*Festuca obtusa.* Panicle, × ½; floret, × 5. (Amer. Gr. Natl. Herb. 490, Md.)

20. Festuca obtúsa Bieler. NODDING FESCUE. (Fig. 62.) Culms solitary or few in a tuft, mostly 50 to 100 cm. tall; blades flat, lax, somewhat glossy, 4 to 7 mm. wide; panicle nodding, very loose and open, the branches spreading, spikelet-bearing toward the ends, the lower usually reflexed at maturity; spikelets 3- to 5-flowered; glumes about 3 and 4 mm. long; lemmas coriaceous, rather turgid, about 4 mm. long, obtuse or acutish, the nerves very obscure. ♃ —Low or rocky woods, Quebec to Manitoba, south to northern Florida and eastern Texas.

21. Festuca paradóxa Desv. (Fig. 63.) Culms few to several in a tuft, 50 to 110 cm. tall, widely leaning; blades flat or subinvolute in drying, lax, 4 to 8 mm. wide; panicle 12 to 20 cm. long, heavily drooping, the slender scabrous branches not so long as in *F. obtusa*, the brownish spikelets somewhat aggregate toward the ends; spikelets 3- to 6-flowered, the lemmas more blunt. ♃ (*F. shortii* Kunth) —Prairies, low open ground, and thickets, Pennsylvania and Delaware to South Carolina, Wisconsin, and eastern Texas.

FIGURE 63.—*Festuca paradoxa.* Panicle, × ½; floret, × 5. (Palmer 34672, Mo.)

FIGURE 64.—*Festuca thurberi.* Panicle, × ½; spikelet, × 5. (Pammel, Colo.)

22. Festuca thúrberi Vasey. THURBER FESCUE. (Fig. 64.) Culms densely tufted, rather stout, erect, 60 to 90 cm. tall; ligule 2 to 4 mm. long; blades involute, scabrous, firm, erect; panicle 10 to 15 cm. long, the branches usually solitary, somewhat remote, ascending or spreading, naked below; spikelets 3- to 6-flowered; glumes rather broad, about 4 and 5 mm. long; lemmas rather firm, faintly nerved, glabrous or nearly so, acute or cuspidate, 7 to 8 mm. long. ♃ —Dry slopes and rocky hills, 2,500 to 3,500 m., Wyoming to New Mexico and Utah.

23. Festuca liguláta Swallen. (Fig. 65.) Culms slender, loosely tufted, erect from a decumbent often rhizomatous base, scabrous below the panicle; sheaths glabrous; blades 6 to 20 cm. long, those of the innovations as much as 30 cm. long, flat and 1 to 2 mm. wide or mostly involute, scabrous, rather firm; ligule 3 to 3.5 mm. long; panicle 6 to 10 cm. long, the 1 or 2 scabrous branches stiffly ascending or spreading, few-flowered, naked below; spikelets 6 mm. long, 2- to 3-flowered, the pedicels (mostly shorter than the spikelets) appressed; glumes acute or acutish, scabrous, the first 3 mm. long, 1-nerved, the second 4 mm. long, 3-nerved; lemmas 4 to 5 mm. long, acutish, scabrous, obscurely nerved, awnless, the paleas slightly longer. ♃ —Moist shady slopes, Guadalupe and Chisos Mountains, Tex.

FIGURE 65.—*Festuca ligulata.* Plant, × ½; floret, × 5. (Type.)

24. Festuca scabrélla Torr. ROUGH FESCUE. (Fig. 66.) Culms densely tufted (rarely producing a slender rhizome), erect, 30 to 90 cm. tall; ligule very short; blades firm, erect, scabrous, involute, or those of the culm sometimes flat but narrow; panicle narrow, 5 to 15 cm. long, the branches solitary or in pairs, the lowermost sometimes in threes, appressed or ascending, naked below;

spikelets 4- to 6-flowered; glumes somewhat unequal, lanceolate, 7 to 9 mm. long; lemmas firm, rather strongly nerved, scaberulous, acute to cuspidate or short-awned, 7 to 10 mm. long. ♃ (*F. hallii* Piper; *F. kingii* var. *rabiosa* (Piper) Hitchc.; *Hesperochloa kingii* var. *rabiosa* (Piper) Swallen.)—Prairies, hillsides, and open woods, up to about 2,000 m. (probably alpine in Colorado), Newfoundland to British Columbia, south to Oregon, North Dakota, and Colorado. FESTUCA SCABRELLA var. MÁJOR Vasey. Culms on the average taller; panicle larger and more spreading; lemmas more strongly nerved. ♃ (*F. campestris* Rydb.)—Hills and dry woods, Michigan (Roscommon), Montana to Washington.

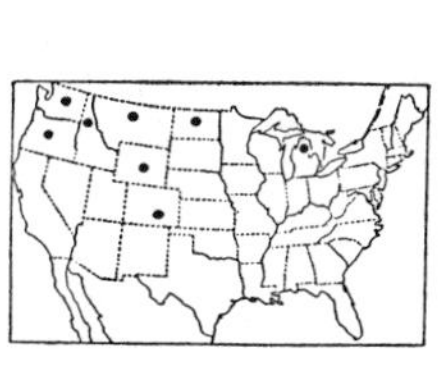

FIGURE 66.—*Festuca scabrella*. Panicle, × ½; floret × 5. (Rydberg 2106, Mont.)

25. Festuca califórnica Vasey. CALIFORNIA FESCUE. (Fig. 67.) Culms tufted, rather stout, 60 to 120 cm. tall; sheaths somewhat scabrous, the collar pubescent or pilose; blades firm, usually involute, sometimes flat, scabrous; panicle open, 10 to 30 cm. long, the rather remote branches usually in pairs, spreading or drooping, naked below; spikelets mostly 4- or 5-flowered; glumes somewhat unequal, 5 to 8 mm. long; lemmas firm, faintly nerved, scaberulous, acuminate or short-awned. ♃ (*F. aristulata* Shear.)—Open dry ground, thickets and open woods, up to about 1,500 m., Oregon and California, west of the Sierra Nevada. A smaller form with pubescent lower sheaths, and shorter, mostly glabrous blades, has been segregated as *F. californica* var. *parishii* (Piper) Hitchc.—Oregon and California (San Bernardino Mountains).

26. Festuca dasýclada Hack. ex Beal. (Fig. 68.) Culms 20 to 40 cm. tall; blades folded, about 2 mm. wide when spread, those of the culm 4 to 6 cm. long, those of the innovations 10 to 15 cm. long; panicle open, 7 to 12 cm. long, the branches rather stiffly and divaricately spreading, softly pubescent; angles ciliate; spikelets pale, long-pediceled, 2-flowered; glumes lanceolate, acuminate, the first about 4 mm., the second about 6 mm. long; lemmas rather thin,

FIGURE 67.—*Festuca californica*. Panicle, × ½; floret, × 5. (Elmer 4431, Calif.)

somewhat keeled, rather strongly nerved, scaberulous, about 6 mm. long; awn about 2 mm. long, from between 2 minute teeth. ♃ —Rocky slopes, rare, Utah.

FESTUCA RIGÉSCENS (Presl) Kunth. Densely tufted, about 30 cm. tall; blades firm, involute, sharp-pointed; panicle narrow, few-flowered, 5 to 10 cm. long; spikelets about 3-flowered, 6 to 7 mm. long; lemmas ovate, thick, convex, awnless or mucronate, 4 to 4.5 mm. long. ♃ —There is a single specimen of this species in the United States National Herbarium, labeled "Arizona, Tracy?" On the sheet is a note made by Professor Piper (Feb. 12, 1904) quoting Tracy, "In open pine woods 4 miles southeast of Flagstaff, about June 20, 1887." This agrees exactly with specimens of this species from Peru, whence originally described. Since the species is not known north of Peru, except from this specimen, it seems probable that the label has been misplaced.

FIGURE 68.—*Festuca dasyclada*. Panicle, × ½; glumes and floret, × 5. (Dupl. type.)

27. Festuca virídula Vasey. GREENLEAF FESCUE. (Fig. 69.) Culms rather loosely tufted, erect, 50 to 100 cm. tall; blades soft, erect, those of the culm flat or loosely involute, those of the innovations slender, involute; panicle open, 10 to 15 cm. long, the branches mostly in pairs, ascending or spreading, slender, somewhat remote, naked below; spikelets 3- to 6-flowered; glumes lanceolate, somewhat unequal, 5 to 7 mm. long; lemmas membranaceous, acute or cuspidate, glabrous, 6 to 8 mm. long. ♃ —Mountain meadows and open slopes, 1,000 to 2,000 m., British Columbia to Alberta, south to central California and Idaho; Colorado (Willow Pass). An important forage grass in the mountains of the Northwestern States. *Festuca howellii* Hack. ex Beal, differing from *F. viridula* in having more scabrous lemmas and awns 2 mm. long, does not seem sufficiently distinct to be recognized as a species. ♃ —Known from a single collection (Josephine County, Oreg.).

FIGURE 69.—*Festuca viridula*. Panicle, × ½; floret, × 5. (Cusick 2431, Oreg.)

28. Festuca rúbra L. RED FESCUE. (Fig. 70.) Culms usually loosely tufted, bent or decumbent at the reddish or purplish base, occasionally closely tufted, erect to ascending, 40 to 100 cm. tall; lower sheaths brown, thin, and fibrillose; blades smooth, soft, usually folded or involute; panicle 3 to 20 cm. long, usually contracted and narrow, the branches mostly erect or ascending; spikelets 4- to 6-flowered, pale green or glaucous, often purple-tinged; lemmas 5 to 7 mm. long, smooth, or scabrous toward apex, bearing an awn about half as long. ♃ —Meadows, hills, bogs, and marshes, in the cooler parts of the northern hemisphere, extending south in the Coast Ranges to Monterey, in the Sierra Nevada to the San Bernardino Mountains, in the Rocky Mountains to Colorado and New Mexico, San Francisco Mountains of Arizona; in the Allegheny Mountains and in the Atlantic coastal marshes to Georgia; Mexico,

FIGURE 70.—*Festuca rubra*. Plant, × ½; spikelet and floret, × 5. (Hitchcock 4201, Alaska.)

Eurasia, North Africa. Occasionally used in grass mixtures for pastures in the Northern States. FESTUCA RUBRA var. LANUGINÓSA Mert. and Koch. Lemmas pubescent. ♃ —Oregon to Wyoming and northward; Michigan, Vermont to Connecticut; Europe. A proliferous form (*F. rubra* var. *prolifera* Piper, *F. prolifera* Fernald) is found in the White Mountains of New Hampshire, in Maine and northward. FESTUCA RUBRA var. COMMUTÁTA Gaud. (*F. fallax* Thuill.). CHEWINGS FESCUE. A form with more erect culms, producing a firmer sod, commonly cultivated in New Zealand and occasionally in the United States. ♃ —FESTUCA RUBRA var. HETEROPHÝLLA (Lam.) Mut. SHADE FESCUE. Densely tufted; basal blades filiform; culm blade flat. ♃ —Used for lawns in shady places. Europe.

29. Festuca occidentális Hook. WESTERN FESCUE. (Fig. 71.) Culms tufted, erect, slender, 40 to 100 cm. tall; blades mostly basal, slender, involute, sulcate, soft, smooth or nearly so; panicle loose, 7 to 20 cm. long, often drooping above, the branches solitary or in pairs; spikelets loosely 3- to 5-flowered, 6 to 10 mm. long, mostly on slender pedicels; lemmas rather thin, 5 to 6 mm. long, scaberulous toward the apex, attenuate into a slender awn about as long or longer. ♃ —Dry rocky wooded slopes and banks, British Columbia to central California, east to Wyoming, northern Michigan, and western Ontario.

FIGURE 71.—*Festuca occidentalis*. Panicle, × ½; spikelet, × 5. (Piper 4908, Wash.)

FIGURE 72.—*Festuca ovina*. Panicle, × ½; floret, × 5. (Robbins 8692, Colo.)

30. Festuca ovína L. SHEEP FESCUE. (Fig. 72.) Culms densely tufted, usually 20 to 40 cm. tall; blades slender, involute, from very scabrous to glabrous, the innovations numerous in a basal cluster, 5 to 10 cm. long or sometimes longer; panicle narrow, sometimes almost spikelike, 5 to 8 cm. long, sometimes longer; spikelets mostly 4- or 5-flowered; lemmas about 4 to 5 mm. long, short-awned. ♃ (*F. saximontana* Rydb.; *F. calligera* Rydb.; *F. minutiflora* Rydb., a rare form with small florets; *F. ovina* var. *pseudovina* Hack. of Piper's revision of *Festuca.*)—Open woods and stony slopes, North Dakota to Washington and Alaska, south to Arizona and New Mexico; introduced eastward through Michigan, Maine, Illinois, and South Carolina; Eurasia. *Festuca ovina*, *F. ovina* var. *duriuscula*, and *F. capillata* are occasionally cultivated in lawn mixtures.

Festuca ovina var. duriúscula (L.) Koch. Hard fescue. Blades smooth, wider and firmer than in *F. ovina.* ♃ —Maine to Iowa and Virginia; introduced from Europe.

Festuca ovina var. brachyphýlla (Schult.) Piper. Alpine fescue. An alpine and high northern form differing in the lower culms, mostly 5 to 20 cm. tall, and the smooth short rather lax blades. ♃ (*F. brachyphylla* Schult.; *F. ovina* var. *supina* Hack. of Piper's revision of *Festuca.*)—Rocky slopes, at high altitudes, mostly above timber line in the United States, arctic regions south to San Bernardino Mountains, San Francisco Mountains, California, and, in the Rocky Mountains, to northern New Mexico; also in the high mountains of Vermont, New Hampshire, and New York.

Festuca ovina var. glaúca (Lam.) Koch. Blue fescue. Blades elongate, glaucous. ♃ (*F. glauca* Lam.)—Cultivated as a border plant.

31. Festuca capilláta Lam. Hair fescue. (Fig. 73.) Densely tufted, more slender and lower than *F. ovina;* blades capillary, flexuous, usually more than half as long as the culm; spikelets smaller; lemmas about 3 mm. long, awnless. ♃ —Lawns and waste places, Newfoundland and Maine to North Carolina and Illinois; Minnesota; Oregon; introduced from Europe.

Figure 73.—*Festuca capillata.* Plant, × ¼; floret, × 5. (Hitchcock 23624, Newf.)

32. Festuca idahoénsis Elmer. Idaho fescue. (Fig. 74.) Culms usually densely tufted in large bunches, 30 to 100 cm. tall; blades numerous, usually elongate, very scabrous, rarely smooth, filiform, involute; panicle narrow, 10 to 20 cm. long, the branches ascending or appressed, somewhat spreading in anthesis; spikelets mostly 5- to 7-flowered; lemmas nearly terete, about 7 mm. long; awn usually 2 to 4 mm. long. ♃ (*F. ovina* var. *ingrata* Beal.)—Open woods and rocky slopes, British Columbia to Alberta, south to central California and Colorado.

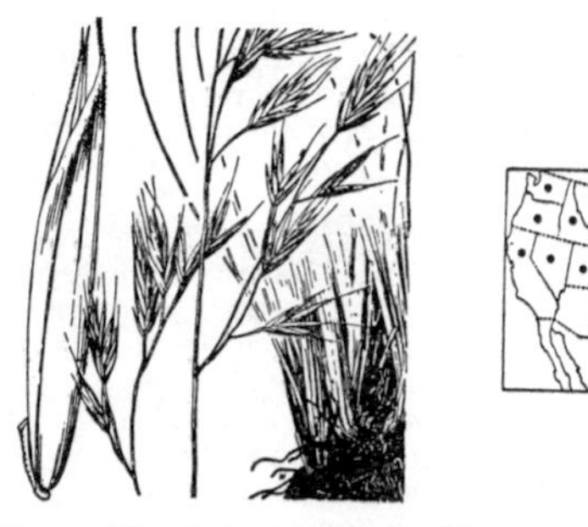

Figure 74.—*Festuca idahoensis.* Plant, × ½; floret, × 5. (Heller 3318, Idaho.)

33. Festuca arizónica Vasey. Arizona fescue. (Fig. 75.) Resembling *F. idahoensis;* differing in the stiffer glaucous foliage, somewhat smaller awnless or nearly awnless lemmas. ♃ —Open pine woods, Nevada and Colorado to Texas and Arizona. Often called pinegrass.

Figure 75.—*Festuca arizonica.* Panicle, × ½; floret, × 5. (Leiberg 5685, Ariz.)

FESTUCA AMETHÝSTINA L. Slender tufted perennial; blades filiform, 15 to 25 cm. long; panicle 5 to 10 cm. long, rather narrow; spikelets about as in *F. ovina*, often purplish. ♃ —Sometimes cultivated for ornament. Europe.

FESTUCA GENICULÁTA (L.) Cav. Annual; culms slender, geniculate below, 20 to 50 cm. tall; panicle 3 to 6 cm. long, rather compact; spikelets awned. ⊙ —Sometimes cultivated for ornament. Portugal.

FESTUCA VALESIACA Schleich. ex Gaud. Slender densely tufted perennial, 15 to 30 cm. tall; blades very slender, sulcate, scabrous, those of the innovations numerous, 10 to 18 cm. long; panicle 4 to 8 cm. long, narrow, the short branches ascending; spikelets similar to those of *F. ovina*, to which this species is closely related. ♃ —Sometimes cultivated in grass gardens. Europe.

5. SCLERÓPOA Griseb.

Spikelets several-flowered, linear, somewhat compressed, the thick rachilla disarticulating above the glumes and between the florets, remaining as a minute stipe to the floret above; glumes unequal, short, acutish, strongly nerved, the first 1-nerved, the second 3-nerved; lemmas nearly terete, obscurely 5-nerved, obtuse, slightly scarious at the tip. Annuals with slightly branched 1-sided panicles. Type species, *Scleropoa rigida*. Name from Greek *skleros*, hard, and *poa*, grass, alluding to the stiff panicle.

1. Scleropoa rígida (L.) Griseb. (Fig. 76.) Culms erect or spreading, 10 to 20 cm. tall; blades flat, 1 to 2 mm. wide; panicles narrow, stiff, condensed, 5 to 10 cm. long, the branches short, floriferous to base, these and the thick pedicels somewhat divaricately spreading in anthesis; spikelets 4- to 10-flowered, 5 to 8 mm. long; glumes about 2 mm. long; lemmas about 2.5 mm. long. ⊙ —Waste places and fields, sparingly introduced from Europe, Massachusetts; Florida to Mississippi; Texas; South Dakota; Washington to California.

FIGURE 76.—*Scleropoa rigida*. Plant, × 1; two views of floret, × 10. (Cocks, Miss.)

6. PUCCINÉLLIA Parl. ALKALI-GRASS

Spikelets several-flowered, usually terete or subterete, the rachilla disarticulating above the glumes and between the florets; glumes unequal, shorter than the first lemma, obtuse or acute, rather firm, often scarious at tip, the first 1-nerved or sometimes 3-nerved, the second 3-nerved; lemmas usually firm, rounded on the back, obtuse or acute, rarely acuminate, usually scarious and often erose at the tip, glabrous or puberulent toward base, rarely pubescent on the nerves, 5-nerved, the nerves parallel, indistinct, rarely rather prominent; palea about as long as the lemma or somewhat shorter. Low pale smooth tufted annuals or perennials with narrow to open panicles. Type species, *Puccinellia distans*. Named for Prof. Benedetto Puccinelli.

The species of the interior are grazed by stock. One, *P. airoides*, furnishes considerable forage in the regions where it is common. A form of this, called Zawadke alkali-grass, is cultivated in Montana.

Lemmas obtuse, pubescent on the nerves for half or three-fourths their length. Dwarf annual .... 1. P. PARISHII.
Lemmas glabrous or, if pubescent, the hairs not confined to the nerves.
  Panicles narrow, strict, the branches appressed, mostly with one spikelet; annual, mostly less than 20 cm. tall; lemmas acute, more or less pubescent .... 2. P. SIMPLEX.
  Panicles narrow or open, not strict; annual or perennial; lemmas glabrous or pubescent only at base.
    Panicles ellipsoid, rather compact, less than 10 cm. long, the branches floriferous nearly to base. Lemmas rather coriaceous; culms rather stout.
      Spikelets 5 to 8 mm. long; lemmas 3 to 3.5 mm. long .... 3. P. RUPESTRIS.
      Spikelets 3 to 4 mm. long; lemmas 2 to 2.5 mm. long .... 4. P. FASCICULATA.
    Panicles pyramidal or elongate, some of the branches naked below, or reduced, narrow, and few-flowered.
      Leaves mostly in a short basal tuft, the blades involute, 5 to 10 cm. long. Panicle 5 to 10 cm. long, open and spreading; lemmas 3.5 mm. long, glabrous, acute. 5. P. LEMMONI.
      Leaves distributed, not in a basal tuft.
        Anthers about 2 mm. long; lemmas 4 to 5 mm. long, pubescent at base. 6. P. MARITIMA.
        Anthers 1 mm. long or less.
          Lemmas about 2 mm. long (2 to 3 mm. in *P. airoides*); panicle open; the slender branches spreading or reflexed.
            Lemmas broad, obtuse or truncate, not narrowed above; lower panicle branches usually reflexed .... 7. P. DISTANS.
            Lemmas narrow, narrowed into an obtuse apex; panicle branches spreading, usually not reflexed .... 8. P. AIROIDES.
          Lemmas 3 to 4 mm. long; panicle narrow, the branches ascending or finally spreading.
            Plants lax, usually 10 to 30 cm. tall; panicle 5 to 10 cm. long, the branches finally spreading, glabrous .... 9. P. PUMILA.
            Plants usually 50 to 90 cm. tall; panicle 10 to 20 cm. long, the branches ascending or appressed, scabrous .... 10. P. GRANDIS.

1. Puccinellia paríshii Hitchc. (Fig. 77.) Annual; culms 3 to 10 cm. tall; blades flat to subinvolute, less than 1 mm. wide; panicle narrow, few-flowered, 1 to 4 cm. long; spikelets 3- to 6-flowered, 3 to 5 mm. long; lemmas about 2 mm. long, obtuse to truncate, scarious and somewhat erose at the tip, pubescent on the mid and lateral nerves nearly to the apex, and on the intermediate nerves about half way. ⊙ —Marshes, California

FIGURE 77.—*Puccinellia parishii.* Panicle, × 1; floret, × 10. (Type.)

(Rabbit Springs, San Bernardino County) and Arizona (Tuba City).

2. Puccinellia símplex Scribn. (Fig. 78.) Annual; culms 7 to 20 cm. tall; blades narrow, soft, flat; panicle narrow, about half the length of the entire plant, the branches few, short, appressed, mostly with 1 spikelet; spikelets 6 to 8 mm. long, appressed; glumes strongly 3-nerved, 1 and 2 mm. long; lemmas 2.5 mm. long, tapering from below the middle to the acute apex, more or less pubescent over the back. ⊙ —Alkaline soil, California; common in alkaline areas of the San Joaquin Valley.

FIGURE 78.—*Puccinellia simplex*. Plant, × 1; floret × 10. (Type.)

3. Puccinellia rupéstris (With.) Fern. and Weath. (Fig. 79.) Annual; culms rather stout, mostly 10 to 20 cm. tall; blades flat, 2 to 6 mm. wide; panicle ellipsoid, glaucous, rather dense, mostly 3 to 6 cm. long, the branches mostly not more than 1.5 cm. long, stiffly ascending, floriferous nearly to base; spikelets 3- to 5-flowered, 5 to 8 mm. long, sessile or nearly so; glumes 3- to 5-nerved, 1.5 and 2.5 mm. long; lemmas 3 to 3.5 mm. long, firm, obscurely nerved, glabrous, obtuse, the apex entire or nearly so. ⊙ —Ballast near New York and Philadelphia. Europe.

FIGURE 79.—*Puccinellia rupestris*. Panicle, × 1; floret, × 10. (Martindale, N. J.)

FIGURE 80.—*Puccinellia fasciculata*. Panicle, × 1; floret, × 10. (Stebbins, Maine.)

4. Puccinellia fasciculáta (Torr.) Bicknell. (Fig. 80.) Apparently perennial; culms rather stout, 20 to 50 cm. tall, sometimes taller; blades flat, folded, or subinvolute, 2 to 4 mm. wide; panicle ellipsoid, 5 to 15 cm. long, the branches fascicled, rather stiffly ascending, some naked at base but with short basal branchlets, all rather densely flowered; spikelets 2- to 5-flowered, 3 to 4 mm. long; glumes ovate, 1 and 1.5 mm. long; lemmas 2 to 2.5 mm. long, firm, obtuse. ♃ (*P. borreri* Hitchc.)—Salt marshes along the coast, Nova Scotia to Virginia; Utah, Nevada and Arizona; Europe.

5. Puccinellia lemmóni (Vasey) Scribn. (Fig. 81.) Perennial; culms erect, slender, 15 to 30 cm. tall; leaves mostly in an erect basal tuft, the slender blades involute, 5 to 10 cm. long; panicle pyramidal, open, 5 to 10 cm. long, the slender flexuous branches fascicled, the lower spreading, the longer ones naked on the lower half; spikelets narrow, 3- to 5-flowered, the rachilla often exposed; glumes about 1 and 2 mm. long; lemmas narrow, acute, glabrous, about 3.5 mm. long; anthers 1.5 mm. long. ♃ —Moist alkaline soil, southern Idaho and Washington to Nevada and California.

FIGURE 82.—*Puccinellia maritima*. Plant, × 1; floret, × 10. (Fernald and Long 20051, Nova Scotia.)

FIGURE 81.—*Puccinellia lemmoni*. Panicle, × 1; floret, × 10. (Jones 4115, Nev.)

6. Puccinellia marítima (Huds.) Parl. (Fig. 82.) Perennial; culms erect, rather coarse, 20 to 40 cm. tall, sometimes taller; blades 1 to 2 mm. wide, usually becoming involute; panicle mostly 10 to 20 cm. long, the branches ascending or appressed, or spreading in anthesis; spikelets 4- to 10-flowered; glumes 3-nerved, 2 to 3 and 3 to 4 mm. long; lemmas 4 to 5 mm. long, pubescent on the base of the lateral nerves and sometimes sparingly between the nerves; anthers 1.5 to 2 mm. long. ♃ —Salt marshes and brackish shores, Nova Scotia to Rhode Island; Washington; on ballast, Philadelphia and Camden; Europe.

7. Puccinellia dístans (L.) Parl. (Fig. 83.) Perennial; culms erect or decumbent at base, 20 to 40 cm. tall, sometimes taller; blades flat or more or less involute, mostly 2 to 4 mm. wide; panicle pyramidal, loose, 5 to 15 cm. long, the branches fascicled, rather distant, the lower spreading or finally reflexed, the longer ones naked half their length or more; spikelets 4- to 6-flowered, 4 to 5 mm. long; glumes 1 and 2 mm. long; lemmas rather thin, obtuse or truncate, 1.5 or usually about 2 mm. long, with a few short

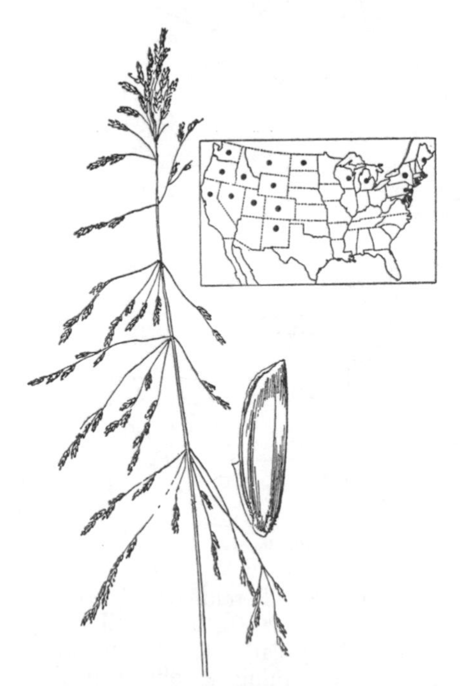

FIGURE 83.—*Puccinellia distans.* Panicle, × ½; floret, × 10. (Schuette, Wis.)

hairs at base; anthers about 0.8 mm. long. ♃ —Moist, more or less alkaline soil, Quebec to British Columbia, south to Maryland, Michigan, Wisconsin, and North Dakota; Washington, south to New Mexico and California; introduced from Eurasia. The more slender specimens are

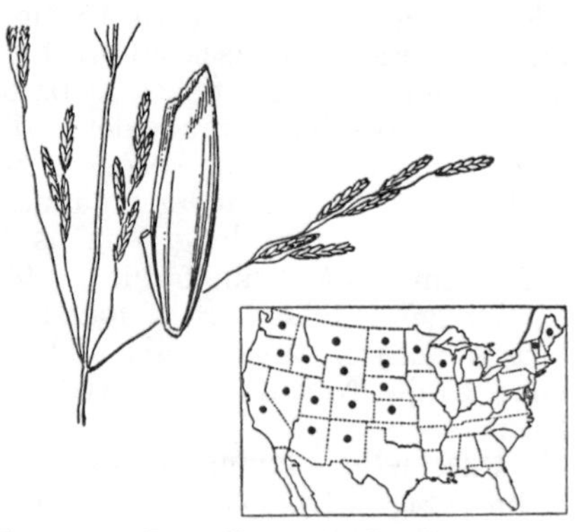

FIGURE 84.—*Puccinellia airoides.* Panicle, × 1; floret, × 10. (Rydberg 2135, Mont.)

the form described as *P. distans* var. *tenuis* (Uechtritz) Fern. and Weath.

8. Puccinellia airoídes (Nutt.) Wats. and Coult. NUTTALL ALKALI-GRASS. (Fig. 84.) Perennial; culms usually erect, slender, rather stiff and firm at base, mostly 30 to 60 cm. rarely to 1 m. tall; blades 1 to 3 mm. wide, flat, or becoming involute; panicle pyramidal, open, mostly 10 to 20 cm. long, the distant scabrous branches fascicled, spreading, naked below, as much as 10 cm. long; spikelets 3- to 6-flowered, 4 to 7 mm. long, the florets rather distant, the rachilla often exposed; pedicels scabrous; glumes 1.5 to 2 mm. long; lemmas 2 to 3 mm. long, rather narrow, somewhat narrowed into an obtuse apex; anthers about 0.7 mm. long. ♃ (*P. nuttalliana* Hitchc.) —Moist, usually alkaline soil, Wisconsin to British Columbia, south to Kansas, New Mexico, and California; introduced in Maine and Vermont. The form with lemmas 2.5 to 3 mm. long has been called *P. cusickii* Weatherby. Alberta to Wyoming and Oregon.

9. Puccinellia púmila (Vasey) Hitchc. (Fig. 85.) Perennial; culms lax, erect or ascending from a de-

FIGURE 85.—*Puccinellia pumila*. Plant, × 1; floret, × 10. (Type.)

cumbent base, 10 to 30 cm. tall; blades rather soft, mostly flat, 1 to 2 mm. wide; panicle pyramidal, open, mostly 5 to 10 cm. long, the lower branches naked below, usually finally spreading or even reflexed; spikelets 4- to 6-flowered; glumes 1.5 and 2.5 mm. long; lemmas 3 to 4 mm. long, rather broad, narrowed toward the obtuse nearly entire apex, obscurely pubescent near base or glabrous; anthers 0.8 to 1 mm. long. ♃ —Salt marshes and shores, Labrador to Connecticut; Alaska to Oregon.

10. Puccinellia grándis Swallen. (Fig. 86.) Culms densely tufted, 50 to 90 cm. tall; sheaths glabrous; ligule 2 to 3 mm. long; blades firm, drying involute, 2 to 3.5 mm. wide, panicles 10 to 20 cm. long, pyramidal, the scabrous branches finally spreading; spikelets 8 to 15 mm. long, 5- to 12-flowered, appressed; lemmas 3 to 4 mm. long, obtuse or subacute, sparsely pilose at the base; anthers 1.3 to 1.5 mm. long. ♃ —Sea beaches, Alaska to central California. This species has been referred to *P. nutkaensis* (Presl) Fern. and Weath., a northern species, not known from the United States.

FIGURE 86.—*Puccinellia grandis*. Panicle, × 1; floret, × 10. (Macoun 66, Br. Col.)

7. GLYCÉRIA R. Br. MANNAGRASS

(*Panicularia* Heist.)

Spikelets few- to many-flowered, subterete or slightly compressed, the rachilla disarticulating above the glumes and between the florets; glumes unequal, short, obtuse or acute, usually scarious, mostly 1-nerved (the second 3-nerved in a few species); lemmas broad, convex on the back, firm, usually obtuse, scarious at the apex, 5- to 9-nerved, the nerves parallel, usually prominent. Usually tall aquatic or marsh perennials, with creeping and rooting bases or with creeping rhizomes, simple culms, mostly closed or partly closed sheaths, flat blades, and open or contracted panicles. Type species, *Glyceria fluitans*. Name from the Greek *glukeros*, sweet, the seed of the type species being sweet.

The species are all palatable grasses but are usually of limited distribution, and most of them are confined to marshes or wet land. *Glyceria elata*, tall mannagrass, is a valuable component of the forage in moist woods of the Northwestern States. *G. striata*, fowl mannagrass, widely distributed, *G. grandis*, American mannagrass, in the Northern States, and *G. pauciflora* of the Northwest are marsh species, but are often grazed.

Spikelets linear, nearly terete, usually 1 cm. long or more, appressed on short pedicels; panicles narrow, erect .... SECTION 1. EUGLYCERIA.
Spikelets ovate or oblong, more or less compressed, usually not more than 5 mm. long; panicles usually nodding .... SECTION 2. HYDROPOA.

Section 1. Euglyceria

Lemmas acute, much exceeded by the palea .... 1. G. ACUTIFLORA.
Lemmas obtuse; palea about as long as the lemma (or slightly longer in *G. septentrionalis* and *G. fluitans*).
  Lemmas glabrous between the slightly scabrous nerves .... 2. G. BOREALIS.
  Lemmas scaberulous or hirtellous between the usually distinctly scabrous nerves.
    Lemmas about 3 mm. long, broadly rounded at the summit.
      First glume 1.5 mm. long; lemmas scaberulous .... 3. G. LEPTOSTACHYA.
      First glume 2 to 2.5 mm. long; lemmas hirtellous .... 4. G. ARKANSANA.
    Lemmas 4 to 7 mm. long.
      Culms more than 60 cm., commonly more than 1 m. tall, flaccid; sheaths closed from below the summit, blades elongate, mostly more than 5 mm. wide.
        Lemmas pale or green, not tinged with purple, about 4 mm. long; palea usually exceeding the lemma; Eastern States .... 5. G. SEPTENTRIONALIS.
        Lemmas slightly tinged with purple near the tip, 5 to 6 mm. long; palea about as long as the lemma, sometimes slightly exceeding it; Northeastern States. 6. G. FLUITANS.
        Lemmas usually tinged with purple near the tip, 4 to 6 mm. long; palea rarely exceeding the lemma; Western States .... 7. G. OCCIDENTALIS.
      Culms 15 to 30 cm. tall, slender but rather firm; sheaths open, the margins overlapping; blades with boat-shaped tip, 3 to 5 cm. long, 2 to 3 mm. wide. 8. G. DECLINATA.

Section 2. Hydropoa

Lemmas with 7 usually prominent nerves; second glume 1-nerved; sheaths, at least the upper, closed from below the summit.
  Panicle contracted, narrow.
    Lemmas 3 to 4 mm. long; panicle oblong, dense, usually not more than 10 cm. long. 11. G. OBTUSA.
    Lemmas 2 to 2.5 mm. long; panicle rather loose, nodding, 15 to 25 cm. long. 12. G. MELICARIA.
  Panicle open, lax.
    Nerves of lemma evident but not prominent .... 13. G. CANADENSIS.
    Nerves of lemma prominent.
      First glume not more than 1 mm. long.
        Blades 2 to 4 mm. wide, sometimes to 8 mm., rather firm, often folded; first glume 0.5 mm. long .... 14. G. STRIATA.
        Blades 6 to 12 mm. wide, flat, thin, lax; first glume about 1 mm. long. 15. G. ELATA.
      First glume more than 1 mm. long, usually about 1.5 mm. long.
        Glumes subequal, blunt, pale, in striking contrast to the purple florets. 9. G. GRANDIS.

Glumes narrow, acute, the second longer than the first; florets olive green. 10. G. NUBIGENA.
Lemmas with 5 prominent nerves; second glume 3-nerved; sheaths open.
Panicle narrow, the branches ascending........ 16. G. ERECTA.
Panicle open, lax.
Culms relatively thick, commonly 1 m. tall; blades mostly 8 to 12 mm. wide.
Panicle branches numerous, many-flowered........ 17. G. PAUCIFLORA.
Panicle branches few, distant, few-flowered........ 18. G. OTISII.
Culms slender, decumbent, weak.
Blades 4 to 8 mm. wide; anthers 1 mm. long........ 19. G. PALLIDA.
Blades 1 to 3 mm. wide; anthers 0.2 to 0.5 mm. long........ 20. G. FERNALDII.

SECTION 1. EUGLYCÉRIA Griseb.

Spikelets linear, nearly terete, usually more than 1 cm. long, appressed on short pedicels; panicles narrow, erect, the branches appressed or ascending after anthesis. The species of Euglyceria, with the exception of *Glyceria acutiflora*, are very closely allied and appear to intergrade.

1. Glyceria acutiflóra Torr. (Fig. 87.) Culms compressed, lax, creeping and rooting below, 50 to 100 cm. long; blades flat, lax, 10 to 15 cm. long, 3 to 6 mm. wide, scabrous on the upper surface; panicle 15 to 35 cm. long, often partly included, the branches rather stiff, bearing 1 or 2 spikelets, or the lower 3 or more; spikelets 5- to 12-flowered, 2 to 4 cm. long, 1 to 2 mm. wide, the lateral pedicels 1 to 3 mm. long; glumes about 2 and 5 mm. long; lemmas 7-nerved, acute, scabrous, 6 to 8 mm. long, exceeded by the acuminate, 2-toothed paleas. ♃ —Wet soil and shallow water, New Hampshire to Virginia and West Virginia, west to Michigan, Missouri, and Tennessee; also northeastern Asia.

FIGURE 87.—*Glyceria acutiflora*. Panicle, × 1; floret, × 10. (Knowlton 866, Mass.)

2. Glyceria boreális (Nash) Batchelder. NORTHERN MANNAGRASS. (Fig. 88.) Culms erect or decumbent at base, slender, 60 to 100 cm. tall, blades flat or folded, usually 2 to 4 mm. wide, sometimes wider; panicle mostly 20 to 40 cm. long, the branches as much as 10 cm. long, bearing several appressed spikelets; spikelets mostly 6- to 12-flowered, 1 to 1.5 cm. long; glumes about 1.5 and 3 mm. long; lemmas rather thin, obtuse, 3 to 4 mm. long, strongly 7-nerved, scarious at the tip, glabrous between the hispidulous nerves. ♃ —Wet places and shallow water, Newfoundland to southeastern Alaska, Pennsylvania to Illinois, Minnesota, and Washington, and in the mountains to New Mexico, Arizona, and central California.

3. Glyceria leptostáchya Buckl. (Fig. 89.) Culms 1 to 1.5 m. tall, rather stout or succulent; sheaths slightly rough; blades flat, scaberulous

FIGURE 88.—*Glyceria borealis.* Panicle, × 1; floret, × 10. (Fernald 193, Maine.)

FIGURE 89.—*Glyceria leptostachya.* Panicle, × 1; floret, × 10. (Heller 5606, Calif.)

on the upper surface, 4 to 7 mm. rarely to 1 cm. wide; panicle 20 to 40 cm. long, the branches ascending, mostly in twos or threes, several-flowered, often bearing secondary branchlets; spikelets 1 to 2 cm. long, 8- to 14-flowered, often purplish; glumes 1.5 and 3 mm. long; lemmas firm, broadly rounded toward apex, about 3 mm. long, 7-nerved, scaberulous on the nerves and between them. ♃ (*Panicularia davyi* Merr.)—Shallow water, up to 1,200 m., rare, Washington to central California.

4. Glyceria arkansána Fernald. (Fig. 90.) Resembling *G. septentrionalis;* first glume 2 to 2.5 mm. long; lemmas 3 to 3.5 mm. long, hirtellous rather than scaberulous. ♃ —Wet ground, Louisiana and Arkansas.[9]

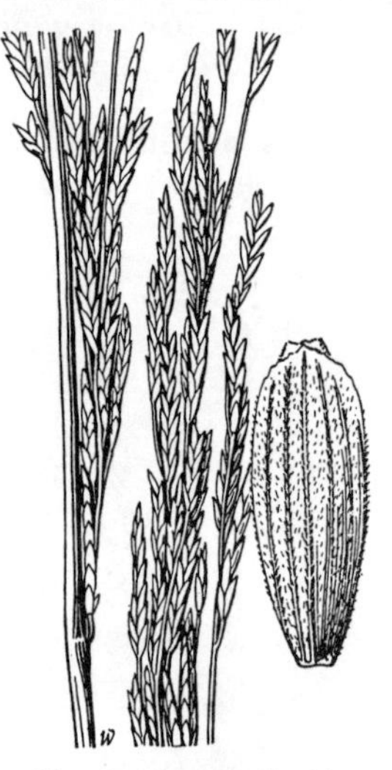

FIGURE 90.—*Glyceria arkansana.* Panicle, × 1; floret, × 10. (Ball 362, La.)

5. Glyceria septentrionális Hitchc. EASTERN MANNAGRASS. (Fig. 91.) Culms 1 to 1.5 m. tall, somewhat succulent; sheaths smooth; blades flat, mostly 10 to 20 cm. long, 4 to 8 mm. wide, usually smooth beneath, slightly scaberulous on the upper surface and margin; panicle 20 to 40 cm. long, somewhat open, the branches as much as 10 cm. long, several-flowered, often spreading at anthesis; spikelets 1 to 2 cm. long, 6- to 12-

[9] A specimen labeled "Western part of New-York," 1840, may have a misplaced label.

flowered, the florets rather loosely imbricate; glumes 2 to 3 and 3 to 4 mm. long; lemmas green or pale, about 4 mm. long, narrowed only slightly at the summit, scaberulous, the paleas usually exceeding them. ♃ —Shallow water and wet places, Quebec to Minnesota, south to Georgia and eastern Texas.

FIGURE 91.—*Glyceria septentrionalis*. Panicle, × 1; floret, × 10. (Deam 3184, Ind.)

6. Glyceria flúitans (L.) R. Br. MANNAGRASS. (Fig. 92.) Resembling *G. septentrionalis* in habit; first glume usually only one-third as long as the first lemma; lemmas scaberulous, the nerves distinct but not raised prominently above the tissue of the internerves; tip of palea usually exceeding its lemma. ♃ (*Panicularia brachyphylla* Nash.)—Shallow water, Newfoundland to Quebec and New York; South Dakota; Eurasia.

7. Glyceria occidentális (Piper) J. C. Nels. (Fig. 93.) Culms flaccid, 60 to 100 cm. tall; blades 3 to 12 mm. wide, smooth beneath, somewhat scabrous on the upper surface; panicle loose, spreading at anthesis, 30 to 50 cm. long; spikelets, 1.5 to 2 cm. long; first glume mostly about 2 mm. long; lemmas usually tinged with purple near the tip, 4 to 6 mm. long, rather strongly scabrous, 7- to 9-nerved, the nerves prominent, raised above the tissue of the internerves; palea about as long as its lemma, sometimes slightly exceeding it. ♃ —Marshes, shallow water, and wet places, Idaho to British Columbia,

FIGURE 92.—*Glyceria fluitans*. Panicle, × 1; floret, × 10. (McIntosh 1076, S. Dak.)

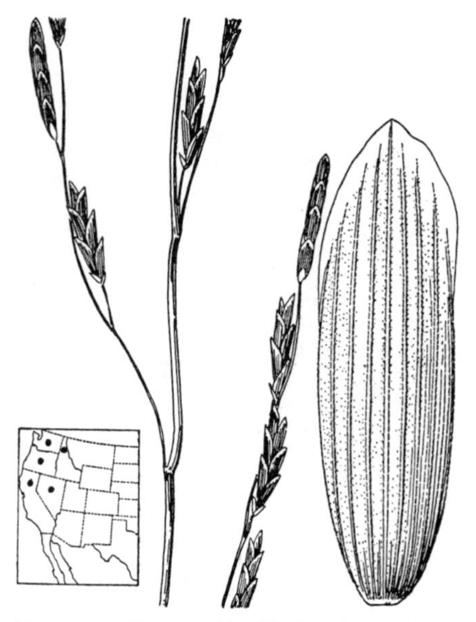

FIGURE 93.—*Glyceria occidentalis*. Panicle, × 1; floret, × 10. (Type.)

northern California and Nevada. The seeds are used for food by the Indians.

8. **Glyceria declináta** Brébiss. (Fig. 94.) Culms 15 to 70 cm. tall, erect from a decumbent branching base; sheaths open, keeled, scaberulous, the margins thin and hyaline; ligule 5 to 7 mm. long; blades 3 to 12 cm. long, 2 to 6 mm. wide, the tip boat-shaped; panicle simple, 6 to 25 cm. long; spikelets 15 to 20 mm. long, appressed; glumes obtuse, the first 1.8 to 2.2 mm. long, the second 3 to 3.5 mm. long; lemma 4 to 5 mm. long, scabrous, 7-nerved, obtuse, irregularly dentate; palea about as long as the lemma, the keels narrowly winged. ♃ —Moist canyons and meadows, Nevada and California; New York (Long Island); Europe, whence probably introduced.

SECTION 2. HYDROPÓA Dum.

Spikelets more or less laterally compressed, ovate to oblong, usually not more than 5 mm. long; panicles open or condensed, but not long and narrow (except in *G. melicaria*).

9. **Glyceria grándis** S. Wats. AMERICAN MANNAGRASS. (Fig. 95.) Culms tufted, stout, 1 to 1.5 m. tall; blades flat, 6 to 12 mm. wide; panicle large, very compound, 20 to 40 cm. long, open, nodding at summit; spikelets 4- to 7-flowered, 5 to 6 mm. long, glumes whitish, about 1.5 and 2 mm. long; lemmas purplish, about 2.5 mm. long; palea rather thin, about as long as the lemma. ♃ (*Panicularia americana* MacM.)—Banks of streams, marshes, and wet places, Prince Edward Island to Alaska, south to Virginia, Tennessee, Iowa, Nebraska, New Mexico, Arizona, and eastern Oregon.

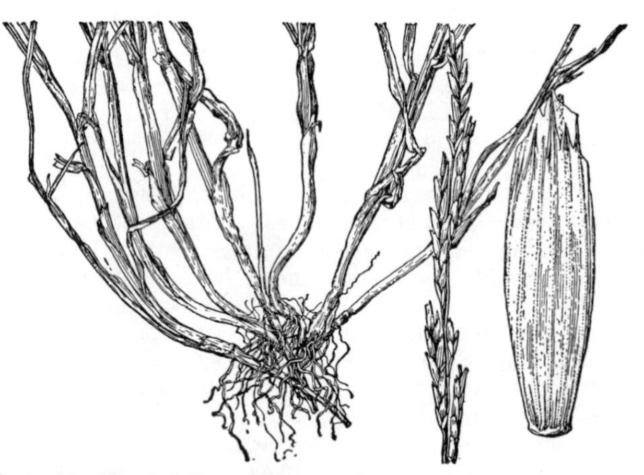

FIGURE 94.—*Glyceria declinata*. Plant, × 1; floret, × 10. (Cooke 15312, Calif.)

FIGURE 95.—*Glyceria grandis*. Panicle, × 1; floret, × 10. (Pearce, N. Y.)

10. Glyceria nubígena W. A. Anderson. (Fig. 96.) Culms 1 to 2 m. tall, slender to rather stout, smooth, shining; sheaths glabrous or scaberulous, the lower much longer than the internodes; ligule truncate, 1 mm. long; blades as much as 45 cm. long, 6 to 10 mm. wide, smooth below, scabrous above; panicles 20 to 30 cm. long, the branches stiffly spreading or reflexed; spikelets 3- to 4-flowered, the florets early deciduous; lemmas about 2.5 mm. long, obtuse or subacute. ♃ —Moist ground, balds and high ridges, Great Smoky Mountains, Tennessee and North Carolina.

11. Glyceria obtúsa (Muhl.) Trin. (Fig. 97.) Culms erect, often decumbent at base, 50 to 100 cm. tall, rather firm; blades elongate, erect, mostly smooth, flat or folded, 2 to 6 mm. wide; panicle erect, oblong or narrowly elliptic, dense, 5 to 15 cm. long, the branches ascending or appressed; spikelets mostly 4- to 7-flowered, 4 to 6 mm. long, green or tawny, the rachilla joints very short; glumes broad, scarious, 1.5 and 2 mm. long; lemmas

FIGURE 96.—*Glyceria nubigena*. Panicle, × 1; floret, × 10. (Barksdale and Jennison 1970, Tenn.)

firm, faintly nerved, smooth, 3 to 4 mm. long, obtuse, the scarious tip narrow, often revolute. ♃ —Bogs and marshy places, Nova Scotia to North Carolina, mostly near the coast.

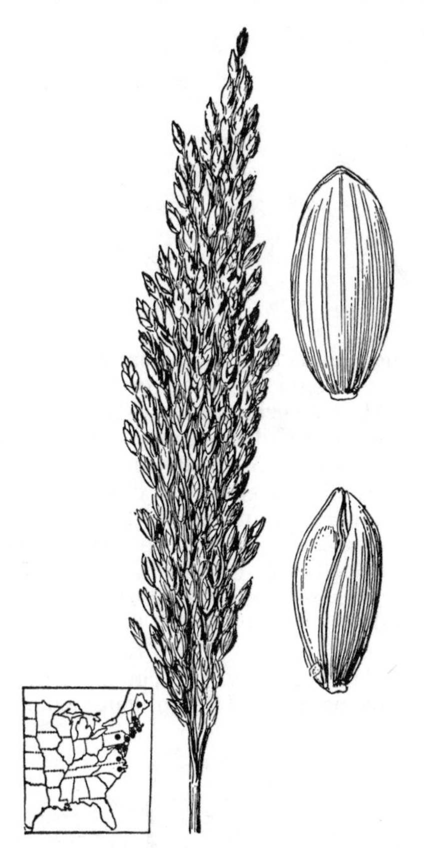

FIGURE 97.—*Glyceria obtusa.* Panicle, × 1; 2 views of floret, × 10. (Miller, N. Y.)

12. Glyceria melicária (Michx.) Hubb. (Fig. 98.) Culms slender, solitary or few, 60 to 100 cm. tall; blades elongate, scaberulous, 2 to 5 mm. wide; panicle narrow but rather loose, nodding, 15 to 25 cm. long, the branches erect, rather distant; spikelets 3- or 4-flowered, about 4 mm. long, green; glumes about 1.5 and 2 mm. long, acutish; lemmas firm, 2 to 2.5 mm. long, acutish, smooth, the nerves rather faint. ♃ (*G. torreyana* Hitchc.; *Panicularia torreyana* Merr.)—Swamps and wet woods, New Brunswick to Ohio, south to the mountains of North Carolina.

13. Glyceria canadénsis (Michx.) Trin. RATTLESNAKE MANNAGRASS. (Fig. 99.) Culms erect, solitary or few in a tuft, 60 to 150 cm. tall; blades scabrous, 3 to 7 mm. wide; panicle open, 15 to 20 cm. long, nearly as wide, the branches rather distant, drooping, naked below; spikelets ovate or oblong, 5- to 10-flowered, 5 to 6 mm. long, the florets crowded, spreading; glumes about 2 and 3 mm. long; lemmas 3 to 4 mm. long, the 7 nerves obscured in the firm tissue of the lemma; palea bowed out on the keels, the floret somewhat tumid. ♃ —Bogs and wet places, Newfoundland to Minnesota, south to Virginia and Illinois.

GLYCERIA CANADENSIS var. LÁXA (Scribn.) Hitchc. On the average taller, with looser panicles of somewhat smaller 3- to 5-flowered spikelets. ♃ (*Panicularia laxa* Scribn.) —Wet places, Nova Scotia to New York, Michigan, Wisconsin, Maryland, West Virginia, North Carolina, and Tennessee.

FIGURE 98.—*Glyceria melicaria.* Panicle, × 1; 2 views of floret, × 10. (Harvey 1322, Maine.)

FIGURE 99.—*Glyceria canadensis*. Panicle, × 1; floret, × 10. (Kneucker, Gram. 464, Conn.)

14. Glyceria striáta (Lam.) Hitchc. FOWL MANNAGRASS. (Fig. 100.) Plants in large tussocks, pale green; culms erect, slender, rather firm, 30 to 100 cm. tall, sometimes taller; blades erect or ascending, flat or folded, moderately firm, usually 2 to 6 mm. wide, sometimes to 9 mm.; panicle ovoid, open, 10 to 20 cm. long, nodding, the branches ascending at base, drooping, naked below; spikelets ovate or oblong, 3- to 7-flowered, 3 to 4 mm. long, often purplish, somewhat crowded toward the ends of the branchlets; glumes about 0.5 and 1 mm. long, ovate, obtuse; lemmas oblong, prominently 7-nerved, about 2 mm. long, the scarious tip inconspicuous; palea rather firm, about as long as the lemma, the smooth keels prominent, bowed out. ♃ (*G. nervata* Trin.)—Moist meadows and wet places, Newfoundland to British Columbia, south to northern Florida, Texas, Arizona, and northern California; Mexico. A low strict northern form has been called *G. striata* var. *stricta* Fernald (*G. nervata* var. *stricta* Scribn.)

15. Glyceria eláta (Nash) Hitchc. TALL MANNAGRASS. (Fig. 101.) Resembling *G. striata;* plants dark green; culms 1 to 2 m. tall, rather succulent; blades flat, thin, lax, 6 to 12 mm. wide; panicle oblong, 15 to 30 cm. long, the branches spreading, the lower often reflexed; spikelets 6- to 8-flowered, 4 to 6 mm. long; glumes and lemmas a little longer than in *G. striata.* ♃ (*Panicularia nervata elata* Piper.)—Wet meadows, springs, and shady moist woods, Montana to British Columbia, south in the mountains to New Mexico and California.

16. Glyceria erécta Hitchc. (Fig. 102.) Culms 10 to 40 cm. tall, sometimes in dense tufts, from slender fragile rhizomes; blades flat, mostly 5 to 12 cm. long, 4 to 9 mm. wide, often equaling the panicle or exceeding it; panicle 3 to 8 cm. long, with ascending or appressed few-flowered

FIGURE 100.—*Glyceria striata*. Plant, × ½; spikelet, × 5; floret, × 10. (V. H. Chase 60, Ill.)

FIGURE 101.—*Glyceria elata*. Plant, × 1; floret, × 10. (Hitchcock 2731, Calif.)

FIGURE 102.—*Glyceria erecta*. Panicle, × 1; floret, × 10. (Hitchcock 3059, Oreg.)

branches; spikelets 3 to 4.5 mm. long; second glume 3-nerved; lemmas 2.5 to 3 mm. long, scaberulous, the tip somewhat erose. ♃ —Springy or boggy places, mostly near or above timber line, Crater Lake, Oreg., to Mount Whitney, Calif., and Glenbrook, Nev.

17. Glyceria pauciflóra Presl. (Fig. 103.) Culms 50 to 120 cm. tall; sheaths open, smooth or scaberulous, sometimes inflated in floating plants; blades thin, flat, lax, scaberulous, mostly 10 to 15 cm. long, 5 to 15 mm. wide; panicle open or rather dense, nodding, 10 to 20 cm. long, the branches ascending or spreading, rather flexuous, the spikelets crowded on the upper half, the lowermost usually 2 to 4; spikelets mostly 5- or 6-flowered, 4 to 5 mm. long, often purplish; glumes broadly ovate or oval, about 1 and 1.5 mm. long, the margins erose-scarious, the second 3-nerved; lemmas oblong, 2 to 2.5 mm. long, with 5 prominent nerves and an outer short faint pair near the margins, scaberulous on the nerves and somewhat so between them, the tip rounded, scarious, somewhat erose. ♃ —Shallow water, marshes and wet meadows, Alaska to South Dakota, south to California and New

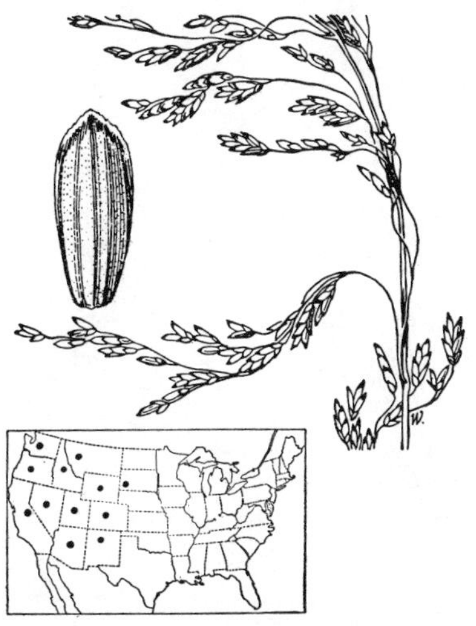

FIGURE 103.—*Glyceria pauciflora*. Panicle, × 1; floret, × 10. (Sandberg, Heller, and McDougal 636, Idaho.)

Mexico, rising in the mountains to timber line.

18. Glyceria otísii Hitchc. (Fig. 104.) Culms about 1.25 m. tall; blades flat, lax, 7 to 16 cm. long, 8 to 12 mm. wide; panicle loosely pyramidal, to 18 cm. long, the branches few, drooping; spikelets scarcely compressed, 5- to 6-flowered; glumes 1 and 1.5 mm. long; lemmas broad, especially at the summit, very scabrous, the prominent hyaline tip contrasting with the purple zone just below, the lower part green. ♃ —Timber, Jefferson County, Wash. Known only from the type collection.

19. Glyceria pállida (Torr.) Trin. (Fig. 105.) Culms slender, lax, ascending from a decumbent rooting base, 30 to 100 cm. long; sheaths open, blades mostly 4 to 8 mm. wide; panicle pale green, open, 5 to 15 cm. long, the

FIGURE 104.—*Glyceria otisii*. Panicle, × 1; floret, × 10. (Type.)

FIGURE 105.—*Glyceria pallida*. Plant, × 1; floret, × 10. (Pearce, N. Y.)

branches ascending, flexuous, finally more or less spreading; spikelets somewhat elliptic, 4- to 7-flowered, 6 to 7 mm. long; glumes 1.5 to 2 and 2 to 2.5 mm. long, the second 3-nerved; lemmas 2.5 to 3 mm. long, scaberulous, obtuse, the scarious tip erose; anthers linear, about 1 mm. long; caryopsis with a crown of erect white hairs 0.2 to 0.25 mm. long. ♃ —Shallow cold water, Maine to Wisconsin, south to North Carolina and Missouri. Resembles species of *Poa.*

20. Glyceria fernáldii (Hitchc.) St. John. (Fig. 106.) Resembling *G. pallida* and appearing to grade into it; culms more slender, 20 to 40 cm. long; blades 1 to 3 mm. wide; panicle on the average smaller, the branches finally spreading or reflexed; spikelets mostly 3- to 5-flowered, 4 to 5 mm. long; glumes and lemmas a little shorter than in *G. pallida;* anthers globose, 0.2 to 0.5 mm. long; crown of hairs of caryopsis 0.1 mm. long. ♃ —Shallow water, Newfoundland to Minnesota, south to Pennsylvania.

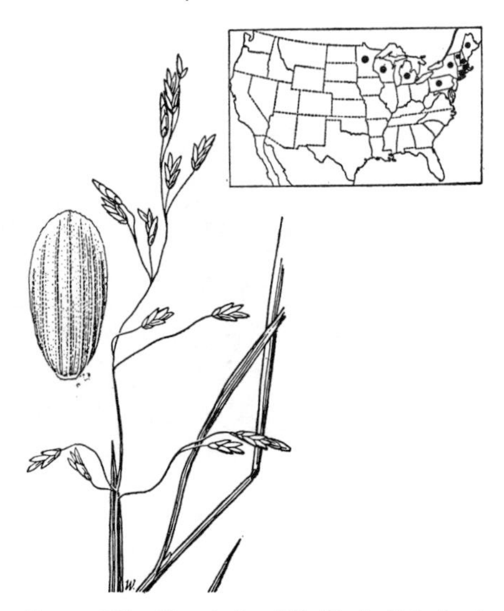

FIGURE 106.—*Glyceria fernaldii.* Plant, × 1; floret, × 10. (Collins, Fernald, and Pease, Quebec.)

8. SCLERÓCHLOA Beauv.

Spikelets 3-flowered, the upper floret sterile; rachilla continuous, broad, thick, the spikelet falling entire; glumes broad, obtuse, rather firm, with hyaline margins, the first 3-nerved, the second 7-nerved; lemmas rounded on the back, obtuse with 5 prominent parallel nerves and hyaline margins; palea hyaline, sharply keeled. Low tufted annual, with broad upper sheaths, folded blades with boat-shaped tips, and dense spikelike racemes, the spikelets subsessile, imbricate in 2 rows on 1 side of the broad thick rachis. Type species, *Sclerochloa dura.* Name from Greek *skleros,* hard, and *chloa,* grass, alluding to the firm glumes.

1. Sclerochloa dúra (L.) Beauv. (Fig. 107.) Culms erect to spreading, 2 to 7 cm. long; foliage glabrous, the lower leaves very small, the upper increasingly larger, with broad overlapping sheaths; blades 7 to 18 mm. long, 1 to 3 mm. wide, the upper exceeding the raceme, the junction with the sheath obscure; raceme 1 to 2 cm. long, nearly half as wide; spikelets 6 to 7 mm. long on very short thick pedicels; first glume about one-third, the second half as long as the spikelets; lower lemma 5 mm. long. ⊙ —Dry sandy or gravelly soil, Washington, Oregon, Idaho, Colorado, Utah, and Texas; New York; introduced from southern Europe.

9. SCOLÓCHLOA Link

(*Fluminea* Fries)

Spikelets 3- or 4-flowered, the rachilla disarticulating above the glumes and between the florets; glumes nearly equal, somewhat scarious and lacerate at summit, the first 3-nerved, the second 5-nerved, about as long as the first lemma; lemmas firm, rounded on the back, villous on the callus, 7-nerved, the

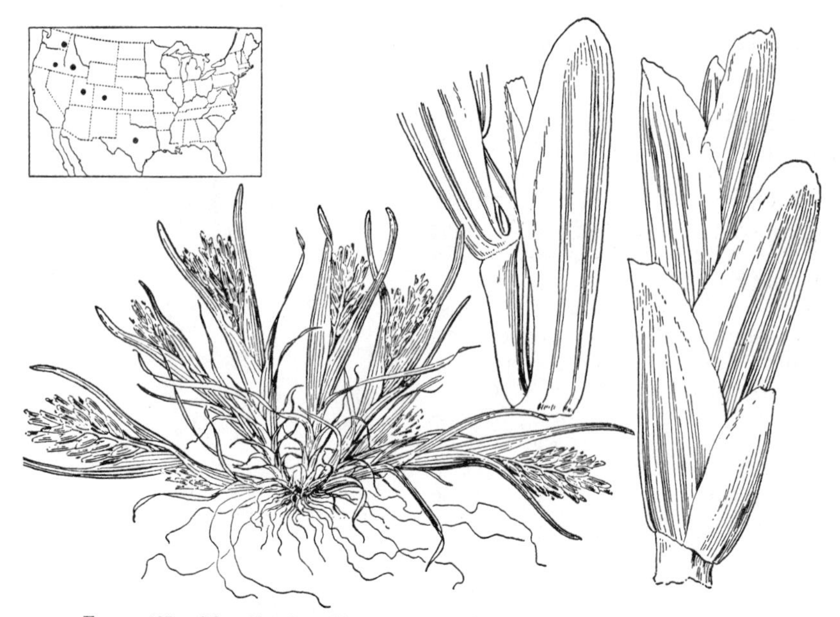

FIGURE 107.—*Sclerochloa dura.* Plant, × 1; spikelet and floret, × 10. (Fallas, Utah.)

nerves rather faint, unequal, extending into a scarious lacerate apex; palea narrow, flat, about as long as the lemma. Tall perennials, with succulent rhizomes, flat blades, and spreading panicles. Type species, *Scolochloa festucacea.* Name from Greek *scolos,* prickle, and *chloa,* grass, alluding to the excurrent nerves of the lemma.

The single species has some value for forage and is often a constituent of marsh hay.

1. Scolochloa festucácea (Willd.) Link. (Fig. 108.) Culms erect, stout, 1 to 1.5 m. tall, from extensively creeping, succulent rhizomes; blades elongate, scabrous on the upper surface, mostly 5 to 10 mm. wide, extending into a fine point; panicle 15 to 20 cm. long, loose, the distant branches fascicled, ascending, naked below, the lowermost nearly as long as the panicle; spikelets about 8 mm. long, the florets approximate; lemmas about 6 mm. long. ♃ —Shallow water and marshes, Manitoba to British Columbia, south to northern Iowa, Nebraska, and eastern Oregon; northern Eurasia.

10. PLEUROPÓGON R. Br. SEMAPHORE-GRASS

Spikelets several- to many-flowered, linear, the rachilla disarticulating above the glumes and between the florets; glumes unequal, membranaceous or subhyaline, scarious at the somewhat lacerate tip, the first 1-nerved, the second obscurely 3-nerved; lemmas membranaceous, 7-nerved, with a round indurate callus, the apex entire or 2-toothed, the midnerve extending into a short mucro or into an awn; keels of the palea winged on the lower half. Soft annuals or perennials, with simple culms, flat blades, and loose racemes of rather large spikelets on a slender flexuous axis. Type species, *Pleuropogon sabinii* R. Br. Name from Greek *pleura,* side, and *pogon,* beard, the palea of the type species having a bristle on each side at the base.

Palatable grasses, but usually too infrequent to be of economic value.

FIGURE 108.—*Scolochloa festucacea*. Plant, × ½; spikelet and floret, × 5. (Griffiths 870, S. Dak.)

FIGURE 109.—*Pleuropogon californicus*. Plant, × ½; spikelet, × 3; floret, × 5. (Bolander 6075, Calif.)

Keels of palea awned about one-third from the base, the awns 2 to 7 mm. long.
5. P. OREGONUS.

Keels of palea awnless.

Lemmas awnless or mucronate, thick, firm, strongly nerved .... 4. P. DAVYI.

Lemmas awned, the awns 1 to 12 mm. long.

Lemmas 4 to 6 mm. long, firm, strongly nerved; wings of palea split about half way to the base forming 2 prominent teeth; culms mostly 30 to 60 cm. tall.
1. P. CALIFORNICUS.

Lemmas 8 to 9 mm. long, relatively thin, the nerves evident but not prominent; culms mostly more than 1 m. tall.

Spikelets reflexed or spreading; awn of the lemma 5 to 12 mm. long.
2. P. REFRACTUS.

Spikelets erect or ascending; awn of the lemma 1 to 2.5 mm. long.
3. P. HOOVERIANUS.

1. Pleuropogon califórnicus (Nees) Benth. ex Vasey. (Fig. 109.) Annual; culms tufted, erect or decumbent at base, 30 to 60 cm. tall; blades flat or folded, seldom more than 10 cm. long, 2 to 5 mm. wide; raceme 10 to 20 cm. long, with 5 to 10 rather distant short-pediceled spikelets; spikelets 6- to 12-flowered, mostly about 2.5 cm. long, erect, or somewhat spreading; glumes obtuse, erose, 4 to 6 mm. long; lemmas scabrous, 5 to 6 mm. long, the nerves prominent, the tip obtuse, scarious, erose, the awn usually 6 to 12 mm. long; wings of palea prominent, cleft, forming a tooth about the middle. ⊙ —Wet meadows and marshy ground, Mendocino County to the San Francisco Bay region, California.

2. Pleuropogon refráctus (A. Gray) Benth. ex Vasey. NODDING SEMAPHORE-GRASS. (Fig. 110.) Perennial; culms 1 to 1.5 m. tall; blades elongate, the uppermost nearly obsolete, 3 to 7 mm. wide; raceme mostly 15 to 20 cm. long, the spikelets as many as 12, about 3 cm. long, 8- to 12-flowered, finally reflexed or drooping; lemmas about 8 mm. long, subacute, less scabrous and the nerves less prominent than in *P. californicus;* awn 5 to 12 mm. long; palea narrow, keeled to about the middle, scarcely or minutely toothed. ♃ —Bogs, wet meadows, and mountain streams, Washington to Mendocino County, Calif., west of the Cascades.

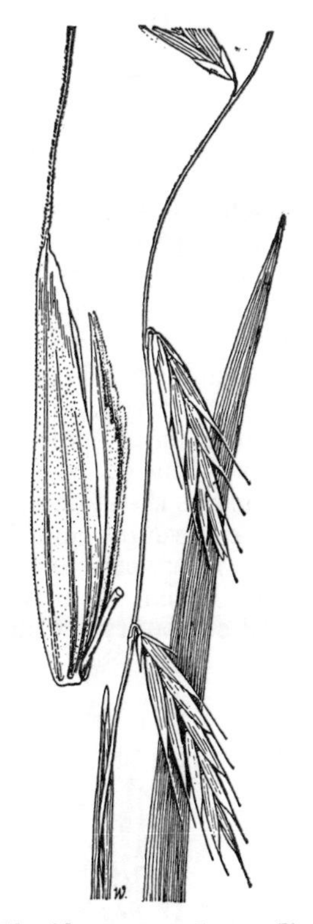

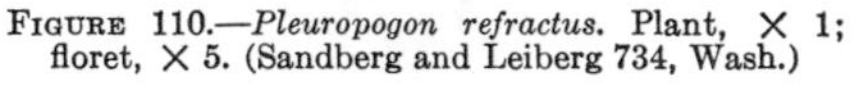
FIGURE 110.—*Pleuropogon refractus.* Plant, × 1; floret, × 5. (Sandberg and Leiberg 734, Wash.)

3. Pleuropogon hooveriánus (Benson) J. T. Howell. (Fig. 111.) Similar to *P. refractus*, but the spikelets erect or ascending; lemmas toothed at the broader hyaline summit, the awn 1 to 2.5 mm. long; wings of palea with a single pointed tooth 1 to 1.5 mm. long; rachilla joints swollen and spongy toward the base. ♃ —Grassy wooded flats, Mendocino and Marin Counties, Calif.

4. Pleuropogon dávyi Benson. (Fig. 112.) Culms erect from short slender rhizomes, 60 to 100 cm. tall; sheaths

FIGURE 111.—*Pleuropogon hooverianus.* Floret and rachilla joint, × 5. (Dupl. type.)

soft, somewhat inflated, transversely veined; blades 10 to 30 cm. long, 6 to 9 mm. wide, glabrous; raceme 20 to 33 cm. long; spikelets 2 to 5.5 cm. long, 8- to 20-flowered, erect or ascending; lemmas 5.5 to 7.5 mm. long, strongly nerved, obtuse, awnless or mucronate; palea oblong, prominently winged, two-thirds to nearly as long as the lemma. ♃ — Wet ground around marshes and creek beds, Sherwood and Walkers Valley (Mendocino County) to Big Valley (Lake County), Calif.

FIGURE 112.—*Pleuropogon davyi.* Floret and rachilla joint, × 5. (Type.)

5. Pleuropogon oregónus Chase. (Fig. 113.) Culms 55 to 90 cm. tall, erect from slender rhizomes, soft, spongy, with long internodes; sheaths overlapping, the lower rather loose; ligule 4 to 5 mm. long, lacerate; blades 8 to 18 cm. long, 4 to 7 mm. wide, mucronate, scaberulous; raceme 6 to 16 cm. long; spikelets 1.5 to 4 cm. long, 7- to 13-flowered, ascending; glumes 2 to 4 mm. long, nerveless; lemmas 5.5 to 7 mm. long, obtuse, erose, awn 6 to 10 mm. long; keels of palea with an awn 2 to 7 mm. long, about one-third from the base. ♃ —Wet meadows, Union (Union County) and Adel (Lake County), Oreg.

FIGURE 113.—*Pleuropogon oregonus.* Plant, × 1; floret, × 10. (Type.)

11. HESPERÓCHLOA (Piper) Rydb.

(Included in *Festuca* L. in Manual, ed. 1)

Spikelets 3- to 5-flowered, the rachilla disarticulating above the glumes and between the florets; glumes subequal or the second longer than the first, shorter than the first floret, lanceolate, acute, the first 1-nerved, the second 3-nerved; lemmas rounded on the back, acute or acuminate, awnless, 5-nerved; palea as long as the lemma, scabrous-ciliate on the keels; stigmas sessile, long and slender; grain beaked, bidentate at the apex. Densely tufted, dioecious, rhizomatous perennial with firm, narrow, flat or loosely involute blades, and narrow erect panicles. Type species, *Hesperochloa kingii*. Name from Greek *esperis*, western, and *chloa*, grass.

1. Hesperochloa kíngii (S. Wats.) Rydb. (Fig. 114.) Culms in large dense clumps, erect, the rhizomes usually wanting in herbarium specimens; sheaths smooth, striate, the lower reddish brown in age; blades firm, flat, or becoming loosely involute, scabrous on the margins, 3 to 6 mm. wide; panicles 7 to 20 cm. long, the branches short, appressed, floriferous nearly to the base, the staminate inflorescences denser with somewhat larger spikelets than the pistillate; spikelets 7 to 12 mm. long; glumes thin, shining, acute or subobtuse, the first 3 to 4 mm. long, the second 4 to 6 mm. long; lemmas 5 to 8 mm. long, acute or acuminate, scabrous. ♃ (*Festuca confinis* Vasey; *F. kingii* Cassidy.)—Dry mountains and hills, 2,000 to 3,500 m., Oregon to southern California, east to Montana, Nebraska, and Colorado.

FIGURE 114.—*Hesperochloa kingii*. Plant, × ½; spikelet, × 5. (Osterhout 1897, Colo.)

12. POA L. Bluegrass

Spikelets 2- to several-flowered, the rachilla disarticulating above the glumes and between the florets, the uppermost floret reduced or rudimentary; glumes acute, keeled, somewhat unequal, the first usually 1-nerved, the second usually 3-nerved; lemmas somewhat keeled, acute or acutish, rarely obtuse, awnless, membranaceous, often somewhat scarious at the summit, 5-nerved (intermediate nerves, that is, the pair between the keel and the marginal nerves, rarely obsolete), the nerves sometimes pubescent, the callus or base of the lemma in many species with scant to copious cottony hairs, termed "web." Low or rather tall slender annuals or usually perennials with spikelets in open or contracted panicles, the relatively narrow blades flat, folded, or involute, ending in a boat-shaped tip. Standard species, *Poa pratensis*. Name from Greek, *poa*, grass.

There are several groups of *Poa* that present many taxonomic difficulties. In the groups containing, for example, *P. nervosa*, *P. arctica*, *P. scabrella*, and *P. nevadensis* many species have been proposed which are not here recognized as valid, because they were based upon trivial or variable characters. The keys are based upon average specimens, but the student may find occasional intermediates between the valid species.

The bluegrasses are of great importance because of their forage value, some species being cultivated for pasture and others forming a large part of the forage on the mountain meadows of the West. The most important is *Poa pratensis*, commonly known as bluegrass or Kentucky bluegrass. In the cooler parts of the United States it is cultivated for lawns and is the standard pasture grass in the humid regions where the soil contains plenty of lime. It has been extensively used in the improvement of badly depleted western mountain ranges. *P. compressa*, Canada bluegrass, is cultivated for pasture in the Northeastern States and Canada, especially on poor soils. *P. trivialis* and *P. palustris* are occasionally grown in meadow mixtures, but are of little agricultural importance. *P. arachnifera*, Texas bluegrass, has been used in some parts of the South for winter pasture and as a lawn grass. *P. annua* is a common weed in lawns and gardens. *P. bulbosa* is cultivated about Medford, Oreg., and elsewhere.

With very few exceptions the bluegrasses are palatable and nutritious and are often the most important grasses in many parts of the West. At high altitudes, *P. alpina*, *P. arctica*, *P. epilis*, and *P. rupicola* are important. In the mountains mostly below timber line are found *P. fendleriana* (mutton grass), *P. longiligula*, *P. nervosa*, *P. secunda* (Sandberg bluegrass), *P. canbyi*, and *P. juncifolia*, all of wide distribution. *P. interior* is most abundant in the Rocky Mountains; *P. scabrella* is probably the most important forage grass of the lower elevations in California; *P. gracillima* and *P. ampla* are mostly in the Northwestern States; *P. arida* is the most valuable bluegrass of the Plains. *P. bigelovii*, an annual, is important in the Southwestern States. *P. macrantha* and *P. confinis* are native sandbinders of the sand dunes on the coast of Washington and Oregon, but are not cultivated.

Spikelets little compressed, narrow, much longer than wide, the lemmas convex on the back, the keels obscure, the marginal and intermediate nerves usually faint. All bunchgrasses.
  Lemmas crisp-puberulent on the back toward the base (the pubescence sometimes obscure or only at the very base .... 7. SCABRELLAE.
  Lemmas glabrous or minutely scabrous, but not crisp-puberulent .... 8. NEVADENSES.
Spikelets distinctly compressed, the glumes and lemmas keeled.
  Plants annual .... 1. ANNUAE.
  Plants perennial.
    Creeping rhizomes present .... 2. PRATENSES.
    Creeping rhizomes wanting.
      Lemmas webbed at base (web sometimes scant or obscure in *P. interior*). 3. PALUSTRES.
      Lemmas not webbed at base (sometimes sparsely webbed in *P. fernaldiana* and *P. pattersoni*).
        Lemmas pubescent on the keel or marginal nerves or both, sometimes pubescent also on the internerves .... 5. ALPINAE.
        Lemmas glabrous (minutely pubescent at base in *P. unilateralis* and sometimes in *P. curta*).
          Blades narrow, usually involute .... 6. EPILES.
          Blades flat, 4 to 8 mm. wide, bright green, often splitting at the apex. Panicles about 15 cm. long with slender spreading branches .... 4. HOMALOPOAE.

1. Annuae

Lemmas glabrous, except the scabrous keel, webbed at base. Sheaths glabrous.
1. P. BOLANDERI.

Lemmas pubescent.
Lemmas pubescent on the back especially toward the base, but not distinctly villous on the keel and nerves, slightly webbed at base. Sheaths usually scabrous; panicle open.
2. P. HOWELLII.

Lemmas pubescent on the nerves, sometimes also on the internerves.
Panicle narrow, contracted, usually interrupted; sheaths scabrous. Lemmas webbed, pubescent on the internerves below........ 3. P. BIGELOVII.

Panicle oblong or pyramidal, the branches spreading; sheaths glabrous.
Lemmas with webby hairs at base, distinctly 3-nerved, the intermediate nerves obscure; anthers 0.1 to 0.2 mm. long........ 4. P. CHAPMANIANA.

Lemmas not webbed at base, distinctly 5-nerved; anthers 0.5 to 1 mm. long.
5. P. ANNUA.

2. Pratenses

1a. Culms strongly flattened, 2-edged........ 6 P. COMPRESSA.
1b. Culms terete or slightly flattened, not 2-edged.
2a. Plants dioecious.
Panicle oblong, the two sexes unlike in appearance, the pistillate spikelets woolly, the staminate glabrous or nearly so. Plains of Texas........ 7. P. ARACHNIFERA.
Panicle oblong or ovoid, the two sexes similar. Seacoast, California and northward.
Glumes and lemmas about 8 mm. long........ 8. P. MACRANTHA.
Glumes and lemmas not more than 6 mm. long.
Panicle densely ovoid; lemmas 6 mm. long, slightly villous below.
9. P. DOUGLASII.
Panicle somewhat open; lemmas 3 mm. long, scaberulous........ 10. P. CONFINIS.
2b. Plants not dioecious, the florets perfect.
3a. Blades involute. Glumes and lemmas 4 to 5 mm. long........ 11. P. RHIZOMATA.
3b. Blades flat or folded.
4a. Lemmas not pubescent nor webbed.
Panicle almost spikelike, erect.
Panicle pale, narrow, linear; lemmas scabrous; leaves crowded toward the base, the blades very firm, conduplicate, pungent, curved. Lower sheaths fibrous.
12. P. FIBRATA.
Panicle tinged with purple, oblong; lemmas glabrous; leaves not crowded toward the base, the blades flat or sometimes folded, straight, erect.
13. P. ATROPURPUREA.
Panicle open, nodding; glumes 3 to 4 mm. long.
Blades broad and short; lower panicle branches reflexed........ 14. P. CURTA.
Blades elongate; panicle branches ascending........ 15. P. NERVOSA.
4b. Lemmas pubescent.
5a. Lemmas glabrous except for the web at base........ 16. P. KELLOGGII.
5b. Lemmas pubescent on the nerves or back, sometimes also webbed at base.
6a. Internerves glabrous, the keel and marginal nerves pubescent.
Lower sheaths retrorsely pubescent, purplish; lemmas pubescent on keel and marginal nerves, not webbed........ 15. P. NERVOSA.
Lower sheaths glabrous (scaberulous in *P. laxiflora*); lemmas webbed at base.
Culms retrorsely scabrous........ 17. P. LAXIFLORA.
Culms glabrous.
Lower panicle branches in a whorl of usually 5; blades mostly shorter than the culm........ 18. P. PRATENSIS.
Lower panicle branches usually in twos, spreading, spikelet-bearing near the ends; blades about as long as the culm........ 19. P. CUSPIDATA.
6b. Internerves pubescent near base, the keel and marginal nerves pubescent.
Panicle contracted, the branches ascending or appressed (sometimes open in *P. glaucifolia*).
First glume 2.5 to 3 mm. long, 1-nerved; first floret about 3 mm. long; anthers 1.5 mm. long. Plains and alkali meadows at medium altitudes.
20. P. ARIDA.
First glume 4 to 5 mm. long, 3-nerved; first floret 5 mm. long; anthers 2.5 mm. long; spikelets mostly shining........ 21. P. GLAUCIFOLIA.
Panicle open, the branches spreading.
Blades broad and short; lower panicle branches reflexed........ 14. P. CURTA.
Blades 2 to 3 mm. wide; panicle pyramidal, the lower branches horizontal
22. P. ARCTICA.

3. Palustres

1a. Lemmas glabrous, or the keel sometimes pubescent.
Sheaths retrorsely scabrous. Culms decumbent and often rooting at base; keel of lemma glabrous or slightly pubescent........ 23. P. TRIVIALIS.
Sheaths glabrous.
Panicle narrow, drooping, the branches appressed or ascending........ 24. P. MARCIDA.
Panicle very open, the few branches slender, naked below, spreading or drooping.
Lemmas villous on the keel; panicle branches mostly in fours or fives.
25. P. ALSODES.
Lemmas glabrous on the keel; panicle branches mostly in twos or threes.
Lemmas obtuse........ 26. P. LANGUIDA.
Lemmas acute........ 27. P. SALTUENSIS.
1b. Lemmas pubescent on keel and marginal nerves.
2a. Sheaths distinctly retrorse-scabrous (sometimes faintly so). Culms usually stout, 40 to 120 cm. tall; panicle usually large and open, mostly more than 15 cm. long.
28. P. OCCIDENTALIS.
2b. Sheaths glabrous or faintly scaberulous.
3a. Lower panicle branches distinctly reflexed at maturity.
Panicle oblong, erect, mostly more than 15 cm. long, the branches several (usually more than 3) in a whorl........ 30. P. SYLVESTRIS.
Panicle nodding, mostly less than 15 cm. long, the branches 1 to 3 together.
31. P. REFLEXA.
3b. Lower panicle branches not reflexed.
4a. Panicle narrowly pyramidal, erect, 15 to 20 cm. long. Lemmas 4 mm. long, pubescent on nerves and internerves; webbed at base; New Mexico.
29. P. TRACYI.
4b. Panicle broadly pyramidal, usually nodding.
5a. Intermediate nerves of lemma distinct........ 32. P. WOLFII.
5b. Intermediate nerves of lemma obscure (distinct in *P. leptocoma*).
6a. Lower panicle branches in pairs, elongate, capillary, bearing a few spikelets near the ends.
Spikelets rather broad, the rachilla joints short, hidden by the florets; sheaths smooth; culms in dense tufts; alpine rocky slopes.
33. P. PAUCISPICULA.
Spikelets narrow, the rachilla joints slender, somewhat elongate, usually not hidden by the florets; sheaths minutely roughened; culms solitary or in small tufts; shady bogs.
Intermediate nerves of lemma distinct; uppermost ligule acute, 3 to 4 mm. long; western mountains below timber line........ 34. P. LEPTOCOMA.
Intermediate nerves of lemma obscure; uppermost ligule truncate, 0.3 to 1.5 mm. long; Great Lakes region at low altitudes.
35. P. PALUDIGENA.
6b. Lower panicle branches often more than 2, if only 2 not capillary and elongate.
Florets usually converted into bulblets with dark purple base; culms swollen and bulblike at base........ 36. P. BULBOSA.
Florets normal; culms not bulblike at base.
Glumes narrow, acuminate, about as long as the first lemma; ligule very short........ 37. P. NEMORALIS.
Glumes lanceolate, acute, shorter than the first lemma; ligules rather prominent, those of the culm leaves 1 to 3 mm. or more long.
Spikelets about 6 mm. long; lemmas 4 mm. long.... 38. P. MACROCLADA.
Spikelets about 4 mm. long; lemmas 2.5 to 3 mm. long.
Culms decumbent at the purplish base; panicle 10 to 30 cm. long, large and open........ 39. P. PALUSTRIS.
Culms erect from a green or tawny base; panicle mostly less than 10 cm. long, comparatively small and few-flowered...... 40. P. INTERIOR.

4. Homalopoae

One species........ 41. P. CHAIXII.

5. Alpinae

Blades folded or involute, firm, rather stiff.
Ligule very short, not noticeable when viewed from the side of sheath.
42. P. FENDLERIANA.

Ligule prominent, easily seen in side view, 5 to 7 mm. long .... 43. P. LONGILIGULA.
Blades flat or, if involute, rather lax or soft.
Panicle branches slender, spreading or drooping, the lower naked and simple for 3 to 4 cm. or more .... 44. P. AUTUMNALIS.
Panicle branches not long and spreading.
Panicle broadly pyramidal, condensed, about as broad as long, the lower branches spreading. Spikelets broad, subcordate .... 45. P. ALPINA.
Panicle longer than broad.
Panicle nodding, the lower branches slender, arcuate-drooping. 46. P. STENANTHA.
Panicle erect, the lower branches short (see also *P. gracillima*).
Panicle rather loose, lower branches naked below, ascending (see also *P. macrolada*).
Plants glaucous, culms flattened; panicle rather narrow.
Spikelets 2- or 3-flowered; panicle 3 to 7 cm. long .... 47. P. GLAUCA.
Spikelets 3- to 6-flowered; panicle 6 to 16 cm. long .... 48. P. GLAUCANTHA.
Plants not glaucous; culms terete, rather lax .... 49. P. FERNALDIANA.
Panicle narrow, condensed, the branches short (see also *P. unilateralis*).
Culms rather lax; ligule minute; glumes about 4 mm. long. 50. P. PATTERSONI.
Culms stiff, ligule about 1.5 mm. long, glumes about 3 mm. long. 51. P. RUPICOLA.

6. Epiles

Panicle open, 10 to 15 cm. long. Blades involute, slender .... 52. P. INVOLUTA.
Panicle contracted or, if open, less than 10 cm. long.
Blades scabrous, filiform, mostly basal.
Spikelets 7 to 9 mm. long; lemmas 4.5 to 6 mm. long, mostly smooth. 53. P. CUSICKII.
Spikelets 6 to 7 mm. long; lemmas about 4 mm. long, scabrous .... 54. P. NAPENSIS.
Blades glabrous.
Lemmas minutely pubescent at base .... 55. P. UNILATERALIS.
Lemmas glabrous.
Blades of the culm 2 to 3 mm. wide, flat, those of the innovations slender and filiform. 56. P. EPILIS.
Blades of the culm and innovations similar. Panicle few-flowered.
Panicle short, open, the capillary branches bearing 1 or 2 spikelets. Culms 10 to 20 cm. tall .... 57. P. VASEYOCHLOA.
Panicle narrow.
Lemmas 5 to 6 mm. long; panicle usually pale or silvery .... 58. P. PRINGLEI.
Lemmas less than 4 mm. long; panicle usually purple.
Glumes about as long as the first and second florets; panicle mostly not exceeding the short soft blades.
Glumes and lemmas smooth, the lemmas erose at summit. 59. P. LETTERMANI.
Glumes and lemmas scabrous, the lemmas acute, scarcely erose. 60. P. MONTEVANSI.
Glumes shorter than the first floret; panicle usually much longer than the usually stiff blades .... 61. P. LEIBERGII.

7. Scabrellae

Sheaths somewhat scabrous .... 62. P. SCABRELLA.
Sheaths glabrous.
Panicle rather open, the lower branches naked at base, ascending or somewhat spreading; culms usually decumbent at base .... 63. P. GRACILLIMA.
Panicle contracted, the branches appressed or at anthesis somewhat spreading.
Culms slender, on the average less than 30 cm. tall; numerous short innovations at base. Blades usually folded .... 64. P. SECUNDA.
Culms stouter, on the average more than 50 cm. tall; innovations usually not numerous. 65. P. CANBYI.

8. Nevadenses

Sheaths scaberulous. Ligule long, decurrent .... 66. P. NEVADENSIS.
Sheaths glabrous.
Ligule prominent; blades broad and short .... 67. P. CURTIFOLIA.
Ligule short; blades elongate.
Blades involute .... 68. P. JUNCIFOLIA.
Blades flat .... 69. P. AMPLA.

1. Ánnuae.—Annuals; culms seldom more than 50 cm. tall; panicles open (contracted in *P. bigelovii*).

1. Poa bolandéri Vasey. (Fig. 115.) Culms erect, 15 to 60 cm. tall; sheaths glabrous; blades relatively short, 3 to 5 mm. wide, abruptly narrowed at tip; panicle about half the length of the entire plant, at first contracted, finally open, the branches few, distant, glabrous, stiffly spreading, naked below; spikelets usually 2- or 3-flowered, the internodes of the rachilla long; glumes broad, 2 and 3 mm. long; lemma scantily webbed at base, acute, the marginal nerves rather indistinct, the intermediate nerves obsolete. ⊙ —Open ground or open woods, 1,500 to 3,000 m., Washington and Idaho to western Nevada and the southern Sierras in California.

FIGURE 115.—*Poa bolanderi*. Panicle, × 1; floret, × 10. (Swallen 799, Calif.)

2. Poa howéllii Vasey and Scribn. HOWELL BLUEGRASS. (Fig. 116.) Culms 30 to 85 cm. tall; sheaths retrorsely scabrous to glabrous; blades wider than in *P. bolanderi*, gradually acuminate; panicle one-third to half the entire height of the plant, open, the branches in rather distant fascicles, spreading, scabrous, naked below, some short branches intermixed; spikelets 3 to 5 mm. long, usually 3- or 4-flowered; glumes narrow, acuminate, 1.5 and 2 mm. long; lemmas webbed at base, 2 to 3 mm. long, ovate-lanceolate, pubescent on the lower part, the nerves all rather distinct. ⊙ —Rocky banks and shaded slopes, mostly less than 1,000 m., Vancouver Island to southern California, especially in the Coast Ranges.

3. Poa bigelóvii Vasey and Scribn. BIGELOW BLUEGRASS. (Fig. 117.) Culms erect, 15 to 35 cm. tall; blades 1 to 5 mm. wide; panicle narrow, interrupted, 7 to 15 cm. long, the branches short, appressed; spikelets about 6 mm. long; glumes acuminate, 4 mm. long, 3-nerved; lemmas about 3 mm. long, sometimes 4 mm., webbed at base, conspicuously pubescent on the lower part of keel and lateral nerves, sometimes sparsely pubescent on lower part of internerves. ⊙ —Open ground, at medium altitudes, Oklahoma and western Texas to Colorado, Nevada, and southern California; northern Mexico.

4. Poa chapmaniána Scribn. (Fig. 118.) Plant drying pale or tawny; culms densely tufted, slender, 10 to 30 cm. tall; blades 1 to 1.5 mm. wide; panicle oblong-pyramidal, 3 to 8 cm. long, open, the lower branches spreading; spikelets 3 to 4 mm. long, mostly 3- to 5-flowered; glumes 2 and 2.5

FIGURE 116.—*Poa howellii*. Panicle, × 1; floret, × 10. (Suksdorf 10464, Wash.)

mm. long; lemmas about 2 mm. long, webbed at base, strongly pubescent on the keel and lateral nerves, the intermediate nerves obscure; anthers 0.1 to 0.2 mm. long. ⊙ —Open ground and cultivated fields, Massachusetts and New York; Delaware to Nebraska, Florida and Texas.

FIGURE 117.—*Poa bigelovii*. Panicle, × 1; floret, × 10. (Fendler 931, N. Mex.)

FIGURE 118.—*Poa chapmaniana*. Panicle, × 1; floret, × 10. (V. H. Chase 3557, Ill.)

5. Poa ânnua L. ANNUAL BLUEGRASS. (Fig. 119.) Tufted, bright green, erect to spreading, sometimes rooting at the lower nodes, usually 5 to 20 cm. tall, sometimes taller, forming mats; culms flattened; blades soft, lax, mostly 1 to 3 mm. wide; panicle pyramidal, open, 3 to 7 cm. long; spikelets crowded, 3- to 6-flowered, about 4 mm. long; first glume 1.5 to 2, the second 2 to 2.5 mm. long; lemmas not webbed at base, distinctly 5-nerved, more or less pubescent on the lower half of all the nerves, the long hairs on the lower part of the keel sometimes simulating a web; anthers 0.5 to 1 mm. long. ☉ —Open ground, lawns, pastures, waste places, and openings in woods, Newfoundland and Labrador to Alaska, south to Florida and California; tropical America at high altitudes; introduced from Europe. In warmer parts of the United States the species thrives in the winter; in intermediate latitudes it is a troublesome weed in lawns, growing luxuriantly in spring, dying in early summer and leaving unsightly patches. Occasionally found in flooded places and stream banks, the culms spreading.

2. **Praténses.**—Perennials with slender creeping rhizomes. Several species dioecious.

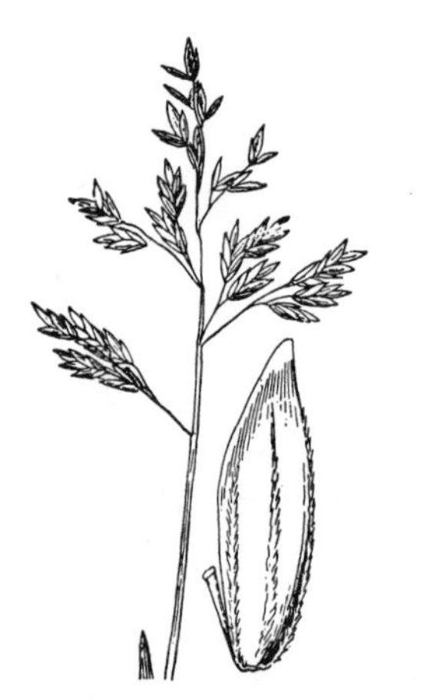

FIGURE 119.—*Poa annua*. Panicle, × 1; floret, × 10. (Hitchcock, D. C.)

FIGURE 120.—*Poa compressa*. Panicle, × 1; floret, × 10. (Gayle 750, Maine.)

6. Poa comprêssa L. CANADA BLUEGRASS. (Fig. 120.) Culms solitary or few together, often gregarious, strongly flattened, wiry, decumbent at base, bluish green, 15 to 70 cm. tall; blades mostly rather short, 1 to 4 mm. wide; panicle narrow, 3 to 10 cm. long, the usually short branches in pairs, spikelet-bearing to the base; spikelets crowded, subsessile, 3- to 6-flowered, 4 to 6 mm. long; glumes 2 to 3 mm. long; lemmas firm, 2 to 3 mm. long, the web at base scant or wanting, the keel and marginal nerves slightly pubescent toward base, the intermediate nerves obscure. ♃ —Open ground, open woods, meadows, and waste places, Newfoundland to Alaska, south to Georgia, Tennessee, Alabama, Oklahoma, New Mexico, and California; introduced from Europe. Cultivated for pastures in poor soil.

7. Poa arachnífera Torr. TEXAS BLUEGRASS. (Fig. 121.) Plants dioecious; culms tufted, 30 to 75 cm. tall; blades mostly 2 to 4 mm. wide, scabrous above; panicle narrow, compact, more or less lobed or interrupted, 5 to 12 cm. long; spikelets mostly 5- to 10-flowered, the pistillate conspicuously cobwebby, the lemmas 5 to 6 mm. long, acuminate, copiously long webby at base, the strongly compressed keel and lateral nerves ciliate-fringed along the lower half; staminate lemmas glabrous or with a scant web at base. ♃ —Prairies and plains, southern Kansas to Texas and Arkansas; introduced eastward to North Carolina and Florida; Idaho. Sometimes cultivated for winter pasture.

FIGURE 121.—*Poa arachnifera.* Plant and pistillate (♀) and staminate (♂) panicles, × 1; pistillate (♀) and staminate (♂) florets, × 10. (Blackman, Tex.)

8. **Poa macrántha** Vasey. (Fig. 122.) Plants dioecious; culms erect from a decumbent base, with extensively creeping rhizomes, and also long runners creeping over the sand, 15 to 40 cm. tall; sheaths tawny, papery; blades involute, subflexuous; panicle contracted, sometimes dense and spikelike, 5 to 12 cm. long, pale or tawny; spikelets about 12 mm. long, about 5-flowered; glumes 3-nerved, or the second indistinctly 5-nerved, about 8 mm. long; lemmas about 8 mm. long, short-webbed at base, pubescent on the keel and marginal nerves below, slightly scabrous on the keel above; pistillate florets with abortive stamens. ♃ —Sand dunes along the coast, Washington to northern California.

FIGURE 122.—*Poa macrantha*. Plant, × 1; floret, × 10. (Hitchcock 2822, Oreg.)

9. Poa douglásii Nees. (Fig. 123.) Plants dioecious, the two kinds similar; culms ascending from a decumbent base, usually less than 30 cm. tall; rhizomes slender; sheaths glabrous, tawny and papery; blades involute, some of them usually exceeding the culm; panicle ovoid, dense, spikelike, 2 to 5 cm. long, 1 to 2 cm. wide, pale or purplish; spikelets 6 to 10 mm. long, about 5-flowered; glumes broad, 3-nerved, 4 to 6 mm. long; lemmas 6 to 7 mm. long, slightly webbed at base, pubescent on the lower part of the keel and marginal nerves, scabrous on the upper part of the keel, usually with 1 to 3 pairs of intermediate nerves. ♃ —Sand dunes near the coast, California, Point Arena to Monterey.

10. Poa confínis Vasey. (Fig. 124.) Plants dioecious, the two kinds similar; culms often geniculate at base, usually less than 15 cm. tall, sometimes as much as 30 cm.; blades involute, those of the innovations numerous; panicle narrow, 1 to 3 cm. long, tawny, the short branches ascending or appressed; spikelets 4 to 5 mm. long, mostly 3- or 4-flowered; glumes unequal, the second 3 mm. long; lemmas 3 mm. long, scaberulous, sparsely webbed at base, the nerves faint; pistillate florets with minute abortive anthers, the staminate often with rudimentary pistil. ♃ —Sand dunes and sandy meadows near the coast, British Columbia to Mendocino County, Calif.

FIGURE 123.—*Poa douglasii*. Plant, × 1; floret, × 10. (Bolander 6074, Calif.)

11. Poa rhizómata Hitchc. (Fig. 125.) Culms tufted with numerous innovations, 40 to 60 cm. tall; lower sheaths usually scaberulous with a puberulent collar; ligule rather prominent on the culm leaves, inconspicuous on the leaves of the innovations; blades involute or sometimes flat, firm, less than 1 mm. thick, flexuous, mostly basal, 2 on the culm, usually puberulent on the upper surface; panicle open, 5 to 8 cm. long, the lower branches mostly in pairs, 2 to 3 cm. long; spikelets, 3- to 5-flowered, 6 to 10 mm. long; glumes 3 to 5 mm. long; lemmas 4 to 5 mm. long, with a rather short web at the base, scaberulous at least on the rather distinct nerves, pubescent on the lower part of keel. ♃ —Dry slopes, southwestern Oregon and northwestern California; apparently rare.

FIGURE 124.—*Poa confinis.* Plant, × 1; floret, × 10. (Piper 4910, Wash.)

FIGURE 125.—*Poa rhizomata.* Plant, × 1; floret, × 10. (Type.)

12. Poa fibráta Swallen. (Fig. 126.) Culms 15 to 35 cm. tall, erect from an ascending base; lower sheaths thin, smooth and shining; ligule 1 to 1.5 mm. long; blades 4 to 8 cm. long, firm, conduplicate, curved, pungent, scabrous; panicles 4 to 10 cm. long, dense, the short appressed branches floriferous to the base; spikelets 3- to 4-flowered, 5 to 6 mm. long; lemmas 2.5 to 3 mm. long, acute or subobtuse, glabrous or obscurely pubescent toward the base. ♃ —Saline flats, Shasta Valley, Siskiyou County, Calif.

13. Poa atropurpúrea Scribn. (Fig. 127.) Culms erect, 30 to 40 cm. tall;

FIGURE 126.—*Poa fibrata*. Plant, × 1; floret, × 10. (Type.)

FIGURE 127.—*Poa atropurpurea*. Plant, × 1; floret, × 10. (Type.)

blades mostly basal, the uppermost culm leaf below the middle of the culm, folded or involute, firm; panicle contracted, almost spikelike, purple-tinged, 3 to 5 cm. long; spikelets 3 to 4 mm. long, rather thick; glumes broad, less than 2 mm. long; lemmas about 2.5 mm. long, broad, glabrous, not webbed at base, the nerves faint. ♃ —Known only from Bear Valley, San Bernardino Mountains, Calif.

14. Poa cúrta Rydb. (Fig. 128.) Culms few in a loose tuft, 40 to 80 cm. tall, rather lax; sheaths glabrous or minutely roughened; ligule truncate, about 1 mm. long; blades 3 to 6 mm. wide; panicle open, 5 to 15 cm. long, nodding, the rather distant branches spreading or reflexed, naked below; spikelets 5 to 10 mm. long, 2- to 6-flowered; lemmas lanceolate, subacute, slightly scaberulous, sometimes slightly pubescent on the back at base, without a web, 4 to 5.5 mm.

FIGURE 128.—*Poa curta*. Panicle, × 1; floret, × 10. (Jones 5573, Utah.)

long, rather strongly nerved or intermediate nerves faint. ♃ —Moist shady places at medium altitudes, western Wyoming, southern Idaho, and Utah.

15. Poa nervósa (Hook.) Vasey. WHEELER BLUEGRASS. (Fig. 129.) Culms erect, 30 to 60 cm. tall; sheaths glabrous or the lower retrorsely pubescent, often purple, the collar often puberulent; ligule 1 to 2 mm. long; blades sometimes folded; panicle open, usually 5 to 10 cm. long, the apex nodding, the branches mostly in twos or threes, naked below; lemmas rather strongly nerved, glabrous or pubescent on the lower part of the nerves. ♃ (*P. wheeleri* Vasey; *P. olneyae* Piper.)—Open woods at medium altitudes, Alberta and British Columbia, south in the mountains to Colorado, New Mexico, and California. Typical *P. nervosa* (including *P. olneyae*) found mostly in Washington and Oregon, has glabrous to scaberulous strongly nerved lemmas, glabrous sheaths, and a loose open panicle, the capillary lower branches in whorls of 3 or 4, drooping, as much as 8 cm. long; typical *P. wheeleri*, originally described from Colorado, has firmer, less strongly nerved lemmas, more or less pubescent on the

FIGURE 129.—*Poa nervosa*. *A*, Plant, × 1. (Suksdorf 10364, Wash.) *B*, Floret, × 10. (Type of *P. wheeleri*.) *C*, Floret, × 10. (Type of *P. nervosa*.)

FIGURE 130.—*Poa kelloggii*. Plant, × 1; floret, × 10. (Kellogg and Bolander 14, Calif.)

lower part of the keel and marginal nerves, and purplish retrorsely pubescent lower sheaths. These characters are not coordinated, and the forms grade into each other, both as to characters and range.

16. Poa kellóggii Vasey. (Fig. 130.) Culms 30 to 60 cm. tall; sheaths slightly scabrous; blades flat or folded, 2 to 4 mm. wide; panicle pyramidal, open, 7 to 15 cm. long, the branches mostly solitary or in twos, spreading or reflexed, bearing a few spikelets toward the ends; spikelets rather loosely flowered, 4 to 6 mm. long; glumes 3 and 4 mm. long; lemmas acute or almost cuspidate, 4 to 5 mm. long, glabrous, rather obscurely nerved, conspicuously webbed at base. ♃ —Moist woods and shady places, Coast Ranges from Corvallis, Oreg., to Santa Cruz County, Calif.

FIGURE 131.—*Poa laxiflora*. Plant, × 1; floret, × 10. (Hitchcock 23468, Wash.)

17. Poa laxiflóra Buckl. (Fig. 131.) Culms retrorsely scabrous, 100 to 120 cm. tall; sheaths slightly retrorse-scabrous; ligule 3 to 5 mm. long; blades lax, 2 to 4 mm. wide; panicle loose, open, nodding or drooping, 10

FIGURE 132.—*Poa pratensis*. Plant, × ½; spikelet, × 5; floret, × 10. (Williams, S. Dak.)

to 15 cm. long, the lower branches in whorls of 3 or 4; spikelets 3- or 4-flowered, 5 to 6 mm. long; lemmas about 4 mm. long, webbed at base, rather sparsely pubescent on lower part of the nerves. ♃ —Moist woods, southeastern Alaska (Cape Fox, Hot Springs), Sol Duc Hot Springs, Olympic Mountains, Wash. Sauvies Island (near Portland), Oreg.

18. Poa praténsis L. KENTUCKY BLUEGRASS. (Fig. 132.) Culms tufted, erect, slightly compressed, 30 to 100 cm. tall; sheaths somewhat keeled; ligule about 2 mm. long; blades soft, flat or folded, mostly 2 to 4 mm. wide, the basal often elongated; panicle pyramidal or oblong-pyramidal, open, the lowermost branches usually in a whorl of 5, ascending or spreading, naked below, normally 1 central long one, 2 shorter lateral ones and 2 short intermediate ones; spikelets crowded, 3- to 5-flowered, 3 to 6 mm. long; lemmas copiously webbed at base, silky-pubescent on lower half or two-thirds of the keel and marginal nerves, the intermediate nerves distinct, glabrous. ♃ —Open woods, meadows, and open ground, widely distributed throughout the United States and northward, except in arid regions, found in all the States (but not common in the Gulf States) and at all altitudes below alpine regions; introduced from Europe. Bluegrass is commonly cultivated for lawns and pasture in the humid northern parts of the United States.

19. Poa cuspidáta Nutt. (Fig. 133.) Culms in large lax tufts, 30 to 50 cm. tall, scarcely longer than the basal blades; blades lax, 2 to 3 mm. wide, abruptly cuspidate-pointed; panicle 7 to 12 cm. long, open, the branches mostly in pairs, distant, spreading, spikelet-bearing near the ends; spikelets 3- or 4-flowered; lemmas 4 to 6 mm. long, tapering to an acute apex, webbed at base, sparingly pubescent on the keel and marginal nerves, the intermediate nerves distinct, glabrous. ♃ (*P. brachyphylla* Schult.) —Rocky woods, New York, New Jersey to Ohio, south to Georgia and Alabama.

20. Poa árida Vasey. PLAINS BLUEGRASS. (Fig. 134.) Culms erect, 20 to 60 cm. tall; blades mostly basal, firm, folded, usually 2 to 3 mm. wide, a single culm leaf usually below the middle of the culm, its blade short;

FIGURE 133.—*Poa cuspidata*. Panicle, × 1; floret, × 10. (Smith 27, Pa.)

FIGURE 134.—*Poa arida*. Panicle, × 1; floret, × 10. (Jones, Colo.)

panicle narrow, somewhat contracted, 2 to 10 cm. long, the branches appressed or ascending; spikelets rather thick, 5 to 7 mm. long, 4- to 8-flowered; lemmas 3 to 4 mm. long, densely villous on the keel and marginal nerves and more or less villous on the lower part of the intermediate nerves. ♃ (*P. sheldoni* Vasey.)—Prairies, plains, and alkali meadows, up to 3,000 m., Manitoba to Alberta, south to western Iowa, Texas, and New Mexico.

21. Poa glaucifólia Scribn. and Will. (Fig. 135.) Plants glaucous; culms in loose tufts, 60 to 100 cm. tall; blades 2 to 3 mm. wide; panicle narrow, open, mostly 10 to 20 cm. long, the branches usually in somewhat distant whorls, mostly in threes, ascending, very scabrous, naked below; spikelets 2- to 4-flowered; glumes

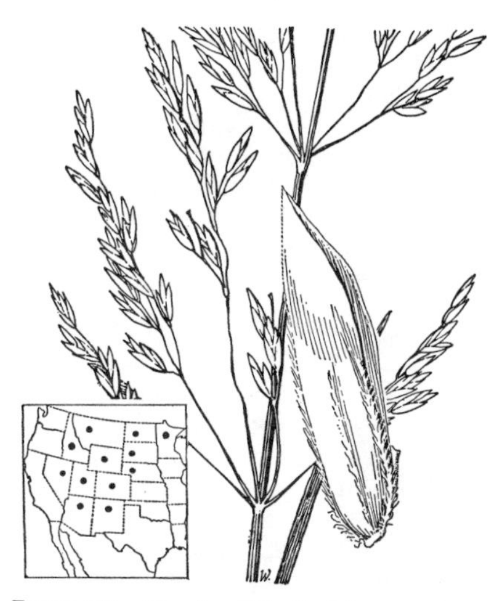

FIGURE 135.—*Poa glaucifolia*. Panicle, × 1; floret, × 10. (Rydberg 3288, Mont.)

4 to 5 mm. long; lemmas about 4 mm. long, villous on the lower half of the keel and marginal nerves and more or less so on the intermediate nerves below. ♃ —Moist places, ditches, and open woods at medium altitudes, British Columbia and Alberta through Idaho to Minnesota, Nebraska, New Mexico, Arizona, and Nevada.

22. Poa árctica R. Br. ARCTIC BLUEGRASS. (Fig. 136.) Culms loosely tufted, erect from a decumbent base,

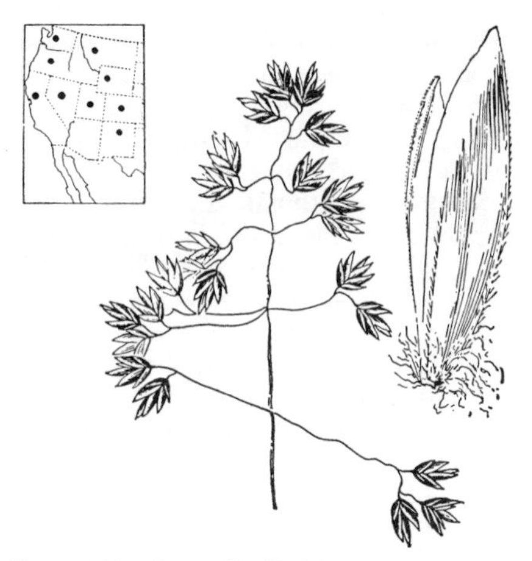

FIGURE 136.—*Poa arctica*. Panicle, × 1; floret, × 10. (Sewall 244, Baffin Land.)

10 to 30 cm. tall; ligule pointed, up to 4 mm. long; blades mostly basal, flat or folded, mostly 2 to 3 mm. wide, one short blade about the middle of the culm; panicle open, pyramidal, 5 to 10 cm. long, the lower branches usually 2, spreading, sometimes reflexed, bearing a few spikelets toward the tip; spikelets 5 to 8 mm. long, 3- or 4-flowered; lemmas densely villous on the keel and marginal nerves and pubescent on the lower part of the internerves, the base often webbed. ♃ (*P. grayana* Vasey; *P. aperta* Scribn. and Merr., a form with pale, rather lax panicles longer than wide.)—Meadows, mostly above timber line, Arctic regions, south to Nova Scotia, in the Rocky Mountains to Nevada and northern New Mexico and in the Cascades to Oregon; California (Inyo County).

3. Palústres.—Perennials without creeping rhizomes; lemmas webbed at base, glabrous, or pubescent on the nerves.

23. Poa triviális L. ROUGH BLUEGRASS. (Fig. 137.) Culms erect from a decumbent base, often rather lax, scabrous below the panicle, 30 to 100 cm. tall; sheaths retrorsely scabrous or scaberulous, at least toward the summit; ligule 4 to 6 mm. long; blades scabrous, 2 to 4 mm. wide; panicle oblong, 6 to 15 mm. long, the lower branches about 5 in a whorl; spikelets usually 2- or 3-flowered, about 3 mm. long; lemma 2.5 to 3 mm. long, glabrous except the slightly pubescent keel, or lateral nerves rarely pubescent, the web at base conspicuous, the nerves prominent. ♃ —Moist places, Newfoundland and Ontario to North Carolina, Minnesota, South Dakota, and Colorado; on the Pacific coast from southern Alaska to northern California; on ballast, Louisiana; introduced from Europe. Sometimes used in mixtures for meadows and pastures under the name rough-stalked meadow grass.

FIGURE 137.—*Poa trivialis*. Panicle, × 1; floret, × 10. (Coville, N. Y.)

24. Poa márcida Hitchc. (Fig. 138.) Culms erect, in small tufts, 40 to 100 cm. tall; ligule very short; blades thin, 1 to 3 mm. wide; panicle drooping, narrow, 10 to 18 cm. long, the capillary branches somewhat distant, solitary or in pairs, ascending or appressed; spikelets mostly 2-flowered; glumes about 3 mm. long; lemmas narrowly lanceolate, acuminate, 4 to 5 mm. long, glabrous, long-webbed at base. ♃ —Bogs and wet shady places, Vancouver Island to the coast mountains of Oregon.

25. Poa alsódes A. Gray. (Fig. 139.) Culms in lax tufts, 30 to 60 cm. tall; blades thin, lax, 2 to 5 mm. wide; panicle 10 to 20 cm. long, very open, the slender branches in distant whorls of threes to fives, finally widely spreading, naked below, few-flowered; spikelets 2- or 3-flowered, about 5 mm. long; lemmas gradually acute, webbed at base, pubescent on the lower part of the keel, otherwise glabrous, faintly nerved. ♃ —Rich or moist woods, Ontario and Maine to Minnesota, south to Delaware and the mountains of North Carolina and Tennessee.

26. Poa lánguida Hitchc. (Fig. 140.) Culms weak, in loose tufts, 30 to 60 or even 100 cm. tall; ligule about 1 mm. long; blades lax, 2 to 4 mm. wide; panicle nodding, 5 to 10 cm. long, the few slender branches mostly in twos or threes, ascending, few-flowered toward the ends; spikelets 2- to 4-flowered, 3 to 4 mm. long; lemmas 2 to 3 mm. long, glabrous except the webbed base, oblong, rather obtuse, at maturity firm. ♃ (*P. debilis* Torr., not Thuill.)—Dry or rocky woods, Newfoundland and Quebec to Wisconsin, south to Pennsylvania, Kentucky, and Iowa.

FIGURE 138.—*Poa marcida*. Panicle, × 1; floret, × 10. (Type.)

27. Poa saltuénsis Fern. and Wieg. (Fig. 141.) Resembling *P. languida;* differing in the thinner, acute, somewhat longer lemmas. ♃ —Woodland thickets, Quebec and Newfoundland to Minnesota, south to Connecticut and Virginia.

28. Poa occidentális Vasey. NEW MEXICAN BLUEGRASS. (Fig. 142.) Culms erect, few in a tuft, usually rather stout, scabrous, as much as 1 to 1.5 m. tall; sheaths somewhat keeled, retrorsely scabrous (sometimes faintly so); ligule 2 to 8 mm. long; blades scabrous, 10 to 20 cm. long, 3 to 6 mm. wide; panicle open, 15 to 30 cm. long, the branches in distant whorls of threes to fives, spreading to reflexed, the lower as much as 10 cm. long, spikelet-bearing toward the ends; spikelets 3- to 6-flowered; lemmas 4.5 to 5 mm. long, conspicuously webbed at base, villous on the lower part of the keel and the marginal nerves and sometimes sparingly pubescent on the internerves below. ♃ —Open woods and moist banks at medium altitudes, Wyoming to New Mexico.

29. Poa trácyi Vasey. (Fig. 143.) Culms erect, 60 to 80 cm. tall; sheaths glabrous, keeled; ligule truncate, about 2 mm. long; blades 3 to 5 mm. wide; panicle narrowly pyram-

FIGURE 139.—*Poa alsodes*. Panicle, × 1; floret, × 10. (Wilson, N. Y.)

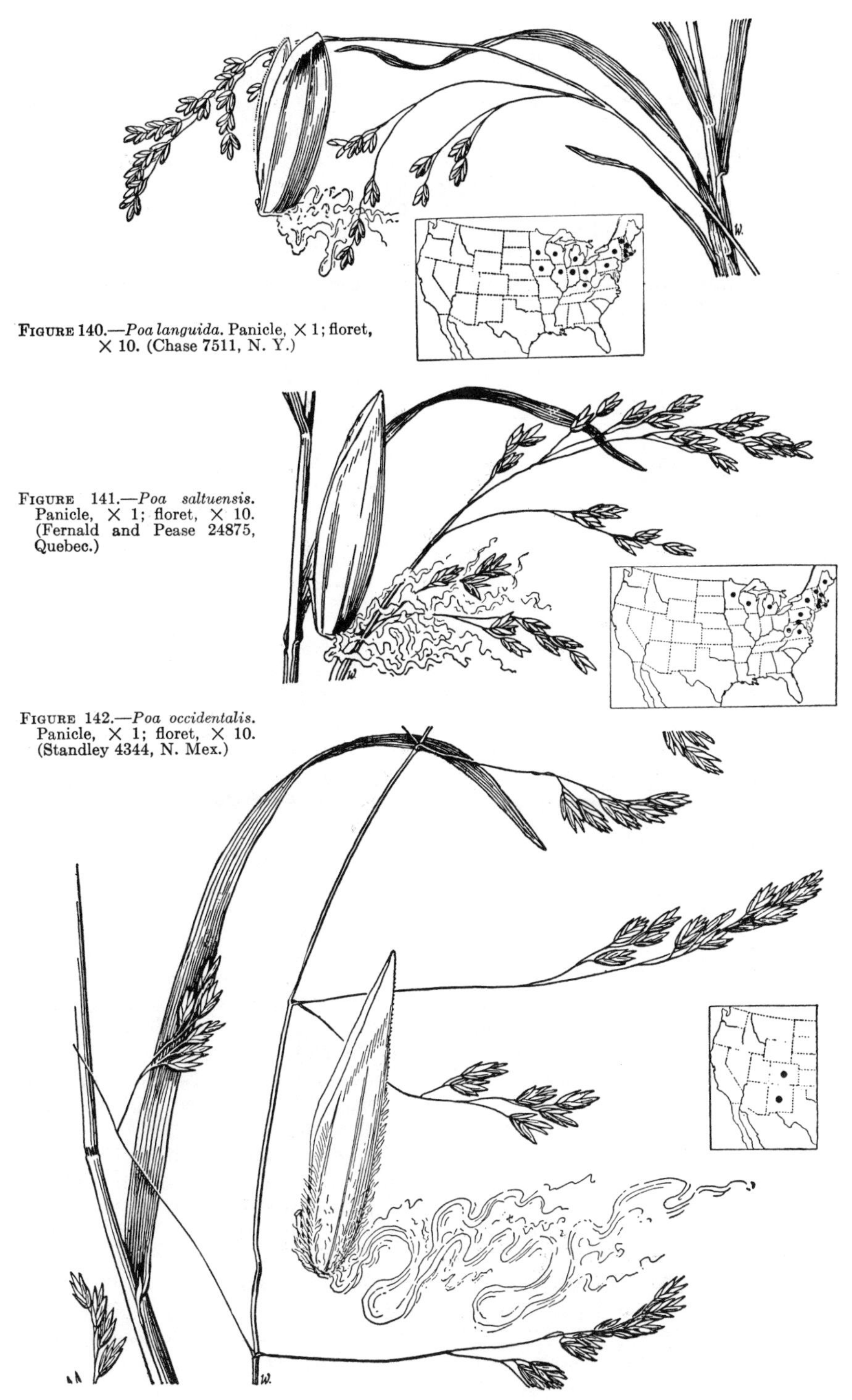

FIGURE 140.—*Poa languida*. Panicle, × 1; floret, × 10. (Chase 7511, N. Y.)

FIGURE 141.—*Poa saltuensis*. Panicle, × 1; floret, × 10. (Fernald and Pease 24875, Quebec.)

FIGURE 142.—*Poa occidentalis*. Panicle, × 1; floret, × 10. (Standley 4344, N. Mex.)

idal, 15 to 20 cm. long, the branches in distant whorls of 2 to 5, spreading, naked on the lower half or two-thirds; spikelets 2- or 3-flowered; lemmas about 3.5 mm. long, oblong-lanceolate or the upper lanceolate, webbed at base, villous on keel and marginal nerves, and more or less so on the internerves below, the intermediate nerves distinct. ♃ —Known only from Raton, N. Mex. May be a form of *P. occidentalis.* Sheaths pubescent in a specimen from St. Louis, Mo.

31. Poa refléxa Vasey and Scribn. Nodding bluegrass. (Fig. 145.) Culms solitary or in small tufts, erect, 20 to 40 cm. tall; blades rather short, 1 to 4 mm. wide; panicle nodding, 5 to 15 cm. long, the branches naked below, solitary, in pairs or in threes, the lower usually reflexed, sometimes strongly so; spikelets 2- to 4-flowered; lemmas about

Figure 143.—*Poa tracyi.* Panicle, × 1; floret, × 10. (Type.)

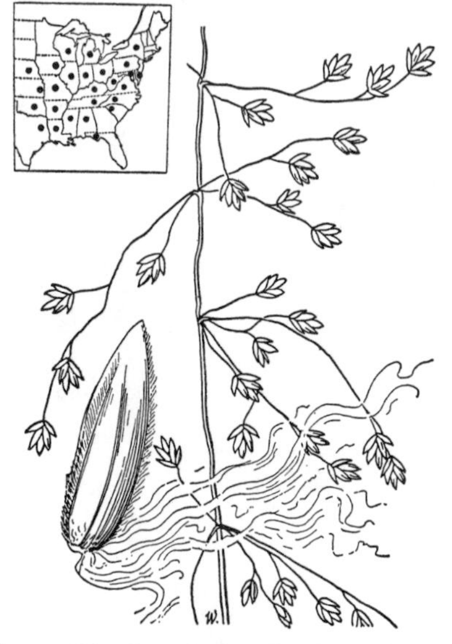

Figure 144.—*Poa sylvestris.* Panicle, × 1; floret × 10. (Wheeler 6, Mich.)

3 mm. long, oblong-elliptic, webbed at base, villous on keel and marginal nerves, sometimes on intermediate nerves. ♃ —Open slopes and alpine meadows, 2,000 to 4,000 m., Montana to eastern British Columbia, south in the mountains to New Mexico and Arizona.

30. Poa sylvéstris A. Gray. (Fig. 144.) Culms tufted, erect, 30 to 100 cm. tall; sheaths glabrous or rarely pubescent, the lower usually antrorsely scabrous; ligule about 1 mm. long; blades lax, 2 to 6 mm. wide; panicle erect, 10 to 20 cm. long, much longer than wide, the slender flexuous branches spreading, usually 3 to 6 at a node, the lower usually reflexed; spikelets 2- to 4-flowered, 3 to 4 mm. long; lemmas 2.5 to 3 mm. long, webbed at base, pubescent on the keel and marginal nerves and more or less pubescent on the internerves. ♃ —Rich, moist, or rocky woods, New York to Wisconsin and Nebraska, south to Florida and Texas.

32. Poa wólfii Scribn. (Fig. 146.) Culms tufted, erect, 40 to 80 cm. tall; sheaths slightly scabrous; blades crowded toward the base of the culms, mostly 1 to 2 mm. wide; panicle drooping, 8 to 15 cm. long, the branches ascending, bearing a few spikelets toward the ends, the lower mostly in pairs; spikelets 2- to 4-flowered, 5 to 6 mm. long; lemmas

3.5 to 4.5 mm. long, acute, webbed at base, pubescent on the keel and marginal nerves, the intermediate nerves distinct. ♃ —Moist woods, Ohio to Minnesota, Nebraska, and Missouri.

33. Poa paucispícula Scribn. and Merr. (Fig. 147.) Culms tufted, leafy, rather lax, 10 to 30 cm. tall, the base often decumbent; blades 1 to 2 mm. wide; panicle lax, few-flowered, 2 to 8 cm. long, the branches in pairs or solitary, naked below; spikelets ovate, purple, 4 to 6 mm. long, 2- to 5-flowered; glumes rather broad, acute, 3 to 4 mm. long; lemmas 3 to 4 mm. long, oblong, obtuse, webbed at base (the web sometimes scant), pubescent on the keel and marginal nerves below. ♃ —Rocky slopes, Alaska to Washington (alpine slopes, Mount Rainier, Mount Baker); Glacier National Park, Mont. More leafy than *P. leptocoma*, more tufted, the panicle branches not so long; spikelets broader.

34. Poa leptocóma Trin. Bog bluegrass. (Fig. 148.) Culms slender, solitary, or few in a tuft, 20 to 50 cm. tall, often decumbent at base; sheaths usually slightly scabrous; ligule acute, the uppermost 3 to 4 mm. long; blades short, lax, mostly 2 to 4 mm. wide; panicle nodding, delicate, few-flowered, the branches capillary, ascending or spreading, subflexuous, the lower mostly in pairs; spikelets narrow, 2- to 4-flowered; glumes narrow, acuminate; lemmas 3.5 to 4.5 mm. long, acuminate, webbed at base, pubescent on the keel and marginal nerves or sometimes nearly glabrous, the intermediate nerves distinct. ♃ —Bogs, Alaska, south in the mountains to northern New Mexico, Colorado, and California (Mount Dana).

35. Poa paludígena Fern. and Wieg. (Fig. 149.) Culms slender, solitary or in small tufts, 15 to 70 cm. tall; sheaths minutely scabrous; ligule short, truncate, the uppermost as much as 1.5 mm. long; blades rather lax, mostly erect, 0.3 to 2 mm. wide; panicle loose and open, mostly 5 to 10 cm. long, the branches long and slender, distant, the lower mostly in twos, spikelet-bearing above the middle; spikelets mostly 4 to 5 mm. long, narrow, 2- to 5-flowered; lemmas 2.5 to 3.5 mm. long, webbed at base with a few long hairs, the keel and lateral nerves pubescent on the lower half or two-thirds, the intermediate nerves glabrous, obscure. ♃ —Bogs and springy places, New York and Pennsylvania to Illinois and Wisconsin.

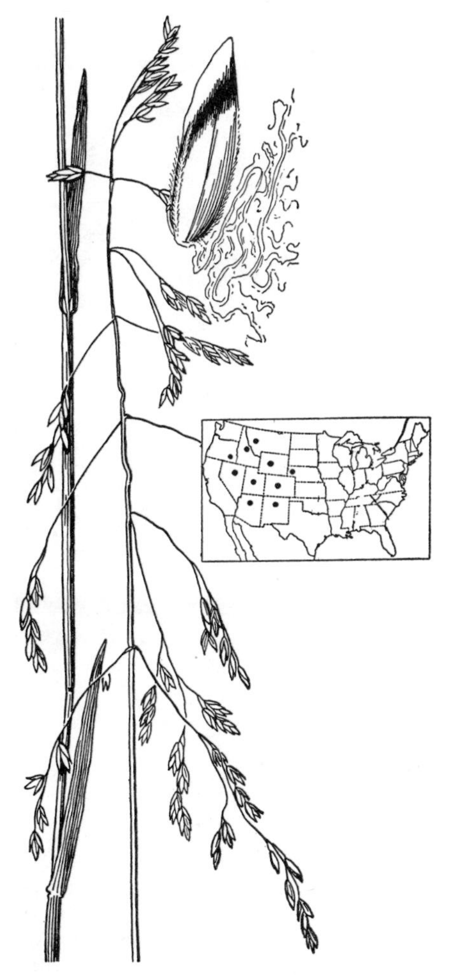

Figure 145.—*Poa reflexa*. Panicle, × 1; floret, × 10. (Clokey 11330, Colo.)

FIGURE 146.—*Poa wolfii*. Panicle, × 1; floret, × 10. (Deam 33821, Ind.)

36. Poa bulbósa L. BULBOUS BLUEGRASS. (Fig. 150.) Culms densely tufted, more or less bulbous at base, 30 to 60 cm. tall; blades flat or loosely involute, 1 to 2 mm. wide; panicle ovoid, mostly 5 to 8 cm. long, somewhat contracted, the branches ascending or appressed, some floriferous to base; spikelets mostly proliferous, the florets converted into bulblets with a dark purple base (about 2 mm. long), the bracts extending into slender green tips 5 to 15 mm. long; unaltered spikelets about 5-flowered, apparently not perfecting seed; lemmas 2.5 mm. long, webbed at base, densely silky on the keel and marginal nerves, the intermediate nerves faint. ♃ —Fields and meadows, New York to North Carolina; North Dakota to British Columbia and California; Utah; Colorado and Oklahoma; introduced from Europe, propagated by bulblets.

37. Poa nemorális L. WOOD BLUEGRASS. (Fig. 151.) Culms tufted, 30 to 70 cm. tall; ligule very short;

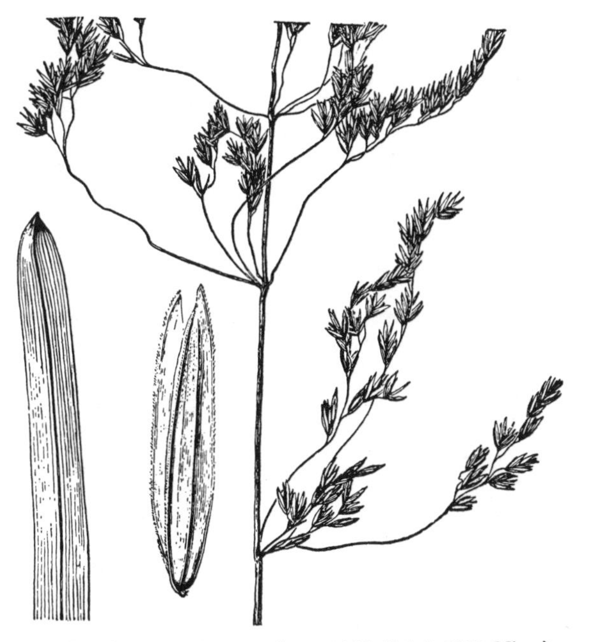

FIGURE 155.—*Poa chaixii*. Panicle, × 1; floret, × 10. (Lakela 2012, Minn.)

Poa cháixii Vill. (Fig. 155.)
s erect or ascending, as much as
tall, soft, flattened, smooth and
g; sheaths compressed, keeled,
us, the lower somewhat
ed; blades mostly 10 to 20 cm.
4 to 8 mm. wide, flat or con-
ate, glabrous with scabrous
s; panicles about 15 cm. long,
ender spreading branches in
of 5, spikelet-bearing above
ddle; spikelets 4 to 6 mm. long,
4-flowered, short-pediceled;
3.5 to 4 mm. long, acute, gla-
or scabrous on the keel, dis-
5-nerved. ♃ —Rich woods,
ota (Hunters Hill near Du-
pparently indigenous); north-
ope.

ae.—Perennials without
eping rhizomes; lemmas not
bbed at base, pubescent on
keel or on the marginal
ves, or both, sometimes also
escent on internerves.

oa fendleriána (Steud.) Va-
TTON GRASS. (Fig. 156.) In-
ly dioecious; culms erect,

FIGURE 156.—*Poa fendleriana*. Panicle, × 1; floret, × 10. (Eggleston 6463, N. Mex.)

tufted, scabrous below the panicle, 30 to 50 cm. tall; sheaths somewhat scabrous; ligule less than 1 mm. long, not noticeable viewed from the side of the sheath; blades mostly basal, folded or involute, firm and stiff; panicle long-exserted, oblong, contracted, pale, 2 to 7 cm. long; spikelets 4- to 6-flowered, about 8 mm. long; glumes broad, 3 to 4 mm. long; lemmas 4 to 5 mm. long, villous on lower part of

blades rather lax, about 2 mm. wide; panicle 4 to 10 cm. long, the branches spreading; spikelets 2- to 5-flowered, 3 to 5 mm. long; glumes narrow, sharply acuminate, about as long as the first floret; lemmas 2 to 3 mm. long, sparsely webbed at base, pubescent on the keel and marginal nerves, the intermediate nerves obscure. ♃ —Labrador to Alaska and British Columbia; occasional in meadows,

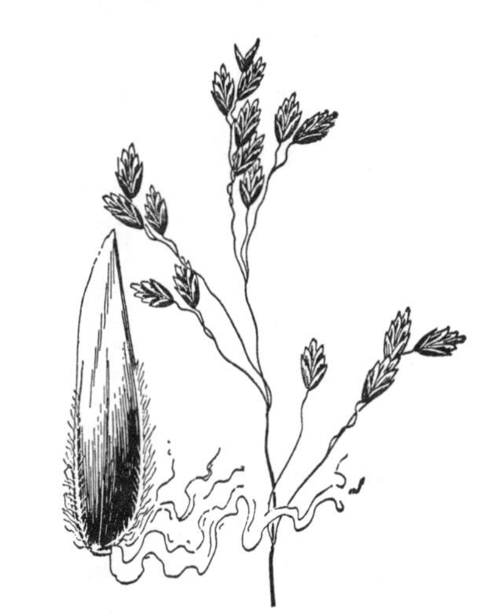

FIGURE 147.—*Poa paucispicula*. Panicle, × 1; floret, × 10. (Hitchcock 11711, Wash.)

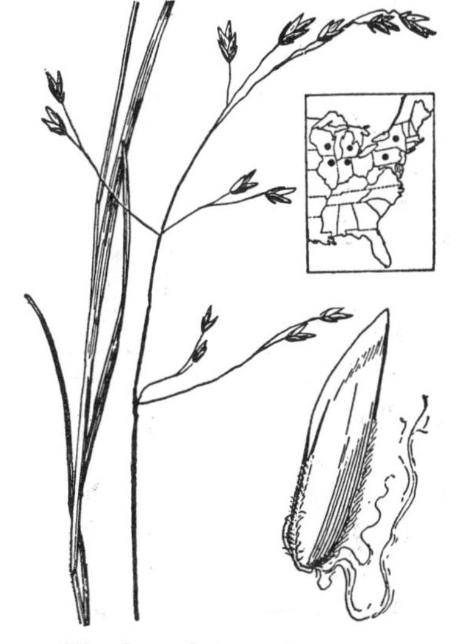

FIGURE 149.—*Poa paludigena*. Panicle, × 1; floret, × 10. (Eames and Wiegand 9250, N. Y.)

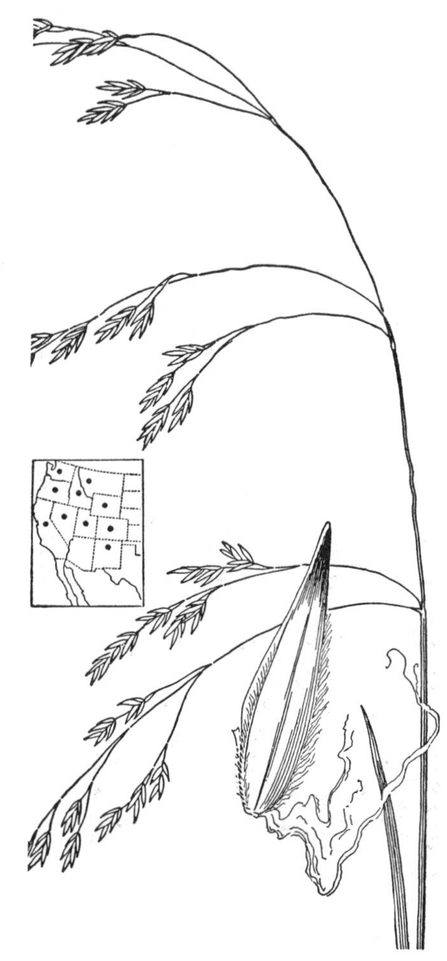

FIGURE 148.—*Poa leptocoma*. Panicle, × 1; floret, × 10. (Arsène and Benedict 15562, N. Mex.)

Maine to Pennsylvania, Michigan, and Minnesota; Wyoming; Washington; Delaware and Virginia; introduced from Europe. Differing from *P. palustris* and *P. interior* in the very short ligule and the narrow acuminate glumes.

38. Poa macrocláda Rydb. (Fig. 152.) Culms 50 to 80 cm. tall, glabrous; ligule prominent, 2 to 3 mm. long; blades 2 to 3 mm. wide; panicle open, 10 to 20 cm. long, pyramidal, the branches spreading, distant, in twos or threes, as much as 8 cm. long, naked on the lower half or

FIGURE 150.—*Poa bulbosa*, × 1. (Henderson 6136, Idaho.)

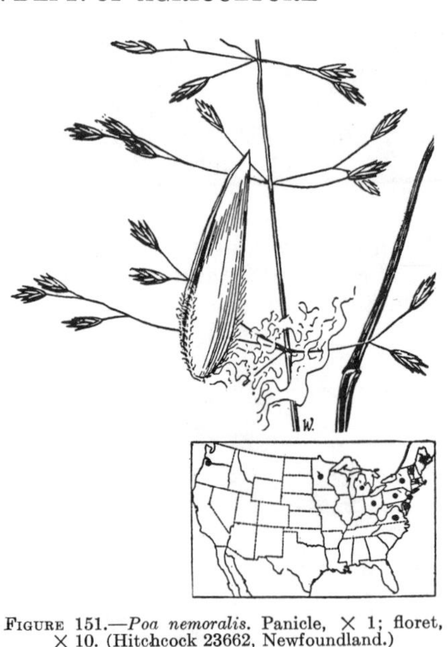

FIGURE 151.—*Poa nemoralis*. Panicle, × 1; floret, × 10. (Hitchcock 23662, Newfoundland.)

two-thirds; spikelets about 6 mm. long, 2- or 3-flowered, purple; glumes 3.5 to 4 mm. long; lemmas 4 to 4.5 mm. long, pubescent on the keel and marginal nerves, the web scant or wanting. ♃ —Moist places, at medium altitudes, Colorado, Montana, and Idaho. A little-known species, allied to *P. palustris*, but with larger spikelets.

39. Poa palústris L. FOWL BLUEGRASS. (Fig. 153.) Culms loosely tufted, glabrous, decumbent at the flattened purplish base, 30 to 150 cm. tall; sheaths keeled, sometimes scaberulous; ligule 3 to 5 mm. long, or only 1 mm. on the innovations; blades 1 to 2 mm. wide; panicle pyramidal or oblong, nodding, yellowish green or purplish, 10 to 30 cm. long, the branches in rather distant fascicles, naked below; spikelets 2- to 4-flowered, about 4 mm. long; glumes lanceolate, acute, shorter than the first floret; lemmas 2.5 to 3 mm. long, usually bronzed at the tip, webbed at base, villous on the keel and marginal nerves. ♃ —Meadows and moist open ground, at low and medium altitudes, Newfoundland and Quebec to Alaska, south to Virginia, Missouri, Nebraska, New Mexico, and California (Sierra Valley, Siskiyou County); Eurasia.

FIGURE 152.—*Poa macroclada*. Panicle, × 1; floret, × 10. (Duplicate type.)

FIGURE 153.—*Poa palustris*. Panicle, × 1; floret, × 10.

40. Poa intérior Rydb. INLAND BLUEGRASS. (Fig. 154.) Culms erect from a usually densely tufted erect base, commonly rather stiff, often scabrous below the panicle, 20 to 50 cm. tall; sheaths slightly keeled or terete; ligule usually less than 1 mm. long; blades 1 to 2 mm. wide; panicle narrowly pyramidal, 5 to 10 cm. long, the branches ascending, the lower 2 or 3 spikelets about 4 mm. long, 2- to 4-flowered; glumes relatively broad, acute to acuminate; lemmas 3 to 3.5 mm. long, webbed at base (the web sometimes scant or obscure), villous on the lower half of the keel and mar-

ginal nerves, the
faint. ♃ —Gr
woods at mediu
not extending
line, Quebec to
Washington, sou
igan, Minnesot
Texas, and Ari

4. Homalopóa
blades fla
a conspic
often spli

FIG

41.
Culm
1 m.
shini
glabr
crowd
long,
duplic
margi
the s
whorl
the mi
2- to
lemma
brous,
tinctly
Minne
luth, a
ern Eu
5. Alpí
cr
we
the
ner
pu
42. P
sey. Mu
complet

keel and marginal nerves, the intermediate nerves obscure; pistillate spikelets with minute stamens, the anthers about 0.2 mm. long. ♃ —Mesas, open dry woods, and rocky hills at medium altitudes, Manitoba to British Columbia, south through western South Dakota (Black Hills), Nebraska, and Idaho to western Texas (Chisos Mountains) and California; northern Mexico. A very small proportion of specimens have been found with well-developed stamens having large anthers, the pistil also developed.

43. Poa longilígula Scribn. and Will. LONGTONGUE MUTTON GRASS. (Fig. 157.) Differing from *P. fendleriana* in the prominent ligule, as much as 5 to 7 mm. long and in the looser, often longer, usually greenish panicle. ♃ —North Dakota to Oregon, south to New Mexico and California.

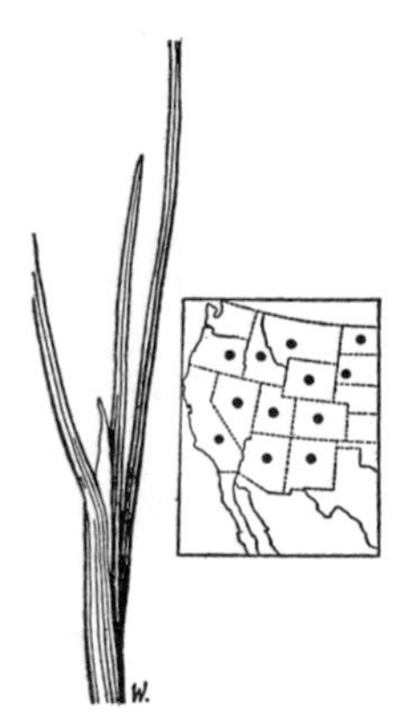

FIGURE 157.—*Poa longiligula.* Ligule, × 1. (Jones 5149, Utah.)

44. Poa autumnális Muhl. ex Ell. (Fig. 158.) Culms in rather large lax tufts, 30 to 60 cm. tall; blades 2 to 3 mm. wide, numerous at base; panicle 10 to 20 cm. long, about as broad, very open, the capillary flexuous branches spreading, bearing a few spikelets near the ends; spikelets 4- to 6-flowered, about 6 mm. long; lemmas oblong, obtusely rounded at the scarious compressed apex, villous on the keel and marginal nerves, pubescent on the internerves below or sometimes

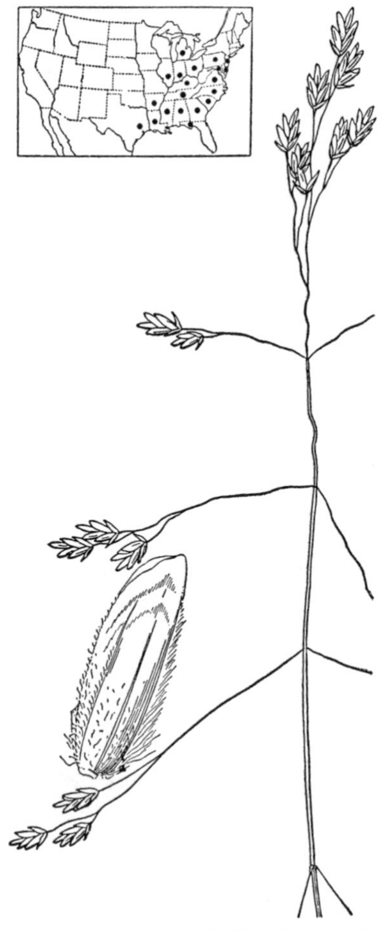

FIGURE 158.—*Poa autumnalis.* Panicle, × 1; floret, × 10. (Curtiss 6787, Ga.)

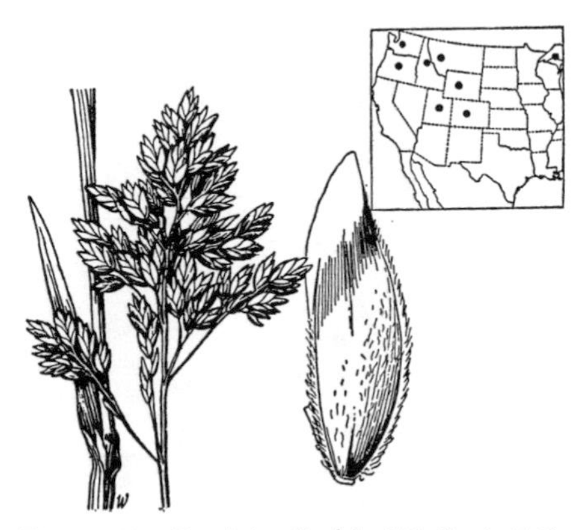

FIGURE 159.—*Poa alpina.* Panicle, × 1; floret, × 10. (Eggleston 11824, Colo.)

nearly to apex. ♃ —Moist woods, New Jersey to Michigan and Illinois, south to Florida and Texas.

45. Poa alpína L. ALPINE BLUEGRASS. (Fig. 159.) Culms erect from a rather thick vertical crown, rather stout, 10 to 30 cm. tall; blades short, 2 to 5 mm. wide, the uppermost about the middle of the culm; panicle ovoid or short-pyramidal, rather compact, 1 to 8 cm. long, the lower branches often reflexed; spikelets broad, purple or purplish; glumes broad, abruptly acute; lemmas 3 to 4 mm. long, strongly villous on the keel and marginal nerves, pubescent on the internerves below, the intermediate nerves faint. ♃ —Mountain meadows, Arctic regions of the Northern Hemisphere, extending south to Quebec, northern Michigan (Keweenaw Point), and the alpine summits of Colorado, Utah, Washington, and Oregon (Wallowa Mountains); Mexico.

46. Poa stenántha Trin. (Fig. 160.) Culms tufted, 30 to 50 cm. tall; ligule prominent, as much as 5 mm. long; blades flat or loosely involute, rather lax, mostly basal, 1 to 2 mm. wide, the uppermost culm leaf below the middle of the culm; panicle nodd ng, 5 to 15 cm. long, the branches in twos or threes, arcuate-drooping, naked below, with a few spikelets at the ends; spikelets 3- to 5-flowered, 6 to 8 mm. long; lemmas about 5 mm. long, pubescent on the lower part of keel and marginal nerves, sparsely pubescent on the internerves below. ♃ —Moist open ground, Alaska, Alberta, and British Columbia, extending into Montana, Colorado (White River Forest), Idaho, Washington (Nooksack River), and Oregon (Crater Lake).

FIGURE 160.—*Poa stenantha*. Panicle, × 1; floret, × 10. (Blankinship, Mont.)

FIGURE 161.—*A*, *Poa glauca*. Panicle, × 1; floret, × 10. (Hitchcock 16053, N. H.) *B*, *P. glaucantha*. Panicle, × 1; floret, × 10. (Butters, Abbe, and Abbe 258, Minn.)

47. Poa glaúca Vahl. (Fig. 161, *A*.) Plants glaucous, in close or loose tufts; culms compressed, stiff, 10 to 30 cm. tall, sometimes taller, naked above, the uppermost leaf usually much below the middle, its ligule about 2 mm. long; blades mostly basal, 3 to 5 cm. long, 1 to 2 mm. wide; panicle 3 to 7 cm. long, narrow, sometimes rather compact, the branches erect or ascending, few-flowered; spikelets mostly 2- or 3-flowered, 5 to 6 mm. long; lemmas 3 to 4 mm. long, strongly pubescent on the lower half of the keel and marginal nerves and often slightly pubescent on the faint intermediate nerves. ♃ —Rocky slopes, Arctic regions south to the alpine summits of New Hampshire; Wisconsin; Minnesota; Colorado. Common in Greenland; Eurasia.

48. Poa glaucántha Gaudin. (Fig. 161, *B*.) Plants mostly glaucous, culms compressed, in tufts, usually 30 to 70 cm. tall, leafy throughout; blades to 12 cm. long; panicle 6 to 16 cm. long, loose, but branches mostly ascending; spikelets 5 to 7 mm. long, 3- to 6-flowered; lemmas pubescent on keel and lateral nerves, sometimes with an obscure web at base. ♃ —Mountain meadows, slopes, and cliffs, Newfoundland to Quebec, Minnesota, Montana, and Wyoming; Europe. Resembles both *Poa nemoralis* and *P. interior*, distinguished from both by the florets without web at base or with very obscure web, from *P. nemoralis* by the flat culms, and from *P. interior* by the more strongly keeled sheaths and larger spikelets. A variable and puzzling species, apparently intermediate between *P. nemoralis* and *P. glauca*. *Poa scopulorum* Butters and Abbe is an unusually slender lax form.

Figure 162.—*Poa fernaldiana*. Panicle, × 1; floret, × 10. (Fernald, Maine.)

49. Poa fernáldiana Nannf. (Fig. 162.) Plants in loose lax bunches; culms weak and slender, 10 to 20 or sometimes 30 cm. tall; ligule truncate, about 1 mm. long; blades mostly basal, lax, mostly about 1 mm. wide; panicle narrow but loose, few-flowered, 2 to 6 cm. long, the branches ascending, naked below; spikelets 2- to 4-flowered, about 5 mm. long; lemmas 3 to 3.5 mm. long, densely villous on the lower half of the keel and marginal nerves, sometimes sparsely webbed at base. (Has been confused with *P. laxa* Haenke, a European species.) ♃ —Rocky slopes, Newfoundland and Quebec to the alpine summits of Maine, New Hampshire, Vermont, and New York. Common on the upper cone of Mount Washington.

Figure 163.—*Poa pattersoni*. Plant, × 1; floret, × 10. (Patterson 154, Colo.)

50. Poa pattersóni Vasey. Patterson bluegrass. (Fig. 163.) Culms loosely tufted with numerous basal leaves, 10 to 20 cm. tall; blades usually folded, rather lax, mostly less than 10 cm. long, about 1 mm. wide; panicle narrow, condensed, purplish,

1 to 4 cm. long; spikelets 2- or 3-flowered, 5 to 6 mm. long; lemmas about 4 mm. long, strongly pubescent on the keel and marginal nerves, short-pubescent on the internerves, sometimes sparsely webbed at base. ♃ —Alpine regions, Montana to Oregon (Mount Hood), Colorado, and Utah.

Figure 164.—*Poa rupicola*. Plant, × 1; floret, × 10. (Swallen 1348, Colo.)

51. Poa rupícola Nash. Timberline bluegrass. (Fig. 164.) Culms densely tufted, erect, rather stiff, often scaberulous below the panicle, 10 to 20 cm. tall; blades short, 1 to 1.5 mm. wide; panicle narrow, purplish, 2 to 4 cm. long, the short branches ascending or appressed; spikelets usually purple, about 3-flowered; lemmas villous below on keel and marginal nerves and some-

Figure 165.—*Poa involuta*. Plant, × 1; floret, × 10. (Swallen 1110, Tex.)

blades rather lax, about 2 mm. wide; panicle 4 to 10 cm. long, the branches spreading; spikelets 2- to 5-flowered, 3 to 5 mm. long; glumes narrow, sharply acuminate, about as long as the first floret; lemmas 2 to 3 mm. long, sparsely webbed at base, pubescent on the keel and marginal nerves, the intermediate nerves obscure. ♃ —Labrador to Alaska and British Columbia; occasional in meadows,

FIGURE 147.—*Poa paucispicula*. Panicle, × 1; floret, × 10. (Hitchcock 11711, Wash.)

FIGURE 149.—*Poa paludigena*. Panicle, × 1; floret, × 10. (Eames and Wiegand 9250, N. Y.)

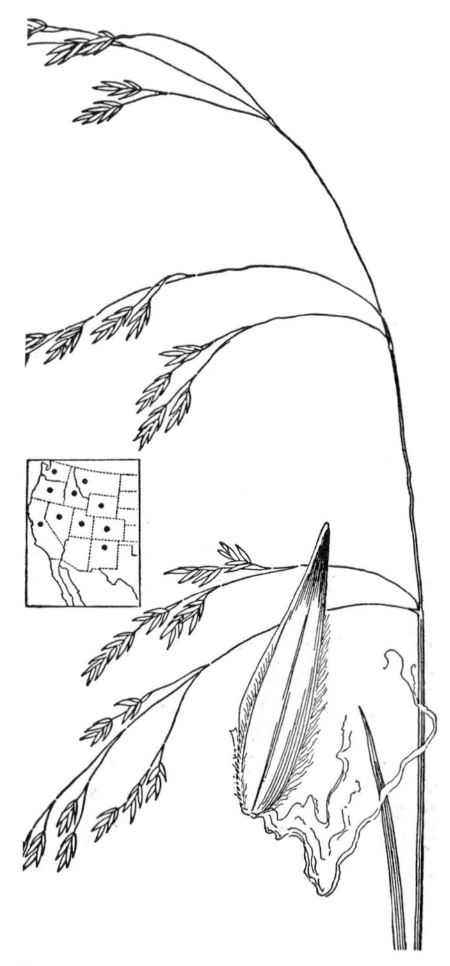

FIGURE 148.—*Poa leptocoma*. Panicle, × 1; floret, × 10. (Arsène and Benedict 15562, N. Mex.)

Maine to Pennsylvania, Michigan, and Minnesota; Wyoming; Washington; Delaware and Virginia; introduced from Europe. Differing from *P. palustris* and *P. interior* in the very short ligule and the narrow acuminate glumes.

38. Poa macrocláda Rydb. (Fig. 152.) Culms 50 to 80 cm. tall, glabrous; ligule prominent, 2 to 3 mm. long; blades 2 to 3 mm. wide; panicle open, 10 to 20 cm. long, pyramidal, the branches spreading, distant, in twos or threes, as much as 8 cm. long, naked on the lower half or

FIGURE 150.—*Poa bulbosa*, × 1. (Henderson 6136, Idaho.)

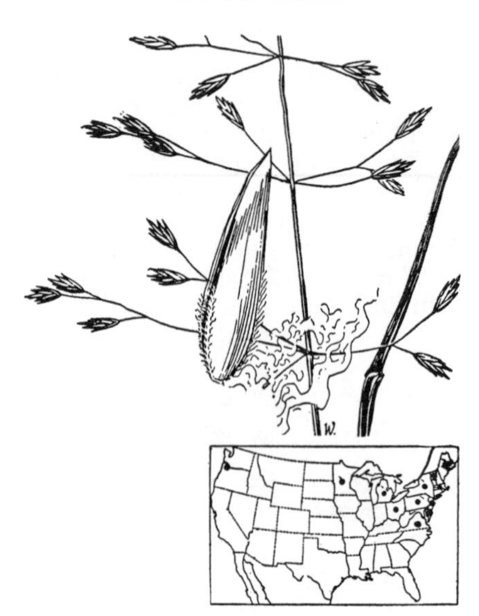

FIGURE 151.—*Poa nemoralis*. Panicle, × 1; floret, × 10. (Hitchcock 23662, Newfoundland.)

two-thirds; spikelets about 6 mm. long, 2- or 3-flowered, purple; glumes 3.5 to 4 mm. long; lemmas 4 to 4.5 mm. long, pubescent on the keel and marginal nerves, the web scant or wanting. ♃ —Moist places, at medium altitudes, Colorado, Montana, and Idaho. A little-known species, allied to *P. palustris*, but with larger spikelets.

39. Poa palústris L. FOWL BLUEGRASS. (Fig. 153.) Culms loosely tufted, glabrous, decumbent at the

FIGURE 152.—*Poa macroclada*. Panicle, × 1; floret, × 10. (Duplicate type.)

flattened purplish base, 30 to 150 cm. tall; sheaths keeled, sometimes scaberulous; ligule 3 to 5 mm. long, or only 1 mm. on the innovations; blades 1 to 2 mm. wide; panicle pyramidal or oblong, nodding, yellowish green or purplish, 10 to 30 cm. long, the branches in rather distant fascicles, naked below; spikelets 2- to 4-flowered, about 4 mm. long; glumes lanceolate, acute, shorter than the first floret; lemmas 2.5 to 3 mm. long, usually bronzed at the tip, webbed at base, villous on the keel and marginal nerves. ♃ —Meadows and moist open ground, at low and medium altitudes, Newfoundland and Quebec to Alaska, south to Virginia, Missouri, Nebraska, New Mexico, and California (Sierra Valley, Siskiyou County); Eurasia.

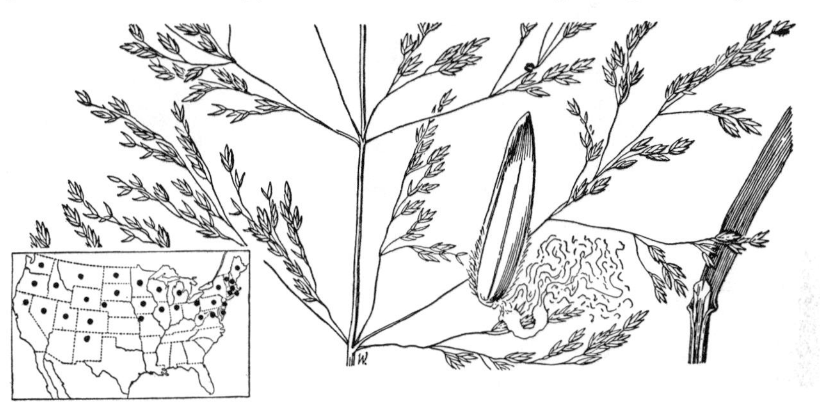

FIGURE 153.—*Poa palustris*. Panicle, × 1; floret, × 10. (Suksdorf 7022, Wash.)

40. Poa intérior Rydb. INLAND BLUEGRASS. (Fig. 154.) Culms erect from a usually densely tufted erect base, commonly rather stiff, often scabrous below the panicle, 20 to 50 cm. tall; sheaths slightly keeled or terete; ligule usually less than 1 mm. long; blades 1 to 2 mm. wide; panicle narrowly pyramidal, 5 to 10 cm. long, the branches ascending, the lower 2 or 3 spikelets about 4 mm. long, 2- to 4-flowered; glumes relatively broad, acute to acuminate; lemmas 3 to 3.5 mm. long, webbed at base (the web sometimes scant or obscure), villous on the lower half of the keel and marginal nerves, the intermediate nerves faint. ♃ —Grassy slopes and open woods at medium altitudes, usually not extending much above timber line, Quebec to British Columbia and Washington, south to Vermont, Michigan, Minnesota, western Nebraska, Texas, and Arizona.

FIGURE 154.—*Poa interior*. Panicle, × 1; floret, × 10. (Clements 297, Colo.)

4. Homalopóae.—Culms flattened; blades flat or conduplicate, with a conspicuous boat-shaped tip, often splitting at the apex.

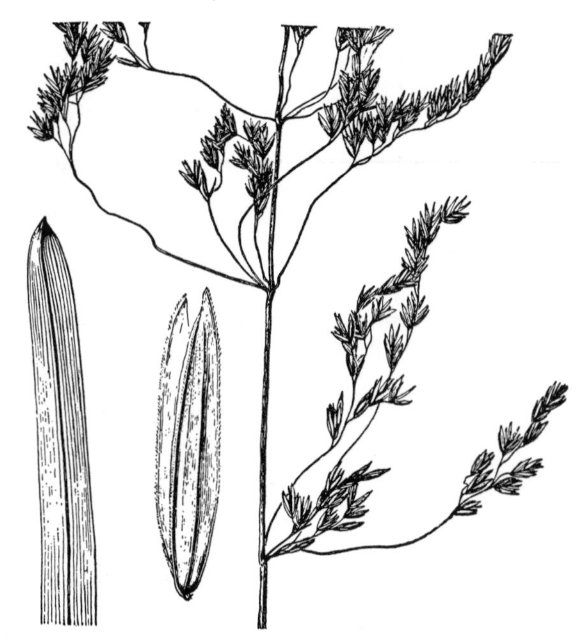

FIGURE 155.—*Poa chaixii*. Panicle, × 1; floret, × 10. (Lakela 2012, Minn.)

41. Poa cháixii Vill. (Fig. 155.) Culms erect or ascending, as much as 1 m. tall, soft, flattened, smooth and shining; sheaths compressed, keeled, glabrous, the lower somewhat crowded; blades mostly 10 to 20 cm. long, 4 to 8 mm. wide, flat or conduplicate, glabrous with scabrous margins; panicles about 15 cm. long, the slender spreading branches in whorls of 5, spikelet-bearing above the middle; spikelets 4 to 6 mm. long, 2- to 4-flowered, short-pediceled; lemmas 3.5 to 4 mm. long, acute, glabrous, or scabrous on the keel, distinctly 5-nerved. ♃ —Rich woods, Minnesota (Hunters Hill near Duluth, apparently indigenous); northern Europe.

5. Alpínae.—Perennials without creeping rhizomes; lemmas not webbed at base, pubescent on the keel or on the marginal nerves, or both, sometimes also pubescent on internerves.

42. Poa fendleriána (Steud.) Vasey. MUTTON GRASS. (Fig. 156.) Incompletely dioecious; culms erect, tufted, scabrous below the panicle, 30 to 50 cm. tall; sheaths somewhat scabrous; ligule less than 1 mm. long, not noticeable viewed from the side of the sheath; blades mostly basal, folded or involute, firm and stiff; panicle long-exserted, oblong, contracted, pale, 2 to 7 cm. long; spikelets 4- to 6-flowered, about 8 mm. long; glumes broad, 3 to 4 mm. long; lemmas 4 to 5 mm. long, villous on lower part of

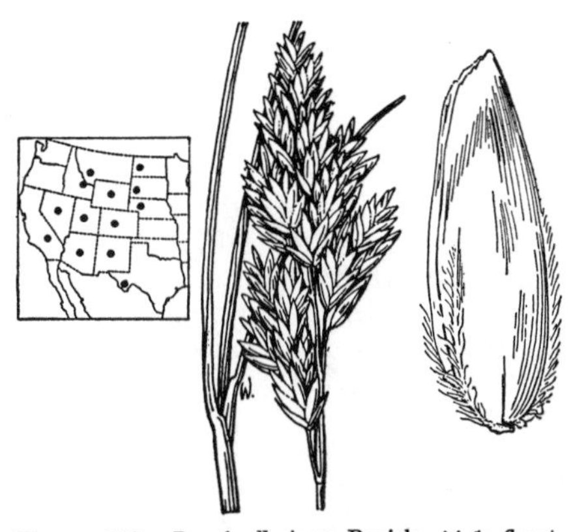

FIGURE 156.—*Poa fendleriana*. Panicle, × 1; floret, × 10. (Eggleston 6463, N. Mex.)

keel and marginal nerves, the intermediate nerves obscure; pistillate spikelets with minute stamens, the anthers about 0.2 mm. long. ♃ —Mesas, open dry woods, and rocky hills at medium altitudes, Manitoba to British Columbia, south through western South Dakota (Black Hills), Nebraska, and Idaho to western Texas (Chisos Mountains) and California; northern Mexico. A very small proportion of specimens have been found with well-developed stamens having large anthers, the pistil also developed.

43. Poa longilígula Scribn. and Will. LONGTONGUE MUTTON GRASS. (Fig. 157.) Differing from *P. fendleriana* in the prominent ligule, as much as 5 to 7 mm. long and in the looser, often longer, usually greenish panicle. ♃ —North Dakota to Oregon, south to New Mexico and California.

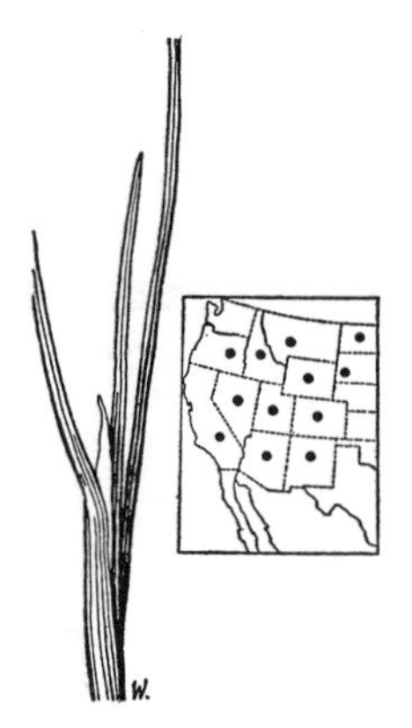

FIGURE 157.—*Poa longiligula*. Ligule, × 1. (Jones 5149, Utah.)

44. Poa autumnális Muhl. ex Ell. (Fig. 158.) Culms in rather large lax tufts, 30 to 60 cm. tall; blades 2 to 3 mm. wide, numerous at base; panicle 10 to 20 cm. long, about as broad, very open, the capillary flexuous branches spreading, bearing a few spikelets near the ends; spikelets 4- to 6-flowered, about 6 mm. long; lemmas oblong, obtusely rounded at the scarious compressed apex, villous on the keel and marginal nerves, pubescent on the internerves below or sometimes

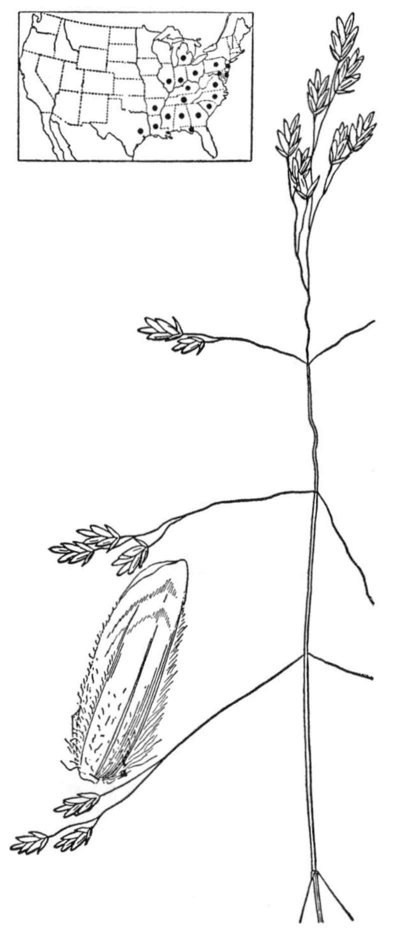

FIGURE 158.—*Poa autumnalis*. Panicle, × 1; floret, × 10. (Curtiss 6787, Ga.)

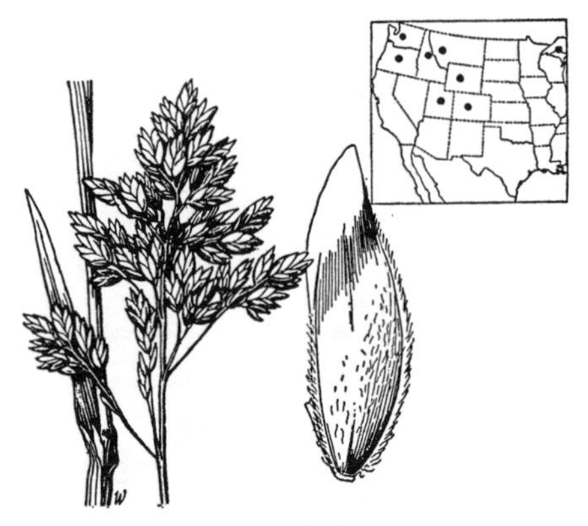

FIGURE 159.—*Poa alpina*. Panicle, × 1; floret, × 10. (Eggleston 11824, Colo.)

nearly to apex. ♃ —Moist woods, New Jersey to Michigan and Illinois, south to Florida and Texas.

45. Poa alpína L. ALPINE BLUEGRASS. (Fig. 159.) Culms erect from a rather thick vertical crown, rather stout, 10 to 30 cm. tall; blades short, 2 to 5 mm. wide, the uppermost about the middle of the culm; panicle ovoid or short-pyramidal, rather compact, 1 to 8 cm. long, the lower branches often reflexed; spikelets broad, purple or purplish; glumes broad, abruptly acute; lemmas 3 to 4 mm. long, strongly villous on the keel and marginal nerves, pubescent on the internerves below, the intermediate nerves faint. ♃ —Mountain meadows, Arctic regions of the Northern Hemisphere, extending south to Quebec, northern Michigan (Keweenaw Point), and the alpine summits of Colorado, Utah, Washington, and Oregon (Wallowa Mountains); Mexico.

46. Poa stenántha Trin. (Fig. 160.) Culms tufted, 30 to 50 cm. tall; ligule prominent, as much as 5 mm. long; blades flat or loosely involute, rather lax, mostly basal, 1 to 2 mm. wide, the uppermost culm leaf below the middle of the culm; panicle nodd ng, 5 to 15 cm. long, the branches in twos or threes, arcuate-drooping, naked below, with a few spikelets at the ends; spikelets 3- to 5-flowered, 6 to 8 mm. long; lemmas about 5 mm. long, pubescent on the lower part of keel and marginal nerves, sparsely pubescent on the internerves below. ♃ —Moist open ground, Alaska, Alberta, and British Columbia, extending into Montana, Colorado (White River Forest), Idaho, Washington (Nooksack River), and Oregon (Crater Lake).

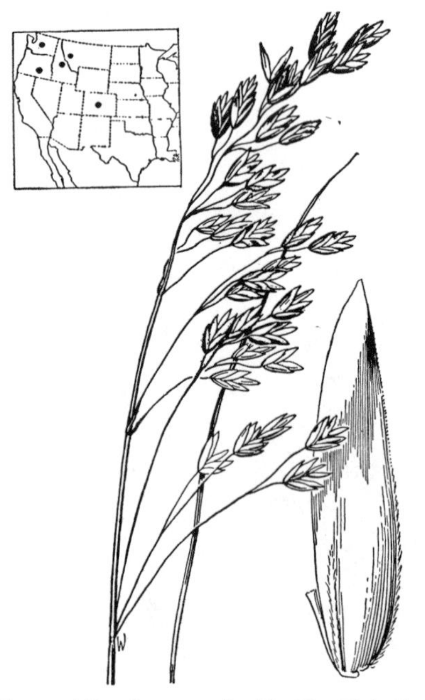

FIGURE 160.—*Poa stenantha.* Panicle, × 1; floret, × 10. (Blankinship, Mont.)

FIGURE 161.—*A*, *Poa glauca.* Panicle, × 1; floret, × 10. (Hitchcock 16053, N. H.) *B*, *P. glaucantha.* Panicle, × 1; floret, × 10. (Butters, Abbe, and Abbe 258, Minn.)

47. Poa glaúca Vahl. (Fig. 161, *A.*) Plants glaucous, in close or loose tufts; culms compressed, stiff, 10 to 30 cm. tall, sometimes taller, naked above, the uppermost leaf usually much below the middle, its ligule about 2 mm. long; blades mostly basal, 3 to 5 cm. long, 1 to 2 mm. wide; panicle 3 to 7 cm. long, narrow, sometimes rather compact, the branches erect or ascending, few-flowered; spikelets mostly 2- or 3-flowered, 5 to 6 mm. long; lemmas 3 to 4 mm. long, strongly pubescent on the lower half of the keel and marginal nerves and often slightly pubescent on the faint intermediate nerves. ♃ —Rocky slopes, Arctic regions south to the alpine summits of New Hampshire; Wisconsin; Minnesota; Colorado. Common in Greenland; Eurasia.

48. Poa glaucántha Gaudin. (Fig. 161, *B.*) Plants mostly glaucous, culms compressed, in tufts, usually 30 to 70 cm. tall, leafy throughout; blades to 12 cm. long; panicle 6 to 16 cm. long, loose, but branches mostly ascending; spikelets 5 to 7 mm. long, 3- to 6-flowered; lemmas pubescent on keel and lateral nerves, sometimes with an obscure web at base. ♃ —Mountain meadows, slopes, and cliffs, Newfoundland to Quebec, Minnesota, Montana, and Wyoming; Europe. Resembles both *Poa nemoralis* and *P. interior*, distinguished from both by the florets without web at base or with very obscure web, from *P. nemoralis* by the flat culms, and from *P. interior* by the more strongly keeled sheaths and larger spikelets. A variable and puzzling species, apparently intermediate between *P. nemoralis* and *P. glauca*. *Poa scopulorum* Butters and Abbe is an unusually slender lax form.

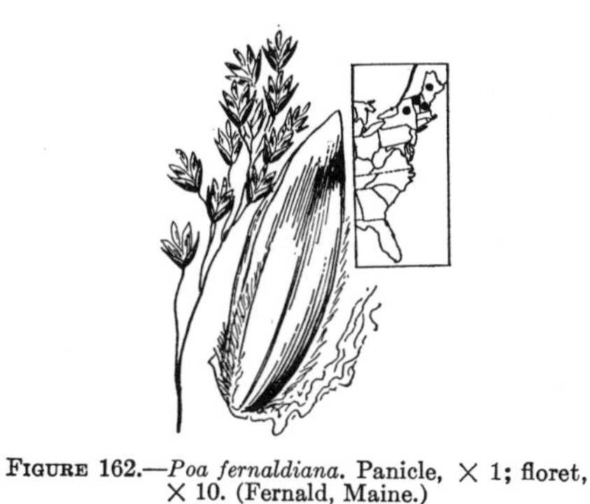

FIGURE 162.—*Poa fernaldiana*. Panicle, × 1; floret, × 10. (Fernald, Maine.)

49. Poa fernáldiana Nannf. (Fig. 162.) Plants in loose lax bunches; culms weak and slender, 10 to 20 or sometimes 30 cm. tall; ligule truncate, about 1 mm. long; blades mostly basal, lax, mostly about 1 mm. wide; panicle narrow but loose, few-flowered, 2 to 6 cm. long, the branches ascending, naked below; spikelets 2- to 4-flowered, about 5 mm. long; lemmas 3 to 3.5 mm. long, densely villous on the lower half of the keel and marginal nerves, sometimes sparsely webbed at base. (Has been confused with *P. laxa* Haenke, a European species.) ♃ —Rocky slopes, Newfoundland and Quebec to the alpine summits of Maine, New Hampshire, Vermont, and New York. Common on the upper cone of Mount Washington.

FIGURE 163.—*Poa pattersoni*. Plant, × 1; floret, × 10. (Patterson 154, Colo.)

50. Poa pattersóni Vasey. PATTERSON BLUEGRASS. (Fig. 163.) Culms loosely tufted with numerous basal leaves, 10 to 20 cm. tall; blades usually folded, rather lax, mostly less than 10 cm. long, about 1 mm. wide; panicle narrow, condensed, purplish,

1 to 4 cm. long; spikelets 2- or 3-flowered, 5 to 6 mm. long; lemmas about 4 mm. long, strongly pubescent on the keel and marginal nerves, short-pubescent on the internerves, sometimes sparsely webbed at base. ♃ —Alpine regions, Montana to Oregon (Mount Hood), Colorado, and Utah.

51. Poa rupícola Nash. TIMBERLINE BLUEGRASS. (Fig. 164.) Culms densely tufted, erect, rather stiff, often scaberulous below the panicle, 10 to 20 cm. tall; blades short, 1 to 1.5 mm. wide; panicle narrow, purplish, 2 to 4 cm. long, the short branches ascending or appressed; spikelets usually purple, about 3-flowered; lemmas villous below on keel and marginal nerves and some-

FIGURE 164.—*Poa rupicola.* Plant, × 1; floret, × 10. (Swallen 1348, Colo.)

FIGURE 165.—*Poa involuta.* Plant, × 1; floret, × 10. (Swallen 1110, Tex.)

times pubescent on the internerves below. ♃ —Rocky slopes, British Columbia, south in the mountains, at high altitudes, South Dakota (Black Hills) and Montana to Oregon (Mount Hood and Wallowa Mountains); New Mexico, and California (Mono Pass, Sheep Mountain). Small specimens of *P. interior*, which resemble this, differ in having a small web at the base of the lemma.

6. Épiles.—Perennials without rhizomes; lemmas not webbed at base, glabrous or scabrous (minutely pubescent in *P. unilateralis*).

52. Poa involúta Hitchc. (Fig. 165.) In dense pale tufts; culms slender, 30 to 40 cm. tall; ligule very short; blades involute, slender, 15 to 25 cm. long, glabrous or slightly scabrous; panicle open, 10 to 15 cm. long, the branches in pairs, few-flowered near the ends; spikelets mostly 3- or 4-flowered, 5 to 6 mm. long; lemmas 3 to 4 mm. long, scabrous. ♃ —Known only from the Chisos Mountains, Tex.

53. Poa cusíckii Vasey. CUSICK BLUEGRASS. (Fig. 166.) Culms in dense often large tufts, erect, 20 to 60 cm. tall; ligule very short; blades filiform, erect, scabrous, mostly basal; panicle usually pale, tawny, or purple-tinged, narrow, oblong, contracted or somewhat open at anthesis, 3 to 8 cm. long; spikelets 7 to 9 mm. long; lemmas 4.5 to 6 mm. long, smooth or scabrous. ♃ —Dry or rocky slopes at medium and high altitudes, Alberta to British Columbia, south to North Dakota, Colorado, and the central Sierras of California. A form with elongate blades and laxer panicle has been differentiated as *P. filifolia* Vasey; Idaho and Washington.

FIGURE 166.—*Poa cusickii.* Panicle, × 1; floret, × 10. (Howell 183, Oreg.)

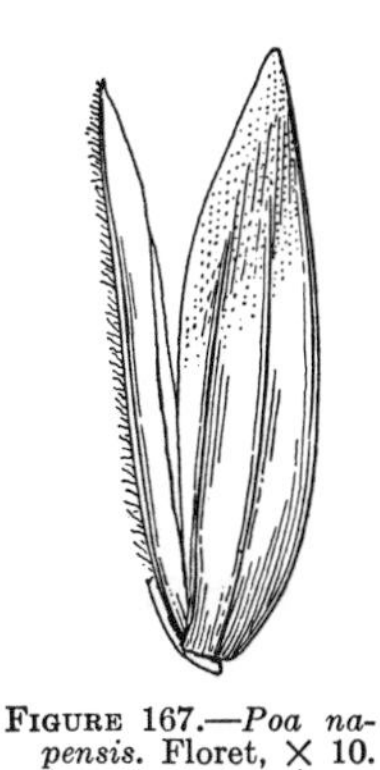

FIGURE 167.—*Poa napensis.* Floret, × 10. (Duplicate type.)

FIGURE 168.—*Poa unilateralis.* Panicle, × 1; floret, × 10. (Chase 5653, Calif.)

54. Poa napénsis Beetle. (Fig. 167.) Resembling *P. cusickii;* ligule about 1 mm. long, decurrent in young leaves; basal blades filiform, the culm blades 1.5 to 2.5 mm. wide; panicle as in *P. cusickii*, the spikelets slightly smaller; glumes 3 and 3.5 mm. long; lemmas about 4 mm. long, slightly to rather strongly scabrous. ♃ —Known only from Myrtledale Hot Springs, Napa County, Calif.

55. Poa unilaterális Scribn. (Fig. 168.) Culms in dense tufts, 10 to 40 cm. tall, sometimes decumbent at base; sheaths tawny, papery; blades flat or folded, shorter than the culms; panicle oblong, dense and spikelike or somewhat interrupted below, 2 to 6 cm. long; spikelets 6 to 8 mm. long; glumes broad, acute; lemmas 3 to 4 mm. long, glabrous except for a few short hairs on the nerves below. ♃ (*P. pachypholis* Piper.)—Cliffs, bluffs, and rocky meadows near the seashore, Washington (Ilwaco), Oregon, and California (Humboldt Bay to Monterey).

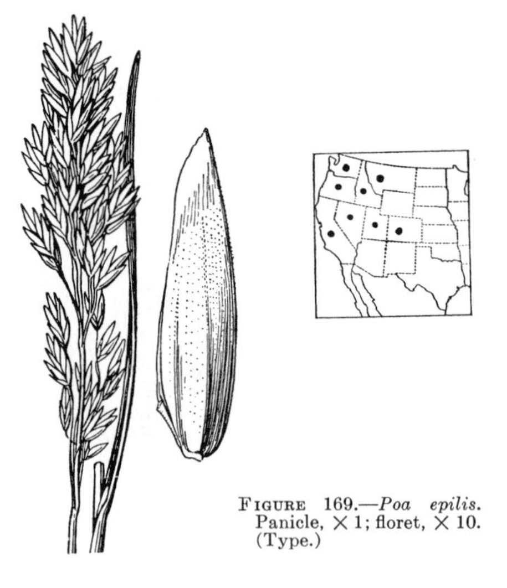

FIGURE 169.—*Poa epilis*. Panicle, × 1; floret, × 10. (Type.)

56. Poa épilis Scribn. SKYLINE BLUEGRASS. (Fig. 169.) Culms compressed, erect in rather loose to dense tufts, 20 to 40 cm. tall; ligule about 3 mm. long; blades of the culm about 3, flat, 3 to 6 cm. long, 2 to 3 mm. wide, of the innovations narrow, longer and usually folded or involute; panicle usually condensed, ovoid, 2 to 6 cm. long, long-exserted, usually purple, the lower branches naked below, ascending or appressed; spikelets 3-flowered, about 5 mm. long; lemmas 4 to 5 or even 6 mm. long, glabrous or minutely scabrous. ♃ —Mountain meadows, mostly above timber line, Alberta to British Columbia, south to Colorado and California.

57. Poa vaseyóchloa Scribn. (Fig. 170.) In small dense soft lax tufts; culms erect, 10 to 20 cm. tall; ligule acute, about 3 mm. long; blades lax, mostly folded or involute, in a basal tuft, mostly less than 5 cm. long, with one or two short ones on the culm, narrow or filiform; panicle ovate, 2 to 4 cm. long, few-flowered, open, the slender branches spreading, bearing 1 or 2 spikelets; spikelets purple, 3- to 6-flowered; glumes 2 to 3 mm. long, rather broad; lemmas smooth or minutely scabrous, 3 mm. long. ♃ —Rocky slopes, Cascade Mountains of Washington and Oregon in the vicinity of Columbia River, and the Wallowa Mountains of Oregon.

FIGURE 170.—*Poa vaseyochloa*. Plant, × 1; floret, × 10. (Type.)

58. Poa prínglei Scribn. (Fig. 171.) Densely tufted; culms 10 to 20 cm. tall; lower sheaths loose, papery; blades mostly basal, involute, mostly 2 to 5 cm. long, sometimes longer, glabrous on the exposed surface, puberulent on inner surface; panicle narrow, condensed, usually pale or silvery, few- to several-flowered, 1 to 5 cm. long; spikelets 3- to 5-flowered, 6 to 8 mm. long; glumes equal, broad, 4 to 5 or rarely 7 mm. long; lemmas 5 to 6, rarely to 8 mm. long, smooth or scabrous. ♃ —Rocky alpine summits, Montana to Washington, south to Nevada (Mount Rose) and California.

Figure 171.—*Poa pringlei*. Plant, × 1; floret, × 10. (Henderson 3080, Idaho.)

59. Poa lettermáni Vasey. (Fig. 172.) In low lax tufts; culms mostly less than 10 cm. tall, usually scarcely exceeding the blades; ligule 1 to 2 mm. long; blades lax, usually not more than 1 mm. wide; panicle narrow, contracted, 1 to 3 cm. long; spikelets 3- or 4-flowered, 4 to 5 mm. long; glumes equal, somewhat acuminate, about as long as the first and second florets; lemmas erose at summit, 2.5 to 3 mm. long. ♃ —Rocky alpine summits, British Columbia, Washington, Wyoming, and Colorado to California.

Figure 172.—*Poa lettermani*. Plant, × 1; floret, × 10. (Letterman, Colo.)

60. Poa montevánsi Kelso. (Fig. 173.) Similar to *P. lettermani*, the culms (in type specimen) only 4.5 cm. tall, differing chiefly in the spikelets, with scabrous glumes and lemmas, the lemmas more acute and scarcely erose. ♃ —Known only from Mount Evans, 14,260 feet altitude, Colo.

Figure 173.—*Poa montevansi*. Plant, × 1; spikelet and floret, × 10. (Type.)

61. Poa leibérgii Scribn. Leiberg bluegrass. (Fig. 174.) Usually densely tufted; culms 5 to 30 cm. tall, erect; ligule 1 to 2 mm. long; blades mostly basal, firm, involute, usually less than 10 cm. long; panicle narrow,

Figure 174.—*Poa leibergii*. Plant, × 1; floret, × 10 (Type.)

2 to 5 cm. long, often purple, the branches short, appressed or ascending; spikelets 2- to 4-flowered, 4 to 6 mm. long; lemmas 3 to 4 mm. long, smooth or scaberulous. ♃ —Alpine meadows and sterile gravelly alpine flats, Idaho, eastern Oregon, and the Sierras of California.

7. Scabréllae.—Perennials, without rhizomes, tufted, with numerous basal leaves; spikelets little compressed, narrow, much longer than wide; lemmas convex, crisp-puberulent on the back towards the base, the keels obscure, the marginal and intermediate nerves usually faint. The whole group of Scabrellae is made up of closely related species which appear to intergrade.

62. Poa scabrélla (Thurb.) Benth. ex Vasey. PINE BLUEGRASS. (Fig. 175.) Culms erect, 50 to 100 cm. tall, usually scabrous, at least below the panicle; sheaths scaberulous; ligule 3 to 5 mm. long; blades mostly basal, 1 to 2 mm. wide, lax, more or less scabrous; panicle narrow, usually contracted, sometimes rather open at base, 5 to 12 cm. long; spikelets 6 to 10 mm. long; glumes 3 mm. long, scabrous; lemmas 4 to 5 mm. long, crisp-puberulent on the back toward base. ♃ —Meadows, open woods, rocks, and hills, at low and medium altitudes, western Montana and Colorado to Washington and California; Baja California. A form like *P. scabrella* in other respects but with smooth lemmas has been differentiated as *P. limosa* Scribn. and Will.—California (Mono Lake and Truckee).

63. Poa gracíllima Vasey. PACIFIC BLUEGRASS. (Fig. 176.) Culms rather loosely tufted, 30 to 60 cm. tall, usually decumbent at base; ligule 2 to 5 mm. long, shorter on the innovations; blades flat or folded, lax, from filiform to 1.5 mm. wide; panicle pyramidal, loose, rather open, 5 to 10 cm. long, the branches in whorls, the lower in twos to sixes, spreading or sometimes reflexed, naked below; spikelets 4 to 6 mm. long; second glume 3 to 4 mm. long; lemmas minutely scabrous, crisp-pubescent near base, especially on the nerves. ♃ —Cliffs and rocky slopes, Alberta to Alaska, south to Colorado and the southern Sierras of California. *Poa tenerrima* Scribn. is a form with open few-flowered panicles; southern Coast Ranges, California; *P. multnomae* Piper is a loose lax form in which the ligules on the innovations are short and truncate; wet cliffs, Multnomah Falls, Oreg.

64. Poa secúnda Presl. SANDBERG BLUEGRASS. (Fig. 177.) Culms erect from a dense, often extensive, tuft of short basal foliage, commonly not more than 30 cm., but sometimes up to 60 cm. tall; ligule acute, rather prominent; blades rather short, soft, flat, folded, or involute; panicle narrow, 2 to 10 cm. long, the branches short, appressed, or somewhat spreading in anthesis; spikelets about as in *P. gracillima.* ♃ (*P. sandbergii* Vasey.)—Plains, dry woods, rocky slopes, at medium and upper altitudes, but not strictly alpine, North Dakota to Yukon Territory, south to Nebraska, New Mexico, and southern California; Chile.

65. Poa cánbyi (Scribn.) Piper. CANBY BLUEGRASS. (Fig. 178.) Green or glaucous; culms 50 to 120 cm. tall; ligule 2 to 5 mm. long; blades flat or folded; panicle narrow, compact or rather loose, 10 to 15 cm. long, sometimes as much as 20 cm., the branches short, appressed; spikelets 3- to 5-flowered; lemmas more or less crisp-pubescent on lower part of back. ♃ (*P. lucida* Vasey; *P. laevigata* Scribn.)—Sandy or dry ground, Michigan (Isle Royale) and Minnesota to Yukon Territory, south to Colorado and eastern Washington to northern California; Quebec. *Poa lucida* has a slender but somewhat loose pale or shining panicle; *P. canbyi* has a denser, compact, dull green panicle, but the two forms grade into each other. *Poa lucida* is

FIGURE 175.—*Poa scabrella*. Plant, × ½; spikelet, × 5; floret, × 10. (Chase 5697, Calif.)

more common in Colorado and Wyoming; *P. canbyi* more common in Montana. The pubescence on the lemma may be obvious or obscure.

rather stiff; panicle narrow, 10 to 15 cm. long, pale, rather loose, the branches short-appressed; spikelets 3- to 5-flowered, 6 to 8 mm. long; glumes narrow, the second about as long as the lowest floret; lemmas 4 to 5 mm. long, rather obtuse at the scarious tip. ♃ —Low meadows and wet places, Montana to eastern Washington and Yukon Territory, south to Colorado, Arizona, and the Sierras and San Bernardino Mountains, California; on wool waste in Maine (North Berwick).

FIGURE 176.—*Poa gracillima*. Plant, × 1; floret, × 10. (Sandberg and Leiberg 747, Wash.)

FIGURE 177.—*Poa secunda*. Plant, × 1; floret, × 10. (Hitchcock 23202, Wyo.)

7. Nevadénses.—Perennials, without rhizomes, tufted; spikelets little compressed, narrow, much longer than wide; lemmas convex on the back, glabrous or minutely scabrous, not crisp-puberulent; keels obscure, marginal and intermediate nerves usually faint.

66. Poa nevadénsis Vasey ex Scribn. NEVADA BLUEGRASS. (Fig. 179.) Culms erect, 50 to 100 cm. tall; sheaths scabrous, sometimes only slightly so; ligule about 4 mm. long, shorter on the innovations, decurrent; blades usually elongate, narrow, involute, sometimes almost capillary,

FIGURE 178.—*Poa canbyi*. Panicle, × 1; floret, × 10. (Williams 2787, Wyo.)

67. Poa curtifólia Scribn. (Fig. 180.) Culms several in a tuft from firm branched crowns, 10 to 20 cm. tall; ligule prominent, the uppermost as much as 5 mm. long; blades short, the lower 1.5 to 2 cm. long, 2 to 3 mm. wide, the upper successively smaller, the uppermost near the panicle, much reduced; panicle narrow, 3 to 6 cm. long; spikelets about 3-flowered; glumes equal, 5 mm. long, the first acuminate, the second broad, rather

FIGURE 180.—*Poa curtifolia.* Panicle, × 1; floret, × 10. (Duplicate type.)

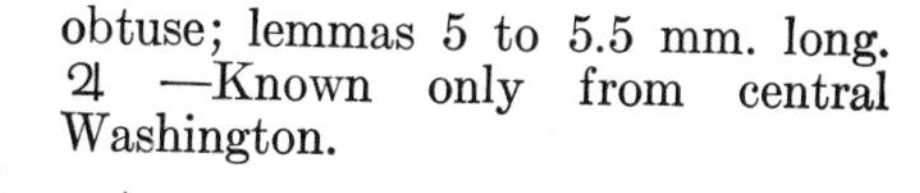

obtuse; lemmas 5 to 5.5 mm. long. ♃ —Known only from central Washington.

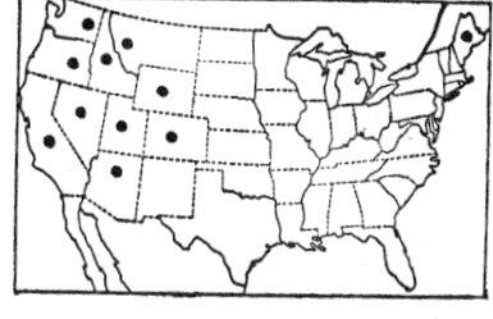

FIGURE 179.—*Poa nevadensis.* Panicle, × 1; floret, × 10. (Parish Bros. 1543, Calif.)

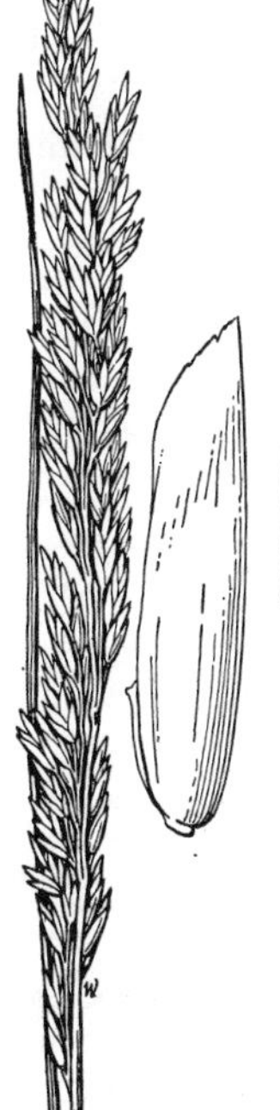

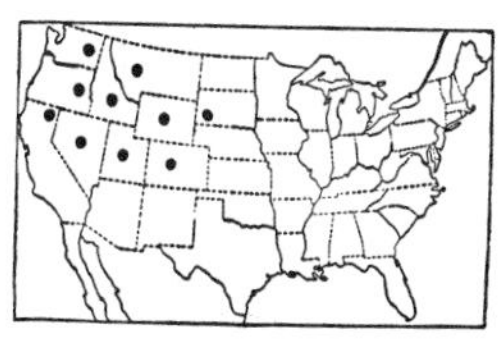

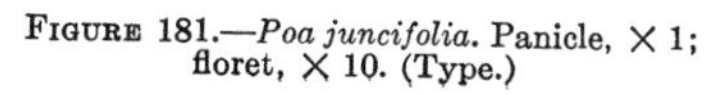

FIGURE 181.—*Poa juncifolia.* Panicle, × 1; floret, × 10. (Type.)

68. Poa juncifólia Scribn. Alkali bluegrass. (Fig. 181.) Pale; culms erect, 50 to 100 cm. tall; ligules short, those of the innovations not visible from the sides; blades involute, smooth, rather stiff; panicle narrow, 10 to 20 cm. long, the branches appressed; spikelets 3- to 6-flowered, 7 to 10 mm. long; glumes about equal; lemmas about 4 mm. long. ♃ (*P. brachyglossa* Piper.)—Alkaline meadows, Montana to British Columbia, south to South Dakota, Colorado, and east of the Cascades to northeastern California.

69. Poa ámpla Merr. Big bluegrass. (Fig. 182.) Green or glaucous; culms 80 to 120 cm. tall; sheaths smooth, rarely scaberulous; ligule short, rounded; blades 1 to 3 mm. wide; panicle narrow, 10 to 15 cm. long, usually rather dense; spikelets 4- to 7-flowered, 8 to 10 mm. long; lemmas 4 to 6 mm. long. ♃ —Meadows and moist open ground or dry or rocky slopes, North Dakota to Yukon Territory, south to Nebraska, New Mexico, and California. The typical form is robust and more or less glaucous; this grades into a smaller green form, more common in the eastern part of the range (*P. confusa* Rydb.). Occasional specimens of the typical form have short rhizomes.

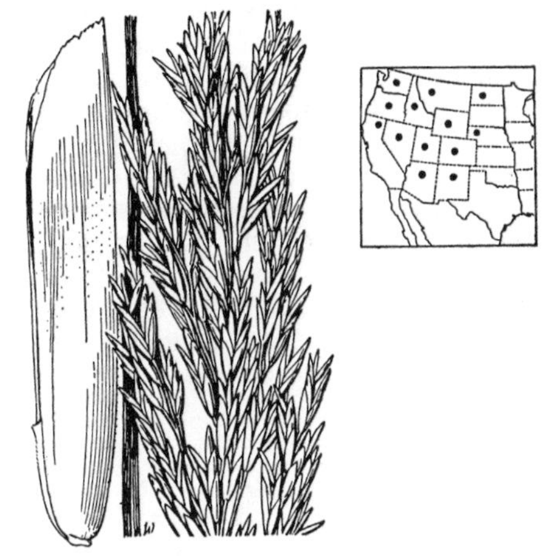

Figure 182.—*Poa ampla*. Panicle, × 1; floret, × 10. (Crandall 205, Colo.)

13. BRÍZA L. Quaking grass

Spikelets several-flowered, broad, often cordate, the florets crowded and spreading horizontally, the rachilla disarticulating above the glumes and between the florets; glumes about equal, broad, papery-chartaceous, with scarious margins; lemmas papery, broad, with scarious spreading margins, cordate at base, several-nerved, the nerves often obscure, the apex in our species obtuse or acutish; palea much shorter than the lemma. Low annuals or perennials, with erect culms, flat blades, and usually open, showy panicles, the pedicels in our species capillary, allowing the spikelets to vibrate in the wind. Standard species, *Briza media*. Name from Greek, *Briza*, a kind of grain, from *brizein*, to nod.

The three species found in this country are introduced from Europe. They are of no importance agriculturally except insofar as *B. minor* occasionally forms an appreciable part of the spring forage in some parts of California. *B. maxima* is sometimes cultivated for ornament, because of the large showy spikelets.

Panicle drooping; spikelets 10 mm. wide .... 1. B. maxima.
Panicle erect; spikelets 4 to 5 mm. wide.
  Plants perennial; upper ligule 1 mm. long; spikelets about 5 mm. long .... 3. B. media.
  Plants annual; upper ligule 5 mm. or more long; spikelets about 3 mm. long. 2. B. minor.

1. Briza máxima L. Big quaking grass. (Fig. 183.) Annual; culms erect or decumbent at base, 30 to 60 cm. tall; panicle drooping, few-flowered; spikelets ovate, 12 mm. long or more, 10 mm. broad, the pedicels slender, drooping; glumes and lemmas usually purple- or brown-margined. ☉ —Sometimes cultivated for ornament; sparingly escaped in California (Monterey County) and Texas.

2. Briza mínor L. LITTLE QUAKING GRASS. (Fig. 184.) Annual; culms erect, 10 to 40 cm. tall; ligule of the upper leaf 5 mm. long or more, acute; blades 2 to 10 mm. wide; panicle 5

FIGURE 183.—*Briza maxima.* × ½. (Baenitz, Dalmatia.)

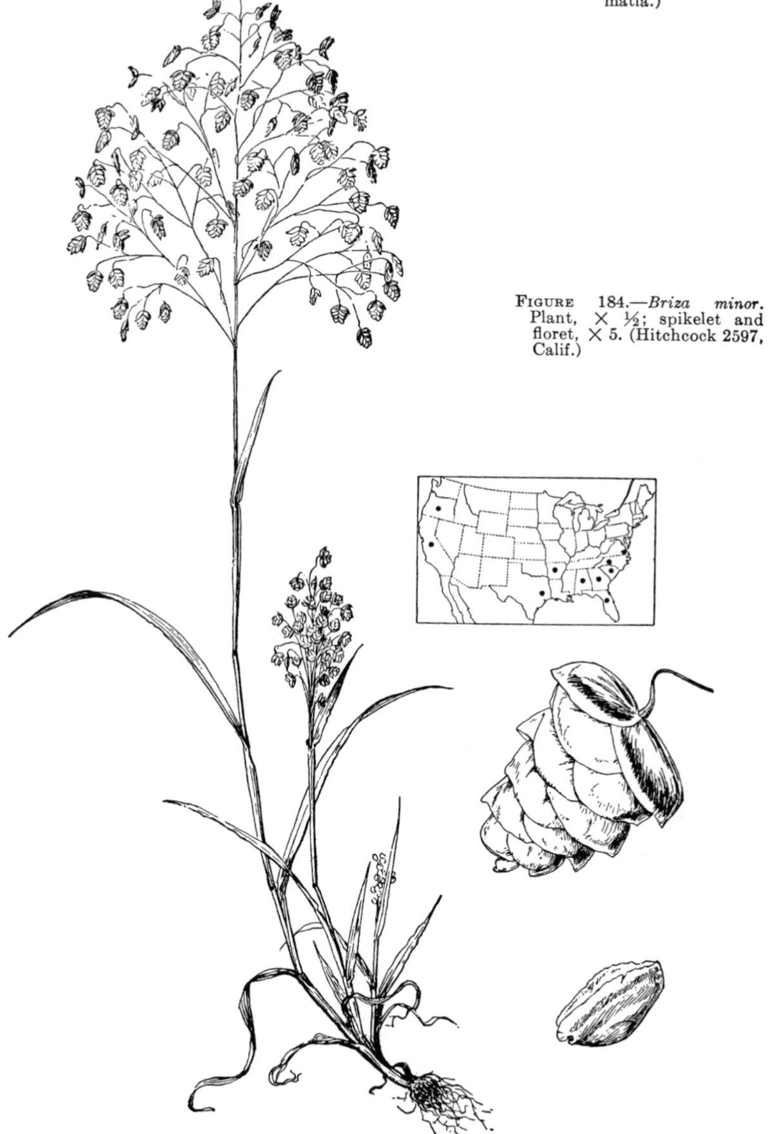

FIGURE 184.—*Briza minor.* Plant, × ½; spikelet and floret, × 5. (Hitchcock 2597, Calif.)

to 12 cm. long, the branches stiffly ascending, the spikelets pendent, triangular-ovate, 3- to 6-flowered, about 3 mm. long. ⊙ —Introduced at several localities in the Eastern States from Canada to Florida, Arkansas, and Texas, becoming common on the Pacific coast, especially in California.

3. Briza média L. (Fig. 185.) Perennial; culms 15 to 60 cm. tall; ligule of the upper leaf about 1 mm. long, truncate; blades 2 to 5 mm. wide; panicle erect, 5 to 10 cm. long, the branches rather stiff, ascending, naked below; spikelets 5- to 12-flowered, orbicular, about 5 mm. long. ♃ —Fields and waste places, sparingly introduced, Ontario to Connecticut and Michigan.

Desmazéria sicula (Jacq.) Dum. Low annual; culms spreading with ascending ends; panicles simple, 3 to 5 cm. long, with large flat 2-ranked spikelets. ⊙ —Occasionally cultivated for ornament. Europe. (Name sometimes spelled *Demazeria.*)

Figure 185.—*Briza media*. Panicle, × ½. (Oakes, Mass.)

14. ERAGRÓSTIS Beauv. Lovegrass

Spikelets few- to many-flowered, the florets usually closely imbricate, the rachilla disarticulating above the glumes and between the florets, or continuous, the lemmas deciduous, the paleas persistent; glumes somewhat unequal, shorter than the first lemma, acute or acuminate, 1-nerved, or the second rarely 3-nerved; lemmas acute or acuminate, keeled or rounded on the back, 3-nerved, the lateral nerves sometimes obscure; palea usually about as long as the lemma, the keels sometimes ciliate. Annuals or perennials of various habit, the inflorescence an open or contracted panicle. Type species, *Eragrostis eragrostis* Beauv. (*E. poaeoides*). Name from the Greek *eros*, love, and *agrostis*, a kind of grass.

Although the species are numerous, they in general appear to have little forage value. *Eragrostis intermedia* is said to furnish forage on the grazing lands of Arizona and New Mexico. Three introduced African species, *E. curvula*, *E. lehmanniana*, and *E. chloromelas*, show promise of being valuable in erosion control in the Southwest.

1a. Plants annual.
 2a. Plants creeping, rooting at the nodes, forming mats.
  Plants with perfect flowers; anthers 0.2 mm. long .... 11. E. hypnoides.
  Plants dioecious; anthers 2 mm. long .... 10. E. reptans.
 2b. Plants often decumbent at base but not creeping and forming mats.
  3a. Palea prominently ciliate on the keels, the cilia usually as long as the width of the lemma.
   Panicle interruptedly spikelike, rarely somewhat open; spikelets usually 3 to 4 mm. long .... 7. E. ciliaris.
   Panicle narrow but open, the pedicels ascending or spreading; spikelets 2 mm. long. 8. E. amabilis.
  3b. Palea scabrous to short-ciliate.
   4a. Panicle long, narrow, rather dense, tawny or stramineous; spikelets 2 to 3 mm. long .... 9. E. glomerata.

4b. Panicle more or less open; spikelets usually more than 3 mm. long.
5a. Spikelets sessile or nearly so .... 12. E. SIMPLEX.
5b. Spikelets pediceled.
6a. Spikelets mostly less than 5-flowered; lemmas obscurely nerved, scarcely keeled.
Panicles two-thirds the entire length of the plant or more, diffuse; pedicels more than 5 mm. long; culms erect, closely tufted .... 14. E. CAPILLARIS.
Panicles less than half the entire length of the plant, oblong, open but scarcely diffuse; pedicels mostly less than 5 mm. long; culms spreading or decumbent at base .... 15. E. FRANKII.
6b. Spikelets mostly more than 5-flowered.
7a. Spikelets ovate to oblong, flat, the florets spreading, closely imbricate. 13. E. UNIOLOIDES.
7b. Spikelets oblong to linear, the florets appressed.
8a. Plants with glandular depressions on the panicle branches, the keel of the lemmas, or on margins of blades or keel of sheaths.
Spikelets 2.5 mm. wide; glands prominent on keel of lemmas. Anthers 0.5 mm. long .... 24. E. CILIANENSIS.
Spikelets not more than 2 mm. wide, mostly less; glandular depressions mostly on panicle branches and leaves.
Panicle narrow, rather dense .... 23. E. LUTESCENS.
Panicle open, at least one-fourth as wide as long.
Spikelets 1.5 to 2 mm. wide, dark drab; panicle branches relatively stout and stiff .... 25. E. POAEOIDES.
Spikelets about 1 mm. wide, pale; panicle branches slender, spreading .... 17. E. PERPLEXA.
8b. Plants not glandular on the branches nor lemmas, sometimes glandular on the sheaths (*E. neomexicana*) and below the nodes (*E. barrelieri*).
Spikelets about 1 mm. wide, linear, slender.
Plant delicate; spikelets 3 to 5 mm. long; lemmas 1 to 1.5 mm. long. 16. E. PILOSA.
Plant rather stout; spikelets 5 to 7 mm. long; lemmas about 2 mm. long. 22. E. ORCUTTIANA.
Spikelets 1.5 mm. wide or wider, ovate to linear.
Panicle narrow, the branches ascending, spikelet-bearing nearly to base, few-flowered; spikelets linear, mostly 10- to 15-flowered. 26. E. BARRELIERI.
Panicle open, often diffuse.
Spikelets linear, mostly 8- to 15-flowered, on slender spreading pedicels mostly longer than the spikelets .... 29. E. ARIDA.
Spikelets ovate to linear, if linear not on spreading pedicels.
Spikelets linear at maturity, appressed along the primary panicle branches, these naked at the base for usually 5 to 10 mm. Lower lemmas 1.5 mm. long.
Primary panicle branches simple or the lower with a branchlet bearing 2 or 3 spikelets; spikelets loosely imbricate or sometimes not overlapping; plants slender, mostly less than 30 cm. tall, the culms slender at base. Chiefly east of the 100th meridian .... 18. E. PECTINACEA.
Primary panicle branches usually bearing appressed branchlets with few to several spikelets, the spikelets thus appearing imbricate or crowded along the primary branches; plants more robust, mostly more than 30 cm. tall, the culms stouter at the base. Chiefly from Texas to southern California .... 19. E. DIFFUSA.
Spikelets ovate to ovate-oblong, rarely linear, if linear not appressed along the primary panicle branches.
Plants comparatively robust, usually more than 25 cm. tall. Texas to southern California.
Panicle large, the branches many-flowered, ascending or drooping. Plant as much as 1 m. tall, with blades as much as 1 cm. wide, but often smaller. 27. E. NEOMEXICANA.
Panicle smaller and more open, the spreading branches few-flowered. Plant usually less than 30 cm. tall. 28. E. MEXICANA

Plants delicate, mostly less than 25 cm. tall; blades mostly not more than 2 mm. wide (see also *E. frankii* var. *brevipes*).
Panicle lax, the branches usually naked at base; spikelets 4 to 7 mm. long.......... 20. E. TEPHROSANTHOS.
Panicle rather stiff, the branches often floriferous nearly to the base; spikelets mostly not more than 3 mm. long. 21. E. MULTICAULIS.

1b. Plants perennial.
9a. Panicle elongate, slender, dense, spikelike.......... 6. E. SPICATA.
9b. Panicle open or contracted, not spikelike.
10a. Plants with stout scaly rhizomes.......... 1. E. OBTUSIFLORA.
10b. Plants without rhizomes.
11a. Spikelets subsessile or nearly so, the lateral pedicels not more than 1 mm. long.
Spikelets subsessile, distant along the few stout panicle branches. 2. E. SESSILISPICA.
Spikelets short-pediceled.
Panicle large, becoming a tumbleweed, the axis and branches viscid. 3. E. CURTIPEDICELLATA.
Panicle narrow (sometimes open in *E. oxylepis*), not a tumbleweed nor viscid; keels of palea forming a thick white band; grain 1 to 1.2 mm. long.
Lemmas 3 mm. long, somewhat abruptly narrowed to the acute apex; panicle usually red brown; anthers 0.2 to 0.3 mm. long.......... 4. E. OXYLEPIS.
Lemmas 3.5 mm. long, tapering to the acuminate apex; panicle pale or slightly pinkish; anthers 0.4 to 0.5 mm. long.......... 5. E. BEYRICHII.
11b. Spikelets with pedicels more than 1 mm. long (appressed along the branches in *E. refracta;* sometimes scarcely more than 1 mm. long in *E. chariis* and *E. bahiensis*). Panicles large and open (sometimes condensed in *E. bahiensis*).
12a. Nerves of lemma obscure; lemma rounded on back, sometimes slightly keeled toward apex.
Axils of main panicle branches usually strongly pilose (rarely glabrous in *E. intermedia*).
Sheaths pilose or hirsute (sometimes glabrous in *E. hirsuta*).
Culms mostly more than 50 cm. tall; blades elongate, flat, not crowded at base of culm.......... 30. E. HIRSUTA.
Culms mostly less than 50 cm. tall; blades rather short and crowded at base of culm.......... 32. E. TRICHOCOLEA.
Sheaths glabrous or nearly so, except the pilose summit.
Spikelets about 1 mm. wide, 3- to 7-flowered, 3 to 5 mm. long; lemmas 1.3 to 1.5 mm. long.......... 31. E. LUGENS.
Spikelets about 1.5 mm. wide; 3- to 8-flowered, 3 to 10 mm. long; lemmas 1.8 to 2 mm. long.......... 35. E. INTERMEDIA.
Axils of main panicle branches glabrous or the lower sparsely pilose.
Pedicels bearing above the middle a glandular band or spot; axils glabrous. 36. E. SWALLENI.
Pedicels without glandular band; lower axils sparsely pilose to glabrous.
Lemmas about 3 mm. long.......... 33. E. EROSA.
Lemmas about 2 mm. long.......... 34. E. PALMERI.
12b. Nerves of lemma evident, usually prominent; lemmas keeled.
Spikelets approximate in a somewhat condensed panicle, or along the main branches of a somewhat spreading panicle; florets mostly 15 to 30.
Panicle branches distant, glabrous or nearly so in the axils.
Paleas readily deciduous.......... 45. E. CHARIIS.
Paleas persistent.......... 46. E. BAHIENSIS.
Panicle branches approximate, villous in the axils. Culms densely cespitose with arcuate blades attentuate to long filiform flexuous tips. 47. E. CURVULA.
Spikelets in an open panicle.
Panicle longer than broad, the branches not horizontally spreading.
Culms not more than 60 cm. tall.
Spikelets 9- to 15-flowered; panicle less than one-third the entire length of culm, the branches not viscid.......... 37. E. TRACYI.
Spikelets 4- to 8-flowered; panicle more than half the entire length of culm, the branches viscid.......... 38. E. SILVEANA.
Culms usually 1 m. or more tall.
Spikelets mostly not more than 6-flowered, purplish. 39. E. TRICHODES.

Spikelets mostly 8- to 15-flowered, stramineous to bronze.
40. E. PILIFERA.

Panicle at maturity about as broad as long.
Panicle purple, the branches slender but rigid........... 41. E. SPECTABILIS.
Panicle green to leaden, the branches capillary, fragile.
Spikelets appressed and distant along the nearly simple panicle branches.
44. E. REFRACTA.
Spikelets on long pedicels.
Lemmas 2 mm. long... 42. E. ELLIOTTII.
Lemmas 3 mm. long... 43. E. ACUTA.

FIGURE 186.—*Eragrostis obtusiflora*. Plant, × ½, two views of floret, × 10. (Toumey, Ariz.)

SECTION 1. CATACLÁSTOS Doell

Rachilla of spikelets disarticulating between the florets at maturity.

1. Eragrostis obtusiflóra (Fourn.) Scribn. (Fig. 186.) Culms erect or ascending, firm, wiry, 30 to 50 cm. tall, from stout creeping rhizomes with closely imbricate hard spiny-pointed scales; sheaths pubescent or pilose at the throat; blades firm, glaucous, flat, becoming involute at least toward the spiny-pointed tip, 5 to 10 cm. long, 2 to 3 mm. wide at base; panicle 5 to 15 cm. long, the rigid simple branches ascending, loosely flowered, 5 to 8 cm. long; spikelets pale or purplish, 6- to 12-flowered, 8 to 12 mm. long, the pedicels about 1 mm. long; glumes acute, 3 and 5 mm. long; lemmas rounded on the back, rather loosely imbricate, obtuse, somewhat lacerate, about 4 mm. long. ♃ — Alkali soil, Arizona, New Mexico (Las Playas); Mexico. "This species is one of the most abundant grasses in the extreme alkaline portions of Sulphur Springs Valley, Arizona, where the large rootstocks in many places bind the shifting sands. It rarely flowers, and its superficial appearance, without flowers, is much the same as our common salt grass (*Distichlis spicata*). It is a hard, rigid grass, but furnishes a large part of the forage of Sulphur Springs Valley, when other grasses are eaten off or are cut short by drought."—Toumey in letter.

2. Eragrostis sessilispíca Buckl. (Fig. 187.) Perennial; culms tufted, erect, 20 to 40 cm. tall, with 1 node above the basal cluster of leaves; sheaths glabrous, strongly pilose at the throat; blades flat to rather loosely involute, 1 to 2 mm. wide; panicle loose, open, pilose in the axils, at first about half the entire length of the culm, elongating toward maturity, the axis curving or loosely spiral, as much as 40 cm. long, the distant branches stiffly spreading, 5 to 15 cm. long, floriferous to base, sometimes bearing below a few secondary branches, the whole panicle finally breaking away and tumbling before the wind; spikelets distant, nearly sessile, appressed, linear, 5- to 12-flowered, 8 to 12 mm. long; glumes acute, about 3 mm. long; lemmas loosely imbricate, acuminate, becoming somewhat indurate, 3 to 3.5 mm. long, the lateral nerves prominent; palea prominently bowed out below. ♃ (*Acamptoclados sessilispica* Nash.)—Plains and sandy prairies, Kansas to Texas, New Mexico, and northern Mexico.

FIGURE 187.—*Eragrostis sessilispica*. Panicle, × 1; floret, × 10. (Swallen 1791, Tex.)

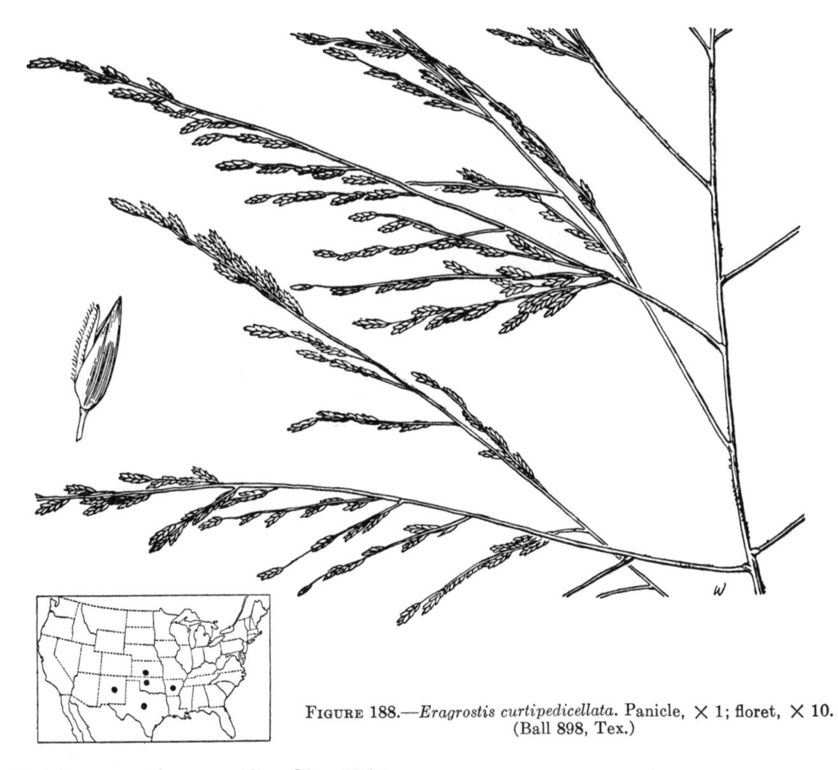

FIGURE 188.—*Eragrostis curtipedicellata.* Panicle, × 1; floret, × 10. (Ball 898, Tex.)

3. Eragrostis curtipedicellāta Buckl. (Fig. 188.) Perennial; culms tufted, erect, 20 to 40 cm. tall; sheaths pilose at the throat; blades flat or loosely involute, 1 to 3 mm. wide; panicle open, spreading, at first 15 to 20 cm. long, the axis and branches viscid, rather sparingly pilose in the axils, finally elongating, breaking away and tumbling before the wind, the branches stiffly ascending or spreading; spikelets oblong or linear, short-pediceled, somewhat appressed on the primary and secondary branches, 6- to 12-flowered, 3 to 6 mm. long; glumes about 1.5 mm. long; lemmas rather closely imbricate, oblong, acute, about 1.5 mm. long; palea ciliate on the keels, not bowed out; grain 0.7 mm. long. ♃ — Plains, open woods, and dry slopes, Colorado and Kansas to Arkansas, Texas, and New Mexico.

4. Eragrostis oxylépis (Torr.) Torr. (Fig. 189.) Perennial; culms tufted, suberect, 20 to 70 cm. tall;

FIGURE 189.—*Eragrostis oxylepis.* Panicle, × 1; floret, × 10. (Reverchon 3501A, Tex.)

sheaths long-pilose at the throat, the foliage otherwise glabrous, the blades flat, more or less involute in drying, 1 to 4, rarely to 5, mm. wide, tapering to a fine point; panicle 5 to 25 cm. long (mostly 10 to 15 cm.) of several to numerous stiff, ascending or spreading densely flowered branches, approximate to distant, the spikelets mostly aggregate on very short branchlets; spikelets usually red brown, strongly compressed, subsessile, linear at maturity, mostly 10- to 40-flowered, 8 to 15 mm. long; lemmas closely imbricate, 3 mm. long, abruptly narrowed to an acute apex, the tip slightly spreading; palea bowed out below, the keels prominent; anthers 0.2 to 0.3 mm. long; grain 1 to 1.2 mm. long. ♃ —Sandy soil, northern Florida to Colorado, New Mexico, and California (San Diego); eastern Mexico to Vera Cruz. Has been confused with *E. secundiflora* Presl, a rather rare species of Mexico, which it closely resembles, but the latter has less strongly compressed spikelets and grains only 0.4 to 0.5 mm. long.

5. Eragrostis beyríchii J. G. Smith. (Fig. 190.) Resembling *E. oxylepis* and possibly only a variety of that species; differing in the softer foliage and panicle, the plant on the average smaller, the panicle mostly smaller, pale or slightly pinkish; spikelets slightly larger; lemmas 3.5 to 4 mm. long (the lower shorter), less firm, tapering to an acuminate apex; palea broader, less bowed out; anthers 0.4 to 0.5 mm. long, yellowish, grain 1 mm. long. ♃ —Sandy soil, Texas and Oklahoma (Wichita Mountains); Mexico.

6. Eragrostis spicáta Vasey. (Fig. 191.) Perennial; culms tufted, erect, about 1 m. tall; blades flat, elongate, more or less involute in drying, tapering to a slender point; panicle pale, slender, dense, spikelike, 10 to 30 cm. long, 3 to 4 mm. thick; spikelets strongly compressed, 2- or 3-flowered, 2 mm. long, the somewhat pubescent pedicels less than 1 mm. long; glumes rather broad, obtuse, unequal, the second about 1 mm. long; lemmas about 2 mm. long, all rising to about the same height, the lateral pair of nerves faint. ♃ —Dry ground, Laredo and Brownsville, Tex.; Baja California; Paraguay, Argentina.

FIGURE 190.—*Eragrostis beyrichii.* Panicle, × 1; floret, × 10. (Tracy 7924, Tex.)

FIGURE 191.—*Eragrostis spicata.* Panicle, × 1; spikelet, × 10. (Swallen 1086, Tex.)

7. Eragrostis ciliáris (L.) R. Br. (Fig. 192.) Annual; culms branching, erect to spreading, slender, wiry, 15 to 30 cm. tall; blades flat to subinvolute, mostly less than 10 cm. long, 1 to 3 mm. wide; panicle often purplish, condensed, interruptedly spikelike, 3 to 10 cm. long, sometimes looser with stiffly ascending short branches; spikelets 6- to 12-flowered, 2 to 4 mm. long; glumes about 1 mm. long; lemmas oblong, 1 to 1.5 mm. long, obtuse, the midnerve slightly excurrent; keels of the palea conspicuously stiffly long-ciliate, the hairs 0.5 to 0.7 mm. long; grain 0.5 mm. long. ⊙ —Sandy shores, rocky soil, and open ground, South

FIGURE 192.—*Eragrostis ciliaris*. Plant, × ½; spikelet, × 5; floret, × 10. (Nash 2104, Fla.)

Carolina to Florida and Mississippi; Texas; New Jersey (ballast); West Indies and Mexico to Brazil and Peru; Africa; Asia. Specimens with laxer panicles of more spreading loosely flowered branches have been differentiated as *E. ciliaris* var. *laxa* Kuntze.

8. Eragrostis amábilis (L.) Wight and Arn. ex Nees. (Fig. 193.) Annual, resembling *E. ciliaris;* blades as much as 5 mm. wide; panicle oblong or oblong-lanceolate, 2 to 4 cm. wide, rather open; spikelets 4- to 8-flowered, about 2 mm. long; glumes less than 1 mm. long; lemmas ovate, obtuse, 1 mm. long; keels of palea long-ciliate, the hairs about 0.3 mm. long. ⊙ (*E. plumosa* Link.)—Gardens and waste places, Georgia and Florida; Texas; tropical America; apparently introduced from the Old World.

9. Eragrostis glomeráta (Walt.) L. H. Dewey. (Fig. 194.) Annual; culms erect, 20 to 100 cm. tall, branching below, the branches erect; blades flat, 3 to 8 mm. wide, tapering to a fine point; panicle narrow, erect, densely flowered, somewhat interrupted, 5 to 50 cm. long, greenish or tawny, the branches ascending or appressed, floriferous to base, many-flowered; spikelets short-pediceled, mostly 6- to 8-flowered, 2 to 3 mm. long; glumes minute; lemmas very thin, about 1 mm. long; grain about

FIGURE 193.—*Eragrostis amabilis.* Panicle, × ½; spikelet, × 10. (Meislahn 10, Fla.)

0.3 to 0.4 mm. long. ⊙ (*E. conferta* Trin.)—Banks of ponds and streams, and low ground, South Carolina to Florida, Missouri, and eastern Texas, south through Mexico and the West Indies to Uruguay.

SECTION 2. PTEROÉSSA Doell

Rachilla of spikelet continuous, not disarticulating at maturity; palea usually persistent for a short time after the fall of the lemma (sometimes falling with it in *E. unioloides* and *E. chariis*).

10. Eragrostis réptans (Michx.) Nees. (Fig. 195.) Annual, dioecious; culms branching, creeping, rooting at the nodes, forming mats; blades flat, usually pubescent, mostly 1 to 3 cm. long; panicles numerous, ovoid, usually rather dense or capitate, few- to

FIGURE 194.—*Eragrostis glomerata.* Panicle, × ½; spikelet and floret, × 10. (Eggert, Ark.)

several-flowered, rarely many-flowered, mostly 1 to 2 cm. long; spikelets several- to many-flowered, linear, at length elongate and more or less curved; lemmas closely imbricate, often sparsely villous, acuminate, about 3 mm. long; palea of pistillate floret about half as long as the lemma,

Figure 195.—*Eragrostis reptans.* Pistillate (♀) and staminate (♂) plants, × ½; floret, × 10. (Bush 1306 (♀) and 1307 (♂), Tex.)

Figure 196.—*Eragrostis hypnoides.* Plant, × ½; floret, × 10. (Mearns 741, Minn.)

of the staminate floret as long as the lemma; grain ovoid, about 0.5 mm. long; anthers before dehiscing, 1.5 to 2 mm. long. ⊙ (*E. capitata* Nash.)—River banks, sandy land, and open ground, Kentucky to South Dakota and Texas; Florida.

11. Eragrostis hypnoídes (Lam.) B. S. P. (Fig. 196.) Annual, branching, creeping, and matlike as in the preceding; blades scabrous or pubescent on the upper surface; panicles elliptic, loosely few-flowered, 1 to 5 cm. long, sometimes somewhat capitate; spikelets several- to many-flowered, linear, mostly 5 to 10 mm. long, sometimes as much as 2 cm. long in a dense cluster; flowers perfect; lemmas glabrous, acute, 1.5 to 2 mm. long; palea about half as long as the lemma; grain 0.5 mm. long; anthers about 0.2 mm. long. ⊙ —Sandy river banks and wet ground, Quebec to Washington, south through Mexico and the West Indies to Argentina; not found in the Rocky Mountains.

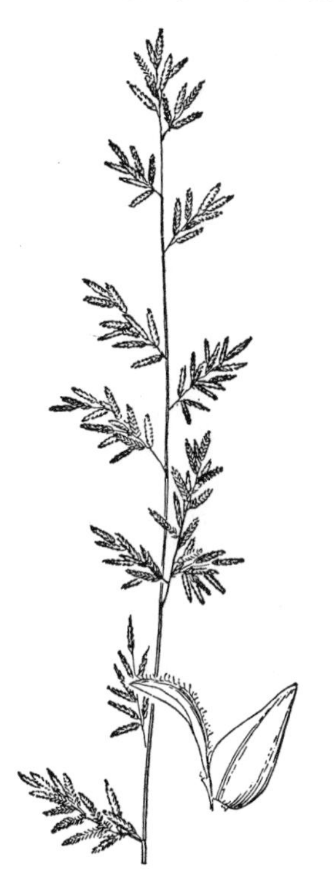

FIGURE 197.—*Eragrostis simplex*. Panicle, × ½; floret, × 10. (Curtiss, Fla.)

12. Eragrostis símplex Scribn. (Fig. 197.) Annual; culms spreading to suberect, 10 to 30 cm. tall; blades flat, 1 to 3 mm. wide; panicle narrow, 5 to 20 cm. long, the main axis often curved, the branches solitary, distant, ascending or spreading, sometimes reflexed, floriferous to base, short, with a few crowded spikelets or as much as 5 cm. long, with short branchlets; spikelets nearly sessile, linear, mostly 20- to 50-flowered, 5 to 20 mm. long; lemmas closely imbricate, ovate, acute, 1.5 to 2 mm. long, the lateral nerves near the margin; grain about 0.5 mm. long, anthers about 0.1 mm. long. ⊙ —Sandy woods, dooryards, and waste places, southern Georgia, Florida, and Alabama.

FIGURE 198.—*Eragrostis unioloides*. Spikelet, × 10. (Curtiss 6898, Fla.)

13. Eragrostis unioloídes (Retz.) Nees. (Fig. 198.) Annual; culms erect or ascending, 20 to 40 cm. tall; blades flat, 2 to 4 mm. wide; panicle elliptic, open, 10 to 15 cm. long, about half as wide, the branches ascending;

spikelets ovate-oblong, strongly compressed, truncate at base, obtuse, 15- to 30-flowered, 5 to 10 mm. long, 3 mm. wide, often pink or purplish; lemmas closely imbricate, nearly horizontally spreading, strongly keeled, acute, 2 mm. long, the lateral nerves prominent; palea falling with the lemma or soon thereafter; grain about 0.7 mm. long. ☉ —Waste ground, Georgia and Florida; introduced from southern Asia.

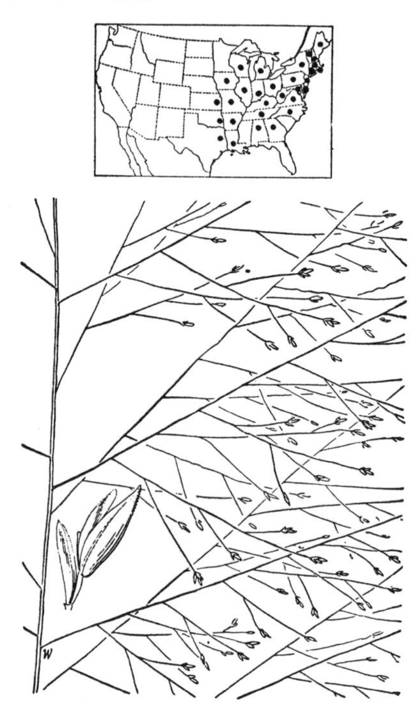

FIGURE 199.—*Eragrostis capillaris.* Panicle, × 1; floret, × 10. (Dewey 35, D. C.)

14. Eragrostis capilláris (L.) Nees. LACEGRASS. (Fig. 199.) Annual; culms erect, 20 to 50 cm. tall, much-branched at base, the branches erect; sheaths pilose, at least on the margin, long-pilose at the throat; blades flat, erect, pilose on upper surface near the base, 1 to 3 mm. wide; panicle oblong or elliptic, open, diffuse, usually two-thirds the entire height of the plant, the branches and branchlets capillary; spikelets long-pediceled, 2- to 4-flowered, 2 to 3 mm. long; glumes acute, 1 mm. long; lemmas acute, about 1.5 mm. long, obscurely nerved, rounded on the back, minutely scabrous toward the tip; grain 0.5 mm. long, somewhat roughened. ☉ —Dry open ground, open woods, and fields, Maine to Wisconsin, south to Georgia, Kansas, and eastern Texas.

15. Eragrostis fránkii C. A. Meyer. (Fig. 200.) Resembling *E. capillaris;* culms usually lower, spreading to erect; sheaths glabrous except the pilose throat; blades glabrous; panicle less than half the entire height of the plant, open but not diffuse, mostly less than half as wide as long, the branches ascending, the shorter pedicels not much longer than the spike-

FIGURE 200.—*Eragrostis frankii.* Panicle, × 1; floret, × 10. (Chase 2005, Ill.)

lets; spikelets 3- to 5-flowered, 2 to 3 mm. long. ☉ —Sandbars, river banks, and moist open ground, New Hampshire to Minnesota, south to Florida and Oklahoma. ERAGROSTIS FRANKII var. BRÉVIPES Fassett. Spikelets 5- to 7-flowered, 3 to 4 mm. long. ☉ —Wisconsin (Glenhaven) and Illinois.

16. Eragrostis pilósa (L.) Beauv. INDIA LOVEGRASS. (Fig. 201.) Weedy annual; culms slender, erect or ascending from a decumbent base, 10 to 50 cm. tall; blades flat, 1 to 3 mm. wide; panicle delicate, open, becoming somewhat diffuse, 5 to 20 cm. long, the branches capillary, flexuous, ascending or spreading, finally somewhat implicate, the lower fascicled, sparsely long-pilose in the axils; spikelets gray to nearly black, linear, scarcely compressed, 3- to 9-flowered, 3 to 5 mm. long, about 1 mm. wide, the pedicels spreading, mostly longer than the spikelets; glumes acute, the first a little less than, the second a little more than, 1 mm. long; lemmas loosely imbricate, the rachilla more or less exposed, rounded on the back, acute, 1.2 to 1.5 mm. long, 0.5 mm. wide from keel to margin, the nerves obscure; grain 0.6 mm. long. ⊙ —Moist open ground and waste places, Maine to Colorado, south to Florida and Texas, south through Mexico and the West Indies to Argentina; California; introduced from Europe.

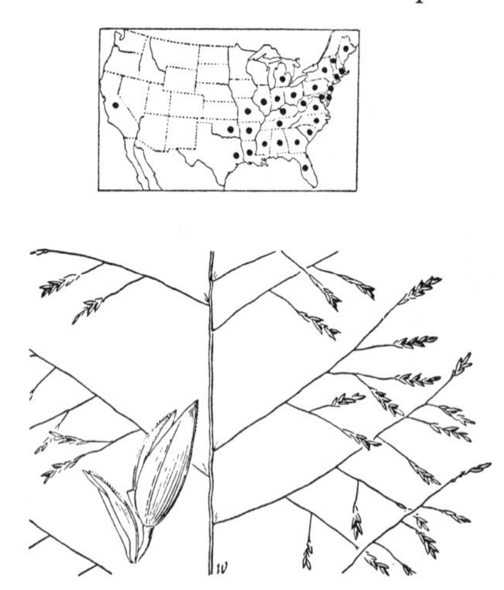

Figure 201.—*Eragrostis pilosa*. Panicle, × 1; floret, and palea, × 10. (Ruth 514, Tex.)

17. Eragrostis perpléxa L. H. Harvey. (Fig. 202.) Annual resembling *E. pilosa*, but mostly less slender; 20 to 50 cm. tall, or in dry ground 12 to 15 cm. tall; blades mostly 3 to 4 mm. wide; panicle less delicate than in *E. pilosa* and without hairs in the axils; culms below the nodes, keels of the sheaths, and panicle branches bearing small glandular depressions, these often obscure in immature plants. ⊙ —Low alkaline areas and buffalo wallows, North Dakota to Kansas; Texas; Colorado.

Eragrostis viréscens Presl. Annual; culms slender, 50 to 60 cm. tall; blades 3 to 6 mm. wide; panicle open, about one third the entire height of the culm, the lower branches mostly solitary, the axils glabrous or nearly so; branchlets and spikelets somewhat appressed along the primary branches; spikelets linear, mostly 7- to 9-flowered, 4 to 5 mm. long, pale or greenish, about 1 mm. wide; lower lemmas scarcely 1.5 mm. long. ⊙ Adventive, Maryland; ballast, Apalachicola, Fla.; Chile. Resembling *E. diffusa;* spikelets smaller.

Figure 202.—*Eragrostis perplexa*. Sheath, × 2; panicle, × 1. (Type.)

18. Eragrostis pectinácea (Michx.) Nees. (Fig. 203.) Resembling *E. pilosa;* panicles less delicate, the axils glabrous or obscurely pilose, the somewhat larger spikelets appressed along the branches and branchlets, often longer than the pedicels; spikelets at maturity mostly linear, 5 to 8 mm. long; lemmas 1.5 to 1.6 mm. long, the rachilla not or scarcely ex-

FIGURE 203.—*Eragrostis pectinacea.* Panicle, × 1; floret, × 10. (V. H. Chase 84, Ill.)

lets, the main panicle branches thus more densely flowered. ☉ —A common weed in fields and open ground, Wyoming, Idaho, Oklahoma, and Texas to Nevada and southern California; introduced occasionally in the Eastern States; Mexico. In some specimens the spikelets are ascending rather than appressed, thus making the panicle more open.

20. Eragrostis tephrosánthos Schult. (Fig. 205.) Annual, rather soft and lax; culms branching at base, erect to decumbent-spreading, 5 to 20 cm. tall, sometimes taller; blades flat, usually 5 to 10 cm. long, 1 to 2 mm. wide; panicle open, mostly 4 to 10 cm. long, about half as wide, the branches ascending or spreading, naked below, the spikelets appressed or ascending along the upper part, the lower axils pilose; spikelets 6- to 12-flowered, 4 to 7 mm. long, about 1.5 mm. wide; glumes about 1 and 1.3 mm. long; lemmas 1.5 to 2 mm. long, the lateral nerves distinct. ☉ —Open ground, fields, and waste places, Florida to southern Texas and south through the lowland Tropics to Brazil.

FIGURE 204.—*Eragrostis diffusa.* Panicle, × 1; floret, × 10. (Reverchon 1614, Tex.)

posed, the nerves evident; grain 0.8 mm. long. ☉ (*E. caroliniana* (Spreng.) Scribn.; *E. purshii* Schrad.) —Fields, waste places, open ground, moist places, Maine to Washington, south to Florida and Arizona, rare in the Western States. The name *E. pectinacea* has been misapplied to *E. spectabilis.*

19. Eragrostis diffúsa Buckl. (Fig. 204.) More robust than *E. pectinacea,* usually 30 to 50 cm. tall, sometimes taller; panicle larger, the primary branches bearing appressed secondary branchlets with few to several spike-

FIGURE 205.—*Eragrostis tephrosanthos.* Panicle, × 1; floret, × 10. (Curtiss 5930, Fla.)

21. Eragrostis multicaúlis Steud. (Fig. 206.) Annual; resembling *E. tephrosanthos*, but the axils of the panicle glabrous; panicle branches spikelet-bearing nearly to base; spikelets mostly 4- to 8-flowered, mostly 3 to 4 mm. long. ⊙ (*E. peregrina* Wiegand.)—Waste places, Maine to Wisconsin, south to Pennsylvania and Virginia; ballast, Portland, Oreg.; introduced from Eurasia.

22. Eragrostis orcuttiána Vasey. (Fig. 207.) Annual; culms ascending from a decumbent base, rather stout, 60 to 100 cm. tall; blades flat, 2 to 6 mm. wide; panicle open, 15 to 30 cm. long, the branches, branchlets, and pedicels slender, spreading, flexuous, finally implicate, the axils glabrous; spikelets linear, 6- to 10-flowered, sometimes a little falcate, 5 to 7 mm. long, about 1 mm. wide; second glume a little more than 1 mm. long; lemmas loosely imbricate (the rachilla often exposed), narrow, acutish, the

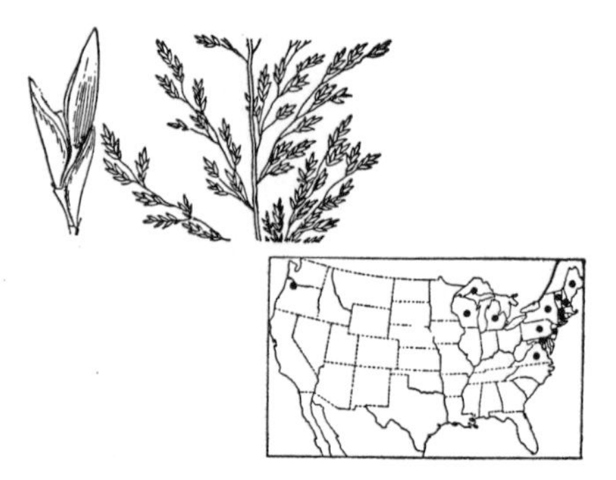

FIGURE 206.—*Eragrostis multicaulis*. Panicle, × 1; floret, × 10. (Hotchkiss 1708, N. Y.)

FIGURE 207.—*Eragrostis orcuttiana*. Panicle, × 1; floret, × 10. (Hitchcock 3063, Calif.)

lower 1.8 mm. long; grain 0.8 mm. long. ⊙ —Fields, waste places, and sandy river banks, Oregon (ballast, Portland); Colorado to Arizona and California.

23. Eragrostis lutéscens Scribn. (Fig. 208.) Annual; culms freely branching at base, erect or ascending, 5 to 20 cm. tall; sheaths and blades with numerous glandular depressions; blades flat; panicles numerous, narrow, erect, pale or yellowish green, 2 to 10 cm. long, the branches ascending or appressed, beset with glandular depressions; spikelets 6- to 10-flowered, 5 to 7 mm. long, compressed; glumes acute, 1.5 and 2 mm. long; lemmas about 2 mm. long, acute, the nerves prominent; palea 1.5 mm. long. ⊙ —Sandy shores, Idaho to Washington, south to Colorado, Arizona, and California; Mexico.

24. Eragrostis cilianénsis (All.) Lutati. STINKGRASS. (Fig. 209.) Weedy annual with disagreeable odor when fresh; culms ascending or spreading, 10 to 50 cm. tall, with a ring of glands below the nodes; foliage sparsely beset with glandular depressions, the sheaths pilose at the throat; blades flat, 2 to 7 mm. wide; panicle erect, dark gray green to tawny, usually rather condensed, sometimes, especially in the Southwest, open, 5 to 20 cm. long, the branches ascending; spikelets oblong, compressed, 10- to 40-flowered, 5 to 15 mm. long, 2.5 to 3 mm. wide; lemmas in side view ovate, acutish, about 2.5 mm. long, 1 mm. wide from keel to margin, the keel scabrous toward apex and beset with a few glands, the lateral nerves prominent; palea about two-thirds as long as the lemma, minutely ciliate on the keels; grain ovoid, plump, 0.7 mm. long; anthers 0.5 mm. long. ⊙ (*E. major* Host; *E. megastachya* Link.)—Cultivated ground, fields, and waste places, Maine to Washington, south throughout the United States, sparingly in the Northwest, absent from the higher mountains; Mexico and West Indies, south to Argentina; introduced from the Old World.

FIGURE 208.—*Eragrostis lutescens*. Plant, × ½; floret, × 10. (Type.)

25. Eragrostis poaeoídes Beauv. ex Roem. and Schult. (Fig. 210.) Annual; resembling *E. cilianensis*, mostly more slender; panicles rather more open, the spikelets smaller, 1.5 to 2 mm. wide, the lemmas about 2 mm. long, the glands sometimes obscure; anthers about 0.2 mm. long. ⊙ (*E. minor* Host; *E. eragrostis* Beauv.)—Waste places, sparingly introduced from Europe, Maine to Wisconsin and Iowa, south to Georgia, Oklahoma, and Texas; California.

26. Eragrostis barreliéri Daveau. (Fig. 211.) Annual; culms erect or decumbent at base, 20 to 50 cm. tall, branching at base, sometimes with a glandular band below the nodes; sheaths pilose at the summit; blades flat, rather short, 2 to 4 mm. wide; panicle erect, open but narrow, 8 to 15 cm. long, the branches ascending or stiffly spreading, few-flowered, spikelet-bearing nearly to base, the

FIGURE 209.—*Eragrostis cilianensis*. Plant, × ½; spikelet, × 5; floret, × 10. (Schuette 155, Wis.)

axils glabrous; spikelets linear, usually 12- to 15-flowered, mostly about 1 cm. long and 1.5 mm. wide; lemmas 2 mm. long or slightly longer. ⊙ —Waste places, Colorado and Kansas to Texas and California; Mexico; introduced from southern Europe.

27. Eragrostis neomexicána Vasey. (Fig. 212.) Annual; culms usually rather stout, often widely spreading, as much as 1 m. tall; sheaths glabrous, pilose at the throat, often with glandular depressions along the keel or nerves; blades flat, often elongate, 5 to 10 mm. wide; panicle 20 to 40 cm. long, smaller in depauperate specimens, open, the branches ascending or spreading but not divaricate, the branchlets at first appressed along the main branches, finally usually spreading, the axils glabrous; spikelets mostly dark grayish green, ovate to ovate-oblong, or rarely linear, mostly 8- to 12-flowered, 5 to 8 mm. long, about 2 mm. wide; lemmas 2 to 2.3 mm. long. ⊙ —Fields, waste places, and wet ground, Texas to southern California, south through Mexico; introduced in Maryland, Indiana, Wisconsin, Iowa, North Dakota, and Missouri.

FIGURE 210.—*Eragrostis poaeoides*. Panicle, × 1 floret, × 10. (Dutton 2235, Vt.)

FIGURE 211.—*Eragrostis barrelieri*. Panicle, × 1; floret, × 10. (Hitchcock 5280, Tex.)

FIGURE 212.—*Eragrostis neomexicana*. Panicle, × 1; floret, × 10. (Type.)

FIGURE 213.—*Eragrostis mexicana.* Panicle, × 1; floret, × 10. (Smith, N. Mex.)

28. Eragrostis mexicāna (Hornem.) Link. MEXICAN LOVEGRASS. (Fig. 213.) Resembling *E. neomexicana*, but lower, erect or spreading, often simple; panicle erect, comparatively small and few-flowered, less compound, the branches and pedicels spreading; spikelets usually not more than 7-flowered. ⊙ —Open ground, Texas to California; Mexico.

29. Eragrostis ārida Hitchc. (Fig. 214.) Annual; culms branching at base, erect or more or less decumbent at base, 20 to 40 cm. tall; sheaths not glandular, the hairs at summit in a dense line part way along the collar; blades mostly flat, glabrous, tapering to a fine point, mostly 4 to 8 cm. long, 1 to 2 mm. wide; panicle mostly one-third to half the entire length of the plant, open, the branches, branchlets, and pedicels flexuous, spreading, the lower axils sparsely pilose, the branches solitary or the lower in pairs; spikelets oblong to linear, stramineous or drab, mostly 8- to 15-flowered, 5 to 10 mm. long, 1.5 to 2 mm. wide, somewhat compressed, the lateral pedicels 2 to 3 mm. long; glumes acute, the first narrow, scarcely 1 mm. long, the second a little longer and wider; lemmas 1.6 to 1.8 mm. long, acutish. ⊙ —Dry soil, Missouri; Texas to California and central Mexico.

FIGURE 214.—*Eragrostis arida.* Panicle, × 1; floret, × 10. (Type.)

30. Eragrostis hirsūta (Michx.) Nees. (Fig. 215.) Perennial; culms erect, tufted, 50 to 120 cm. tall; sheaths hirsute to glabrous, pilose at the throat and especially along the collar at each side; blades flat, elongate, 5 to 10 mm. wide, becoming more or less involute, tapering to a fine point, scabrous on the upper surface; panicle diffuse, more than half the entire height of the plant, pilose in the axils, branching 4 or 5

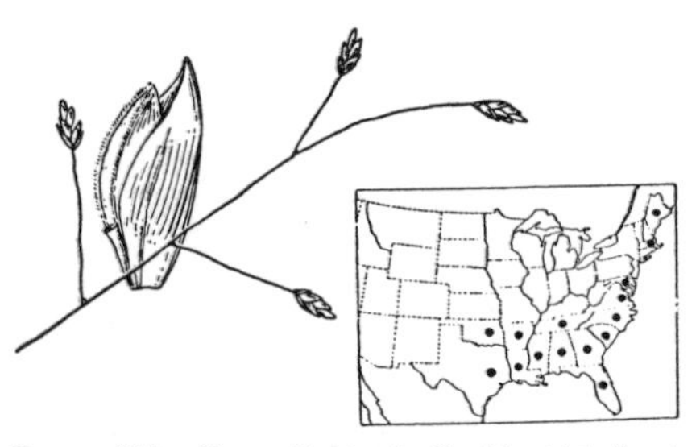

FIGURE 215.—*Eragrostis hirsuta.* Panicle, × 1; floret, × 10. (Curtiss 3499, Fla.)

FIGURE 216.—*Eragrostis lugens*. Plant, × 1; floret, × 10. (Reverchon 16, Tex.)

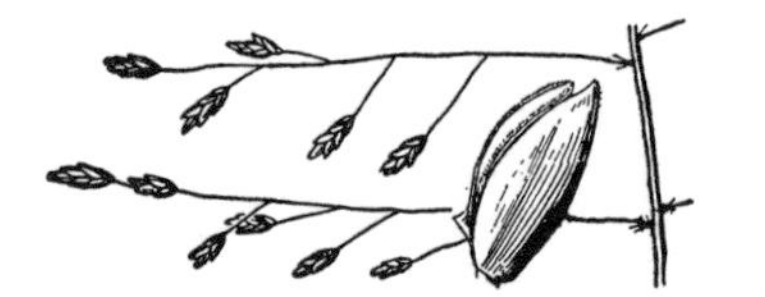

FIGURE 217.—*Eragrostis trichocolea*. Panicle, × 1; floret, × 10. (Curtiss, Fla.)

times; spikelets on long flexuous pedicels, ovate to ovate-oblong, 2- to 6-flowered (rarely to 8-flowered), 3 to 4 mm. long; glumes acuminate, 1.5 and 2 mm. long; lemmas rather turgid, 2 mm. long, acute, the nerves obscure; grain oblong, 1 mm. long, minutely striate and pitted. ♃ —Dry soil, fields and open woods, Maryland to Oklahoma, south to Florida and eastern Texas; British Honduras; introduced in Maine and Massachusetts. Plants with glabrous sheaths have been segregated as *E. hirsuta* var. *laevivaginata* Fern.

31. Eragrostis lúgens Nees. (Fig. 216.) Perennial; culms tufted, rather wiry, sometimes geniculate below, sparingly branching; sheaths pilose in the throat, sometimes along the margin and on sides at summit; blades subinvolute, 10 to 25 cm. long, 1.5 to 3 mm. wide, pilose on the upper surface toward base, rarely beneath; panicle rather diffuse, 15 to 30 cm. long, about two-thirds as wide, the axis and ascending to spreading branches capillary, flexuous, the lower branches in pairs or verticils, the axils, except upper, conspicuously long pilose; spikelets on long pedicels, mostly glossy drab, 3- to 7-flowered, 3 to 5 mm. long, 1 to 1.2 mm. wide; glumes thin, 0.7 and 1.2 mm. long, falling early; lemmas closely imbricate, 1.3 to 1.5 mm. long, abruptly acute; grain about 0.7 mm. long. ♃ —Dry prairie, Florida, Louisiana, and Texas; also on ballast, Mobile, Ala.; Mexico and Venezuela to Argentina.

32. Eragrostis trichocólea Hack. and Arech. (Fig. 217.) Perennial; culms erect, 30 to 60 cm. tall, the leaves rather short, mostly crowded at the base; sheaths, at least the lower, spreading, pilose; blades spreading, flat or, especially on the innovations, involute, mostly 8 to 12 cm. long, 2 to 4 mm. wide, pilose; panicle diffuse, 15 to 20 cm. long, nearly or quite as wide, the branches stiffly and widely spreading, pilose in the axils; pedicels 2 or 3 times as long as the spikelets; spikelets 3- to 5-flowered, 3 to 4 mm. long, about 1.5 mm. wide; glumes 1 to 1.2 and 1.3 to 1.5 mm. long; lemmas about 1.5 mm. long. ♃ —Sandy woods, Florida (Tampa, Lakeland) and Texas; Mexico to Uruguay.

33. Eragrostis erósa Scribn. (Fig. 218.) Perennial; culms tufted, erect, 50 to 90 cm. tall; blades mostly involute; panicle diffuse, less than half the entire height of the plant, usually about one-third, mostly more than half as wide as long, branching 2 or 3 times, sparsely pilose or glabrous in the axils; spikelets mostly 8- to 9-flowered, 5 to 10 mm. long, 1.8 to 2 mm. wide; lemmas 2.5 to 3 mm. long, hyaline-margined toward summit, the tip erose. ♃ —Rocky

FIGURE 218.—*Eragrostis erosa*. Panicle, × 1 (Skehan 58, N. Mex.); floret, × 10. (Type.)

hills, western Texas to New Mexico and northern Mexico.

34. Eragrostis palméri S. Wats. (Fig. 219.) Perennial; culms tufted, erect, about 70 cm. tall; blades involute, elongate, erect; panicle open, oblong, 15 to 20 cm. long, 5 to 7 cm. wide, glabrous in the axils; spikelets 5 to 7 mm. long, mostly 7- to 9-flowered, brownish; first glume about 1 mm. long; second glume 1.5 to 2 mm. long; lemmas rounded on the back, bronze-tipped, about 2 mm. long. ♃ —Alkaline banks, Texas; Mexico (Juárez, Coahuila). Differs from *E. erosa* in the oblong panicle and smaller spikelets and lemmas.

FIGURE 219.—*Eragrostis palmeri*. Panicle, × 1; floret, × 10. (Silveus 851, Tex.)

35. Eragrostis intermédia Hitchc. PLAINS LOVEGRASS. (Fig. 220.) Perennial; culms erect, tufted, mostly 40 to 80 cm. tall; sheaths glabrous or the lowermost sparsely pilose, conspicuously pilose at the throat, the hairs extending in a line across the collar; blades flat to subinvolute, pilose on the upper surface near the base, otherwise glabrous or with a few scattered hairs, 10 to 25 cm. long, 1 to 3 mm. wide; panicle erect, open, often diffuse, 15 to 35 cm. long, at maturity mostly about three-fourths as wide, the axils pilose, sometimes sparsely so or rarely glabrous, the branches slender but rather stiff, the lower in pairs or verticils, all spreading, often horizontal; spikelets usually 3- to 8-flowered, 3 to 10 mm. long, about 1.5 mm. wide, grayish or brownish green, the pedicels somewhat flexuous, 1 to 3 times as long as the spikelet; glumes acute, 1 to 1.2 and 1.2 to 1.4 mm. long; lemmas turgid, obscurely nerved, 1.8 to 2 mm. long, usually bronze-tipped, not hyaline-margined; grain oblong, about 0.7 mm. long. ♃ —Dry or sandy prairies, Georgia; Louisiana and Missouri to Arizona and south to Central America. A few specimens from New Mexico have long spikelets (as much as 13-flowered) and glabrous axils.

FIGURE 220.—*Eragrostis intermedia*. Panicle, × 1; floret, × 10. (Type.)

FIGURE 221.—*Eragrostis swalleni*. Plant and panicle, × 1; floret and glandular band, × 10. (Type.)

36. Eragrostis swalléni Hitchc. (Fig. 221.) Perennial; culms in dense tufts, erect, 20 to 50 cm. tall, an obscure glandular band below the nodes; sheaths sparingly pilose at the throat; blades involute, glabrous, arching-recurved, 10 to 30 cm. long; panicle erect, open, 10 to 20 cm. long, the branches ascending or spreading, glabrous, stiffly flexuous; spikelets oblong to linear, stramineous or grayish green, 7 to 10 mm. long, about 2 mm. wide, mostly 8- to 12-flowered, the slender pedicels bearing above the middle a glandular band or spot; glumes acutish, rather broad, about 1.2 and 1.8 mm. long; lemmas rather closely imbricate, acutish, about 2 mm. long; palea minutely scabrous on the keels; grain nearly smooth, slightly narrowed toward the summit, 1 mm. long. ♃ —Sandy prairies, southern Texas; northern Mexico.

37. Eragrostis trácyi Hitchc. (Fig. 222.) Apparently perennial; culms erect, tufted, 30 to 80 cm. tall; sheaths rather sparsely pilose at the throat; blades flat or, especially of the innovations, involute, 5 to 25

FIGURE 222.—*Eragrostis tracyi*. Panicle, × 1; floret, × 10. (Type.)

FIGURE 223.—*Eragrostis silveana*. Panicle, × 1; spikelet, × 10. (Type.)

cm. long, 1 to 3 mm. wide; panicle erect, open, 10 to 15 cm. long, 5 to 8 cm. wide, the axils glabrous or nearly so, the branches ascending to spreading, flexuous; spikelets linear, mostly 9- to 15-flowered, 5 to 10 mm. long, about 1.5 mm. wide, pinkish or purplish, the flexuous pedicels spreading, 2 to 5 mm. long; glumes acutish, about 1 mm. and 1.5 mm. long; lemmas 1.5 to 2 mm. long, rather soft, loosely imbricate, the lateral nerves distinct; palea somewhat persistent; grain about 0.7 mm. long. ♃ —Sandy soil, known only from Sanibel Island, Fla.

39. Eragrostis trichódes (Nutt.) Wood. (Fig. 224.) Perennial; culms tufted, erect, 60 to 120 cm. tall; sheaths pilose at the summit, sometimes on the upper half; blades flat to subinvolute, elongate, 2 to 6 mm. wide, tapering to a slender point, scabrous on the upper surface; panicle usually purplish, diffuse, oblong, usually about half the entire height of the culm, branching 3 or 4 times, the branches capillary, loosely ascending, sparsely pilose in the axils; spikelets long-pediceled, lanceolate to ovate-oblong, mostly 4- to 6-flowered, 4 to 7 mm. long; glumes acuminate, nearly equal, 2.5 to 3 mm. long, about as long as the first floret; lemmas 2.5 to 3 mm. long, acute, subcompressed, the keel and lateral nerves strong; grain 1 mm. long, minutely pitted; anthers a little more than 1 mm. long. ♃ —Sand barrens and open sandy woods, Illinois to Colorado and Texas.

FIGURE 224.—*Eragrostis trichodes*. Panicle, × 1; floret, × 10. (Reverchon, Tex.)

38. Eragrostis silveána Swallen. (Fig. 223.) Perennial; culms densely tufted, erect from a knotty base, 40 to 50 cm. tall; sheaths glabrous; blades flat or loosely involute in drying, elongate, 3 mm. wide, attenuate to a fine point, glabrous; panicle 25 to 35 cm. long, 10 to 15 cm. wide, the viscid scabrous branches stiffly ascending or spreading, naked at base, sparsely pilose in the axils; spikelets purplish, 4- to 8-flowered, 2.5 to 4 mm. long, the ultimate pedicels short, usually appressed; glumes about 1 mm. long; lemmas acute, about 1.3 mm. long, the lateral nerves prominent. ♃ —Open ground, southern Texas.

40. Eragrostis pilífera Scheele. (Fig. 225.) Resembling *E. trichodes*, often in smaller tufts and taller; panicle stramineous or golden bronze; spikelets linear, 8- to 15-flowered, 8 to 12 mm. long; glumes and lemmas about 3 mm. long. ♃ (*E. grandiflora* Smith and Bush.)—Sand hills and sand barrens, Illinois and Nebraska to Louisiana and Texas.

41. Eragrostis spectábilis (Pursh) Steud. PURPLE LOVEGRASS. (Fig. 226.) Perennial, in dense tufts, rarely producing short or slender rhizomes; culms stiffly erect to spreading, 20 to 60 cm. tall; sheaths glabrous or pilose, conspicuously hairy at the throat; blades flat or folded, rather firm, stiffly ascending, tapering to a fine point, glabrous or rarely pilose, mostly 3 to 8 mm. wide; panicle at first included at base, two thirds the entire height of the culm, diffuse, bright purple, rarely pale, branching 3 or 4 times, the axis stiff, the branches stiffly spreading toward maturity, rarely pilose, strongly pilose in the axils, the lower shorter than the middle ones, finally reflexed, the whole panicle finally breaking away and tumbling before the wind; spikelets long-pediceled, short-pediceled toward the ends of the branches, oblong to linear, 6- to 12-flowered, 4 to 8 mm. long; glumes acute, a little more than 1 mm. long; lemmas acute, about 1.5 mm. long, slightly scabrous toward the tip, the lateral nerves prominent toward the base; palea somewhat bowed out, exposing the rather prominently short-ciliate keels; grain oval, dark-brown, 0.6 mm. long. ♃ —Sandy soil, Maine to Minnesota, south to Florida and Arizona; Mexico (San Luis Potosí). This species was formerly generally called *E. pectinacea*.

42. Eragrostis ellióttii S. Wats. (Fig. 227.) Perennial; culms tufted. stiffly erect or spreading, 40 to 80 cm. tall; sheaths glabrous, pilose at the throat; blades flat, elongate, scabrous on the upper surface, 2 to 4 mm. wide; panicle diffuse, fragile, usually more than half the entire height of the plant, branching 3 or 4 times, the branches capillary, spreading; spikelets on long capillary spreading pedicels, linear, mostly 8- to 15-flowered, 5 to 12 mm. long, about 2 mm. wide, pale or gray; glumes acute, 1 and 1.5 mm. long; lemmas closely imbricate, acute, about 2 mm. long, bowed out below, fitting into the angles of the zigzag rachilla; grain oval, 0.7 mm. long. ♃ —Low ground, wet meadows, and low pine woods, Coastal Plain, North Carolina to Florida and eastern Texas; West Indies and eastern Mexico.

FIGURE 225.—*Eragrostis pilifera*. Panicle, × 1; floret, × 10. (Rydberg 1831, Nebr.)

43. Eragrostis acúta Hitchc. (Fig. 228.) Perennial; culms erect, 40 to 60 cm. tall; sheaths glabrous, pilose at the throat; blades flat, becoming more or less involute, 2 to 4 mm. wide; panicle diffuse, more than half

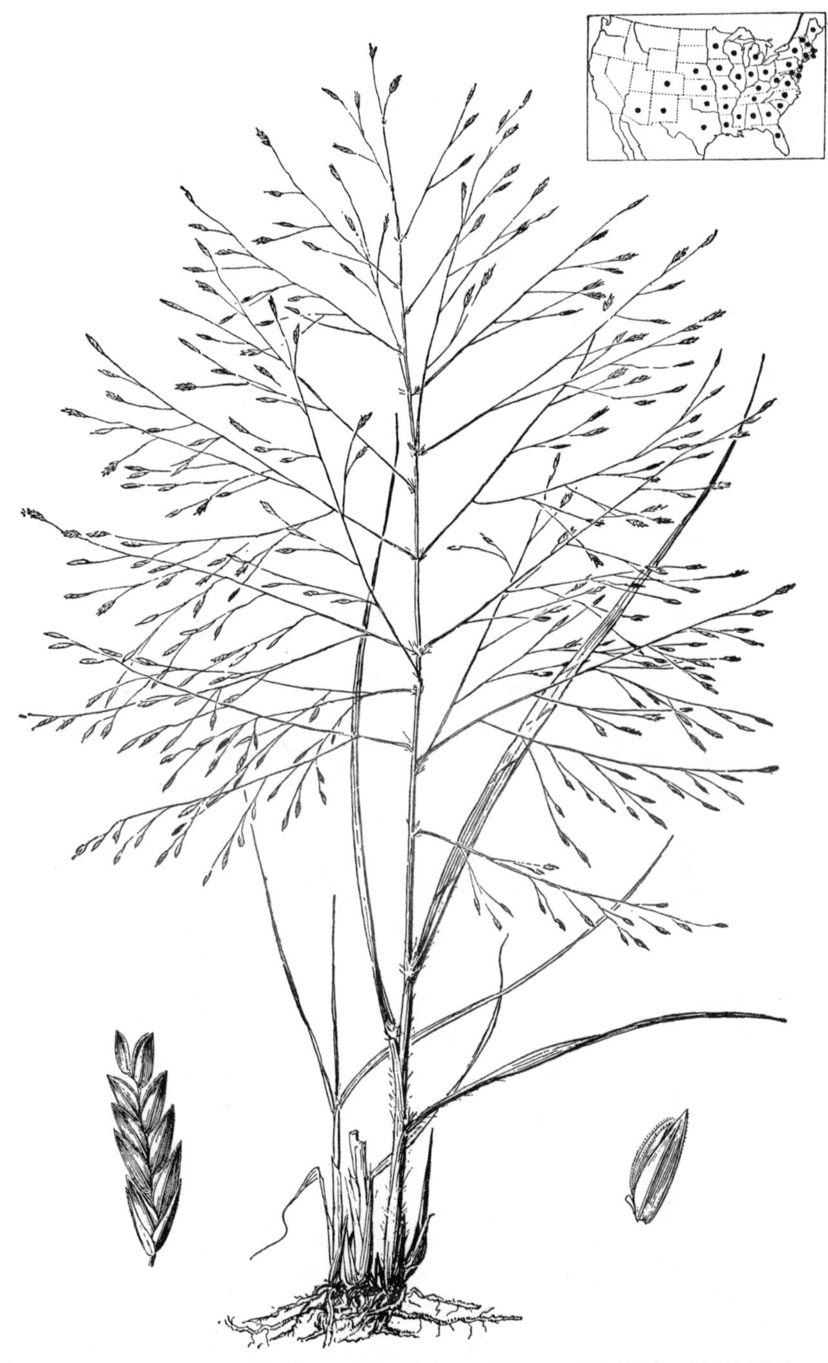

FIGURE 226.—*Eragrostis spectabilis*. Plant, × ½; spikelet, × 5; floret, × 10. (Hitchcock 7849, Md.)

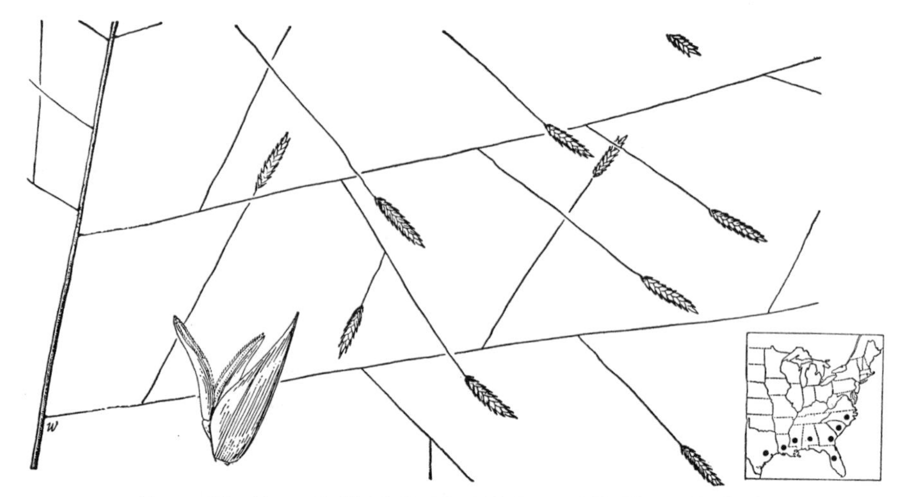

FIGURE 227.—*Eragrostis elliottii.* Panicle, × 1; floret, × 10. (Tracy 7384, Fla.)

FIGURE 228.—*Eragrostis acuta.* Panicle, × 1; floret, × 10. (Type.)

the entire height of the plant, branching 3 or 4 times, the branches less fragile than in *E. elliottii;* spikelets on long spreading pedicels, oblong-elliptic, 10- to 20-flowered, 8 to 14 mm. long, 3 mm. wide, pale or stramineous; glumes acuminate, 2.5 and 3 mm. long; lemmas acuminate, 3 mm. long; grain 0.8 mm. long. ♃ —Low pine woods and moist sandy soil, peninsular Florida.

44. Eragrostis refrácta (Muhl.) Scribn. (Fig. 229.) Resembling *E. elliottii;* blades more or less pilose on

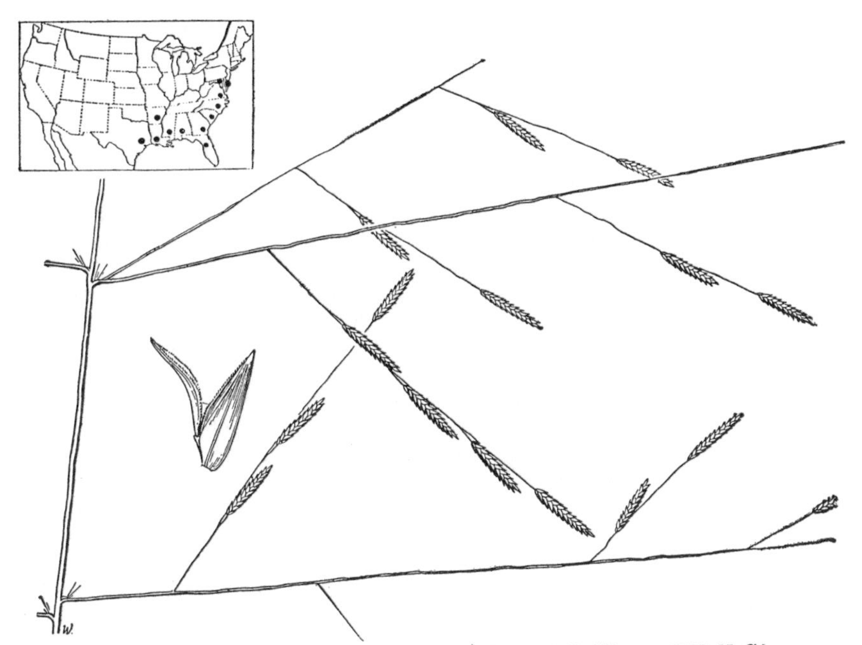

FIGURE 229.—*Eragrostis refracta.* Panicle, × 1; floret, × 10. (Kearney 1922, N. C.)

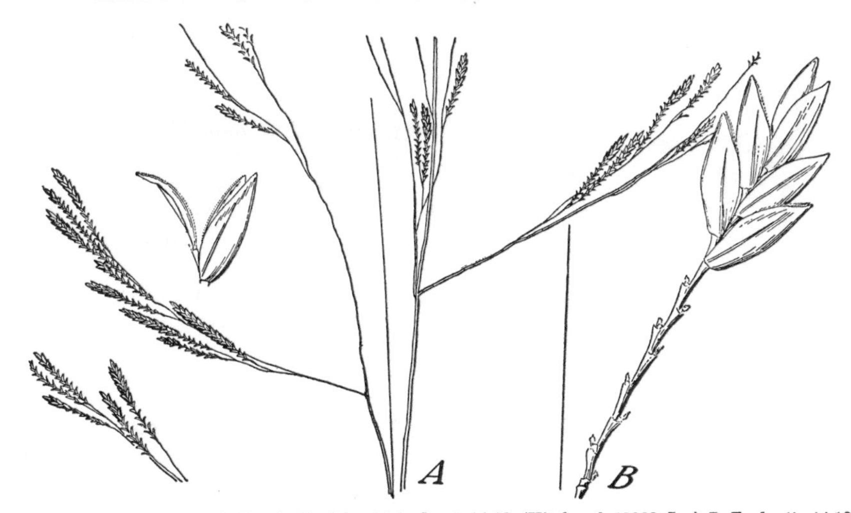

FIGURE 230.—*A, Eragrostis bahiensis.* Panicle, × 1; floret, × 10. (Hitchcock 19862, La.) *B, E. chariis,* × 10. (Weatherwax 822, Fla.)

the upper surface near base; lower panicle branches usually finally reflexed, long-pilose in the axils; spikelets short-pediceled, appressed and distant along the nearly simple panicle branches, the lemmas on the average shorter than in *E. elliottii.* ♃ —Low sandy soil, Coastal Plain, Delaware to Florida, Arkansas, and eastern Texas.

45. Eragrostis cháriis (Schult.) Hitchc. (Fig. 230, *B.*) Perennial; culms erect or ascending at base, 60 to 120 cm. tall; panicle open, 7 to 15 cm. long, nodding, the branches glabrous or with a few hairs in the axils, ascending, solitary, rather distant, naked below, rather closely flowered with ascending or appressed branchlets; spikelets linear, 5 to 10 mm. long, 8- to 20-flowered; glumes about 1.3 and 1.7 mm. long; lemmas 1.5 to 2 mm. long, imbricate; palea persistent only a short time after the fall of the lemma, the naked rachilla persisting. ♃ —Sandy roadsides, Florida (St. Petersburg); introduced from southeastern Asia.

46. Eragrostis bahiénsis Schrad. (Fig. 230, *A*.) Resembling *E. chariis;* panicle often more or less condensed; spikelets as much as 30-flowered; lemmas about 2 mm. long; palea persistent. ♃ —Introduced, Florida (Milton, Pensacola), Alabama (Mobile), and Louisiana (Avery Island); Brazil.

FIGURE 231.—*Eragrostis curvula*. Panicle, × 1; floret, × 10. (Silveus 2156, cult., Tex.)

47. Eragrostis cúrvula (Schrad.) Nees. WEEPING LOVEGRASS. (Fig. 231.) Culms 60 to 120 cm. tall, densely tufted, erect, simple or sometimes branching at the lower nodes; sheaths narrow, keeled, glabrous or sparsely hispid, the lower densely hairy toward the base; blades elongate, involute, attenuate to a fine point, arcuate spreading, scabrous; panicles 20 to 30 cm. long, the branches solitary or in pairs, ascending, naked at the base, at least the lower densely pilose in the axils; spikelets 7- to 11-flowered, 8 to 10 mm. long, gray green; lemmas about 2.5 mm. long, obtuse or subacute, the nerves prominent. ♃ —Cultivated for ornament; spontaneous in Florida, Texas, and Arizona. Useful in erosion control and showing promise of being valuable in revegetation of grasslands in the Southern States.

Eragrostis lehmanniána Nees. LEHMANN LOVEGRASS. Perennial; culms finally prostrate, 30 to 80 cm. long, the nodes rooting and producing tufts of branches; panicles 10 to 15 cm. long, open; spikelets linear, 10 to 12 mm. long. ♃ —Introduced from Africa, drought-resistant and proving effective in erosion control, Texas, Oklahoma, and Arizona (well established near Tucson).

Eragrostis stenophýlla Hochst. Erect smooth annual, 30 to 40 cm. tall, with loosely involute blades and rather loose panicle with ascending branches, the linear spikelets several-flowered, the lemmas 1.3 mm. long. ☉ —Florida, Mississippi (Biloxi), probably escaped from grass garden; India.

Eragrostis cyperoídes (Thunb.) Beauv. Stiff stout stoloniferous perennial with sharp-pointed blades and narrow elongate interrupted panicles, the distant branches with naked thornlike tips; spikelets coriaceous, crowded. ♃ —Oregon (Linnton), on ballast; South Africa.

ERAGROSTIS TEF (Zuccagni) Trotter. TEFF. Annual; culms branching and spreading, 30 to 100 cm. tall; panicle large and open; spikelets 5- to 9-flowered, 6 to 8 mm. long. ☉ (*E. abyssinica* (Jacq.) Link.)—Occasionally cultivated for ornament. Africa, where the seed is used for food.

ERAGROSTIS OBTÚSA Munro. Low branching perennial; panicles open, 5 to 10 cm. long; spikelets gray olivaceous, broadly ovate, the lemmas almost horizontally spreading. ♃ —Occasionally cultivated for ornament. South Africa.

Eragrostis chloromélas Steud. Boer lovegrass. Erect branching perennial, 40 to 90 cm. tall, forming dense clumps; blades elongate, subinvolute; panicle 10 to 20 cm. long, loose; spikelets dark olivaceous. ♃ —Introduced from Africa, drought-resistant and promising in erosion control in the Southwest.

15. CATABRÓSA Beauv.

Spikelets mostly 2-flowered, the florets rather distant, the rachilla disarticulating above the glumes and between the florets; glumes unequal, shorter than the lower floret, flat, nerveless, irregularly toothed at the broad truncate apex; lemmas broad, prominently 3-nerved, the nerves parallel, the broad apex scarious; palea about as long as the lemma, broad, scarious at apex. Aquatic perennials, with creeping bases, flat soft blades, and open panicles. Type species, *Catabrosa aquatica*. Name from Greek *katabrosis*, an eating up or devouring, referring to the toothed or erose glumes.

1. Catabrosa aquática (L.) Beauv. Brookgrass (Fig. 232.) Glabrous throughout; culms 10 to 40 cm. long;

Figure 232.—*Catabrosa aquatica*. Plant, × ½; spikelet and floret, × 5. (Williams and Fernald, Quebec.)

FIGURE 233.—*Molinia caerulea*. Plant, × ½; spikelet and floret, × 5. (Kirk 157, Vt.)

blades mostly less than 10 cm. long, 2 to 8 mm. wide; panicle erect, 10 to 20 cm. long, oblong or pyramidal, yellow to brown, the branches spreading in somewhat distant whorls; spikelets short-pediceled, about 3 mm. long; glumes about 1.5 and 2 mm. long; lemmas 2.5 to 3 mm. long. ♃ —Mountain meadows, around springs and along streams, Newfoundland and Labrador to Alberta, south through Wisconsin, North Dakota, South Dakota, and eastern Oregon to northern Arizona; Eurasia. Sometimes 1-flowered spikelets occur in panicles with 2-flowered ones.

Cutándia memphítica (Spreng.) Richt. Low annual; blades flat; panicle few-flowered; spikelets on short pedicels, finally divergent on the zigzag branches. ⊙ —San Bernardino Mountains, Calif.; introduced from the Mediterranean region.

16. MOLÍNIA Schrank

Spikelets 2- to 4-flowered, the florets distant, the rachilla disarticulating above the glumes, slender, prolonged beyond the upper floret and bearing a rudimentary floret; glumes somewhat unequal, acute, shorter than the first lemma, 1-nerved; lemmas membranaceous, narrowed to an obtuse point, 3-nerved; palea bowed out below, equaling or slightly exceeding the lemma. Slender tufted perennials, with flat blades and narrow, rather open panicles. Type species, *Molinia caerulea.* Named for J. I. Molina.

1. Molinia caerúlea (L.) Moench. (Fig. 233.) Culms erect, 50 to 100 cm. tall; blades 2 to 7 mm. wide, erect, tapering to a fine point; panicle 10 to 20 cm. long, purplish, the branches ascending, rather densely flowered, mostly floriferous to the base; spikelets short-pediceled, 4 to 7 mm. long; lemmas about 3 mm. long. ♃ —Meadows and fields, introduced in a few localities, Maine to Pennsylvania; Eurasia.

17. DIARRHÉNA Beauv.

(*Diarina* Raf.)

Spikelets few-flowered, the rachilla disarticulating above the glumes and between the florets; glumes unequal, acute, shorter than the lemmas, the first 1-nerved, the second 3- to 5-nerved; lemmas chartaceous, pointed, 3-nerved, the nerves converging in the point, the upper floret reduced; palea chartaceous, obtuse, at maturity the lemma and palea widely spread by the large turgid beaked caryopsis with hard shining pericarp; stamens 2 or 3. Perennials, with slender rhizomes, broadly linear, flat blades, long-tapering below, and narrow, few-flowered panicles. Type species, *Diarrhena americana.* Name from Greek *dis*, twice, and *arren*, male, alluding to the two stamens.

1. Diarrhena americána Beauv. (Fig. 234.) Culms slender, about 1 m.tall, arched-l eaning, leaves approximate below the middle of the culm; sheaths pubescent toward the summit; blades elongate, 1 to 2 cm. wide, scabrous to pubescent beneath; panicle long-exserted, drooping, 10 to 30 cm. long, the branches few, appressed, the lower distant; spikelets 10 to 18 mm. long, at first narrow, the florets expanded at maturity; lemmas 6 to 10 mm. long. ♃ (*Diarina festucoides* Raf.)—Rich or moist woods, Virginia to Michigan and South Dakota, south to Tennessee, Arkansas, Oklahoma, and eastern Texas.

18. DISSANTHÉLIUM Trin.

Spikelets mostly 2-flowered, the rachilla slender, disarticulating above the glumes and between the florets; glumes firm, nearly equal, acuminate, much longer than the lower floret, mostly exceeding all the florets, the first 1-nerved, the second 3-nerved; lemmas strongly compressed, oval or elliptic, acute, 3-nerved, the lateral nerves near the margin; palea some-

FIGURE 234.—*Diarrhena americana.* Plant, × ½; spikelet and floret, × 5. (Wilcox 66, Ill.)

what shorter than the lemma. Annuals or perennials with narrow panicles. Type species, *Dissanthelium supinum* Trin. Name from Greek, *dissos*, double, and *anthelion*, a small flower, alluding to the two small florets.

1. Dissanthelium califórnicum (Nutt.) Benth. (Fig. 235.) Annual, lax; culms more or less decumbent or spreading, about 30 cm. tall; blades flat, 10 to 15 cm. long, 2 to 4 mm. wide; panicle 10 to 15 cm. long, narrow but rather loose, the branches in fascicles, ascending, slender, flexuous, some of them floriferous to base; glumes narrow, acute, nearly equal, about 3 mm. long; lemmas pubescent, nearly 2 mm. long. ⊙ —Open ground, islands off the southern coast of California and of Baja California.

19. REDFIÉLDIA Vasey

Spikelets compressed, mostly 3- or 4-flowered, the rachilla disarticulating above the glumes and between the florets; glumes somewhat unequal, 1-nerved, acuminate; lemmas chartaceous, 3-nerved, the nerves parallel, densely villous at base; palea as long as the lemma; grain free. A rather tall perennial, with extensive rhizomes, and a large panicle with diffuse capillary branches. Type species, *Redfieldia flexuosa.* Named for J. H. Redfield.

1. Redfieldia flexuósa (Thurb.) Vasey. Blowout grass. (Fig. 236.) Culms tough, 60 to 100 cm. tall, the rhizomes long, slender; blades glabrous, involute, elongate, flexuous, tapering to a fine point; panicle oblong, one-third to half the entire length of the culm; spikelets 5 to 7 mm. long, broadly V-shaped, the glumes acuminate, about half as long as the spikelet; lemmas acute, sometimes mucronate, 4 to 5 mm. long. ♃ —Sand hills, North Dakota to Oklahoma, west to Utah and Arizona (Moki Reservation). A sand-binding grass.

Figure 235.—*Dissanthelium californicum.* Plant, × ½; spikelet and floret, × 10. (Trask 324, Calif.)

FIGURE 236.—*Redfieldia flexuosa*. Plant, × ½; spikelet and floret, × 5. (Over 2429, S. Dak.)

20. MONANTHÓCHLOË Engelm.

Plants dioecious; spikelets 3- to 5-flowered, the uppermost florets rudimentary, the rachilla disarticulating tardily in pistillate spikelets; glumes wanting; lemmas rounded on the back, convolute, narrowed above, several-nerved, those of the pistillate spikelets like the blades in texture; palea narrow, 2-nerved, in the pistillate spikelets convolute around the pistil, the rudimentary uppermost floret enclosed between the keels of the floret next below. Creeping wiry perennial, with clustered short subulate blades, the spikelets inconspicuous at the ends of the short branches, only a little exceeding the leaves. Type species, *Monanthochloë littoralis*. Name from Greek *monos*, single, *anthos*, flower, and *chloe*, grass, alluding to the unisexual flowers.

1. Monanthochloë littorális Engelm. (Fig. 237.) Culms tufted, extensively creeping, the short branches erect; blades falcate, mostly less than 1 cm. long, conspicuously distichous in distant to approximate clusters; spikelets 1 to few, nearly concealed in the leaves. ♃ —Muddy seashores and tidal flats, southern Florida, especially on the keys; Texas (Galveston and southward); southern California (Santa Barbara and southward); Mexico, Cuba.

21. DISTÍCHLIS Raf. SALTGRASS.

Plants dioecious; spikelets several to many-flowered, the rachilla of the pistillate spikelets disarticulating above the glumes and between the florets; glumes unequal, broad, acute, keeled, 3- to 7-nerved, the lateral nerves sometimes faint; lemmas closely imbricate, firm, the pistillate coriaceous, acute or subacute, with 9 to 11 mostly faint nerves (nerves fewer in *D. texana*); palea as long as the lemma or shorter, the margins bowed out near the base, the pistillate coriaceous, enclosing the grain. Low perennials, with extensively creeping scaly rhizomes, sometimes stolons, erect, rather rigid culms, and dense, rather few-flowered panicles. Type species, *Distichlis spicata*. Name from Greek *distichos*, 2-ranked, alluding to the distichous leaves.

The species of *Distichlis* in general have little value for forage, but in the interior basins, such as the vicinity of Great Salt Lake, *D. stricta* is grazed when better grasses are not available.

Plants mostly more than 30 cm. tall; blades not conspicuously distichous, mostly 20 to 40 cm. long; panicle more than 10 cm. long; stolons present, long and stout .... 3. D. TEXANA.
Plants mostly less than 30 cm. tall; blades conspicuously distichous, mostly less than 10 cm. long; panicle rarely more than 5 cm. long.
  Panicles condensed, the spikelets imbricate, mostly 5- to 9-flowered; keels of pistillate paleas with narrow entire wings .... 1. D. SPICATA.
  Panicles looser, the spikelets less imbricate, the individual spikelets plainly visible; keels of pistillate paleas with broader serrate-erose wings .... 2. D. STRICTA.

1. Distichlis spicáta (L.) Greene. SEASHORE SALTGRASS. (Fig. 238.) Culms 10 to 40 cm. tall, sometimes taller; leaves numerous, the sheaths closely overlapping, the spreading blades conspicuously distichous, flat to involute, sharp-pointed, mostly less than 10 cm. long; panicle usually pale or greenish, 1 to 6 cm. long, rarely longer; spikelets mostly 5- to 9-flowered, mostly 6 to 10 mm. long, compressed; lemmas 3 to 6 mm. long, the pistillate more coriaceous and more closely imbricate than the staminate; palea rather soft, narrow, the keels narrowly winged, entire; anthers about 2 mm. long. ♃ — Seashores, forming dense colonies, Nova Scotia to Florida and Texas; British Columbia to California, Mexico, and Cuba; Pacific slope of South

FIGURE 237.—*Monanthochloë littoralis.* Plant, × ½; pistillate spikelet and floret, × 5. (Hitchcock 623, Fla.)

America. Occasional plants produce runners above ground as well as below. Such specimens have been segregated as *D. spicata* var. *stolonifera* Beetle. DISTICHLIS SPICATA var. NÁNA Beetle. Culms slender from slender rhizomes; blades 1 to 8 cm. long, subinvolute, slender; panicles of 2 to 5 spikelets, the spikelets slightly narrower than in the species; keels of the palea densely short-ciliate. ♃ —Alkaline boggy or sandy soil, Stanislaus and Kern Counties, Calif. Insufficiently known.

2. Distichlis strícta (Torr.) Rydb. DESERT SALTGRASS. (Fig. 239.) Resembling *D. spicata;* panicles less congested, the individual spikelets easily distinguished; staminate panicles stramineous, the spikelets 8- to 15-flowered; pistillate spikelets greenish leaden, mostly 7- or 9-flowered, broader; lemmas firm, the palea a little shorter, much broader below, the keels with wide serrulate erose or lacerate wings. ♃ (*D. dentata* Rydb., the pistillate plant.) — Alkaline soil of the interior, Saskatchewan to eastern Washington, south to Texas and California; Mexico. This and *D. spicata* appear to be distinct for the most part, but the staminate plants are sometimes difficult to distinguish.[10]

3. Distichlis texána (Vasey) Scribn. (Fig. 240.) Culms erect from a decumbent base, 30 to 60 cm. tall, producing extensively creeping rhizomes and long stout stolons; blades flat, firm, glabrous beneath, scabrous on the upper surface, mostly 20 to 40 cm. long, 2 to 6 mm. wide; panicle narrow, pale, 10 to 25 cm. long, somewhat interrupted, the branches appressed; spikelets somewhat compressed, 4- to 8-flowered, 1 to 1.5 cm. long; glumes 5 and 7 mm. long, acute; lemmas of pistillate spikelets closely imbricate and appressed, about 8 mm. long with 3 strong nerves, the intermediate nerves obscure, acute, the margins broad, hyaline; palea of pistillate spikelets shorter than the lemma, strongly bowed out below, closely convolute around the pistil, the keels with narrow erose or toothed wings; lemmas of staminate spikelets more spreading, about 6 mm. long, 3-nerved; palea about as long as the lemma, not bowed out, not convolute, the keels minutely scabrous, not winged; anthers 3 mm. long. ♃ —Sand flats, Presidio and Brewster Counties, Tex., and northern Mexico.

FIGURE 238.—*Distichlis spicata.* Plant, × 1; floret, × 5. (Hitchcock 2826, Oreg.)

[10] REEDER, J. R. STATUS OF DISTICHLIS DENTATA. Torrey Bot. Club Bul. 70: 53–57. 1943.

FIGURE 239.—*Distichlis stricta.* Staminate plant, × ½; staminate spikelet and floret, × 5 (Mearns 3132, Calif.); pistillate panicle, × 1; pistillate floret, × 5 (Sandberg and Leiberg 463, Wash.).

22. UNÍOLA L.

Spikelets 3- to many-flowered, the lower 1 to 6 lemmas empty, the rachilla disarticulating above the glumes and between the florets; glumes compressed-keeled, rigid, usually narrow, 3- to 7-nerved, acute or acuminate, rarely mucronate; lemmas compressed, sometimes conspicuously flattened, chartaceous, many-nerved, the nerves sometimes obscure, acute or acuminate, the empty ones at the base and the uppermost usually reduced; palea rigid, strongly keeled, bowed out at base, weakly so in *Uniola paniculata;* stamen 1. Rather tall, erect perennials, with flat or sometimes convolute blades and narrow or open panicles of compressed, sometimes very broad and flat spikelets. Type species, *Uniola paniculata.* Ancient Latin name of a plant.

The inland species are not abundant enough to be of value for forage. *Uniola latifolia* is worthy of cultivation as an ornamental; *U. paniculata* is a sand binder along the southern seacoast; the seeds of *U. palmeri* Vasey of Mexico are used for food by the Cocopa Indians.

Rhizomes extensively creeping; blades firm, flat at base, tapering into a long flexuous involute point; empty lemmas about 4; coastal dunes........................ 1. U. PANICULATA.
Rhizomes wanting or short and knotty; blades thin, flat; empty lemma 1 (2 or 3 in *U. ornithorhyncha*); rich or moist woods.
  Spikelets 8- to 12-flowered on slender pedicels; panicle nodding or drooping. 2. U. LATIFOLIA.
  Spikelets 3- to 7-flowered, nearly sessile; panicle erect, nearly simple, the branches stiff.
    Spikelets more than 10 mm. (usually more than 12 mm.) wide, with 5 to 7 fertile florets.
      Sterile lemma 1; panicle 10 to 15 cm. long, the lower branches with 2 to 5 rather distant spikelets........................ 3. U. NITIDA.
      Sterile lemmas 2 or 3; panicle 3 to 8 cm. long, the branches very short with approximate spikelets........................ 4. U. ORNITHORHYNCHA.
    Spikelets rarely as much as 8 mm. wide at maturity, V-shaped, with 1 to 4 fertile florets (rarely more), and 1 sterile lemma.
      Collar of sheath pubescent, the sheaths commonly loosely long-pubescent, rarely glabrous........................ 5. U. SESSILIFLORA.
      Collar and sheaths glabrous or nearly so .... 6. U. LAXA.

1. Uniola paniculáta L. SEA OATS. (Fig. 241.) Culms stout, about 1 m. tall, from extensively creeping rhizomes; blades flat, firm, elongate,

FIGURE 240.—*Distichlis texana.* Panicle, × 1; lemma and palea, × 5. (Nealley, Tex.)

FIGURE 241.—*Uniola paniculata.* Plant, × 1/10; spikelets, × 1. (Kearney 2134, Va.)

FIGURE 242.—*Uniola latifolia*. Plant, × ½; spikelet and floret, × 3. (Chase 5874, Md.)

becoming involute toward the long, fine flexuous point; panicle pale, narrow, condensed, heavy and nodding, 20 to 40 cm. long, the branches arching and drooping, as much as 12 cm. long; spikelets very flat, 10- to 20-flowered, mostly 2 to 2.5 cm. long, 1 cm. wide, the first 4 to 6 lemmas empty, the slender pedicels shorter than the spikelets; lemmas about 9-nerved, strongly compressed-keeled about 1 cm. long, acute; palea acute, as long as the lemma, the strong wings of the keels ciliate. ♃ —Sand dunes of the seacoast, Northampton County, Va., to Florida and Texas; northern West Indies; eastern Mexico. Spikelets apparently sterile, no caryopses nor stamens found.

2. Uniola latifólia Michx. BROADLEAF UNIOLA. (Fig. 242.) Culms 1 to 1.4 m. tall, with short strong rhizomes, forming colonies; blades flat, narrowly lanceolate, 10 to 20 cm. long, mostly 1 to 2 cm. wide; panicle open, drooping, 10 to 20 cm. long, the branches bearing a few large, very flat spikelets, the pedicels capillary; spikelets 8- to 12-flowered, 2 to 3.5 cm. long, 1 to 1.5 cm. wide, green or finally tawny, the first lemma empty; lemmas lanceolate, strongly compressed-keeled, acute, about 1 cm. long, striate-nerved, the keel ciliate with soft ascending hairs, the callus pilose; palea shorter than the lemma, wing-keeled; anther minute, the flower cleistogamous; caryopsis flat, oval, black, 5 mm. long. ♃ —Rich woods, Pennsylvania and New Jersey to Illinois and Kansas, south to Florida and Texas; Arizona (Pinal County).

3. Uniola nítida Baldw. (Fig. 243.) Culms slender, 50 to 75 cm. tall, erect, loosely tufted, with short rhizomes; blades flat, spreading, mostly less than 15 cm. long, 4 to 8 mm. wide; panicle open, few-flowered, 10 to 15 cm. long, with a few spreading branches 3 to 8 cm. long, bearing 2 to 5 nearly sessile spikelets; spikelets 4- to 7-flowered, 1 to 1.5 cm. long, about 1 cm. wide, the first lemma empty; lemmas spreading, 7 to 10 mm. long, compressed-keeled, gradually acuminate, striate-nerved; palea equaling the lemma, acuminate, 2-toothed, the keels prominently winged; anther 1.5 mm. long. ♃ —Moist woods, South Carolina to Florida.

4. Uniola ornithorhyncha Steud. (Fig. 244.) Culms slender, 30 to 50 cm. tall, loosely tufted with short rhizomes; sheaths pubescent on the collar; blades flat, thin, mostly less than 15 cm. long, 3 to 6 mm. wide; panicle narrow, 3 to 9 cm. long, the short approximate branches with 1 to 3 nearly sessile spikelets or the lower somewhat distant with 4 to 6 spikelets, pubescent in the axils; spikelets very flat, with 3 or 4 widely spreading fertile florets, the 2 or 3 lower lemmas empty, appressed; fertile lemmas about 8 mm. long, narrow, gradually acuminate, striate-nerved; palea as long as or longer than the lemma, acuminate, 2-toothed, strongly bowed out below, the keels rather narrowly winged; anther 1 to 1.8 mm. long. ♃ —Low woods or hummocks in swamps, Alabama to Louisiana.

5. Uniola sessiliflóra Poir. (Fig. 245.) Culms erect, 0.5 to 1.5 m. tall, in loose tufts with short rhizomes; sheaths pilose, at least toward the summit; blades elongate, firm, mostly sparsely pilose on the upper surface toward the base, 5 to 10 mm. wide, tapering to base; panicle long-exserted, 20 to 50 cm. long, narrow, the branches distant, stiffly ascending or appressed, the lower as much as 7 cm. long, the upper short, somewhat capitate; spikelets nearly sessile, aggregate in clusters, flat, usually 3- to 5-flowered, broadly V-shaped at maturity, the first lemma empty; glumes about 2 mm. long; lemmas spreading, about 5 mm. long, acuminate, beaked, especially before maturity, striate-nerved; palea shorter than the lemma, acute, broad, the keels narrowly winged; grain black, 3 mm. long, at maturity spreading the lemma and

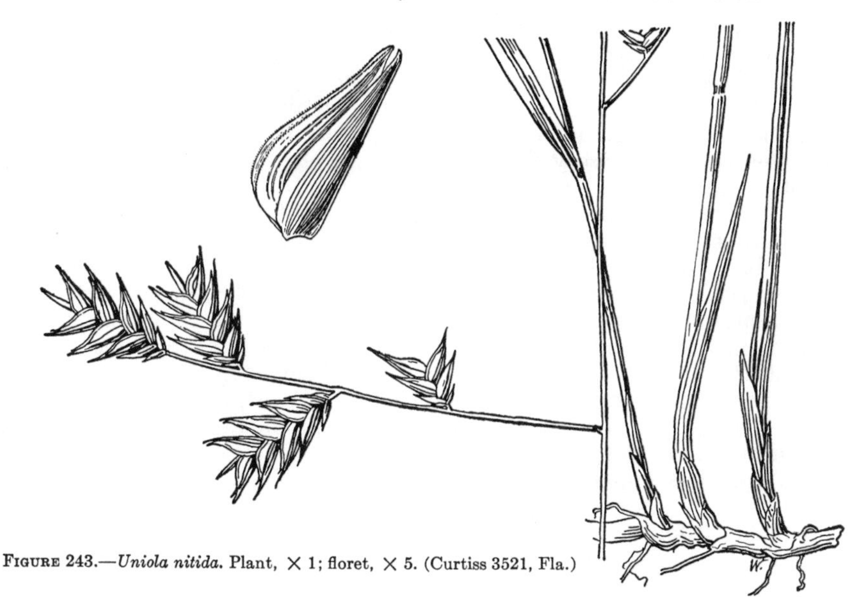

FIGURE 243.—*Uniola nitida.* Plant, × 1; floret, × 5. (Curtiss 3521, Fla.)

palea; anther 1.3 mm. long. ♃ (*U. longifolia* Scribn.)—Rich woods, southeastern Virginia to Tennessee and Oklahoma, south to Florida and eastern Texas.

6. Uniola láxa (L.) B. S. P. (Fig. 246.) Culms slender, 60 to 100 cm. tall, erect to nodding from a loosely tufted sometimes knotty base; blades elongate, flat to sometimes loosely involute, 3 to 6 mm. wide; panicle narrow, slender, 15 to 30 cm. long, the branches short, appressed, approximate, the lower sometimes 3 cm. long and distant; spikelets nearly sessile, approximate, flat, usually 3- to 4-flowered, the first lemma empty; lemmas spreading, 4 to 5 mm. long, gradually acuminate, striate-nerved; palea broad, the keels narrowly winged; grain black, 2.5 mm. long, at maturity spreading the lemma and palea; anther 1.2 mm. long. ♃ —Moist woods, Coastal Plain, Long Island to Florida and Texas, extending to western North Carolina, Kentucky, Arkansas, and Oklahoma.

23. DÁCTYLIS L. ORCHARD GRASS

Spikelets few-flowered, compressed, finally disarticulating between the florets, nearly sessile in dense 1-sided fascicles, these borne at the ends of the few branches of a panicle; glumes unequal, carinate, acute, hispid-ciliate on the keel; lemmas compressed-keeled, mucronate, 5-nerved, ciliate on the keel. Perennials, with flat blades and fascicled spikelets. Type species, *Dactylis glomerata.* Name from Greek *dactulos*, a finger, alluding to the stiff branches of the panicle.

1. Dactylis glomeráta L. ORCHARD GRASS. (Fig. 247.) Culms in large tussocks, 60 to 120 cm. tall; blades elongate, 2 to 8 mm. wide; panicles 5 to 20 cm. long, the few distant stiff solitary branches ascending, or spreading at anthesis, appressed at maturity, the lowermost sometimes as much as 10 cm. long; lemmas about 8 mm. long, mucronate or short-awned. ♃ —Fields, meadows, and waste places, Newfoundland to southeastern Alaska; south to Florida and central California; Eurasia. Commonly cultivated as a meadow and pasture grass. In England called cocksfoot. A variegated form (called by gardeners var. *variegata*) is occasionally cultivated for borders.

FIGURE 245.—*Uniola sessiliflora.* Plant, × 1; floret, × 5. (Tracy, Miss.)

FIGURE 244.—*Uniola ornithorhyncha.* Plant, × 1; floret, × 5. (Tracy and Lloyd 448, Miss.)

24. CYNOSÚRUS L. DOGTAIL

Spikelets of two kinds, sterile and fertile together, the fertile sessile, nearly covered by the short-pediceled sterile one, these pairs imbricate in a dense 1-sided spikelike panicle; sterile spikelets consisting of 2 glumes and several narrow, acuminate, 1-nerved lemmas on a continuous rachilla; fertile spikelets 2- or 3-flowered, the glumes narrow, the lemmas broader, rounded on the back, awn-tipped, the rachilla disarticulating above the glumes. Annuals or perennials with narrow flat blades and dense spikelike or subcapitate panicles. Type species, *Cynosurus cristatus.* Name from Greek *kuon* (*kun*-) dog, and *oura*, tail.

Plants perennial; panicles narrow, spikelike; awns inconspicuous............ 1. C. CRISTATUS.
Plants annual; panicles subcapitate; awns conspicuous............................ 2. C. ECHINATUS.

1. Cynosurus cristátus L. CRESTED DOGTAIL. (Fig. 248.) Perennial; culms tufted or geniculate at base, erect, 30 to 60 cm. tall; panicle spikelike, linear, more or less curved, 3 to 8 cm.

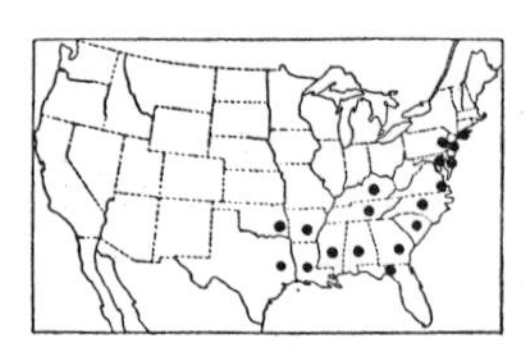

FIGURE 246.—*Uniola laxa*. Plant, × 1; floret, × 5. (Van Eseltine and Moseley 178, D. C.)

long; pairs of spikelets about 5 mm. long; lemmas with awns mostly not more than 1 mm. long. ♃ —Fields and waste places, Newfoundland to Michigan and North Carolina; Idaho, Washington to California; introduced from Europe. Occasionally cultivated in mixtures for meadows, but of little value.

2. Cynosurus echinátus L. (Fig. 249.) Annual; culms 20 to 40 cm. tall; blades short; panicle subcapitate, 1 to 4 cm. long, bristly; pairs of spikelets 7 to 10 mm. long; lemmas with awns 5 to 10 mm. long. ⊙ —Open ground, British Columbia; Oregon to central California; Maryland; North Carolina; Arkansas and Oklahoma; introduced from Europe.

25. LAMÁRCKIA Moench

(*Achyrodes* Boehmer)

Spikelets of two kinds, in fascicles, the terminal one of each fascicle fertile, the others sterile; fertile spikelet with 1 perfect floret on a slender stipe and a rudimentary floret on a long rachilla-joint, both awned, the glumes narrow, acuminate or short-awned, 1-nerved; lemma broader, scarcely nerved, bearing just below the apex a delicate awn; sterile spikelets linear, 1 to 3 in each fascicle, consisting of 2 glumes similar to those of the fertile spikelet, and numerous imbricate, obtuse, awnless, empty lemmas, a reduced spikelet similar to the fertile one borne on the pedicel with one of the sterile ones.—Low annual with flat blades and oblong, 1-sided, dense panicles, the crowded fascicles drooping, the fertile being hidden, except the awns, by the numerous sterile ones; fascicles falling entire. Type species, *Lamarckia aurea*. Named for J. B. Lamarck.

1. Lamarckia aúrea (L.) Moench. GOLDENTOP. (Fig. 250.) Culms erect or decumbent at base, 10 to 40 cm. tall; blades soft, 3 to 7 mm. wide; panicle dense, 2 to 7 cm. long, 1 to 2 cm. wide, shining, golden yellow to purplish, the branches short, erect, the branchlets capillary, flexuous; pedicels fascicled, pubescent, with a tuft of long whitish hairs at the base; fertile spikelet about 2 mm. long, the awn of lemma about twice as long as the spikelet; sterile spikelet 6 to 8 mm. long. ⊙ —Open ground and waste places, Texas, Arizona, southern California, and northern Mexico; introduced from the Mediterranean region. Sometimes cultivated for ornament.

26. ARÚNDO L.

Spikelets several-flowered, the florets successively smaller, the summits of all about equal, the rachilla glabrous, disarticulating above the glumes and between the florets; glumes somewhat unequal, membranaceous, 3-nerved, narrow, tapering into a slender point, about as long as the spikelet; lemmas thin, 3-nerved, densely and softly long-pilose, gradually narrowed at the summit, the nerves ending in slender teeth, the middle one extending into a straight awn. Tall perennial reeds, with broad linear blades and large plumelike terminal panicles. Type species, *Arundo donax*. *Arundo*, the ancient Latin name.

1. Arundo dónax L. GIANT REED. (Fig. 251.) Culms stout, in large

FIGURE 247.—*Dactylis glomerata*. Plant, × ½; spikelet and floret, × 5. (Wilson 1334, Conn.)

FIGURE 248.—*Cynosurus cristatus*. Plant, × ½; fertile spikelet and floret, × 5. (Waghorne 23, Newf.)

clumps, 2 to 6 m. tall, sparingly branching, from thick knotty rhizomes; blades numerous, elongate, 5 to 7 cm. wide on the main culm, conspicuously distichous, spaced rather evenly along the culm, the margin scabrous; panicle dense, erect, 30 to 60 cm. long; spikelets 12 mm. long. ♃ —Along irrigation ditches, Arkansas and Texas to southern California, occasionally established eastward from Maryland south; tropical America; introduced from the warm regions of the Old World. Frequently cultivated for ornament, including var. VERSÍCOLOR (Miller) Stokes, with white-striped blades. In the Southwest the culms are used for lattices, mats, and screens, and in the construction of adobe huts. In Europe the culms are used for making the reeds of clarinets and organ pipes. If kept cut down the culms branch; in this form used for hedges. Planted in southeastern Texas to prevent wind erosion.

FIGURE 249.—*Cynosurus echinatus*. Panicle, × 1; fertile floret, × 5. (Macoun 80976, Vancouver Island.)

GYNÉRIUM Willd. ex Beauv.

Plants dioecious; spikelets several-flowered, the pistillate with long-attenuate glumes and smaller long-silky lemmas, the staminate with shorter glumes and glabrous lemmas.

FIGURE 250.—*Lamarckia aurea.* Plant, × ½; fertile spikelet and floret, × 5. (Baker 5275, Calif.)

Tall perennial reeds with plumelike panicles. Type species, *Gynerium saccharoides* (*G. sagittatum*). Name from Greek *gune*, female, and *erion*, wool, referring to the woolly pistillate spikelets.

Gynerium sagittátum (Aubl.) Beauv. UVA GRASS. Culms as much as 10 or 12 m. tall, clothed below with the overlapping old sheaths, the blades fallen; blades sharply serrulate, commonly 2 m. long, 4 to 6 cm. wide, forming a great fan-shaped summit to the sterile culms, panicle pale, plumelike, densely flowered, 1 m. or more long, the main axis erect, the branches

Figure 251.—*Arundo donax*. Plant, × 1/3; spikelet and floret, × 3. (Biltmore Herb. 7514, N. C.)

drooping. ♃ —Occasionally cultivated for ornament in greenhouses. River banks and wet ground, tropical America; soil binder.

27. CORTADÉRIA Stapf

PAMPASGRASS

Spikelets several-flowered; rachilla internodes jointed, the lower part glabrous, the upper bearded, forming a stipe to the floret; glumes longer than the lower florets; lemmas of pistillate spikelets clothed with long hairs. Large tussock grasses, with leaves crowded at the base, the blades elongate, narrow, attenuate, the margins usually serrulate; panicle large, plumelike. Type species, *Cortaderia argentea* (*C. selloana*). Name from the Argentine native name *cortadera*, cutting, because of the cutting edges of the blades.

1. Cortaderia selloána (Schult.) Aschers. and Graebn. PAMPASGRASS. (Fig. 252.) Dioecious perennial reed, in large bunches; culms stout, erect 2 to 3 or more m. tall; panicle feathery, silvery white to pink, 30 to 100 cm. long; spikelets 2- to 3-flowered, the pistillate silky with long hairs, the staminate naked; glumes white, papery, long, slender; lemmas bearing a long slender awn. ♃ (*Gynerium argenteum* Nees.)—Plains and open slopes, Brazil to Argentina and Chile. Cultivated as a lawn ornamental in the warmer parts of the United States; in southern California grown commercially for the plumes which are used for decorative purposes, the culms here being sometimes as much as 7 m. tall. Recently planted by Soil Conservation Service for supplementary dry-land pasture in Ventura and Los Angeles Counties, Calif., cattle reported to be thriving on it.

FIGURE 252.—*Cortaderia selloana*. Pistillate (♀) and staminate (♂) panicles, × 1. (Silveus 308, Tex.)

CORTADERIA RUDIÚSCULA Stapf. Differing from *C. selloana* in the looser yellowish or purplish panicle; spikelets somewhat smaller. ♃ —Occasionally cultivated for ornament; Argentina. Has been called *C. quila* Stapf, but that name is ultimately based on *Arundo quila* Molina, which is a bamboo, *Chusquea quila* (Molina) Kunth.

Ampelodésmos mauritánicus (Poir.) Dur. and Schinz. Robust perennial in large clumps, culms solid, 2 to 3 m. tall; blades elongate, wiry, curved at base, bending forward across the culm, the upper surface downward; panicle 20 to 50 cm. long, many-flowered, the slender, flexuous, very scabrous branches naked at base, drooping, the spikelets crowded toward the ends, 2- to 5-flowered, 12 to 15 mm. long, the lower part of lemma and rachilla joints densely pilose with white hairs. ♃ —Occasionally cultivated as an ornamental; escaped and established in Napa County, Calif. Mediterranean region. Generic name often incorrectly spelled *Ampelodesma.*

28. PHRAGMÍTES Trin.

Spikelets several-flowered, the rachilla clothed with long silky hairs, disarticulating above the glumes and at the base of each segment between the florets, the lowest floret staminate or neuter; glumes 3-nerved, or the upper 5-nerved, lanceolate, acute, unequal, the first about half as long as the upper, the second shorter than the florets; lemmas narrow, long-acuminate, glabrous, 3-nerved, the florets successively smaller, the summits of all about equal; palea much shorter than the lemma. Perennial reeds, with broad, flat, linear blades and large terminal panicles. Type species, *Arundo phragmites* L. (*Phragmites communis*). Name from the Greek, in reference to its growth like a fence (*phragma*) along streams.

1. Phragmites commúnis Trin. Common reed. (Fig. 253.) Culms erect, 2 to 4 m. tall, with stout creeping rhizomes and often also with stolons; blades flat, 1 to 5 cm. wide; panicle tawny or purplish, 15 to 40 cm. long, the branches ascending, rather densely flowered; spikelets 12 to 15 mm. long, the florets exceeded by the hairs of the rachilla. ♃ (*P. phragmites* Karst.)—Marshes, banks of lakes and streams, and around springs, Nova Scotia to British Columbia, south to Maryland, North Carolina, Illinois, Louisiana, and California; Florida; Mexico and West Indies to Chile and Argentina; Eurasia, Africa, Australia.

In the Southwest this, in common with *Arundo donax*, is called by the Mexican name carrizo and is used for lattices in the construction of adobe huts. The stems were used by the Indians for shafts of arrows and in Mexico and Arizona for mats and screens, for thatching, cordage, and carrying nets.

29. NEYRAÚDIA Hook. f.

Spikelets 4- to 8-flowered; rachilla jointed about half way between the florets, the part below the joint glabrous, the part above bearded, forming a stipe below the mature floret; glumes unequal, 1-nerved; lemmas narrow, 3-nerved, acuminate, conspicuously long-pilose on the margins, awned from between 2 fine teeth, the awn recurved. Tall perennial with large open many-flowered panicles. Type species, *Neyraudia madagascariensis* (Kunth) Hook. f. (*N. arundinacea* (L.) Henr.) Name an anagram of *Reynaudia*, a genus of Cuban grasses.

1. Neyraudia reynaudiána (Kunth) Keng. (Fig. 254.) Reedlike perennial, 1 to 3 m. tall, resembling *Phragmites communis;* sheaths woolly at the throat and on the collar; blades flat, 1 to 2 cm. wide or sometimes narrow and subinvolute; panicle nodding, 30 to 60 cm. long, rather densely flowered; spikelets 4- to 8-flowered, the lowest 1 or 2 lemmas empty, 6 to 8 mm. long, rather short-pediceled along the numerous panicle branches; lemmas somewhat curved, slender, the awn flat, recurved. ♃ —Planted in testing garden at Coconut Grove, Fla., and occasionally escaped; native of southern Asia.

30. MÉLICA L. Melicgrass

Spikelets 2- to several-flowered (rarely with 1 perfect floret), the rachilla disarticulating above the glumes and between the fertile florets (in some species spikelets falling entire), prolonged beyond the perfect florets and bearing 2 or 3 approximate gradually smaller empty lemmas, each enclosing the

FIGURE 253.—*Phrag mites communis.* Plant, × 1/3; spikelet and floret, × 3. (Hitchcock 5078, N. Dak.)

one above; glumes somewhat unequal, thin, often papery, scarious-margined, obtuse or acute, sometimes nearly as long as the lower floret, 3- to 5-nerved, the nerves usually prominent; lemmas convex, several-nerved, membranaceous or rather firm, scarious-margined, sometimes conspicuously so, awnless or sometimes awned from between the teeth of the bifid apex, the callus not bearded. Rather tall perennials, the base of the culm often swollen into a corm, with closed sheaths, usually flat blades, narrow or sometimes open, usually simple panicles of relatively large spikelets. Type species, *Melica nutans* L. *Melica*, an Italian name for a kind of sorghum, probably from the sweet juice (mel, honey).

The species are in general palatable grasses but, not being gregarious, do not furnish much forage. Important species are *M. porteri*, *M. imperfecta*, and *M. subulata*.

Spikelets narrow; lemmas acute (obtuse in *M. harfordii*) or awned. SECTION 1. BROMELICA.
Spikelets broad; lemmas obtuse, awnless ..... SECTION 2. EUMELICA.

Section 1. Bromelica

Lemmas long-awned from a bifid apex.
  Branches of panicle few, distant, spreading, naked on the lower half ..... 1. M. SMITHII.
  Branches of panicle short, appressed, spikelet-bearing from near the base. 2. M. ARISTATA.
Lemmas awnless or minutely awned.
  Culms not bulbous at base; lemmas obtuse, mucronate or awn-tipped. 3. M. HARFORDII.
  Culms bulbous at base; lemmas acute or acuminate.
    Lemmas acuminate, usually pilose; panicle narrow, the branches short, usually appressed ..... 4. M. SUBULATA.
    Lemmas acute; panicle broad, the branches long and spreading ..... 5. M. GEYERI.

Section 2. Eumelica

1a. Culms bulbous at base (see also *M. californica*).
  Pedicels capillary, flexuous or recurved; panicle narrow ..... 6. M. SPECTABILIS.
  Pedicels stouter, appressed.
    Rachilla soft, enlarged, wrinkled in drying, usually brownish ..... 8. M. FUGAX.
    Rachilla firm, whitish, not wrinkled.
      Panicle rather dense, the branches short, appressed, usually imbricate; glumes thin, indistinctly nerved ..... 7. M. BULBOSA.
      Panicle loosely flowered, the branches, or some of them, stiffly ascending-spreading in anthesis, usually somewhat distant, scarcely imbricate; glumes firm, distinctly nerved ..... 9. M. INFLATA.
1b. Culms not distinctly bulbous at base (somewhat swollen in *M. californica*.)
  2a. Spikelets falling entire, nodding to pendulous on capillary pedicels.
    Spikelets 4- or 5-flowered, reflexed; panicle narrow (open in *M. porteri* var. *laxa*).
      Spikelets V-shaped; glumes 10 to 15 mm. long ..... 10. M. STRICTA.
      Spikelets narrow; glumes not more than 7 mm. long ..... 11. M. PORTERI.
    Spikelets 1- to 3-flowered, nodding; panicle open, the lower branches spreading.
      Spikelets with 1 perfect floret; lemma with a few flat, twisted golden hairs on the back about the middle ..... 14. M. MONTEZUMAE.
      Spikelets with 2 perfect florets, lemmas without hairs.
        Glumes nearly as long as the usually 2-flowered spikelet; apexes of the 2 florets about the same height; panicle simple or nearly so ..... 12. M. MUTICA.
        Glumes shorter than the usually 3-flowered spikelet; apex of second floret a little higher than that of the first; panicle compound ..... 13. M. NITENS.
  2b. Spikelets not falling entire, not pendulous.
    Spikelets 4 to 6 mm. long; fertile florets 1 or 2.
      Fertile lemmas pubescent; fertile florets often 2 ..... 15. M. TORREYANA.
      Fertile lemmas glabrous; fertile floret usually 1 ..... 16. M. IMPERFECTA.
    Spikelets 8 to 15 mm. long; fertile florets 2 to several.
      Spikelets silvery white; glumes about as long as the spikelet; plant tall, somewhat woody ..... 17. M. FRUTESCENS.
      Spikelets tawny to purplish; glumes shorter than the spikelet; plant lower, herbaceous ..... 18. M. CALIFORNICA.

Section 1. Bromélica Thurb.

Spikelets narrow; glumes usually narrow, scarious-margined (papery in *M. geyeri*); sterile lemmas similar to the acute (obtuse in *M. harfordii*) or awned fertile lemmas.

1. Melica smíthii (Porter) Vasey. Smith melic. (Fig. 255.) Culms slender, 60 to 120 cm. tall; sheaths retrorsely scabrous; blades lax, scabrous, 10 to 20 cm. long, 6 to 12 mm. wide; panicle 12 to 25 cm. long, the branches solitary, distant, spreading, naked below, sometimes reflexed, as much as 10 cm. long; spikelets 3- to 6-flowered, 18 to 20 mm. long, sometimes purplish; glumes acute; lemmas about 10 mm. long, with an awn 3 to 5 mm. long. ♃ (*Avena smithii* Porter.)—Moist woodlands, western Ontario and northern Michigan to British Columbia, south to

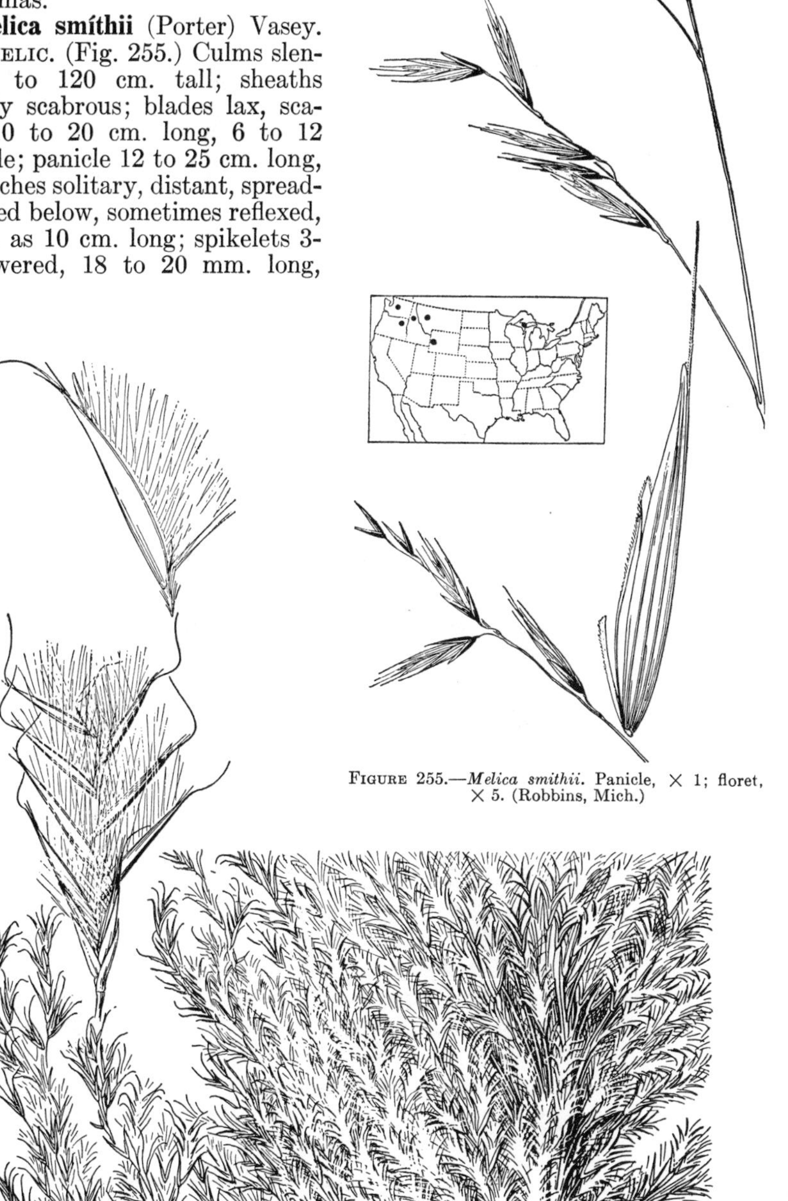

Figure 255.—*Melica smithii*. Panicle, × 1; floret, × 5. (Robbins, Mich.)

Figure 254.—*Neyraudia reynaudiana*. Panicle, × 1; spikelet, × 5; floret, × 10. (Moldenke 432, Fla.)

FIGURE 256.—*Melica aristata*. Plant, × ½; spikelet and floret, × 5. (Cusick 2888, Oreg.)

Wyoming (Teton Mountains) and Oregon (Wallowa Mountains).

2. **Melica aristáta** Thurb. ex Boland. (Fig. 256.) Culms erect or de-

cumbent below, 60 to 100 cm. tall; sheaths scabrous to pubescent; blades 3 to 5 mm. wide, more or less pubescent; panicle narrow, 10 to 15 cm. long, the branches short, mostly appressed or ascending; spikelets, excluding awns, about 15 mm. long; glumes 10 to 12 mm. long; lemmas 7-nerved, scabrous, awned, the awn 6 to 10 mm. long. ♃ —Dry woods, meadows, and open slopes, Montana and Washington to the central Sierras of California.

3. Melica harfórdii Boland. HARFORD MELIC. (Fig. 257.) Culms tufted,

FIGURE 257.—*Melica harfordii.* Panicle, × 1; floret, × 5. (Yates 457, Calif.)

60 to 120 cm. tall, often decumbent below; sheaths scabrous to villous; blades scabrous, firm, flat to subinvolute, 1 to 4 mm. wide; panicle narrow, 10 to 15 cm. long, the

FIGURE 258.—*Melica subulata.* Panicle, × 1; floret, × 5. (Hitchcock 11631, Wash.)

branches appressed; spikelets 1 to 1.5 cm. long, short-pediceled; glumes 7 to 9 mm. long, obtuse; lemmas rather faintly 7-nerved, hispidulous below, pilose on the lower part of the margin, the apex emarginate, mucronate, or with an awn less than 2 mm. long. ♃ —Open dry woods and slopes, British Columbia to the Cascade Mountains of Oregon, south to Monterey County and Yosemite National Park, Calif. A smaller form with narrow involute blades has been segregated as *M. harfordii* var. *minor* Vasey.

4. Melica subuláta (Griseb.) Scribn. ALASKA ONIONGRASS. (Fig. 258.) Culms 60 to 125 cm. tall, mostly bulbous at base; sheaths retrorsely scabrous, often pilose; blades thin,

FIGURE 259.—*Melica geyeri*. Plant, × 1; floret, × 5. (Heller 11932, Calif.)

usually 2 to 5 mm. wide, sometimes wider; panicle usually narrow, mostly 10 to 20 cm. long, the branches appressed or sometimes spreading; spikelets narrow, 1.5 to 2 cm. long, loosely flowered; glumes narrow, obscurely nerved, the second about 8 mm. long; lemmas prominently 7-nerved, tapering to an acuminate point, awnless, the nerves more or less pilose-ciliate. ♃ —Meadows, banks, and shady slopes, western Wyoming and Montana to Alaska, south in the mountains to Mount Tamalpais and Lake Tahoe, Calif.

5. Melica géyeri Munro. GEYER ONIONGRASS. (Fig. 259.) Culms 1 to 1.5 m. tall, bulbous at base; sheaths usually glabrous, sometimes slightly scabrous or pubescent; blades scabrous (rarely puberulent), mostly less than 5 mm. wide; panicle 10 to 20 cm. long, open, the branches slender, rather distant, spreading, bearing a few spikelets above the middle; spikelets 12 to 20 mm. long; glumes broad, smooth, papery, the second about 6 mm. long; lemmas 7-nerved, scaberulous or nearly glabrous, narrowed to an obtuse point, awnless. ♃ —Open dry woods and rocky slopes, at medium altitudes, western Oregon to central California in the Coast Range; infrequent in the Sierras to Placer County; Nevada; Yellowstone Park, Wyo.

MELICA GEYERI var. ARISTULÁTA J. T. Howell. Lemma with an awn 0.5 to 2 mm. long from a toothed apex. ♃ —Known only from Marin County, Calif.

SECTION 2. EUMÉLICA Aschers.

Spikelets broad; glumes broad, papery; lemmas awnless; sterile lemmas small, aggregate in a rudiment more or less hidden in the upper fertile lemmas.

6. Melica spectábilis Scribn. PURPLE ONIONGRASS. (Fig. 260.) Culms 30 to 100 cm. tall, bulbous at base, rarely with a short rhizome; sheaths pubescent; blades flat to subinvolute, 2 to 4 mm. wide; panicle mostly 10 to 15 cm. long, narrow, the branches appressed; spikelets purple-tinged, rather turgid, 10 to 15 mm. long, the pedicels capillary, flexuous; glumes broad, papery; lemmas strongly 7-nerved, obtuse, scarious-margined, imbricate. ♃ —Rocky or open woods and thickets, Montana to British Columbia, south to Colorado and northern California.

7. Melica bulbósa Geyer ex Port. and Coult. ONIONGRASS. (Fig. 261.) Culms 30 to 60 cm. tall, bulbous at base, resembling *M. spectabilis;* sheaths and blades flat to involute, 2 to 4 mm. wide, glabrous, scabrous, or pubescent; panicle narrow, rather densely flowered, the branches short, appressed, rather stiff, mostly imbricate; spikelets papery with age, mostly 7 to 15 mm. long, the short pedicels stiff, erect; lemmas obscurely nerved, obtuse or slightly emarginate. ♃ (*M. bella* Piper.)—Rocky woods and hills, Montana to British Columbia, south to Colorado and California; western Texas (Jeff Davis County). Specimens with pubescent foliage have been differentiated as *M. bella intonsa* Piper.

8. Melica fúgax Boland. Little oniongrass. (Fig. 262.) Culms mostly 20 to 60 cm. tall, in loose tufts, the bulbs prominent; sheaths retrorsely scabrous; blades 1.5 to 4 mm. wide, scabrous, usually pubescent on the upper surface; panicle 8 to 15 cm. long, the branches stiffly spreading or reflexed at anthesis, the lower 2 to 4 cm. long; spikelets 8 to 14 mm. long, the florets somewhat distant, usually purple-tinged, the rachilla soft, wrinkled in drying, often brownish; second glume nearly as long as the lower lemma; lemmas obscurely nerved, obtuse or emarginate. ♃ —Dry hills and open woods, Washington to Nevada and central California.

9. Melica infláta (Boland.) Vasey. (Fig. 263.) Culms 60 to 100 cm. tall, bulbous at base; sheaths glabrous or pubescent; blades flat, 2 to 4 mm.

Figure 260.—*Melica spectabilis*. Plant, × 1; floret, × 5. (Tweedy 85, Wyo.)

Figure 261.—*Melica bulbosa*. Plant, × 1; floret, × 5. (Tidestrom 1252, Utah.)

FIGURE 262.—*Melica fugax*. Plant, × 1; floret, × 5. (Vasey 9, Wash.)

wide; panicle 15 to 20 cm. long, narrow, the rather distant branches, or some of them, stiffly ascending-spreading in anthesis, the lower as much as 5 cm. long; spikelets somewhat inflated, 12 to 20 mm. long, pale green; glumes scabrous on the strong nerves; lemmas strongly nerved, scabrous, acutish. ♃ —California (Yosemite National Park and Mount Shasta), Washington (Chelan County, the sheaths and blades pubescent).

10. Melica strícta Boland. ROCK MELIC. (Fig. 264.) Culms 15 to 60 cm. tall, densely tufted, the base somewhat thickened but not bulbous; sheaths scaberulous, sometimes pu-

FIGURE 263.—*Melica inflata*. Plant, × 1; floret, × 5. (Hall and Babcock 3334, Calif.)

FIGURE 264.—*Melica stricta*. Plant, × 1; floret, × 5. (Swallen 720, Calif.)

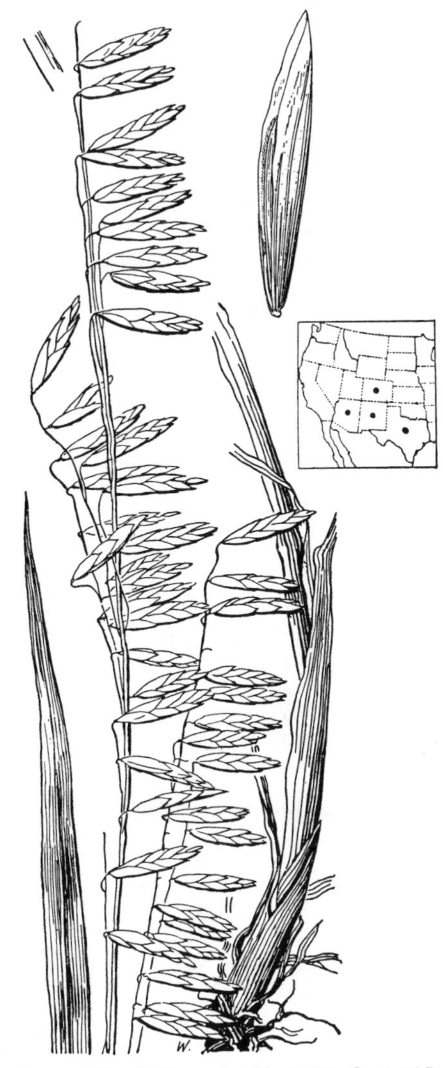

FIGURE 265.—*Melica porteri*. Plant, × 1; floret, × 5. (Shear 726, Colo.)

bescent; blades mostly 1 to 3 mm. wide, scabrous, pubescent on the upper surface; panicle narrow, simple or with 1 or 2 short branches at base; spikelets 12 to 16 mm. long, 4- or 5-flowered, broadly V-shaped, reflexed on capillary pedicels, falling entire; glumes thin, shining, nearly as long as the spikelet; lemmas faintly nerved, scabrous, and obtuse. ♃ —Rocky slopes and banks, at medium alti-

FIGURE 266.—*Melica mutica*. Plant, × ½; spikelet and floret, × 5. (Chase 3695, Va.)

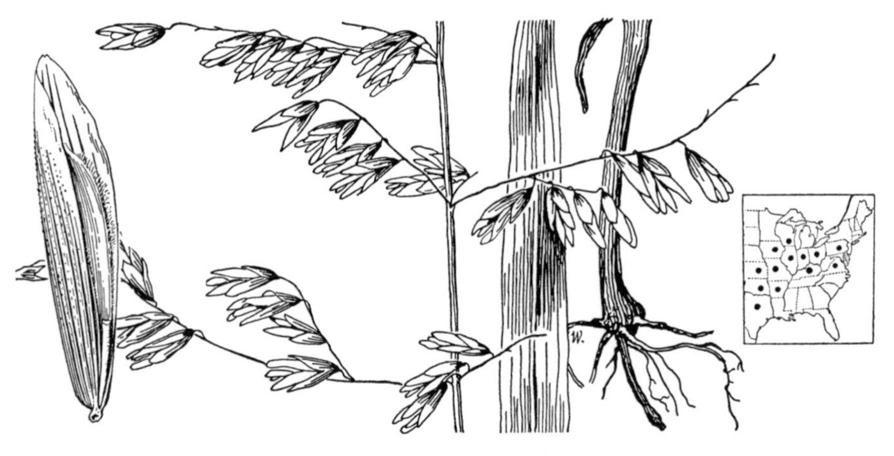

FIGURE 267.—*Melica nitens*. Plant, × 1; floret, × 5. (McDonald 15, Ill.)

tudes, Utah and Nevada to Oregon (Steins Mountains), the Sierras, and the mountains of southern California.

11. Melica portéri Scribn. PORTER MELIC. (Fig. 265.) Culms 50 to 100 cm. tall, tufted; sheaths smooth or scabrous; blades 2 to 5 mm. wide; panicle green or tawny, narrow, 1-sided, 15 to 20 cm. long, the branches short, appressed, few-flowered; spikelets 10 to 15 mm. long, 4- or 5-flowered, narrow, reflexed on capillary pubescent pedicels, falling entire; glumes half to two-thirds as long as the spikelet; lemmas with 5 strong nerves and several faint ones, scaberulous. ♃ —Canyons, open woods, and moist places, mostly at 2,000 to 3,000 m., Colorado and Texas to Arizona; Mexico.

MELICA PORTERI var. LÁXA Boyle. Panicles open, the branches 4 to 9 cm. long, spreading to ascending, the glumes often purplish. ♃ —Rocky slopes, Chisos Mountains, Tex., to Arizona. Resembles *M. nitens*, but blades narrower, spikelets 4- or 5-flowered, and rudiment slender.

12. Melica mútica Walt. TWO-FLOWER MELIC. (Fig. 266.) Culms 60 to 100 cm. tall, erect, loosely tufted; sheaths scabrous or somewhat pubescent; blades flat, 2 to 5 mm. wide; panicle 10 to 20 cm. long, nearly simple, with 1 to few short, spreading, few-flowered branches below; spikelets broad, pale, 7 to 10 mm. long, usually 2-flowered, the florets spreading, pendulous on slender pedicels, pubescent at the summit, the spikelets falling entire; glumes nearly as long as the spikelet; lemmas scaberulous, strongly nerved, the two florets about the same height; rudiment obconic. ♃ —Rich or rocky woods, Maryland to Iowa, south to Florida and Texas.

13. Melica nítens (Scribn.) Nutt. THREE-FLOWER MELIC. (Fig. 267.) Resembling *M. mutica;* on the average culms taller; sheaths glabrous or scabrous; blades 7 to 15 mm. wide; panicle more compound with several spreading branches; glumes shorter than the usually 3-flowered narrower spikelet; apex of the second floret a little higher than that of the first; lemmas acute; rudiment mostly minute. ♃ —Rocky woods, Pennsylvania to Iowa and Kansas, south to Virginia, Arkansas, Oklahoma, and Texas.

14. Melica montezúmae Piper. (Fig. 268.) Culms 50 to 100 cm. tall, erect, tufted; sheaths scaberulous; ligule thin, 5 to 10 mm. long; blades flat or subinvolute, 2 to 3 mm. wide; panicle 10 to 20 cm. long, the branches simple or nearly so, distant, the lower 5 to 8 cm. long, spreading to ascend-

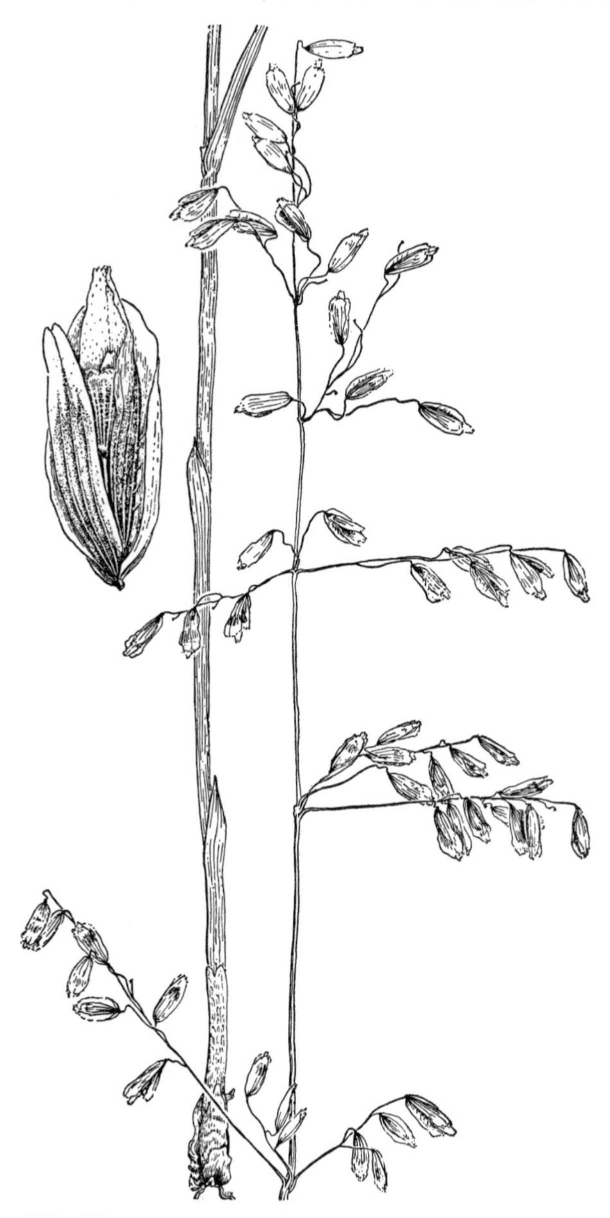

FIGURE 268.—*Melica montezumae*. Panicle, × 1; spikelet, × 5. (Pringle 430, Mexico.)

ing; spikelets pale; falling entire, 7 to 8 mm. long, more or less pendulous on filiform pedicels; glumes exceeding the florets, hyaline toward the summit, the first 4 mm. broad, expanded at maturity, the second slightly shorter and narrower; fertile floret 1, the lemma scabrous, strongly nerved and with a few flat twisted golden hairs about the middle; rudiment obconic. ♃ —Shaded mountain slopes and canyons, Pecos and Brewster Counties, Tex., and northern Mexico.

15. Melica torreyána Scribn. Torrey melic. (Fig. 269.) Culms 30 to 100 cm. tall, ascending from a loose decumbent not bulbous base; blades lax, 1 to 3 mm. wide; panicle narrow, rather loose, 8 to 20 cm. long, the branches more or less fascicled, appressed or ascending, the lower fascicles distant; spikelets 4 to 6 mm. long, with 1 or 2 perfect florets and a minute obovoid, long-stiped rudiment; glumes strongly nerved, as long as the spikelet or nearly so; lemmas pubescent, subacute. ♃ —Thickets and banks at low altitudes, central California, especially in the bay region.

Figure 269.—*Melica torreyana.* Panicle, × 1; floret, × 5. (Chase 5686, Calif.)

16. Melica imperfécta Trin. California melic. (Fig. 270.) Resembling *M. torreyana;* culms erect or ascending; the base sometimes decumbent or stoloniferous; panicle 5 to 30 cm. long, the lower branches commonly ascending to spreading; spikelets usually with 1 perfect floret and an oblong, short-stiped rudiment appressed to the palea; glumes indistinctly nerved; lemma a little longer than the glumes, glabrous, indistinctly nerved, obtuse. ♃ —Dry open woods and rocky hillsides, at low and medium altitudes, central and southern California, especially in the Coast Ranges; Baja California.

Figure 270.—*Melica imperfecta.* Panicle, × 1; spikelet, × 5. (Elmer 4710, Calif.)

A few forms have been distinguished as varieties.

Melica imperfecta var. refrácta Thurb. Lower branches of panicle spreading or reflexed; blades pubescent. ♃ —Southern California. Melica imperfecta var. flexuósa Boland. Like the preceding but blades glabrous. ♃ —Central and southern California. Melica imperfecta var. mínor Scribn. Culms less than 30 cm. tall; blades glabrous, 1 to 2 mm. wide. ♃ —Southern California.

17. Melica frutéscens Scribn. (Fig. 271.) Culms 0.75 to 2 m. tall, sparingly branching, rather woody below, not bulbous at base; sheaths retrorsely scabrous; blades rather firm, 2 to 4 mm. wide, those of the innova-

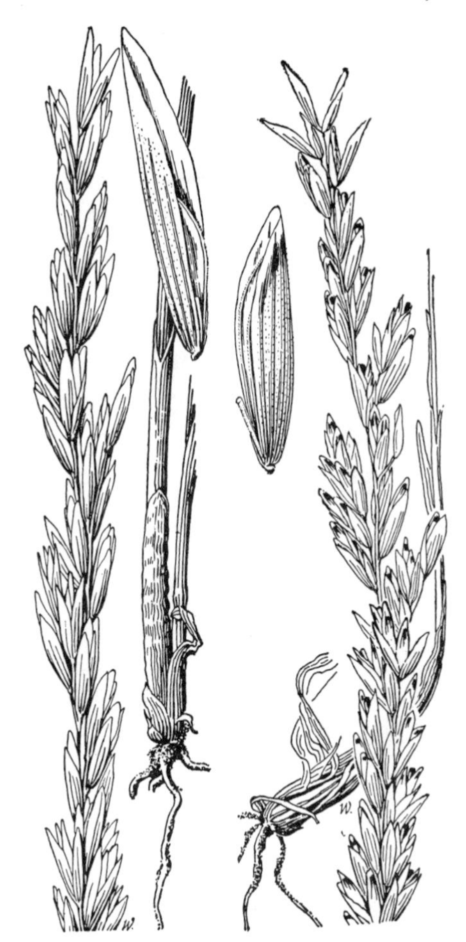

FIGURE 271.—*Melica frutescens.* Plant, × 1; floret, × 5. (Munz, Johnston, and Harwood 4143, Calif.)

FIGURE 272.—*Melica californica.* Plant, × 1; floret, × 5. (Hoffman 37, Calif.)

tions, 1 to 2 mm. wide, subinvolute; panicle silvery-shining, narrow, rather dense, 10 to 30 cm. long, the branches short, appressed; spikelets short-pediceled, 12 to 15 mm. long; glumes nearly as long as the spikelet, prominently 5-nerved; lemmas subacute, faintly 7-nerved. ♃ —Hills and canyons, at low and medium altitudes, Arizona and southern California (Inyo County and southward); Baja California.

18. Melica califórnica Scribn. (Fig. 272.) Culms 60 to 120 cm. tall, the base usually decumbent, often more or less bulbous; sheaths glabrous or pubescent, the lower persistent, brown and shredded; blades 1 to 4 mm. wide; panicle narrow, rather dense, 10 to 20 cm. long, tawny to purplish, not silvery; spikelets short-pediceled, 10 to 12 mm. long (rarely shorter) with 2 to 4 florets besides the rudiment; glumes scaberulous, a little shorter than the spikelets; lemmas rather prominently 7-nerved, scaberulous, subacute to obtuse, often emarginate. ♃ (*M. bulbosa* Geyer ex Thurb., not *M. bulbosa* of this work.)—Mountain meadows and rocky woods, at low and medium altitudes, Oregon (Malheur County) and California.

MELICA CALIFORNICA var. NEVADÉNSIS Boyle. Spikelets mostly 2-flowered, 7 to 8 mm. long, the glumes about equaling the upper floret. ♃ —In the lower Sierra Nevada, California.

MELICA ALTÍSSIMA L. Tall perennial; blades 15 to 20 cm. long, 5 to 10 mm. wide; panicle narrow, dense, tawny to purple; spikelets about 12 mm. long; glumes and lemmas broad, papery. ♃ —Sometimes cultivated for ornament. Eurasia.

MELICA CILIÁTA L. Panicle pale, narrow, condensed, silky. ♃ —Occasionally cultivated for ornament. Europe.

31. SCHIZÁCHNE Hack.

Spikelets several-flowered, disarticulating above the glumes and between the florets, the rachilla glabrous; glumes unequal, 3- and 5-nerved; lemmas lanceolate, strongly 7-nerved, long-pilose on the callus, awned from just below the teeth of the prominently bifid apex; palea with softly pubescent, thickened submarginal keels, the hairs longer toward the summit. Rather tall perennial with simple culms and open rather few-flowered panicle. Type species, *Schizachne fauriei* Hack. (*S. purpurascens*). Name from Greek *schizein*, to split, and *achne*, chaff, alluding to the b fid lemma.

1. Schizachne purpuráscens (Torr). Swallen. FALSE MELIC. (Fig. 273.) Culms erect from a loosely tufted

FIGURE 273.—*Schizachne purpurascens.* Plant, × ½; lemma, palea, and caryopsis, × 5. (Chase 7444, N. Y.)

FIGURE 274.—*Vaseyochloa multinervosa*. Plant, × ½; spikelet and floret, × 5. (Swallen 1854, Tex.)

decumbent base, 50 to 100 cm. tall; sheaths closed; blades flat, narrowed at the base, 1 to 5 mm. wide; panicle about 10 cm. long, the branches single or in pairs, more or less drooping, bearing 1 or 2 spikelets; spikelets 2 to 2.5 cm. long; glumes purplish, less than half as long as the spikelet; lemmas about 1 cm. long, the awn as long as the lemma or longer. ♃ (*Melica striata* Hitchc.; *M. purpurascens* Hitchc.; *Avena torreyi* Nash.)—Rocky woods, Newfoundland to southern Alaska, south to Maryland, Kentucky, South Dakota, and Montana, and in the mountains from British Columbia to New Mexico; Siberia and Japan.

32. VASEYÓCHLOA Hitchc.

Spikelets subterete or slightly compressed, several-flowered, the rachilla disarticulating above the glumes and between the florets, the joints very short; glumes rather firm, unequal, much shorter than the lemmas, the first 3- to 5-nerved, the second 7- to 9-nerved; lemmas rounded on the back, firm, closely imbricate, 7- to 9-nerved, broad, narrowed to an obtuse entire apex and with a stipelike hairy callus, pubescent on the lower part of the back and margins; palea shorter than the lemma, splitting at maturity, the arcuate keels strongly wing-margined; caryopsis concavo-convex, oval, black, the base of the styles persistent as a 2-toothed crown. Slender perennial with elongate blades and somewhat open panicles. Type species, *Vaseyochloa multinervosa.* Named from Vasey and Greek, *chloa*, grass.

1. Vaseyochloa multinervósa (Vasey) Hitchc. (Fig. 274.) Culms erect, loosely tufted, 40 to 100 cm. tall, with slender rhizomes; sheaths scaberulous, pilose at the throat; blades flat to loosely involute, 1 to 4 mm. wide; panicle narrow, loose, 5 to 20 cm. long, the branches few, at first appressed, later spreading, the lower as much as 8 cm. long, bearing a few spikelets from about the middle; spikelets 12 to 18 mm. long, 6- to 12-flowered, purple-tinged; glumes acute, the first narrow, 4 mm. long, the second broad, 5 mm. long; lemmas narrowed to an obtuse point, about 6 mm. long, the nerves becoming rather obscure toward maturity; grain 2.5 to 3 mm. long, 1.5 to 2 mm. wide, deeply concave on the ventral side. ♃ (*Melica multinervosa* Vasey; *Distichlis multinervosa* Piper.)—Sandy open woods or open ground, southeastern Texas; rare. The rhizomes appear to break off readily, most herbarium specimens being without them.

32A. ECTOSPERMA Swallen

(See pp. 860, 995)

33. TRÍDENS Roem. and Schult.

(Included in *Triodia* R. Br. in Manual, ed. 1.)

Spikelets several-flowered, the rachilla disarticulating above the glumes and between the florets; glumes membranaceous, often thin, nearly equal in length, the first sometimes narrower, 1-nerved, the second rarely 3- to 5-nerved, acute to acuminate; lemmas broad, rounded on the back, the apex from minutely emarginate or toothed to deeply and obtusely 2-lobed, 3-nerved, the lateral nerves near the margin, the midnerve usually excurrent between the lobes as a minute point or as a short awn, the lateral nerves often excurrent as minute points, all the nerves pubescent below (subglabrous in 1 species), the lateral nerves sometimes conspicuously so throughout; palea broad, the 2 nerves near the margin, sometimes villous; grain concavo-convex. Erect, tufted perennials, rarely rhizomatous or stoloniferous, the blades usually flat, the inflorescence an open to contracted or capitate panicle. Type species,

T. quinquifidus Roem. and Schult. (*T. flavus*). Name from Latin, *tria*, thrice, and *dens*, tooth, referring to the 3-toothed lemma.

In general the species of *Tridens* are of little importance economically, *T. grandiflorus*, *T. elongatus*, and *T. pilosus* being the most useful on the range. *Tridens pulchellus* is often abundant, but is not relished by stock, the little dry plants seldom being eaten.

1a, Panicle capitate, exceeded by fascicles of leaves; low creeping plants. 1. T. PULCHELLUS.
1b. Panicle exserted, open or spikelike; plants not creeping.
  2a. Panicle open, or loose, not dense or spikelike.
    Pedicels of the lateral spikelets less than 1 mm. long .... 8. T. AMBIGUUS.
    Pedicels all slender, more than 1 mm. long (some short in *T. buckleyanus*).
      Lateral nerves not excurrent.
        Spikelets not more than 5 mm. long; lemmas 2 mm. long. 9. T. ERAGROSTOIDES.
        Spikelets 6 to 8 mm. long; lemmas 4 to 5 mm. long .... 6. T. BUCKLEYANUS.
      Lateral nerves excurrent as short points.
        Rhizomes developed, scaly and creeping .... 7. T. CAROLINIANUS.
        Rhizomes wanting.
          Panicle 5 to 15 cm. long; blades 1 to 3 mm. wide .... 13. T. TEXANUS.
          Panicle 15 to 30 cm. long, the branches viscid; blades 3 to 10 mm. wide.
            Panicle rather dense, the branches narrowly ascending, floriferous nearly to the base .... 11. T. OKLAHOMENSIS.
            Panicle open, the branches widely spreading, loosely flowered, naked at the base.
              Panicle erect, the branches stiffly spreading; pulvini hairy, extending entirely around the base of the branches .... 12. T. CHAPMANI.
              Panicle drooping; pulvini confined to the upper surface at the base of the branches .... 10. T. FLAVUS.
  2b. Panicle narrow, contracted or spikelike, the branches appressed. (See also *T. carolinianus*.)
    Panicle dense, oval or oblong, mostly less than 10 cm. long.
      Lemmas deeply 2-lobed.
        Lobes of lemma 1.5 to 2.5 mm. long, firm, scarcely shining; awn longer than the lobes; panicles mostly oval, not more than 6 cm. long, usually less, often purple tinged .... 2. T. GRANDIFLORUS.
        Lobes of lemma 1 to 1.5 mm. long, obtuse, thin, shining; awn scarcely longer than the lobes; panicles oblong, 5 to 8 cm. long, very dense, tawny. 3. T. NEALLEYI.
      Lemmas minutely notched, not lobed.
        Panicle 1 to 2 cm. long; lemma margins densely long-ciliate; palea half as long as the lemma .... 4. T. PILOSUS.
        Panicle 4 to 10 cm. long; lemma margins short-pilose near base; palea about as long as the lemma .... 5. T. CONGESTUS.
    Panicle slender, spikelike (long and dense in *T. strictus*).
      Lemmas glabrous. Panicle whitish .... 15. T. ALBESCENS.
      Lemmas pilose on the margins.
        Lemmas mucronate; panicle dense .... 14. T. STRICTUS.
        Lemmas not mucronate (rarely lowest lemma obscurely so); panicle not dense.
          Glumes acuminate, longer than the lowest floret, the second 3-nerved; blades mostly flat, some of them 2 to 4 mm. wide .... 17. T. ELONGATUS.
          Glumes obtuse, short, the second 1-nerved; blades mostly folded or involute, mostly about 1 mm. wide .... 16. T. MUTICUS.

1. Tridens pulchéllus (H. B. K.) Hitchc. FLUFFGRASS. (Fig. 275.) Low, tufted, usually not more than 15 cm. high; culms slender, scabrous or puberulent, consisting of 1 long internode, bearing at the top a fascicle of narrow leaves, the fascicle finally bending over to the ground, taking root and producing other culms, the fascicles also producing the inflorescence; sheaths striate, papery-margined, pilose at base; blades involute, short, scabrous, sharp-pointed; panicle capitate, usually not exceeding the blades of the fascicle, consisting of 1 to 5 nearly sessile relatively large white woolly spikelets; glumes

FIGURE 275.—*Tridens pulchellus.* Plant, × ½; spikelet and floret, × 5. (Chase 5511, Ariz.)

FIGURE 276.—*Tridens grandiflorus*. Plant, × ½; floret, × 5. (Eggleston 10973, Ariz.)

glabrous, subequal, broad, acuminate, awn-pointed, 6 to 8 mm. long, nearly as long as the spikelet; lemmas 4 mm. long, conspicuously long-pilose below, cleft about halfway, the awn scarcely exceeding the obtuse lobes, divergent at maturity. ♃ (*Dasyochloa pulchella* Willd.)—Mesas and rocky hills, especially in arid or semiarid regions, Texas to Nevada and southern California to southern Mexico.

2. Tridens grandiflórus (Vasey) Woot. and Standl. LARGE-FLOWERED TRIDENS. (Fig. 276.) Culms tufted, erect or geniculate below, 10 to 50 cm. tall, often pubescent at the nodes; blades flat or folded, rather firm, white-margined, appressed-pubescent, 1 to 2 mm. wide, those of the culm less than 10 cm. long; panicle dense, oblong, purplish, 2 to 6 cm. long, cleistogamous spikelets borne in the lower sheaths; spikelets 4- to 8-flowered, 5 to 12 mm. long; glumes acuminate, about as long as the first floret; lemmas 4 to 6 mm. long, conspicuously long-pilose on the margins, densely pilose on the back below, deeply lobed, the awn as long as the lobes, or exceeding them. ♃ —Rocky slopes, western Texas to southern Arizona and northern Mexico. This has been referred to *Triodia avenacea* H. B. K., a Mexican species with stolons and smaller purple panicles.

3. Tridens néalleyi (Vasey) Woot. and Standl. (Fig. 277.) Culms erect, 20 to 40 cm., or sometimes as much as 60 cm., tall, glabrous or the lower internodes pilose, at least some of the nodes, especially the lower ones, conspicuously bearded; leaves mostly crowded at the base in a dense cluster, the culm leaves rather distant; blades firm, flat or conduplicate, with thick white midnerve and margins, pilose on both surfaces, 5 to 10 cm. long, about 2 mm. wide, the uppermost usually reduced; panicles 4 to 6 cm. long, pale, very densely flowered, the individual spikelets obscured; spikelets 6 to 8 mm. long; glumes equal, acuminate, as long as or somewhat shorter than the spikelet; lemmas 4 to 6 mm. long, the lobes broad, hyaline, obtuse, more or less erose, spreading at maturity; awn as long as or only slightly exceeding the lobes of the lemma. ♃ —Rocky slopes, southwestern Texas and New Mexico (Las Cruces); northern Mexico.

FIGURE 277.—*Tridens nealleyi*. Floret, × 5. (Nealley 153, Tex.)

4. Tridens pilósus (Buckl.) Hitchc. HAIRY TRIDENS. (Fig. 278.) Culms erect, densely tufted, 10 to 30 cm. tall, usually only 1 node showing, the tufts easily pulled up; sheaths pilose at the throat; blades 1 to 1.5

mm. wide, flat or folded, mostly in a short basal cluster, somewhat pilose, the margins thick, white, the culm blades 1 to 2 cm. long; panicle long-exserted, ovoid, 1 to 2 cm. long, pale or purplish, of 3 to 10 large short-pediceled spikelets; spikelets 6- to 12-flowered, 1 to 1.5 cm. long, compressed, glumes about two-thirds as long as the lower florets; lemmas about 6 mm. long, densely pilose toward the base, pilose on the margin toward the tip, acute, minutely 2-toothed, the awn 1 to 2 mm. long; palea half as long as the lemma, pilose on the back and margins below.

♃ (*Triodia acuminata* Vasey; *Tricuspis pilosa* Nash; *Erioneuron pilosum* Nash.)—Plains and rocky hills, western Kansas to Nevada, south to Texas, Arizona, and central Mexico.

5. Tridens congéstus (L. H. Dewey) Nash. (Fig. 279.) Culms erect, tufted, 30 to 60 cm. tall; blades flat, 2 to 3

FIGURE 279.—*Tridens congestus*. Panicle, × 1; floret, × 5. (Tracy 8879, Tex.)

mm. wide, tapering to a fine point; panicle mostly dense, pale or pinkish, 4 to 10 cm. long, sometimes interrupted below; spikelets rather turgid, 6- to 12-flowered, 5 to 10 mm. long; lemmas 3 to 4 mm. long, broad, obtuse, short-pilose on the midnerve and margin below, the apex slightly notched, the awn less than 1 mm. long; palea about as long as the lemma, broad, abruptly bowed out below. ♃ —Sandy or dry plains, southern Texas.

6. Tridens buckleyánus (L. H. Dewey) Nash. (Fig. 280.) Culms erect, tufted, 30 to 60 cm. tall; sheaths scaberulous, sometimes sparsely pilose; blades flat, 1 to 3 mm. wide, tapering to a fine point; panicle 10 to 20 cm. long, the few branches distant, ascending to spreading, as much as 7 cm. long; spikelets pale to dark purple, short-pediceled, appressed, rather few and somewhat distant along the simple branches, 3- to

FIGURE 278.—*Tridens pilosus*. Plant, × ½; floret, × 5. (Griffiths 6427, Tex.)

FIGURE 280.—*Tridens buckleyanus*. Panicle, × 1; floret, × 5. (Tharp 2996, Tex.)

5-flowered, 6 to 8 mm. long; glumes slightly shorter than the lower florets; lemmas 4 to 5 mm. long, pubescent on the callus and on the lower two-thirds of the midnerve and margin, the apex obtuse, entire, the midnerve not or scarcely excurrent; palea a little shorter than the lemma, pubescent along the margins; grain elliptic, 3 mm. long. ♃ —Rocky wooded slopes, southern Texas.

FIGURE 281.—*Tridens carolinianus*. Plant, × 1; floret, × 5. (Bartlett 3224, Ala.)

7. Tridens caroliniánus (Steud.) Henr. (Fig. 281.) Culms slender, erect, 1 to 1.5 m. tall, with creeping scaly rhizomes; lower sheaths pubescent; blades flat, elongate, 2 to 7 mm. wide; panicle purplish, narrow, rather loose, nodding, 10 to 20 cm. long, the branches appressed or narrowly ascending; spikelets short-pediceled, 3- to 5-flowered, 7 to 10 mm. long; glumes broad, mucronate from a notched apex; lemmas about 5 mm. long, pilose on the callus and on the lower half of the midnerve and margins, the summit lobed, the 3 nerves excurrent less than 1 mm.; palea glabrous, a little shorter than the lemma, bowed out below. ♃ (*Triodia drummondii* Scribn. and Kearn., *Tridens drummondii* Nash.)—Sandy woods, Coastal Plain, South Carolina to Florida and Louisiana.

8. Tridens ambíguus (Ell.) Schult. (Fig. 282.) Culms slender, erect, 60 to 100 cm. tall; lower sheaths glabrous; blades flat or loosely involute, 1 to 5 mm. wide; panicle open, ovoid, pale or purplish, 8 to 20 cm. long, the branches ascending, 3 to 8 cm. long; spikelets on pedicels less than 1 mm. long along the simple branches, 4- to 7-flowered, 4 to 6 mm. long, nearly as broad, the florets crowded; glumes broad, subacute; lemmas 3 to 4 mm. long, mucronate from a minutely lobed apex, the lateral nerves scarcely or barely exserted, pilose on the midnerve and margins on the lower half; palea nearly as long as the lemma, the keels bowed out below. ♃ (*Triodia langloisii* (Nash) Bush.)—Wet pine barrens, on the coast, South Carolina to Florida and Texas.

9. Tridens eragrostoídes (Vasey and Scribn.) Nash. (Fig. 283.) Culms slender, erect, densely tufted, 50 to 100 cm. tall; blades flat, 1 to 4 mm. wide, setaceous-tipped; panicle open, 10 to 30 cm. long, the branches rather distant, slender, flexuous, spreading or drooping, 5 to 15 cm. long, nearly simple, rather few-flowered; spikelets on slender pedicels 1 to 10 mm. long, oblong, mostly 6- to 10-flowered, scarcely 5 mm. long; glumes acuminate; lemmas about 2 mm. long, obtuse, obscurely pubescent along the midnerve on the lower half, the margins pubescent, the midnerve minutely excurrent. ♃ —Dry ground among shrubs, Florida Keys, Texas, Arizona, and northern Mexico; Cuba.

10. Tridens flávus (L.) Hitchc. PURPLETOP. (Fig. 284.) Culms erect, tufted, 1 to 1.5 m. tall; basal sheaths compressed-keeled; blades elongate, 3 to 10 mm. wide, very smooth; panicle open, 15 to 35 cm. long, usually purple or finally nearly black, rarely yellowish, the branches distant, spreading to drooping, naked below, as much as 15 cm. long, with slender divergent branchlets, the axils pubescent, the axis, branches, branchlets, and pedicels viscid; spikelets oblong, mostly 6- to 8-flowered, 5 to 8 mm. long; glumes subacute, mucronate; lemmas 4 mm. long, obtuse, pubescent on the callus and lower half of keel and margins, the 3 nerves excurrent; palea a little shorter than the lemma, somewhat bowed out below. ♃ (*Tricuspis seslerioides* Torr.)—Old fields and open woods, New Hampshire to Nebraska, south to Florida and Texas. The type specimen is the rare form with yellowish panicle. In some Florida specimens the excurrent nerves of the lemma are as much as 1 mm. long.

11. Tridens oklahoménsis (Feath.) Feath. (Fig. 285.) Culms 120 to 150 cm. tall, densely tufted, stout, erect, more or less viscid, especially at and below the nodes; blades to 60 cm. long and 12 mm. wide, flat, glabrous or sparsely pilose on the upper surface at the base; panicles terminal and axillary, purple, the terminal ones 20 to 25 cm. long, the long branches narrowly ascending, floriferous nearly to the base; spikelets 6 to 8 mm. long,

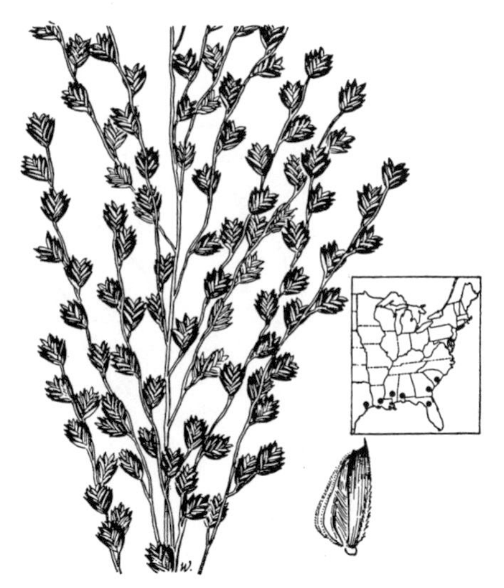

FIGURE 282.—*Tridens ambiguus*. Panicle, × 1; floret, × 5. (Curtiss 5020, Fla.)

7- to 9-flowered, short-pediceled; glumes equal, acute, about 4 mm. long; lowest lemma 4 mm. long. ♃ —Wet meadows, near Stillwater, Okla.

12. Tridens chapmáni (Small) Chase. (Fig. 286.) Culms 60 to 160 cm. tall, slender or occasionally rather

FIGURE 283.—*Tridens eragrostoides*. Panicle, × 1; two views of floret, × 5. (Swallen 1471, Tex.)

coarse; lower leaves crowded toward the base, the sheaths narrow, spreading from the culm, keeled, glabrous, densely villous on the collar; blades flat or loosely rolled, elongate, attenuate, 3 to 7 mm. wide, narrowed toward the base; panicles 15 to 25 cm. long, usually erect, the branches

FIGURE 284.—*Tridens flavus*. Plant, × ½; spikelet and floret, × 5. (Dewey 350, Va.)

and branchlets stiffly spreading, the bases of the principal ones surrounded by glandular hairy pulvini; spikelets long-pediceled, divergent, 7 to 10 mm. long, pale or purple-tinged. ♃ — Dry pine and oakwoods, New Jersey, Virginia, Missouri, and Oklahoma, south to Florida and Texas.

13. Tridens texânus (S. Wats.) Nash. (Fig. 287.) Culms erect, densely tufted, 20 to 40 cm. tall; sheaths pubescent at throat and on the collar; blades flat or subinvolute, 1 to 4 mm. wide, tapering to a slender point; panicle open, 5 to 15 cm. long, nodding, the branches rather distant, flexuous, drooping, few-flowered; spikelets oblong, 6- to 10-flowered, 6 to 10 mm. long, rather turgid, pink or purplish, more or less nodding on short pedicels; glumes broad, acute to obtuse; lemmas 4 to 5 mm. long, obtuse, minutely lobed, the margins densely pilose near the base, the keel glabrous or sparsely pilose below, the 3 nerves short-excurrent; palea about as long as the lemma, strongly bowed out at base. ♃ —Plains and dry slopes, central and southern Texas, and northern Mexico.

FIGURE 285.—*Tridens oklahomensis.* Panicle, × 1; floret, × 5. (Wade 77, Okla.)

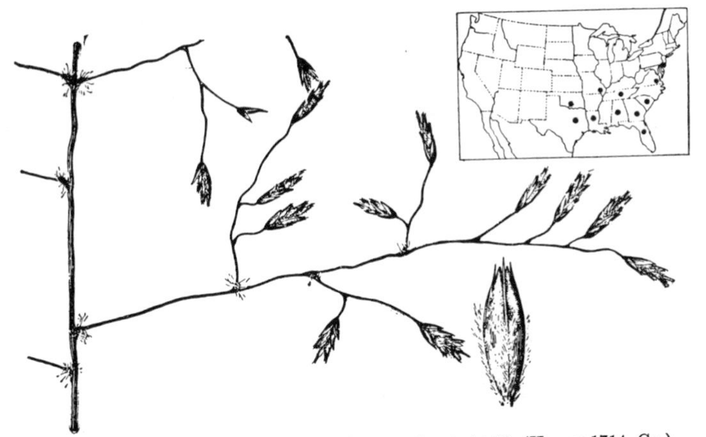

FIGURE 286.—*Tridens chapmani.* Panicle, × 1; floret, × 10. (Harper 1714, Ga.)

14. Tridens stríctus (Nutt.) Nash. (Fig. 288.) Culms rather stout, erect, 1 to 1.5 m. tall; blades elongate, flat or loosely involute, 3 to 8 mm. wide; panicle dense, spikelike, more or less interrupted below, narrowed above, 10 to 30 cm. long; spikelets short-pediceled, 4- to 6-flowered, about 5 mm. long, the florets closely imbricate; glumes as long as the spikelet, or nearly so, the apex spreading, the keel glandular viscid toward maturity; lemmas about 3 mm. long, obtuse, the keel and margins pilose on the lower half to two-thirds, the midnerve ex-

FIGURE 287.—*Tridens texanus*. Panicle, × 1; floret, × 5. (Wooton, Tex.)

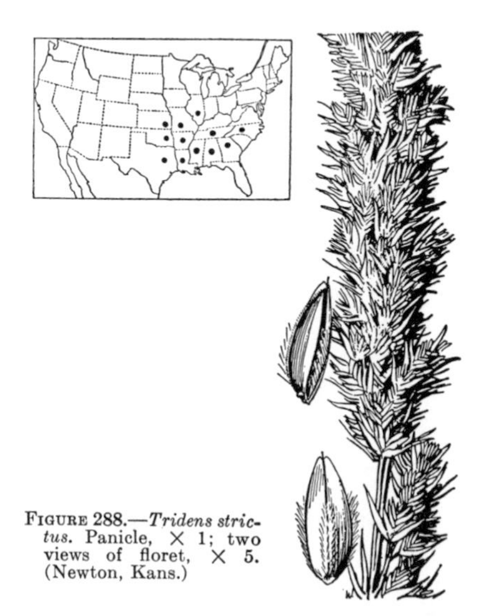

FIGURE 288.—*Tridens strictus*. Panicle, × 1; two views of floret, × 5. (Newton, Kans.)

current as a minute awn; palea about as long as the lemma, short-ciliate on the sharp keels, not strongly bowed out. ♃ (*Tricuspis stricta* A. Gray.)—Low moist ground and low woods, Illinois and Kansas to North Carolina, Alabama, and Texas.

15. Tridens albéscens (Vasey) Woot. and Standl. WHITE TRIDENS. (Fig. 289.) Culms erect, tufted, 30 to 80 cm. tall; blades flat to loosely involute, elongate, 2 to 4 mm. wide, tapering to a fine point; panicle narrow, rather dense, greenish to nearly white, 10 to 20 cm. long; spikelets short-pediceled, 8- to 12-flowered, 5 to 7 mm. long, the florets closely imbricate; glumes a little longer than the first lemma, subacute; lemmas 3 mm. long, obscurely pubescent on the callus, otherwise glabrous, obtuse, the midnerve minutely or not at all excurrent; palea a little shorter than the lemma, bowed out below. ♃ (*Rhombolytrum albescens* Nash.)—Plains and open woods, Kansas and Colorado to Texas and New Mexico; northern Mexico.

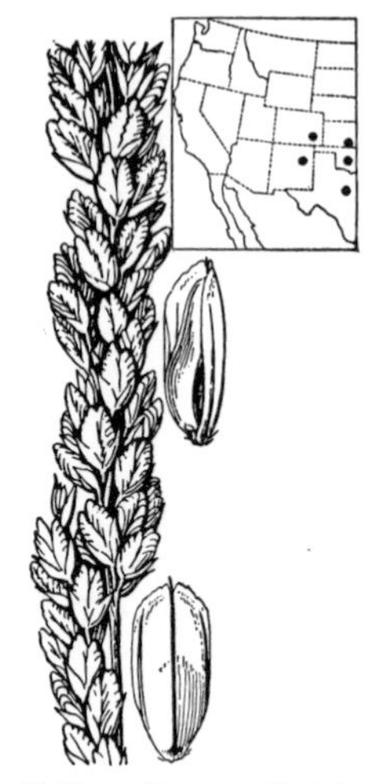

FIGURE 289.—*Tridens albescens*. Panicle, × 1; two views of floret, × 5. (Ball 1652, Tex.)

16. Tridens múticus (Torr.) Nash. SLIM TRIDENS. (Fig. 290.) Culms slender, densely tufted, 30 to 50 cm. tall; sheaths and blades scaberulous, the sheaths usually loosely pilose, more densely so at the summit; blades flat or subinvolute, 1 to 3 mm. wide, sometimes sparsely pilose; panicle narrow, rather dense, interrupted, the branches short, appressed; spikelets

6- to 8-flowered, about 1 cm. long, pale to purplish, nearly terete; glumes scaberulous, about as long as the lower florets; lemmas about 5 mm. long, densely pilose on the lower half of the nerves and on the callus, obtuse, entire or minutely notched, the midnerve not exserted; palea half or two-thirds as long as the lemma, densely pilose on the keels and puberulent on the back. ♃ —Plains and rocky slopes, Texas to southeastern California, north to Nevada and Utah; Mexico.

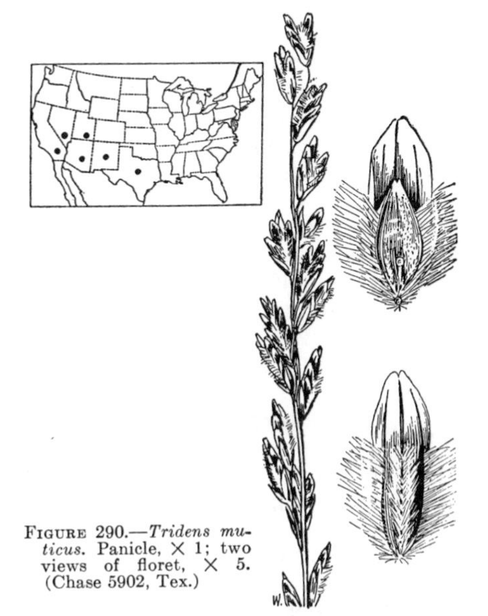

FIGURE 290.—*Tridens muticus*. Panicle, × 1; two views of floret, × 5. (Chase 5902, Tex.)

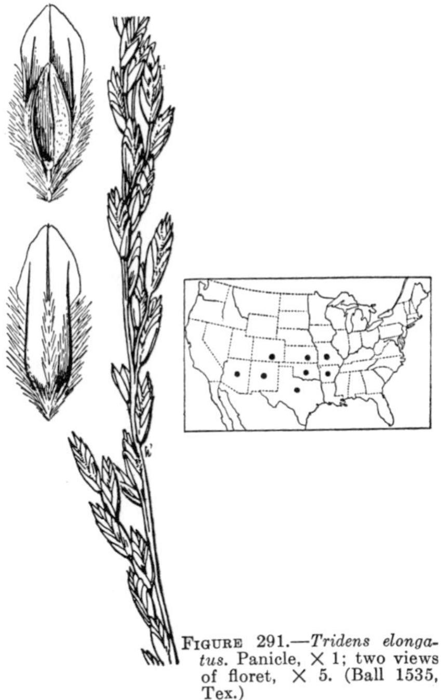

FIGURE 291.—*Tridens elongatus*. Panicle, × 1; two views of floret, × 5. (Ball 1535, Tex.)

17. Tridens elongâtus (Buckl.) Nash. ROUGH TRIDENS. (Fig. 291.) Culms erect, tufted, 40 to 80 cm. tall; sheaths and blades scaberulous, sometimes sparsely pilose, the blades mostly flat, 2 to 4 mm. wide, tapering to a fine point; panicle elongate; erect, pale or purple-tinged, loosely flowered, 10 to 25 cm. long, the branches rather distant, appressed, scarcely or not at all overlapping; spikelets similar to those of *T. muticus*, the glumes longer, the hairs on the florets not so long. ♃ (*Tricuspis elongata* Nash.) —Plains, sandy prairies, and rocky slopes, Missouri to Colorado, Texas, and Arizona.

34. TRÍPLASIS Beauv.

Spikelets few-flowered, V-shaped, the florets remote, the rachilla slender, disarticulating above the glumes and between the florets; glumes nearly equal, smooth, 1-nerved, acute; lemmas narrow, 3-nerved, 2-lobed, the nerves parallel, silky-villous, the lateral pair near the margin, the midnerve excurrent as an awn, as long as the lobes or longer; palea shorter than the lemma, the keels densely long-villous on the upper half. Slender tufted annuals or perennials, with short blades, short, open, few-flowered, purple, terminal panicles and cleistogamous narrow panicles in the axils of the leaves. Both species have, in addition to the small panicles of cleistogamous spikelets in the upper sheaths, additional cleistogamous spikelets, usually reduced to a single large floret, at the bases of the lower sheaths. The culms break at the nodes, the mature cleistogenes remaining within the sheaths. Type species, *Triplasis americana*. Name from Greek *triplasios*, triple, alluding to the awn and the two subulate lobes of the lemma. The species are of no importance except as they tend to hold sandy soil.

Lobes of lemma not subulate-pointed; awn shorter than the lemma; annual.
1. T. PURPUREA.

Lobes of lemma subulate-pointed; awn longer than the lemma; perennial.
2. T. AMERICANA.

1. Triplasis purpúrea (Walt.) Chapm. PURPLE SANDGRASS. (Fig. 292.) Annual, often purple; culms ascending to widely spreading, pubescent at the several to many nodes, 30 to 100 cm. tall, rarely taller; blades flat or loosely involute, 1 to 3 mm. wide, mostly 4 to 8 cm. long; panicle 3 to 5 cm. long, with few spreading few-flowered branches, the axillary more or less enclosed in the sheaths; spikelets short-pediceled, 2- to 4-flowered, 6 to 8 mm. long; lemmas 3 to 4 mm. long, the lobes broad, rounded or truncate, the nerves and callus densely short-villous, the awn about as long as the lobes or somewhat exceeding them; palea conspicuously silky-villous on the upper half of the keels; grain about 2 mm. long. ⊙ —Dry sand, Ontario, Maine, and New Hampshire to Minnesota and Nebraska, south to Florida and Texas; Colorado (introduced?); Honduras. In autumnal culms the numerous short joints with sheaths swollen at the base, containing cleistogenes, are conspicuous. Plants with awns exceeding the lobes of the lemma have been differentiated as *T. intermedia* Nash.

2. Triplasis americána Beauv. (Fig. 293.) Perennial; culms slender, tufted, mostly erect, 30 to 60 cm. tall; blades flat or subinvolute, mostly 15 to 18 cm. long; panicle 2 to 5 cm. long, the few slender ascending branches with 1 or 2 spikelets; spikelets mostly 2- or 3-flowered, about 1 cm. long; lemmas 5 to 6 mm. long, the lobes about half as long as the entire lemma, subulate-pointed, the nerves with a narrow stripe of silky hairs, the awn 5 to 8 mm. long, pubescent below; keels of the palea long-villous, the hairs erect. ♃ —Dry sand, Coastal Plain, North Carolina to Florida and Mississippi.

35. NEOSTÁPFIA Davy

(Included in *Anthochloa* Nees in Manual, ed. 1)

Spikelets few-flowered, subsessile, closely imbricate around a simple axis, the rachilla disarticulating between the florets; glumes wanting; lemmas flabellate, prominently many-nerved; palea much narrower and a little shorter than the lemma, obtuse, hyaline. Low annual with loose sheaths merging into rather broad flat blades without definite junction and dense cylindric panicles, the axis prolonged beyond the spikelets, this portion naked or bearing small bracts. Type species, *Neostapfia colusana*. Named for Otto Stapf. (Distinguished from *Anthochloa* Nees, of the Andes, in which the axis is not prolonged, the short-pediceled spikelets have well-developed persistent glumes, the lemmas are not strongly nerved, and the sheaths and blades are distinctly differentiated.)

1. Neostapfia colusána (Davy) Davy. (Fig. 294.) Culms 7 to 30 cm. long, ascending from a decumbent base; leaves overlapping, loosely folded around the culm, 5 to 10 cm. long, 6 to 12 mm. wide at the middle, tapering toward both ends, minutely ciliate, with raised viscid glands on the nerves and margins; panicles pale green, at first partly included, later short-exserted, 3 to 7 cm. long, 8 to 12 mm. thick; spikelets usually 5-flowered, 6 to 7 mm. long; lemmas flabellate, very broad, 5 mm. long, ciliolate-fringed, the many nerves viscid-glandular at maturity. ⊙ (*Anthochloa colusana* (Davy) Scribn.) —Bordering rain pools on hard alkali

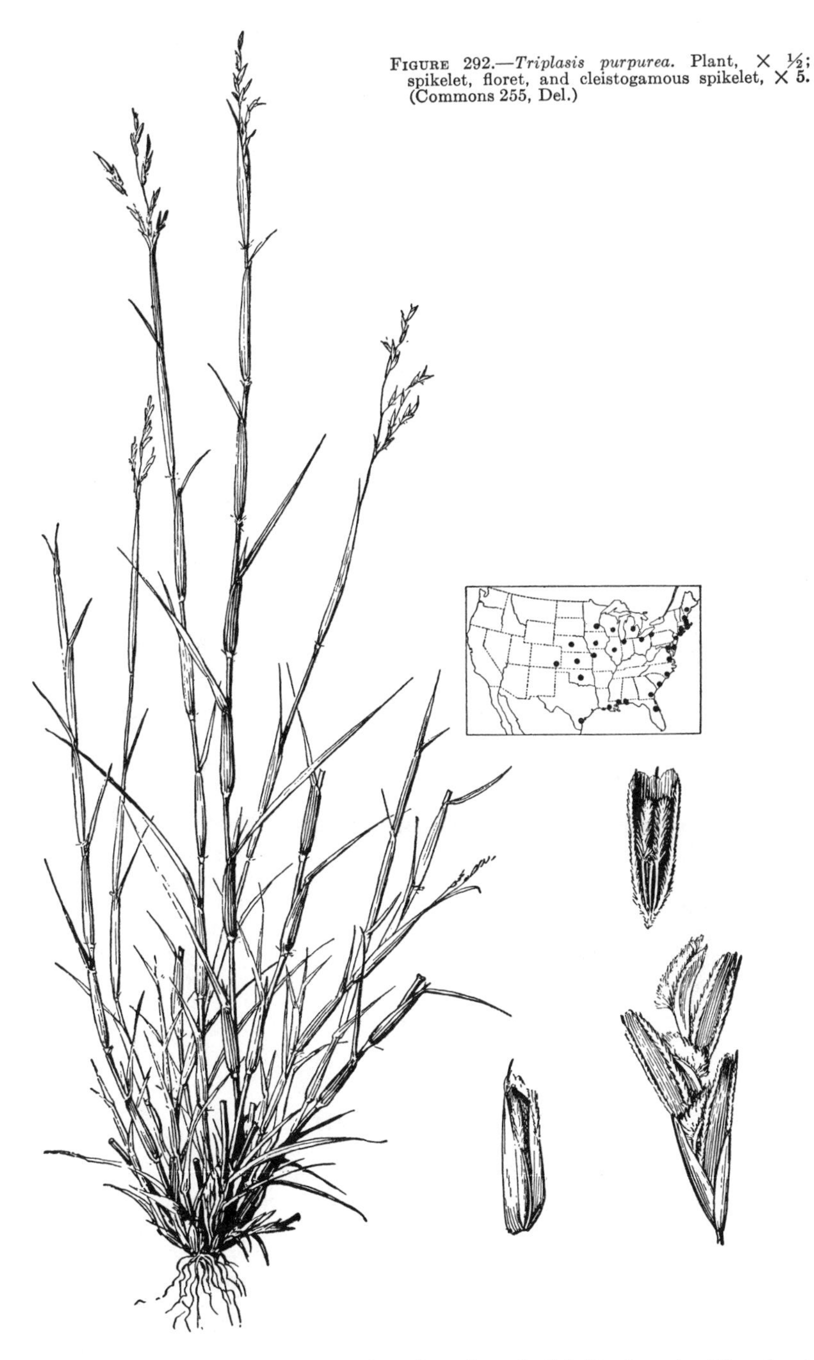

FIGURE 292.—*Triplasis purpurea*. Plant, × ½; spikelet, floret, and cleistogamous spikelet, × 5. (Commons 255, Del.)

soil, Colusa, Stanislaus, and Merced Counties, Calif. At maturity the entire plant is thickly beset with minute raised viscid glands.

36. ORCÚTTIA Vasey

Spikelets several-flowered, the upper florets reduced, the rachilla continuous, the spikelets persistent even after maturity; glumes nearly equal, shorter than the lemmas, broad, irregularly 2- to 5-toothed, many-nerved, the nerves extending into the teeth; lemmas firm, prominently 13- to 15-nerved, the broad summit toothed; palea broad, as long as the lemma. Low annuals with short culm blades, solitary spikes or spikelike racemes, the subsessile spikelets relatively large, the upper aggregate, the lower more or less remote. With the exception of *O. greenei*, the young plants produce elongate juvenile leaves before the development of the culms. Type species, *Orcuttia californica*. Named for C. R. Orcutt.

Lemmas with 7 to 11 very short teeth .... 1. O. GREENEI.
Lemmas with 5 relatively long acuminate or awn-tipped teeth.
  Racemes 2 to 5 cm. long, often capitate, the spikelets usually crowded toward the summit, remote toward the base; teeth of lemma unequal, the middle longer than the lateral ones; nerves of lemma relatively faint .... 2. O. CALIFORNICA.
  Racemes 5 to 10 cm. long, narrow, not capitate, the spikelets rather evenly distributed (the lower distant in *O. tenuis*); teeth of lemma equal; nerves of lemma prominent.
    Blades 1 to 2 mm. wide; spikelets mostly 2- to 10-flowered, glabrous .... 3. O. TENUIS.
    Blades 2 to 6 mm. wide; spikelets mostly 10- to 40-flowered, pilose .... 4. O. PILOSA.

1. Orcuttia greénei Vasey. (Fig. 295.) Culms 15 to 20 cm. tall, suberect; blades 2 to 3 cm. long, subinvolute; raceme 3 to 7 cm. long, pale; spikelets 10 to 15 mm. long, loosely papillose-pilose; glumes 4 to 5 mm. long; lemmas 6 mm. long, the obtuse or truncate tip spreading, 7- to 11-toothed, the teeth mucronate but not awned. ⊙ —Moist open ground, Sacramento and San Joaquin Valleys, Butte and San Joaquin Counties, southeast to Tulare County, Calif. At maturity foliage and spikelets minutely viscid-glandular.

2. Orcuttia califórnica Vasey. (Fig. 296.) Culms 5 to 15 cm. long, spreading with ascending ends, forming little mats; foliage thin, pilose, the sheaths loose, the blades 2 to 4 cm. long; raceme loose below, dense or subcapitate at the summit; spikelets 8 to 12 mm. long, densely to sparsely pilose; glumes sharply toothed; lemmas about 6 mm. long, deeply cleft into 5 awn-tipped teeth. The whole plant at maturity more or less viscid-glandular. ⊙ —Drying mud flats, near Murrietta, Riverside County, Calif.; Baja California.

ORCUTTIA CALIFORNICA var. INAEQUÁLIS (Hoover) Hoover. Resembling the species, but differing in having usually shorter capitate inflorescences

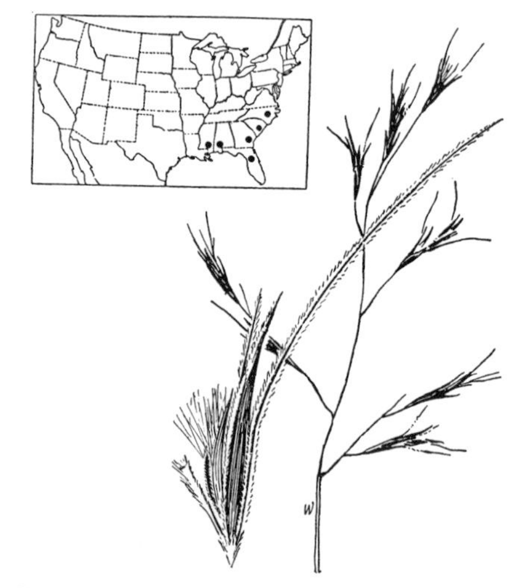

FIGURE 293.—*Triplasis americana*. Panicle, × 1; floret, × 5. (Curtiss 5570, Fla.)

and unequally toothed lemmas; culms ascending or prostrate. Sacramento and San Joaquin Valleys, Sacramento to Tulare County, Calif.

ORCUTTIA CALIFORNICA var. VÍSCIDA Hoover. Plants very viscid; teeth of lemma awned, giving the capitate inflorescence a distinctly bristly appearance. Near the Sierra Nevada foothills, Sacramento County, Calif.

3. Orcuttia ténuis Hitchc. (Fig. 297.) Culms in small tufts, slender,

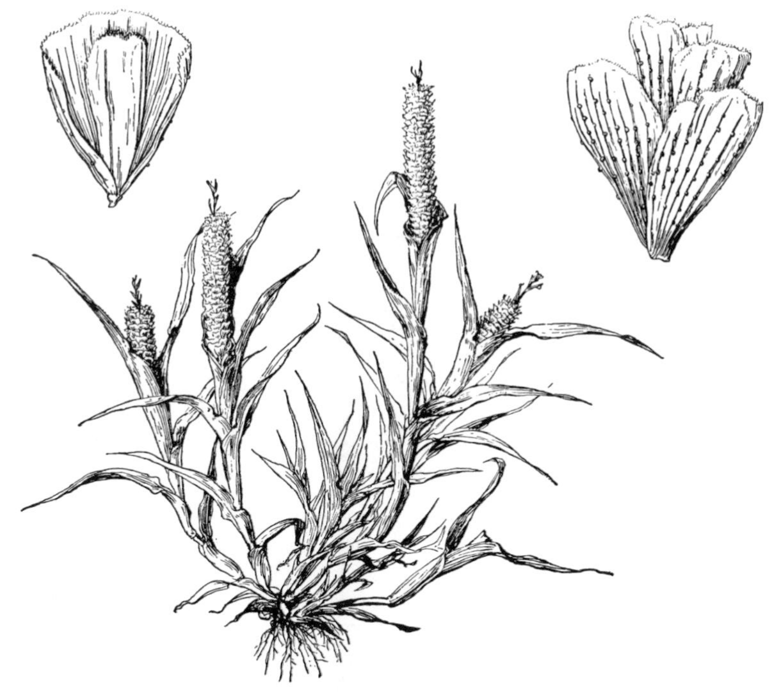

FIGURE 294.—*Neostapfia colusana*. Plant, × ½; spikelet and floret, × 5. (Type.)

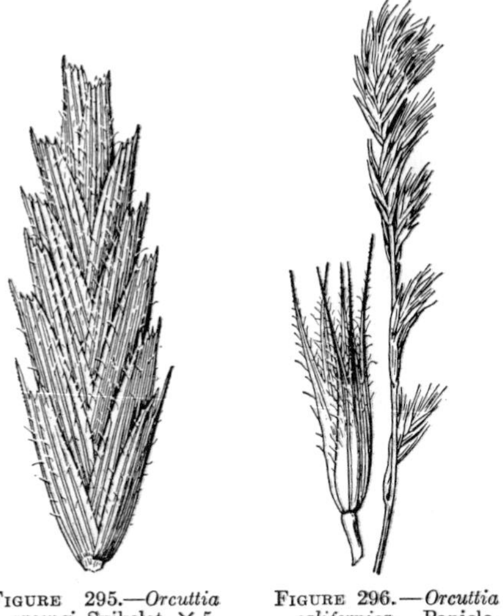

FIGURE 295.—*Orcuttia greenei*. Spikelet, × 5. (Type.)

FIGURE 296.—*Orcuttia californica*. Panicle, × 1; floret, × 5. (Munz 10804, Calif.)

erect, 5 to 12 cm. tall; leaves mostly basal, the blades strongly nerved, 1 to 2 cm. long; raceme more than half the entire height of the plant, the lower spikelets distant, the upper approximate but not crowded; spikelets purple-tinged, 12 to 15 mm. long; glumes and lemmas scabrous, sometimes with a few hairs toward the base of the lemmas; glumes 3 to 4 mm. long, sharply toothed; lemmas 5 mm. long, 5-toothed, the teeth acuminate, awn-tipped, the rigid tips spreading or slightly recurved. ⊙ —Beds of vernal pools, Shasta and Tehama Counties, east of the Sacramento River, Calif.

4. Orcuttia pilósa Hoover. (Fig. 298.) Culms densely tufted, 5 to 20 cm. tall, erect or geniculate-decumbent at base, viscid at maturity; sheaths and blades pilose or the blades nearly glabrous beneath; racemes 5 to 10 cm. long; spikelets 10- to 40-flowered, appressed or somewhat spreading, the upper crowded, the lower approximate; glumes about 3 mm. long, irregularly 3-toothed;

FIGURE 297.—*Orcuttia tenuis*. Plant, × ½; spikelet and floret, × 5. (Type.)

FIGURE 298.—*Orcuttia pilosa*. Plant, × ½; floret, × 5. (Hoover 1298, Calif.)

lemmas 4 to 5 mm. long, the teeth equal, acute or awn-tipped, strongly viscid-glandular at maturity; anthers 2.5 to 3 mm. long. ⊙ —San Joaquin Valley, Calif., from Stanislaus County to Madera County.

37. BLEPHARIDÁCHNE Hack.

Spikelets compressed, 4-flowered, the rachilla disarticulating above the glumes, but not between the florets; glumes nearly equal, compressed, 1-nerved, thin, smooth; lemmas 3-nerved, the nerves extending into awns, deeply 3-lobed, conspicuously ciliate, the first and second sterile, containing a palea but no flower, the third fertile, the fourth reduced to a 3-awned rudiment. Low annuals or perennials, with short, dense, few-flowered panicles scarcely exserted from the subtending leaves. Type species, *Blepharidachne kingii*. Name from Greek *blepharis* (blepharid-), eyelash, and *achne*, chaff, alluding to the ciliate lemma.

Glumes a little longer than the florets, acuminate; foliage scaberulous.......... 1. B. KINGII.
Glumes a little shorter than the florets, subacute; foliage densely grayish harsh-puberulent. 2. B. BIGELOVII.

1. Blepharidachne kíngii (S. Wats.) Hack. (Fig. 299.) Low tufted perennial with the aspect of *Tridens pulchellus*, but not rooting at upper nodes; culms mostly less than 10 cm. tall; sheaths with broad hyaline margins; blades less than 1 mm. wide, involute, curved, sharp-pointed, 1 to 3 cm. long; panicles subcapitate, pale or purplish, 1 to 2 cm. long, exceeded by the upper blades; spikelets flabellate; glumes about 8 mm. long, acuminate, exceeding the florets; sterile lemmas about 6 mm. long, all the lemmas about the same height, long-ciliate on the margins, pilose at the base and on the callus, cleft nearly to the middle, the lateral lobes narrow, obtuse, the nerve at one

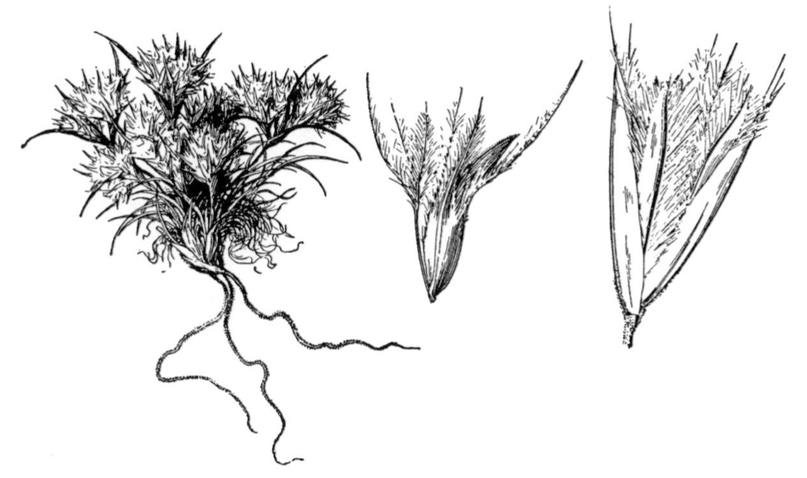

FIGURE 299.—*Blepharidachne kingii*. Plant, × 1; spikelet and perfect floret, × 5. (Jones 4094, Nev.)

margin, awn-tipped, the central lobe consisting of the awn, ciliate below, somewhat exceeding the lateral ones; palea much narrower and somewhat shorter than the lemma; fertile lemma similar to the sterile ones, the palea broad and as long as the lemma; upper sterile lemma on a rachilla segment about 3 mm. long, reduced to 3 plumose awns; grain compressed, 2 mm. long. ♃ —Deserts, Utah, Nevada, and California (Death Valley), apparently rather rare, but reported as common and sometimes the dominant grass in desert regions in Elko and White Pine Counties, Nev.

2. Blepharidachne bigelóvii (S. Wats.) Hack. (Fig. 300.) Perennial, culms stiff, 10 to 20 cm. long, the culms and foliage harsh-puberulent; sheaths broad, firm; blades coarser than in *B. kingii;* panicles dense, oblong, 1 to 3 cm. long, the blades not exceeding the panicle; glumes about 6 mm. long, subacute, shorter than the florets; sterile lemmas ciliate and awned as in *B. kingii*, cleft about 1 mm. ♃ —Rocky slopes, Pecos and El Paso Counties, Tex.

FIGURE 300.—*Blepharidachne bigelovii*. Plant, × 1; fertile floret, × 5. (Type.)

38. CÓTTEA Kunth

Spikelets several-flowered, the uppermost reduced, the rachilla dis-

FIGURE 301.—*Cottea pappophoroides*. Plant, × ½; spikelet, floret, and cleistogene, × 5. (Griffiths 5946, Ariz.)

articulating above the glumes and between the florets; glumes about equal, nearly equaling the lower lemma, with several parallel nerves; lemmas rounded on the back, villous below, prominently 9- to 11-nerved, some of the nerves extending into awns of irregular size and some into awned teeth; palea a little longer than the body of the lemma, the keels near the margin. An erect tufted branching perennial with flat blades and oblong loose panicle. Type species, *Cottea pappophoroides*. Named for Heinrich Cotta.

1. Cottea pappophoroídes Kunth. (Fig. 301.) Softly pubescent throughout; culms 30 to 50 cm. tall; blades 3 to 7 mm. wide; panicle 8 to 15 cm. long, the branches loosely ascending; spikelets 4- to 7-flowered, 5 to 7 mm. long, about 5 mm. wide, green or purplish; glumes 4 to 5 mm. long; lemmas 3 to 4 mm. long, the basal hairs conspicuous, at least the middle awn spreading. ♃ —Plains and dry hills, western Texas to southern Arizona, south to central Mexico; Ecuador to Argentina. Cleistogamous spikelets, usually reduced to a single floret, are found in the lower sheaths, and often large, very turgid ones at the very base. Not abundant enough to have economic importance.

39. PAPPÓPHORUM Schreb. PAPPUSGRASS

Spikelets 4- to 6-flowered, the lower 1 to 3 fertile, the upper reduced, the rachilla disarticulating above the glumes, but not or only tardily between the florets, the internodes very short; glumes nearly equal, keeled, thin-membranaceous, as long as the body of the florets, 1-nerved, acute; lemmas rounded on the back, firm, obscurely many-nerved, dissected above into numerous spreading, unequal awns, the florets falling together, the awns of all forming a pappuslike crown; palea as long as the body of the lemma, the nerves near the margin. Erect tufted perennials, with narrow or spikelike whitish to tawny or purplish panicles. Type species, *Pappophorum alopecuroideum* Vahl. Name from Greek *pappos*, pappus, and *phoros*, bearing, alluding to the pappuslike crown of the lemma. Our species are of minor economic importance.

Panicle spikelike, tawny or whitish .... 1. P. MUCRONULATUM.
Panicle narrow but rather loose, pinkish .... 2. P. BICOLOR.

1. Pappophorum mucronulátum Nees. (Fig. 302.) Culms erect, 60 to 100 cm. tall; blades flat to subinvolute, 2 to 5 mm. wide; panicle spikelike, tawny or whitish, tapering at summit, 10 to 20 cm. long; spikelets short-pediceled with 1 or 2 fertile florets and 2 or 3 sterile reduced ones, the rachilla disarticulating below the fertile floret and tardily above it; glumes 1-nerved; fertile lemma subindurate, the nerves obscure, villous toward base, dissected into numerous unequal awns 2 to 5 mm. long, the body about 3 mm. long. ♃ (*P. apertum* Munro.)—Low places on plains and in valleys, Texas, Arizona, and northern Mexico; South America; wool waste, Maine.

2. Pappophorum bícolor Fourn. (Fig. 303.) Culms erect, 30 to 80 cm. tall; blades flat to subinvolute, 1 to 5 mm. wide; panicle mostly 10 to 15 cm. long, usually pink-tinged, rather loose, the branches 1 to 4 cm. long; spikelets on pedicels 1 to 5 mm. long, with 2 or 3 fertile florets and 1 or 2 sterile reduced ones, all about the same height in the spikelet, the rachilla not separating between the florets; glumes 1-nerved; lemmas somewhat indurate, obscurely nerved, pilose on the callus and on the lower half to two-thirds of the midnerve and margins, dissected into about 12 somewhat unequal scabrous awns 2 to 4 mm. long, the body about 3 mm. long, the awns about as long. ♃ —Open valley land, Texas, Arizona (La Noria, near Monument 111), and Mexico.

FIGURE 302.—*Pappophorum mucronulatum.* Plant, × ½; spikelet and perfect floret, × 5. (Pringle, Ariz.)

FIGURE 303.—*Pappophorum bicolor*, × 1. (Griffiths 6291, Tex.)

40. ENNEAPÓGON Desv. ex Beauv.

(Included in *Pappophorum* Schreb. in Manual, ed. 1)

Spikelets 3-flowered, the first floret fertile, the second smaller, sterile, the third rudimentary; glumes strongly 7-nerved; lemmas rounded on the back, firm, the truncate summit bearing 9 plumose equal awns; palea a little longer than the body of the lemma, the keels near the margin. Slender tufted perennials, with narrow feathery panicles. Type species *Enneapogon desvauxii* Beauv. Name from *ennea*, nine, and *pogon*, beard, alluding to the 9 plumose or bearded awns. A single species in America.

1. Enneapogon desvaúxii Beauv. SPIKE PAPPUSGRASS. (Fig. 304.) Culms numerous, slender, decumbent-spreading, 20 to 40 cm. tall, the nodes pubescent; blades flat to subinvolute, about 1 mm. wide; panicle spikelike, gray green or drab, mostly 2 to 5 cm. long, sometimes interrupted below; glumes longer than the body of the lemmas, 7-nerved, acuminate, pubescent; lemma of first floret (including awns) 4 to 5 mm. long, the body about 1.5 mm. long, villous, 9-nerved, the awns plumose, except at the apex. ♃ (*Pappophorum wrightii* S. Wats.)[11]—Dry plains and stony hills, Utah and Texas to Arizona, south to Oaxaca, Peru, Bolivia, and Argentina. Cleistogamous spikelets are produced in the lower sheaths, the cleistogenes larger than the normal florets, but the awns almost wanting. The culms disarticulate at the lower nodes, carrying the cleistogenes with them. Furnishes a fair proportion of forage on sterile hills.

41. SCLEROPÓGON Phil.

Plants monoecious or dioecious. Staminate spikelets several-flowered, pale, the rachilla not disarticulating; glumes about equal, membranaceous, long-acuminate, 1-nerved or obscurely 3-nerved, nearly as long as the first lemma; lemmas similar to the glumes, somewhat distant, 3-nerved or obscurely 5-nerved, mucronate; palea obtuse, shorter than the lemma. Pistillate spikelets subtended by a narrow bract on the pedicel, several-flowered, the upper florets reduced to awns, the rachilla disarticulating above the glumes but not separating between the florets or only tardily so; glumes acuminate, 3-nerved, with a few fine additional nerves, the first about half as long as the second; lemmas narrow, 3-nerved, the nerves extending into slender, scabrous, spreading awns, the florets falling together, forming a cylindric many-awned fruit, the lowest floret with a sharp-bearded callus as in *Aristida;* palea narrow, the 2 nerves near the margin, produced into short awns. Stoloniferous perennial, with short flexuous blades and narrow few-flowered racemes or simple panicles, the staminate and pistillate panicles strikingly different in appearance. Staminate and pistillate panicles may occur on the same plant, or rarely the 2 kinds of spikelets may be found in the same panicle. It may be that the seedlings produce 2 kinds of branches, each kind then re-

[11] For an account of the genus and the identity of this species, see *Chase, A.*, Madroña 7:187–189. 1946.

FIGURE 304.—*Enneapogon desvauxii*. Plant, × ½; spikelet, perfect floret, and cleistogene, × 5. (Purpus 8272, Ariz.)

producing its own sex. This should be investigated. Type species, *Scleropogon brevifolius*. Name from Greek *skleros*, hard, and *pogon*, beard, alluding to the hard awns.

1. Scleropogon brevifólius Phil. BURRO GRASS (Fig. 305.) Culms erect, 10 to 20 cm. tall, tufted, producing

FIGURE 305.—*Scleropogon brevifolius*. Pistillate and staminate plants, × ½; pistillate spikelet, × 2; pistillate and staminate florets, × 5. (Zuck, Ariz.)

wiry stolons with internodes 5 to 15 cm. long; leaves crowded at the base, the blades flat, 1 to 2 mm. wide, sharp-pointed; racemes, excluding awns, 1 to 5 cm. long; staminate spikelets 2 to 3 cm. long; body of pistillate spikelets 2.5 to 3 cm. long, the awns 5 to 10 cm. long, loosely twisted. ♃ (*S. karwinskyanus* Benth.)—Semiarid plains and open valley lands, Texas to Colorado, Nevada, and Arizona; south to central Mexico; Argentina. The mature pistillate spikelets break away and with their numerous long spreading awns form "tumbleweeds" that are blown before the wind, the pointed barbed callus readily penetrating clothing or wool, the combined florets acting like the single floret of long-awned aristidas. Spikelets rarely staminate below and pistillate above. On overstocked ranges, where it tends to become established, it is useful in preventing erosion. Often important as a range grass, especially when young.

TRIBE 3. HORDEAE

42. AGROPÝRON Gaertn. Wheatgrass

Spikelets several-flowered, solitary (rarely in pairs), sessile, placed flatwise at each joint of a continuous (rarely disarticulating) rachis, the rachilla disarticulating above the glumes and between the florets; glumes equal, firm, several-nerved, rarely 2-nerved, 1-nerved, or nerveless, usually shorter than the first lemma, acute or awned, rarely obtuse or notched; lemmas convex on the back, rather firm, 5- to 7-nerved, acute or awned from the apex; palea about as long as the lemma. Perennials (our species except *Agropyron triticeum*), often with creeping rhizomes, with usually erect culms and green or purplish, usually erect, spikes. Type species, *Agropyron triticeum* Gaertn. Name from Greek *agrios*, wild, and *puros*, wheat, the two original species being weeds in wheatfields.

Most of the species of *Agropyron* furnish forage, and a few are among the most valuable range grasses of the Western States. In the valleys some species may grow in sufficient abundance to produce hay.

Agropyron trachycaulum (*A. tenerum*, *A. pauciflorum*) has been cultivated in the Northwestern States on a commercial scale under the name slender wheatgrass, and the seed has been carried by seedsmen in that region. *A. smithii*, western wheatgrass, sometimes called Colorado bluestem, is a source of hay in alkaline meadows through the Western States. *A. spicatum*, or bluebunch wheatgrass, and *A. dasystachyum* are important range grasses in the Northwestern States. *A. trachycaulum* and *A. subsecundum* (*A. caninum*, so-called), because of their abundance in the mountain grazing regions, are also important. *A. repens*, quackgrass, is a good forage grass, but, because of its creeping rhizomes, is a troublesome weed, especially in the Eastern States where it is widely introduced. The species with strong creeping rhizomes are valuable for holding embankments and sandy soils.

The divisions of the species into those with rhizomes and those without is convenient and usually definite when the entire base is present, but some species normally without rhizomes (as *A. spicatum*) may rarely produce them and species in which rhizomes occur may not show them in herbarium specimens.

1a. Plants with creeping rhizomes.
  Lemmas awned, the awn divergent at maturity.
    Lemmas pubescent .... 9. A albicans.
    Lemmas glabrous .... 10. A. griffithsii.
  Lemmas awnless or with a short straight awn.
    Glumes rigid, gradually tapering into a short awn .... 5. A. smithii.
    Glumes not rigid, acute or abruptly awn-pointed.

Lemmas glabrous (sometimes pubescent in *A. riparium*).
Blades lax, flat.
Glumes shorter than the spikelets; rachilla glabrous.................. 2. A. REPENS.
Glumes nearly as long as the spikelet; rachilla pubescent.
4. A. PSEUDOREPENS.
Blades firm, stiff, often involute.
Spikelets much compressed, closely imbricate, the spike dense.
3. A. PUNGENS.
Spikelets not much compressed, somewhat distant, the spike slender.
8. A. RIPARIUM.
Lemmas pubescent.
Spike 6 to 12 cm. long; spikelets 1 to 1.5 cm. long; glumes 6 to 9 mm. long.
6. A. DASYSTACHYUM.
Spike as much as 25 cm. long; spikelets as much as 2.5 cm. long; glumes to 13 mm. long.................. 7. A. ELMERI.
1b. Plants without creeping rhizomes.
Spikelets much compressed, crowded on the rachis.................. 1. A. DESERTORUM.
Spikelets not much compressed nor divergent.
Spikelets awnless or awn-tipped only.
Glumes 2 to 2.5 mm. wide, nearly as long as the spikelet; rachilla villous.
Glumes with a broad subhyaline margin, unsymmetrical at the summit; lemmas commonly pubescent; spike rarely more than 7 cm. long, the spikelets closely imbricate.................. 14. A. LATIGLUME.
Glumes not thin-margined; lemmas glabrous; spike 10 to 25 cm. long, the spikelets mostly scarcely or slightly imbricate.................. 13. A. TRACHYCAULUM.
Glumes narrower, much shorter than the spikelet; rachilla scaberulous.
Blades involute (rarely flat).................. 19. A. INERME.
Blades flat.................. 21. A. PARISHII.
Spikelets awned.
Culms prostrate-spreading.................. 17. A. SCRIBNERI.
Culms erect (decumbent at base in *A. pringlei*).
Rachis finally disarticulating.
Glumes narrow, 2-nerved; awns of lemmas spreading, out-curved or recurved.
22. A. SAXICOLA.
Glumes broader, with usually 3 to 5 distinct scabrous nerves; awn straight, 2 to 5 cm. long.................. 23. A. SAUNDERSII.
Rachis continuous.
Awn straight or nearly so.
Spikelets about as long as the internodes of the rachis...... 21. A. PARISHII.
Spikelets imbricate, longer than the internodes of the rachis.
Lemmas coarsely pubescent.................. 11. A. VULPINUM.
Lemmas glabrous or scabrous toward summit only.
12. A. SUBSECUNDUM.
Awn divergent, when dry.
Spikelets imbricate.................. 15. A. BAKERI.
Spikelets distant.
Spikelets 3 to 7 in a spike, about twice as long as the internode; spike 4 to 7 cm. long.................. 16. A. PRINGLEI.
Spikelets mostly more than 7 in a spike, usually shorter than the internode; spike mostly more than 8 cm. long.
Spike 8 to 15 cm. long; blades 1 to 2 mm. wide.......... 18. A. SPICATUM.
Spike 15 to 30 cm. long; blades 4 to 6 mm. wide...... 20. A. ARIZONICUM.

1. Agropyron desertórum (Fisch.) Schult. (Fig. 306.) Culms slender, erect or geniculate at base, in dense tufts, 25 to 100 cm. tall; sheaths glabrous or the lower spreading-hirsute; blades 2 to 4 mm., occasionally to 5 mm. wide; spike 5 to 9 cm. long, 7 to 11 mm. wide, somewhat bristly, the short-jointed rachis pubescent; spikelets closely spaced on the rachis, 8 to 12 mm. long, 5- to 7-flowered, somewhat spreading; glumes and lemmas firm, glabrous to sparsely ciliate on the keel, both abruptly narrowed into an awn 2 to 3 mm. long, the lemma about 6 mm. long, the awn commonly slightly bent to one side. ♃ ("*A. cristatum*" of Manual, ed. 1)—Grown in experiment stations and found here and there in grainfields, Ontario, North Dakota, South Dakota, Montana, Wyoming, Colorado, Utah, Nevada, Arizona, and California; adventive, Albany Port, N. Y. Introduced from Russia, extensively planted in the northern Great Plains area, and spreading readily by reseeding.

Agropyron cristátum (L.) Gaertn. CRESTED WHEATGRASS. Spike 2 to 7 cm. long; spikelets more widely spreading, the glumes somewhat contorted, gradually tapering into the awns, these curved, 2 to 5 mm. long. ♃ —Adventive on barrier beach, Fishers Island, N. Y.; Barton, N. Dak. Introduced from Russia, grown in experiment stations, and a valuable dry-land grass for soil conservation and forage in the northern Great Plains. Sometimes found mixed in plantings of *A. desertorum.*

FIGURE 306.—*Agropyron desertorum,* × 1. (Ball 1768, Colo.)

Agropyron sibíricum (Willd.) Beauv. Rather smaller with relatively scant foliage; spike 6 to 10 cm. long, the rachis glabrous or nearly so; spikelets somewhat spreading, about as in *A. desertorum,* the glumes and lemmas mucronate or with an awn 1 to 2 mm. long. ♃ —Introduced from Russia, grown in a few experiment stations, spontaneous in Idaho (near Boise) and New Mexico (near Gallup). Better suited to dry soils.

Agropyron tritíceum Gaertn. Annual, branching at base; culms slender, erect or usually decumbent, mostly 10 to 30 cm. tall; blades flat, mostly less than 10 cm. long, 2 to 3 mm. wide; spike oval or ovate, 1 to 1.5 cm. long, thick; spikelets crowded, about 7 mm. long; glumes and lemmas acuminate. ⊙ —Absaroka Forest, Mont., Wyoming, Mountain Home, Idaho; Corfu, Wash. Sparingly introduced from southern Russia.

2. Agropyron répens (L.) Beauv. QUACKGRASS. (Fig. 307, *A.*) Green or glaucous; culms erect or curved at base, 50 to 100 cm. tall, sometimes taller, with creeping yellowish rhizomes; sheaths of the innovations often pubescent; blades relatively thin, flat, usually sparsely pilose on the upper surface, mostly 6 to 10 mm. wide; spike 5 to 15 cm. long, the rachis scabrous on the angles; spikelets mostly 4- to 6-flowered, 1 to 1.5 cm. long, the rachilla glabrous or scaberulous; glumes 3- to 7-nerved, awn-pointed; lemmas mostly 8 to 10 mm. long, the awn from less than 1 mm. to as long as the lemma; palea obtuse, nearly as long as the lemma, scabrous on the keels. ♃ —Waste places, meadows and pastures, Newfoundland to Alaska (Skagway), south to North Carolina, Arkansas, Utah, and California; Mexico; introduced from Eurasia. Common in the Northern States; a troublesome weed in cultivated ground. Called also quitch grass and couch grass. Awned specimens have been described as *Agropyron leersianum* (Wulf.) Rydb.; also referred to *A. repens* f. *aristatum* (Schum.) Holmb.

3. Agropyron púngens (Pers.) Roem. and Schult. (Fig. 307, *B.*) Glaucous, culms 50 to 80 cm. tall,

FIGURE 307.—*A*, *Agropyron repens*. Plant, × ½; spikelet and floret, × 3. *B*, *A. pungens*, × 3. (Scribner, Maine.)

with pale or brownish rhizomes; blades firm, mostly involute, scabrous on the upper surface; spikelets awnless, compressed, often as much as 10-flowered, the florets closely imbricate; glumes firm, acute, obscurely nerved, scabrous on the keel. ♃ —Seacoast, Maine (Cape Elizabeth), Massachusetts (Harwich); ballast, New Jersey and Oregon; introduced from Europe.

4. Agropyron pseudorépens Scribn. and Smith. (Fig. 308.) Resembling *A. repens*, often stouter, the rhizomes not yellow; blades commonly narrower; spike 10 to 20 cm. long, the spikelets contracted and appressed, the flat or scarcely keeled glumes 2 to 2.5 mm. wide, nearly equaling the spikelets; lemmas scaberulous to minutely hispidulous, rachilla villous. ♃ —Mostly in bottom lands or valleys, Alberta; Michigan (south shore of Lake Superior); South Dakota and Nebraska to Washington, south to New Mexico and Arizona. Specimens without rhizomes resemble *A. trachycaulum*.

FIGURE 308.—*Agropyron pseudorepens*, × 1. (Chase 5389, Colo.)

5. Agropyron smíthii Rydb. WESTERN WHEATGRASS. (Fig. 309.) Usually glaucous; culms erect, 30 to 60 cm. tall, sometimes taller, with creeping rhizomes; sheaths glabrous; blades firm, stiff, mostly flat when fresh, involute in drying, strongly nerved, scabrous or sometimes sparsely villous on the upper surface, mostly 2 to 4 mm. wide, tapering to a sharp point; spike erect, mostly 7 to 15 cm. long, the rachis scabrous on the angles; spikelets rather closely imbricate, occasionally two at a node, 6- to 10-flowered, 1 to 2 cm. long, the rachilla scabrous or scabrous-pubescent; glumes rigid, tapering to a short awn, rather faintly nerved, 10 to 12 mm. long; lemmas about 1 cm. long, firm, glabrous, often pubes-

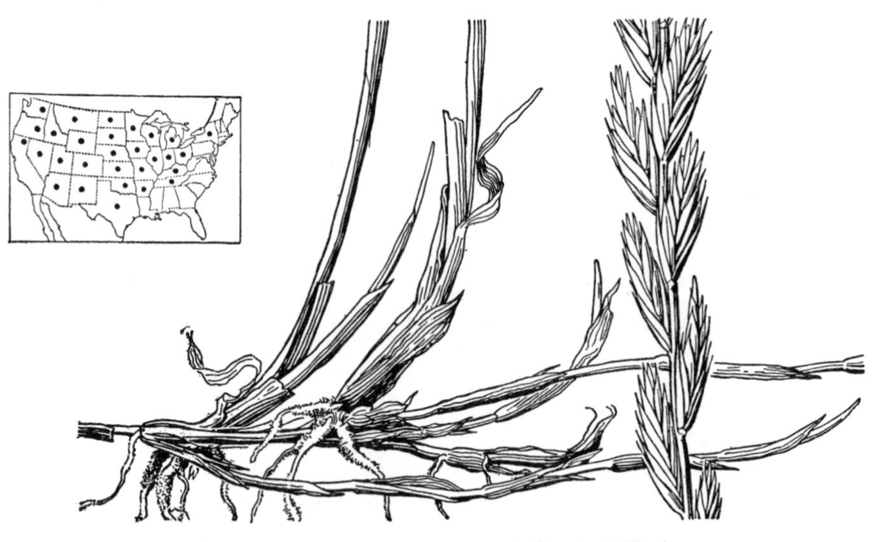

FIGURE 309.—*Agropyron smithii*, × 1. (Nelson 3918, Wyo.)

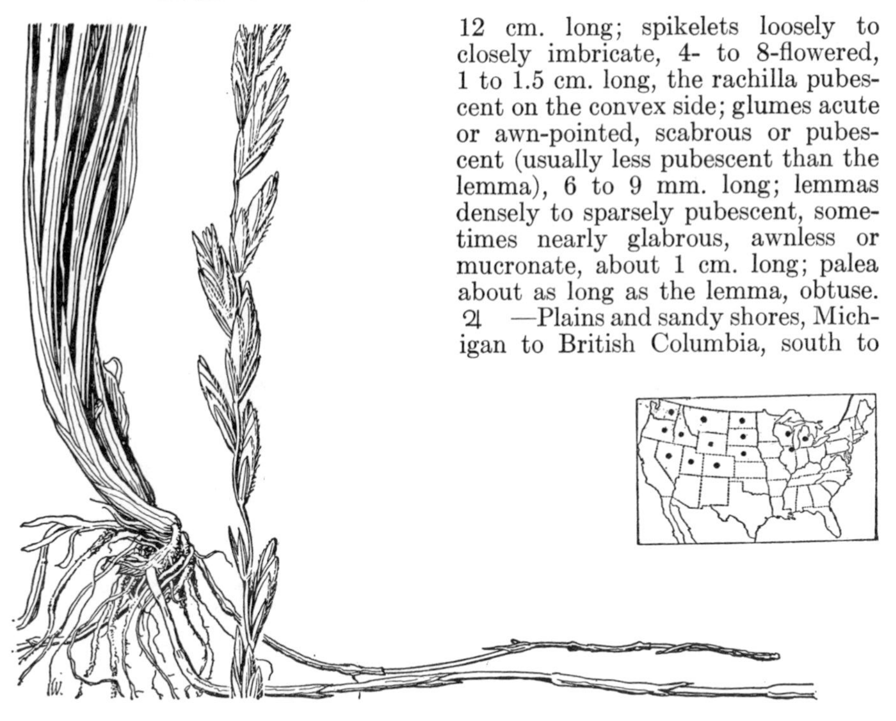

FIGURE 310.—*Agropyron dasystachyum*, × 1. (Griffiths 488, Wash.)

cent near the base, obscurely nerved, acuminate, mucronate, sometimes short-awned; palea scabrous-pubescent on the keels. ♃ —Moist, usually alkaline soil, Ontario to Alberta and British Columbia; New York; Michigan to Washington, south to Tennessee, Texas, Arizona, and northeastern California; mostly introduced east of Iowa and Kansas. Two varieties have been recognized. AGROPYRON SMITHII var. MÓLLE (Scribn. and Smith) Jones. Lemmas and sometimes glumes more or less pubescent. ♃ —About the same range as the species. AGROPYRON SMITHII var. PALMÉRI (Scribn. and Smith) Heller. Lower sheaths pubescent. ♃ —Colorado to Utah, south to New Mexico and Arizona.

6. Agropyron dasystáchyum (Hook.) Scribn. THICKSPIKE WHEATGRASS. (Fig. 310.) Often glaucous; culms mostly 40 to 80 cm. tall, with creeping rhizomes; blades flat to involute, 1 to 3 mm. wide; spike mostly 6 to 12 cm. long; spikelets loosely to closely imbricate, 4- to 8-flowered, 1 to 1.5 cm. long, the rachilla pubescent on the convex side; glumes acute or awn-pointed, scabrous or pubescent (usually less pubescent than the lemma), 6 to 9 mm. long; lemmas densely to sparsely pubescent, sometimes nearly glabrous, awnless or mucronate, about 1 cm. long; palea about as long as the lemma, obtuse. ♃ —Plains and sandy shores, Michigan to British Columbia, south to

FIGURE 311.—*Agropyron elmeri*, × 1. (Type.)

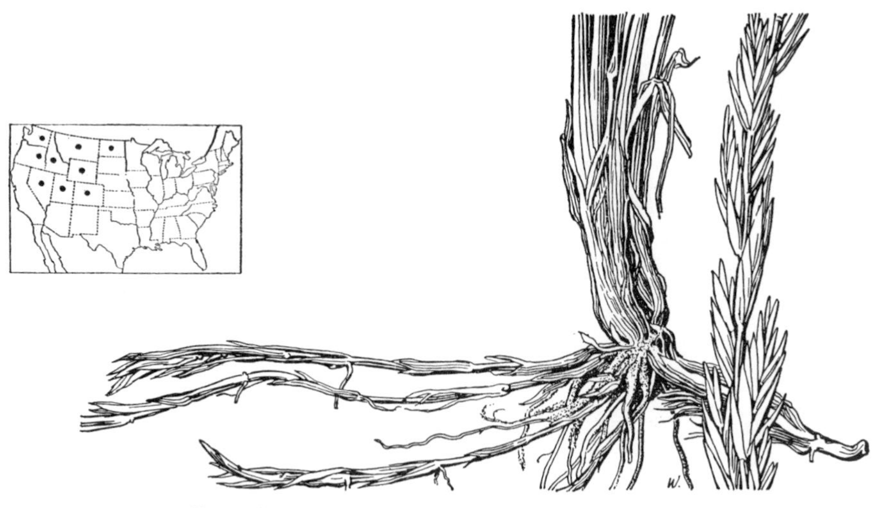

FIGURE 312.—*Agropyron riparium*, × 1. (Nelson 3965, Wyo.)

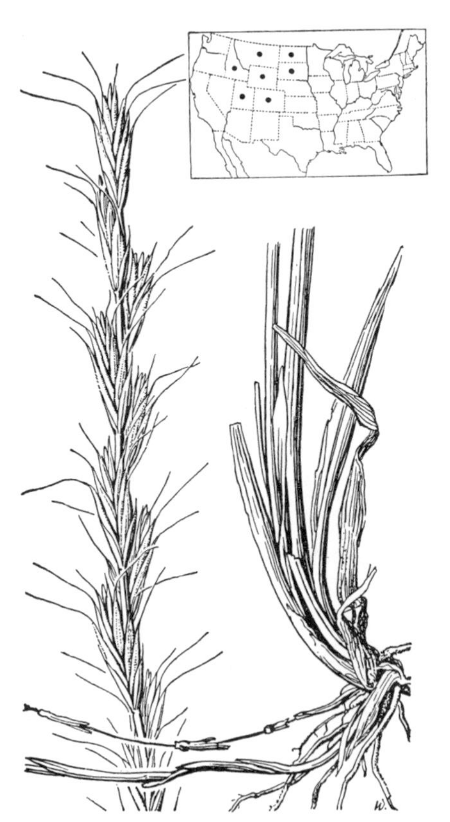

FIGURE 313.—*Agropyron albicans*, × 1. (Griffiths 3013, Wyo.)

Illinois, Nebraska, Colorado, Nevada, and Oregon. In the form growing on the sandy shores of Lake Michigan the lemmas are densely villous, but villous forms occur in other parts of the range of the species.

This and the four following species appear to intergrade, forming a polymorphous group.

7. Agropyron elméri Scribn. (Fig. 311.) Resembling *A. dasystachyum*; culms on the average taller, more robust, the spike longer (as much as 25 cm. long), the spikelets larger (as much as 10-flowered and 2.5 cm. long); glumes and lemmas usually longer (as much as 12 mm. and 15 mm., respectively); lemmas pubescent, sometimes sparsely so or scabrous only or pubescent only on the margins at base. ♃ —Dry or sandy soil, British Columbia to Oregon.

8. Agropyron ripárium Scribn. and Smith. STREAMBANK WHEATGRASS. (Fig. 312.) Resembling *A. dasystachyum*, with vigorous rhizomes; blades usually narrower; spikelets usually more imbricate; lemmas glabrous or somewhat pubescent along the edges of the lower part of the lemma. ♃ —Dry or moist meadows and hills, North Dakota to Alberta and Washington, south to Oregon and Colorado.

9. Agropyron álbicans Scribn. and Smith. (Fig. 313.) Similar to *A. dasystachyum;* glumes awn-pointed, about 1 cm. long; awn of lemma 1 to 1.5 cm. long, divergent when dry. ♃ —Plains and dry hills, South Dakota to Alberta and Idaho, Colorado and Utah.

10. Agropyron griffíthsi Scribn. and Smith ex Piper. (Fig. 314.) Resembling *A. albicans,* differing chiefly in having glabrous lemmas, the rachis rarely disarticulating. ♃ —Open, dry, sandy or alkaline soil, western North Dakota to Washington, south to Wyoming and Colorado. In the type specimen the lemmas are smooth, but in several other specimens the lemmas are scabrous. Possibly only a glabrous form of *A. albicans.*

Agropyron intermédium (Host) Beauv. Blades short, involute, acutish; glumes about 5-nerved; lemmas awnless. ♃ —Ballast at Camden, N. J.; adventive from Europe. Planted in the Northwest for pastures and for revegetating range lands.

Agropyron trichóphorum (Link) Richt. Blades flat; spikelets pubescent, awnless; glumes several-nerved, acutish. ♃ —Lynn, Mass.; adventive from Europe. Planted to some extent in the Northwest.

Agropyron júnceum (L.) Beauv. Blades loosely involute; spikelets glabrous; glumes 9-nerved, acutish. ♃ —Ballast near Portland, Oreg.; dunes, San Francisco, Calif.; adventive from Europe.

11. Agropyron vulpínum (Rydb.) Hitchc. (Fig. 315.) Culms 50 to 75 cm. tall, somewhat geniculate at base; blades drying loosely involute, 10 to 12 cm. long, 2 to 4 mm. wide; spike nodding, 10 to 15 cm. long, the rachis stiffly scabrous-ciliate on the angles; spikelets imbricate but not appressed, some toward the base two at a node, 3- to 5-flowered, the rachilla appressed-pubescent; glumes scabrous, strongly 5-nerved, awn-tipped; lemmas 5-nerved toward the

FIGURE 314.—*Agropyron griffithsi,* × 1. (Williams and Griffiths 164, Wyo.)

FIGURE 315.—*Agropyron vulpinum,* × 1. (Type.)

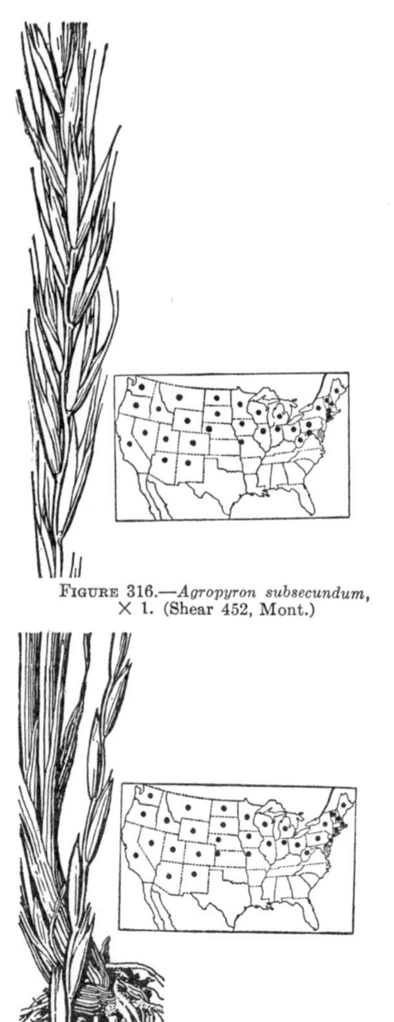

FIGURE 316.—*Agropyron subsecundum*, × 1. (Shear 452, Mont.)

FIGURE 317.—*Agropyron trachycaulum*, × 1. (Shear 404.)

minutely toothed apex, coarsely pubescent, the scabrous awn 8 to 10 mm. long. ♃ (*Elymus vulpinus* Rydb.) —Moist ground, Grant County, Nebr. and Livingston, Mont.

12. Agropyron subsecúndum (Link) Hitchc. BEARDED WHEATGRASS. (Fig. 316.) Green or glaucous, without creeping rhizomes; culms erect, tufted, 50 to 100 cm. tall; sheaths glabrous or rarely pubescent; blades flat, 3 to 8 mm. wide; spike erect or slightly nodding, 6 to 15 cm. long, sometimes unilateral from twisting of the spikelets to one side, the rachis scabrous or scabrous-ciliate on the angles, sometimes disarticulating; spikelets rather closely imbricate, few-flowered, the rachilla villous, the callus of the florets short-pilose; glumes broad, rather prominently 4- to 7-nerved, nearly as long as the spikelet, tapering into an awn; lemmas obscurely 5-nerved, the nerves becoming prominent toward the tip, the awn straight or nearly so, usually 1 to 3 cm. long. ♃ —Moist meadows and open woods, Newfoundland to Alaska, south to the mountains of Maryland, west to Washington and California, and south to New Mexico and Arizona. Said by Malte to be self-pollinated. This is the species which has generally been called by American botanists *A. caninum* (L.) Beauv.; that is a European species, differing in having 3-nerved glumes.

AGROPYRON SUBSECUNDUM var. ANDÍNUM (Scribn. and Smith) Hitchc. Culms mostly not more than 50 cm. tall, loosely tufted, usually geniculate at base; lower sheaths pale, usually papery; spike short; awns mostly 5 to 10 mm. long, often curved. An alpine form of mountain meadows. ♃ —Montana to Washington, south to Colorado and Nevada.

Agropyron caninum (L.) Beauv. Glumes 3-nerved. ♃ —Ballast near Portland, Oreg.; adventive from Europe.

13. Agropyron trachycaúlum (Link) Malte. SLENDER WHEATGRASS. (Fig. 317.) Resembling *A. subsecundum;* sheaths glabrous or rarely pubescent; blades mostly 2 to 4 mm. wide; spike usually more slender, 10 to 25 cm. long, sometimes unilateral; spikelets from rather remote to closely imbricate; glumes and lemmas awnless or nearly so. ♃ (*A. tenerum* Vasey, *A. pauciflorum* (Schwein.) Hitchc.)—Labrador to Alaska, south to the mountains of West Virginia, Missouri, New Mexico, and California; northwestern Mexico. Alpine plants lower, and with shorter denser commonly purplish spikes, resemble *A. subsecundum* var. *andinum*, but the spikelets are awnless. They have been referred to *A. violaceum* (Hornem.) Lange, an Arctic species, and to *A. biflorum* (Brignoli) Roem. and Schult.

Figure 318.—*Agropyron latiglume*, × 3. (Type.)

14. Agropyron latiglúme (Scribn. and Smith) Rydb. (Fig. 318.) Culms loosely tufted, curved or geniculate below, 20 to 50 cm. tall; blades flat, short, 3 to 5 mm. wide, short-hirsute on both surfaces, rarely glabrous or nearly so beneath; spike mostly 3 to 7 cm. long, rarely longer; spikelets usually closely imbricate; glumes broad, flat, thin-margined, unsymmetrical and slightly notched at summit, awn-tipped; lemmas commonly appressed-pubescent, awnless or awn-tipped. ♃ —Alpine meadows, open slopes, mostly at high altitudes, Montana, Wyoming, and Colorado to Labrador and Alaska.

15. Agropyron bakéri E. Nels. Baker wheatgrass. (Fig. 319.) Resembling *A. subsecundum;* culms erect, mostly 50 to 100 cm. tall, rather loosely tufted; spike mostly 5 to 12 cm. long, the spikelets rather loosely imbricate; awns divergently curved when dry, 1 to 4 cm. long. ♃ —Open slopes, upper altitudes, northern Michigan; Alberta to Washington, Oregon, and New Mexico.

16. Agropyron prínglei (Scribn. and Smith) Hitchc. (Fig. 320.) Culms tufted, decumbent at base, 30 to 50 cm. tall, the basal sheaths soft and papery; blades flat or loosely involute, mostly less than 10 cm. long, 1 to 3 mm. wide; spike more or less flexuous, 4 to 7 cm. long, the rachis scabrous on the angles, slender, the middle internodes usually 8 to 10 mm. long; spikelets mostly 3 to 7 in each spike, rather distant, the lower and middle ones (excluding awns) about as long as two internodes, mostly 3- to 5-flowered, the rachilla joints minutely

Figure 319.—*Agropyron bakeri*, × 1. (Hitchcock 1686, Colo.)

FIGURE 320.—*Agropyron pringlei*, × 1. (Pringle 504, Calif.)

scabrous, about 2 mm. long; glumes rather narrow, about 3-nerved on the exposed side, 7 to 8 mm. long, tapering into a straight awn about 5 mm. long; lemmas tapering into a scabrous, strongly divergent awn 1.5 to 2.5 cm. long; palea 10 to 12 mm. long. ♃ —Stony slopes, 2,500 to 3,500 m., in the Sierra Nevada, Calif.

17. Agropyron scribnéri Vasey. SPREADING WHEATGRASS. (Fig. 321) Culms tufted, prostrate or decumbent-spreading, often flexuous, 20 to 40 cm. long; blades flat or, especially on the innovations, loosely involute, more or less pubescent, mostly basal, the 2 or 3 culm blades usually less than 5 cm. long, 1 to 3 mm. wide; spike long-exserted, often nodding or flexuous, dense, 3 to 7 cm. long, the rachis disarticulating at maturity, the internodes glabrous, 3 to 5 mm. long, or the lowermost longer; spikelets 3- to 5-flowered, the rachilla internodes minutely scabrous, about 2 mm. long; glumes narrow, one obscurely nerved, the other with 2 or 3 distinct nerves, tapering into a divergent awn similar to the awns of the lemmas; lemmas nerved toward the tip, tapering to a strongly divergent awn 1.5 to 2.5 cm. long; palea a little longer than the body of the lemma, the apex with 2 short slender teeth. ♃ —Alpine slopes, 3,000 to 4,000 m., Montana and Idaho to New Mexico and California. Characterized by the hard leafy basal tussock with slender spreading flexuous culms.

18. Agropyron spicátum (Pursh) Scribn. and Smith. BLUEBUNCH WHEATGRASS (Fig. 322.) Green or glaucous; culms tufted, often in large bunches, erect, 60 to 100 cm. tall; sheaths glabrous; blades flat to loosely involute, 1 to 2 mm., sometimes to 4 mm., wide, glabrous beneath, pubescent on the upper surface; spike slender, mostly 8 to 15 cm. long, the rachis scaberulous on the angles, the internodes 1 to 2 cm. long, or the

FIGURE 321.—*Agropyron scribneri*, × 1. (Shear 1179, Colo.)

lowermost 2.5 cm.; spikelets distant, not as long (excluding the awns) as the internodes or slightly longer, mostly 6- to 8-flowered, the rachilla joints scaberulous, 1.5 to 2 mm. long; glumes rather narrow, obtuse to acute, rarely short-awned, about 4-nerved, usually about half as long as the spikelet, glabrous or scabrous on the nerves; lemmas about 1 cm. long, the awn strongly divergent, 1 to 2 cm. long; palea about as long as the lemma, obtuse. ♃ —Plains, dry slopes, canyons and dry open woods, northern Michigan to Alaska, south to western South Dakota, New Mexico, and California. A smaller form with smaller spikelets, found in desert regions of the Great Basin has been differentiated as *A. vaseyi* Scribn. and Smith. A. SPICATUM var. PUBÉSCENS Elmer. Culms and foliage pubescent. ♃ —Washington and Idaho.

FIGURE 322.—*Agropyron spicatum*, × 1. (Vasey, Wash.)

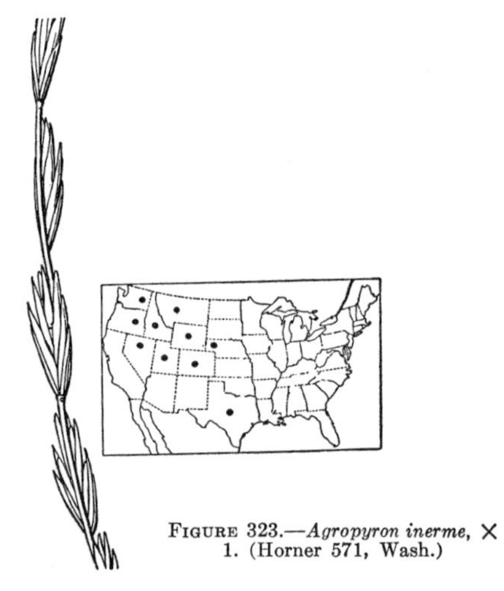

FIGURE 323.—*Agropyron inerme*, × 1. (Horner 571, Wash.)

19. Agropyron inérme (Scribn. and Smith) Rydb. BEARDLESS WHEATGRASS. (Fig. 323.) Differing from *A. spicatum* in the awnless spikelets. ♃ (*A. spicatum* var. *inerme* Heller.)—Dry plains and hills, Montana to British Columbia, south to Utah, Wyoming, western Nebraska, and eastern Oregon; Texas. Closely related to *A. spicatum*, but very different in appearance because awnless.

FIGURE 324.—*Agropyron arizonicum*, × 1. (Type.)

20. Agropyron arizónicum Scribn. and Smith. (Fig. 324.) Resembling *A. spicatum*, usually taller and coarser;

FIGURE 325.—*Agropyron parishii*, × 1. (Type.)

FIGURE 326.—*Agropyron saxicola*, × 1. (Type.)

blades commonly 4 to 6 mm. wide; spike 15 to 30 cm. long, flexuous, the rachis more slender; spikelets distant, mostly 3- to 5-flowered; glumes short-awned; awns of the lemmas stouter, mostly 2 to 3 cm. long. ♃ —Rocky slopes, western Texas, New Mexico, Arizona, Nevada, California (Eel Ridge), and Chihuahua, Mexico.

Agropyron semicostátum (Steud.) Nees ex Boiss. Blades flat; spike nodding, 10 to 20 cm. long; spikelets several-flowered, imbricate; glumes several-nerved, much shorter than the spikelet, acute but scarcely awned, awn of lemma flexuous or finally divergent, 1.5 to 3 cm. long. ♃ —Ballast near Portland, Oreg. Native of Asia. Cultivated in experiment plots in California, Washington, D. C., and Mississippi in the last century under the unpublished name *Agropyrum japonicum*. Tracy used the name in print in economic notes. (See Synonymy.)

21. Agropyron paríshii Scribn. and Smith. (Fig. 325.) Culms 70 to 100 cm. tall, the nodes retrorsely pubescent; blades flat or loosely involute, 2 to 4 mm. wide; spike slender, nodding, 10 to 25 cm. long, the internodes of the rachis 1.5 to 2.5 cm. long; spikelets 4- to 7-flowered, mostly about 2 cm. long, narrow, appressed, the rachilla joints scaberulous, about 2 mm. long; glumes 3- to 5-nerved, 1 to 1.5 cm. long, acute; lemmas acute or with a slender awn 1 to 8 mm. long; palea as long as the lemma, obtuse. ♃ —Canyons and rocky slopes, California (Monterey and San Benito Counties and San Bernardino Mountains); rare. AGROPYRON PARISHII var. LAÉVE Scribn. and Smith. Nodes glabrous; awns usually 1 to 2 cm. long. ♃ —California, more widespread than the species.

22. Agropyron saxícola (Scribn. and Smith) Piper. (Fig. 326.) Culms tufted, erect, 30 to 80 cm. tall; sheaths glabrous or sometimes pubescent; blades flat to loosely involute, glabrous or sometimes pubescent, 1 to 4 mm. wide; spike 5 to 12 cm. long, the rachis tardily disarticulating, the internodes more or less scabrous on the angles, 5 to 10 mm. long; spikelets imbricate, sometimes in pairs, about twice as long as the internodes of the rachis, 4- to 6-flowered, the rachilla minutely scabrous; glumes narrow, 2-nerved, the nerves sometimes obscure, sometimes with a third faint nerve, awned, the awn divergent, 5 to 20 mm. long, sometimes with a tooth or short awn at the base of the main awn; lemmas about 8 mm. long, the awn divergent, mostly 2 to 5 cm. long, sometimes with 1 or 2 short additional awns; palea about as long as the lemma, obtuse or truncate. ♃ —Dry or rocky slopes and plains, western South Dakota to Washington, south to Utah, Arizona, and California.

23. Agropyron saundérsii (Vasey) Hitchc. (Fig. 327.) Culms erect, 60 to 100 cm. tall; blades flat or loosely involute; spike erect, 8 to 15 cm. long, mostly purplish, the rachis tardily disarticulating; spikelets sometimes in pairs near the middle of the spike, 1 to 1.5 cm. long (excluding awns), 2- to 5-flowered; glumes variable, narrow with 2 nerves or wider with 3 to 5 nerves, the nerves strong and at least the midnerve scabrous, the awn 1 to 5 cm. long, sometimes with a short lateral awn near the base; lemmas scabrous, the awn straight, 2 to 5 cm. long. ♃ (*Elymus saundersii* Vasey.)—Dry slopes, Colorado, Wyoming, Idaho, Utah, Arizona, and California. Only the 5 specimens of the type collection from Veta Pass, Colo., have spikelets with awns to 5 cm. long. In some specimens the awns of the glumes vary from 5 to 16 mm. and those of the lemmas from 7 to 30 mm. (*Elymus saundersii* var. *californicus* Hoover), and in others from 10 to 20 mm. on the glumes and 15 to 35 mm. on the lemmas.

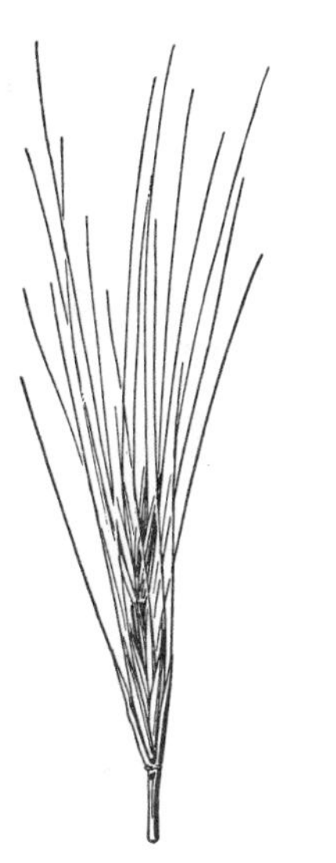

FIGURE 327.—*Agropyron saundersii*, × 1. (Type.)

43. TRÍTICUM L.

Spikelets 2- to 5-flowered, solitary, placed flatwise at each joint of a continuous or articulate rachis, the rachilla disarticulating above the glumes and between the florets or continuous; glumes rigid, keeled, 3- to several-nerved, the apex abruptly mucronate or toothed or with one to several awns; lemmas broad, keeled, very asymmetric, many-nerved, abruptly pointed or awned. Low or rather tall annuals, with flat blades and thick spikes. Standard species, *Triticum aestivum*. *Triticum*, the old Latin name for wheat.

1. Triticum aestívum L. WHEAT. (Fig. 328.) Culms erect, freely branching at base, 60 to 100 cm. tall; blades 1 to 2 cm. wide; spike mostly 5 to 12 cm. long; internodes of rachis 3 to 6 mm. long; spikelets broad, glabrous or pubescent, long-awned to awnless; glumes usually strongly keeled toward one side, the keel extending into a mucro, the other side usually obtusely angled at apex. ⊙ (*T. vulgare* Vill.; *T. sativum* Lam.)—Commonly cultivated; fields and waste places in the vicinity of cultivated fields or grain elevators, but not established.

Spelt (*T. spelta* L.) and emmer (*T. dicoccum* Schrank) are sometimes cultivated for the grain, used for stock feed, and for forage. In these two species the rachis breaks up, each joint bearing a spikelet which remains entire, each floret permanently enclosing the grain. In spelt the spikelets are somewhat distant, exposing the rachis, in emmer the spikelets are closely imbricate, scarcely exposing the rachis. A large number of varieties of wheat are in cultivation; the lemmas may be glabrous or pubescent, the awns long or nearly or quite wanting.

On the basis of the number of chromosomes the wheats and their

FIGURE 328.—*Triticum aestivum.* Plant with awned spikes (bearded wheat) and a nearly awnless spike (beardless wheat), × ½; spikelet and floret, × 3. (Cult.)

allies may be divided into three groups. The group with 7 chromosomes (probably the most primitive) includes einkorn (*T. monococcum* L.). The group with 14 chromosomes includes durum wheat (*T. durum* Desf.), poulard wheat (*T. turgidum* L.), Polish wheat (*T. polonicum* L.), emmer (*T. dicoccum* Schrank), and also *T. pyramidale* Perciv., *T. orientale* Perciv. (not Biebers. 1806), *T. persicum* Vavilov (not Aitch. and Hemsl. 1888), *T. dicoccoides* Koern. and *T. timopheevi* (Zhukov.) Zhukov.[12] The group with 21 chromosomes includes spelt and the commonly cultivated wheats referred to as *T. vulgare* Vill. and *T. compactum* Host, also *T. macha* Dekap. and Menab. and *T. sphaerococcum* Perciv.[12] Alaska wheat is a variety of poulard wheat with branched heads. It is also known by several other names, such as Egyptian, miracle, and mummy. This variety is considered inferior commercially to standard varieties of wheat. Stories of varieties originating from seed found with mummies 3,000 years old have no basis in fact.

The origin of wheat is not known, as there is no native species like any of the cultivated forms. Some botanists have suggested species of *Aegilops* and others *T. dicoccoides* Koern., a wild species of Palestine, as the possible ancestor.

44. AÉGILOPS L. Goatgrass

Spikelets 2- to 5-flowered, solitary, turgid or cylindric, placed flatwise at each joint of the rachis and fitting into it, the joints thickened at the summit, the spikelets usually not reaching the one above on the same side, exposing the rachis; spike usually disarticulating near the base at maturity, falling entire, or finally disarticulating between the spikelets. Annuals with flat blades and usually awned spikes. Type species, *Aegilops ovata*. Name from *Aegilops*, an old Greek name for a kind of grass.

The species of *Aegilops* have been recently introduced into the United States and in some places are becoming troublesome weeds. At maturity the spikes fall entire, the lowest rachis joint serving as a pointed callus to the 2- to several-jointed, strongly barbed fruits, which work their way into the mouths and noses of grazing animals and into the wool of sheep.

Spikelets subovate; rachis not disarticulating .... 3. A. ovata.
Spikelets cylindric; rachis finally disarticulating.
  Glumes with 1 awn .... 1. A. cylindrica.
  Glumes with 3 awns .... 2. A. triuncialis.

1. Aegilops cylíndrica Host. Jointed goatgrass. (Fig. 329.) Culms erect, branching at base, 40 to 60 cm. tall; blades 2 to 3 mm. wide; spike cylindric, 5 to 10 cm. long; internodes of rachis 6 to 8 mm. long; spikelets 8 to 10 mm. long, glabrous to hispid; glumes several-nerved, keeled at 1 side, the keel extending into an awn, the main nerve of the other side extending into a short tooth; lemmas mucronate, those of the uppermost spikelets awned like the glumes; awns very scabrous, those of the upper spikelets about 5 cm. long, those of the lower spikelets progressively shorter. ⊙ —Weed in wheatfields, and waste places, New York, and Pennsylvania; Indiana to Wyoming and Utah, south to Texas and New Mexico; Washington; recently introduced from Europe.

2. Aegilops triunciális L. Barb goatgrass. (Fig. 330.) Culms branching and spreading at base, 20 to 40 cm. tall; blades rather rigid, sharp-pointed, spreading; spike 3 to 4 cm. long, 2 or 3 of the lower spikelets often reduced, the fertile spikelets 3 to 5; glumes with 3 strong scabrous, somewhat spreading awns, 4 to 8

[12] These names supplied by W. J. Sando, geneticist.

FIGURE 329.—*Aegilops cylindrica*, × ½. (Bush 72148, Mo.)

cm. long; lemmas with three rigid unequal awns. ⊙ —Troublesome weed on range land, California; adventive in Pennsylvania; introduced from Europe.

3. Aegilops ovāta L. Culms tufted, geniculate at base, 15 to 25 cm. tall; blades short, sharp-pointed; spike thick, of 2 to 4 subovate spikelets, the upper sterile; glumes with 4 stiff scabrous spreading awns 2 to 3 cm. long; lemmas usually with 1 long and 2 short awns. ⊙ —Weed in fields, California and Virginia; introduced from Europe.

45. SECĀLE L. RYE

Spikelets usually 2-flowered, solitary, placed flatwise against the rachis, the rachilla disarticulating above the glumes and produced beyond the upper floret as a minute stipe; glumes narrow, rigid, acuminate or subulate-pointed; lemmas broader, sharply keeled, 5-nerved, ciliate on the keel and exposed margins, tapering into a long awn. Erect, mostly annual grasses, with flat blades and dense spikes. Type species, *Secale cereale*. *Secale*, the old Latin name for rye.

1. Secale cereāle L. RYE. (Fig. 331.) In habit resembling wheat, but usually taller, the spike more slender, somewhat nodding, on the average longer. ⊙ —Commonly cultivated; escaped from cultivation, in fields and waste places. This species is thought to be derived from *S. montanum* Guss., a perennial native in the mountains of southwestern Asia.

Secale montānum Guss. Culms in rather large dense clumps, erect or geniculate at the base, mostly 100 to 135 cm. tall; blades flat, stiffly spreading; spikes somewhat drooping, 10 to 13 cm. long, the rachis rather readily disarticulating; awns 1 to 2 cm. long, slender, scabrous. ♃ —Persisting along roadsides around the experiment station at Pullman, Wash. Introduced from southwestern Asia.

FIGURE 330.—*Aegilops triuncialis*, × ½. (Cole, Calif.)

46. ÉLYMUS L. WILD-RYE

Spikelets 2- to 6-flowered, in pairs (3 or more or solitary sometimes in a few species) at each node of a usually continuous rachis, placed as in *Agropyron* but the rachilla distorted at base, bringing the florets more or less dorsiventral to the rachis; rachilla disarticulating above the glumes and between the florets; glumes equal, somewhat asymmetric, usually rigid, sometimes indurate below, narrow to subulate, 1- to several-nerved, acute to aristate; lemmas rounded on the back or nearly terete, obscurely 5-nerved, acute or usually

FIGURE 331.—*Secale cereale*. Plant, × ½; spikelet, × 3; floret, × 5. (Hill, Ill.)

awned from the tip. Erect, usually rather tall perennials (one annual), with flat or rarely convolute blades and slender or bristly spikes, the spikelets usually crowded, sometimes somewhat distant. Type species, *Elymus sibiricus* L. Name from *Elumos,* an old Greek name for a kind of grain. The species in which the spikelets are mostly solitary can be distinguished from *Agropyron* by the narrow or subulate glumes. The seed of certain species (e.g., *E. mollis* and *E. canadensis*) have been used for food by the Indians.

The species of *Elymus* are for the most part good forage grasses and in some localities form a part of the native hay. In the wooded areas of the Northwest, *E. glaucus* is one of the valuable secondary grasses of the ranges. The species with creeping rhizomes are likely to be of value as soil or sand binders. *E. mollis* is a natural sea-dune grass, and *E. arenicola* and *E. flavescens* are common on inland shifting dunes. *E. triticoides* is to be recommended for holding embankments. On the western ranges *E. cinereus* and *E. triticoides* are important.

1a. Plants annual; spike long-awned, nearly as broad as long........ 1. E. CAPUT-MEDUSAE.
1b. Plants perennial; spike much longer than broad.
  2a. Rhizomes present, slender, creeping.
    Glumes lanceolate, awnless or awn-pointed. Plants of coastal dunes.
      Glumes and lemmas papery, distinctly nerved........ 2. E. MOLLIS.
      Glumes and lemmas firm, faintly nerved (lemmas nerved at apex).
        3. E. VANCOUVERENSIS.
    Glumes subulate or very narrow.
      Spikelets glabrous.
        Lemmas acute or awn-pointed, brownish or tan-colored; spikelets paired or solitary, crowded.
          Spikelets usually in pairs, or paired and solitary in a single spike; culms 60 to 120 cm. tall........ 8. E. TRITICOIDES.
          Spikelets solitary in short spikes; culms 10 to 20 cm. tall...... 9. E. PACIFICUS.
        Lemmas awned, the awns 3 to 14 mm. long; spikelets usually solitary, rather distant, pale........ 10. E. SIMPLEX.
      Spikelets densely villous to coarsely, sometimes sparsely, pubescent.
        Lemmas awned or awn-tipped; spike 5 to 15 cm. long.
          Lemmas copiously villous; awn 1 to 4 mm. long........ 6. E. INNOVATUS.
          Lemmas hirsute or hirtellous; awn 5 to 10 mm. long........ 7. E. HIRTIFLORUS.
        Lemmas awnless; spike 10 to 25 cm. long.
          Glumes pubescent; lemmas soft, densely villous........ 4. E. FLAVESCENS.
          Glumes glabrous or nearly so; lemmas relatively firm, coarsely pubescent, sometimes sparsely so........ 5. E. ARENICOLA.
            Lemmas glabrous to sparsely strigose; culms glabrous; spikes usually compound; blades 15 to 35 mm. wide........ 13. E. CONDENSATUS.
            Lemmas more or less pubescent; culms harsh-puberulent, at least about the nodes; spikes not or scarcely compound; blades 5 to 15 mm. wide.
              14. E. CINEREUS.
  2b. Rhizomes wanting (or short and stout in *E. condensatus*). Plants tufted.
    3a. Rachis tardily disjointing; glumes and lemmas awned.
      Spike mostly 5 to 7 mm. wide; spikelets mostly in twos; blades subinvolute.
        18. E. MACOUNII.
      Spike 8 to 10 mm. wide; spikelets often in threes; blades flat, 5 to 10 mm. wide.
        19. E. ARISTATUS.
    3b. Rachis continuous.
      4a. Glumes subulate to subsetaceous, not broadened above the base, the nerves obscure except in *E. villosus.*
        Lemmas awnless or awn-tipped, the awn shorter than the body.
          Spike thick, sometimes compound; spikelets commonly in twos to fours.
            Lemmas glabrous to sparsely strigose; culms glabrous; spikes usually compound; blades 15 to 35 mm. wide........ 13. E. CONDENSATUS.
            Lemmas more or less pubescent; culms harsh-puberulent at least about the nodes; spikes not or scarcely compound; blades 5 to 15 mm. wide.
              14. E. CINEREUS.
          Spike slender; some or most of the spikelets solitary at the nodes, the paired spikelets near the middle.

Culms numerous in a close tuft, the leaves mostly basal; lemmas mostly awnless ..... 12. E. SALINUS.
Culms few, loosely tufted, the leaves scattered along the usually taller culms; lemmas awn-tipped, the awn 2 to 5 mm. long ..... 11. E. AMBIGUUS.
Lemmas awned, the awn as long as the body or longer.
Awns straight; lemmas about 1.2 mm. wide across the back. 20. E. VILLOSUS.
Awns flexuous-divergent; lemmas about 2 mm. wide across the back. 21. E. INTERRUPTUS.
4b. Glumes lanceolate or narrower, broadened above the base, strongly 3- to several-nerved.
Glumes relatively thin, flat, several-nerved, not indurate at base.
Lemmas sparsely long-hirsute on the margins toward the summit. 17. E. HIRSUTUS.
Lemmas glabrous or scabrous.
Lemmas awned ..... 15. E. GLAUCUS.
Lemmas awnless or minutely awn-tipped ..... 16. E. VIRESCENS.
Glumes firm, indurate at base.
Awns divergently curved when dry; base of glumes not terete. 22. E. CANADENSIS.
Awns straight; base of glumes terete.
Glumes about 1 mm. wide about the middle, the bases not bowed out; palea much shorter than the lemma ..... 23. E. RIPARIUS.
Glumes 1.5 to 2 mm. wide about the middle, the bases bowed out; palea as long as the lemma ..... 24. E. VIRGINICUS.

FIGURE 332.—*Elymus caput-medusae*, × 1. (Vasey 3076, Wash.)

1. Elymus cáput-medúsae L. (Fig. 332.) Annual; culms ascending from a decumbent, branching base, slender, 20 to 60 cm. tall; blades narrow, short; spike very bristly, 2 to 5 cm. long (excluding the long spreading awns); glumes subulate, smooth, indurate below, tapering into a slender awn 1 to 2.5 cm. long; lemmas lanceolate, 3-nerved, 6 mm. long, very scabrous, tapering into a flat awn 5 to 10 cm. long. ⊙ —Open ground, Idaho and Washington to California; a bad weed, spreading on the ranges in northern California; introduced from Europe.

2. Elymus móllis Trin. AMERICAN DUNEGRASS. (Fig. 333.) Culms stout, pubescent below the spike, glaucous, 60 to 120 cm. tall, with numerous overlapping basal leaves, the rhizomes widely creeping; blades firm, 7 to 12 mm. wide, often involute in drying; spike erect, dense, thick, soft, pale, 7 to 25 cm. long; glumes lanceolate, flat, many-nerved, scabrous or pubescent, 12 to 25 mm. long, acuminate, about as long as the spikelet; lemmas scabrous to felty-pubescent, acuminate or mucronate. ♃ —Sand dunes along the coast, Alaska to Greenland, south to Long Island, N.Y., and central California; along Lakes Superior and Michigan; also eastern Siberia to Japan. Closely related to the European *E. arenarius* L. with culm smooth below the spike and glabrous glumes. A form found along the coast of Washington with somewhat compound spikes has been differentiated as *E. arenarius* var. *compositus* (Abrom.) St. John, but the plants are found to be diseased.

FIGURE 333.—*Elymus mollis*, × 1. (Henderson 2169, Wash.)

3. Elymus vancouverénsis Vasey. (Fig. 334.) Resembling *E. mollis*, less leafy; spike somewhat interrupted, purplish; glumes narrowly lanceolate, firm, gradually acuminate, 1 to 1.5

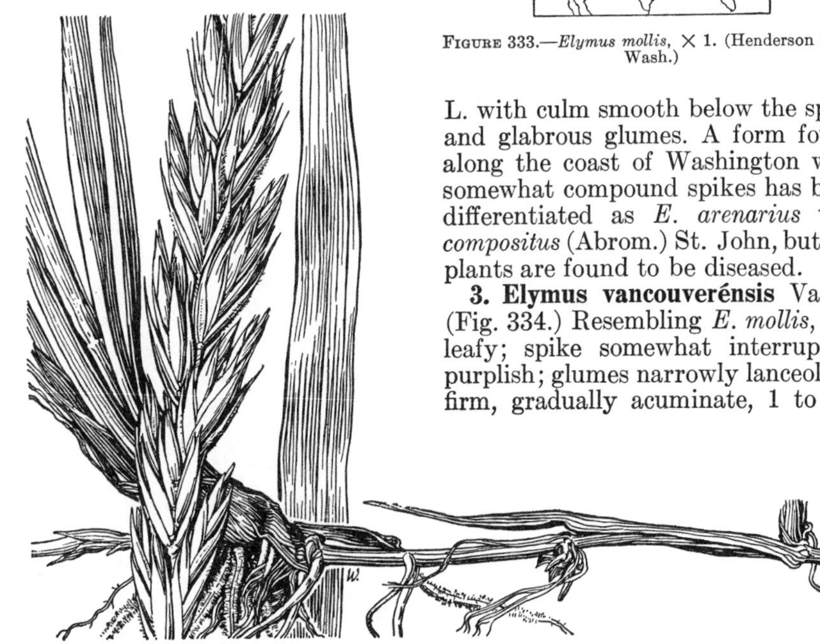

FIGURE 334.—*Elymus vancouverensis*, × 1. (Piper 812, Wash.)

FIGURE 335.—*Elymus flavescens*, × 1. (Merrill and Wilcox 160, Idaho.)

cm. long, sparsely long-villous, especially toward the apex; lemmas firm, 1 to 1.5 cm. long, tapering into a short awn. ♃ —Dunes and sandy shores, British Columbia to northern California.

4. Elymus flavéscens Scribn. and Smith. (Fig. 335.) Culms erect, slender, glabrous, 50 to 100 cm. tall, the rhizomes slender, nearly vertical from deep slender horizontal rhizomes with brown scales; sheaths glabrous; blades firm, glabrous beneath, scabrous above, 2 to 5 mm. wide, flat, or involute in drying; spike 10 to 25 cm. long, sometimes with short branches, somewhat nodding; spikelets 2 to 3 cm. long, several-flowered, approximate or somewhat distant; glumes very narrow or subulate, pubescent, nerveless, mostly unequal, 1 to 1.5 cm. long; lemmas awnless, densely silky-villous, the hairs long, yellowish or brownish. ♃ —Sand dunes, eastern Washington and Oregon, Idaho; South Dakota (Black Hills).

5. Elymus arenícola Scribn. and Smith. (Fig. 336.) Resembling *E. flavescens* to which it is closely related; glumes glabrous or nearly so; lemmas firmer, coarsely pubescent, sometimes sparsely so, or the pubescence confined to the base or margins, the pubescence grayish rather than yellow. ♃ —Sandy valleys, often in drifting sand, Washington, Oregon, and Idaho.

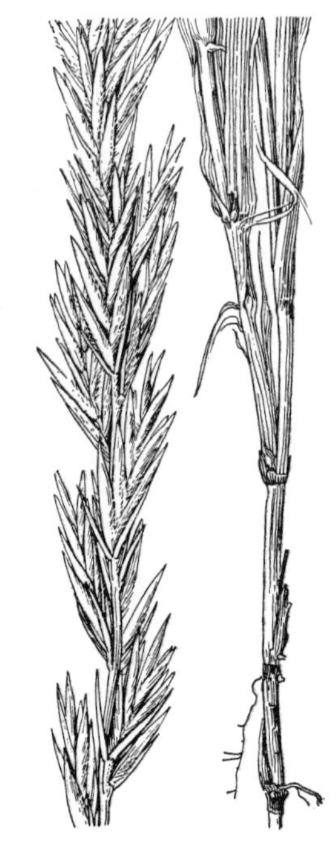

FIGURE 336.—*Elymus arenicola*, × 1. (Palmer 356, Idaho.)

FIGURE 337.—*Elymus innovatus*, × 1. (Hayward 2719, S. Dak.)

6. Elymus innovátus Beal. (Fig. 337.) Resembling *E. flavescens;* spike rather dense, 5 to 12 cm. long, the rachis villous; spikelets 1 to 1.5 cm. long, the narrow glumes and the lemmas densely purplish or grayish-villous, the lemmas with an awn mostly 1 to 4 mm. long. ♃ —Open woods and gravelly flats, Alaska to British Columbia; Montana, Wyoming, and South Dakota (Black Hills).

7. Elymus hirtiflórus Hitchc. (Fig. 338.) Culms erect, tufted, 40 to 90 cm. tall, with slender creeping rhizomes; blades firm, flat or usually involute, glabrous beneath, 5 to 20 cm. long, 1 to 4 mm. wide when flat; spike erect, 5 to 15 cm. long; spikelets 4- to 6-flowered; glumes firm, hirsute, narrow, tapering into an awn about as long as the body, the entire length 1 to 1.5 cm.; lemmas hirsute, sometimes sparingly so, the lower 8 to 9 mm. long, with an awn 5 to 10 mm. long. ♃ —River banks, Wyoming; Alberta.

8. Elymus triticoídes Buckl. BEARDLESS WILD-RYE. (Fig. 339.) Culms usually glaucous, rarely pubescent below spike, 60 to 120 cm. tall, commonly in large colonies from extensively creeping scaly rhizomes; ligule a truncate rim about 1 mm.

FIGURE 338.—*Elymus hirtiflorus.* Spike, × 1; spikelet, × 5. (Type.)

long; blades mostly 2 to 6 mm. wide, flat or soon involute; spike erect, slender to rather dense, rarely compound; spikelets mostly 12 to 20 mm. long; glumes very narrow to subulate, firm, nerveless or 1- to 3-nerved, awn-

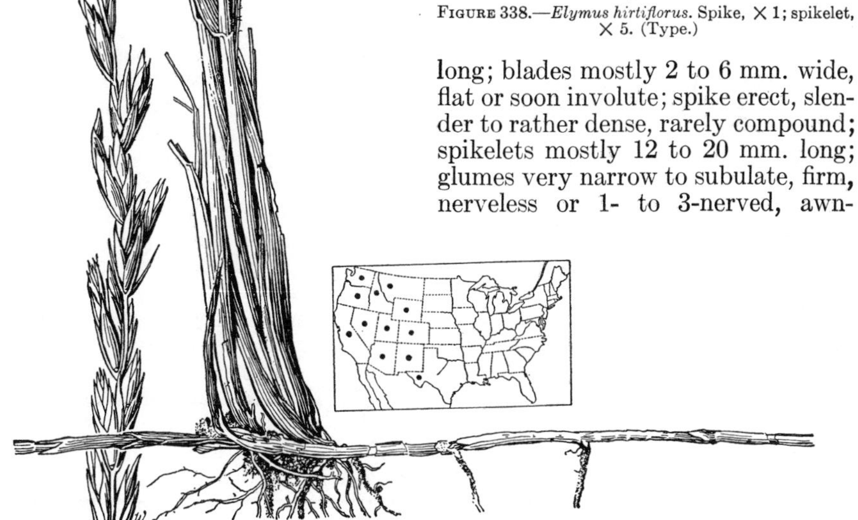

FIGURE 339.—*Elymus triticoides,* × 1. (Cusick 763, Oreg.)

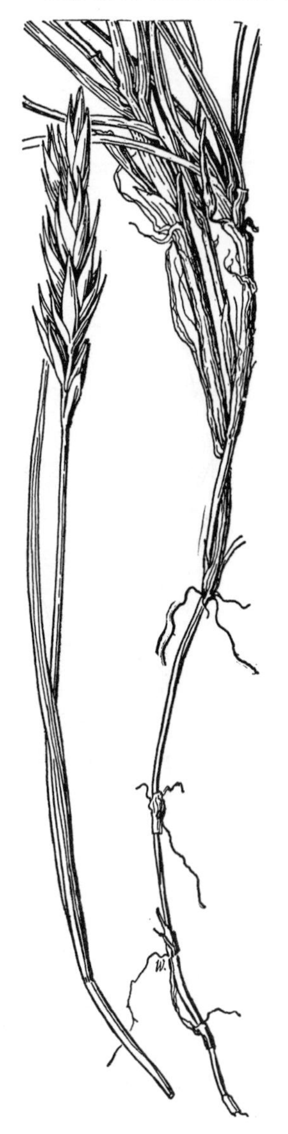

FIGURE 340.—*Elymus pacificus*, × 1. (Davy 6781, Calif.)

tipped, 5 to 15 mm. long, those of the upper spikelets usually reduced or obsolete; lemmas 6 to 10 mm. long, glabrous, firm, brownish, purplish or tawny, awn-tipped. ♃ —Moist or alkaline soil, at low and medium elevations, Montana to Washington, south to western Texas and Baja California. ELYMUS TRITICOIDES var. PUBÉSCENS Hitchc. Sheaths and involute blades pubescent. ♃ —Oregon, California, Nevada; rare.

ELYMUS TRITICOIDES subsp. MULTIFLÓRUS Gould. Plants robust; blades 6 to 12 mm. wide; spike compound, the branches mostly short, congested, but sometimes to 5 cm. long; spikelets 1.5 to 2.5 cm. long. ♃ —Wyoming to Washington, Nevada, and California. Intergrades with the species.

9. Elymus pacíficus Gould. (Fig. 340.) Culms low, more or less spreading, 10 to 20 cm. tall, with slender extensively creeping rhizomes; blades involute, mostly longer than the culms, pungent-pointed; spike 2 to 5 cm. long, the rachis glabrous; spikelets solitary, few-flowered, 12 to 15 mm. long; glumes nerveless, firm, tapering into a short awn; lemmas about 1 cm. long, obscurely nerved, pointed or awn-tipped, the margin very narrowly hyaline. (*Agropyron arenicola* Davy, not *Elymus arenicola* Scribn. and Smith.) ♃ —Sandy seacoast, middle California.

10. Elymus símplex Scribn. and Williams. (Fig. 341.) More extensively creeping than *E. triticoides*, the rhizomes sometimes as much as 5 m. long; culms ascending, 50 to 90 cm. tall; sheaths crowded, the lower often becoming reddish and papery; blades firm, flat or loosely rolled, strongly nerved; spikes 5 to 20 cm. long; spikelets as much as 2.5 cm. long, usually distant, solitary or sometimes paired; glumes subulate-aristate, 1 to 2 cm. long; rachilla villous; lemmas glabrous, the margins hyaline, awned, the awn 3 to 14 mm. long. ♃ —River banks, alkaline flats, drifting sands, and rocky slopes, southern Wyoming, Colorado, and Utah. Valuable in erosion control.

11. Elymus ambíguus Vasey and Scribn. (Fig. 342.) Culms few, loosely tufted, erect, 30 to 70 cm. tall; sheaths glabrous; blades flat to subinvolute, 2 to 5 mm. wide, scabrous; spike erect, rather dense, 5 to 15 cm. long; spikelets solitary toward the base and apex of the spike, mostly 2- to 4-flowered; glumes subulate, scabrous toward the awned tip; lemmas glabrous or scabrous on the back, about 1 cm. long, short-awned, the awn 2 to 5 mm. long. ♃ —Open slopes at medium altitudes in the mountains, Montana, Colorado, and Utah. ELYMUS AMBIGUUS var. STRIGÓSUS (Rydb.) Hitchc. Lemmas strigose or pubescent. ♃ (*E. strigosus* Rydb., lemmas strigose; *E. villiflorus* Rydb.) lemmas pubescent.)—Wyoming, Colorado.

12. Elymus salínus Jones. SALINA WILD-RYE. (Fig. 343.) Culms erect, 30 to 80 cm. tall, sometimes scabrous below nodes and below spike; sheaths scabrous; blades firm, involute, scabrous, or rarely softly pubescent; spike slender, erect, 5 to 12 cm. long; spikelets mostly solitary, often rather distant, 1 to 1.5 cm. long; glumes subulate, 4 to 8 mm. long, sometimes reduced, glabrous or scabrous; lemmas about 1 cm. long, awnless or rarely awn-tipped, glabrous or scabrous, rarely sparsely strigose, the nerves obscure. ♃ —Rocky slopes and sagebrush hills, Wyoming and Colorado to Idaho, Nevada, and southern California.

13. Elymus condensátus Presl. GIANT WILD-RYE. (Fig. 344.) Culms robust, in large tufts, usually 2 to 3 m. tall, with short thick rhizomes; ligule 2 to 5 mm. long; blades firm, strongly nerved, flat, as much as 3 cm. wide; spike erect, dense, 15 to 50 cm. long, usually more or less compound, the branches erect, 2 to 7 cm. long; spikelets often in threes to fives, commonly distorted by pressure; glumes subulate, awn-pointed, usually 1-nerved or nerveless, about as long as the first lemma, sometimes longer; lemmas glabrous to sparsely strigose, with a hyaline margin, awnless or mucronate. ♃ —Sand dunes, sandy or rocky slopes, moist ravines, mostly near the coast, Alameda County to San Diego County, Calif., and on the adjacent islands off the coast.

FIGURE 341.—*Elymus simplex*, × 1. (Type.)

FIGURE 342.—*Elymus ambiguus*, × 1. (Hitchcock 10990, Colo.)

FIGURE 343.—*Elymus salinus*, × 1. (Rydberg 2041, Wyo.)

FIGURE 344.—*Elymus condensatus*, × 1. (Pringle in 1882, Calif.)

14. Elymus cinéreus Scribn. and Merr. (Fig. 345.) Culms robust, but less so than in *E. condensatus*, typically without rhizomes, harsh-puberulent, at least about the nodes; sheaths and blades glabrous to densely harsh-puberulent, the blades mostly less than 15 mm. wide; spikes 10 to 25 cm. long (mostly 12 to 20 cm.), thick and dense but typically not branched, or with 1 of the 3 to 5 spikelets at a node pedicellate; glumes and lemmas like those of *E. condensatus*, but the lemmas more or less pubescent. ♃ (*E. condensatus* var. *pubens* Piper.)—River banks, ravines, moist or dry slopes and plains, mostly at higher altitudes than the preceding, Minnesota to British Columbia, south to Colorado, and California. On the whole this appears to be distinct from *E. condensatus*, but a rather large number of specimens from Wyoming to California have branched spikes, some with blades to 15 mm. wide, a few with rhizomes. These intermediate specimens are more or less harshly puberulent, at least about the nodes. The seeds are sometimes used for food by the Indians.

FIGURE 345.—*Elymus cinereus*, × 1. (Butler 839, Calif.)

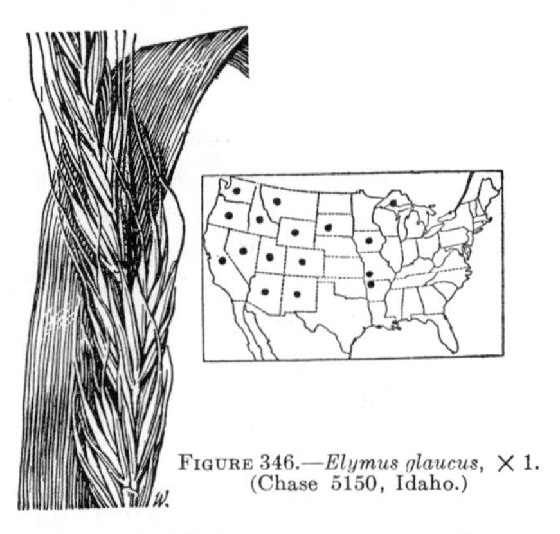

FIGURE 346.—*Elymus glaucus*, × 1. (Chase 5150, Idaho.)

15. Elymus glaúcus Buckl. BLUE WILD-RYE. (Fig. 346.) Culms in loose to dense tufts, often bent at base, erect, 60 to 120 cm. tall, without rhizomes, leafy; sheaths smooth or scabrous; blades flat, usually lax, mostly 8 to 15 mm. wide, usually scabrous on both surfaces, sometimes narrow and subinvolute; spike long-exserted, from erect to somewhat nodding, usually dense, commonly 5 to 20 cm. long, occasionally longer; glumes lanceolate at base, 8 to 15 mm. long, with 2 to 5 strong scabrous nerves, acuminate or awn-pointed; lemmas awned, the awn 1 to 2 times as long as the body, erect to spreading. ♃ —Open woods, copses, and dry hills at low and medium altitudes, Ontario and Michigan to southern Alaska, south through South Dakota and Colorado to New Mexico and California; Iowa, Missouri, and Arkansas. Exceedingly variable, the commonest form is loosely tufted, with lax blades 10 to 15 mm. wide and somewhat nodding spike, but plants with narrower blades and stiff spikes are frequent, the extreme form differentiated as *E. angustifolius* Davy. The original specimen described by Buckley is a rather small plant intermediate in blades and spike. ELYMUS GLAUCUS var. JEPSÓNI Davy. Sheaths and blades pubescent. ♃ —British Columbia to California; Montana and Nevada.

FIGURE 347.—*Elymus virescens*, × 1. (Flett, Wash.)

FIGURE 348.—*Elymus hirsutus*, × 5. (Thompson 7332, Wash.)

16. Elymus virḗscens Piper. (Fig. 347.) Resembling *E. glaucus* and nearly as variable in habit, often decumbent at base; sheaths from glabrous to retrorsely pubescent, blades 2 to 12 mm. wide, glabrous to harsh-puberulent; spike 5 to 15 cm. long, dense, spikelets imbricate; glumes flat, 1 to 2 mm. wide, strongly nerved, pointed or awn-tipped; lemmas glabrous to scabrous, barely awn-tipped or with an awn 1 to 4 mm. long. ♃ Moist woods, southern Alaska to California.

17. Elymus hirsū́tus Presl. (Fig. 348.) Culms solitary or in small tufts, 50 to 140 cm. tall, rather weak; blades flat, lax, 4 to 10 mm. wide, scabrous; spike drooping, mostly loose, the rachis exposed; spikelets mostly about 15 mm. long; glumes about 1 mm. wide, strongly nerved, awned; lemmas sparsely long-hirsute along the margin toward the summit, sometimes coarsely pubescent on the back, the slender awn flexuous or divergent, 1.5 to 2 cm. long. ♃ —Moist woods or open ground, Alaska to Oregon.

18. Elymus macoū́nii Vasey. MACOUN WILD-RYE. (Fig. 349.) Culms

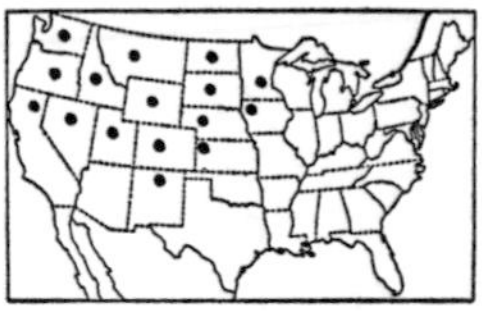

FIGURE 349.—*Elymus macounii*. Disarticulating spike, × 1. (Anderson, Mont.)

densely tufted, erect, slender, 50 to 100 cm. tall; sheaths glabrous or rarely pubescent; blades erect, rather firm, subinvolute, usually scabrous on both surfaces, 10 to 20 cm. long, mostly 2 to 5 mm. wide; spike slender, erect or somewhat nodding, 4 to 12 cm. long, usually about 5 mm. thick (excluding awns), the slender rachis tardily disarticulating; spikelets imbricate, appressed, mostly 2-flowered, about 1 cm. long, excluding the awns; glumes very narrow, scabrous, slightly divergent but not bowed out at base, the midnerve usually distinct; lemmas scabrous toward the apex, extending into slender straight awns 1 to 2 cm. long. ♃ —Meadows and open ground, Minnesota to Alaska and eastern Washington, south to Iowa, Kansas, New Mexico, and California. (Said by Stebbins to be a hybrid between *Agropyron trachycaulum* and species of *Hordeum*.)

19. Elymus aristátus Merr. (Fig. 350.) Culms tufted, rather leafy, erect, 70 to 100 cm. tall; sheaths glabrous, blades flat, 5 to 10 mm. wide; spike erect, dense, 6 to 14 cm. long, 5 to 10 mm. thick, the rachis tardily disarticulating; spikelets closely imbricate, often in threes, 1- to 2-flowered, about 1 cm. long, excluding the awns; glumes subsetaceous, scabrous, 10 to 20 mm. long; lemmas slightly wider than in *E. macounii*, sparsely scabrous at least on the upper half, the slender straight awn 10 to 20 mm. long. ♃ —Meadows and open slopes, at middle altitudes, Wyoming to Washington, south to Nevada and California.

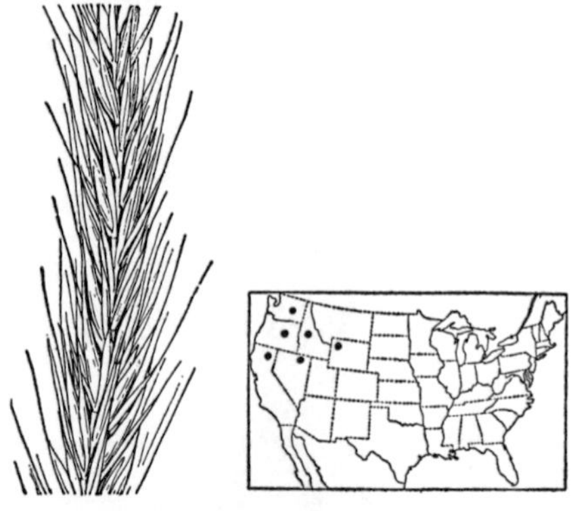

FIGURE 350.—*Elymus aristatus*, × 1. (Chase 4762, Idaho.)

20. Elymus villósus Muhl. (Fig. 351.) Culms in small tufts, ascending, slender, 60 to 100 cm. tall; sheaths glabrous to pilose; blades flat, lax, pubescent on upper surface, glabrous and glossy to scabrous beneath; spike drooping, dense, 5 to 12 cm. long; glumes subsetaceous, spreading, distinctly nerved above the firm cylindric nerveless divergent or somewhat bowed-out base, hirsute, 12 to 20 mm. long; lemmas nerved toward the tip, hispidulous to hirsute, 7 to 9 mm. long, about 1.2 mm. across the back, the straight slender awn 1 to 3 cm. long. ♃ (*E. striatus*, American authors, not Willd.) Moist or dry woods and shaded slopes, Canada and Vermont to North Dakota and Wyoming, south to South Carolina, Alabama, and Texas. E. ARKANSÁNUS Scribn. and Ball (*E. villosus* forma *arkansanus* Fernald), a relatively rare form with usually slightly stouter culms, the spikes mostly less drooping, scabrous glumes, and glabrous to scabrous lemmas, is found sparingly in Illinois, North

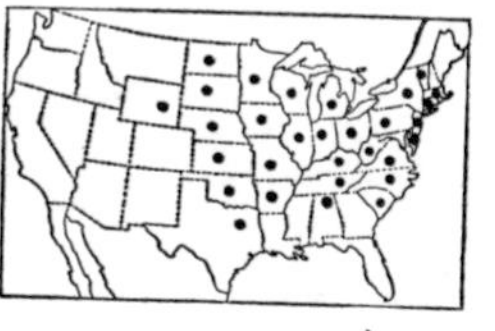

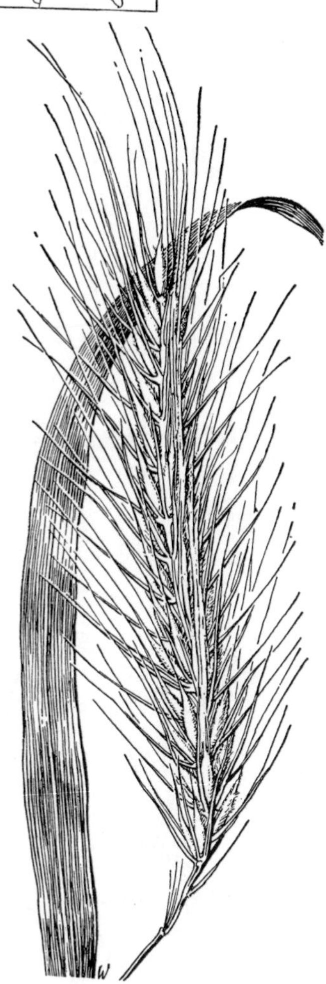

FIGURE 351.—*Elymus villosus*, × 1. (Commons 163, Del.)

FIGURE 352.—*Elymus interruptus*, × 1. (Grant 3071, Minn.)

Dakota, South Dakota, Nebraska, Missouri, Maryland, Virginia, North Carolina, Kentucky, Tennessee, Arkansas, Texas, and Wyoming. Large specimens resemble *E. riparius*, but the palea reaches the base of the awn.

21. Elymus interrúptus Buckl. (Fig. 352.) Culms erect, 70 to 130 cm. tall; sheaths glabrous; blades flat scabrous, 5 to 12 mm. wide; spike flexuous or nodding, 8 to 20 cm. long; glumes setaceous or nearly so, 1 to 3 cm. long, one or both reduced in occasional spikelets, mostly flexuous or spreading, the nerves obscure at least toward the base; lemmas hirsute to scabrous, or glabrous, about 1 cm. long, about 2 mm. across the back, the awn flexuous or divergent, 1 to 3 cm. long. ♃ (*E. diversiglumis* Scribn. and Ball.)—

FIGURE 353.—*Elymus canadensis*. Plant, × ½; spikelet and floret, × 5. (Lansing 3240, Mich.)

Rich, open moist soil, Michigan to North Dakota and Wyoming; Tennessee, Arkansas, Oklahoma, Texas, New Mexico.

22. Elymus canadénsis L. CANADA WILD-RYE. (Fig. 353.) Green or often glaucous; culms erect, tufted, mostly 1 to 1.5 m. tall; sheaths glabrous or rarely pubescent; blades flat, scabrous or sparsely hispid on the upper surface, mostly 1 to 2 cm. wide; spike thick and bristly, nodding or drooping, often interrupted below, 10 to 25 cm. long, sometimes glaucous; spikelets commonly in threes or fours, slightly spreading; glumes narrow, mostly 2- to 4-nerved, scabrous, sometimes hispid but less so than the lemmas, the bases somewhat indurate and divergent but scarcely bowed out, the awn about as long as the body; lemmas scabrous-hirsute to hirsute-pubescent, rarely glabrous, strongly nerved above, the awn divergently curved when dry, 2 to 3 cm. long. ♃ —River banks, open ground, and sandy soil, Quebec to southern Alaska, south to North Carolina, Missouri, Texas, Arizona, and northern California. *E. wiegandii* Fernald has been differentiated on lax inflorescence, shorter glumes, and thin flat blades, pilose on the nerves. These characters are found to be rarely coordinated, loose flexuous spikes being not infrequent in humid regions, rarer in dry areas; pilose blades are very rare. ELYMUS CANADENSIS var. ROBÚSTUS (Scribn. and Smith) Mackenz. and Bush. Differing in the stouter and denser only slightly nodding very bristly spikes. ♃ —Prairies, Massachusetts to Montana, south to Kentucky, Missouri, Texas, and Arizona. ELYMUS CANADENSIS var. BRACHÝSTACHYS (Scribn. and Ball) Farwell. Lemmas glabrous or nearly so. ♃ —Moist open or partly shaded ground, Arkansas, Oklahoma, Texas, and New Mexico; Mexico. Grades into *E. canadensis;* many specimens of *E. canadensis* from Kansas to North Dakota have sparingly hirsute lemmas, showing a transition to this variety.

23. Elymus ripárius Wiegand. (Fig. 354.) Culms rather slender, erect, 1 to 1.5 m. tall; sheaths glabrous; blades rather thin, flat, 5 to 15 mm. wide, scabrous; spike somewhat nodding, 7 to 20 cm. long; glumes narrow, about 1 mm. wide at the middle, 2- to 4-nerved, somewhat indurate but scarcely bowed out at base; lemmas minutely hispidulous to glabrous, the awn straight, mostly 2 to 3 cm. long. ♃ —River banks and low ground, Quebec and Maine to Wisconsin and Nebraska, south to North Carolina, Arkansas, and Kansas. Differing from *E. virginicus* var. *glabriflorus* in the nodding spike and less indurate glumes; from *E. canadensis* in the straight awns and narrower and somewhat more indurate glumes. When the ranges of *E. riparius* and *E. canadensis* coincide the latter may be distinguished by the hirsute lemmas.

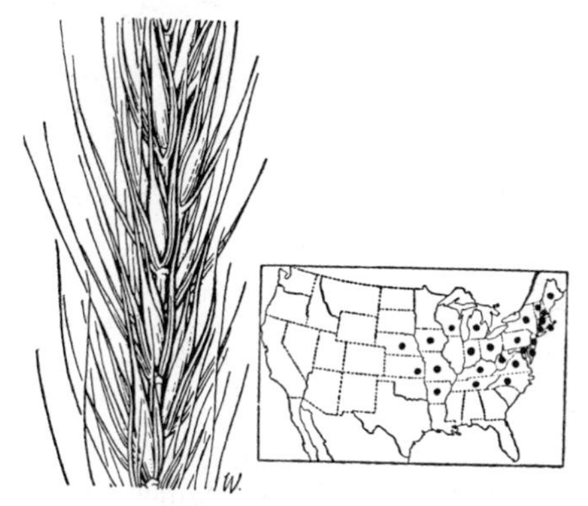

FIGURE 354.—*Elymus riparius*, × 1. (Woodward, Conn.)

24. Elymus virgínicus L. VIRGINIA WILD-RYE. (Fig. 355.) Culms tufted, erect, 60 to 120 cm. tall; sheaths glabrous; blades flat, scabrous, mostly 5 to 15 mm. wide; spike usually erect, often partly included, 5 to 15 cm. long; glumes strongly nerved, firm, indurate, yellowish, nerveless and bowed out at base leaving a rounded sinus, broadened above (1.5 to 2 mm. wide), scabrous, the apex somewhat curved, tapering into a straight awn, about as long as the body or shorter; lemmas glabrous and nerveless below, scabrous and nerved above, tapering into a straight awn usually about 1 cm. long. ♃ —

FIGURE 355.—*Elymus virginicus*, × 1. (Hitchcock 79, Va.)

Moist ground, low woods, and along streams, Newfoundland to Alberta, south to Florida and Arizona. Sometimes called Terrell grass. A variable species of which the following intergrading varieties may be distinguished.

ELYMUS VIRGINICUS var. GLABRIFLÓRUS (Vasey) Bush. Glumes mostly less bowed out; lemmas glabrous; awns mostly 2 to 3 cm. long, the spike more bristly. ♃ —Maine to Kansas, south to Florida and New Mexico.

ELYMUS VIRGINICUS var. HALÓPHILUS (Bickn.) Wiegand. More slender, usually glaucous; blades narrower, often becoming involute; spikes and spikelets somewhat smaller. ♃ —Brackish marshes and moist sand along the coast, Maine to Virginia.

ELYMUS VIRGINICUS var. SUBMÚTICUS Hook. Glumes and lemmas awnless or nearly so. ♃ —Woods and open ground, Quebec to Washington, south to Rhode Island; Ohio and Kentucky to Oklahoma and Montana; Utah.

ELYMUS VIRGINICUS var. INTERMÉDIUS (Vasey) Bush. Glumes, lemmas, and rachis more or less hirsute, the awns about as in *E. virginicus*. ♃ (*E. hirsutiglumis* Scribn.)—Thickets and low ground, Maine to Iowa, south to Florida and Texas.

ELYMUS VIRGINICUS var. AUSTRÁLIS (Scribn. and Ball) Hitchc. Differing from *E. virginicus* var. *intermedius* in the stouter, bristly spike and longer awns; differing from *E. virginicus* var. *glabriflorus* in the hirsute or strongly scabrous glumes and lemmas. ♃ —Prairies, rocky hills, and open woods, Vermont to Iowa, south to Florida, Kentucky, and Texas.

ELYMUS GIGANTÉUS Vahl. Robust perennial from stout rhizomes; blades numerous at base, elongate; spike dense, 15 to 20 cm. long, about 2 cm. thick; glumes and lemmas sharp-pointed, the glumes glabrous, the lemmas pubescent below. ♃ —Occasionally cultivated for ornament. Siberia.

47. SITÁNION Raf. SQUIRRELTAIL

Spikelets 2- to few-flowered, the uppermost floret reduced, usually 2 at each node of a disarticulating rachis, the rachis breaking at the base of each joint, remaining attached as a pointed stipe to the spikelets above; glumes narrow or setaceous, 1- to 3-nerved, the nerves prominent, extending into one to several awns, these (when more than one) irregular in size, sometimes mere lateral appendages of the long central awn, sometimes equal, the glume being bifid; lemmas firm, convex on the back, nearly terete, 5-nerved, the nerves obscure, the apex slightly 2-toothed, the central nerve extending into a long, slender, finally spreading awn, sometimes one or more of the lateral nerves also extending into short awns; palea firm, nearly as long as the body of the lemma, the two keels serrulate. Low or rather tall tufted perennials, with bristly spikes. Type species, *Sitanion elymoides* Raf. (*S. hystrix*). Name from Greek *sitos*, grain.

The species are exceedingly variable, being glabrous to densely pubescent and green to glaucous; the glumes and lemmas vary in division and length of awns. Some 15 to 25 variations have been recognized as species, but study of extensive collections shows that most of the characters used in differentiating the forms are inconstant and combine in various ways.

The species are widespread in the Western States but do not form complete stands. They have forage value when young but at maturity the disarticulating joints of the spike, with their pointed rachis joints and long-awned spikelets, are blown about by the wind and often cause injury to stock, penetrating the mouth, nose, and ears, working in by means of the forwardly roughened awns, and causing inflammation. Grazed also after the heads are blown off. The commonest species is *S. hystrix.*

Spike much longer than broad; glumes narrowly lanceolate, 2- to 4-nerved.
1. S. HANSENI.

Spike as broad as long or broader; glumes bristlelike, 1- or obscurely 2-nerved.
- Glumes cleft into at least 3 fine divisions........2. S. JUBATUM.
- Glumes entire or 2-cleft........3. S. HYSTRIX.

1. Sitanion hanséni (Scribn) J. G. Smith. HANSEN SQUIRRELTAIL. (Fig. 356.) Culms 60 to 100 cm. tall; sheaths and blades glabrous or scabrous to softly pubescent, the blades flat to subinvolute, 2 to 8 mm. wide; spike somewhat nodding or flexuous, 8 to 20 cm. long; glumes narrowly lanceolate, sometimes bifid, 2- to 3-nerved, long-awned, lower lemmas about 8 mm. long, the awn 4 to 5 cm. long, divergent when dry and mature. ♃ —Open woods and rocky slopes, Wyoming to eastern Washington, Utah, and California. Pubescent plants have been differentiated as *S. anomalum* J. G. Smith. (*S. hanseni* is said by Stebbins to consist of a series of hybrids between *Elymus glaucus* and *Sitanion jubatum* or *S. hystrix.*)

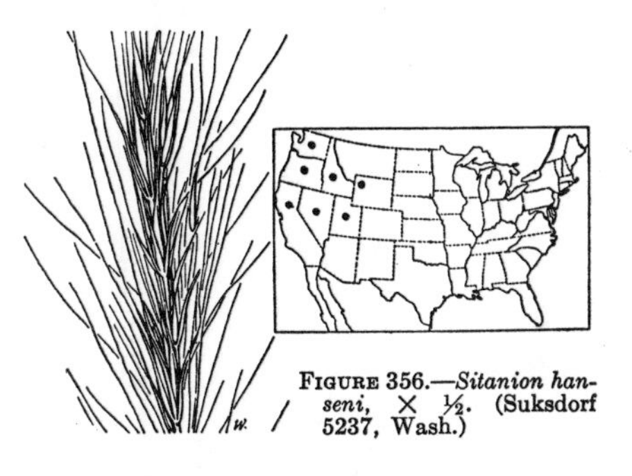

FIGURE 356.—*Sitanion hanseni*, × ½. (Suksdorf 5237, Wash.)

2. Sitanion jubâtum J. G. Smith. BIG SQUIRRELTAIL. (Fig. 357.) Culms erect to ascending, 20 to 60 cm. tall, rarely taller; foliage glabrous or scabrous to white-villous, the blades flat, often becoming involute, mostly not more than 4 mm. wide; spike erect, dense, 3 to 10 cm. long, thick and bushy from the numerous long slender spreading awns; glumes split into 3 or more long awns; lemmas mostly 8 to 10 mm. long, smooth, or scabrous toward apex, the awns and those of the glumes spreading, 3 to 10 cm. long, rarely shorter. ♃ —Rocky or brushy hillsides and open dry woods and plains, Idaho to eastern Washington, south to Utah, Nevada, Arizona, and Baja California. Occasionally a few of the glumes in a spike are divided into only 2 awns. Short-awned plants have been differentiated as *S. breviaristatum* J. G. Smith and the more densely pubescent plants as *S. villosum* J. G. Smith.

3. Sitanion hŷstrix (Nutt.) J. G. Smith. SQUIRRELTAIL. (Fig. 358.) Culms erect to spreading, rather stiff, 10 to 50 cm. tall; foliage from glabrous or puberulent to softly and densely white-pubescent, the blades flat to involute, rather stiffly ascending to spreading, 5 to 20 cm. long, 1 to 3 mm. wide, rarely as much as 5 mm. wide; spike mostly short-exserted or partly included, erect, 2 to 7 cm., rarely 10 cm., long or longer, the glumes very narrow, 1- to 2-nerved, the nerves extending into scabrous awns, sometimes bifid to the middle, or bearing a bristle or awn along one margin; lemmas convex, smooth or scabrous to appressed pubescent, sometimes glaucous, the awns of glumes and lemmas widely spreading, 2 to 10 cm. long. ♃ —Dry hills, plains, open woods, and rocky slopes, South Dakota to British Columbia, south to Missouri, Texas, California, and Mexico. At high altitudes plants often dwarf. Softly pubescent plants have been differentiated as *S. cinereum* J. G. Smith (the pubescence whitish) and *S. velutinum* Piper; short-awned plants as *S. insulare* J. G. Smith and *S. marginatum* Scribn. and Merr.; rather small plants with unusually slender awns as *S. minus* J. G. Smith, and tall plants with coarse spikes as *S. brevifolium* J. G. Smith, *S. longifolium* J. G. Smith, and *S. montanum* J. G. Smith.

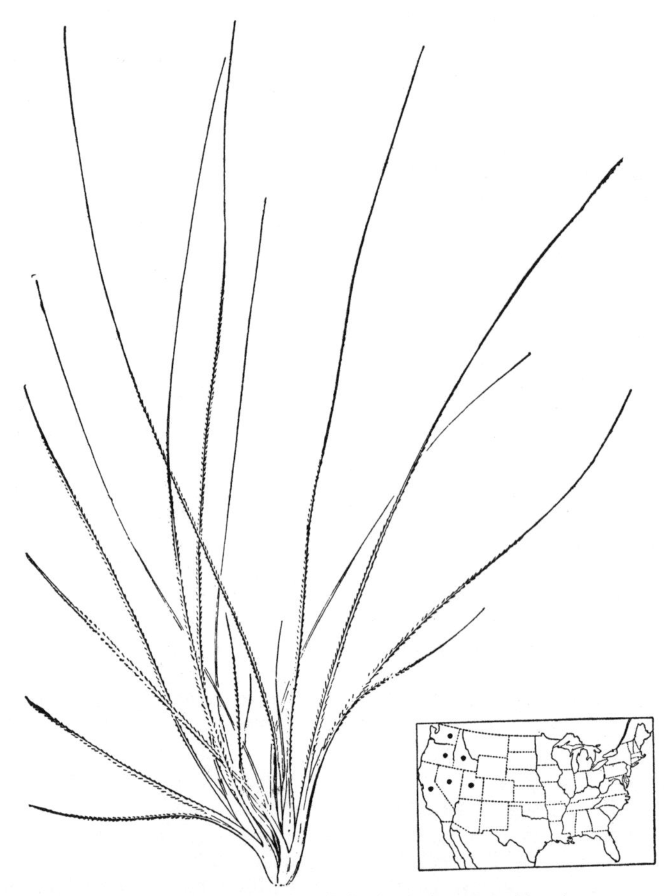

FIGURE 357.—*Sitanion jubatum*. Pair of spikelets, × 2. (Type.)

48. HÝSTRIX Moench

Spikelets 2- to 4-flowered, 1 to 4 at each node of a continuous flattened rachis, horizontally spreading or ascending at maturity; glumes reduced to short or minute awns, the first usually obsolete, both often wanting in the upper spikelets; lemmas convex, rigid, tapering into long awns, 5-nerved, the nerves obscure except toward the tip; palea about as long as the body of the lemma. Erect perennials, with flat blades and bristly, loosely flowered spikes. Type species, *Elymus hystrix* L. (*Hystrix patula*). *Hustrix*, Greek name for the porcupine, alluding to the bristly spikes. The species have little forage value, as

FIGURE 358.—*Sitanion hystrix*. Plant, × ½; spikelet and floret, × 3. (Hitchcock 2289, Colo.)

they are nowhere abundant. The first species is worthy of cultivation for ornament.

Spikelets soon divergent; lemmas glabrous or pubescent, not hispid.......... 1. H. PATULA.
Spikelets ascending or appressed; lemmas appressed-hispid................ 2. H. CALIFORNICA.

FIGURE 359.—*Hystrix patula.* Plant, × ½; spikelet and floret, × 3. (Moyer, Minn.)

1. Hystrix pátula Moench. BOTTLEBRUSH. (Fig. 359.) Culms slender, 60 to 120 cm. tall; sheaths glabrous or scabrous, rarely retrorsely pubescent; blades mostly 7 to 15 mm. wide; spike nodding, 8 to 15 cm. long, the internodes of the slender rachis 5 to 10 mm. long; spikelets mostly in pairs, 1 to 1.5 cm. long, horizontally spreading toward maturity; lemmas glabrous or sometimes coarsely pubescent, the awns 1 to 4 cm. long, slender, straight. ♃ (*H. hystrix* Millsp.)—Moist or rocky woods, Nova Scotia to North Dakota, south to Georgia and Arkansas. Plants with pubescent lemmas have been differentiated as *H. patula* var. *bigeloviana* (Fernald) Deam. Such plants occur throughout the range, except from Delaware, Maryland, and southward.

2. Hystrix califórnica (Boland.) Kuntze. (Fig. 360.) Culms stout, 1 to 2 m. tall; sheaths hispid or the upper smooth; blades as much as 2 cm. wide; spike 12 to 25 cm. long; spikelets usually 3 or 4 at a node, 1.2 to 1.5 cm. long, thicker than in *H. patula*, ascending at maturity; lemmas hispidulous, the awn about 2 cm. long. ♃ —Woods and shaded banks, near the coast, Sonoma County to Santa Cruz County, Calif. In addition to the sessile spikelets there may be a short branch bearing 1 or 2 spikelets.

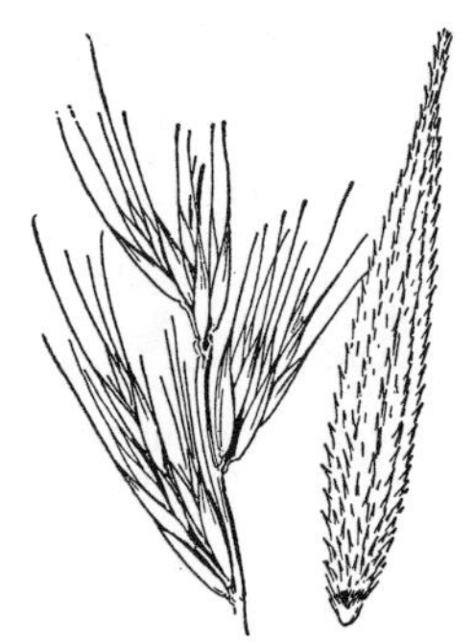

FIGURE 360.—*Hystrix californica*. Spike, × ½; floret, × 3. (Vasey, Calif.)

49. HÓRDEUM L. BARLEY

Spikelets 1-flowered (rarely 2-flowered), 3 (sometimes 2) together at each node of the articulate rachis (continuous in *Hordeum vulgare*), the back of the lemma turned from the rachis, the middle spikelet sessile, the lateral ones pediceled (except in *H. vulgare* and *H. montanense*); rachilla disarticulating above the glumes and, in the central spikelet, prolonged behind the palea as a bristle and sometimes bearing a rudimentary floret; lateral spikelets usually imperfect, sometimes reduced to bristles; glumes narrow, often subulate and awned, standing in front of the spikelet; lemmas rounded on the back, 5-nerved, usually obscurely so, tapering into a usually long awn. Annual or perennial low or rather tall grasses, with flat blades and dense bristly spikes, disarticulating at the base of the rachis segment, this remaining as a stipe below the attached triad of spikelets. Type species, *Hordeum vulgare. Hordeum*, the old Latin name for barley.

Aside from the well-known cultivated barley, *H. vulgare*, the species are of relatively minor value. All furnish forage when young, but many species are aggressive weeds and some (especially *H. jubatum*) at maturity are injurious to stock because of the sharp-pointed joints of the mature spikes, which pierce the nose and mouth parts. The auricle at the base of the blades, characteristic of Hordeae, is wanting in some species of this genus.

Plants perennial; awns slender; auricle wanting.
  Lateral spikelets sessile; central spikelet usually 2-flowered .... 1. H. MONTANENSE.
  Lateral spikelets pedicellate.
    Spike, including awns, as broad as long or nearly so (narrower in var. *caespitosum*); awns 2 to 5 cm. long .... 2. H. JUBATUM.
    Spike, including awns, much longer than broad, awns not more than 1 cm. long.
      Floret of lateral spikelet evident, from staminate to reduced and empty; spike 6 to 10 mm. wide; blades 3 to 8 mm. wide .... 3. H. BRACHYANTHERUM.
      Floret of lateral spikelets scarcely distinct from its awn; spike about 5 mm. wide; blades 2 to 3 mm. wide .... 4. H. CALIFORNICUM.
Plants annual, branching at base; awns mostly stouter.
  Blades with prominent auricles at base.
    Rachis continuous, the 3 spikelets sessile .... 11. H. VULGARE.

Rachis disarticulating; lateral spikelets pedicellate.
Floret of lateral spikelets longer and broader than that of central spikelet; rachis internodes mostly 3 mm. long .... 9. H. LEPORINUM.
Floret of lateral spikelets not larger than that of central spikelet; rachis internodes mostly 2 mm. long .... 10. H. STEBBINSII.
Blades without auricles.
Glumes of the fertile spikelet dilated above the base .... 5. H. PUSILLUM.
Glumes of the fertile spikelet not dilated.
Awns slender, 1.5 to 2 cm. long, fragile; one glume of lateral spikelets slightly dilated. 6. H. ARIZONICUM.
Awns relatively stout.
Floret of lateral spikelets awnless; glumes slender, not rigid, not bowed out. 7. H. DEPRESSUM.
Floret of lateral spikelets awned; glumes thickened and slightly bowed out below, rigid .... 8. H. HYSTRIX.

1. Hordeum montanénse Scribn. (Fig. 361.) Culms 60 to 100 cm. tall; sheaths glabrous; blades flat, lax, scabrous, 5 to 8 mm. wide; spike nodding, 8 to 17 cm. long; central spikelets usually 2-flowered, with a rudiment of a third floret; lateral spikelets sessile, usually well developed; glumes slightly broadened above the base, 1 to 3.5 cm. long including awns; lower floret of central spikelet about 8 mm. long, the awn 1.5 to 3.5 cm. long. ♃ (*H. pammeli* Scribn. and Ball.)—Prairies, Illinois, Iowa, South Dakota, Montana, and Wyoming. Variable and somewhat anomalous; lateral spikelets sometimes with 2 florets. Approaches *Elymus;* specimens referred by geneticists to hybrid *Hordeum jubatum* × *Elymus virginicus.*

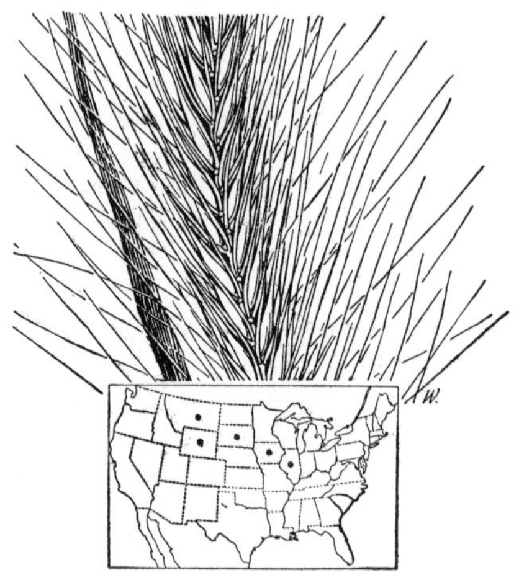

FIGURE 361.—*Hordeum montanense*, × 1. (V. H. Chase 1467, Ill.)

2. Hordeum jubátum L. FOXTAIL BARLEY. (Fig. 362.) Perennial, tufted; culms erect, or decumbent at base, 30 to 60 cm. tall; blades 2 to 5 mm. wide, scabrous; spike nodding, 5 to 10 cm. long, about as wide, soft, pale; lateral spikelets reduced to 1 to 3 spreading awns; glumes of perfect spikelet awnlike, 2.5 to 6 cm. long, spreading; lemma 6 to 8 mm. long with an awn as long as the glumes. ♃ —Open ground, meadows and waste places, Newfoundland and Labrador to Alaska, south to Maryland, Missouri, Texas, California, and Mexico; introduced in the Eastern States. A troublesome weed in the Western States, especially in irrigated meadows. HORDEUM JUBATUM var. CAESPITÓSUM (Scribn.) Hitchc. BOBTAIL BARLEY. Awns 1.5 to 3 cm. long. (*H. caespitosum* Scribn.) North Dakota to Alaska, south to California and Arizona; Mexico.

3. Hordeum brachyántherum Nevski. MEADOW BARLEY. (Fig. 363.) Perennial, tufted; culms erect or ascending, 20 to 70 cm., sometimes to 100 cm., tall; lower sheaths thin, often shredded, softly retrorse-pubescent to glabrous; blades 3 to 8 mm., mostly 3 to 6 mm., wide, spike erect or slightly nodding, 8 to 10 cm. long, rarely longer, sometimes purplish; floret of central spikelet usually 7 to 10 mm. long, typically 1.5 mm. wide, the awn about 1 cm. long, the glumes slightly shorter; glumes of lateral spikelets usually unequal, somewhat shorter, the floret from well developed and staminate to much reduced and empty (occasionally a staminate and

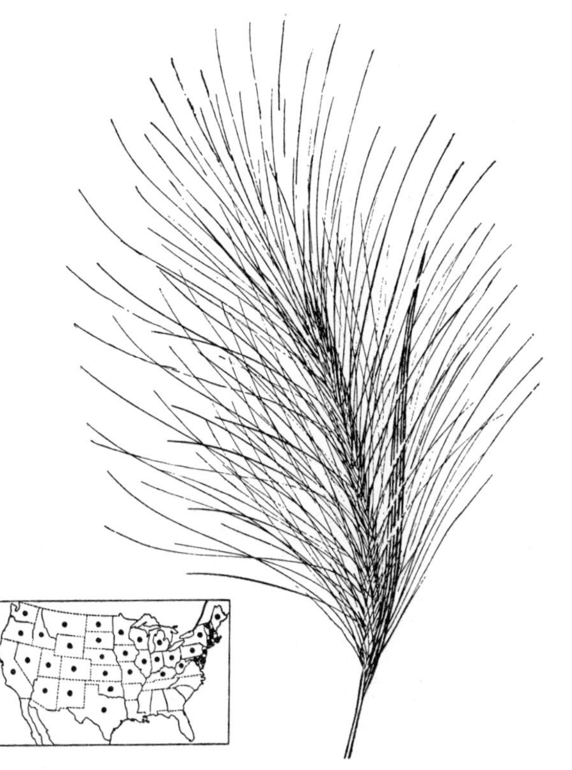

FIGURE 362.—*Hordeum jubatum*, × 1. (Blankinship 189, Mont.)

an empty lateral floret in the same triad), the awn 2 to 5 mm. long; spikelets extremely variable, the spike sometimes slender, the perfect floret 5 to 6 mm. long, the awn 5 to 6 mm. (The name *H. nodosum* L. has been misapplied to this species.) ♃ —Meadows, bottom lands, salt marshes, grassy slopes up to 3,000 m., Aleutian Islands and Alaska to California; Labrador, Newfoundland; Montana to New Mexico and Arizona to California; adventive Maine, Indiana, Mississippi.

4. Hordeum califórnicum Covas and Stebbins. Densely tufted perennial; culms slender, 30 to 55 cm. tall; lower sheaths softly retrorse-pubescent to glabrous; blades 2 to 3 mm. wide, the auricle wanting; spike erect, 2.5 to 6 cm. long, mostly purplish; floret of central spikelet 6 to 7 (rarely 8) mm. long, the awn 4 to 10 mm. long, the rachilla behind the palea often wanting; floret of lateral spikelet much reduced, scarcely distinct from the awn. ♃ —Meadows, dried creek beds, and brushy flats and slopes, Oregon and California; scarce, probably depauperate dry ground plants of the preceding.

5. Hordeum pusíllum Nutt. LITTLE BARLEY. (Fig. 364.) Annual; culms 10 to 35 cm. tall; blades erect, flat, the auricle wanting; spike erect, 2 to 7 cm. long, 10 to 14 mm. wide; first glume of the lateral spikelets and both glumes of the fertile spikelet dilated above the base, attenuate into a slender awn 8 to 15 mm. long, the glumes very scabrous; lemma of central spikelet awned, of lateral spikelets awn-pointed. ⊙ —Plains and open, especially alkaline, ground, Delaware to Washington, south to Florida, southern California, and northern Mexico;

FIGURE 363.—*Hordeum brachyantherum.* Plant, × ½; group of spikelets and floret, × 3. (Whited 433, Wash.)

adventive in Maine and Pennsylvania; common westward, rare in the Atlantic States; also southern South America. HORDEUM PUSILLUM var. PÚBENS Hitchc. Spike broader; spikelets pubescent; dilated glumes wider. ⊙ —Texas to Utah and Arizona.

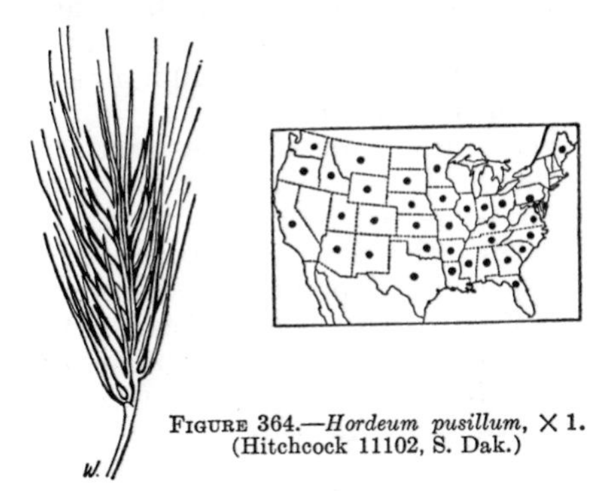

FIGURE 364.—*Hordeum pusillum*, × 1. (Hitchcock 11102, S. Dak.)

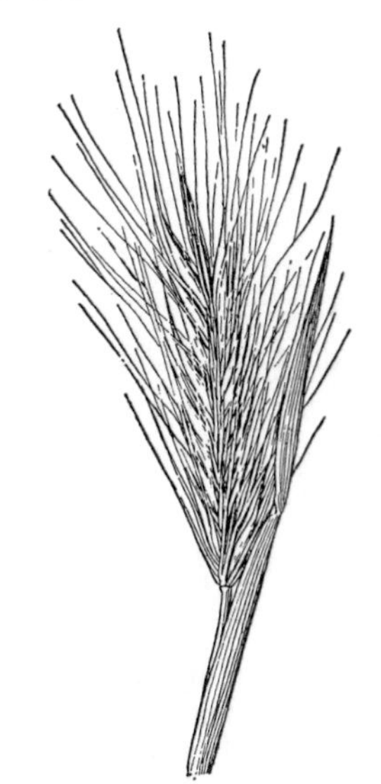

FIGURE 365.—*Hordeum arizonicum*, × 1. (Thornber 536, Ariz.)

6. Hordeum arizónicum Covas. (Fig. 365.) Annual; culms geniculate at base, 20 to 60 cm. tall; lower sheaths pubescent, the upper more or less inflated; blades 3 to 5 mm. wide, sparsely pubescent, the auricle wanting; spike erect, 3 to 12 cm. long; floret of central spikelet 8 to 9 mm. long, 1.5 mm. wide, the awn 15 to 22 mm. long, the glumes slightly shorter; glumes of lateral florets nearly as long, one slightly dilated (all awns scabrous, slender, fragile, readily breaking); floret reduced to a small short-awned lemma. (The name *H. adscendens* has been misapplied to this species.) ⊙ —Dry open ground (large plants found along irrigation ditches), Arizona and California (Bard).

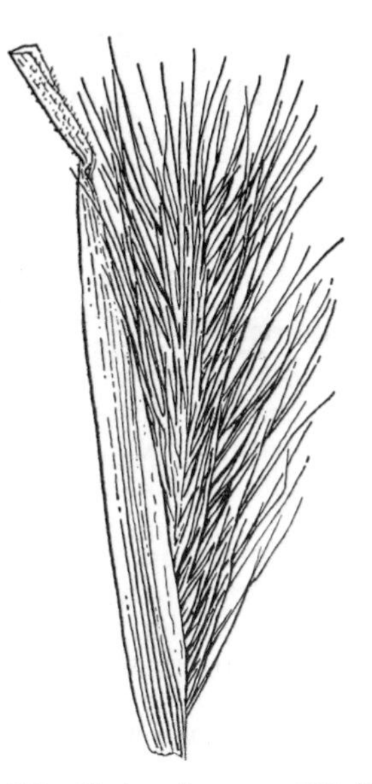

FIGURE 366.—*Hordeum depressum*, × 3. (Type.)

7. Hordeum depréssum (Scribn. and Smith) Rydb. (Fig. 366.) Annual; culms geniculate at base, commonly spreading with ascending ends, 6 to 45 cm. long; upper sheaths often inflated; blades pubescent, mostly not more than 5 cm. long (rarely to 15 cm.), 2 to 4 mm. wide, the auricle wanting; spike erect, 4 to 7 cm. long; floret of central spikelet 7 to 8 mm. long, nearly terete, the awn about 10 mm. long; awns of the glumes and of the glumes of lateral spikelets nearly equal, the whole triad usually about 2 cm. long; floret of lateral spikelet awnless. ⊙ —Mostly in moist alkaline soil or along rivers, also in arid or sterile ground, sea level to 600 m., Idaho and Washington to California.

FIGURE 367.—*Hordeum hystrix*, × 1. (Hitchcock 2688, Calif.)

8. Hordeum hýstrix Roth. MEDITERRANEAN BARLEY. (Fig. 367.) Annual; culms freely branching and spreading or geniculate at base, 15 to 40 cm. tall; sheaths and blades, especially the lower, more or less pubescent, the auricle wanting; spike erect, 1.5 to 3 cm. long, 10 to 15 mm. wide, the axis usually not readily breaking; glumes setaceous, rigid, nearly glabrous to scabrous, about 12 mm. long; lemma of central spikelet 5 mm. long, the awn somewhat longer than the glumes; floret of lateral spikelets reduced, short-awned. ⊙ (*H. gussonianum* Parl.)—Fields and waste places, Utah to British Columbia, Arizona, and California; adventive in Massachusetts, New Jersey, and Pennsylvania; introduced from Europe.

Hordeum marínum Huds. Differing from *H. hystrix* in the glabrous dissimilar glumes of the lateral spikelets, the outer subulate, the inner somewhat broader. ⊙ (*H. marítimum* With.)—On ballast, Camden, N. J.; Europe.

9. Hordeum leporínum Link. (Fig. 368.) Annual; branching at base, spreading; sheaths glabrous, blades pilose to glabrous; auricle at base of blade well developed; spike 5 to 9 cm. long, often partly enclosed by the inflated uppermost sheath, the rachis internodes mostly 3 mm. long; glumes of the central spikelet lanceolate, 3-nerved, long-ciliate on both margins, the nerves scabrous, the awn 2 to 2.5 cm. long; floret 1 to 1.2 cm. long, raised on a rachilla segment 1 mm. long, the awn 3 to 4 cm. long; lateral spikelets usually staminate, the glumes much shorter, unlike, the inner similar to those of the central one, the outer setaceous, not ciliate, the lemma broad, 10 to 20 mm. long, the awn 2 to 4 cm. long. ⊙ —Weed, fields, waste places and open ground, introduced from southern Europe; here and there in the Eastern States, Massachusetts to Georgia; Vancouver Island and Washington to California, Utah, and Texas. This and *H. stebbinsii* have been confused with *H. murinum* L., of Europe, not known from America.

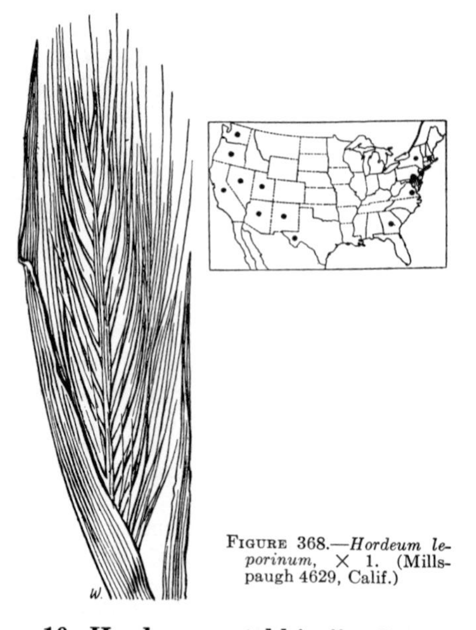

FIGURE 368.—*Hordeum leporinum*, × 1. (Millspaugh 4629, Calif.)

10. Hordeum stebbínsii Covas. Similar to the preceding, the culms often shorter and more geniculate; spikes narrower, mostly 9 to 15 mm. wide before beginning to break up, the triads closely ascending and slightly more crowded, the rachis internodes mostly 2 mm. long; florets of lateral spikelets not larger than that of the middle spikelet; all awns mostly shorter and slightly more

FIGURE 369.—*Hordeum vulgare*. Plant, × ½; group of spikelets and floret, × 3; spike of beardless barley (*a*), × ½. (Cult.)

slender. ⊙ —Weed, fields, waste places, and open, mostly arid ground, introduced from the Old World, ballast, Mobile, Ala.; adventive, Oklahoma; Idaho and Washington; New Mexico to California. Often difficult to distinguish from the preceding.

11. Hordeum vulgáre L. BARLEY. (Fig. 369.) Annual; culms erect, 60 to 120 cm. tall; blades flat, mostly 5 to 15 mm. wide, the auricle well developed; spike erect or nearly so, 2 to 10 cm. long, excluding awns, the 3 spikelets sessile; glumes divergent at base, narrow, nerveless, gradually passing into a stout awn; awn of lemma straight, erect, mostly 10 to 15 cm. long. ⊙ —Cultivated for the grain, sometimes spontaneous in fields and waste places but not persistent. There are two groups of the cultivated barleys. In the 2-rowed forms (*H. distichon* L.) the lateral spikelets are fairly well developed but sterile. The probable ancestor for at least a part of these is *H. spontaneum* Koch, of Asia. In the second group all the spikelets produce large seed. These are called 6-rowed (*H. hexastichon* L.) or, if the lateral florets overlap, 4-rowed barleys (in European literature). In some varieties the caryopsis is naked. The ancestor of the 6-rowed barleys is not known but probably was similar to some of our cultivated varieties of this group. HORDEUM VULGARE var. TRIFURCÁTUM (Schlecht.) Alefeld, BEARDLESS BARLEY. Awns suppressed or variously deformed, commonly 3-cleft, the central division converted into a hooded lobe. Adventive or occasional in grainfields and along roads, Connecticut to New Jersey; South Dakota, Montana; Colorado, Utah, New Mexico; California.

50. LÓLIUM L. RYEGRASS

Spikelets several-flowered, solitary, placed edgewise to the continuous rachis, one edge fitting to the alternate concavities, the rachilla disarticulating above the glumes and between the florets; first glume wanting (except on the terminal spikelet and rarely in 1 or 2 spikelets in a spike), the second outward, strongly 3- to 5-nerved, equaling or exceeding the second floret; lemmas rounded on the back, 5- to 7-nerved, obtuse, acute, or awned. Annuals or perennials, with flat blades and slender, usually flat spikes. Type species, *Lolium perenne*. *Lolium*, an old Latin name for darnel.

Lolium perenne, perennial or English ryegrass, was the first meadow grass to be cultivated in Europe as a distinct segregated species, the meadows and pastures formerly being native species. This and *L. multiflorum*, Italian ryegrass, are probably the most important of the European forage grasses. Both species are used in the United States to a limited extent for meadow, pasture, and lawn. They are of importance in the South for winter forage. In the Eastern States the ryegrasses are often sown in mixtures for parks or public grounds, where a vigorous early growth is required. The young plants can be distinguished from bluegrass by the glossy dark-green foliage. *L. temulentum*, darnel, is occasionally found as a weed in grainfields and waste places. It is in bad repute, because of the presence in the grain of a narcotic poison, said to be due to a fungus. Darnel is supposed to be the plant referred to as the tares sown by the enemy in the parable of Scripture.

Glume shorter than the spikelet.
  Lemmas nearly or quite awnless; culms subcompressed .... 1. L. PERENNE.
  Lemmas, at least the upper, awned; culms cylindric .... 2. L. MULTIFLORUM.
Glume as long as or longer than the spikelet. Annuals.
  Spike flat; spikelets much wider than the rachis.
    Florets plump, 6 to 8 mm. long .... 3. L. TEMULENTUM.
    Florets dorsally compressed, 9 to 10 mm. long .... 4. L. PERSICUM.
  Spike subcylindric; spikelets scarcely wider than the rachis .... 5. L. SUBULATUM.

1. Lolium perénne L. PERENNIAL RYEGRASS. (Fig. 370, *B*.) Short-lived perennial; culms erect or decumbent at the commonly reddish base, 30 to 60 cm. tall; auricles at summit of sheath, minute or obsolete; foliage glossy, the blades 2 to 4 mm. wide; spike often subfalcate, mostly 15 to 25 cm. long; spikelets mostly 6- to 10-flowered; lemmas 5 to 7 mm. long, awnless or nearly so. ♃ —Meadows and waste places, Newfoundland to Alaska and south to Virginia and California, occasionally farther south; cultivated in meadows, pastures, and lawns, introduced from Europe. Also called English ryegrass. LOLIUM PERENNE var. CRISTÁTUM Pers. Spikes ovate, the spikelets crowded, horizontally spreading. ♃ —Open ground, Wilmington, Del., and Washington, D. C.; ballast, Salem and Eola, Oreg.; adventive from Europe.

2. Lolium multiflórum Lam. ITALIAN RYEGRASS. (Fig. 370, *A*.) Differing from *L. perenne* in the more robust habit, to 1 m. tall, pale or yellowish at base; auricles at summit of sheaths prominent; spikelets 10- to 20-flowered, 1.5 to 2.5 cm. long; lemmas 7 to 8 mm. long, at least the upper awned. ♃ (*L. italicum* A. Br.)—About the same range as *L. perenne*, especially common on the Pacific coast where it is often called Australian ryegrass. Introduced from Europe. Closely related to *L. perenne*, but generally recognized as distinct agriculturally. A much reduced form has been called forma *microstachyum* Uechtritz.—California.

LOLIUM MULTIFLORUM var. RAMÓSUM Guss. A peculiar form, the spike transformed into a narrow many-flowered panicle. ♃ —Linn County, Oreg., waif. Europe.

3. Lolium temuléntum L. DARNEL. (Fig. 371.) Annual; culms 60 to 90 cm. tall; blades mostly 3 to 6 mm. wide; spike strict, 15 to 25 cm. long; glume about 2.5 cm. long, as long as or longer than the 5- to 7-flowered spikelet, firm, pointed; florets plump, the lemmas as much as 8 mm. long, obtuse, awned, the awn 6 to 12 mm. long. ⊙ —Grainfields and waste places, occasional throughout the eastern United States and rather common on the Pacific coast; introduced from Europe. LOLIUM TEMULENTUM var. LEPTOCHAÉTON A. Br. Lemmas awnless. ⊙ —Washington to California, occasional on the Atlantic coast, Maine to Texas; introduced from Europe.

4. Lolium pérsicum Boiss. and Hohen. Annual, resembling small plants of *L. temulentum*, branching at the lower nodes; spike 8 to 12 cm. long; spikelets mostly more distant than in *L. temulentum*, the glume three-fourths to as long as the spikelet, the florets mostly 9 to 10 mm. long, not plump, the awn slender, commonly flexuous, the palea slightly exceeding the lemma. ⊙ —A weed in wheatfields and waste ground, Ontario to Alberta, and in North Dakota, becoming a bad weed. Introduced, probably in wheat seed from Russia.

5. Lolium subulátum Vis. (Fig. 372.) Annual; culms freely branching at base, stiffly spreading or prostrate; foliage scant, blades short; spike subcylindric, rigid, often curved; spikelets sunken in the excavations of the rachis, the florets partly hidden by the appressed obtuse strongly nerved glume; lemmas 5 mm. long. ⊙ —On ballast, near Portland, Oreg.; introduced from Europe.

Lolium stríctum Presl. Annual; branched and spreading at base, 10 to 30 cm. tall; spike thickish, 5 to 10 cm. long, the rachis thick but flattish and angled. ⊙ —Ballast, Linnton, Oreg., Berkeley, Calif.; Mohave County, Ariz. Introduced from Europe. Resembles *L. subulatum*, but the spikelets not sunken in a cylindric rachis.

LOLIUM REMÓTUM Schrank. Leafy annual; spike slender, spikelets more or less remote; glume half to two-thirds as long as the spikelets; florets 3 to 4 mm. long, plump, awnless. ⊙ —Weed in flax field, North Dakota, the seed from Russia.

FIGURE 370.—*A*, *Lolium multiflorum*. Plant, × ½; spikelet, × 3; floret, × 5. (Suksdorf 5142, Wash.) *B*, *L. perenne*, × ½. (Kimball, D. C.)

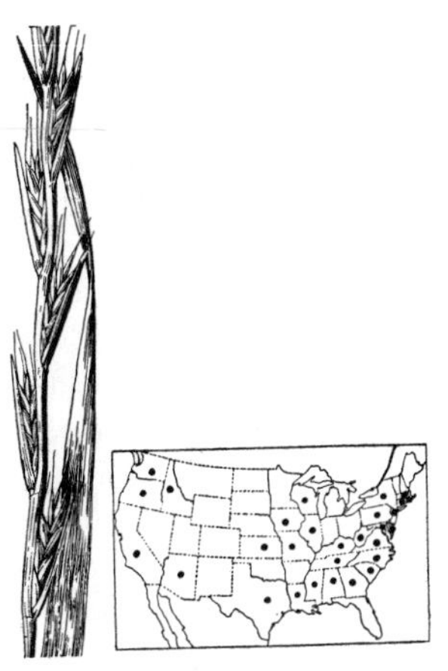

FIGURE 371.—*Lolium temulentum*, × ½. (Leiberg 771, Oreg.)

Nárdus strícta L. Slender, tufted perennial; sheaths crowded at the base; blades slender, involute, rather stiff; spike slender, 1-sided, 3 to 8 cm. long; spikelets 1-flowered; first glume wanting; second glume minute; lemma narrow, acuminate or short-awned, scabrous. ⊙ —Introduced in Newfoundland and Quebec, and sparingly in dry open ground in New Hampshire, New York, and Michigan; Europe.

51. MONÉRMA Beauv.

(Included in *Lepturus* R. Br. in Manual, ed. 1)

Spikelets 1-flowered, embedded in the hard, cylindric articulate rachis and falling attached to the joints; first glume wanting except on the terminal spikelet, the second glume closing the cavity of the rachis and flush with the surface, indurate, nerved, acuminate, longer than the joint of the rachis; lemma with its back to the rachis, hyaline, shorter than the glume, 3-nerved; palea a little shorter than the lemma, hyaline.

Low annual, with slender cylindric spikes. Type species, *M. monandra* Beauv. (*M. cylindrica* (Willd.) Coss. and Dur.) Name from Greek *monos*, one, and *erma*, support, referring to the single spike.

FIGURE 372.—*Lolium subulatum*, × ½. (Sheldon, Oreg.)

1. Monerma cylíndrica (Willd.) Coss. and Dur. THINTAIL. (Fig. 373.) Annual; culms bushy-branched, spreading or prostrate, 10 to 30 cm. tall; spike curved, narrowed upward; glume 6 mm. long, acuminate; lemma 5 mm. long, pointed; rachis disarticulating at maturity, the spikelets remaining attached to the joints. ⊙ (*Lepturus cylindricus* Trin.)—Salt marshes, San Francisco Bay, Calif., south to San Diego and Santa Catalina Island; introduced from the Old World.

52. PARÁPHOLIS C. E. Hubb.

(Included in *Pholiurus* Trin. in Manual, ed. 1)

Spikelets 1-or 2-flowered, embedded in the cylindric articulate rachis and falling attached to the joints; glumes 2, placed in front of the spikelet and enclosing it, coriaceous, 5-nerved, acute, asymmetric, appearing like halves of a single split glume; lemma with its back to the rachis, smaller than the glumes, hyaline, 1-nerved; palea a little shorter than the lemma, hyaline. Low annuals, with slender cylindric spikes. Type species, *P. incurva* (L.) C. E. Hubb. Name from Greek *para*, beside, and *pholis*, scale, referring to the 2 glumes side by side.

FIGURE 373.—*Monerma cylindrica*. Plant, × ½; rachis joint and spikelet, × 5. (Parish 4446, Calif.)

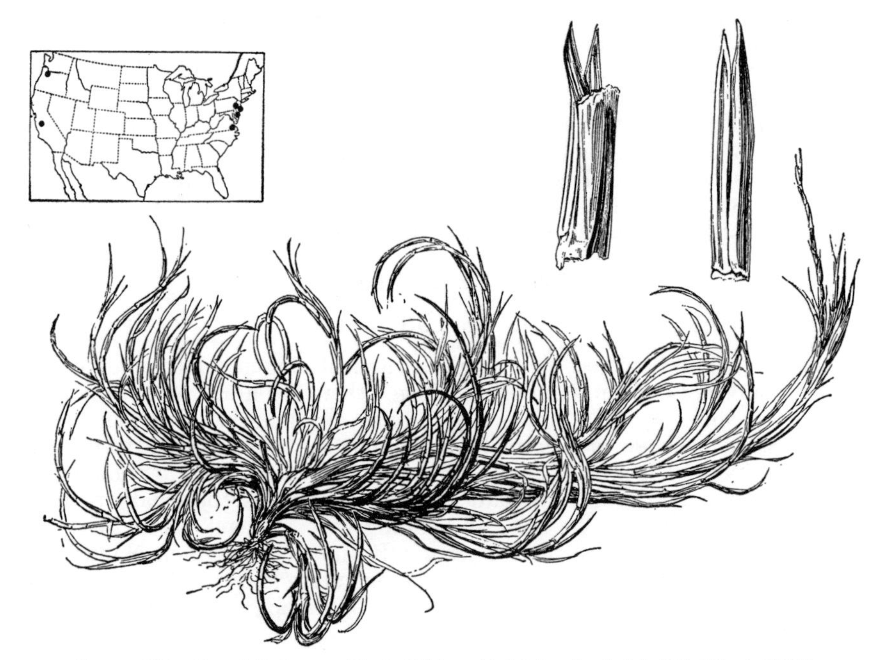

FIGURE 374.—*Parapholis incurva*. Plant, × ½; rachis joint and spikelet, × 5. (Trask, Calif.)

1. Parapholis incúrva (L.) C. E. Hubb. SICKLE GRASS. (Fig. 374.) Culms tufted, decumbent at base, 10 to 20 cm. tall; blades short, narrow; spike 7 to 10 cm. long, cylindric, curved; spikelets 7 mm. long, pointed. ⊙ (*Pholiurus incurvus* (L.) Schinz and Thell.)—Mud flats and salt marshes along the coast, New Jersey and Pennsylvania to Virginia; California; Portland, Oreg.; introduced from Europe.

53. SCRIBNÉRIA Hack.

Spikelets 1-flowered, solitary, laterally compressed, appressed flatwise against the somewhat thickened continuous rachis, the rachilla disarticulating above the glumes, prolonged as a very minute hairy stipe; glumes equal, narrow, firm, acute, keeled on the outer nerves, the first 2-nerved, the second 4-nerved; lemma shorter than the glumes, membranaceous, obscurely nerved, the apex short-bifid, the faint midnerve extending as a slender awn; palea about as long as

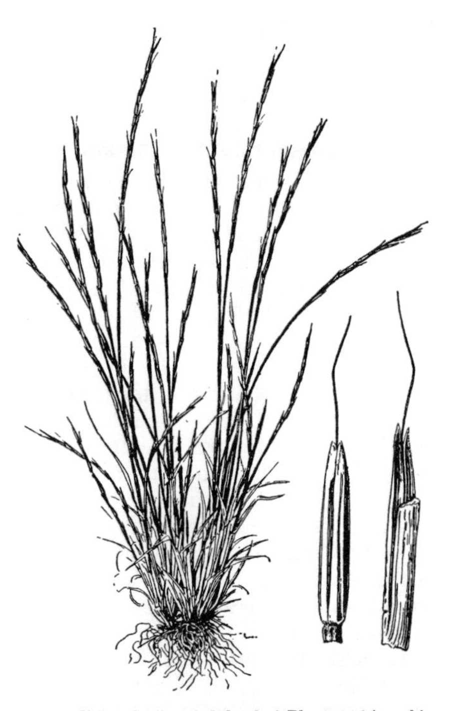

FIGURE 375.—*Scribneria bolanderi*. Plant, × ½; rachis joint and spikelet, × 5. (Suksdorf 217, Wash.)

the lemma; stamen 1. Low annual, with slender cylindric spikes. Type species, *Scribneria bolanderi*. Named for F. Lamson-Scribner.

1. Scribneria bolandéri (Thurb.) Hack. (Fig. 375.) Culms branching at base, erect or ascending, 7 to 30 cm. tall; foliage scant, the blades subfiliform; ligule about 3 mm. long; spike about 1 mm. thick, usually one-third to half the entire height of the plant, the internodes 4 to 6 mm. long; spikelets about 7 mm. long; lemmas pubescent at base, the awn erect, 2 to 4 mm. long. ⊙ —Sandy or sterile ground, in the mountains, Washington to California; rare or overlooked, very inconspicuous.

TRIBE 4. AVENEAE

54. SCHÍSMUS Beauv.

Spikelets several-flowered, the rachilla disarticulating above the glumes and between the florets; glumes subequal, longer than the first floret, usually as long as the spikelet, with white membranaceous margins; lemmas broad, rounded on the back, several-nerved, pilose along the lower part of the margin, the summit hyaline, bidentate; palea broad, hyaline, the nerves at the margin. Low tufted annuals with filiform blades and small panicles, the slender pedicels finally disarticulating at the base and falling with the spikelet or with the glumes. Type species, *Schismus marginatus* Beauv. (*S. barbatus*). Name from Greek, *schismos*, a splitting, referring to the bidentate lemmas. This genus has usually been placed in the tribe Festuceae, but its characters place it more naturally in the tribe Aveneae.

Glumes 4 to 5 mm. long; lemmas about 2 mm. long, rounded and emarginate at apex; palea rounded, as long as the lemma .... 1. S. BARBATUS.
Glumes 5 to 6 mm. long; lemmas 2.5 to 3 mm. long, the apex with 2 acute hyaline lobes; palea acute, shorter than the lemma .... 2. S. ARABICUS.

1. Schismus barbátus (L.) Thell. (Fig. 376.) Culms tufted, erect to prostrate-spreading, 5 to 35 cm. tall; blades usually less than 10 cm. long; panicle oval to linear, 1 to 5 cm. long, usually rather dense, pale or purplish; spikelets about 5-flowered; glumes 4 to 5 mm. long, shorter than the spikelet, 5- to 7-nerved, acute; lemmas about 2 mm. long, 9-nerved, the margin appressed-pilose on the lower half, the teeth minute, sometimes with a mucro between, the rachilla joints slender, flexuous; palea concave, as broad as the lemma and about as long. ⊙ —Open ground in yards, along roadsides, and in dry river beds; Utah to California and southern Arizona; Argentina, Chile. Introduced from the Mediterranean region; India to South Africa.

FIGURE 376.—*Schismus barbatus*. Plant, × ½; spikelet and florets, × 5. (Peebles and Harrison 846, Ariz.)

2. Schismus arábicus Nees. (Fig. 377.) Resembling *S. barbatus*, culms widely spreading, the spikelets a little larger, 5- to 7-flowered; lemmas 2.5 to

3 mm. long, longer pilose on the margins and back, the apex cleft into 2 acute lobes, the acute palea reaching the base of the cleft or a little longer. ☉ —Dry open ground, southern Arizona, Nevada (Clark County), and California; Chile; introduced from southwestern Asia or Africa. Locally dominant in Maricopa County, Ariz., and an excellent forage grass in winter; apparently spreading rapidly.

FIGURE 377.—*Schismus arabicus.* Spikelet, × 10; florets, × 5. (Peebles 9098, Ariz.)

55. KOELÉRIA Pers.

Spikelets 2- to 4-flowered, compressed, the rachilla disarticulating above the glumes and between the florets, prolonged beyond the perfect florets as a slender bristle or bearing a reduced floret at the tip; glumes usually about equal in length, unlike in shape, the first narrow, sometimes shorter, 1-nerved, the second wider than the first, broadened above the middle, 3- to 5-nerved; lemmas somewhat scarious, shining, the lowermost a little longer than the glume, obscurely 5-nerved, acute or short-awned, the awn, if present, borne just below the apex. Slender, low or rather tall annuals or perennials, with narrow blades and shining spikelike panicles. Type species, *Koeleria cristata.* Named for G. L. Koeler.

Koeleria cristata is a good forage grass and is a constituent of much of the native pasture throughout the Western States. The plants, however, are rather scattering.

Plants perennial .... 1. K. CRISTATA.
Plants annual .... 2. K. PHLEOIDES.

1. Koeleria cristáta (L.) Pers. JUNEGRASS. (Fig. 378.) Tufted perennial; culms erect, puberulent below the panicle, 30 to 60 cm. tall; sheaths, at least the lower, pubescent; blades flat or involute, glabrous or, especially the lower, pubescent, 1 to 3 mm. wide; panicle erect, spikelike, dense (loose in anthesis), often lobed, interrupted, or sometimes branched below, 4 to 15 cm. long, tapering at the summit; spikelets mostly 4 to 5 mm. long; glumes and lemmas scaberulous, 3 to 4 mm. long, sometimes short-awned, the rachilla joints very short. ♃ —Prairie, open woods, and sandy soil, Ontario to British Columbia, south to Delaware, Missouri, Louisiana, California, and Mexico; widely distributed in the temperate regions of the Old World. Variable; several American varieties have been proposed, but the forms are inconstant and intergrading, and it is not practicable to distinguish definite varieties. On the Pacific coast there is a rather large loosely tufted form (*K. cristata* var. *longifolia* Vasey) with long narrow or involute blades and somewhat open panicle.

2. Koeleria phleoídes (Vill.) Pers. (Fig. 379.) Annual; culms 15 to 30 cm. tall, smooth throughout; sheaths

FIGURE 378.—*Koeleria cristata*. Plant, × ½; glumes and floret, × 10. (Bebb 2862, Ill.)

and blades sparsely pilose; panicle dense, spikelike, 2 to 7 cm. long, obtuse; spikelets 2 to 4 mm. long; glumes acute; lemmas short-awned from a bifid apex; glumes and lemmas in the typical form papillose-hirsute on the back, but commonly papillose only. ⊙ —Introduced from Europe at Pensacola, Fla., Mobile, Ala., Cameron County, Tex., Portland, Oreg., and at several points in California. Cultivated in nursery plots at Beltsville, Md., and Tucson, Ariz.

56. SPHENÓPHOLIS Scribn. WEDGEGRASS

Spikelets 2- or 3-flowered, the pedicel disarticulating below the glumes, the rachilla produced beyond the upper floret as a slender bristle; glumes unlike in shape, the first narrow, usually acute, 1-nerved, the second broadly obovate, 3- to 5-nerved, the nerves sometimes obscure, mostly somewhat coriaceous, the margin scarious; lemmas firm, scarcely nerved, awnless or rarely with an awn from just below the apex, the first a little shorter or a little longer than the second glume; palea hyaline, exposed. Slender perennials (rarely annual) with usually flat blades and narrow shining panicles. Type species, *Sphenopholis obtusata*. Name from Greek *sphen*, wedge, and *pholis*, horny scale, alluding to the hard obovate second glume.

All the species are forage grasses but are usually not abundant. The most important are *S. intermedia* and *S. obtusata*.

Panicle dense, usually spikelike, erect or nearly so; second glume subcucullate. 1. S. OBTUSATA.
Panicle not dense, lax, nodding, from very slender to many-flowered, but not spikelike.
  Spikelets awned 6. S. PALLENS.
  Spikelets awnless (rarely awned in *S. filiformis*).
    Lemmas glabrous; second glume acute or subacute; panicle many-flowered.
      Second glume about 2.5 mm. long 2. S. INTERMEDIA.
      Second glume about 3.5 mm. long 3. S. LONGIFLORA.
    Lemmas scabrous; second glume broadly rounded at the summit; panicle relatively few-flowered.
      Blades rarely more than 10 cm. long, flat, 2 to 5 mm. wide 4. S. NITIDA.
      Blades elongate, flat to subinvolute, mostly less than 2 mm. wide 5. S. FILIFORMIS.

1. Sphenopholis obtusáta (Michx.) Scribn. PRAIRIE WEDGEGRASS. (Fig. 380.) Culms erect, tufted, 30 to 100 cm. tall; sheaths glabrous to finely retrorsely pubescent; blades flat, glabrous, scabrous, or pubescent, mostly 2 to 5 mm. wide; panicle erect or nearly so, dense, spikelike to interrupted or lobed, rarely slightly looser, 5 to 20 cm. long; spikelets 2.5 to 3.5 mm. long, the two florets closer together than in the other species; second glume very broad, subcucullate, somewhat inflated at maturity, 5-nerved, scabrous; lemmas minutely papillose, rarely mucronate or with a short straight awn, the first about 2.5 mm. long. ♃ —Open woods, old fields, moist ground, and prairies, Maine to British Columbia, south to Florida, Arizona, and California; Mexico; Dominican Republic. Variable in size and in denseness of panicle. Sometimes annual or flowering the first season. Specimens with less dense and lobed panicles may be distinguished from denser panicled specimens of *S. intermedia* by the broader, firmer, subcucullate second glume and more approximate florets.

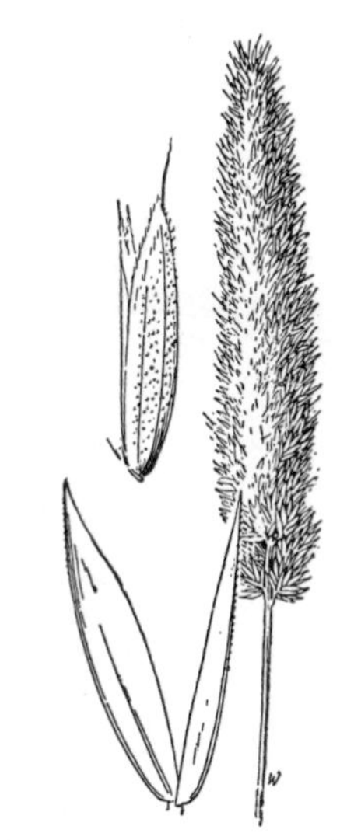

FIGURE 379.—*Koeleria phleoides*. Panicle, × 1; glumes and floret, × 10. (Heller 11417, Calif.)

2. Sphenopholis intermédia (Rydb.) Rydb. SLENDER WEDGEGRASS. (Fig. 381.) Culms erect in small tufts, 30 to 120 cm. tall; sheaths glabrous or pubescent; blades flat, often elongate, lax, mostly 2 to 6 mm. wide, sometimes wider, mostly sca-

FIGURE 380.—*Sphenopholis obtusata*. Plant, × ½; glumes and floret, × 10. (Hitchcock 1453, N. C.)

berulous, occasionally sparsely pilose; panicle nodding, from rather dense to open, mostly 10 to 20 cm. long, the branches spikelet-bearing from base; spikelets 3 to 4 mm. long; second glume relatively thin, acute or subacute, about 2.5 mm. long; lemmas subacute, rarely mucronate, smooth or rarely very minutely roughened, mostly 2.5 to 3 mm. long. ♃ —

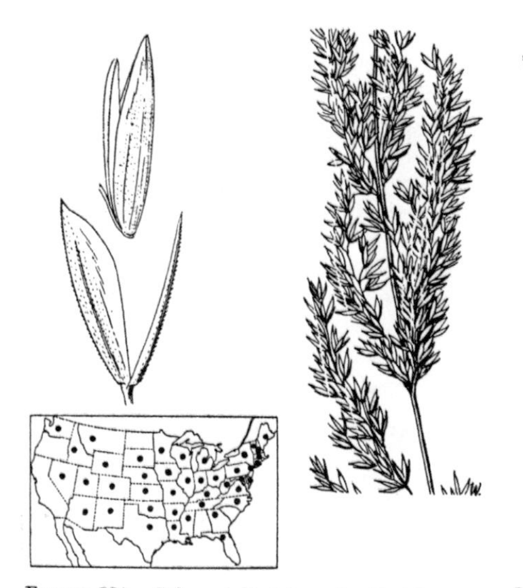

FIGURE 381.—*Sphenopholis intermedia*. Panicle, × 1; glumes and floret, × 10. (Clark 1785, Ind.)

Damp or rocky woods, slopes, and moist places, Newfoundland to British Columbia, south to Florida and Arizona; Tanana Hot Springs, Alaska. Delicate plants with small panicles resembling *S. nitida* may be distinguished by the very narrow first glume, the acute to subacute second glume and lemmas, and usually by the glabrous foliage. Plants with rather dense panicles resembling *S. obtusata* may be distinguished by the thinner, less rounded, more compressed second glume. This is the species called *Sphenopholis pallens* (Spreng.) Scribn. in some manuals. Bieler's description of *Aira pallens* shows that Scribner misapplied the name (see no. 6).

3. Sphenopholis longiflóra (Vasey) Hitchc. (Fig. 382.) Culms relatively stout, erect from a decumbent base, 40 to 70 cm. tall; lower sheaths puberulent, the others glabrous; blades thin, flat, scaberulous, 5 to 18 cm. long, 3 to 8 mm. wide; panicle many-flowered, rather loose, slightly nodding, 10 to 18 cm. long; spikelets mostly 2-flowered, the rachilla hispidulous; glumes very scabrous on the green part, the second thin, acute,

FIGURE 382.—*Sphenopholis longiflora*. Panicle, × 1; glumes and floret, × 10. (Nealley, Tex.)

about 3.5 mm. long; lemmas smooth, scaberulous toward the tip, the first about 4 mm. long. ♃ —Wooded banks, Arkansas and Texas. Differing from *S. intermedia* in the larger spikelets, broader blades, and more tapering lemmas.

4. Sphenopholis nítida (Bieler) Scribn. (Fig. 383.) Culms tufted, leafy at base, slender, shining, 30 to 70 cm. tall; sheaths and blades mostly softly pubescent, occasionally glabrous, the blades 2 to 5 mm. wide, 3 to 10 cm. long, the basal sometimes longer; panicle rather few-flowered, mostly 8 to 12 cm. long, the filiform branches distant, ascending, spreading in anthesis; spikelets 3 to 3.5 mm. long; glumes about equal in length, usually nearly as long as the first floret, the first glume broader than in the other species, the second broadly rounded at summit, at least the second lemma scabrous-papillose. ♃ —Dry or rocky woods, Massachusetts to North Dakota, south to Florida and Texas.

5. Sphenopholis filifórmis (Chapm.) Scribn. (Fig. 384.) Culms erect, very

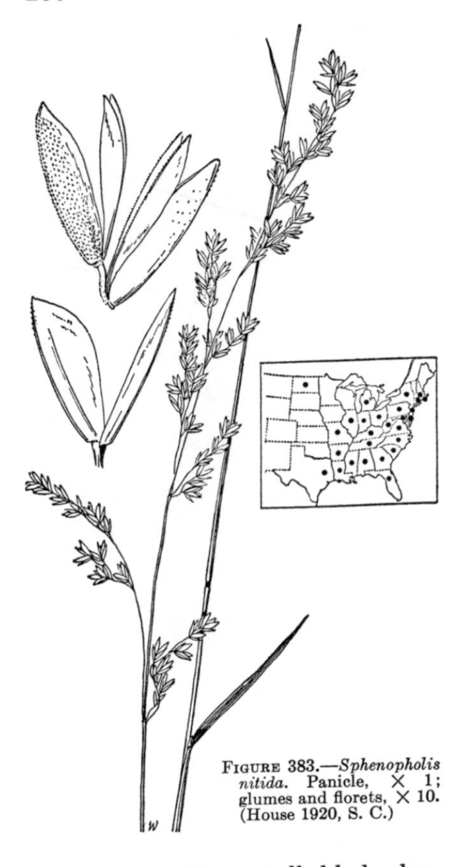

FIGURE 383.—*Sphenopholis nitida*. Panicle, × 1; glumes and florets, × 10. (House 1920, S. C.)

slender, 30 to 60 cm. tall; blades lax, flat to subinvolute, mostly less than 2 mm. wide; panicle slender, often nodding, 5 to 15 cm. long, the short branches rather distant, erect or ascending; spikelets 3 to 4 mm. long, the 2 florets rather distant; second glume broadly rounded at summit, about 2 mm. long; lemmas obtuse to subacute, rarely with a short spreading awn; the first smooth, the second minutely roughened. ♃ —Dry soil, Coastal Plain, southeastern Virginia to Florida, Tennessee, and eastern Texas. Awned lemmas, either the first or second, are occasionally found in some panicles.

6. Sphenopholis pállens (Bieler) Scribn. (Fig. 385.) Culms erect, about 60 cm. tall; lower sheaths minutely pubescent, the upper glabrous; blades flat, glabrous, 1 to 2 mm. wide; panicle narrow, nodding, loose or somewhat compact, 15 to 25 cm. long, the branches ascending, the lower distant; spikelets 2- or 3-flowered, 3 to 3.5 mm. long; second floret scaberulous, usually awned just below the apex, the awn scabrous, geniculate, 1 to 2 mm. long. ♃ (*Eatonia aristata* Scribn. and Merr.)—Rich wooded slopes, Southampton County, Va., to South Carolina. The type of *Aira pallens* Bieler has not been examined, but it was received from

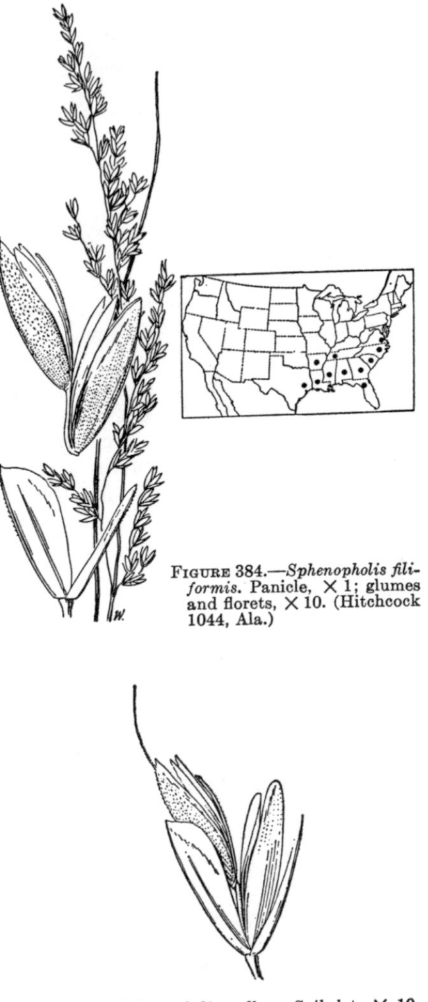

FIGURE 384.—*Sphenopholis filiformis*. Panicle, × 1; glumes and florets, × 10. (Hitchcock 1044, Ala.)

FIGURE 385.—*Sphenopholis pallens*. Spikelet, × 10. (Curtiss, S. C.)

Muhlenberg and may be assumed to be the same as the specimen in the Muhlenberg Herbarium described under *Aira pallens* by Muhlenberg.

57. TRISÉTUM Pers. Trisetum

Spikelets usually 2-flowered, sometimes 3- to 5-flowered, the rachilla prolonged behind the upper floret, usually villous; glumes somewhat unequal, acute, the second usually longer than the first floret; lemmas usually short-bearded at base, 2-toothed at apex, the teeth often awned, bearing from the back below the cleft apex a straight and included or usually bent and exserted awn (awnless or nearly so in *Trisetum melicoides* and *T. wolfii*). Tufted perennials (except *Trisetum interruptum*), with flat blades and open or usually contracted or spikelike shining panicles. Type species, *Trisetum flavescens*. Name from Latin *tri*, three, and *setum*, bristle, alluding to the awn and two teeth of the lemma.

Several of the species are valuable for grazing. *Trisetum spicatum* constitutes an important part of the forage on alpine and subalpine slopes and *T. wolfi* at medium altitudes.

Spikelets disarticulating below the glumes.
  Plants perennial; panicle lax, somewhat open .... 9. T. PENNSYLVANICUM.
  Plants annual; panicle narrow, dense, interrupted .... 10. T. INTERRUPTUM.
Spikelets disarticulating above the glumes.
  Awn included within the glumes, or wanting.
    Panicle rather lax, nodding .... 1. T. MELICOIDES.
    Panicle rather dense, erect .... 2. T. WOLFII.
  Awn exserted.
    Awn straight (see also *T. montanum* var. *shearii*) .... 3. T. ORTHOCHAETUM.
    Awn geniculate.
      Panicle dense, spikelike, sometimes slightly interrupted below; plants densely tufted .... 5. T. SPICATUM.
      Panicle loose and open to contracted, but not spikelike; plants in small tufts or solitary.
        Panicle relatively few-flowered, loose, lax or drooping, the filiform branches naked below; florets distant .... 4. T. CERNUUM.
        Panicle many-flowered, from rather loose to dense and interrupted; florets not distant.
          Panicle yellowish; spikelets mostly 3- or 4-flowered; introduced. 8. T. FLAVESCENS.
          Panicle pale green, sometimes purplish-tinged; spikelets usually 2-flowered.
            Spikelets about 8 mm. long .... 6. T. CANESCENS.
            Spikelets 5 to 6 mm. long .... 7. T. MONTANUM.

1. Trisetum melicoídes (Michx.) Scribn. (Fig. 386.) Culms 50 to 100 cm. tall; sheaths pubescent or scabrous; blades 2 to 8 mm. wide, scabrous, sometimes pubescent on the upper surface; panicle somewhat open, nodding, 10 to 20 cm. long, the branches slender, ascending, lax or drooping, as much as 7 cm. long, rather closely flowered above the middle; spikelets scaberulous, 6 to 7 mm. long; glumes 4 to 6 mm. long, the second longer and broader; lemmas acute, 5 to 6 mm. long, rarely with a minute awn just below the tip, the rachilla and callus hairs 1 to 2 mm. long. ♃ —River banks, lake shores, mostly in gravelly ground,

Figure 386.—*Trisetum melicoides*. Panicle, × 1; glumes and floret, × 5. (Pringle, Vt.)

Newfoundland to Vermont, Michigan, and Wisconsin.

FIGURE 387.—*Trisetum wolfii.* Panicle, × 1; glumes and floret, × 5. (Swallen 809, Calif.)

2. Trisetum wólfii Vasey. WOLFS TRISETUM. (Fig. 387.) Culms erect, 50 to 100 cm. tall, loosely tufted, sometimes with short rhizomes; sheaths scabrous, rarely the lower pilose; blades flat, scabrous, rarely pilose on the upper surface, 2 to 4 mm. wide; panicle erect, rather dense but scarcely spikelike, green or pale, sometimes a little purplish, 8 to 15 cm. long; spikelets 5 to 7 mm. long, 2-flowered, sometimes 3-flowered; glumes nearly equal, acuminate, about 5 mm. long; lemmas obtusish, scaberulous, 4 to 5 mm. long, awnless or with a minute awn below the tip, the callus hairs scant, about 0.5 mm. long, the rachilla internode about 2 mm. long, rather sparingly long-villous. ♃ —Meadows and moist ground, at medium altitudes in the mountains, Montana to Washington, south to New Mexico and California.

3. Trisetum orthochaétum Hitchc. (Fig. 388.) Culms solitary, erect, slender, 110 cm. tall; sheaths glabrous; blades flat, scabrous, 8 to 20 cm. long, 3 to 7 mm. wide; panicle slightly nodding, lax, pale, about 18 cm. long, the filiform branches loosely ascending, naked below, the lower fascicled, as much as 8 cm. long; spikelets short-pediceled, somewhat appressed, mostly 3-flowered, 8 to 9 mm. long excluding awns, the rachilla appressed-silky; glumes acuminate, about 6 mm. long, the second wider; lemmas rounded on the back, minutely scaberulous on the upper part, obscurely 5-nerved, the callus short-pilose, the apex acute, erose-toothed, awned about 2 mm. below the tip, the awn straight or nearly so, exceeding the lemma about 3 mm. ♃ —Known only from boggy meadows, Lolo Hot Springs, Bitterroot Mountains, Mont.

FIGURE 388.—*Trisetum orthochaetum.* Panicle, × 1; glumes and floret, × 5. (Type.)

4. Trisetum cérnuum Trin. NODDING TRISETUM. (Fig. 389.) Culms rather lax, 60 to 120 cm. tall; sheaths glabrous to sparsely pilose; blades thin, flat, lax, scabrous, 6 to 12 mm. wide; panicle open, lax, drooping, 15 to 30 cm. long, the branches verticillate, filiform, flexuous, spikelet-bearing toward the ends; spikelets 6 to 12 mm. long, with usually 3 distant florets, the first longer than the second glume; first glume narrow, acuminate, 1-nerved, 0.5 to 2 mm. long, the second broad, 3-nerved, 3 to 4 mm. long, occasionally reduced; lemma 5 to 6 mm. long, the teeth setaceous, the hairs of the callus 0.5 to 1 mm. long, of the rachilla as much as 2 mm. long, the awns slender, curved, flexuous or loosely spiral, mostly 5 to 10 mm. long, attached 1 to 2 mm. below tip. ♃ —Moist woods, Alberta to southeastern Alaska, south to western Montana and northern California.

5. Trisetum spicâtum (L.) Richt. SPIKE TRISETUM. (Fig. 390.) Culms densely tufted, erect, 15 to 50 cm. tall, glabrous to puberulent; sheaths and usually the blades puberulent; panicle dense, usually spikelike, often interrupted at base, pale or often dark purple, 5 to 15 cm. long; spikelets 4 to 6 mm. long; glumes somewhat unequal in length, glabrous or scabrous except the keels, or sometimes pilose, the first narrow, acuminate, 1-nerved, the second broader, acute, 3-nerved; lemmas scaberulous, 5 mm. long, the first longer than the glumes, the teeth setaceous; awn attached about one-third below the tip, 5 to 6 mm. long, geniculate, exserted. ♃ —Alpine meadows and slopes, Arctic America, southward to Connecticut, Pennsylvania, northern Michigan and Minnesota, in the mountains to New Mexico and California; also on Roan Mountain, N. C.; high mountains through Mexico to the Antarctic regions of South America; Arctic and alpine regions of the Old World. In northern regions the species descends to low altitudes. Exceedingly variable; several varieties have been proposed, but the characters used to differentiate them are variable and are not correlated. Two rather more outstanding varieties, both intergrading with the species are: *T. spicatum* var. *molle* (Michx.) Beal, with densely pubescent foliage, and *T. spicatum* var. *congdoni* (Scribn. and Merr.) Hitchc., a nearly glabrous alpine form with slightly larger spikelets.

FIGURE 389.—*Trisetum cernuum.* Panicle, × 1; glumes and floret, × 5. (Elmer 1946, Wash.)

6. Trisetum canéscens Buckl. TALL TRISETUM. (Fig. 391.) Culms erect, or decumbent at base, 60 to 120 cm. tall; sheaths, at least the lower, sparsely to densely and softly retrorse-pilose, rarely scabrous only; blades flat, scabrous or canescent, sometimes sparsely pilose, mostly 2 to 7 mm. wide; panicle narrow, usually loose, sometimes interrupted and spikelike, 10 to 25 cm. long; spikelets about 8 mm. long, 2- or 3-flowered, the florets not so distant as in *T. cernuum;* glumes smooth, except the keel, the first narrow, acuminate, the second broad, acute, 3-nerved, 5 to 7 mm. long; lemmas rather firm, scaberulous, the upper exceeding the glumes, 5 to 6 mm. long, the teeth aristate, the callus hairs rather scant, the rachilla hairs copious; awn geniculate, spreading, loosely twisted below, attached one-third below the tip, usually about 12 mm. long. ♃ —Mountain meadows, moist ravines and along streams, Montana to British Columbia, south to central California. Plants with less pubescent sheaths and looser panicles resemble *T. cernuum* but in that the spikelets are commonly 3-flowered, the florets distant. Plants with more velvety foliage and narrow panicles with short densely flowered

FIGURE 390.—*Trisetum spicatum*. Plant, × ½; spikelet and floret, × 5. (Rydberg and Bessey 3593, Mont.)

branches, the lower in distant fascicles, have been differentiated as *T. projectum* Louis-Marie. Intergrading specimens are more numerous than the extreme described.

FIGURE 391.—*Trisetum canescens*. Panicle, × 1; glumes and floret, × 5. (Hitchcock 3409, Calif.)

FIGURE 392.—*Trisetum montanum*. Panicle, × 1; glumes and floret, × 5. (Type.)

7. Trisetum montánum Vasey. (Fig. 392.) Resembling *T. canescens*, on the average smaller, the blades narrower; sheaths from nearly glabrous to softly retrorsely pubescent; panicles smaller than usual in *T. canescens*, more uniformly rather dense, often purple-tinged; spikelets 5 to 6 mm. long, the glumes and lemmas thinner than in *T. canescens*, the awn more delicate, 5 to 8 mm. long. ♃ —Mountain meadows, gulches and moist places on mountain slopes, between 2,000 and 3,300 m., Colorado, Utah, New Mexico, and Arizona. A form with purplish panicles and erect awns only 2 to 3 mm. long, known from a single collection near Silverton, Colo., has been differentiated as *T. montanum* var. *shearii* Louis-Marie.

8. Trisetum flavéscens (L.) Beauv. (Fig. 393.) Resembling *T. canescens;* sheaths glabrous or the lower sparsely pilose; panicle usually yellowish, many-flowered, somewhat condensed; spikelets mostly 3- or 4-flowered; lemmas 4 to 6 mm. long. ♃ —Waste places, Vermont, New York, Missouri, Colorado, Washington, California, and probably other States; introduced from Europe.

Trisetum aúreum (Ten.) Ten. Annual; culms 10 to 20 cm. tall; panicle ovate, contracted, 2 to 3 cm. long; spikelets 3 mm. long; awns 2 to 3 mm. long. ⊙ —Ballast, Camden, N. J.; Europe.

9. Trisetum pennsylvánicum (L.) Beauv. ex Roem. and Schult. (Fig. 394.) Culms slender, weak, usually subgeniculate at base, 50 to 100 cm. tall; sheaths glabrous or rarely scabrous; blades flat, scabrous, 2 to 5 mm. wide; panicle narrow, loose, nodding, 10 to 20 cm. long; pedicels disarticulating about the middle or toward the base; spikelets 5 to 7 mm.

FIGURE 393.—*Trisetum flavescens*. Panicle, × 1; floret, × 5. (Grant 26, Wash.)

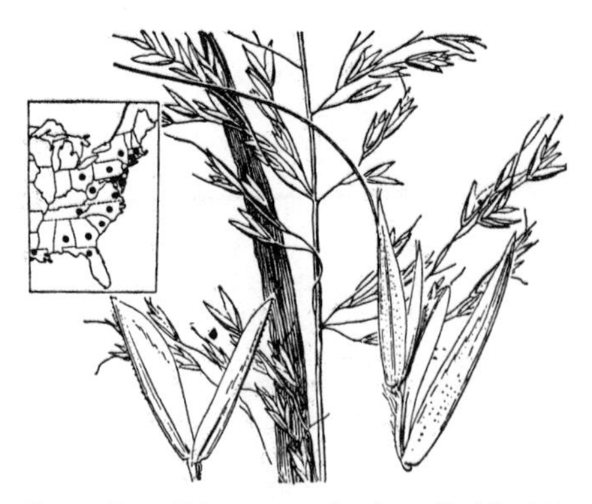
FIGURE 394.—*Trisetum pennsylvanicum.* Panicle, × 1; glumes and florets, × 5. (Heller 4800, Pa.)

FIGURE 395.—*Trisetum interruptum.* Panicle, × 1; glumes and floret, × 5. (Jermy, Tex.)

long, 2-flowered, the long rachilla internodes slightly hairy; glumes mostly 4 to 5 mm. long, acute, the second wider; lemmas acuminate, the first usually awnless, the second awned below the 2 setaceous teeth, the awn horizontally spreading, 4 to 5 mm. long. ♃ —Swamps and wet places, Massachusetts to Ohio and West Virginia, south on the Coastal Plain to Florida and west to Tennessee and Louisiana.

10. Trisetum interrúptum Buckl. (Fig. 395.) Annual; culms tufted, sometimes branching, erect or spreading, 10 to 40 cm. tall; sheaths often scabrous or pubescent; blades flat, sometimes pubescent, 1 to 4 mm. wide, mostly 3 to 10 cm. long; panicle narrow, interrupted, from slender to rather dense but scarcely spikelike, 5 to 12 cm. long, sometimes with smaller axillary panicles; pedicels disarticulating a short distance below the summit; spikelets about 5 mm. long, 2-flowered, the second floret sometimes rudimentary; glumes about equal in length, acute, 4 to 5 mm. long, the first 3-nerved, the second a little broader, 5-nerved; lemmas acuminate with 2 setaceous teeth, the awns attached above the middle, flexuous, 4 to 8 mm. long, that of the first lemma often shorter and straight. ⊙ —Open dry ground, Texas to Colorado and Arizona.

58. DESCHÂMPSIA Beauv. HAIRGRASS

Spikelets 2-flowered, disarticulating above the glumes and between the florets, the hairy rachilla prolonged beyond the upper floret and sometimes bearing a reduced floret; glumes about equal, acute or acutish, membranaceous; lemmas thin, truncate and 2- to 4-toothed at summit, bearded at base, bearing a slender awn from or below the middle, the awn straight, bent or twisted. Low or moderately tall annuals or usually perennials, with shining pale or purplish spikelets in narrow or open panicles. Standard species, *Deschampsia caespitosa.* Included in *Aira* by some authors. Named for Deschamps.

Deschampsia caespitosa is often the dominant grass in mountain meadows, where it furnishes excellent forage.

Plants annual; foliage very scant .... 1. D. DANTHONIOIDES.
Plants perennial; foliage not scant, one-third to half the entire length of the culm.
  Panicle narrow, the distant branches appressed.
    Glumes 4 to 6 mm. long; lemma smooth, not deeply toothed .... 2. D. ELONGATA.
    Glumes 7 mm. long; lemma scaberulous, deeply toothed or lacerate.
      3. D. CONGESTIFORMIS.
  Panicle open or contracted, if narrow, not more than one-fourth the length of the culm.
    Blades thin, flat; glumes exceeding the florets .... 4. D. ATROPURPUREA.

Blades firm or filiform; glumes not exceeding the upper floret.
Blades filiform, flexuous; awn exserted, geniculate, twisted........ 5. D. FLEXUOSA.
Blades flat or folded, stiff; awn included or slightly exserted, straight.
Panicle open, usually nodding or drooping................................ 6. D. CAESPITOSA.
Panicle narrow, condensed, erect.. 7. D. HOLCIFORMIS.

1. Deschampsia danthonioídes (Trin.) Munro ex Benth. ANNUAL HAIRGRASS. (Fig. 396.) Annual; culms slender, erect, 15 to 60 cm. tall; blades few, short, narrow; panicle open, 7 to 25 cm. long, the capillary branches commonly in twos, stiffly ascending, naked below, bearing a few short-pediceled spikelets toward the ends; glumes 4 to 8 mm. long, 3-nerved, acuminate, smooth except the keel, exceeding the florets; lemmas smooth and shining, somewhat indurate, 2 to 3 mm. long, the base of the florets and the rachilla pilose, the awns geniculate, 4 to 6 mm. long. ⊙ —Open ground, Alaska to Montana and Baja California; also Chile.

FIGURE 396.—*Deschampsia danthonioides.* Panicle, × 1; glumes and floret, × 10. (Parish 3300, Calif.)

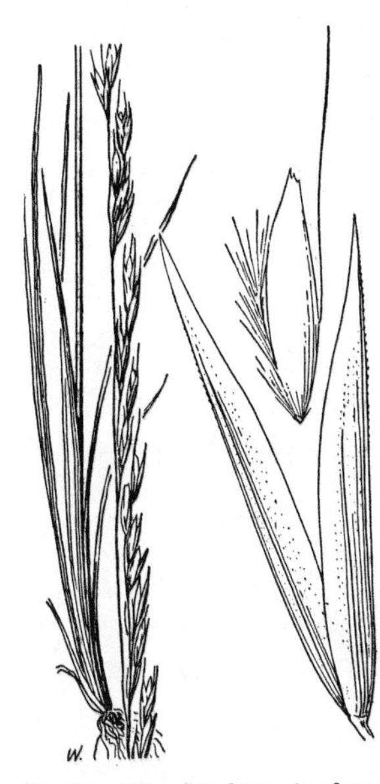

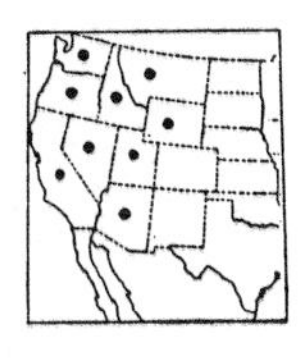

FIGURE 397.—*Deschampsia elongata.* Panicle, × 1 glumes and floret, × 10. (Swallen 780, Calif.)

Variable in the size of the spikelets. A form described from southern California as *D. gracilis* Vasey, with somewhat laxer panicles, the rather more numerous spikelets only 4 to 5 mm. long, grades into the usual form.

2. Deschampsia elongáta (Hook.) Munro ex Benth. SLENDER HAIRGRASS. (Fig. 397.) Culms densely tufted, slender, erect, 30 to 120 cm. tall; blades soft, 1 to 1.5 mm. wide, flat or folded, those of the basal tuft filiform; panicle narrow, as much as 30 cm. long, the capillary branches appressed; spikelets on short appressed pedicels; glumes 4 to 6 mm. long, 3-nerved, equaling or slightly exceeding the florets; lemmas 2 to 3 mm. long, similar to those of *D. danthonioides*, the awns shorter, straight. ♃ —Open ground, Alaska to Wyoming, south to Arizona and California; Mexico; Chile.

—Only known from Gallatin Valley, Bozeman, Gallatin County, and from Cooke, Park County, Mont.

4. Deschampsia atropurpúrea (Wahl.) Scheele. MOUNTAIN HAIRGRASS. (Fig. 399.) Culms loosely tufted, erect, purplish at base, 40 to 80 cm. tall; blades flat, rather soft, ascending or appressed, 5 to 10 cm. long, 4 to 6 mm. wide, acute or abruptly acuminate; panicle loose, open, 5 to 10 cm. long, the few capillary drooping branches naked below; spikelets mostly purplish, broad; glumes about 5 mm. long, broad, the second 3-nerved, exceeding the florets; lemmas scabrous, about 2.5 mm. long, the callus hairs one-third to half as long, the awn of the first straight, included, of the second, geniculate, exserted. ♃ —Woods and wet meadows, Newfound-

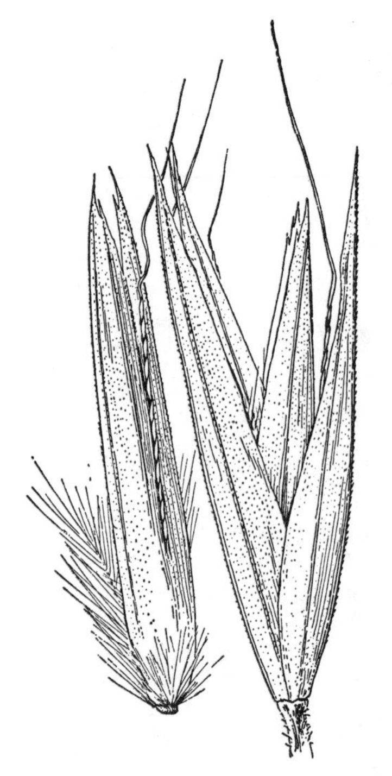

FIGURE 398.—*Deschampsia congestiformis.* Spikelet and floret, × 10. (Type.)

3. Deschampsia congestifórmis Booth. (Fig. 398.) Culms in small tufts, slender, 45 to 70 cm. tall, scaberulous above; sheaths scaberulous toward the summit; ligule 1.5 to 3 mm. long; blades flat or folded, scabrous on both surfaces, 2 to 3 mm. wide, the basal 10 to 30 cm. long, those of the culm 3 to 8 cm. long, those of the innovations subfiliform; panicle long-exserted, 6.5 to 10 cm. long, narrow, condensed, the short branches erect, the axis and branches slender, hirtellous; spikelets short-pediceled, appressed, 7 to 10 mm. long; glumes about 7 mm. long, scabrous, especially on the midnerve; lemmas 7 to 8 mm. long, awned from near the base, toothed or lacerate at the apex, sometimes splitting down the back at maturity, the awn twisted and geniculate, exceeding the spikelets 3 to 4 mm., the callus hairs about 0.5 to 1 mm. long, those of the rachilla 1 to 2 mm. long. ♃

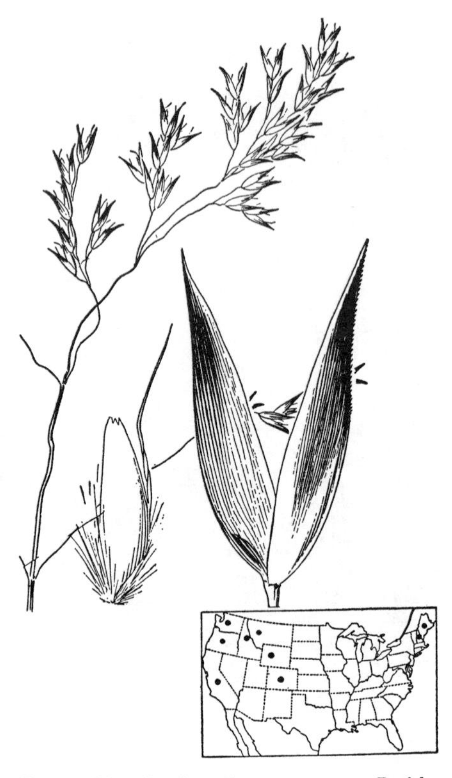

FIGURE 399.—*Deschampsia atropurpurea.* Panicle, × 1; glumes and floret, × 10. (Leiberg 2952, Idaho.)

land and Labrador to Alaska, south to the White Mountains of New Hampshire; Colorado and California; northern Eurasia.

5. Deschampsia flexuósa (L.) Trin. CRINKLED HAIRGRASS. (Fig. 400.) Culms densely tufted, erect, slender, 30 to 80 cm. tall; leaves mostly in a basal tuft, numerous, the sheaths scabrous, the blades involute, slender or setaceous, flexuous; panicle loose, open, nodding, 5 to 12 cm. long, the capillary branches naked below, the branchlets spikelet-bearing toward the ends; spikelets 4 to 5 mm. long, purplish or bronze, the florets approximate; glumes 1-nerved, acute, shorter than the florets; lemmas scabrous, the callus hairs about 1 mm. long, the awn attached near the base, geniculate, twisted, 5 to 7 mm. long. ♃ —Dry or rocky woods, slopes, and open ground, Greenland to Alaska, south to Georgia, Michigan, and Wisconsin; Arkansas and Oklahoma (Le Flore County); Mexico; Eurasia. A form with yellow-striped foliage (called by gardeners *Aira foliis variegatis*) is occasionally grown for ornament.

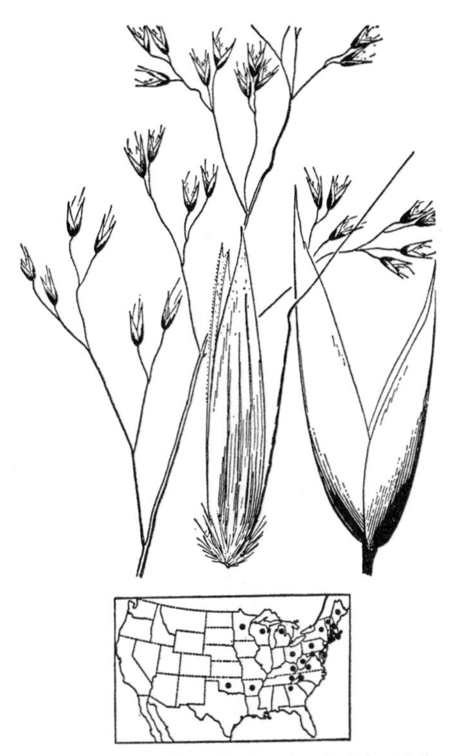

FIGURE 400.—*Deschampsia flexuosa.* Panicle, × 1; glumes and floret, × 10. (Hitchcock 16059, N. H.)

6. Deschampsia caespitósa (L.) Beauv. TUFTED HAIRGRASS. (Fig. 401.) Culms in dense tufts, leafy at base, erect, 60 to 120 cm. tall; sheaths smooth; blades 1.5 to 4 mm. wide, often elongate, rather firm, flat or folded, scabrous above; panicle loose, open, nodding, 10 to 25 cm. long, the capillary scabrous branches and branchlets spikelet-bearing toward the ends; spikelets 4 to 5 mm. long, pale or purple-tinged, the florets distant, the rachilla internode half the length of the lower floret; glumes 1-nerved or the second obscurely 3-nerved, acute, about as long as the florets; lemmas smooth, the callus hairs short; awn from near the base, from straight and included in the glumes to weakly geniculate and twice as long as the spikelet. ♃ —Bogs and wet places, Greenland to Alaska, south to New Jersey, West Virginia, North Carolina, Illinois, North Dakota, New Mexico, and California; Arctic and temperate regions of the Old World. Variable in size, in width and texture of blades, in shape of the panicle, and in length of awn. The forms which have been segregated as species and varieties are inconstant, and the characters used to distinguish them are not correlated. Rarely with proliferous spikelets. Large plants from Oregon and California have been described under *Deschampsia caespitosa* subsp. *beringensis* (Hultén) Lawr., but are not *D. beringensis* Hultén, of the Aleutians. Tall plants, with long flat blades, elongate panicles, and spikelets, 3 to 4 mm. long, found in Connecticut, have been referred to D. CAESPITOSA var. PARVIFLÓRA (Thuill.) Coss. and Germ. They agree with

FIGURE 401.—*Deschampsia caespitosa*. Plant, × ½; glumes and floret, × 10. (Nelson 3623, Wyo.)

FIGURE 402.—*Deschampsia holciformis.* Panicle, × 1; glumes and floret, × 10. (Bolander, Calif.)

specimens from Germany and are probably introduced.

7. Deschampsia holcifórmis Presl. (Fig. 402.) Culms in dense tufts with numerous basal leaves, erect, relatively robust, 50 to 125 cm. tall; blades mostly folded, 20 to 50 cm. long, 2 to 4 mm. wide, rather firm; panicle 10 to 25 cm. long, condensed, many-flowered, the branches appressed to subflexuous-ascending, purplish to brownish; spikelets 6 to 8 mm. long; glumes and lemmas scaberulous, the glumes about equaling

FIGURE 403.—*Aira praecox.* Panicle, × 1; glumes and floret, × 10. (Amer. Gr. Natl. Herb. 375, Del.)

the spikelets or shorter, 3-nerved, the lateral nerves of the first often obscure; lemmas awned from below the middle, the awns erect, exceeding the spikelet, the callus hairs short. ♃ —Marshes and sandy soil near the coast, Vancouver Island to central California.

59. AÍRA L.

(*Aspris* Adans.)

Spikelets 2-flowered, disarticulating above the glumes, the rachilla not prolonged; glumes boat-shaped, about equal, 1-nerved or obscurely 3-nerved, acute, membranaceous or subscarious; lemmas firm, rounded on the back, tapering into 2 slender teeth, bearing on the back below the middle a slender geniculate, twisted, usually exserted, awn, this sometimes wanting in the lower floret or reduced; callus minutely bearded. Delicate annuals with lax, subfiliform blades and open or contracted panicles of small spikelets. Type species, *Aira praecox. Aira,* an old Greek name for a weed, probably darnel. Weedy grasses of no economic importance, introduced from Europe.

Panicle dense, spikelike .... 1. A. PRAECOX.
Panicle open.
  Lower floret with awn as long as that of the upper floret .... 2. A. CARYOPHYLLEA.
  Lower floret awnless or nearly so .... 3. A. ELEGANS.

1. Aira praécox L. (Fig. 403.) Culms tufted, 10 to 20 cm. tall, usually erect; panicle narrow, dense, 1 to 3 cm. long; spikelets yellowish, shin-

FIGURE 404.—*Aira caryophyllea.* Plant, × ½; spikelet and floret, × 10. (Heller 3889, Wash.)

ing, 3.5 to 4 mm. long; lemmas with awns 2 to 4 mm. long, that of the lower floret the shorter. ⊙ —Sandy open ground, along the coast, New Jersey to Virginia; Vancouver to California.

2. Aira caryophylléa L. SILVER HAIRGRASS. (Fig. 404.) Culms solitary or in small tufts, erect, 10 to 30 cm. tall; panicle open, the silvery shining spikelets 3 mm. long, clustered toward the ends of the spreading capillary branches; both lemmas with awns about 4 mm. long. ⊙ —Open dry ground, Coastal Plain, Massachusetts to Florida and Louisiana; Ohio; common on the Pacific coast from British Columbia to California; southern South America.

3. Aira élegans Willd. ex Gaudin. (Fig. 405.) Resembling *A. caryophyllea;* panicle more diffuse; spikelets 2.5 mm. long, scattered at the ends of the branches; lemma of lower floret awnless or with a minute awn just below

FIGURE 405.—*Aira elegans.* Panicle, × 1; spikelet and florets, × 10. (Davis 2016, S. C.)

the apex, that of the upper floret with an awn 3 mm. long. ⊙ (*A. capillaris* Host, not Savi).—Open ground, Coastal Plain, Maryland to Florida; Tennessee; Arkansas and Texas; Oregon and California.

60. CORYNÉPHORUS Beauv.

Spikelets 2-flowered, disarticulating above the glumes; glumes nearly equal, 1-nerved, acute, membranaceous; lemmas thin, acute, awned from near the base, the awn jointed about the middle, the joint with a minute ring of hairs, the lower part straight, brown, the upper slender, club-shaped. Slender annuals with subfiliform blades and narrow panicles. Type species *Corynephorus canescens.* Name from Greek *korynephoros*, club-bearing. One species introduced from Europe.

FIGURE 406.—*Corynephorus canescens.* Spikelet and florets, × 10. (Bicknell, Mass.)

1. Corynephorus canéscens (L.) Beauv. (Fig. 406.) Culms tufted, 20 to 35 cm. tall, branching and leafy at base; panicle 5 to 10 cm. long, pale or purplish; spikelets about 3.5 mm. long; florets about 1.7 mm. long, faintly nerved, the callus and rachilla softly pilose, the awns equaling or slightly exceeding the glumes. ⊙ —Waste ground and ballast, British Columbia. Marthas Vineyard and Long Island, N. Y., New Jersey, and Pennsylvania.

61. AVÉNA L. OATS

Spikelets 2- or 3-flowered, the rachilla bearded, disarticulating above the glumes and between the florets; glumes about equal, membranaceous or papery, 7- to 9-nerved, longer than the lower floret, usually exceeding the upper floret; lemmas indurate, except toward the summit, 5- to 9-nerved, bidentate, bearing a dorsal bent and twisted awn (straight and reduced in *Avena sativa*), the awn in age commonly breaking at the bend. Low or moderately tall annuals, with narrow or open, usually rather few-flowered panicles of large spikelets. Type species, *Avena sativa*. *Avena*, the old Latin name for oats.

The most important species of the genus is *A. sativa*, the familiar cultivated oat. Two other introduced species, *A. fatua* and *A. barbata*, are known as wild oats because of their close resemblance to the cultivated oat. These two species are common on the Pacific coast where they are often utilized for hay. Much of the grain hay of that region is made from either cultivated or wild oats. The varieties of cultivated oat are derived from three species of *Avena*. The common varieties of this country and of temperate and mountain regions in general are derived from *A. fatua*. The Algerian oat grown in North Africa and Italy and the red oat of our Southern States (*A. byzantina* K. Koch) are derived from *A. sterilis*. A few varieties adapted to dry countries are derived from *A. barbata*.

Teeth of lemma setaceous; pedicels curved, capillary .... 3. A. BARBATA.
Teeth of lemma acute, not setaceous; pedicels stouter.
Spikelets mostly 2-flowered, the florets not readily separating; awn usually straight or wanting; lemmas glabrous .... 2. A. SATIVA.
Spikelets mostly 3-flowered, the florets readily separating; awn stout, geniculate, twisted; lemmas clothed with stiff brown hairs (hairs sometimes white or scant). 1. A. FATUA.

1. Avena fátua L. WILD OAT. (Fig. 407, *A*.) Culms 30 to 75 cm. tall, erect, stout; leaves numerous, the blades flat, usually 4 to 8 mm. wide, scabrous; panicle loose and open, the slender branches usually horizontally spreading; spikelets usually 3-flowered; glumes about 2.5 cm. long; rachilla and lower part of the lemma clothed with long stiff brownish, or sometimes whitish, hairs, these sometimes scant; florets readily falling from the glumes; lemmas nerved above, about 2 cm. long, the teeth acuminate, not setaceous; awn stout, geniculate, twisted below, 3 to 4 cm. long. ⊙ —Cultivated soil and waste places; introduced from Europe; rare in the Eastern States; Maine to Pennsylvania, Missouri and westward, a common weed on the Pacific coast. Seed used for food by the Indians.

Avena stérilis L. ANIMATED OATS. Resembling *A. fatua*, the spikelets 3.5 to 4.5 cm. long, the awns 5 to 7 cm. long. ⊙ —Sometimes cultivated as a curiosity, occasionally spontaneous. When laid on a moist surface the fruits twist and untwist as the awns lose or absorb moisture. Sometimes used as flies in fishing, the spikelets jerking as the awns untwist.

2. Avena satíva L. OAT. (Fig. 407, *B*.) Differing from *A. fatua* in having mostly 2-flowered spikelets, the florets not readily separating from the glumes; lemmas glabrous; awn usually straight, often wanting. ⊙ —Commonly cultivated and occasionally escaped. In *A. nuda* L., NAKED OAT, the caryopsis readily separates from the lemma and palea. *A. brevis* Roth is a form with smaller spikelets, the lemmas plump, awned. *A. strigosa* Schreb. has a 1-sided panicle, the lemmas scabrous toward the apex, both florets awned.

3. Avena barbáta Brot. SLENDER OAT. (Fig. 408.) Differing from *A. fatua* in the somewhat smaller, mostly 2-flowered spikelets on curved capillary pedicels; lemmas clothed with stiff red hairs, the teeth ending in fine points 4 mm. long. ⊙ —A common weed in fields and waste places, Washington and Oregon to Arizona and California.

FIGURE 407.—*A*, *Avena fatua*. Plant, × ½; spikelet and floret, × 2. (Umbach, Ill.) *B*, *A. sativa*, × 2. (Deam, Ind.)

Cultivated oats fall into three groups, according to the number of chromosomes. Group 1, 7 chromosomes, *A. brevis*, *A. strigosa*. Group 2, 14 chromosomes, *A. barbata*. Group 3, 21 chromosomes, *A. sativa*, *A. fatua* (including *A. orientalis* Schreb.), *A. nuda*, *A. sterilis*, *A. byzantina* (including *A. sterilis* var. *algeriensis* Trabut).

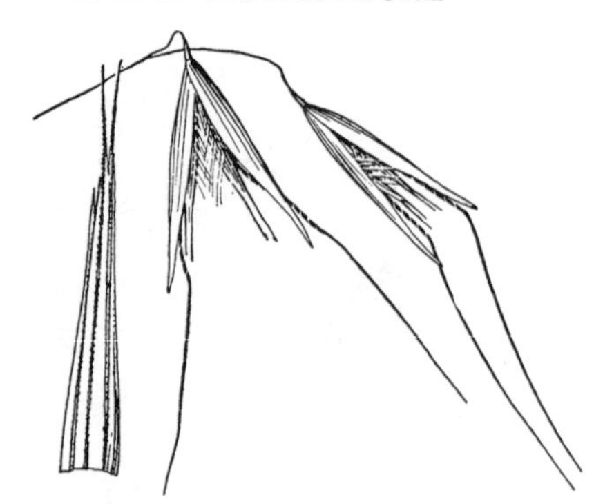

FIGURE 408.—*Avena barbata*. Spikelets, × 1; tip of lemma, × 5. (Davy 5023, Calif.)

62. HELICTOTRÍCHON Besser

(*Avena* sec. *Avenastrum* Koch; included in *Avena* L. in Manual, ed. 1)

Spikelets 3- to several-flowered, the rachilla bearded, disarticulating above the glumes and between the florets; glumes about equal, 3- to 5-nerved, subhyaline except toward the base; lemmas convex, the lower half subindurate and several-nerved, the upper part subhyaline, awned from about the middle, the awns twisted and geniculate, much exceeding the spikelets. Tufted perennials with rather narrow panicles of shining spikelets. Type species, *H. sempervirens* (Vill.) Pilger. Name from *helictos*, twisted, and "trichon," apparently referring to the awn, which is twisted. Perennials, numerous in Eurasia, 1 introduced and 2 native in western North America.

Blades involute; panicle 2 to 5 cm. long .... 3. H. MORTONIANUM.
Blades flat or folded; panicle 5 to 15 cm. long.
  Sheaths and blades glabrous .... 2. H. HOOKERI.
  Sheaths, at least the lower, and blades pubescent .... 1. H. PUBESCENS.

1. **Helictotrichon pubéscens** (Huds.) Pilger. (Fig. 409.) Culms erect, 50 to 80 cm. tall; sheaths pubescent; blades flat, pubescent; panicle narrow, open, 10 to 15 cm. long, the flexuous branches ascending; spikelets mostly 3-flowered, 12 to 15 mm. long, glumes and lemmas thin, shining, the rachilla with long white hairs; first glume 1- or 3-nerved, the second 3-nerved; lemmas about 1 cm. long; awn attached about the middle, 1.5 to 2 cm. long. ♃ —Waste places, Connecticut and Vermont; introduced from Europe.

2. **Helictotrichon hookéri** (Scribn.) Henr. SPIKE OAT. (Fig. 410.) Culms densely tufted, 20 to 40 cm. tall; blades firm, flat or folded, 1 to 3 mm. wide, the margins somewhat thickened; panicle long-exserted, narrow, 5 to 10 cm. long, the branches erect or ascending, 1-flowered, or the lower 2-flowered; spikelets 3- to 6-flowered, about 1.5 cm. long; glumes very thin, slightly shorter than the spikelet; lemmas firm, brown, scaberulous, 1 to 1.2 cm. long, the callus short-bearded, the rachilla white-villous; awn 1 to 1.5 cm. long. ♃ Dry slopes and prairies, Manitoba to Alberta, Minnesota, Montana, and New Mexico.

3. **Helictotrichon mortoniánum** (Scribn.) Henr. ALPINE OAT. (Fig. 411.) Culms densely tufted, 10 to 20 cm. tall; blades erect, firm, usually involute; panicle short-exserted, purplish, narrow, 2 to 5 cm. long, the short branches erect, bearing usually a single spikelet, 10 to 12 mm. long, mostly 2-flowered; glumes exceeding the florets; lemmas firm, glabrous, the apex with 4 soft teeth, the callus with a tuft of stiff hairs about 2 mm. long, the rachilla long-villous; awn 1 to 1.5

FIGURE 409.—*Helictotrichon pubescens.* Glumes and floret, × 5. (Weatherby and Harger 4249, Conn.)

FIGURE 410.—*Helictotrichon hookeri.* Panicle, × 1; floret, × 5. (Scribner 372, Mont.)

cm. long. ♃ —Alpine meadows, Colorado, Utah, and New Mexico.

63. ARRHENÁTHERUM Beauv.

Spikelets 2-flowered, the lower floret staminate, the upper perfect, the rachilla disarticulating above the glumes and produced beyond the florets; glumes rather broad and papery, the first 1-nerved, the second a little longer than the first and about as long as the spikelet, 3-nerved; lemmas 5-nerved, hairy on the callus, the lower bearing near the base a twisted, geniculate, exserted awn, the upper bearing a short straight slender awn just below the tip. Rather tall perennials, with flat blades and narrow panicles. Type species, *Arrhenatherum avenaceum* Beauv. (*A. elatius*). Name from Greek *arren*, masculine, and

FIGURE 411.—*Helictotrichon mortonianum.* Panicle, × 1; floret, × 5. (Type.)

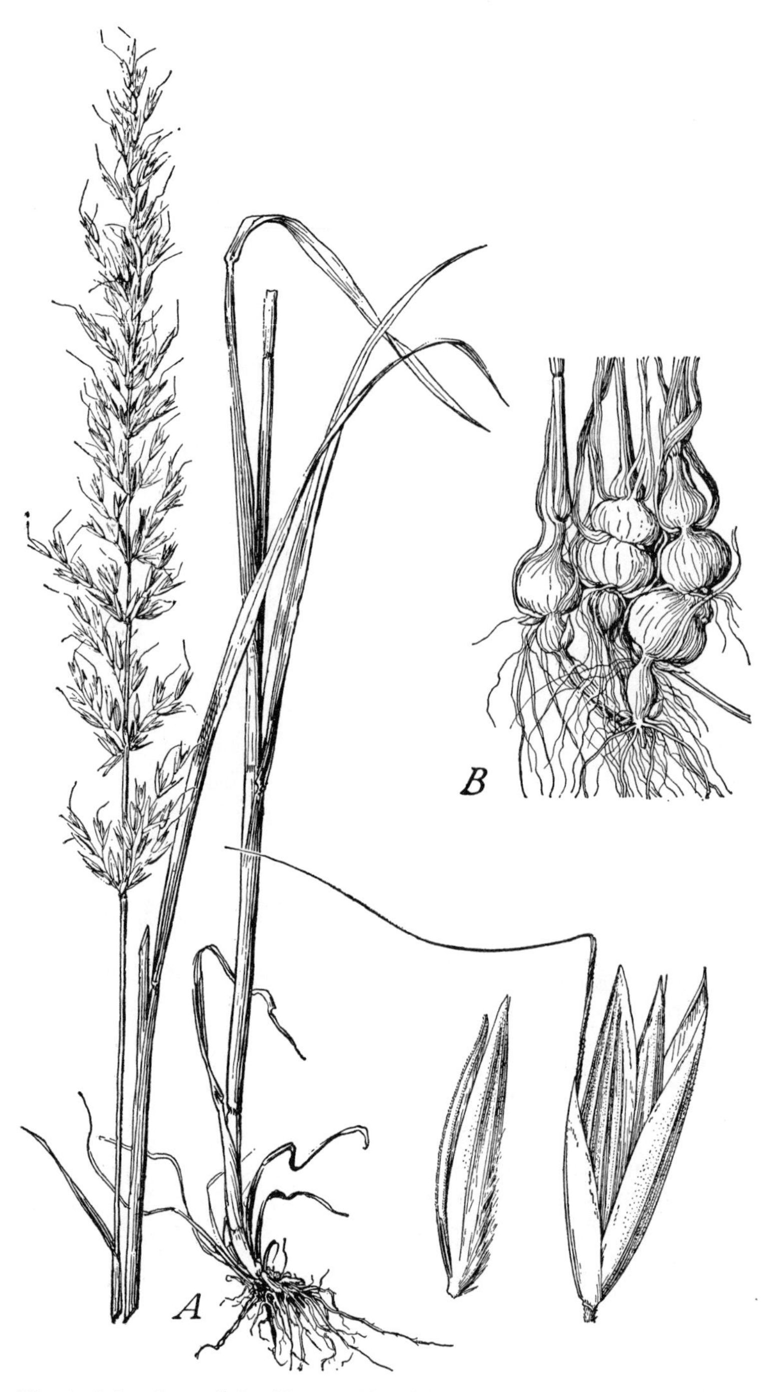

FIGURE 412.—*A*, *Arrhenatherum elatius*. Plant, × ½; spikelet and upper floret, × 5. (McDonald 46, Ill.) *B*, Var. *bulbosum*. Basal corms, × 1. (Harper, Ala.)

ather, awn, referring to the awned staminate floret.

1. Arrhenatherum elátius (L.) Presl. TALL OATGRASS. (Fig. 412, *A*.) Culms erect, 1 to 1.5 m. tall; blades flat, scabrous, 5 to 10 mm. wide; panicle pale or purplish, shining, 15 to 30 cm. long, the short branches verticillate, spreading in anthesis, usually spikelet-bearing from the base; spikelets 7 to 8 mm. long; glumes minutely scabrous; lemmas scabrous, the awn of the staminate floret about twice as long as its lemma. ♃ —Meadows, open ground, and waste places, Newfoundland to British Columbia, south to Georgia, Tennessee, Iowa, Idaho, Utah, Arizona, and California; frequent in the Northern and Eastern States; introduced from Europe and escaped from cultivation. Cultivated in the northern humid regions as a meadow grass.

ARRHENATHERUM ELATIUS var. BULBÓSUM (Willd.) Spenner. TUBER OATGRASS. (Fig. 412, *B*.) Base of culm consisting of a series of closely approximate corms (short subglobose internodes) 5 to 10 mm. in diameter. ♃ —Occasionally introduced, Michigan, Virginia, and West Virginia to Alabama; California; Europe.

ARRHENATHERUM ELATIUS var. BIARISTÁTUM (Peterm.) Peterm. Both lemmas with well-developed awns. ♃ —Ithaca, N. Y., and Delaware County, Pa.; Europe.

64. HÓLCUS L.

(*Notholcus* Nash)

Spikelets 2-flowered, the pedicel disarticulating below the glumes, the rachilla curved and somewhat elongate below the first floret, not prolonged above the second floret; glumes about equal, longer than the 2 florets; first floret perfect, the lemma awnless; second floret staminate, the lemma bearing on the back a short awn. Perennials with flat blades and contracted panicles. Standard species, *Holcus lanatus*. *Holcus*, an old Latin name for a kind of grain.

Rhizomes wanting .... 1. H. LANATUS.
Rhizomes present .... 2. H. MOLLIS.

1. Holcus lanátus L. VELVET GRASS. (Fig. 413.) Plant grayish, velvety-pubescent; culms erect, 30 to 100 cm. tall, rarely taller; blades 4 to 8 mm. wide; panicles 8 to 15 cm. long, contracted, pale, purple-tinged; spikelets 4 mm. long; glumes villous, hirsute on the nerves, the second broader than the first, 3-nerved; lemmas smooth and shining, the awn of the second hooklike. ♃ —Open ground, meadows, and moist places, Maine to Kansas and Colorado, south to Georgia and Louisiana; common on the Pacific coast, British Columbia, and Montana to Arizona and California; introduced from Europe; occasionally cultivated as a meadow grass on light or sandy land.

2. Holcus móllis L. (Fig. 414.) Culms glabrous, 50 to 100 cm. tall, with vigorous slender rhizomes; sheaths, except the lower, glabrous; blades villous or velvety, 4 to 10 mm. wide; panicle ovate or oblong, rather loose, 6 to 10 cm. long; spikelets 4 to 5 mm. long; glumes glabrous; awn of the second floret geniculate, exserted, about 3 mm. long. ♃ —Damp places, recently introduced from Europe and apparently spreading, Washington to California; Lewis County, N. Y.; ballast, Camden, N. J., Delaware County, Pa.

65. SIEGLÍNGIA Bernh.

Spikelets 4- to 5-flowered, the rachilla disarticulating above the glumes and between the florets; glumes equal, acute, the first 1- to 3-nerved, the second 3- to 5-nerved; lemmas firm, 7- to 9-nerved, bifid, the midnerve excurrent from between

FIGURE 413.—*Holcus lanatus*. Plant, × ½; spikelet, florets, and mature fertile floret, × 5. (Griffiths 4449 Calif.)

the short teeth in a short flat mucro, the margins densely pilose toward the base. Densely tufted perennial with short narrow blades and narrow, simple, few-flowered panicle. Type species, *Sieglingia decumbens*. Named for Siegling.

1. Sieglingia decúmbens (L.) Bernh. (Fig. 415.) Culms 20 to 50 cm. tall, erect, densely tufted; leaves crowded toward the base; blades 5 to 15 cm. long or those of the innovations elongate, 2 to 3 mm. wide; panicles 2 to 7 cm. long, the short few-flowered branches appressed; spikelets 8 to 12 mm. long; lemmas 5 to 6 mm. long. ♃ —Open woods, Long Beach, Wash.; escaped from cultivation, Berkeley, Calif.; Newfoundland and Nova Scotia; Europe. Cleistogamous spikelets sometimes developed in the lower sheaths.

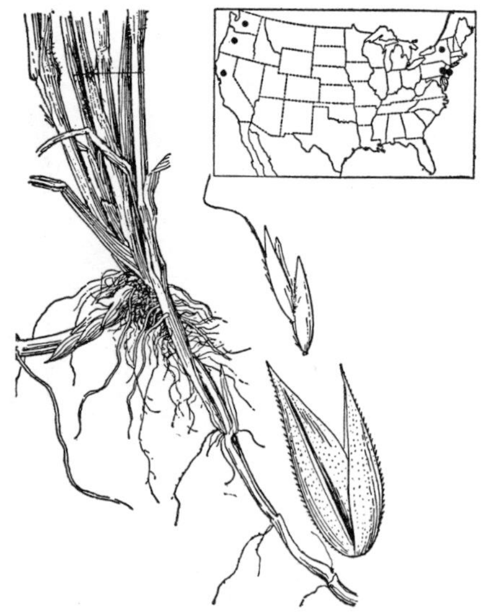

FIGURE 414.—*Holcus mollis*. Plant, × 1; glumes and floret, × 5. (Tracy 2646, Calif.)

66. DANTHÓNIA Lam. and DC. OATGRASS

Spikelets several-flowered, the rachilla readily disarticulating above the glumes and between the florets; glumes about equal, broad, papery, acute, mostly exceeding the uppermost floret; lemmas rounded on the back, obscurely several-nerved, the apex bifid, the lobes acute, usually extending into slender awns, a stout flat, twisted, geniculate awn arising from between the lobes. Tufted low or moderately tall perennials, with few-flowered open or spikelike panicles of rather large spikelets. All our species produce cleistogenes (enlarged fertile, 1- or 2-flowered, cleistogamous spikelets) in the lower sheaths, the culms finally disarticulating at the lower nodes. Type species, *Danthonia spicata*. Named for Etienne Danthoine.

The species are found in grassland and contribute somewhat toward the forage value of the range but usually are not abundant. In California *D. californica* is considered a nutritious grass; *D. compressa* is important in the mountains of North Carolina and Tennessee.

Lemmas glabrous on the back, pilose on the margin only.
  Panicle narrow, the pedicels appressed .... 4. D. INTERMEDIA.
  Panicle open, the slender pedicels spreading or reflexed.
    Panicle usually of a single spikelet .... 7. D. UNISPICATA.
    Panicle of few to several spikelets .... 6. D. CALIFORNICA.
Lemmas pilose on the back, sometimes sparsely so.
  Glumes mostly 20 to 22 mm. long .... 5. D. PARRYI.
  Glumes 10 to 17 mm. long.
    Sheaths pilose (rarely glabrous); glumes 12 to 17 mm. long. Culms 50 to 100 cm. tall. 3. D. SERICEA.
    Sheaths glabrous or nearly so; glumes rarely more than 15 mm. long.
      Panicle simple or nearly so, usually contracted after anthesis; blades rarely more than 15 cm. long, commonly less .... 1. D. SPICATA.
      Panicle usually compound and somewhat open; blades or some of them more than 15 cm., often as much as 25 cm. long .... 2. D. COMPRESSA.

1. Danthonia spicáta (L.) Beauv. ex Roem. and Schult. POVERTY OATGRASS. (Fig. 416.) Culms 20 to 70 cm. tall, mostly not more than 50

FIGURE 415.—*Sieglingia decumbens*. Panicle, × 1; glumes and floret, × 5. (Robinson and Schrenk 206, Newfoundland.)

cm., slender, terete; leaves numerous in a basal cluster, the blades usually curled or flexuous; sheaths glabrous or pilose above the nodes, with a tuft of long hairs in the throat; blades usually not more than 12 cm. long, filiform, to 2 mm. wide, occasionally a few blades 15 to 20 cm. long, subinvolute or in damp weather flat, glabrous or sparsely pilose; panicle 2 to 5 cm. long, rarely longer, the stiff short branches bearing a single spikelet, or the lower longer with 2 (rarely 3 or 4), usually erect after anthesis; glumes 10 to 12 mm. long (rarely longer); lemmas 3.5 to 5 mm. long, sparsely villous except the 2-toothed summit, the teeth acuminate to subsetaceous; terminal segment of awn about 5 mm. long; palea broad, flat, obtuse, ciliolate, reaching to the base of the awn. ♃ —Dry and sterile or rocky soil, Newfoundland to British Columbia, south to Florida, eastern Texas, and eastern Kansas, in the mountains to New Mexico and Oregon. Variable; tall specimens with longer blades and setaceous teeth resemble *D. compressa*. A rather stiff western form with subsetaceous teeth has been described as *D. thermale* Scribn. Very slender plants with narrow pilose blades and spikelets only 8 to 9 mm. long have been differentiated as var. *longipila* Scribn. and Merr. *D. spicata* var. *pinetorum* (Piper) Piper has been differentiated on variable characters. The basal blades, said to be slightly if at all curling, are closely curled in the type specimen.

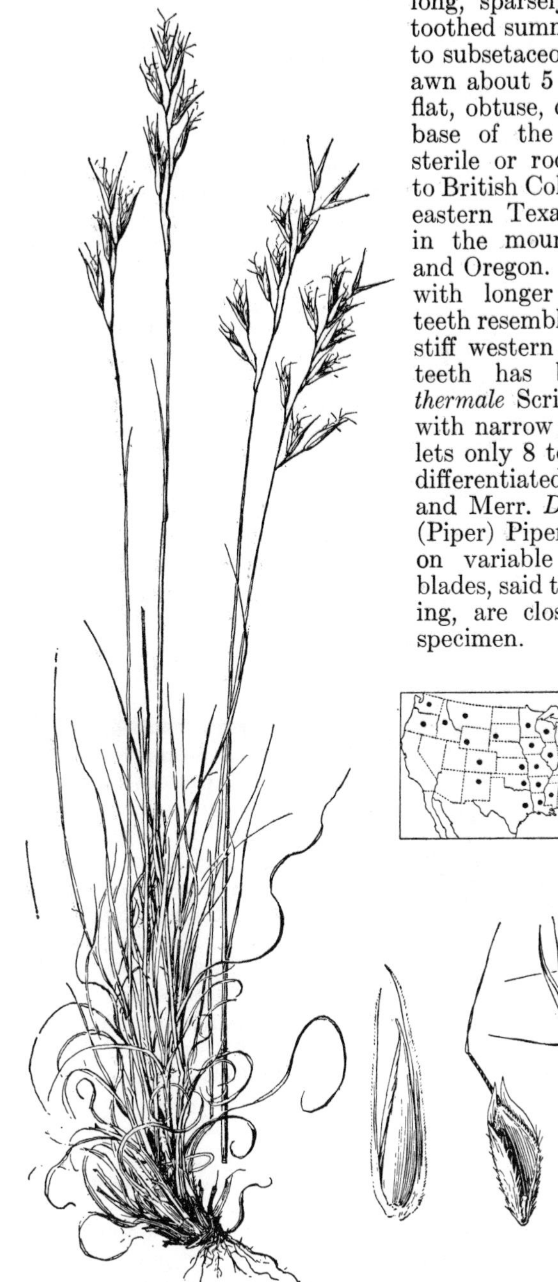

FIGURE 416.—*Danthonia spicata*. Plant, × ½; spikelet, floret, and cleistogene, × 5. (Gayle 787, Maine.)

FIGURE 417.—*Danthonia compressa.* Panicle, × 1; floret, × 5. (Hitchcock 103, Tenn.)

FIGURE 418.—*Danthonia sericea.* Panicle, × 1; floret, × 5. (Kearney 1219, Va.)

2. Danthonia compréssa Austin. (Fig. 417.) Culms on the average stouter and taller than in *D. spicata,* compressed, rather loosely tufted, sometimes decumbent or with short rhizomes, 40 to 80 cm. tall; sheaths reddish above the nodes, glabrous, or sparsely pubescent on the collar, a conspicuous tuft of white hairs in the throat; blades elongate, some of them commonly 20 to 25 cm. long, 2 to 3 mm. wide, usually flat, sometimes involute and subfiliform, scabrous; panicle 5 to 8 cm. long (rarely to 10 cm.), the slender branches bearing 2 or 3 spikelets, contracted after anthesis but looser than in *D. spicata;* glumes 10 to 14 mm. (usually about 12 mm.) long; lemma and palea as in *D. spicata* but the teeth of the lemma aristate, 2 to 3 mm. long. ♃ —Meadows, and open woods, Nova Scotia to Quebec, Maine to Ohio and south to the mountains of North Carolina and Georgia. Appears to intergrade with *D. spicata.* Taller stouter plants with panicles of 9 to 20 spikelets with glumes 10 to 13 mm. long have been differentiated as *D. alleni* Austin.

3. Danthonia serícea Nutt. DOWNY OATGRASS. (Fig. 418.) Culms erect, densely tufted, 50 to 100 cm. tall; sheaths, especially the lower, villous (rarely glabrous); blades 10 to 25 cm. long, 2 to 4 mm. wide, those of the innovations mostly involute, those of the culm mostly flat; panicle 5 to 10 cm. long, relatively many-flowered, the branches bearing 2 to 6 spikelets, rather open or contracted after anthesis; glumes 12 to 17 mm. long; lemmas densely long-pilose, especially along the margin, about 10 mm. long, including the slender aristate teeth, the teeth about half the entire length; palea concave, narrowed toward the 2-toothed apex. ♃ —Sand barrens, chiefly Coastal Plain, Massachusetts (Sherborn); New Jersey to northern Florida, Kentucky, and Louisiana. A rare form with nearly glabrous foliage has been differentiated as *D. epilis* Scribn. (*D. glabra* Nash, not Phil.) Virginia to Georgia.

4. Danthonia intermédia Vasey. TIMBER OATGRASS. (Fig. 419.) Culms 10 to 50 cm. tall; sheaths glabrous (the lower rarely pilose) with long hairs in the throat; blades subinvolute, or those of the culm flat, glabrous or sparsely pilose; panicle purplish, narrow, few-flowered, 2 to 5 cm. long, the branches appressed, bearing a single spikelet; glumes about 15 mm. long; lemmas 7 to 8 mm. long, appressed-pilose along the margin below and on the callus, the summit scaberulous, the teeth acuminate, aristate-tipped; terminal segment of awn 5 to 8 mm. long; palea narrowed above, notched at the apex. ♃ —Meadows and bogs, northern and alpine regions. Newfoundland and Quebec to Alaska, south to northern Michigan, New Mexico, and California.

5. Danthonia párryi Scribn. PARRY OATGRASS. (Fig. 420.) Culms rather stout, in tough clumps, 30 to 60 cm. tall, somewhat enlarged at base from the numerous overlapping firm persistent sheaths; sheaths glabrous, somewhat pilose at the throat, a glabrous or pubescent line or ridge on the collar, the lower blades falling from the sheaths; blades erect-flexuous, mostly 15 to 25 cm. long, narrow or filiform, flat or involute, glabrous; panicle 3 to 7 cm. long, usually with 3 to 8 spikelets, the branches more or less pubescent, ascending or appressed, the lowermost 1 to 2 cm. long, with 1 or 2 spikelets; glumes 20 to 22 mm. long, rarely less; lemmas about 1 cm. long, rather densely to sparsely pilose over the back, strongly pilose on the callus at the sides, the rachilla glabrous, the teeth more or less aristate; terminal segment of awn 8 to 12 mm. long; palea narrowed above, nearly as long as the lemma, 2-toothed. ♃ —Open grassland, open woods, and rocky slopes, in the mountains, mostly be-

FIGURE 420.—*Danthonia parryi*. Panicle, × 1; floret, × 5. (Hitchcock 19087, Colo.)

FIGURE 421.—*Danthonia californica*. Panicle, × 1; floret, × 5. (Eastwood 27, Calif.)

FIGURE 419.—*Danthonia intermedia*. Panicle, × 1; floret, × 5. (Hitchcock 11288, Mont.)

low timber line, Alberta and Montana to New Mexico.

6. Danthonia califórnica Boland. CALIFORNIA OATGRASS. (Fig. 421.) Culms 30 to 100 cm. tall, glabrous, tending to disarticulate at the nodes; sheaths glabrous, pilose at the throat; blades mostly 10 to 20 cm. long, flat or, especially those of the innovations, involute, glabrous; panicle bearing mostly 2 to 5 spikelets, the pedicels slender, spreading or somewhat reflexed, more or less flexuous, 1 to 2 cm. long, a rather prominent pulvinus at the base of each; glumes 15 to 20 mm. long (rarely less or more); lemmas, excluding awns, 8 to 10 mm. long, pilose on the lower part of the margin and on the callus, otherwise glabrous, the teeth long-aristate; terminal segment of awn 5 to 10 mm. long; palea subacute, usually extending beyond base of awn. ♃ —Meadows and open woods, Montana to British Columbia, south to Colorado, New Mexico, and California.

DANTHONIA CALIFORNICA var. AMERICÁNA (Scribn.) Hitchc. Culms on the average shorter, the tufts usually more spreading; foliage sparsely to conspicuously spreading-pilose; spikelets on the average smaller, but large plants with large spikelets occur, with conspicuously pilose foliage. ♃ —Montana and Wyoming to British Columbia, south to California; Chile. *D. macounii* Hitchc. appears to belong here, differing in having lemmas sparsely pilose on the back. Known only from Nanaimo, Vancouver Island (*Macoun* 78825).

7. Danthonia unispicáta (Thurb.) Munro ex Macoun. ONE-SPIKE OATGRASS. (Fig. 422.) Culms 15 to 25 cm. tall, in dense spreading tufts; sheaths and blades pilose, the hairs on the sheaths spreading or reflexed; panicle reduced to a single spikelet or sometimes 2, rarely 3, spikelets, the lower usually reduced, their pedicels appressed or ascending, the long pedicel of the terminal spikelet jointed with the culm; spikelets on the average smaller than in *D. californica;* lemmas usually glabrous, the callus hairy. ♃ —Open or rocky ground, Montana to British Columbia, south to Colorado and California.

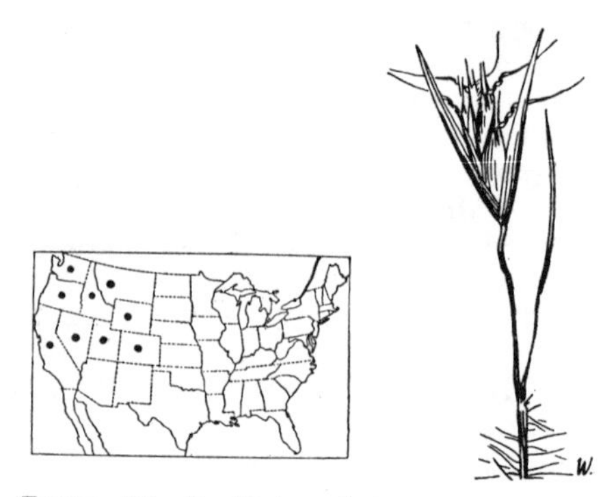

FIGURE 422.—*Danthonia unispicata*, × 2. (Davy, Calif.)

DANTHONIA PILÓSA R. Br. Tufted, 30 to 60 cm. tall, the foliage loosely pilose; panicle narrow, several-flowered; spikelets about 6-flowered; glumes 13 to 14 mm. long; florets disarticulating with a sharp hairy callus, the lemma pilose at base and on the margin, often with a few hairs in the middle of the back; teeth with slender awns 6 to 8 mm. long, the central awn 12 to 15 mm. long. ♃ —Introduced from Australia, escaped in Humboldt, Alameda, and Santa Barbara Counties, Calif.

DANTHONIA SEMIANNULÁRIS (Labill.) R. Br. Tufted, 40 to 100 cm. tall, often rather robust; foliage glabrous or nearly so; panicle many-flowered; glumes mostly 10 to 15 mm. long; florets with a slender hairy callus, the lemma pilose at base and with a conspicuous row of long tufted hairs across the middle; teeth tipped with slender awns, 5 to 8 mm. long, the central awn 10 to 20 cm. long. ♃ —Introduced from Australia; planted on range lands in California and escaped in several localities in the State. Extremely variable with several varieties.

DANTHONIA PURPUREA (Thunb.) Beauv. ex Roem. and Schult. Densely tufted perennial, forming thick mats of filiform curly pilose leaves; culms very slender, 1 to 2 cm. tall, with few short blades; panicle subcapitate, of few to several spikelets on short slender pedicels; spikelets about 8 mm. long; glumes dark purple fading to brown; florets about 4 mm. long, with a slender hairy callus, the lemma pilose at base and with small tufts of white hairs across the middle of the back; awn 2 to 3 mm. long, ♃ —Introduced from South Africa, grown in the grass garden of University of California, Berkeley.

TRIBE 5. AGROSTIDEAE

67. CALAMAGRÓSTIS Adans. REEDGRASS

Spikelets 1-flowered, the rachilla disarticulating above the glumes, prolonged behind the palea (in our species, except *Calamagrostis epigeios*) as a short, commonly hairy bristle; glumes about equal, acute or acuminate; lemma shorter and usually more delicate than the glumes, usually 5-nerved, the midnerve exserted as an awn, the callus bearing a tuft of hairs, these often copious and as long as the lemma. Perennial, usually moderately tall grasses, mostly with creeping rhizomes, with small spikelets in open or usually narrow, sometimes spikelike, panicles. Type species, *Arundo calamagrostis* L. Name from Greek *kalamos*, a reed, and *agrostis*, a kind of grass, the type species being a reedy grass. American species belong to the Section Deyeuxia, in which the rachilla is prolonged. In Section Epigeios, of the Old World (one species introduced), the rachilla is not prolonged.

Several species are important native forage grasses. Pinegrass, *C. rubescens*, is a leading range grass in the mountains of Oregon and Washington. Bluejoint, *C. canadensis*, is a source of much of the wild hay of Wisconsin and Minnesota. On the plains and bench lands of Wyoming and northward, *C. montanensis* furnishes forage, especially when young. In low wet lands of the Northern States *C. inexpansa* is grazed especially by horses and cattle.

1a. Awn longer than the glumes, geniculate.
  2a. Panicle open, the branches spreading, naked below.
    Blades scattered, 5 to 9 mm. broad, flat; plant mostly more than 1 m. tall. 1. C. BOLANDERI.
    Blades mostly basal, mostly not more than 2 mm. wide, often involute.
      Awn about 1 cm. long, much longer than the glumes; blades nearly or quite as long as the flowering culms .... 2. C. HOWELLII.
      Awn only a little exceeding the glumes; blades much shorter than the culms, capillary, sulcate, folded .... 3. C. BREWERI.
  2b. Panicle compact, the branches appressed, floriferous from base.
    Blades scattered, broad and flat, 6 to 10 mm. wide .... 4. C. TWEEDYI.
    Blades mostly basal, firm, narrow, becoming involute.
      Glumes about 1 cm. long, gradually long-acuminate; awn nearly 1 cm. long above the bend .... 5. C. FOLIOSA.
      Glumes 6 to 8 mm. long, abruptly acute or acuminate; awn usually less than 5 mm. long above the bend .... 6. C. PURPURASCENS.
1b. Awn included or scarcely longer than the glumes, straight or geniculate.
  3a. Awn geniculate, protruding sidewise from the glumes; callus hairs rather sparse, shorter than the lemma.
    Plants tufted, not rhizomatous, less than 40 cm. tall; blades 1 to 2 mm. wide, soon involute, at least toward the tip.
      Panicles compact, spikelike; northwestern .... 7. C. MONTANENSIS.
      Panicles loose, open, relatively few-flowered; Tennessee .... 8. C. CAINII.
    Plants rhizomatous, mostly more than 60 cm. tall; blades mostly more than 4 mm. wide, flat.
      Sheaths, or some of them, pubescent on the collar.
        Callus hairs one-third as long as lemma; western species .... 9. C. RUBESCENS.
        Callus hairs half to three-fourths as long as lemma; eastern species.
          Palea about as long as the lemma .... 10. C. PORTERI.
          Palea three-fourths as long as the lemma .... 11. C. PERPLEXA.
      Sheaths glabrous on the collar.
        Culms stout, mostly more than 1 m. tall.
          Panicles loose, the branches ascending or spreading .... 17. C. NUTKAENSIS.
          Panicles compact .... 18. C. DENSA.
        Culms slender, mostly less than 1 m. tall.
          Hairs on callus and rachilla scant, less than 1 mm. long.
            Spikelets 5 mm. long; panicle spikelike .... 19. C. KOELERIOIDES.
            Spikelets 4 mm. long; panicles scarcely spikelike, some of the branches naked below .... 16. C. PICKERINGII.
          Hairs on callus and rachilla rather prominent, at least half as long as the lemma.

FIGURE 423.—*Calamagrostis bolanderi*. Panicle, × 1; glumes and floret, × 10. (Bolander, Calif.)

Callus hairs in 2 tufts, at sides of lemma.
Plants with creeping rhizomes; spikelets 4 to 5.5 mm. long.
Blades thin, glabrous on the upper surface, scaberulous beneath; panicle pale, rather loose; glumes relatively thin, 5 to 5.5 mm. long, scaberulous on the keel toward the summit............ 12. C. INSPERATA.
Blades firm, scabrous; panicle tawny to purplish, rather dense; glumes firm, 4 to 4.5 mm. long, scabrous throughout..... 13. C. LACUSTRIS.
Plants tufted; spikelets 3.5 to 4 mm. long. .... 14. C. FERNALDII.
Callus hairs surrounding base of lemma.................................. 15. C. NUBILA.
3b. Awn straight (somewhat bent in *C. epigeios* and *C. lactea*), included; callus hairs usually not much shorter than the lemma.
Sheaths pubescent on the collar (see *C. inexpansa* var. *barbulata*). 20. C. SCRIBNERI.
Sheaths glabrous on the collar.
Panicle rather loose and open.
Callus hairs copious, about as long as the lemma; awn delicate, straight.
21. C. CANADENSIS.
Callus hairs rather scant, about half as long as the lemma; awn stronger, weakly geniculate... 22. C. LACTEA.
Panicle more or less contracted.
Blades flat, rather lax.
Awn attached near the base; rachilla not prolonged................ 29. C. EPIGEIOS.
Awn attached at or about middle; rachilla prolonged.
Glumes scabrous; plant green... 23. C. CINNOIDES.
Glumes nearly smooth; plant pale.................................... 24. C. SCOPULORUM.

Blades involute or, if flat, rigid and becoming involute.
Blades broad and short, as much as 5 mm. wide, nearly smooth.
28. C. CRASSIGLUMIS.
Blades elongate, smooth or scabrous.
Blades firm, scabrous, rather rigid; ligule 4 to 6 mm. long; panicle firm, dense.
25. C. INEXPANSA.
Blades relatively soft, smooth beneath; ligule 1 to 3 cm. long.
Spikelets 3.9 to 4.2 mm. long; panicle 18 to 22 cm. long.
26. C. CALIFORNICA.
Spikelets 3 to 3.5 mm. long; panicle 5 to 15 cm. long.... 27. C. NEGLECTA.

FIGURE 424.—*Calamagrostis howellii*. Panicle, × 1; glumes and floret, × 10. (Chase 4846, Oreg.)

1. Calamagrostis bolandéri Thurb. (Fig. 423.) Culms erect, 1 to 1.5 m. tall, with slender rhizomes; sheaths scabrous; ligule 4 to 5 mm. long; blades flat, 5 to 9 mm. wide, scattered, nearly smooth; panicle open, 10 to 20 cm. long, the branches verticillate, spreading, naked below, the longer 5 to 10 cm. long; glumes 3 to 4 mm. long, purple, scabrous, acute; lemma very scabrous, about as long as the glumes, the awn from near the base, geniculate, exserted, about 2 mm. long above the bend, the callus hairs short; rachilla pilose, 1 to 2 mm. long. ♃ —Bogs and moist ground, prairie or open woods, near the coast, Mendocino and Humboldt Counties, Calif.

2. Calamagrostis howéllii Vasey. (Fig. 424.) Culms densely tufted, rather slender, ascending, 30 to 60

FIGURE 425.—*Calamagrostis breweri.* Plant, × 1; glumes and floret, × 10. (Bolander 6098, Calif.)

cm. tall; sheaths smooth or slightly scabrous; ligule 2 to 8 mm. long; blades slender, scabrous on the upper surface, flat or soon involute, especially toward the tip, about as long as the culms, the two cauline shorter, about 1 mm. wide; panicle pyramidal, 5 to 15 cm. long, rather open, the lower branches in whorls, ascending, naked below, 3 to 5 cm. long; spikelets pale or tinged with purple; glumes acuminate, 6 to 7 mm. long; lemma acuminate, a little shorter than the glumes, the awn attached about 2 mm. above the base, geniculate, exserted about 1 cm.; callus hairs and those of the rachilla about half as long as the lemma. ♃ —Perpendicular cliffs, near Columbia River and its tributaries, Washington and Oregon.

3. Calamagrostis brewéri Thurb. SHORTHAIR. (Fig. 425.) Culms densely tufted, slender, erect, 15 to 30 cm. tall; leaves mostly basal, usually involute-filiform; panicle ovate, purple, 3 to 8 cm. long, the lower branches slender, spreading, few-flowered, 1 to 2 cm. long; glumes 3 to 4 mm. long, smooth, acute; lemma nearly as long as glumes, cuspidate-toothed, the awn from near the base, geniculate, exserted, twisted below, about 2 mm. long above the bend, the callus hairs short, scant; rachilla long-pilose, about half as long as the lemma. ♃ —Mountain meadows of the high Sierra Nevada, Calif., where it is an important range grass.

4. Calamagrostis tweédyi (Scribn.) Scribn. (Fig. 426.) Culms erect, 1 to 1.5 m. tall, smooth, with short rhizomes; sheaths smooth, the lower becoming fibrous; blades flat, somewhat scabrous, the cauline 5 to 15 cm. long, as much as 1 cm. wide, those of the innovations narrower and longer; panicle oblong, rather compact, or interrupted below, about 10 cm. long; glumes abruptly acuminate, purple-tinged, 6 to 7 mm. long; lemma about as long as the glumes, the awn exserted about 5 mm., the callus hairs scant, scarcely 1 mm. long; rachilla pilose, 2 mm. long. ♃ —Moist open alpine slopes, Idaho and Cleland Counties, Idaho, and Kittitas County and Cascade Mountain, Wash.

5. Calamagrostis foliósa Kearney. (Fig. 427.) Culms tufted, erect, 30 to 60 cm. tall; leaves numerous, crowded toward the base, the sheaths overlapping, the blades involute, firm, smooth, nearly as long as the culm; panicle pale, dense, spikelike, 5 to 12 cm. long; glumes about 1 cm. long, acuminate; lemma 5 to 7 mm. long, acuminate, the apex with 4 setaceous teeth, the awn from near base, geniculate, about 8 mm. long above the bend, the callus hairs numerous, 3 mm. long; rachilla pilose, nearly as long as lemma. ♃ —Humboldt and Mendocino Counties, Calif.

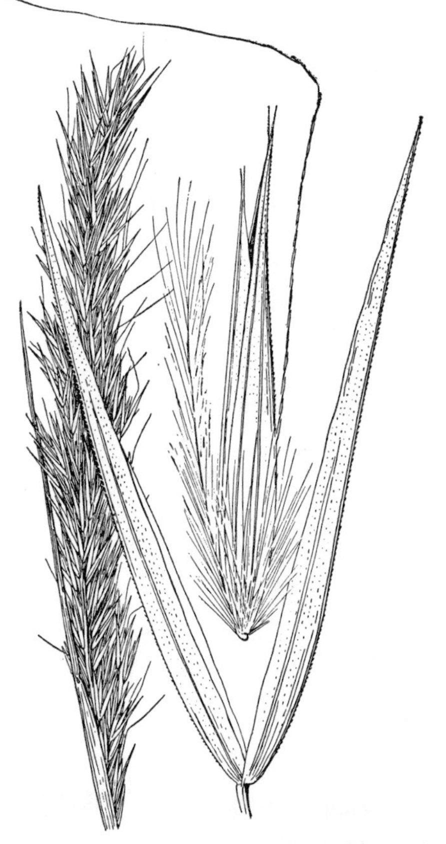

FIGURE 427.—*Calamagrostis foliosa*. Panicle, × 1; glumes and floret, × 10. (Davy 6602, Calif.)

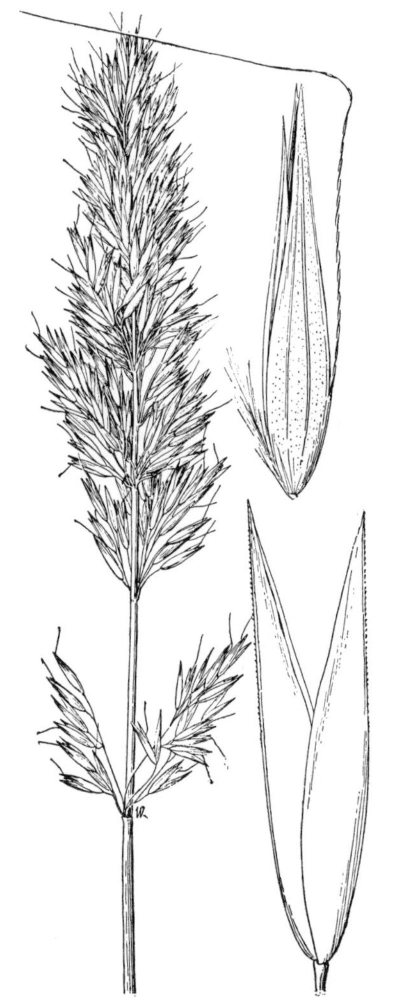

FIGURE 426.—*Calamagrostis tweedyi*. Panicle, × 1; glumes and floret, × 10. (Vasey, Wash.)

6. Calamagrostis purpuráscens R. Br. PURPLE REEDGRASS. (Fig. 428.) Culms tufted, sometimes with short rhizomes, erect, 40 to 60 cm. or even 100 cm. tall; sheaths usually scabrous, the old sheaths persistent and fibrous; blades 2 to 4 mm. wide, flat or more or less involute, rather thick, scabrous; panicle dense, usually pinkish or purplish, spikelike, 5 to 12 cm. long, rarely longer; glumes 6 to 8 mm. long, scabrous; lemma nearly as long as glumes, the apex with 4 setaceous teeth, the awn from near base, finally geniculate, exserted about 2 mm.; hairs of callus and rachilla about one-

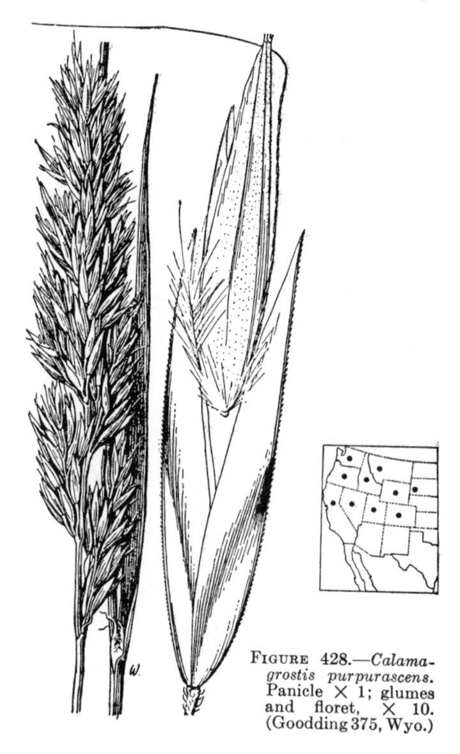

FIGURE 428.—*Calamagrostis purpurascens.* Panicle × 1; glumes and floret, × 10. (Goodding 375, Wyo.)

third as long as the lemma. ♃ (*C. vaseyi* Beal.)—Rocks and cliffs, Greenland to Alaska, south to Quebec, South Dakota (Black Hills), Colorado, and California.

7. Calamagrostis montanénsis Scribn. PLAINS REEDGRASS. (Fig. 429.) Culms stiffly erect, scabrous below the panicle, usually 20 to 40 cm. tall, sometimes taller, with slender creeping rhizomes; lower sheaths rather papery, smooth; blades erect, mostly less than 2 mm. wide, more or less involute, scabrous, sharp-pointed; panicle dense, erect, more or less interrupted, usually pale, 5 to 10 cm. long; spikelets 4 to 5 mm. long, the pedicels very scabrous; glumes acuminate, scabrous; lemma nearly as long as the glumes, finely 4-toothed, the awn attached about 1 mm. above base, about equaling the lemma, slightly geniculate and protruding from side of glumes; palea nearly as long as the lemma; hairs of callus and rachilla rather abundant, about half as long as the lemma. ♃ —Plains and dry open ground, Manitoba to Alberta, south to Minnesota, Wyoming, Colorado, and Idaho.

8. Calamagrostis cáinii Hitchc. (Fig. 430.) Culms 30 to 60 cm. tall, slender, erect; blades as much as 35 cm. long, 1 to 2 mm. wide, flat or loosely involute, attenuate, scabrous above; panicles 6 to 10 cm. long, pale or purple-tinged, the slender ascending branches 1 to 2 cm. long, few-flowered; glumes narrow, acuminate, 5 to 6 mm. long; lemma acuminate or minutely dentate, the nerves sometimes extending into short mucros, the callus hairs about 1 mm. long; awn attached about 1 mm. above the base, geniculate, a little longer than the glumes; rachilla very short, the hairs 1 to 2 mm. long. ♃ —Shrubby summit and open slopes of Mount LeConte, above 5,000 feet, Tenn.

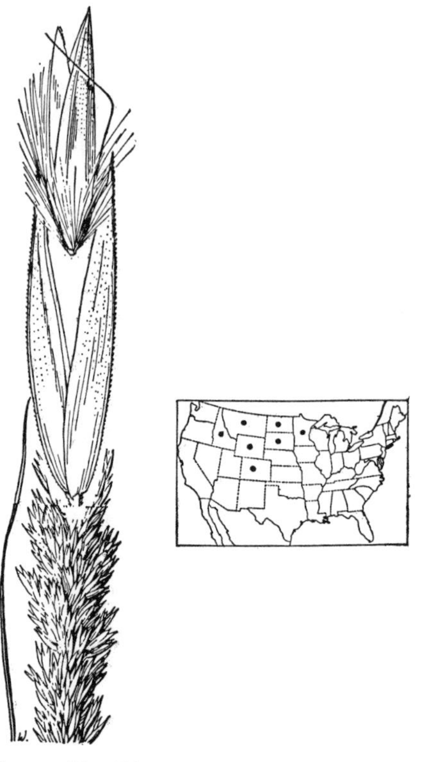

FIGURE 429.—*Calamagrostis montanensis.* Panicle, × 1; glumes and floret, × 10. (Scribner 363, Mont.)

9. Calamagrostis rubéscens Buckl. PINEGRASS. (Fig. 431.) Culms slender, tufted, 60 to 100 cm. tall, with creeping rhizomes; sheaths smooth, but pubescent on the collar, sometimes obscurely so; blades erect, 2 to 4 mm. wide, flat or somewhat involute, scabrous; panicle narrow, spikelike or somewhat loose or interrupted, pale or purple, 7 to 15 cm. long; glumes 4 to 5 mm. long, narrow, acuminate; lemma pale, thin, about as long as glumes, smooth, the nerves obscure, the awn from near base, geniculate, exserted from side of glumes, 1 to 2 mm. long above the bend, the callus hairs scant, about one-third as long as the lemma; rachilla 1 mm. long, the sparse hairs extending to 2 mm. ♃ —Open pine woods, prairies, and banks, British Columbia, south to northern Colorado and central California. A valuable range grass. A large form with dense lobed panicle has been differentiated as *C. cusickii* Vasey.

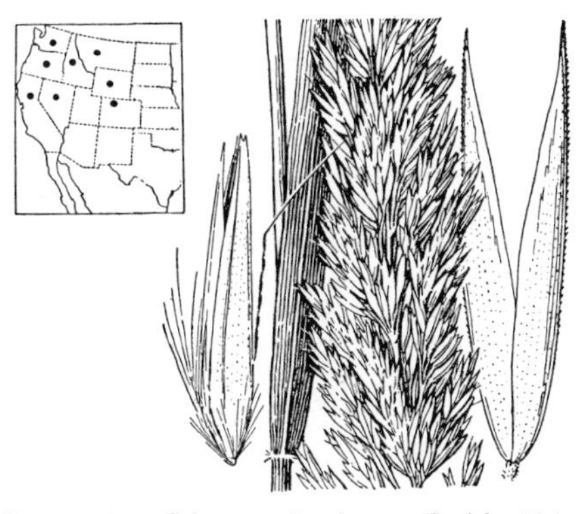

FIGURE 431.—*Calamagrostis rubescens*. Panicle, × 1; glumes and floret, × 10. (Sandberg and Leiberg Wash.)

FIGURE 430.—*Calamagrostis cainii*. Panicle, × 1; glumes and floret, × 10. (Underwood 1210, Tenn.)

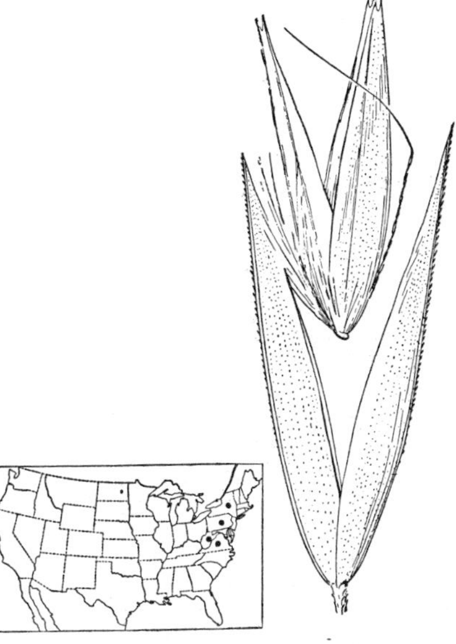

FIGURE 432.—*Calamagrostis porteri*. Glumes and floret, × 10. (Porter, Pa.)

10. Calamagrostis portéri A. Gray. (Fig. 432.) Culms slender, 60 to 120 cm. tall, with slender rhizomes; sheaths pubescent on the collar; blades flat, spreading, lax, 4 to 8 mm. wide; panicle narrow but rather loose, erect or somewhat nodding, 10 to 15

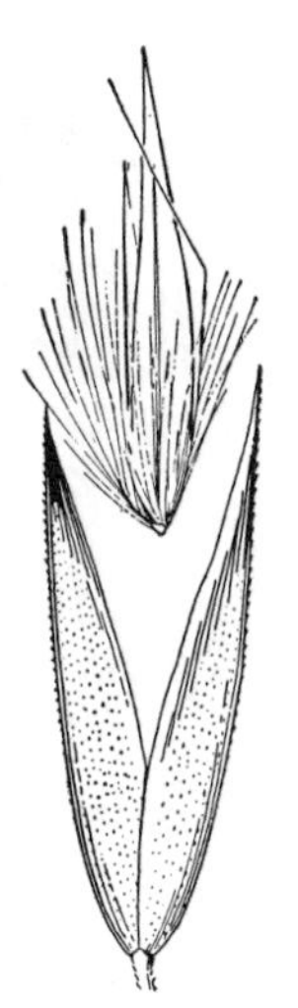

FIGURE 433.—*Calamagrostis perplexa.* Glumes and floret, × 10. (Metcalf 5668, N. Y.)

cm. long; glumes 4 to 6 mm. long, scaberulous; lemma slightly shorter than the glumes, toothed at apex, the awn from near base, about as long as the lemma, bent and protruding from side of glumes; palea about as long as the lemma; callus hairs in tufts at the sides, rather scant, nearly half as long as the lemma; rachilla hairs scant, extending to about 3 mm. ♃ —Dry rocky soil, New York, Pennsylvania, Virginia (Luray), and West Virginia. Apparently flowering irregularly or rarely.

11. Calamagrostis perpléxa Scribn. (Fig. 433.) Culms slender, 90 to 100 cm. tall, with slender rhizomes; lower sheaths overlapping and with reduced blades, the others shorter than the internodes, minutely scaberulous, tomentose at the sides of the collar; ligule 3 to 5 mm. long; blades (except the lower) 15 to 35 cm. long, 3 to 6 mm. wide, scabrous; panicle 10 to 15 cm. long, 2 to 3 cm. wide, many-flowered but rather loose, the axis smooth except toward the apex; spikelets 3.5 to 4 mm. long, the glumes nearly equal, acuminate, scaberulous; lemma 3.5 mm. long, acuminate, the awn from near the base, about as long as the lemma; palea and callus hairs about three-fourths as long as the lemma, the hairs in 2 rather dense

FIGURE 434.—*Calamagrostis insperata.* Panicle, × 1; glumes and floret, × 10. (Type.)

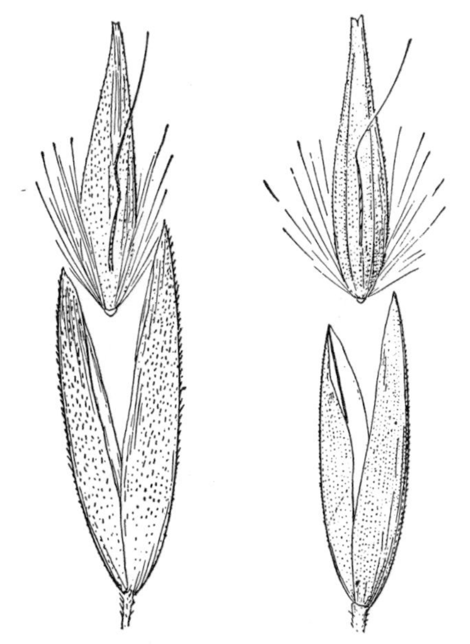

FIGURE 435.—*Calamagrostis lacustris.* Glumes and floret, × 10. (Type.)

FIGURE 436.—*Calamagrostis fernaldii.* Glumes and floret, × 10. (Fernald 427, Maine.)

tufts at the sides, the hairs of the rachilla scarcely as long, scant. ♃ —Wet rocks, New York (Thatcher's Pinnacle, near Ithaca, type locality).

12. Calamagrostis insperáta Swallen. (Fig. 434.) Culms 85 to 95 cm. tall, erect from slender creeping rhizomes; sheaths glabrous on the collar; ligule 5 mm. long; blades flat, rather thin, 4 to 8 mm. wide, 10 to 22 cm. long, acuminate, glabrous, the margins scabrous; panicles 12 to 14 cm. long, the branches narrowly ascending, at least some of them naked at the base; spikelets 5 to 5.5 mm. long; lemma 4 mm. long, scaberulous on the keel, the callus hairs in tufts at the sides, rather dense, some of them half to three-fourths as long as the lemma; rachilla 0.5 mm. long, the hairs as much as 2 mm. long; awn from about one-fourth above the base, about as long as the lemma, geniculate. ♃ —Known only from Ofer Hollow, Jackson County, Ohio.

13. Calamagrostis lacústris (Kearn.) Nash. (Fig. 435.) Culms rather slender from short rhizomes, 35 to 100 cm. tall; sheaths and blades scabrous, the blades firm, 2 to 4 mm. wide; panicle 8 to 15 cm. long, 1 to 2.5 cm. wide, relatively dense, or with one of the lower fascicle of branches naked at base, the axis scabrous; spikelets 4 to 4.5 mm. long; glumes firm, rather broad, scabrous; lemma about 3.5 mm. long, scabrous, the awn from near the base, about as long as the lemma, geniculate; callus hairs about half to two-thirds as long as the lemma, in 2 tufts at the sides; rachilla minute, its hairs exceeding those of the callus. ♃ —Mossy rocks, marshy meadows, and sandy shores, Ontario, Vermont, eastern New York, northern Michigan, and eastern Minnesota.

14. Calamagrostis fernáldii Louis-Marie. (Fig. 436.) Culms loosely tufted, about 80 cm. tall; sheaths glabrous on the collar; blades elongate, 2 to 4 mm. wide, scabrous on both surfaces; panicle 8 to 9.5 cm. long, narrow, pale; glumes 3.5 to 4 mm. long; lemma 3.2 to 3.6 mm. long, scabrous, minutely toothed, the awn from near the base, scarcely as long as the lemma, the palea about two-thirds as long; callus hairs in tufts at the sides, half to two-thirds as long as the lemma; rachilla hairs two-thirds to three-fourths as long as the lemma. ♃ —Wet cliffs, only known from Boarstone Mountain, Piscataquis County, Maine.

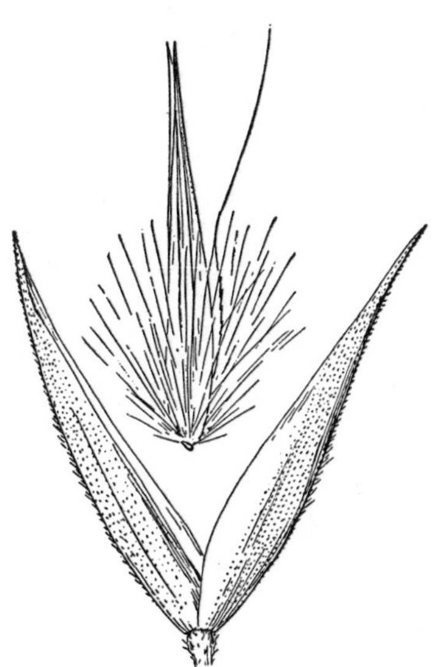

FIGURE 437.—*Calamagrostis nubila.* Glumes and floret, × 10. (Boott, N. H.)

15. Calamagrostis núbila Louis-Marie. (Fig. 437.) Culms tufted, erect, 55 cm. tall; sheaths mostly overlapping, scaberulous toward the summit; ligule 3 to 5 mm. long; blades flat, 12 to 18 cm. long, 4 to 5 mm. wide, long-attenuate, scabrous on both surfaces, the upper exceeding the inflorescence; panicle pale, 13 to 14 cm. long, about 4 cm. wide, many-flowered but rather loose, probably nodding, the axis and branches flexuous, scabrous; spikelets on short scabrous pedicels; glumes 4.5 to 5.2 mm. long, scabrous, the second indistinctly 3-nerved; lemma 4.5 mm. long, toothed at the acuminate apex, the awn from near base, about as long as the lemma, bent and protruding from side of glumes; palea about two-thirds as long as the lemma; callus and rachilla hairs rather copious, three-fourths to nearly as long as the lemma. ♃ —Only known from Lake of the Clouds, Mount Washington, N.H.

16. Calamagrostis pickeríngii A. Gray. (Fig. 438.) Culms solitary or few in tufts, rather rigid, scabrous below the panicle, 30 to 60 cm. tall, with creeping rhizomes; blades erect, flat, 4 to 5 mm. wide; panicle purplish, erect, contracted and rather dense, 7 to 12 cm. long; glumes acute, about 4 to 4.5 mm. long; lemma a little shorter than the glumes, scaberulous, narrowed to an obtuse point, the awn attached about 1 mm. above the base, about as long as the lemma, slightly bent and protruding somewhat from the side of the glumes; callus hairs in 2 tufts, scant, about 0.5 mm. long; rachilla about 1 mm. long, the hairs short, rather scant. ♃ —Bogs, wet meadows, and sandy beaches, Newfoundland and Labrador to the mountains of Massachusetts and New York; Isle Royale, Mich. Slender plants with slightly smaller spikelets have been differentiated as *C. pickeringii* var. *debilis* (Kearney) Fern. and Wieg.

FIGURE 438.—*Calamagrostis pickeringii*. Panicle, × 1; glumes and floret, × 10. (Hubbard 634, Mass.)

17. Calamagrostis nutkaénsis (Presl) Steud. PACIFIC REEDGRASS. (Fig. 439.) Culms stout, 1 to 1.5 m. tall with short rhizomes (not usually present in herbarium specimens); ligule 3 to 8 mm. long; blades elongate, 6 to 12 mm. wide, flat, becoming involute, gradually narrowed into a long point, scabrous; panicle usually purplish, narrow, rather loose, 15 to 30 cm. long, the branches rather stiffly ascending; glumes 5 to 7 mm. long, acuminate; lemma about 4 mm. long, indistinctly nerved, the awn rather stout, from near the base, slightly geniculate, about equaling the lemma or shorter; hairs of callus and rachilla scarcely half as long ♃ —Along the coast in moist soil or wet wooded hills, from Alaska to central California.

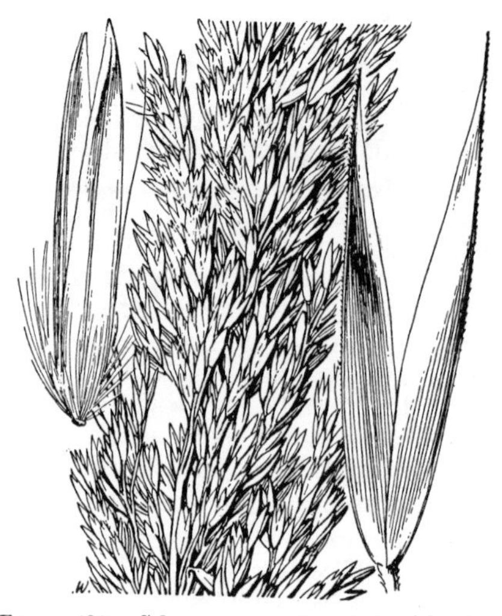

FIGURE 439.—*Calamagrostis nutkaensis*. Panicle, × 1; glumes and floret, × 10. (Hitchcock 23576, Oreg.)

18. Calamagrostis dénsa Vasey. CUYAMACA REEDGRASS. (Fig. 440.) Culms rather stout, densely tufted, smooth or scabrous just below the panicle, mostly more than 1 m. tall, with rather stout rhizomes; sheaths slightly scabrous; ligule 3 to 5 mm. long; blades flat, or subinvolute, scabrous, 15 to 25 cm. long, 3 to 8 mm. wide, the uppermost shorter; panicle spikelike, dense, pale, 10 to 15 cm. long; glumes 4.5 to 5 mm. long, acuminate, scaberulous; lemma 3.5 to 4 mm. long, the awn bent, about as long as the lemma, more or less exserted at the side, the hairs of callus and ra-

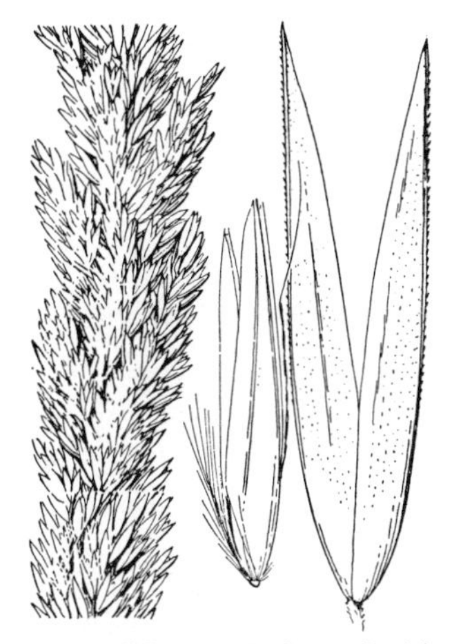

FIGURE 440.—*Calamagrostis densa.* Panicle, × 1; glumes and floret, × 10. (Hitchcock 13163, Calif.)

chilla scant, about 1 mm. long. ♃ —Dry hills, among shrubs, mountains east of San Diego, Calif.

19. Calamagrostis koelerioídes Vasey. (Fig. 441.) Differs from *C. densa* in the more slender culms and (often purplish) panicles; lemma nearly as long as the glumes. ♃ —Dry hills, banks, and meadows, Wyoming to Washington, south to southern California. Possibly a form of *C. densa.*

20. Calamagrostis scribnéri Beal. SCRIBNER REEDGRASS. (Fig. 442.) Culms tufted, with numerous creeping rhizomes, slender, 60 to 100 cm. tall; lower sheaths loose, thin, upper scabrous, retrorsely pubescent on the collar; ligule about 5 mm. long; blades thin, elongate, 4 to 7 mm. wide, scabrous; panicle pale or purplish, narrow but rather lax, 10 to 15 cm. long (rarely longer); glumes about 4 mm. long, acuminate; lemma a little shorter than the glumes, sharply toothed, the awn about as long as the glumes or a little longer, feebly bent, the callus hairs about half as long as the lemma; rachilla minute, its hairs nearly as long as the lemma. ♃ —Moist meadows, Montana and Washington to New Mexico; infrequent.

21. Calamagrostis canadénsis (Michx.) Beauv. BLUEJOINT. (Fig. 443, *A.*) Culms suberect, tufted, 60 to 150 cm. tall, with numerous creeping rhizomes; sheaths glabrous or rarely obscurely pubescent; blades numerous, elongate, flat, rather lax, scabrous, 4 to 8 mm. wide; panicle nodding, from narrow and rather dense to loose and relatively open, especially at base, 10 to 25 cm. long; glumes usually 3 to 4 mm. long, smooth or more commonly scabrous, acute to acuminate; lemma nearly as

FIGURE 441.—*Calamagrostis koelerioides.* Glumes and floret, × 10. (Hitchcock 23558, Oreg.)

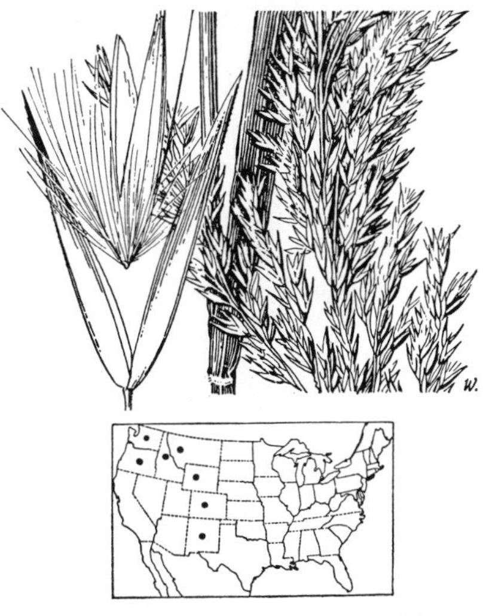

FIGURE 442.—*Calamagrostis scribneri.* Panicle, × 1; glumes and floret, × 10. (Rydberg 3083, Mont.)

FIGURE 443.—*A*, *Calamagrostis canadensis*. Plant, × ½; glumes and floret, × 10. (Chase 5077, Mont.) *B*, Var. *scabra*, × 10. (Pringle, N. H.) *C*, Var. *macouniana*, × 10. (Pammel 891, Minn.)

long as the glumes, smooth, thin in texture, the awn delicate, straight, attached just below the middle and extending to or slightly beyond its tip, the callus hairs abundant, about as long as lemma; rachilla delicate, sparsely long-pilose. ♃ —Marshes wet places, open woods, and meadows, Greenland to Alaska, south to West Virginia and North Carolina (Roan Mountain), Missouri, Kansas, to New Mexico and California. A widely distributed and exceedingly variable species. Characters used to differentiate the many proposed varieties are not correlated in the larger proportion of specimens. The panicle varies in density and the glumes in size and scabridity. The following varieties are recognizable but are connected with the species by many intergrading specimens.

Calamagrostis canadensis var. scábra (Presl) Hitchc. (Fig. 443, *B.*) Differing in having spikelets 4.5 to 6 mm. long, the glumes rather firm, hispidly short-ciliate on the keel, strongly scabrous otherwise, but the greater scabridity not constant. ♃ —Mountains of New England, New York, and northward, and along the Pacific coast from Washington to Alaska. This form has been referred to *C. langsdorfii* (Link) Trin., which proves to be an Old World species not found in America.

Calamagrostis canadensis var. macouniána (Vasey) Stebbins. (Fig. 443, *C.*) Differing from *C. canadensis* in the smaller spikelets, about 2 mm. long. Scarcely a distinct variety. ♃ —Saskatchewan (*Macoun* 44, 45), Minnesota (Bemidji), South Dakota (Chamberlain, Redfield), Iowa, Nebraska (Central City), Missouri (Lake City, Little Blue), Montana (Manhattan), Yellowstone Park, Washington (Spokane County), Oregon (Crook County).

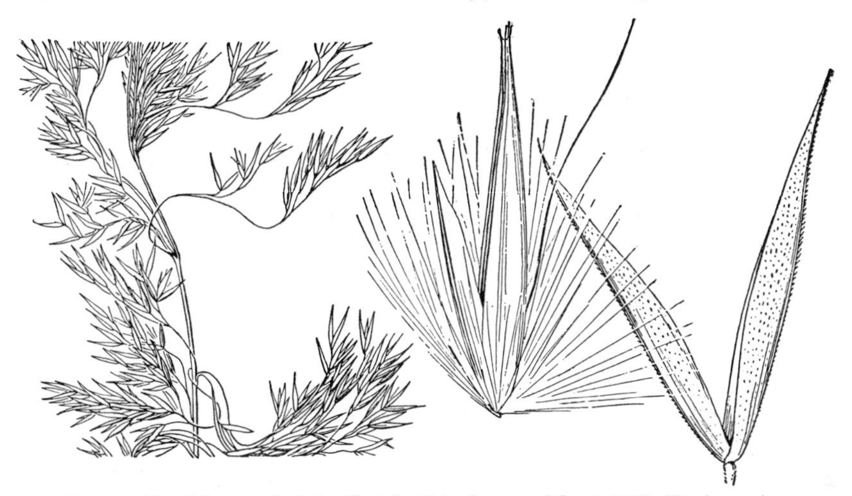

Figure 444.—*Calamagrostis lactea.* Panicle, × 1; glumes and floret, × 10. (Dupl. type.)

22. Calamagrostis láctea Beal. (Fig. 444.) Culms ascending, 80 to 150 cm. tall, weak, the nodes subgeniculate, with a short knotty rhizome; sheaths scaberulous; ligule rather firm, 3 to 5 mm. long; blades elongate, flat, lax, scabrous, 6 to 12 mm. wide; panicle pale, narrowly pyramidal, 12 to 20 cm. long, loosely flowered; glumes 5 to 6 mm. long, scabrous, acuminate; lemma shorter than the glumes, scabrous, the apex setaceous-toothed, the awn attached near the base, about equaling the lemma, weakly geniculate; palea slightly exceeding the lemma, the callus hairs about half as long; rachilla minute, sparsely pilose. ♃

—Mountain slopes, Washington to California; apparently rare.

23. Calamagrostis cinnoídes (Muhl.) Barton. (Fig. 445.) Glaucous; culms rather stout, erect, 80 to 150 cm. tall, with slender rhizomes readily broken off; sheaths and blades very scabrous, sometimes sparsely hirsute, the blades flat, 5 to 10 mm. wide; panicle erect, dense, more or less lobed (somewhat open at anthesis), 8 to 20 cm. long, purple-tinged; glumes 6 to 7 mm. long, scabrous, long-acuminate or awn-pointed; lemma firm, acuminate, scabrous, shorter than the glumes, the awn attached about one-fourth below the tip, not much exceeding the lemma, the callus hairs copious, about two-thirds as long; rachilla about 1 mm. long, glabrous below, with a brush of long white hairs at the tip about equaling the lemma. ♃ —Bogs and moist ground, Maine to New York, south to Alabama and Louisiana.

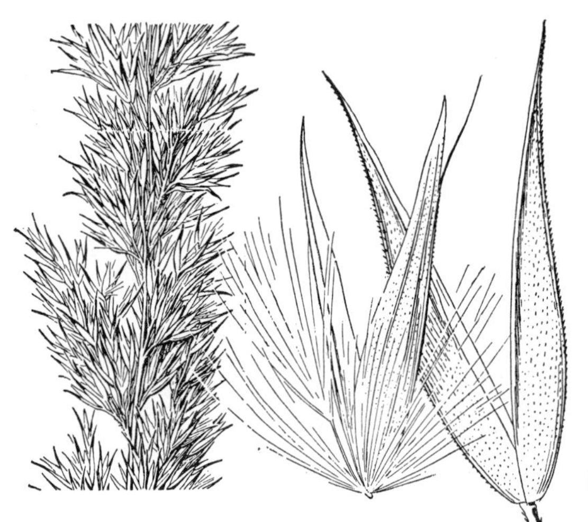

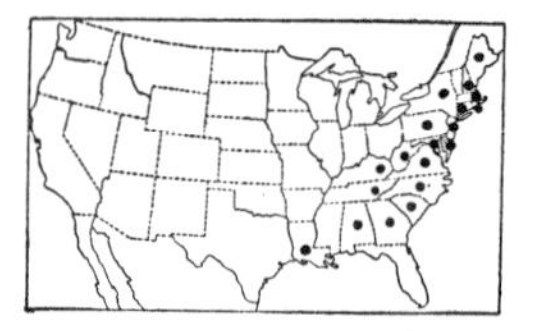

FIGURE 445.—*Calamagrostis cinnoides.* Panicle, × 1; glumes and floret, × 10. (Chase 7518, Md.)

24. Calamagrostis scopulórum Jones. (Fig. 446.) Pale, glaucous; culms erect, 50 to 80 cm. tall, with short rhizomes; blades elongate, flat, scabrous, 3 to 7 mm. wide; panicle pale to purplish, contracted, sometimes spikelike, 8 to 15 cm. long; glumes 4 to 6 mm. long, somewhat scabrous, acute or acuminate, not awn-pointed; lemma about as long as the glumes, minutely pilose, the awn attached above the middle, straight, about as long as the lemma, the callus hairs about two-thirds as long; rachilla rather sparsely long-pilose, especially on the upper part. ♃ —Moist soil in gulches, Montana, Wyoming (Wild Cat Peak), Colorado, Utah, New Mexico, and Arizona.

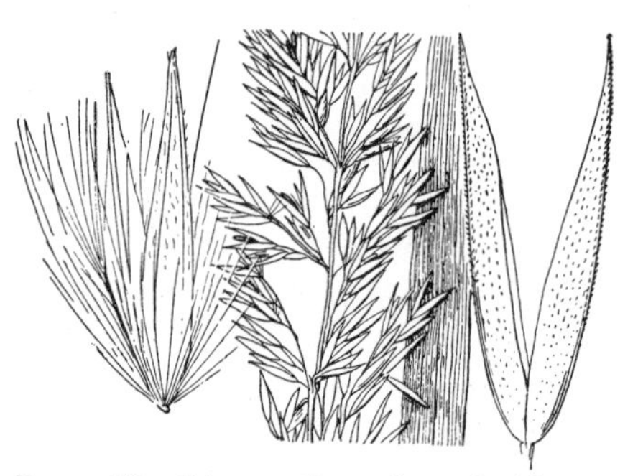

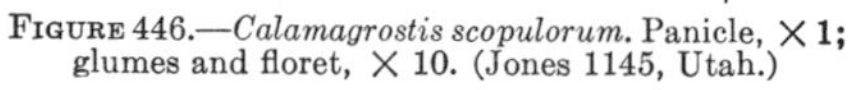

FIGURE 446.—*Calamagrostis scopulorum.* Panicle, × 1; glumes and floret, × 10. (Jones 1145, Utah.)

25. Calamagrostis inexpánsa A. Gray. NORTHERN REEDGRASS. (Fig. 447.) Culms tufted, 40 to 120 cm. tall, with rather slender rhizomes, often scabrous below the panicle; sheaths smooth, or somewhat scabrous, the basal ones numerous, withering but persistent; ligule 4 to 6 mm. long; blades firm, rather rigid, flat or loosely involute, very scabrous, 2 to 4 mm. wide; panicle narrow, dense, the branches mostly erect and spikelet-bearing from the base; 5 to 15 cm. long; glumes 3 to 4 mm. long, abruptly acuminate, scaberulous; lemma as long as glumes, scabrous, the awn attached about the middle, straight or nearly so, about as long as glumes, the callus

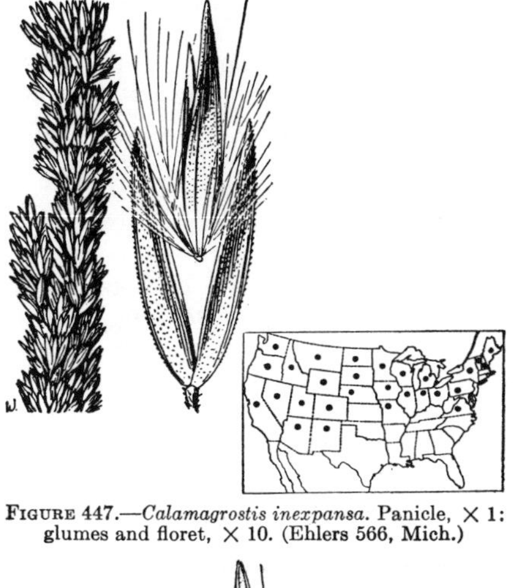

FIGURE 447.—*Calamagrostis inexpansa*. Panicle, × 1: glumes and floret, × 10. (Ehlers 566, Mich.)

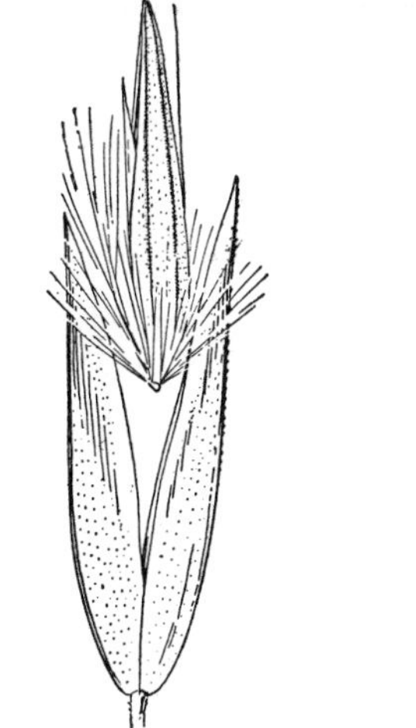

FIGURE 448.—*Calamagrostis californica*. Glumes and floret, × 10. (Type.)

hairs half to three-fourths as long; rachilla 0.5 mm. long, some of the hairs reaching to tip of lemma. ♃ —Meadows, marshes, and wet places, Greenland to Alaska, south to Maine, Virginia (Mountain Lake), Washington, New Mexico, and California. CALAMAGROSTIS INEXPANSA var. NÓVAE-ÁNGLIAE Stebbins. Panicle more loosely flowered, the longer branches naked below. ♃ —Wet granite ledges, Maine to Vermont. CALAMAGROSTIS INEXPANSA var. BARBULÁTA Kearney. Culms robust, puberulent below the nodes; collar of sheaths

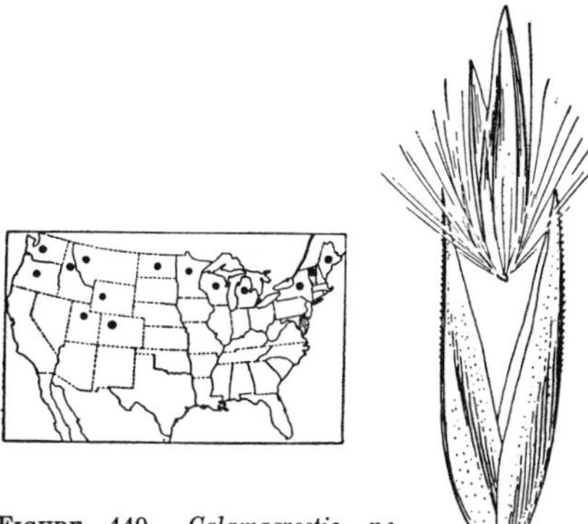

FIGURE 449.—*Calamagrostis neglecta*. Glumes and floret, × 10. (Fernald 182, Maine.)

puberulent; awn minute or obsolete, callus hairs nearly as long as the lemma. ♃ —Known only from Mason County, Wash.

26. Calamagrostis califórnica Kearney. (Fig. 448.) Related to *C. inexpansa*, but foliage softer and panicle longer and looser; ligule 2 to 3 mm. long; blades elongate, 1 to 4 mm. wide, mostly involute, scabrous on the upper surface, smooth beneath; panicle 18 to 22 cm. long, the densely flowered branches in rather distant fascicles, some of them naked at base for 1 to 2.5 cm., the axis glabrous; spikelets 3.9 to 4.2 mm. long; glumes acuminate, scabrous; lemma nearly as long as the glumes, strongly nerved, scabrous, the awn attached a little below the middle, straight, scarcely equaling the lemma, the callus hairs scarcely half as long as the lemma, the palea and the hairs of the rachilla about three-fourths as long. ♃ —Only known from a single collection from the Sierra Nevada, particular locality not known.

27. Calamagrostis neglécta (Ehrh.) Gaertn. Mey. and Schreb. (Fig. 449.) Resembling *C. inexpansa*, on the average smaller; ligule 1 to 3 mm. long; blades smooth or nearly so, lax and soft, narrow, often filiform; panicles on the average smaller; glumes rather thinner in texture, often smooth ♃ —Marshes, sandy shores, and wet places, Greenland to Alaska, south to Maine, Vermont, New York, Michigan to Washington, Colorado, and Oregon; northern Eurasia.

FIGURE 450.—*Calamagrostis crassiglumis.* Panicle, × 1; glumes and floret, × 10. (Suksdorf 1024, Wash.)

28. Calamagrostis crassiglúmis Thurb. (Fig. 450.) Culms rather rigid, 15 to 40 cm. tall, with short rhizomes; lower sheaths overlapping, somewhat papery; blades flat, or somewhat involute, smooth, firm, about 4 to 5 mm. wide; panicle narrow, dense, spikelike, 2 to 5 cm. long, dull purple; glumes 3 to 4 mm. long, ovate, rather abruptly acuminate, purple, scaberulous, firm or almost indurate; lemma about as long as glumes, broad, obtuse or abruptly pointed, the awn attached about the middle, straight, about as long as lemma, the callus hairs abundant, about 3 mm. long; rachilla 1 mm. long, the hairs reaching to apex of lemma. ♃ —Swampy soil, Vancouver Island, Washington (Whatcom Lake), California (Mendocino County). A rare species allied to *C. inexpansa* and *C. neglecta.*

29. Calamagrostis epigeíos (L.) Roth. (Fig. 451.) Culms 1 to 1.5 m. tall, with extensively creeping rhizomes; ligule about 4 mm. long, rather firm; blades elongate, 4 to 8, sometimes to 13 mm. wide, scabrous; panicle pale, erect, narrow, rather dense, 25 to 35 cm. long; spikelets crowded; glumes subequal, mostly 5 to 6 mm., sometimes to 8 mm., long, narrowly lanceolate, attenuate; lemma scarcely half as long as the glumes, 2-toothed at the apex, the awn mostly from below the middle, delicate, often obscure, slightly bent, about as long as

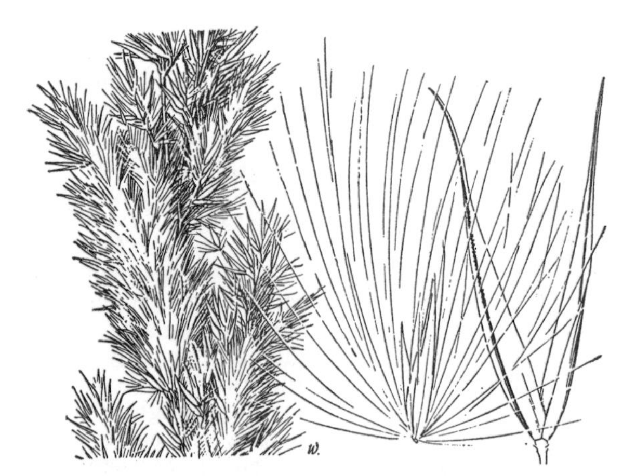

FIGURE 451.—*Calamagrostis epigeios.* Panicle, × 1; glumes and floret, × 10. (Fernald 757, Mass.)

the lemma to equaling the glumes; callus hairs rather copious, about equaling the glumes; rachilla obsolete. ♃ —Sandy woods, salt marshes, fields, and waste ground, near the coast of Massachusetts, Long Island and Saratoga County, N. Y., Montgomery County, Pa., North Dakota to Iowa and Kansas; becoming a weed. Introduced from Eurasia.

68. AMMÓPHILA Host. BEACHGRASS

Spikelets 1-flowered, compressed, the rachilla disarticulating above the glumes, produced beyond the palea as a short bristle, hairy above; glumes about equal, chartaceous; lemma similar to and a little shorter than the glumes, the callus bearded; palea nearly as long as the lemma. Tough, rather coarse, erect perennials, with hard, scaly, creeping rhizomes, long, tough, involute blades, and pale, dense spikelike panicles. Type species, *Ammophila arenaria*. Named from the Greek *ammos*, sand, and *philos*, loving, alluding to the habitat.

The species of *Ammophila* are important sand-binding grasses, *A. arenaria* being used in northern Europe to hold the barrier dunes along the coast. In this country it has been tried with success on Cape Cod and at Golden Gate Park, San Francisco. Called also marram, psamma, and sea sandreed.

Ligule thin, 10 to 30 mm. long .... 2. A. ARENARIA.
Ligule firm, 1 to 3 mm. long .... 1. A. BREVILIGULATA.

1. Ammophila breviliguláta Fernald. AMERICAN BEACHGRASS. (Fig. 452.) Culms in tufts, commonly 70 to 100 cm. tall with deep strong extensively creeping rhizomes, the base of the culms clothed with numerous broad overlapping sheaths; ligule firm, 1 to 3 mm. long; blades elongate, firm, soon involute, curved forward past the culm, the scaberulous upper surface downward; panicle pale, 15 to 30 cm. long, nearly cylindrical; spikelets 11 to 14 mm. long; glumes scaberulous, the first 1-nerved, the second 3-nerved; lemma scabrous, the callus hairs about 2 mm. long, the rachilla about 3 mm. long. ♃ —Sand dunes along the coast from Newfoundland to North Carolina, and on the shores of the Great Lakes from Lake Ontario to Lake Superior and Lake Michigan.

2. Ammophila arenária (L.) Link. EUROPEAN BEACHGRASS. (Fig. 453.) Like the preceding in habit, the culms sometimes thicker; ligule thin, 1 to 3 cm. long; panicle often thicker in the middle, tapering to the summit; spikelets 1.2 to 1.5 cm. long; callus hairs about 3 mm. long, the rachilla 2 mm. long. ♃ —Sand dunes along the coast from San Francisco to Washington. Introduced as a sand binder in the vicinity of San Francisco and now established at several places to the north; coast of Europe.

69. CALAMOVÍLFA Hack.

Spikelets 1-flowered, the rachilla disarticulating above the glumes, not prolonged behind the palea; glumes unequal, chartaceous, 1-nerved, acute; lemma a little longer than the second glume, chartaceous, 1-nerved, awnless, glabrous or pubescent, the callus bearded; palea about as long as the lemma. Rigid, usually tall perennials, with narrow or open panicles, some species with creeping rhizomes. Type species, *Calamovilfa brevipilis*. Name from Greek *kalamos*, reed, and *Vilfa*, a genus of grasses. *Calamovilfa longifolia* is of some value for forage, but is rather coarse and woody; a variety of this and also *C. gigantea* are inland sand binders.

Rhizomes short and thick.
Panicle narrow, contracted .... 1. C. CURTISSII.

Panicle subpyramidal, rather open .... 2. C. BREVIPILIS.
Rhizomes extensively creeping.
Lemma glabrous (except for the callus hairs) .... 3. C. LONGIFOLIA.
Lemma villous on the back above the callus hairs .... 4. C. GIGANTEA.

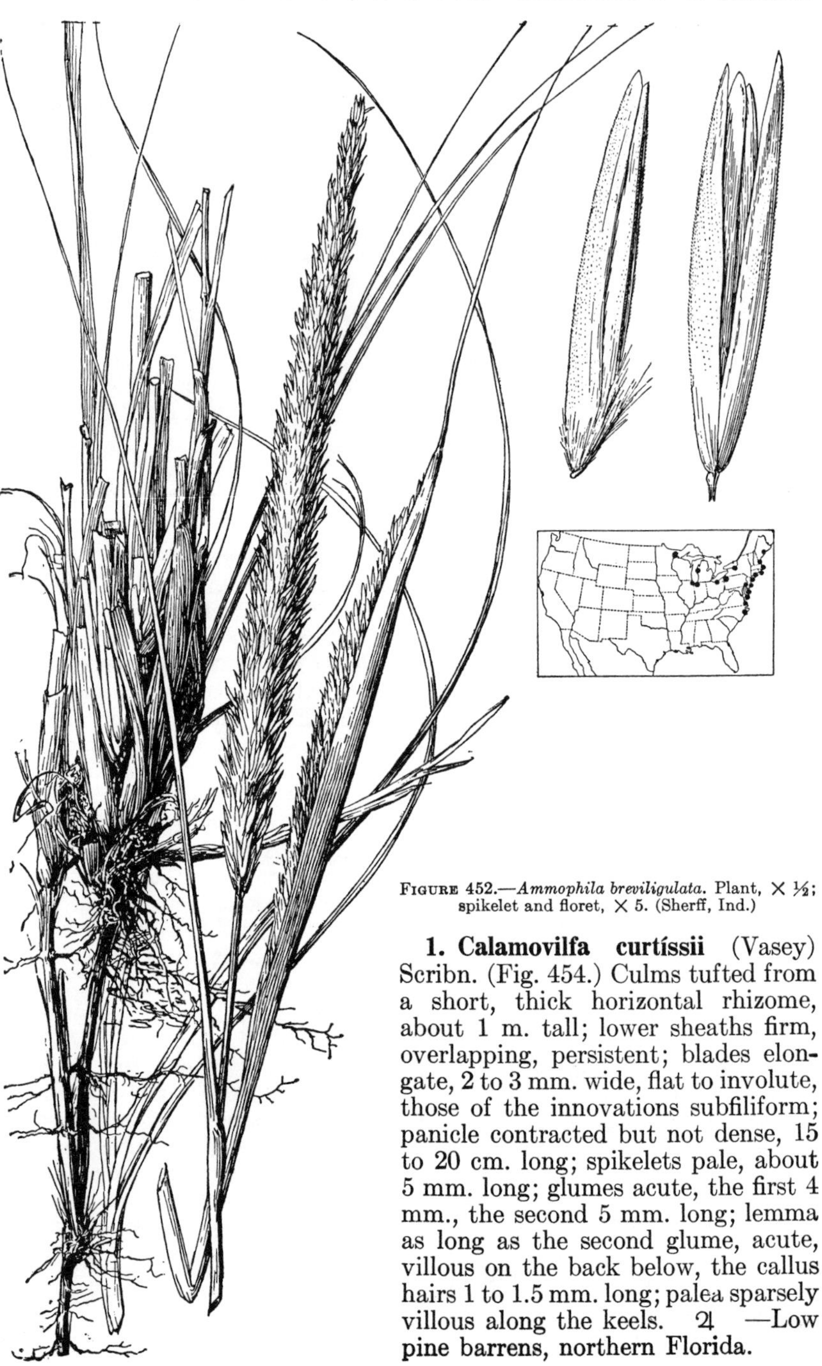

FIGURE 452.—*Ammophila breviligulata*. Plant, × ½; spikelet and floret, × 5. (Sherff, Ind.)

1. Calamovilfa curtíssii (Vasey) Scribn. (Fig. 454.) Culms tufted from a short, thick horizontal rhizome, about 1 m. tall; lower sheaths firm, overlapping, persistent; blades elongate, 2 to 3 mm. wide, flat to involute, those of the innovations subfiliform; panicle contracted but not dense, 15 to 20 cm. long; spikelets pale, about 5 mm. long; glumes acute, the first 4 mm., the second 5 mm. long; lemma as long as the second glume, acute, villous on the back below, the callus hairs 1 to 1.5 mm. long; palea sparsely villous along the keels. ♃ —**Low pine barrens, northern Florida.**

2. Calamovilfa brevípilis (Torr.) Scribn. (Fig. 455.) Culms solitary or few, compressed, 60 to 120 cm. tall, the base as in *C. curtissii;* blades elongate, 2 to 3 mm. wide, flat to subinvolute; panicle subpyramidal, rather open, 10 to 25 cm. long, the branches ascending, flexuous, naked below; pedicels sparsely pilose at the summit; spikelets brownish, 5 to 6 mm. long; glumes acuminate, the first 2 to 2.5 mm. long, the second about 4 mm. long; lemma villous on the back below, the callus hairs 1.5 mm. long; palea exceeding the lemma, villous on the back. ♃ —Marshes and river banks, New Jersey.

CALAMOVILFA BREVIPILIS var. CÁLVIPES Fernald. Very similar to the species; panicles looser, more open; pedicels glabrous; spikelets 4 to 5 mm. long, the lemma and palea about equal. ♃ —Sphagnous bog, Greensville County, Va.

FIGURE 454.—*Calamovilfa curtissii.* Plant, × ½; glumes and floret, × 5. (Garber, Fla.)

FIGURE 453.—*Ammophila arenaria.* Glumes, floret, and ligule, × 5. (Heller 5670.)

CALAMOVILFA BREVIPILIS var. HETERÓLEPIS Fernald. Panicles somewhat narrower; pedicels with a few short hairs at summit; spikelets more crowded toward the ends of the branches, 5.5 to 6 mm. long, the palea slightly shorter than the lemma. ♃ —Edge of swamps and moist savannas, Virginia to South Carolina.

3. Calamovilfa longifólia (Hook.) Scribn. (Fig. 456.) Culms mostly solitary, 50 to 180 cm. tall, with strong scaly creeping rhizomes; sheaths usually more or less appressed-villous, especially near the summit; blades firm, elongate, flat or soon involute, 4 to 8 mm. wide near base, tapering to a long fine point; panicle 15 to 35 cm. long, rather narrow or contracted,

FIGURE 455.—*Calamovilfa brevipilis*. Plant, × ½; glumes and floret, × 5. (Brinton, N. J.)

the branches ascending or appressed, sometimes slightly spreading; spikelets pale, 6 to 7 mm. long; glumes acuminate, the first about 2 mm. shorter than the second; lemma somewhat shorter than the second glume, glabrous, the callus hairs copious, more than half as long as the lemma. ♃ —Sand hills and sandy prairies or open woods, Michigan to Alberta, south to Indiana, Colorado, and Idaho. CALAMOVILFA LONGIFOLIA var. MÁGNA Scribn. and Merr. Panicle more open and spreading. ♃ —Sandy ridges and dunes along Lakes Huron and Michigan.

4. Calamovilfa gigantéa (Nutt.) Scribn. and Merr. (Fig. 457.) Culms robust, mostly solitary, usually 1.5 to 2 m. tall, as much as 6 mm. thick at base, with strong creeping rhizomes; sheaths glabrous; blades elongate, 5 to 10 mm. wide at base, tapering to a long involute tip; panicle open, as much as 60 cm. long, the branches rather stiffly spreading, as much as 25 cm. long; spikelets similar to those of *C. longifolia*, but somewhat larger; lemma and palea villous along the back; callus hairs copious, half as long as the lemma. ♃ —Sand dunes, Kansas to Utah, Texas, and Arizona.

70. APÉRA Adans.

(Included in *Agrostis* L. in Manual, ed. 1)

Spikelets 1-flowered, disarticulating above the glumes, the rachilla prolonged back of the palea as a naked bristle; glumes subequal, acuminate; lemma firm, subindurate at maturity, acute, bearing a long delicate straight awn just below the tip; palea nearly as long as the lemma, strongly 2-nerved. Annuals with flat blades and loose or narrow panicles. Type species, *Apera spica-venti* (L.) Beauv. Name from Greek *a*, not, and *peros*, maimed, apparently alluding to the long awn, this nearly wanting in *Calamagrostis calamagrostis* (L.) Karst. (*C. lanceolata* Roth), from which Adanson differentiated the genus.

Panicle open, the branches naked below .... 1. A. SPICA-VENTI.
Panicle narrow, contracted, interrupted, the branches, or some of them floriferous from the base .... 2. A. INTERRUPTA.

1. Apera spíca-vénti (L.) Beauv. (Fig. 458.) Annual; culms branched at base, mostly 40 to 60 cm. tall; ligule as much as 6 mm. long; blades flat, 1 to 3 mm. wide; panicle 10 to

FIGURE 456.—*Calamovilfa longifolia*. Plant, × ½; spikelet and floret, × 5. (Babcock, Ill.)

FIGURE 457.—*Calamovilfa gigantea.* Panicle, × ½; glumes and floret, × 5. (White, Okla.)

20 cm. long, usually less than half as broad, the branches capillary, spreading, whorled, naked at base; spikelets 2 to 2.5 mm. long; glumes somewhat unequal, the first shorter and narrower; lemma about as long as the second glume, scaberulous, with a slender awn from below the apex, the awn about twice as long as the glumes; palea about as long as the lemma; rachilla less than 0.5 mm. long. ⊙ —Introduced at a few points from Maine to Maryland; Ohio; Missouri; Portland, Oreg.; Europe.

2. Apera interrúpta (L.) Beauv. (Fig. 459.) Similar to *A. spica-venti;* panicle narrower, more condensed, interrupted, the branches or some of them floriferous from the base; awn of lemma about 1 cm. long. ⊙ —Introduced in Missouri (St. Louis), Washington (Spokane), Oregon (Portland), Idaho (Nezperce Forest), and British Columbia (Okanogan); Europe.

71. AGRÓSTIS L. Bentgrass

Spikelets 1-flowered, disarticulating above the glumes, the rachilla usually not prolonged; glumes equal or nearly so, acute, acuminate, or sometimes awn-pointed, usually scabrous on the keel and sometimes on the back; lemma obtuse, usually shorter and thinner than the glumes, mostly 3-nerved, awnless or dorsally awned, often hairy on the callus; palea usually shorter than the lemma, 2-nerved in only a few species, usually small and nerveless or obsolete. Delicate to moderately tall annuals or usually perennials, with flat or sometimes involute, scabrous blades, and open to contracted panicles of small spikelets. Type species, *Agrostis stolonifera.* Name from Greek *agrostis,* a kind of grass, from *agros,* a field; the word agrostology is from the same root. The rachilla is regularly prolonged in a few species and in occasional spikelets of other species.

Most of the species are important forage plants, either under cultivation or in the mountain meadows of the Western States. The three important cultivated species are redtop, *Agrostis alba,* used for meadows, pastures, lawns, and sports turf, Colonial bent, *A. tenuis,* used for pastures, lawns, and sports turf, and creeping bent, *A. palustris,* used for lawns and golf greens. Velvet bent, *A. canina,* is sometimes used for putting greens. Recently forms of *A. palustris,* called Washington bent and Metropolitan bent, have come into use for lawns and especially for golf greens. They are propagated by the stolons. Fiorin is a name applied in England to *A. palustris.*

The native species abundant enough to be of importance as forage plants are *A. exarata,* throughout the western part of the United States, *A. oregonensis* in Oregon, and *A. variabilis* in alpine regions of the Northwest.

1a. Palea evident, 2-nerved, at least half as long as the lemma.

FIGURE 459.—*Apera interrupta*. Panicle, × ½; glumes and floret, × 5. (Bonser 3, Wash.)

FIGURE 458.—*Apera spica-venti*. Plant, × ½; glumes and floret, × 5. (Martindale, N. J.)

2a. Rachilla prolonged behind the palea as a minute bristle.
Lemma pubescent........ 1. A. AVENACEA.
Lemma glabrous.
Spikelets 2 mm. long........ 2. A. THURBERIANA.
Spikelets 3 mm. long........ 3. A. AEQUIVALVIS.
2b. Rachilla not prolonged.
Glumes scabrous on the keel and on the back; panicle contracted, lobed, the short branches densely verticillate........ 4. A. SEMIVERTICILLATA.
Glumes scabrous on the keel only; panicle open or, if contracted, not lobed nor with densely verticillate branches.
Plants tufted; dwarf alpine species........ 10. A. HUMILIS.
Plants with rhizomes or stolons; taller species of low and medium altitudes.
Branches of panicle naked at base, the panicle open and delicate; ligule as much as 2 mm. long on culm leaves, less than 1 mm. on the innovations.
9. A. TENUIS.
Branches of panicle or some of them floriferous from base; ligule as much as 6 mm. long.
Panicle contracted, the branches appressed; long stolons developed in isolated plants. Culms decumbent at base........ 6. A. PALUSTRIS.
Panicle open, the branches ascending, no long stolons developed.
Culms producing rather stout creeping leafy stolons........ 7. A. NIGRA.
Culms decumbent at base; rhizomes wanting........ 5. A. STOLONIFERA.
Culms erect; rhizomes developed........ 8. A. ALBA.
1b. Palea obsolete, or a minute nerveless scale (in *A. exarata* and *A. californica* as much as 0.5 mm. long or more).
3a. Plants annual, lemma with a slender awn, geniculate or flexuous.
Lemma awnless........ 11. A. ROSSAE.
Lemma with a slender geniculate or flexuous awn.
Awn flexuous, delicate; Southeastern States........ 12. A. ELLIOTTIANA.
Awn geniculate; Pacific coast.
Spikelets about 1.5 mm. long; lemma awned below the tip........ 13. A. EXIGUA.
Spikelets at least 2.5 mm. long; lemma awned from the middle.
Apex of lemma obscurely toothed or nearly entire; lemma 1.7 to 1.9 mm. long.
16. A. MICROPHYLLA.
Apex of lemma bearing 2 or 4 delicate awns.
Lemma pilose; glumes 3.5 to 4 mm. long........ 15. A. KENNEDYANA.
Lemma glabrous except on the callus; glumes 5 to 6 mm. long.
Lemma relatively firm, scabrous, 3.2 to 3.5 mm. long; palea nearly ⅓ as long as the lemma........ 17. A. ARISTIGLUMIS.
Lemma thin, glabrous, 3 mm. long; palea obsolete........ 14. A. HENDERSONI.
3b. Plants perennial; lemma awned or awnless, the awn when present not much exserted.
4a. Plants spreading by creeping rhizomes (those of *A. lepida* short).
Hairs at base of lemma 1 to 2 mm. long........ 18. A. HALLII.
Hairs at base of lemma minute or wanting.
Rhizomes short; alpine tufted plants........ 19. A. LEPIDA.
Rhizomes long and slender.
Panicle spikelike........ 20. A. PALLENS.
Panicle open........ 21. A. DIEGOENSIS.
4b. Plants without rhizomes, stolons sometimes developed.
5a. Panicle narrow, contracted, at least some of the lower branches spikelet-bearing from the base.
Culms slender, not more than 20 cm. tall, in dense tufts with numerous basal leaves; blades not more than 7 cm. long, mostly less, less than 2 mm. wide; panicles seldom more than 5 mm. wide.
Culms spreading; panicles strict, greenish; lemma with a minute awn or the midnerve ending below the summit........ 22. A. BLASDALEI.
Culms erect; panicle narrow but loose, purple; lemma awnless, the midnerve reaching the summit........ 23. A. VARIABILIS.
Culms taller, stouter, not in tufts with dense basal foliage; blades or some of them at least 8 to 10 cm. long and 3 to 5 mm. wide, commonly much larger; glumes scabrous on the keel.
Panicle from loose to dense; lemma acute, not toothed; palea minute.
Panicle loose, the branches verticillate, not densely flowered at base; awn of lemma twisted, geniculate........ 25. A. AMPLA.
Panicle dense to loose, the branches crowded and densely flowered at base; lemma awnless or (in vars. *pacifica* and *monolepis*) awned.
24. A. EXARATA.

Panicle dense and spikelike; lemma minutely 4-toothed; palea ¼ to ⅓ as long as the lemma........ 26. A. CALIFORNICA.

5b. Panicle open, sometimes diffuse; branches very slender, scabrous, the lower branches not spikelet-bearing at the base.

Lemma awned from near the base.

Blades elongate, 3 to 5 mm. wide; panicle branches flexuous; spikelets about 3.5 mm. long........ 28. A. HOWELLII.

Blades about 1 mm. wide or less; panicle branches straight; spikelets 2 to 2.5 mm. long........ 27. A. HOOVERI.

Lemma awnless or awned from the middle or above.

Panicle very diffuse, the capillary branches branching toward the end or (in *A. scabra* var. *geminata*) above the middle.

Spikelets 1.5 to 1.7 mm. long, very densely clustered at the ends of the branchlets; lemma 1 to 1.2 mm. long, scarcely longer than the caryopsis; anthers about 0.2 mm. long........ 29. A. HIEMALIS.

Spikelets 2 to 2.7 mm. long, loosely arranged at the ends of the branchlets; lemma 1.5 to 1.7 mm. long, distinctly longer than the caryopsis; anthers 0.4 to 0.5 mm. long........ 30. A. SCABRA.

Panicle open but not diffuse, the branches branching at or below the middle.

Lemma awnless (occasional plants with awned lemmas).

Spikelets about 2 mm. long; plants of high altitudes, delicate, 10 to 30 cm. tall........ 31. A. IDAHOENSIS.

Spikelets 2 to 3 mm. long; more robust plants of low and medium altitudes.

Panicle rather lax, sometimes delicate and divaricately spreading; blades flat, as much as 6 mm. wide; eastern United States.

Spikelets mostly 2.2 to 2.7 mm. long, not aggregate or but slightly so at the ends of the panicle branches........ 32. A. PERENNANS.

Spikelets mostly 2.7 to 3.5 mm. long, aggregate towards the ends of the panicle branches........ 33. A. ALTISSIMA.

Panicle rather stiff, the branches whorled and rather stiffly ascending; Pacific coast........ 34. A. OREGONENSIS.

Lemma awned.

Spikelets about 2 mm. long; introduced........ 35. A. CANINA.

Spikelets 2.5 to 3 mm. long; native.

Ligule 1 to 2 mm. long........ 36. A. BOREALIS.

Ligule 5 to 8 mm. long........ 37. A. LONGILIGULA.

FIGURE 460.—*Agrostis avenacea.* Panicle, × ½; glumes and floret, × 10. (Tracy and Earle 403, Tex.)

1. Agrostis avenácea Gmel. (Fig. 460.) Perennial; culms tufted, erect or decumbent at base, 20 to 60 cm. tall; sheaths smooth; ligule of culm leaves 3 to 5 mm. long; blades flat, scabrous, 1 to 2 mm. wide; panicle diffuse, 15 to 30 cm. long, the branches in distant whorls, capillary, reflexed at maturity, divided above the middle; glumes acuminate, 3 to 4 mm. long; lemma about half as long as the glumes, thin, pubescent, short-bearded on the callus, and bearing about the middle a slender geniculate and twisted awn exserted about the length of the glumes; palea nearly as long as the lemma; rachilla slender, pilose, from half to as long as the lemma. ♃ (*A. retrofracta* Willd.)—Introduced in central California (15 miles south of Stockton), Texas (Kent), and Ohio (Painesville); common in Hawaiian Islands and Polynesia.

FIGURE 461.—*Agrostis thurberiana*. Panicle, × 1; glumes and floret, × 5. (Type.)

FIGURE 462.—*Agrostis aequivalvis*. Panicle, × 1; glumes and floret, × 5. (Howell 1712, Alaska.)

2. Agrostis thurberiána Hitchc. THURBER BENT. (Fig. 461.) Culms slender, in small tufts, erect, 20 to 40 cm. tall; leaves somewhat crowded at base, the blades about 2 mm. wide; panicle rather narrow, lax, more or less drooping, 5 to 7 cm. long; spikelets green, pale, or purple, 2 mm. long; lemma nearly as long as the glumes, the palea about two-thirds as long; rachilla hairy, 0.3 mm. long. ♃ —Bogs and moist places, at medium and upper altitudes, Colorado to British Columbia and south in the Sierras to central California.

3. Agrostis aequiválvis (Trin.) Trin. (Fig. 462.) Similar to *A. thurberiana;* culms on the average taller, blades longer; panicle usually purple, 5 to 15 cm. long; spikelets about 3 to 4.5 mm. long; palea nearly as long as the lemma; rachilla minutely pubescent, one-fifth to half as long as the lemma. ♃ —Wet meadows and bogs, Alaska, southward (rare) in the Cascade Mountains to Oregon.

4. Agrostis semiverticilláta (Forsk.) C. Christ. WATER BENT. (Fig. 463.) Culms usually decumbent at base, sometimes with long creeping and rooting stolons; blades firm, mostly relatively short and broad, but in luxuriant specimens elongate; panicle contracted, 3 to 10 cm. long, densely flowered, lobed, with short verticillate branches, especially at base, the branches spikelet-bearing from the base; spikelets usually falling entire; glumes equal, narrowed to an obtuse tip, scabrous on back and keel, 2 mm. long; lemma 1 mm. long, awnless, truncate and toothed at apex; palea nearly as long as the lemma. ♃ (*A. verticillata* Vill.)—Moist ground at low altitudes, especially along irrigation ditches (in irrigated regions), Texas to California, north to Utah and Washington; on ballast at some Atlantic ports. Introduced in America, south to Argentina; warmer parts of the Eastern Hemisphere.

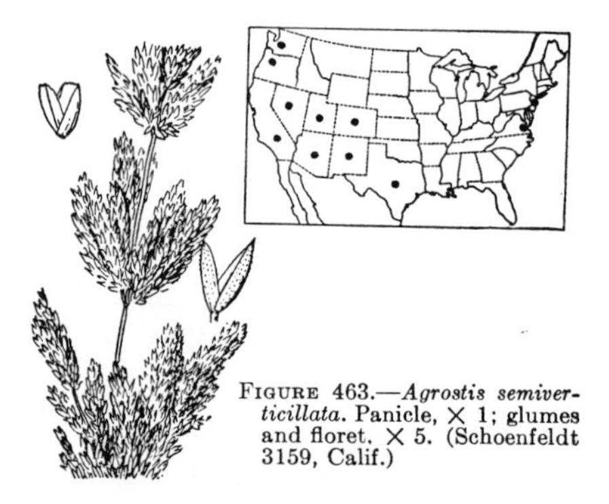

FIGURE 463.—*Agrostis semiverticillata*. Panicle, × 1; glumes and floret, × 5. (Schoenfeldt 3159, Calif.)

5. Agrostis stolonífera L. (Fig. 464.) Culms ascending from a spreading base, the decumbent portion rooting in wet soil, 20 to 50 cm. tall; ligule as much as 6 mm. long; blades flat, mostly 1 to 3 mm. wide; panicle oblong, 5 to 15 cm. long, pale or purple, somewhat open, the branches or some of them spikelet-bearing from near the base; spikelets 2 to 2.5 mm. long; glumes acute, glabrous except the scabrous keel; lemma shorter than the glumes, awnless or rarely awned from the back; palea usually half to two-thirds as long as the lemma. ♃ —Moist grassy places, Newfoundland to Alaska, south to Virginia (adventive in South Carolina) in the East and to Washington in the West; northern Europe. This species appears to be native in northern North America.

6. Agrostis palústris Huds. CREEPING BENT. (Fig. 465.) Differing from *A. stolonifera* chiefly in the long stolons, the narrow stiff appressed blades, and the condensed (sometimes somewhat open) panicle. ♃ (*A. maritima* Lam.)—Marshes along the coast, from Newfoundland to Virginia; British Columbia to northern California; sometimes occupying extensive areas, as at Coos Bay, Oreg.; introduced at various places in the interior of southern Canada and northeastern United States to Virginia and Wisconsin, and occasionally southward, Texas to Arizona, especially along ditches; Idaho and Washington to Colorado and California; Eurasia. Forms of this species, known as seaside, Coos Bay, and Cocoos bents (propagated by seed), and Metropolitan and Washington

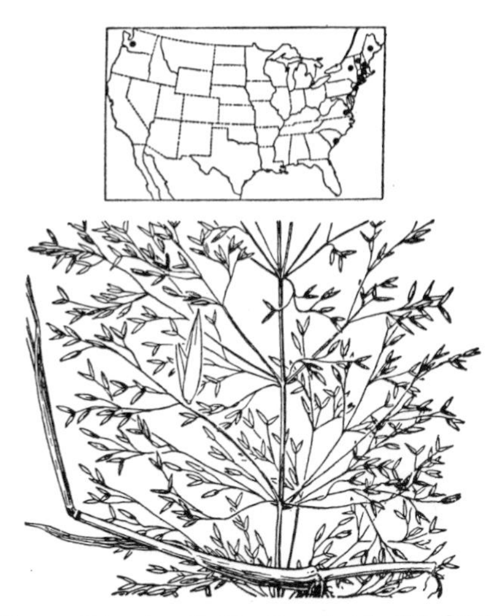

FIGURE 464.—*Agrostis stolonifera*. Panicle, × 1; floret, × 5. (Hitchcock 23899, Newfoundland.)

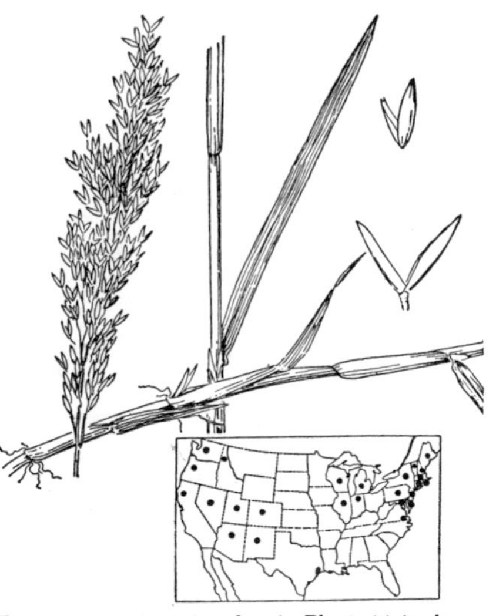

FIGURE 465.—*Agrostis palustris*. Plant, × 1; glumes and floret, × 5. (Hitchcock 11713, Wash.)

FIGURE 466.—*Agrostis nigra*. Plant, × 1; floret, × 5. (Moore 47, cult. Mo. Bot. Gard.)

FIGURE 467.—*Agrostis alba*. Plant, × ½; 2 spikelets and floret, × 5. (Chase 5191, Mont.)

bents (propagated by stolons and formerly called carpet bent), are used for lawns and extensively for putting greens.

7. Agrostis nígra With. Black bent. (Fig. 466.) Culms long-decumbent at base, also with rather stout leafy stolons, the fertile branches ascending or erect, 20 to 30 cm. tall; ligule as in *A. alba;* panicle brownish, open as in *A. alba*, but on the average more condensed along the branches, the base usually partly included. ♃ —Sometimes found mixed with "South German" bent (creeping bent), hence may be a constituent of lawns grown from imported seed; Europe.

8. Agrostis álba L. Redtop. (Fig. 467.) Differing from *A. stolonifera* in its usually erect more robust culms, sometimes as much as 1 to 1.5 m. tall, the base erect or decumbent, with strong creeping rhizomes; blades flat, 5 to 10 mm. wide; panicle pyramidal-oblong, reddish, as much as 20 cm. long, the branches spreading in anthesis, sometimes contracting later; lemmas rarely awned ♃ (*A. gigantea* Roth.)—This is the common redtop cultivated for meadows, pastures, and lawns, extensively escaped in all the cooler parts of the United States; Eurasia. This form appears not to be native in America. Plants growing without cultivation often have pale panicles and may tend to take on the aspect of *A. stolonifera*. This and the two preceding are closely allied and appear to intergrade. The name *A. palustris* has been erroneously applied to this species.

Figure 468.—*A*, *Agrostis tenuis*. Panicle, × 1; glumes, floret, and ligule, × 5. (Waghorne, Newfoundland.) *B*, Var. *aristata*. Floret, × 5. (Gayle 786, Maine.)

9. Agrostis ténuis Sibth. Colonial bent. (Fig. 468, *A*.) Culms slender, erect, tufted, usually 20 to 40 cm. tall, with short stolons but no creeping rhizomes; ligule short, less than 1 mm. or on the culm as much as 2 mm. long; blades mostly 5 to 10 cm. long, 1 to 3 mm. wide; panicle mostly 5 to 10 cm. long, open, delicate, the slender branches naked below, the spikelets not crowded. ♃ (*A. vulgaris* With.)—Cultivated for pastures and lawns in the northeastern United States; escaped and well established throughout those regions; Newfoundland south to North Carolina, West Virginia, and Michigan; British Columbia to Montana and California; Europe. This species appears not to be native in America; it has been referred to *A. capillaris* L., a distinct species of Europe. In older works this has been called Rhode Island bent. Forms of this species are sometimes called Prince Edward Island, New Zealand, Rhode Island Colonial, Astoria, and Colonial bent. Highland bent is an aberrant form which may be a distinct species.

Agrostis tenuis var. aristáta (Parnell) Druce. (Fig. 468, *B*.) Differing from *A. tenuis* in having lemma awned from near the base, the awn usually geniculate and exceeding the glumes. ♃ —Fields and open woods, Nova Scotia and Quebec to North Carolina; Alaska to Vancouver Island; northern California; Europe. This form appears to be native, at least in the more northerly part of its range.

10. Agrostis húmilis Vasey. (Fig. 469.) Culms low, tufted, mostly not more than 15 cm. tall; leaves mostly basal, the blades flat or folded, usually not more than 1 mm. wide; panicle narrow, purple, 1 to 3 cm. long, the branches appressed to somewhat spreading; spikelets about 2

FIGURE 469.—*Agrostis humilis.* Panicle, × 1; glumes and floret, × 5. (Type.)

mm. long; lemma nearly as long as the glumes, awnless; palea about two-thirds as long as lemma. ♃ —Bogs and alpine meadows at high altitudes, Wyoming and Colorado to Washington, Oregon, and Nevada.

FIGURE 470.—*Agrostis rossae.* Panicle, × 1; glumes and floret, × 5. (V. H. Chase 5740, Yellowstone Natl. Park, Wyo.)

11. Agrostis róssae Vasey. (Fig. 470.) Annual, erect, leafy and branching at base, 10 to 19 cm. tall; sheaths rather loose; blades flat, 1 to 2.5 cm. long, 1 to 2 mm. wide; panicle 3.5 to 6 cm. long, usually contracted, the capillary scabrous purplish branches in relatively distant fascicles, narrowly ascending, naked at base; spikelets 2 to 2.5 mm. long; glumes acuminate; lemma 1.5 to 1.6 mm. long, minutely toothed, awnless; palea very minute. ⊙ —Alkali soil near hot springs, Upper Geyser Basin and along Fire Hole River, Yellowstone Park, Wyo.

12. Agrostis elliottiána Schult. (Fig. 471.) Annual; culms slender, erect or decumbent at base, 10 to 40 cm. tall; blades flat, about 1 mm. wide; panicle finally diffuse, about half the entire height of the plant, the branches capillary, fascicled, the spikelets toward the ends of the branchlets, the whole panicle breaking away at maturity; spikelets 1.5 to 2 mm. long; glumes acute; lemma

FIGURE 471.—*Agrostis elliottiana.* Panicle, × 1; glumes and floret, × 5. (Johnson, Miss.)

1 to 1.5 mm. long, minutely toothed, awned below the tip, the awn very slender, flexuous, delicately short-pilose, 5 to 10 mm. long, sometimes falling at maturity; palea wanting. ⊙ —Fields, waste places, and open ground, Maryland to Kansas, south to Georgia and eastern Texas; introduced in Maine and Massachusetts; Yucatan.

FIGURE 472.—*Agrostis exigua.* Panicle, × 1; glumes and floret, × 5. (Type.)

13. Agrostis exígua Thurb. (Fig. 472.) Annual; culms delicate, 3 to 10 cm. tall, branching from the base; blades 5 to 20 mm. long, subinvolute, scabrous; panicle half the length of the plant, finally open; glumes 1.5 mm. long, scaberulous; lemma equaling the glumes, scaberulous toward the 2-toothed apex, bearing below the tip a delicate bent awn 4 times as long; palea wanting. ⊙ —Foothills and rocky plains, upper Sacramento Valley, and muddy pond border, Howell Mountain, Napa County, Calif.

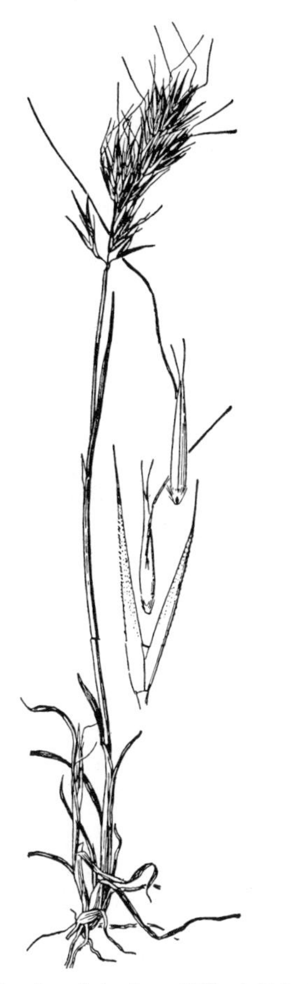

FIGURE 473.—*Agrostis hendersonii.* Plant, × 1; glumes and 2 views of floret, × 5. (Type.)

14. Agrostis hendersónii Hitchc. (Fig. 473.) Annual; culms about 10 cm. tall; ligule 2 to 3 mm. long; blades flat or loosely involute, 1 to 3 cm. long, about 1 mm. wide; ligule delicate, about 2 mm. long; panicle condensed, about 2.5 cm. long, purplish; spikelets short-pedi-

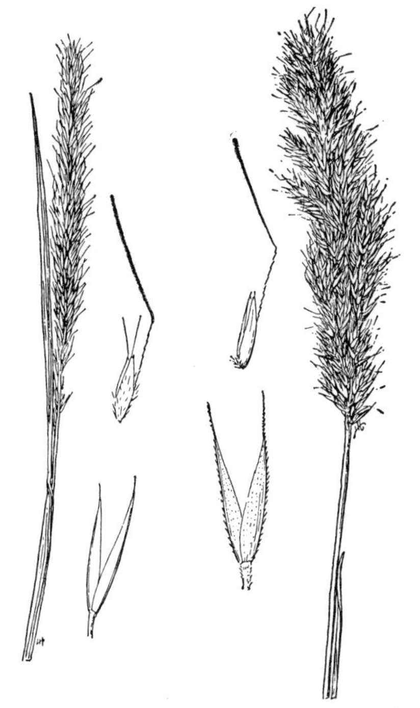

FIGURE 474.—*Agrostis kennedyana.* Panicle, × 1; glumes and floret, × 5. (Type collection.)

FIGURE 475.—*Agrostis microphylla.* Panicle, × 1; glumes and floret, × 5. (Bolander 1512, Calif.)

celed, 5 to 6 mm. long; glumes subequal, setaceous-tipped; lemma about 3 mm. long, finely 2-toothed, the delicate awns of the teeth readily breaking off, awned from the middle, the awn about 1 cm. long, geniculate, the callus pubescent; palea obsolete. ⊙ —Wet ground, known only from Sams Valley, near Gold Hill, Jackson County, Oreg., and Shasta County, Calif.

15. Agrostis kennedyána Beetle. (Fig. 474.) Annual; culms very slender, 15 to 23 cm. tall; ligule about 2 mm. long; blades flat or loosely involute, 2 to 4 cm. long, 1 to 1.5 mm. wide, or the basal blades slightly

FIGURE 476.—*Agrostis aristigluma*. Plant, × ½; glumes and two views of floret, × 5. (Type.)

longer; panicle spikelike, 2 to 5 cm. long, pale; spikelets short-pediceled; glumes narrow, acuminate, the first 3.5 to 4 mm., the second 3 to 3.2 mm. long; lemma delicate, about 1.7 mm. long, awned from about the middle, the delicate awn about 5 mm. long, geniculate, the lemma loosely pilose except at the 2-toothed summit, the teeth bearing delicate awns about 1 mm. long; palea obsolete. ⊙ —Known only from San Diego County, Calif.

16. Agrostis microphýlla Steud. (Fig. 475.) Annual; culms branching at base, slender, erect or ascending, 8 to 40 cm. tall, commonly short and tall culms in the same tuft; blades 2 to 15 cm. long, rarely longer, 1.5 to 3 mm. wide, scabrous; panicle mostly 2 to 8 cm. long (exceptionally less or to 10 cm.), narrow, dense, often lobed; glumes subequal, 3 to 4.4 mm. long, acuminate to awn-tipped; lemma 1.7 to 1.9 mm. long, minutely toothed, awned from about the middle, the awn geniculate, 3.5 to 6 mm. long, rarely longer; palea wanting. ⊙ —Moist open ground, Vancouver Island, Oregon, California, and Baja California. Variable, occasionally small and delicate; glumes rarely only 2 to 2.5 mm. long. A short, densely tufted form with rather thick panicle has been differentiated as *A. inflata* Scribn. The type, from Vancouver Island, is a young plant, the panicles partly included in the slightly inflated upper sheaths. A. MICROPHYLLA var. MÁJOR Vasey is a taller form, 40 to 55 cm. tall, the pale panicles to 15 cm. long; glumes 2.5 to 3 mm. long; lemma 1.6 to 1.7 mm. long. Only known from Humboldt Mountains, Nev.

17. Agrostis aristiglúmis Swallen. (Fig. 476.) Annual; culms sparingly branching at base, erect, 5 to 15 cm. tall; ligule 2 to 2.5 mm. long, decurrent; blades flat, 2 to 15 cm. long, rarely longer, 1.5 to 3 mm. wide; panicle mostly 3 to 6 cm. long, 5 to 8 mm. wide, dense; glumes 5 to 6 mm. long, attenuate into an awn 1 to 2 mm. long, the first glume 1-nerved, the second 3-nerved; lemma 3.2 to 3.5 mm. long, relatively firm, scabrous, 5-nerved, awned from the back, the awn geniculate, 6 to 7 mm. long, the lateral nerves excurrent as delicate awns, the inner pair very minute; palea nearly one-third as long as the lemma, nerveless. ⊙ —Only known from a "slope of loose gravelly soil on an outcrop of diatomaceous shale of the Monterey series," west of Mount Vision, Point Reyes Peninsula, Marin County, Calif.

18. Agrostis hállii Vasey. (Fig. 477.) Culms erect, 60 to 90 cm. tall, with creeping rhizomes; ligule usually conspicuous, 2 to 7 mm. long; blades flat, 2 to 5 mm. wide; panicle 10 to 15 cm. long, narrow but loose, the branches verticillate; glumes about 4 mm. long; lemma awnless, 3 mm. long, with a tuft of hairs at base about half as long; palea obsolete. ♃ —Mostly in woods near the coast from Oregon to Santa Barbara, Calif. AGROSTIS HALLII var. PRÍNGLEI (Scribn.) Hitchc. Branching, foliage stramineous; blades narrow, usually involute; panicle narrow, compact. ♃ —Near the coast, in sand, Mendocino County, Calif.

FIGURE 477.—*Agrostis hallii*. Panicle, × 1; glumes and floret, × 5. (Bioletti 110, Calif.)

19. Agrostis lépida Hitchc. (Fig. 478.) Culms tufted, 30 to 40 cm. tall, erect, with numerous short rhizomes; ligule, at least on the innovations, as much as 4 mm. long; leaves mostly basal, the blades firm, erect, flat or folded, the upper culm leaf below the middle of the culm, the blade 3 cm. long or less; panicle purple, 10 to 15 cm. long, the branches verticillate, becoming divaricately spreading, the lowermost 2 to 5 cm. long; glumes 3 mm. long, smooth or nearly so; lemma 2 mm. long; palea obsolete. ♃ —Meadows and open woods, Sequoia National Park and San Bernardino Mountains, Calif., at upper altitudes.

FIGURE 478.—*Agrostis lepida*. Plant, × ½; glumes and floret, × 5. (Type.)

20. Agrostis pállens Trin. DUNE BENT. (Fig. 479.) Culms erect, 20 to 40 cm. tall, with creeping rhizomes; ligule rather firm, 2 to 3 mm. long; blades flat or somewhat involute, 1 to 4 mm. wide; panicle contracted, almost spikelike, 5 to 10 cm. long; glumes 2.5 to 3 mm. long; lemma a little shorter than the glumes, awnless; palea obsolete. ♃ —Sand dunes along the coast, Washington to central California.

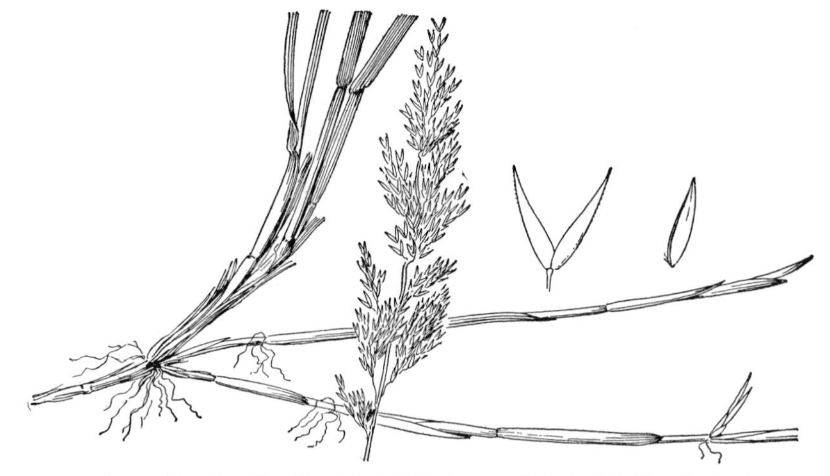

FIGURE 479.—*Agrostis pallens*. Plant, × 1; glumes and floret, × 5. (Howell, Oreg.)

FIGURE 480.—*Agrostis diegoensis*. Plant, × 1; glumes and floret, × 5. (Orcutt, Calif.)

21. Agrostis diegoénsis Vasey. THINGRASS. (Fig. 480.) Culms erect, as much as 1 m. tall with creeping rhizomes; blades flat, lax, 2 to 6 mm. wide; panicle narrow, open, 10 to 15 cm. long, the branches ascending, rather stiff, some of them naked below; spikelets about as in *A. pallens*, awned or awnless. ♃ —Meadows and open woods at low and medium altitudes, Montana and British Columbia to southern California and Nevada.

22. Agrostis blasdálei Hitchc. (Fig. 481.) Culms 10 to 15 cm. tall, densely tufted; blades narrow or filiform, rigid, involute, 2 to 4 cm. long; panicle strict, narrow, almost spikelike, 2 to 3 cm. long, the short branches closely appressed; spikelets 2.5 to 3 mm. long; lemma about 1.8 mm. long, awnless or with a very short awn just above the middle; palea about 0.3 mm. long, nerveless. ♃ —Cliffs and dunes, Mendocino and Marin Counties, Calif. Previously referred to *A. breviculmis* Hitchc. of Peru.

FIGURE 481.—*Agrostis blasdalei*. Panicle, × 1; glumes and floret, × 5. (Type.)

23. Agrostis variábilis Rydb. MOUNTAIN BENT. (Fig. 482.) Culms 10 to 25 cm. tall, densely tufted; blades flat, mostly not more than 1 mm. wide; panicle, 2 to 6 cm. long, the branches ascending; spikelets purple, about 2.5 mm. long; lemma 1.5 mm. long, awnless; palea minute. ♃ —Rocky creeks and mountain slopes at high altitudes; British Columbia and Alberta to Colorado and California. Included in *A. rossae* Vasey in Manual, ed. 1.

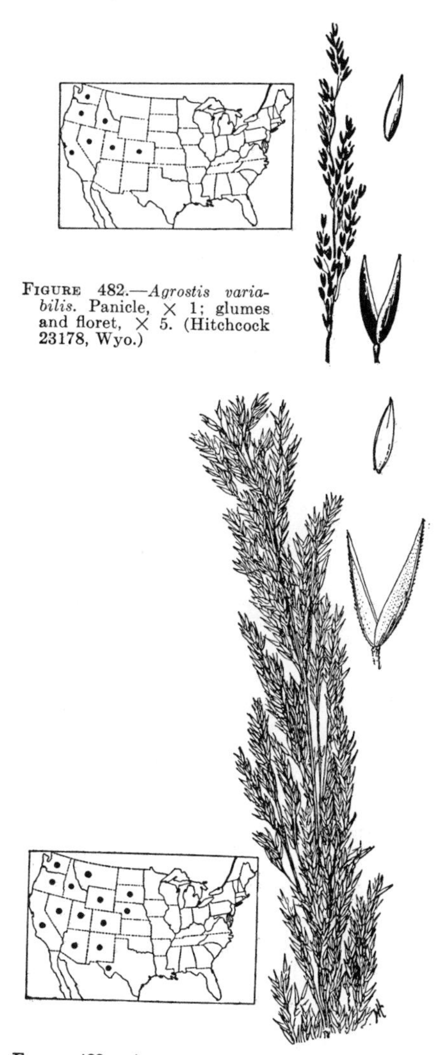

FIGURE 482.—*Agrostis variabilis.* Panicle, × 1; glumes and floret, × 5. (Hitchcock 23178, Wyo.)

FIGURE 483.—*Agrostis exarata.* Panicle, × 1; glumes and floret, × 5. (Davy 4357, Calif.)

24. Agrostis exaráta Trin. SPIKE BENT. (Fig. 483.) Culms 20 to 120 cm. tall, slender to relatively stout, mostly tufted; sheaths smooth to somewhat scabrous; ligule to 6 mm. long; blades flat, 2 to 10 mm. wide, usually scabrous; panicle narrow, from somewhat open to dense and interrupted, 5 to 30 cm. long; glumes subequal, 2.5 to 4 mm. long, acuminate to awn-tipped, scabrous on the keel, nearly smooth to scabrous on the back; lemma 1.7 to 2 mm. long, the midnerve ending above the middle or excurrent as a prickle or short awn, sometimes the nearly straight awn exceeding the glumes; palea minute. ♃ —Moist open ground, at low and medium altitudes, South Dakota and Nebraska to Alberta and Alaska, south to Texas, California, and Mexico. Common and extremely variable, ranging from slender plants with narrow blades and few-flowered panicles (*A. scouleri* Trin.) to robust plants a meter or more tall, with dense panicles as much as 30 cm. long (*A. grandis* Trin.). The specimens in the Trinius Herbarium from Unalaska (type) and Sitka, with culms 25 to 60 cm. tall and narrow but not dense panicles, the lemmas awnless, represent about the center of the range of variation. Awnless and awned spikelets are found in the same panicle.

AGROSTIS EXARATA var. PACÍFICA Vasey. Lemma with a straight or weakly geniculate awn exceeding the glumes; habit of the plant, height, and foliage as in the species, the variations similar. ♃ —Frequent from Vancouver Island and Washington to California, rare elsewhere: Canada, the Aleutians, Nebraska, Idaho, Arizona.

AGROSTIS EXARATA var. MONOLÉPIS (Torr.) Hitchc. Panicle narrow, dense, often interrupted; glumes mostly awn-tipped; awn of lemma exceeding the glumes 1.5 to 2 mm. ♃ —Washington to California.

25. Agrostis ámpla Hitchc. (Fig. 484.) Resembling *A. exarata* var. *pacifica*, the panicle looser, the branches verticillate, some of them 5 to 9 cm. long, the spikelets less crowded at the base; glumes 3.5 to 4.5 mm. (the first exceeding the second), acuminate to awn-tipped; lemma about 2.5 mm. long, awned from about the middle, the awn twisted, geniculate; anthers 0.8 to 1.8 mm. long. ♃ —Moist or wet places, Pacific slope, Oregon and California; infrequent.

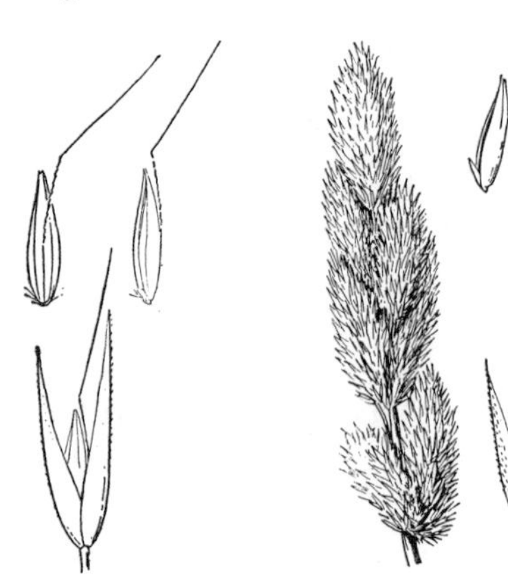

FIGURE 484.—*Agrostis ampla*. Spikelet, and two views of floret, × 5. (Type.)

FIGURE 485.—*Agrostis californica*. Panicle, × 1; glumes and floret, × 5. (Anderson, Calif.)

26. Agrostis califórnica Trin. (Fig. 485.) Culms tufted, usually rather stout, erect or somewhat spreading at base, 15 to 60 cm. tall; sheaths sometimes slightly scabrous; ligule truncate, usually shorter than in *A. exarata*, puberulent; blades flat, firm, strongly nerved on the upper surface, usually not more than 10 cm. long, those of the culm comparatively broad and short, often 3 to 5 cm. long and 3 to 5 mm. wide, rarely as much as 10 mm. wide; panicle dense, spikelike, sometimes slightly interrupted, mostly 2 to 10 cm. long and 5 to 15 mm. wide; spikelets about 3 mm. long; glumes acute or acuminate, prominently scabrous on the keel and strongly scabrous on the sides; lemma a little shorter than the glumes, awnless or with a straight awn from minute to somewhat exceeding the glumes; palea one-fourth to one-third as long as the lemma. ♃ (*A. densiflora* Vasey.)—Sandy soil and cliffs near the sea, Mendocino County to Santa Cruz, Calif. This species has been confused with *A. exarata* and with *A. glomerata* (Presl) Kunth of Peru.

27. Agrostis hoóveri Swallen. (Fig. 486.) Culms densely tufted, very slender, erect, 55 to 75 cm. tall; ligule 3 to 3.5 mm. long, lacerate, decurrent; blades lax, mostly 10 to 15 cm. long, not or scarcely more than 1 mm. wide; panicle 7 to 17 cm. long, loose, the branches ascending; spikelets slightly purplish, 2 to 2.5 mm. long, the second glume slightly shorter than the first; lemma 2 mm. long, minutely erose, 5-nerved, scaberulous, bearing from near the base a bent awn slightly exceeding the glumes; palea obsolete. ♃ —Dry, mostly sandy open woodland, San Luis Obispo and Santa Barbara Counties, Calif.

FIGURE 486.—*Agrostis hooveri*. Panicle × 1; glumes and floret, × 5. (Type.)

28. Agrostis howéllii Scribn. (Fig. 487.) Culms erect or decumbent at base, 40 to 60 cm. tall; ligule 3 to 4 mm. long, lacerate; blades lax, as much as 30 cm. long, 3 to 5 mm. wide; panicle loose and open, 10 to 30 cm. long, the branches flexuous; spikelets pale, clustered toward the ends of the branches; glumes acuminate, rather narrow and firm, somewhat scabrous on the keel, the first about 3.5 mm. long, the second a little shorter; lemma acute, 2.5 mm. long, 4-toothed, faintly 3- to 5-nerved, bearing from

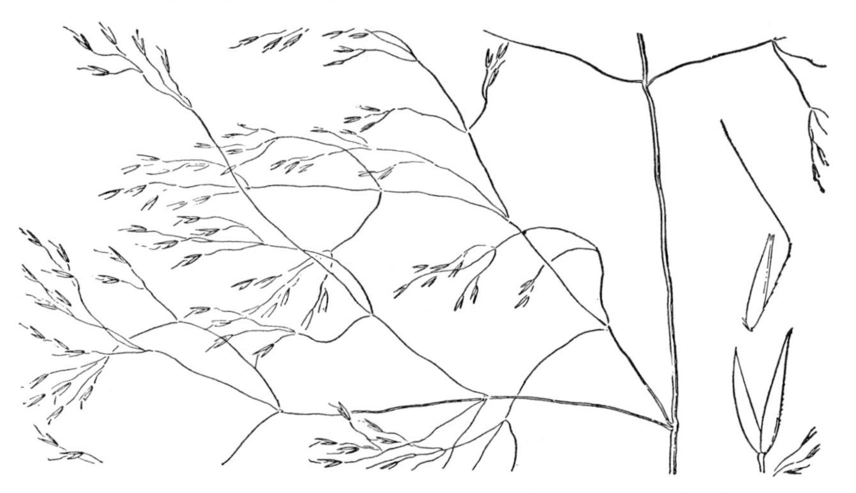

FIGURE 487.—*Agrostis howellii*. Panicle, × 1; glumes and floret, × 5. (Type.)

near the base an exserted bent awn about 6 mm. long; palea obsolete. ♃ —Known only from Oregon (Multnomah and Hood River Counties).

29. Agrostis hiemális (Walt.) B. S. P. (Fig. 488.) Culms mostly 30 to 40 cm. tall, erect in small tufts, glabrous; blades crowded toward the base in a dense cluster, 3 to 5 cm. long, less than 1 mm. wide, flat or subfiliform; panicles fragile, the slender filiform branches in rather distant whorls, widely spreading or drooping, unbranched below the middle, spikelet-bearing only at the ends of the branchlets; spikelets 1.5 to 1.7 mm. long, clustered, short-pediceled, appressed; glumes subequal, acute, scabrous on the keels; lemma 1 to 1.2 mm. long, the callus glabrous; anthers 0.2 mm. long. ♃ —Open ground, fields, and waste places, Massachusetts to Florida, west to Wisconsin, Kansas, Oklahoma, and Texas.

30. Agrostis scábra Willd. (Fig. 489.) Culms 30 to 85 cm., rarely to 100 cm., tall, erect in small dense tufts; sheaths shorter than the internodes, glabrous; ligule hyaline, 2 to 5 mm. long; blades flat, 8 to 20 cm. long, 1 to 3 mm. wide, scabrous, the basal ones often subfiliform; panicles 15 to 25 cm. long, rarely longer, the brittle scabrous branches in rather distant verticils, ascending or spreading, sometimes drooping, branching above the middle; spikelets 2 to 2.7 mm. long, loosely arranged at the ends of the branchlets; glumes unequal, acuminate, scabrous on the keels; lemma 1.5 to 1.7 mm. long, distinctly longer than the caryopsis, the callus sparsely pilose; anthers 0.4 to 0.5 mm. long. ♃ —Mountain meadows, fields, and open woods, Newfoundland and Alaska, south to Florida, Texas, and California; probably introduced in the Southern States. (Included in *A. hiemalis* in Manual, ed. 1.)

AGROSTIS SCABRA var. GEMINÁTA (Trin.) Swallen. Branches of panicle short and divaricate; lemma awned or awnless. The type specimen, from Alaska, is awned; a large number of specimens over a wide range agree in other respects, but are awnless. ♃ —At high latitudes and altitudes, Newfoundland to Alaska, south to New Hampshire, North Dakota, Colorado, and California.

31. Agrostis idahoénsis Nash. IDAHO REDTOP. (Fig. 490.) Culms slender, tufted, 10 to 30 cm. tall; leaves mostly basal, the blades narrow; panicle loosely spreading, 5 to 10 cm. long, the branches capillary,

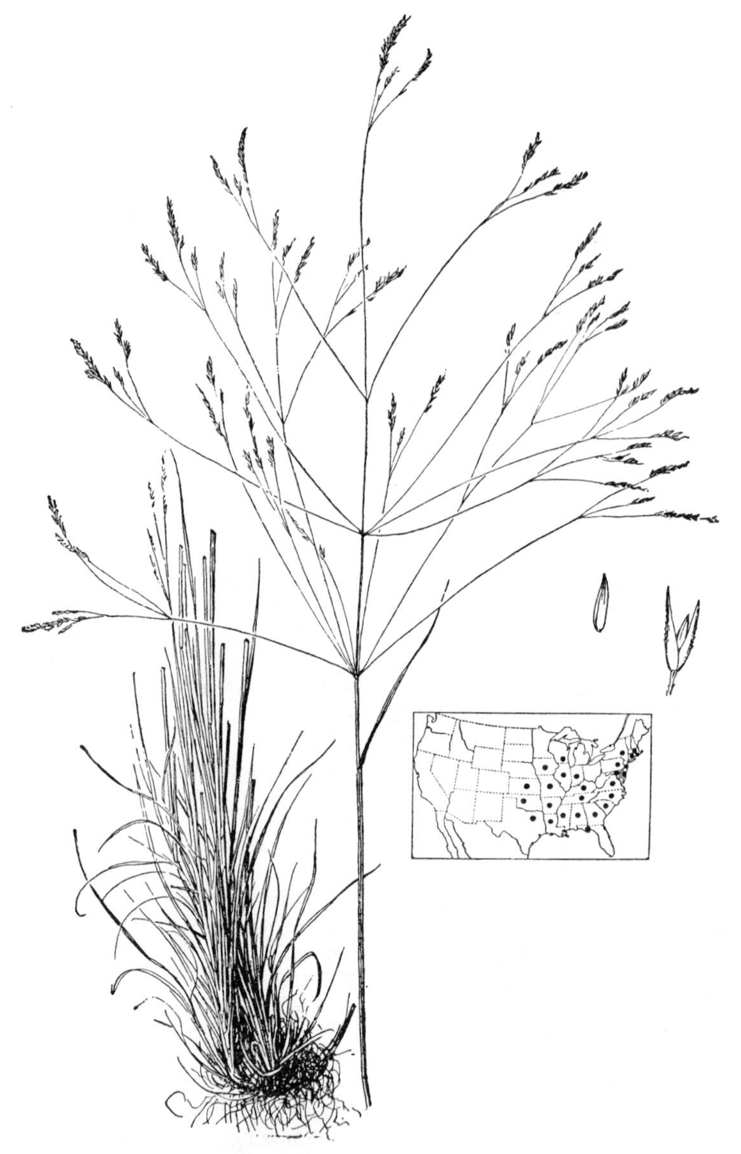

FIGURE 488.—*Agrostis hiemalis*. Plant, × ½; glumes and floret, × 5. (Deam 6514, Ind.)

flexuous, minutely scabrous; spikelets 1.5 to 2.5 mm. long; lemma about 1.3 mm. long, awnless; palea minute. ♃ —Mountain meadows, at medium and high altitudes, western Montana to Washington, south to New Mexico, Arizona, and the high mountains of California; Fairbanks, Alaska. Differs from *A. scabra* in the smaller spikelets and in the narrower panicle with shorter flexuous branches.

32. Agrostis perénnans (Walt.) Tuckerm. AUTUMN BENT. (Fig. 491, *A*.) Culms erect to somewhat decumbent at base, varying from weak and lax to relatively stout, 30 to 100 cm. tall, often with lax leafy shoots at base; leaves rather numerous, the

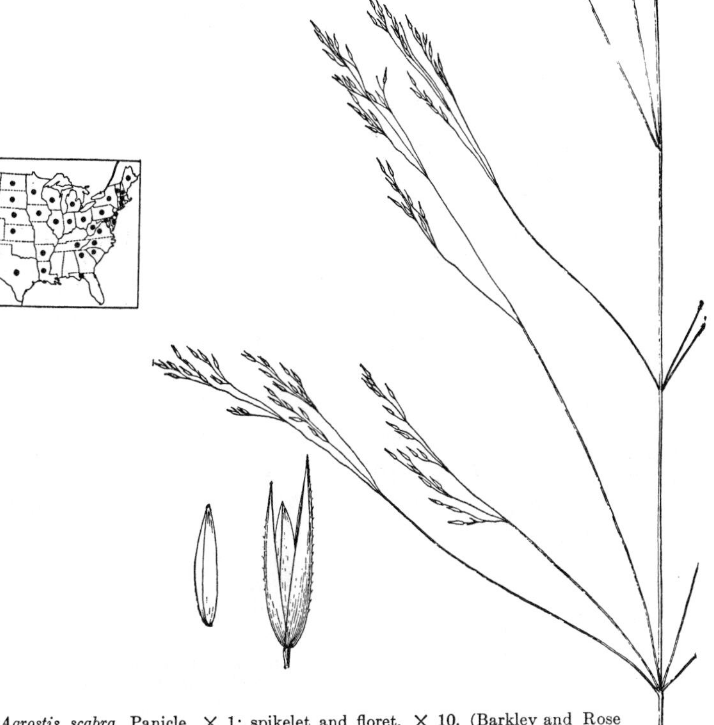

FIGURE 489.—*Agrostis scabra*. Panicle, × 1; spikelet and floret, × 10. (Barkley and Rose 1881, Mont.)

blades from lax to stiffly upright, corresponding to the culms, 10 to 20 cm. long, 1 to 6 mm. wide; panicle pale to tawny, open, oblong, the branches verticillate, mostly lax, ascending, branching about the middle; spikelets 2 to 3.2, mostly 2.2 to 2.7 mm. long, the pedicels spreading, but the spikelets sometimes somewhat aggregate towards the ends of the branchlets; glumes acute or acuminate, the first slightly longer; lemma 1.5 to 2 mm. long, rarely awned (*A. perennans* forma *chaetophora* Fernald); palea obsolete or nearly so. ♃ —Open ground, old fields, open woods, in rather dry soil from sea level to mountain tops, flowering in late summer or autumn, Quebec to Minnesota, south to Florida and eastern Texas; Mexico. Extremely variable, in dry open ground erect and rather stout; in shady places weak, with lax pale panicle and divaricate branchlets and spikelets 2 mm. long (*A. perennans* var. *aestivalis* Vasey). Intergrades with the following, the intermediate specimens (*A. scribneriana* Nash) rather numerous in the Eastern States.

33. Agrostis altíssima (Walt.) Tuckerm. (Fig. 491, *B*.) Culms mostly stouter than in the preceding, erect or ascending; panicle branches usually ascending, the spikelets more or less aggregate toward the ends; spikelets 2.3 to 3.7, mostly 2.7 to 3.5 mm. long. ♃ —Mostly in marshy ground, pine barren bogs, and wooded swamps, coastal plain, New Jersey and Maryland to Alabama and Mississippi.

34. Agrostis oregonénsis Vasey. OREGON REDTOP. (Fig. 492.) Culms 60 to 90 cm. tall; blades 2 to 4 mm. wide; panicle oblong, 10 to 30 cm. long, open, the branches verticillate, rather stiff and ascending, numerous in the lower whorls, the longer 5 to 10 cm. long, branching above the middle; glumes 2.5 to 3 mm. long; lemma 1.5 mm. long, awnless; palea about 0.5 mm. long. ♃ —Marshes, bogs, and wet meadows, Montana to British Columbia, south to Wyoming and California.

35. Agrostis canína L. VELVET BENT. (Fig. 493.) Culms tufted, 30 to 50 cm. tall; blades mostly short and narrow, those of the culm 3 to 6 cm. long, usually not more than 2 mm. wide; panicle loose and spreading, mostly 5 to 10 cm. long; glumes equal, acute, 2 mm. long, the lower minutely scabrous on the keel; lemma a little shorter than the glumes, awned about the middle, the awn exserted, bent; callus minutely hairy; palea minute. ♃ —Meadows and open ground, Newfoundland to Quebec, south to Delaware, West Virginia, Tennessee, and Michigan; pos-

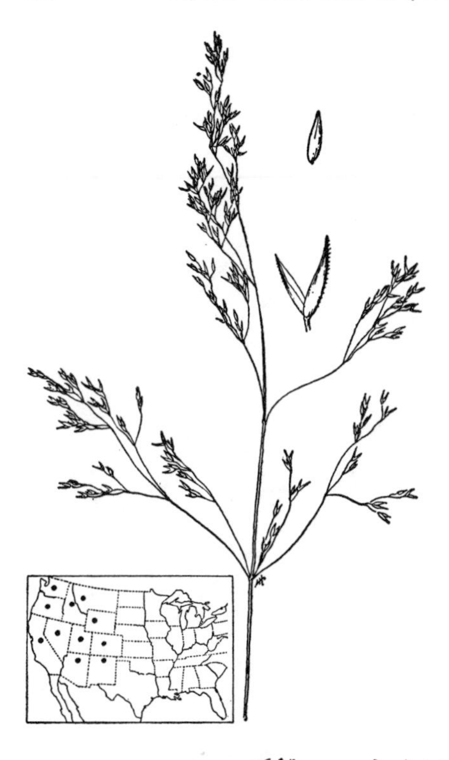

FIGURE 490.—*Agrostis idahoensis*. Panicle, × 1; glumes and floret, × 5. (Chase 5040, Idaho.)

FIGURE 491.—*A*, *Agrostis perennans*. Panicle, × 1; glumes and floret, × 5. (Millspaugh 53, W. Va.) *B*, *A. altissima*. Glumes and two views of floret, × 5. (A. Gray, N. J., in Trinius Herb.)

sibly native northward but introduced in the United States; Europe. Sometimes cultivated for putting greens.

FIGURE 492.—*Agrostis oregonensis*. Panicle, × 1; glumes and floret, × 5. (Hitchcock 23524, Oreg.)

FIGURE 493.—*Agrostis canina*. Panicle, × 1; glumes and floret, × 5. (Commons 99, Del.)

36. Agrostis boreális Hartm. (Fig. 494.) Culms tufted, 20 to 40 cm. tall, or, in alpine or high northern plants, dwarf; leaves mostly basal, the blades 5 to 10 cm. long, 1 to 3 mm. wide; panicle pyramidal, 5 to 15 cm. long, the lower branches whorled and spreading; glumes 2.5 to 3 mm. long, acute; lemma a little shorter than the glumes, awned, the awn usually bent and exserted; palea obsolete or nearly so. ♃ (*A. bakeri* Rydb., lemma with a straight awn or awnless.)—Rocky slopes and moist banks at high latitudes and altitudes,

FIGURE 494.—*Agrostis borealis*. Panicle, × 1; glumes and floret, × 5. (Faxon 99, N. H.)

Newfoundland and Greenland to Alaska, south to the high mountains of New England and New York; West Virginia; summit of Roan Mountain, N. C.; Alberta and Washington to Wyoming, Colorado, and Utah; northern Europe.

FIGURE 495.—*Agrostis longiligula*. Panicle, × 1; glumes and floret, × 5. (Type.)

37. Agrostis longilígula Hitchc. (Fig. 495.) Culms erect, about 60 cm. tall; ligule 5 to 6 mm. long; blades 10 to 15 cm. long, 3 to 4 mm. wide, scabrous; panicle narrow, but loosely flowered, bronze purple, 10 to 15 cm. long, the branches very scabrous; glumes 4 mm. long; lemma 2.5 mm. long, bearing at the middle a bent exserted awn; palea minute. ♃ —Bogs and marshes at low altitudes, Tillamook County, Oreg., to Marin County, Calif.

Agrostis longiligula var. austrális J. T. Howell. Ligule 4 to 11 mm. long; awn of lemma straight, about 1 mm. long or obsolete. ♃ —Wet places, Marin, Sonoma, and Mendocino Counties, Calif.

Agrostis nebulósa Boiss. and Reut. Cloudgrass. Culms slender, branching, about 30 cm. tall; foliage scant; panicle delicate, oblong, half as long as the plant, the branches in verticils; spikelets 1 mm. long. ⊙ (Sometimes called *A. capillaris*, not *A. capillaris* L.)—Cultivated for dry bouquets. Spain.

72. PHÍPPSIA (Trin.) R. Br.

Spikelets 1-flowered, the rachilla disarticulating above the glumes, not prolonged; glumes unequal, minute, the first sometimes wanting; lemma thin, somewhat keeled, 3-nerved, abruptly acute; palea a little shorter than the lemma, dentate. Dwarf, tufted perennial, with narrow, few-flowered panicles of small spikelets. Type species, *Phippsia algida*. Named for C. J. Phipps.

1. Phippsia álgida (Phipps) R. Br. (Fig. 496.) Culms densely tufted, 2 to 10 cm. tall; blades soft, narrow, with boat-shaped tip; lemma about 1.5 mm. long. ♃ —Summit of Grays Peak, Colo.; Arctic regions of both hemispheres.

73. COLEÁNTHUS Seidel

Spikelets 1-flowered; glumes wanting; lemma ovate, hyaline, terminating in a short awn; palea broad, 2-toothed, the keels awn-tipped. Dwarf annual, with short flat blades and small panicles. Type species, *Coleanthus subtilis*. Name from Greek *koleos*, sheath, and *anthos*, flower, alluding to the sheaths enclosing the base of the panicles.

1. Coleanthus súbtilis (Tratt.) Seidel. (Fig. 497.) Culms spreading, forming little mats, mostly less than 5 cm. long; panicle 5 to 10 mm. long, the short branches verticillate; lemma about 1 mm. long, the awn about equaling the dark caryopsis. ⊙ —Mud flats along the lower Columbia River, Oregon and Washington, well established but probably introduced; northern Eurasia.

Mibóra mínima (L.) Desv. Delicate annual, 3 to 10 cm. tall with short narrow blades and slender racemes of 6 to 8 appressed purple spikelets, 2 mm. long, the glumes obtuse, the lemma and palea shorter, pubescent. ⊙ —Plymouth, Mass.; introduced from Europe.

Figure 496.—*Phippsia algida*. Plant, × ½; glumes and floret, × 10. (Oldmixon, Alaska.)

FIGURE 497.—*Coleanthus subtilis*. Plant, × 1; lemma and palea and two views of spikelet with ripe caryopsis, × 20. (Howell, Oreg.)

74. CÍNNA L. WOODREED

Spikelets 1-flowered, disarticulating below the glumes, the rachilla forming a stipe below the floret and produced behind the palea as a minute bristle; glumes equal or subequal, 1- to 3-nerved; lemma similar to the glumes, nearly as long, 3-nerved, bearing a minute, short, straight awn just below the apex (rarely awnless); palea 1-keeled. Tall perennials with flat blades and close or open panicles. Type species, *Cinna arundinacea*. *Cinna* (kinna) an old Greek name for a grass.

Our two species furnish highly palatable forage but usually are not abundant enough to be of much importance.

Spikelets 5 mm. long; panicle rather dense, the branches ascending.... 1. C. ARUNDINACEA.
Spikelets 3.5 to 4 mm. long; panicle loose, the branches spreading or drooping.
2. C. LATIFOLIA.

1. Cinna arundinácea L. STOUT WOODREED. (Fig. 498.) Culms erect, usually 1 to 1.5 m. tall, often somewhat bulbous at base, solitary or few in a tuft; sheaths glabrous; ligule rather prominent, thin; blades flat, scabrous, mostly less than 1 cm. wide; panicle many-flowered, nodding, grayish, 15 to 30 cm. long, the branches ascending; spikelets 5 to 6 mm. long; glumes somewhat unequal, acute, the second 3-nerved; lemma usually a little longer than the first glume, bearing below the tip a minute straight awn; palea apparently 1-nerved. ♃ —Moist woods, Maine to South Dakota, south to Georgia and eastern Texas. CINNA ARUNDINACEA var. INEXPÁNSA Fern. and Grisc. Panicle narrower, the shorter branches ascending; spikelets 3.7 to 4.2 mm. long. ♃ —Margin of swamps and moist woods, southeast Virginia.

2. Cinna latifólia (Trevir.) Griseb. DROOPING WOODREED. (Fig. 499.) Resembling *C. arundinacea;* blades shorter and on the average wider, as much as 1.5 cm. wide; panicle green, looser, the branches fewer, spreading or drooping, naked at base for as much as 5 cm.; spikelets about 4 mm. long; awn of lemma sometimes as much as 1 mm. long (rarely wanting); palea 2-nerved, the nerves very close together. ♃ —Moist woods, Newfoundland and Labrador to Alaska, south to Connecticut, in the mountains to North Carolina and Tennessee, to Michigan, Illinois, South Dakota, in the Rocky Mountains to northern New Mexico, to Utah and central California; northern Eurasia.

75. LIMNÓDEA L. H. Dewey

Spikelets 1-flowered, disarticulating below the glumes, the rachilla prolonged behind the palea as a short slender bristle; glumes equal, firm; lemma membranaceous, smooth,

FIGURE 498.—*Cinna arundinacea*. Plant, × ½; glumes and floret, × 10. (Dewey 336, Va.)

FIGURE 499.—*Cinna latifolia*. Panicle, × 1; glumes and floret, × 10. (Sandberg 713, Minn.)

nerveless, 2-toothed at the apex, bearing from between the teeth a slender bent awn, twisted at base; palea a little shorter than the lemma. Slender annual with flat blades and narrow panicles. Type species, *Limnodea arkansana*. Name altered from *Limnas*, a genus of grasses.

FIGURE 500.—*Limnodea arkansana*. Plant, × ½; glumes and floret, × 10. (Orcutt 5910, Tex.)

1. Limnodea arkansána (Nutt.) L. H. Dewey. (Fig. 500.) Culms branching at base, 20 to 40 cm. tall; blades more or less pubescent on both surfaces; panicle 5 to 15 cm. long, narrow but loose; spikelets 3.5 to 4 mm. long; glumes hispidulous or pilose; awn 8 to 10 mm. long. ♃ —Dry soil, prairies and river banks, Coastal Plain, Florida to Texas, Arkansas, and Oklahoma. The form with pilose glumes has been called *L. arkansana* var. *pilosa* (Trin.) Scribn.

76. ALOPECÚRUS L. Foxtail

Spikelets 1-flowered, disarticulating below the glumes, strongly compressed laterally; glumes equal, usually united at base, ciliate on the keel; lemma about as long as the glumes, 5-nerved, obtuse, the margins united at base, bearing from below the middle a slender dorsal awn, this included or exserted two or three times the length of the spikelet; palea wanting. Low or moderately tall perennials or some annuals, with flat blades and soft, dense, spikelike panicles. Type species, *Alopecurus pratensis.* Name from Greek *alopex*, fox, and *oura*, tail, alluding to the cylindric panicle.

The species of *Alopecurus* are all palatable and nutritious forage grasses, but usually are not found in sufficient abundance to be of great importance. *A. pratensis*, meadow foxtail, is sometimes used as a meadow grass in the eastern United States; *A. aequalis* is the most common on the western ranges.

Spikelets 5 to 6 mm. long. Introduced perennials.
  Panicle slender, tapering at each end; glumes scabrous on the keel. 1. A. MYOSUROIDES.
  Panicle cylindric, dense; glumes conspicuously ciliate on the keel........ 2. A. PRATENSIS.
Spikelets 2 to 4 mm. long (rarely 5 mm. in *A. saccatus*, annual). Native species.
  Plants perennial.
    Spikelets densely woolly all over; panicle oblong, 1 to 5 cm. long, about 1 cm. thick. 3. A. ALPINUS.
    Spikelets not woolly; panicle linear or oblong-linear, less than 1 cm. thick.
      Awn scarcely exceeding the glumes........ 5. A. AEQUALIS.
      Awn exserted 2 mm. or more.
        Awn exserted 2 to 3 mm.; panicle 3 to 4 mm. thick; spikelets 2.5 mm. long. 6. A. GENICULATUS.
        Awn exserted 3 to 5 mm.; panicle 4 to 6 mm. thick; spikelets about 3 mm. long. 4. A. PALLESCENS.
  Plants annual.
    Spikelets 4 to 5 mm. long; panicle relatively loose........ 9. A. SACCATUS.
    Spikelets 2 to 3.5 mm. long; panicle dense.
      Spikelets 2 to 2.5 mm. long; anthers 0.5 mm. long........ 7. A. CAROLINIANUS.
      Spikelets 3 to 3.5 mm. long; anthers about 1 mm. long........ 8. A. HOWELLII.

1. Alopecurus myosuroídes Huds. (Fig. 501.) Annual; culms tufted, slightly scabrous, 10 to 50 cm. tall, erect or decumbent at base; blades usually 2 to 3 mm. wide; panicle slender, somewhat tapering at each end, 4 to 10 cm. long, 3 to 5 mm. wide; glumes 6 mm. long, pointed, whitish with 3 green nerves, glabrous, scabrous on the keel, short-ciliate at base; lemma about as long as the glumes, the awn bent, exserted 5 to 8 mm. ⊙ (*A. agrestis* L.)—Fields, waste places, and ballast ground, Maine to North Carolina, Kansas, Texas, Washington, to California; introduced, rare; Eurasia.

2. Alopecurus praténsis L. Meadow foxtail. (Fig. 502.) Perennial; culms erect, 30 to 80 cm. tall; blades 2 to 6 mm. wide; panicle 3 to 7 cm. long, 7 to 10 mm. thick; glumes 5 mm. long, villous on the keel and pubescent on the sides; awn exserted 2 to 5 mm. ♃ —Fields and waste places, Newfoundland and Labrador to Alaska, south to Delaware and Missouri; Montana, Idaho, and Oregon.

Introduced; Eurasia. Occasionally cultivated as a meadow grass.

3. Alopecurus alpínus J. E. Smith. ALPINE FOXTAIL. (Fig. 503.) Perennial; culms erect or often decumbent at base, rather stiff and rushlike, 10 to 80 cm. tall, with slender rhizomes; sheaths glabrous, often inflated; blades 3 to 5 mm. wide; panicle ovoid or oblong, 1 to 4 cm. long, about 1 cm. wide, woolly; glumes 3 to 4 mm. long, woolly; lemma awned near the base, the awn exserted slightly or as much as 5 mm. ♃ —Mountain meadows and along brooks, Greenland to Alaska, south in the Rocky Mountains to Colorado and Utah; Arctic regions and northern Eurasia.

4. Alopecurus palléscens Piper. WASHINGTON FOXTAIL. (Fig. 504.) Perennial, tufted, pale green; culms 30 to 50 cm. tall, erect, or lower nodes geniculate; sheaths somewhat inflated; panicle pale, dense, 2 to 7 cm. long, 4 to 6 mm. thick; glumes about 3 mm. long, ciliate on the keel, appressed-pubescent on the sides; lemma awned near the base, the awn exserted 3 to 5 mm.; anthers about 2 mm. long. ♃ —Edges of ponds and wet places, British Columbia and Montana to Washington and northern California.

5. Alopecurus aequális Sobol. SHORT-AWN FOXTAIL. (Fig. 505.) Perennial; culms erect or spreading, usually not rooting at the nodes, 15 to 60 cm. tall; blades 1 to 4 mm. wide; panicle slender, 2 to 7 cm. long, about 4 mm. thick; spikelets 2 mm. long; awn of lemma scarcely exserted; anthers about 0.5 mm. long. ♃ (*A. aristulatus* Michx.)—In water and wet places, Greenland to Alaska, south to Pennsylvania, Illinois, Kansas, New Mexico, and California; Eurasia.

6. Alopecurus geniculátus L. WATER FOXTAIL. (Fig. 506.) Differing from *A. aequalis* chiefly in the usually more decumbent culms rooting at the nodes and the longer awn exserted 2 to 3 mm., giving the panicle a softly bristly appearance; spikelets about 2.5 mm. long, the tip dark purple;

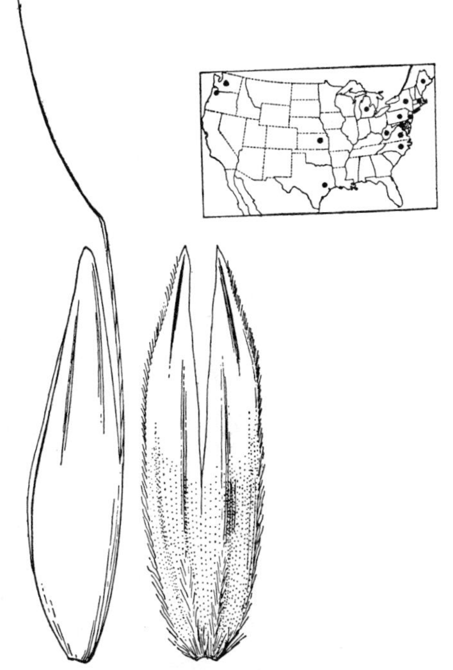

FIGURE 501.—*Alopecurus myosuroides*. Glumes and floret, × 10. (Commons, 14, Del.)

awn of lemma about as long again as the spikelet; anthers about 1.5 mm. long. ♃ —In water and wet places, Newfoundland to Saskatchewan and British Columbia; Maine to Virginia; Pennsylvania, Michigan, Wisconsin; Kansas and Wyoming to Utah; Montana; Washington to California and Arizona; Eurasia.

7. Alopecurus caroliniánus Walt. (Fig. 507.) Annual; culms tufted, much branched at base, 10 to 50 cm. tall; similar to *A. geniculatus* and *A. aequalis,* but panicle more slender than in the former; spikelets 2 to 2.5 mm. long, pale, the awn as in *A. geniculatus;* anthers about 0.5 mm. long. ⊙ (*A. ramosus* Poir.)—Moist open ground, old fields, and wet places, British Columbia; Long Island, N. Y., to Florida, Washington, and California, except West Virginia, Nevada, and New Mexico.

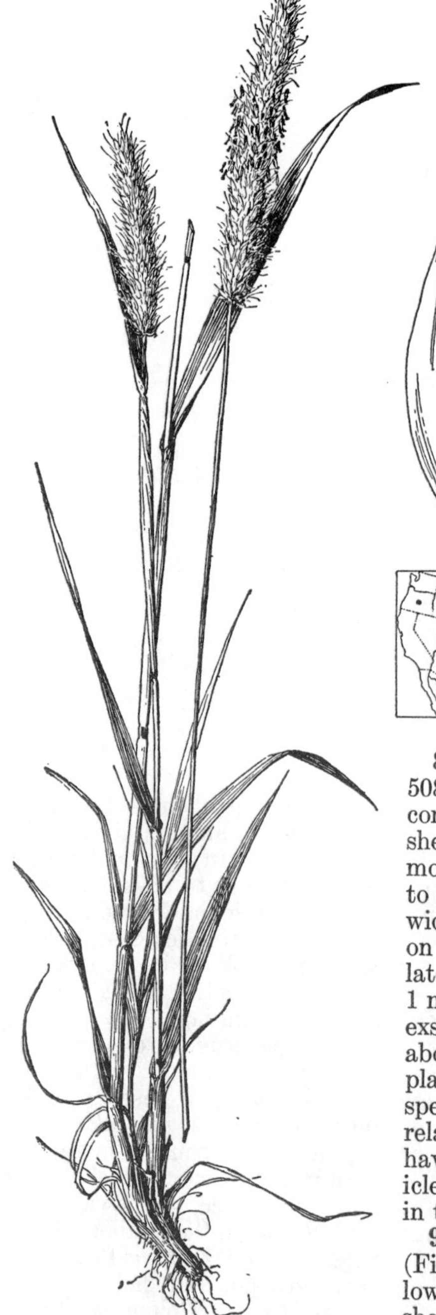

FIGURE 502.—*Alopecurus pratensis*. Plant, × ½; glumes and floret, × 10. (Henderson, Oreg.)

8. **Alopecurus howéllii** Vasey. (Fig. 508.) Annual; culms 15 to 30 cm. tall, commonly geniculate at lower nodes; sheaths, especially the uppermost, more or less inflated; panicle oblong to linear, 2 to 6 cm. long, 4 to 7 mm. wide; glumes 3 to 3.5 mm. long, ciliate on the keel, appressed-pilose on the lateral nerves; awn attached less than 1 mm. from the base of lemma, bent, exserted 3 to 5 mm.; anthers orange, about 1 mm. long. ⊙ —Wet places, Oregon and California. This species and the following are closely related and may not be distinct. Both have dwarf specimens with small panicles short-exserted or partly included in the inflated upper sheath.

9. **Alopecurus saccátus** Vasey. (Fig. 509.) On the average somewhat lower than *A. howellii*, the upper sheaths inflated, the panicle 2 to 4 cm. long, rather less dense, short exserted or partly included; spikelets 4 to 5 mm. long, the awn exserted 5 to

8 mm.; anthers 1 mm. long. ⊙ — Wet places, along the Columbia River, Washington and Oregon; California (Colusa County).

Alopecurus créticus Trin. Annual, 10 to 40 cm. tall; panicle dense; spikelets wedge-shaped, 4 mm. long; glumes firm, the keels broadly winged toward the summit, ciliate; lemma truncate, the awn from near the base. Waif, ballast, Philadelphia, Pa.; Europe.

Alopecurus réndlei Eig. Annual; culms 15 to 30 cm. tall, geniculate; upper sheaths inflated; panicle 1.5 to 2 cm. long, 7 to 9 mm. wide; spikelets 5 to 6 mm. long, almost diamond-shaped, the glumes inflated-gibbous

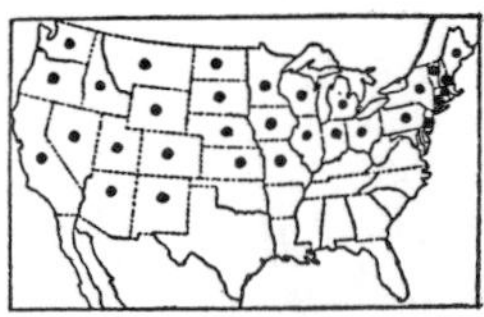

FIGURE 505.—*Alopecurus aequalis.* Panicle, × 1; glumes and floret, × 10. (Fernald, Maine.)

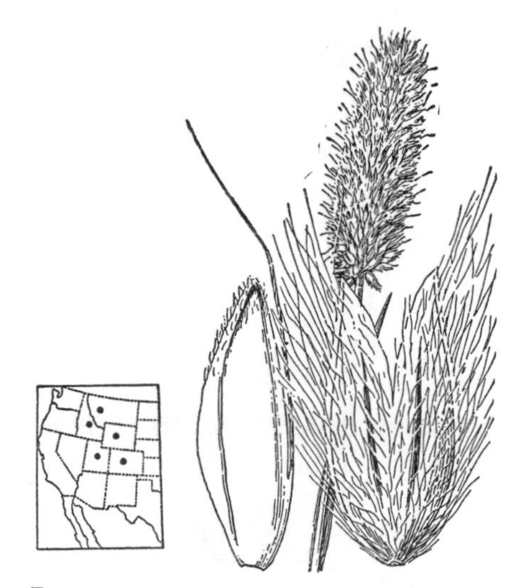

FIGURE 503.—*Alopecurus alpinus.* Panicle, × 1; glumes and floret, × 10. (Hall and Harbour 682, Colo.)

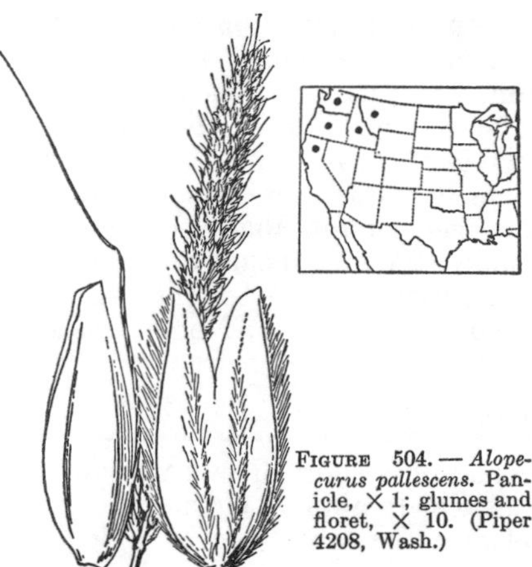

FIGURE 504. — *Alopecurus pallescens.* Panicle, × 1; glumes and floret, × 10. (Piper 4208, Wash.)

FIGURE 506.—*Alopecurus geniculatus.* Panicle, × 1; glumes and floret, × 10. (Weatherby 3394, Mass.)

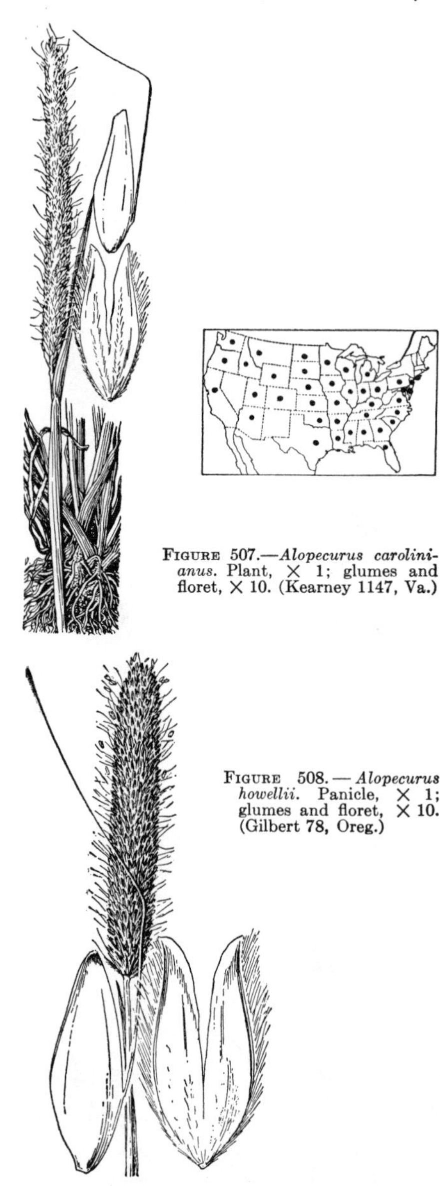

FIGURE 507.—*Alopecurus carolinianus.* Plant, × 1; glumes and floret, × 10. (Kearney 1147, Va.)

FIGURE 508. — *Alopecurus howellii.* Panicle, × 1; glumes and floret, × 10. (Gilbert 78, Oreg.)

FIGURE 509.—*Alopecurus saccatus.* Panicle, × 1; glumes and floret, × 10. (Suksdorf 188, Wash.)

and indurate on the back about the middle; awn 5 to 10 mm. long. ⊙ —Waif, ballast, old Navy Yard, Philadelphia, Pa.; Europe.

Alopecurus arundináceus Poir. Tall rhizomatous perennial; blades 3 to 10 mm. wide; panicle 4 to 10 cm. long, 7 to 8 mm. thick, often purplish; spikelets 4 to 5 mm. long; glumes sparsely pubescent, long-ciliate on the keel; lemma about equaling the glumes, the awn included or exserted 1 to 3 mm. ♃ —Adventive in hay meadows, Labrador; North Dakota; Eurasia.

77. POLYPÓGON Desf.

Spikelets 1-flowered, the pedicel disarticulating a short distance below the glumes, leaving a short-pointed callus attached; glumes equal, entire or 2-lobed, awned from the tip or from between the lobes, the awn slender, straight; lemma much shorter than the glumes, hyaline, usually bearing a slender straight awn shorter than the awns of the glumes. Usually decumbent annuals or perennials with flat scabrous blades and dense, bristly, spikelike panicles. Type species, *Polypogon monspeliensis*. Name from Greek *polus*, much, and *pogon*, beard, alluding to the bristly inflorescence.

One species, *P. monspeliensis*, is palatable to stock and is sometimes sufficiently abundant on low meadows to be of importance in the West.

Plants annual.
  Glumes slightly lobed, the lobes not ciliate........ 1. P. MONSPELIENSIS.
  Glumes prominently lobed, the lobes ciliate-fringed........ 2. P. MARITIMUS.
Plants perennial.
  Glumes gradually narrowed into the awn........ 5. P. ELONGATUS.
  Glumes abruptly rounded at summit.
    Awns rather stiff and straight; glumes 2.5 to 3 mm. long........ 3. P. INTERRUPTUS.
    Awns delicate, flexuous; glumes 1.5 to 2 mm. long........ 4. P. AUSTRALIS.

1. Polypogon monspeliénsis (L.) Desf. RABBITFOOT GRASS. (Fig. 510.) Annual; culms erect or decumbent at base, 15 to 50 cm. tall (sometimes depauperate or as much as 1 m. tall); ligule 5 to 6 mm. long; blades in average plants 4 to 6 mm. wide; panicle dense, spikelike, 2 to 15 cm. long, 1 to 2 cm. wide, tawny yellow when mature; glumes hispidulous, about 2 mm. long, the awns 6 to 8 mm. long, rarely longer; lemma smooth and shining, about half as long as the glumes, the delicate awn slightly exceeding them. ⊙ —Ballast and waste places, New Brunswick to Georgia, Oklahoma, and Texas, west to Alaska and California, infrequent in the East, mostly confined to the coastal States, a common weed in the Western States; at low altitudes, south to Argentina; introduced from Europe.

2. Polypogon marítimus Willd. (Fig. 511.) Annual; culms 20 to 30 cm. tall, upright or spreading; ligule as much as 6 mm. long; blades usually less than 5 cm. long, 2 to 4 mm. wide; panicle mostly smaller and less dense than in *P. monspeliensis;* glumes about 2.5 mm. long, hispidulous below, the deep lobes ciliate-fringed, the awns 7 to 10 mm. long; lemma awnless. ⊙ —Introduced, Georgia (Tybee Island); Nebraska, California (Napa and New York Falls, Amador County); Mediterranean region.

3. Polypogon interrúptus H. B. K. DITCH POLYPOGON. (Fig. 512.) Perennial; culms tufted, geniculate at base, 30 to 80 cm. tall; ligule 2 to 5 mm. long or the uppermost longer; blades commonly 4 to 6 mm. wide; panicle oblong, 5 to 15 cm. long, more or less interrupted or lobed; glumes equal, 2.5 to 3 mm. long, scabrous, the awns 3 to 5 mm. long; lemma smooth and shining, 1 mm. long, minutely toothed at the truncate apex, the awn exceeding the glumes. ♃ (*P. lutosus* of Manual, ed. 1, a doubtful species of Europe.)—Ditches and wet places at low altitudes, British Columbia to California, east to Louisiana; Nebraska; Oklahoma; south to Argentina.

4. Polypogon austrális Brongn. (Fig. 513.) Perennial; culms as much as 1 m. tall; ligule 2 to 3 mm. long, fragile; blades commonly 5 to 7 mm. wide; panicle soft, lobed or interrupted, mostly 8 to 15 cm. long, the numerous awns purplish; glumes 1.5 to 2 mm. long, hispidulous, the awn flexuous, delicate, 4 to 6 mm. long; lemma about two-thirds as long as the glumes, the awn about 3 mm. long. ♃ (*P. crinitus* Trin., not Nutt.)—Introduced at Bingen, Wash.; Chile and Argentina.

5. Polypogon elongátus H. B. K. (Fig. 514.) Perennial; culms rather coarse, as much as 1 m. tall, erect or decumbent at base; sheaths glabrous; ligule prominent, as much as 8 mm. long, lacerate, decurrent; blades 10 to 20 cm. long, 6 to 8 mm. or as much as 10 mm. wide, very scabrous; panicle erect or nodding, loose, interrupted, 15 to 30 cm. long, the branches clustered, densely flowered to the base; glumes about 3 mm. long,

FIGURE 510.—*Polypogon monspeliensis*. Plant, × ½; glumes and floret, × 10. (Chase 5584, Calif.)

hispidulous, gradually narrowed to an awn 2 to 3 mm. long; lemma 1.5 mm. long, the awn 1 to 2 mm. long. ♃ —Wet places, along streams and ditches, Arizona (Santa Rita Mountains); Mexico to Argentina.

78. LYCÚRUS H. B. K.

Spikelets 1-flowered; glumes awned, the first usually 2-awned; lemma narrow, firm, longer than the glumes, tapering into a slender awn. Slender perennial, with grayish, bristly spikelike panicles, the spikelets borne in pairs, the lower of the pair sterile, the two falling together. Type species, *Lycurus phleoides*. Name for Greek *lukos*, wolf, and *oura*, tail, alluding to the spikelike panicles.

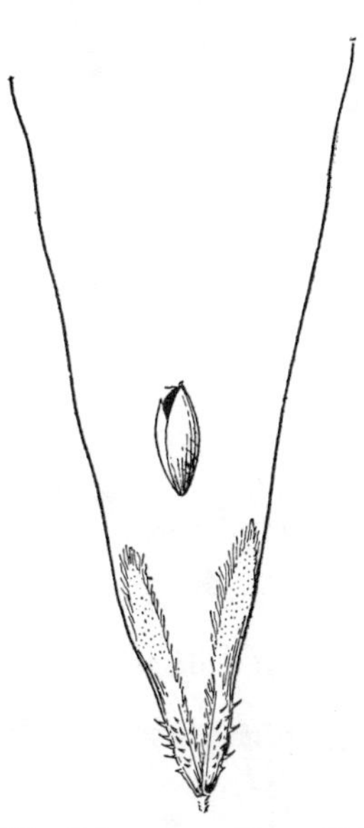

FIGURE 511.—*Polypogon maritimus*, × 10. (Hansen 607, Calif.)

FIGURE 512.—*Polypogon interruptus*. Panicle, × 1; glumes and floret, × 10. (Hitchcock 2686, Calif.)

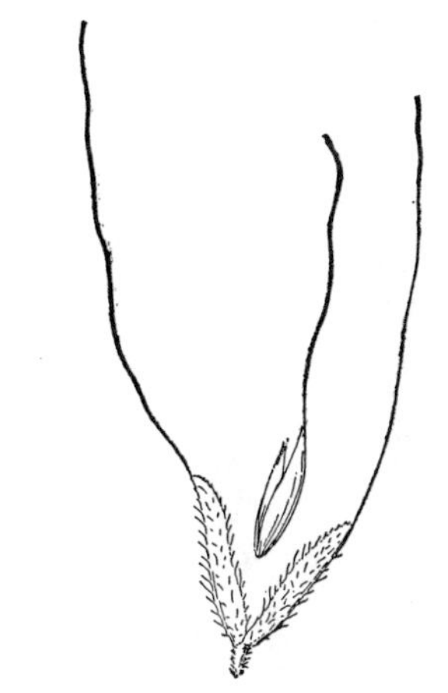

FIGURE 513.—*Polypogon australis*, × 10. (Suksdorf 10091, Wash.)

FIGURE 514.—*Polypogon elongatus*. Glumes and floret, × 10. (Silveus 3488, Ariz.)

1. Lycurus phleoídes H. B. K. WOLFTAIL. (Fig. 515.) Culms densely tufted, 20 to 60 cm. tall, compressed, erect or decumbent at base; blades flat or folded, 1 to 2 mm. wide, those of the culm mostly less than 10 cm. long; panicle 3 to 6 cm. long, about 5 mm. thick; spikelets including awns about 5 mm. long, the glumes shorter than the lemma, the first 2- or 3-

FIGURE 515.—*Lycurus phleoides*. Plant, × ½; glumes and floret, × 10. (Rydberg 2363, Colo.)

FIGURE 516.—*Phleum pratense*. Plant, × ½; glumes and floret, × 10. (Mearns 2209, Wyo.)

awned, the second usually 1-awned, the awns slightly spreading; lemma 3-nerved, pubescent on the margins, the awn 2 to 3 mm. long; palea about as long as the lemma, pubescent. ♃ —Plains and rocky hills, Colorado and Utah to Texas and Arizona, south to southern Mexico. Adventive in wool waste, Maine. An important southwestern forage grass.

79. PHLÉUM L. Timothy

Spikelets 1-flowered, laterally compressed, disarticulating above the glumes; glumes equal, membranaceous, keeled, abruptly mucronate or awned or gradually acute; lemma shorter than the glumes, hyaline, broadly truncate, 3- to 5-nerved; palea narrow, nearly as long as the lemma. Annuals or perennials, with erect culms, flat blades, and dense, cylindric panicles. Type species, *Phleum pratense*. Name from Greek *phleos*, an old name for a marsh reed.

The common species, *P. pratense*, or timothy, is our most important hay grass. It is cultivated in the humid regions, the Northeastern States, south to the Cotton Belt, and west to the 100th meridian, and also in the humid region of Puget Sound and in mountain districts. The native species, *P. alpinum*, alpine timothy, furnishes forage in mountain meadows of the Western States.

Panicle cylindric, several times longer than wide.. 1. P. pratense.
Panicle ovoid or oblong, usually not more than twice as long as wide........ 2. P. alpinum.

1. Phleum praténse L. Timothy. (Fig. 516.) Culms 50 to 100 cm. tall, from a swollen or bulblike base, forming large clumps; blades elongate, mostly 5 to 8 mm. wide; panicle cylindric, commonly 5 to 10 cm. long, often longer, the spikelets crowded, spreading; glumes about 3.5 mm. long, truncate with a stout awn 1 mm. long, pectinate-ciliate on the keel. ♃ —Commonly escaped from cultivation along roadsides and in fields and waste places throughout the United States; Eurasia. In some localities known as herd's grass.

2. Phleum alpínum L. Alpine timothy. (Fig. 517.) Culms 20 to 50 cm. tall, from a decumbent, somewhat creeping, densely tufted base; blades mostly less than 10 cm. long, 4 to 6 mm. wide; panicle ellipsoid or short-cylindric, bristly; glumes about 5 mm. long, hispid-ciliate on the keel, the awns 2 mm. long. ♃ —Common in mountain meadows, in bogs and wet places, Greenland to Alaska, south in the mountains of Maine and New Hampshire; northern Michigan; in the mountains of the Western States to New Mexico and California; also on the seacoast at Fort Bragg, Calif., and northward; Mexico; Eurasia and Arctic and alpine regions of the Southern Hemisphere.

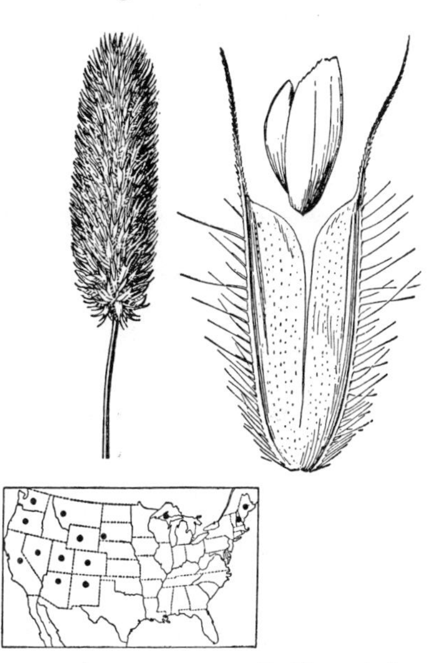

Figure 517.—*Phleum alpinum*. Panicle, × 1; glumes and floret, × 10. (Clements 337, Colo.)

Phleum arenárium L. Annual; culms tufted, 5 to 30 cm. tall; foliage scant, mostly basal, the blades 2 to 4 cm. long; panicle 1 to 3 cm. long, somewhat tapering at each end; glumes acuminate, strongly ciliate on

FIGURE 518.—*Gastridium ventricosum*. Plant, × ½; glumes and floret, × 10. (Davy and Blasdale 5340, Calif.)

the keel. ⊙ —Ballast near Portland, Oreg.; coast of Europe and North Africa.

Phleum subulátum (Savi) Aschers. and Graebn. Annual; culms 10 to 20 cm. tall; blades 2 to 5 cm. long; panicle linear-oblong, mostly 3 to 8 cm. long, 4 to 5 mm. thick; glumes 2 mm. long, scaberulous, subacute, the tips approaching. ⊙ —Ballast, Philadelphia, Pa., and near Portland, Oreg.; Mediterranean region.

Phleum paniculátum Huds. Annual; culms 10 to 30 cm. tall; foliage scabrous; panicle cylindric, 2 to 5 cm. long, 3 to 6 mm. thick; glumes 2 mm. long, glabrous, hard, widened upward to a truncate swollen summit, with a hard awn-point at the tip. ⊙ —Ballast near Portland, Oreg.; Mediterranean region.

80. GASTRÍDIUM Beauv.

Spikelets 1-flowered, the rachilla disarticulating above the glumes, prolonged behind the palea as a minute bristle; glumes narrow, unequal, somewhat swollen at the base; lemma much shorter than the glumes, hyaline, broad, truncate, awned or awnless; palea about as long as the lemma. Annual with flat blades and pale, shining, spikelike panicles. Type species, *Milium lendigerum* L. (*G. ventricosum*). Name from Greek *gastridion*, a small pouch, alluding to the slightly saccate glumes.

1. Gastridium ventricósum (Gouan) Schinz and Thell. NITGRASS. (Fig. 518.) Culms 20 to 40 cm. tall; foliage scant, blades scabrous; panicle 5 to 8 cm. long, dense, spikelike; spikelets slender, about 5 mm. long; glumes tapering into a long point, the second about one-fourth shorter than the first; floret minute, plump, pubescent, the delicate awn 5 mm. long, somewhat geniculate. ⊙ —Open ground and waste places, Oregon to California; Texas; also Boston, Mass.; introduced from Europe. A common weed on the Pacific coast, of no economic value.

81. LAGÚRUS L.

Spikelets 1-flowered, the rachilla disarticulating above the glumes, pilose under the floret, produced beyond the palea as a bristle; glumes subequal, thin, 1-nerved, villous, gradually tapering into a plumose awn-point; lemma shorter than the glumes, thin, glabrous, bearing on the back above the middle a slender, exserted, somewhat geniculate, awn, the summit bifid, the divisions delicately awn-tipped; palea narrow, thin, the two keels ending in minute awns. Annual, with pale, dense, ovoid or oblong woolly heads. Type species, *Lagurus ovatus.* Name from Greek *lagos,* hare, and *oura,* tail, alluding to the woolly heads.

1. Lagurus ovátus L. (Fig. 519.) Culms branching at the base, 10 to 30 cm. tall, slender, pubescent; sheaths and blades pubescent, the sheaths somewhat inflated, the blades flat, lax; panicle 2 to 3 cm. long, nearly as thick, pale and downy, bristling with dark awns; glumes very narrow, 10 mm. long, the awns of the lemmas much exceeding them. ⊙ —Cultivated for ornament and sparingly escaped; New Jersey; Pacific Grove, San Francisco, and Berkeley, Calif.; ballast, Beaufort, N. C.; Mediterranean region.

82. MUHLENBÉRGIA Schreb. Muhly

Spikelets 1-flowered (occasionally 2-flowered), the rachilla disarticulating above the glumes; glumes usually shorter than the lemma, sometimes as long, obtuse to acuminate or awned, keeled or convex on the back, the first sometimes small, rarely obsolete; lemma firm-membranaceous, 3-nerved (the nerves sometimes obscure or rarely an obscure additional pair), with a very short callus, rarely long-pilose, usually minutely pilose, the apex acute, awned from the tip or just below it, or from between very short lobes, sometimes only mucronate, the awn straight or flexuous. Perennial, or rarely annual, low or moderately tall or rarely robust grasses, tufted or rhizomatous, the culms simple or much-branched, the inflorescence a narrow (sometimes spikelike) or open panicle. Type species, *Muhlenbergia schreberi.* Named for G. H. E. Muhlenberg.

Many of the western species are important range grasses, forming a considerable proportion of the grass flora of the arid and semiarid regions, and long ago dubbed "muhly" by forest rangers. The most important of these are *M. montana* on mesas and rocky hills of the Western States, *M. pauciflora, M. emersleyi,* and *M. wrightii* in the Southwest.

1a. Plants annual.
  2a. Lemma awned.
    Awn of lemma 0.5 to 3 mm. long; glumes acuminate, hirsute.
      Spikelets 1.5 to 1.8 mm. long; relatively long pediceled and spreading along the panicle branches .... 5. M. texana.
      Spikelets 2 to 2.5 mm. long; short pediceled and mostly appressed along the panicle branches .... 6. M. eludens.
    Awn of lemma more than 5 mm. long.
      Second glume 3-nerved and often 3-toothed .... 9. M. pulcherrima.
      Second glume 1-nerved (rarely 2-nerved).
        First glume 2-nerved and usually bidentate.
          Glumes equal to or slightly longer than the floret; lemma about 3 mm. long; awn 2 to 10 mm. long .... 11. M. depauperata.
          Glumes shorter than the floret, sometimes minute, but usually about half as long as the lemma; lemma 4 to 5 mm. long; awn 10 to 20 mm. long. 12. M. brevis.
        First glume 1-nerved (rarely 2-nerved), entire or erose, but not bidentate.
          Glumes acuminate or aristate. Lateral nerves of lemma often ciliate. 10. M. pectinata.

FIGURE 519.—*Lagurus ovatus*. Plant, × ½; spikelet and floret, × 5. (Heller 5340, Calif.)

Glumes obtuse.

Panicle open, the branches spreading; lemma 2.5 to 3.5 mm. long.

7. M. MICROSPERMA.

Panicle very narrow, the branches appressed; lemma 4.5 to 6 mm. long.

8. M. APPRESSA.

2b, Lemma awnless (see also *M. texana*). Culms branching and panicle-bearing at base.

Pedicels capillary, elongate.
Panicles very diffuse; pedicels straight; glumes glabrous............ 3. M. FRAGILIS.
Panicles open but scarcely diffuse; glumes pilose.
Pedicels sinuous and tangled; glumes long-pilose........................ 4. M. SINUOSA.
Pedicels straight or subflexuous; glumes minutely pilose.... 2. M. MINUTISSIMA.
Pedicels short, appressed; glumes glabrous.
Panicles loose, delicate; spikelets 1 to 1.2 mm. long.......................... 1. M. WOLFII.
Panicles narrow, contracted; spikelets 2 mm. long.................. 13. M. FILIFORMIS.
Culms simple, compressed.. 29. M. UNIFLORA.
1b. Plants perennial.
3a. Rhizomes developed, usually prominent, scaly, creeping, often branching.
4a. Blades 2 mm. wide or less, mostly short and involute.
5a. Panicles open, the spikelets on slender pedicels.
Spikeless awned, 4 to 5 mm. long; blades involute. Panicle branches in stiffly spreading fascicles.. 50. M. PUNGENS.
Spikelets awnless, acutish or mucronate, 1 to 2 mm. long; blades flat.
Sheaths compressed keeled; panicle oblong; eastern species.
28. M. TORREYANA.
Sheaths rounded; panicle as broad as long; western species.
Ligule 1 to 2 mm. long, auricled... 26. M. ARENACEA.
Ligule minute, not auricled... 27. M. ASPERIFOLIA.
5b. Panicles narrow, more or less condensed, the spikelets on short pedicels.
Culms tall, stout, somewhat woody at base, as much as 6 mm. thick, 1 to 3 m. tall.
30. M. DUMOSA.
Culms lower, slender.
Lemma and palea glabrous.
Culms smooth, widely creeping, the blades fine, conspicuously recurved, spreading.
Spikelets about 3 mm. long.. 14. M. REPENS.
Spikelets about 2 mm. long.. 15. M. UTILIS.
Culms nodulose-roughened, erect or decumbent at base, sometimes spreading, but not widely creeping.. 16. M. RICHARDSONIS.
Lemma and palea pilose or villous on the lower half.
Awns 6 to 10 mm. long.
Panicles densely flowered; glumes as long as the floret.
21. M. POLYCAULIS.
Panicles loosely flowered; glumes about half as long as the floret.
23. M. ARSENEI.
Awns 1 to 3 mm. long or the lemma mucronate only.
Blades 5 to 10 cm., rarely 15 cm. long, flat......................... 20. M. GLAUCA.
Blades 1 to 3 cm. long, involute or pungently pointed.
Glumes about half as long as the floret; lemma 2 to 2.5 mm. long.
17. M. VILLOSA.
Glumes nearly as long as the floret; lemma 3 to 4 mm. long.
Culms glabrous below the nodes; sheaths glabrous (rarely pubescent below the summit); ligule 1 mm. long, short lacerate; lemma loosely villous on the margins on lower half and at the very base, mucronate to short awned.................................. 18. M. THURBERI.
Culms strigose below the nodes; sheaths often strigose to hirsute; ligule 0.5 to 1 mm. long; lemma densely villous on lower half; awn 1 to 3 mm. long... 19. M. CURTIFOLIA.
4b. Blades flat, at least some of them more than 3 mm., usually 5 mm. wide or more.
6a. Panicles loosely flowered, slender, much exceeding the leaves (see also *M. sylvatica*); glumes broad below, abruptly pointed, shorter than the body of the lemma.
Culms slender, rather weak, becoming much branched, glabrous or slightly scabrous below the nodes. Lemma acuminate, 2.5 to 3.5 mm. long, awned.
37. M. BRACHYPHYLLA.
Culms erect, simple or sparingly branched.
Spikelets 1.5 to 2.5 mm. long; lemma awnless or awn-tipped; blades commonly not more than 5 to 7 mm. wide...................................... 35. M. SOBOLIFERA.
Spikelets 3 to 4 mm. long; lemma with an awn 2 to 5 times as long as the body; blades commonly 8 mm. or more wide......................... 36. M. TENUIFLORA.
6b. Panicles usually densely flowered (sometimes loose in *M. sylvatica*); glumes tapering from base to apex. Culms commonly freely branching (often simple or nearly so in *M. glomerata*).
Hairs at base of floret copious, as long as the body of the lemma.... 31. M. ANDINA.
Hairs at base of floret inconspicuous, not more than half as long as the lemma.

Glumes with stiff scabrous awn-tips, much exceeding the awnless lemma; panicles terminal on the culm or leafy branches, compact, interrupted, bristly.
Culms mostly simple or branching at base; internodes minutely puberulent; sheaths not or scarcely keeled.......... 32. M. GLOMERATA.
Culms subcompressed, mostly branching from the middle nodes; internodes smooth and glossy except at summit; sheaths keeled. 33. M. RACEMOSA.
Glumes acuminate, sometimes awn-tipped but not stiff and exceeding the lemma; panicles terminal and axillary, numerous, not bristly.
Culms glabrous below the nodes; panicles not compact, the branches ascending; plants sprawling, top-heavy, the branchlets geniculate-spreading. 38. M. FRONDOSA.
Culms strigose below the nodes; panicles compact or if not the branches erect or nearly so; plants often bushy-branching but not sprawling with geniculate branchlets.
Callus hairs wanting; lemma nearly smooth, awnless. 39. M. GLABRIFLORA.
Callus hairs present; lemma pubescent below.
Panicles not compactly flowered; lemma with awn as much as 10 mm. or more long (nearly awnless in forma *attenuata*); some of the blades 10 to 15 cm. or more long.......... 40. M. SYLVATICA.
Panicles compactly flowered or, if not, lemma awnless; blades commonly less than 10 cm. long, but sometimes longer.
Sheaths glabrous.......... 41. M. MEXICANA.
Sheaths scabrous.......... 34. M. CALIFORNICA.

3b. Rhizomes wanting, the culms tufted, usually erect.
7a. Culms decumbent and rooting at the nodes.
Spikelets awnless; panicles open, diffuse.......... 29. M. UNIFLORA.
Spikelets awned; panicles narrow, the branches ascending or appressed.
Glumes minute, the first sometimes wanting.......... 42. M. SCHREBERI.
Glumes evident, as much as 3 mm. long (see also *M. schreberi* var. *palustris*).
Awns 1 to 2 mm. long.......... 43. M. CURTISETOSA.
Awns 5 to 20 mm. long.......... 22. M. PAUCIFLORA.
7b. Culms erect or spreading, but not rooting at the nodes.
Second glume 3-toothed (rarely not toothed in *M. filiculmis*).
Lemma 4 mm. long; culms relatively stout, 15 to 60 cm. tall.... 45. M. MONTANA.
Lemma 2.5 to 3 mm. long; culms filiform, 10 to 20 cm. tall.... 46. M. FILICULMIS.
Second glume usually acute or awned, sometimes erose-toothed, not distinctly 3-toothed.
8a. Panicle narrow or spikelike, the branches floriferous from the base or nearly so (see also *M. metcalfei*).
9a. Lemma acute, acuminate, mucronate or short-awned.
Blades involute.
Panicle elongate and spikelike.
Glumes and lemma or some of them awn-tipped.......... 70. M. MARSHII.
Glumes acute to blunt or erose; lemma not awn-tipped.
Ligule 2 to 3 mm. long; lower panicle branches sometimes 5 to 10 cm. long.......... 68. M. RIGENS.
Ligule 1 to 2 mm. long; lower panicle branches seldom more than 3 cm. long.......... 69. M. MUNDULA.
Panicle narrow but scarcely spikelike, the branches loosely flowered.
Blades mostly in a short basal cluster; panicle 5 to 8 cm. long. 44. M. JONESII.
Blades not in a short basal cluster; panicle 10 to 30 cm. long. 58. M. DUBIA.
Blades flat, folded, or loosely involute.
Panicle more or less spikelike.
Glumes obtuse; culms delicate. Ligule about 2 mm. long. 13. M. FILIFORMIS.
Glumes acute or acuminate; culms wiry.
Glumes gradually acute; culms minutely pubescent; ligule about 0.5 mm. long.......... 24. M. CUSPIDATA.
Glumes abruptly acute, usually awn-pointed or awned; culms hispidulous; ligule 1 to 3 mm. long.......... 25. M. WRIGHTII.
Panicle narrow, but not spikelike.
Lemma villous below.......... 67. M. EMERSLEYI.
Lemma glabrous or obscurely pubescent.

Lower sheaths compressed keeled........................ 65. M. LINDHEIMERI.
Lower sheaths not compressed keeled................ 64. M. LONGILIGULA.

9b. Lemma with an awn usually more than 5 mm. long, or some of the awns less in *M. dubioides* and *M. metcalfei.*
Old sheaths becoming flat and more or less coiled at base of plant. 47. M. VIRESCENS.
Old sheaths not flat and coiled.
Panicle mostly 20 to 40 cm. long.
Ligule 1 to 2 mm. long; glumes acute or awn-pointed. 59. M. DUBIOIDES.
Ligule 4 to 5 mm. long; glumes obtuse to subobtuse. 57. M. METCALFEI.
Panicle mostly 5 to 10 cm. long.
10a. Lemma pilose or villous on lower part.
Culms loosely tufted, hard and wiry at base.
Glumes and floret about equal; lemma 2.5 to 3 mm. long, villous below... 21. M. POLYCAULIS.
Glumes about half as long as floret; lemma 4 to 5 mm. long, sparsely pilose.. 23. M. ARSENEI.
Culms closely or somewhat loosely tufted, slender but not hard and wiry at base.. 48. M. MONTICOLA.
10b. Lemma scaberulous, not pilose.
Glumes less than 1 mm. long.................................. 49. M. PARVIGLUMIS.
Glumes 2 to 4 mm. long.. 22. M. PAUCIFLORA.

8b. Panicle open, or at least loose, the branches naked at base (sometimes shortly so in *M. metcalfei*).
Plants widely spreading, much branched, wiry, the base knotty. 51. M. PORTERI.
Plants erect, not widely spreading and much branched.
Blades flat, the midnerve and margins white-cartilaginous. 52. M. ARIZONICA.
Blades folded or involute, or occasionally some of them flat.
Blades short in a basal cluster.
Panicle mostly less than 15 cm. long; blades 1 to 3 cm. long, involute, curled or falcate... 53. M. TORREYI.
Panicle mostly more than 20 cm. long; blades commonly 5 to 8 cm. long, flat or usually folded.. 54. M. ARENICOLA.
Blades elongate.
11a. Panicle open or diffuse, if narrow, the branches slender; capillary, more or less flexuous.
Awn of lemma less than 5 mm. long; panicle usually not more than twice as long as wide at maturity, the branches and pedicels stiff.
Plants fibrous at the base; lemma awnless or with an awn to 2 mm., rarely to 5 mm., long... 60. M. EXPANSA.
Plants not fibrous at base; lemma with an awn 2 to 5 mm. long. 61. M. REVERCHONI.
Awn of lemma usually more than 10 mm. long (sometimes awnless in *M. emersleyi*); panicle elongate, usually at least 4 times as long as wide at maturity.
Panicle diffuse, the branches more than 10 cm. long; pedicels usually much longer than the spikelets.................... 62. M. CAPILLARIS.
Panicle open but not diffuse.
Panicle deep purple; blades relatively coarse, some of them usually flat.. 63. M. RIGIDA.
Panicle pale or tawny; blades involute, scabrous.
Ligule 4 to 10 mm. long; glumes obtuse to subacute. 55. M. SETIFOLIA.
Ligule 1 to 3 mm. long; glumes acute to mucronate. 56. M. XEROPHILA.
11b. Panicle narrow, elongate, the branches rather stiffly ascending or appressed.
Lower sheaths rounded.. 57. M. METCALFEI.
Lower sheaths compressed-keeled.
Glumes as long as the floret; lemma villous below. 67. M. EMERSLEYI.
Glumes distinctly shorter than the floret; lemma pubescent on the margins toward the base.................................. 66. M. INVOLUTA.

FIGURE 520.—*Muhlenbergia wolfii*. Plant, × 1; spikelet and floret, × 10. (Hitchcock 7661, Mex.)

1. **Muhlenbergia wólfii** (Vasey) Rydb. (Fig. 520.) Annual; culms spreading, branching at base, 6 to 25 cm. tall; blades flat, mostly 1 to 3 cm. long, 1 mm. wide or less; panicle 2 to 6 cm. long, the simple branches ascending, the short, stiff pedicels appressed along the branches; spikelets 1 to 1.2 mm. long; glumes glabrous, about half as long as the spikelet; lemma rather turgid, minutely white-silky along the margins. ⊙ (*Sporobolus ramulosus* of Manual, ed. 1.)—Open or wooded slopes, mostly in thin soil, Colorado to northern Mexico and Arizona.

2. **Muhlenbergia minutíssima** (Steud.) Swallen. (Fig. 521.) Annual; culms erect to spreading, branching at base, 10 to 35 cm. tall; blades flat, mostly less than 10 cm. long, about 1 mm. wide; panicle half to three-fourths the length of the entire plant, the slender pedicels ascending; spikelets 1.2 to 1.5 mm. long, the glumes half to two-thirds as long, minutely pilose; lemma minutely silky-pubescent along the midnerve and margins. ⊙ (*Sporobolus microspermus* of Manual, ed. 1.)—Moist sandy or rocky slopes, Montana to Washington south to Texas, California, and northern Mexico.

3. **Muhlenbergia frágilis** Swallen. (Fig. 522.) Annual; culms geniculate-ascending, freely branching at base, 10 to 30 cm. tall; blades flat, mostly 2 to 6 cm. long, 1 to 1.5 mm. wide; panicle very diffuse, the capillary branches, branchlets, and pedicels widely spreading or reflexed, fragile; spikelets 1 to 1.1 mm. long, the glumes half to two-thirds as long, glabrous; lemma silky-pubescent on the keel and margins, the palea silky-pubescent between the nerves. ⊙ —Moist sandy soil and rocky hills, western Texas to southern Arizona, south to central Mexico.

4. **Muhlenbergia sinuósa** Swallen. (Fig. 523.) Annual; culms geniculate-ascending, freely branching at base; blades flat, mostly 4 to 10 cm. long, 1 to 1.5 mm. wide, minutely pubescent on both surfaces; panicle many-flowered, 14 to 22 cm. long, 2 to 6 cm. wide, the scabrous branches ascending, the elongate, capillary pedicels sinuous and tangled; spikelets often purple-tinged, 1.5 to 2 mm. long, the glumes about half as long, usually conspicuously pilose; lemma obtuse, delicately silky-pubescent below on the midnerve and margins, the broad palea equal. ⊙ —Moist canyon walls and borders of marshes, New Mexico and Arizona.

5. **Muhlenbergia texána** Buckl. (Fig. 524.) Annual, culms delicate, erect or ascending, branching at base, 10 to 30 cm. tall, the culms strongly

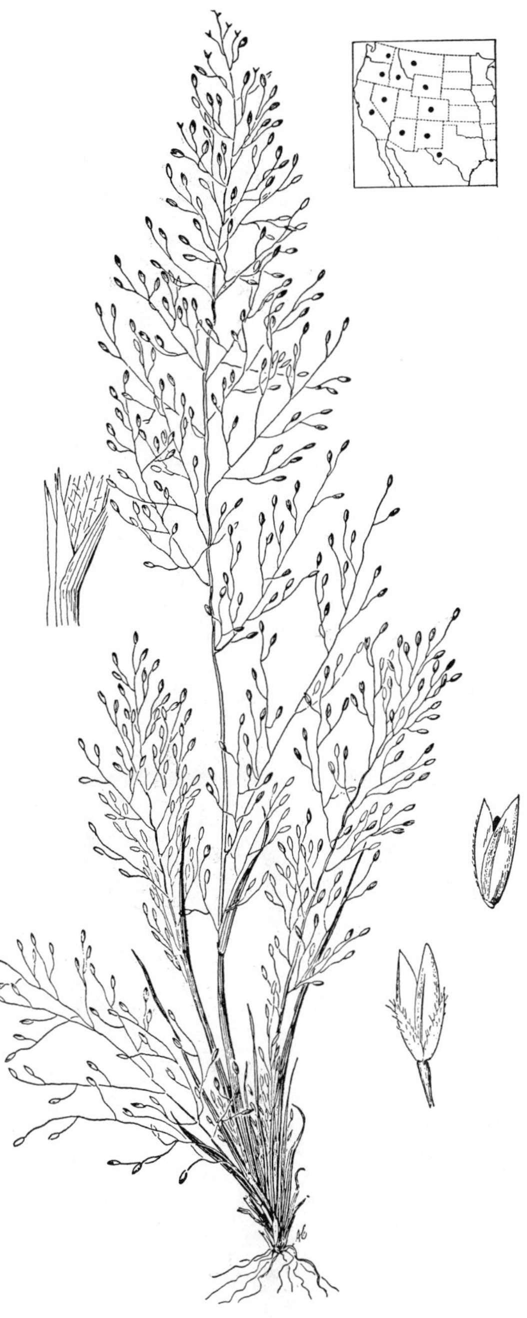

FIGURE 521.—*Muhlenbergia minutissima.* Plant, × 1; spikelet, floret, and ligule, × 10. (Metcalfe 1431, N. Mex.)

unequal; foliage scant, ligule about 2 mm. long, erose, decurrent down the sheath; blades 2 to 5 cm. long, about 1 mm. wide; panicle half to two-thirds

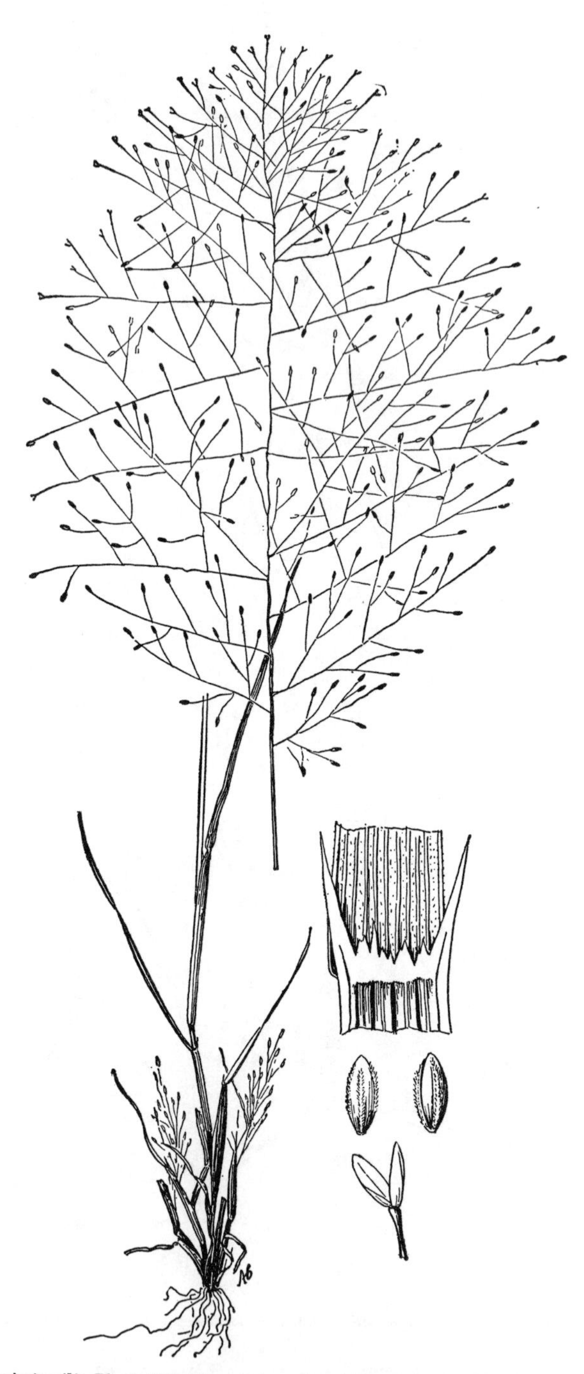

FIGURE 522.—*Muhlenbergia fragilis*. Plant, × 1; glumes, two views of floret, and ligule, × 10. (Type.)

FIGURE 523.—*Muhlenbergia sinuosa.* Plant, × 1; spikelet and ligule, × 10. (Type.)

FIGURE 524.—*Muhlenbergia texana.* Plant, × 1; spikelet and floret, × 10. (Wright 736, western Texas.)

the length of the plant, the delicate branches ascending or spreading; spikelets about 1.5 mm. long, on capillary mostly spreading pedicels 2 to 5 mm. long; glumes 1 and 1.5 mm. long, sparsely hirsute; lemma 1.6 to 1.8 mm. long, minutely silky on the nerves below, slightly notched and with a delicate awn 1 to 1.3 mm. long, the awns sometimes fallen in overmature specimens. ⊙ —Rocky canyons and slopes, western Texas to Arizona, northern Mexico, and Baja California; rare or overlooked.

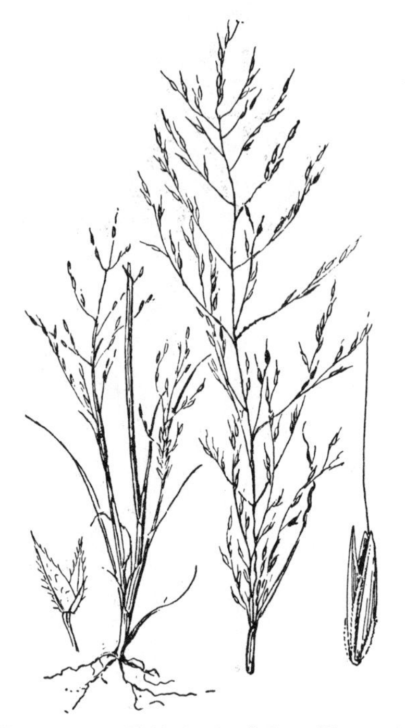

FIGURE 525.—*Muhlenbergia eludens*. Plant, × 1; glumes and floret, × 8. (Pringle 399, Mex.)

6. Muhlenbergia elúdens C. G. Reeder. (Fig. 525.) Annual, branching at base, culms slender, erect, 15 to 35 cm. tall, the culms strongly unequal; foliage scant, scabrous; ligule 2 to 2.5 mm. long; blades mostly 4 to 7 cm. long to 1.5 mm. wide, involute upward; panicle half to three-fourths the length of the plant, the slender branches relatively stiffly spreading; spikelets 2.2 to 2.5 mm. long, on short pedicels, mostly closely appressed to the branches; glumes about 1 to 1.5 mm. long, hirsute; lemma 2.3 mm. long, silky on the midnerve and margins, slightly notched and with an awn 2 to 2.5 mm. long. ⊙ (Included in *M. texana* in Manual, ed. 1.)—Rocky woods and wet ledges and gravel bars, to 2,400 m. altitude, New Mexico, Arizona, and northern Mexico.

7. Muhlenbergia microspérma (DC.) Kunth. LITTLESEED MUHLY. (Fig. 526.) Annual; culms densely tufted, branching and spreading at base, often purple, 10 to 30 cm. tall; blades mostly less than 3 cm. long, 1 to 2 mm. wide, scabrous; panicles narrow, 5 to 15 cm. long, the branches rather distant, ascending; spikelets on short thick pedicels; glumes broad, obtuse, subequal, less than 1 mm. long; lemma narrow, 2 to 4 mm. long, scabrous, the slender awn 1 to 3 cm. long. ⊙ —Open dry ground, Nevada, Arizona, and southern California to Peru. Cleistogamous spikelets are developed at the base of lower sheaths, solitary or few in a fascicle in each axil, each spikelet included in an indurate thickened, tightly rolled narrowly conical reduced sheath, which readily disarticulates from the plant at maturity. The glumes are wanting and awn of lemma reduced, but the grain is larger than that of the spikelets in the terminal inflorescence, being about the same length (2 mm.) but much thicker.

FIGURE 526.—*Muhlenbergia microsperma*. Plant, × 1; glumes and floret, × 10. (Mearns 2780, Ariz.)

8. Muhlenbergia appréssa C. O. Goodding. (Fig. 527.) Culms 10 to 40 cm. tall, erect or decumbent at base, much branched below; ligule lacerate, 2 to 3 mm. long; blades flat or folded, 1 to 4 cm. long, scabrous or puberulent; panicles numerous, as much as 20 cm. long, very narrow, loosely flowered, the branches appressed; glumes 1 to 2 mm. long or sometimes less, obtuse; lemma 4.5 to 6 mm. long, scabrous above, densely pilose on the callus and margins at the base; awn 10 to 30 mm. long. ⊙ —Canyons and slopes, southern Arizona. Cleistogamous spikelets similar to those in *M. microsperma* are common in the lower reduced sheaths.

FIGURE 527.—*Muhlenbergia appressa*. Plant, × 1; glumes and floret, × 10. (Type.)

9. Muhlenbergia pulchérrima Scribn. (Fig. 528.) Culms 10 to 25 cm. tall, erect, freely branching at the base; sheaths scabrous, longer than the internodes; ligule thin, 2 to 3 mm. long; blades flat, pubescent on the upper surface, mostly less than 5 cm. long and 1 mm. wide; panicles 3 to 5 cm. long, the branches ascending or appressed; first glume 0.5 to 1 mm. long, acute or notched, the second 2 mm. long, 2- or 3-toothed; lemma 3 to 4 mm. long, narrow, acuminate, minutely bifid, scabrous, pubescent on the lower half of the margins; awn slender, flexuous, mostly 10 to 15 mm. long, or sometimes only 5 mm. long. ⊙ —Rocky ledges and open ground, Arizona (Apache County); Chihuahua, Mexico.

FIGURE 528.—*Muhlenbergia pulcherrima*. Plant, × 1; glumes and floret, × 10. (Schroeder, Ariz.)

10. Muhlenbergia pectináta C. O. Goodding. (Fig. 529.) Culms 10 to 25 cm. long, erect to decumbent, sometimes rooting at the lower nodes, freely branching, angular; sheath margins often ciliate; ligule erose to ciliate, about 0.5 mm. long; blades flat to involute, 1 to 6 cm. long, 1 to 2 mm. wide, pubescent or sparsely pilose; panicles numerous, narrow, 2 to 12 cm. long; spikelets 3.5 to 4.5 mm. long; glumes abruptly acute or acuminate, commonly aristate, 1.5 to 2 mm. or sometimes 3 mm. long, the awn about half the entire length; lemma 3- to 5-nerved, scabrous to prominently ciliate on the lateral nerves, the callus appressed-pubescent; awn 10 to 30 mm. long. ⊙ —Moist rocky hillsides, southern Arizona; Mexico.

FIGURE 529.—*Muhlenbergia pectinata*. Plant, × 1; glumes and floret, × 10. (Type.)

11. Muhlenbergia depauperáta Scribn. (Fig. 530.) Culms 2 to 15 cm. tall, densely tufted, erect, scabrous to hispidulous below the nodes; blades 1 to 1.5 cm. long (rarely 3 cm.), 1 to 1.5 mm. wide, scabrous, puberulent on the upper surface, with white cartilaginous midnerve and margins; panicles narrow, spikelike, often included, 1 to 4 cm. long (rarely to 6 cm.), the branches and pedicels closely appressed; glumes narrow, scabrous, about equal to or slightly longer than the floret, the tips often spreading; first glume 2-nerved, bidentate or entire, 2.5 to 3.5 mm. long; second glume 1-nerved, acuminate-aristate, 3 to 4 mm. long; lemma 3 to 3.5 mm. long, prominently 3-nerved, scabrous above, sparsely pubescent on the internerves, the straight awn 2 to 10 mm. long, rarely less. ⊙ —Open gravelly places, Arizona and New Mexico; northern Mexico.

12. Muhlenbergia brévis C. O. Goodding. (Fig. 531.) Culms 3 to 20 cm. tall, erect, tufted, much branched below; ligule 1 to 3 mm. long, lacerate; blades flat to involute, 0.5 to 4 cm. long, scabrous or puberulent above, scabrous below; panicles 1 to 2 cm. long, narrow, rather densely flowered, the branches erect; glumes scabrous, variable, shorter than the floret; first glume 1 to 3 mm. long, 2-nerved, minutely to deeply bifid; second glume 1.5 to 4 mm. long (usu-

FIGURE 530.—*Muhlenbergia depauperata*. Plant, × 1; glumes and floret, × 10. (Hitchcock 13560, N. Mex.)

ally 2 to 3 mm.), 1-nerved, acuminate; lemma 4 to 5 mm. long, 3- to 5-nerved, scabrous, especially on the nerves, sparsely to rather densely appressed-pubescent on the internerves toward the base; awn 10 to 20 mm. long (rarely less). ⊙ (*M. depauperata* of Manual, ed. 1.)—Open ground at higher elevations, Colorado and Texas to Arizona; Mexico.

13. Muhlenbergia filifórmis (Thurb.) Rydb. PULL-UP MUHLY. (Fig. 532.) Annual, or sometimes appearing perennial, loosely tufted, rather soft and lax, erect or somewhat spreading; culms filiform, usually 5 to 15 cm. tall, sometimes as much as 30 cm.; ligule about 2 mm. long; blades flat, usually less than 3 cm. long; panicle narrow, interrupted, few-flowered, usually less than 5 cm. long; glumes ovate, 1 mm. long; lemma lanceolate, acute, mucronate, 2 mm. long, minutely pubescent, scaberulous at tip. ⊙ —Open woods and mountain meadows, South Dakota and Kansas to British Columbia, south to New Mexico and California. A somewhat stouter form with thicker panicles has been differentiated as *M. simplex* Rydb.

14. Muhlenbergia répens (Presl) Hitchc. CREEPING MUHLY. (Fig. 533.) Perennial with widely creeping scaly rhizomes; culms decumbent, branching, spreading, the flowering branches 5 to 20 cm. long; blades mostly 1 to 3

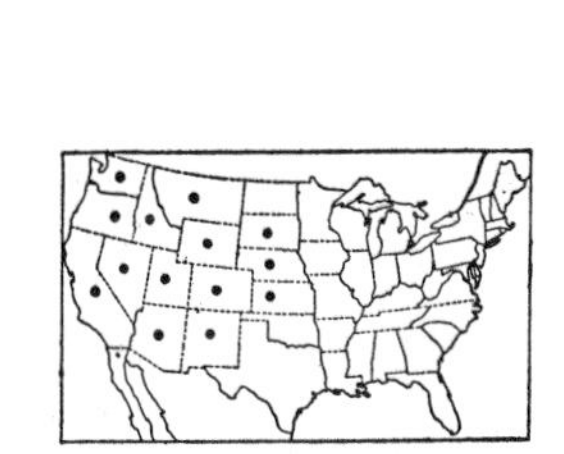

FIGURE 532.—*Muhlenbergia filiformis.* Plant, × 1; glumes and floret, × 10. (Nelson 4011, Wyo.)

cm. long, flat or soon involute; panicle narrow, 1 to 4 cm. long, sometimes longer, interrupted; spikelets about 3 mm. long; glumes more than half as long as the lemma or a little more, acutish; lemma narrowed to a more or less apiculate summit, minutely roughened, usually darker than the glumes, the lateral nerves obscure. ♃ —Dry rocky or sandy open ground, Texas to Arizona; Mexico.

15. Muhlenbergia útilis (Torr.) Hitchc. APAREJO GRASS. (Fig. 534.) Similar to *M. repens;* usually more delicate and more widely spreading with finer leaves, the blades mostly 1 mm. wide or less; spikelets about 2 mm. long, less pointed, the glumes

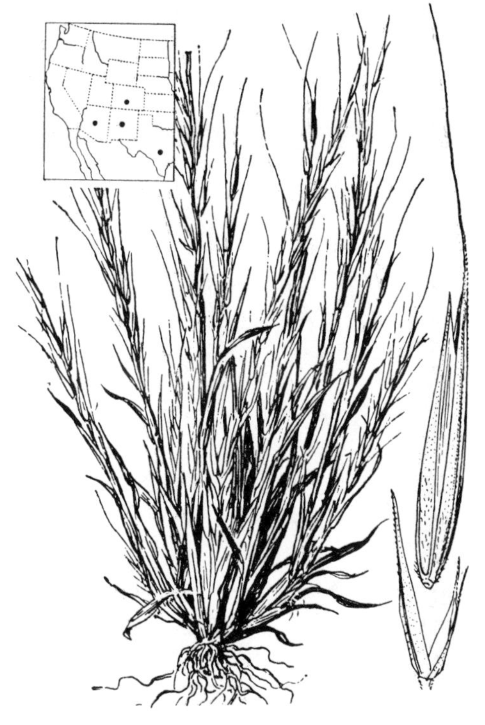

FIGURE 531.—*Muhlenbergia brevis.* Plant, × 1; glumes and floret, × 10. (Type.)

FIGURE 533.—*Muhlenbergia repens*. Plant, × 1; glumes and floret, × 10. (Silveus 831, Tex.)

sometimes less than half as long as the paler lemma. ♃ (*Sporobolus utilis* Scribn.)—Wet places, marshy soil, and along ditches and streams, Texas, southern California, Nevada, and Mexico. Used for stuffing pack saddles.

16. Muhlenbergia richardsónis (Trin.) Rydb. MAT MUHLY. (Fig. 535.) Perennial from numerous hard creeping rhizomes; culms wiry, nodulose-roughened, erect or decumbent at base, from 5 to 60 cm. tall; ligule 2 to 3 mm. long; blades usually involute, 1 to 5 cm. long, rarely longer; panicle narrow, interrupted, or sometimes rather close and spikelike, 2 to 10 cm. long; spikelets 2 to 3 mm. long, the glumes about half as long, ovate; lemma lanceolate, acute, mucronate. ♃ —Dry or moist open often alkaline soil, New Brunswick and Maine to Alberta, south to Michigan and Nebraska and in the mountains to New Mexico, through eastern Washington to California and Arizona; Baja California. There are two intergrading forms of this species; one with rather stout decumbent or somewhat spreading culms (*M. squarrosa* (Trin.) Rydb.), the other with slender erect culms (*M. richardsonis* (Trin.) Rydb.).

17. Muhlenbergia villósa Swallen. (Fig. 536.) Culms 10 to 20 cm. tall, wiry, freely branching, erect from creeping rhizomes, puberulent, obscurely nodulose; blades 2.5 to 3.5 cm. long, firm, involute, glabrous beneath, pubescent above; panicles 2 to 4 cm. long, the branches appressed or spreading, closely flowered; spikelets 2 to 2.5 mm. long, appressed; glumes subequal, 1 to 1.6 mm. long, acute or

FIGURE 534.—*Muhlenbergia utilis*. Plant, × 1; glumes and floret, × 10. (Lindheimer 559, Tex.)

FIGURE 535.—*Muhlenbergia richardsonis*. Plant, × ½; glumes and lemma, × 10. (Jones 5743, Utah.)

subobtuse; lemma and palea villous on the lower half, the lemma acute or mucronate. ♃ —Known only from south of Stanton, Tex. The type of this species was previously referred to *M. thurberi* Rydb.

18. Muhlenbergia thurbéri Rydb. (Fig. 537.) Perennial, with creeping rhizomes; culms slender, 10 to 20 cm. tall, branched at base, the branches erect, tufted, the tufts on branches of the rhizome; sheaths glabrous; blades involute, slender, mostly 1 to 3 cm. long; panicle pale, narrow, slender, 3 to 7 cm. long, the branches short, appressed, few-flowered; spikelets 3.5 to 4 mm. long; glumes nearly as long as the lemma, acute; lemma and palea villous on lower half, the lemma mucronate to short-awned. ♃ —Dry hills, New Mexico and Arizona; rare.

19. Muhlenbergia curtifólia Scribn. (Fig. 538.) Perennial, with creeping rhizomes; culms 10 to 20 cm. tall, loosely tufted, few from the branches of the rhizome; sheaths glabrous or pubescent; blades 1 to 2.5 cm. long, 2 to 3 mm. wide or less, rigidly spreading, pungently pointed, more or less pubescent; panicle 4 to 8 cm. long, slender, the branches appressed; spikelets 3 to 3.5 mm. long; glumes acute, a little shorter than the floret; lemma and palea villous on the lower half, scabrous above, tapering into an awn 1 to 4 mm. long. ♃ —Rocky soil, southern Utah, southern Nevada, and northern Arizona.

20. Muhlenbergia glaúca (Nees) Mez. (Fig. 539.) Perennial, from a slender creeping branching woody rhizome; culms slender, wiry, erect

FIGURE 536.—*Muhlenbergia villosa.* Plant, × 1; glumes and floret, × 10. (Type.)

or ascending, 20 to 60 cm. tall, branching from the lower nodes; blades flat to subinvolute, mostly 5 to 10 cm. long, 1 to 2 mm. wide; panicle 5 to 12 cm. long, narrow, contracted, interrupted, the branches short, appressed; spikelets 3 to 4 mm. long, the glumes nearly as long, acuminate; lemma sparsely pilose on the lower part, acuminate into an awn usually 1 to 3 mm. (rarely as much as 8 mm.) long. ♃ (*M. lemmoni* Scribn.)—Deserts, western Texas to southern California (Jamacha) and northern Mexico.

21. Muhlenbergia polycaúlis Scribn. (Fig. 540.) Perennial, from a firm crown; culms numerous, wiry, decumbent and scaly at base, 30 to

FIGURE 537.—*Muhlenbergia thurberi.* Plant, × 1; glumes and floret, × 10. (Standley 7345, Ariz.)

FIGURE 538.—*Muhlenbergia curtifolia.* Plant, × 1; glumes and floret, × 10. (Type.)

FIGURE 539.—*Muhlenbergia glauca.* Plant, × 1; glumes and floret, × 10. (Nealley 726, Tex.)

50 cm. tall; blades mostly flat and less than 5 cm. long, about 1 mm. wide; panicle narrow, contracted, interrupted, 3 to 8 cm. long; spikelets, excluding awns, 2.5 to 3 mm. long, the glumes a little shorter, tapering to slender awn tips; lemma and palea loosely villous below, the lemma tapering into a delicate awn 1 to 2 cm. long. ♃ —Shaded ledges and grassy slopes, western Texas to southern Arizona and central Mexico.

22. Muhlenbergia pauciflóra Buckl. NEW MEXICAN MUHLY. (Fig. 541.) Perennial; culms loosely tufted, wiry, erect, branching at the lower nodes, 30 to 60 cm. tall; blades 1 mm. wide or less; panicle narrow, contracted, interrupted, 5 to 12 cm. long, the branches erect or ascending; spike-

FIGURE 540.—*Muhlenbergia polycaulis.* Plant, × 1; glumes and floret, × 10. (Type.)

FIGURE 541.—*Muhlenbergia pauciflora*. Plant, × 1; glumes and floret, × 10. (Wright 732, Tex.)

lets, excluding awn, about 4 mm. long, the glumes about half as long, acuminate to awn-tipped; lemma scaberulous only, tapering into a slender flexuous awn, 5 to 20 mm. long. ♃ —Rocky hills and canyons, western Texas and Colorado, Utah, and Arizona, south to northern Mexico.

23. Muhlenbergia arsénei Hitchc. (Fig. 542.) Perennial, without rhizomes but the spreading base sometimes rhizomatous in appearance, loosely tufted; culms wiry, 10 to 45 cm. tall, branched below, the branches erect; leaves crowded toward the base, the blades slender, involute, sharp-pointed, 1 to 3 cm. long; panicle narrow, rather loose, purplish, 2 to 10 cm. long, the branches ascending, floriferous from base; spikelets, excluding the awns, 4 to 5 mm. long, the glumes shorter, acute or subacute, awnless; lemma sparsely pubescent below, tapering into a flexuous awn 6 to 10 mm. long. ♃ —Arid slopes, northern New Mexico and southeastern Utah; southern California (Clark Mountains).

24. Muhlenbergia cuspidáta (Torr.) Rydb. PLAINS MUHLY. (Fig. 543.) Culms slender, wiry, 20 to 40 cm.

tall, erect, in dense tufts with hard bulblike scaly bases; ligule minute; blades flat or loosely involute, erect or ascending, 1 to 2 mm. wide; panicle narrow, somewhat spikelike, 5 to 10 cm. long, the short branches appressed; spikelets about 3 mm. long; glumes subequal, acuminate-cuspidate, about two-thirds as long as the spikelet; lemma acuminate-cuspidate, minutely pubescent. ♃ —Prairies and gravelly or stony slopes, Michigan and Wisconsin to Alberta, south to Ohio, Kentucky, and New Mexico.

25. Muhlenbergia wríghtii Vasey. SPIKE MUHLY. (Fig. 544.) Culms closely tufted from a hard crown, erect, wiry, 20 to 60 cm. tall; sheaths compressed-keeled; ligule 1 to 3 mm. long, sometimes longer; blades flat, 1 to 3 mm. wide; panicle spikelike, interrupted below, 5 to 10 cm. long; spikelets about 2.5 mm. long, the

FIGURE 542.—*Muhlenbergia arsenei*. Plant, × 1; glumes and floret, × 10. (Type.)

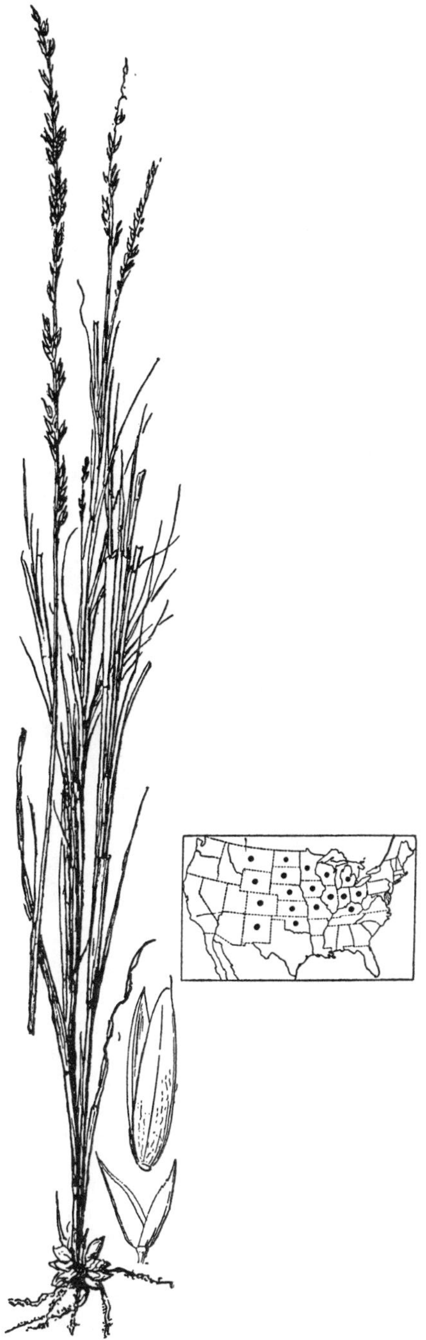

FIGURE 543.—*Muhlenbergia cuspidata*. Plant, × 1; glumes and floret, × 10. (Crattv, Iowa.)

glumes rather thin, mostly about half as long as the spikelet, broad at base, tapering to an awn point; lemma glabrous, acuminate, awn-tipped. ♃ —Plains and open slopes at medium altitudes, Oklahoma, Colorado, Utah, New Mexico, Arizona, and northern Mexico.

26. Muhlenbergia arenácea Buckl. Hitchc. (Fig. 545.) Perennial, with creeping rhizomes; culms tufted from the branches of the rhizomes, sometimes decumbent at base, 10 to 35 cm. tall; ligule prominent, decurrent,

FIGURE 544.—*Muhlenbergia wrightii.* Plant, × 1; glumes and floret, × 10. (Standley 8249, N. Mex.)

1 to 2 mm. long, the margins usually split away, forming an erect auricle at each side; blades flat, wavy, mostly 1 to 3 cm. long, about 1 mm. wide, sharp-pointed, the margins and midnerve white and cartilaginous; panicle diffuse, 7 to 12 cm. long, about as broad, the branches and pedicels capillary; spikelets about 2 mm. long, rarely 2-flowered; the glumes about half as long, abruptly apiculate or subacute; lemma glabrous, abruptly mucronate. ♃ (*Sporobolus auriculatus* Vasey.)—Low places in mesas, Texas and Colorado to Arizona and Sonora. This species and the next three are placed in *Muhlenbergia* because of the 3-nerved mucronate lemma. The caryopsis does not fall from the lemma and palea as in most species of *Sporobolus*, nor can the pericarp be separated from the grain by moistening it.

27. Muhlenbergia asperifólia (Nees and Mey.) Parodi. SCRATCHGRASS. (Fig. 546.) Perennial, pale or glaucous, with slender scaly rhizomes; culms branching at base, spreading, slender, compressed, 10 to 50 cm. tall, the branches ascending or erect; sheaths somewhat compressed-keeled, usually overlapping; ligule minute, erose-toothed; blades flat, crowded, scabrous, mostly 2 to 5 cm. long, 1 to 2 mm. wide; panicle diffuse, 5 to 15 cm. long, about as wide, the capillary scabrous branches finally widely spreading, the panicle at maturity breaking away; spikelets 1.5 to 2 mm. long, occasionally 2-flowered, the pedicels capillary; glumes acute, from half to nearly as long as the spikelet; lemma thin, broad, minutely mucronate from an obtuse apex. ♃ (*Sporobolus asperifolius* Nees and Mey.)—Damp or marshy, often alkaline soil, along irrigation ditches and banks of streams, New York, Indiana and Alberta to British Columbia, south to Texas, California, and Mexico; southern South America. The caryopsis is frequently affected by a fungus (*Tilletia asperifolia* Ell. and Everh.) which produces a large globular body.

28. Muhlenbergia torreyána (Schult.) Hitchc. (Fig. 547.) Perennial, strongly compressed at base, with short very scaly rhizomes; culms simple, or sparingly branching at base, erect, 30 to 60 cm. tall; blades elongate, rather firm, flat or folded, 1 to 3 mm. wide; panicle oblong, open, 10 to 20 cm. long, the capillary branches and pedicels ascending; spikelets about 2 mm. long, the glumes subequal, slightly shorter; lemma and palea minutely sca-

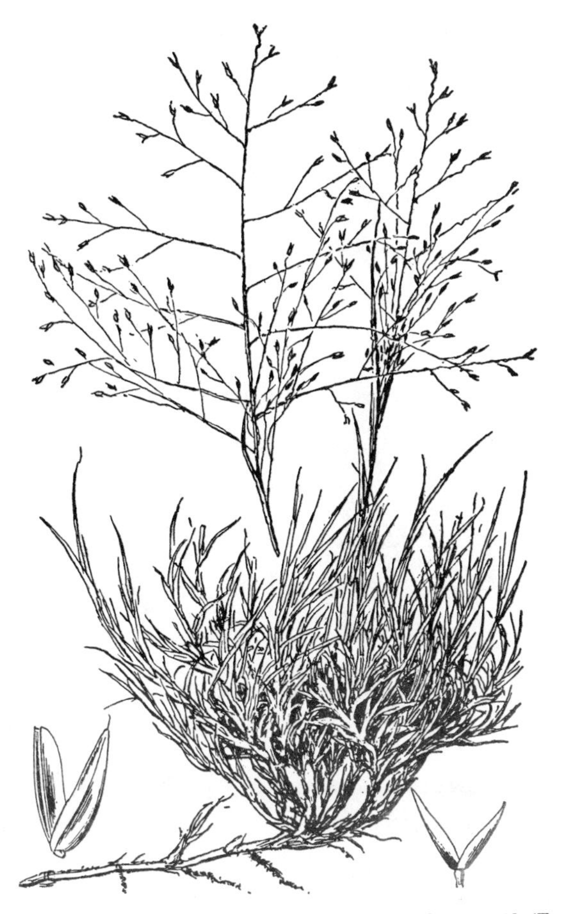

FIGURE 545.—*Muhlenbergia arenacea*. Plant, × 1; glumes and floret, × 10. (Tracy 7909, Tex.)

FIGURE 546.—*Muhlenbergia asperifolia*. Plant, × 1; glumes and floret, × 10. (Griffiths 212, S. Dak.)

FIGURE 547.—*Muhlenbergia torreyana.* Plant, × 1; glumes and floret, × 10. (Vasey, N. J.)

berulous-puberulent. ♃ (*Sporobolus compressus* Kunth; *S. torreyanus* Nash.)—Moist pine barrens and meadows, New Jersey and Delaware; Georgia (Sumter County), Kentucky, and Tennessee.

29. Muhlenbergia uniflóra (Muhl.) Fernald. (Fig. 548.) Perennial, but often appearing like an annual, tufted, often with decumbent bases; culms slender, erect, 20 to 40 cm. tall, the base and lower sheaths compressed; blades flat, crowded along the lower part of the culm, about 1 mm. wide; panicle loose, open, oblong, 7 to 20 cm. long, 2 to 4 cm. wide, the branches and pedicels capillary; spikelets dark purplish, about 1.5 mm. long, rarely 2-flowered; glumes scarcely half as long as the spikelet, subacute; lemma faintly 3-nerved, acutish. ♃ (*Sporobolus serotinus* A. Gray; *S. uniflorus* Scribn. and Merr.)—Bogs and wet meadows, Newfoundland to Michigan and New Jersey.

30. Muhlenbergia dumósa Scribn. (Fig. 549.) Perennial, with short, stout creeping scaly rhizomes; culms robust, solid, thick, and scaly at base (here as much as 6 mm. thick), the main culm erect or leaning, 1 to 3 m. tall, the lower part clothed with bladeless sheaths, freely branching at the middle and upper nodes, the branches numerous, fascicled, spreading, decompound, the ultimate branchlets filiform; blades

FIGURE 548.—*Muhlenbergia uniflora.* Plant, × 1; glumes and floret, × 10. (Chamberlain 147, Maine.)

Figure 549.—*Muhlenbergia dumosa*. Plant, × 1; glumes and floret, × 10. (Pringle, Ariz.)

flat or soon involute, smooth, those of the branches mostly less than 5 cm. long and 1 mm. wide; panicles numerous on the branches, commonly exceeded by the leaves, 1 to 3 cm. long, narrow, somewhat flexuous; spikelets, excluding the awn, about 3 mm. long, the glumes scarcely half as long, thin, pale with a green midnerve, usually minutely awn-tipped or with an awn as much as 9 mm. long; lemma narrow, pubescent about the base and margin, pale with green nerves, the awn from the slightly notched apex, flexuous, 3 to 5 mm. long. ♃ —Canyons and valley flats, southern Arizona to Jalisco, Mexico. Has the aspect of a miniature bamboo.

31. Muhlenbergia andína (Nutt.) Hitchc. Foxtail muhly. (Fig. 550.) Perennial, with numerous scaly rhizomes; culms erect or sometimes spreading, scabrous-puberulent below the nodes and the panicle, 50 to 100 cm. tall; sheaths smooth or slightly scabrous, keeled; ligule 1 mm. long, membranaceous, short-ciliate; blades flat, 2 to 6 mm. wide, scabrous; panicle narrow, spikelike, usually more or less lobed or interrupted, grayish, silky, often purple-tinged, 7 to 15 cm. long; glumes narrow, acuminate, ciliate-scabrous on the keels, 3 to 4 mm. long; lemma 3 mm. long, tapering into a capillary awn 4 to 8 mm. long, the hairs at base

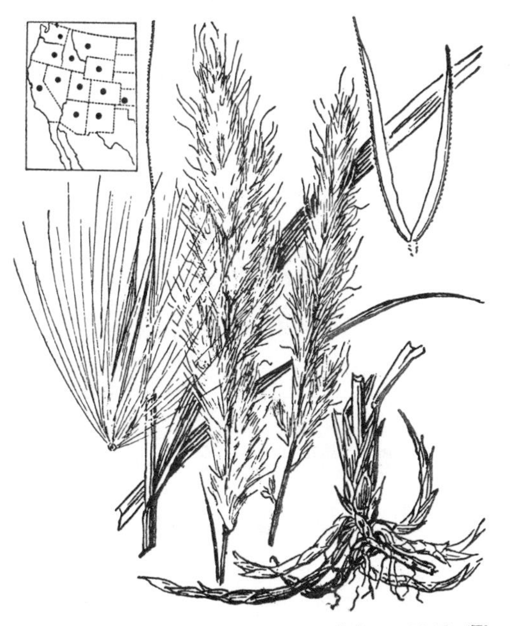

Figure 550.—*Muhlenbergia andina*. Plant, × 1; glumes and floret, × 10. (Elmer 558, Wash.)

FIGURE 551.—*Muhlenbergia glomerata*. Plant, × 1; glumes and floret, × 8. (Macoun 26241, Ontario.)

FIGURE 552.—*Muhlenbergia racemosa*. Panicle, × 1; glumes and floret, × 10. (V. H. Chase 940, Ill.)

of floret copious, nearly as long as the body of the lemma. ♃ (*M. comata* Benth.)—Meadows, moist thickets, gravelly river beds, and open ground, at medium altitudes, Montana to eastern Washington, south to Kansas, New Mexico, and central California.

32. Muhlenbergia glomeráta (Willd.) Trin. (Fig. 551.) Perennial from creeping branching scaly rhizomes; culms slender, erect or suberect, 30 to 90 cm. tall, simple or with a few erect branches at base, the internodes minutely puberulent; sheaths rounded on the back; ligule minute; blades flat, 5 to 15 cm. long, lax, 2 to 5 mm. wide, ascending; panicle narrow, compact, lobed, mostly interrupted at base, often purplish, 3 to 10 cm. long; spikelets 5 to 6 mm. long, the narrow, attenuate subequal glumes stiffly awn-tipped; lemma about 3 mm. long, pointed, pilose on the lower part. ♃ —Sphagnum bogs, swamps, and moist ground, Newfoundland to British Columbia, Maine to Wisconsin, Virginia, and Indiana; Nebraska. Has been confused with *M. racemosa;* occasionally difficult to distinguish. Internodes are sometimes glabrous, but are roughish to the fingernail.

33. Muhlenbergia racemósa (Michx.) B. S. P. (Fig. 552.) Perennial from creeping scaly branching rhizomes, these and culms usually somewhat stouter than in the preceding; culms erect or ascending, subcompressed, 30 to 100 cm. tall, usually finally branching from the middle nodes, the branches mostly erect, the internodes smooth and shining except toward the summit; sheaths loose, keeled; ligule 1 to 1.5 mm. long; blades flat, 4 to 18 cm. long, 2 to 7 mm. wide, commonly somewhat firmer than those of *M. glomerata,* erect to ascending; panicle 3 to 14 cm. long, narrow, compact, often lobed, less commonly purple and thicker than in *M. glomerata;* spikelets 5 (rarely 4.5) to 7 mm. long, the narrow attenuate subequal glumes stiffly awn-tipped; lemma 2.5 to 3.5 mm. long, acuminate, rarely with a short awn, pilose on the lower part. ♃ Meadows, prairies, alluvial soil along rivers, irrigation ditches, rocky slopes, dry ground and waste places, occasionally in wet meadows, swamps, and moist canyon bottoms, found in a wide range of habitats; Manitoba to Alberta; Michigan and Indiana to Washington, Oklahoma, and Arizona. Specimens from Orono, Maine, and Washington, D. C., were doubtless from cultivated plants.

34. Muhlenbergia califórnica Vasey. (Fig. 553.) Perennial, pale, leafy, the base more or less creeping and rhizomatous; culms ascending, somewhat woody below, 30 to 60 cm. tall, branching below; sheaths scaberulous; blades flat, 3 to 6 mm. wide, scabrous, usually short; panicle narrow, dense but interrupted, 7 to 15 cm. long; spikelets 3 to 4 mm. long, the glumes slightly shorter, scabrous, acuminate, awn-tipped; lemma scabrous, acuminate, awn-tipped, with sparse callus hairs about half as long as the lemma. ♃—Stream borders and gullies, foothills and mountain slopes up to 2,000 m., confined to southern California.

FIGURE 553.—*Muhlenbergia californica.* Plant, × 1; glumes and floret, × 10. (Parish 2113, Calif.)

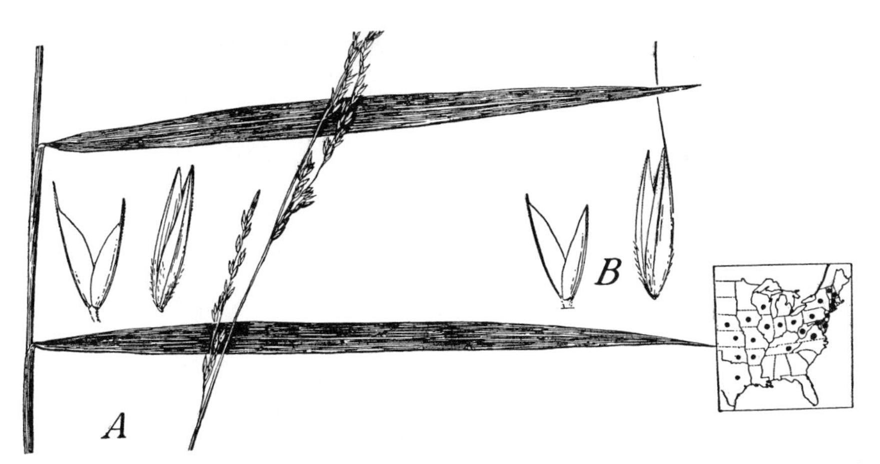

FIGURE 554.—*A*, *Muhlenbergia sobolifera.* Plant, × 1; glumes and floret, × 10. (Metcalf 1589, N. Y.) *B*, Var. *setigera*, × 10. (Reverchon 1049, Tex.)

35. Muhlenbergia sobolífera (Muhl.) Trin. (Fig. 554, *A*.) Perennial, with numerous creeping scaly rhizomes 2 to 3 mm. thick; culms erect, slender, solitary or few in a tuft, glabrous, 60 to 100 cm. tall, sparingly branching, the branches erect; blades flat, spreading, scabrous, those of the main culm 5 to 15 cm. long, 3 to 8 mm. wide, occasionally larger, at time of flowering aggregate along the middle part of

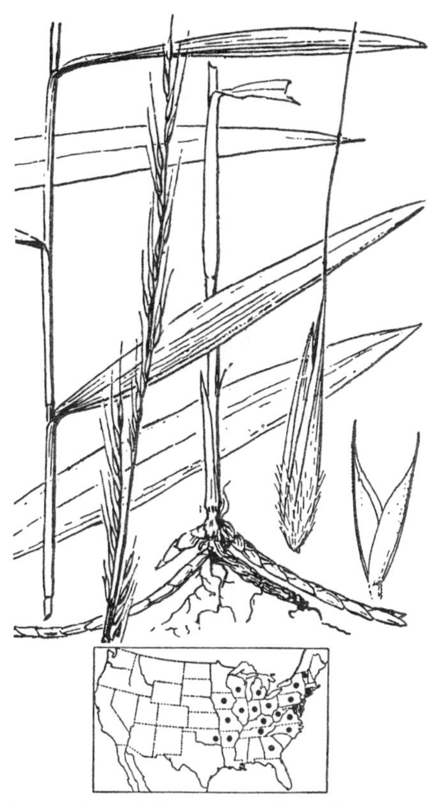

FIGURE 555.—*Muhlenbergia tenuiflora*. Plant, × 1; glumes and floret, × 10. (Mosley, Ohio.)

the culm; panicles slender, somewhat nodding, mostly 5 to 15 cm. long, the distant branches appressed, floriferous from base, overlapping or the lower more distant; spikelets mostly 2 to 2.5 mm. long, the glumes about two-thirds as long, abruptly acuminate or awn-tipped; lemma elliptic, bluntish, pubescent on the lower part, usually apiculate. ♃ —Dry rocky woods and cliffs, New Hampshire to Nebraska, south to Virginia, Tennessee, and Texas.

MUHLENBERGIA SOBOLIFERA var. SETÍGERA Scribn. (Fig. 554, *B*.) Branching more freely in the later stages; lemma with an awn 1 to 3 mm. long. ♃ —Dry woods, Arkansas and Texas.

36. Muhlenbergia tenuiflóra (Willd.) B. S. P. (Fig. 555.) Similar to *M. sobolifera* in habit; culms often more robust; blades mostly 10 to 18 cm. long and 6 to 10 mm. wide; panicles on the average longer; culms retrorsely puberulent at least around the nodes; sheaths puberulent or scaberulous toward the summit; spikelets (excluding the awns) 3 to 4 mm. long, the glumes about half as long, broad at base, abruptly acuminate, scaberulous; lemma narrow, pubescent toward the base, tapering into a slender straight awn 3 to 10 mm. long. ♃ —Rocky woods, Ontario and Vermont to Iowa, south to Georgia, Tennessee, and Oklahoma.

37. Muhlenbergia brachyphýlla Bush. (Fig. 556.) Perennial, with numerous slender scaly rhizomes; culms slender, suberect, freely branching at the middle nodes, the branches lax, glabrous or obscurely scabrous below the nodes; blades flat, spreading, scaberulous, mostly 7 to 15 cm. long and 3 to 5 mm. wide; panicles on filiform peduncles, very slender, lax, relatively few-flowered, mostly 8 to 15 cm. long; spikelets, excluding the awn, about 3 mm. long, the glumes about two-thirds as long, awn-tipped; lemma minutely pubescent toward the base, tapering into a slender awn 3 to 6 mm. long, rarely shorter. ♃ —Low woods, Maryland to North Carolina; Indiana and Wisconsin to Nebraska, south to Texas. Resembling *M. tenuiflora*, but with numerous filiform branches and more slender panicles.

38. Muhlenbergia frondósa (Poir.) Fernald. WIRESTEM MUHLY. (Fig. 557.) Perennial, with creeping scaly rhizomes; culms often relatively stout, glabrous below the nodes, finally decumbent, often rooting at the geniculate lower nodes, freely branching from all the nodes (occasionally simple below), the branches ascending or somewhat spreading, the plants becoming top-heavy and bushy, 40 to 100 cm. long; blades flat, scabrous, usually not more than 10 cm. long, sometimes as much as 15 cm., 3 to 7

FIGURE 556.—*Muhlenbergia brachyphylla.* Plant, × 1; glumes and florets, × 10. (V. H. Chase 3759, Ill.)

mm. wide; panicles numerous, short-exserted or partly included, terminal and axillary, the larger as much as 10 cm. long (the axillary shorter), narrow, sometimes rather loose, the branches ascending, mostly densely flowered from the base; glumes 2 to 3 mm., rarely to 4 mm., long, tapering into an awned tip, subequal or unequal, shorter than the floret, or the second glume exceeding it; lemma 2 to 3 mm. long, pointed, short-pilose at base. ♃ (Described under *M. mexicana* in Manual, ed. 1.)—Thickets, low ground, and waste places, New Brunswick to North Dakota, south to Georgia and Texas.

MUHLENBERGIA FRONDOSA forma COMMUTÁTA (Scribn.) Fernald. Lemmas awned. ♃ —Quebec and Maine to South Dakota, south to Virginia and Missouri. May be distinguished from the awned forms of *M. mexicana* by the culms smooth below the nodes.

FIGURE 557.—*Muhlenbergia frondosa.* Plant, × 1; glumes and floret, × 10. (V. H. Chase 1166, Ill.)

39. Muhlenbergia glabriflóra Scribn. (Fig. 558.) In habit resembling *M. frondosa*, freely branching; culms scaberulous below the nodes as in *M. sylvatica;* blades numerous, short, narrow, appressed; panicles on the average shorter and narrower than in *M. frondosa;* spikelets about as in *M. frondosa* but the lemma glabrous. ♃ —Low woods, Maryland to North Carolina; Indiana to Missouri, Arkansas, and Texas.

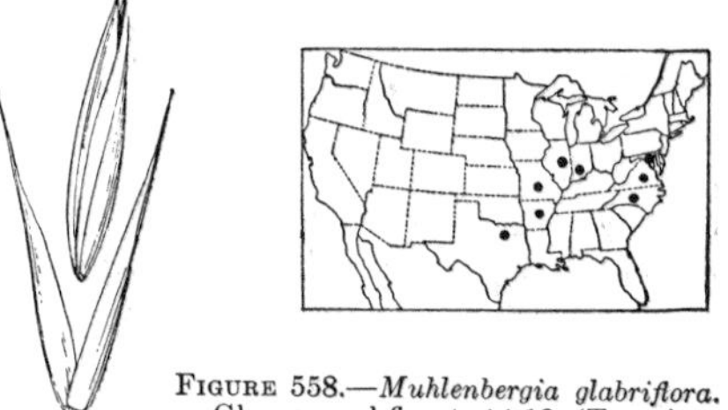

FIGURE 558.—*Muhlenbergia glabriflora.* Glumes and floret, × 10. (Type.)

40. Muhlenbergia sylvática (Torr.) Torr. (Fig. 559.) Perennial with creeping scaly rhizomes, culms slender, retrorsely scaberulous below the nodes, rather sparingly branching from the middle and upper nodes, finally leaning, the subfiliform branches often elongate, drooping, the plant 40 to 100 cm. tall; blades flat, lax, ascending to spreading, 0.5 to 18, commonly 8 to 15 cm., long, 2 to 8 mm. wide; panicles slender, nodding, the slender branches appressed, slightly overlapping; glumes lanceolate, acuminate or awn-tipped, 2 to 3 mm. long; lemma slightly exceeding the glumes, pilose below, tapering into a slender awn 5 to 10 mm. long. ♃ (*M. umbrosa* Scribn.)—Moist woods and thickets, Quebec and Maine to South Dakota, south to Alabama and Texas; Arizona.

MUHLENBERGIA SYLVATICA forma ATTENUÁTA (Scribn.) Palmer and Steyermark. Lemmas short-awned or nearly awnless. ♃ —Ontario, Maine, Connecticut, Indiana, Illinois, Michigan, South Dakota, Missouri, District of Columbia, and Oklahoma.

MUHLENBERGIA SYLVATICA var. ROBÚSTA Fernald. Culm stiffer, blades somewhat firmer, some of them 7 to 10 mm. wide; panicles with more densely flowered branches; glumes slightly broader. ♃ —Maine, Connecticut, New York, New Jersey, and Indiana.

41. Muhlenbergia mexicána (L.) Trin. (Fig. 560.) Resembling *M. frondosa*, the culms erect or ascending, usually simple below, less freely branching, scaberulous below the nodes; blades lax, often 10 to 20 cm. long, mostly 2 to 4 mm. wide; panicles mostly long-exserted, narrow, the upper often 10 to 15 cm. long, of numerous short appressed densely flowered somewhat aggregate branches; spikelets 2 to 3 mm. long, glumes narrow, attenuate, awn-

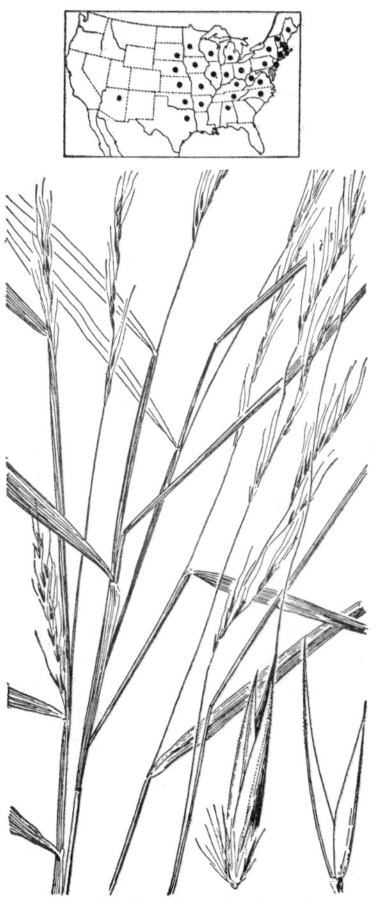

FIGURE 559.—*Muhlenbergia sylvatica.* Plant, × 1; glumes and floret, × 10. (Conant, Mass.)

FIGURE 560.—*Muhlenbergia mexicana.* Plant, × 1; glumes and floret, × 10. (Deam 19225, Ind.)

tipped, about equaling the pointed or awn-tipped lemma, the lemma long-pilose below. ♃ (Described under *M. foliosa* in Manual, ed. 1. The name *M. mexicana* had long been misapplied to the recently recognized *M. frondosa* (Poir.) Fernald.)—Moist thickets, low woods, and low open ground, Quebec and Maine to British Columbia and Washington, south to North Carolina, New Mexico, and California.

MUHLENBERGIA MEXICANA forma AMBÍGUA (Torr.) Fernald. Lemmas with an awn 4 to 10 mm. long. ♃ —Range of the species to North Dakota; intergrading with forma *setiglumis* in Indiana and westward.

MUHLENBERGIA MEXICANA forma SETIGLÚMIS (S. Wats.) Fernald. ♃ —Glumes with an awn 1 to 2 mm. long; lemma awned as in the preceding, the two scarcely distinct. ♃ —Iowa and South Dakota to Washington, south to New Mexico and California.

42. Muhlenbergia schrebéri Gmel. NIMBLEWILL. (Fig. 561.) Culms slender, branching, spreading and decumbent at base, usually rooting at the lower nodes, but not forming definite creeping rhizomes, the flowering branches ascending, 10 to 30 cm. long; blades flat, mostly less than 5 cm. long, and 2 to 4 mm. wide; panicles terminal and axillary, slender, loosely flowered, lax, nodding, 5 to 15 cm. long; glumes minute, the first often obsolete, the second rounded, 0.1 to 0.2 mm. long; lemma narrow, somewhat pubescent around the base, the body about 2 mm. long, the slender awn 2 to 5 mm. long. ♃ —Damp shady places, New Hampshire to Wisconsin and eastern Nebraska, south to Florida and Texas; eastern Mexico. In spring and early summer the culms are short and erect with spreading blades, the plants being very different in appearance from the flowering phase of fall. MUHLENBERGIA SCHREBERI var. PALÚSTRIS (Scribn.) Scribn. Glumes developed as much as 1 mm. long. ♃ —Washington, D. C.; Bull Run Mountains, Va.

43. Muhlenbergia curtisetósa (Scribn.) Bush. (Fig. 562.) A little-known form, differing from *M. schreberi* in having stouter culms, coarser panicles, the glumes evident, rarely as much as 2 mm. long, the lemma 2.5 to 3 mm. long, the awn 1 to 2 mm. long. ♃ —Delaware County, Pa., Illinois (Clinton), Missouri (Eagle Rock).

44. Muhlenbergia jonésii (Vasey) Hitchc. (Fig. 563.) Perennial, closely tufted; culms erect, 20 to 40 cm. tall; leaves mostly basal, the numerous lower sheaths finally flattened and loose; ligule 2 to 4 mm. long; blades subfiliform, involute, scabrous; panicle narrow, 5 to 15 cm. long, the branches ascending, rather loosely flowered; spikelets 3 to 4 mm. long; glumes broad, scabrous-puberulent,

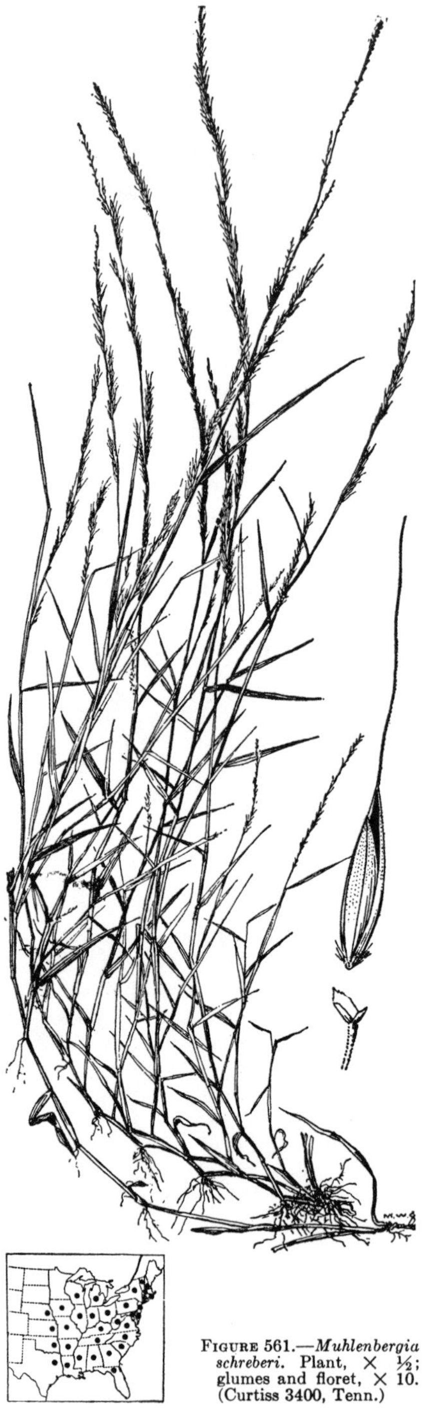

FIGURE 561.—*Muhlenbergia schreberi*. Plant, × ½; glumes and floret, × 10. (Curtiss 3400, Tenn.)

about one-third as long as the spikelet, obtuse, often erose; lemma obscurely pubescent below, tapering to an acuminate or awned tip. ♃ — Open ground, northeastern California.

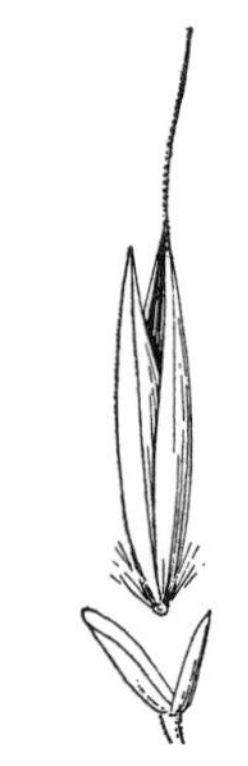

FIGURE 562.—*Muhlenbergia curtisetosa*. Glumes and floret, × 10. (Wolf 30, Ill.)

FIGURE 563.—*Muhlenbergia jonesii*. Plant, × 1; glumes and floret, × 10. (Austin 1230, Calif.)

45. Muhlenbergia montána (Nutt.) Hitchc. MOUNTAIN MUHLY. (Fig. 564.) Perennial; culms densely tufted, erect, 15 to 60 cm. tall; sheaths glabrous, mostly basal, becoming flat and loose; blades flat to involute, 1 to 2 mm. wide; panicle narrow, rather

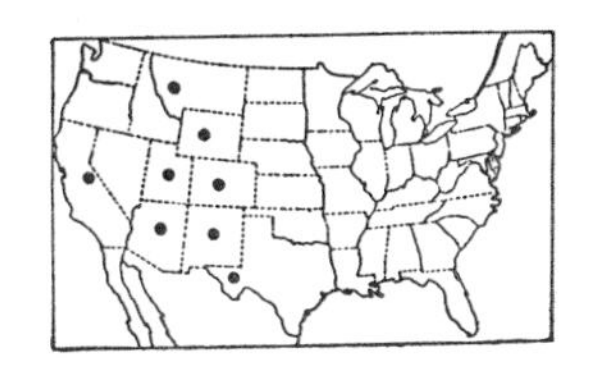

FIGURE 564.—*Muhlenbergia montana*. Plant, × 1; glumes and floret, × 10. (Patterson 156, Colo.)

loose, 5 to 15 cm. long, the branches ascending or appressed, floriferous from base; first glume acute, 1.5 mm. long, the second longer, broader, 3-nerved, 3-toothed; lemma 3 to 4 mm. long, pilose below, scaberulous above, the awn slender, flexuous, 1 to 1.5 cm. long, sometimes shorter. ♃ (*M. trifida* Hack., *M. gracilis* of authors, not Kunth.)—Canyons, mesas, and rocky hills, 2,000 to 3,000 m., Montana to Utah and central California, south to western Texas and southern Mexico.

46. Muhlenbergia filicúlmis Vasey. SLIMSTEM MUHLY. (Fig. 565.) Culms densely tufted, erect, filiform, 10 to 20 cm. tall, the leaves in a short basal cluster; ligule prominent; blades involute, filiform, mostly less than 5 cm. long; panicle slender, the branches erect, mostly 2 to 5 cm. long, sometimes as much as 10 cm.; spikelets about 2.5 to 3 mm. long, the glumes about half as long, awn-tipped, the first rather narrow, acuminate, the second broader, 3-nerved, sharply 3-toothed, rarely entire or erose only; lemma pubescent on the lower half, tapering to an awned tip, or rarely with an awn as much as 4 mm. long. ♃ —Open sandy or

FIGURE 565.—*Muhlenbergia filiculmis*. Panicle, × 1; glumes and floret, × 10. (Type.)

rocky soil, 2,000 to 3,000 m. altitude, Wyoming, Colorado, New Mexico, and Utah.

47. Muhlenbergia virescéns (H. B. K.) Kunth. SCREWLEAF MUHLY. (Fig. 566.) Perennial; culms densely tufted, erect, 40 to 60 cm. tall, the old basal sheaths flattened and more or less coiled; ligule, except the margin, delicate, 3 to 10 mm. long; blades flat or those of the innovations involute, mostly elongate and flexuous; panicle narrow but rather loose, 5 to 15 cm. long, the branches erect; spikelets, excluding awns, about 5 mm. long, the glumes slightly shorter, acute, the second 3-nerved; lemma and palea pubescent on the lower half, the lemma tapering into a slender flexuous awn 1 to 2 cm. long. ♃ —Canyons, rocky hills, and mesas, New Mexico and Arizona to central Mexico.

48. Muhlenbergia montícola Buckl. MESA MUHLY. (Fig. 567.) Perennial; culms tufted, slender, erect or decumbent at base, 30 to 50 cm. tall, branching at the lower and middle nodes, leafy throughout; blades 3 to 7 cm. long, narrow, flat, or soon involute; panicle soft, narrow, contracted, 5 to 10, sometimes to 20 cm. long, the branches appressed or slightly spreading; spikelets, excluding awns, about 3 mm. long, the glumes about two-thirds as long, subacute to obtuse and erose at tip; lemma pubescent at base and on lower half of margin, tapering into a delicate flexuous awn 1 to 2 cm. long. ♃ —Rocky hills and canyons, western Texas to Arizona and central Mexico.

49. Muhlenbergia parviglúmis Vasey. (Fig. 568.) Perennial, with the habit of *M. monticola;* blades on the average somewhat longer, 1 to 3 mm. wide; panicle looser, the branches filiform, longer; glumes minute, erose, subacute to truncate; lemma scaberulous only, tapering in-

FIGURE 566.—*Muhlenbergia virescens*. Plant, × 1; glumes and floret, × 10. (Palmer 565, Ariz.)

FIGURE 567.—*Muhlenbergia monticola*. Plant, × 1; glumes and floret, × 10. (Nealley 399, Tex.)

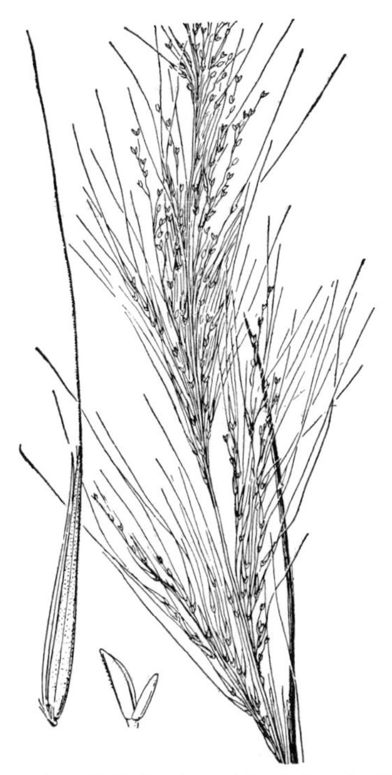

FIGURE 568.—*Muhlenbergia parviglumis*. Panicle, × 1; glumes and floret, × 10. (Vasey, Tex.)

to a delicate awn 2 to 3 cm. long. ♃ —Canyons, Texas, New Mexico, and northern Mexico; Cuba.

50. Muhlenbergia púngens Thurb. (Fig. 569.) Perennial, with strong creeping rhizomes; culms tufted, erect from a decumbent leafy base, 20 to 40 cm. tall, sometimes taller; blades short, involute, sharp-pointed; panicle long-exserted, open, oblong, 5 to 15 cm. long; the main branches 3 to 5, these dividing into fascicles of capillary finally spreading or divaricate very scabrous branchlets; spikelets purple to brownish, 4 to 5 mm. long, the glumes about one-third as long, scabrous, often erose or toothed, the midnerve extending into a short awn; lemma terete, tapering into an awn about 1 mm. long; palea about as long as the lemma, the keels awn-tipped. ♃ —Dry hills and sandy plains, South Dakota and Nebraska to Wyoming, New Mexico, and Arizona.

51. Muhlenbergia portéri Scribn. BUSH MUHLY. (Fig. 570.) Perennial; culms woody or persistent at base, numerous, wiry, widely spreading or ascending through bushes, scaberulous, mostly branching from all the nodes, 30 to 100 cm. tall or more; sheaths smooth, spreading away from the branches, the prophylla conspicuous; blades mostly about 1 mm. wide, flat, 2 to 8 cm. long, early deciduous from the sheaths; panicle 5 to 10 cm. long, open, the slender branches and branchlets brittle, widely spreading, bearing rather few long-pediceled spikelets; glumes narrow, acuminate, slightly unequal, the second about 2 mm. long; lemma purple, acuminate, sparsely pubescent, 3 to 4 mm. long, with a delicate awn 5 to 12 mm. long. ♃ —Dry mesas and hills, canyons, and rocky deserts, western Texas to Colorado,

FIGURE 569.—*Muhlenbergia pungens*. Plant, × 1; glumes and floret, × 10. (Jones 6046, Utah.)

Nevada, and southern California, south to northern Mexico. Known also as mesquite grass and black grama.

52. Muhlenbergia arizónica Scribn. (Fig. 571.) Perennial, in close tufts; culms slender, erect or decumbent at base, 15 to 40 cm. tall; sheaths keeled; ligule thin, 1 to 2 mm. long, decurrent; blades flat or folded, mostly less than 5 cm. long, 1 to 2 mm. wide, the margins and midnerve white, cartilaginous; panicle open, 5 to 12 cm. long 4 to 8 cm. wide, the branches capillary, compound; spikelets long-pedicellate, about 3 mm. long, the glumes about one-third as long, ovate, subacute; lemma narrowly lanceolate, minutely pubescent along the midnerve and margins below, the awn about 1 mm. long, from a minutely notched apex. ♃ —Stony hills, southern Arizona and northwestern Mexico.

53. Muhlenbergia torréyi (Kunth) Hitchc. ex Bush. RINGGRASS. (Fig. 572.) Perennial in loose tufts, with numerous innovations, the base decumbent or forming short rhizomes, the plants usually gregarious, sometimes forming large patches or "fairy rings"; culms slender, 10 to 30 cm. tall; leaves in a short basal cluster; blades closely involute, usually 2 to 3 cm. long, falcate or flexuous, forming a crisp curly cushion; panicle open, usually about half the entire length of the culm, commonly purple, the capillary branches finally spreading, the pedicels mostly as long as the spikelets or longer; spikelets about 3 mm. long, the glumes, including the awn-tip, about two-thirds as long; lemma nearly glabrous, tapering into a delicate awn about 3 mm. long. ♃ (*M. gracillima* Torr.)—Plains, mesas, and dry hills, western Kansas and Wyoming to Texas and Arizona.

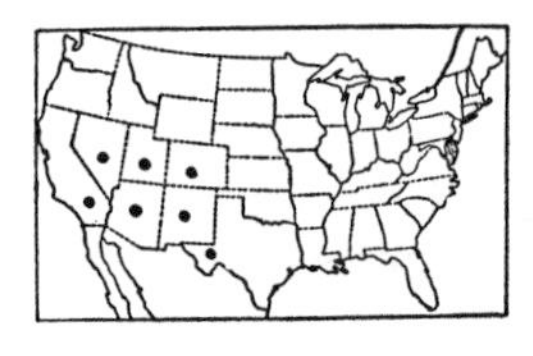

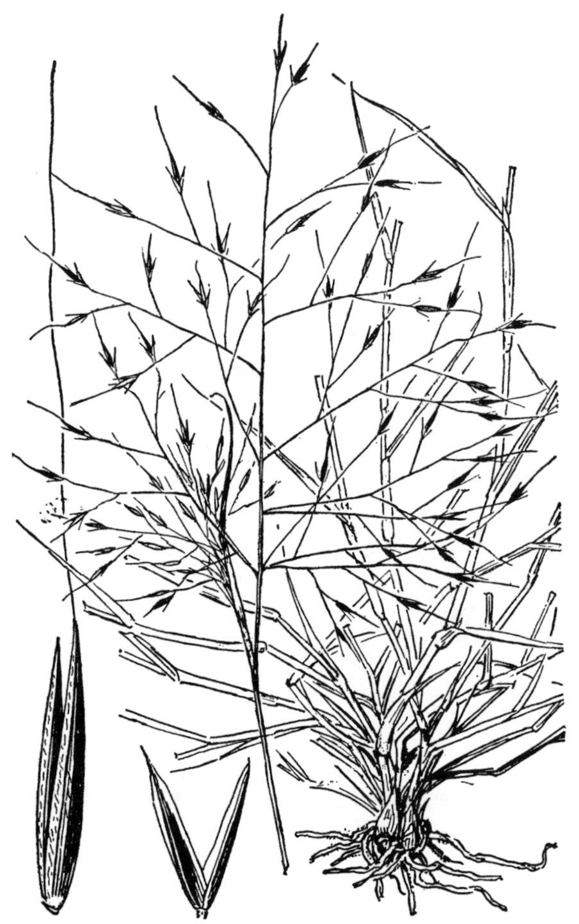

FIGURE 570.—*Muhlenbergia porteri.* Plant, × 1; glumes and floret, × 10. (Chase 5887, Tex.)

54. Muhlenbergia arenícola Buckl. (Fig. 573.) Resembling *M. torreyi;* culms mostly 30 to 50 cm. tall; blades usually straight and on the average longer; panicle larger, mostly pale, the branchlets and pedicels appressed; spikelets slightly longer, the lemma scabrous, the awn 1 to 2 mm. long. ♃ —Sandy plains and mesas, western Kansas to Arizona, south to northern Mexico.

55. Muhlenbergia setifólia Vasey. (Fig. 574.) Perennial, tufted; culms erect, hard, wiry, 50 to 80 cm. tall; sheaths with erect auricles, 2 to 10 mm. long; blades involute, fine, scarcely 0.5 mm. thick, very scabrous, flexuous, as much as 20 cm. long; panicle narrow, open, 10 to 30 cm. long, the capillary branches ascending, flexuous; spikelets, excluding awns, about 5 mm. long, the glumes one-third to half as long, obtuse to subacute; lemma hairy on the callus, otherwise smooth, tapering into a flexuous awn 1.5 to 2 cm. long. ♃ —Rocky hills, western Texas and northern Mexico.

56. Muhlenbergia xeróphila C. O. Goodding. (Fig. 575.) Culms 45 to 90 cm. tall, densely tufted, glabrous or scaberulous; sheaths scaberulous; ligule 2 to 4 mm. long, obtuse; blades involute, 15 to 50 cm. long, 1 to 1.5 mm. wide; panicle open (contracted at maturity), 15 to 35 cm. long, with cap-

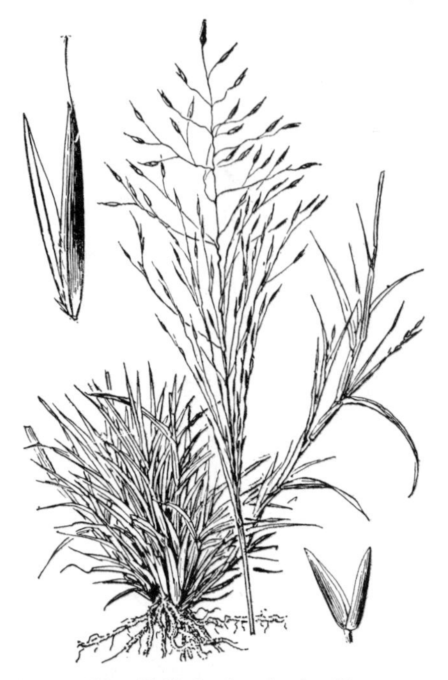

FIGURE 571.—*Muhlenbergia arizonica*. Plant, × 1; glumes and floret, × 10. (Griffiths 3368, Ariz.)

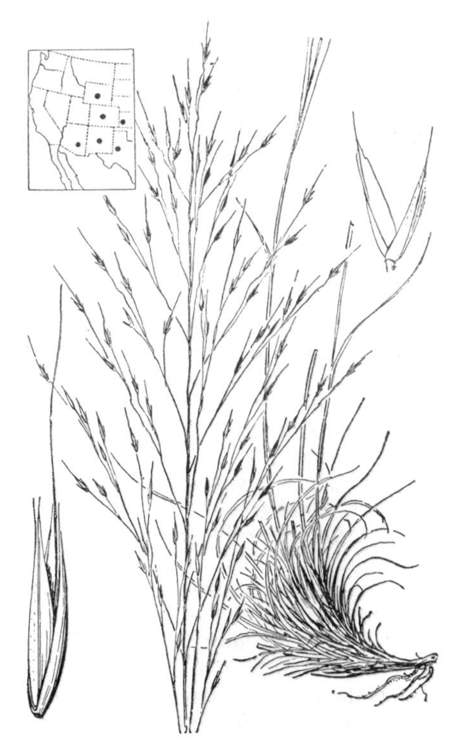

FIGURE 572.—*Muhlenbergia torreyi*. Plant, × 1; glumes and floret, × 10. (Chase 5298, Colo.)

illary, flexuous, spreading branches; spikelets about 4 mm. long; glumes equal or subequal, 2 to 2.5 mm. or sometimes as much as 3 mm. long, acute or acuminate, scabrous or pubescent; lemma 4 mm. long, scabrous, the callus appressed-pilose, the hairs about 1 mm. long, the delicate capillary awn 10 to 35 mm. long. ♃ —Canyons and rocky slopes, southern Arizona.

57. Muhlenbergia metcálfei Jones. (Fig. 576.) Perennial, in close tufts; culms erect, 50 to 80 cm. tall; ligule 3 to 15 mm. long, sometimes longer; blades involute, slender, flexuous, scabrous, sometimes only slightly so, not crowded at base; panicle narrow but somewhat loose, pale or slightly purplish, 15 to 40 cm. long, the branches usually naked at base; spikelets tapering to summit, about 4 mm. long; glumes nearly equal, obtuse, a little less than half as long as spikelet; lemma scaberulous toward summit, the awn 3 to 10 mm. long. ♃ —Rocky hills, Texas and New Mexico.

58. Muhlenbergia dúbia Fourn. PINE MUHLY. (Fig. 577.) Perennial, closely tufted; culms erect, hard and wiry at base, 30 to 100 cm. tall; sheaths with erect firm auricles, 4 to 10 mm. long, rarely longer; blades involute, scabrous; panicle narrow, sometimes almost spikelike, grayish, 10 to 30 cm. long, rarely longer; spikelets about 4 mm. long; glumes about half as long as the spikelet, minutely scaberulous, obtuse; lemma minutely scaberulous, with an awn as much as 4 mm. long, rarely acuminate only. ♃ (*M. acuminata* Vasey; *Sporobolus ligulatus* Vasey and Dewey.)—Canyons and rocky hills, up to 7,000 feet elevation, western Texas, New Mexico, and northern Mexico.

59. Muhlenbergia dubioídes C. O. Goodding. (Fig. 578.) Culms 50 to 100 cm. tall, densely tufted, erect;

FIGURE 573.—*Muhlenbergia arenicola.* Plant, × 1; glumes and floret, × 10. (Hitchcock 13602, Tex.)

ligule truncate, 1 to 2 mm. long; blades 15 to 50 cm. long, 1 to 2 mm. wide, involute, glabrous, or scaberulous below; panicle 15 to 35 cm. long, 2 to 4 cm. wide, densely flowered, the branches appressed; spikelets about 4 mm. long; glumes subequal, 2 to 3 mm. long, acute, more or less erose, scaberulous; lemma 3.5 to 4 mm. long, the callus appressed-pilose with hairs 1 to 1.5 mm. long; awn straight, scabrous, 3 to 10 mm. long. ♃ —Canyons and rocky slopes, Santa Cruz and Pima Counties, southern Arizona.

60. Muhlenbergia expánsa (DC.) Trin. (Fig. 579.) Resembling *M. capillaris,* in denser tufts, the old basal sheaths forming a curly fibrous mass; blades narrow, flat, becoming involute; panicle relatively smaller, narrower, the capillary branches and branchlets mostly straight; spikelets 3.5 to 5 mm. long, the glumes one-third to two-thirds as long, acute to acuminate; lemma scaberulous, nearly glabrous at base, awnless or with an awn 2 to 3 mm. long, rarely longer. ♃ (*M. trichopodes* Chapm.)—Moist pine barrens near the coast, Virginia to Florida and Texas.

61. Muhlenbergia reverchóni Vasey and Scribn. (Fig. 580.) Resembling *M. expansa,* culms more slender, foliage finer; glumes less than half as long as the lemma, subacute or erose; lemma with an awn 2 to 5 mm. long. ♃ —Rocky prairies, Texas and Oklahoma.

62. Muhlenbergia capilláris (Lam.) Trin. (Fig. 581.) Perennial, in tufts; culms rather slender, erect, 60 to 100 cm. tall; sheaths scaberulous, at least toward the summit, and with auricles mostly 3 to 5 mm. long; blades elongate, flat or involute, 1 to 4 mm. wide, those of the innovations narrower, involute; panicle purple, oblong, diffuse, one-third to half the entire height of the culm, the branches capillary, flex-

FIGURE 574.—*Muhlenbergia setifolia.* Plant, × 1; glumes and floret, × 10. (Hitchcock 13507, N. Mex.)

uous, the branchlets and pedicels finally spreading; spikelets, excluding awns, 3 to 4 mm. long, the glumes one-fourth to two-thirds as long, acute, the second often short-awned; lemma scaberulous, minutely hairy on the callus and with a delicate awn 5 to 15 mm. long. ♃ —Rocky or sandy woods, Massachusetts to Indiana and Kansas, south to Florida and Texas; West Indies, eastern Mexico.

MUHLENBERGIA CAPILLARIS var. FÍLIPES (M. A. Curtis) Chapm. ex Beal. Culms stouter; blades mostly involute; glumes with delicate awns, mostly longer than the lemma; lemma with a delicate setaceous tooth each side of the awn. ♃ (*M. filipes* M. A. Curtis.)—Moist pine barrens near the coast, North Carolina, Florida, Mississippi, and Texas.

63. Muhlenbergia rígida (H. B. K.) Kunth. PURPLE MUHLY. (Fig. 582.) Perennial, densely tufted; culms erect, 60 to 100 cm. tall; leaves crowded at base, old sheaths persistent, the sheaths with auricles 2 to 5 mm., rarely longer; blades flat or soon involute, flexuous, those of the innovations involute; panicle dark purple, narrow, finally loose and open, 15 to 30 cm. long, the capillary branches ascending, the lower as much as 10 cm. long; spikelets, excluding awns, about 4 mm. long, the glumes from minute to about one-fourth as long, acute to erose-obtuse; lemma strongly nerved, hairy on the callus and with a

FIGURE 575.—*Muhlenbergia xerophila*. Panicle, × 1; glumes and floret, × 10. (Silveus 3477, Ariz.)

FIGURE 576.—*Muhlenbergia metcalfei*. Panicle, × 1; glumes and floret, × 10. (Metcalfe, N. Mex.)

flexuous awn 1 to 1.5 cm. long. ♃ (*M. berlandieri* Trin.)—Rocky or gravelly soil, Texas to Arizona and northern Mexico.

64. Muhlenbergia longilígula Hitchc. (Fig. 583.) Culms erect, about 1 m. tall, the base hard, wiry, cylindric, the lower sheaths expanded; ligule (or auricle of sheath) firm, usually about 1 cm. long; blades as much as 50 cm. long, 2 to 5 mm. wide, flat to subinvolute, very scabrous, usually drying involute; panicle narrow, somewhat loose, erect, 20 to 40 cm. long, the branches ascending or appressed; spikelets 2 to 3 mm. long; glumes subequal, acutish, usually glabrous; lemma usually about as long as the glumes, glabrous, awnless, rarely with a minute awn. ♃ (*Epi-*

FIGURE 577.—*Muhlenbergia dubia*. Plant, × 1; glumes and floret, × 10. (Hitchcock 3775, N. Mex.)

FIGURE 578.—*Muhlenbergia dubioides*. Panicle, × 1; glumes and floret, × 10. (Type.)

FIGURE 579.—*Muhlenbergia expansa.* Panicle, × 1; glumes and floret, × 10. (Tracy 3701, Miss.)

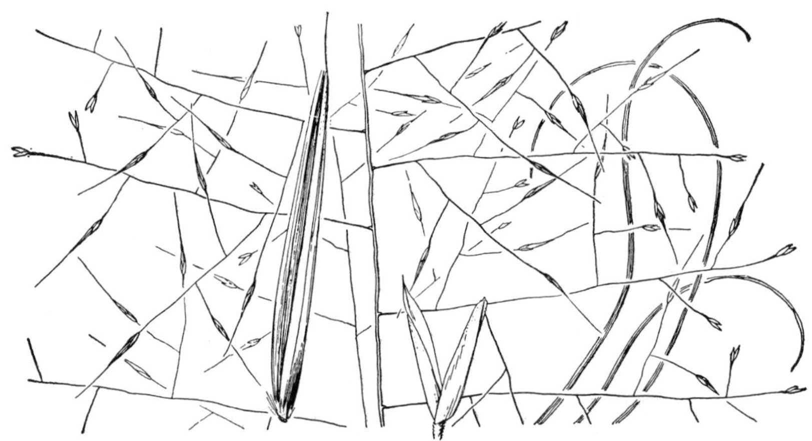

FIGURE 580.—*Muhlenbergia reverchoni.* Panicle, × 1; glumes and floret, × 10. (Reverchon, Tex.)

campes ligulata Scribn., not *Muhlenbergia ligulata* Scribn. and Merr.)—Canyons and rocky slopes, western New Mexico, Arizona, southern Nevada, and northern Mexico.

65. Muhlenbergia lindheímeri Hitchc. (Fig. 584.) Culms erect, 1 to 1.5 m. tall, the numerous overlapping lower sheaths keeled; ligule rather thin, elongate, mostly hidden in the folded base of the blade; blades elongate, firm, flat or usually folded, about 3 mm. wide, scaberulous or glabrous; panicle narrow, pale, somewhat loose, erect, 20 to 40 cm. long, the branches ascending or appressed; spikelets 2.5 to 3 mm. long; glumes acute to rather obtuse, scabrous-puberulent; lemma a little shorter to a little longer than the glumes, 3-nerved, glabrous or obscurely pubescent, awnless or rarely with an awn as much as 3 mm. long. ♃ —Rocky slopes, Texas.

66. Muhlenbergia involúta Swallen. (Fig. 585.) Culms erect, densely tufted, 60 to 135 cm. tall; sheaths compressed-keeled, scabrous; ligule about 10 mm. long; blades elongate, involute, wiry, scabrous; panicle erect, narrow, 30 to 40 cm. long, the subcapillary branches ascending or appressed, naked toward the base, the lower as much as 20 cm. long; spikelets 3 to 4.5 mm. long; glumes acute or somewhat erose, scabrous, 2 to 2.5 mm. long; lemma densely pubescent on the margin toward the very base, the minutely toothed apex awned from just below the teeth, the awn

FIGURE 581.—*Muhlenbergia capillaris*. Plant, × ½; glumes and floret, × 10. (Scribner, Tenn.)

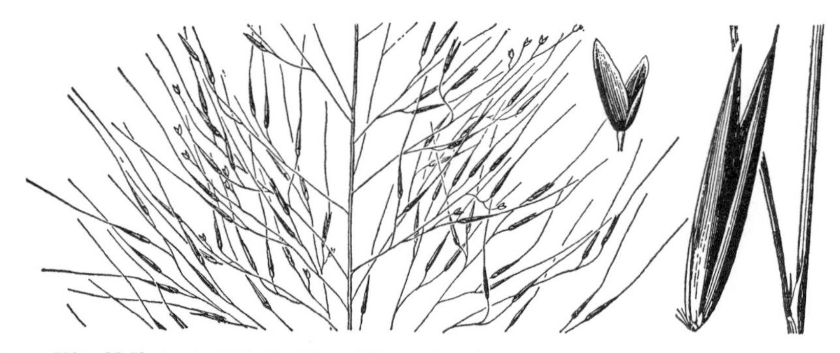

FIGURE 582.—*Muhlenbergia rigida*. Panicle and ligule, × 1; glumes and floret, × 10. (Metcalfe 1447, N. Mex.)

FIGURE 583.—*Muhlenbergia longiligula*. Panicle and ligule, × 1; glumes and floret, × 10. (Jones, Ariz.)

slender, 1.5 to 2 mm. long. ♃ — Canyons and ravines, southern Texas.

67. Muhlenbergia emersléyi Vasey. BULLGRASS. (Fig. 586.) Culms in large clumps, erect, 50 to 100 cm. tall; sheaths glabrous, slightly scabrous, compressed-keeled, especially those of the innovations; ligule softly membranaceous, 1 to 2 cm. long; blades flat or folded, scabrous, 1 to 4 mm. wide, the lower as much as 50 cm. long; panicle narrow but rather loose, erect or nodding, mostly 20 to 40 cm. long, the branches ascending, more or less fascicled or whorled, naked below; spikelets 2.5 to 4 mm. long, often purplish; glumes thin, equal, acutish, scabrous; lemma about as long as the glumes, narrowed and scabrous above, villous below, with a delicate flexuous awn, about 1.5 cm. long, or sometimes awnless. ♃ — Rocky woods and ravines, Texas to Arizona and Mexico. A good soil binder on steep slopes.

68. Muhlenbergia rígens (Benth.) Hitchc. DEERGRASS. (Fig. 587.) Culms rather slender, stiffly erect, in small bunches, with a hard tough base, 1 to 1.5 m. tall; sheaths smooth

FIGURE 584.—*Muhlenbergia lindheimeri*. Panicle, × 1; glumes and floret, × 10. (Type.)

FIGURE 585.—*Muhlenbergia involuta*. Panicle and ligule, × 1; spikelet and floret, × 10. (Type.)

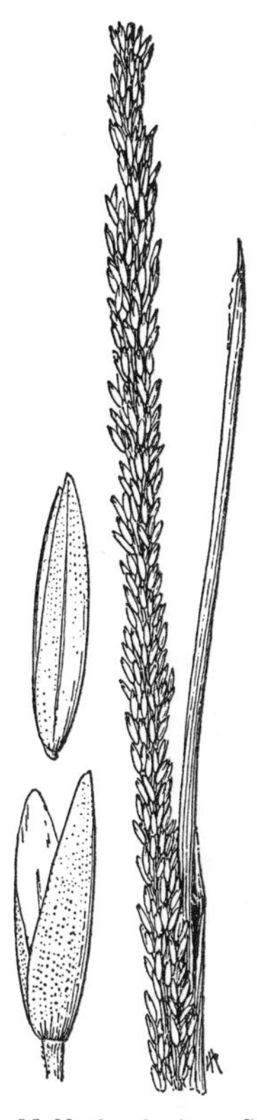

FIGURE 587.—*Muhlenbergia rigens*. Spikelet and floret, × 10. (Type collection.)

or slightly scabrous, mostly overlapping, the lower crowded, expanded, somewhat papery; ligule firm, truncate, 2 to 3 mm. long; blades scabrous, elongate, involute, tapering into a long slender point; panicle grayish or

FIGURE 586.—*Muhlenbergia emersleyi*. Panicle, × 1; glumes and floret, × 10. (Wooton and Standley, N. Mex.)

pale, slender, mostly spikelike, 20 to 60 cm. long or more, the lower branches sometimes 5 to 10 cm. long; spikelets 2.5 to 3.5 mm. long, the glumes shorter than the lemma, from acute to obtuse or somewhat erose, scabrous-puberulent, rarely faintly 3-nerved; lemma scaberulous, sparsely pilose at base, 3-nerved toward the narrowed summit, awnless. ♃ (*Epicampes rigens* Benth.)—Dry or open ground, hillsides, gullies, and

FIGURE 588.—*Muhlenbergia mundula*. Plant, × 1; glumes and floret, × 10. (Metcalfe 10, N. Mex.)

open forest, southern California. Used by Indians in basket making.

69. Muhlenbergia múndula I. M. Johnston. (Fig. 588.) Similar to the preceding; ligule 1 to 2 mm. long; panicle similar, but lower branches not more than 4 cm. long; spikelets 3 to 4 mm. long, the glumes shorter than the lemma or sometimes about equaling it. ♃ (This and the next species included in *M. rigens* in Manual, ed. 1.)—Rocky canyons and gullies, Nevada, New Mexico, Arizona, and northern Mexico. This and the following doubtfully distinct from *M. rigens*. Many intermediates are found.

70. Muhlenbergia márshii I. M. Johnston. (Fig. 589.) Often smaller than *M. rigens*, differing in the minute ligule and narrower, usually awn-tipped glumes and lemma. ♃ —Rocky stream banks and canyons, Texas and northern Mexico.

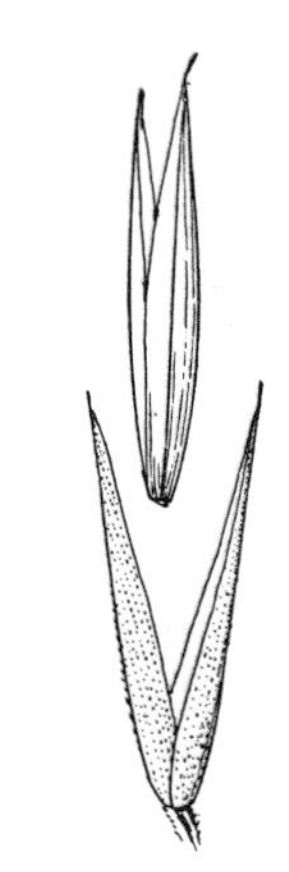

FIGURE 589.—*Muhlenbergia marshii*. Glumes and lemma, × 10. (Type collection.)

83. SPORÓBOLUS R. Br. DROPSEED

Spikelets 1-flowered, the rachilla disarticulating above the glumes; glumes 1-nerved, usually unequal, the second often as long as the spikelet; lemma membranaceous, 1-nerved, awnless; palea usually prominent and as long as the lemma or longer; caryopsis free from the lemma and palea, falling readily from the spikelet at maturity, the pericarp free from the seed, usually thin and closely enveloping it, but readily slipping away when moist. Annuals or perennials, with small spikelets in open or contracted panicles. Type species, *Sporobolus indicus*. Name from Greek *spora*, seed, and *ballein*, to throw, alluding to the free seeds. In some species of this genus the palea splits at maturity, giving the impression of an extra lemma. The first glume is early deciduous in some species. The size of the spikelets is often variable in the same panicle.

Most of the perennial species are palatable forage grasses, but few of them are abundant enough to be of importance. Two species of the Southwest, *S. airoides* and *S. wrightii*, are valuable grasses in the arid and semiarid regions; *S. interruptus* is common on the Arizona Plateau; and the widely distributed *S. cryptandrus* is also important. The seed of *S. flexuosus* and *S. cryptandrus* have been used for food by the Indians.

1a. Plants annual.
Panicles pyramidal, many-flowered, the lower branches verticillate.
Spikelets appressed, short-pediceled, 1.5 to 1.7 mm. long; panicle branches densely flowered .... 1. S. PULVINATUS.
Spikelets spreading, long-pediceled, 1.8 to 2 mm. long; panicle branches loosely few-flowered .... 2. S. PATENS.
Panicles narrow, spikelike, few-flowered, usually included in the sheaths.
Lemma pubescent .... 3. S. VAGINIFLORUS.
Lemma glabrous .... 4. S. NEGLECTUS.
1b. Plants perennial.
2a. Plants producing creeping rhizomes. Panicle narrow or spikelike.
Rhizomes extensively creeping; leaves numerous, crowded, the blades involute, conspicuously distichous; panicle spikelike .... 10. S. VIRGINICUS.

Rhizomes short; leaves not numerous nor crowded nor involute; panicle narrow but loose .... 6. S. MACER.
2b. Plants without creeping rhizomes.
3a. Glumes nearly equal, much shorter than the lemma. Panicle narrow or spikelike.
Panicle branches short and appressed, the panicle spikelike .... 8. S. POIRETII.
Panicle branches slender, ascending, the panicle scarcely spikelike .... 9. S. INDICUS.
3b. Glumes unequal or if equal as long as the spikelet.
4a. Spikelets mostly 3 to 7 mm. long. Plants usually less than 1 m. tall.
Second glume shorter than the lemma; panicle contracted, more or less included in the sheath.
Lemma glabrous, the palea not exceeding it .... 5. S. ASPER.
Lemma pubescent, the palea acuminate, exceeding it ...... 7. S. CLANDESTINUS.
Second glume about as long as the lemma; panicle open (contracted in *S. purpurascens*), not included.
Branches of the narrow panicle in distinct whorls, usually less than 4 cm. long.
Branches 2 to 3 cm. long, somewhat distant, more or less spreading, the panicle open .... 17. S. JUNCEUS.
Branches 1 to 2 cm. long, ascending or appressed, overlapping, the panicle contracted .... 18. S. PURPURASCENS.
Branches of the open panicle not in distinct whorls, usually more than 4 cm. long.
Spikelets short-pediceled and appressed along the main panicle branches.
Spikelets about 4 mm. long, purplish .... 14. S. CURTISSII.
Spikelets about 3 mm. long, pale .... 30. S. THARPII.
Spikelets not appressed, the branches and pedicels somewhat spreading.
Blades terete .... 15. S. TERETIFOLIUS.
Blades flat or folded.
Glumes about equal, as long as the lemma .... 16. S. FLORIDANUS.
Glumes unequal.
Panicles 30 to 50 cm. long, purple; culms mostly more than 1 m. tall. 13. S. SILVEANUS.
Panicles 10 to 20 cm. long, gray or lead-colored; culms 30 to 70 cm. tall.
Blades elongate .... 12. S. HETEROLEPIS.
Blades mostly less than half as long as culm .... 11. S. INTERRUPTUS.
4b. Spikelets 1 to 2.5 mm. long (sometimes 3 mm. in *S. giganteus*).
5a. Lower panicle branches in distinct whorls, the mature panicle pyramidal; spikelets about 1 mm. long .... 19. S. PYRAMIDATUS.
5b. Lower panicle branches not in distinct whorls (occasionally whorled in *S. domingensis*); spikelets 1.5 to 2.5 mm. long.
6a. Basal sheaths compressed-keeled. Panicle branches few, widely spreading, naked for about one-third their length; spikelets 1.5 mm. long. 26. S. BUCKLEYI.
6b. Basal sheaths not compressed-keeled.
7a. Sheaths with a conspicuous tuft of white hairs at summit.
Culms robust, 1 to 2 m. tall; spikelets 2.5 to 3 mm. long. 25. S. GIGANTEUS.
Culms more slender, mostly less than 1 m. tall; spikelets 2 to 2.5 mm. long.
Panicle open, often large, the branches and branchlets flexuous, the spikelets loosely arranged .... 22. S. FLEXUOSUS.
Panicle open or compact, if open the spikelets crowded on the branchlets.
Panicle, or the exserted portion, somewhat open, the branches naked below (sometimes entirely enclosed).
Base of plant a close tuft .... 21. S. CRYPTANDRUS.
Base of plant a cluster of knotty rhizomes. Culms erect, slender, mostly less than 30 cm. tall; blades short, involute, spreading. 23. S. NEALLEYI.
Panicle compact, spikelike, usually exserted .... 24. S. CONTRACTUS.
7b. Sheaths naked or nearly so at the summit.
Pedicels elongate, capillary .... 29. S. TEXANUS.
Pedicels short.
Panicle 1 to 2 times as long as wide, loose, the branches not crowded; blades mostly involute .... 27. S. AIROIDES.
Panicle more than 3 times as long as wide, relatively dense; blades mostly flat.
Panicle not more than 20 cm. long, usually smaller. 20. S. DOMINGENSIS.
Panicle commonly 50 cm. long, rarely as small as 25 or 30 cm. 28. S. WRIGHTII.

FIGURE 590.—*Sporobolus pulvinatus*. Panicle, × 1; glumes and floret, × 10. (Type.)

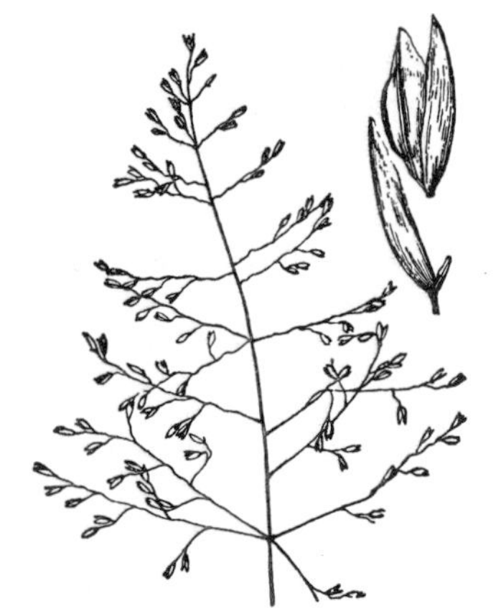

FIGURE 591.—*Sporobolus patens*. Panicle, × 1; glumes and floret, × 10. (Type.)

1. Sporobolus pulvinátus Swallen. (Fig. 590.) Culms 5 to 30 cm. tall in small erect or spreading tufts; blades mostly 4 to 7 cm. long, 2 to 5 mm. wide, lanceolate-acuminate, scabrous, the uppermost much reduced; panicles 2 to 5 or rarely to 8 cm. long, pyramidal, the branches erect to spreading, densely flowered, usually naked at the base; spikelets 1.5 to 1.7 mm. long, appressed; first glume minute, the second as long as the spikelet, abruptly acute or subobtuse; lemma acute or subobtuse; palea broad, conspicuous, as long as the lemma. ⊙ —Sandy land, Texas, New Mexico, and Arizona; northern Mexico.

2. Sporobolus pátens Swallen. (Fig. 591.) Culms 10 to 25 cm. tall, slender, erect; sheaths glabrous, sparsely hispid at the throat, the uppermost elongate, almost bladeless; blades 1 to 3.5 cm. long, 1 to 2 mm. wide, flat, scabrous on the margins; panicles pyramidal, 2.5 to 5 cm. long, the slender branches spreading or even reflexed, few-flowered, the branchlets abruptly spreading; spikelets 1.8 to 2 mm. long, the pedicels slender, spreading, as much as 3 mm. long; first glume minute; second glume and lemma equal, acute; palea shorter than the lemma, truncate, minutely

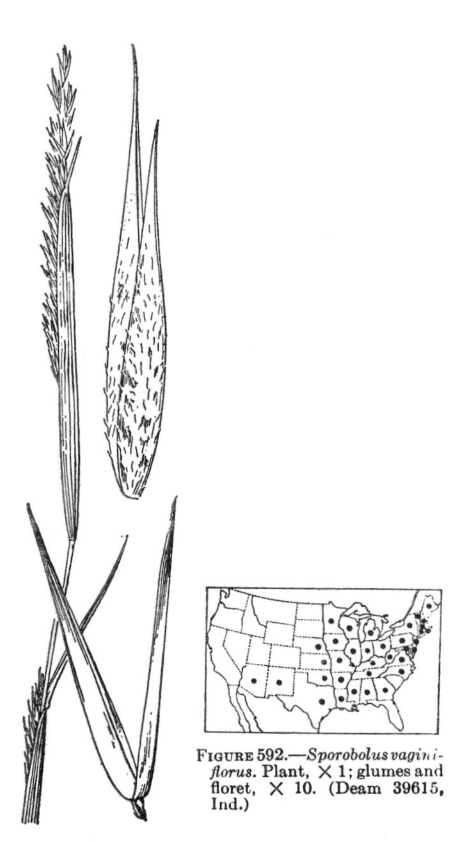

FIGURE 592.—*Sporobolus vaginiflorus*. Plant, × 1; glumes and floret, × 10. (Deam 39615, Ind.)

dentate. ⊙ —Open dry ground, southern Arizona.

3. Sporobolus vaginiflórus (Torr.) Wood. (Fig. 592.) Annual, branching from base; culms erect to spreading, mostly 20 to 40 cm. tall, sometimes as much as 75 cm.; blades slender, subinvolute, the lower elongate; panicles terminal and axillary, slender, mostly not more than 3 cm. long, the terminal exserted or partly included, the axillary included in the sheaths or slightly exserted, late in the season the sheaths swollen and containing cleistogamous spikelets; glumes acute, about equal, 3 to 5 mm. long; lemma as long as the glumes or exceeding them, acute or acuminate, rather sparsely pubescent, sometimes mottled with dark spots; palea acuminate, sometimes longer than the lemma. ⊙ —Sandy soil or open waste ground, Maine and Ontario to Minnesota and Nebraska, south to Georgia, Texas, and Arizona.

Figure 593.—*Sporobolus neglectus*. Plant, × 1; spikelet and floret, × 10. (Deam 33426, Ind.)

Figure 594.—*Sporobolus asper*. Plant × 1; glumes and floret, × 10. (Deam 42707, Ind.)

4. Sporobolus negléctus Nash. (Fig. 593.) Differing from *S. vaginiflorus* chiefly in the smaller, paler, plumper spikelets, 2 to 3 mm. long, and in the glabrous lemma; lower blades often sparsely pilose; panicles usually entirely hidden in the more swollen sheaths. ⊙ —Dry open ground and sandy fields, Quebec and Maine to Montana, south to Virginia, Tennessee, and Texas; also Washington and Arizona. A form from Missouri (Ozark Mountains), with rather strongly pilose leaves, has been differentiated as *S. ozarkanus* Fernald.

5. Sporobolus ásper (Michx.) Kunth. (Fig. 594.) Perennial; culms erect, often rather stout, solitary or in small tufts, 60 to 120 cm. tall; blades elongate, flat, becoming involute, 1 to 4 mm. wide at base, tapering to a fine point; panicle terminal and axillary, pale or whitish, sometimes purplish, contracted, more or less spikelike, usually enclosed at base or sometimes entirely in the inflated upper sheath, 5 to 15 cm. long; spikelets 4 to 6 mm. long; glumes rather broad, keeled, subacute, the first about half as long as the spikelet, the second two-thirds to three-fourths as long; lemma and palea subequal, glabrous, the tip boat-shaped. ♃ —Prairies and sandy meadows, Vermont to Montana, south to Louisiana and Arizona; eastern Washington.

Sporobolus asper var. pilósus (Vasey) Hitchc. Sheaths and blades more or less pilose. ♃ (*S. pilosus* Vasey.)—Prairies and rocky hills, Kansas (Saline County and westward), Texas (Del Rio), and Montana.

Sporobolus asper var. hookéri (Trin.) Vasey. Less robust, the more slender, fewer flowered, panicle looser; spikelets usually smaller, 3 to 5 mm. long. ♃ (*S. attenuatus* Nash; *S. drummondii* Vasey.)—Plains, Missouri, Kansas, Mississippi, Texas, and Oklahoma. Foliage rarely somewhat villous.

6. Sporobolus mácer (Trin.) Hitchc. (Fig. 595.) Perennial, with short scaly rhizomes; culms erect, 50 to 70 cm. tall; blades flat, 10 to 20 cm. long, 1 to 2 mm. wide, sometimes wider, pilose on the upper surface near base and at the throat of the sheath; panicle narrow, often enclosed at base, 5 to 15 cm. long, the branches erect; spikelets 4 to 5 mm.

Figure 595.—*Sporobolus macer*. Plant, × ½; glumes and floret, × 10. (Chase 4341, Miss.)

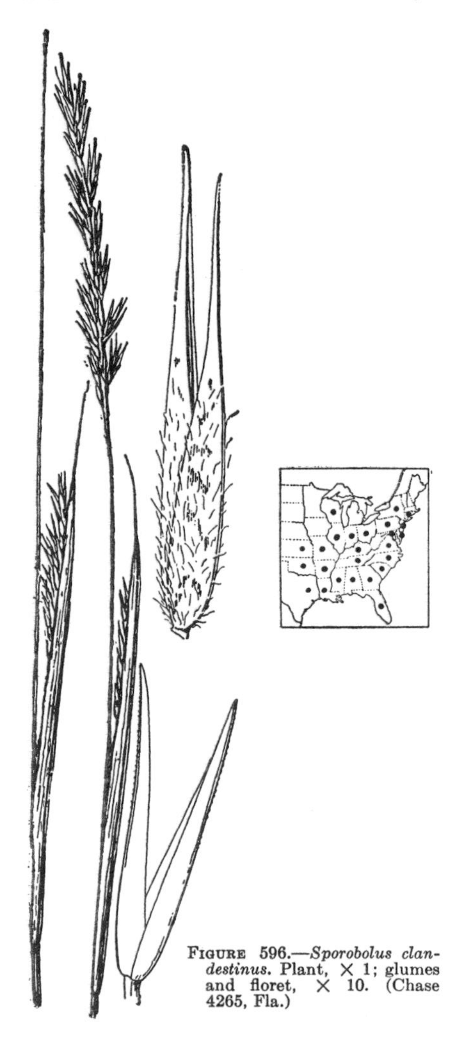

FIGURE 596.—*Sporobolus clandestinus*. Plant, × 1; glumes and floret, × 10. (Chase 4265, Fla.)

long, the glumes keeled, the first about two-thirds as long, the second a little longer than the first; lemma and palea subequal, the tips boat-shaped. ♃ —Wet pineland, Oklahoma, Mississippi, Louisiana, and Texas. Except for the rhizomes this species resembles *S. asper* var. *hookeri*.

7. Sporobolus clandestínus (Bieler.) Hitchc. (Fig. 596.) Perennial; culms relatively stout to slender, erect to spreading, 50 to 100 cm. tall; lower sheaths sometimes pilose; blades flat, becoming involute, with a long fine point; panicle narrow, contracted, 5 to 10 cm. long, usually partly enclosed; spikelets 5 to 7 mm. long, the glumes keeled, acute or subacute, the first more than half as long as the spikelet, the second longer than the first; lemma sparsely appressed-pubescent, acuminate, the palea longer, sometimes as much as 10 mm. long. ♃ (*S. canovirens* Nash.)—Sandy fields, pine barrens, hills, and prairies, Connecticut to Wisconsin and Kansas, south to Florida and Texas.

8. Sporobolus poirétii (Roem. and Schult.) Hitchc. SMUTGRASS. (Fig. 597.) Perennial; culms erect, solitary or in small tufts, 30 to 100 cm. tall; blades flat to subinvolute, rather firm, 2 to 5 mm. wide at base, elongate, tapering to a fine point; panicle usually spikelike but more or less interrupted, 10 to 40 cm. long, the branches appressed or ascending; spikelets about 2 mm. long; glumes obtuse, somewhat unequal, about half as long as the spikelet or less; lemma acutish. ♃ (*Sporobolus berteroanus* (Trin.) Hitchc. and Chase.)—Open ground and waste places, Virginia to Tennessee and Oklahoma, south to Florida, Texas, and the warmer parts of America to Argentina; on ballast in Oregon and New Jersey; tropical Asia, apparently introduced in America. At maturity the extruded reddish caryopses remain for some time sticking to the panicle by the mucilaginous pericarp. Often affected with a black fungus. This species has been referred to the Australian *S. elongatus* R. Br., which seems to be distinct, differing in its looser panicle.

9. Sporobolus índicus (L.) R. Br. (Fig. 598.) Resembling *S. poiretii*, but the blades more slender, especially at base, and the panicle branches longer, more slender, less densely flowered, loosely ascending to somewhat spreading, the panicle not spikelike. ♃—Punta Gorda, Fla.; ballast, Mobile, Ala.; tropical America.

10. Sporobolus virgínicus (L.) Kunth. (Fig. 599.) Perennial, with

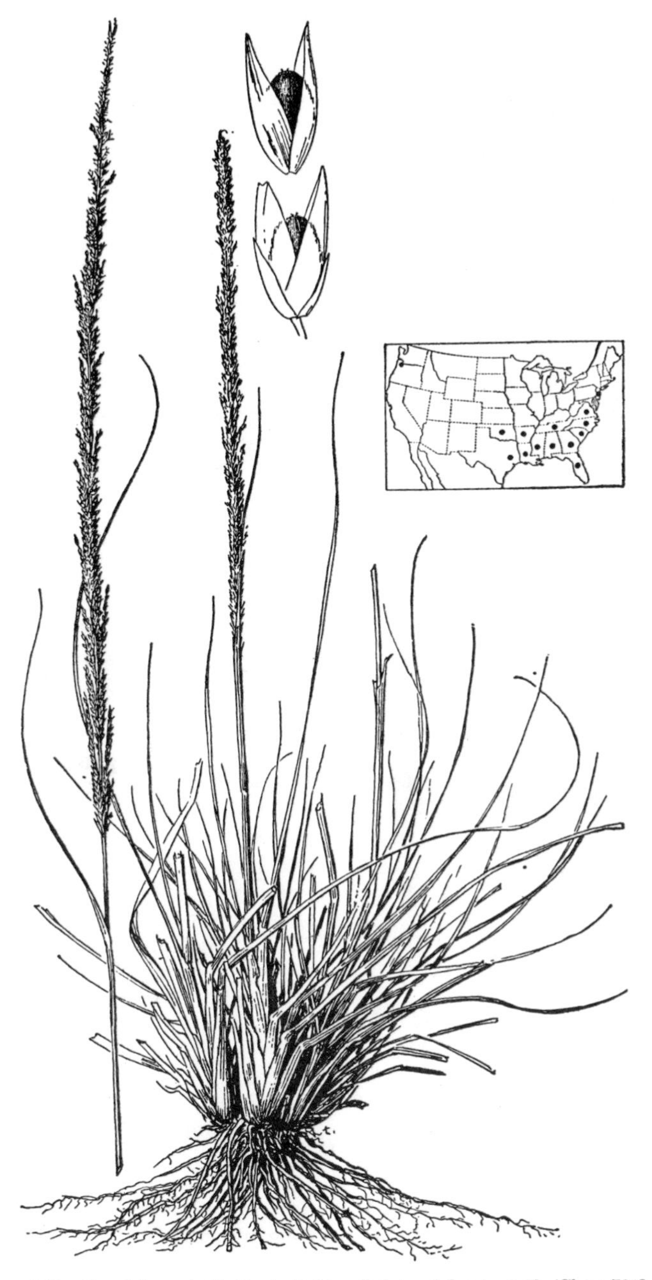

FIGURE 597.—*Sporobolus poiretii.* Plant, × ½; spikelet and floret, × 10. (Chase 7043, Fla.)

numerous branching widely creeping slender rhizomes (yellowish in drying); culms erect, 10 to 40 cm. tall; sheaths overlapping, more or less pilose at the throat; blades flat or becoming involute especially toward the fine point, conspicuously distichous, mostly less than 5 cm. long or

FIGURE 598.—*Sporobolus indicus*. Panicle, × 1; spikelet and floret, × 10. (Léon 867, Cuba.)

on the innovations longer; panicle pale, contracted or spikelike, 2 to 8

FIGURE 599.—*Sporobolus virginicus*. Plant, × 1; glumes and floret, × 10. (Nash 2467, Fla.)

cm. long, 5 to 10 mm. thick; spikelets 2 to 2.5 mm. long; glumes and lemma about equal. ♃ —Sandy or muddy seashores and saline marshes, forming extensive colonies, with relatively few flowering culms, southeastern Virginia (Gronovius, Fl. Virg.) to Florida and Texas, south through the West Indies to Brazil. Readily grazed where available. A robust form (called *S. littoralis* (Lam.) Kunth), with culms as much as 1 m. tall and panicles as much as 15 cm. long, is found in the West Indies and extends into Florida. Complete intergradations are found, and the type specimen is not the robust form.

11. Sporobolus interrúptus Vasey. BLACK DROPSEED. (Fig. 600.) Perennial, densely tufted; culms erect, 30 to 60 cm. tall, the leaves crowded at base, about 2 on the culm; sheaths more or less pilose; blades flat or folded, sparsely pilose to glabrous, 1 to 2 mm. wide; panicle 10 to 20 cm. long, brownish-leaden, the branches distant, finally spreading, naked at base; spikelets about 6 mm. long, short-pediceled; glumes acute, the first 2 to 3 mm., the second 4 to 6 mm. long; lemma and palea acute, about equal. ♃ —Grassy plains and hills, Arizona. The second glume and lemma may have wrinkles toward the summit that look like nerves.

12. Sporobolus heterólepis (A. Gray) A. Gray. PRAIRIE DROPSEED. (Fig. 601.) Perennial, in dense tufts; culms erect, slender, 30 to 70 cm. tall; sheaths somewhat pilose at the throat, the lower sometimes sparsely pilose on the back; blades elongate, flat, becoming involute at the slender attenuate tip, 2 mm. or less wide; panicle, 5 to 20 cm. long, the branches ascending or spreading, 3 to 6 cm. long, naked below, few-flowered above; spikelets grayish; glumes acuminate, the first 2 to 4 mm. long, the second 4 to 6 mm. long; lemma shorter than the second glume, palea slightly longer than the lemma; caryopsis globose, nutlike, nearly 2 mm. thick, finally splitting the palea. ♃ —

Prairies, Quebec to Saskatchewan, south to Connecticut, eastern Texas, and Colorado.

13. Sporobolus silveánus Swallen. (Fig. 602.) Culms 85 to 115 cm. tall, densely tufted, erect, scabrous; sheaths glabrous or scaberulous, pubescent on the collar, the uppermost elongate, the lower shiny, becoming more or less papery with age; blades as much as 45 cm. long, 1 to 2 mm. wide, usually involute, curved or flexuous; panicles 30 to 50 cm. long, the ascending branches rather distant, few-flowered, naked at the base; spikelets 5 to 6 mm. long, purple; first glume 3 to 4.5 mm. long, the second 4.5 to 6 mm. long; lemma subacute; palea as long as the lemma, the keels obscure. ♃ —Open woods, western Louisiana and eastern Texas.

14. Sporobolus curtíssii (Vasey) Small ex Scribn. (Fig. 603.) Perennial, in dense tufts; culms slender, 30 to 70 cm. tall; basal sheaths pilose at the throat; blades flat or folded, flexuous, about 1 mm. wide, pilose on the upper surface near the base; panicle pyramidal, open, 7 to 20 cm. long, the branches solitary or in twos, ascending; spikelets appressed along the main branches, bronze or purplish, about 4.5 mm. long; glumes about equal, acuminate, as long as or longer than the lemma and palea. ♃ —Dry pine barrens, North Carolina to Florida.

15. Sporobolus teretifólius Harper. (Fig. 604.) Perennial, in tufts; culms erect, wiry, 60 to 80 cm. tall, sheaths pilose at the throat; blades elongate, slender, terete, wiry, flexuous, pilose on the upper surface at base; panicle pyramidal, open, 15 to 20 cm. long, the capillary branches, branchlets, and pedicels ascending to spreading; spikelets purplish brown, 4 to 5 mm. long; glumes acute, the first half as long, the second as long as the equal lemma and palea. ♃ —Moist pine barrens, North Carolina and Georgia.

16. Sporobolus floridánus Chapm. (Fig. 605.) Plants more robust than *S. curtissii*, as much as 1 m. tall; sheaths keeled, the basal ones somewhat pilose at throat, the base indurate and shining, blades folded at base, usually flat above, 2 to 5 mm. wide, abruptly narrowed at apex; panicle narrow, open, 15 to 35 cm. long, the branches and branchlets ascending; spikelets 4 to 5 mm. long;

FIGURE 600.—*Sporobolus interruptus*. Plant, × 1; glumes and floret, × 10. (Rusby, Ariz.)

FIGURE 601.—*Sporobolus heterolepis*. Plant, × 1; spikelet and floret with caryopsis and split palea, × 10. (McDonald, Ill.)

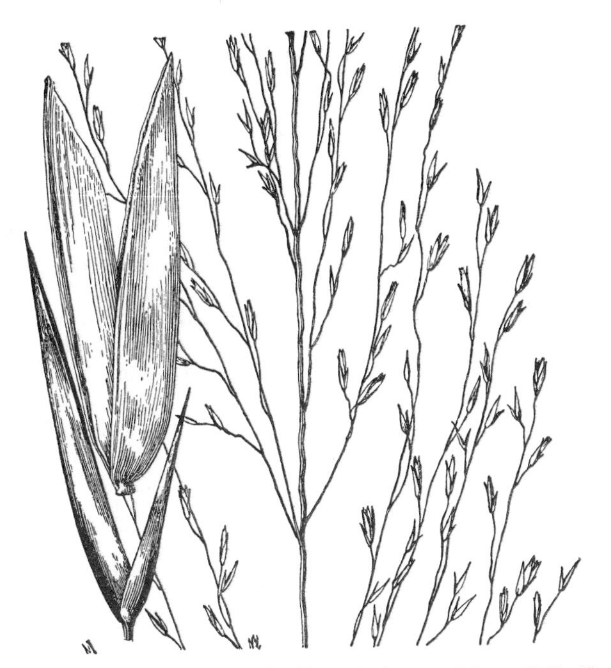

FIGURE 602.—*Sporobolus silveanus*. Panicle, × 1; glumes and floret, × 10. (Type.)

FIGURE 603.—*Sporobolus curtissii*. Panicle, × 1; glumes and floret, × 10. (Bitting 1050, Fla.)

glumes acute, subequal, about as long as the lemma and palea. ♃ —Low pine barrens, North Carolina to Florida.

17. Sporobolus júnceus (Michx.) Kunth. (Fig. 606.) Perennial, in dense bunches; culms erect, slender, about 3-noded, 30 to 60 cm. tall; blades folded or involute, slender, glabrous; panicle mostly bronze brown, oblong or narrowly pyramidal, open, 7 to 15 cm. long, 2 to 5 cm. wide, the flexuous branches (2 to 3 cm. long) in rather regular whorls 1 to 3 cm. apart, widely spreading to ascending, naked at base, the short-pediceled spikelets appressed along the upper part; spikelets about 3 mm. long; first glume about half as long, the second glume as long as the acute lemma or a little longer. ♃ (*S. gracilis* (Trin.) Merr.)—Pine barrens of the Coastal Plain, southeastern Virginia to Florida and Texas. Common in the high pineland of Florida.

18. Sporobolus purpuráscens (Swartz) Hamilt. (Fig. 607.) Re-

FIGURE 604.—*Sporobolus teretifolius.* Plant, × 1; glumes and floret, × 10. (Harper 677, Ga.)

sembling *S. junceus;* blades flat or folded, 1 to 3 mm. wide; panicle 10 to 15 cm. long, more contracted than in *S. junceus,* the shorter branches numerous in the whorls, ascending or appressed, floriferous nearly to the base; spikelets about as in *S. junceus,* greenish purple. ♃ —Sandy prairies, southern Texas and eastern Mexico; West Indies to Brazil.

19. Sporobolus pyramidátus (Lam.) Hitchc. (Fig. 608.) Perennial, in spreading or prostrate tufts; culms 10 to 40 cm. tall; leaves crowded at the base, the sheaths pilose at the throat; blades flat, mostly less than 10 cm. long, 2 to 4 mm. wide, sparsely long-ciliate toward the base; panicle pale, pyramidal, 3 to 7 cm. long, rarely longer, the branches spreading, somewhat viscid, 1 to 3 cm. long, naked below, closely flowered above, the lowermost in a distinct whorl; spikelets a little more than 1 mm.

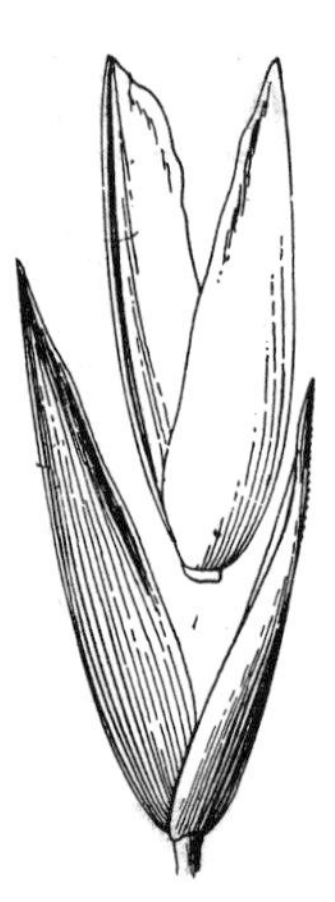

FIGURE 605.—*Sporobolus floridanus.* × 10. (Curtiss 4054, Fla.)

FIGURE 606.—*Sporobolus junceus.* Panicle, × 1; glumes and floret, × 10. (Curtiss 4056, Fla.)

long; first glume minute, the second as long as the lemma and palea. ♃ (*S. argutus* Kunth.) —Sandy or gravelly soil, especially along streets and along the seashore and in the interior in alkaline soil, Kansas and Colorado to Louisiana and Texas; southern Florida; tropical America.

20. Sporobolus domingénsis (Trin.) Kunth. (Fig. 609.) Perennial; culms erect, 20 to 100 cm. tall; leafy at base; blades rather firm, mostly 5 to 20 cm. long, 3 to 8 mm. wide, drying subinvolute, panicle pale, mostly 10 to 15 cm. long, the branches ascending or appressed; spikelets about 2 mm. long, the first glume half as long. ♃ —Coral sand and rocks along the coast of southern Florida, mostly on the Keys, north to Sanibel Island; West Indies.

21. Sporobolus cryptándrus (Torr.) A. Gray. SAND DROPSEED. (Fig. 610.) Perennial, usually in rather small tufts; culms erect or spreading, sometimes prostrate, 30 to 100 cm. tall; sheaths with a conspicuous tuft of long white hairs at summit; blades flat, 2 to 5 mm. wide, more or less involute in drying, tapering to a fine point; panicles terminal and axillary, usually included at base, sometimes entirely included, the well-

FIGURE 608.—*Sporobolus pyramidatus.* Panicle, × 1; glumes and floret, × 10. (Hitchcock 5343, Tex.)

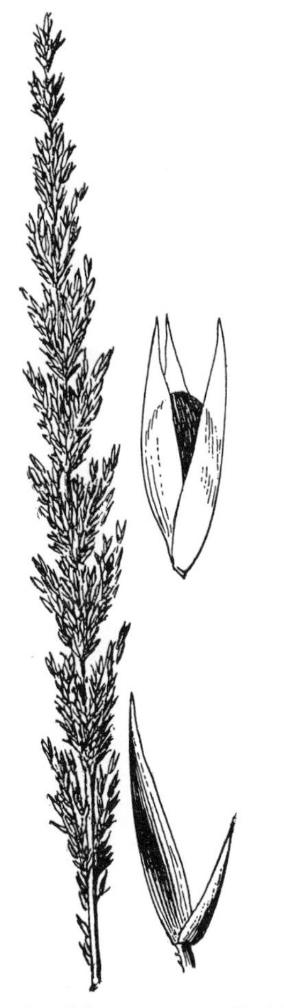

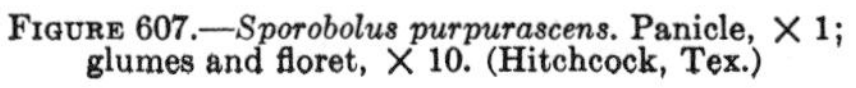

FIGURE 607.—*Sporobolus purpurascens.* Panicle, × 1; glumes and floret, × 10. (Hitchcock, Tex.)

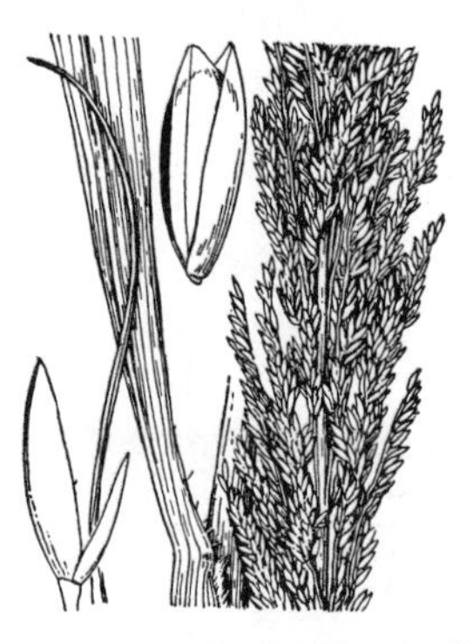

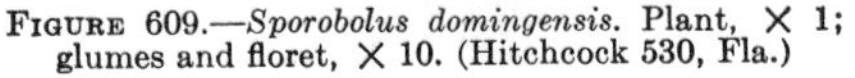

FIGURE 609.—*Sporobolus domingensis.* Plant, × 1; glumes and floret, × 10. (Hitchcock 530, Fla.)

FIGURE 610.—*Sporobolus cryptandrus.* Plant, × ½; glumes and floret, × 10. (Shear 253, Nebr.)

developed terminal panicles open, as much as 25 cm. long, the branches spreading or sometimes reflexed, rather distant, naked at base, as much as 8 cm. long or even more, the spikelets crowded along the upper part of the main branches; spikelets from pale to leaden, 2 to 2.5 mm. long; first glume one-third to half as long, the second about as long as the acute lemma and palea. ♃ —Sandy open ground, Maine and Ontario to Alberta and Washington, south to North Carolina, Indiana, Louisiana, southern California, and northern Mexico.

22. Sporobolus flexuósus (Thurb.) Rydb. MESA DROPSEED. (Fig. 611.) Resembling *S. cryptandrus*, differing in the more open often elongate panicles, the slender branches and branchlets spreading or drooping, flexuous, loosely flowered. ♃ —Mesas, western Texas to southern Utah, Nevada, southern California, and northern Mexico.

23. Sporobolus nealléyi Vasey. NEALLEY DROPSEED. (Fig. 612.) Resembling dwarf forms of *S. cryptandrus*, but differing in the loose rhizomatous base; culms slender, erect, 15 to 40 cm. tall; blades slender, involute, squarrose-spreading, mostly less than 5 cm. long; panicle delicate, open, 3 to 8 cm. long, sometimes enclosed in the sheaths, the branches and branchlets spreading, the spikelets less crowded than in *S. cryptandrus*. ♃ —Gypsum sands, western Texas, Nevada, New Mexico and Arizona.

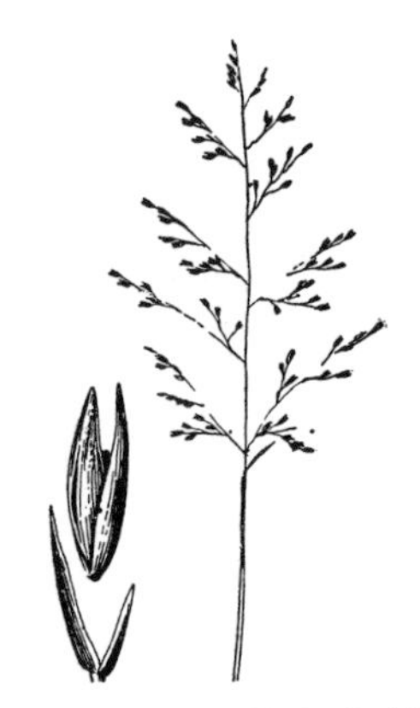

FIGURE 612.—*Sporobolus nealleyi*. Panicle, × ½; glumes and floret, × 10. (Nealley, Tex.)

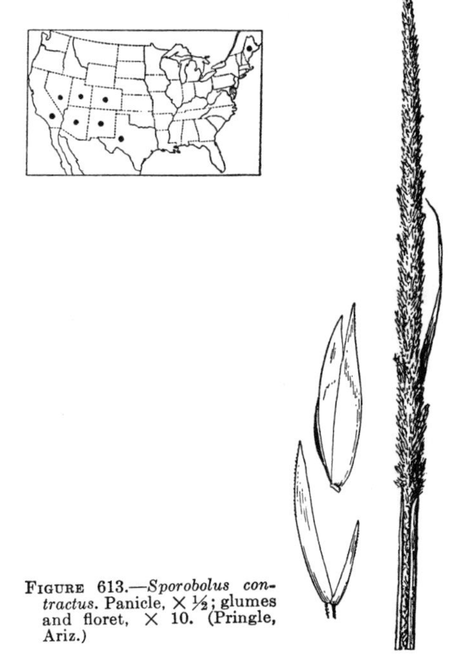

FIGURE 613.—*Sporobolus contractus*. Panicle, × ½; glumes and floret, × 10. (Pringle, Ariz.)

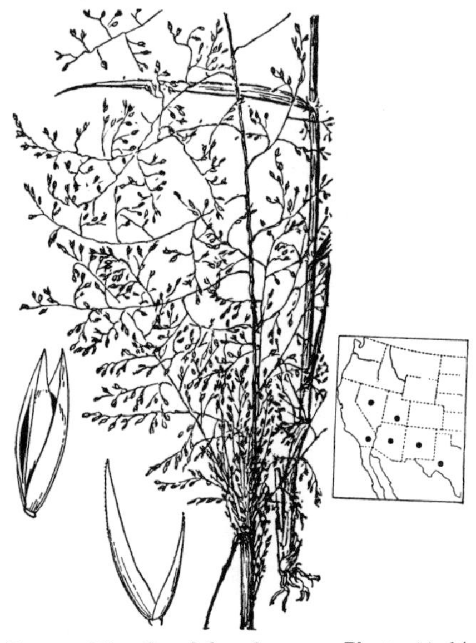

FIGURE 611.—*Sporobolus flexuosus*. Plant, × ½; glumes and floret, × 10. (Vasey, N. Mex.)

24. Sporobolus contráctus Hitchc. SPIKE DROPSEED. (Fig. 613.) Differing from *S. cryptandrus* in the spikelike panicle as much as 50 cm. long, usually

FIGURE 614.—*Sporobolus giganteus.* Panicle, × ½; glumes and floret, × 10. (Nealley, Tex.)

included at the base, rarely entirely included in the sheath. ♃ (*S. strictus* Merr.)—Mesas, dry bluffs, and sandy fields, Arkansas, Colorado to Nevada, south to western Texas, southeastern California, and Sonora; adventive in Maine.

25. Sporobolus gigantéus Nash. GIANT DROPSEED. (Fig. 614.) Resembling *S. cryptandrus* and *S. contractus;* culms 1 to 2 m. tall, erect, robust; blades as much as 1 cm. wide; panicle usually thicker than in *S. contractus,* less spikelike; spikelets 2.5 to 3 mm. long. ♃ —Mesas and sandhills, Oklahoma and western Texas to Colorado and Arizona.

26. Sporobolus bucklėyi Vasey. (Fig. 615.) Perennial, the base strongly compressed; culms erect, slender, 40 to 80 cm. tall; sheaths keeled, pubescent on the margin and collar; blades flat, 4 to 7 mm. wide; panicle open, 10 to 30 cm. long, the slender branches widely spreading, as much as 10 cm. long, solitary, rather distant, naked below, with closely flowered short-appressed branchlets above; spikelets about 1.5 mm. long; glumes narrow, the first a little shorter, the second a little longer than the acute lemma; palea about as long as the lemma, splitting as the grain (1 mm. long) ripens. ♃ —Texas and eastern Mexico.

27. Sporobolus airoídes (Torr.) Torr. ALKALI SACATON. (Fig. 616.) Perennial, in large tough bunches; culms erect to spreading, 50 to 100 cm. tall; sheaths pilose at the throat; ligule pilose; blades elongate, flat, soon becoming involute, usually less than 4 mm. wide, often flexuous; panicle nearly half the entire height of the plant, at maturity half to two-thirds as wide as long, the stiff slender branches and branchlets finally widely spreading, naked at base, the spikelets aggregate along the upper half to two-thirds; spikelets 2 to 2.5 mm. long, the first glume about half as long, commonly falling toward

FIGURE 615.—*Sporobolus buckleyi.* Panicle, × ½; glumes and floret, × 10. (Nealley, Tex.)

FIGURE 616.—*Sporobolus airoides*. Plant, × ½; glumes and floret, × 10. (Metcalfe, N. Mex.)

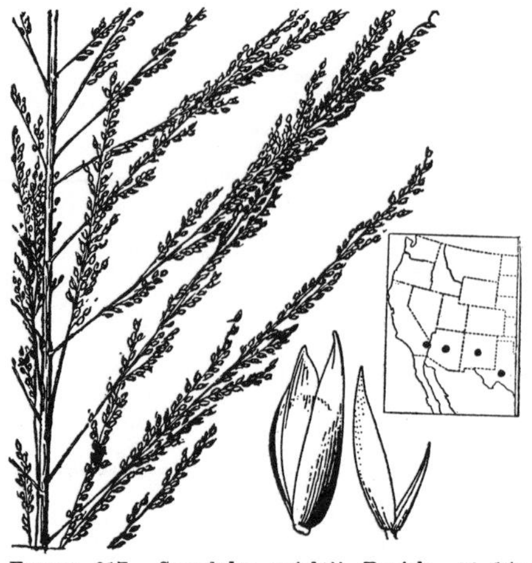

FIGURE 617.—*Sporobolus wrightii.* Panicle, × ½; glumes and floret, × 10. (Hitchcock 3648, Ariz.)

maturity; second glume, lemma, and palea about equal, the palea splitting as the grain ripens. ♃ —Meadows and valleys, especially in moderately alkaline soil, South Dakota and Missouri to eastern Washington, south to Texas and southern California; Mexico. Mature spikelets with the first glume fallen and the palea split to the base are puzzling to the beginner. Less mature complete spikelets will usually be found at the base of the panicle. A good forage grass in alkaline regions; often called bunchgrass.

28. Sporobolus wríghtii Munro ex Scribn. SACATON. (Fig. 617.) Perennial, in large dense tufts; culms robust, erect, firm and hard, 1 to 2 m. tall; sheaths sparsely pilose at the throat; ligule pilose; blades elongate, flat, involute in drying, 3 to 6 mm. wide; panicle pale, narrow, open, mostly 30 to 60 cm. long, the branches crowded, straight, stiffly ascending, the branchlets appressed, closely flowered from the base or nearly so; spikelets 2 to 2.5 mm. long, the first glume about one-third as long, the second two-thirds to three-fourths as long, acute; lemma and palea about equal. ♃ —Mesas and valleys, southern and western Texas and Oklahoma to southern California and central Mexico. Useful for grazing when young; also furnishes hay and makes good winter range.

29. Sporobolus texánus Vasey. (Fig. 618.) Perennial, in close hemispherical tufts; culms erect to spreading, slender, wiry, 30 to 50 cm. tall; sheaths pilose at the throat, the lower often papillose-pilose on the surface; blades flat, involute in drying, mostly less than 10 cm. long, 1 to 4 mm. wide; panicle open, rather diffuse, breaking away at maturity, 15 to 30 cm. long, about as wide, the capillary scabrous branches, branchlets, and long pedicels stiffly spreading; spikelets about 2.5 mm. long, the first glume acute, one-third to half as long, the second, acuminate, slightly exceeding the acute lemma and palea, the palea early splitting. ♃ —Mesas, valleys, and salt marshes, Kansas and Colorado to Texas and Arizona.

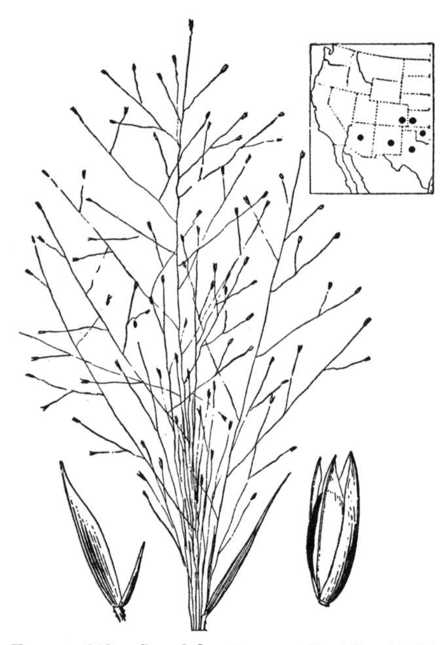

FIGURE 618.—*Sporobolus texanus.* Panicle, × ½; glumes and floret with caryopsis, × 10. (Nealley, Tex.)

30. Sporobolus thárpii Hitchc. (Fig. 619.) Perennial, densely tufted; culms 60 to 100 cm. tall; sheaths glabrous, the lower firm, loose, shining;

blades elongate, involute, flexuous, about 1 mm. thick, tapering to a long

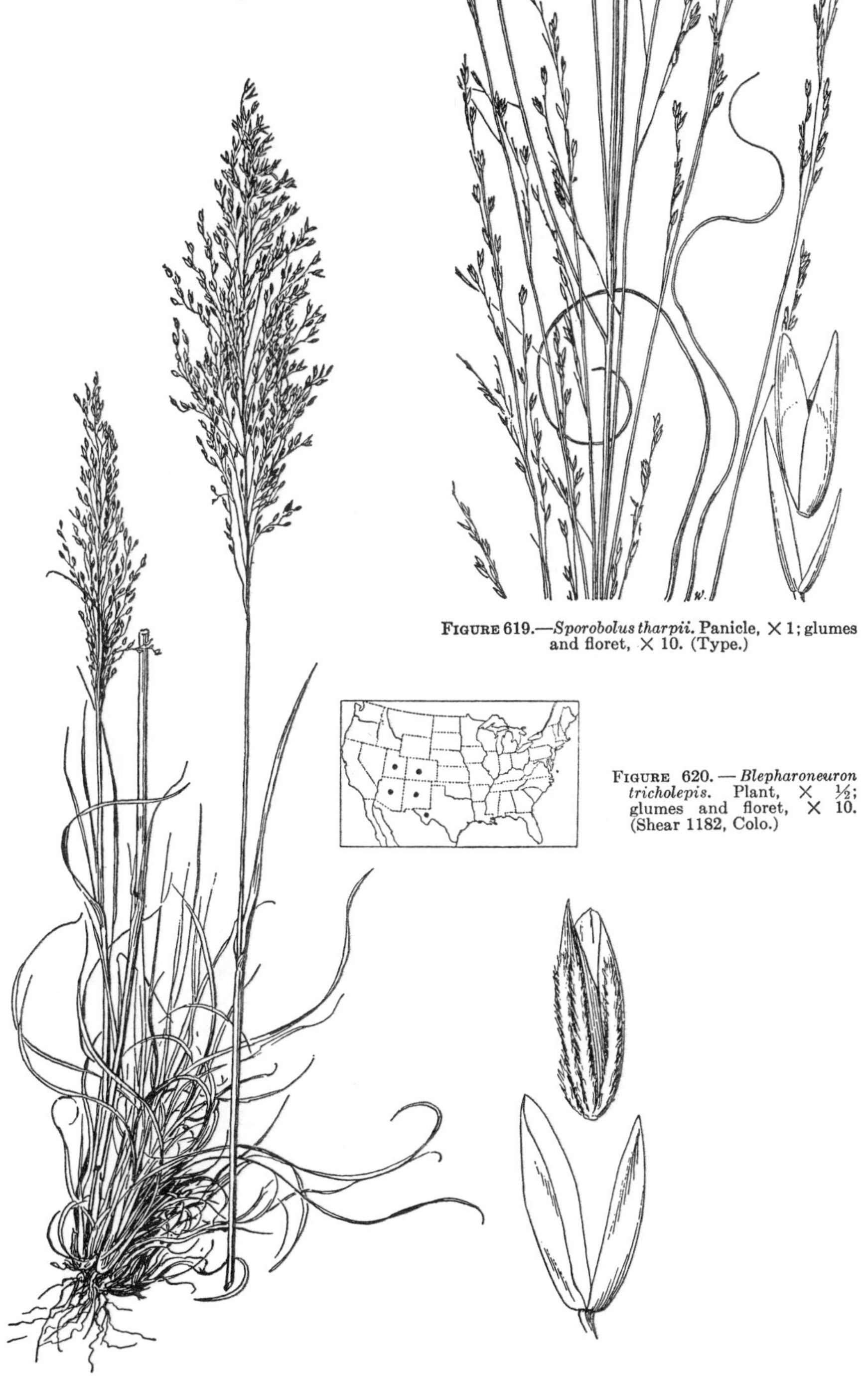

FIGURE 619.—*Sporobolus tharpii*. Panicle, × 1; glumes and floret, × 10. (Type.)

FIGURE 620. — *Blepharoneuron tricholepis*. Plant, × ½; glumes and floret, × 10. (Shear 1182, Colo.)

fine point, long-ciliate at base; panicle open, as much as 30 cm. long, the branches stiffly ascending, the lower as much as 15 cm. long; spikelets appressed along the nearly simple branches and branchlets, about 3 mm. long; first glume narrow, acuminate, about half as long as the spikelet, the second glume, lemma, and palea acute, about equal. ♃ —Known only from Padre Island, Tex.

84. BLEPHARONEÚRON Nash

Spikelets 1-flowered, the rachilla disarticulating above the glumes; glumes subequal, rather broad; lemma 3-nerved, the nerves densely silky villous; palea densely villous between the two nerves. Tufted perennial, with open, narrow panicles. Type species, *Blepharoneuron tricholepis.* Name from Greek *blepharis,* eyelash, and *neuron,* nerve, alluding to the villous nerves of the lemma.

1. Blepharoneuron trichólepis (Torr.) Nash. Hairy dropseed (Fig. 620.) Culms erect, densely tufted, slender, 20 to 60 cm. tall; leaves crowded on the innovations, mostly less than half as long as the culm, the slender blades flat, soon becoming involute, often flexuous; panicle grayish, elliptic, 5 to 20 cm. long, 2 to 5 cm. wide, many-flowered, the branches ascending, the pedicels capillary, flexuous; spikelets 2.5 to 3 mm. long; glumes obtuse or subacute, a little shorter than the abruptly pointed lemma; palea slightly exceeding the lemma. ♃ —Rocky slopes and dry open woods, 2,000 to 3,500 m., Colorado to Utah, south to Texas, Arizona, and Mexico. Palatable and sufficiently abundant in places to be of importance.

85. CRÝPSIS Ait.

Spikélets 1-flowered, disarticulating below the glumes; glumes about equal, narrow, acute; lemma broad, thin, 1-nerved; palea similar to the lemma, about as long, splitting between the nerves; fruit readily falling from the lemma and palea, the seed free from the thin pericarp (easily removed when wet). Spreading annual, with capitate inflorescences in the axils of a pair of broad spathes, these being enlarged sheaths with short rigid blades. Type species, *Crypsis aculeata* (L.) Ait. Name from Greek *krupsis,* concealment, alluding to the partially hidden inflorescence.

Figure 621.—*Crypsis niliaca.* Plant, × ½; glumes and floret, × 10. (Brandegee, Calif.)

1. Crypsis nilíaca Fig. and De Not. (Fig. 621.) Freely branching, prostrate, the mats to 30 cm. in diameter, often depauperate, 2 to 3 cm. wide; sheaths tuberculate, the summit bearded; blades flat, involute toward the apex, 2 to 5 cm. long, spreading, readily falling from the sheaths, mature plants mostly bladeless; glumes about 3 mm. long, minutely pilose; lemma and palea about as long as the glumes, the broad palea readily splitting between the nerves. (Described under *C. aculeata* in Manual, ed. 1.) ⊙ —Overflowed land, dried mud flats, sand bars, and wet alkali ground, Sacramento and San Joaquin Valleys and in Humboldt, Santa Clara, and Los Angeles Counties, Calif. Introduced; first found at Norman, Glenn County, and in alkali hollow, Colusa County, in May 1898, the source of the seed not known. The grass is slowly spreading, the latest collection being made in Santa Clara County in 1942. Egypt and southwestern Asia.

86. HELEÓCHLOA Host ex Roemer

Spikelets 1-flowered, the rachilla mostly disarticulating above the glumes; glumes about equal, narrow, acute; lemma broader, thin, 1-nerved, a little longer than the glumes; palea nearly as long as the lemma, readily splitting between the nerves. Low spreading tufted annuals with oblong, dense, spikelike panicles, the subtending leaves with inflated sheaths and reduced blades. Type species, *Heleochloa alopecuroides*. Name from Greek *helos*, marsh, and *chloa* grass, alluding to the habitat of the type species.

1. Heleochloa schoenoídes (L.) Host. (Fig. 622, *A*.) Culms tufted, branching, erect to spreading and geniculate, 10 to 30 cm. long; sheaths often somewhat inflated; blades flat, with involute slender tips, mostly less than 10 cm. long, 2 to 4 mm. wide; panicle pale, 1 to 4 cm. long, 8 to 10 mm. thick; spikelets about 3 mm. long; pericarp readily separating. ⊙ —Waste places, Massachusetts to Wisconsin, south to Delaware, Ohio, Illinois, and Iowa; California; introduced from Europe.

Heleochloa alopecuroídes (Pill. and Mitterp.) Host. (Fig. 622, *B*.) Differing from *H. schoenoides* in the more slender panicles, 4 to 5 mm. thick, exserted at maturity; spikelets about 2 mm. long. ⊙ —Ballast, Philadelphia, Pa., and near Portland, Oreg.; Europe.

87. BRACHYÉLYTRUM Beauv.

Spikelets 1-flowered, the rachilla disarticulating above the glumes, prolonged behind the palea as a slender naked bristle; glumes minute, the first often obsolete, the second sometimes awned; lemma firm, narrow, 5-nerved, the base extending into a pronounced oblique callus, the apex terminating in a long straight scabrous awn. Erect, slender perennials with short slender knotty rhizomes, flat blades, and narrow, rather few-flowered panicles. Type species, *Brachyelytrum erectum*. Name from Greek *brachus*, short, and *elutron*, cover or husk, alluding to the short glumes.

1. Brachyelytrum eréctum (Schreb.) Beauv. (Fig. 623.) Culms 60 to 100 cm. tall; sheaths sparsely retrorse-hispid, rarely glabrous; blades mostly 7 to 15 cm. long, 1 to 1.5 cm. wide, scabrous, sparingly pilose beneath, at least on the nerves and margin; panicle 5 to 15 cm. long, the short branches appressed; second glume 0.5 to 2 mm. long; lemma subterete, about 1 cm. long, scabrous, the nerves sometimes hispid, the awn 1 to 3 cm. long. ♃ —Moist or rocky woods, Newfoundland to Minnesota, south to Georgia, Louisiana, and Oklahoma. Plants with lemmas scabrous only toward the summit and on the nerves have been named *B. erectum* var. *septentrionale* Babel.

FIGURE 622.—*A*, *Heleochloa schoenoides*. Plant, × ½; spikelet and floret, × 5. (Smith, Pa.) *B*, *H. alopecuroides*, × 5. (Burk, Pa.)

88. MÍLIUM L.

Spikelets 1-flowered, disarticulating above the glumes; glumes equal, obtuse, membranaceous, rounded on the back; lemma a little shorter than the glumes, obtuse, obscurely nerved,

FIGURE 623.—*Brachyelytrum erectum*. Plant, × ½; branchlet with glumes of two spikelets, and floret, × 5. (Bissell, Conn.)

rounded on the back, dorsally compressed, in fruit becoming indurate, smooth and shining, the margins enclosing the lemma as in *Panicum*. Moderately tall grasses with flat blades and open panicles. Type species, *Milium effusum*. *Milium*, old Latin name for millet.

1. Milium effúsum L. (Fig. 624.) Smooth perennial, somewhat succulent; culms slender, erect from a bent base, 1 to 1.5 m. tall; blades mostly 10 to 20 cm. long, flat, lax, 8 to 15 mm. wide; panicle 10 to 20 cm. long, the slender branches in remote spreading or drooping pairs or fascicles, naked below; spikelets pale, 3 to 3.5 mm. long; glumes scaberulous. ♃ —Damp or rocky woods, Quebec and Nova Scotia to Minnesota, south to Maryland and Illinois; Eurasia. A handsome grass, sometimes cultivated as an annual.

FIGURE 624.—*Milium effusum*. Plant, × ½; spikelet and floret, × 5. (Phillips, Maine.)

89. ORYZÓPSIS Michx. RICEGRASS

Spikelets 1-flowered, disarticulating above the glumes; glumes about equal, obtuse to acuminate; lemma indurate, usually about as long as the glumes, broad, oval or oblong, nearly terete, usually pubescent, with a short, blunt, oblique callus, and a short deciduous, sometimes bent and twisted awn; palea enclosed by the edges of the lemma. Mostly slender perennials, with flat or often involute blades and terminal narrow or open panicles. Type species, *Oryzopsis asperifolia*. Name from *oruza*, rice, and *opsis*, appearance, alluding to a fancied resemblance to rice.

Nearly all the species are highly palatable to stock, but are usually not in sufficient abundance to be of importance, except *O. hymenoides* (Indian ricegrass), which is common in the arid and semiarid regions of the West and furnishes much feed. The seed has been used for food by the Indians. Locally important may be *O. micrantha* in the Black Hills region and *O. kingii* in the high Sierras. *O. miliacea* is cultivated for forage in California.

As the result of study of several species of *Oryzopsis* and *Stipa*, Johnson and Rogler[13] conclude that the types of *Oryzopsis caduca* and *O. bloomeri* are hybrids between *O. hymenoides* and *Stipa viridula* and *O. hymenoides* and *S. occidentalis*, respectively. For these the generic name *Stiporyzopsis* is proposed. Other hybrids between *O. hymenoides* and six other species of *Stipa*—*S. elmeri*, *S. thurberiana*, *S. californica*, *S. scribneri*, *S. robusta*, and *S. columbiana*—are described, but not transferred to *Stiporyzopsis*.

Lemma smooth (rarely pubescent in *O. micrantha*).
 Blades flat, 5 mm. wide or more. Spikelets numerous, about 3 mm. long. 1. O. MILIACEA.
 Blades more or less involute, less than 2 mm. wide.
  Panicle branches spreading or reflexed; fruit about 2 mm. long, pale. 2. O. MICRANTHA.
  Panicle branches ascending or appressed; fruit about 4 mm. long, dark brown. 3. O. HENDERSONI.
Lemma pubescent.
 Pubescence on lemma long and silky.
  Panicle branches and the capillary pedicels divaricately spreading. 12. O. HYMENOIDES.
  Panicle branches and pedicels erect or ascending.
   Awn 6 mm. long; culms usually not more than 30 cm. tall ..... 11. O. WEBBERI.
   Awn 12 mm. long; culms 30 to 60 cm. tall ..... 10. O. BLOOMERI.
 Pubescence on lemma short, appressed.
  Spikelets, excluding awn, 6 to 9 mm. long; blades flat.
   Basal blades elongate, uppermost not more than 1 cm. long ..... 8. O. ASPERIFOLIA.
   Basal blades reduced, upper elongate ..... 9. O. RACEMOSA.
  Spikelets, excluding awn, 5 mm. long or less; blades involute or subinvolute.
   Panicle branches erect or appressed.
    Blades and panicle stiff, erect; awns about 5 mm. long ..... 4. O. EXIGUA.
    Blades flexuous, the panicle somewhat so; awns at least 10 mm. long. 7. O. KINGII.
   Panicle branches loosely ascending or spreading.
    Awn not more than 2 mm. long, straight or nearly so ..... 5. O. PUNGENS.
    Awn 10 to 20 mm. long, weakly twice-geniculate ..... 6. O. CANADENSIS.

1. Oryzopsis miliácea (L.) Benth. and Hook. ex Aschers. and Schweinf. SMILO GRASS. (Fig. 625.) Culms relatively stout, sometimes branching, erect from a decumbent base, 60 to 150 cm. tall; ligule about 2 mm. long; blades flat, 8 to 10 mm. wide; panicle 15 to 30 cm. long, loose, the branches spreading with numerous short-pediceled spikelets beyond the middle; glumes acuminate, 3 mm. long; lem-

[13] Amer. Jour. Bot. 30: 49–56. f. 1–40. 1943; JOHNSON, B. L., Amer. Jour. Bot. 32: 599–608. f. 1–71. 1945; Bot. Gaz. 107: 1–32. 1945.

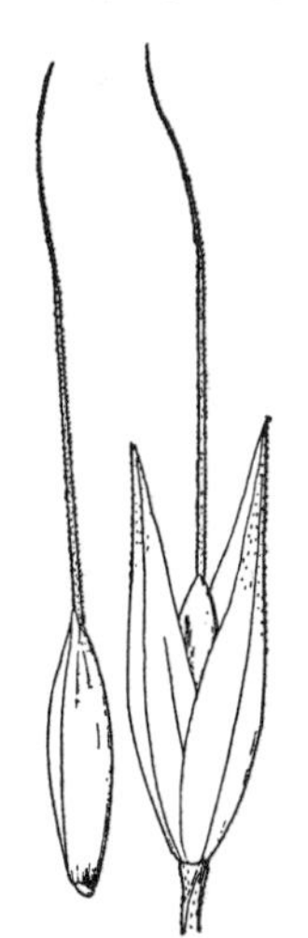

FIGURE 625.—*Oryzopsis miliacea*, × 5. (Kralik, Europe.)

ma smooth, 2 mm. long, the straight awn about 4 mm. long. ♃ —Introduced in California; ballast, Camden, N. J., and Philadelphia, Pa.; Mediterranean region.

2. Oryzopsis micrántha (Trin. and Rupr.) Thurb. LITTLESEED RICEGRASS. (Fig. 626.) Culms densely tufted, erect, slender, 30 to 70 cm. tall; ligule about 1 mm. long; blades scabrous, flat or involute, 0.5 to 2 mm. wide; panicle open, 10 to 15 cm. long, the branches distant, single or in pairs, spreading or finally reflexed, 2 to 5 cm. long, with short-pediceled appressed spikelets toward the ends; glumes thin, acuminate, 3 to 4 mm. long; lemma elliptic, glabrous, or rarely appressed-pilose, 2 to 2.5 mm. long, yellow or brown, the straight awn 5 to 10 mm. long. ♃ —Open dry woods and rocky slopes, medium altitudes, Saskatchewan to North Dakota and Montana, south to Nevada, New Mexico, Arizona, and California (Mohave Desert). The form with pilose lemmas is found from Colorado to Arizona.

FIGURE 626.—*Oryzopsis micrantha*. Panicle, × 1; floret, × 5. (Hitchcock 22993, N. Mex.)

3. Oryzopsis hendersóni Vasey. (Fig. 627.) Culms densely tufted, scabrous, 10 to 40 cm. tall; leaves mostly basal, the sheaths broad, papery, glabrescent; ligule very short; blades subfiliform, involute, scabrous, firm, mostly less than 10 cm. long, the one or two culm blades 4 to 5 cm. long; panicle few-flowered, 5 to 12 cm. long, the few scabrous branches appressed or ascending, spikelet-bearing toward the ends, the lower as much as 8 cm. long; spikelets short-pediceled; glumes abruptly acute, 5 to 6 mm. long; lemma nearly as long as the glumes, glabrous, dark brown at maturity, the awn early deciduous, nearly straight, 6 to 10 mm. long. ♃ —Dry or gravelly soil. Known only from Mount Clements, Wash., and from the Ochoco National Forest, Oreg.

4. Oryzopsis exígua Thurb. LITTLE RICEGRASS. (Fig. 628.) Culms densely tufted, stiffly erect, scabrous, 15 to 30 cm. tall; sheaths smooth or somewhat scabrous; ligule 2 to 3 mm. long; blades involute-filiform, stiffly erect, scabrous, 5 to 10 cm. long, the culm blades about 2, shorter; panicle narrow, 3 to 6 cm. long, the branches appressed, the lower 1 to 2 cm. long; spikelets short-pediceled, glumes abruptly acute, 4 mm. long;

FIGURE 627.—*Oryzopsis hendersoni*. Plant, × ½; spikelet and floret, × 5. (Type.)

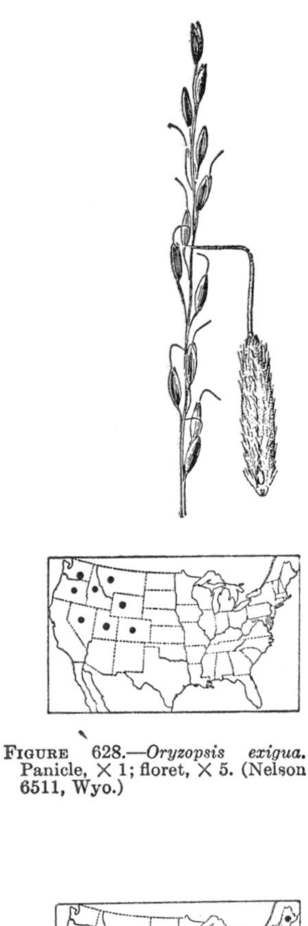

FIGURE 628.—*Oryzopsis exigua*. Panicle, × 1; floret, × 5. (Nelson 6511, Wyo.)

lemma appressed-pilose, about as long as the glumes, the awn about 5 mm. long, not twisted, geniculate. ♃ —Dry open ground or open woods, at moderately high altitudes, Montana to Washington, south to Colorado, Nevada, and Oregon.

5. Oryzopsis púngens (Torr.) Hitchc. (Fig. 629.) Culms tufted, erect, slender, 20 to 50 cm. tall; blades elongate, slender, flat or involute, less than 2 mm. wide; panicle narrow, 3 to 6 cm. long, the branches erect or ascending or spreading in anthesis; spikelets long-pediceled; glumes 3 to 4 mm. long, obscurely 5-nerved, obtuse; lemma about as long as the glumes, rather densely pubescent, the awn usually 1 to 2 mm. long. ♃ —Sandy or rocky soil, Labrador to British Columbia, south to Connecticut, Indiana, South Dakota, and Colorado.

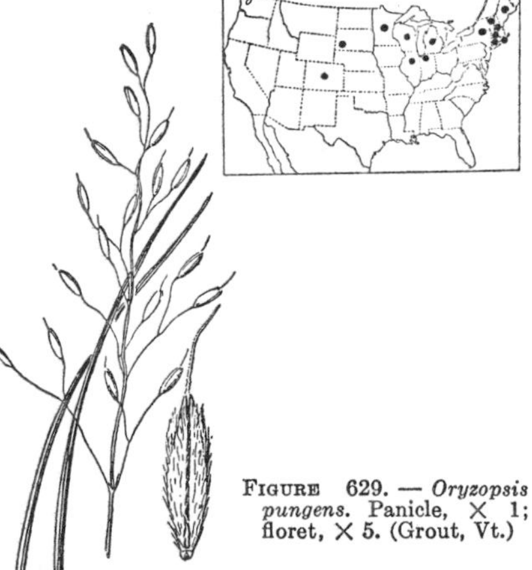

FIGURE 629. — *Oryzopsis pungens*. Panicle, × 1; floret, × 5. (Grout, Vt.)

6. Oryzopsis canadénsis (Poir.) Torr. (Fig. 630.) Culms slender, tufted, erect, 30 to 70 cm. tall; ligule about 2 mm. long; blades flat

FIGURE 630.—*Oryzopsis canadensis*. Panicle, × 1; floret, × 5. (Rand, Maine.)

to involute, scabrous; panicle open, 5 to 10 cm. long, the slender flexuous branches ascending or spreading, naked below, few-flowered above; spikelets long-pediceled; glumes 4 to 5 mm. long, abruptly acute; lemma about 3 mm. long, rather sparsely appressed-pilose, the awn 1 to 2 cm. long, weakly twice geniculate. ♃ —Woods and thickets, Newfoundland to Alberta, south to New Hampshire, New York, West Virginia (Panther Knob, Pendleton County), northern Michigan, Wisconsin, northern Minnesota, and Wyoming.

7. Oryzopsis kíngii (Boland.) Beal. (Fig. 631.) Culms tufted, slender, 20 to 40 cm. tall; leaves numerous at the base, the blades involute, filiform, flexuous; ligule about 1 mm. long; panicle narrow, loose, the short slender branches appressed or ascending, few-flowered; spikelets rather short-pediceled; glumes broad, papery, nerveless, obtuse, purple at base, the first about 3.5 mm. long, the second a little longer; lemma elliptic, 3 to 3.5 mm. long, rather sparingly appressed-pubescent; awn bent in a wide curve or indistinctly geniculate below the middle, not twisted, minutely pubescent, about 12 mm. long, not readily deciduous. ♃ —Meadows at upper altitudes, central Sierra Nevada, Calif.

8. Oryzopsis asperifólia Michx. (Fig. 632.) Culms tufted, the innovations erect, the fertile culms widely spreading or prostrate, 20 to 70 cm. long, nearly naked, the two or three sheaths bearing reduced or obsolete blades; basal blades erect, firm, scabrous, flat to somewhat revolute, elongate, 3 to 8 mm. wide, tapering toward each end, glaucous beneath; panicle nearly simple, rather few-flowered, 5 to 8 cm. long, the branches appressed; spikelets on appressed pedicels 3 to 6 mm. long; glumes 6 to 8 mm. long, somewhat obovate, about 7-nerved, abruptly pointed or apiculate; lemma about as long as the glumes, sparingly pubescent, more densely so on the callus, pale or yellowish at maturity, the awn 5 to 10 mm. long. ♃ —Wooded slopes and dry banks, Newfoundland to British Columbia; Maine to West Virginia (Panther Knob, Pendleton

FIGURE 631.—*Oryzopsis kingii*. Plant, × 1; floret × 5. (Bolander 6097, Calif.)

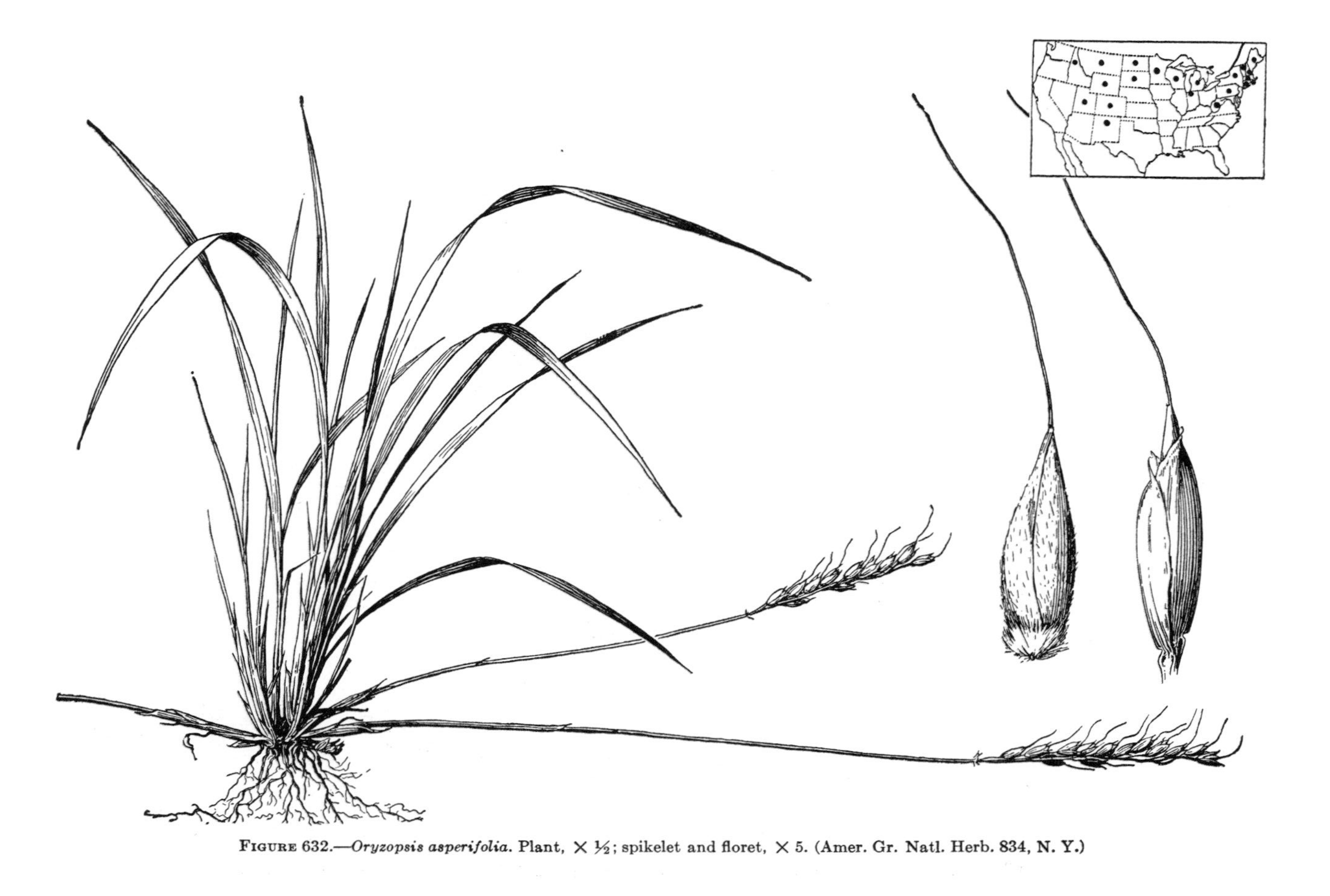

FIGURE 632.—*Oryzopsis asperifolia.* Plant, × ½; spikelet and floret, × 5. (Amer. Gr. Natl. Herb. 834, N. Y.)

County), Indiana to Idaho, south in the mountains to Utah and New Mexico.

FIGURE 633.—*Oryzopsis racemosa*. Panicle, × ½; floret, × 5. (Sartwell, N. Y.)

9. **Oryzopsis racemósa** (J. E. Smith) Ricker. (Fig. 633.) Culms tufted, from a knotty rhizome, erect, 30 to 100 cm. tall; culm leaves several, the lowermost blades reduced, the others elongate, flat, 5 to 15 mm. wide, tapering at both ends, rather thin, scabrous above, pubescent beneath; panicle 10 to 20 cm. long, the branches distant, the lower spreading or reflexed at maturity, bearing a few spikelets toward the end; glumes 7 to 9 mm. long, about 7-nerved, abruptly acuminate; lemma slightly shorter than the glumes, sparsely pubescent, nearly black at maturity, the awn 1.5 to 2.5 cm. long, slightly flexuous. ♃ —Rocky woods, Quebec to Minnesota and South Dakota, south to Virginia, Kentucky, and Iowa.

10. **Oryzopsis blooméri** (Boland.) Ricker. (Fig. 634.) Culms tufted, 30 to 60 cm. tall; leaves crowded at the base; ligule about 1 mm. long; blades narrow, involute, firm; panicle 7 to 15 cm. long, the branches slender, rather stiffly ascending, the longer 5 to 7 cm. long, spikelet-bearing from about the middle; spikelets rather long-pediceled; glumes broad, indistinctly 3- to 5-nerved, rather abruptly acuminate, 8 to 10 mm. long; lemma elliptic, 5 mm. long, densely long-villous; awn about 12 mm. long, tardily deciduous, slightly twisted and appressed-villous below, weakly geniculate. ♃ —Dry ground, medium altitudes, North Dakota to eastern Washington, south to New Mexico and California, rather rare.

FIGURE 634.—*Oryzopsis bloomeri*. Panicle, × 1; floret, × 5. (Sandberg and Leiberg 231, Wash.)

11. **Oryzopsis webbéri** (Thurb.) Benth. ex Vasey. (Fig. 635.) Culms densely tufted, erect, 15 to 30 cm. tall; blades involute, filiform, scabrous; panicle narrow, 2.5 to 5 cm. long, the branches appressed; glumes about 8 mm. long, narrow, obscurely 5-nerved, minutely scaberulous, acuminate; lemma narrow, 6 mm. long, densely long-pilose, the awn about 6 mm. long, straight or bent, not

twisted. ♃ —Deserts and plains, Idaho, Colorado, Nevada, and California.

12. Oryzopsis hymenoídes (Roem. and Schult.) Ricker. INDIAN RICE-GRASS. (Fig. 636.) Culms densely tufted, 30 to 60 cm. tall; ligule about 6 mm. long, acute; blades slender, involute, nearly as long as the culms; panicle diffuse, 7 to 15 cm. long, the slender branches in pairs, the branchlets dichotomous, all divaricately spreading, the ultimate pedicels capillary, flexuous; glumes about 6 to 7 mm. long, puberulent to glabrous, rarely hirsute, papery, ovate, 3- to 5-nerved, abruptly pointed; lemma fusiform, turgid, about 3 mm. long, nearly black at maturity, densely long-pilose with white hairs 3 mm. long; awn about 4 mm. long, straight, readily deciduous. ♃ —Deserts and plains, medium altitudes, Manitoba to British Columbia, south to Texas, California, and northern Mexico.

ORYZOPSIS HYMENOIDES var. CONTRÁCTA B. L. Johnson. Panicles narrow, the branches ascending; lemmas less turgid and less copiously pilose. ♃ —Dry soil, Wyoming.

Nassélla chiléensis (Trin. and Rupr.) E. Desv. Slender tufted perennial; blades narrow, flat or loosely involute; panicle narrow, 3 to 5 cm. long, the few branches appressed, 1 to 1.5 cm. long; glumes 4 mm. long, awn-pointed; mature lemma flattish, obovate-oblong, gibbous at apex, smooth and shining, 2 mm. long; awn geniculate, 1 cm. long, soon deciduous. ♃ (*N. major* (Trin. and Rupr.) E. Desv.)—Ballast, Portland, Oreg. Introduced from Chile.

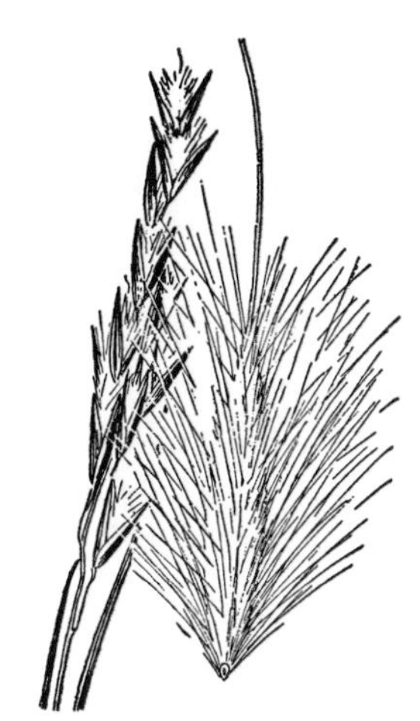

FIGURE 635.—*Oryzopsis webberi*. Panicle, × 1; floret, × 5. (Hillman, Nev.)

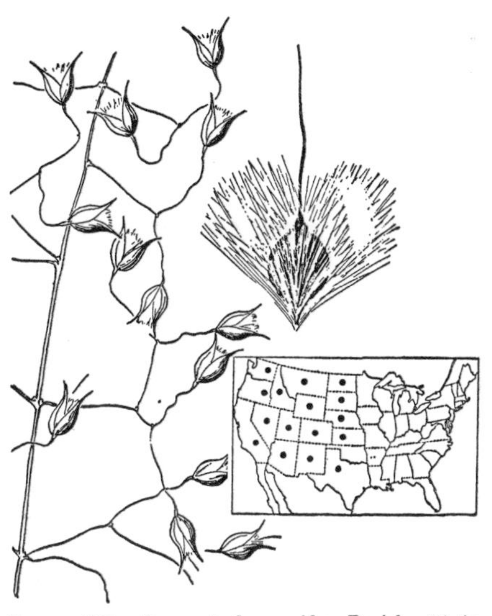

FIGURE 636.—*Oryzopsis hymenoides*. Panicle, × 1; floret, × 5. (Mearns 2583, Wyo.)

90. PIPTOCHAÉTIUM Presl

Spikelets 1-flowered, disarticulating above the glumes, the callus of the floret short, acutish, usually bearded; glumes about equal, broad, ovate, convex on the back, thin, abruptly acuminate; fruit brown or dark gray, coriaceous, obovate, shorter than the glumes, glabrous or hispid above the callus, often minutely striate, sometimes tuberculate near the summit, the lemma turgid, usually somewhat compressed and keeled on the back, gibbous near the summit back of the awn, the edges not meeting but clasping the sulcus of the palea, the summit sometimes expanded into a crown; awn deciduous or persistent, curved,

FIGURE 637.—*Piptochaetium fimbriatum*. Plant, × ½; glumes, floret, and palea, × 5. (Hitchcock 13511, N. Mex.)

flexuous or geniculate, often twisted below; palea narrow, indurate, except toward the margins, central keel consisting of two nerves and a narrow channel or sulcus between, the apex of the keel projecting above the summit of the lemma as a minute point. Tufted perennials with narrow usually involute blades and rather few-flowered panicles. Type species, *Piptochaetium setifolium* Presl. Name from Greek *piptein*, to fall, and *chaite*, bristle, alluding to the deciduous awns of the type species.

1. Piptochaetium fimbriátum (H. B. K.) Hitchc. PINYON RICEGRASS. (Fig. 637.) Culms densely tufted, erect, slender, 40 to 80 cm. tall; blades involute-filiform, flexuous, elongate; panicle open, 5 to 15 cm. long, the slender branches spreading, few-flowered toward the ends; spikelets long-pediceled; glumes about 5 mm. long, abruptly acuminate, 7-nerved; lemma a little shorter than the glumes, appressed-pubescent, especially on the callus, dark brown at maturity with a circular ridge at the base of the awn; awn weakly twice geniculate, 1 to 2 cm. long. ♃ (*Oryzopsis fimbriata* Hemsl.)—Open rocky woods, Colorado to western Texas, Arizona, and Mexico. A fine forage grass. Specimens from the United States and most of those from northern Mexico have pale glumes (*P. fimbriatum* var. *confine* I. M. Johnston), while those of middle and southern Mexico have purple or brown glumes, as in the type of *P. fimbriatum*. In that, 1 panicle is open and 2 are narrow, as in var. *confine*.

91. STÍPA L. NEEDLEGRASS

Spikelets 1-flowered, disarticulating above the glumes, the articulation oblique, leaving a bearded, sharp-pointed callus attached to the base of the floret; glumes membranaceous, often papery, acute, acuminate, or even aristate, usually long and narrow; lemma narrow, terete, firm or indurate, strongly convolute, rarely the margins only meeting, terminating in a prominent awn, the junction of body and awn evident, the awn twisted below, geniculate, usually persistent; palea enclosed in the convolute lemma. Tufted perennials, with usually convolute blades and mostly narrow panicles. Type species, *Stipa pennata* L. Name from Greek *stupe*, tow, alluding to the feathery awns of the type species.

The species are for the most part valuable forage plants. Several, all western, such as *Stipa comata*, *S. occidentalis*, *S. lemmoni*, and *S. neomexicana*, are grazed chiefly when young. *Stipa lettermani* is important at high altitudes, in the mountains of the West; *S. columbiana* at medium altitudes; *S. viridula* in the Rocky Mountains; *S. pulchra*, *S. thurberiana*, and *S. speciosa* in California. Some of the species, when mature, particularly *S. spartea* and *S. comata*, are injurious, especially to sheep, because of the hard sharp points to the fruits which penetrate the skin. Sleepy grass, *S. robusta*, acts as a narcotic (see p. 458). One of the Old World species, *S. tenacissima* L., furnishes a part of the esparto or alfa grass of Spain and Algeria that is used in the manufacture of paper and cordage.

1a. Terminal segment of awn plumose.
  Awn 12 to 18 cm. long .... 1. S. NEOMEXICANA.
  Awn 1.2 to 1.5 cm. long .... 16. S. PORTERI.
1b. Terminal segment of awn not plumose, or somewhat plumose in *S. occidentalis*.
  2a. First segment of the once-geniculate awn strongly plumose, the ascending hairs 5 to 8 mm. long .... 2. S. SPECIOSA.
  2b. First segment of awn sometimes plumose but the hairs not more than 2 mm. long.
    3a. Mature lemma 2 to 3 mm. long. Awn capillary, flexuous, about 5 cm. long. 34. S. TENUISSIMA.
    3b. Mature lemma at least 5 mm. long.

4a. Lemma densely appressed-villous with white hairs 3 to 4 mm. long, rising above the summit in a pappuslike crown.
Culms 1 to 2 m. tall; spikelets about 2 cm. long; awns 4 to 5 cm. long. 5. S. CORONATA.
Culms not more than 50 cm. tall; spikelets less than 1 cm. long; awns about 2 cm. long .... 32. S. PINETORUM.
4b. Lemma often villous but the hairs not more than 1 mm. long, or sometimes those at the summit as much as 2 mm. long.
5a. Summit of mature lemma smooth, cylindric, whitish, forming a ciliate crown 0.5 to 1 mm. long (see also *S. pulchra*) .... 3. S. LEUCOTRICHA.
5b. Summit of mature lemma not forming a crown.
6a. Lemma 2-lobed at summit, the lobes extending into awns 2 to 3 mm. long on each side of the central awn .... 4. S. STILLMANII.
6b. Lemma not lobed at summit or only obscurely so.
7a. Awn plumose below, the hairs ascending or spreading (compare *S. pulchra*, with appressed-hispid awn).
Awns once or obscurely twice-geniculate, hairs at summit of lemma longer. 23. S. CURVIFOLIA.
Awns distinctly twice geniculate.
Ligule 3 to 6 mm. long, hyaline .... 17. S. THURBERIANA.
Ligule minute, mostly hairy.
Lemma 8 to 10 mm. long; glumes firm .... 19. S. LATIGLUMIS.
Lemma 6 to 8 mm. long; glumes thin.
Hairs on upper part of lemma longer than those below; culms 60 to 125 cm. tall.
Sheaths pubescent .... 18. S. ELMERI.
Sheaths glabrous .... 22. S. CALIFORNICA.
Hairs short all over the lemma; culms 25 to 40 cm. tall. 20. S. OCCIDENTALIS.
7b. Awn scabrous or nearly glabrous, rarely appressed-hispid, not plumose.
8a. Lemma more than 7 mm. (often 1 to 2 cm.) long, glabrous or sparsely pubescent above the callus, mostly cylindric (somewhat fusiform in *S pulchra*).
Mature lemma pale or finally brownish, sparsely pubescent to summit, mostly more than 1 cm. long .... 10. S. COMATA.
Mature lemma dark.
Lemma 8 to 10 mm. long.
Glumes 3-nerved; summit of lemma hispidulous-ciliate, the hairs erect, nearly 1 mm. long.
Lemma slender, cylindric; basal blades usually numerous, narrow, involute, glaucous, pilose .... 12. S. CERNUA.
Lemma fusiforme; blades green .... 11. S. PULCHRA.
Glumes 5- to 9-nerved.
Lemmas glabrous above the base, minutely roughened at apex; callus with fine sharp point .... 8. S. AVENACEA.
Lemmas sparsely pubescent to apex; callus rather blunt. 13. S. PRINGLEI.
Lemma 12 to 25 mm. long, cylindric.
Mature lemma glabrous above the callus .... 7. S. AVENACIOIDES.
Mature lemma more or less pubescent above the callus. 9. S. SPARTEA.
8b. Lemma less than 7 mm. long, or if as long as 7 to 8 mm., distinctly pubescent on the upper part (see also *S. cernua*).
Panicle open, the branches spreading or ascending, naked at base.
Panicle diffuse, the branches divergent, drooping; lemma about 5 mm. long; awn about 2 cm. long .... 6. S. RICHARDSONI.
Panicle open but not diffuse.
Ligule 3 to 6 mm. long; awn about 5 cm. long, the terminal segment flexuous .... 14. S. EMINENS.
Ligule 1 mm. long or less; awn 2.5 to 4 cm. long .... 15. S. LEPIDA.
Panicle narrow, the branches appressed.
Hairs on lemma copious, at least at summit, 2 mm. long.
Lemmas evenly villous all over; summit with lobes 0.8 to 1.5 mm. long .... 21. S. LOBATA.
Lemmas conspicuously villous above, less so below; summit not lobed or obscurely so.
Lemma about 8 mm. long, villous at summit, pubescent below. 24. S. SCRIBNERI.

Lemma about 5 mm. long, villous all over but more so above.
32. S. PINETORUM.
Hairs not copious, usually not more than 1 mm. long at summit.
Glumes broad, abruptly acuminate, rather firm, the first 5-nerved.
25. S. LEMMONI.
Glumes narrow, gradually acuminate, usually hyaline, the first usually 3-nerved.
Awn 4 to 6 cm. long, obscurely geniculate, the terminal segment flexuous........ 33. S. ARIDA.
Awn mostly less than 5 cm. long, if as much as 4 cm. long, twice-geniculate and the terminal segment straight or nearly so.
Sheaths, at least the lowermost, pubescent.
30. S. WILLIAMSII.
Sheaths glabrous.
Sheaths villous at the throat; fruit rather turgid, the callus broad and short; lower nodes of panicle villous.
Glumes thin, papery; plants rather slender, mostly less than 1 m. tall; panicle rather slender, loose.
26. S. VIRIDULA.
Glumes firm, the nerves inconspicuous; plants robust, mostly more than 1 m. tall; panicle larger, more compact........ 27. S. ROBUSTA.
Sheaths not villous at the throat or only slightly so; fruit slender, the callus narrow, sharp-pointed; nodes of panicle glabrous or nearly so.
Culms densely pubescent below the nodes.
31. S. DIEGOENSIS.
Culms glabrous throughout.
Awn mostly more than 2 cm. long; hairs at summit of lemma about as long as the others.
28. S. COLUMBIANA.
Awn mostly less than 2 cm. long; hairs at summit of lemma longer than those on the body, 1 to 1.5 mm. long........ 29. S. LETTERMANI.

1. Stipa neomexicána (Thurb.) Scribn. NEW MEXICAN FEATHER-GRASS. (Fig. 638.) Culms mostly 40 to 80 cm. tall; sheaths glabrous or the lower minutely pubescent; ligule very short, ciliate; blades slender, firm, convolute, glabrous beneath, the basal 10 to 30 cm. long, scarcely 1 mm. wide when unrolled; panicle narrow, 3 to 10 cm. long; spikelets pale, more or less shining; glumes 3 to 5 cm. long, tapering to a fine point; lemma about 15 mm. long including the pilose callus 4 to 5 mm. long; awn readily deciduous, 12 to 18 cm. long, the lower one-fourth to one-third straight, strongly twisted, appressed-villous, the middle segment 1 to 2 cm. long, the terminal segment flexuous, plumose, the hairs about 3 mm. long. ♃ —Mesas, canyons, and rocky slopes, western Texas, Oklahoma, Wyoming, and Colorado to Utah and Arizona.

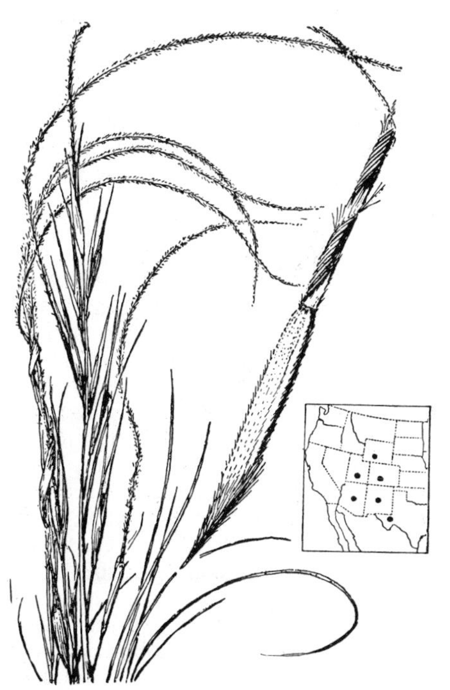

FIGURE 638.—*Stipa neomexicana.* Plant, × ½; lemma, × 5. (Jones 5377, Utah.)

FIGURE 639.—*Stipa speciosa*. Panicle, × ½; floret, × 5. (Reed 4853, Calif.)

2. Stipa speciósa Trin. and Rupr. DESERT NEEDLEGRASS. (Fig. 639. Culms numerous, 30 to 60 cm. tall; sheaths brownish, smooth or the lower pubescent or even felty at the very base, the throat densely short-villous; ligule short; blades elongate, involute-filiform, mostly basal, more or less deciduous from the outer and older persistent sheaths; panicle narrow, dense, 10 to 15 cm. long, not much exceeding the leaves, white or tawny, feathery from the plumose awns; glumes smooth, 14 to 16 mm. long, 3-nerved, long-acuminate, papery; lemma 7 to 9 mm. long, narrow, densely short-pubescent, the callus sharp and smooth below; awn with one sharp bend, the first section 1.5 to 2 cm. long, densely long-pilose on the lower two-thirds or more, the hairs 5 to 8 mm. long, the remaining portion of the awn scabrous, the second segment about 2.5 cm. long. ♃ —Deserts, canyons, and rocky hills, Colorado and Arizona to southern California; southern South America.

3. Stipa leucótricha Trin. and Rupr. TEXAS NEEDLEGRASS. (Fig. 640.) Culms 30 to 60 cm. tall, the nodes pubescent; blades 10 to 30 cm. long, flat, often becoming involute, hispidulous beneath, 2 to 4 mm. wide; panicle narrow, mostly not more than 10 cm. long; glumes 12 to 18 mm. long; lemma about 1 cm. long, the slender callus about 4 mm. long, the body oblong, brownish, appressed-pubescent on the lower part, papillose-roughened at least toward the summit, abruptly narrowed into a cylindric smooth neck about 1 mm. long, the crown ciliate with short stiff hairs; awn 6 to 10 cm. long, rather stout, twice-geniculate, the first segment hispidulous, twisted, 2 to 3.5 cm. long. ♃ —Dry, open grassland, Oklahoma and Texas to central Mexico. Cleistogamous spikelets with glumes obsolete and lemma nearly awnless are borne in basal sheaths just after maturity of panicle.

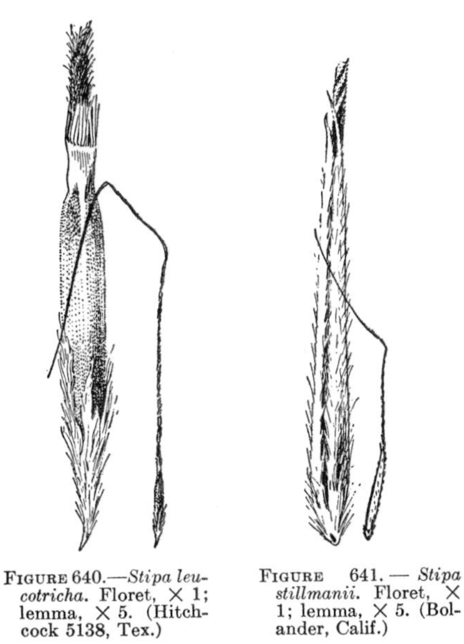

FIGURE 640.—*Stipa leucotricha*. Floret, × 1; lemma, × 5. (Hitchcock 5138, Tex.)

FIGURE 641.—*Stipa stillmanii*. Floret, × 1; lemma, × 5. (Bolander, Calif.)

4. Stipa stillmánii Boland. (Fig. 641.) Culms stout, 60 to 100 cm. tall; sheaths smooth, puberulent at the throat and collar; ligule very short; blades elongate, scattered, folded or involute, firm, the uppermost filiform; panicle 10 to 20 cm. long, narrow, dense or interrupted at base, the branches short, fascicled; glumes equal, 14 to 16 mm. long, papery, minutely scabrous, acuminate into a scabrous awn-point, the first 3-nerved, the second 5-nerved; lemma 9 mm. long, short-pilose, bearing 2 slender teeth at the apex, the callus short; awn about 2.5 cm. long, once- or indistinctly twice-geniculate, scabrous. ♃ —Rocky slopes, Sierra Nevada, from Lassen National Forest to Tahoe National Forest, Calif.; apparently rare.

5. Stipa coronáta Thurb. (Fig. 642.) Culms stout, 1 to 2 m. tall, as much as 6 mm. thick at base, smooth or pubescent below the nodes; sheaths smooth, the margin and throat villous; ligule about 2 mm. long, ciliate; blades elongate, 4 to 6 mm. wide, flat to subinvolute with a slender involute point; panicle 30 to 40 cm. long, contracted, erect, purplish; glumes gradually acuminate, 3-nerved, the first about 2 cm. long, the second 2 to 4 mm. shorter; lemma about 8 mm. long, densely villous with long appressed hairs 3 to 4 mm. long; awn usually 4 to 5 cm. long, scabrous, twice-geniculate, the first and second segments about 1 cm. long. ♃ —Open ground in the Coast Range, California, from Monterey to Baja California; Grand Canyon, Ariz.

Stipa coronata var. depauperáta (Jones) Hitchc. Culms usually 30 to 50 cm. tall; blades 10 to 20 cm. long; panicle 10 to 15 cm. long, rather few-flowered, the spikelets commonly smaller than in the species, the lemma 6 to 7 mm. long, the awn about 2.5 cm. long, once-geniculate, the first segment twisted and scabrous-pubescent, about 1 cm. long, the second segment bent about horizontally. ♃ —Dry or rocky slopes, Utah and Nevada to Arizona and southern California. Many intermediates occur between the variety and the species.

6. Stipa richardsóni Link. Richardson needlegrass. (Fig. 643.) Culms 50 to 100 cm. tall; blades mostly basal, usually 15 to 25 cm. long, involute, subfiliform, scabrous; panicle 10 to 20 cm. long, open, the

Figure 642.—*Stipa coronata*. Floret, × 1; lemma × 5. (Orcutt 1068, Calif.)

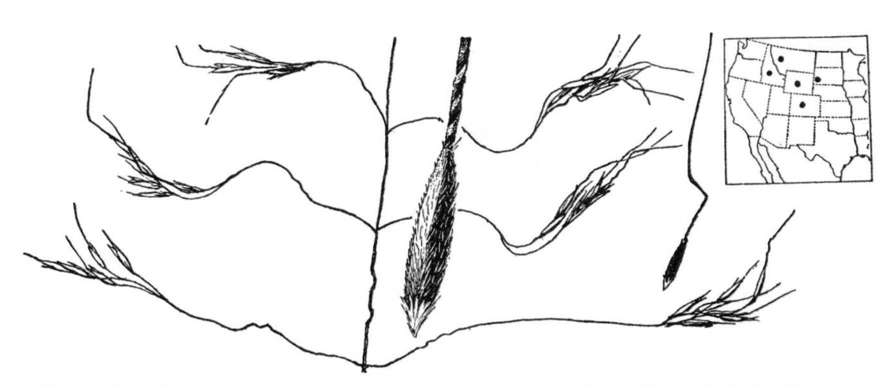

Figure 643.—*Stipa richardsoni*. Panicle, × ½; floret, × 1; lemma, × 5. (Hitchcock 11468, Alberta.)

branches slender, distant, spreading or drooping, naked below; glumes 8 to 9 mm. long; lemma about 5 mm. long, subfusiform, brown at maturity; awn 2.5 to 3 cm. long. ♃ — Bottom lands and wooded slopes, Saskatchewan to South Dakota, Colorado, Idaho, and British Columbia.

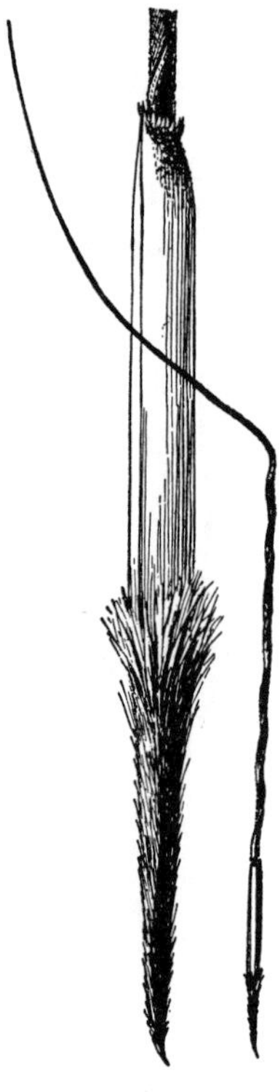

FIGURE 644.—*Stipa avenacioides.* Floret, × 1; lemma, × 5. (Curtiss 5834, Fla.)

7. Stipa avenacioídes Nash. (Fig. 644.) Culms about 1 m. tall; ligule 2 to 3 mm. long; blades elongate, involute, subfiliform; panicle 10 to 25 cm. long, open, the branches slender, spreading, naked below; glumes about 2 cm. long; lemma brown, linear, 1.5 to 2 cm. long including the callus 7 mm. long, the body glabrous, minutely papillose at the slightly contracted summit, slightly hispidulous on the crown; awn 8 to 11 cm. long, scabrous, twice geniculate. ♃ — Dry pine woods, peninsular Florida.

8. Stipa avenácea L. BLACKSEED NEEDLEGRASS. (Fig. 645.) Culms 60 to 100 cm. tall; ligule about 3 mm. long; blades 20 to 30 cm. long, 1 mm. wide, flat or involute; panicle 10 to 15 cm. long, open, the slender branches 2 to 4 cm. long, bearing 1 or 2 spikelets; glumes 1.5 cm. long; lemma dark brown, 9 to 10 mm. long, the callus 2 mm. long, the body glabrous, papillose-roughened toward the summit, awn scabrous, 4.5 to 6 cm. long, twice-geniculate. ♃ — Dry or rocky open woods, Massachusetts to Michigan south to Florida and Texas, mostly on the Coastal Plain.

FIGURE 645.—*Stipa avenacea.* Floret, × 1; lemma, × 5. (Kneucker, Gram. 564, Md.)

9. Stipa spártea Trin. PORCUPINE GRASS. (Fig. 646.) Culms about 1 m. tall; ligule rather firm, 4 to 5 mm. long; blades 20 to 30 cm. long, 3 to 5 mm. wide, flat, involute in drying; panicle 15 to 20 cm. long, narrow, nodding, the few slender branches bearing 1 or 2 spikelets; glumes 3 to 4 cm. long; lemma subcylindric, brown, 1.6 to 2.5 cm. long, the callus about 7 mm. long, the body pubescent below, glabrous above except for a line of pubescence on one side, the crown erect-ciliate; awn stout, 12 to 20 cm. long, twice geniculate. ♃ —Prairies, Ontario to British Columbia; Pennsylvania to Montana, Missouri, and New Mexico. STIPA SPARTEA var. CURTISÉTA Hitchc. Glumes

FIGURE 646.—*Stipa spartea*. Plant, × ½; glumes and floret, × 2. (McDonald 16, Ill.)

2 to 3 cm. long; lemma 12 to 15 mm. long; awn mostly not more than 7 or 8 cm. long. ♃ —Manitoba to Alberta, Montana, South Dakota, and Wyoming.

10. Stipa comáta Trin. and Rupr. NEEDLE-AND-THREAD. (Fig. 647.) Culms 30 to 60 cm. tall, sometimes taller; ligule thin, 3 to 4 mm. long; blades 10 to 30 cm. long, 1 to 2 mm. wide, flat or involute, panicle commonly included at base, narrow, 10 to 20 cm. long; glumes 1.5 to 2 cm. long, the attenuate tips subhyaline; lemma 8 to 12 mm. long, mostly about 1 cm., pale or finally brownish, the callus about 3 mm. long, the body sparsely pubescent or glabrate toward the summit; awn 10 to 15 cm. long, indistinctly twice-geniculate, very slender, loosely twisted below, flexuous above, often deciduous. ♃ —Prairies, plains, and dry hills, Indiana to Yukon Territory, south to Texas and California. A form from Washington with pubescent foliage has been differentiated as *S. comata* var. *intonsa* Piper. STIPA COMATA var. INTERMÉDIA Scribn. and Tweedy. Differing from *S. comata* in the shorter straight third segment of the awn; glumes and lemma on the average a little longer; panicle usually exserted. —Canada; Montana to Washington, south to New Mexico and California.

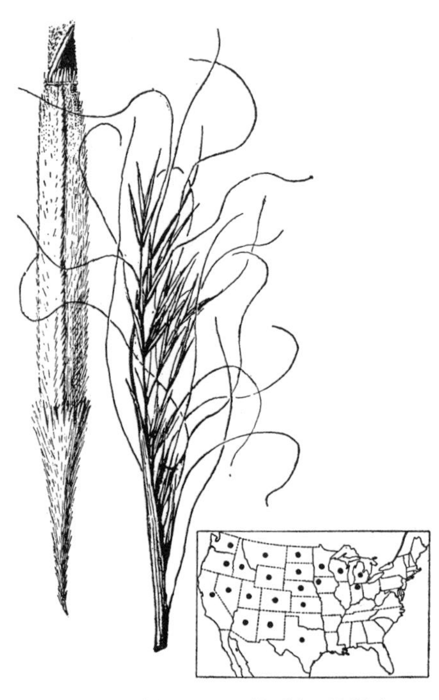

FIGURE 647.—*Stipa comata*. Panicle, × ½; lemma, × 5. (Hitchcock 1700, Colo.)

FIGURE 648.—*Stipa pulchra*. Panicle, × ½; lemma, × 5. (Chase 5598, Calif.)

11. Stipa púlchra Hitchc. PURPLE NEEDLEGRASS. (Fig. 648.) Culms 60 to 100 cm. tall; blades long, narrow, flat or involute; ligule about 1 mm. long; panicle nodding, about 15 to 20 cm. long, loose, the branches spreading, slender, some of the lower 2.5 to 5 cm. long; glumes narrow, long-acuminate, purplish, 3-nerved, the first about 20 mm. long, the second 2 to 4 mm. shorter; lemma 7.5 to 13 mm. long, fusiform, sparingly pilose, sometimes only in lines above, minutely papillose-roughened, the callus about 2 mm. long, the summit sometimes with a smooth neck and a ciliate crown (as in *S. leucotricha*); awn 7 to 9 cm. long, short-pubescent to the second bend, the first segment 1.5 to 2 cm. long, the second shorter, the third 4 to 6 cm. long. ♃ —Open ground, northern California to Baja California, mostly in the Coast Ranges.

the branches ascending, few-flowered, naked below; glumes about 1 cm. long, broad, rather abruptly narrowed into a short point, 7- to 9-nerved; lemma 7 to 8 mm. long, oblong-elliptic, brown, minutely papillose and brownish pubescent, the callus 1 mm. long; awn about 3 cm. long, obscurely twice-geniculate. ♃

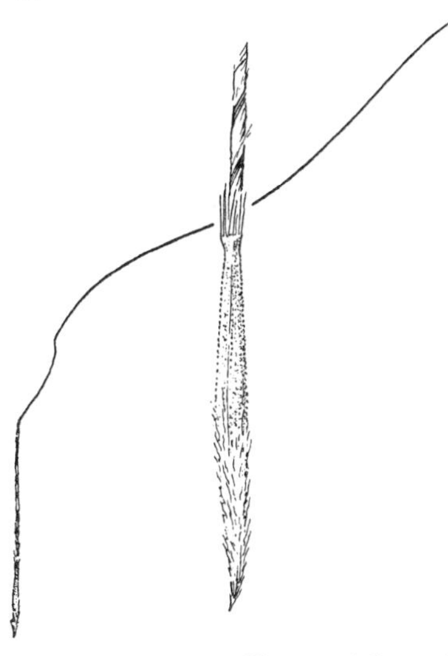

FIGURE 64 .—*Stipa cernua*. Glumes and floret, × 5. (Hall 2921, Calif.)

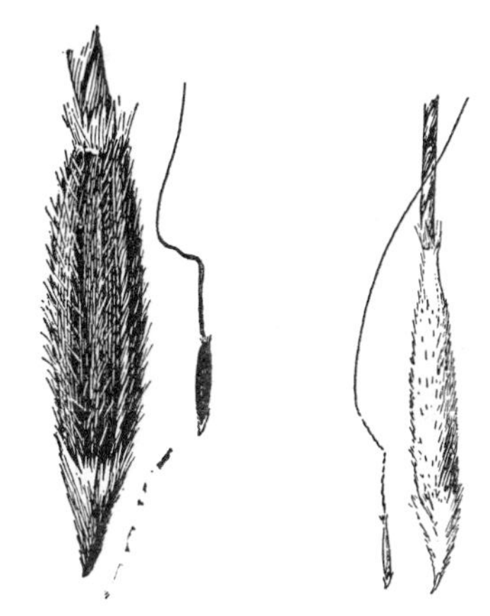

FIGURE 650. — *Stipa pringlei*. Floret, × 1; lemma, × 5. (Hitchcock 7691, Mexico.)

FIGURE 651.—*Stipa eminens*. Floret, × 1; lemma, × 5. (Palmer 523, Mexico.)

12. Stipa cérnua Stebbins and Love. (Fig. 649.) Culms mostly 60 to 90 cm. tall, in rather large clumps; basal blades numerous, narrow, glaucous, those of the culm 1.2 to 2.4 mm. wide; panicle open with slender flexuous branches; glumes acuminate, the first 12 to 19 mm. long, the second a little shorter; lemma 5 to 10.5 mm. long, papillose, silky-pilose below and on the nerves, the callus acute, densely bearded; awn 6 to 11 cm. long, the terminal segment flexuous. ♃ —Foothills of Sierra Nevada and Coast Ranges, Calif.

13. Stipa príngleí Scribn. PRINGLE NEEDLEGRASS. (Fig. 650.) Culms, about 1 m. tall; ligule about 2 mm. long; blades 10 to 30 cm. long, 1 to 3 mm. wide, flat or those of the innovations involute, firm, erect, scabrous, panicle nodding, 10 to 15 cm. long, —Rocky woods and slopes, Texas, New Mexico, and Arizona to Chihuahua, Mex.

14. Stipa éminens Cav. (Fig. 651.) Culms slender, rather wiry, 80 to 120 cm. tall; ligule 3 to 6 mm. long; blades mostly elongate, flat or involute, 1 to 4 mm. wide; panicle nodding, open, 10 to 20 cm. long, usually densely pilose on the lower node, the branches slender, spreading, often flexuous, usually 3 to 4 or even more at the node; glumes about 1.5 cm. long; lemma pale, 5 to 7 mm. long, pubescent; awn 3 to 6 cm. long, obscurely twice-geniculate, the third segment flexuous. ♃ —Rocky hills, Texas to Arizona and central Mexico.

15. Stipa lépida Hitchc. FOOTHILL NEEDLEGRASS. (Fig. 652.) Culms slender, puberulent below the nodes, 60

FIGURE 652.—*Stipa lepida*. Floret, × 1; lemma, × 5. (Chase 5609, Calif.)

FIGURE 653.—*Stipa porteri*. Floret, × 1; lemma, × 5. (Wolf 1109, Colo.)

to 100 cm. tall; sheaths smooth, rarely puberulent, sparingly villous at throat; ligule very short; blades 10 to 30 cm. long, flat, 2 to 4 mm. wide, pubescent on upper surface near base; panicle rather loose and open, usually 15 to 20 cm. long, sometimes more than 30 cm. long, the branches distant, slender; glumes 3-nerved, smooth, acuminate, the first 6 to 10 mm. long, the second about 2 mm. shorter; lemma about 6 mm. long, brown, sparingly villous, nearly glabrous toward the hairy-tufted apex; awn indistinctly twice-geniculate, about 2.5 to 4 cm. long, scabrous. ♃ —Dry hills, open woods, and rocky slopes, central California to Baja California, in the Coast Range. STIPA LEPIDA var. ANDERSÓNII (Vasey) Hitchc. Differing only in the more slender culms, the slender involute blades, and in the narrow or reduced panicle.—Same range as the species.

FIGURE 654.—*Stipa thurberiana*. Floret, × 1; lemma, × 5. (Chase 4689, Idaho.)

16. Stipa portéri Rydb. (Fig. 653.) Culms 20 to 35 cm. tall; ligule 2 to 3 mm. long; blades 2 to 12 cm. long, involute, subfiliform, sulcate, scaberulous; panicle mostly 5 to 10 cm. long, open, the branches distant, capillary, flexuous, few-flowered; glumes 5 to 6 mm. long; lemma about 5 mm. long, oblong-elliptic, softly pilose on the lower half, scaberulous above, lobed at summit; awn 12 to 15 mm. long, plumose with hairs 1 to 2 mm. long, with a single bend one-third from the base, the first segment weakly twisted. ♃ —High mountains of Colorado.

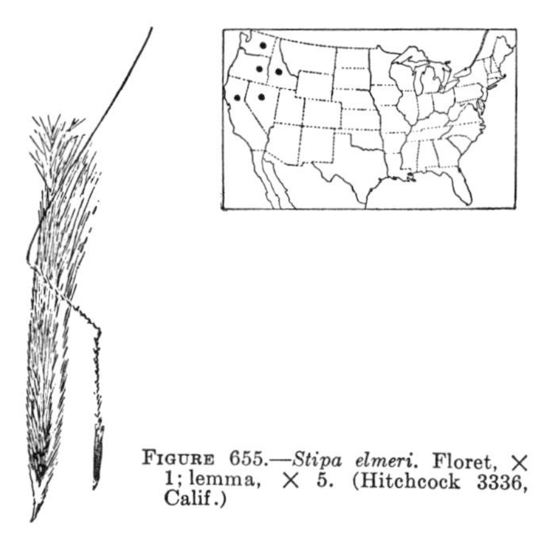

FIGURE 655.—*Stipa elmeri*. Floret, × 1; lemma, × 5. (Hitchcock 3336, Calif.)

17. Stipa thurberiána Piper. THURBER NEEDLEGRASS. (Fig. 654.) Culms mostly 30 to 60 cm. tall; sheaths scaberulous or the upper glabrous; ligule hyaline, 3 to 6 mm. long; blades 10 to 25 cm. long, filiform, involute, scabrous to densely soft-pubescent, flexuous; panicle mostly 8 to 15 cm. long, narrow, the ascending branches few flowered; glumes 11 to 13 mm. long, the acuminate summit hyaline; lemma 8 to 9 mm. long, appressed-pubescent, callus about 1 mm. long; awn 4 to 5 cm. long, twice-geniculate, the first and second segments plumose with hairs 1 to 2 mm. long. ♃ —Mesas and rocky slopes, Idaho to Washington and central California.

18. Stipa elméri Piper and Brodie ex Scribn. (Fig. 655.) Culms 60 to 100 cm. tall, more or less puberulent, especially at the nodes; sheaths pubescent; ligule very short; blades 15 to 30 cm. long, 2 to 4 mm. wide, flat or becoming involute, pubescent on the upper surface, or those of the innovations also on the lower surface; panicle narrow, 15 to 35 cm. long, rather loose; glumes 12 to 14 mm. long, long-acuminate, hyaline except toward base; lemma about 7 mm. long, appressed-pubescent, the

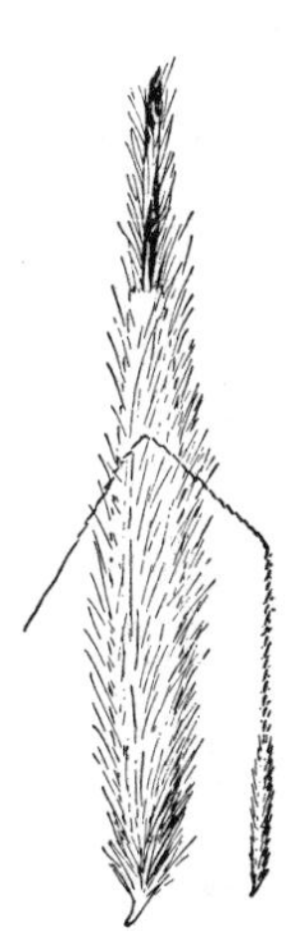

FIGURE 656.—*Stipa latiglumis.* Floret, × 1; lemma, × 5. (Type.)

callus 1 mm. long; awn 4 to 5 cm. long, distinctly twice-geniculate, the segments nearly equal, the first and second finely plumose. ♃ —Dry hills, sandy plains, and open woods, Washington and Idaho to California and Nevada.

19. Stipa latiglúmis Swallen. (Fig. 656.) Culms slender, erect, strigose below, 50 to 110 cm. tall; sheaths, at least the lower, pubescent; blades flat or loosely involute, pilose on the upper surface, glabrous beneath; ligule 1 to 4 mm. long; panicle narrow, loosely flowered, 15 to 30 cm. long, the branches distant, slender, the

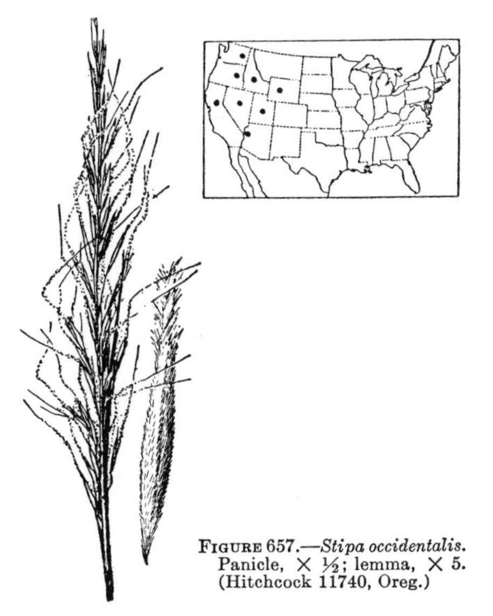

FIGURE 657.—*Stipa occidentalis.* Panicle, × ½; lemma, × 5. (Hitchcock 11740, Oreg.)

lower as much as 10 cm. long; glumes about equal, firm, rather abruptly acute or acuminate, 3-nerved, tinged with purple, 13 to 15 mm. long, 1.5 mm. wide from keel to margin; lemma densely pubescent, 8 to 9 mm. long, the sharp callus 1 mm. long; awn twice-geniculate, 3.5 to 4.5 cm. long, the first and second segments plumose. ♃ —Sierras of central California at medium altitudes.

20. Stipa occidentális Thurb. WESTERN NEEDLEGRASS. (Fig. 657.) Culms mostly 25 to 40 cm. tall;

FIGURE 658.—*Stipa lobata.* Floret, × 1; lemma, × 5; summit of lemma, × 15. (Type.)

FIGURE 659.—*Stipa californica.* Floret, × 1; lemma, × 5. (Hall 2556, Calif.)

sheaths glabrous to pubescent; blades 10 to 20 cm. long, 1 to 2 mm. wide, usually involute, glabrous beneath, white-puberulent on the upper surface; panicle 10 to 20 cm. long, lax, the few slender branches narrowly ascending; glumes about 12 mm. long, the attenuate tips hyaline; lemma pale brown, about 7 mm. long, rather sparsely appressed-pubescent; awn 3 to 4 cm. long, twice-geniculate, plumose, the hairs on first and second segments about 1 mm. long, shorter on third segment. ♃ —Plains, rocky hills, and open woods, Wyoming to Washington, Arizona, and California.

21. Stipa lobáta Swallen. (Fig. 658.) Culms densely tufted, erect, scaberulous below the panicle, 35 to 85 cm. tall; blades flat or loosely folded toward the base, tapering into a fine point, as much as 50 cm. long, 1 to 4 mm. wide at the base, scabrous on the upper surface, glabrous beneath; ligule less than 0.5 mm. long; panicle narrow, 10 to 18 cm. long, the branches appressed; glumes about equal, acuminate, 3-nerved, scabrous, 9 to 10 mm. long; lemma brownish, 6 mm. long, densely pubescent with hairs 1 to 2 mm. long, the callus very short, blunt, the summit 2-lobed, the lobes 0.8 to 1.5 mm. long, awned from between the lobes; awn twice-geniculate, 12 to 16 mm. long, the first and second segments appressed-hispid. ♃ —Rocky hills at medium altitudes, western Texas and New Mexico.

22. Stipa califórnica Merr. and Davy. (Fig. 659.) Culms 75 to 125 cm. tall; ligule rather firm, 1 to 2 mm. long; blades 10 to 25 cm. long, 1 to 4 mm. wide, flat, becoming involute, those of the innovations slender and involute; panicle 15 to 30 cm., sometimes to 50 cm., long, slender, pale; glumes about 12 mm. long; lemma 6 to 8 mm. long, rather sparsely villous with ascending white hairs, those at the summit about 1.5 mm. long; awn 2.5 to 3.5 cm. long, twice-geniculate, the first and second segments plumose. ♃ —Dry open ground, Idaho and Washington to California and western Nevada.

FIGURE 660.—*Stipa curvifolia.* Floret, × 1; lemma, × 5. (Type.)

23. Stipa curvifólia Swallen. (Fig. 660.) Culms densely tufted, erect, about 35 cm. tall; leaves clustered toward the base, the lowermost sheaths pubescent, the blades involute, becoming curved with age; panicle 7 to 8 cm. long, dense, the branches short, appressed; glumes about 10 mm. long; lemma 5.5 mm. long, light brown, evenly white pilose; awn once or obscurely twice-geniculate, 22 to 25 mm. long, twisted and densely plumose below the bend.

♃ —Known only from limestone cliffs, Guadalupe Mountains, N. Mex.

24. Stipa scribnéri Vasey. SCRIBNER NEEDLEGRASS. (Fig. 661.) Culms 30 to 70 cm. tall; sheaths villous at the throat; ligule less than 1 mm. long; blades 15 to 25 cm. long, 2 to 4 mm. wide, flat or sometimes involute; panicle 10 to 25 cm. long, contracted, the rather short stiff branches erect; glumes 10 to 15 mm. long, relatively firm, attenuate; lemma about 8 mm. long, pale, narrow-fusiform, villous with white hairs, those at the summit about 2 mm. long, forming a brushlike tip; awn 14 to 20 mm. long, twice-geniculate. ♃ —Mesas and rocky slopes, Colorado, Utah, New Mexico, and Arizona.

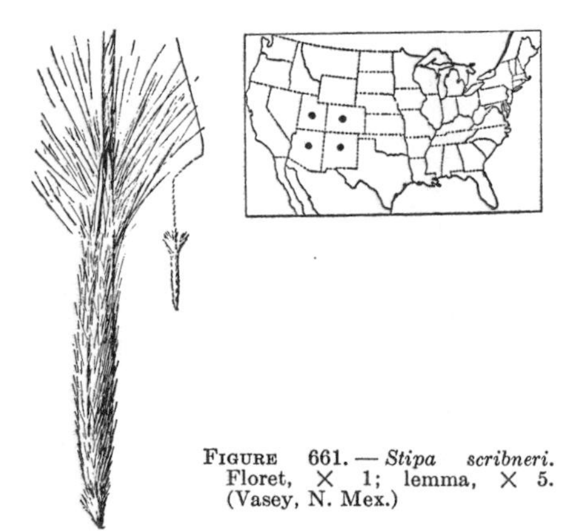

FIGURE 661. — *Stipa scribneri.* Floret, × 1; lemma, × 5. (Vasey, N. Mex.)

25. Stipa lemmóni (Vasey) Scribn. LEMMON NEEDLEGRASS. (Fig. 662.) Culms 30 to 80 cm. tall, scaberulous, usually puberulent below the nodes; ligule 1 to 3 mm. long; blades 10 to 20 cm. long, flat or involute, 1 to 2 mm. wide, or those of the innovations very narrow; panicle 5 to 12 cm. long, narrow, pale or purplish; glumes 8 to 10 mm. long, rather broad and firm, somewhat abruptly acuminate, the first 5-nerved, the second 3-nerved; lemma 6 to 7 mm. long, pale or light brown, the callus rather blunt, the body fusiform, 1.2 mm. wide, villous with appressed hairs; awn 20 to 35 mm. long, twice-geniculate, appressed-pubescent to

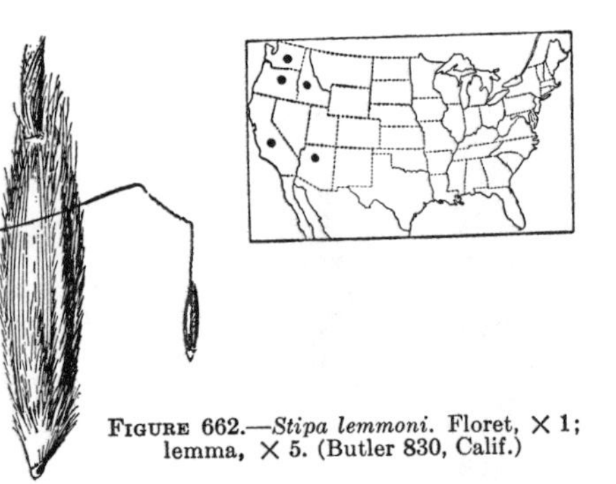

FIGURE 662.—*Stipa lemmoni.* Floret, × 1; lemma, × 5. (Butler 830, Calif.)

the second bend. ♃ —Dry open ground and open woods, British Columbia to Idaho and California.

26. Stipa virídula Trin. GREEN NEEDLEGRASS. (Fig. 663.) Culms 60 to 100 cm. tall; sheaths villous at the throat, often rather sparingly so, more or less hispidulous in a line across the collar; ligule about 1 mm. long; blades 10 to 30 cm. long, 1 to 3 or even 5 mm. wide, flat or, especially on the innovations, involute; panicle 10 to 20 cm. long, narrow, rather closely flowered, greenish or tawny at maturity; glumes 7 to 10 mm. long, hyaline-attenuate; lemma 5 to 6 mm. long, fusiform, at maturity plump, more than 1 mm. wide, the body at maturity brownish, appressed-pubescent, the callus rather blunt; awn 2 to 3 cm. long, twice-geniculate. ♃ —Plains and dry slopes, Alberta and Saskatchewan to Wisconsin and Illinois, west to Montana and Arizona; New York (near Rochester); east of the Mississippi, found near railways.

FIGURE 663.—*Stipa viridula.* Floret, × 1; lemma and summit of sheath, × 5. (Griffiths 201, S. Dak.)

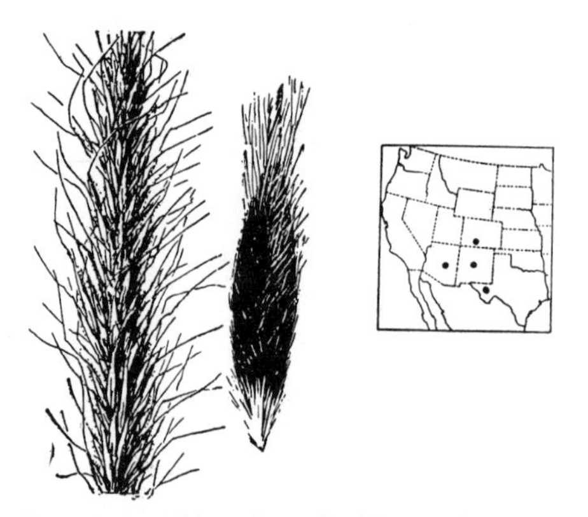

FIGURE 664.—*Stipa robusta*. Panicle, × ½; lemma, × 5. (Hitchcock 13280, N. Mex.)

27. Stipa robústa (Vasey) Scribn. SLEEPY GRASS. (Fig. 664.) Culms robust, mostly 1 to 1.5 m. tall; sheaths villous at the throat and on the margin, a strong hispidulous line across the collar; ligule 2 to 4 mm. long; blades elongate, flat or on the innovations involute, those of the culm as much as 8 mm. wide; panicle narrow, compact, often more or less interrupted below, as much as 30 cm. long and 2 cm. thick; glumes about 1 cm. long, attenuate into a fine soft point; lemma 6 to 8 mm. long, about as in *S. viridula;* awn 2 to 3 cm. long, rather obscurely twice-geniculate. ♃ (*S. vaseyi* Scribn.)—Dry plains and hills and dry open woods, Colorado to western Texas, Arizona, and northern Mexico. Said to act as a narcotic on animals that graze upon it, especially affecting horses.

28. Stipa columbiána Macoun. COLUMBIA NEEDLEGRASS. (Fig. 665.) Culms mostly 30 to 60 cm. tall, sometimes as much as 1 m.; sheaths naked at the throat; ligule 1 to 2 mm. long; blades 10 to 25 cm. long, 1 to 3 mm. wide, mostly involute, especially on the innovations, those of the culm sometimes flat; panicle 7 to 20 cm. long, narrow, mostly rather dense, often purplish; glumes about 1 cm. long; lemma 6 to 7 mm. long, pubescent as in *S. viridula*, the body narrower, the callus sharper; awn 2 to 2.5 cm. long, twice-geniculate. ♃ (*S. minor* Scribn.)—Dry plains, meadows, and open woods, at medium and high altitudes, South Dakota to Yukon Territory, south to Texas and California. Differing from *S. viridula* in the glabrous throat of the sheath and in the shape of the fruit.

STIPA COLUMBIANA var. NELSÓNI (Scribn.) Hitchc. Differing in its usually larger size, often as much as 1 m. tall, the broader culm blades, and the larger and denser panicle; lemma 6 to 7 mm. long; awn as much as 3.5 cm. long, sometimes longer. ♃ —Alberta to Washington, south to Colorado and Arizona.

FIGURE 665.—*Stipa columbianai*. Panicle, × ½; lemma, × 5. (Nelson 7478, Wyo.)

29. Stipa lettermáni Vasey. LETTERMAN NEEDLEGRASS. (Fig. 666.) Resembling small forms of *S. columbiana;* culms often in large tufts, 30 to 60 cm. tall; blades slender, involute; panicle slender, narrow, loose, 10 to 15 cm. long; glumes about 6 mm. long; lemma 4 to 5 mm. long, slender and more copiously hairy than in *S. columbiana;* awn 1.5 to 2 cm. long. ♃ —Open ground or open woods at upper altitudes, Wyoming to Montana and Oregon, south to New Mexico and California.

30. Stipa williámsii Scribn. WILLIAMS NEEDLEGRASS. (Fig. 667.) Differing from *S. columbiana* chiefly in having more or less pubescent culms, sheaths, and blades; culms

60 to 100 cm. tall; panicle 10 to 20 cm. long; lemma about 7 mm. long; awn usually 3 to 5 cm. long. ♃ —Dry hills and plains, Montana to Washington, south to Colorado and California.

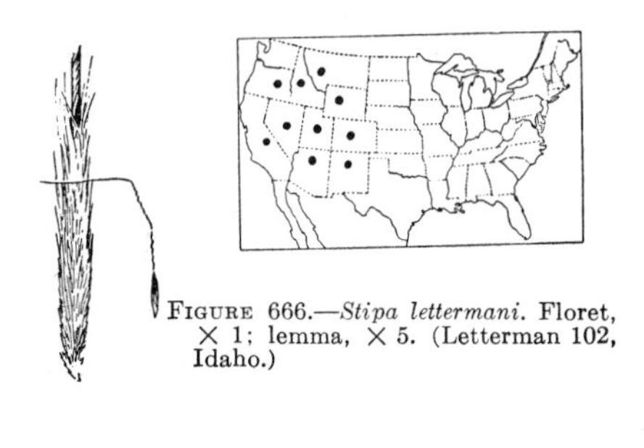

FIGURE 666.—*Stipa lettermani*. Floret, × 1; lemma, × 5. (Letterman 102, Idaho.)

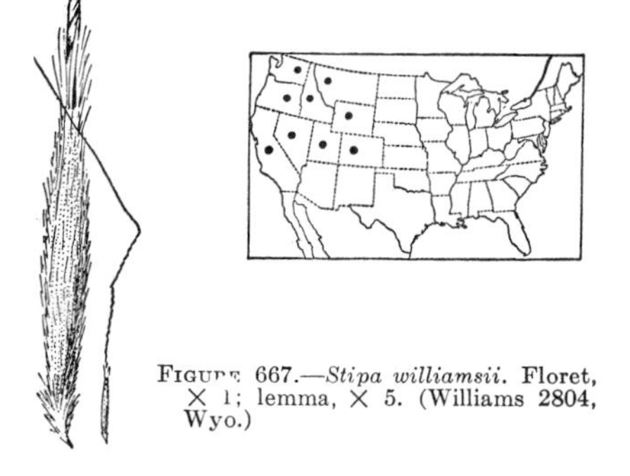

FIGURE 667.—*Stipa williamsii*. Floret, × 1; lemma, × 5. (Williams 2804, Wyo.)

31. Stipa diegoénsis Swallen. (Fig. 668.) Culms 70 to 100 cm. tall, scaberulous, densely pubescent below the nodes; sheaths glabrous or scaberulous; ligule 1 to 2 mm. long, obtuse or truncate; blades 15 to 40 cm. long, 2 to 4 mm. wide, flat or involute, scabrous below, pubescent above; panicle 15 to 30 cm. long, dense, the branches appressed; glumes acuminate, the first 9 to 10 mm. long, 1-nerved, the second 8 to 9 mm. long, 3-nerved; lemma 6.5 to 7.5 mm. long, the hairs at the summit 1 to 2 mm. long, the callus 0.5 mm. long, sharp-pointed; awn 2 to 3.3 cm. long, twice-geniculate, scabrous. ♃ —Along streams in chaparral. Known only from San Diego County (Jamul), Calif., and northern Baja California.

32. Stipa pinetórum Jones. (Fig. 669.) Culms in large tufts, 30 to 50

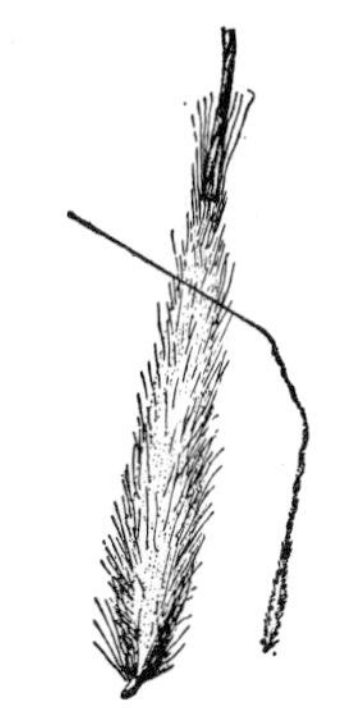

FIGURE 668.—*Stipa diegoensis*. Floret, × 1; lemma × 5. (Type.)

cm. tall; ligule very short; leaves mostly basal, the blades 5 to 12 cm. long, involute-filiform, more or less flexuous, slightly scabrous; panicle narrow, 8 to 10 cm. long; glumes about 9 mm. long; lemma 5 mm. long, narrowly fusiform, clothed especially on the upper half with hairs 2 mm. long, forming a conspicuous tuft exceeding the body of the lemma, and bearing 2 hyaline teeth 1 mm. long at the summit; awn about 2 cm. long, twice-geniculate, nearly glabrous. ♃ —Open pine woods at high altitudes, rare, Colorado to Montana, Idaho, and California.

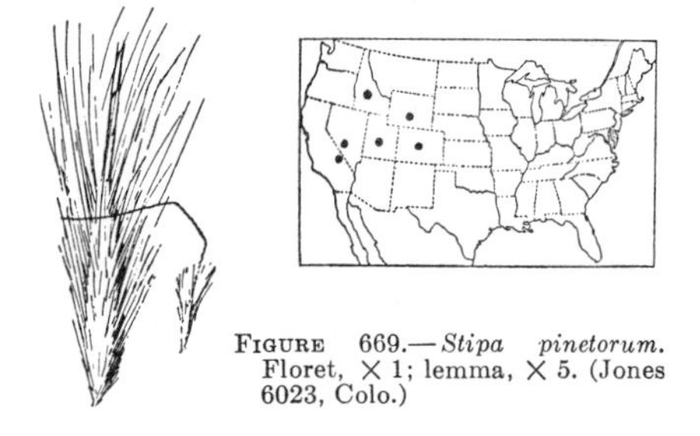

FIGURE 669.—*Stipa pinetorum*. Floret, × 1; lemma, × 5. (Jones 6023, Colo.)

33. Stipa árida Jones. (Fig. 670.) Culms 40 to 80 cm. tall; blades 10 to 20 cm. long, 1 to 2 mm. wide, flat or involute, scabrous; panicle 10 to 15 cm. long, narrow, compact, pale or silvery; glumes 8 to 12 mm. long; lemma 4 to 5 mm. long; appressed-pubescent on the lower half and along the margin, slightly roughened toward the summit; awn 4 to 6 cm. long, capillary, scaberulous, loosely twisted for 1 or 2 cm., flexuous beyond. ♃ —Rocky slopes, Texas, Colorado to Arizona and California (Funeral Mountains).

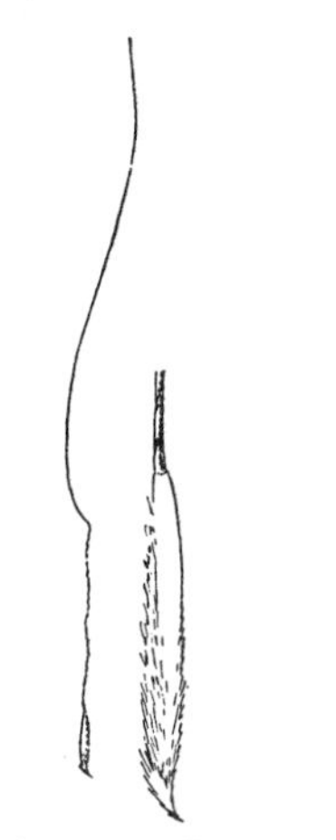

FIGURE 670.—*Stipa arida.* Floret, × 1; lemma, × 5. (Jones 5377, Utah.)

34. Stipa tenuíssima Trin. (Fig. 671.) Culms in large tufts, slender, wiry, 30 to 70 cm. tall; ligule 2 mm. long; blades 15 to 30 cm. long, sometimes longer, filiform, wiry, closely involute; panicle 10 to 30 cm. long, narrow, soft, nodding; glumes about 1 cm. long; lemma 2 to 3 mm. long, oblong-elliptic, glabrous, minutely papillose-roughened, the short callus densely pilose; awn about 5 cm. long, capillary, flexuous, obscurely geniculate about the middle. ♃ —Dry open ground, rocky slopes, and open dry woods, Texas and New Mexico to central Mexico; Argentina.

Stipa neesiána Trin. and Rupr. Related to *S. leucotricha* but with shorter lemma with thickened erose crown. ♃ —Ballast, Mobile, Ala.; South America.

Stipa brachychaéta Godr. Blades firm, flat, or loosely involute; panicle narrow, open, the few spikelets on slender pedicels; glumes 8 mm. long; lemma 5 mm. long, brown, pubescent in lines; awn 12 mm. long. ♃ —Ballast near Portland, Oreg.; Argentina.

STIPA ELEGANTÍSSIMA Labill. Tufted perennial; foliage scant; panicle commonly half the height of the plant, the filiform spreading branches conspicuously feathery; spikelets purple, long-awned. ♃ —Sometimes cultivated for ornament; Australia.

STIPA PENNÁTA L. Tufted perennial; blades elongate, involute; panicle few-flowered, the large spikelets with awns 25 to 35 cm. long, conspicuously feathery above the bend. ♃ —Sometimes cultivated for ornament; Europe.

STIPA TENACÍSSIMA L. ESPARTO. Tufted perennial with tough branching base; blades elongate, involute, tomentose at base and with erect auricles 3 to 10 mm. long; panicle narrow, dense; awns 4 to 6 cm. long, feathery below the bend. ♃ —Sometimes cultivated for ornament; Spain and Algeria, where it is gathered for making paper and cordage; also in Portugal and Morocco.

STIPA SPLÉNDENS Trin. Robust perennial, 1.2 to 2 m. tall; foliage scabrous; panicle 30 to 50 cm. long, many-flowered, but loose; spikelets 5 to 6 mm. long; lemma as long as the glumes, silky; awn weakly geniculate, 10 to 15 mm. long. ♃ —Introduced from Siberia under the name "chee grass," sparingly cultivated. Seed of *Calamagrostis epigeios* was mixed with the first introduction and "chee grass" was erroneously applied to that, which thrived more vigorously than the *Stipa.*

92. ARÍSTIDA L. THREE-AWN

Spikelets 1-flowered, the rachilla disarticulating obliquely above the glumes; glumes equal or unequal, narrow, acute, acuminate, or awn-tipped; lemma indurate, narrow, terete, convolute, with a hard, sharp-pointed, usually minutely bearded callus, terminating above in a usually trifid awn (the lateral divisions reduced or obsolete in Section Streptachne), the base sometimes undivided, forming a column. Annual or perennial, mostly slender tufted grasses, with narrow, frequently convolute blades and narrow or sometimes open panicles. Type species, *Aristida adscensionis* L. Name from Latin *arista,* awn.

The species are of distinctly minor importance for forage except in the Southwest, where several, such as *A. longiseta,* are eaten by stock before the

FIGURE 671.—*Stipa tenuissima.* Plant, × ½; spikelet, × 2; glumes and floret, × 5. (Bailey 694, Tex.)

flowers are produced. The ripe fruits of several species are troublesome to stock on the plains because of the sharp hard points. These fruits are produced sometimes in vast numbers and are carried far and wide by the wind in open country. *Aristida adscensionis* is one of the annuals that make up the "six-weeks" grasses of the Southwest.

Lemma articulate with the column of the awns; awns nearly equal. SECTION 1. ARTHRATHERUM.
Lemma not articulate.
  Lateral awns minute (less than 1 mm. long) or wanting........ SECTION 2. STREPTACHNE.
  Lateral awns more than 1 mm. long (rarely obsolete in *A. ramosissima*), usually well developed........ SECTION 3. CHAETARIA.

Section 1. Arthratherum

Plants annual.
  Column very short........ 1. A. DESMANTHA.
  Column 10 to 15 mm. long, twisted........ 2. A. TUBERCULOSA.
Plants perennial.
  Culms pubescent........ 3. A. CALIFORNICA.
  Culms glabrous........ 4. A. GLABRATA.

Section 2. Streptachne

Awn (column) twisted at base........ 7. A. ORCUTTIANA.
Awn not twisted.
  Branches of panicle distant, spreading, mostly more than 5 cm. long, naked at base; awn straight or abruptly divergent........ 5. A. TERNIPES.
  Branches of panicle short, approximate, 3 to 5 cm. long, floriferous nearly to base; awn curved and flexuous........ 6. A. FLORIDANA.

Section 3. Chaetaria

1a. Central awn spirally coiled at base, the lateral straight. Plants annual. (Group DICHOTOMAE.)
  Lateral awns half to two-thirds as long as the central, somewhat spreading. 8. A. BASIRAMEA.
  Lateral awns much shorter than the central, 1 to 3 mm. long, erect.
    Glumes nearly equal, 6 to 8 mm. long; lemma sparsely appressed-pilose, 5 to 6 mm. long........ 9. A. DICHOTOMA.
    Glumes unequal, the second longer, about 1 cm. long; lemma glabrous except the keel, scabrous toward the apex, about 1 cm. long........ 10. A. CURTISSII.
1b. Central awn not spirally coiled (in a few species all the awns loosely contorted in the lower part).
  2a. Plants annual. (Group ADSCENSIONES.)
    Awns mostly 4 to 7 cm. long, about equal, divergent........ 11. A. OLIGANTHA.
    Awns mostly less than 2 cm. long, often unequal.
      Central awn with a semicircular bend at base, spreading or reflexed.
        Lateral awns much reduced; lemma about 2 cm. long........ 12. A. RAMOSISSIMA.
        Lateral awns one-third to half as long as the central; lemma 4 to 5 mm. long. 13. A. LONGESPICA.
      Central awn not sharply curved, the awns about equally divergent.
        Glumes unequal; awns flat at base, 10 to 15 mm. long........ 14. A. ADSCENSIONIS.
        Glumes about equal; awns terete, 15 to 20 mm. long........ 15. A. INTERMEDIA.
  2b. Plants perennial.
    3a. Panicle open, the branches spreading (in *A. pansa* ascending), naked at base. (Group DIVARICATAE.)
      Panicle branches stiffly and abruptly spreading or reflexed at base.
        Branchlets divaricate and implicate........ 16. A. BARBATA.
        Branchlets appressed.
          Summit of lemma narrowed into a twisted neck 2 to 5 mm. long. 17. A. DIVARICATA.
          Summit of lemma somewhat narrowed but not twisted........ 18. A. HAMULOSA.
      Panicle branches drooping or ascending, not abruptly spreading at base.
        Lateral awns one-fourth to half as long as the central one........ 19. A. PATULA.
        Lateral awns about as long as the central, at least more than half as long. 20. A. PANSA.
    3b. Panicle narrow, the branches ascending or appressed (branches sometimes somewhat spreading in *A. parishii* and *A. purpurea*).
      Column 1 cm. or more long, twisted; glumes awned........ 21. A. SPICIFORMIS.
      Column less than 1 cm. long.

Creeping rhizomes present. Glumes unequal, awned; awns loosely twisted at base, the central a little longer, 18 to 24 mm. long.................. 31. A. RHIZOMOPHORA.
Creeping rhizomes wanting (sometimes short ones in *A. stricta*).
4a. First glume about half as long as the second (as much as two-thirds as long in *A. glauca*). (Group PURPUREAE.)
Lemma tapering into a slender somewhat twisted beak 5 to 6 mm. long; awns 1.5 to 2.5 cm. long, widely spreading.................................. 22. A. GLAUCA.
Lemma beakless or only short-beaked.
Branches of the rather loose and nodding panicle slender and flexuous (see also *A. longiseta* var. *rariflora*).
Lemma about 1 cm. long; awns 3 to 5 cm. long........ 23. A. PURPUREA.
Lemma 7 to 8 mm. long; awns about 2 cm. long.... 24. A. ROEMERIANA.
Branches of the erect panicle stiff and appressed, or the lowermost sometimes somewhat flexuous.
Panicle mostly more than 15 cm. long, the branches several-flowered; awns about 2 cm. long. Sheaths with a villous line across the collar. 25. A. WRIGHTII.
Panicle mostly less than 15 cm. long, the branches few-flowered; awns 2 to several cm. long.
Lemma gradually narrowed above, scaberulous on the upper half; leaves mostly in a short curly cluster at the base of the plant. 27. A. FENDLERIANA.
Lemma scarcely narrowed above, scaberulous only at the tip; leaves not conspicuously basal....................................... 26. A. LONGISETA.
4b. First glume more than half as long as the second. (Usually the glumes about equal or the first sometimes a little longer.)
Sheaths lanate-pubescent. Panicle branched, somewhat spreading; central awn 1.5 to 2.5 cm. long, spreading or reflexed from a curved base. 28. A. LANOSA.
Sheaths not lanate-pubescent.
Column of awn at maturity 3 to 5 mm. long, distinctly twisted. 29. A. ARIZONICA.
Column of awn less than 3 mm. long, or if so long, not twisted.
Blades villous on upper surface near base, involute...... 30. A. STRICTA.
Blades not involute and villous at base.
Awns at maturity about equally divergent, sometimes slightly twisted but not spirally contorted at base.
Lemma about 7 mm. long; awns horizontally spreading; panicle usually more than 20 cm. long............... 32. A. PURPURASCENS.
Lemma 10 to 12 mm. long; awns somewhat spreading but scarcely horizontal; panicle mostly 10 to 15 cm. long. 33. A. PARISHII.
Awns at maturity unequally divergent or spirally contorted at base.
Awns not spirally contorted at base; central awn more spreading than the others, curved at base, sometimes reflexed.
Lateral awns erect, two-thirds to three-fourths as long as the central.
Glumes about 12 mm. long.................................. 34. A. AFFINIS.
Glumes about 6 mm. long.................................. 35. A. VIRGATA.
Lateral awns spreading or reflexed. Panicles nearly simple.
Glumes 6 to 7 mm. long; spikelets mostly in pairs. 36. A. SIMPLICIFLORA.
Glumes about 1 cm. long; spikelets solitary.... 37. A. MOHRII.
Awns spirally contorted at base, spreading.
Blades flat (sometimes subinvolute in *A. condensata*).
Panicle slender, the branches short, rather distant, few-flowered. 38. A. TENUISPICA.
Panicle rather thick, the branches as much as 10 cm. long, rather densely many-flowered............ 39. A. CONDENSATA.
Blades involute... 40. A. GYRANS.

SECTION 1. ARTHRÁTHERUM (Beauv.) Reichenb.

Lemma articulate with the column of the awns, the latter finally deciduous; glumes 1-nerved; awns nearly equal.

1. Aristida desmántha Trin. and Rupr. (Fig. 672.) Annual; branching,

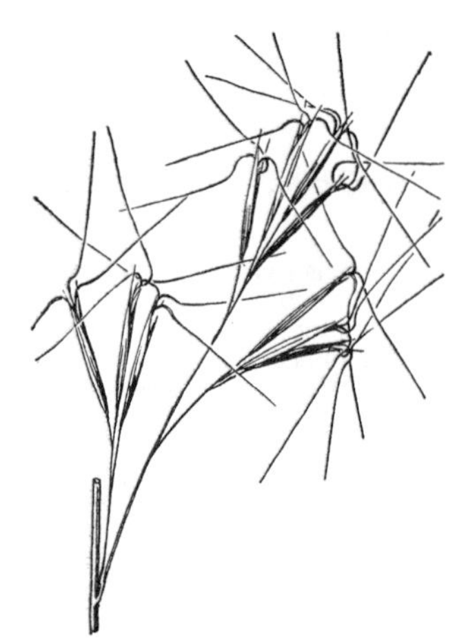

FIGURE 672.—*Aristida desmantha*, × 1. (Reverchon 3428, Tex.)

as much as 80 cm. tall; sheaths often woolly; blades folded or involute, 2 to 3 mm. wide; panicle as much as 20 cm. long, the branches stiffly ascending, very scabrous, bearing 1 to few spikelets; glumes slightly unequal, the body about 1 cm. long, tapering into an awn about half as long; lemma 7 to 8 mm. long, glabrous below,

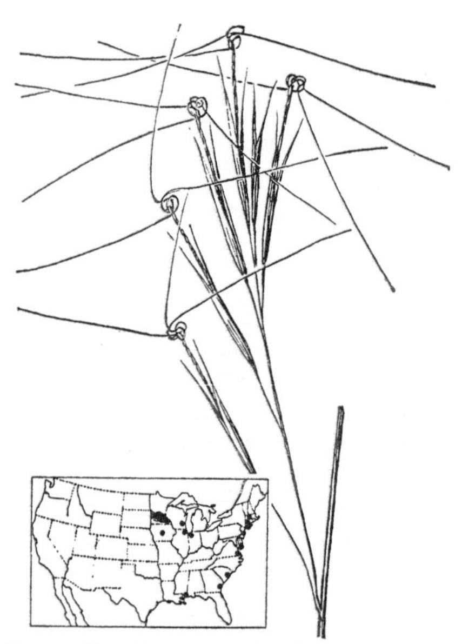

FIGURE 673.—*Aristida tuberculosa*, × 1. (V. H. Chase 322, Ind.)

somewhat laterally compressed and slightly twisted at summit, the densely pubescent callus about 2 mm. long; awns 2 to 2.5 cm. long, united for 1 to 2 mm., the bases curved in a semicircular somewhat contorted bend, the upper part thus usually deflexed. ⊙ —Open sandy soil or sandy woods, Illinois, Nebraska, and Texas.

2. Aristida tuberculósa Nutt. (Fig. 673.) Annual; culms branching, 30 to 60 cm. or even 1 m. tall; blades involute, 2 to 4 mm. wide when flat; panicle 10 to 20 cm. tall, the branches stiffly ascending; glumes about equal, gradually narrowed into an awn, about 2.5 cm. long, including the awn; lemma 11 to 13 mm. long, glabrous, except for the slightly scabrous summit, extending downward into a densely pubescent callus 3 to 4 mm. long; column of awns twisted, 10 to 15 mm. long, the upper 2 or 3 mm. twisted but not united, above this forming a semicircular bend, the terminal straight part of the awns usually deflexed, 3 to 4 cm. long. ⊙ —Open sandy woods, Massachusetts to Georgia and Mississippi near the coast; around the southern end of Lake Michigan and in other localities in Wisconsin, Indiana, Illinois, Iowa, and Minnesota.

3. Aristida califórnica Thurb. (Fig. 674.) Perennial, tufted, much branched at base; culms pubescent, 10 to 30 cm. tall; blades mostly involute and less than 5 cm. long; panicles numerous, mostly reduced to few-flowered racemes; first glume about 8 mm. long, the second about 12 mm. long; lemma 5 to 7 mm. long, glabrous below, scaberulous toward the summit, the strongly pubescent callus 1.5 to 2 mm. long; column 15 to 20 mm. long, the awns about equal, 2.5 to 3.5 cm. long, spreading horizontally, the bases arcuate and slightly contorted. ♃ —Dry sandy or gravelly soil, deserts of southern California, southwestern Arizona, and northern Mexico.

4. Aristida glabráta (Vasey) Hitchc. (Fig. 675.) Perennial; culms erect, branched, glabrous, 20 to 40 cm. tall; blades mostly involute, those of the culm 1 to 3 cm. long; panicle narrow, 3 to 6 cm. long; first glume 5 to 6 mm., the second 10 to 12 mm. long; lemma 5 to 7 mm. long, the twisted column 6 to 14 mm. long; awns about equal, divergent, 2 to 3 cm. long. ♃ —Open dry ground, southern Arizona to Baja California.

SECTION 2. STREPTÁCHNE (R. Br.) Domin (Sect. *Uniseta* Hitchc.)

Lateral awns minute (less than 1 mm. long) or wanting (see also *A. dichotoma* and *A. ramosissima* of Section Chaetaria); lemma not articulate with the column of the awn.

5. Aristida térnipes Cav. SPIDER GRASS. (Fig. 676.) Perennial; culms erect, 50 to 100 cm. tall; blades flat, involute toward the end and tapering into a fine point, as much as 40 cm. long, 2 to 3 mm. wide; panicle open, one-third to half the entire height of the plant, the branches few, distant, spreading, scabrous, mostly naked at base; spikelets appressed at the ends of the branches; glumes about equal, 8 to 10 mm. long; lemma glabrous, often strongly scabrous on the keel, gradually narrowed into a laterally compressed scabrous falcate beak, 1-nerved on each side, this extending into a single straight or divergent scabrous nearly terete awn, the obsolete

FIGURE 675.—*Aristida glabrata*, × 1. (Griffiths 7312, Ariz.)

FIGURE 674.—*Aristida californica*, × 1. (Kearney 3524, Ariz.)

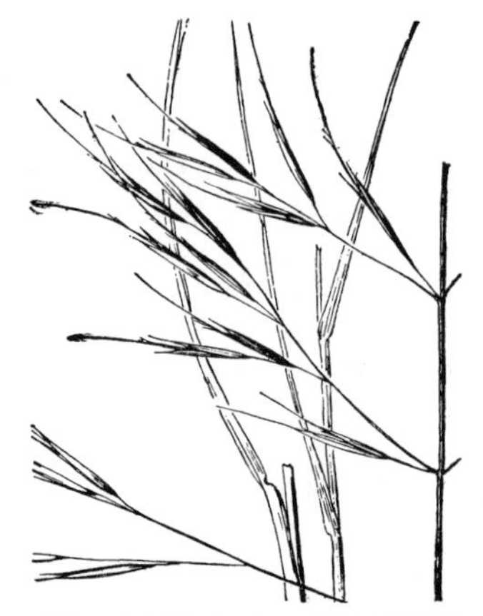

FIGURE 676.—*Aristida ternipes*, × 1. (Griffiths 7271, Ariz.)

or minute lateral awns about 1.7 mm. above the lemma, the central awn 10 to 15 mm. long. ♃ (*A. scabra* Kunth.)—Rocky hills and dry plateaus, Texas, New Mexico, and Arizona to northern South America; Bahamas, Cuba. ARISTIDA TERNIPES var. MÍNOR (Vasey) Hitchc. Smaller and often prostrate or ascending, the panicle usually more than half the length of the entire plant, less diffuse, the shorter branches usually stiffly spreading or somewhat deflexed. ♃ (*A. divergens* Vasey.)—Rocky hills and plains, Texas to Arizona; Nicaragua.

FIGURE 677.—*Aristida floridana*, × 1. (Blodgett, Fla.)

6. Aristida floridâna (Chapm.) Vasey. (Fig. 677.) Resembling *A. ternipes*, but differing in having a narrow panicle with ascending branches 3 to 5 cm. long, spikelet-bearing nearly to the base; awns sickle-shaped, the column somewhat twisted. ♃ —Known only from the original collection from Key West, Fla.

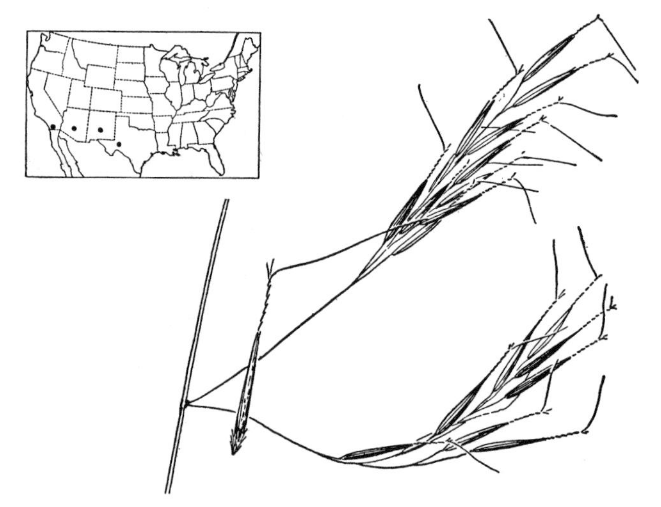

FIGURE 678.—*Aristida orcuttiana*. Panicle, × 1; floret, × 2. (Smith, N. Mex.)

7. Aristida orcuttiána Vasey. BEGGARTICK GRASS. (Fig. 678.) Perennial; culms erect, 30 to 60 cm. or even 1 m. tall; blades flat or the upper involute, as much as 3 mm. wide; panicle open, as much as 30 cm. long, nodding or drooping, the branches few, distant, spreading or drooping, as much as 20 cm. long; glumes equal or nearly so, 10 to 15 mm. long; lemma 8 to 10 mm. long, gradually narrowed into a scabrous twisted column, the total length to the bend 10 to 17 mm.; central awn divergent, 5 to 10 mm. long, the lateral awns from obsolete to as much as 1 to 2 mm. long, erect. ♃ —Rocky hills and plains, Texas to southern California (San Diego), and northwestern Mexico.

SECTION 3. CHAETÁRIA (Beauv.) Trin.

Lateral awns more than 1 mm. long, usually well developed; lemma not articulate with the column of the awns.

FIGURE 679.—*Aristida basiramea*, × 1. (Pammel 174, Iowa.)

8. Aristida basirámea Engelm. ex Vasey. (Fig. 679.) Annual; branching at base, 30 to 50 cm. tall; blades flat, as much as 15 cm. long and 1.5 mm. wide; panicles terminal and axillary, the terminal 5 to 10 cm. long, the

FIGURE 680.—*Aristida dichotoma*, × 1. (Jackson 1829, Del.)

axillary mostly enclosed in the sheaths; glumes somewhat unequal, 12 to 15 mm. long; lemma about 1 cm. long; central awn coiled at base, 10 to 15 mm. long, the lateral awns half to two-thirds as long, somewhat spreading. ⊙ —Open barren or sandy soil, Maine to North Dakota, south to Kentucky, Oklahoma, and Colorado; introduced in Maine.

9. Aristida dichótoma Michx. (Fig. 680.) Annual; culms branched at base, 20 to 40 cm. tall; blades short, the lower mostly flat, scarcely 1 mm. wide, the upper involute; panicles terminal and axillary, the terminal usually less than 10 cm. long, the lateral small; glumes about equal, 6 to 8 mm. long; lemma 5 to 6 mm. long; central awn spirally coiled, horizontally bent, 3 to 6 mm. long, the lateral awns erect, about 1 mm. long. ⊙ —Dry open ground, Maine to Wisconsin and eastern Kansas, south to Florida and Texas.

10. Aristida curtíssii (A. Gray) Nash. (Fig. 681.) Annual; similar to *A. dichotoma*, differing in the less branching habit, the longer and more

FIGURE 681.—*Aristida curtissii*, × 1. (Waite, Ill.)

conspicuous blades, the looser panicles of larger spikelets, the more unequal glumes, the longer second glume (about 1 cm. long), the longer smooth lemma (about 1 cm. long) and central awn, and the usually longer lateral awns; central awn about 1 cm. long, the lateral awns 2 to 4 mm. long. ⊙ —Open dry ground, Maryland and Virginia to South Dakota, Wyoming, Colorado, and Kentucky to Oklahoma; Florida.

11. Aristida oligántha Michx. PRAIRIE THREE-AWN. (Fig. 682.) Annual, much branched; culms 30 to 50 cm. tall; blades flat or loosely involute, usually not more than 1 mm. wide; panicle loose, 10 to 20 cm. long; spikelets short-pediceled, the lower often in pairs; glumes about equal, 2 to 3 cm. long, tapering into an awn, the first 3- to 5-nerved; lemma about 2 cm. long, the awns about equal, divergent, 4 to 7 cm. long, somewhat spirally curved at base. ⊙ —Open dry ground, Massachusetts to South Dakota, south to Florida and Texas; Oregon to Arizona.

12. Aristida ramosíssima Engelm. ex A. Gray. (Fig. 683.) Annual, much branched; culms 30 to 50 cm. tall; blades flat or involute, about 1 mm. wide; panicle narrow, 8 to 12 cm. long; glumes 3- to 5-nerved, the first about 15 mm., the second about 2 cm. long, including an awn 3 to 5 mm. long; lemma about 2 cm. long, tapering into a neck about 5 mm. long; central awn with a semicircular bend or part of a coil at base, 15 to 20 mm. long, spreading, the lateral awns reduced or as much as 6 mm. long, rarely longer. ⊙ —Open sterile soil, Indiana to Iowa, south to Tennessee, Louisiana, Oklahoma, and Texas.

13. Aristida longespíca Poir. (Fig. 684.) Annual, branched; culms 20 to 40 cm. tall; blades flat or involute, about 1 mm. wide; panicles narrow, slender, the terminal 10 to 15 cm. or even 20 cm. long; glumes about equal, 5 mm. long; lemma 4 to 5 mm. long; central awn sharply curved at base, spreading, 5 to 15 mm. long, the lateral awns erect, one-third to half as long as the central, sometimes only 1 mm. long. ⊙ (*A. gracilis* Ell.)—Sterile or sandy soil, New Hampshire to Michigan and Kansas, south to Florida and Texas, especially on the Coastal Plain. In the typical form the lateral awns are short; in var. *geniculata* Fernald (*A. geniculata* Raf.) the lateral awns are more than one-third as long as the central one.

14. Aristida adscensiónis L. SIX-WEEKS THREE-AWN. (Fig. 685.) Annual, branched at base, erect or spreading; culms 10 to 80 cm. tall; panicle narrow and usually rather compact, 5 to 10 cm. long, or longer in large plants; first glume 5 to 7

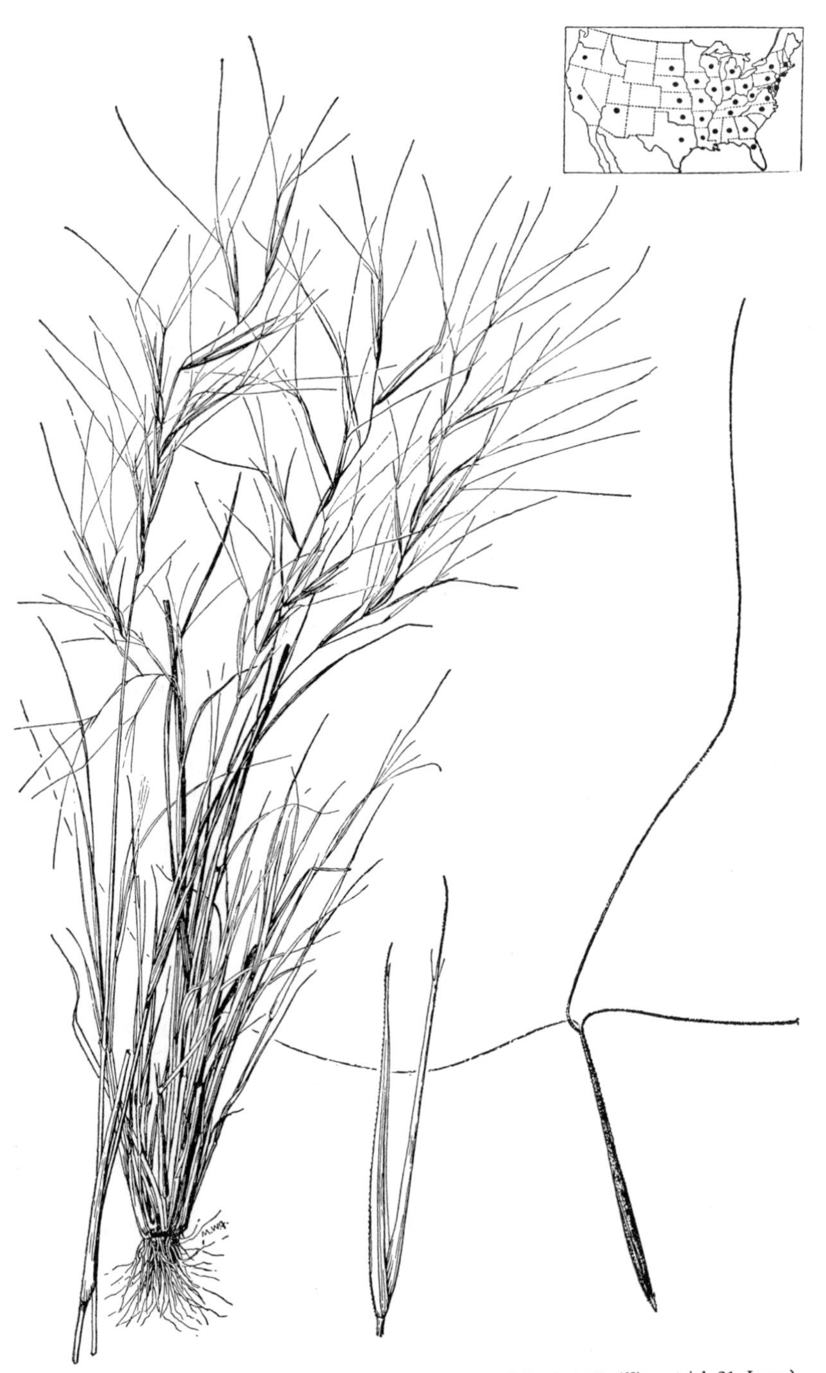

FIGURE 682.—*Aristida oligantha*. Plant, × ½; glumes and floret, × 2. (Fitzpatrick 21, Iowa.)

FIGURE 683.—*Aristida ramosissima*, × 1. (Deam 18549, Ind.)

mm. long, the second 8 to 10 mm. long; lemma 6 to 9 mm. long, compressed toward the scarcely beaked summit, scabrous on the upper part of the keel; awns about equal (the lateral occasionally shorter), mostly 10 to 15 mm. long, about equally divergent at an angle of as much as 45°, flat and without torsion at base. ⊙ —Dry open ground, Missouri (Courtney); southern Kansas to Texas, west to Nevada and southern California, southward to Argentina; a common weed in the American tropics; warmer parts of the Old World. Originally described from Ascension Island. Variable in size from depauperate plants a few centimeters tall with shorter contracted panicle (*A. bromoides* H. B. K.) to tall slender plants with large open panicle (*A. fasciculata* Torr.).

15. Aristida intermédia Scribn. and Ball. (Fig. 686.) Annual, simple or branched, 20 to 40 cm. tall; blades flat or involute, mostly less than 10 cm. long and 2 mm. wide; panicle narrow, slender, loosely flowered, 10 to 20 cm. long; glumes about equal, 1 cm. long; lemma 8 mm. long; awns about equal, all somewhat divergent, 1.5 to 2 cm. long. ⊙ —Low sandy soil, Indiana and Michigan to Nebraska, south to Florida (Pensacola), Mississippi, and Texas. The measurements of the spikelet are sometimes less than those given, especially in plants attacked by smut.

16. Aristida barbáta Fourn. HAVARD THREE-AWN. (Fig. 687.) Perennial, forming hemispherical tufts as much as 30 cm. in diameter, the culms rather stiffly radiating in all directions, 15 to 30 cm. long; blades closely involute, mostly less than 10 cm. long and 0.5 mm. thick; panicles about half the length of the entire plant, open, the branches divaricately spreading or somewhat reflexed, mostly 3 to 6 cm. long, in pairs or with short basal branchlets, but without long naked base, the branchlets and pedicels implicate or flexuous, the whole panicle fragile at maturity, breaking away and rolling before the wind; glumes about equal, 1 cm. long; lemma gradually narrowed into a straight or twisted scaberulous beak, the entire length 8 to 10 mm.; awns somewhat di-

FIGURE 684.—*Aristida longespica*, × 1. (Vasey, D. C.)

FIGURE 685.—*Aristida adscensionis*, × 1. (Earle 559, N. Mex.)

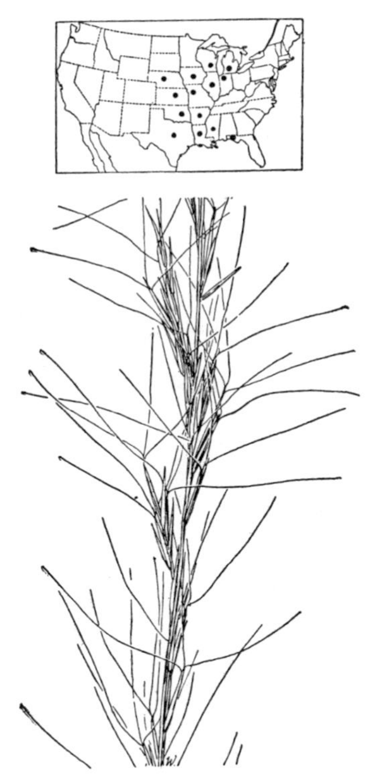

FIGURE 686.—*Aristida intermedia*, × 1. (Kearney 236, Miss.)

vergent, nearly equal, 15 to 20 mm. long. ♃ (*A. havardii* Vasey.)—Hills and plains, western Texas to Arizona and central Mexico.

17. Aristida divaricáta Humb. and Bonpl. ex Willd. POVERTY THREE-AWN. (Fig. 688.) Perennial; culms erect or prostrate-spreading, usually 30 to 60 cm. long, sometimes longer; blades flat or usually loosely involute, or the basal closely involute, mostly less than 3 mm. wide; panicle large, diffuse, usually as much as half the entire length of the culm, the branches spreading or reflexed, naked below; glumes nearly equal, 1 cm. long; lemma 1 cm. long, narrowed into a twisted beak 2 to 5 mm. long; awns about equal, 10 to 15 mm. long. ♃ —Dry hills and plains, Kansas to southern California, south to Texas and Guatemala.

18. Aristida hamulósa Henr. (Fig. 689.) Resembling *A. divaricata;* lemma somewhat narrowed at summit but not twisted, central awn a little longer than the two lateral ones. ♃ —Dry hills and plains, western Texas to southern California, south

FIGURE 687.—*Aristida barbata*, × 1. (Wooton, N. Mex.)

FIGURE 688.—*Aristida divaricata*, × 1. (Talbot, N. Mex.)

to Guatemala. In Arizona more common than *A. divaricata*.

19. Aristida pátula Chapm. ex Nash. (Fig. 690.) Perennial, erect, as much as 1 m. tall; blades flat, becoming involute especially at the slender tip, elongate, 2 to 4 mm. wide; panicle loose and open, one-third to half the entire length of the culm, the branches drooping, naked below, as much as 20 cm. long; glumes 12 to 15 mm. long, nearly equal; lemma 10 to 12 mm. long; central awn straight, 2 to 2.5 cm. long, the lateral scarcely diverging, 5 to 10 mm. long. ♃ —Moist sandy pine barrens and low open ground, peninsular Florida.

20. Aristida pánsa Woot. and Standl. WOOTON THREE-AWN. (Fig. 691.) Perennial; culms stiffly erect, slender, wiry, 20 to 40 cm. tall; blades closely involute, 0.5 mm. thick, often flexuous; panicle rather nar-

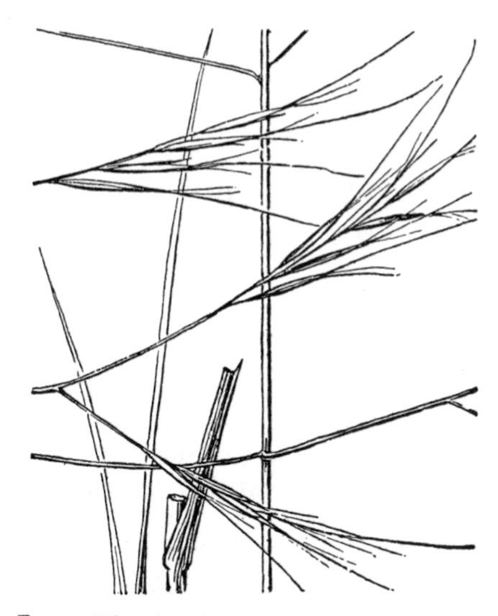

FIGURE 690.—*Aristida patula*, × 1. (Hitchcock, Fla.)

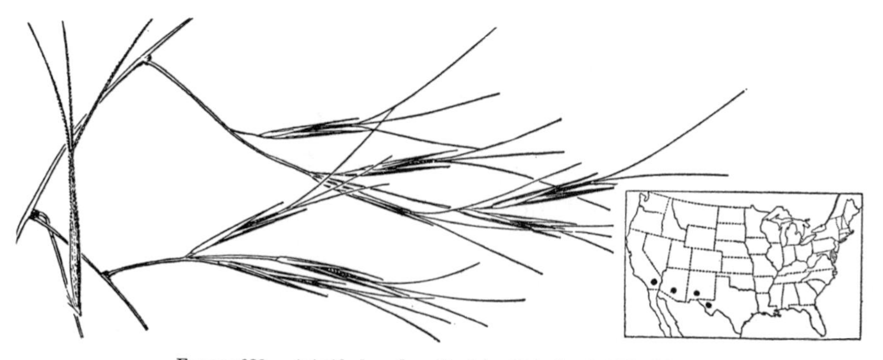

FIGURE 689.—*Aristida hamulosa*. Panicle, × 1; floret, × 3. (Type.)

row, open, rather stiffly upright, 10 to 20 cm. long, the branches stiffly ascending, 4 to 8 cm. long; spikelets erect or narrowly ascending on the branchlets; first glume 5 to 7 mm. long, the second 7 to 10 mm. long; lemma about as long as the second glume, or slightly longer, tapering into a scabrous slightly twisted beak about 2 mm. long; awns about equal, divergent or finally nearly horizontally spreading, 10 to 20 mm. long, the bases finally somewhat curved or warped. ♃ —Plains and open ground, western Texas to Arizona; northern Mexico.

FIGURE 691.—*Aristida pansa*, × 1. (Wooton, N. Mex.)

21. Aristida spicifórmis Ell. (Fig. 692.) Perennial; culms strictly erect, 50 to 100 cm. tall; blades erect, flat or usually involute, elongate, 1 to 3 mm. wide; panicle erect, dense and spikelike, 10 to 15 cm. long, more or less spirally twisted; glumes unequal, abruptly long-awned, the first 4 mm. long, the second 8 to 10 mm. long, the awns usually 10 to 12 mm. long; lemma 5 to 6 mm. long, extending into a slender twisted column 1 to 3 cm. long; awns about equal, 2 to 3 cm. long, divergent or horizontally spreading, more or less curved or warped at base. ♃ —Pine barrens along the coast, South Carolina to Florida and Mississippi; Cuba, Puerto Rico.

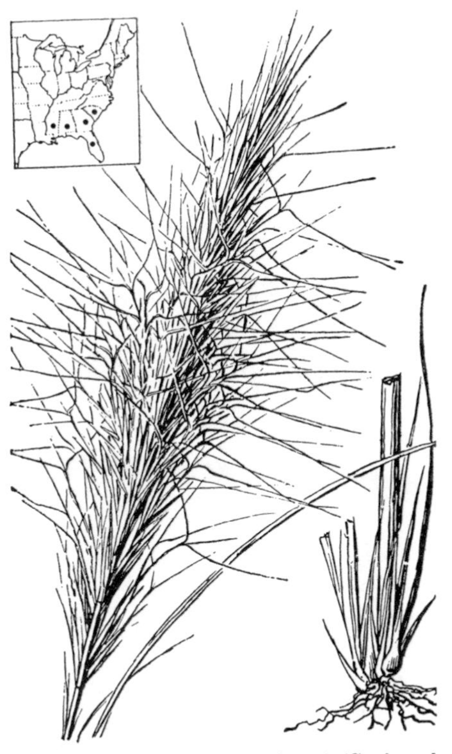

FIGURE 692.—*Aristida spiciformis*, × 1. (Combs and Baker 1115, Fla.)

22. Aristida glaúca (Nees) Walp. REVERCHON THREE-AWN. (Fig. 693.) Perennial; culms erect, 20 to 40 cm. tall; blades involute, mostly curved or flexuous, 5 to 10 cm. long, about 1 mm. thick; panicle narrow, erect, rather few-flowered, mostly 8 to 15 cm. long, the branches stiffly appressed; first glume 5 to 8 mm. long, the second about twice as long; lemma 10 to 12 mm. long, tapering into a minutely scabrous, slender, somewhat twisted beak about half the total length of the lemma; awns equal, divergent or horizontally spreading, 1.5 to 2.5 cm. long. ♃ (*A. reverchoni* Vasey.)—Dry or rocky hills and plains, Texas to Utah, Nevada, and southern California, south to Puebla, Mexico.

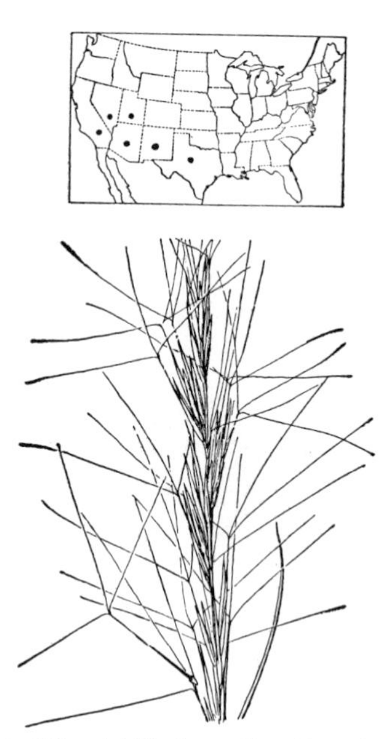

FIGURE 693.—*Aristida glauca*, × 1. (Reverchon 1237, Tex.)

23. Aristida purpúrea Nutt. PURPLE THREE-AWN. (Fig. 694.) Perennial, often in large tufts; culms 30 to 50 cm. tall; blades usually involute and less than 10 cm. long, 1 to 1.5 mm. wide when unrolled; panicle narrow, nodding, rather lax and loose, usually purplish, 10 to 20 cm. long, the branches and longer pedicels capillary, more or less curved or flexuous; first glume 6 to 8 mm. long, the second about twice as long; lemma about 1 cm. long, the body tapering to a scarcely beaked summit, tuberculate-scabrous in lines from below the middle to the summit; awns nearly equal, spreading, 3 to 5 cm. long. ♃ —Dry hills and plains, Arkansas and Kansas to Utah and Texas to southern California; northern Mexico. ARISTIDA PURPUREA var. LAXIFLÓRA Merr. Panicle few-flowered, the capillary branches bearing 1 or 2 spikelets. ♃ —Texas to Arizona.

24. Aristida roemeriána Scheele. (Fig. 695.) Differing from *A. purpurea* chiefly in the smaller spikelets; first glume 4 to 5 mm. long; lemma 7 to 8 mm. long, the awns about 2 cm. long. ♃ (*A. micrantha* Nash.) —Texas, New Mexico, and northern Mexico.

25. Aristida wríghtii Nash. (Fig. 696.) Perennial; culms tufted, erect, 30 to 60 cm. tall; sheaths villous at the throat and with a more or less hispid or villous line across the collar; blades involute, curved or flexuous; panicle erect, narrow, 15 to 20 cm. long; first glume 6 to 7 mm. long, the second about twice as long; lemma 10 to 12 mm. long; awns nearly equal, about 2 cm. long, divergent. ♃ —Dry plains and hills, Oklahoma, Texas, Colorado, and Utah to southern California and central Mexico.

26. Aristida longiséta Steud. RED THREE-AWN. (Fig. 697.) Perennial, often in large bunches; culms 20 to 30 cm. tall; blades involute, curved or flexuous, usually less than 15 cm. long; panicle narrow, erect but not stiff, few-flowered, the axis only a few cm. long, the branches ascending or appressed, or the lower more or less curved or flexuous; first glume 8 to 10 mm. long, the second about twice as long; lemma terete, 12 to 15 mm. long, only slightly narrowed above, glabrous or the upper part scaberulous but scarcely tuberculate-scabrous in lines as in *A. purpurea;* awns about equal, divergent, 6 to 8 cm. long. ♃ —Plains and foothills, North Dakota and Iowa to Montana and British Columbia, south to Texas, Arizona, and northern Mexico. ARISTIDA LONGISETA var. RARIFLÓRA Hitchc. Differing in the few-flowered panicles with capillary flexuous branches bearing 1 or 2 spikelets.

FIGURE 694.—*Aristida purpurea*, × 1. (Bush 665, Tex.)

FIGURE 695.—*Aristida roemeriana*, × 1. (Swallen 1585, Tex.)

FIGURE 696.—*Aristida wrightii*, × 1. (Ball 1511, Tex.)

♃ —Texas to Colorado and Arizona.

ARISTIDA LONGISETA var. ROBÚSTA Merr. Taller and more robust, 30 to 50 cm. tall, the blades longer and not in conspicuous basal tufts, the panicle longer, stiffer, and the branches more stiffly ascending, the awns mostly 4 to 5 cm. long. ♃ —Same range but more common northward, extending east to Minnesota and west to Washington and California.

27. Aristida fendleriána Steud. FENDLER THREE-AWN. (Fig. 698.) Resembling *A. longiseta;* differing in the numerous short curly blades at the base of the plant, the shorter glumes (the first about 7 mm. long), the gradually narrowed lemma, scaberulous on the upper half, and the shorter awns (2 to 5 cm. long). ♃ —Dry plains and hills, North Dakota and Montana, south to Texas, Nevada, and southern California; Mexico.

28. Aristida lanósa Muhl. ex Ell. (Fig. 699.) Perennial; culms solitary or few in a tuft, rather robust, 1 to 1.5 m. tall; sheaths lanate-pubescent or rarely glabrous; blades flat, elon-

FIGURE 697.—*Aristida longiseta*, × 1. (Thompson 63, Kans.)

gate, as much as 4 mm. wide; panicle narrow, rather loose, as much as 40 cm. long; first glume 12 to 14 mm. long, the second about 10 mm.; lemma 8 to 9 mm. long; central awn horizontally spreading or reflexed from a curved base, 1.5 to 3 cm. long, the lateral half to two-thirds as long, erect or spreading. ♃ —Dry sandy soil of the Coastal Plain, New Jersey and West Virginia to Florida and Texas; Tennessee; Oklahoma and Missouri. A slender form 65 cm. tall, with fewer-flowered panicle, the lemma 10 mm. long, the central awn 2.5 to 3 cm. long, has been differentiated as *A. lanosa* var. *macera* Fern. and Grisc. ♃ —Cape Henry, Va.

FIGURE 699.—*Aristida lanosa*, × 1. (Canby, Md.)

FIGURE 698.—*Aristida fendleriana*, × 1. (Coville 1089, Ariz.)

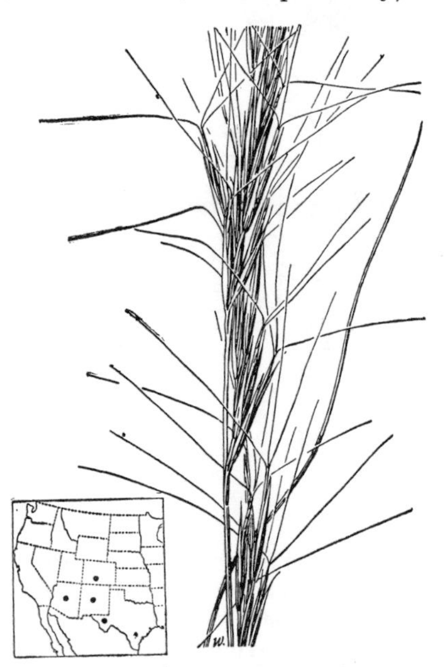

FIGURE 700.—*Aristida arizonica*, × 1. (Rusby, Ariz.)

29. Aristida arizónica Vasey. ARIZONA THREE-AWN. (Fig. 700.) Perennial; culms erect, 30 to 120 cm. tall; blades flat, narrowed to a fine involute point or some of them involute throughout, 1 to 4 mm. wide, the old ones usually curled or flexuous; panicle narrow, erect, closely flowered or more or less interrupted at base, 10 to 25 cm. long; glumes equal or nearly so, awn-pointed, 10 to 15 mm. long; lemma 1 to 1.5 cm. long, including the more or less twisted beak of about 3 to 5 mm.; awns about equal, ascending, 1 to 2 cm. long. ♃ —Dry plains, stony hillsides, and open forest, mostly at 1,500 to 2,500 m. altitude, southern Colorado and western Texas to Arizona.

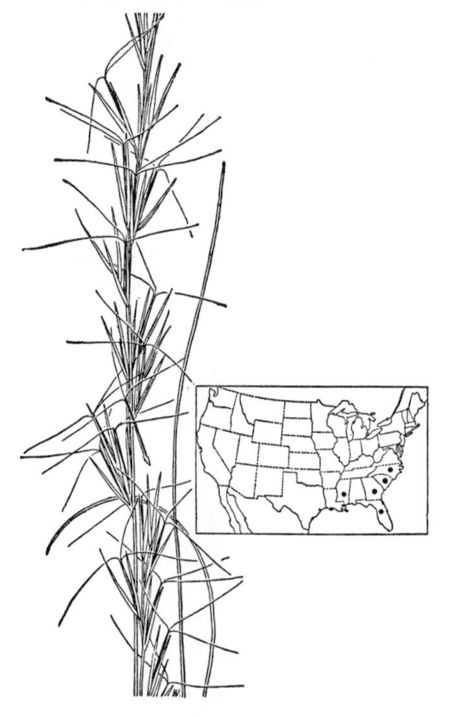

FIGURE 701.—*Aristida stricta*, × 1. (Chase 4565, N. C.)

30. Aristida stricta Michx. PINELAND THREE-AWN. (Fig. 701.) Perennial; culms erect, 50 to 100 cm. tall; blades closely involute, villous on the upper surface above the base (the hairs visible without unrolling the blade), elongate, 1 mm. thick; panicle slender, as much as 30 cm. long; glumes about equal, 7 to 10 mm. long; lemma 6 to 8 mm. long, scarcely beaked; awns divergent, the central 1 to 1.5 cm. long, the lateral a little shorter. ♃ —Common in pine barrens, North Carolina to Florida, west to Mississippi.

31. Aristida rhizomóphora Swallen. (Fig. 702.) Perennial; culms tufted, erect, 65 to 80 cm. tall, producing well-developed scaly rhizomes; blades firm, flat or folded, 7 to 10 cm. long, 1 to 2 mm. wide, those of the innovations flexuous, as much as 30 cm. long; panicle flexuous, 20 to 30 cm. long, the distant branches somewhat spreading, few-flowered, spikelet-bearing from near the base; glumes acuminate, usually awned, the first 8 to 14 mm. long, the second 12 to 17 mm. long (including the awn); lemma 9 to 12 mm. long, the callus 1 mm. long, the awns flexuous, curved or loosely twisted at base, spreading, the central often reflexed by a semicircular bend, 18 to 28 mm. long, the lateral 15 to 20 mm. long. ♃ —Prairies, peninsular Florida.

32. Aristida purpuráscens Poir. ARROWFEATHER. (Fig. 703.) Perennial; culms tufted from a rather thin, weak, sometimes decumbent base, slender, 40 to 70 cm. or even 1 m. tall; blades flat, rather lax and flexuous (especially the old ones), usually less than 2 mm. wide; panicle narrow, rather lax and nodding, one-third to half the entire length of the plant; glumes about equal, mostly 8 to 12 mm. long; lemma about 7 mm. long; awns about equal, divergent or somewhat reflexed, 1.5 to 2.5 cm. long. ♃ —Dry sandy soil, Massachusetts to Wisconsin and Kansas, south to Florida and Texas; British Honduras.

33. Aristida paríshii Hitchc. (Fig. 704.) Perennial; culms erect, 30 to 50 cm. tall; blades more or less involute, sometimes flat, 1 to 2 mm. wide; panicle narrow, 15 to 30 cm. long; glumes short-awned, the first 12 mm. long, the second 1 or 2 mm. longer; lemma about 12 mm. long, tapering into a short, straight or obscurely twisted beak; awns about equal, divergent, about 2.5 cm. long. ♃ —

FIGURE 702.—*Aristida rhizomophora.* Plant, × ½; spikelet, × 2; two views of callus, × 10. (Type.)

Dry or rocky soil, Nevada, Arizona, and southern California.

34. Aristida affínis (Schult.) Kunth. (Fig. 705.) Perennial; culms tufted from a hard thickened base, stiffly erect, rather stout, 1 to 1.5 m. tall; blades flat, becoming loosely involute, elongate, as much as 3 mm. wide; panicle narrow, virgate, as much as 50 cm. long; glumes equal, about 12 mm. long, the first with a distinct nerve on one side (thus 2-nerved); lemma 8 mm. long, the straight beak about 1 mm. long; central awn horizontally spreading, 1.5 to 3 cm. long, the lateral awns erect, two-thirds to three-fourths as long. ♃ (*A. palustris* Vasey.)—Low pine barrens and flatwoods, North Carolina and Kentucky to Florida and Texas, mostly on the Coastal Plain.

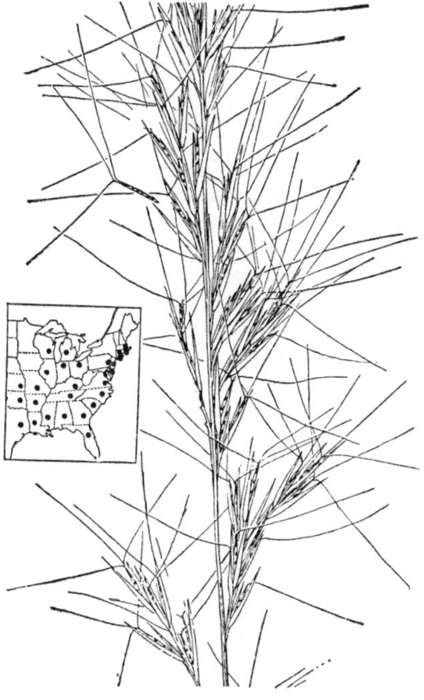

FIGURE 703.—*Aristida purpurascens,* × 1. (Chase 4563, N. C.)

FIGURE 704.—*Aristida parishii*, × 1. (Parish 1029A, Calif.)

35. Aristida virgáta Trin. (Fig. 706.) Perennial; culms tufted from a rather slender soft base, erect, 50 to 80 cm. tall; blades flat, rather lax, usually not more than 2 mm. wide; panicle slender, erect, though not very stiff, rather loosely flowered, one-third to half the entire length of the culm; glumes about equal, 6 to 7 mm. long; lemma 4 to 5 mm. long; central awn horizontally spreading or somewhat reflexed, 1.5 to 2 cm. long, the lateral awns erect, about two-thirds as long as the central. ♃ (*A. chapmaniana* Nash.)—Moist sandy soil of the Coastal Plain, New Jersey to Florida and Texas.

36. Aristida simpliciflóra Chapm. (Fig. 707.) Perennial; culms erect from a rather delicate base, slender, 30 to 60 cm. tall; blades flat, 5 to 15 cm. long, 1 mm. wide; panicle slender, somewhat nodding, 10 to 20 cm. long, few-flowered, the spikelets mostly in pairs; glumes equal, 6 to 7 mm. long; lemma a little shorter than the glumes; central awn finally reflexed by a semicircular bend, 1 to 1.5 cm. long, the lateral awns horizontally spreading, a little shorter than the central one. ♃ —Moist pine woods, rare, western Florida; Mississippi (McNeill).

37. Aristida móhrii Nash. (Fig. 708.) Perennial; culms erect, 40 to 60 cm. tall; blades flat or those of the innovations involute, 10 to 15 cm. long, 1 to 2 mm. wide, the uppermost reduced; panicle slender, strict, as much as 30 cm. long; spikelets solitary, appressed, distant, even the upper not overlapping; glumes equal, firm, rather broad toward the mucronate apex, 1 cm. long; lemma terete, a little shorter than the glumes; awns divergent, the central one reflexed by a semicircular bend near the base, 1.5 to 2 cm. long, the lateral ones scarcely shorter than the central, horizontally spreading or re-

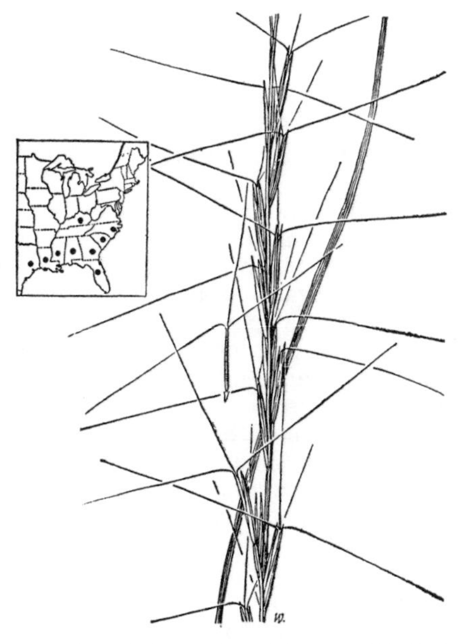

FIGURE 705.—*Aristida affinis*, × 1. (Combs 688, Fla.)

flexed. ♃ —Sterile soil, South Carolina, Florida, and Alabama.

38. Aristida tenuispíca Hitchc. (Fig. 709.) Perennial; culms slender, 60 to 100 cm. tall; blades flat, 10 to 20 cm. long, 1 to 2 mm. wide, bearing scattered long hairs on the upper surface; panicle slender, about half the entire length of the culm; glumes nearly equal, about 8 mm. long; lemma 7 mm. long including a 1-mm. long beak; awns equal, 12 to 15 mm. long, spreading or reflexed, somewhat spirally contorted at base. ♃ —Low pine barrens, peninsular Florida; British Honduras.

39. Aristida condensáta Chapm. (Fig. 710.) Perennial; culms rather robust, a meter or more tall; lower sheaths usually appressed pubescent; blades firm, flat, becoming involute, elongate, 2 to 3 mm. wide; panicle narrow, as much as 30 cm. long, the branches 5 to 12 cm. long, ascending, closely flowered; glumes equal, 8 to 9 mm. long; awns equal, divergent, 10 to 15 mm. long, the base more or less contorted, finally forming a loose spiral. ♃ —Sandy pine or oak barrens, North Carolina, Georgia, Florida, and Alabama, on the Coastal Plain. Specimens with glabrous lower sheaths have been differentiated as *A. condensata* var. *combsii* (Scribn. and Ball) Heur.

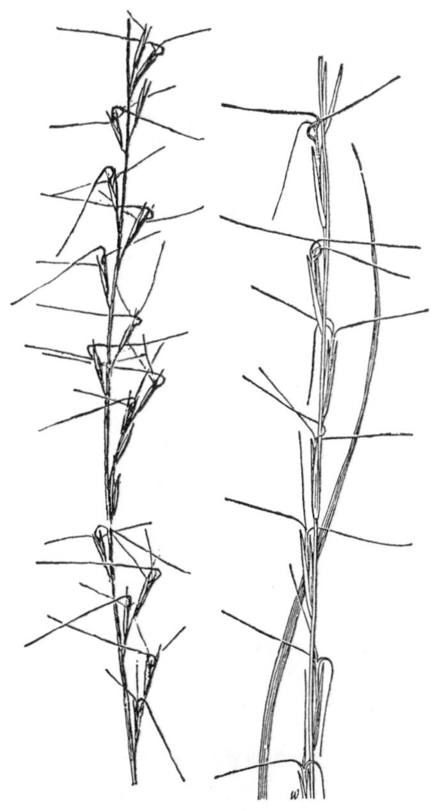

FIGURE 707.—*Aristida simpliciflora*, × 1. (Chapman, Fla.)

FIGURE 708.—*Aristida mohrii*, × 1. (Mohr 53, Ala.)

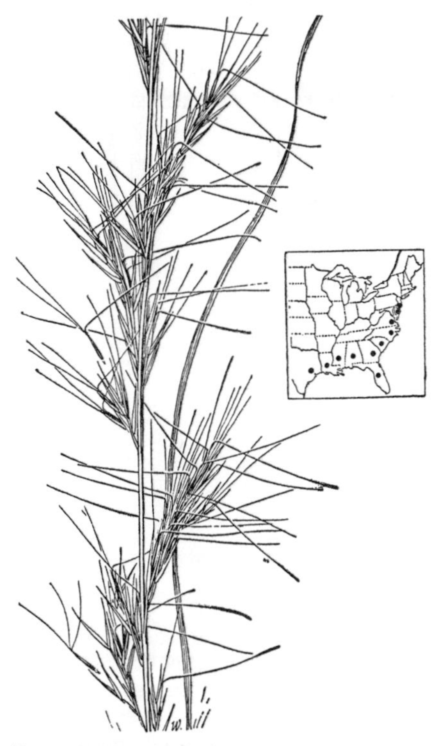

FIGURE 706.—*Aristida virgata*, × 1. (Tracy 4667, Miss.)

40. Aristida gýrans Chapm. (Fig. 711.) Perennial; culms erect, slender, 40 to 70 cm. tall; blades involute, 10 to 15 cm. long, 1 mm. wide; panicle slender, rather lax, 15 to 30 cm. long, the branches appressed, not at all or only slightly overlapping, bearing mostly 1 to 3 spikelets; first glume 7 to 8 mm. long, the second 10 to 11 mm. long; lemma about 6 mm. long, the callus 1.5 mm. long, sharp; awns equal, divergent, 1 to 1.5 cm. long, about equally contorted at base in a loose spiral. ♃ —Dry sandy soil, Georgia and Florida.

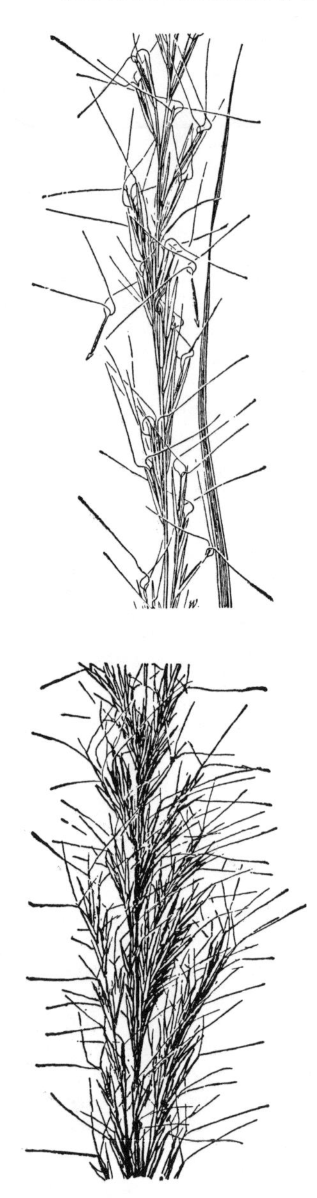

FIGURE 709.—*Aristida tenuispica*, × 1. (Tracy 7104, Fla.)

FIGURE 711.—*Aristida gyrans*, × 1. (Combs 1289, Fla.)

FIGURE 710.—*Aristida condensata*, × 1. (Chapman, Fla.)

TRIBE 6. ZOYSIEAE

93. TRÁGUS Hall.

(*Nazia* Adans.)

Spikelets 1-flowered, in small spikes of 2 to 5, the spikes subsessile, falling entire, the spikelets sessile on a very short zigzag rachis, the first glumes small, thin, or wanting, appressed to the rachis, the second glumes of the 2 lower spikelets strongly convex with 3 thick nerves bearing a row of squarrose, stout hooked prickles along each side, the 2 second glumes forming the halves of a little bur, the upper 1 to 3 spikelets reduced and sterile; lemma and palea thin, the lemma flat, the palea strongly convex. Low annuals, with flat blades and terminal inflorescence, the burs or spikes rather closely arranged along an elongate, slender axis. Type species, *Tragus racemosus*. Name from Greek *tragos*, he-goat, applied by Plinius to a plant.

Spikelets 2 to 3 mm. long, the apex scarcely projecting beyond the spines, the bur nearly sessile........ 1. T. BERTERONIANUS.
Spikelets 4 to 4.5 mm. long, the acuminate apex projecting beyond the spines, the bur pediceled........ 2. T. RACEMOSUS.

1. Tragus berteroniánus Schult. (Fig. 712.) Culms branched at base, spreading, 10 to 40 cm. long; blades firm, mostly less than 5 cm. long, 2 to 4 mm. wide, the cartilaginous margin bearing stiff white hairs or short slender teeth; raceme dense, 4 to 10 cm. long, 4 to 5 mm. thick; burs 2 to 3 mm. long, nearly sessile, the apex scarcely exceeding the spines. ⊙ (The name *Nazia aliena* Scribn. has been erroneously applied to the species.)—Dry open ground, probably introduced, Texas to Arizona, south to Argentina; also in the warmer parts of the Old World; on ballast at Boston and on wool waste in Maine.

FIGURE 712.—*Tragus berteronianus*. Plant, × ½; bur and spikelet, × 5. (Hitchcock 3745, N. Mex.)

FIGURE 713.—*Tragus racemosus*, × 1. (Griffiths 1529, Ariz.)

2. Tragus racemósus (L.) All. (Fig. 713.) Differing from *T. berteronianus* in the larger burs, the spikelets 4 to 4.5 mm. long, in the acuminate apex projecting beyond the spines, and in the pediceled burs. ⊙ (*Nazia racemosa* Kuntze.)—Waste ground and on ballast at a few places from Maine to North Carolina; Texas to Arizona; introduced from the Old World.

ANTHÉPHORA Schreb.

Spikelets with 1 perfect floret and a sterile lemma below, in clusters of 4, the indurate first glumes united at base, forming a pitcher-shaped pseudo-involucre, the clusters subsessile and erect on a slender, flexuous, continuous axis, deciduous at maturity. Type species, *Anthephora elegans* Schreb. (*A. hermaphrodita*). Name from *anthe*, blossom, and *pherein*, to bear.

Anthephora hermaphrodíta (L.) Kuntze. Leafy ascending or decumbent annual; culms mostly 20 to 50 cm. tall; blades flat, thin, 5 to 10 mm. wide; spikes erect, 5 to 10 cm. long; first glume 5 to 7 mm. long, about 9-nerved; second glume narrow, acuminate, shorter than the first, pubescent; sterile lemma 5-nerved, about as long as the fertile floret. ⊙ —Escaped from experiment station plots, Florida (Gainesville); a common weed in tropical America.

94. ZOÝSIA Willd.

(*Osterdamia* Neck.)

Spikelets 1-flowered, laterally compressed, appressed flatwise against the slender rachis, glabrous, disarticulating below the glumes; first glume wanting; second glume coriaceous, mucronate, or short-awned, completely infolding the thin lemma and palea, the palea sometimes obsolete. Low perennials, with creeping rhizomes, short, pungently pointed blades, and terminal spikelike racemes, the spikelets on short appressed pedicels. Type species, *Zoysia pungens* Willd. Named for Karl von Zois.

Several years ago a species of this genus was introduced into the United States as a lawngrass under the names Korean lawngrass and Japanese lawngrass. It was recommended for the Southern States and was said to be hardy as far north as Connecticut. The species then introduced appears to be *Zoysia japonica* Steud. Recently a fine-leaved species, *Zoysia tenuifolia* Willd. ex Trin. (Mascarene grass), has been introduced in Florida and southern California (called in the latter region Korean velvet grass) and has given favorable results. These species may escape from cultivation. The original species, *Z. matrella* (L.) Merr. (*Z. pungens* Willd.), Manila grass (fig. 714.) common in the Philippine Islands, has been used in recent years for lawns from the Gulf States to Long Island, propagated by cuttings. The spikelets are about 2.5 mm. long and 0.8 mm. wide. But little seed is produced. Sometimes called "Flawn."

In *Z. japonica* (Japanese lawngrass) the blades are flat and rather stiff, 2 to 4 mm. wide, the spikelets about 3 mm. long and a little more

FIGURE 714.—*Zoysia matrella.* Plant, × ½; spikelet and floret, × 10. (Whitford 1303, P. I.)

than 1 mm. wide. The rhizomes are underground. In *Z. tenuifolia* the blades are involute-capillary, the spikelets much narrower than in *Z. japonica,* and the stolons are at or near the surface of the soil.

95. HILÃRIA H. B. K.

Spikelets sessile, in groups of 3, the groups falling from the axis entire, the central spikelet (next the axis) fertile, 1-flowered (occasionally 2-flowered), the 2 lateral spikelets staminate, 2-flowered (occasionally 3-flowered); glumes coriaceous, those of the 3 spikelets forming a false involucre, in some species connate at the base, more or less asymmetric, usually bearing an awn on one side from about the middle (extension of the midnerve of the asymmetric glume); lemma and palea hyaline, about equal in length. Perennials, with stiff, solid culms and narrow blades, the groups of spikelets appressed to the axis, in terminal spikes. Type species, *Hilaria cenchroides* H. B. K. Named for Auguste St. Hilaire.

All the species are important range grasses and resist close grazing. Curly mesquite is the dominant "short grass" of the Texas plains. The larger species are well known on the range in the arid and semiarid regions of the Southwest.

Culms white felty-pubescent .... 5. H. RIGIDA.
Culms not felty-pubescent.
  Cluster of spikelets not flabellate; glumes of lateral spikelets narrowed toward summit. 4. H. JAMESII.
  Cluster of spikelets flabellate; glumes (at least the outer one) of lateral spikelets broadest toward summit.
    Glumes subhyaline and fimbriate at summit; plants tufted, not stoloniferous. 3. H. MUTICA.
    Glumes firm, not fimbriate; plants stoloniferous (except in *H. belangeri* var. *longifolia*).
      Glumes of lateral spikelets much shorter than the florets, pale; group of spikelets mostly 5 mm. long .... 1. H. BELANGERI.
      Glumes of lateral spikelets about equaling the florets, blackish; group of spikelets 7 to 8 mm. long .... 2. H. SWALLENI.

1. Hilaria belangéri (Steud.) Nash. CURLY MESQUITE. (Fig. 715.) Plants in tufts, sending out slender stolons, these producing new tufts, the internodes of the stolons wiry, 5 to 20

FIGURE 715.—*Hilaria belangeri*. Plant, × ½; two views of group of spikelets, × 5; fertile spikelet, staminate spikelet, and fertile floret, × 5. (Hitchcock, Tex.)

cm. long; culms erect, slender, 10 to 30 cm. tall, villous at the nodes; blades flat, 1 to 2 mm. wide, scabrous, more or less pilose, usually short, crowded at base, often forming a curly tuft, but sometimes longer and erect; spike usually 2 to 3 cm. long, with mostly 4 to 8 clusters of spikelets, the axis flat, the internodes alternately curved, 3 to 5 mm. long; group of spikelets 5 to 6 mm. long; lateral spikelets attenuate at base, the glumes united below, firm, scabrous, the outer lobe broadened upward, 2- to 3-nerved, the inner much reduced, the midnerve of both glumes extending into short awns, the first glume smaller, the lateral nerves sometimes excurrent into awns or teeth (the glumes variable in a single spike); fertile spikelet usually shorter than the sterile, rounded at base; glumes firm with deeply lobed thinner upper part, the midnerves extending into awns mostly exceeding the staminate spikelets; lemma compressed, narrowed above, awnless ♃ (*H. texana* Nash.)—Mesas and plains, Texas to Arizona and northern Mexico. *H. cenchroides* H. B. K., to which this species has commonly been referred, is confined to Mexico. H. BELANGERI var. LONGIFÓLIA (Vasey) Hitchc. Stolons wanting; blades elongate. ♃ —Arizona and Sonora.

2. Hilaria swálleni Cory. (Fig. 716.) Resembling *H. belangeri*, culms to 35 cm. tall; blades usually 2 mm. wide, scarcely curled; spike 2 to 4.5 cm. long, with 3 to 8 clusters of spikelets, the internodes of the flat axis 4 to 6 mm. long; glumes of lateral spikelets similar, oblong, narrowed at base, about equaling the florets, firm and strongly pigmented except toward the summit, the nerves often rather obscure; awns of all glumes slightly longer than those of the preceding; fertile spikelet about equaling the sterile, the fertile floret slightly larger than in *H. belangeri*. ♃ —Mesas and rocky plains, western Texas and northern Mexico. Said to be better forage than *H. belangeri*.

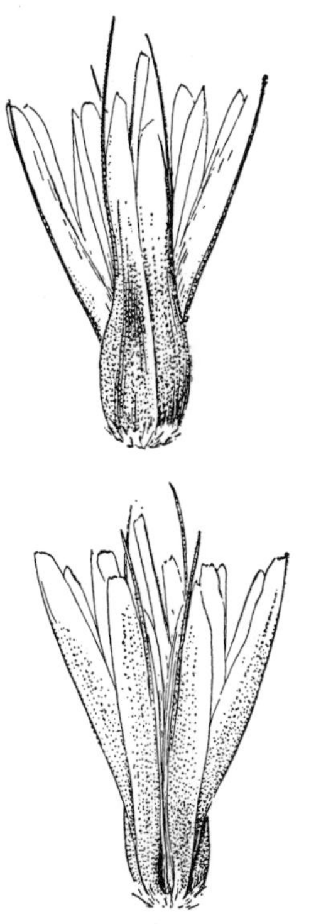

FIGURE 716.—*Hilaria swalleni*. Two views of group of spikelets, × 5. (Young 46, Tex.)

FIGURE 717.—*Hilaria mutica*, × 1. (Toumey, Ariz.)

3. Hilaria mútica (Buckl.) Benth. TOBOSA GRASS. (Fig. 717.) Culms from a tough rhizomatous base, 30

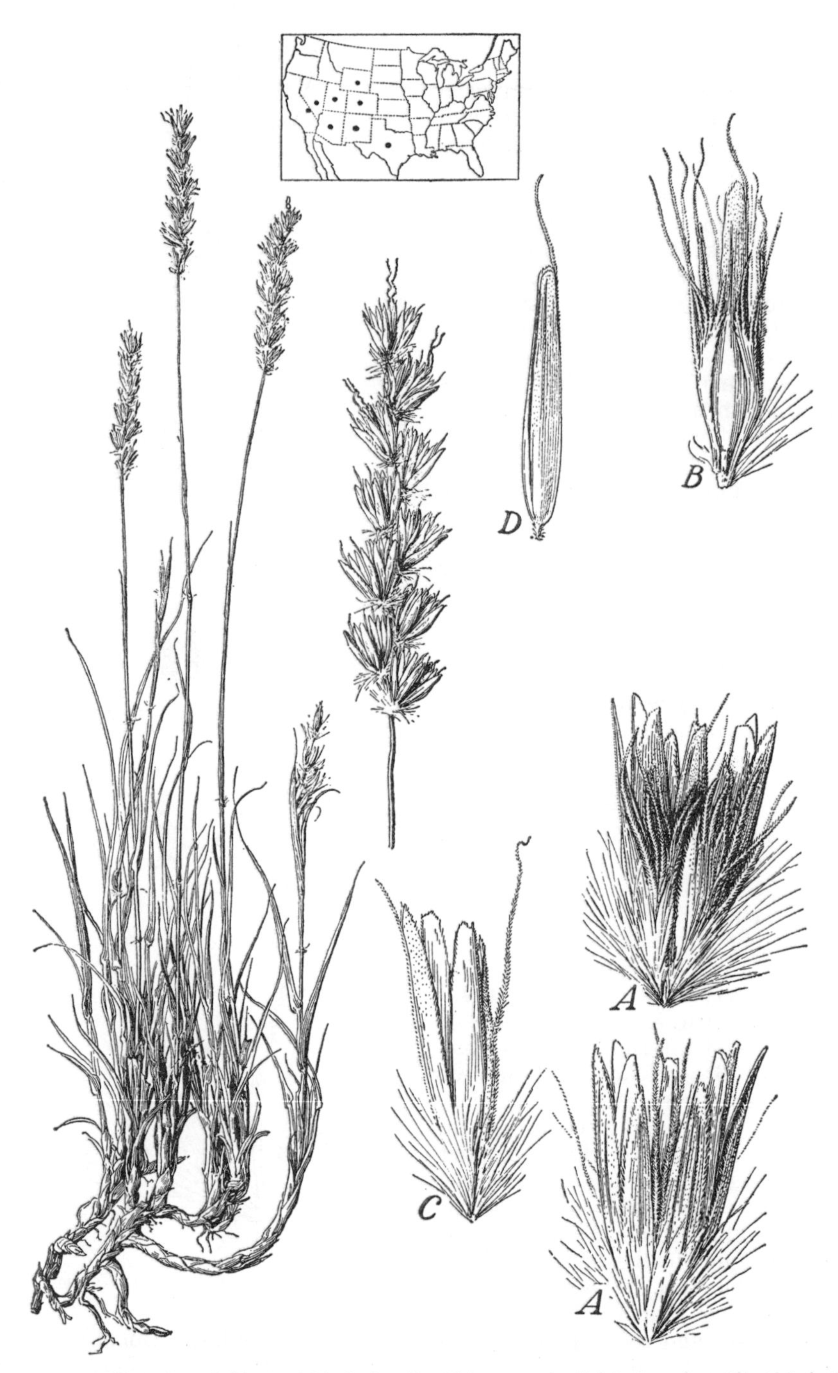

FIGURE 718.—*Hilaria jamesii*. Plant, × ½; single spike, × 1; group of spikelets, two views (*A*), × 5; fertile spikelet (*B*), staminate spikelet (*C*), and fertile floret (*D*), × 5. (Tidestrom 1449, Utah.)

to 60 cm. tall, glabrous, the nodes pubescent; blades flat or somewhat involute, rather rigid, 2 to 3 mm. wide; spikes 4 to 6 cm. long; group of spikelets about 7 mm. long; bearded at base; glumes of lateral spikelets very unsymmetrical, widened toward the ciliate summit, the nerves flabellate, not excurrent or barely so; fertile spikelet about equaling the lateral ones, its glumes strongly keeled, cleft into few to several narrow ciliate lobes and slender awns; lemma exceeding the glumes, mucronate between 2 rounded lobes. ♃ (*Pleuraphis mutica* Buckl.)—Dry plains and hills, Texas to Arizona and northern Mexico.

4. Hilaria jamésii (Torr.) Benth. GALLETA. (Fig. 718.) Plants erect, the base often decumbent or rhizomatous, bearing also tough scaly rhizomes; culms glabrous, the nodes villous; sheaths glabrous or slightly scabrous, sparingly villous around the short membranaceous ligule; blades mostly 2 to 5 cm. long, 2 to 4 mm. wide, rigid, soon involute, the upper reduced; group of spikelets 6 to 8 mm. long, long-villous at base, similar to those of *H. rigida,* but the glumes of lateral spikelets acute, usually with a single awn; lemma of the fertile spikelet exceeding its glumes. ♃ (*Pleuraphis jamesii* Torr.)—Deserts, canyons, and dry plains, Wyoming and Utah to Texas and Inyo County, Calif.

5. Hilaria rígida (Thurb.) Benth. ex Scribn. BIG GALLETA. (Fig. 719.) Plants rather robust at base, branching, the branches mostly erect or ascending, the base rather woody, decumbent or rhizomatous; culms numerous, rigid, felty-pubescent, glabrate and scabrous above, 50 to 100 cm. tall; leaves felty or glabrous, usually woolly at the top of the sheath; blades spreading, 2 to 5 cm. long, or longer on sterile shoots, 2 to 4 mm. wide, more or less involute, acuminate into a rigid coriaceous point; group of spikelets about 8 mm. long, densely bearded at base; glumes of lateral spikelets thin, long-ciliate, about 7-nerved, usually 2- to 4-lobed at the broad summit and with 1 to 3 nerves excurrent into slender awns, nerves sometimes obscure and scarcely excurrent (variable in a single spike); fertile spikelet about equaling the lateral ones, its narrow glumes deeply cleft into few to several acuminate ciliate lobes and slender awns; lemma scarcely exceeding the glumes, thin, ciliate, 2-lobed, the midnerve excurrent into a short awn. ♃ (*Pleuraphis rigida* Thurb.)—Deserts, southern Utah and Nevada to Arizona, southern California, and Sonora.

FIGURE 719.—*Hilaria rigida,* × 1. (Palmer 494, Utah.)

96. AEGOPÓGON Humb. and Bonpl. ex Willd.

Spikelets on short flat pedicels, in groups of 3, the group short-pedunculate, spreading, the peduncle disarticulating from the axis and forming a pointed stipe below the group, this falling entire; central spikelet shorter pedicellate, fertile, the two lateral ones longer pedicellate and staminate or neuter; glumes membranaceous, notched at the apex, the

FIGURE 720.—*Aegopogon tenellus*. Plant, × ½; group of spikelets, × 5; lateral spikelets and central spikelet, × 10. (Pringle 1407, Mexico.)

midnerve extending into a delicate awn; lemma and palea thinner than the glumes, extending beyond them, the lemma 3-nerved, the central nerve and sometimes also the lateral ones extending into awns, the palea 2-awned. Low, lax annuals, with short, narrow, flat blades and loose racemes of delicate groups of spikelets. Type species, *Aegopogon cenchroides* Humb. and Bonpl. Name from Greek *aix*, goat, and *pogon*, beard, alluding to the fascicle of awns of the spikelets.

1. Aegopogon tenéllus (DC.) Trin. (Fig. 720.) Culms 10 to 20 cm. long, usually spreading or decumbent; blades 1 to 2 mm. wide; racemes 3 to 5 cm. long; spikelets, excluding awns, about 2 mm. long; lemma and palea of lateral spikelets broad and rounded at summit with a single delicate awn, those of the fertile spikelet narrower, with one long and 2 short awns. ☉ —Open ground, mountains of southern Arizona, south to northern South America. Lateral spikelets sometimes reduced or rudimentary (var. *abortivus* (Fourn.) Beetle), but such spikelets and also central spikelets with reduced awns are found in plants with normal spikelets.

TRIBE 7. CHLORIDEAE

97. LEPTÓCHLOA Beauv. SPRANGLETOP

Spikelets 2- to several-flowered, sessile or short-pediceled, approximate or somewhat distant along one side of a slender rachis, the rachilla disarticulating above the glumes and between the florets; glumes unequal or nearly equal, awnless or mucronate, 1-nerved, usually shorter than the first lemma; lemmas obtuse or acute, sometimes 2-toothed and mucronate or short-awned from between the teeth, 3-nerved, the nerves sometimes pubescent. Annuals or perennials, with flat blades and numerous usually slender spikes or racemes borne on a common axis forming a long or sometimes short panicle. Type species, *Leptochloa virgata.* Name from Greek *leptos,* slender, and *chloa,* grass, alluding to the slender spikes.

The only species of *Leptochloa* important as a forage grass is *L. dubia,* or sprangletop, of the Southwest, useful for grazing and for hay.

Plants perennial.
  Lemmas broad, notched at apex, the lateral nerves glabrous........................ 1. L. DUBIA.
  Lemmas acute or awned, the lateral nerves pubescent.
    Lemmas about 3 mm. long; panicle flabellate, the axis short.... 2. L. CHLORIDIFORMIS.
    Lemmas about 1.5 mm. long; panicle oblong, the axis relatively long.
      Sheaths and blades glabrous; lemmas awnless or nearly so................ 3. L. VIRGATA.
      Sheaths and blades sparsely pilose; lemmas awned..................... 4. L. DOMINGENSIS.
Plants annual.
  Sheaths papillose-pilose; first floret not longer than the second glume; spikelets mostly 1 to 2 mm. long.. 5. L. FILIFORMIS.
  Sheaths smooth or scabrous, not pilose; spikelets more than 2 mm. long.
    Lemmas awned, awns sometimes minute. Culms freely branching.
      Lemmas viscid on the back; panicle oval, usually less than 10 cm. long, the longer branches usually less than 5 cm. long; second glume 1.5 mm. long. 6. L. VISCIDA.
      Lemmas not viscid; panicle more than 10 cm. long, the longer branches usually as much as 10 cm. long; second glume 3 mm. long................ 7. L. FASCICULARIS.
    Lemmas awnless or mucronate only.
      Lemmas obtuse, sometimes mucronate.
        Spikelets 5 to 7 mm. long, 6- to 9-flowered, lead color.............. 8. L. UNINERVIA.
        Spikelets 2 to 3 mm. long, 3- to 4-flowered, pale.......................... 9. L. NEALLEYI.
      Lemmas acuminate.
        Sheaths scabrous, keeled and compressed... 10. L. SCABRA.
        Sheaths smooth or slightly scabrous near apex, scarcely keeled or compressed. 11. L. PANICOIDES.

1. Leptochloa dúbia (H. B. K.) Nees. GREEN SPRANGLETOP. (Fig. 721.) Perennial; culms wiry, erect, 50 to 100 cm. tall; sheaths glabrous; blades flat or sometimes folded or loosely involute, scabrous, as much as 1 cm. wide, usually narrower; panicle of few to many spreading or ascending racemes 3 to 12 cm. long, approximate or somewhat distant on an axis as much as 15 cm. long; spikelets 5- to 8-flowered (or in reduced specimens only 2-flowered), 5 to 10 mm. long; lemmas broad, glabrous on the internerves, obtuse or emarginate, the midnerve sometimes extending into a short point, the florets at maturity widely spreading, very different in appearance from their early phase. ♃ —Rocky hills and canyons and sandy soil, southern Florida; Oklahoma and Texas to Arizona, south through Mexico; Ar-

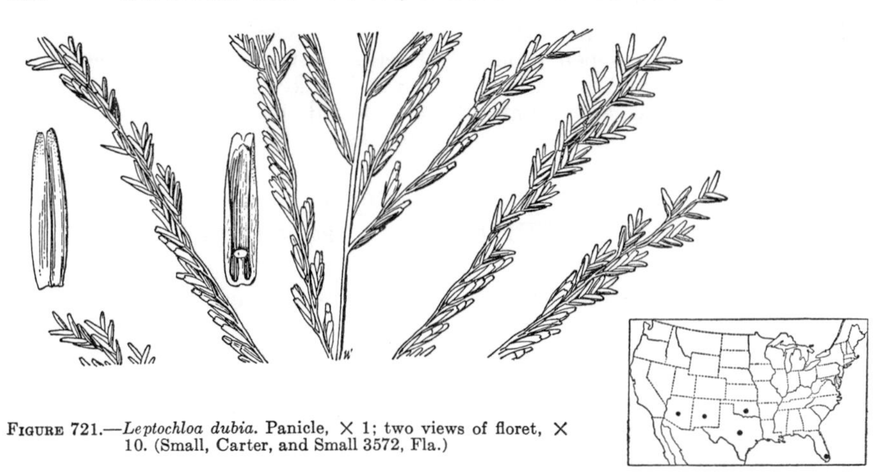

FIGURE 721.—*Leptochloa dubia*. Panicle, × 1; two views of floret, × 10. (Small, Carter, and Small 3572, Fla.)

gentina. Racemes of cleistogamous spikelets are often found in the sheaths.

2. Leptochloa chloridifórmis (Hack.) Parodi. (Fig. 722.) Robust tufted perennial, somewhat glaucous; culms erect, 80 to 150 cm. tall; sheaths scaberulous; ligule a dense line of white hairs, 1 to 2 mm. long; blades erect, elongate, flat, rather firm, 3 to 4 mm. wide, villous on the upper surface near the base, the margins scabrous, long-attenuate; panicle long-exserted; spikes numerous (usually 10 to 15), pale or stramineous, erect at base, flabellate or outcurved above, 10 to 15 cm. long, aggregate in 2 or 3 whorls on an axis 3 to 4 cm. long; spikelets closely imbricate on a rachis 0.5 mm. wide, 4-flowered, about 4 mm. long; glumes acute, the first 1.5 mm. long, the second 2.5 to 3 mm. long; lemmas keeled, pilose on the margins nearly to apex, the midnerve extending beyond the obtuse tip as a minute mucro, the first and second florets about 3 mm. long, the other shorter, not extending much beyond the first two. ♃ —Dry open ground, Cameron County, Tex.; Paraguay and Argentina.

3. Leptochloa virgáta (L.) Beauv. (Fig. 723.) Perennial; culms wiry, erect, 50 to 100 cm. tall; blades flat; racemes several to many, slender, laxly ascending, 5 to 10 cm. long, the lower distant, the others often aggregate; spikelets nearly sessile, mostly 3- to 5-flowered; lemmas 1.5 to 2 mm. long, awnless or the lower with a short awn. ♃ —Open ground and grassy slopes, southern Florida and southern Texas; tropical America.

4. Leptochloa domingénsis (Jacq.) Trin. (Fig. 724.) Resembling *L. virgata;* sheaths and blades sparsely pilose; panicle more elongate, the racemes shorter and more numerous; lemmas appressed-pubescent on the internerves, awned, the awn of the lower florets 1 to 3 mm. long. ♃ —Open ground and grassy slopes, southern Florida; Texas; tropical America.

5. Leptochloa filifórmis (Lam.) Beauv. RED SPRANGLETOP. (Fig. 725.) Annual; the foliage and panicles often reddish or purple; culms erect or branching and geniculate below, 40 to 70 cm. tall, or often dwarf; sheaths papillose-pilose, sometimes sparsely so; blades flat, thin, as much as 1 cm. wide; panicle somewhat viscid, of numerous approximate slender racemes 5 to 15 cm. long, on an axis mostly about half the entire length of the culm; spikelets 3- to 4-flowered, 1 to 2 mm. long, rather distant on the rachis; glumes acuminate, longer than the first floret, often as long as the spikelet; lemmas awnless, pubescent on the nerves, 1.5 mm. long. ☉

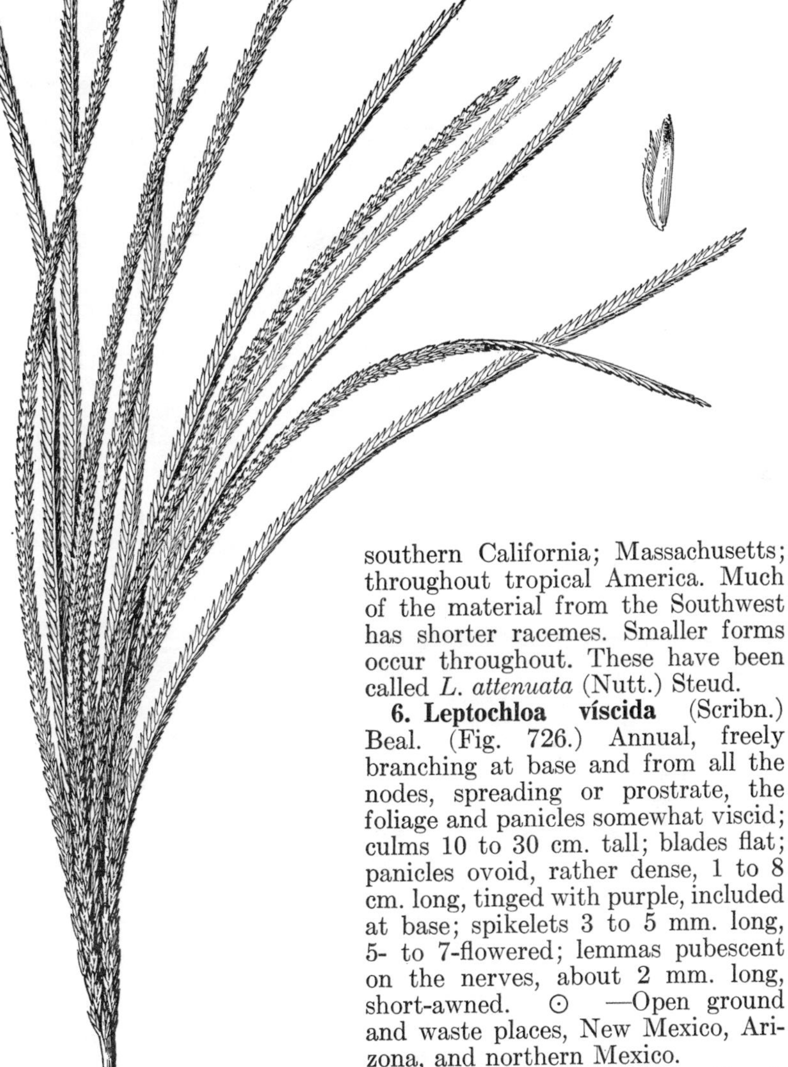

FIGURE 722.—*Leptochloa chloridiformis*. Panicle, × 1; floret, × 10. (Silveus 622, Tex.)

(*L. mucronata* Kunth.)—Open or shady ground, a common weed in gardens and fields, Virginia to southern Indiana and eastern Kansas, south to Florida and Texas, west to southern California; Massachusetts; throughout tropical America. Much of the material from the Southwest has shorter racemes. Smaller forms occur throughout. These have been called *L. attenuata* (Nutt.) Steud.

6. Leptochloa víscida (Scribn.) Beal. (Fig. 726.) Annual, freely branching at base and from all the nodes, spreading or prostrate, the foliage and panicles somewhat viscid; culms 10 to 30 cm. tall; blades flat; panicles ovoid, rather dense, 1 to 8 cm. long, tinged with purple, included at base; spikelets 3 to 5 mm. long, 5- to 7-flowered; lemmas pubescent on the nerves, about 2 mm. long, short-awned. ⊙ —Open ground and waste places, New Mexico, Arizona, and northern Mexico.

7. Leptochloa fasciculáris (Lam). A. Gray. (Fig. 727.) Annual, somewhat succulent; culms erect to spreading or prostrate, freely branching, 30 to 100 cm. tall; blades flat to loosely involute; panicles more or less included, mostly 10 to 20 cm. long, often smaller, occasionally longer, the racemes several to numerous, as much

FIGURE 723.—*Leptochloa virgata*. Panicle, × 1; floret, × 10. (Wilson 9402, Cuba.)

as 10 cm. long, usually ascending or appressed, or at maturity spreading; spikelets usually overlapping, 7 to 12 mm. long, 6- to 12-flowered; lemmas 4 to 5 mm. long, the lateral nerves pubescent below, acuminate, the awn from short to as long as the body. ⊙ (*Diplachne fascicularis* Beauv.) —Brackish marshes along the coast, New Hampshire and New York to Florida and Texas and in alkali flats, ditches, and marshes, Ohio to North Dakota; Washington and Colorado to New Mexico, Arizona, and California; south through tropical America to Argentina. A prostrate form has been called *Diplachne procumbens* (Muhl.) Nash and *D. maritima* Bickn.

8. Leptochloa uninérvia (Presl) Hitchc. and Chase. (Fig. 728.) Resembling *L. fascicularis*, rather sparingly branching, usually strictly erect, the panicle more oblong in outline, with shorter, denser-flowered racemes; spikelets 5 to 7 mm. long, 6- to 9-flowered, lead-color; glumes broader, more obtuse; lemmas scarcely narrowed toward tip, apiculate but not awned, the lateral nerves more or less excurrent. ⊙ (*L. imbricata* Thurb.)—Ditches and moist places, North Carolina; Mississippi to Texas; Colorado and New Mexico to Oregon and California, south to Mexico; Peru to Argentina; introduced in Maine, Massachusetts, and New Jersey.

FIGURE 724.—*Leptochloa domingensis*. Panicle, × 1; floret, × 10. (Hitchcock 10055, Trinidad.)

9. Leptochloa nealléyi Vasey. (Fig. 729.) Annual, usually erect and rather robust; culms mostly 1 to 1.5 m. tall, simple or sparingly branching at base; sheaths glabrous or slightly scabrous, mostly keeled; blades elongate, flat to loosely involute; panicle commonly 25

FIGURE 725.—*Leptochloa filiformis*. Plant, × ½; spikelet and floret, × 10. (Ruth 51, Tenn.)

FIGURE 726.—*Leptochloa viscida*. Panicle, × 1; floret, × 10. (Mearns 833, Ariz.)

to 50 cm. long, not more than 4 cm. wide, the racemes subverticillate, overlapping, 2 to 4 cm. long, appressed or ascending; spikelets crowded, 3- or 4-flowered, 2 to 3 mm. long; lemmas about 1.5 mm. long, obtuse, the nerves sparingly pubescent, the lateral close to the margin. ⊙ —Marshes, mostly near the coast, Louisiana (Cameron) and Texas; also eastern Mexico.

10. Leptochloa scábra Nees. (Fig. 730.) Annual; culms erect, about 1 m. tall, somewhat robust and succulent, sparingly branching; sheaths and blades scabrous, the blades elongate, 8 to 12 mm. wide; panicle 20 to 40 cm. long, not more than 7 cm. wide, usually less, the slender racemes crowded, 4 to 8 cm. long, ascending or somewhat drooping, usually curved or flexuous; spikelets crowded, mostly 3-flowered, about 3 mm. long; lemmas acute, awnless, the nerves pubescent. ⊙ —Marshes and ditches, Louisiana (near New Orleans) and tropical America.

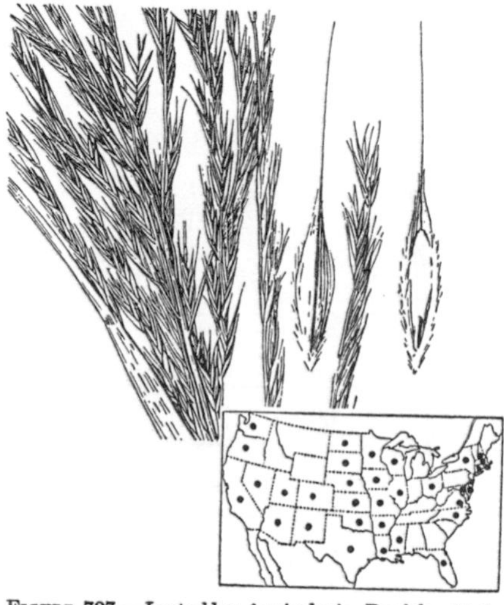

FIGURE 727.—*Leptochloa fascicularis*. Panicle, × 1; two views of floret, × 10. (Hitchcock 7876, Md.)

11. Leptochloa panicoídes (Presl) Hitchc. (Fig. 731.) Annual; culms erect or spreading, 50 to 100 cm. tall, branching; sheaths glabrous; blades thin, 5 to 10 mm. wide, scaberulous; panicle oblong, 10 to 20 cm. long, 3 to 5 cm. wide, the racemes approximate, 3 to 5 cm. long, ascending, rather lax; spikelets 5- to 7-flowered, 4 to 5 mm. long; lemmas 2.5 mm. long, apiculate, the lateral nerves minutely pubescent at base. ⊙ (*L. floribunda* Doell.)—Indiana (Posey County) and Missouri to Mississippi (Holmes County), Arkansas, and Texas; Brazil.

FIGURE 728.—*Leptochloa uninervia*. Panicle, × 1; two views of floret, × 10. (Tharp 3123, Tex.)

98. TRICHONEŬRA Anderss.

Spikelets few-flowered, the rachilla disarticulating above the glumes, the internodes pilose at base, disarticulating near their summit, the upper part forming a short callus below the floret; glumes about equal, 1-nerved, long-acuminate, mostly as long as the spikelet or longer; lemmas bidentate, 3-nerved, the lateral nerves near the margin, the midnerve usually excurrent as a short awn, the margins long-ciliate; palea broad, the nerves near the margin. Annuals or perennials with simple panicles, the spikelets short-pediceled along one side of the main branches. Type species, *Trichoneura hookeri* Anderss. Name from Greek *thrix*, hair, and *neuron*, nerve, alluding to the ciliate nerves of the lemma.

FIGURE 729.—*Leptochloa nealleyi*. Panicle, × 1; two views of floret, × 10. (Fisher 25, Tex.)

1. Trichoneura élegans Swallen. (Fig. 732.) Annual, branching at base; culms erect, rather robust, or ascending, 40 to 110 cm. tall, several-noded; sheaths scaberulous; blades flat, or subinvolute toward the tip, scabrous, elongate, 3 to 7 mm. wide; panicle erect, 10 to 18 cm. long, the axis angled, scabrous; branches numerous, stiffly ascending, the lower 5 to 8 cm. long, rather densely flowered; spikelets mostly 5- to 8-flowered, 9 to 10 mm. long; glumes about equaling the spikelet, the setaceous tips slightly

FIGURE 730.—*Leptochloa scabra*. Panicle, × 1; two views of floret, × 10. (Tracy 8388, La.)

spreading; lemmas scaberulous toward the obtuse minutely lobed summit, the awn minute, the margins conspicuously ciliate on the lower half to two-thirds, the hairs as much as 1 mm. long. ⊙ —Sandy soil, southern Texas.

99. TRIPÓGON Roth

Spikelets several-flowered, subsessile, appressed in 2 rows along one

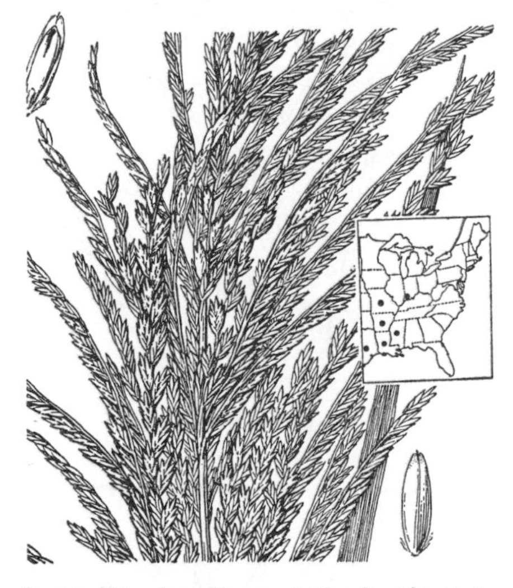

FIGURE 731.—*Leptochloa panicoides*. Panicle, × 1; two views of floret, × 10. (Tracy 7451, Miss.)

FIGURE 732.—*Trichoneura elegans*. Plant, × 1; spikelet and floret, × 10. (Type.)

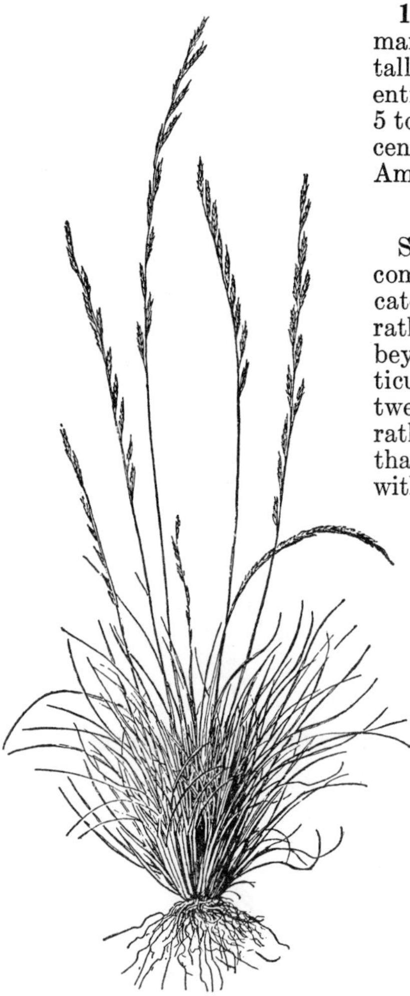

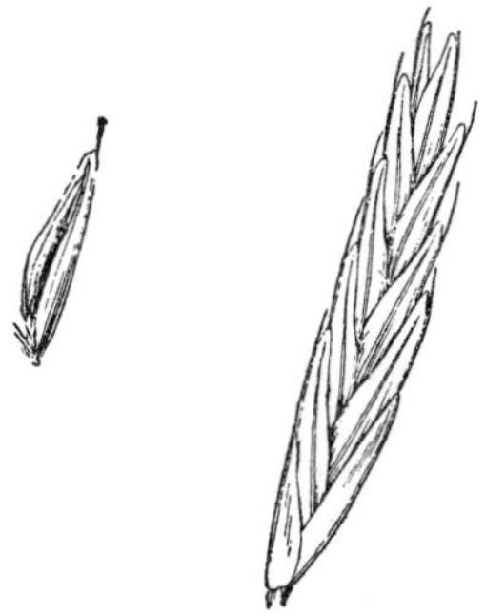

side of a slender rachis, the rachilla disarticulating above the glumes and between the florets; glumes somewhat unequal, acute or acuminate, narrow, 1-nerved; lemmas narrow, 3-nerved, bearing at base a tuft of long hairs, the apex bifid, the midnerve extending as a short awn. Our species a low, tufted perennial, with capillary blades and slender solitary spikes, the spikelets somewhat distant. Type species, *Tripogon bromoides* Roth. Name from Greek *treis*, three, and *pogon*, beard, alluding to the hairs at the base of the three nerves of the lemma.

1. Tripogon spicátus (Nees) Ekman. (Fig. 733.) Culms 10 to 20 cm. tall; spike from one-fourth to half the entire height of the plant; spikelets 5 to 8 mm. long. ♃ —Rocky hills, central Texas, Mexico; Cuba; South America.

FIGURE 733.—*Tripogon spicatus*. Plant, × ½; spikelet and floret, × 5. (Nealley 78, Tex.)

100. ELEUSÍNE Gaertn.

Spikelets few to several-flowered, compressed, sessile and closely imbricate, in 2 rows along one side of a rather broad rachis, not prolonged beyond the spikelets; rachilla disarticulating above the glumes and between the florets; glumes unequal, rather broad, acute, 1-nerved, shorter than the first lemma; lemmas acute, with 3 strong green nerves close together, forming a keel, the uppermost somewhat reduced; seed dark brown, roughened by fine ridges, loosely enclosed in the thin pericarp. Annuals, with 2 to several rather stout spikes, digitate at the summit of the culms, sometimes with 1 or 2 a short distance below, or rarely with a single spike. Type species, *Eleusine coracana*. Name from Eleusis, the town where Demeter was worshipped.

1. Eleusine índica (L.) Gaertn. GOOSEGRASS. (Fig. 734.) Branching at base, ascending to prostrate, very smooth; culms compressed, usually

FIGURE 734.—*Eleusine indica.* Plant, × ½; spikelet, floret, and seed (without pericarp), × 5. (Fredholm 5331, Fla.)

less than 50 cm. long, but sometimes as much as 1 m.; blades flat or folded, 3 to 8 mm. wide; spikes mostly 2 to 6, rarely more, or but 1 in depauperate plants, flat, 4 to 15 cm. long. ☉ —Waste places, fields, and open ground, Massachusetts to South Dakota and Kansas, south to Florida and Texas; occasional in Oregon, Utah, Arizona, and California; introduced; a common weed in the warmer regions of both hemispheres.

Eleusine tristáchya (Lam.) Lam. Spikes 1 to 3, rarely more, 1 to 2.5 cm. long, 8 to 10 mm. thick; resembling *E. indica*, but the spikes short and thick. ☉ —On ballast, Camden, N. J. and Mobile, Ala.; Portland, Oreg. and elsewhere; tropical Africa; introduced in tropical South America.

Eleusine coracána (L.) Gaertn. African millet. More robust than *E. indica;* spikes thicker, heavier, sometimes incurved at the tip, brownish at maturity. A cultivated form of *E. indica*; the seed used for food among primitive peoples in Africa and southern Asia. ☉ —Occasionally grown at experiment stations. Called also ragi, coracan millet, and finger millet.

101. DACTYLOCTÉNIUM Willd.

Spikelets 3- to 5-flowered, compressed, sessile and closely imbricate, in two rows along one side of the rather narrow flat rachis, the end projecting in a point beyond the spikelets; rachilla disarticulating above the first glume and between the florets; glumes somewhat unequal, broad, 1-nerved, the first persistent upon the rachis, the second mucronate or short-awned below the tip, deciduous; lemmas firm, broad, keeled, acuminate or short-awned, 3-nerved, the lateral nerves indistinct, the upper floret reduced; palea about as long as the lemma; seed subglobose, ridged or wrinkled, enclosed in a thin, early-disappearing pericarp. Annuals or perennials with flat blades and 2 to several short thick spikes, digitate and widely spreading at the summit of the culms. Type species, *Dactyloctenium aegyptium.* Name from Greek *daktulos*, finger, and *ktenion,* a little comb, alluding to the pectinate arrangement of the spikelets.

1. Dactyloctenium aegýptium (L.) Beauv. (Fig. 735.) Culms compressed, spreading with ascending ends, rooting at the nodes, branching, commonly forming radiate mats, usually 20 to 40 cm. long, sometimes as much as 1 m.; blades flat, ciliate; spikes 1 to 5 cm. long. ☉ —Open ground, waste places, and fields, Coastal Plain, North Carolina to Florida and Texas; also occasional at more northern points (Maine to New Jersey; Illinois); Colorado, Arizona, and California; tropical America; introduced from Old World Tropics.

102. MICROCHLÓA R. Br.

Spikelets 1-flowered, awnless, sessile in 2 rows along one side of a narrow flattened rachis, the rachilla disarticulating above the glumes; glumes subequal, longer than the floret, acute, 1-nerved; floret with a soft, pointed callus; lemma thin, 3-nerved, flabellate; palea narrow, a little shorter than the lemma. Slender perennials with simple culms and slender solitary falcate spikes. Type species, *Microchloa setacea* R. Br. Name from the Greek *micros*, small, and *chloe*, grass.

1. Microchloa kúnthii Desv. (Fig. 736.) Perennial; culms very slender, erect in small dense tufts, 10 to 30 cm. tall; sheaths, except the lowermost, much shorter than the internodes, scaberulous; ligule ciliate, 1 to 1.5 mm. long; blades firm, flat or usually folded, with thick white scabrous margins, those of the culm 1 to 2.5 cm. long, those of the innovations to 6 cm. long, 1 to 1.5 mm. wide; spike 6 to 15 cm. long, falcate, the rachis ciliate; spikelets 2.5 to 3.5 mm. long; lemma 2 to 2.5 mm. long, pilose on the midnerve, the margins densely ciliate with hairs about 1 mm. long. ♃ —Granitic outcrop on rocky slope, Carr Canyon, Huachuca Mountains,

FIGURE 735.—*Dactyloctenium aegyptium*. Plant, × ½; spikelet, floret, and seed (without pericarp), × 5. (Small and Heller 378, N. C.)

southern Arizona; Mexico and Guatemala.

103. CÝNODON L. Rich.

(*Capriola* Adans.)

Spikelets 1-flowered, awnless, sessile in 2 rows along one side of a slender continuous rachis and appressed to it, the rachilla disarticulating above the glumes and prolonged behind the palea as a slender naked bristle, sometimes bearing a rudimentary lemma; glumes narrow, acuminate, 1-nerved, about equal, shorter than the floret; lemma firm, strongly compressed, pubescent on the keel, 3-nerved, the lateral nerves close to the margins. Perennial, usually low grasses, with creeping stolons or rhizomes, short blades, and several slender spikes digitate at the summit of the upright culms. Type species, *Cynodon dactylon.* Name from *kuon* (*kun-*), dog, and *odous*, tooth, alluding to the sharp hard scales of the rhizome.

1. Cynodon dáctylon (L.) Pers. BERMUDA GRASS. (Fig. 737.) Extensively creeping by scaly rhizomes or by strong flat stolons, the old bladeless sheaths of the stolon and the lowest one of the branches often forming conspicuous pairs of "dog's teeth"; flowering culms flattened, usually erect or ascending, 10 to 40 cm. tall; ligule a conspicuous ring of white hairs; blades flat, glabrous or pilose on the upper surface, those of the innovations often conspicuously distichous; spikes usually 4 or 5, 2.5 to 5 cm. long; spikelets imbricate, 2 mm. long, the lemma boat-shaped, acute. ♃ (*Capriola dactylon* Kuntze.)—Open ground, grassland, fields, and waste places, common, Maryland to Oklahoma, south to Florida and Texas, west to California; also occasional north of this region (Massachusetts to Michigan, Oregon); warm regions of both hemispheres, introduced in America. Bermuda grass is the most important pasture grass of the Southern States, and is also widely utilized there as a lawngrass. On alluvial ground it may grow sufficiently rank to be cut for hay. It propagates readily by its rhizomes and stolons, and on this account may become a troublesome weed in cultivated fields. This grass is known also as wire-grass (especially the weedy form in fields). A more robust form,

FIGURE 736.—*Microchloa kunthii.* Plant, × ½. (Conzatti 3605, Mexico.)

found along the seacoast of Florida, has been called *C. maritimus* H. B. K., though the type of that (from Peru) is characteristic *C. dactylon.* There are large areas of Bermuda grass around the Roosevelt Dam,

FIGURE 737.—*Cynodon dactylon.* Plant, × ½; spikelet and two views of floret, × 5. (Kearney, Tenn.)

Ariz., where it survives submergence and furnishes grazing at low water.

CYNODON TRANSVAALÉNSIS Davy. Extensively creeping with fine foliage, the blades rarely more than 1 mm. wide; spikes mostly 2 or 3, the spikelets a little narrower and the glumes shorter than in *C. dactylon.* ♃ —Coming into cultivation as a lawngrass, escaped, Ames, Iowa, and Bard, Calif. Introduced from South Africa.

104. WILLKÓMMIA Hack.

Spikelets 1-flowered, dorsally compressed, sessile in 2 rows on one side of a slender rachis and appressed to it, the rachilla somewhat lengthened below and above the second glume, disarticulating just above it, not prolonged above the floret; glumes thin, unequal, the first narrow, nerveless, the second 1-nerved; lemma awnless, 3-nerved, the lateral nerves near the margin, the back of the lemma sparingly pubescent between the nerves, the margins densely covered with silky hairs; nerves of the palea densely silky hairy. Annuals or perennials, with several short spikes racemose on a slender axis; our species a low tufted perennial. Type species, *Willkommia sarmentosa* Hack. Named for H. M. Willkomm.

1. Willkommia texána Hitchc. (Fig. 738.) Culms erect to spreading, 20 to 40 cm. tall; blades flat or more or less involute, short; spikes few to several, 2 to 5 cm. long, somewhat overlapping or the lower distant, appressed, the axis 4 to 15 cm. long; spikelets about 4 mm. long, narrow, acute; first glume about two-thirds as long as the second, obtuse; second glume subacute; lemma about as long as the second glume. ♃ — Spots of hardpan, central and southern Texas. A stoloniferous form has been found in Argentina.

105. SCHEDONNÁRDUS Steud.

Spikelets 1-flowered, sessile and somewhat distant in 2 rows on one side of a slender, continuous 3-angled rachis, appressed to its slightly concave sides, the rachilla disarticulating above the glumes, not prolonged; glumes narrow, stiff, somewhat unequal, acuminate, 1-nerved; lemmas narrow, acuminate, a little longer than the glumes, 3-nerved. Low,

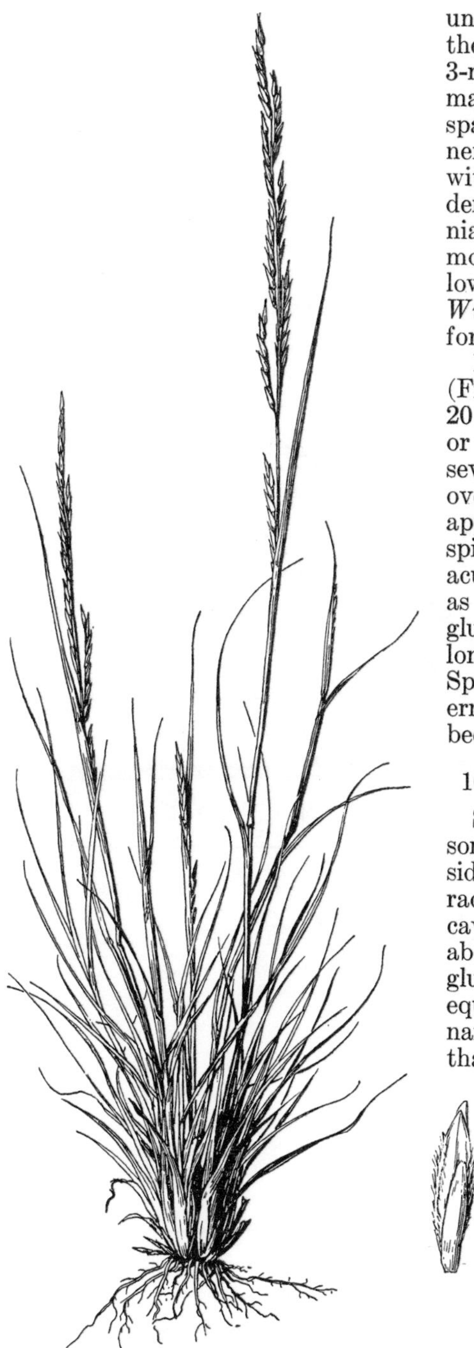

FIGURE 738.—*Willkommia texana*. Plant, × ½; two views of spikelet and floret, × 5. (Tracy 8903, Tex.)

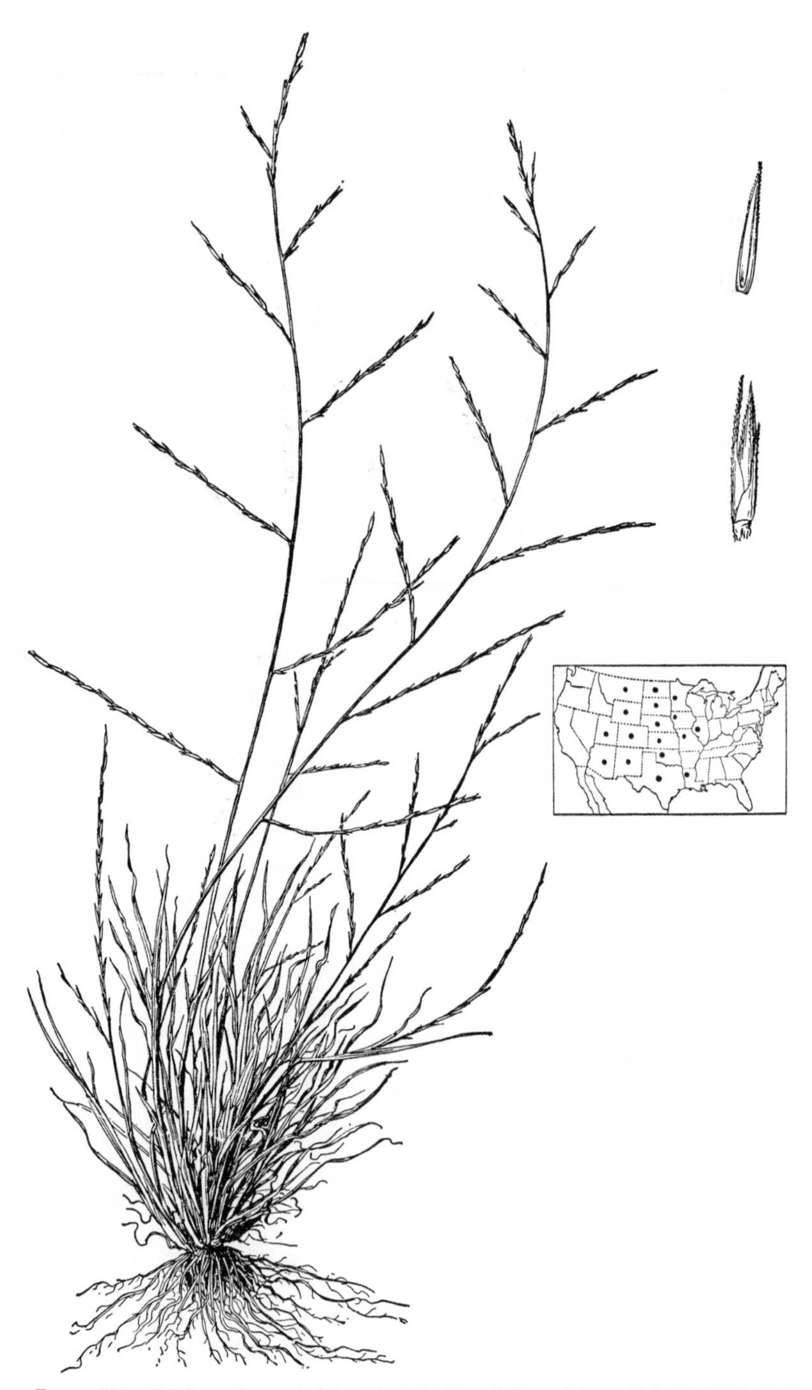

FIGURE 739.—*Schedonnardus paniculatus*. Plant, × ½; spikelet and floret, × 5. (Hall 797, Tex.)

FIGURE 740.—*Beckmannia syzigachne.* Plant, × ½; spikelet and floret, × 5. (Hitchcock 4668, Alaska.)

tufted perennial, with stiff, slender, divergent spikes rather remote along a common axis. Type species, *Schedonnardus texanus* Steud. (*S. paniculatus*). Name from Greek *schedon*, near, and *Nardus*, a genus of grasses (Steudel places *Schedonnardus* next to *Nardus* in his classification).

1. Schedonnardus paniculátus (Nutt.) Trel. TUMBLEGRASS. (Fig. 739.) Culms 20 to 40 cm. tall; leaves crowded at the base; blades flat, mostly 2 to 5 cm. long, about 1 mm. wide, wavy; spikes 2 to 10 cm. long; spikelets narrow, acuminate, about 4 mm. long. The axis of the inflorescence elongates after flowering, becoming 30 to 60 cm. long, curved in a loose spiral; the whole breaks away at maturity and rolls before the wind as a tumbleweed. ♃ —Prairies and plains, Illinois to Saskatchewan and Montana, south to Louisiana and Arizona; Argentina. This species forms an inconsiderable part of the forage on the Great Plains.

106. BECKMÁNNIA Host
SLOUGHGRASS

Spikelets 1- or 2-flowered, laterally compressed, subcircular, nearly sessile and closely imbricate, in 2 rows along one side of a slender continuous rachis, disarticulating below the glumes, falling entire; glumes equal, inflated, obovate, 3-nerved, rounded above but the apex apiculate; lemma narrow, 5-nerved, acuminate, about as long as the glumes; palea nearly as long as the lemma. Erect, rather stout annuals with flat blades and numerous short appressed or ascending spikes in a narrow more or less interrupted panicle. Type species, *Beckmannia erucaeformis* (L.) Host, to which our species was formerly referred. Named for Johann Beckmann.

1. Beckmannia syzigáchne (Steud.) Fernald. AMERICAN SLOUGHGRASS. (Fig. 740.) Light green; culms 30 to 100 cm. tall; panicle 10 to 25 cm. long, the erect branches 1 to 5 cm. long; spikes crowded, 1 to 2 cm. long; spikelets 1-flowered, 3 mm. long; glumes transversely wrinkled and with a deep keel, the acuminate apex of the lemma protruding. ⊙ —Marshes and ditches, Manitoba to Alaska; New York and Ohio to the Pacific coast, south to Kansas and New Mexico; Asia. The European *B. erucaeformis* (L.) Host has 2-flowered spikelets. Our species is palatable to stock, sometimes sufficiently abundant locally to be an important forage grass, and is frequently cut for hay.

107. SPARTÍNA Schreb. CORDGRASS

Spikelets 1-flowered, much flattened laterally, sessile and usually closely imbricate on one side of a continuous rachis, disarticulating below the glumes, the rachilla not produced beyond the floret; glumes keeled, 1-nerved, or the second with a second nerve on one side, acute or short-awned, the first shorter, the second often exceeding the lemma; lemma firm, keeled, the lateral nerves obscure, narrowed to a rather obtuse point; palea 2-nerved, keeled and flattened, the keel between or at one side of the nerves. Erect, often stout tall perennials, with usually extensively creeping, firm, scaly rhizomes (wanting in *Spartina spartinae*, *S. bakeri*, and sometimes in *S. caespitosa*), long tough blades, and 2 to many appressed or sometimes spreading spikes racemose on the main axis, the slender tips of the rachises naked, often prolonged. Type species, *Spartina schreberi* Gmel. Name from Greek *spartine*, a cord made from *spartes* (*Spartium junceum*), probably applied to *Spartina* because of the tough leaves.

The species with rhizomes often form extensive colonies to the exclusion of other plants. They are important soil binders and soil builders in coastal and interior marshes. A European species, *S. townsendi* H. and J. Groves, has in recent years assumed much importance, especially in southern England, the Netherlands, and northern France, as a soil builder along the coast where it is reclaiming extensive areas of marsh land. The marsh hay of the Atlantic coast, much used for packing and formerly for bedding, often consists largely of *S. patens*.

Blades usually more than 5 mm. wide, flat when fresh, at least at base, the tip involute; plants mostly robust and more than 1 m. tall.
  First glume nearly as long as the floret, slender-acuminate, the second with an awn as much as 7 mm. long; spikes somewhat distant, mostly more or less spreading. 1. S. PECTINATA.
  First glume shorter than the floret, acute, the second acute or mucronate but not slender-awned; spikes approximate, usually appressed.
    Blades very scabrous on the margins; glumes strongly hispid-scabrous on the keels. 2. S. CYNOSUROIDES.
    Blades glabrous throughout or minutely scabrous on the margins; glumes glabrous or usually softly hispidulous or ciliate on the keels.
      Inflorescence dense and spikelike, the spikes closely imbricate; the spikelets mostly somewhat curved, giving a slightly twisted effect; blades mostly comparatively short .... 3. S. FOLIOSA.
      Inflorescence less dense, the spikes more slender, less crowded, the spikelets not curved, the inflorescence with no suggestion of a twist ...... 4. S. ALTERNIFLORA.
Blades less than 5 mm. wide (rarely more in *S. gracilis*); involute (sometimes flat in *S. gracilis*); plants mostly slender and less than 1 m. tall (taller in *S. bakeri*).
  Inflorescence dense, cylindric; spikes numerous .... 5. S. SPARTINAE.
  Inflorescence not cylindric; spikes not more than 10, usually fewer.
    Creeping rhizomes absent (see also *S. caespitosa*); plants in large hard tufts with culms 1.5 to 2 m. tall and long slender blades .... 6. S. BAKERI.
    Creeping rhizomes present (except occasionally in *S. caespitosa*); plants usually less than 1 m. tall.
      Second glume 12 to 16 mm. long, aristate .... 7. S. CAESPITOSA.
      Second glume less than 10 mm. long, acute.
        Blades usually flat; glumes conspicuously hispid-ciliate on the keels; spikes several, appressed .... 8. S. GRACILIS.
        Blades usually involute; glumes scabrous on the keels; spikes few, ascending to spreading .... 9. S. PATENS.

1. Spartina pectináta Link. PRAIRIE CORDGRASS. (Fig. 741.) Culms 1 to 2 m. tall, firm or wiry; blades elongate, flat when fresh, soon involute in drying, as much as 1.5 cm. wide, very scabrous on the margins; spikes mostly 10 to 20, sometimes fewer or as many as 30, mostly 4 to 8 cm. long, ascending, sometimes appressed, rarely spreading, on rather slender peduncles; glumes hispid-scabrous on the keel, the first acuminate or short-awned, nearly as long as the floret, the second exceeding the floret, tapering into an awn as much as 7 mm. long; lemma glabrous except the scabrous keel, 7 to 9 mm. long, the apex with 2 rounded teeth; palea usually a little longer than the lemma. ♃ (*S. michauxiana* Hitchc.)—Fresh-water marshes, Newfoundland and Quebec to eastern Washington and Oregon, south to North Carolina, Arkansas, Texas, and New Mexico; in the Eastern States extending into brackish marshes along the coast.

2. Spartina cynosuroídes (L.) Roth. BIG CORDGRASS. (Fig. 742.) Culms 1 to 3 m. tall, stout, the base sometimes as much as 2 cm. thick; blades flat, 1 to 2.5 cm. wide, very scabrous on the margins; spikes numerous, ascending, approximate, often dark-colored, usually more or less peduncled, mostly 3 to 8 cm. long; spikelets about 12 mm. long; glumes acute, hispid-scabrous on the keel, the first much shorter than the floret, the second longer than the floret, sometimes rather long-acuminate; lemma not toothed at apex; palea a little longer than the lemma. ♃ (*S. polystachya* (Michx.) Beauv. (*S. cynosuroides* var. *polystachya* Beal) has been differentiated on its strictly maritime habitat, but morphological

FIGURE 741.—*Spartina pectinata*. Plant, × ½; spikelet and floret, × 5. (Worthern, Mass.)

characters are not coordinated with habitat.)—Salt or brackish marshes along the coast, and margins of tidal streams, Massachusetts to Florida and Texas.

3. Spartina foliósa Trin. (Fig. 743.) Culms 30 to 120 cm. tall, stout, as much as 1 cm. thick at base, somewhat spongy, usually rooting at the lower nodes; blades 8 to 12 mm. wide at the flat base, gradually narrowed to a long involute tip, smooth throughout; inflorescence dense, spikelike, about 15 cm. long; spikes numerous, approximate, closely appressed, 3 to 5 cm. long; spikelets very flat, 9 to 12 mm. long, occasionally longer; glumes firm, glabrous or hispid-ciliate on the keel, acute, the first narrow, half to two-thirds as long as the second, smooth, the second sparingly hispidulous and striate-nerved; lemma hispidulous on the sides, mostly smooth on the keel, shorter than the second glume; palea thin, longer than the lemma. ♃ (*S. leiantha* Benth.) —Salt marshes along the coast from San Francisco Bay, Calif., to Baja California.

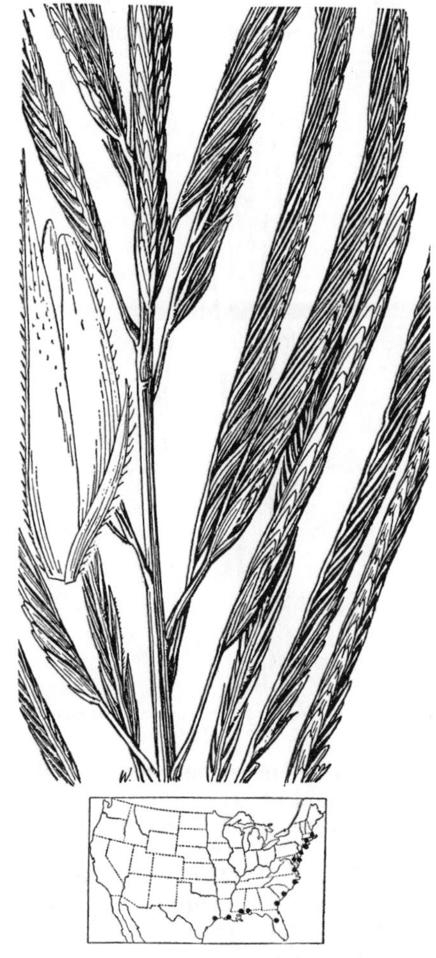

FIGURE 742.—*Spartina cynosuroides*. Panicle, × 1; spikelet, × 5. (Boettcher 444, Va.)

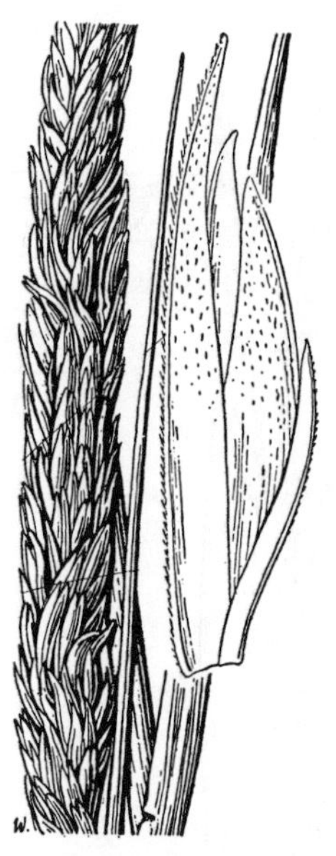

FIGURE 743.—*Spartina foliosa*. Panicle, × 1; spikelet × 5. (Heller 13871, Calif.)

4. Spartina alterniflóra Loisel. SMOOTH CORDGRASS. (Fig. 744.) Smooth throughout or the margins of the blades minutely scabrous, 0.5 to 2.5 m. tall; culms soft and spongy or succulent at base, often 1 cm. or more thick; blades flat, tapering to a long involute tip, 0.5 to 1.5 cm. wide; spikes appressed, 5 to 15 cm. long; spikelets somewhat remote, barely overlapping or sometimes more imbricate, mostly 10 to 11 mm. long; glumes glabrous or hispid on the keel, the first acute, narrow, shorter than the lemma, the second obtusish,

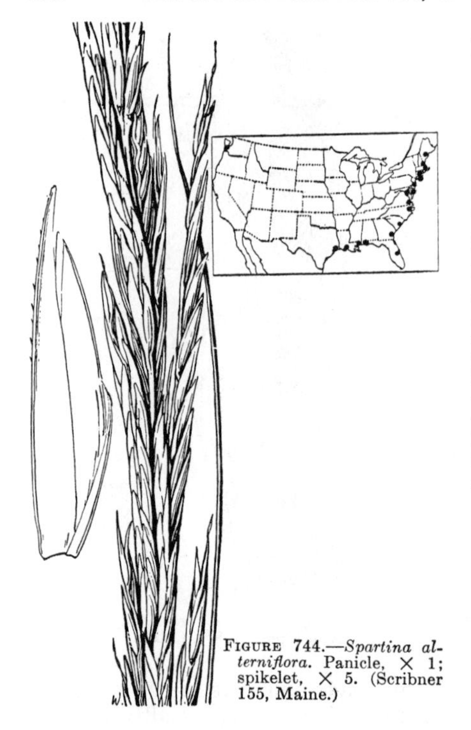

FIGURE 744.—*Spartina alterniflora.* Panicle, × 1; spikelet, × 5. (Scribner 155, Maine.)

a little longer than the lemma; floret sparingly pilose or glabrous. ♃ —Salt marshes along the coast, often growing in the water, Quebec and Newfoundland to Florida and Texas; recently introduced in oyster culture, Pacific County, Wash., and spreading; Atlantic coast of Europe. Through the southern part of the range of the species the spikelets are often more imbricate. The imbricate form with glabrous spikelets has been differentiated as *S. alterniflora* var. *glabra* (Muhl.) Fernald; that with sparsely pilose spikelets as *S. alterniflora* var. *pilosa* (Merr.) Fernald.

5. Spartina spartínae (Trin.) Merr. (Fig. 745.) In large dense tufts without rhizomes; culms stout, 1 to 2 m. tall; blades narrow, firm, strongly involute; spikes short and appressed, closely imbricate, forming a dense cylindric inflorescence 10 to 30 cm. long; spikelets closely imbricate, 6 to 8 mm. long; glumes hispid-ciliate on the keel, the first shorter than the lemma, the second usually a little longer. ♃ (*S. junciformis* Engelm. and Gray.)—Marshes, swamps, and moist prairies near the coast, Florida to Texas and eastern Mexico.

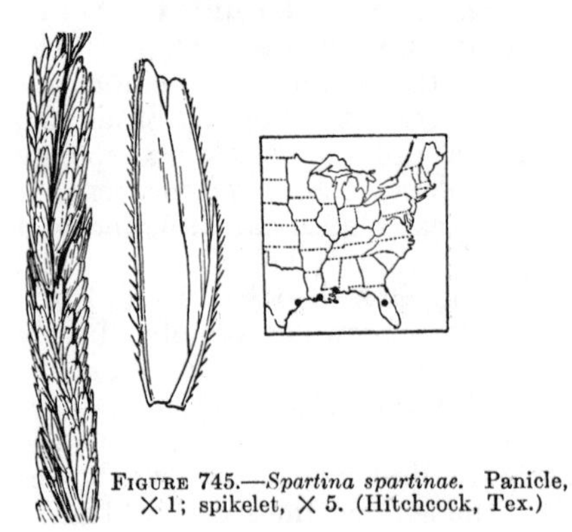

FIGURE 745.—*Spartina spartinae.* Panicle, × 1; spikelet, × 5. (Hitchcock, Tex.)

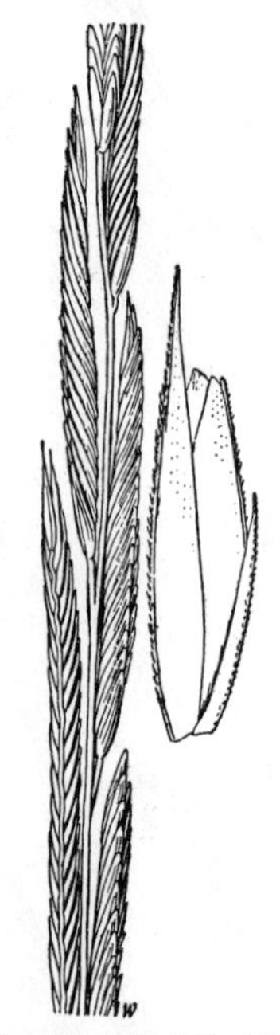

FIGURE 746.—*Spartina bakeri.* Panicle, × 1; spikelet, × 5. (Type.)

6. Spartina bakéri Merr. (Fig. 746.) In large dense tufts without rhizomes; culms stout, 1 to 2 m. tall; blades 4 to 8 mm. wide, involute or occasionally flat; inflorescence 12 to 18 cm. long, the spikes 5 to 12, 3 to 6 cm. long, appressed; spikelets closely appressed, 6 to 8 mm. long; glumes scabrous, hispid-ciliate on the keel, the first about half as long as the lemma, the second longer, acuminate. ♃ —Sandy soil, South Carolina, Georgia, and Florida.

7. Spartina caespitósa A. A. Eaton. (Fig. 747.) Culms 70 to 100 cm. tall, erect, from coarse widely spreading rhizomes or tufted, the rhizomes nearly wanting; blades 10 to 40 cm. long, 3 to 7 mm. wide, flat or becoming involute, scabrous on the upper surface and margins; spikes 2 to 7, 3 to 9 cm. long, finally spreading, rather distant; glumes acuminate, aristate, conspicuously hispid-ciliate on the keels, the second 12 to 16 mm. long; lemma about 8 mm. long, minutely lobed. ♃ —Salt marshes near the coast, New Hampshire to Maryland.

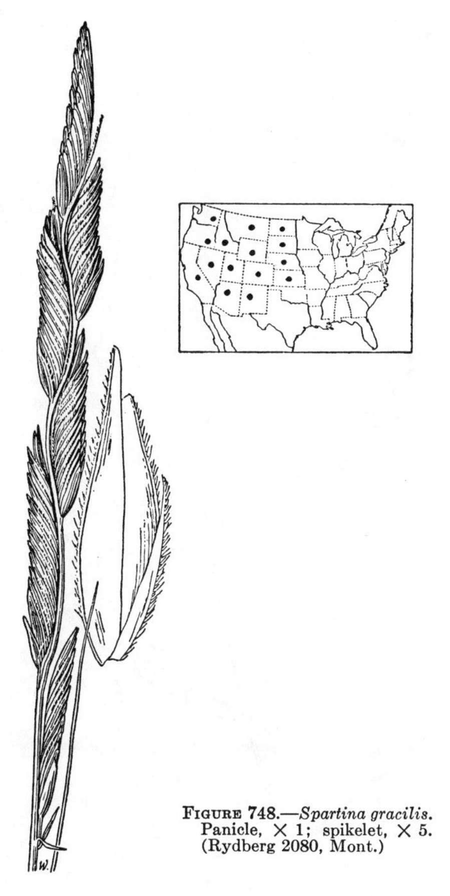

Figure 748.—*Spartina gracilis*. Panicle, × 1; spikelet, × 5. (Rydberg 2080, Mont.)

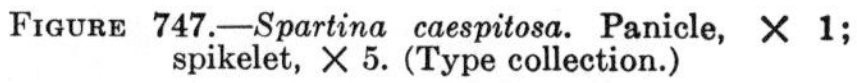

Figure 747.—*Spartina caespitosa*. Panicle, × 1; spikelet, × 5. (Type collection.)

8. Spartina grácilis Trin. Alkali cordgrass. (Fig. 748.) Culms 60 to 100 cm. tall; blades flat, becoming involute, 15 to 20 cm. long, very scabrous above, mostly less than 5 mm. wide; spikes 4 to 8, closely appressed, 2 to 4 cm. long; spikelets 6 to 8 mm. long; glumes ciliate on the keel, acute, the first about half as long as the second; lemma nearly as long as second glume, ciliate on the keel; palea as long as lemma, obtuse. ♃ —Alkaline meadows and plains, Saskatchewan to British Columbia, south to Kansas and New Mexico,

and through eastern Washington to Arizona.

9. Spartina pâtens (Ait.) Muhl. SALTMEADOW CORDGRASS. (Fig. 749.) Culms slender, mostly less than 1 m. tall, with long slender rhizomes; blades sometimes flat but mostly involute, less than 3 mm. wide; spikes 2 to several, appressed to somewhat spreading, 2 to 5 cm. long, rather remote on the axis; spikelets 8 to 12 mm. long; first glume about half as long as the floret, the second longer than the lemma; lemma 5 to 7 mm. long, emarginate at apex; palea a little longer than the lemma. ♃ —Salt marshes and sandy meadows along the coast, Quebec to Florida and Texas, and in saline marshes inland, New York and Michigan. SPARTINA PATENS var. MONÓGYNA (M. A. Curtis) Fernald. Often taller and coarser, commonly with 4 to 8 spikes, the spikelets slightly smaller and more closely imbricate. Intermediate specimens rather frequent. ♃ (*S. juncea* Willd., *S. patens* var. *juncea* Hitchc.)—Along the coast, New Jersey to Texas.

FIGURE 749.—*Spartina patens*. Panicle, × 1; spikelet, × 5. (Killip 6359, Md.)

108. CTÉNIUM Panzer

(*Campulosus* Desv.)

Spikelets several-flowered but with only 1 perfect floret, sessile and pectinately arranged on one side of a continuous rachis, the rachilla disarticulating above the glumes; first glume small, hyaline, 1-nerved, the second about as long as the lemmas, firm, 3- to 4-nerved, bearing on the back a strong divergent awn; lemmas rather papery, 3-nerved, with long hairs on the lateral nerves and a short straight or curved awn on the back just below the apex, the first and second lemmas empty, the third enclosing a perfect flower, the upper 1 to 3 empty and successively smaller. Erect, slender, rather tall perennials, with usually solitary, often curved spikes. Type species, *Ctenium carolinianum* Panzer. (*C. aromaticum*). Name from Greek *ktenion*, a little comb, alluding to the pectinate arrangement of the spikelets.

Plants forming dense tussocks; second glume with a row of prominent glands on each side of the midnerve; awn stout, at maturity horizontal or nearly so; ligule about 1 mm. long. 1. C. AROMATICUM.

Plants with slender scaly rhizomes; second glume glandless or with obscure glands; awn rather slender, not horizontally spreading; ligule 2 to 3 mm. long.... 2. C. FLORIDANUM.

FIGURE 750.—*Ctenium aromaticum*. Plant, × ½; spikelet and fertile floret, × 5. (McCarthy, N. C.)

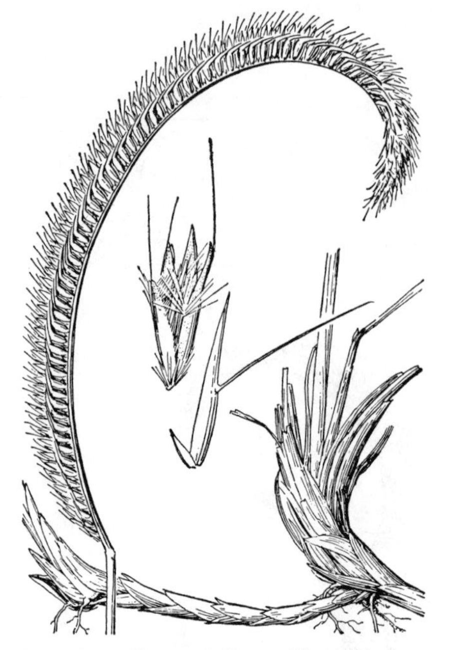

FIGURE 751.—*Ctenium floridanum.* Plant, × 1; glumes and florets, × 5. (Combs 702a, Fla.)

1. Ctenium aromáticum (Walt.) Wood. TOOTHACHE GRASS. (Fig. 750.) Culms 1 to 1.5 m. tall, the old sheaths persistent and fibrillose at base; ligule about 1 mm. long; blades flat or involute, stiff; spike 5 to 15 cm. long; spikelets 5 to 7 mm. long. ♃ (*Ctenium carolinianum* Panzer.)—Wet pine barrens, Coastal Plain, Virginia to Florida and Louisiana. The roots spicy when freshly dug. Furnishes fair cattle forage in moist pine barrens of Florida.

2. Ctenium floridánum (Hitchc.) Hitchc. (Fig. 751.) Differs from *C. aromaticum* in having creeping scaly rhizomes, ligule 2 to 3 mm. long, second glumes with longer, more slender awns and without glands or with only obscure ones. ♃ (Erroneously referred by American authors to *Campulosus chapadensis* Trin.)—Moist pine barrens, Florida.

109. GYMNOPÓGON Beauv.

Spikelets 1- or rarely 2- or 3-flowered, nearly sessile, appressed and usually remote in 2 rows along one side of a slender continuous rachis, the rachilla disarticulating above the glumes and prolonged behind the 1 or more fertile florets as a slender stipe, bearing a rudiment of a floret, this sometimes with 1 or 2 slender awns; glumes narrow, acuminate, 1-nerved, usually longer than the floret; lemmas narrow, 3-nerved, the lateral nerves near the margin, the apex minutely bifid, bearing between the teeth a slender awn, rarely awnless. Perennials or rarely annuals (ours perennial), with short, stiff, flat blades, often folded in drying, numerous long slender divergent or reflexed spikes, approximate on a slender stiff axis. Type species, *Gymnopogon racemosus* Beauv. (*G. ambiguus*). Name from Greek *gumnos*, naked, and *pogon*, beard, alluding to the naked prolongation of the rachilla.

Awn 4 to 6 mm. long, longer than the lemma .... 1. G. AMBIGUUS.
Awn 1 to 3 mm. long, usually shorter than the lemma.
  Spikelets 1-flowered; spikes floriferous only in the upper half .... 2. G. BREVIFOLIUS.
  Spikelets 2- to 3-flowered; spikes floriferous to the base.
    Spikes stiffly ascending, usually more than 20; glumes widely spreading even on young spikelets .... 3. G. CHAPMANIANUS.
    Spikes spreading or reflexed, usually fewer than 15; glumes not spreading, even in mature spikelets .... 4. G. FLORIDANUS.

1. Gymnopogon ambíguus (Michx.) B. S. P. (Fig. 752.) Culms 30 to 60 cm. tall in small clumps with short scaly rhizomes, suberect to spreading, rigid, sparingly branching; leaves numerous, approximate with overlapping sheaths, or the lower rather distant; blades spreading, 5 to 15 mm., mostly about 10 mm. wide, the base

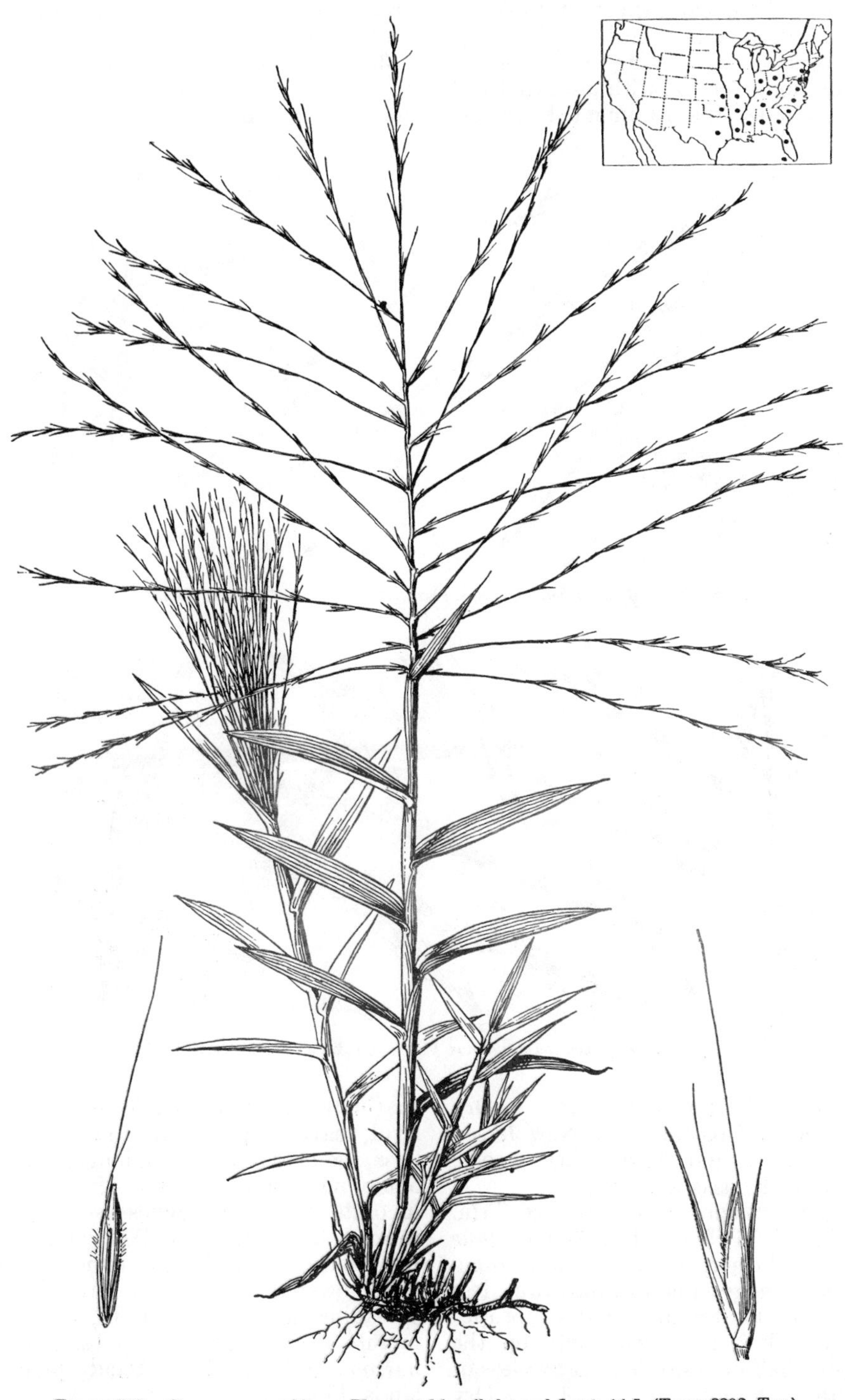

FIGURE 752.—*Gymnopogon ambiguus*. Plant, × ½; spikelet and floret, × 5. (Tracy 8292, Tex.)

rounded-truncate; spikes 10 to 20 cm. long, floriferous from base, the lower spikelets often remote; glumes 4 to 6 mm. long; lemma with an awn 4 to 6 mm. long, the rudiment bearing a delicate shorter awn. ♃ —Dry pinelands, Coastal Plain, New Jersey to Florida and Texas; dry woods, Ohio to Kansas and south.

2. Gymnopogon brevifólius Trin. (Fig. 753.) Differing from *G. ambiguus* in the longer, more slender, somewhat straggling culms, narrower, less crowded blades, and in the subcapillary spikes, floriferous only on the upper half or third; lemma awnless or with a minute awn. ♃ —Dry ground, Coastal Plain, New Jersey to Florida and Louisiana.

3. Gymnopogon chapmaniánus Hitchc. (Fig. 754.) Culms 30 to 40 cm. tall, in small tufts, ascending, sparingly branching from lower nodes, rigid; leaves approximate toward the base, the blades 5 to 6 cm. long, about 5 mm. wide, sharp-pointed, often subinvolute in drying; spikes ascending to spreading (not reflexed), floriferous from base, spikelets not remote, 2- or 3-flowered, the florets somewhat spreading; lemmas pubescent, with a minute awn or awnless; palea very narrow, arched. ♃ —Sandy pinelands, Florida.

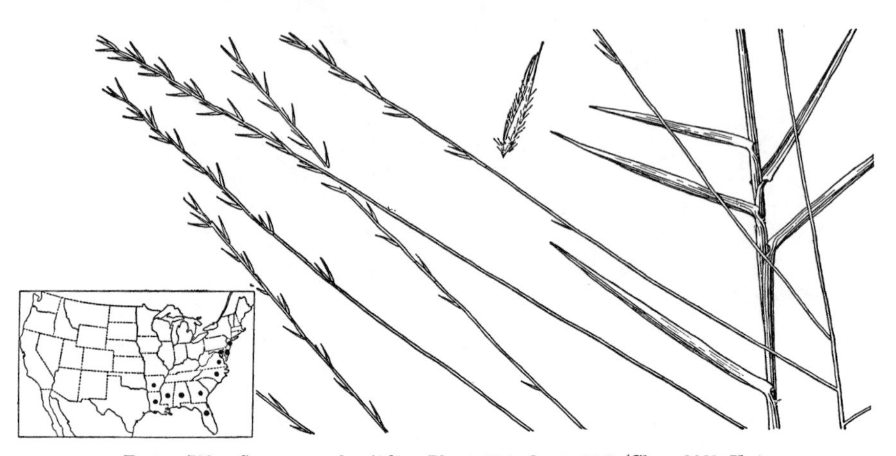

FIGURE 753.—*Gymnopogon brevifolius*. Plant, × 1; floret, × 5. (Chase 3669, Va.)

FIGURE 754.—*Gymnopogon chapmanianus*. Plant, × 1; florets, × 5. (Tracy 7102, Fla.)

4. Gymnopogon floridánus Swallen. (Fig. 755.) Plants in small tufts, commonly purple below; culms 15 to 45 cm. tall; sheaths glabrous, overlapping, and crowded toward the base, minutely hairy in the throat, the uppermost elongate; blades firm, mostly about 3 cm. long, 2 to 4 mm. wide, sometimes to 6 cm. long and 6 mm. wide, flat, stiffly spreading; spikes 5 to 20, very slender, 10 to 15 cm. long, spreading or reflexed, spikelet-bearing to the base or nearly so; spikelets 2- or 3-flowered, 3 to 5 mm. long; glumes about equal, acuminate, as long as the florets, not spreading; lemma 2 to 2.2 mm. long. ♃ —Sandy prairies and pine barrens, peninsular Florida.

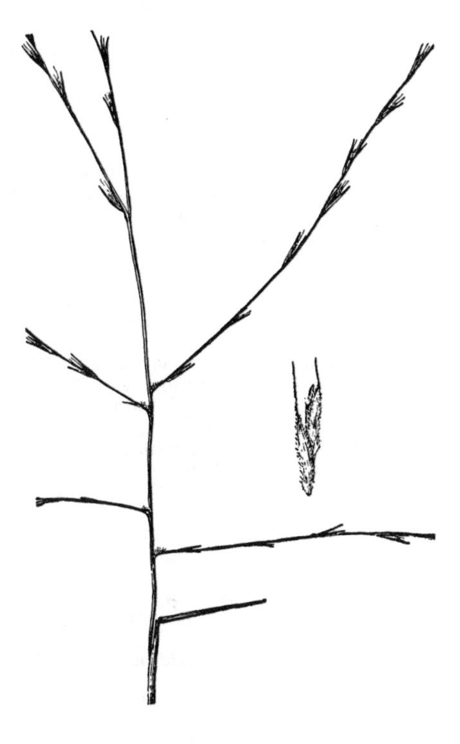

FIGURE 755.—*Gymnopogon floridanus*. Panicle, × 1; florets, × 5. (Type.)

110. CHLÓRIS Swartz. FINGERGRASS

Spikelets with 1 perfect floret, sessile, in 2 rows along one side of a continuous rachis, the rachilla disarticulating above the glumes, produced beyond the perfect floret and bearing 1 to several reduced florets consisting of empty lemmas (a few species occasionally with a second fertile floret), these often truncate, and, if more than 1, the smaller ones usually enclosed in the lower, forming a somewhat club-shaped rudiment; glumes somewhat unequal, the first shorter, narrow, acute; lemma keeled, usually broad, 1- to 5-nerved, often villous on the callus and villous or long-ciliate on the keel or marginal nerves, awned from between the short teeth of a bifid apex, the awn slender or sometimes reduced to a mucro, the sterile lemmas awned or awnless. Tufted perennials or sometimes annuals with flat or folded scabrous blades and 2 to several, sometimes showy and feathery, spikes aggregate at the summit of the culms. Type species, *Chloris cruciata* (L.) Swartz. Named for Greek *Chloris*, the goddess of flowers.

Several species are found on the plains of Texas, where they form part of the forage for grazing animals. *C. virgata* is a rather common annual weed in the Southwest, especially in alfalfa fields. It may be locally abundant and then furnishes considerable forage. *C. gayana*, Rhodes grass, is cultivated in the irrigated regions of the Southwest, where it is valuable as a meadow grass. It is also used in the Hawaiian Islands on some ranches in the drier regions. In a few species 2 or 3 internodes of the culm may be greatly reduced, bringing the nodes and sheaths close together.

Lemmas firm, dark brown, awnless or mucronate. Perennials with strongly compressed

culms and sheaths, and firm flat or folded blades abruptly rounded at the tip.
SECTION 1. EUSTACHYS.
Lemmas distinctly awned (awn very short in *C. cucullata*), pale or fuscous.
SECTION 2. EUCHLORIS.

Section 1. Eustachys

Spikes numerous, usually more than 10 .... 1. C. GLAUCA.
Spikes usually not more than 6.
Spikelets 2 mm. long; lemmas dark .... 2. C. PETRAEA.
Spikelets 3 mm. long; lemmas pale to golden brown until maturity.
Spikes 2, sometimes 1 or 3 .... 3. C. FLORIDANA.
Spikes 4 to 6 .... 4. C. NEGLECTA.

Section 2. Euchloris

Rudiment narrow, oblong, acute, often inconspicuous. (Second rudiment truncate in *C. gayana*).
Plant producing long, stout stolons .... 5. C. GAYANA.
Plant not stoloniferous (occasionally with short stolons in *C. andropogonoides*).
Fertile lemma about 2.5 mm. long; plants mostly less than 50 cm. tall; spikes mostly less than 10 cm. long .... 7. C. ANDROPOGONOIDES.
Fertile lemma 4 to 7 mm. long; plants 40 to 100 cm. or more tall; spikes mostly more than 10 cm. long.
Blades folded, abruptly acute or rounded; spikes whorled, naked at base.
8. C. TEXENSIS.
Blades flat, long-acuminate; spikes racemose on a short axis, solitary or in small fascicles .... 6. C. CHLORIDEA.
Rudiment truncate-broadened at apex, usually conspicuous (rather narrow in *C. virgata*).
Lemma conspiculusly ciliate-villous, the spikes feathery.
Plants annual. Lemma long-ciliate on the lateral nerves near apex .... 9. C. VIRGATA.
Plants perennial.
Spikes flexuous, nodding, mostly 10 to 15 cm. long; hairs much exceeding the spikelets .... 10. C. POLYDACTYLA.
Spikes straight or subflexuous, 5 to 7 cm. long; hairs about equaling the spikelets.
11. C. CILIATA.
Lemma minutely ciliate on the nerves or glabrous, the spikes not feathery.
Awn of fertile lemma usually 3 to 8 mm. long; spikes mostly 7 to 12 cm. long, the spikelets not closely crowded .... 12. C. VERTICILLATA.
Awn of fertile lemma usually less than 3 mm. long; spikes usually less than 6 cm. long, the spikelets crowded.
Awns about 1 mm. long; rudiment prominent, inflated, broadly triangular-truncate, about 1.5 mm. wide as folded at summit .... 15. C. CUCULLATA.
Awns 2 to 3 mm. long; rudiment not inflated, not more than 1 mm. wide as folded at summit.
Rudiment oblong-cuneate, about 0.6 mm. wide as folded at summit.
13. C. SUBDOLICHOSTACHYA.
Rudiment triangular-truncate, about 1 mm. wide as folded at summit.
14. C. LATISQUAMEA.

SECTION 1. EÚSTACHYS (Desv.) Reichenb.

Lemmas firm, brown to blackish, awnless or mucronate only; glumes scabrous, the second mucronate from a notched or truncate summit. Perennials.

1. Chloris glaúca (Chapm.) Wood. (Fig. 756.) Glaucous; culms erect, compressed, stout, 70 to 150 cm. tall; basal sheaths several, broad, compressed, keeled, overlapping and equitant, those of the succeeding 1 or 2 distant nodes similar, 2 to 4 leaves aggregate; blades flat or folded, as much as 1 cm. wide, the tip abruptly rounded; spikes several to many (as many as 20), ascending, 7 to 12 cm. long; spikelets about 2 mm. long; lemma glabrous or scaberulous on the nerves. ♃ (*Eustachys glauca* Chapm.)—Brackish marshes, wet prairies, and swamps, North Carolina (Wilmington), Georgia (Baker County), and Florida.

2. Chloris petraéa Swartz. (Fig. 757.) Often glaucous, sometimes purplish; culms slender, 50 to 100 cm. tall, more or less decumbent and root-

FIGURE 756.—*Chloris glauca.* Plant, × 1; florets, × 5. (Combs and Baker 1143, Fla

ing or producing distinct stolons; sheaths compressed, strongly keeled, usually 2 to 4 aggregate below; blades 3 to 8 mm. wide, often short and numerous on the stolons; spikes mostly 4 to 6, 4 to 10 cm. long; spikelets 2 mm. long; lemma mucronate, short-ciliate on the nerves. ♃ (*Eustachys petraea* Desv.)—Strands, sandy fields, and open pine woods, Coastal Plain, North Carolina to Florida and Texas; tropical America.

3. Chloris floridána (Chapm.) Wood. (Fig. 758.) Culms slender, 40 to 80 cm. tall; sheaths compressed, crowded at base but not paired or aggregate at succeeding nodes; blades 3 to 7 mm. wide, somewhat narrowed toward the acutish tip; spikes mostly 2, sometimes 1 or 3, 5 to 10 cm. long; spikelets 3 mm. long; second glume with an awn about 1 mm. long; lemma with a slender mucro 0.5 to 1 mm. long, stiffly ciliate on keel and lateral nerves. ♃ (*Eustachys floridana* Chapm.)—Dry sandy woods and open ground, Georgia and Florida.

4. Chloris neglécta Nash. (Fig. 759.) Differing from *C. floridana* in having usually taller, stouter culms, the leaves sometimes paired at the lower nodes; spikes 3 to 8, mostly 4 to 6. ♃ (*Eustachys neglecta* Nash.) —Open sandy woods and swamps, Florida.

Chloris distichophýlla Lag. Culms about 1 m. tall; spikes several (as many as 20), drooping, feathery; lemma ciliate with silky hairs 1 mm. long. ♃ —Escaped from cultivation in southern California. A specimen from Bastrop, Tex., is probably also an escape from cultivation; South America.

CHLORIS ARGENTÍNA (Hack.) Lillo and Parodi. Culms erect, compressed, 30 to 90

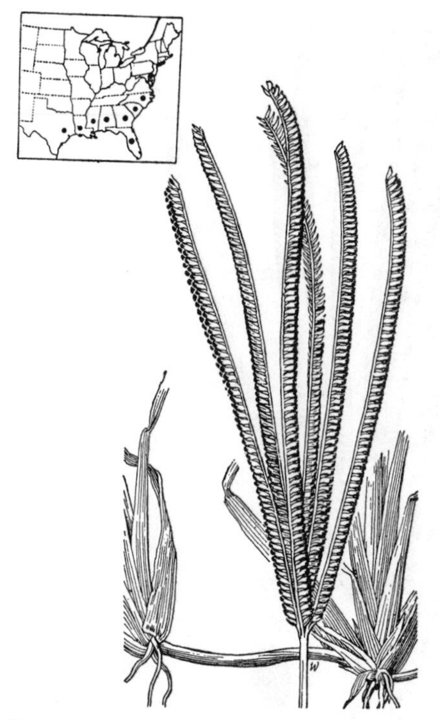

FIGURE 757.—*Chloris petraea.* Plant, × 1; florets, × 5. (Curtiss, Fla.)

FIGURE 758.—*Chloris floridana.* Panicle, × 1; florets, × 5. (Nash 2198, Fla.)

cm. tall; leaves mostly crowded toward the base, the sheaths compressed, keeled, the blades short, 4 to 10 mm. wide; racemes 7 to 12, mostly 5 to 10 cm. long, erect or ascending, crowded, brown, appearing feathery from the cilia on the margins of the lemma; spikelets about 2 mm. long. ♃ —Introduced from Argentina. Roadsides near Tifton, Ga. Probably escaped from cultivation.

CHLORIS CAPÉNSIS (Houtt.) Thell. Stoloniferous perennial; culms 40 to 75 cm. tall; blades obtuse; spikes few to several, finally

FIGURE 759.—*Chloris neglecta.* Panicle, × 1; florets, × 5. (Curtiss 3445, Fla.)

arcuate-spreading; spikelets about 2.5 mm. long, the glumes short-awned, the brown lemmas white-ciliate on the keel and margin, awnless. ♃ —Introduced from South Africa. Levy County, Fla. Probably escaped from cultivation.

FIGURE 760.—*Chloris gayana*. Plant, × ½; florets, × 5. (Hitchcock 13667, Ariz.)

SECTION 2. EUCHLÓRIS Endl.

Lemmas tawny to grayish or fuscous, awned; glumes acute to acuminate. Mostly perennial.

5. Chloris gayâna Kunth. RHODES GRASS. (Fig. 760.) Culms 1 to 1.5 m. tall with long, stout, leafy stolons, the internodes compressed, tough and wiry; blades 3 to 5 mm. wide, tapering to a fine point; spikes several to numerous, erect or ascending, 5 to 10 cm. long; spikelets crowded, pale-tawny; lemma 3 mm. long, hispid on the margin near the summit, more or less hispidulous below, the awn 1 to 5 mm. long; rudiment commonly of 2 florets, the lower occasionally fertile, rather narrow, the awn usually somewhat shorter than that of the fertile lemma, the upper minute, broad, truncate. ♃ —Cultivated for forage in warmer regions, escaped into fields and waste places, North Carolina and from Florida to southern California and in tropical America. Introduced from Africa. A promising meadow grass in irrigated regions.

6. Chloris chlorídea (Presl) Hitchc. (Fig. 761.) Culms slender, 60 to 100 cm. tall; blades flat, 3 to 7 mm. wide, long-acuminate; spikes slender, few to several, mostly 8 to 15 cm. long, approximate on an axis 2 to 10 cm. long; spikelets appressed, not crowded; lemma narrow, glabrous, somewhat scaberulous toward the tip, about 6 mm. long, the awn 10 to 12 mm. long; rudiment very narrow, awned. ♃ (*C. clandestina* Scribn. and Merr.)—Open ground, Texas (Brownsville), Arizona, Mexico, and Honduras. Large cleistogamous spikelets are borne on slender underground branches, rather rare in herbarium specimens, either infrequent or readily broken off.

7. Chloris andropogonoídes Fourn. (Fig. 762.) Culms densely tufted, 20 to 40 cm. tall, the leaves mostly basal; blades about 1 mm. wide as folded; spikes slender, few to several, 5 to 10 cm. long, whorled, divergent, floriferous from base; spikelets scarcely overlapping; lemma minutely pubescent on midnerve and margin or

FIGURE 761.—*Chloris chloridea.* Terminal and subterranean inflorescences, × 1; florets, × 5. (Silveus 379, Tex.)

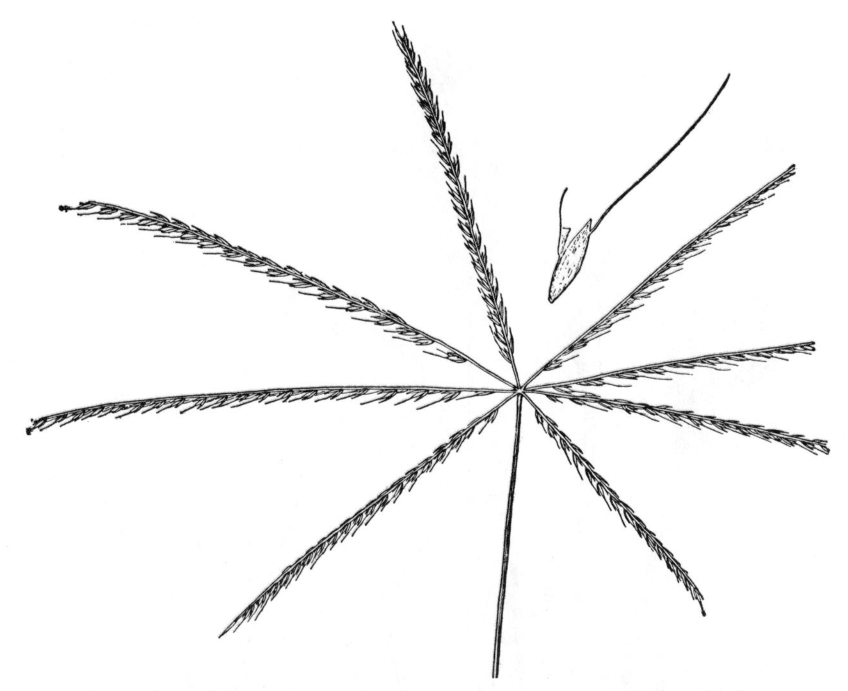

FIGURE 762.—*Chloris andropogonoides*. Panicles, × 1; florets, × 5. (Chase 6067, Tex.)

glabrous, 2 to 3 mm., usually about 2.5 mm. long, awned below the tip, the awn about 5 mm. long; rudiment narrow, the awn usually shorter than that of the lemma. ♃ (*C. tenuispica* Nash.)—Plains, Texas and northern Mexico.

8. **Chloris texénsis** Nash. (Fig. 763.) Culms taller and stouter than in *C. andropogonoides;* blades 2 to 3 mm. wide as folded; spikes slender, mostly about 15 to 18 cm. long, naked for 1 to 4 cm. at the base; spikelets appressed, not crowded; lemma about 4 mm. long, naked on the midnerve, minutely pilose on margin toward summit; awn about 1 cm. long. ♃ (*C. nealleyi* Nash.) —Plains, Texas, rare.

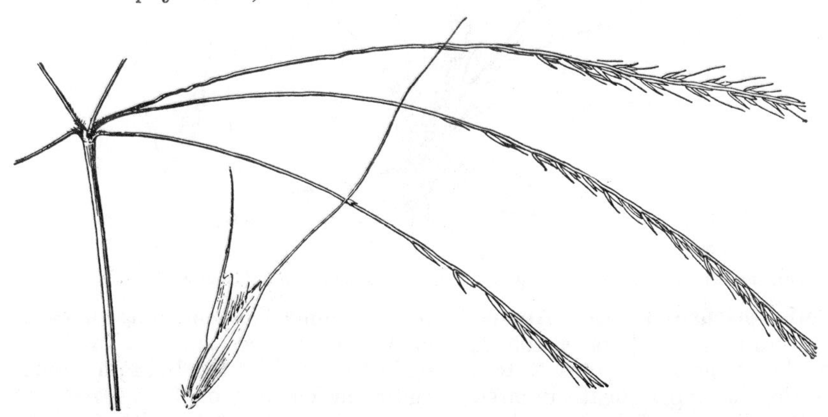

FIGURE 763.—*Chloris texensis*. Panicle, × 1; florets, × 5. (Thurow 8, Tex.)

FIGURE 764.—*Chloris virgata.* Plant, × ½; glumes and florets, × 5. (Tracy 8173, Tex.)

Chloris prieúrii Kunth. Annual; culms 30 to 60 cm. tall, often rooting at the lower nodes; blades 2 to 6 mm. wide, the upper sheath inflated; spikes 2 to 8, erect, 5 to 8 cm. long; fertile lemma 2.5 mm. long, narrow, ciliate near the summit, with a delicate awn 7 to 10 mm. long; rudiment narrow, of 3 or 4 reduced sterile lemmas each with a long delicate erect awn. ⊙ —Ballast, Wilmington, N. C., and Mobile, Ala.; West Africa.

9. Chloris virgáta Swartz. FEATHER FINGERGRASS. (Fig. 764.) Annual; culms ascending to spreading, 40 to 60 or even 100 cm. tall; upper sheaths often inflated; blades flat, 2 to 6 mm. wide; spikes several, 2 to 8 cm. long, erect, whitish or tawny, feathery or silky; spikelets crowded; lemma 3 mm. long, somewhat humpbacked on the keel, long-ciliate on the margins near the apex, the slender awn 5 to 10 mm. long; rudiment narrowly cuneate, truncate, the awn as long as that of the lemma. ⊙ (*C. elegans* H. B. K.)—Open ground, a common weed in fields and waste places; Nebraska to Texas and southern California; Maine and Massachusetts, on wool waste; introduced in a few localities in the Eastern States, Ohio, Indiana, and North Carolina to Florida; Louisiana and Missouri; tropical America.

10. Chloris polydáctyla (L.) Swartz. (Fig. 765.) Culms erect, wiry, 50 to 100 cm. tall; blades as much as 1 cm. wide; spikes several to many, mostly 10 to 15 cm. long, flexuous, nodding, tawny, feathery; spikelets crowded; lemma ciliate with long silky hairs; rudiment oblong, obliquely truncate, awns of lemma and rudiment about 3 mm. long. ♃ —Open sandy soil, southern Florida; West Indies to Paraguay.

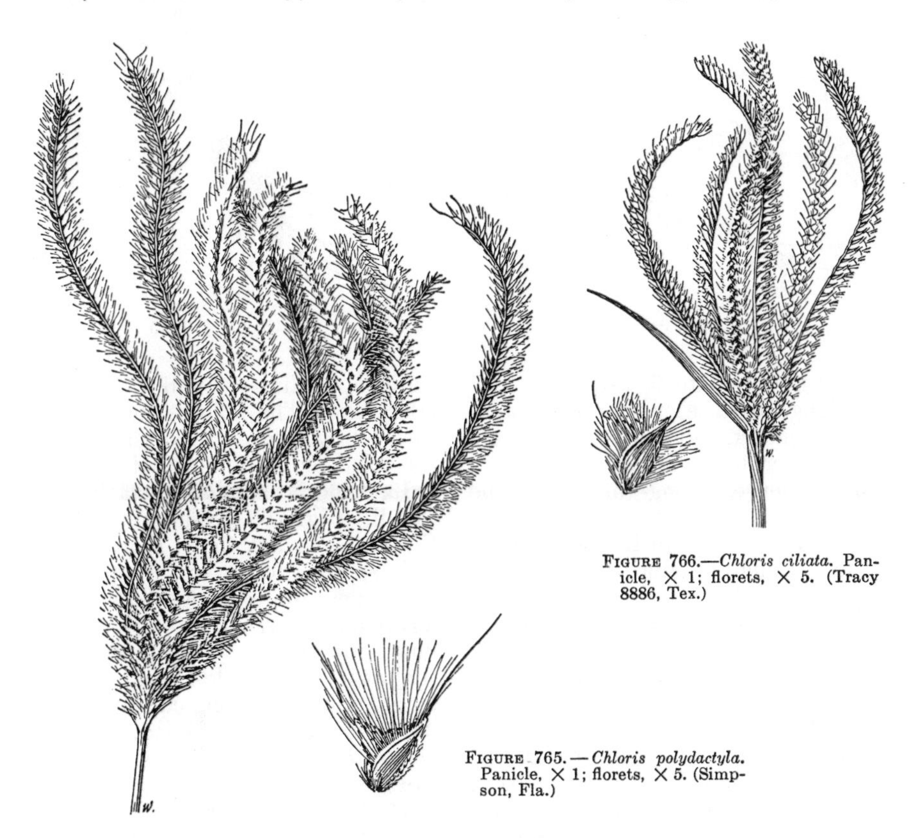

FIGURE 766.—*Chloris ciliata*. Panicle, × 1; florets, × 5. (Tracy 8886, Tex.)

FIGURE 765.—*Chloris polydactyla*. Panicle, × 1; florets, × 5. (Simpson, Fla.)

11. Chloris ciliáta Swartz. (Fig. 766.) Perennial; culms erect or ascending, 50 to 100 cm. tall; leaves not aggregate toward the base, sheaths not much compressed; blades 3 to 5 mm. wide, sharply acuminate;

FIGURE 767.—*Chloris verticillata.* Panicle, × 1; florets, × 5. (Ball 1112, Tex.)

spikes mostly 3 to 6, usually 5 to 7 cm. long, digitate or nearly so, erect to spreading, somewhat flexuous; spikelets crowded, about 3 mm. long; lemma densely long-villous on the keel and the middle of the margin, the awn shorter than the body; rudiment triangular-cuneate, about 2 mm. wide. ♃ (*C. nashii* Heller.) —Open grassland, southern Texas and Mexico.

12. Chloris verticillāta Nutt. WINDMILL GRASS. (Fig. 767.) Culms tufted, 10 to 40 cm. tall, erect or decumbent at base, sometimes rooting at the lower nodes; leaves crowded at base, 2 to 4, sometimes aggregate at lower nodes; sheaths compressed, blades 1 to 3 mm. wide, obtuse; spikes slender, 7 to 10 or even 15 cm. long, in 1 to 3 whorls, finally widely spreading; spikelets about 3 mm. long; fertile lemma pubescent on the nerves, the awn mostly 5 to 8 mm. long; rudiment (rarely fertile), cuneate-oblong, rather turgid, about 0.7 mm. wide as folded, truncate, the awn about 5 mm. long. ♃ —Plains, Missouri to Colorado, south to Louisiana and Arizona; introduced in Maryland, Indiana, Illinois, and California (Berkeley). The inflorescence at maturity breaks away and rolls before the wind as a tumbleweed.

13. Chloris subdolichostáchya C. Muell. (Fig. 768.) Similar to *C. verticillata*, but not more than 20 cm. tall, spikes mostly less than 6 cm. long, these more condensed and usually in one whorl or irregularly approximate; lemma 2 to 2.5 mm. long, the awns mostly less than 3 mm. long; rudiment oblong-cuneate, about 0.6 mm. wide as folded. ♃ (*C. brevispica* Nash.)—Plains, Kansas, Texas.

14. Chloris latisquámea Nash. (Fig. 769.) Culms densely tufted, 20 to 60 cm. tall, very leafy at base, sometimes rooting at the lower nodes; sheaths compressed, 2 to 4 often aggregate at the lower node; blades 2 to 4 mm. wide; spikes mostly 8 to 12, relatively broad, 4 to 10 cm. long, in 1 or 2 whorls, spreading; spikelets rather crowded, pale, turning fuscous at maturity; lemma about 2.5 mm. long, pubescent on the nerves, the awn 2 to 2.5 mm. long; rudiment (rarely fertile) triangular cuneate,

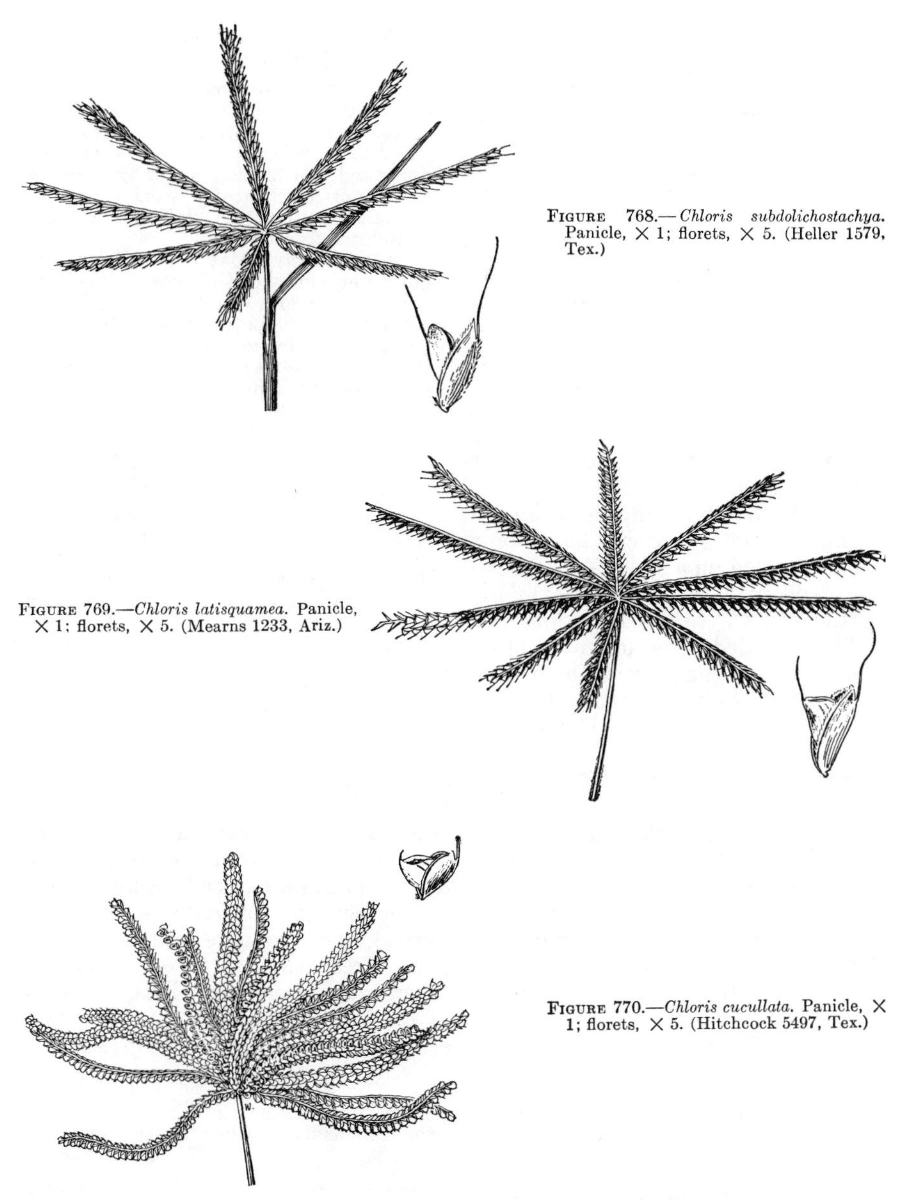

FIGURE 768.—*Chloris subdolichostachya.* Panicle, × 1; florets, × 5. (Heller 1579, Tex.)

FIGURE 769.—*Chloris latisquamea.* Panicle, × 1; florets, × 5. (Mearns 1233, Ariz.)

FIGURE 770.—*Chloris cucullata.* Panicle, × 1; florets, × 5. (Hitchcock 5497, Tex.)

about 1 mm. wide at summit as folded. ♃ —Plains, Texas, Arizona. Resembling *C. cucullata,* but commonly taller with longer spikes, the rudiment longer than broad, less inflated, the awns 2 to 2.5 mm. long.

15. Chloris cucullâta Bisch. (Fig. 770.) Culms tufted, erect or somewhat spreading at base, 20 to 50 cm. tall; sheaths compressed; blades 1 to 2 mm. wide as folded, the uppermost often much reduced; spikes numerous, 2 to 5 cm. long, digitate, radiating, flexuous or curled; spikelets crowded, stramineous, turning fuscous at maturity, triangular, about 2 mm. long and about as broad; rudiment prominent, compressed-cup-shaped, about 1.5 mm. wide, the awns of lemma and rudiment about 1 mm. long. ♃ —Plains and sandy barrens, Texas, Oklahoma, and New Mexico.

Chloris radiáta (L.) Swartz. Weedy branching annual; culms 30 to 40 cm. long, decumbent; blades thin, 2 to 3 mm. wide; spikes slender, several to many, 3 to 8 cm. long; lemma narrow, 2.5 mm. long, the narrow rudiment mostly included in its margins; awns of lemma and rudiment very slender, 5 to 10 mm. long. ⊙ —Ballast, near Portland, Oreg.; tropical America.

Chloris submútica H. B. K. Sparingly stoloniferous, culms 30 to 65 cm. tall; sheaths compressed-keeled; spikes 5 to 14, 3 to 8 cm. long, somewhat whorled on a short axis, spreading; spikelets 3 to 3.5 mm. long; fertile floret 3 to 3.5 mm. long, the callus bearded, the lemma obtuse, pilose toward the summit, awnless or mucronate; rudiment truncate, awnless ♃ —Dona Ana County, N. Mex., probably escaped from cultivation. Mexico.

Chloris bérroi Arech. Densely tufted, culms 40 to 65 cm. tall, leafy; spikes and spikelets much like those of *C. ciliata*, but the 2 to 5 spikes closely and permanently appressed, the rachises adhering, forming a subcylindrical silky inflorescence. ♃ —Occasionally cultivated, Oklahoma and Texas, introduced from Uruguay.

Chloris ventricósa R. Br. Culms straggling and rooting at the nodes, 40 to 90 cm. long; spikes 3 to 5, 7 to 10 cm. long, flexuous, spreading or drooping; spikelets about 5 mm. long; fertile lemma subindurate, brown, truncate, glabrous except for the pubescent callus, awn 4 to 5 mm. long, that of the truncate rudiment 1 to 2 mm. long. ♃ —Occasionally cultivated, Virginia and Oklahoma; introduced from Australia.

Chloris cantérai Arech. Perennial, resembling *C. polydactyla*, but blades only 2 to 5 mm. wide; spikes 2 to 4; spikelets slightly larger. ♃ —Spontaneous along roadsides and in uncultivated ground, Bexar County, Texas, introduced from Paraguay.

Chloris truncáta R. Br. Stoloniferous perennial; culms erect, 10 to 30 cm. tall; spikes 6 to 10, 7 to 15 cm. long, horizontal or reflexed; spikelets 3 mm. long, the awns 6 to 12 mm. long. ♃ —Occasionally cultivated for ornament under the name stargrass. Australia.

111. TRICHLÓRIS Fourn.

Spikelets 2- to 5-flowered, nearly sessile, in 2 rows along one side of a continuous slender rachis, the rachilla disarticulating above the glumes and prolonged behind the uppermost perfect floret, bearing a reduced, usually awned floret; glumes unequal, acuminate, or short-awned, the body shorter than the lower lemma; lemmas narrow, 3-nerved, the midnerve and usually the lateral nerves extending into slender awns. Erect, slender, tufted perennials, with flat scabrous blades and numerous erect or ascending spikes, aggregate but scarcely digitate at the summit of the culms. Type species, *Trichloris pluriflora*. Name from Latin *tri*, three, and *Chloris*, a genus of grasses, the lemmas being 3-awned.

Spikelets 2-flowered, both lemmas with 3 long awns .... 1. T. crinita.
Spikelets 3- to 5-flowered, the lateral awns of the lemmas more or less reduced, sometimes obsolete .... 2. T. pluriflora.

1. Trichloris crinita (Lag.) Parodi. (Fig. 771, *A*.) Culms 40 to 100 cm. tall; blades 2 to 4 mm. wide; inflorescence dense, feathery, the spikes 5 to 10 cm. long; spikelets crowded; fertile lemma about 3 mm. long, the second lemma much reduced, both with delicate awns about 1 cm. long. ♃ (*T. mendocina* (Phil.) Kurtz.)—Plains, canyons, and rocky hills, western Texas to Arizona and northern Mexico; southern South America. Rarely cultivated for ornament (as *T. blanchardiana* Fourn.).

2. Trichloris pluriflóra Fourn. (Fig. 771, *B*.) Culms 50 to 100 cm. tall; blades 5 to 10 mm. wide; inflorescence looser and less feathery than in *T. crinita;* spikes 7 to 15 cm. long; fertile

FIGURE 771.—*A*, *Trichloris crinita*. Plant, × ½; glumes and florets, × 5. (Nealley, Tex.) *B*, *T. pluriflora*. Glumes and florets, × 5. (Griffiths 6484, Tex.)

lemma about 4 mm. long, the others successively shorter, the middle awns of all 5 to 15 mm. long, somewhat spreading, the lateral awns short or obsolete. ♃ —Plains and dry woods, southern Texas and Mexico; southern South America.

112. BOUTELÓUA Lag. GRAMA

Spikelets 1-flowered, with the rudiments of 1 or more florets above, sessile, in 2 rows along one side of the rachis; glumes 1-nerved, acuminate or awn-tipped, the first shorter and narrower; lemma as long as the second glume or a little longer, 3-nerved, the nerves extending into short awns or mucros, the internerves usually extending into lobes or teeth; palea sometimes 2-awned; rudiment various, usually 3-awned, the awns usually longer than those of the fertile lemma, a second rudimentary floret sometimes present. Perennial or sometimes annual, low or rather tall grasses, with 2 to several or many spikes racemose on a common axis, or sometimes solitary, the spikelets few to many in each spike, rarely solitary, pectinate or more loosely arranged and appressed, the rachis of the spike usually naked at the tip. The sterile florets forming the rudiment are variable in all the species and commonly in individual specimens. The general pattern of rudiment is fairly constant for each species, the variability being in the reduction or increase in number and size of the sterile florets, the reduction from 3 awns to 1, and in the amount of pubescence. Type species, *Bouteloua racemosa* Lag. (*B. curtipendula*). Named for the brothers, Boutelou, Claudio, and Esteban. The genus was originally published as *Botelua*.

The many species are among our most valuable forage grasses, forming an important part of the grazing on the western ranges. *B. gracilis*, blue grama, and *B. hirsuta*, hairy grama, are prominent in "short grass" regions of the Great Plains; *B. eriopoda*, black grama, and *B. rothrockii*, Rothrock grama, are prominent in Arizona. Two annuals, *B. barbata* and *B. parryi*, form a part of the sixweeks grasses of the Southwest; *B. curtipendula* is widely distributed and is much used for grazing and for hay; *B. trifida* is important from Texas to Arizona.

Spikelets not pectinately arranged (except in *B. chondrosioides*), the spikes falling entire at maturity .... SECTION 1. ATHEROPOGON.
Spikelets pectinately arranged, the spikes persistent, the florets falling from the persistent glumes .... SECTION 2. CHONDROSIUM.

Section 1. Atheropogon

Plants annual .... 1. B. ARISTIDOIDES.
Plants perennial.
  Spikes usually 20 to 50; awns short, inconspicuous.
    Spikes of 1 or 2 spikelets; culms very slender .... 2. B. UNIFLORA.
    Spikes of few to several spikelets; culms mostly stouter .... 3. B. CURTIPENDULA.
  Spikes fewer; awns conspicuous.
    Glumes pubescent.
      Spikes rhomboid-oblong, as much as 2 cm. long, the spikelets somewhat pectinately arranged .... 6. B. CHONDROSIOIDES.
      Spikes cuneate-triangular, about 1 cm. long (including the awns), the spikelets appressed, not pectinately arranged.
        Culms 20 to 30 cm. tall; leaves crowded at base; spikes mostly 6 to 8. 4. B. RIGIDISETA.
        Culms mostly 30 to 50 cm. tall, leafy throughout; spikes mostly more than 10. 5. B. ELUDENS.
    Glumes glabrous or scabrous, not pubescent.
      Base of plants hard, rhizomatous; culms mostly simple; spikes 2 to 3 cm. long. 7. B. RADICOSA.
      Base of plants not rhizomatous; culms branching; spikes usually about 1.5 cm., sometimes 2 cm., long .... 8. B. FILIFORMIS.

Section 2. Chondrosium

Plants annual (see also *B. rothrockii*); densely tufted, spreading.
  Spike 1 .... 9. B. SIMPLEX.
  Spikes 2 or more.
    Rachis papillose-pilose .... 11. B. PARRYI.
    Rachis not pilose .... 10. B. BARBATA.
Plants perennial.
  Plants decumbent or stoloniferous; culms white-lanate .... 17. B. ERIOPODA.
  Plants erect or nearly so; culms tufted, not lanate.
    Spikes normally 2, sometimes 1 or 3.
      Rachis prolonged beyond the spikelets as a naked point; glumes tuberculate.
        Culms retrorsely hirsute below the nodes .... 13. B. GLANDULOSA.
        Culms glabrous .... 14. B. HIRSUTA.
      Rachis not prolonged; glumes not tuberculate (slightly so in *B. gracilis*).
        Culms herbaceous, the base not woody .... 15. B. GRACILIS.
        Culms woody and perennial at base .... 16. B. BREVISETA.
    Spikes normally 4 or more (see also *B. gracilis* var. *stricta*).
      Culms 25 to 50 cm. tall; awn 1 to 2 mm. long; glumes scabrous; spikes spreading. 12. B. ROTHROCKII.
      Culms 10 to 20 cm. tall; awn about 5 mm. long; glumes glabrous; spikes usually appressed .... 18. B. TRIFIDA.

SECTION 1. ATHEROPÓGON (Muhl.) Endl.

Spikes deciduous from the main axis; spikelets not pectinately arranged (somewhat so in *B. chondrosioides*). (*Atheropogon* Muhl. based on *A. apludoides* Muhl. (*Bouteloua curtipendula*).)

1. Bouteloua aristidoídes (H. B. K.) Griseb. NEEDLE GRAMA. (Fig. 772.) Annual, erect or spreading, branching; culms slender, 10 to 30 cm. tall; blades small and few, in vigorous plants as much as 15 cm. long; spikes mostly 8 to 14 on a slender axis, reflexed, readily falling, the base of the rachis forming a sharp, bearded point; spikelets 2 to 4, narrow, appressed; rudiment of 3 scabrous awns about 5 mm. long, exceeding the fertile floret. ⊙ (*Triathera aristidoides* Nash.)—Mesas, deserts, and foothills in open ground, Texas to Nevada, southern California, and northern Mexico; Argentina.

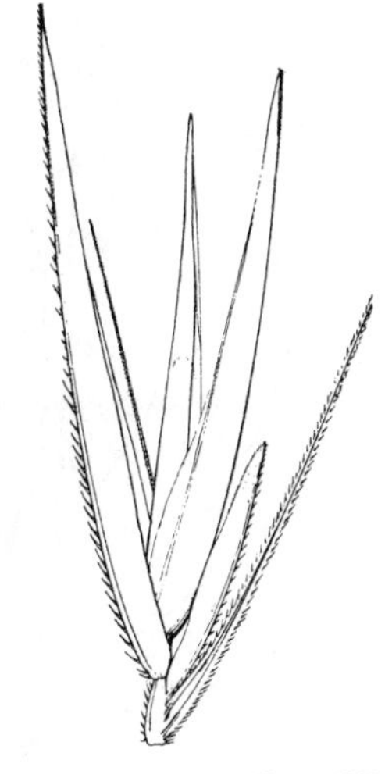

FIGURE 773.—*Bouteloua uniflora*, × 7. (Type.)

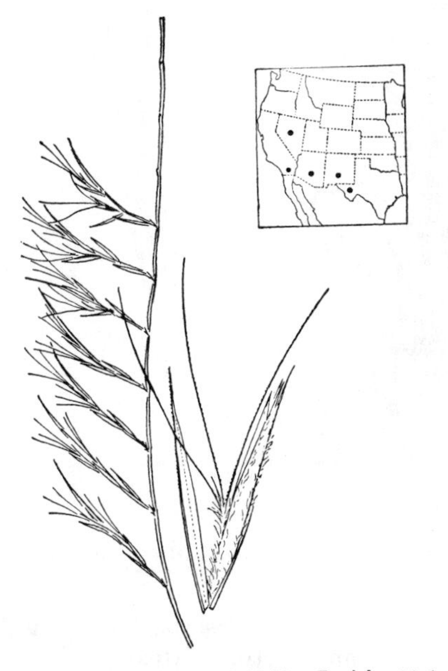

FIGURE 772.—*Bouteloua aristidoides*. Panicle, × 1; spikelet, × 5. (Griffiths 7308, Ariz.)

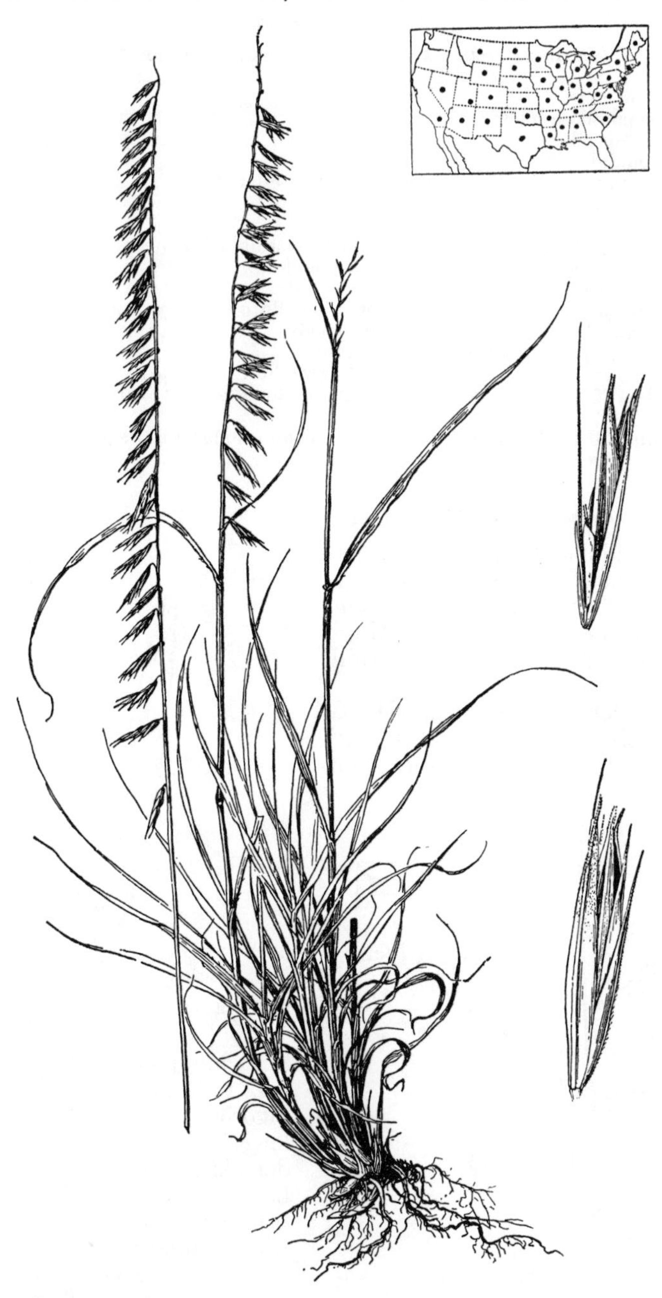

FIGURE 774.—*Bouteloua curtipendula.* Plant, × ½; spikelet and florets, × 5. (Chase 5408, Colo.)

BOUTELOUA ARISTIDOIDES var. ARIZÓNICA Jones. Spikes arcuate, to 2.5 cm. long, with 5 to 10 spikelets. ⊙ —Mesas and deserts, southern Arizona and northern Mexico.

2. Bouteloua uniflóra Vasey. (Fig.

773.) Resembles slender forms of *B. curtipendula*, culms slender, wiry, sometimes with slender stolons, the slender blades subinvolute, the spikes 8 to 9 mm. long, with 1 or 2 spikelets, the scabrous rachis mostly longer than the first glume; lemma awnless; rudiment reduced to a single awn appressed to the back of the palea. ♃ —Rocky hills and valleys, central and western Texas.

3. Bouteloua curtipéndula (Michx.) Torr. SIDE-OATS GRAMA. (Fig. 774.) Perennial, with scaly rhizomes; culms erect, tufted, 50 to 80 cm. tall; blades flat or subinvolute, 3 to 4 mm. wide, scabrous; spikes 35 to 50, 1 to 2 cm. long, purplish, spreading or pendulous and mostly twisted to one side of the slender axis, this 15 to 25 cm. long; spikelets 5 to 8, appressed or ascending, 6 to 10 mm. long; fertile lemma acute, mucronate; rudiment with 3 awns and subacute intermediate lobes, often reduced and inconspicuous. ♃ (*Atheropogon curtipendulus* Fourn.)—Plains, prairies, and rocky hills, Maine and Ontario to Montana, south to Virginia, Alabama, Texas, Arizona, and southern California; South Carolina (introduced); Mexico to Argentina.

4. Bouteloua rigidiséta (Steud.) Hitchc. (Fig. 775.) Perennial, tufted, leafy at base; culms erect, 20 to 30 cm. tall; blades narrow, flat or somewhat involute, 1 to 1.5 mm. wide, sparingly papillose-pilose; spikes 6 to 8, triangular-cuneate, spreading, about 1 to 1.2 cm. long including the awns; spikelets mostly 2 to 4, crowded, ascending; glumes pubescent; fertile lemma with 3 spreading awns, the intermediate lobes acute; rudiment with stout spreading awns, much exceeding those of the fertile lemma, the intermediate lobes firm, pointed, a second similar but smaller rudiment commonly developed. ♃ (*B. texana* S. Wats.; *Polyodon texanus* Nash.)—Plains and rocky hills, Oklahoma, Texas, and northern Mexico.

5. Bouteloua elúdens Griffiths. (Fig. 776.) Perennial, densely tufted, leafy at base; culms erect, 25 to 60 cm. tall; blades mostly 1 to 1.5 mm. wide; axis slender, flexuous, 6 to 8 cm. long; spikes 10 to 20, triangular, spreading, about 1 cm. long including the awns; spikelets about 5; rachis and glumes densely pubescent; fertile lemma pubescent toward the summit, the apex 3-cleft, the divisions awn-tipped; rudiment with stout pubescent awns about 5 mm. long, the long narrow intermediate lobes glabrous; a second similar but smaller rudiment usually developed. ♃ —Rocky hills, southern Arizona and Sonora, Mexico.

FIGURE 775.—*Bouteloua rigidiseta*. Panicle, × 1; spikelet, × 7; lemma and florets, × 5. (Griffiths 6370, Tex.)

FIGURE 776.—*Bouteloua eludens*. Panicle, × 1; spike and spikelet, × 5. (Type.)

6. Bouteloua chondrosioídes (H. B. K.) Benth. ex S. Wats. (Fig. 777.) Perennial, tufted, leafy at base; culms erect, 20 to 50 cm. tall; blades 2 to 3 mm. wide; axis 4 to 6 cm. long; spikes 4 to 6, rhomboid-oblong, ascending, 1 to 2 cm. long, the rachis densely pubescent, the tip 3-cleft; spikelets several, subpectinate; rachis broad, densely pubescent on the margin; glumes and fertile lemma densely pubescent, the lemma 3-cleft, the divisions awn-tipped; rudiment cleft nearly to the base, the middle awn broadly winged, the lateral ones slender, all spreading. ♃ —Mesas and rocky hills, western Texas to southern Arizona; Mexico and Guatemala.

7. Bouteloua radicósa (Fourn.) Griffiths. PURPLE GRAMA. (Fig. 778.) Perennial, tufted, from a stout rhizomatous base; culms erect, 60 to 80 cm. tall; blades 2 to 3 mm. wide, sparsely papillose-ciliate on the margin, mostly aggregate toward the lower part of the culm, the upper part naked; axis 10 to 15 cm. long; spikes mostly 7 to 12, oblong, 2 to 3 cm. long; spikelets mostly 8 to 11; glumes broader than in other species; fertile lemma indurate down the center, with 3 awns, the middle longest, and no intermediate lobes; rudiment with 3 awns 5 to 8 mm. long and no intermediate lobes, usually containing a palea and staminate flower sometimes a perfect flower, the lower floret being staminate. ♃ —Rocky hills, southern New Mexico to southern California and Mexico.

8. Bouteloua filifórmis (Fourn.) Griffiths. SLENDER GRAMA. (Fig. 779.) Resembling *B. radicosa;* culms erect or geniculate-spreading, sparingly branching, the base not rhizomatous; spikes ascending to spreading, mostly about 1.5 cm. long, sometimes as much as 2 cm.; spikelets mostly 6 to 10, very like those of *B. radicosa.* ♃ —Rocky hills, Texas to Arizona and Mexico; Panama.

FIGURE 778.—*Bouteloua radicosa.* Panicle, × 1; spikelet, × 5. (Griffiths 7181, Ariz.)

SECTION 2. CHONDRÓSIUM (Desv.) Benth.

Spikes persistent; spikelets crowded (looser in *B. eriopoda*), pectinate; florets falling from the glumes. (*Chondrosium* Desv. based on *C. procumbens* Durand (*B. simplex*).

FIGURE 777.—*Bouteloua chondrosioides.* Panicle, × 1; spikelet, × 5. (Type.)

FIGURE 779.—*Bouteloua filiformis.* Panicle, × 1; spikelet, × 5. (Griffiths 7199, Ariz.)

9. Bouteloua símplex Lag. MAT GRAMA. (Fig. 780.) Annual, tufted, prostrate or ascending; foliage scant; blades 2 to 3 cm. long, about 1.5 mm. wide; spike solitary, 1.5 to 2.5 cm.

FIGURE 780.—*Bouteloua simplex*. Plant, × 1; spikelet, × 5. (Griffiths 7362, Ariz.)

long, strongly arcuate at maturity; spikelets mostly 20 to 30, about 5 mm. long; fertile lemma pilose at base with stout awns and subacute intermediate lobes; rudiment bearded at summit of rachilla-joint, cleft to the base or nearly so, the awns equal, a second rudiment, broad and awnless, sometimes developed. ☉ (*B. procumbens* Griffiths.)—Open ground, Texas to Colorado, Utah, Arizona, and Mexico; wool waste, Maine; Ecuador to Argentina.

10. Bouteloua barbáta Lag. SIX-WEEKS GRAMA. (Fig. 781.) Annual, tufted, branching, erect to prostrate, often forming mats with ascending ends, the culms as much as 30 cm. long; foliage scant; blades 1 to 4 cm. long, 1 to 1.5 mm. wide; spikes 4 to 7, 1 to 2 cm. long; spikelets 25 to 40, 2.5 to 4 mm. long, nearly as broad; fertile lemma densely pilose at least along the sides, usually throughout, the awns from minute to as long as the body, the intermediate lobes subacute to obtuse; rudiment from obscurely to conspicuously bearded at summit of rachilla joint, cleft nearly to the base, the intermediate lobes broad, subcucullate, the awns of rudiment and fertile lemma reaching about the same height, a second rudiment, broad and awnless, often developed. ☉ (*B. microstachya* L. H. Dewey.)—Open ground, mesas, and rocky hills, Texas and Colorado to Nevada and southeastern California; Mexico. The awns vary in length. The form with shorter awns is that described as *B. pumila* Buckl.; the longer awned form is that described as *B. arenosa* Vasey.

11. Bouteloua párryi (Fourn.) Griffiths. PARRY GRAMA. (Fig. 782.)

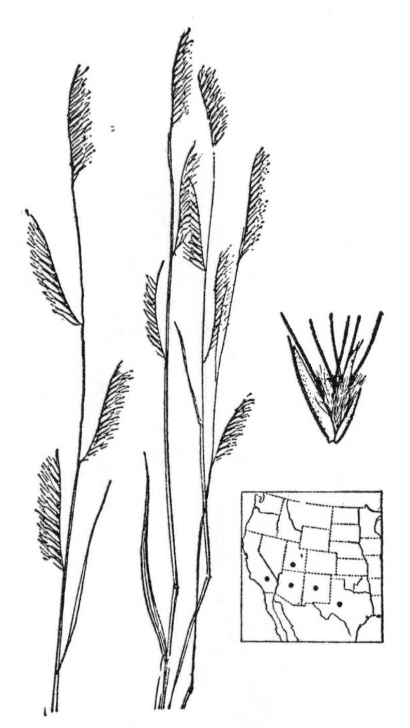

FIGURE 781.—*Bouteloua barbata*. Plant, × 1; spikelet, × 5. (Griffiths 6095, Ariz.)

Annual, resembling *B. rothrockii;* culms erect or geniculate-spreading, sometimes branching; blades papillose-pilose; spikes 4 to 8, often flexuous, commonly grayish purple, 2 to 3.5 cm. long; rachis papillose-pilose; spikelets 40 to 65, about 6 mm. long; second glume awned from a bifid tip, the keel papillose-pilose with spreading hairs; fertile lemma densely pilose, deeply cleft, the awns spreading, the oblong intermediate lobes fimbriate; rudiment densely bearded at summit of rachilla, cleft nearly to the base, the lobes obovate, fimbriate, the awns exceeding those of the fertile lemma; a second rudiment, broad, awnless or with a single awn, usually developed. ⊙ —Mesas and rocky hills, New Mexico, Arizona, and northern Mexico.

12. Bouteloua rothróckii Vasey. ROTHROCK GRAMA. (Fig. 783.) Perennial, sometimes appearing to be annual; culms tufted, erect, 25 to 50 cm. tall; blades 2 to 3 mm. wide; axis 10 to 25 cm. long; spikes 4 to 12, 2.5 to 3 cm. long, straight to subarcuate; spikelets 40 to 50, about 5 mm. long; fertile lemma pilose at base, deeply cleft, the awns (1 to 2 mm. long) spreading, the intermediate and lateral lobes fimbriate; rudiment densely bearded at summit of rachilla joint, cleft nearly to the base, the lobes broad and rounded, the awns mostly exceeding those of the fertile lemma; a second rudiment, broad and awnless, usually developed. ♃ —Mesas, canyons, and rocky hills, in open ground, or among brush, Arizona and southern California (Jamacha), to northern Mexico.

FIGURE 783.—*Bouteloua rothrockii.* Panicle, × 1; spikelet, × 4. (Griffiths 7185, Ariz.)

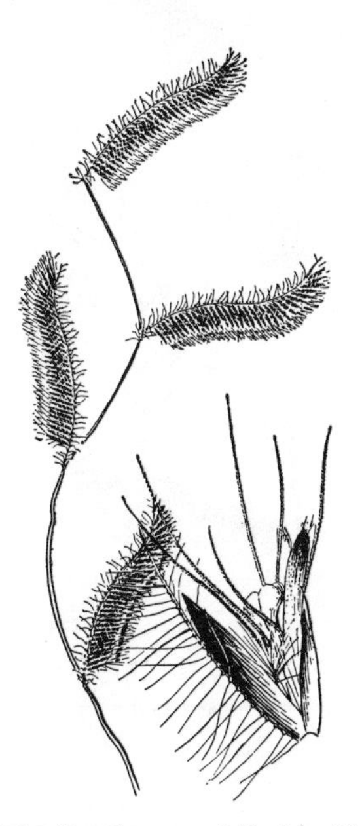

FIGURE 782.—*Bouteloua parryi.* Panicle, × 1; spikelet, × 5. (Griffiths 7277, Ariz.)

13. Bouteloua glandulósa (Cervant.) Swallen. (Fig. 784.) Similar to *B. hirsuta;* lower part of the culms and the lower sheaths conspicuously papillose-hirsute with ascending or spreading hairs; blades flat, attenuate, 2 to 3 mm. wide, more or less ciliate or hairy toward the base; spikes 1 to 3, ascending to reflexed, the rachis prolonged beyond the spikelets as a prominent bristle, commonly 1 to 1.5 cm. long; spikelets similar to those of *B. hirsuta*, but the awns of the rudiment somewhat longer, the spikes more bristly. ♃ *B. hirticulmis* Scribn.—Rocky hills, prairies, and open ground, Arizona (Santa Cruz County); Mexico.

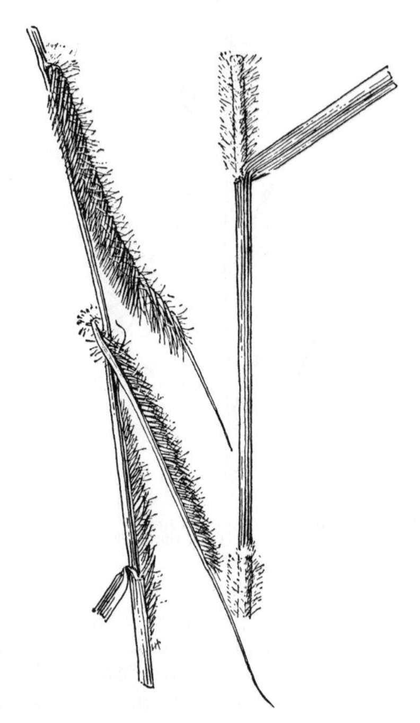

FIGURE 784.—*Bouteloua glandulosa*. Panicle, × 1. (Type of *B. hirticulmis*.)

14. Bouteloua hirsúta Lag. HAIRY GRAMA. (Fig. 785.) Perennial, densely tufted; culms erect, 20 to 60 cm. tall, leafy at base; blades flat or subinvolute, about 2 mm. wide, flexuous; spikes 1 to 4, usually 2, 2.5 to 3.5 cm. long, the rachis extending beyond the spikelets as a slender point 5 to 8 mm. long; spikelets 35 to 45, about 5 mm. long, second glume tuberculate-hirsute with spreading hairs, the tubercles black; fertile lemma 3-cleft, the divisions and margins of lemma pubescent, awn-tipped; rudiment from puberulent to bearded at summit of rachilla, cleft nearly to the base, the lobes firm, broad, spreading, the awns black. ♃ —Plains and rocky hills, Wisconsin and North Dakota to Texas, Colorado, Arizona, and California (Jamacha), south through Mexico; also peninsular Florida. *Bouteloua pectinata* Featherly was differentiated from *B. hirsuta* by taller more robust culms and by a rudimentary spikelet at the end of the rachis. Such a spikelet is rarely developed in *B. hirsuta*, but it is not correlated with robust plants.

15. Bouteloua grácilis (H. B. K.) Lag. ex Steud. BLUE GRAMA. (Fig. 786.) Perennial; densely tufted; culms erect, 20 to 50 cm. tall, leafy at base; blades flat or loosely involute, 1 to 2 mm. wide; spikes usually 2, sometimes 1 or 3, rarely more, 2.5 to 5 cm. long, falcate-spreading at maturity, the rachis not projecting beyond the spikelets; spikelets numerous, as many as 80, about 5 mm. long; fertile lemma pilose, the awns slender, the intermediate lobes acute; rudiment densely bearded at summit of

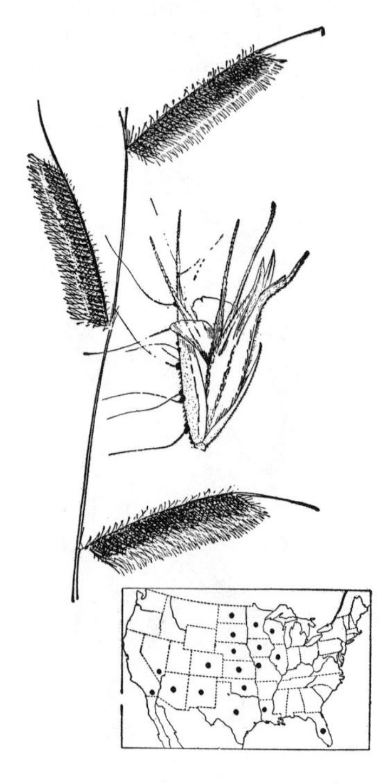

FIGURE 785.—*Bouteloua hirsuta*. Panicle, × 1; spikelet, × 5. (Griffiths 3371, Ariz.)

rachilla, cleft to the base, the lobes rounded, the awns slender, about equaling the tip of fertile lemma; one or two additional rudiments, broad and awnless, sometimes developed. ♃ (*B. oligostachya* Torr.) —Plains, Wisconsin to Manitoba and

FIGURE 787.—*Bouteloua breviseta.* Panicle, × 1; spikelet, × 5. (Nealley 669, Tex.)

Alberta, south to Arkansas, Texas, and southern California; Mexico; introduced in a few places in the Eastern States.

BOUTELOUA GRACILIS var. STRÍCTA (Vasey) Hitchc. Spikes 4 to 6, usually ascending or appressed. ♃ —Rare, Texas and Arizona.

16. Bouteloua brevisēta Vasey. (Fig. 787.) Perennial, wiry, the base perennial, woody, loosely tufted; culms branching, 25 to 40 cm. tall; blades 3 to 6 cm. long, 1 to 1.5 mm. wide, flat or becoming involute, sharp-pointed; spikes mostly 2, sometimes 1, rarely 3, 2 to 3 cm. long; spikelets 30 to 45, about 4 mm. long; fertile lemma pubescent, with 3 awns and acuminate intermediate

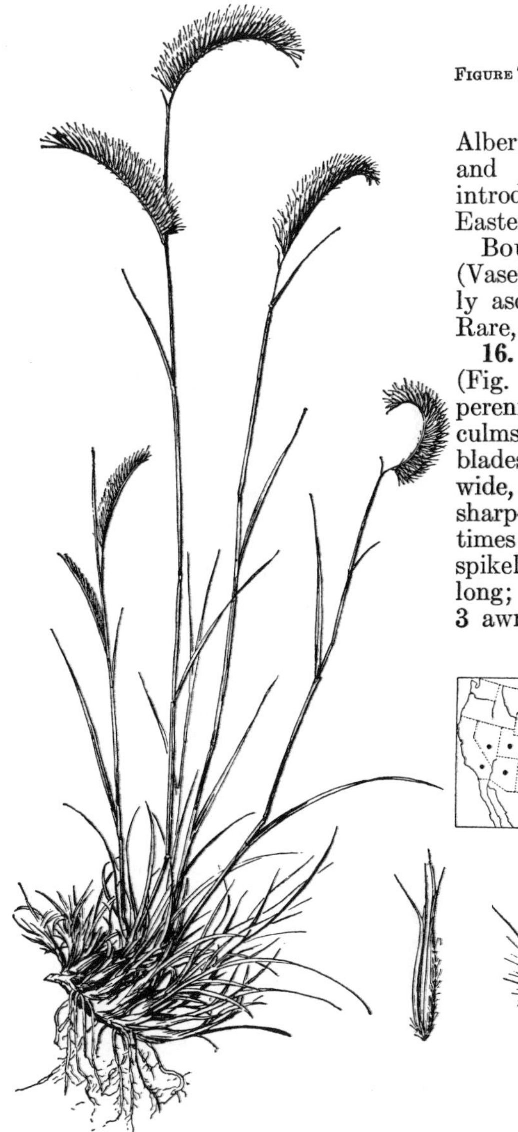

FIGURE 786.—*Bouteloua gracilis.* Plant, × ½; glumes and florets, × 5. (Amer. Gr. Natl. Herb. 384, Nev.)

FIGURE 788.—*Bouteloua eriopoda*. Plant, × 1; spikelet, × 5. (Hitchcock 13357, Tex.)

lobes; rudiment densely bearded at summit of rachilla joint, cleft nearly to the base, the rounded lobes obscured in the dense hairs. ♃ (*B. ramosa* Scribn.)—Gypsum sands and calcareous rocks, western Texas, New Mexico, and northern Mexico. Resembling *B. gracilis* but with loose, woody base and wiry culms; rachis prolonged and bearing a rudimentary spikelet at the tip.

17. Bouteloua eriopóda (Torr.) Torr. BLACK GRAMA. (Fig. 788.) Perennial; culms tufted, with swollen bases, slender, wiry, widely spreading with arched internodes or stoloniferous, white-lanate, 40 to 60 cm. long; blades 1 to 1.5 mm. wide, flexuous; spikes 3 to 8, commonly 4 or 5, loosely ascending, 2 to 3 cm. long; spikelets 12 to 20, not crowded and pectinate, 7 to 10 mm. long, narrow; fertile lemma acuminate, with a terminal awn, the lateral minute or obsolete; rudiment slender, cleft nearly to the base, the awns equaling the awn of the fertile lemma, the lobes minute, narrow. ♃ —Mesas, hills, and dry open ground, Oklahoma and Texas to Colorado, Utah, southern California, and northern Mexico.

18. Bouteloua trífida Thurb. (Fig. 789.) Perennial, tufted, leafy at base, rather delicate; culms erect, 10 to 20 cm. tall; blades usually only 1 to 2 cm. long; spikes 3 to 7, 1 to 2 cm. long, ascending or appressed; spikelets about 12, purplish, 7 to 10 mm. long; fertile lemma pubescent toward base, cleft more than half its length, with awns (5 mm. long) winged toward base and no intermediate lobes; rudiment cleft to the base, the awns similar to those of the fertile lemma, about as long. ♃ (*B. trinii* Griffiths; *B. burkii* Scribn.)—Mesas, ravines, and rocky hills, Texas to Nevada and Arizona; California (Death Valley); northern Mexico. Variable in length of the awns, the type of *B. trifida* being the longer awned form.

FIGURE 789.—*Bouteloua trifida*. Panicle, × 1; spikelet, × 5. (Amer. Gr. Natl. Herb. 669, Tex.)

FIGURE 790.—*Cathestecum erectum*. Plant, × ½; group of spikelets, central spikelet, and fertile floret, × 5. (Palmer 161, Mex.)

113. CATHÉSTECUM Presl

Spikes consisting of 3 spikelets, the upper or central perfect, the 2 lateral staminate or rudimentary, the spike falling entire; central spikelet with 1 perfect floret below and 1 or more reduced florets above; glumes unequal, the first a short, thin, nerveless scale in the central spikelet, narrow and acuminate in the lateral spikelets, the second about as long as the lemma, acuminate, all usually villous; lemma 3-nerved, the nerves extending into awns and the internerves into teeth; nerves of the palea extending into short awns; second and third floret with a fairly well developed lemma and palea, the fourth floret, if present, usually reduced. Low tufted or stoloniferous annuals or perennials, with short blades, and several to many short deciduous spikes approximate on a slender flexuous axis. Type species, *Cathestecum prostratum* Presl. Name from Greek *kathestekos*, set fast, stationary, the application not obvious.

1. Cathestecum eréctum Vasey and Hack. (Fig. 790.) Perennial with wiry stolons having arched internodes and hairy nodes; culms slender, 10 to 30 cm. tall; blades flat, about 1 mm. wide, mostly basal; spikes 4 to 8, ovoid, about 5 mm. long; lateral spikelets about two-thirds as long as the central spikelet; lemmas of all spikelets similar, the sterile ones more deeply lobed; awns from about as long as the lobes to twice as long, hairy at base. ♃ —Dry hills, western Texas, southern Arizona, and northern Mexico.

114. MUNRÓA Torr.

Spikelets in pairs or threes on a short rachis, the lower 1 or 2 larger, 3- or 4-flowered, the upper 2- or 3-flowered, the group (reduced spikes) enclosed in the broad sheaths of short leaves, usually about 3 in a fascicle, forming a cluster or head at the ends of the branches; rachilla disarticulating above the glumes and between the florets; glumes of the lower 1 or 2 spikelets equal, 1-nerved, narrow, acute, a little shorter than the lemmas, those of the upper spikelet unequal, the first much shorter or obsolete; lemmas 3-nerved, those of the lower spikelet coriaceous, acuminate, the points spreading, the midnerve extended into a mucro, those of the upper spikelet mem-

FIGURE 791.—*Munroa squarrosa*. Plant, × ½; group of spikelets, spikelet, and floret, × 5. (Zuck 43, Ariz.)

branaceous; palea narrow, enclosing the oval, dorsally compressed caryopsis. Low-spreading, much-branched annual, the short, flat, pungent leaves in fascicles. Type species, *Munroa squarrosa*. Named for William Munro.

1. Munroa squarrósa (Nutt.) Torr. FALSE BUFFALO GRASS. (Fig. 791.) Forming mats as much as 50 cm. in diameter, the internodes of the prostrate culms scabrous, as much as 10 cm. long, the fascicles at the nodes consisting of several short leafy branches, with 1 or 2 longer branches with slender internodes; blades stiff, mostly less than 3 cm. long, 1 to 3 mm. wide; fascicles of spikelets about 7 mm. long; lemmas with a tuft of hairs on the margin about the middle. ⊙ —Open ground, plains, and hills, at medium altitudes, common in old fields and recently disturbed soil, Alberta and North Dakota to Montana, south to Texas, Arizona, and Nevada. Occasional plants are found with a white floccose covering, the remains of egg cases of a species of woolly aphid. The variety *floccuosa* Vasey was described from such a specimen.

115. BŬCHLOË Engelm.

(*Bulbilis* Raf.)

Plants dioecious or monoecious. Staminate spikelets 2-flowered, sessile and closely imbricate, in 2 rows on one side of a slender rachis, forming a short spike; glumes somewhat unequal, rather broad, 1-nerved, acutish; lemmas longer than the glumes, 3-nerved, rather obtuse, whitish; palea as long as its lemma. Pistillate spikelets mostly 4 or 5 in a short spike or head, this falling entire, usually 2 heads to the inflorescence, the common peduncle short and included in the somewhat inflated sheaths of the upper leaves, the thickened indurate rachis and broad outer (second) glumes forming a rigid white obliquely globular structure crowned by the green-toothed summits of the glumes; first glume (inside) narrow, thin, mucronate, well developed to obsolete in a single head; second glume firm, thick and rigid, rounded on the back, obscurely nerved, expanded in the middle, with inflexed margins, enveloping the floret, abruptly contracted above, the summit with 3 green rigid acuminate lobes; lemma firm-membranaceous, 3-nerved, dorsally compressed, broad below, narrowed into a 3-lobed green summit, the middle lobe much the larger; palea broad, obtuse, about as long as the body of the lemma, enveloping the caryopsis. A low stoloniferous perennial with short curly blades, the staminate flowers in 2 or 3 short spikes on slender, erect culms, the pistillate in sessile heads partly hidden among the leaves. Type species, *Buchloë dactyloides*. Name contracted from Greek *boubalos*, buffalo, and *chloë*, grass, a Greek rendering of the common name, "buffalo grass."

1. Buchloë dactyloídes (Nutt.) Engelm. BUFFALO GRASS. (Fig. 792.) Gray green, forming a dense sod, the curly blades forming a covering 5 to 10 cm. thick; blades rather sparsely pilose, 1 to 2 mm. wide; staminate culms slender, 5 to 20 cm. tall, the spikes 5 to 15 mm. long; pistillate heads 3 to 4 mm. thick. ♃ —Dry plains, western Minnesota to central Montana, south to northwestern Iowa, Texas, western Louisiana, Arizona, and northern Mexico. Buffalo grass forms, when unmixed with other species, a close soft grayish-green turf. It is dominant over large areas on the uplands of the Great Plains, colloquially known as the "short-grass country," and is one of the most important grazing grasses of this region. The foliage cures on the ground and furnishes nutritious feed during the winter. The sod houses of the early settlers were made mostly from the sod of this grass. In 1941 it was planted at Boyce Thompson Institute, Yonkers, N. Y., and is proving to be an excellent cover for exposed dry banks.

FIGURE 792.—*Buchloë dactyloides.* Pistillate and staminate plants, × ½; pistillate spike and floret, × 5; staminate spikelet, × 5. (Ruth 156, Tex.)

TRIBE 8. PHALARIDEAE

116. HIERÓCHLOË R. Br.

(*Savastana* Schrank; *Torresia* Ruiz and Pav.)

Spikelets with 1 terminal perfect floret and 2 staminate florets, disarticulating above the glumes, the staminate florets falling attached to the fertile one; glumes equal, 3-nerved, broad, thin and papery, smooth, acute; staminate lemmas about as long as the glumes, boat-shaped, hispidulous, hairy along the margin; fertile lemma somewhat indurate, about as long as the others, smooth or nearly so, awnless; palea 3-nerved, rounded on the back. Perennial, erect, slender, sweet-smelling grasses, with small panicles of broad, bronze-colored spikelets. Type species, *Hierochloë antarctica* (Labill.) R. Br. Name from Greek *hieros*, sacred, and *chloë*, grass, holy grass; *H. odorata* was used in parts of Europe for "strewing before the doors of churches on festival days."

Flowering culms with short blades only (rarely to 10 cm. long) with few to many long-leaved sterile shoots at base.
  Staminate lemmas bearing exserted awns........ 1. H. ALPINA.
  Staminate lemmas awnless or nearly so........ 2. H. ODORATA.
Flowering culms with blades 25 to 50 cm. long........ 3. H. OCCIDENTALIS.

1. Hierochloë alpína (Swartz) Roem. and Schult. (Fig. 793.) Culms 10 to 40 cm. tall, tufted, with leafy shoots at base and short rhizomes; blades 1 to 2 mm. wide, the basal ones elongate, those of the culm shorter and wider; panicle contracted, 3 to 4 cm. long; spikelets short-pediceled, 6 to 8 mm. long; staminate lemmas ciliate on the margin, awned below the tip, the awn of the second lemma 5 to 8 mm. long, bent, twisted below, that of the first a little shorter, straight; fertile lemma acute, appressed-pubescent toward apex. ♃ —Arctic regions, Greenland to Alaska, south to Newfoundland and Quebec; alpine meadows and rocky slopes, high mountains, Maine, New Hampshire, Vermont, New York, and Montana; Europe.

FIGURE 793.—*Hierochloë alpina*. Plant, × 1; spikelet and floret, × 5. (Hitchcock 16058, N. H.)

2. Hierochloë odoráta (L.) Beauv. SWEETGRASS. (Fig. 794.) Culms 30 to 60 cm. tall, with few to several leafy shoots and slender, creeping rhizomes; blades 2 to 5 mm. wide, sometimes wider, those of the sterile shoots elongate, those of the culm mostly less than 5 cm. long, rarely to 10 cm. long; panicle pyramidal, 4 to 12 cm. long, from somewhat compact to loose with slender drooping branches; spikelets mostly short-pediceled, 5 mm. long; staminate lemmas awnless or nearly so, fertile lemma pubescent toward the apex. ♃ —Meadows, bogs, and moist places, Labrador to Alaska, south to New Jersey, Indiana, Iowa, Oregon, and in the mountains to New Mexico and Arizona; Eurasia. The Indians use the grass, known as Seneca grass, to make fragrant baskets. Also called holy grass and vanilla grass. A tall form with culm blades 12 to 17 cm. long, and a very loose lax panicle,

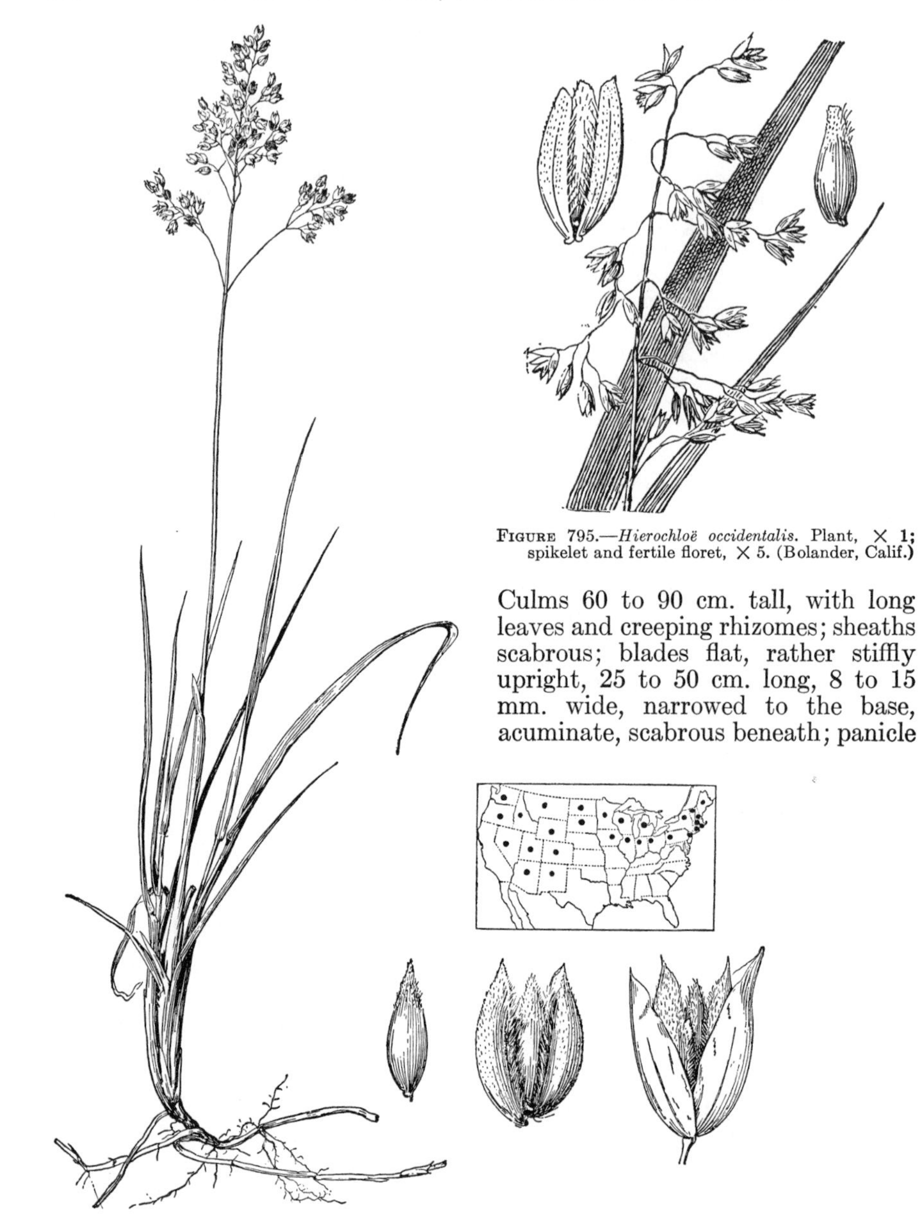

FIGURE 795.—*Hierochloë occidentalis*. Plant, × 1; spikelet and fertile floret, × 5. (Bolander, Calif.)

FIGURE 794.—*Hierochloë odorata*. Plant, × ½; spikelet, florets, and fertile floret, × 5. (Shear 437, Mont.)

found in Van Cortlandt Park, New York City, has been described as *Hierochloë nashii* Kaczmarek (*Savastana nashii* Bickn.).

3. Hierochloë occidentális Buckl. CALIFORNIA SWEETGRASS. (Fig. 795.) Culms 60 to 90 cm. tall, with long leaves and creeping rhizomes; sheaths scabrous; blades flat, rather stiffly upright, 25 to 50 cm. long, 8 to 15 mm. wide, narrowed to the base, acuminate, scabrous beneath; panicle mostly open, 7 to 15 cm. long, the subcapillary branches drooping, loosely flowered or the spikelets aggregate toward the ends, the lower branches 2.5 to 7 cm. long; spikelets 4 to 5 mm. long, the glumes with a pale shining margin; staminate lemmas awnless or nearly so; fertile lemma appressed-pubescent toward apex. ♃ (*H. macrophylla* Thurb.)—Forests in the redwood belt, Oregon to Monterey, Calif.; Bingen, Wash.

117. ANTHOXÁNTHUM L. VERNALGRASS

Spikelets with 1 terminal perfect floret and 2 sterile lemmas, the rachilla disarticulating above the glumes, the sterile lemmas falling attached to the fertile floret; glumes unequal, acute or mucronate; sterile lemmas shorter than the glumes, empty, awned from the back; fertile lemma shorter than the sterile ones, awnless; palea 1-nerved, rounded on the back, enclosed in the lemma. Sweet-smelling annuals or perennials, with flat blades and spikelike panicles. Type species, *Anthoxanthum odoratum*. Name from Greek *anthos*, flower, and *xanthos*, yellow, alluding to the yellow inflorescence.

Plants perennial........ 1. A. ODORATUM.
Plants annual........ 2. A. ARISTATUM.

1. Anthoxanthum odorátum L. SWEET VERNALGRASS. (Fig. 796, *A*.) Culms tufted, erect, slender, 30 to 60 cm. tall, rarely to 1 m. tall; blades 2 to 5 mm. wide; panicle long-exserted, brownish yellow, acute, 2 to 6 cm. long; spikelets 8 to 10 mm. long; glumes scabrous, the first about half as long as the second; sterile lemmas subequal, appressed-pilose with golden hairs, the first short-awned below the apex, the second awned from near the base, the awn twisted below, geniculate, slightly exceeding the second glume; fertile lemma about 2 mm. long, brown, smooth and shining. ♃ —Meadows, pastures, and waste places, Greenland and Newfoundland to Louisiana and Michigan, and on the Pacific coast from British Columbia to California; introduced from Eurasia. Sometimes included in meadow mixtures to give fragrance to the hay, but the grass has little forage value.

2. Anthoxanthum aristátum Boiss. (Fig. 796, *B*.) Differing from *A. odoratum* in being annual, the culms lower, often geniculate and bushy branching; panicles looser; spikelets a little smaller. ⊙ —Waste places in several localities from Maine to Iowa; West Virginia; North Carolina; Florida; Mississippi and Arkansas; Vancouver Island to California; introduced from Europe.

ANTHOXANTHUM GRÁCILE Bivon. Tufted annual; culms 20 cm. tall; blades pubescent; panicle silvery; spikelets about 12 mm. long, conspicuously awned. ⊙ —Occasionally cultivated for dry bouquets. Italy.

EHRHÁRTA Thunb.

Spikelets laterally compressed with 1 fertile floret and 2 large sterile lemmas below enclosing the fertile floret; rachilla disarticulating above the glumes, the fertile floret and sterile lemmas falling together; glumes ovate, rather obscurely keeled; sterile lemmas indurate, compressed, 3- to 5-nerved; fertile lemma indurate, ovate, 5-nerved, obtuse. Erect or decumbent spreading annuals or perennials with flat blades and narrow panicles. Type species, *Ehrharta capensis* Thunb. Named for Friedrich Ehrhart.

Ehrharta eréсta Lam. Culms erect or ascending from a decumbent base, branching, mostly 30 to 50 cm. tall; blades 5 to 12 cm. long, 4 to 9 mm. wide; panicles 6 to 15 cm. long, the branches narrowly ascending or sometimes spreading; spikelets 3 to 3.5 mm. long; sterile lemmas awnless, the first smooth, the second cross-wrinkled. ♃ —Escaped, Berkeley, Calif. Introduced from South Africa. Shows considerable competitive ability and may become of value in re-

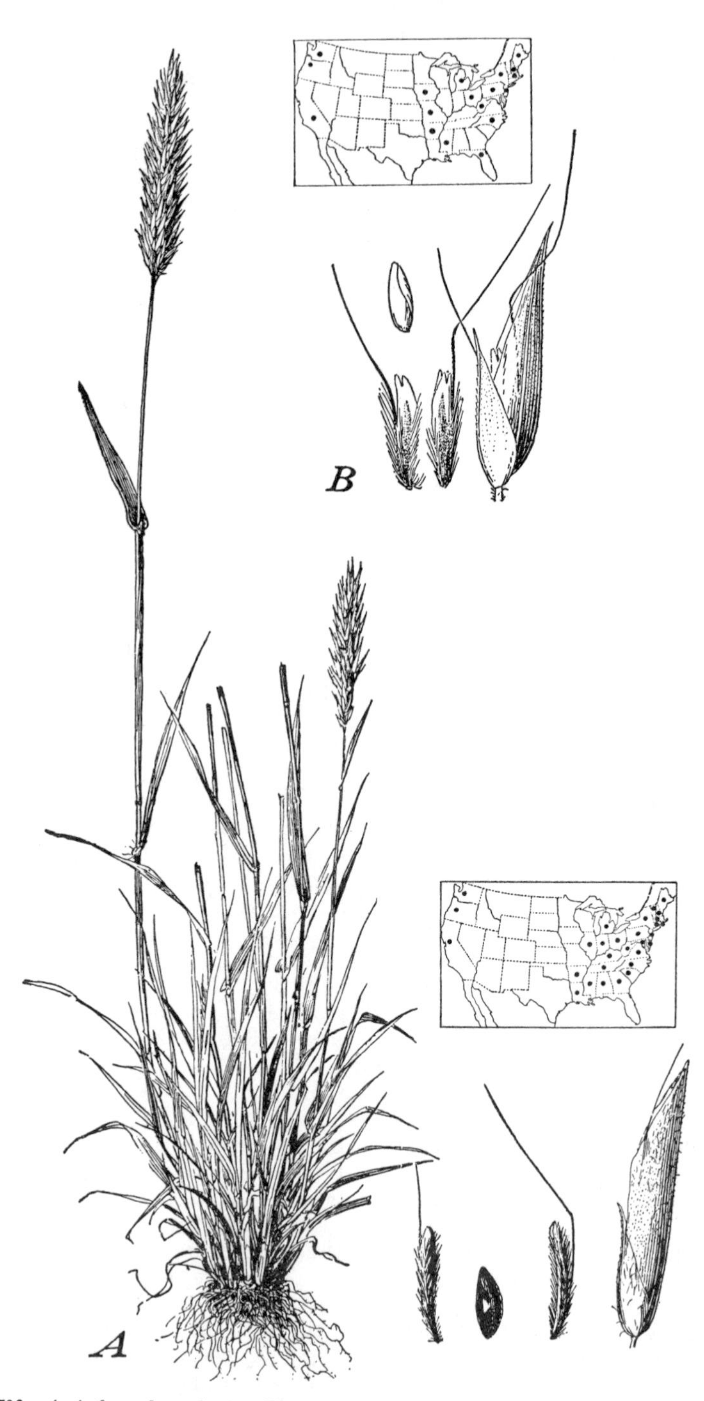

FIGURE 796.—*A*, *Anthoxanthum odoratum*. Plant, × ½; spikelet, sterile lemmas, and fertile floret, × 5. (Biltmore Herb. 74b, N. C.) *B*, *A. aristatum*. Spikelet, sterile florets, and fertile floret, × 5, (White 1591, N. Y.)

placing some of the troublesome weeds.

Ehrharta calycina J. E. Smith. Erect leafy perennial to 75 cm. tall; panicle 10 to 15 cm. long, branchlets and pedicels subcapillary; spikelets 7 to 8 mm. long, purplish; glumes nearly as long as the lemmas; sterile lemmas thinly silky-villous; fertile lemma silky on the nerves. ♃ —Grown at Davis, Calif., as a promising drought-resistant grass for nonirrigated range lands. Introduced; South Africa.

118. PHÁLARIS L. Canary grass

Spikelets laterally compressed, with 1 terminal perfect floret and 2 sterile lemmas below (obsolete in *Phalaris paradoxa*), the rachilla disarticulating above the glumes, the usually inconspicuous sterile lemmas falling closely appressed to the fertile floret; glumes equal, boat-shaped, often winged on the keel; sterile lemmas reduced to 2 small, usually minute, scales (rarely only 1); fertile lemma coriaceous, shorter than the glumes, enclosing the faintly 2-nerved palea. Annuals or perennials, with numerous flat blades, and narrow or spikelike panicles. Type species, *Phalaris canariensis*. *Phalaris*, an old Greek name for a grass.

Spikelets in groups of 7, 1 fertile surrounded by 6 sterile, the group falling entire. 1. P. paradoxa.
Spikelets all alike, not in groups falling entire.
  Plants perennial.
    Rhizomes wanting; panicle dense, ovate or oblong .... 8. P. californica.
    Rhizomes present; panicle narrow, spreading during anthesis .... 9. P. arundinacea.
  Plants annual.
    Glumes broadly winged; panicle ovate or short-oblong.
      Sterile lemma solitary; fertile lemma 3 mm. long .... 4. P. minor.
      Sterile lemmas 2, fertile lemma 4 to 6 mm. long.
        Sterile lemmas 0.6 mm. long or less .... 3. P. brachystachys.
        Sterile lemmas half as long as fertile .... 2. P. canariensis.
    Glumes wingless or nearly so; panicles oblong or linear, dense.
      Glumes wingless, acuminate; fertile lemma turgid, the acuminate apex smooth. 7. P. lemmoni.
      Glumes narrowly winged toward summit, acute or abruptly pointed; fertile lemma less turgid, villous to the acute apex.
        Panicle tapering to each end, mostly 2 to 6 cm. long (occasionally longer). 5. P. caroliniana.
        Panicle subcylindric, mostly 6 to 15 cm. long (occasionally smaller). 6. P. angusta.

1. Phalaris paradóxa L. (Fig. 797.) Annual, tufted, more or less spreading at base; culms 30 to 60 cm. tall; panicle dense, oblong, narrowed at base, 2 to 6 cm. long, often enclosed at base in the uppermost enlarged sheath; spikelets finally falling from the axis in groups of 6 or 7, those of the upper part of the panicle slender-pediceled, the central spikelet fertile, the subulate-acuminate glumes with a prominent toothlike wing near the middle of the keel, the others sterile, with smaller pointed glumes with toothed-winged keels; fertile lemma 3 mm. long, with only a few hairs toward the summit, the sterile lemmas obsolete; spikelets of lower part of panicle short-pediceled, the glumes of the outer 4 spikelets deformed, cuneate-clavate. ⊙ —Occasional in grainfields and waste places, California and Arizona; ballast, Philadelphia, New Orleans; introduced from Mediterranean region.

Phalaris paradoxa var. praemórsa (Lam.) Coss. and Dur. Panicle mostly smaller, all the spikelets short-pediceled and with outer sterile spikelets having deformed clavate glumes, as in the lower part of panicle of the species; glumes of all spikelets subindurate. ⊙ —Fields and waste

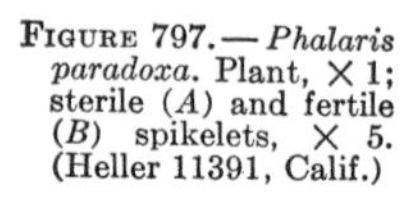
FIGURE 797.—*Phalaris paradoxa*. Plant, × 1; sterile (*A*) and fertile (*B*) spikelets, × 5. (Heller 11391, Calif.)

places, Washington to California and Arizona; ballast, Philadelphia; introduced from Mediterranean region.

2. **Phalaris canariénsis** L. CANARY GRASS. (Fig. 798.) Annual; culms erect, 30 to 60 cm. tall; panicle ovate to oblong-ovate, dense, 1.5 to 4 cm. long; spikelets broad, imbricate, pale with green stripes; glumes 7 to 8 mm. long, abruptly pointed, the green keel with a prominent pale wing, broadened upward; fertile lemma 5 to 6 mm. long, acute, densely appressed-pubescent; sterile lemmas at least half as long as fertile. ⊙ —Waste places, infrequent, Nova Scotia to Alaska, south to Virginia, Kansas, Wyoming, Arizona, and California, and occasionally southward; introduced from the western Mediterranean region. This species furnishes the canary seed of commerce.

3. **Phalaris brachýstachys** Link. (Fig. 799.) Differing from *P. canariensis* in having smaller spikelets, the glumes about 6 mm. long, the fertile lemma 4 to 5 mm. long, and especially in the short sterile lemmas not more than 0.6 mm. long. ⊙ —Texas (Asherton); California (Butte County); Oregon (ballast, near Portland); introduced from the Mediterranean region.

4. **Phalaris mínor** Retz. (Fig. 800.) Resembling *P. canariensis*; panicle ovate-oblong, 2 to 5 cm. long; spikelets narrower, not so conspicuously striped; glumes 4 to 6 mm. long, the wing of the keel narrower; fertile lemma lance-ovate, about 3 mm. long, acute; sterile lemma solitary, about 1 mm. long. ⊙ —Fields and waste places, New Brunswick to New Jersey, rare; Louisiana and Texas; Colorado; ballast, near Portland, Oreg.; Arizona; frequent in California; Mexico; introduced from the Mediterranean region.

5. **Phalaris caroliniána** Walt. (Fig. 801.) Annual; culms erect, 30 to 60

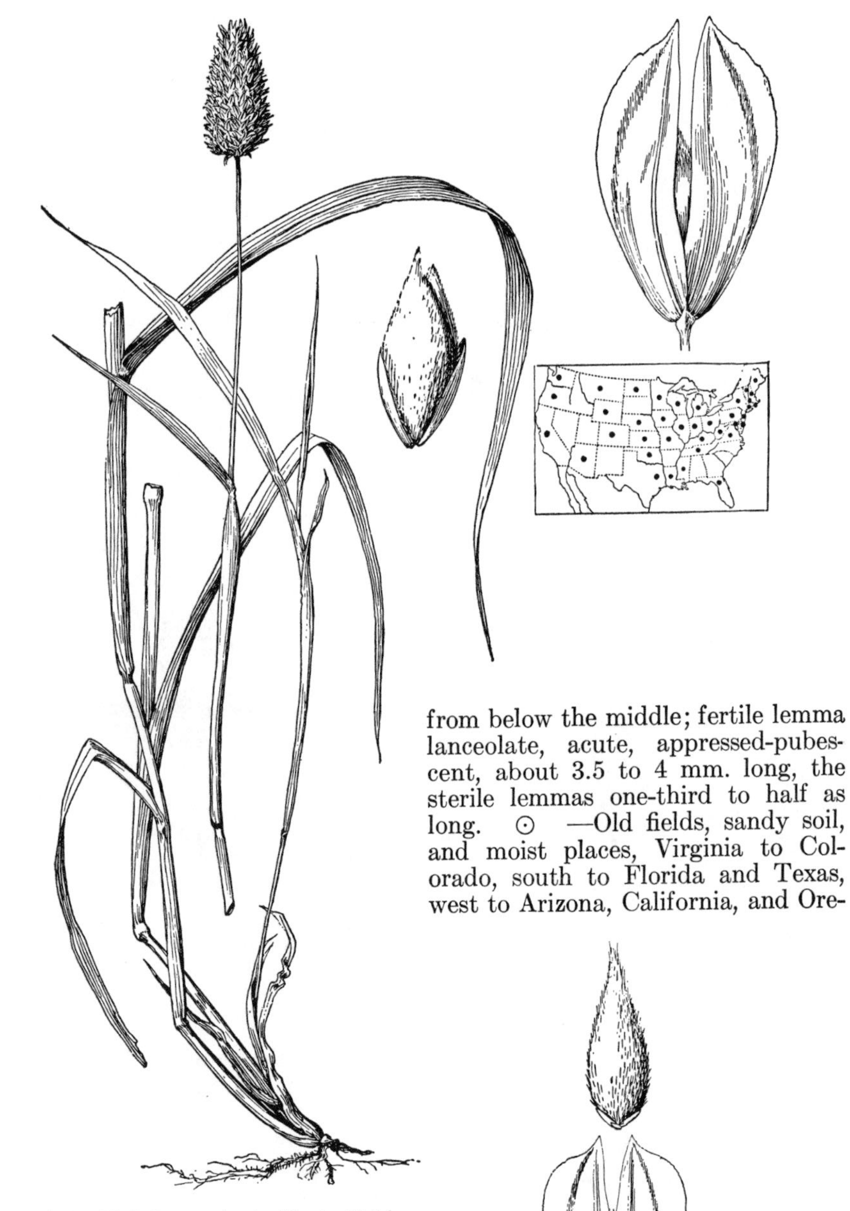

FIGURE 798.—*Phalaris canariensis*. Plant, × ½; spikelet and floret, × 5. (Mearns 3376, Wyo.)

cm. tall or even more; panicle oblong, 2 to 6 cm. long, occasionally longer, tapering to each end; glumes 5 to 6 mm. long, oblong, rather abruptly narrowed to an acute apex, the keel scabrous and narrowly winged above from below the middle; fertile lemma lanceolate, acute, appressed-pubescent, about 3.5 to 4 mm. long, the sterile lemmas one-third to half as long. ⊙ —Old fields, sandy soil, and moist places, Virginia to Colorado, south to Florida and Texas, west to Arizona, California, and Ore-

FIGURE 799.—*Phalaris brachystachys*. Spikelet and floret, × 5. (Suksdorf 1904, Oreg.)

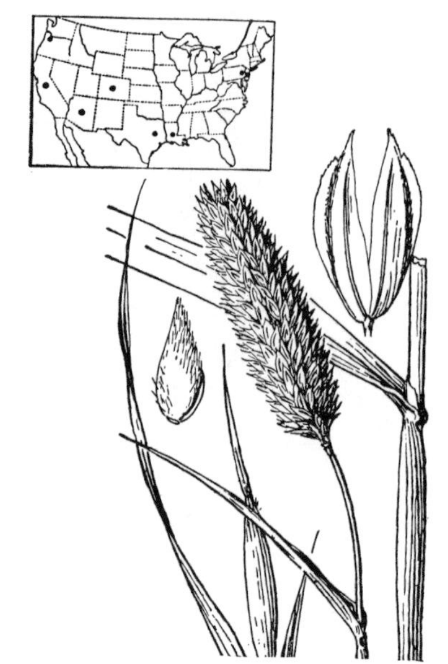

FIGURE 800.—*Phalaris minor*. Plant, × 1; glumes and floret, × 5. (Ball 1932, Calif.)

gon. A few specimens from the Pacific coast are relatively robust, up to 80 cm. tall, with panicles 3 to 8 cm. long,

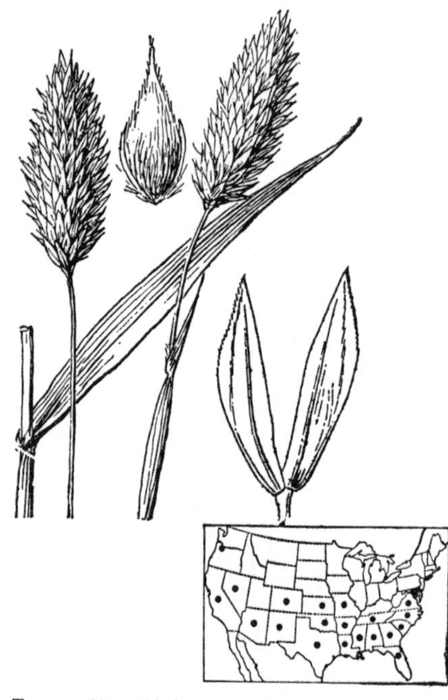

FIGURE 801.—*Phalaris caroliniana*. Plant, × 1; glumes and floret, × 5. (Hitchcock 1074, Miss.)

some of them slightly lobed and not tapering to the base, the spikelets 6 to 6.5 mm. long.

6. Phalaris angústa Nees ex Trin. (Fig. 802.) Annual; culms 1 to 1.5 m. tall; panicle subcylindric, mostly 6 to 15 cm. long, about 8 mm. thick; glumes 3.5 to 4 mm. long, narrow, abruptly pointed, the keel scabrous and narrowly winged toward the summit; fertile lemma ovate-lanceolate, acute, appressed-pubescent, 3 mm. long; sterile lemmas about one-third as long. ⊙ —Open ground at low altitudes, Mississippi, Louisiana, and Texas; Arizona and California; southern South America.

FIGURE 802.—*Phalaris angusta*. Plant, × 1; glumes and floret, × 5. (Suksdorf 32, Calif.)

7. Phalaris lemmóni Vasey. (Fig. 803.) Annual; culms 30 to 90 cm. tall; panicle 5 to 15 cm. long, subcylindric or lobed toward base, often purplish; glumes about 5 mm. long, narrow, acuminate, scabrous, not winged on the keel; fertile lemma ovate-lanceolate, acuminate, 3.5 to 4 mm. long, brown at maturity, appressed-pubescent, except the acuminate tip, sterile lemmas (1 or 2) less than one-third as long. ⊙ —Moist places, at low altitudes, in the coastal valleys, central and southern California.

8. Phalaris califórnica Hook. and Arn. (Fig. 804.) Perennial, often in dense tussocks; culms erect, 75 to 160 cm. tall; blades rather lax, 8 to 15 mm. wide; panicle ovoid or oblong, 2 to 5 cm. long, 2 to 2.5 cm. thick, often purplish-tinged; glumes 6 to 8 mm. long, narrow, tapering from below the middle to an acute apex, the keel smooth or nearly so, sharp but not winged; fertile lemma ovate-lanceolate, about 4 mm. long, rather sparsely appressed-pubescent, the palea often exposed, the sterile lemmas half to two-thirds as long. ♃ —Ravines and open moist ground in the Coast Range, southwestern Oregon to San Luis Obispo County, Calif.

Figure 803.—*Phalaris lemmoni*. Glumes and floret, × 5. (Type.)

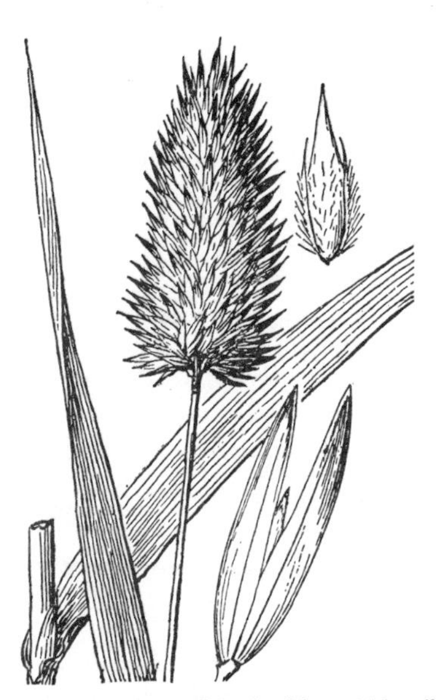

Figure 804.—*Phalaris californica*. Plant, × 1; spikelet and floret, × 5. (Heller 6677, Calif.)

Figure 805.—*Phalaris arundinacea*. Plant, × 1; glumes and floret, × 4. (Chase 7583, Md.)

Figure 806.—*Phalaris tuberosa* var. *stenoptera*, × 5. (McCrary, N. C.)

9. Phalaris arundinácea L. Reed canary grass. (Fig. 805.) Perennial, with creeping rhizomes, glaucous; culms erect, 60 to 150 cm. tall; panicle 7 to 18 cm. long, narrow, the branches spreading during anthesis, the lower as much as 5 cm. long; glumes about 5 mm. long, narrow, acute, the keel scabrous, very narrowly winged; fertile lemma lanceolate, 4 mm. long, with a few appressed hairs; sterile lemmas villous, 1 mm. long. ♃ —Marshes, river banks, and moist places, New Brunswick to southeastern Alaska (also at Tanana Hot Springs, Alaska), south to North Carolina, Kentucky, Oklahoma, New Mexico, Arizona, and northeastern California; Eurasia. An important constituent of lowland hay from Montana to Wisconsin. PHALARIS ARUNDINACEA var. PÍCTA L. RIBBON GRASS. Blades striped with white. ♃ —Grown for ornament in gardens; also called gardener's garters.

PHALARIS TUBERÓSA var. STENÓPTERA (Hack.) Hitchc. (Fig. 806.) Perennial, with a loose branching, rhizomatous base; culms stout, as much as 1.5 m. tall; panicle 5 to 15 cm. long, 1.5 cm. wide, slightly lobed; glumes 5 to 6 mm. long, the keel scabrous, rather narrowly winged on the upper two-thirds; fertile lemma 4 mm. long, ovate-lanceolate, acute, appressed-pubescent; sterile lemma usually solitary, about one-third as long as fertile lemma. ♃ —About 1902 there appeared in Queensland, Australia, the source unknown, a species of *Phalaris* which gave promise of being a valuable forage grass. About 1907 it was distributed from the Toowoomba Botanic Gardens, Queensland. Stapf, of Kew Gardens, identified this grass as *P. bulbosa* L. Hackel described it as a distinct species, *P. stenoptera*. It has been grown at the California Experiment Station from seed from South Africa. It has also been cultivated in Oregon, in Washington, D. C., and in North Carolina, and is spontaneous in Humboldt County, Calif. This differs from typical *P. tuberosa* of the Mediterranean region in having short vertical or ascending, sometimes branching, rhizomes, the base of the culms little or not at all swollen. It has been called Harding grass. Burbank distributed it as *P. stenophylla* (error for *stenoptera*), calling it Peruvian wintergrass. The name *P. bulbosa* has been misapplied to *P. tuberosa* L., but true *P. bulbosa* L. is a species of *Phleum* (*P. tenue* Schrad.; *P. bulbosum* (L.) Richt.).

TRIBE 9. ORYZEAE

119. ORÝZA L. RICE

Spikelets 1-flowered, laterally compressed, disarticulating below the glumes; glumes 2, much shorter than the lemma, narrow; lemma rigid, keeled, 5-nerved, the outer nerves near the margin, the apex sometimes awned; palea similar to the lemma, narrower, keeled, with a median bundle but with no strong midnerve on the back, 2-nerved close to the margins. Annual or sometimes perennial swamp grasses, often tall, with flat blades and spikelets in open panicles. Type species, *Oryza sativa*. Name from *oruza*, old Greek name for rice. The spikelet in *Oryza* and *Leersia* is interpreted by Stapf, Arber, and some others as consisting of 2 greatly reduced glumes and 2 subulate sterile lemmas below the single fertile floret. The true glumes, according to this interpretation, are represented by the minute cuplike expansion, sometimes distinctly 2-lobed, at the summit of the pedicel, persistent and showing no line of demarcation from the pedicel, the articulation of the spikelet being below the sterile lemmas, the latter wanting in *Leersia*. The problem deserves further study.

1. Oryza satíva L. RICE. (Fig. 807.) Annual, or in tropical regions sometimes perennial; culms erect, 1 to 2 m. tall; blades elongate; panicle rather dense, drooping, 15 to 40 cm. long; spikelets 7 to 10 mm. long, 3 to 4 mm. wide; lemma and palea papillose-roughened and with scattered appressed hairs, the lemma from mucronate to long-awned. ⊙ —Cultivated in all warm countries at low altitudes where there is sufficient moisture; one of the world's most important food plants; sometimes adventive near the coast from Virginia to Florida and Texas.

FIGURE 807.—*Oryza sativa*. Plant, × ½; spikelet, × 5. (Cult.)

120. LEÉRSIA Swartz

(*Homalocenchrus* Mieg.)

Spikelets 1-flowered, strongly compressed laterally, disarticulating from the pedicel; glumes wanting; lemma chartaceous, broad, oblong to oval, boat-shaped, usually 5-nerved, the lateral pair of nerves close to the margins, these and the keel often hispid-ciliate, the intermediate nerves sometimes faint; palea as long as the lemma, much narrower, usually 3-nerved, the keel usually hispid-ciliate, the lateral nerves close to the margins, the margins firmly held by the margins of the lemma; stamens 6 or fewer. Perennials, usually with creeping rhizomes, flat, scabrous blades, and mostly open panicles. Type species, *Leersia oryzoides*. Named for J. D. Leers.

Spikelets broadly oval, 3 to 4 mm. wide .... 1. L. LENTICULARIS.
Spikelets elliptic, not more than 2 mm. wide.
  Panicle narrow, the branches ascending or appressed .... 4. L. HEXANDRA.
  Panicle open, the capillary branches finally spreading.
    Spikelets glabrous, about 2 mm. long; culms tufted, erect; rhizomes wanting. 5. L. MONANDRA.
    Spikelets hispidulous; culms decumbent at base; rhizomes present.
      Lower panicle branches solitary; spikelets 3 mm. long, 1 mm. wide. 3. L. VIRGINICA.
      Lower panicle branches fascicled; spikelets 5 mm. long, 1.5 to 2 mm. wide. 2. L. ORYZOIDES.

1. Leersia lenticuláris Michx. CATCHFLY GRASS. (Fig. 808.) Culms straggling, 1 to 1.5 m. tall, with creeping scaly rhizomes; sheaths scabrous at least toward the summit; blades lax, 1 to 2 cm. wide; panicle open, drooping, 10 to 20 cm. long, the branches ascending or spreading, naked below, branched above, branchlets bearing closely imbricate spikelets along one side; spikelets pale, broadly oval, very flat, 4 to 5 mm. long, sparsely hispidulous, the keels bristly ciliate. ♃ —Ditches and swamps, Maryland to Minnesota, south to Florida and Texas.

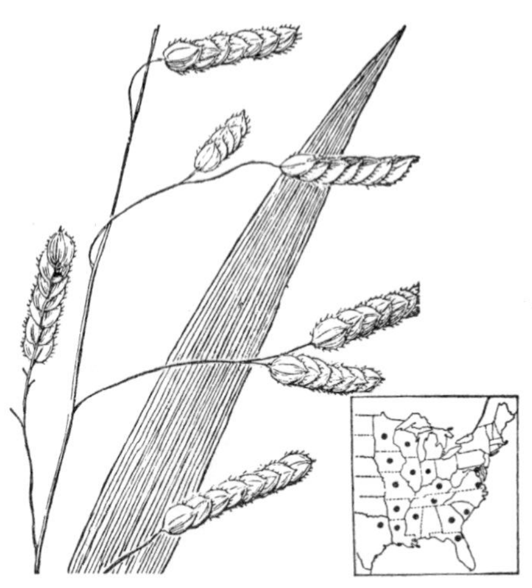

FIGURE 808.—*Leersia lenticularis*, × 1. (McDonald 68, Ill.)

2. Leersia oryzoídes (L.) Swartz. RICE CUTGRASS. (Fig. 809.) Culms slender, weak, often decumbent at base, 1 to 1.5 m. tall, with slender creeping rhizomes; sheaths and blades strongly retrorsely scabrous, the blades mostly 8 to 10 mm. wide; panicles terminal and axillary, 10 to 20 cm. long, the flexuous branches finally spreading, the spikelets more loosely imbricate than in *L. lenticularis;* spikelets elliptic, 5 mm. long, 1.5 to 2 mm. wide, sparsely hispidulous, the keels bristly ciliate; axillary panicles reduced, partly included in the sheaths, the spikelets cleistogamous. ♃ —Marshes, river banks, and wet places, often forming a zone around ponds and lakes, Quebec and Maine to British Columbia and eastern Washington south to northern Florida, Texas, Colorado, Arizona, and southeastern California; Europe. The late cleistogamous phase has been described as *L. oryzoides* forma *inclusa* (Wiesb.) Dörfl.

3. Leersia virgínica Willd. WHITEGRASS. (Fig. 810.) Culms slender,

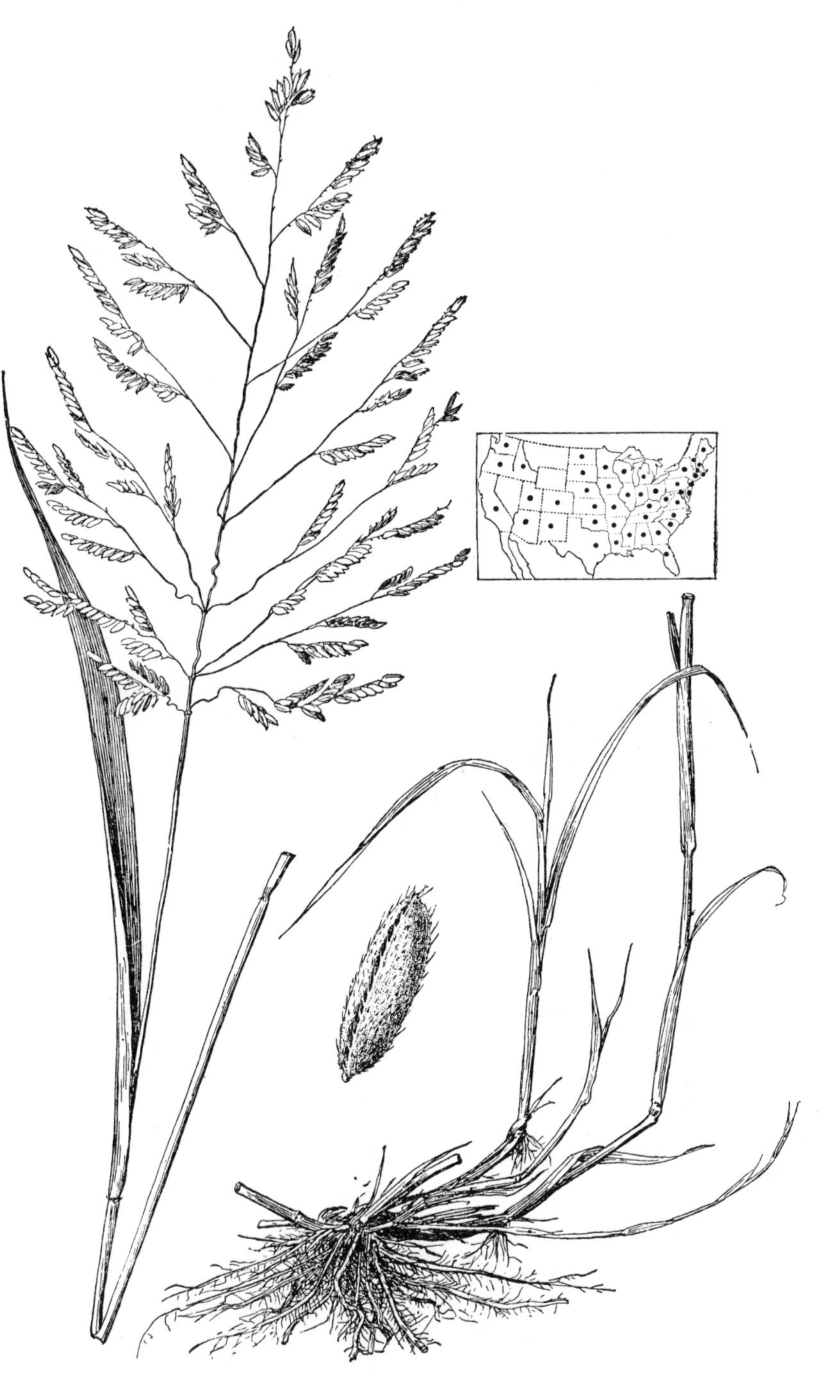

FIGURE 809.—*Leersia oryzoides*. Plant, × ½; spikelet, × 5. (Hitchcock 5317, Tex.)

FIGURE 810.—*Leersia virginica*, × 1. (French, Iowa.)

weak, branching, 50 to 120 cm. tall, with clusters of very scaly rhizomes much stouter than the culm base; blades relatively short, 6 to 12 mm. wide; panicle open, 10 to 20 cm. long, the capillary branches rather distant, stiffly spreading, naked below, those of the branches smaller, sometimes included in the sheath; spikelets oblong, closely appressed to the branchlets, about 3 mm. long and 1 mm. wide, sparsely hispidulous, the keels short-hispid. ♃ —Low woods and moist places, Quebec to South Dakota, south to Florida and Texas.

4. Leersia hexándra Swartz. (Fig. 811.) Culms slender, weak, usually long-decumbent from a creeping and rooting base, with slender rhizomes and extensively creeping leafy stolons; the flowering culms upright; blades rather stiff, 2 to 5 mm. wide; panicle narrow, 5 to 10 cm. long, the branches ascending or appressed, floriferous nearly to the base; spikelets oblong, about 4 to 5 mm. long, a little more than 1 mm. wide, often purplish, sparsely hispidulous, the keels bristly ciliate. ♃ —Shallow water, ditches, and wet places near the coast, Virginia to Florida and Texas; widely distributed in the tropics of both hemispheres.

FIGURE 811.—*Leersia hexandra*, × 1. (Wurzlow, La.)

FIGURE 812.—*Leersia monandra*, × 1. (Nealley, Tex.)

5. Leersia monándra Swartz. (Fig. 812.) Culms tufted, erect, wiry, 50 to 100 cm. tall, without rhizomes; sheaths smooth or nearly so; blades elongate, 1 to 5 mm. wide; panicle open, the capillary solitary branches spreading, naked below, the small spikelets near the ends; spikelets pale, broadly ovate, glabrous, about

2 mm. long. ♃ —Rocky woods and prairies, Florida Keys, southern Florida, and southern Texas; West Indies.

TRIBE 10. ZIZANIEAE

121. ZIZÁNIA L. Wildrice

Spikelets unisexual, 1-flowered, disarticulating from the pedicel; glumes obsolete, represented by a small collarlike ridge; pistillate spikelet terete, angled at maturity; lemma chartaceous, 3-nerved, tapering into a long slender awn; palea 2-nerved, closely clasped by the lemma; grain cylindric, 1 to 2 cm. long; staminate spikelet soft; lemma 5-nerved, membranaceous, linear, acuminate or awn-pointed; palea about as long as the lemma, 3-nerved; stamens 6. Tall aquatic annuals or perennials, with flat blades and large terminal panicles, the lower branches ascending or spreading, bearing the pendulous staminate spikelets, the upper branches ascending, at maturity erect, bearing appressed pistillate spikelets, the staminate spikelets early deciduous, the pistillate spikelets tardily deciduous. Type species, *Zizania aquatica.* Name from *Zizanion,* an old Greek name for a weed growing in grain, the tares of the Scripture parable.

The seeds of wildrice were used by the aborigines for food and are still used to some extent by some of the northern tribes of Indians. Wildrice is important as a food and as shelter for waterfowl and is sometimes planted for this purpose in marshes on game preserves. The Chinese cultivate the Asiatic species, *Z. latifolia* (Griseb.) Turcz., as the source of a vegetable which they call *kau sun.* This consists of a thickened portion of the base of the culm, the point of incipient fruiting of a smut fungus, *Ustilago edulis.*

Plants annual, erect........ 1. Z. aquatica.
Plants perennial, long-decumbent at base........ 2. Z. texana.

1. Zizania aquática L. Annual wildrice. (Fig. 813, *B*.) Annual; culms robust, usually 2 to 3 m. tall; blades elongate, 1 to 4 cm. wide, scaberulous; ligule 10 to 15 mm. long; panicles mostly 30 to 50 cm. long, the branches mostly 15 to 20 cm. long; lemma and palea of pistillate spikelet about 2 cm. long, thin, hispid throughout. ⊙ —Marshes and borders of streams and ponds, usually in shallow water, Maine to Michigan and Illinois, south to Florida and Louisiana; Idaho.

Zizania aquatica var. angustifólia Hitchc. Culms usually not more than 1.5 m. tall; ligule 3 to 8 mm. long; blades usually not more than 1 cm. wide; lemma and palea of pistillate spikelet mostly larger, firm, shining, hispid only on the margin and nerves. ⊙ —Shallow water, Quebec and New Brunswick to North Dakota, south to New York and Nebraska.

Zizania aquatica var. intérior Fassett. (Fig. 813, *A*.) Closely resembling the species, or the blades narrower; pistillate spikelet as in var. *angustifolia;* intergrades in the Middle West. ⊙ —Michigan and Indiana to North and South Dakota; Idaho.

2. Zizania texána Hitchc. Texas wildrice. (Fig. 814.) Perennial; culm long-decumbent and rooting at base, 1 to 3 m. long; blades elongate, 3 to 15 or even 20 mm. wide; panicle 20 to 30 cm. long, narrow, the lower (staminate) branches ascending, 5 to 10 cm. long; staminate spikelets 7 to 9 mm. long, 1.5 mm. wide; pistillate spikelets about 1 cm. long, tapering into an awn 1 to 2 cm. long. ♃

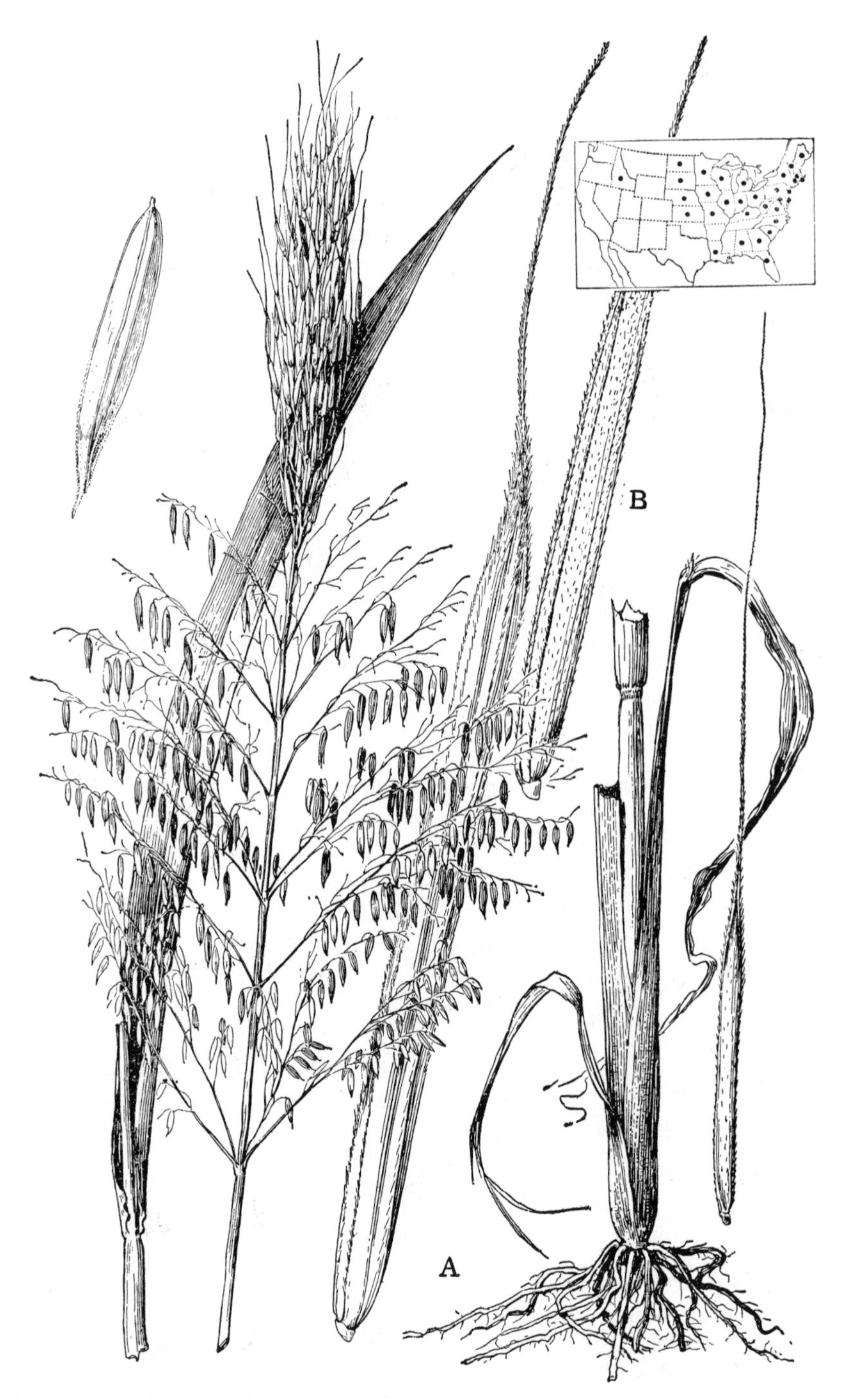

FIGURE 813.—*A*, *Zizania aquatica* var. *interior*. Plant, × ½; pistillate spikelet, × 2; second view, × 5. (Fink, Iowa.) *B*, *Z. aquatica*. Pistillate spikelet, × 5. (Hitchcock, Va.)

—Growing in rapidly flowing water, San Marcos, Tex. The grass grows in water 30 to 120 cm. deep, the lower part of the plant prostrate or floating on the water, the upper part erect. Flowers from April to November and at warm periods during winter. Said to be troublesome in irrigation ditches.

122. ZIZANIÓPSIS Doell and Aschers.

Spikelets unisexual, 1-flowered, disarticulating from the pedicel, mixed on the same branches of the panicle, the staminate below; glumes wanting; lemma 7-nerved, short-awned in the pistillate spikelets; palea 3-nerved; staminate spikelets with 6 stamens; styles rather long, united; fruit obovate, free from the lemma and palea, coriaceous, smooth and shining, beaked with the persistent style; seed free from the pericarp. Robust perennial marsh grasses, with stout creeping rhizomes, broad flat blades, and large open panicles. Type species, *Zizaniopsis microstachya* (Nees) Doell and Aschers. Name from *Zizania*, a generic name, and Greek *opsis*, appearance, alluding to the similarity to *Zizania*.

1. Zizaniopsis miliácea (Michx.) Doell and Aschers. (Fig. 815.) SOUTHERN WILDRICE. Culms 1 to 3 m. tall or even taller; blades glabrous except the very scabrous margins, 1 to 2 cm. wide, the midrib stout; panicle rather narrow, nodding, 30 to 50 cm. long, the numerous branches fascicled, as much as 15 to 20 cm. long, naked at base; spikelets 6 to 8 mm. long, short-awned, the staminate slender, the pistillate turgid at maturity. ♃ —Marshes, creeks, and river banks, Maryland to Kentucky and Oklahoma, south to Florida and Texas.

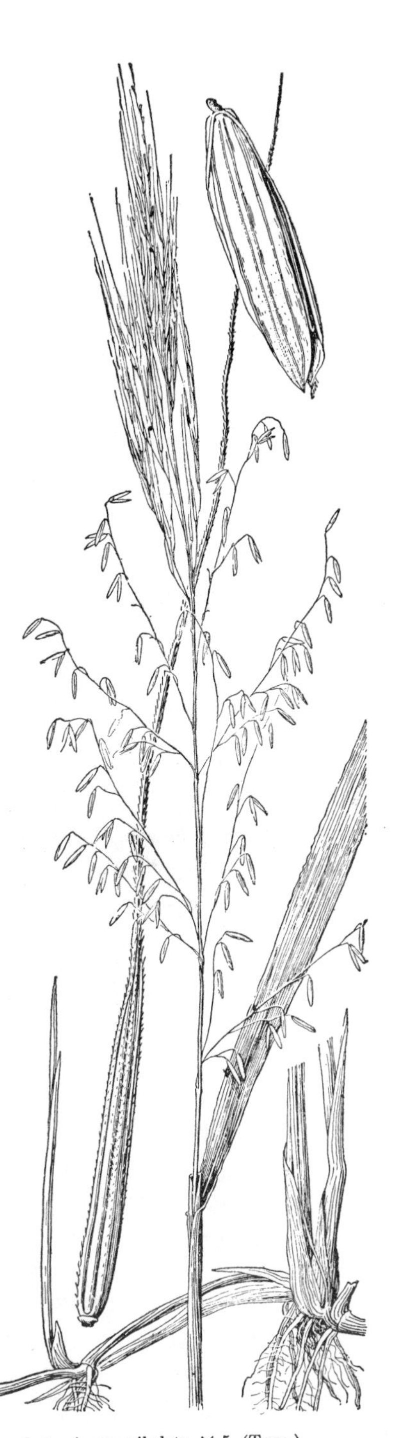

FIGURE 814.—*Zizania texana*. Plant, × ½; pistillate and staminate spikelets, × 5. (Type.)

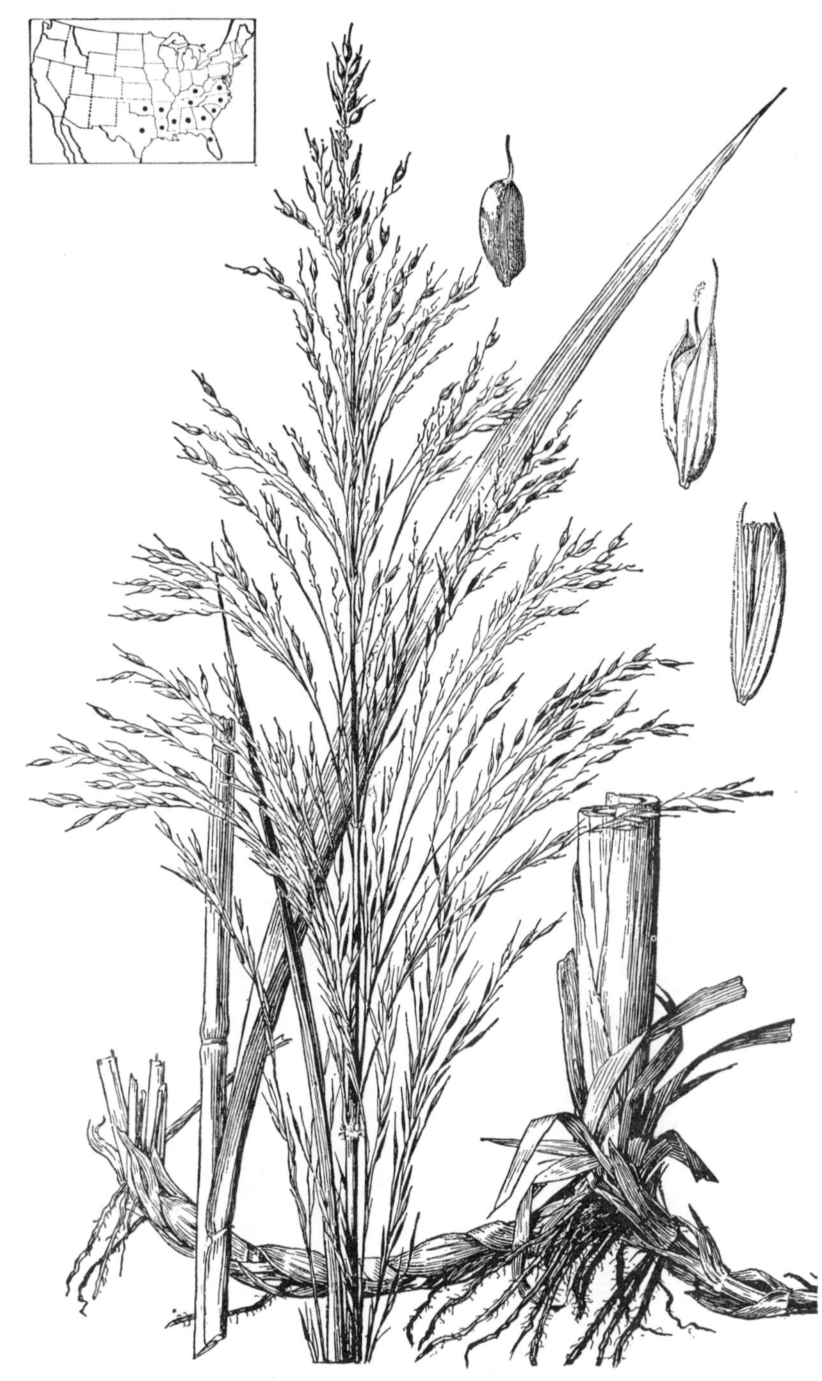

FIGURE 815.—*Zizaniopsis miliacea.* Plant, × ½; staminate spikelet, pistillate spikelet, and ripe caryopsis, × 5. (Chase 7121, S. C.)

123. LUZÍOLA Juss.

Spikelets unisexual, 1-flowered, disarticulating from the pedicel, the staminate and pistillate spikelets in separate panicles on the same plant; glumes

FIGURE 816.—*Luziola peruviana*. Plant, × ½; pistillate and staminate spikelets, × 5. (Curtiss 6871, Fla.)

wanting; lemma and palea about equal, thin, several to many-nerved, lanceolate or oblong; stamens 6 or more; stigmas long, plumose; grain free, globose, finely striate. Creeping, low or delicate perennials, with narrow flat blades and terminal and axillary panicles. Type species, *Luziola peruviana.* Name modified from *Luzula*, a genus of Juncaceae.

Pistillate spikelets ovoid, about 2 mm. long; staminate and pistillate panicles on the same shoot........ 1. L. PERUVIANA.
Pistillate spikelets oblong-lanceolate, 4 to 5 mm. long; staminate and pistillate panicles on different shoots........ 2. L. BAHIENSIS.

1. Luziola peruviána Gmel. (Fig. 816.) Culms slender, branching, the flowering shoots ascending, 10 to 40 cm. tall; blades 1 to 4 mm. wide, exceeding the panicles; staminate panicles terminal, narrow, the spikelets about 7 mm. long; pistillate panicles terminal and axillary, 3 to 6 cm. long, about as wide, the spikelets about 2 mm. long, ovoid at maturity, abruptly pointed. ♃ —Muddy ground and wet meadows, Florida (Pensacola) and Louisiana (vicinity of New Orleans); Mexico and Cuba, south to Argentina.

2. Luziola bahiénsis (Steud.) Hitchc. (Fig. 817.) Extensively stoloniferous, the flowering shoots not more than 15 cm. tall, mostly less; blades 2 to 4 mm. wide, much exceeding the panicles; panicles mostly terminal, the staminate few-flowered, the spikelets about 5 mm. long; pistillate panicles 4 to 6 cm. long, the few stiff branches finally spreading, with a few appressed oblong-lanceolate spikelets 4 to 5 mm. long, the lemma and palea much exceeding the caryopsis. ♃ —Lagoons and banks of streams, southern Alabama; Cuba, Venezuela, Brazil.

FIGURE 817.—*Luziola bahiensis*, × 1. (Mohr, Ala.)

124. HYDRÓCHLOA Beauv.

Spikelets unisexual, 1-flowered, disarticulating from the pedicel, the staminate and pistillate spikelets in separate panicles on the same plant; glumes wanting; staminate spikelets with a thin 7-nerved lemma, a 2-nerved palea, and 6 stamens; pistillate spikelets with a thin 7-nerved lemma and 5-nerved palea, the stigmas long and slender. A slender, branching, aquatic grass, probably perennial, the leaves floating; staminate spikelets in small few-flowered terminal racemes; pistillate spikelets in few-flowered racemes in the axils of the leaves. Type species, *Hydrochloa caroliniensis.* Name from Greek *hudor*, water, and *chloa*, grass, alluding to the habitat.

1. Hydrochloa caroliniénsis Beauv. (Fig. 818.) Culms up to 1 m. or more long, freely branching, leafy; blades flat, 1 to 3 cm. long, 1 to 2 mm. wide, in vigorous shoots as much as 6 cm. long and 5 mm. wide; spikelets inconspicuous and infrequent, the staminate about 4 mm. long, the pistillate about 2 mm. ♃ —Ponds and slow-flowing streams, sometimes in sufficient abundance to become troublesome. North Carolina to Florida and Louisiana. Eaten by livestock. Lemma 5- or 7-nerved; palea 4- to 7-nerved. (Weatherwax.)

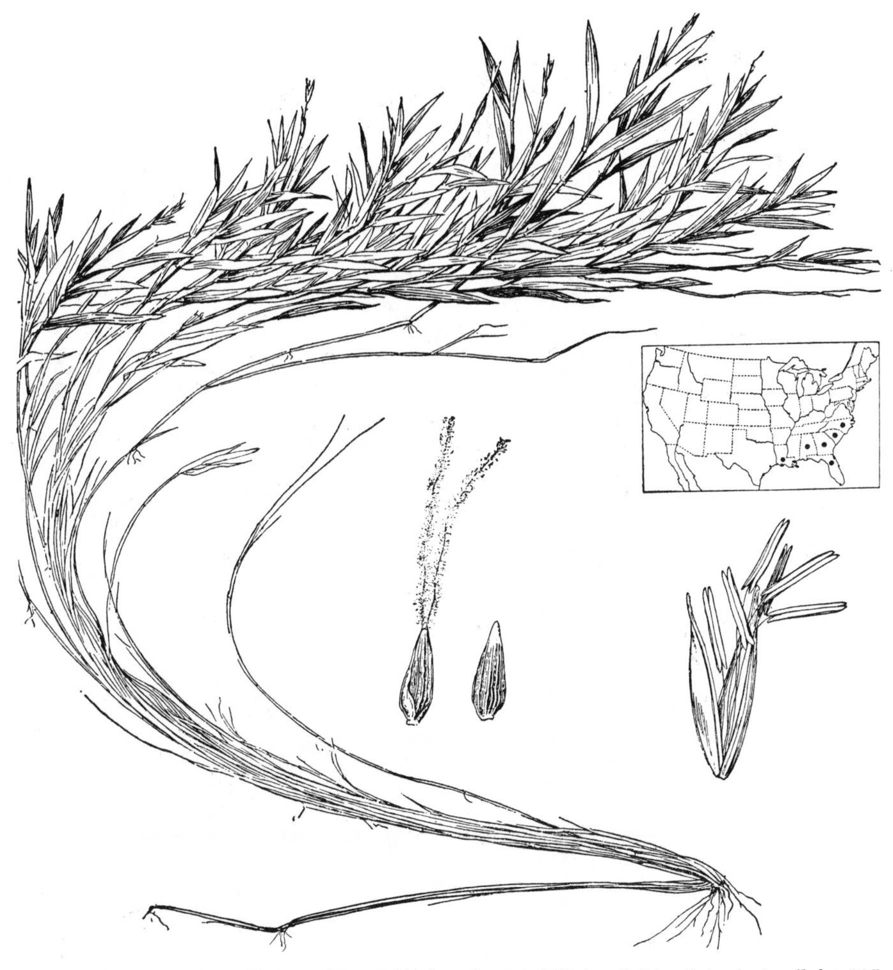

FIGURE 8 18.—*Hydrochloa caroliniensis.* Plant, × ½; two views of pistillate spikelet and staminate spikelet, × 5. (Nash 1152, Fla.)

125. PHÁRUS L.

Spikelets in pairs, appressed along the slender spreading, nearly simple panicle branches, one pistillate, subsessile, the other staminate, pediceled, much smaller than the pistillate spikelet; fertile lemma subindurate, terete, clothed, at least toward the beaked apex, with thick uncinate hairs; blades petioled (the petiole with a single twist reversing the upper and under surfaces of the blade), the nerves running from midnerve to margin, with fine transverse veins between the nerves. Perennials with broad flat elliptic or oblanceolate blades and terminal panicles with rather few stiffly spreading branches breaking readily at maturity, the terete pistillate spikelets appressed, the uncinate fruits acting like burs. Type species, *Pharus latifolius* L. Name from Greek *pharos*, cloth or mantle, possibly alluding to the broad blades.

1. Pharus parvifólius Nash. (Fig. 819.) Culms long-decumbent and rooting at base, the flowering shoot 30 to 50 cm. tall; blades elliptic,

FIGURE 819.—*Pharus parvifolius*, × ½. (Miller 1231, Dominican Republic.)

abruptly acuminate, 10 to 20 cm. long, 2 to 4 cm. wide; panicles mostly 10 to 20 cm. long, about as wide; pistillate spikelets about 1 cm. long, the glumes thin, brown, less than half as long as the lemma; staminate spikelets about 3 mm. long, the slender pedicels appressed to the pistillate spikelets. ♃ —Rocky woods, Florida, rare (Pineola; Orange Lake); West Indies to Brazil.

TRIBE 11. MELINIDEAE

126. MELÍNIS Beauv.

Spikelets small, dorsally compressed, 1-flowered with a sterile lemma below the fertile floret, the rachilla disarticulating below the glumes; first glume minute; second glume and sterile lemma similar, membranaceous, strongly nerved, slightly exceeding the fertile floret; fertile lemma and palea subhyaline toward summit. Perennials with slender, branching, decumbent culms and narrow many-flowered panicles, with capillary branchlets and pedicels. Type species, *Melinis minutiflora*. Name from Greek *meline*, millet.

1. Melinis minutiflóra Beauv. Molasses grass. (Fig. 820.) Culms ascending from a tangled much-branched base, as much as 1 m. tall; the foliage viscid-pubescent; blades flat, 5 to 15 cm. long, 5 to 10 mm. wide; panicle 10 to 20 cm. long, purplish; spikelets about 2 mm. long; sterile lemma 2-lobed, with a delicate awn 1 to 10 mm. long from between the lobes. ♃ —Introduced from Brazil, though native of Africa. Cultivated for forage and spreading in open ground through Central and South America and the West Indies. It has been tried successfully in southern Florida. The grass has a heavy sweetish odor when fresh. Called in Brazil capím gordura.

Figure 820.—*Melinis minutiflora*. Plant, × 1; spikelet, × 10. (Moldenke 453, Fla.)

Thysanolaéna máxima (Roxb.) Kuntze. Robust perennial, 1 to 3 m. tall; blades 3 to 7 cm. wide; panicle commonly 1 m. long, the slender flat densely flowered branches drooping; spikelets about 2 mm. long, pointed; fertile lemma long-ciliate. ♃ —Introduced in southern Florida and southern California as an ornamental.